The Legislative History of the Federal Antitrust Laws and Related Statutes

Other parts of this set (in preparation)

Part II
The Hart-Scott-Rodino Antitrust Improvements
Act of 1976

Part III
Antitrust Exemptions, Regulated Industries,
and FTC-Enforced Statutes

The Legislative History of the Federal Antitrust Laws and Related Statutes

Part I
The Antitrust Laws

Volume 2

Edited by Earl W. Kintner

Senior Partner
Arent, Fox, Kintner, Plotkin & Kahn
Washington, D.C.

Former Chairman and General Counsel
Federal Trade Commission

CHELSEA HOUSE PUBLISHERS
New York London
1978

Ref
KF1635.8
1978
pt. 1
v. 2

Project Editor   Jeanette Morrison
Associate Editor   Judy Susman
Editorial Staff   Karyn Browne, Don Coulter, Maxine Krasnow, Deborah Weiss
Design   Susan Lusk, Jeanette Morrison

©1978 by Earl W. Kintner
All rights reserved.
Printed and bound in the United States of America.

Published 1978 by Chelsea House Publishers

Library of Congress Cataloging in Publication Data (Revised)

Kintner, Earl W
    The Federal antitrust laws.

    His Legislative history of the Federal antitrust laws and related statutes; pt. 1, v. 1—
    1. Antitrust law—United States. I. United States. Laws, statutes, etc. 1977. II. Title.
KF1635.8 1977. pt. 1. vol. 1 343'.73'072s
ISBN 0-87754-101-9 (v. 1) [343'.73'072] 77-21143

Kintner, Earl W.
    Legislative history of the Federal antitrust laws and related statutes.
    CONTENTS: pt. 1. The Federal antitrust laws.
    1. Antitrust law—United States. I. United States. Law, statutes, etc. 1977. II. Title.
KF1635.8 1977 343'.73'072 77-21144
ISBN 0-87754-100-0

CHELSEA HOUSE PUBLISHERS

Harold Steinberg, Chairman & Publisher   Andrew E. Norman, President
A Division of Chelsea House Educational Communications, Inc.
70 West 40th Street, New York, N.Y. 10018

*To Jerrold G. Van Cise—
peerless student, teacher and practitioner of antitrust law—
and to all other students of antitrust law.*

Guide to the use of this set

1. The materials are arranged statute by statute, each chapter bearing the name of the statute whose legislative history is covered therein. In a few cases, chapters include subsections setting forth the history of amendatory statutes (*e.g.*, Chapter 15, Expediting Act of 1903 and Amendments).

2. The following reference material appears at the beginning of each chapter:
    A detailed table of contents for each chapter.
    An *Introduction* covering the legislative, social, and economic context and history of the statute, its provisions, and its significance.
    A *Chronological Synopsis* of the significant events in the statute's history, with an emphasis on congressional consideration.
    A *Table of Reprinted Documents,* arranged by document type for ready reference.

For additional information see the *Introductory editorial note* on page xv.

Summary of the contents

Part I
The Antitrust Laws

A. THE SHERMAN ACT

Chapter 1 / Sherman Act of 1890

B. THE FAIR TRADE AMENDMENTS

Chapter 2 / Miller-Tydings Resale Price Maintenance Act of 1937
Chapter 3 / McGuire Resale Price Maintenance Act Amendment of 1952
Chapter 4 / Consumer Goods Pricing Act of 1975 (Fair Trade Repealer)

C. THE CLAYTON ACT AND AMENDMENTS

Chapter 5 / Clayton Act of 1914
Chapter 6 / Robinson-Patman Price Discrimination Act of 1936
Chapter 7 / Celler-Kefauver Act of 1950

D. THE FTC ACT AND AMENDMENTS

Chapter 8 / Federal Trade Commission Act of 1914
Chapter 9 / Wheeler-Lea Act of 1938
Chapter 10 / Antitrust Amendments of 1973
Chapter 11 / Federal Trade Commission Improvement Act of 1975

E. ACTS RELATING TO FOREIGN COMMERCE

Chapter 12 / Wilson Tariff Act of 1894 and Amendment
Chapter 13 / Section 11, Panama Canal Act of 1912
Chapter 14 / Section 337, Tariff Act of 1930 and Amendments

F. ACTS RELATING TO PROCEDURE AND ENFORCEMENT

Chapter 15 / Expediting Act of 1903 and Amendments
Chapter 16 / Antitrust Immunity Act of 1903 and Amendments
Chapter 17 / Publicity in Taking Evidence Act of 1913
Chapter 18 / Antitrust Civil Process Act of 1962
Chapter 19 / Antitrust Procedures and Penalties Act of 1974

Part II
The Hart-Scott-Rodino Antitrust Improvements Act of 1976

Part III
Antitrust Exemptions, Regulated Industries, and FTC-Enforced Statutes

Contents of Volume 2

Guide to the use of this set / **vi**
Summary of the contents / **vii**
Preface to Part I / **xi**
Acknowledgments / **xiii**
Introductory editorial note / **xv**

C. THE CLAYTON ACT AND AMENDMENTS

Chapter 5 / Clayton Act of 1914 / **985**
       (Continued in Volume 3)

A detailed table of contents appears at the beginning of the chapter.

Preface to Part I

During my years first as General Counsel and later as Chairman of the Federal Trade Commission, I came to the conclusion that the antitrust and trade regulation laws are violated more often through ignorance than through intent. I learned that many businessmen and lawyers had a thirst for knowledge concerning those laws but were bewildered by their complexity and by the jargon all too often used in articles and books intended to explain the antitrust laws. Since then I have devoted a substantial amount of my time to explaining the antitrust and trade regulation laws by means of seven books, numerous legal articles, and over 400 speeches.

I was delighted when Chelsea House asked me to produce a legislative history of the federal antitrust laws. The absence of a comprehensive, authoritative compilation of the legislative histories of the federal antitrust statutes has long been a hindrance to an understanding of these laws by lawyers, courts, and businessmen. Although the labor involved in compiling such an exhaustive set of books is truly herculean, several colleagues in my law firm and I gladly undertook it as a service to our profession, to law libraries and law students, and to the innumerable businessmen whose plans and decisions are pervasively affected by the antitrust laws. Not the least of our compilation problems has been that of locating long out-of-print materials, sometimes available only in the dog-eared copy in an agency's library or archives.

The 19 statutes covered in the first part of this set are both substantive and procedural and range from the Sherman Act, which the Supreme Court has described as "a comprehensive charter of economic liberty aimed at preserving free and unfettered competition as the rule of trade,"* to the little-known and never-used antitrust provision of the Panama Canal Act. My intent in these first volumes has been to present a comprehensive history of the 19 federal statutes pertaining directly to the federal antitrust laws. Future volumes to be published by Chelsea House will cover the Hart-Scott-Rodino Antitrust Improvements Act of 1976 and the more than 40 statutes relating to antitrust exemptions, regulated industries, and FTC-enforced statutes.

For this set of books the primary source materials are the actual congressional bills, reports, and debates. In addition, materials such as presidential messages and addresses, annual and special agency reports, and letters and other documents from executive departments and congressional committees have been included to clarify statutory provisions and to document the concerns that motivated passage. The background and importance of each statute is explained in an introduction, which is extensively footnoted with references to pertinent materials. Major federal court decisions construing the legislative history or examining the nature of the statutes are also included, with explanatory commentaries where necessary.

The Introductions, Commentaries, and editorial selection of documents and cases are intended to give the reader an objective, well-informed view of the origins, congressional intent, and developments pertinent to each law. I have consciously avoided making any value judgments as to the efficacy or wisdom of the statutes. The documents are intended to speak for themselves. It is hoped that the product of our labors will serve as a useful tool, previously wholly lacking, to those interested in antitrust law and legislation in this country.

E.W.K.

---

* Northern Pac. Ry. v. United States, 356 U.S. 1, 4, 78 S. Ct. 514, 517, 2 L. Ed. 2d 545, 549 (1958).

Acknowledgments

As I noted in the Preface, the labor involved in researching, compiling, and editing the 19 legislative histories contained in the first part of this set was truly herculean. A number of colleagues in my law firm made significant contributions to these volumes and I gratefully acknowledge their assistance.

At the outset two of my colleagues deserve special thanks for their substantial contributions to this project. Joseph P. Griffin served as coordinator and managing editor for the project as a whole. Mark R. Joelson made substantial editorial and substantive contributions to each of the Introductions and Commentaries. I would also like to thank Jeanette Morrison, project editor at Chelsea House, for her substantial editorial assistance, and Judy Susman, her associate editor.

Grateful acknowledgment is also made to my colleagues below for their major contributions to individual chapters:

1 / Sherman Act   *John C. Filippini*
2 / Miller-Tydings Resale Price Maintenance Act   *Alan R. Malasky*
3 / McGuire Resale Price Maintenance Act Amendment   *Alan R. Malasky*
4 / Consumer Goods Pricing Act   *David B. Goldston*
5 / Clayton Act   *Robert W. Green*
6 / Robinson-Patman Price Discrimination Act   *Salvatore A. Romano*
7 / Celler-Kefauver Act   *Eugene J. Meigher, Robert B. Weintraub*
8 / Federal Trade Commission Act   *Stephen T. Phelps, Christopher Smith*
9 / Wheeler-Lea Act   *Christopher Smith*
10 / Antitrust Amendments of 1973   *Douglas G. Green*
11 / Federal Trade Commission Improvement Act   *Christopher Smith*
12 / Wilson Tariff Act and Amendment   *Marc L. Fleischaker*
13 / Section 11, Panama Canal Act   *Joseph P. Griffin*
14 / Section 337, Tariff Act of 1930   *Bruce E. Aitken, Joseph P. Griffin*
15 / Expediting Act and Amendments   *Marc L. Fleischaker*
16 / Antitrust Immunity Act and Amendments   *Paul F. Donahue, Joseph P. Griffin*
17 / Publicity in Taking Evidence Act   *Thomas J. Tourish, Jr.*
18 / Antitrust Civil Process Act   *David L. Cohen*
19 / Antitrust Procedures and Penalties Act   *Lee Calligaro*

Professor Bernie R. Burrus, Bruce V. Bordelon, David L. Carden, John Cushing, Paul F. Donahue, Debra Goldstein, Jeremy Mathis, Sherrill A. Sherman, Brison S. Shipley, and Daniel P. Sternberg, as well as several librarians at the Library of Congress and the Federal Trade Commission, provided valuable research assistance. Finally I would like to thank Inge Vogel for her skill and patience.

E.W.K.

Introductory editorial note

Part I of this set covers developments to January 1, 1977; significant later developments have been included where possible.

ORGANIZATION OF THE MATERIAL

This set is divided into three Parts:
Part I / The Antitrust Laws
Part II / The Hart-Scott-Rodino Antitrust Improvements Act of 1976
Part III / Antitrust Exemptions, Regulated Industries, and FTC-Enforced Statutes

Where appropriate, parts are subdivided into sections reflecting traditional topical groupings. For example, Part I is divided as follows:
  A. The Sherman Act
  B. The Fair Trade Amendments
  C. The Clayton Act and Amendments
  D. The FTC Act and Amendments
  E. Statutes Relating to Foreign Commerce
  F. Statutes Relating to Procedure and Enforcement

EDITORIAL METHOD

In reprinting these documents, every effort has been made to preserve the integrity of the original texts.

Original pagination. An inverted T-bar system (employing the symbol⊥) has been used to provide the original page numbers of all reprinted documents except the *United States Code* (always cited to section numbers).

Bill prints. All bill prints are reproduced line for line, together with the original line numbers.

Footnotes. Original document footnotes reprinted herein are separated from the text by a short, one-inch line that begins at the left margin. The original note numbers have been retained.
Footnotes added by the editor appear below any original footnotes and are separated from them or from the text by a line drawn across the entire page. Editor's footnotes are numbered consecutively throughout each chapter and each note number is preceded by the chapter number as a prefix. For example, the editor's footnotes in Chapter 1 are numbered 1.1, 1.2, 1.3, etc.

Case citations. Full citations to all significant cases named, partially cited, or otherwise referred to in the documents have been footnoted at the first appearance of each case in each chapter and as many times thereafter as would be helpful to the reader.

Deletions. The printed record of congressional hearings regarding the statutes covered in this series runs into the tens of thousands of pages, much of which is now only of historic interest. The editor has therefore limited such material to representative exhibits and to statements made by individuals who were directly responsible for the drafting of the legislation in question and/or its subsequent passage. The only other material excluded was that which was clearly irrelevant, procedural, or unnecessarily duplicative.

All deletions made by the editor have been indicated by ellipsis points. Since the original pagination has been provided, the omission of full paragraphs has been indicated by ellipsis points at the end of the paragraph preceding the omitted part, rather than by a full line of ellipsis points.

Congressional Record. In reprinting the congressional debate, the permanent, bound edition of the *Congressional Record* has been used except in the case of the most recent statutes, where only the daily edition of the *Record* was available at the time of compilation. Where the daily edition has been used, this is indicated in the title to the document.

The first name, state, and party affiliation of each Congressperson has been supplied in brackets at his or her first appearance in each chapter.

General style. Capitalization, abbreviation, and typographical style (insofar as possible) have all been retained.

Apparent errors in the original texts have been treated in several ways. In general, *sic* has been inserted in brackets to indicate "so in original" following obvious typographical errors, inadvertent grammatical slips that could mistakenly be attributed to typographical errors made in reprinting, incorrect spellings of proper names, and obvious factual discrepancies. *Sic* has not been used for every odd expression or spelling variation, or to indicate inconsistent capitalization, etc.

Missing punctuation has been added in brackets where needed for clarity.

C THE CLAYTON ACT AND AMENDMENTS

Chapters
5   **Clayton Act of 1914**
6   **Robinson-Patman Price Discrimination Act of 1936**
7   **Celler-Kefauver Act of 1950**

5 CLAYTON ACT OF 1914

989   Introduction
1025   Chronological Synopsis
1039   Table of Reprinted Documents

CURRENT VERSION

1043   Clayton Antitrust Act as amended
15 U.S.C. §§ 12, 13, 14-21, 22-27
29 U.S.C. §§ 52-53

ORIGINAL VERSION

1061   Clayton Antitrust Act, October 15, 1914

The Origins

1071   Representative lease and license agreement of the United Shoe Machinery Co.

1074   Tentative antitrust bills ordered printed by Rep. Henry D. Clayton
63d Cong., 2d Sess.
1914

1080   H.R. 15657, 63d Cong., 2d Sess.
April 14, 1914

House Consideration

1089   Report of the House Committee on the Judiciary
H.R. Rep. No. 627, Pt. 1, 63d Cong., 2d Sess.
May 6, 1914

1125   Minority Views, H.R. Rep. No. 627, Pt. 2
May 12, 1914

1152   Minority Views, H.R. Rep. No. 627, Pt. 3
May 13, 1914

1160   Minority Views, H.R. Rep. No. 627, Pt. 4
May 13, 1914

1163   H.R. 15657 as reported by the House Committee on the Judiciary
May 6, 1914

House Debate, 63d Cong., 2d Sess.
1181   May 6, 1914
1182   May 22, 1914
1233   May 23, 1914
1317   May 25, 1914
1330   May 26, 1914
1390   May 28, 1914
1448   May 29, 1914
1506   June 1, 1914
1661   June 2, 1914

1728   H.R. 15657 as agreed upon in the Committee of the Whole House
        63d Cong., 2d Sess.
        June 2, 1914

1738   House Debate, 63d Cong., 2d Sess.
        June 5, 1914

Senate Consideration

Senate Debate, 63d Cong., 2d Sess.
1743   June 6, 1914
1743   July 22, 1914

1744   Report of the Senate Committee on the Judiciary
        S. Rep. No. 698, 63d Cong., 2d Sess.
        July 22, 1914

1753   H.R. 15657 as reported by the Senate Committee on the Judiciary
        July 22, 1914

Senate Debate, 63d Cong., 2d Sess.
1767   August 5, 1914
1768   August 12, 1914
1768   August 13, 1914
1791   August 17, 1914
1823   August 18, 1914
1877   August 19, 1914
1925   August 20, 1914
1985   August 21, 1914
2011   August 25, 1914
2078   August 26, 1914
2136   August 27, 1914
2186   August 28, 1914
2219   August 29, 1914
2236   August 31, 1914
2294   September 1, 1914
2366   September 2, 1914

2423   H.R. 15657 as amended and passed by the Senate
        63d Cong., 2d Sess.
        September 2 (legislative day, August 25), 1914

2438   H.R. 15657 with Senate amendments numbered
        63d Cong., 2d Sess.
        September 3, 1914

Conference Consideration

2454 House Debate, 63d Cong., 2d Sess.
September 4, 1914

Senate Debate, 63d Cong., 2d Sess.
2454 September 4, 1914
2455 September 23, 1914
2456 September 24, 1914

2456 Report of the Conference Committee
H.R. Rep. No. 1168, 63d Cong., 2d Sess.
September 25, 1914

Senate Debate, 63d Cong., 2d Sess.
2470 September 25, 1914
2472 September 26, 1914
2474 September 28, 1914
2504 September 29, 1914
2533 September 30, 1914
2586 October 1, 1914
2642 October 2, 1914
2683 October 3, 1914
2695 October 5, 1914

House Debate, 63d Cong., 2d Sess.
2758 October 6, 1914
2760 October 7, 1914
2789 October 8, 1914

Presidential Comment

2837 Letter from President Woodrow Wilson to Rep. Oscar W. Underwood
October 17, 1914

THE DECISIONS

2841 Commentary

2857 Standard Oil Co. of California v. United States, 337 U.S. 293 (1949)

2865 Emich Motors Corp. v. General Motors Corp., 340 U.S. 558 (1951)

2868 United States v. E. I. du Pont de Nemours & Co., 353 U.S. 586 (1957)

2874 Northern Pacific Railway Co. v. United States, 356 U.S. 1 (1958)

2879 Tampa Electric Co. v. Nashville Coal Co., 365 U.S. 320 (1961)

2885 Citizen Publishing Co. v. United States, 394 U.S. 131 (1969)

Introduction

CLAYTON ACT OF 1914

Based upon 24 years of practical experience under the Sherman Act, Congress sought in the Clayton Act to remedy certain perceived weaknesses in the existing law and to expand its coverage.

During this same period, however, Congress was also forging a novel approach to trade regulation, ultimately embodied in legislation creating the Federal Trade Commission.[5.1]

The bills proposing the Clayton Act[5.2] and the FTC Act[5.3] were introduced at approximately the same time in early 1914 and were considered substantially concurrently, although they were reported out by different committees in each House.[5.4] Because of the interrelationships between these two proposals, the final language of each was tempered by the existence of the other. For example, the Senate's passage of the FTC Act prior to opening deliberations on the Clayton bill was the major reason for the ultimate rejection of criminal penalties for violations of sections 2 and 3 of the Clayton Act.[5.5]

While there was a consensus that the Sherman Act needed supplementation, two competing approaches were recommended. On the one hand, there were advocates of supplementing that Act by declaring certain practices unlawful. On the other hand, there were those who believed such statutory attempts futile, since the trusts could

---

[5.1] Federal Trade Commission Act of 1914, ch. 311, 38 Stat. 717, *as amended,* 15 U.S.C. §§ 41-46, 47-58 (1976), the legislative history of which appears *infra* at chapter 8.

[5.2] H.R. 15657, 63d Cong., 2d Sess. (introduced by Representative Henry D. Clayton (D., Ala.) on April 14, 1914), *infra* at 1080-88.

[5.3] H.R. 15613, 63d Cong., 2d Sess. (introduced by Representative J. Harry Covington (D., Md.) on April 13, 1914).

[5.4] The Clayton bills were assigned to the House Judiciary Committee, chaired by Representative Henry D. Clayton, and to the Senate Judiciary Committee, chaired by Senator Charles A. Culberson (D., Tex.). The FTC bills were assigned to the Senate Committee on Interstate Commerce and to the House Committee on Interstate and Foreign Commerce.

[5.5] See discussion *infra* at 1010-12, 1019.

simply adopt new methods of achieving their goals. This group advocated creation of a trade commission, with power to declare individual trade practices unfair.[5.6]

The result of this competition was that the Clayton Act limited its thrust to certain broad, enumerated trade and commercial practices which were declared unlawful, while the Federal Trade Commission Act established a new commission with power to review all trade practices and to order a respondent to cease and desist from using those particular practices that it determined to be unfair.

As finally enacted, the Clayton Act limited its amendment of the Sherman Act to: (1) expanding its venue provisions (adding the words "or has an agent"), (2) giving final judgments of antitrust violations in government cases effect as prima facie evidence in private actions arising from the same fact situation, and (3) providing for the tolling of the statute of limitations for private actions during the pendency of a government case. Beyond these changes, the Clayton Act concentrated upon enumerating additional unlawful acts and practices and prescribed rules for the granting and enforcement of injunctive relief. Moreover, the Act clarified the intent of Congress that the labor of a human being did not constitute a commodity or article of commerce and that nonprofit labor and agricultural organizations, in their exercise of lawful activities, could not be illegal combinations or conspiracies under the antitrust laws.

There have been only two significant amendments to the Clayton Act since 1914, both designed to strengthen original provisions that were proving ineffective from an enforcement standpoint. The first such amendment, in 1936, substituted the language of the Robinson-Patman Act[5.7] for original section 2 provisions prohibiting sellers from discriminating in price between different purchasers of commodities. The second such change was effected in 1950 by the Celler-Kefauver Act,[5.8] which amended original section 7 to remove a notorious loophole in the merger context. Under the Clayton Act as passed in 1914, only stock mergers were covered, and companies could avoid its proscriptions through structuring mergers as asset acquisitions. The 1950 amendment eliminated this possibility.

THE ORIGINS

Enforcement Experience Under the Sherman Law Prior to 1914

Although consideration has already been given to the early enforcement of the Sherman Act in chapter 1,[5.9] a further analysis of these early cases is helpful in understanding the genesis of the Clayton Act.

Before looking at specific early cases brought under the Sherman Act, however, reference to a contemporary assessment of early enforcement efforts is appropriate. In a January 1903 letter, Senator George F. Edmunds (R., Vt.), one of the principal architects of the Sherman Act, wrote as follows:

> The only difficulty with the bill we reported and which became law was the want of administration, that is to say, that the law was and is entirely capable of putting an end to such so-called trusts and such combinations as interfere with or restrain commerce among the States, etc., if the officers of the Government having charge of the enforcement of law understand their duty and are willing to do it, being, of course, supplied with sufficient means to put it into force. . . . What is needed is not, so much, more legislation as competent and earnest administration of the laws that exist.[5.10]

[5.6] For a brief general review of the historical background of these Acts see G. HENDERSON, THE FEDERAL TRADE COMMISSION: A STUDY IN ADMINISTRATIVE LAW AND PROCEDURE (1924).

[5.7] Act of June 19, 1936, ch. 592, 49 Stat. 1526, 15 U.S.C. §§ 13–13b, 21a (1976), the legislative history of which appears *infra* at chapter 6. As the discussion in chapter 6 points out, only section 1 of the Robinson-Patman Act (15 U.S.C. § 13) is considered an amendment of the Clayton Act.

[5.8] Act of Dec. 29, 1950, ch. 1184, 64 Stat. 1125, *amending* Clayton Act §§ 7, 11, 15 U.S.C. §§ 18, 21 (1976), the legislative history of which appears *infra* at chapter 7.

[5.9] See the *Commentary* in chapter 1, *Sherman Act of 1890, supra*.

[5.10] Letter from George F. Edmunds to John A. Sleicher, Esq., Feb. 7, 1903, as reproduced in H. THORELLI, THE FEDERAL ANTITRUST POLICY 369 (1955).

There appear to have been several reasons for this relatively lackluster early performance by the Department of Justice in enforcing the Sherman Act. First, with the exception of some comparatively minor deficiency appropriations to permit employment of special assistants in several cases, Congress granted no special funds for antitrust enforcement before 1903. Responding to the perceived need for more effective enforcement, Congress in 1903 appropriated $500,000 to be used specifically for antitrust enforcement,[5.11] and it also passed other legislation ameliorating the Department's administrative burdens in prosecuting antitrust violations, including passage of the Expediting Act[5.12] permitting direct and speedy appeals of antitrust cases to the Supreme Court, and the addition of a rider to the antitrust appropriations bill providing for limited immunity for witnesses in such cases.[5.13]

Second, the broad language of the Sherman Act and the lack of definitive judicial interpretations offered a further deterrent to vigorous enforcement by individual district attorneys, who could not have been unaware of the indifference to the trust problem of Presidents Benjamin Harrison, Grover Cleveland, and William McKinley and their respective Attorneys General.[5.14] Evincing his own unfavorable attitude toward the Sherman Act, Attorney General Richard Olney reported in 1893:

> There has been, and probably still is, a widespread impression that the aim and effect of this statute are to prohibit and prevent those aggregations of capital which are so common at the present day, and which are sometimes on so large a scale as to control practically all the branches of an extensive industry. It would not be useful, even if it were possible, to ascertain the precise purposes of the framers of the statute. It is sufficient to point out what small basis is for the popular impression referred to.[5.15]

Finally, the hoped-for contribution of private plaintiffs to enforcement of the new law did not materialize to any substantial degree before 1903.

In this context, the government's loss in 1895 of its first antitrust case to reach the Supreme Court, the *Sugar Trust* case,[5.16] was especially disheartening. In that case, a company having approximately 65 percent of the domestic sugar refining and sales capacity purchased four smaller Pennsylvania sugar refining companies that together had about 33 percent of the domestic refining and sales capacity.

Although the complaint averred that the major company monopolized the manufacture and sale of refined sugar in the United States, controlling the price of sugar, and that the making of the purchase contracts was with intent to monopolize and constituted a combination and conspiracy to restrain trade, the Supreme Court affirmed the circuit court's (now known as the district court) dismissal of the complaint for failure to allege a violation of the Sherman Act.

Given the Justice Department's earlier unsuccessful attempts to prosecute the *Whiskey Trust* case,[5.17] one would have anticipated that great care would be taken in drafting the complaint and preparing the evidence against the so-called sugar trust. A careful review of the Supreme Court's opinion, however, suggests that the fatal flaw in the complaint was that no proof was offered that the combinations complained of

---

[5.11] H. THORELLI, *supra* note 5.10, at 369, 560–61, 588.

[5.12] Act of Feb. 11, 1903, ch. 544, 32 Stat. 823, *as amended*, 15 U.S.C. §§ 28, 29 (Supp. IV, 1974), the legislative history of which appears *infra* at chapter 15. The Justice Department put this new law to prompt use in filing the *Northern Securities* case. Northern Sec. Co. v. United States, 193 U.S. 197, 24 S. Ct. 436, 48 L. Ed. 679 (1904).

[5.13] Antitrust Immunity Act of 1903, ch. 755, 32 Stat. 904, the legislative history of which appears *infra* at chapter 16. *See* H. THORELLI, *supra* note 5.10, at 534-38, 551–54. Creation in 1903 of the Bureau of Corporations within the Department of Commerce and Labor also provided an important assist in the systematic collection and analysis of data concerning corporations. *Id.*

[5.14] H. THORELLI, *supra* note 5.10, at 370. Thorelli's discussion of early antitrust enforcement, analyzed by particular presidential administration and each Attorney General, is informative, as is his review of both government and private antitrust actions filed between 1890 and 1903. *See id.* at 369-431, 477–99.

[5.15] 1893 ATT'Y GEN. ANN. REP. xxvi f., as reproduced in H. THORELLI, *supra* note 5.10, at 385.

[5.16] United States v. E.C. Knight Co., 156 U.S. 1, 15 S. Ct. 249, 39 L. Ed. 325 (1895), *aff'g* 60 F. 934 (3d Cir. 1894).

[5.17] United States v. Greenhut, 50 F. 469 (D. Mass. 1892).

constituted a restraint upon interstate trade or commerce. Analyzing the combination complained of under the Sherman Act, the Court stated:

> ... What the law struck at was combinations, contracts, and conspiracies to monopolize trade and commerce among the several states or with foreign nations; but the contracts and acts of the defendants related exclusively to the acquisition of the Philadelphia refineries and the business of sugar refining in Pennsylvania, and bore no direct relation to commerce between the states or with foreign nations. The object was manifestly private gain in the manufacture of the commodity, but not through the control of interstate or foreign commerce. It is true that the bill alleged that the products of these refineries were sold and distributed among the several states, and that all the companies were engaged in trade or commerce with the several states and with foreign nations; but this was no more than to say that trade and commerce serve manufacture to fulfill its function. Sugar was refined for sale, and sales were probably made at Philadelphia for consumption, and undoubtedly for resale by the first purchasers throughout Pennsylvania and other states, and refined sugar was also forwarded by the companies to other states for sale. Nevertheless, it does not follow that an attempt to monopolize, or the actual monopoly of, the manufacture was an attempt, whether executory or consummated, to monopolize commerce, even though, in order to dispose of the product, the instrumentality of commerce was necessarily invoked. *There was nothing in the proofs to indicate any intention to put a restraint upon trade or commerce,* and the fact, as we have seen, that trade or commerce might be indirectly affected was not enough to entitle complainants to a decree.[5.18]

Unfortunately for antitrust enforcement, the *Knight* opinion was commonly accepted as enunciating the rule that manufacture by itself was a purely local activity and not subject to the reach of the Sherman Act, whose scope is constitutionally limited to activities occurring in interstate commerce. Although the government secured several notable Supreme Court decisions in its favor in the next several years,[5.19] not until the Court decided the *Northern Securities* case[5.20] in 1904 was this unfortunate precedent disposed of and the business community put on notice that mergers of competitors would fare no better under the Sherman Act than informal or formal combinations or agreements among the same competing companies to restrain interstate commerce.

The unfortunate effect of the *Knight* case was further exacerbated by three more Supreme Court decisions in the succeeding four-year period: *United States v. Trans-Missouri Freight Association*,[5.21] *United States v. Joint Traffic Association*,[5.22] and *United States v. Addyston Pipe & Steel Co.*[5.23] In these cases, agreements among competing railway companies to maintain uniform and reasonable rates were declared unlawful, and an association of pipe manufacturers which allocated sales territories among its members was also held to be unlawful. Given the apparent judicial approval of the merger of sugar companies comprising some 98 percent of domestic production in the *Knight* case, it is understandable that many businessmen and lawyers believed at that time that the only prudent way for competing businessmen to associate or combine for any commercial purpose was through the medium of an actual merger of their businesses.[5.24]

Any remaining confusion on the part of businessmen as to the reach of the Sherman Act under section 1 was largely laid to rest by the decision in the *Northern Securities* case. Involving as it did a complaint against a holding company,[5.25] this case

---

[5.18] 156 U.S. at 17 (emphasis added). Several historians have independently suggested that the government's prosecution of this case may have been compromised. The failure of the attorneys involved to put in any of the available evidence proving the trust's purpose to dominate interstate commerce in sugar is at best inexplicable. *See* H. THORELLI, *supra* note 5.10, at 384-88, where he reproduces materials written by several others.

[5.19] *See, e.g.,* cases cited *infra* at notes 5.21–.23.

[5.20] 193 U.S. 197, 24 S. Ct. 436, 48 L. Ed. 679 (1904).

[5.21] 166 U.S. 290, 17 S. Ct. 540, 41 L. Ed. 1007 (1897), *rev'g* 58 F. 58 (8th Cir. 1893).

[5.22] 171 U.S. 505, 19 S. Ct. 25, 43 L. Ed. 259 (1898), *rev'g* 89 F. 1020 (2d Cir. 1897). Portions of this decision are reprinted *supra* at Chapter 1.

[5.23] 175 U.S. 211, 20 S. Ct. 96, 44 L. Ed. 136 (1899), *aff'g* 85 F. 271 (6th Cir. 1898) (Taft, J.).

[5.24] *See* H. THORELLI, *supra* note 5.10, at 604-09.

[5.25] The *Northern Securities* case involved the acquisition in 1901 by a holding company of all shares of stock in the Great Northern Railway Co. and the Northern Pacific Railway Co., which operated

did not present as starkly restraining a combination as that presented in the *Knight* case; nevertheless, the Supreme Court sustained a judgment on the evidence presented that such a combination was unlawful. Although this decision was rendered by a narrow five-to-four majority, it laid to rest the then popular notion that the particular form of a combination or agreement could be the decisive factor as to its legality under the antitrust law.

Other Pressures for Extension of the Sherman Act

During the period 1895-1904, when the efficacy of the Sherman Act to reach corporate mergers and holding companies was in doubt, several other developments further encouraged corporate consolidation. In 1889 New Jersey amended its incorporation statute to permit a corporation to purchase and hold the stock of other corporations.[5.26] Given the intensifying competition among the states to serve as a corporation's domicile and gain the right to levy taxes on its operations, other states shortly followed New Jersey's lead.[5.27]

Beginning in this period and extending through the 1914 congressional debates on the Clayton Act, the great industrial trusts grew, prospered, and gained the economic strength to exert almost unlimited power over labor and prices.[5.28] Injunctions against labor organizations were secured from federal district court judges under the Sherman Act, and the power of the federal courts was used to crush strikes and otherwise limit the ability of workers to organize.[5.29] Although the Supreme Court in 1895 upheld the conviction of Eugene Debs for contempt of court in his action in relation to the Pullman strike without relying upon the Sherman Act,[5.30] in the period between 1890 and 1914 at least 101 cases were filed in which federal judges issued injunctions against labor organizations under the Sherman Act,[5.31] notwithstanding the clear legislative history that it was not intended to apply to such combinations.[5.32]

In addition to the general powerlessness of labor organizations to bargain effectively with the great trusts under these circumstances, other trust activities had harmful effects. For example, the operation of the money trust and the power it gained through control over the issuance of currency is well detailed in the Pujo committee investigation in 1912.[5.33] Passage of the Federal Reserve Act in 1913 was directly

---

parallel rail lines between the Great Lakes and the Pacific Ocean. Prior to 1901, these companies had engaged in active competition. This case also established other important precedents, which are not discussed herein.

[5.26] Laws of the State of New Jersey, 1889, ch. 265, § 4, 414. Cited in H. THORELLI, *supra* note 5.10, at 84.

[5.27] *Eg.*, New York in 1892, Delaware in 1899, and Maine in 1901. H. THORELLI, *supra* note 5.10, at 256.

[5.28] On August 25, 1914, Senator William H. Thompson (D., Kan.) inserted in the debates a lengthy table listing 628 trusts, formed from 9,877 independent companies, and having total capitalization of almost $25 billion. He testified that the greatest amount of trust formation took place between 1898 and 1908. 51 CONG. REC. 14218-21 (1914), *infra* at 2051-62.

[5.29] *See, e.g.*, Loewe v. Lawlor, 208 U.S. 274, 28 S. Ct. 301, 52 L. Ed. 488 (1908) (the *Danbury Hatters* case); United States v. Debs, U.S. DEP'T OF JUSTICE, 1 DECREES AND JUDGMENTS IN FEDERAL ANTI-TRUST CASES 1890-1918, at 13 (1918) (C.C.N.D. Ill., filed July 2, 1894) (issuing injunction in the Pullman strike of 1894); United States v. Elliott, 62 F. 801 (C.C.E.D. Mo. 1894).

[5.30] *In re* Debs, 158 U.S. 564, 15 S. Ct. 900, 39 L. Ed. 1092 (1895). For a good brief discussion of the circumstances surrounding the action against Eugene Debs, including correspondence between Attorney General Olney and his special attorney in Chicago, Edwin Walker, see H. THORELLI, *supra* note 5.10, at 389-94.

[5.31] A tabulation of these 101 cases was introduced in both Houses during floor debates on the Clayton bills. *See* 51 CONG. REC. 9173-74, 13665-66 (1914), *infra* at 1278-81, 1778-80.

[5.32] An excellent general review of the legislative history of the Sherman Act on this point was presented on August 13, 1914, by Senator Henry F. Ashurst (D., Ariz.) on the floor of the Senate during debates on the Clayton bill, 51 CONG. REC. 13662-64 (1914), *infra* at 1771-74.

[5.33] *See* REPORT ON INVESTIGATION OF CONDITIONS IN U.S. BANKS AND BANKING, H.R. REP. NO. 1593, 62d Cong., 3d Sess. (1913); *Investigation of Financial and Monetary Conditions in the United States under H.R. 429 and 504 Before the Subcomm. to Investigate the Concentration of Control of Money and Credit of the House Banking and Currency Comm.*, 62d Cong., 2d-3d Sess. (1912-1913) (29 pts.).

responsive to this evil.[5.34] In January 1912, the Stanley committee commenced an investigation of the steel trust,[5.35] which served to further define the nature of the large trust and to refute on economic grounds the myth that efficiency is directly related to corporate size.

In each of these hearings and in the three major House and Senate trust legislation hearings conducted between 1911 and 1914,[5.36] a consummate attack on the evils of the trust was offered by Louis D. Brandeis, an attorney in private practice in Boston who had gained wide repute for his effective support of public and social causes.[5.37] Brandeis had had an intimate involvement with the shoe machinery trust from 1899 through January 1907, serving as an incorporator, attorney, and director of the United Shoe Machinery Co. and the United Shoe Machinery Corp.[5.38] Based upon his knowledge of this trust, its use of certain tying clauses in its equipment leases,[5.39] and its aggressive policy of buying out competing shoe machinery manufacturers, Brandeis constructed an irresistible case for the inclusion of anti-tying provisions in the legislation that ultimately became the Clayton Act.[5.40]

In addition to conditioning the lease of certain of its machinery upon the explicit condition that the supplies necessary to the functioning of those machines be purchased only from the company, the United Shoe Machinery Co. also inserted certain tying clauses in its leases for its fundamental, so-called bottoming machines, requiring (1) that the lessee utilize these machines solely in finishing the shoes upon which certain intermediate manufacturing processes had been done on other machines leased to him by United, (2) that the lessee use these machines to their full capacity, and (3) that the lessee pay to United a royalty for each pair of shoes on which the soles had been welted or stitched by machine, without regard to whether United's machinery had been utilized in their manufacture. The lease also provided that the failure of the lessee to use exclusively certain classes of machinery leased to him by United would constitute grounds for immediate termination of the leases, and that, upon termination of the leases, the lessee would be further obligated to pay United the sum of $150 per machine returned. These provisions, coupled with United's lease-only policy on its machinery and its efforts to buy out competing manufacturers of shoe machinery and to buy up new shoe machinery patents from independent inventors, had by 1911 given

---

[5.34] *See, e.g.,* discussion of President Wilson's support for the Federal Reserve Act in A. MASON, BRANDEIS: A FREE MAN'S LIFE 397-99 (1946).

[5.35] *See* INVESTIGATION OF UNITED STATES STEEL CORP., H.R. REP. NO. 1127, 62d Cong., 2d Sess. (1912); *Hearings Before the Special Comm. to Investigate Violations of the Antitrust Act of 1890 and Other Acts,* 62d Cong., 2d Sess. (1912) (8 pts.).

[5.36] *Hearings on H.R. 11380, H.R. 11381, H.R. 15926, and H.R. 19959 Before the House Comm. on the Judiciary,* 62d Cong., 2d Sess. (1912) [hereinafter cited as *Hearings on H.R. 11380*], discussed *infra* at 997-99; *Hearings Pursuant to S. Res. 98 Before the Senate Comm. on Interstate Commerce,* 62d Cong., 3d Sess. (1913) [hereinafter cited as *Hearings Pursuant to S. Res. 98*], discussed *infra* at 999-1000; and *Hearings on Trust Legislation Before the House Comm. on the Judiciary,* 63d Cong., 2d Sess. (1914) [hereinafter cited as *1914 House Hearings*], discussed *infra* at 1000-03.

[5.37] Some measure of Brandeis' effectiveness in these hearings and other matters can be gauged from the severity and rancor of the attacks made on him by businessmen and prominent lawyers following his nomination by President Wilson to the Supreme Court in 1916. Confirmation hearings on his appointment lasted four months, from his nomination on January 28, 1916, to a vote on June 1, 1916, when he was confirmed, 47-22. Brandeis took the oath of office as an Associate Justice on June 5, 1916, and served until his retirement on February 13, 1939, at age 82. For a good description of the nomination fight see A. MASON, *supra* note 5.34, chs. 30-31, at 465-508.

[5.38] Brandeis' relationship with these companies was uncharacteristic and placed him in the compromising position of supporting the shoe machinery trust as a "good" monopoly while otherwise opposing monopoly as repugnant to the American way of life. A. MASON, *supra* note 5.34, at 214. This former relationship was to come back and haunt Brandeis during the 1911-1914 trust legislation hearings, where he roundly attacked the monopolistic practices of this trust, and in the 1916 hearings on his confirmation as an Associate Justice of the Supreme Court. Copies of highly critical and factually misleading correspondence concerning Brandeis from the president of the United Shoe Machinery Co. were incorporated at several points in the three trust hearings from 1911-1914, cited at note 5.36 *supra.*

[5.39] Representative extracts from a United Shoe Machinery Co. lease from this period are reproduced *infra* at 1071-73.

[5.40] *See* Clayton Act § 3.

the company a virtual monopoly over the manufacture of shoe machinery in the United States.[5.41]

Although it appears clear that United's initial incentive for the adoption of its lease-only system was to foster competition among shoe manufacturers (by encouraging and permitting a new company to enter the business at no capital expense for the essential machinery), this policy led directly to the establishment of monopoly power by United in the manufacture of shoe machinery, with disastrous consequences for competition in that industry. After extensively reviewing United's leasing practices in the latter part of 1906, Brandeis determined to resign as a director in December of that year, and following a series of conferences early in January 1907 at which the company declined to accept his recommendation against continued use of these methods, Brandeis ceased to act as counsel for the company.[5.42] Responding to the activities of United between 1906 and 1911, Brandeis determined in 1911 to mount an attack upon these methods during the congressional hearings on trust legislation.[5.43]

Further impetus for legislation to bar tying contracts was provided in 1912 by the Supreme Court's decision in the *A. B. Dick Co.* case. [5.44] In that case, the issue was the legality of a patentee's practice of licensing his patented duplicating machine for use only with inks, stencils, and supplies of the patentee's own manufacture. The opinion in this case pointed out that such licensing provisions were lawful under the existing patent laws and expressed the opinion that only Congress had the power to change the law to make such practices illegal.[5.45] This precedent also received prominent attention during the Clayton Act debates in 1914.[5.46]

Two other cases decided under the Sherman Act in 1911 and 1913 concerning the legality of manufacturers' efforts to maintain minimum retail prices upon trademarked products also figured prominently in testimony during the hearings on trust legislation, and many witnesses advocated passage of fair-trade legislation, but no provisions relative to this topic were ultimately incorporated in the Clayton Act. The first of these cases, *Dr. Miles Medical Co. v. John D. Park & Sons Co.*, involved a complicated price maintenance scheme which operated after the manufacturer had parted with dominion and risk of loss over his trademarked goods;[5.47] the second case, known as the

---

[5.41] According to testimony given by Mr. Charles H. Jones, President of the Commonwealth Shoe & Leather Co., Boston, Mass., during the *Hearings Pursuant to S. Res. 98, supra* note 5.36, the government's bill of equity filed against the United Shoe Machinery Co. in December 1911 alleged that that company then controlled more than 98% of the manufacture, sale, and lease of all the essential and auxiliary shoe manufacturing machines and devices. *Id.* at 2258; *cf.* United States v. United Shoe Mach. Co., 247 U.S. 37, 38 S. Ct. 473, 62 L. Ed. 968 (1918).

[5.42] Letter from Louis D. Brandeis to Hon. Moses E. Clapp, Chairman, Senate Committee on Interstate Commerce, Feb. 24, 1912. Reproduced in *Hearings Pursuant to S. Res. 98, supra* note 5.36, at 2615, and in *Hearings on H.R. 11380, supra* note 5.36, ser. 2 and 3, app. at 17.

[5.43] Brandeis appeared at both the Senate and House hearings of 1911-1913 cited at note 5.36 *supra*. He explained his representation thus: "I represent primarily myself, Mr. Chairman, but I have also acted for a certain number of gentlemen known as the Shoe Manufacturers' Alliance." *Hearings on H.R. 11380, supra* note 5.36, ser. 2, at 13.

[5.44] Henry v. A.B. Dick Co., 224 U.S. 1, 32 S. Ct. 364, 56 L. Ed. 645 (1912).

[5.45] 224 U.S. at 35. The Court summed up the issue as follows:
> . . . It must not be forgotten that we are dealing with a constitutional and statutory monopoly. An attack upon the rights under a patent because it secures a monopoly to make, to sell, and to use, is an attack upon the whole patent system. We are not at liberty to say that the Constitution has unwisely provided for granting a monopolistic right to inventors, or that Congress has unwisely failed to impose limitations upon the inventor's exclusive right to use. And if it be that the ingenuity of patentees in devising ways in which to reap the benefit of their discoveries requires to be restrained, Congress alone has the power to determine what restraint shall be imposed. As the law now stands it contains none, and the duty which rests upon this and upon every other court is to expound the law as it is written. Arguments based upon suggestions of public policy not recognized in the patent laws are not relevant. The field to which we are invited by such arguments is legislative, not judicial. The decisions of this court, as we have construed them, do not so limit the privilege of the patentee, and we could not so restrict a patent grant without overruling the long line of judicial decisions from circuit courts and circuit courts of appeal, heretofore cited, thus inflicting disastrous results upon individuals who have made large investments in reliance upon them.

Id.

[5.46] *See, e.g.,* 51 CONG. REC. 14091-95, 14200-03 (1914), *infra* at 1992-2001, 2012-20.

[5.47] 220 U.S. 373, 31 S. Ct. 376, 55 L. Ed. 502 (1911).

Sanatogen case, involved the attempt by the manufacturer of a patented product to utilize a license notice on the package to effect resale price control.[5.48]

Early Congressional Efforts to Strengthen the Sherman Act

In 1900 Congress reacted to the *Knight* case[5.49] by considering, among other things, a joint resolution proposing a constitutional amendment giving the Congress full power to regulate any corporation engaged in interstate commerce, through the creation of a federal incorporation system.[5.50] In addition to this proposed constitutional amendment, the Republican majority in the House also reported favorably a bill to amend the Sherman Act, first, by providing heavier mandatory penalties and mandatory terms of imprisonment in criminal cases, and second, by adding new provisions to bar trust goods from interstate transportation, to deny the use of the mails to convicted combinations, to penalize any common carrier which knowingly transported the goods of a trust, to grant broader subpoena powers in both civil and criminal cases, and to invest private citizens with the right to proceed against combinations on behalf of the government.[5.51]

Both of these legislative proposals were responsive to the Supreme Court's distinction in the *Knight* case between the local manufacture of goods and the distribution of manufactured products in interstate commerce, only the latter of which was held subject to congressional authority under the commerce clause. The committee report on the joint resolution[5.52] in particular was written under the Republican majority's assumption that the *Knight* case had unequivocally announced the rule that manufacturing was a purely local function, amenable to control by the states alone under the reservation of powers clause contained in article 10 of the Bill of Rights.[5.53] According to this analysis, Congress had virtually exhausted its powers to regulate corporations under the commerce clause, and a constitutional amendment was therefore necessary if Congress was to reach all corporate activities that might affect interstate commerce.

The Democratic minority strongly protested that the proposed constitutional amendment was both not necessary to reach the trusts effectively and that it would, if adopted, unnecessarily interfere with and supersede the states' right to control corporations within their borders. During the debates on the joint resolution, Representative Henry D. Clayton (D., Ala.) maintained that what was needed instead was effective enforcement of the Sherman Act. He complained:

> The Attorney-General can see no difference between ordinary business and an act which was a crime at common-law and has remained a crime for centuries. If larceny were treated as a matter of ordinary business, it would be very difficult to deal with it. If these crimes against trade are treated as matters of ordinary business, then it is impossible to stop them. If the Attorney-General would quit treating these illegal acts as affairs of ordinary business and treat them as serious offenses, which the law declares them to be, the trouble of enforcing the law would be at an end.[5.54]

The joint resolution ultimately failed on a vote of 154 in favor, 132 opposed—less than the required two-thirds majority.[5.55]

Although criticized by the Democrats as not going far enough, the companion bill

---

[5.48] Bauer & Cie v. O'Donnell, 229 U.S. 1, 35 S. Ct. 616, 57 L. Ed. 1041 (1913). Legislation permitting creation of state fair-trade laws was ultimately enacted in 1937 as the Miller-Tydings Resale Price Maintenance Act. The Miller-Tydings Act was repealed in 1975. See chapter 2 for a discussion of this later legislation.

[5.49] United States v. E.C. Knight Co., 156 U.S. 1 (1895).

[5.50] H.R.J. Res. 138, 56th Cong., 1st Sess. (introduced by Representative Jenkins (R., Wis.) on Jan. 26, 1900). See also H.R. REP. No. 1501, 56th Cong., 1st Sess. (May 15, 1900).

[5.51] H.R. 10539, 56th Cong., 1st Sess. (introduced by Representative Littlefield (R., Me.) on April 7, 1900). See also H.R. REP. No. 1506, 56th Cong., 1st Sess. (1900).

[5.52] H.R. REP. No. 1501, *supra* note 5.50.

[5.53] U.S. CONST. amend. X.

[5.54] 33 CONG. REC. A330 (1900).

[5.55] *Id.* at 6426.

was ultimately approved by the House on June 2, 1900, by the overwhelming vote of 274 to 1.[5.56] The bill reached the Senate on June 5, just prior to adjournment, and the Senate voted to refer the bill to the Senate Judiciary Committee.[5.57] Finally, on March 2, 1901, Senator James K. Jones (D., Ark.) submitted a resolution that the Judiciary Committee be discharged from further consideration of this bill and that the Senate proceed to its consideration. His resolution was rejected and the bill was not subsequently reported for consideration by the Senate.[5.58]

With the decision of the Supreme Court in the *Northern Securities* case in 1904, the unfortunate precedential effect of the *Knight* case was removed, and the pressures in Congress for reform or amendment of the Sherman Act remained relatively quiescent until 1911. Nevertheless, between 1908 and the announcement of the Supreme Court's decision in the *Standard Oil* case in 1911,[5.59] several bills were introduced proposing that the Sherman Act be amended so as not in the future to "be construed or held to prohibit any contract, agreement, or combination that is not in *unreasonable restraint* of trade or commerce with foreign nations or among the several States."[5.60]

CONGRESSIONAL ACTION

The Sixty-second Congress

House Hearings on Trust Legislation, 1912

Shortly after the Supreme Court's announcement of its decision in the *Standard Oil* case in 1911,[5.61] pressure to strengthen the Sherman Act revived and culminated initially in the introduction by Senator Robert M. La Follette (R., Wis.) on August 19, 1911, of a bill to supplement the antitrust law.[5.62] A companion bill was introduced in the House on December 15, 1911, by Representative Irvine L. Lenroot (R., Wis.),[5.63] and an amended successor bill was introduced by Senator La Follette on January 30, 1912, shortly after the beginning of the second session of the 62d Congress.[5.64]

The facts surrounding the drafting and introduction of these proposals make clear that they constituted an integrated and coordinated legislative effort to strengthen and make more effective the existing antitrust law. Testimony provided by Louis D. Brandeis before the House Judiciary Committee during hearings on trust legislation in 1912 provides essential background information on this legislation.[5.65] According to Brandeis' testimony, Senator La Follette called a conference of 10 to 15 persons in May of 1911 to discuss the need for trust legislation in the aftermath of the *Standard Oil* decision.[5.66]

In response to Chairman Clayton's assertion during these hearings that Brandeis was the author of the pending legislation, Mr. Brandeis stated:

> Just one word which I wanted to say to avoid any misapprehension as to the chairman's statement as to the authorship of the bill. This bill did not in the proper sense originate with me. It originated in this way: Shortly after the Standard Oil decision, Senator La Follette called

---

[5.56] *Id.* at 6502.

[5.57] *Id.* at 6670.

[5.58] 34 CONG. REC. 3438-39 (1901).

[5.59] Standard Oil Co. v. United States, 221 U.S. 1, 31 S. Ct. 502, 55 L. Ed. 619 (1911). Portions of this decision are reprinted *supra* at chapter 1.

[5.60] S. 6331, 60th Cong., 1st Sess. (introduced by Senator Joseph B. Foraker (R., Ohio) on March 25, 1908) (emphasis added). Other bills introduced contained substantially identical provisions.

[5.61] Standard Oil Co. v. United States, 221 U.S. 1 (decided May 15, 1911).

[5.62] S. 3276, 62d Cong., 1st Sess. (1911).

[5.63] H.R. 15926, 62d Cong., 2d Sess. (1911).

[5.64] S. 4931, 62d Cong., 2d Sess. (1912).

[5.65] *Hearings on H.R. 11380, supra* note 5.36, ser. 2, at 104-05, 129-30.

[5.66] *Id.* at 129-30. The following individuals were listed as having attended this conference: Senators La Follette, Clapp, and Bourne; Representative Lenroot; Brandeis; Mr. Gifford Pinchot; and several others from Philadelphia and Washington.

a conference of quite a very large number of gentlemen, Members of both Houses of Congress, and quite a number of whom were not and to which I was invited, to consider what further legislation, if any, ought to be drafted in view of the decision of the Supreme Court. At that conference views were expressed by a number of persons, including myself; and Mr. Lenroot, and I were asked by the conference to submit to the conference a draft for consideration. That was afterwards taken up with Senator La Follette, and there were many conferences with many people at that time, and what is now embodied in the Lenroot bill plus those additional provisions which I referred to, are the outgrowth of that conference and of the contributions in thought and suggestions of a very large number of people, and I do not want to have it appear upon this record, in view of what the chairman said, that I had been alone the author or responsible for the outcome.[5.67]

The following colloquy later ensued:

Mr. BRANDEIS. . . .
I had known nothing about the conference at all, except that I received word from Senator La Follette that he wanted to consider the question of proper trust legislation in the face of the Supreme Court decisions and various questions in Congress at that time, and there were 10 or 15 persons whom—I do not know just why; some, perhaps, happened to be here. I had been asked specially to come to consider some questions in regard to the trust law. I knew nothing of the conference.

Mr. HOWLAND. It had no political significance?

Mr. BRANDEIS. Absolutely none. The question was how to deal with this matter. Some businessmen and some Members of Congress were discussing it. Either then or soon afterwards Francis J. Heeney and then Senator La Follette and I sat down to try the first draft of the bill. I happened to see Mr. Heeney on the street and I said I wished he would look it over.

The CHAIRMAN. The committee are very much obliged to you, Mr. Brandeis.

Mr. BRANDEIS. Quite a lot of others and a little later a good many people were consulted in regard to the measure, and made suggestions that were of value. The last provisions were prepared as the result of the questions which were put to me by Senator Townsend when I appeared before the Senate Committee on Interstate Commerce.

Mr. HIGGINS. You finally resolved in favor of this bill?

Mr. BRANDEIS. I can not say everybody agreed to it—not to the bill in its present shape. The bill is one of growth, certain provisions of which were introduced by Senator La Follette in August and others that were introduced by him in December, and still others were prepared and submitted in January. It was a matter of development and thought and change; many of the provisions were changed.[5.68]

The general provisions of this proposed legislation had been put into roughly final form by the end of January 1912. The bills proposed to leave the Sherman Act unchanged and supplement it by adding new sections 9 through 19. As proposed, section 9 would have changed the burden of proof in restraint cases from the government to the defendant. Once the existence of a restraint on commerce had been established, the defendant would have had the burden of proving that restraint to be reasonable.

Section 10 provided for the establishment of nine separate categories of trade practices "conclusively deemed to have been or to be unreasonable."

Section 11 provided that where any corporation represented 40 percent or more of a particular industry and was involved in a restraint of commerce, a rebuttable presumption would arise that such restraint had been or was unreasonable.

Section 12 provided that final judgments in favor of the government concerning the existence of an unlawful restraint of commerce or unlawful monopoly would constitute conclusive evidence as to the same issues of law in favor of a private party injured by the combination.

Section 13 gave to private parties the right to intervene in government cases for the purpose of recovering the damages they had sustained.

Section 14 provided a new statute of limitations for private actions under the Sherman Act, permitting such actions to be filed within three years after a final decree or judgment had been entered in favor of the government.

[5.67] *Id.* at 104-05.

[5.68] *Id.* at 129-30. Mr. Brandeis' appearance before the Senate Interstate Commerce Committee has been memorialized in *Hearings Pursuant to S. Res. 98, supra* note 5.36, and his colloquy with Senator Townsend is found at 1265-67. These hearings are discussed *infra* at 999-1000.

Section 15 provided that when a combination found to have been unlawful controlled the market in some essential article for which no other article was reasonably substitutable, the court would be empowered to require the combination to continue furnishing the articles under reasonable conditions.

Section 16 specified in detail that a combination found to be unlawful in a government civil action was subject to having its property partitioned by a court, which might further prescribe conditions for dissolution of the unlawful combination.

Section 17 granted to private parties and to the states the right to intervene on their own behalf in any government suit and to seek redress from the court upon a finding of violation of the Sherman Act.

Section 18 prohibited the United States from dealing with any combination against which a government action had commenced, except in cases of necessity.

Finally, section 19 provided that any patent used in violation of the Act would be forfeited to the United States and annulled.

None of these bills were enacted. Following the election of President Wilson in 1912, the new Democratic majority in Congress devoted its major legislative efforts during 1913 to passage of the Federal Reserve Act[5.69] and to reduction of the protective tariffs.[5.70]

Senate Hearings on Trust Legislation, 1911–1913

On July 26, 1911, the Senate adopted a resolution authorizing and directing its Committee on Interstate Commerce to conduct an investigation as to what changes were necessary or desirable in the laws relating to control over corporations engaged in interstate commerce.[5.71] Acting pursuant to this resolution, the Senate Interstate Commerce Committee commenced hearings on August 4, 1911, and filed its report with the Senate on February 26, 1913.[5.72]

The Senate committee's concern with the decision of the Supreme Court in the *Standard Oil* case is best summarized in the following statement from the committee's report:

The fair conclusion is that it is now the settled doctrine of the Supreme Court that only undue or unreasonable restraints of trade are made unlawful by the anti-trust act, and that in each instance it is for the court to determine whether the established restraint of trade is a due restraint or an undue restraint.

Whatever may be the opinion of the several members of the committee with respect to the soundness of the rule as now established, the committee as a whole accepts it as the present law of the land. It is profoundly convinced that, in view of the rule and its necessary effect upon the business of the country, the inherent rights of the people, and upon the execution of the statute it has become imperative to enact additional legislation.

The committee has full confidence in the integrity, intelligence, and patriotism of the Supreme Court of the United States, but it is unwilling to repose in that court, or any other court, the vast and undefined power which it must exercise in the administration of the statute under the rule which is has promulgated. It substitutes the court in the place of Congress, for whenever the rule is invoked the court does not administer the law, but makes the law. If it continues in force, the Federal courts will, so far as restraint of trade is concerned, make a common law for the United States just as the English courts have made a common law for England.

The people of this country will not permit the courts to declare a policy for them with respect to this subject. If we do not promptly exercise our legislative power, the courts will suffer immeasureable injury in the loss of that respect and confidence so essential to their usefulness. It is inconceivable that in a country governed by a written Constitution and statute law the courts can be permitted to test each restraint of trade by the economic standard which the individual members of the court may happen to approve. If we do not speedily prescribe in so far as we can a legislative rule by which to measure the forms of contract and combination in restraint of trade with which we are familiar or which we can anticipate, we cease to be a

---

[5.69] Act of Dec. 23, 1913, Sess. II, ch. 6, 38 Stat. 251, *as amended*, 12 U.S.C. § 221 (1976).

[5.70] Act of Oct. 3, 1913, Sess. I, ch. 16, 38 Stat. 114.

[5.71] S. Res. 98, 62d Cong., 1st Sess., 47 CONG. REC. 2695 (1911).

[5.72] SENATE COMM. ON INTERSTATE COMMERCE, CONTROL OF CORPORATIONS, PERSONS, AND FIRMS ENGAGED IN IN-

Government of law and become a Government of men, and, moreover, of a very few men, and they appointed by the President.[5.73]

Notwithstanding this stirring call for additional legislation, and after taking testimony from more than 100 witnesses and compiling a written transcript nearly 2,800 pages in length,[5.74] the committee reported as follows:

> It is not yet ready to report any of the bills which are now before it, and which propose specific modifications of or additions to the existing statute; nor is it prepared at this time to report a substitute for them. It hopes that it may be able before the close of the present session to act finally upon these bills and recommend in definite form the legislation which it may think necessary or wise to meet modern business conditions. It is, however, prepared to answer the general inquiries propounded in the resolution, and in view of the overwhelming importance of the subject it ventures to add to the direct response some observations upon the origin, purpose, and effect of the enactment commonly known as the anti-trust law, to indicate wherein it is inadequate, and to suggest the general scope of further regulation.[5.75]

Although the La Follette bill had been specifically considered by the committee, and Louis D. Brandeis and other witnesses had testified at some length concerning that measure, the report focused primarily upon proposals looking toward the creation of a federal trade commission. Included in the materials submitted by counsel for the United Shoe Machinery Co., however, were copies of 22 form leases used by that company containing the tying clauses so important to the enactment of section 3 of the Clayton Act.[5.76]

No trust legislation was subsequently enacted in this Congress, however.

The Sixty-third Congress

House Consideration of H.R. 15657

Hearings and Introduction of the Clayton Bill. On January 20, 1914, President Wilson presented a special message before a joint session of Congress, stressing the need for certainty in the antitrust laws and endorsing the creation of an interstate trade commission.[5.77] Meanwhile, Chairman Clayton of the House Judiciary Committee had already commenced hearings on trust legislation on December 9, 1913.[5.78] On January 29, 1914, Chairman Clayton noted that this was the date the committee had set to begin consideration of the proposed antitrust measures.[5.79]

During the early course of these hearings, Chairman Clayton had committee prints of four tentative bills prepared for consideration by the committee.[5.80] In general, these bills proposed supplementing the Sherman Act with provisions: (1) to restrict price discriminations between different purchasers, (2) to bar the use of exclusive sales or dealing agreements, (3) to provide that final judgments in government cases would constitute conclusive evidence against the same defendant in a subsequent private action, (4) to permit any person to sue for injunctive relief against threatened loss by a violation of the Act, (5) to enumerate certain additional prohibited practices, (6) to impose individual guilt upon the officers of a corporation that violated the Act, (7) to prohibit certain intercorporate directorships, (8) to prohibit stock acquisitions by one

---

TERSTATE COMMERCE, S. REP. NO. 1326, 62d Cong., 3d Sess. (1913), reproduced herein in chapter 8. Although this report states that the "hearings began of the 15th day of November, 1911," *id.* at 1, the committee had held a hearing on August 4, 1911. *Hearings Pursuant to S. Res. 98, supra* note 5.36, at 1–23.

[5.73] S. REP. NO. 1326, *supra* note 5.72, at 10–11.

[5.74] *Hearings Pursuant to S. Res. 98, supra* note 5.36.

[5.75] S. REP. NO. 1326, *supra* note 5.72, at 2.

[5.76] *Hearings Pursuant to S. Res. 98, supra* note 5.36, at 2170-250. Representative extracts from one of these leases are reproduced *infra* at 1071-73.

[5.77] 51 CONG. REC. 1963 (1914), reproduced herein in chapter 8.

[5.78] *1914 House Hearings, supra* note 5.36. These hearings ultimately ran to 35 parts and comprise 2055 pages.

[5.79] *Id.* at 54.

[5.80] These bills are reproduced *infra* at 1074-80.

corporation of a competitor, and (9) to prohibit acquisition of the stock of two competing firms by a third corporation.

One important witness appearing during these hearings was Louis D. Brandeis, who had contributed materially to the drafting of the La Follette-Lenroot bills in the preceding Congress.[5.81] Although Mr. Brandeis had appeared before the same House committee in 1912 both for himself and as counsel for the Shoe Manufacturers' Alliance—an association of shoe manufacturers—his appearance in 1914, ostensibly as a private citizen, was in fact as a spokesman for the Wilson administration's antitrust program.[5.82] Since Mr. Brandeis completed his testimony on February 25, 1914—prior to the introduction of Chairman Clayton's bill, H.R. 15657[5.83]—most of the Brandeis testimony was devoted to discussion of provisions that had originally appeared in the La Follette-Lenroot bills two years earlier.

In the course of his appearance, Brandeis did advocate one new proposal: adding a provision which would make any antitrust violation by a company a complete defense to a second company in any suit against it by the first company, either on a contract or for patent infringement.[5.84] In addition, Brandeis noted his general opposition to giving an individual the right to file a bill for dissolution of an unlawful combination,[5.85] and in response to a question whether either the proposed trade commission or the Attorney General should be given the power to advise a businessman on a particular course of conduct, he replied, "I do not think it would be safe at this time to give such power either to a commission or to the Attorney General."[5.86]

Testifying in favor of his proposed provision barring the use of the federal courts to enforce contracts or patents used in violation of the Sherman Act, Brandeis made the following classic argument for the enforcement of antitrust prohibitions by creating substantial business risks for violators rather than harsh criminal penalties which the courts do not enforce:

Mr. BRANDEIS. Well, there is practically to-day a position almost of irony in the law, that here we go on with the greatest solemnity and declare a corporation illegal. It has conducted its business year in and year out within the law, and then at the end of a long proceeding we declare it illegal and say, "Do not do it again." Now, if it be, or if it should happen, that

---

[5.81] *1914 House Hearings, supra* note 5.36, at 637-95, 921-52, 1317-18.

[5.82] From October 9, 1913, until the latter part of 1914, Brandeis was also serving the government directly as Special Counsel to the Interstate Commerce Commission in the *Advance Rate* case, and on January 28, 1916, he was nominated by President Wilson to fill a vacancy on the Supreme Court. A. MASON, *supra* note 5.34, at 687.

[5.83] H.R. 15657, 63d Cong., 2d Sess. (introduced by Representative Henry D. Clayton on April 14, 1914), *infra* at 1080-88. The actual framing of this bill was done by a three-man subcommittee of the Judiciary Committee, comprised of Representatives Clayton (D., Ala.), Carlin (D., Va.), and Floyd (D., Ark.). The circumstances surrounding the framing were reported by Mr. Floyd as follows during the debates:

> . . . My colleague in the committee, Mr. VOLSTEAD, the senior member of the Judiciary Committee on the minority side, who filed a minority report, intimated last night in his speech, if he did not say it, that this bill had in some way been framed in secret. I desire to say that no bill that was ever brought into this House has been more openly considered, both by the committee and by the country at large and by everyone who desired to consider it, than has this bill. It is true that the Judiciary Committee assigned the work of framing the bill to a subcommittee composed of the chairman [Mr. CLAYTON], the gentleman from Virginia [Mr. CARLIN], and myself. We worked for hours, for days, and for weeks formulating the provisions of this measure when no one else was present, but whenever we formulated a proposition we brought it into the spotlight, laid it not only before the members of the committee but before the country. This legislation was in response to the message of the President delivered January 20, 1914.
>
> . . . When the tentative bills were first prepared they were printed and notice was issued through the press to the country, inviting criticism, and people interested in the legislation came from all parts of the country and all sections of the country and criticized various provisions in the bills and suggested amendments. We had public hearings for weeks. I want to say that many of these criticisms proved valuable to the committee; many suggestions made were finally incorporated in the bill as it was finally submitted to the House.

51 CONG. REC. 9156 (1914), *infra* at 1240.

[5.84] *1914 House Hearings, supra* note 5.36, at 669.

[5.85] *Id.* at 649-50.

[5.86] *Id.* at 677.

there had been some handicap upon that corporation as the result of its illegal conduct of its business; that it had contracts which the court would not lend its aid to enforce, or if it had patents which the court would not lend its aid to enforce because it was engaged in illegal business, it seems to me that would far more comport with the dignity of the law.

Mr. VOLSTEAD. But, is not this true, Mr. Brandeis, that a great many of those contracts might be very innocent and have no relation to the illegal business complained of? Would not this be broad enough to practically wipe them out? Now, wherever it is relieved of its illegal restraint of trade, and as a result of that a contract was entered into or depended upon an illegal act, of course, I think it would be perfectly proper—

Mr. BRANDEIS (interposing). That is true, but we are undertaking here pretty ineffectually to punish—we put in all sorts of threats which are merely threats—they do not amount to anything—to punish people with fines and imprisonment, when the fine is inconsiderable, and if it is large it is set aside and the imprisonment does not occur. We have got an idea that we ought to use the deterrent power of the court to prevent people from taking all the chances of breaking the law, and if they do it it does not do any harm. Now, if we want to put teeth into this law let us do it in a way that will amount to something. Do not let us write some penalties and imprisonments into it that will not be enforced, but let us point [out] to people that if they do business in a way where they go to the border line of illegality they are going to run some risks of loss as well as a mighty good chance of gain.[5.87]

Shortly after making this observation, Brandeis responded as follows to a hypothetical case in which the government bought products from a corporation presently being sued by the government and thereafter sought to set up the antitrust illegality provision to bar payment to the corporation:

The Government can do that with any contract because it is sovereign. What I have endeavored to accomplish in both of those provisions is this: It is to help overcome these various anomalous positions in which we are to-day in regard to the Sherman law, and have been for the last 23 or 24 years, where a man did not stand to lose anything by taking the law into his own hands or resolving doubts into his own favor and making the combination. It seems that we ought to arrange our legislation so that there would be a risk in doing these things, so that a man, in respect to the Sherman law as in respect to a great many other things, would keep away from the danger line. The question was once put to me, "Would you advise a man safely under the Sherman law?" I said, "It depends altogether upon what you mean by safely. If you point to a great precipice and ask me, 'How near can I go to the edge of that precipice without falling over?' I would have to answer, 'No, sir; I can not, for you may go near to that precipice and there may be a loose stone or a protruding root that you may stumble and go over,' but if you ask me, 'How near can I go that precipice and be safe?' I could tell you that, 'If you keep on this side of a certain line you will be absolutely safe, but in between here and there it is very dangerous and you had better not go there.' " Now, under the Sherman law as it exists to-day, men have been going near the danger line because apparently there was no danger to it. There was absolutely all the time a chance of sure winning. There was no chance of losing at all, because nothing happened except the declaration when a final decree came, "Do not do it again." That is all that happened. Now, it seems to me that what we should do in perfecting this machinery and in devising this machinery is to make it so that men should have something to lose if they take the risks and are actually found afterwards to be in the wrong.[5.88]

The last witness in these hearings was heard on April 6, 1914, but Chairman Clayton's bill was not formally introduced until eight days later.[5.89] On May 6, 1914, his bill was favorably reported, with certain amendments, by the House Committee on the Judiciary.[5.90] Among the major provisions of the bill as reported were its

---

[5.87] *Id.* at 670.

[5.88] *Id.* at 674.

[5.89] *See* note 5.83 *supra*.

[5.90] H.R. REP. No. 627, 63d Cong., 2d Sess. (1914). This report is composed of four parts: Part 1 containing the majority report (incorporating the majority reports from H.R. REPS. NOS. 612 and 613, 62d Cong., 2d Sess. (1912) relating to regulation of injunctions and procedure in contempt cases); part 2 containing one minority report (incorporating the minority reports from the same two 1912 reports referenced *supra*); and parts 3 and 4 containing two separate, additional minority reports. The 1912 materials incorporated in this report contain the most exhaustive legal analysis of injunctive and contempt powers attempted during the Clayton Act hearings and debates. The House report has been reproduced in its entirety *infra* at 1089-1163 except for its reprint of the Clayton bill as reported, which is reproduced in its original format *infra* at 1163-81.

prohibitions against certain price discriminations in commerce,[5.91] prohibitions against mineowners' arbitrary discrimination in selling the product of such mines,[5.92] prohibition against certain exclusive dealing and tying contracts,[5.93] prohibition against certain mergers by competing companies or use of holding companies to own the stock of competing companies,[5.94] and prohibitions against interlocking directorates.[5.95] Each of these provisions contained a criminal penalty against violation.[5.96]

In addition to these primary antitrust features, the bill also included provisions seeking to eliminate use of the antitrust laws in labor disputes, establishing detailed rules for the federal courts to follow in exercising their injunctive and contempt powers, and giving private parties the right to sue for injunctive relief from threatened violations of the antitrust law.[5.97] Also included to encourage private lawsuits was the important provision making a final judgment as to violation in a government case conclusive evidence in a private suit filed thereafter against the same unlawful combination.[5.98]

Action on the Wilson administration's proposals in the House was complicated by the fact that H.R. 12120, the trade commission bill,[5.99] was referred to the House Committee on Interstate Commerce and not to the Judiciary Committee, which was considering Chairman Clayton's antitrust bill, H.R. 15657.[5.100] Accordingly, although Clayton was the sponsor of both of these bills, his committee dealt solely with the question of substantive and procedural changes to the Sherman Act, and attempts to better coordinate these two proposals were deferred until the floor debates on the measures.[5.101] The House debates were conducted concurrently—but separately—and both bills were passed by the House on June 5, 1914.[5.102]

Debates (May 22–June 5, 1914). Having successfully shepherded his bill through the Judiciary Committee, having reported it to the House on May 6, 1914, and having secured a special rule for its consideration, Chairman Clayton tendered his resignation

---

[5.91] H.R. 15657 as reported by the House Committee on the Judiciary, 63d Cong., 2d Sess. § 2 (May 6, 1914). [Clayton Act § 2.]

[5.92] *Id.* at § 3. [Rejected by the Senate and not included in the Clayton Act.]

[5.93] *Id.* at § 4. [Clayton Act § 3.]

[5.94] *Id.* at § 8. [Clayton Act § 7.]

[5.95] *Id.* at § 9. [Clayton Act § 8.]

[5.96] *Id.* at §§ 2–4, 8, 9. All but section 9 provided maximum penalties of $5,000 and one year's imprisonment or both. Section 9 set its penalty at $100 for *each day* the violation continued, as well as providing for imprisonment for up to one year, or both.

[5.97] *Id.* at §§ 7, 15–23. [Clayton Act §§ 6, 14–22.]

[5.98] *Id.* at § 6. [Clayton Act § 5.]

[5.99] H.R. 12120, 63d Cong., 2d Sess. (1914). This bill was supplanted by H.R. 15613, introduced by Representative Covington (D., Md.), chairman of the House Committee on Interstate and Foreign Commerce, and reported favorably by that committee on April 14, 1914. H.R. REP. No. 533, 63d Cong., 2d Sess. (1914), *infra* at chapter 8.

[5.100] H.R. 15657, 63d Cong., 2d Sess. (1914), *infra* at 1080–88.

[5.101] Several of the minority reports contained in H.R. REP. No. 627, *supra* note 5.90, make specific and critical reference to this manner of dealing with such closely interrelated legislation. Representative of this complaint is the following statement by Representative Dick T. Morgan (R., Okla.):

In my judgment it is unfortunate that one committee should not have had exclusive judisdiction over the proposed legislation to create a Federal trade commission and all antitrust legislation. The creation of a Federal commission with certain jurisdiction over industrial corporations engaged in interstate trade will mark an epoch in our national policy in Federal control of private business. Manifestly all legislation for the supervision, regulation, and control of private business engaged in interstate commerce will and should center in and around the national commission, whether its jurisdiction and power be great or small. So it seems to me, if the Sherman law is to be amended, the new statutory provisions should be drawn with the trade commission and its power in view. Because we are entering upon a new field of Federal activity in the control of private business; all our enactments should be suited to our new enforcing agency—the proposed Federal commission. But over this proposed legislation the Judiciary Committee has no jurisdiction, and it is not proper for me to discuss any of the provisions relative thereto.

Id., pt. 4, at 5, *infra* at 1162–63.

[5.102] 51 CONG. REC. 9910–11 (1914), *infra* at 1739–42. H.R. 15613 (the trade commission bill) was passed on a voice vote, H.R. 15657 on a rollcall, by 277 to 54.

to the House, effective May 25, 1914,[5.103] to accept appointment as a federal district court judge for the Northern and Middle Districts of Alabama. The House accordingly took up consideration of H.R. 15657 on May 22, 1914, with Representative Edwin Y. Webb (D., N.C.) serving as its floor manager in his capacity as the new chairman of the Judiciary Committee.[5.104]

Under the procedure adopted, the House resolved itself into the Committee of the Whole House on the State of the Union for consideration of this legislation. General debate on the Clayton bill took place until May 26, 1914, when section 1 of the bill was first read for amendment.[5.105]

Opening the general debate on May 22, 1914, Representative Webb presented an overview of the bill and its intent, concluding with a statement on the contempt power of federal judges and Congress' power to regulate it.[5.106] Representative Andrew J. Volstead (R., Minn.), who had charge of scheduling the minority's time, followed with a general statement opposing the legislation.[5.107]

Continuing the general debate on May 23, 1914, Representative John C. Floyd (D., Ark.), one of the three framers of the bill, offered detailed comments on sections 2 and 4, which concerned price discrimination and exclusive dealing and tying contracts.[5.108] During his presentation, Representative George C. Scott (R., Iowa) raised an important question regarding the provisions in section 5 relating to the conclusive effect on subsequent private party litigants of a judgment granted in a government case. Floyd conceded that under this provision the judgment, whether favorable or unfavorable to the government, would be conclusive as to the private party suing upon the same facts. In response to Scott's question concerning interference with the constitutional rights of private parties, Floyd asked that the question be passed and debated later under the five-minute rule.[5.109]

Following a general statement by Representative John M. Nelson (R., Wis.), who opposed the bill on the grounds that it would not help the small businessman and would not hinder private monopoly,[5.110] Representative Isaac R. Sherwood (D., Ohio) offered a detailed discussion of the treatment of labor organizations under the Sherman Act, concluding with a tabulation of 101 cases in which federal judges had issued injunctions against labor organizations.[5.111]

Foreshadowing the ultimate rejection of section 3 concerning limitations upon a mineowner's right to sell the products of his mine, Representative Samuel B. Avis (R., W. Va.) delivered a strong attack on this proposed section, arguing that it raised constitutional issues concerning impairment of contracts and fifth amendment rights.[5.112]

The final statement of the day was made by Representative Clement C. Dickinson (D., Mo.), who requested that the jurisdictional provisions in section 10 relating to

---

[5.103] 51 CONG. REC. 9195 (1914). During the Senate debates on this bill, Senator James A. Reed (D., Mo.) made the following statement in discussing the House bill:

> I call your attention now to another thing. It was stated publicly that Congressman Clayton, who was appointed to a high judicial position, would not take his office because, at the request of the President, he chose to remain in his seat in Congress long enough to perfect this particular bill, and he sat there as the representative of the President—at least as the man in whom the President had special confidence—for some considerable time after his appointment to the bench, in order that he might complete this work and bring it here to Congress. He therefore was one of the men speaking, I think, for the President, who, in pursuit of the President's express recommendation, singled out certain practices that were well known and sought to meet those practices by a specific statutory provision.

Id. at 14268, infra at 2118.

[5.104] 51 CONG. REC. 9068, 9073 (1914), infra at 1182, 1192.

[5.105] Id. at 9273, infra at 1390.

[5.106] Id. at 9068-77, infra at 1182-1201.

[5.107] Id. at 9077-81, infra at 1201-09.

[5.108] Id. at 9156-66, infra at 1240-63.

[5.109] Id. at 9164-65, infra at 1258-59.

[5.110] Id. at 9166-70, infra at 1263-72.

[5.111] Id. at 9171-74, infra at 1272-81.

[5.112] Id. at 9175-80, infra at 1284-94.

corporations be broadened further to permit an injured private citizen to sue wherever a corporation committed a wrong or had an agent, officer, or employee.[5.113]

Debate resumed on May 25, 1914, with discussion of the provisions of section 2 relating to price discriminations.[5.114]

On May 26, 1914, the final day of general debate on the Clayton bill, Representatives William J. MacDonald (Prog., Mich.) and James M. Graham (D., Ill.) opened the debate with a further discussion of the need of labor for an exemption from the Sherman Act.[5.115] Representative Charles C. Carlin (D., Va.), another framer of the Clayton bill, closed the general debate with a fairly detailed statement concerning the objects of the various provisions contained in the bill.[5.116]

Although the reading of the bill for amendment commenced on May 26, 1914, the Committee of the Whole rose immediately after the reading of section 1 and no amendments were considered on that day.[5.117] When debate resumed on May 28, 1914, Representative Dick T. Morgan (R., Okla.), who believed that the bill would unnecessarily impede small business, offered an amendment to section 1 which would have exempted organizations having an aggregate capital of less than $5 million from the prohibitions of sections 2, 4, and 8 of the bill.[5.118] This amendment was opposed by Mr. Floyd and was rejected on a voice vote.[5.119]

Following the reading of section 2, relating to price discriminations, 12 separate amendments were offered and 11 were rejected. The one amendment accepted was to eliminate a split infinitive in the first sentence of the section.[5.120] Among the amendments rejected was one by Representative George S. Graham (R., Pa.) which would have exempted price discrimination made "in lawfully meeting competition."[5.121] Nevertheless, such a "meeting competition" defense was ultimately incorporated in section 2 of the Clayton Act.[5.122]

Because section 3 of the bill, relating to the sale of mine products, was not ultimately included in the Clayton Act or any other subsequent legislation, the further debates and amendments relating to this section are not discussed herein.[5.123]

After the reading of section 4, relating to exclusive dealing practices, Representative Walter I. McCoy (D., N.J.) proposed an amendment to limit the prohibition to those transactions made "with the intent of obtaining or establishing a monopoly or of destroying the business of a competitor."[5.124] Although his amendment was defeated after extensive discussion concerning the need for this provision, this section was ultimately modified to incorporate a similar provision during the Senate-House conference to resolve differences between the bills as originally passed in the separate Houses.[5.125] One amendment was accepted, broadening the phrase "condition or understanding" to read "condition, agreement or understanding."[5.126]

Representative Dickinson proposed the final amendment of the day, to add, in section 5 (the jurisdiction provision), after the words "in which the defendant resides

---

[5.113] *Id.* at 9189-90, *infra* at 1314-16.

[5.114] *Id.* at 9195-202, *infra* at 1317-30.

[5.115] *Id.* at 9245-52, *infra* at 1330-46.

[5.116] *Id.* at 9268-73, *infra* at 1380-89.

[5.117] *Id.* at 9273, *infra* at 1389-90.

[5.118] *Id.* at 9388, *infra* at 1390.

[5.119] *Id.* at 9389, *infra* at 1391.

[5.120] *Id.* at 9389-96, *infra* at 1391-1406. The amendment of Representative Gardner (R., Mass.), which was accepted, changed the words "to thereby destroy" to "thereby to destroy." *Id.* at 9393, *infra* at 1400.

[5.121] *Id.* at 9389-91, *infra* at 1392-95.

[5.122] See discussion *infra* at 1014.

[5.123] Portions of the debates relating to section 3 are reproduced in full herein, however, in the interest of comprehensiveness and completeness.

[5.124] 51 CONG. REC. 9398-410 (1914), *infra* at 1410-32.

[5.125] See discussion *infra* at 1019-20, 1021-22.

[5.126] 51 CONG. REC. 9411 (1914), *infra* at 1434.

or is found," the words "doing business and the cause of action may accrue."[5.127] Extensive discussion on this topic ensued, carrying over into the next day's debates.[5.128] On May 29, 1914, Mr. Dickinson withdrew his amendment to permit Mr. Floyd to offer a committee amendment adding the words "or has an agent" after the word "found," and this amendment was adopted.[5.129]

After the reading of section 6, Representative Volstead, in response to the earlier suggestion of Mr. Scott, offered an amendment to change this section so that only final judgments in favor of the government would be conclusive evidence in a later suit on the same facts by a private party.[5.130] After extensive discussion and debate, his amendment was accepted.[5.131]

Although debates on section 7, relating to the labor exemption, commenced on May 29, 1914,[5.132] most of the debates on this section took place three days later, on June 1.[5.133] The only amendment to this section ultimately accepted by the House was one proposed by Chairman Webb of the Judiciary Committee at the request of several members, to make clear that Congress intended to exempt labor organizations from the operation of the antitrust laws.[5.134] This amendment added the following language to the first paragraph of section 7: "Nor shall such organizations, orders, or associations, or members thereof, be held or construed to be illegal combinations or conspiracies in restraint of trade under the antitrust laws." The final vote on this amendment was 207 in favor and none opposed.[5.135]

No amendments to section 8 were accepted, although several were debated.[5.136]

Several amendments were offered immediately following the reading of section 9.[5.137] Of these, only one was accepted, changing the civil penalty from "$100 a day" to "not exceeding $100 a day."[5.138]

After amending section 10, dealing with corporate jurisdiction, by adding the words "or has an agent,"[5.139] and some debate on sections 12, 15, 17, and 18, further debate was carried over until the next day.

On June 2, following the debate on section 18, Representative William A. Cullop (D., Ind.) offered an amendment to add a new section 18a, which would have granted concurrent jurisdiction to the state courts for actions arising under the Clayton bill. This proposal was debated at some length and only narrowly rejected by a vote of 32 in favor, 34 opposed.[5.140]

After the reading of section 20, dealing with the procedure to be followed in contempt cases, the purpose and intent of this provision was discussed at some length.[5.141] During this debate, Representative James W. Bryan (Prog., Wash.) offered an amendment which would have barred trial of the contempt by the judge whose injunction or order had been disobeyed.[5.142] In urging rejection of this amendment, Mr. Webb expressed the opinion that section 23 of the Judicial Code already provided for the nondiscretionary removal of a judge upon the filing by a party of an affidavit "that the judge before whom the action or proceeding is to be tried or heard has a personal

---

[5.127] *Id.* at 9414, *infra* at 1440-41.

[5.128] *Id.* at 9414-17, 9466, *infra* at 1441-49.

[5.129] *Id.* at 9466-67, *infra* at 1449-52.

[5.130] *Id.* at 9487, *infra* at 1487.

[5.131] *Id.* at 9487-95, *infra* at 1487-1503.

[5.132] *Id.* at 9495-96, *infra* at 1504-06.

[5.133] *Id.* at 9538-86, *infra* at 1506-1610.

[5.134] *Id.* at 9538-66, *infra* at 1506-68.

[5.135] *Id.* at 9566, *infra* at 1568.

[5.136] *Id.* at 9591-600, *infra* at 1620-36.

[5.137] *Id.* at 9600-07, *infra* at 1636-51.

[5.138] *Id.* at 9606-07, *infra* at 1650.

[5.139] *Id.* at 9607, *infra* at 1651-52.

[5.140] *Id.* at 9662-64, *infra* at 1682-86.

[5.141] *Id.* at 9664-68, *infra* at 1686-95.

[5.142] *Id.* at 9666, *infra* at 1689.

bias or prejudice either against him or in favor of any opposite party to the suit."[5.143] Upon receiving this assurance, Mr. Bryan withdrew his amendment.[5.144]

After the entire bill had been read for amendment the first time, Representative Dick T. Morgan offered a new section 24, under which a corporation possessing a virtual monopoly in the sale of any commodity would, upon court order, be subject to being treated as a "quasi-public corporation and made subject to the control of the Commissioner of Corporations or . . . [his] successor . . . , in all its practices, prices, and charges."[5.145] After a brief debate, the amendment was rejected.[5.146]

Following acceptance of two corrective amendments to section 9 offered by the committee,[5.147] a further committee amendment to section 11 was adopted, providing the following limitation on the scope of the subpoena power accorded by it:

Provided, That no writ of subpoena shall be issued to run for more than 100 miles from the trial court without the permission of the court being first had, upon proper application, and cause shown.[5.148]

Debate was again resumed on section 12, which had been passed over previously. As reported by the committee, this section read as follows:

SEC. 12. That whenever a corporation shall be guilty of the violation of any of the provisions of the antitrust laws, the offense shall be deemed to be also that of the individual directors, officers, or agents of such corporation; and upon the conviction of the corporation any director, officer, or agent who shall have authorized, ordered, or done any of such prohibited acts shall be deemed guilty of a misdemeanor, . . .

As the ensuing series of amendments and substitutes and amendments to amendments made clear, there was substantial consensus that the original language would require the actual conviction of the corporation itself before the officers of the corporation could be convicted for acts in violation of the antitrust laws.[5.149]

The House resolved this issue by accepting Representative Lenroot's amendment to the committee amendment, changing the language of the bill to read as follows:

That whenever a corporation shall violate any of the provisions of the antitrust laws, such violation shall be deemed to be also that of the individual directors, officers, or agents of such corporation who shall have authorized, ordered, or done any of the acts constituting in whole or in part such violation, and shall be deemed a misdemeanor; and upon conviction therefor of any such director, officer, or agent he shall be punished by a fine of not exceeding $5,000 or by imprisonment for not exceeding one year, or by both, in the discretion of the court.[5.150]

The final amendment offered and accepted corrected the earlier amendment to section 11 to provide that the 100-mile limit on the scope of the subpoena applied to persons residing outside the district, and that subpoenas would continue to issue to any person residing within the district, without regard to the number of miles from his residence to the trial court.[5.151] Mr. Webb's motion that the bill as amended be laid aside with a favorable recommendation was agreed to.[5.152]

On Friday, June 5, 1914, the bill as amended in the debates was called up for a vote immediately following the favorable vote on the trade commission bill. The Clayton bill was passed on a rollcall vote, 277 votes in favor, 54 opposed, 3 "present," and 99 not voting.[5.153]

[5.143] *Id.* at 9667-68, *infra* at 1693.
[5.144] *Id.* at 9668, *infra* at 1694.
[5.145] *Id.* at 9672, *infra* at 1703-04.
[5.146] *Id.* at 9674, *infra* at 1708.
[5.147] *Id.* at 9674-75, *infra* at 1708.
[5.148] *Id.* at 9675, *infra* at 1709-10.
[5.149] *Id.* at 9675-82, *infra* at 1710-23.
[5.150] *Id.* at 9681-82, *infra* at 1721-23.
[5.151] *Id.* at 9682, *infra* at 1724-25.
[5.152] *Id., infra* at 1725.
[5.153] *Id.* at 9911, *infra* at 1739-41.

H.R. 15657 as Reported by the Senate Committee on the Judiciary

On July 22, 1914, Chairman Charles A. Culberson (D., Tex.) of the Senate Committee on the Judiciary submitted his committee's report on the Clayton bill.[5.154] The report sums up the purpose of this proposed legislation as follows:

> It is well, at the outset, to state the theory of the bill, both as it passed the House of Representatives and as it is proposed to be amended, for the general scope of the House measure is unchanged. It is not proposed by the bill or amendments to alter, amend, or change in any respect the original Sherman Antitrust Act of July 2, 1890. The purpose is only to supplement that Act and the other antitrust acts referred to in section 1 of the bill. Broadly stated, the bill, in its treatment of unlawful restraints and monopolies, seeks to prohibit and make unlawful certain trade practices which, as a rule, singly and in themselves, are not covered by the Act of July 2, 1890, or other existing antitrust acts, and thus, by making these practices illegal, to arrest the creation of trusts, conspiracies, and monopolies in their incipiency and before consummation.[5.155]

Before turning to discussion of this bill as reported to the Senate, a cautionary note is appropriate. Because of the Senate's rejection of original section 3 of the House bill and the addition of several intermediate sections first proposed by the Senate, the section numbers as used in this discussion will, in most cases, not be the same as the section numbers of the same provisions as they were ultimately enacted.

For ease of reference, the Senate Judiciary Committee reprinted H.R. 15657 in comparative format, with the proposed additional language shown in italics and the language proposed to be deleted shown lined through.[5.156]

As reported to the Senate, the bill proposed a number of changes from the version passed by the House on June 5. Beginning with section 1, language was added to exempt the Philippine Islands from the operation of the act in response to a request from the War Department.[5.157]

Certain language changes were proposed for section 2 to make clear that it was not intended to apply to purely local transactions. In addition, the criminal penalties were deleted, and a "discrimination in price . . . made in good faith to meet competition and not intended to create monopoly" defense was added. Finally, a proviso was added limiting the unilateral right to select customers, requiring that such selections be made "in *bona fide* transactions and not in restraint of trade."[5.158]

Section 3 was deleted in its entirety, with the following explanation:

> The proposed Senate amendment is to strike out this section altogether, because, in the opinion of the [C]ommittee, it would be unwise to enact such legislation as is contained in it. It would, primarily, deny freedom of contract to one of the parties, and consequently would be of doubtful constitutional validity. Passing from this consideration, the Committee believe that such an enactment, which would practically compel owners of the products named to sell to anyone or else decline to do so at the peril of incurring heavy penalties, would project us into a field of legislation at once untried, complicated and dangerous.[5.159]

Section 4 was amended by deleting the criminal penalty, by broadening the language to include contracts for sale as well as sales, and by adding after the word "commodities" the words "whether patented or unpatented."[5.160]

No changes to section 5 were proposed.[5.161]

5.154 S. REP. NO. 698, 63d Cong., 2d Sess. (1914), *infra* at 1744-52. Pages 2 through 42 reproduce verbatim most of the House Judiciary Committee's majority report on H.R. 15657. H.R.REP. NO. 627, 63d Cong., 2d Sess., pt. 1, 7-46 (1914), *infra* at 1089-1121, including the incorporated majority reports from H.R. REPS. NOS. 612 and 613, 62d Cong., 2d Sess. (1912), relating to regulation of injunctions and procedure in contempt cases. See note 5.90 *supra*.

5.155 S. REP. NO. 698, *supra* note 5.154, at 1.

5.156 Reproduced *infra* at 1753-67.

5.157 S. REP. NO. 698, *supra* note 5.154, at 42-43.

5.158 *Id.* at 43-44.

5.159 *Id.* at 44.

5.160 *Id.*

5.161 *Id.*

INTRODUCTION

Based upon a brief review of the constitutionality of making a judgment in a government case conclusive evidence in a subsequent private case, the committee proposed a substitute for section 6, under which a final judgment for the government would constitute prima facie evidence against the defendant in a subsequent private action. In addition, the committee proposed establishing a six-year statute of limitations for antitrust actions and incorporated the House provision tolling the statute of limitations during the pendency of a government action.[5.162]

Section 7 was changed by striking out the words "fraternal," "consumers," and "orders, or associations," as well as striking out the second paragraph in its entirety. In addition, a restriction was added making this exemption applicable only to those groups enumerated that "lawfully" carried out their activities. The committee explained its changes on the basis that the original language broadened the exemption to cover groups which should not be covered and that the language in some cases was capable of overly broad construction by the courts.[5.163]

Section 8 contained a number of minor language changes, in addition to the substantive change of deleting the criminal penalty provision.[5.164]

Section 9 was deleted in its entirety and new proposed language substituted therefor. As the committee explained, it proposed limiting this section to industrial corporations, with railroads to be regulated by the Interstate Commerce Commission, and banks and trust companies eliminated on the grounds that their regulation should be made through amendments to the national bank laws, with enforcement by the Comptroller of the Currency and the Federal Reserve Board. In addition, the general criminal penalty was deleted, with a new penalty provided for violations committed by common carriers.[5.165]

A new section 9a was added, creating a criminal penalty for any officer or director of a common carrier who unlawfully appropriated properties of such carrier.[5.166]

In place of the criminal penalties stricken from sections 2, 4, 8, and 9, the committee proposed a new section 9b, granting the authority to enforce compliance with these sections to the Interstate Commerce Commission, in the case of common carriers, and to the Federal Trade Commission in respect to all other types of organizations.[5.167]

Section 10 on jurisdiction was broadened to reach a corporation wherever it transacted any business and to provide that service of process could be had in any district where it resided or might be found.[5.168]

Section 11, dealing with subpoenas, was changed by deleting the proviso which limited the scope of subpoenas for persons residing outside the district to 100 miles from the place of trial.[5.169]

Section 12, the personal guilt provision, was broadened to make additional acts of directors, officers, and agents of a corporation unlawful.[5.170]

Section 13 was not changed.[5.171]

Section 14 was changed to make clear that its remedy was in addition to the remedies provided in section 9b for violations of sections 2, 4, 8, and 9 of the bill.[5.172]

Sections 15 through 23 were also changed in some particulars, the most important of which were the elimination from section 18 of the right to picket the home of a

---

[5.162] *Id.* at 45.
[5.163] *Id.* at 46.
[5.164] *Id.* at 46–47.
[5.165] *Id.* at 47–48.
[5.166] *Id.* at 48.
[5.167] *Id.* at 48–49.
[5.168] *Id.* at 49.
[5.169] *Id.*
[5.170] *Id.* at 50.
[5.171] *Id.*
[5.172] *Id.*

person,[5.173] and the addition to section 20 of a provision permitting the judge in a contempt case, for a good cause shown, to order a person arrested and brought promptly before the court.[5.174]

Senate Consideration of H.R. 15657

Hearings. Apparently in view of the extensive hearings on trust legislation conducted by the Senate Committee on Interstate Commerce from 1911 through 1913,[5.175] the Senate Judiciary Committee published in 1914 a *Hearings* volume comprised of the Clayton bill as passed by the House, House Report No. 627, a compilation of the Sherman Act and its amendments, a table of cases instituted under that Act (with a brief description of each), a list of court decisions, the reprint of 1908 Senate hearings on S. 6331 and S. 6440, and reprints of three sets of hearings from previous years concerning federal injunctions.[5.176] While this material is of some historic interest, it does not contribute to the legislative history of the Clayton Act and will not be further discussed herein.

Debates. As previously noted, the House bill with amendments was favorably reported by the Senate Judiciary Committee on July 22, 1914.[5.177] Although the Senate on August 5, 1914, agreed to proceed with consideration of the bill,[5.178] substantive debate did not begin until August 13.[5.179]

After the bill had been read, Senator Henry F. Ashurst (D., Ariz.) presented a detailed discussion of court decisions in labor disputes.[5.180] No other statements were made on this first day of debate.

When debate resumed on August 17, 1914, Senator William H. Thompson (D., Kan.) contributed a further detailed discussion concerning court decisions in labor cases,[5.181] after which Chairman Culberson of the Senate Judiciary Committee offered brief remarks and consideration of the committee amendments was opened.[5.182] Section 1 was thereupon amended to exclude coverage of the Philippine Islands, without debate.[5.183]

Mr. Culberson then noted that the federal trade commission bill had passed the Senate and was in conference. Because that bill had in the meantime been amended to give the commission power to restrain unfair trade practices, Culberson stated that the Judiciary Committee had now authorized abandonment of the amendments proposed to section 2, and he moved to strike section 2 in its entirety "for the reason that the general subject embraced in that section can be dealt with by the Federal trade commission, as provided for in the trade commission bill."[5.184] This amendment was accepted without further debate.

The amendment striking section 3 was next agreed to,[5.185] and then the committee's substituted amendment to strike section 4 for the same reasons stated in regard to section 2 was agreed to without debate.[5.186] Although there was no amendment pending to section 5, Senator Wesley L. Jones (R., Wash.) posed the

---

[5.173] *Id.* at 51.

[5.174] *Id.*

[5.175] *Hearings Pursuant to S. Res. 98, supra* note 5.36, discussed in detail *supra* at 999-1000.

[5.176] *Hearings on H.R. 15657 Before the Senate Comm. on the Judiciary,* 63d Cong., 2d Sess. (1914).

[5.177] 51 CONG. REC. 12468 (1914), *infra* at 1743.

[5.178] *Id.* at 13319, *infra* at 1767.

[5.179] *Id.* at 13658, *infra* at 1768. The bill had been briefly laid before the Senate on August 12, 1914, but no debate was conducted on that date. *Id.* at 13633, *infra* at 1768.

[5.180] *Id.* at 13661-68, *infra* at 1769-86.

[5.181] *Id.* at 13844-48, *infra* at 1791-1800.

[5.182] *Id.* at 13848, *infra* at 1800-01.

[5.183] *Id.* at 13849, *infra* at 1801.

[5.184] *Id., infra* at 1801.

[5.185] *Id., infra* at 1801-02.

[5.186] *Id., infra* at 1802.

INTRODUCTION

question as to whether section 5 would apply to violations of the trade commission bill. Mr. Culberson responded that, as drafted, neither the trade commission bill nor the Clayton bill provided that the FTC Act was to be included within the definition of antitrust laws.[5.187] Debate then turned to the committee amendment to section 6, with Senator Charles S. Thomas (D., Colo.) suggesting that the committee amendment be amended to permit judgments rendered in the past to serve as prima facie evidence. Extensive debate on the whole section then ensued, with the amendment to the amendment finally being adopted.[5.188]

When debate resumed on August 18, 1914, Senator Nathan P. Bryan (D., Fla.) proposed a further amendment to the section 6 committee amendment to extend the prima facie evidence rule to cover judgments in criminal proceedings as well. His amendment was agreed to.[5.189] An extended discussion of the legal effect of the prima facie evidence rule then ensued, culminating in a rollcall vote agreeing to the amendment as amended.[5.190] Senator Atlee Pomerene (D., Ohio) then opened up a general discussion on the labor provisions of the bill, which carried over for two more days, during which time many members spoke and the committee amendments to section 7 were agreed upon.[5.191] The remainder of the debate on August 20 was devoted to the committee amendments to sections 8, 9, and 9a.[5.192]

On August 21 and 25 there was extensive debate, led by Senator James A. Reed (D., Mo.), in support of a motion to reconsider the vote whereby sections 2 and 4 were stricken from the bill.[5.193] At the close of these debates, the motion to reconsider the deletion of section 4 was agreed to.[5.194] Further debate on sections 2 and 4 ensued, culminating on August 26 in another vote on the committee amendment to strike section 4. The committee amendment was again agreed to, on a vote of 27 in favor, 26 opposed.[5.195]

Immediately after this vote, Senator Thomas J. Walsh (D., Mont.), on behalf of the Judiciary Committee, offered an amendment adding a new section 4, making unlawful the insertion of any tying provisions in a contract for the sale or lease of a patented product.[5.196] Mr. Reed put forward an amendment to this amendment, adding criminal penalties for its violation, and his amendment was agreed to.[5.197] Mr. Walsh's amendment as amended was then agreed to.[5.198]

During the debate on Mr. Reed's amendment, Senator Francis G. Newlands (D., Nev.) made a statement which indicated the fundamental philosophical differences between those Senators who believed that a federal trade commission was the answer to unfair trade practices and those who believed that supplementing the Sherman Act was the better method:

> Mr. President, this paragraph relates to tying contracts. In my judgment, without any such amendment as is suggested by the Senator from Montana [Mr. Walsh] or such a provision as was urged by the Senator from Missouri [Mr. Reed], it would be within the jurisdiction of the Federal trade commission to issue an order upon proof compelling a defendant to cease and desist from such a practice, under the unfair-competition clause of the trade-commission bill.
>
> The trade commission is called upon to enforce the provisions with reference to unfair competition. The trade commission can be invoked to enforce the provision which the Senator

---

[5.187] *Id., infra* at 1802.

[5.188] *Id.* at 13849-59, *infra* at 1802-23. The final vote was 24 in favor, 23 opposed, with the Vice President casting the deciding vote. *Id* at 13858-59, *infra* at 1822-23.

[5.189] *Id.* at 13897-98, *infra* at 1824-25.

[5.190] *Id.* at 13898-902, 13906-07, *infra* at 1825-36.

[5.191] *Id.* at 13907-25, 13963-83 (August 19), 14010-28 (August 20), *infra* at 1836-1954.

[5.192] *Id.* at 14029-42, *infra* at 1954-84.

[5.193] *Id.* at 14088-100, 14200-23, *infra* at 1986-2065.

[5.194] *Id.* at 14223, *infra* at 2065. The motion so far as it pertained to section 2 had been withdrawn. *Id.*

[5.195] *Id.* at 14272-73, *infra* at 2128-29.

[5.196] *Id.* at 14273, *infra* at 2129.

[5.197] *Id.* at 14273-75, *infra* at 2130-33.

[5.198] *Id.* at 14276, *infra* at 2136.

from Montana seeks to have incorporated in this bill. If the trade commission makes an order to cease and desist, and the practice is not discontinued by the defendant, the trade commission can enforce its order through an application to the court, which will issue an injunction, which, if violated, would result in the punishment of the recalcitrant defendant, either by imprisonment or fine, and certainly by imprisonment if the practice was not discontinued.

I regard that as a much better method of accomplishing the discontinuance of these obnoxious practices than a resort to grand juries and trial juries. I believe that all these complicated questions relating to trade should be enforced so far as practicable through the trade commission, with the aid of the courts, and not by criminal process. For 20 years we have endeavored to enforce the Sherman antitrust law through resort to criminal prosecutions, and they have not been successful. They have certainly not been half so successful as the courts themselves through the process of injunction. So I am opposed to adding a penal clause to this provision.

... I am not opposed to the legislation suggested by the Senator from Montana. I am opposed to adding to it penal provisions, because I think we can get at these things much more efficiently through the trade commission and through the civil courts.[5.199]

On August 27, 1914, the committee amendment proposing to strike the criminal penalty from section 8 was debated and agreed to.[5.200] Immediately thereafter, the committee amendment to strike the criminal penalties from section 9 was also debated and agreed to.[5.201] The committee amendments involving sections 9b, 10, 11, 12, 14, 15, 16, 17, and all but the final clause of 18 were then debated, most of them being agreed to with little or no discussion.[5.202] The day's debate closed in the middle of a discussion concerning the desirability of limiting section 18 by adding the language "to be violations of the antitrust laws."

When debate resumed on August 28, Mr. Culberson proposed an amendment to the amendment adding instead the language "of any law of the United States."[5.203] This amended language was agreed to.[5.204] In between the adoption of the two final committee amendments, those to sections 19 and 20, an extended debate developed concerning the interaction of sections 19, 20, and 22, the effect of which was that in cases involving actions constituting a criminal offense under any United States statute or state law, an individual violating an order of a court in a legal action involving private parties was entitled to a jury trial, while an individual or organization defendant in an action by the United States was not entitled to a jury trial in a contempt action founded upon violation of an injunction issued in such cases.[5.205]

The committee amendments having been disposed of, the bill as amended was opened for further debate and amendment on August 28.[5.206] Senator Thomas thereupon proposed an amendment to add a new section 24, containing a savings clause, which was thereupon agreed to.[5.207]

During the debate on August 31, Senator Reed offered an amendment to section 8 changing the word "is" to the words "may be," making the effect clause read: "where the effect of such acquisition may be to eliminate or substantially lessen competition."[5.208] His amendment was accepted by Chairman Culberson and agreed to.[5.209] Senator John K. Shields (D., Tenn.) then offered an amendment striking the word "substantially" in the second paragraph, making the test of violation: "may be to lessen competition." His amendment was agreed to.[5.210] Shortly thereafter, Mr.

[5.199] *Id.* at 14274, *infra* at 2131-32. Senator Newlands was the principal architect of the Federal Trade Commission Act.

[5.200] *Id.* at 14312-19, *infra* at 2136-50.

[5.201] *Id.* at 14319-21, *infra* at 2150-56.

[5.202] *Id.* at 14321-31, *infra* at 2156-78.

[5.203] *Id.* at 14364, *infra* at 2186.

[5.204] *Id.* at 14367, *infra* at 2193.

[5.205] *Id.* at 14367-77, *infra* at 2193-2216.

[5.206] *Id.* at 14377, *infra* at 2216.

[5.207] *Id., infra* at 2216.

[5.208] *Id.* at 14463, *infra* at 2260.

[5.209] *Id.* at 14464, *infra* at 2261.

[5.210] *Id., infra* at 2262.

Culberson moved the conforming elimination of the words "substantially" and "eliminate or substantially" from other sentences in section 8. His amendments were agreed to.[5.211]

An interesting debate on Mr. Reed's proposal to grant state attorneys general the right to initiate suits at their cost in the name of the United States began on August 31 and carried over to September 1, when it was defeated.[5.212] Mr. Reed then offered several other amendments, only one of which was accepted. That amendment added a new section providing that when a corporation had merged and had been found to be a monopoly or combination in restraint of trade, the court in which the adverse judgment had been rendered was to decree a dissolution of the corporation and retain jurisdiction as necessary to accomplish that purpose.[5.213]

On September 1 also, Senator Albert B. Cummins (R., Iowa) proposed an amendment to section 9, the effect of which would have been to remove the limitation that prohibitions against interlocking directors only applied where one or both corporations had "capital, surplus, and undivided profits" of more than $1 million. This amendment, which prompted strong and lengthy debate, was ultimately rejected by a substantial margin.[5.214]

On September 2, several amendments were offered to section 7, most of which were not agreed to, although Senator Culberson successfully proposed adding a new first sentence to the section: "That the labor of a human being is not a commodity or article of commerce."[5.215] Mr. Cummins next offered an amendment to add the following words in section 18: "or from attending at any place where any such person or persons may lawfully be for the purpose of peacefully obtaining or communicating information." His amendment was agreed to.[5.216] An amendment to create a limited informer's award was debated at some length and rejected.[5.217] After several other amendments were acted upon, the bill as amended was reported out from the Committee of the Whole and all previous amendments not reserved were concurred in.[5.218]

Once again, an attempt was made to revive section 2. Senator Moses E. Clapp (R., Minn.) offered a new section to the same effect as a substitute for section 2, but his amendment was rejected and the action of the committee in striking this section was concurred in by a vote of 40 to 20.[5.219] Following the presentation of several unsuccessful amendments to the substitute section 4 approved by the Committee of the Whole, agreement to the substitute section was concurred in.[5.220] On September 2, 1914, the bill as amended was read a third time and passed on a rollcall vote of 46 in favor and 16 opposed.[5.221]

Conference Consideration and Final Passage of H.R. 15657

On September 4, 1914, the House disagreed to the Senate amendments and asked for a conference.[5.222] The conferees appointed to represent the House were Mr. Webb, Mr. Carlin, Mr. Floyd of Arkansas, Mr. Volstead, and Mr. Nelson. Later that day, this House action was laid before the Senate, which moved to insist upon its amendments and to agree to the conference.[5.223] Mr. Culberson, Mr. Lee S. Overman (D., N.C.),

---

[5.211] *Id.* at 14473, *infra* at 2281.
[5.212] *Id.* at 14476–79, 14513-26, *infra* at 2287-2323.
[5.213] *Id.* at 14527, *infra* at 2324-25.
[5.214] *Id.* at 14534-43, *infra* at 2340-58.
[5.215] *Id.* at 14590-91, *infra* at 2378-79.
[5.216] *Id.* at 14591, *infra* at 2379-80.
[5.217] *Id.* at 14591-96, *infra* at 2380-89.
[5.218] *Id.* at 14597, *infra* at 2392.
[5.219] *Id.* at 14597-99, *infra* at 2393-96.
[5.220] *Id.* at 14599-606, *infra* at 2396-2413.
[5.221] *Id.* at 14609-10, *infra* at 2421-23.
[5.222] *Id.* at 14737, *infra* at 2454.
[5.223] *Id.* at 14718, *infra* at 2454.

Mr. William E. Chilton (D., W. Va.), Mr. Clarence D. Clark (R., Wyo.), and Mr. Knute Nelson (R., Minn.) were appointed to represent the Senate.

The conference report was first submitted to the Senate on September 23, 1914,[5.224] but then withdrawn for corrections and reissued the next day with a new number.[5.225] On September 25, 1914, the House conferees submitted their report, which included a detailed statement by the managers on the part of the House concerning the amendments accepted.[5.226]

The conference committee considered a total of 95 amendments, and its disposition of the more important ones is discussed below. In the following analysis, the first section reference in each paragraph is to the section number assigned in H.R. 15657 as passed by the House on June 5, 1914.[5.227]

On section 1, the exemption of the Philippine Islands was accepted.[5.228]

On section 2, substitute language was agreed upon, preserving the prohibitions contained in the original House bill while eliminating the criminal penalty provision and incorporating the meeting competition defense originally proposed in the bill reported by the Senate Committee on the Judiciary.[5.229]

Section 3 as passed by the House and rejected by the Senate was eliminated.[5.230] In lieu of the stricken section 3, a new section 3 was created from House section 4 and the substitute section 4 adopted in the Senate, retaining much of the House language, adding "whether patented or unpatented," and striking the criminal penalty.[5.231]

A conforming amendment was made in section 5 and it was renumbered section 4.[5.232]

Section 6, renumbered section 5, was modified substantially along the lines proposed by the Senate, establishing a prima facie evidence rule but limiting its reach so as not to apply to consent judgments or certain pending suits in equity which might thereafter be closed by consent judgments. In addition, the House provision as to the tolling of the statute of limitations during the pendency of a government case was accepted without the Senate provision extending the statute of limitations generally to six years.[5.233]

Section 7 was changed to comport substantially with the Senate version and renumbered section 6.[5.234]

Section 8 was changed to reflect most of the language of the Senate, with the notable exception that the words "substantial" and "substantially" were restored and the phrase "or to restrain such commerce in any section or community" and the word "tend" were added at several points. Finally, this section was renumbered section 7.[5.235]

[5.224] S. Doc. No. 583, 63d Cong., 2d Sess. (1914), withdrawn for corrections. Printed also at 51 Cong. Rec. 15588-91 (1914).

[5.225] S. Doc. No. 585, 63d Cong., 2d Sess. (1914). Printed also at 51 Cong. Rec. 15637-40 (1914).

[5.226] H.R. Rep. No.1168, 63d Cong., 2d Sess. (1914). This conference report is reproduced *infra* at 2456-69, for ease of reference. For those wishing to make a detailed study of the conference changes, reference is suggested to the final Senate version of H.R. 15657, printed on September 3, 1914, with the Senate amendments numbered and reproduced *infra* at 2438-53. On August 28, 1914, the Senate had ordered H.R. 15657 to be reprinted with all committee amendments agreed upon through that date. 51 Cong. Rec. 14378 (1914), *infra* at 2218. On August 27, 1914, discussion had taken place concerning the intent to renumber sections upon completion of the amendment process, with a unanimous consent motion to that effect being adopted. *Id.* at 14322, *infra* at 2158. Accordingly, the section numbers appearing in the bill which passed the Senate do not correspond to those in the bill adopted by the House.

[5.227] The bill as originally passed by the House is reproduced *infra* at 1753-67 as part of the Senate Judiciary Committee's comparative print of the House bill with proposed Senate amendments.

[5.228] H.R. Rep. No. 1168, *supra* note 5.226, at 1.

[5.229] *Id.* at 1-2, 11. Representative Graham had earlier proposed adding a meeting competition defense, but his amendment was rejected by the House. See discussion *supra* at 1005.

[5.230] *Id.* at 1.

[5.231] *Id.* at 2, 11.

[5.232] *Id.* at 1, 11.

[5.233] *Id.* at 2-3, 11-12.

[5.234] *Id.* at 1, 3, 12.

[5.235] *Id.* at 1, 3, 12-14.

Section 9 was changed by striking out the first paragraph from the House version and by adding thereafter the language proposed by the Senate, with the further change of substituting $5,000,000 for $2,500,000 in the House version and changing the city size in the banking provision from 100,000 to 200,000. Finally, the criminal penalty provided in the House version was stricken and the section renumbered section 8.[5.236]

A new section 9 was added, based upon the language in Senate section 9a, with the addition of the words "or used in" after the words "arising or accruing from."[5.237]

A new section 10 was added, based primarily upon the language the Senate proposed to replace the first paragraph in original section 9.[5.238]

A new section 11 was added, based in large part upon the provisions passed in the Senate as section 9b.[5.239] This section, which had no counterpart in the House, vested authority to enforce compliance with new sections 2, 3, 7, and 8 of the Act in the Interstate Commerce Commission where applicable to common carriers, in the Federal Reserve Board where applicable to banks, etc., and in the Federal Trade Commission where applicable to any other activities in commerce.

Section 10 was changed to reinstate the original House language, with the exception of the words "has an agent," which were replaced by "transacts business; and all process in such cases may be served in the district of which it is an inhabitant, or wherever it may be found." Finally, the section was renumbered section 12.[5.240]

Section 11 was restored to the original House version, reincorporating the 100-mile limitation on service of subpoenas upon persons living outside the district. The section was renumbered section 13.[5.241]

Section 12 was changed to reinstate the original House language in lieu of the Senate proposal by the insertion of the word "penal" in the second line, and the section was renumbered section 14.[5.242]

Section 13 was retained in its original form, but renumbered section 15.[5.243]

Section 14 was reinstated as originally passed by the House and the words "including sections two, three, seven, and eight of this Act" were added after the words "violation of the antitrust laws."[5.244] As changed, this section was renumbered section 16.

Section 15 was changed to correspond to the minor language changes adopted in the Senate and renumbered section 17.[5.245]

Section 16 was left as it had passed the House, with a minor conforming reference change, and renumbered section 18.[5.246]

Section 17 was changed slightly by adding three words adopted by the Senate and renumbered section 19.[5.247]

Section 18 was changed to incorporate some of the new words adopted by the Senate, including the substitution of the words "to be violations of any law of the United States" for the final word "unlawful."[5.248] As changed, this section was renumbered section 20.

Section 19 was changed to incorporate the Senate amendment substituting the

---

[5.236] *Id.* at 1, 4, 14. In the course of the Senate's renumbering, *see* note 5.226 *supra*, the portion of its new section 9 relating to common carriers was separated out and assigned its own section number, section 10. In that form, it was accepted by the conferees with changes as new section 10. *See* text accompanying note 5.239 *infra*.

[5.237] *Id.* at 4, 15.

[5.238] *Id.* at 6–7, 15.

[5.239] *Id.* at 4–6, 15.

[5.240] *Id.* at 1, 7, 15.

[5.241] *Id.* at 1, 8, 15.

[5.242] *Id.* at 8, 15–16.

[5.243] *Id.* at 8, 16.

[5.244] *Id.* at 1, 8, 16.

[5.245] *Id.*

[5.246] *Id.* at 8–9, 16.

[5.247] *Id.* at 9, 16.

[5.248] *Id.* at 1, 9, 16–17.

words "under the laws of any State in which the act was committed" for the words "at common law," and, as changed, renumbered section 21.[5.249]

Section 20 was changed to correspond to the Senate version and renumbered section 22.[5.250]

Section 21 remained unchanged save for being renumbered section 23.[5.251]

Section 22 likewise remained unchanged except for conforming an internal reference and being renumbered section 24.[5.252]

Section 23 also remained unchanged save for being renumbered section 25.[5.253]

Of the remaining three new sections proposed by the Senate, the first, which would have directed the court in certain cases to decree the dissolution of a monopoly in restraint of trade, and the second, which would have made it unlawful for any corporation in interstate commerce to do any business in any state contrary to the laws of either that state or the state in which the corporation was domiciled, were rejected.[5.254]

The third section adopted by the Senate contained the savings clause, providing that a finding of illegality as to any element of the Act would relate solely to that element and that the rest of the Act would remain valid. The House conferees accepted this paragraph, which was numbered section 26.[5.255]

Senate Debate on Conference Report. On September 28, 1914, the Senate proceeded to actively consider and debate the conference report on H.R. 15657.[5.256] Senator Reed opened the debate with a general discussion of the bill as reported by the conference committee, expressing strong criticism of the deletion of the criminal penalties for violations of sections 2, 3, 7, and 8.[5.257] He also criticized the conferees' removal from section 5 of the word "heretofore," the effect of which was to extend prima facie evidence treatment only to those cases decided after the passage of the Clayton Act.[5.258] He further enumerated "the 82 great trust cases which have been heretofore decided against the trusts."[5.259]

Mr. Reed then opened an extended debate upon the conferees' substitution of certain language in sections 2, 3, 7, and 8, a debate which continued on September 29 and September 30.[5.260] In the course of this debate, there was much discussion concerning the final incorporation of the word "substantially" and the words "or tend to create a monopoly in any line of commerce," with Mr. Reed and some others contending that this language materially weakened the bill and made its enforcement more difficult.[5.261]

Midway through this discussion, Senator Walsh pointed out to Mr. Reed that the conferees had accepted the latter's proposal to substitute the words "may be" for "is" in these same provisions.[5.262] Continuing this debate on September 30, Senator Chilton argued strongly that these language changes in section 2 strengthened the bill and lessened the burden of proof for the parties seeking to establish an unlawful price discrimination.[5.263] Senator Nelson asserted that the language "any line of commerce"

[5.249] *Id.* at 1, 9, 17.

[5.250] *Id.*

[5.251] *Id.* at 10, 17.

[5.252] *Id.*

[5.253] *Id.*

[5.254] *Id.* at 1, 10, 17–18.

[5.255] *Id.* at 10, 18.

[5.256] 51 CONG. REC. 15818 (1914), *infra* at 2474.

[5.257] *Id.* at 15818-21, *infra* at 2474-80.

[5.258] *Id.* at 15821-27, *infra* at 2481-95.

[5.259] *Id.* at 15821-22, *infra* at 2481-84.

[5.260] *Id.* at 15827-31, 15854-68 (Sept. 29), 15934-40 (Sept. 30), *infra* at 2495-2545.

[5.261] *Id.* at 15830-31, 15855-57, *infra* at 2501-04, 2506-09.

[5.262] *Id.* at 15859, *infra* at 2515.

[5.263] *Id.* at 15935, *infra* at 2535.

meant a line of commerce in general and that to have the proscribed effect, the restraint challenged must have a measurable effect upon the general commerce.[5.264] Mr. Reed had urged the same construction of this clause in passing on September 28.[5.265] In response to the hypothetical question whether a local fuel-oil dealer who had been put out of business by the discriminatory pricing of the Standard Oil Co. could make out a cause of action under this section, the following colloquy took place:

Mr. NELSON.
... He is utterly obliterated from the map as a dealer in oil. Yet that poor fellow, if he comes into court and seeks relief under the provisions of this bill as amended by the conference committee, must show that the effect of obliterating him in the little town of Alexandria is to substantially lessen competition, or that it tends to create a monopoly in that line of commerce.
Mr. OVERMAN. If he is destroyed, would not that lessen competition or tend to lessen competition?
Mr. NELSON. It would be so slight that it would be very difficult to prove. It would be like a dipper of water poured into the Potomac.
Mr. OVERMAN. There is a competitor put out of business. That is lessening competition, is it not?
Mr. NELSON. Well, it would be so slight that it would not be appreciable. It would not be a substantial lessening of competition or the creation of a monopoly.
Mr. OVERMAN. How would it be slight when the man was absolutely driven out of business?[5.266]

During Mr. Nelson's discourse, Senator Chilton again pointed to the conferees' acceptance of the words "may be" in lieu of "is" in this section and expressed the opinion that this change made violations of the section easier to prove.[5.267] Debate then turned to other sections and became more general.

On October 1, Senators William E. Borah (R., Idaho) and John W. Weeks (R., Mass.) presented statements to the effect that passage of the Clayton bill would engender new uncertainties on the part of businessmen until its provisions had been interpreted and given substance in the courts.[5.268] Speaking about the probable effects of the Clayton bill, Mr. Weeks stated:

After 20 years of trials of cases following the advice of attorneys and followed by the decisions of the courts, business has finally come to a reasonably sound conclusion, as far as the Sherman Antitrust Act is applicable. It will take as many years of doubt to determine what this law means, multiplied by the increased number of cases which will be covered by the provisions of this law as compared with those which are affected by the Sherman Antitrust Act.[5.269]

Senator Weeks then sought to rehabilitate the reputation of the United Shoe Machinery Co., which he characterized as "the bogy [sic] man which has been set up by almost all those who have discussed [the Clayton bill]."[5.270] During this effort, Mr. Weeks was asked by Senator Reed for the name of the attorney who worked out the legal problems in consolidating three separate machinery companies into the United Shoe Machinery Co. Mr. Weeks responded that one of the attorneys involved in the consolidation was Louis D. Brandeis, and he indicated that Mr. Brandeis had drawn the original shoe machinery leases which that company was still using.[5.271] Senator Weeks buttressed his argument that United's commercial practices were unobjectionable

---

[5.264] *Id., infra* at 2535.

[5.265] *Id.* at 15830, *infra* at 2501-03. *See also id.* at 15936, *infra* at 2537.

[5.266] *Id.* at 15935, *infra* at 2535.

[5.267] *Id.* at 15936-37, *infra* at 2538.

[5.268] *Id.* at 15983-96, *infra* at 2587-2617.

[5.269] *Id.* at 15990, *infra* at 2602.

[5.270] *Id., infra* at 2604.

[5.271] *Id.* at 15992, *infra* at 2608. Documents contained in the various 1911–1914 trust hearings, including correspondence from Mr. Brandeis himself, indicate that he served as an incorporator and director of the United Shoe Machinery Co. from 1899 to December 6, 1906, and served as an outside counsel to the company from 1899 to January 7, 1907. *See, e.g., Hearings on H.R. 11380, supra* note 5.36, ser. 2 and 3, app. at

by citing a statement in which Mayor James M. Curley of Boston reported that his investigation indicated the company's activities were beneficial to its local community, the state, and the nation.[5.272]

When debate resumed on October 2, Senators George W. Norris (R., Neb.), Clapp, and Reed again debated the meaning of "in any line of commerce" and "substantially."[5.273] Following some general debate on October 3, Senator Thomas Sterling (R., S.D.) briefly turned the debate back to the use of the word "substantially" and referred to the incorporation in the final bill of an exemption for price discriminations "made in good faith to meet competition."[5.274] He, too, criticized these changes as having weakened the bill.

On October 5, Senator Walsh responded to the questions raised by others concerning addition of the word "substantially."[5.275] In his view, addition of "substantially" did not materially alter the test which a court would apply in determining whether commerce had been affected to the requisite degree to constitute a violation.

> ... If it were out, the language would receive the same construction, because no court would find that competition was lessened unless it was "substantially" lessened. The Sherman Act denounces all combinations in restraint of commerce, but no combination falls under the ban of the statute unless commerce is restrained to a "substantial" extent. De minimis non curat lex. How much reason there is to dread disastrous results from such a construction is exhibited by the decision in the Union Pacific-Southern Pacific case, in which the traffic affected by the combination amounted only to eighty-eight one-hundredths of 1 per cent of the total tonnage of the Southern Pacific. Yet the court held that the restraint of trade was substantial enough to bring the combination under the condemnation of the law.[5.276]

Following additional debate, Senator Reed moved that the bill be recommitted to the conference committee and that the conferees be instructed to insist upon the inclusion of the criminal penalties substantially as passed by the House and that, further, the word "heretofore" be inserted in section 5.[5.277] His motion was defeated on a rollcall by a vote of 25 in favor, 35 opposed.[5.278] Immediately thereafter, the conference report was agreed to on a rollcall vote, with 35 in favor, 24 opposed, and 37 not voting.[5.279] The date of final approval was October 5, 1914.

House Debate on Conference Report. Although the House received the conference report on September 25, 1914, it did not begin actual consideration of the report until October 7.[5.280] Immediately following the reading of the conference report, Representative James R. Mann (R., Ill.) raised a point of order concerning the manner in which the conferees had dealt with the differing versions of the bill as passed by the

---

17. His actual authorship of the leases in question could not be substantiated from other available sources, but it is clear from such things as his written statements and other materials that he was not convinced that these leases were objectionable from a legal or economic standpoint until 1906 at the earliest. The lease program permitted small companies to enter the shoe manufacturing industry with very little capital, and thereby fostered competition in that industry. Extracts from a lease used by this company at that time are reproduced *infra* at 1071-73.

5.272 51 CONG. REC. 15994-95 (1914), *infra* at 2613. Mayor Curley later achieved notoriety in his own right by being elected to a new term as mayor of Boston in 1945 after having been indicted on federal mail fraud charges stemming from an alleged war contracts brokerage scheme in which he participated while serving as a Representative to Congress from Massachusetts. He was subsequently convicted and served a four-month term of imprisonment, while continuing to hold the office of mayor, and was later granted executive clemency by President Truman. Prior to this conviction, Curley had served other terms as a United States Representative and had been governor of Massachusetts. See, *e.g.,* N.Y. Times, June 8, 1947, § 4, at 11, col. 1.

5.273 51 CONG. REC. 16044-48, 16057-58 (1914), *infra* at 2647-54, 2674-76.

5.274 *Id.* at 16115-16, *infra* at 2688-90.

5.275 *Id.* at 16149, *infra* at 2709-10.

5.276 *Id., infra* at 2709-10.

5.277 *Id.* at 16167, *infra* at 2751.

5.278 *Id.* at 16169-70, *infra* at 2754-56.

5.279 *Id.* at 16170, *infra* at 2756-57.

5.280 *Id.* at 16264, *infra* at 2760.

separate Houses. Specifically, he charged that the conferees had exceeded their jurisdiction by changing certain portions of the text as to which there had been no disagreement and which were accordingly not properly before the conference committee.[5.281] After some debate, his point of order was rejected.[5.282]

Representative Webb then opened the debate on the conference report with these words:

> Mr. Speaker, there has been a great deal of misinformation and misrepresentation about the meaning and effect of the antitrust bill, both as it passed the House and as it passed the Senate and as it came from conference. Some of this misinformation is pitiful ignorance; other of it is downright, deliberate misrepresentation. . . .
>
> . . . Now for just a little while, I want to tell the House in plain, straightforward, undisguised language what has taken place in both the House, Senate, and conference.[5.283]

Speaking of sections 2 and 4, Mr. Webb described the events leading to the final, compromise language:

> Now, there were those who insisted that we ought to have criminal penalties attached to these two sections, 2 and 4. Others, however, took the position that the sections ought to go out entirely, because we had in the meantime passed the Trade Commission bill with section 5 in it which denounced as unlawful unfair methods of competition, and that the Trade Commission could and would take up all the acts denounced in sections 2 and 4, and prevent their further commission. So, between those two ideas the battle raged for nearly three weeks. We finally agreed to the Senate amendments striking out the criminal penalties, but to retain sections 2 and 4 as they went from the House, with an amendment which denounced as unlawful the tying contract and the discrimination in price. But as originally drawn they were criminal sections, and section 2 made it a crime to discriminate in price for the purpose of destroying or injuring a competitor. We thought that was probably too restricted. We agreed, instead of retaining the language "with purpose or intent thereby to destroy or wrongfully injure the business of a competitor," and so forth, to insert this language: "Where the effect of such discrimination may be to substantially lessen competition or tend to create a monopoly in any line of commerce." We felt that that would tend to give the section more elasticity and breadth. That is the reason we accepted this amendment, and forbade discriminating in price when the effect of such discrimination might be to substantially lessen competition or tend to create a monopoly.
>
> We did the same thing with reference to section 4, which forbade the tying contract.[5.284]

In response to Representative William H. Stafford's (R., Wis.) question whether section 3 as agreed to by the conferees was as strong as Senator Walsh's amendment (Senate section 2), the following colloquy took place:

> Mr. WEBB. Yes, sir; in civil remedies.
>
> Mr. STAFFORD. That it will prevent, for instance, the United Shoe Machinery Co. from entering into such binding contracts as now exist with the users of their machinery, that they will be forbidden to use machinery of other competitors, and keep companies, for instance the Dick Co., from forbidding the use of their mimeograph machines with stationery and supplies not furnished by that company.
>
> Mr. WEBB. I will say to my friend that, in my opinion, immediately after the President signs this bill with section 3 in it every such contract made by the United Shoe Machinery Co. will become unlawful, because they may not only lessen substantial competition, but they do it. They not only tend to create monopoly, but they do it.
>
> Mr. STAFFORD. And it is also the gentleman's opinion that it will correct the conditions referred to by Chief Justice White in the Dick case?
>
> Mr. WEBB. I think so. It was intended to do it, and I believe it will.
>
> Mr. STAFFORD. Of course there is no question but that the language of the Walsh amendment would do it. The language of that amendment is clear and positive and would cover such cases. The language of the amendment agreed to by the conferees I do not believe is as clear and forceful as the Walsh amendment.
>
> Mr. WEBB. We can be certain of nothing until the Supreme Court passes upon it, but I will

---

[5.281] *Id.* at 16269, *infra* at 2760.

[5.282] *Id.* at 16273, *infra* at 2768.

[5.283] *Id., infra* at 2768.

[5.284] *Id., infra* at 2769-70.

say that Senator WALSH, who introduced the amendment, is satisfied that the section as the conference presents it will cover the case it is intended to cover, and I hope it will. I am in favor of repealing the opinion in the case of Dick against Henry. Those are the sections around which such a war has been waged in the last few weeks in the other branch of the Congress.

Now, let us see if these sections are "toothless." It is contended that we have extracted the teeth because we have left out the criminal penalties. But I will tell you, my friends—

Mr. HARDY. Will the gentleman yield for just one question?

Mr. WEBB. Yes, sir.

Mr. HARDY. If I caught your expressions correctly—and I will ask if I have—one essential change, as I understand it, is that you let the unlawfulness of these contracts hinge not on the purpose of them but on the effect of them?

Mr. WEBB. Yes sir; and tendency.

Mr. HARDY. Effect and tendency?

Mr. WEBB. Yes.

Mr. HARDY. Does not that make the law stronger than if it depended upon the purpose being shown?

Mr. WEBB. Yes. I believe it will be easier to prove a violation in a civil suit.[5.285]

Mr. Webb proceeded to enumerate the "teeth" of the bill, "five different distinct civil remedies that are given to individuals, to the Department of Justice, and to the Trade Commission" to prevent and restrain violations of sections 2 and 3.[5.286] In pointing out these civil penalties, he cited the acquittal of the individuals indicted in the *Beef Trust* case[5.287] for the proposition that juries are "disinclin[ed] . . . to convict men under these criminal sections [of the Sherman Act]."[5.288] Mr. Webb stated:

. . . Now, the next thing is to give the individual who is harmed by these practices—not necessarily restraints of trade or monopolies, but things that lead up to restraints of trade and monopolies—the right to bring suit for any amount he pleases.[5.289]

That debate led to this discussion of the purpose of the Clayton bill:

Mr. ALEXANDER. This bill undertakes to prohibit those acts which lead to monopoly which the Sherman antitrust law does not reach. This bill makes those specific acts unlawful, and they may be restrained by civil remedies.

Mr. WEBB. Exactly.

Mr. ALEXANDER. But if they culminate in violation of the Sherman antitrust law, then they may be prosecuted civilly and criminally.

Mr. WEBB. Exactly. That is a fair statement of it, and that is what led a great many Members of the House and Senate to the conclusion that those acts that did not violate the Sherman law should not be denounced as criminal acts in the first instance in a new law. If a number of small links in the chain finally result in violation of the Sherman law, then the person who constructs the chain becomes subject to the pains and penalties of the Sherman law. A person who only builds one link in the chain is denounced here. There are people, and honest people, who thought that we ought not to put a man in jail for making one link, but that we should forbid him from forging other links. The Sherman law takes care of restraints of trade and monopoly. This bill is intended to prevent those individual acts which, if multiplied and persisted in, may lead to a violation of the Sherman law.[5.290]

During the further debate on the civil remedies available under the Clayton bill, Representative Ellsworth R. Bathrick (D., Ohio) pointed out that section 16 required any private party seeking an injunction against threatened damage by violation of the antitrust laws to execute "a proper bond against damages for an injunction, improvidently granted."[5.291] He suggested that this was a weakness in the bill, in that a defendant would seek to prove very large potential damages, in such amount as to preclude the plaintiff from making bond and securing his injunction.[5.292]

[5.285] *Id.* at 16274, *infra* at 2770.

[5.286] *Id.* at 16274-75, *infra* at 2770-72.

[5.287] Swift & Co. v. United States, 196 U.S. 375, 25 S. Ct. 276, 49 L. Ed. 518 (1905).

[5.288] 51 CONG. REC. 16274 (1914), *infra* at 2771.

[5.289] *Id.*, *infra* at 2771.

[5.290] *Id.* at 16275, *infra* at 2774.

[5.291] *Id.* at 16276, *infra* at 2774.

[5.292] *Id.*, *infra* at 2774.

Mr. BATHRICK. . . . There is the weakness of the injunction remedy, as it seems to me. I would like to get the gentleman's opinion on it.

Mr. WEBB. The size of the bond is within the discretion of the court. The gentleman would not give everybody the right to go into court and ask for an injunction without some bond covering the possible damage.

Mr. BATHRICK. The gentleman from North Carolina is familiar enough with the practice to know that plaintiffs are often deterred from applying for injunctions because of the necessity of putting up a bond. That is the weakness of the process.

Mr. WEBB. My friend knows that a bond in individual cases could not under the court's ruling be very large, because it would apply only to the individual's damage, and would not be like an injunction stopping the whole business of the defendant in all sections and States. It would be only in reference to a particular locality, and the damages could not be very great.

Mr. BATHRICK. Oh, yes; but the defendants would come in and try to show that the damages were going to be very large and that they required a very large bond.

Mr. WEBB. Then that is a weakness of our whole judicial system. A sensible judge can adjust that trouble. But a man that alleges a thing must prove it.

Mr. BATHRICK. As compared with a threatened term in jail or a fine under a criminal prosecution, the injunctive process is very weak, in my opinion.

Mr. WEBB. Well, that is the gentleman's opinion, and there are other men who agree with him.

Mr. BARTLETT. If the gentleman from North Carolina will pardon me, I call attention to the fact that the bond is only conditioned on the ground that the injunction was improvidently granted.

Mr. WEBB. Exactly.[5.293]

Representative Volstead closed out debate on October 7 with a long statement summing up the defects of the bill, noting, among other things, the inclusion of the word "substantially" and its weakening effect on this legislation.[5.294]

Opening the debate on October 8, Representative Floyd of Arkansas, a House conferee and a framer of the original Clayton bill, furnished the following explanation of the origins of the word "substantially" and the reason for its use in the bill agreed to by the conferees:

. . . I desire to take up now briefly that part of the report covering sections 2, 3, and 7. The first relates to discriminatory contracts, the second relates to tying or exclusive contracts, and the third to holding companies. It will be observed that these sections deal with contractual relations in commercial dealings. After the penalties were stricken out, the provisions of sections 2 and 3 were modified, because as criminal sections they were drafted with all the particularity of criminal statutes, the intent and purpose being included. But that is not the rule applicable to contracts. So when we decided that the acts forbidden, instead of being made penal and criminal, should be simply condemned as unlawful, a modification was made in harmony with principles governing the construction and interpretation of contracts.

We have been criticized for injecting or inserting certain words into sections 2 and 3 in conference. Where did those mysterious words "substantially lessen competition or tend to create a monopoly" originate? They were incorporated in section 8, the holding-company provision of the bill, as it passed this House. They passed muster in the Senate of the United States and were retained in the holding-company provision as it passed the Senate and were retained in conference. In modifying and changing sections 2 and 3, so as to make the acts prohibited therein unlawful, without making them penal, it became necessary to change the wording of

---

[5.293] *Id., infra* at 2774. There was no substantive debate in 1914 concerning the meaning of the words "improvidently granted" in this section. Clayton Act section 16 is based upon section 266a of H.R. 23635, 62d Cong., 2d Sess. (1912), which was passed by the House but not acted on by the Senate. The House report on H.R. 23635 (House Report No. 612, cited at note 5.90 *supra*) was incorporated in the House report on the Clayton bill and is reproduced *infra* at 1101-16. The original language of section 266a was:

SEC. 266a. That no restraining order or interlocutory order of injunction shall issue except upon the giving of security by the applicant in such sum as the court or judge may deem proper, conditioned upon the payment of such costs and damages as may be incurred or suffered by any party who may be found to have been wrongfully enjoined or restrained thereby.

H.R. REP. NO. 627, 63d Cong., 2d Sess., pt. 1, 39 (1914), *infra* at 1116.

The intended purpose of this section was to eliminate the discretion of the court as to requiring the giving of security under the Act of June 1, 1872, ch. 255, § 7, 17 Stat. 197. *Id.* at 26. The present language of rule 65(c) of the Federal Rules of Civil Procedure tracks the language of proposed section 266a almost exactly.

[5.294] 51 CONG. REC. 16280-84 (1914), *infra* at 2780-89.

each, in other respects. We took the language that had been already approved by both the House and the Senate in another section, the one relating to holding companies, and applied it to sections 2 and 3, the latter corresponding to our section 4, so that the three sections, namely, sections 2, 3, and 7 of the conference report, are in harmony now, all dealing with the question of contracts, the same principle being applied to each one of them.

The gentleman from Minnesota [Mr. VOLSTEAD] criticizes this language and criticizes these provisions, claiming that we are in some way interfering with the operations of the Sherman antitrust law; at least he fears we are. Not at all. That language did not originate with our committee. That language originated from a discussion in the opinion of the Supreme Court of the United States in the case of the Addyston Pipe & Steel Co. against United States. The court, in discussing this very question of contracts, uses this language. I quote:

"But it has never been, and in our opinion ought not to be, held that the word included the right of an individual to enter into private contracts upon all subjects, no matter what their nature and wholly irrespective, among other things, of the fact that they would, if performed, result in the regulation of interstate commerce and in the violation of an act of Congress upon that subject. The provision in the Constitution does not, as we believe, exclude Congress from legislating with regard to contracts of the above nature while in the exercise of its constitutional right to regulate commerce among the States. On the contrary, we think the provision regarding the liberty of the citizen is, to some extent, limited by the commerce clause of the Constitution, and that the power of Congress to regulate interstate commerce comprises the right to enact a law prohibiting the citizen from entering into these private contracts which directly and substantially, and not merely indirectly, remotely, incidentally, and collaterally, regulate to a greater or less degree commerce among the States."[5.295]

Here is the origin of the application of that word "substantially" in the several sections referred to. And yet some criticisms have been published in the press to the effect that some sinister influence was brought to bear upon the conferees after the bill was sent to conference in order to induce the conferees to write those words into those sections after the penalties originally provided had been stricken out. *Why the necessity of restoring these sections without penalties?* In justice to the Senate of the United States let it be said that after section 5 of the Trade Commission bill had passed that body and had been approved by the House, condemning as unlawful all unfair methods of competition, the theory of the Senators was that these unfair methods would be included and cared for under the provisions of the Trade Commission bill. But that was not the view of your managers on the part of the House. *Your conferees believed that in dealing with these contractual relations, the Supreme Court having held that Congress has the power to declare null and void any contract that substantially interfered with interstate commerce, but that the courts have no such power in the absence of an act of Congress condemning them, such contracts would be upheld in the future, not only by the commission but by the courts, until the legislative power of this Government declared them to be unlawful. We insisted that those three provisions be placed back in the bill, and finally they were placed back in the bill without the penalties.* In answer to the gentleman from Ohio [Mr. BATHRICK] I will say for the things condemned in these sections, namely, the making of discriminatory contracts, the making of tying or exclusive contracts, and the making of contracts for unlawful acquisition of stock under section 7 no criminal penalty attaches, because those are not penal provisions of the antitrust laws; but they are still provisions of the antitrust laws, and every civil remedy that is applicable to any antitrust law may be invoked for their enforcement.[5.296]

Mr. Floyd also provided the following explanation concerning the interrelationship of the Sherman Act and the Clayton bill:

Mr. COOPER. The title of this act is "An act to supplement existing laws against unlawful restraint and monopolies, and for other purposes." If I understand the gentleman, it is his contention, in supporting this conference report, that the criminal clauses of the Sherman law are still in force and that this act simply supplements them?

Mr. FLOYD of Arkansas. Certainly; that is correct.

Mr. COOPER. And that those criminal clauses are not repealed?

Mr. FLOYD of Arkansas. They are not repealed in any sense, and I thank the gentleman for asking the question.[5.297]

Representative Nelson, the minority member of the House conferees, stated that he could not agree to the conference report "for the sole reason that [he was] heartily in

---

[5.295] 175 U.S. 211, 228-29 (1899).

[5.296] 51 CONG. REC. 16317-18 (1914), *infra* at 2790-92 (emphasis added).

[5.297] *Id.* at 16319, *infra* at 2795.

favor of real antitrust legislation that shall make it impossible for private monopoly to exist in this country."[5.298] He characterized use of the word "substantially" as "dangerous," criticized use of the phrase "or tend to create a monopoly in any line of commerce," and termed the defenses incorporated in section 2 "loopholes."[5.299]

During Chairman Webb's summation for the majority, Mr. Nelson engaged him in further brief debate on the defenses provided in section 2 and the deletion of criminal penalties from this section.[5.300] Mr. Webb reiterated his earlier statement that sections 2 and 3 were supplemental to the Sherman Act, and that this bill was designed to reach practices not individually in themselves violative of the Sherman Act, except when done to such extent and with such persistence as to restrain trade or create a monopoly.[5.301]

On October 8, 1914, the House accepted the conference report on a rollcall vote, 245 in favor, 52 opposed, 5 "present," and 126 not voting.[5.302]

[5.298] *Id.* at 16324, *infra* at 2803.

[5.299] *Id., infra* at 2804.

[5.300] *Id.* at 16341, *infra* at 2830.

[5.301] *Id., infra* at 2830-31.

[5.302] *Id.* at 16344-45, *infra* at 2833-36.

Chronological Synopsis

CLAYTON ACT OF 1914

[NOTE: During the initial Senate and House debates, the section numbers of H.R. 15657 do not correspond to the section numbers of the Act as passed. The chart below corresponds the section numbers of H.R. 15657 to those of the Clayton Act. During the debate on the Conference Report on H.R. 15657, section numbers conform to those of the Act as passed.]

H.R. 15657 Senate & House debates	Clayton Act
§ 2	§ 2
§ 3 (deleted by Senate)	
§ 4	§ 3
§ 5	§ 4
§ 6	§ 5
§ 7	§ 6
§ 8	§ 7
§ 9	§ 8
§ 9a (added by Senate)	§§ 9 and 10
§ 9b (added by Senate)	§ 11
§ 10	§ 12
§ 11	§ 13
§ 12	§ 14
§ 13	§ 15
§ 14	§ 16
§ 15	§ 17
§ 16	§ 18
§ 17	§ 19
§ 18	§ 20
§ 19	§ 21
§ 20	§ 22
§ 21	§ 23
§ 22	§ 24
§ 23	§ 25
§ 24 (added by Senate)	§ 26

62d Congress, 1st Session

July 26, 1911

Senate adopted S. Res. 98, directing the Interstate Commerce Committee to investigate what changes were necessary or desirable in the laws relating to control of corporations engaged in interstate commerce [47 Cong. Rec. 3225-26].
   [Printed in Senate Report No. 1326, at 1] ....Chap. 8

August 4, 1911; November 15, 1911 to February 9, 1912

Senate Interstate Commerce Committee hearings pursuant to S. Res. 98.

62d Congress, 3d Session

February 26, 1913

Senate Interstate Commerce Committee filed its report pursuant to S. Res. 98 (Cummins report).
[Senate Report No. 1326] ....Chap. 8

63d Congress, 2d Session

December 9, 1913 to April 6, 1914

House Judiciary Committee hearings on trust legislation.

January 20, 1914

President Wilson announced his antitrust program in a message to Congress stressing the need for certainty in the antitrust laws and endorsing the creation of an interstate trade commission [51 Cong. Rec. 1963].
[House Document No. 625] ....Chap. 8

April 14, 1914

H.R. 15657 was introduced by Rep. Clayton and referred to the House Judiciary Committee [51 Cong. Rec. 6714].
[Bill print] 1080

May 6, 1914

H.R. 15657 was reported favorably, with amendments, by the House Judiciary Committee.
[House Report No. 627] 1089
[Bill print] 1163

May 12, 1914

Minority views of Rep. Graham, Rep. Danforth, and Rep. Dyer submitted.
[House Report No. 627, part 2] 1125

May 13, 1914

Minority views of Rep. Nelson and Rep. Volstead submitted.
[House Report No. 627, part 3] 1152

Minority views of Rep. Morgan of Oklahoma submitted.
[House Report No. 627, part 4] 1160

May 22, 1914

House, sitting in Committee of the Whole, commenced debate on H.R. 15657 [51 Cong. Rec. 9068-91] 1182

May 23, 1914

House continued general debate on H.R. 15657 [51 Cong. Rec. 9153-90] 1233

May 25, 1914

House continued general debate on H.R. 15657 [51 Cong. Rec. 9195-202] 1317

May 26, 1914

House concluded general debate on H.R. 15657 and began reading the bill for amendment [51 Cong. Rec. 9245-73] 1330

CHRONOLOGICAL SYNOPSIS 1027

May 28, 1914

House continued consideration of H.R. 15657 [51 Cong. Rec. 9388-417] 1390

    Morgan amendment to section 1, exempting organizations with aggregate capital of less than $5 million from the prohibitions of sections 2, 4, and 8 of the bill, was rejected [51 Cong. Rec. 9389]..1391

    Section 2 (dealing with price discrimination) was debated. Eleven amendments were proposed and rejected. One technical amendment was adopted [51 Cong. Rec. 9389-96]..............1391

    Section 3 (dealing with refusals to deal by mineowners and operators) was debated [51 Cong. Rec. 9396-98] 1406

        Bathrick amendment extending the section to oil deposits was adopted [51 Cong. Rec. 9398]..1408

        Decker amendment requiring that the refusal to deal be done with the intent to injure the business of another was rejected [51 Cong. Rec. 9398] 1409

    Section 4 (concerning exclusive dealing practices) was debated [51 Cong. Rec. 9398-414] 1410

        McCoy amendment to limit the section's prohibition to exclusive dealing arrangements made "with the intent of obtaining or establishing a monopoly or of destroying the business of a competitor" was defeated [51 Cong. Rec. 9410]..............................1432

        Morgan amendment extending the section's penalties to persons whose agents violated the section was rejected [51 Cong. Rec. 9411] 1433

        Towner amendment to insert the words "in commerce," making the first line of the section read: "That any person who shall lease or make a sale in commerce of goods," was rejected [51 Cong. Rec. 9411] 1433

        Towner amendment changing the section's requirements of either a lease or sale, or the fixing of a price from the disjunctive to the conjunctive was rejected [51 Cong. Rec. 9411]..1434

        Towner amendment changing the phrase "condition or understanding" to "condition, agreement or understanding" was accepted [51 Cong. Rec. 9411] 1434

    Section 5 (pertaining to jurisdiction in private actions and placing venue in districts where the defendant resided or was found) was debated. Rep. Dickinson proposed an amendment extending venue to districts in which the defendant did business and the action accrued. Rep. Cullop offered an amendment to the amendment so as to make the venue phrase read "in which the defendant resides or has an agency doing business and the cause of action may accrue." (House adjourned before taking action on these amendments.) [51 Cong. Rec. 9414-17] 1440

May 29, 1914

House continued consideration of H.R. 15657 [51 Cong. Rec. 9466-96] 1448

    Pending Dickinson and Cullop amendments were withdrawn [51 Cong. Rec. 9466] 1450

    Committee amendment to section 5, adding the words "or his agent" to the venue provision, was offered by Rep. Floyd and accepted [51 Cong. Rec. 9466-67] 1450

    Section 3 was debated and amended [51 Cong. Rec. 9468-85] 1452

    Morgan amendment to add a new section 3a dealing, in general terms, with discrimination between purchasers, lessors, or communities, was rejected [51 Cong. Rec. 9486] 1486

    Towner amendment to section 5, adding the words "or declared to be unlawful," was rejected [51 Cong. Rec. 9487] 1487

    Section 6 (dealing with the res judicata effect of a final judgment in a government action) was debated [51 Cong. Rec. 9487-95]..1487

        Volstead amendment providing that the final judgment would only be res judicata if the defendant lost was accepted [51 Cong. Rec. 9495] 1503

        Levy amendment to add at the end of the first paragraph the words "that nothing herein contained shall interfere with legitimate business or commercial enterprises, and no citizen shall be deprived of his liberty or happiness while pursuing the same" was rejected [51 Cong. Rec. 9495] 1503

    Debate on section 7 (exempting labor and agricultural organizations) began. Rep. Madden offered an amendment to strike the second paragraph [51 Cong. Rec. 9495-96] 1504

June 1, 1914

House continued consideration of H.R. 15657 [51 Cong. Rec. 9538-611] 1506

    Debate on section 7 was resumed [51 Cong. Rec. 9538-86] 1506

        Webb amendment adding the words "Nor shall such organizations, orders, or associations, or members thereof, be held or construed to be illegal combinations or conspiracies in restraint of trade under the antitrust laws" was accepted [51 Cong. Rec. 9566] 1568

        Thomas amendment to strike the entire first paragraph and insert in lieu thereof: "The provisions of the antitrust law shall not apply to agricultural, labor, consumers, fraternal, or horticultural orders or associations" was rejected. Rep. MacDonald's proposal to modify the Thomas amendment so as to retain the language of the Webb amendment was also rejected [51 Cong. Rec. 9569] 1574

        Nelson amendment exempting cooperative agricultural associations was rejected [51 Cong. Rec. 9579] 1596

        Bryan amendment to add the sentence "There shall be no abridgement of the right of wage earners and producers to organize for the protection of wages and improvement of labor conditions" was rejected [51 Cong. Rec. 9579] 1596

        Hulings amendment to the second paragraph, requiring ICC approval before agreements between common carriers are immunized from the antitrust laws, was accepted [51 Cong. Rec. 9581] 1600

        Madden amendment (proposed May 29) was rejected [51 Cong. Rec. 9585] 1609

        Fowler amendment providing that common carrier agreements shall be open to inspection by Congress was rejected [51 Cong. Rec. 9586] 1610

        Platt amendment excluding manufacturers' associations from the Act (apparently offered in jest) was rejected [51 Cong. Rec. 9586]..1610

    Ferris amendment to add a new section 7a, requiring persons transporting various natural resources in commerce to become common carriers subject to the Interstate Commerce Act, was ruled out of order as not germane [51 Cong. Rec. 9589] 1617

    Towner amendment to add a new section prohibiting discrimination in purchase price for agricultural products for the purpose of injuring cooperative associations was rejected [51 Cong. Rec. 9591] 1620

    Section 8 (dealing with stock acquisitions by corporations) was debated [51 Cong. Rec. 9591-600] 1620

        Volstead amendment proposing numerous changes in the section was rejected [51 Cong. Rec. 9597] 1633

        Vaughan amendment partially exempting the acquisition of local telephone exchanges from the antitrust laws was rejected [51 Cong. Rec. 9599] 1635

        Brown amendment to clarify the legality of public utility holding companies under certain circumstances was rejected [51 Cong. Rec. 9600] 1636

    Section 9 (dealing with interlocking directorates) was debated [51 Cong. Rec. 9600-07] 1636

        Cline amendment to the proviso to the section's prohibition against interlocking bank directorates was defeated [51 Cong. Rec. 9604] 1646

        McCoy substitute for the section's provision regarding interlocking bank directorates was rejected [51 Cong. Rec. 9606] 1650

        Bartlett amendment changing the civil penalty for violation of the section from "$100 a day" to "not exceeding $100 a day" was accepted [51 Cong. Rec. 9607] 1650

        Gardner amendment to the interlocking bank directorates provision, authorizing the Federal Reserve Board to allow such interlocking directorates under certain circumstances, was rejected [51 Cong. Rec. 9607] 1650

        Reilly amendment to change the city size in the banking provision from 100,000 to 200,000 was rejected [51 Cong. Rec. 9607]...1650

    Section 10 (providing that actions may be brought in the judicial districts where the defendant corporation "is an inhabitant" or "may be found") was debated [51 Cong. Rec. 9607-08] ...1651

        Webb amendment providing for venue in districts in which the corporation "has an agent" was accepted [51 Cong. Rec. 9607] 1652

        Sumners amendment providing for venue in districts "where the cause of action or any part thereof arises" was rejected [51 Cong. Rec. 9608] 1652

CHRONOLOGICAL SYNOPSIS

    Section 12 (personal guilt section, providing that upon the conviction of a corporation for violation of the antitrust laws, directors, officers, and agents who participated in the unlawful acts would be deemed guilty of a misdemeanor) was debated [51 Cong. Rec. 9608-10] 1654

        Volstead amendment, eliminating the prerequisite of a corporate conviction before individuals may be found guilty of antitrust violations, was passed over [51 Cong. Rec. 9610] 1657

    Section 15 (dealing with preliminary injunctions and temporary restraining orders) was debated [51 Cong. Rec. 9610-11] 1657

        MacDonald substitute, limiting the availability of injunctions in labor disputes, was rejected [51 Cong. Rec. 9611] 1660

    Section 17 (detailing the form of injunctions and restraining orders and specifying which parties were to be bound by such orders) was debated [51 Cong. Rec. 9611] 1660

June 2, 1914

House concluded debate on H.R. 15657 [51 Cong. Rec. 9652-98] 1661

    Section 18 (limiting the use of injunctions and restraining orders in labor disputes) was debated [51 Cong. Rec. 9652-62] 1661

        Webb amendment adding at the end of the section the words "nor shall any of the acts specified in this paragraph be considered or held unlawful" was adopted after a Volstead amendment to add a proviso that "nothing in this act shall be construed to permit a secondary boycott" was rejected [51 Cong. Rec. 9662] 1680

        Clarifying amendments offered by Rep. MacDonald and Rep. Hulings were rejected [51 Cong. Rec. 9662] 1681

        Technical amendment offered by Rep. Fowler was rejected [51 Cong. Rec. 9662] 1682

    Cullop amendment to add a new section 18a, granting state courts concurrent jurisdiction with federal courts over cases arising under the Act, was rejected [51 Cong. Rec. 9664] 1686

    Section 20 (dealing with procedure in contempt cases) was debated [51 Cong. Rec. 9664-68] 1686

        Bryan amendment barring the judge whose injunction or order had been disobeyed from trying the contempt case was proposed but withdrawn upon Rep. Webb's assurance that existing law so provided [51 Cong. Rec. 9666-68] 1689

    Section 21 (providing for appeals from contempt convictions) was debated [51 Cong. Rec. 9668-69] 1695

        Murray amendment to add a proviso that the procedure provided would not supersede the writ of habeas corpus was rejected [51 Cong. Rec. 9669] 1696

    Section 22 (providing that section 19 did not apply to contempts committed in the presence of the court, nor to contempts involving disobedience to orders entered in cases brought by the United States) was debated [51 Cong. Rec. 9669-72] 1696

        Murray amendment to add a proviso that in all contempt cases the accused has the right to trial was rejected [51 Cong. Rec. 9671] 1700

    Section 23 (providing that a contempt proceeding must be instituted within one year of the contemptuous "act" and that a contempt proceeding was not a bar to a criminal prosecution for the same "act") was debated [51 Cong. Rec. 9672] 1702

    Morgan amendment to add a new section 24, providing that any corporation possessing a virtual monopoly in the sale of any commodity could be judged a quasi-public corporation and made subject to the control of the Commissioner of Corporations, was rejected [51 Cong. Rec. 9674] 1708

    House returned to section 9 and adopted two corrective amendments but rejected Murray amendment lowering the jurisdictional threshold for the interlocking bank directorates provision from $2.5 million to $1 million [51 Cong. Rec. 9674-75] 1708

    House returned to section 11 and accepted Graham amendment placing a geographical limitation upon the scope of the subpoena power [51 Cong. Rec. 9675] 1709

    House returned to section 12 (personal guilt provision) [51 Cong. Rec. 9675-82] 1710

        Volstead substitute (introduced June 1) was rejected [51 Cong. Rec. 9678] 1716

June 2, 1914 — Cont.

Several other substitutes seeking to remove the conviction of a corporation as a condition precedent to the conviction of individual directors, officers, or agents were considered, one of which was adopted [51 Cong. Rec. 9682] 1723

Corrective amendment to Graham amendment to section 11 was adopted [51 Cong. Rec. 9682] 1724

Committee of the Whole House laid aside bill as amended with a favorable recommendation [51 Cong. Rec. 9682] 1725
[Bill print] 1728

June 5, 1914

House passed H.R. 15657 by a vote of 277-54 [51 Cong. Rec. 9909-12] 1738

June 6, 1914

H.R. 15657 received by the Senate and referred to the Judiciary Committee [51 Cong. Rec. 9929] 1743

July 22, 1914

H.R. 15657 was reported favorably, with amendments, by the Senate Judiciary Committee [51 Cong. Rec. 12468] 1743
[Senate Report No. 698] 1744
[Bill print] 1753

August 5, 1914

Senate agreed to consider H.R. 15657 [51 Cong. Rec. 13319] 1767

August 12, 1914

H.R. 15657 made the pending Senate business [51 Cong. Rec. 13633] 1768

August 13, 1914

Senate, sitting as the Committee of the Whole, began debate on H.R. 15657 [51 Cong. Rec. 13658-70] 1768

August 17, 1914

Senate continued debate on H.R. 15657. Consideration of proposed committee amendments began [51 Cong. Rec. 13844-59] 1791

Committee amendment to section 2, making the Act inapplicable to the Philippine Islands, was agreed to [51 Cong. Rec. 13849] 1801

Section 2 (relating to price discrimination) was struck on the ground that the subject was covered by the FTC Act (then in conference) [51 Cong. Rec. 13849] 1801

Section 3 (relating to refusals to deal in the mining and energy industries) was struck in its entirety [51 Cong. Rec. 13849] 1801

Section 4 (relating to exclusive dealing practices) was struck on the ground that the subject was covered by the FTC Act [51 Cong. Rec. 13849] 1802

Section 5 (granting a private right of action for violations of the antitrust laws) was discussed [51 Cong. Rec. 13849] 1802

Section 6 (making final judgments in government suits conclusive evidence in subsequent private suits and tolling the statute of limitations during the pendency of government action) was debated. Committee amendment, making the final judgment only prima facie evidence and adding a six-year statute of limitations for antitrust laws, was proposed. Sen. Thomas offered an amendment to the committee amendment, extending the section to suits then pending, which was accepted [51 Cong. Rec. 13849-59] 1802

August 18, 1914

Senate continued consideration of H.R. 15657 [51 Cong. Rec. 13897-925] 1823

CHRONOLOGICAL SYNOPSIS 1031

    Debate on section 6 was resumed [51 Cong. Rec. 13897-907] 1824

        Bryan amendment to the committee amendment, extending the prima facie evidence rule to judgments in criminal prosecutions, was agreed to [51 Cong. Rec. 13897-98] 1824

        Committee amendment as amended was debated and adopted [51 Cong. Rec. 13898-907] ..1825

    Section 7 (exempting labor and agricultural organizations) was debated [51 Cong. Rec. 13907-25] 1836

        Committee amendments removing fraternal and consumer organizations from the exemption and limiting the labor exemption to *lawful* actions were proposed [51 Cong. Rec. 13918] 1859

        Committee amendment striking fraternal organizations from the exemption was agreed to [51 Cong. Rec. 13925] 1877

August 19, 1914

Senate continued consideration of H.R. 15657, resuming debate on section 7 [51 Cong. Rec. 13963-83] 1877

    Committee amendment striking consumer organizations from the exemption was agreed to [51 Cong. Rec. 13963-64] 1877

    Committee amendment striking the words "orders, or associations" from the section at their first two appearances was agreed to [51 Cong. Rec. 13979] 1910

August 20, 1914

Senate continued consideration of H.R. 15657 [51 Cong. Rec. 14010-42] 1925

    Debate on section 7 was resumed [51 Cong. Rec. 14010-28] 1925

        Committee amendment inserting the word "lawfully" was agreed to [51 Cong. Rec. 14028] 1953

        Committee amendment striking the third occurrence of the words "orders, or associations" was adopted [51 Cong. Rec. 14028] 1953

        Committee amendment striking the second paragraph (antitrust exemption for associations of common carriers) was agreed to [51 Cong. Rec. 14028] 1954

    Committee amendments to section 8 (dealing with stock acquisitions by corporations) were adopted [51 Cong. Rec. 14029-30] 1954

    Committee amendments to section 9 (dealing with interlocking directorates) were adopted [51 Cong. Rec. 14030-31] 1957

    Committee proposal to insert a new section 9a, making it a felony for officers and directors of a common carrier to embezzle or willfully misapply the firm's assets, was debated. Sen. Kenyon offered an amendment extending this prohibition to intentional or negligent misapplication of assets [51 Cong. Rec. 14031-42] 1960

August 21, 1914

Senate continued consideration of H.R. 15657 [51 Cong. Rec. 14087-100] 1985

    Debate on the proposed new section 9a was resumed [51 Cong. Rec. 14087-88] 1985

        Kenyon amendment (offered Aug. 20) was rejected [51 Cong. Rec. 14087-88] 1985

        Additional amendments to the proposed section were considered but not acted upon at this time [51 Cong. Rec. 14088] 1986

    Motion to reconsider the deletion of sections 2 and 4 was debated [51 Cong. Rec. 14088-100] 1986

August 25, 1914

Senate continued consideration of H.R. 15657 [51 Cong. Rec. 14200-29] 2011

    Debate on the motion to reconsider sections 2 and 4 was resumed [51 Cong. Rec. 14200-23] 2012

        Senate agreed to reconsider the vote whereby section 4 was stricken (that part of the motion pertaining to section 2 was withdrawn) [51 Cong. Rec. 14223] 2065

August 25, 1914 — Cont.

Senate returned to section 9a and agreed to amend the committee amendment to require that the misapplied assets arise or accrue from commerce [51 Cong. Rec. 14223] 2065

Committee amendment to add a new section 9b, vesting jurisdiction to enforce sections 2, 4, 8, and 9 in the ICC as to common carriers and in the FTC as to all other commerce, and detailing the procedures to be followed by the Commissions, was debated. Sen. Walsh (on behalf of the committee) offered an amendment to the amendment, changing the procedural provision to conform to that established by section 5 of the FTC Act and authorizing the ICC and FTC to order divestiture of stock (for section 8 violations) or the replacement of directors (for section 9 violations) [51 Cong. Rec. 14223-29] 2066

August 26, 1914

Senate debated sections 2 and 4 of H.R. 15657 [51 Cong. Rec. 14249-76] 2078

Reed substitute for section 4 was adopted with minor changes [51 Cong. Rec. 14271-72] 2125

Senate again voted to adopt the committee amendment striking section 4 [51 Cong. Rec. 14272-73] 2128

Sen. Walsh (on behalf of the committee) offered an amendment adding a new section 4, prohibiting exclusive dealing or tying provisions in contracts for the sale or lease of patented products, which was agreed to with the addition of a criminal penalty proposed by Sen. Reed [51 Cong. Rec. 14273-76] 2129

August 27, 1914

Senate continued consideration of H.R. 15657 [51 Cong. Rec. 14312-43] 2136

Committee amendments deleting the criminal penalty provisions from sections 8 and 9 were debated and agreed to [51 Cong. Rec. 14312-21] 2136

Proposed new section 9b was debated [51 Cong. Rec. 14321-23] 2156

Walsh amendment (proposed Aug. 25) was agreed to [51 Cong. Rec. 14321-22] 2156

Walsh amendment to proposed section 9b, striking references to sections 2 and 4, was agreed to [51 Cong. Rec. 14323] 2159

Section 9b as amended was adopted [51 Cong. Rec. 14323] 2161

Committee amendment to section 10, placing venue in any district where a corporation "transacts any business" and providing for service of process in any district where it resides or might be found, was agreed to [51 Cong. Rec. 14324] 2161

Committee amendment to section 11, deleting the proviso placing a geographical limitation on subpoenas, was agreed to [51 Cong. Rec. 14324] 2162

Committee amendment to section 12 (personal guilt provision), clarifying that directors, officers, and agents of a corporation may be liable in their individual capacities for antitrust violations, was debated and adopted after Jones amendment to make the section applicable to violations of all, rather than just the penal, provisions of the antitrust laws was rejected [51 Cong. Rec. 14324-29] 2162

Section 14 was amended to specify that the right to a private cause of action (previously included in H.R. 15657) specifically applies to all violations of sections 4, 8, and 9 [51 Cong. Rec. 14329] 2173

Proviso to section 14, disallowing private suits for injunctive relief against common carriers in respect to matters subject to the jurisdiction of the Interstate Commerce Commission, was deleted [51 Cong. Rec. 14329] 2173

Committee amendment to section 15 (dealing with preliminary injunctions and temporary restraining orders) was agreed to, making irreparable injury to the applicant, rather than to his "property" or "property rights," a condition precedent to the granting of a temporary restraining order [51 Cong. Rec. 14329-30] 2174

A number of minor and perfecting committee amendments to sections 15, 16, 17, and 18 were agreed to without debate [51 Cong. Rec. 14330-31] 2176

Committee amendment to section 18 (dealing with injunctions in labor disputes), exempting various specified labor activities only from the antitrust laws, rather than from all laws, was debated [51 Cong. Rec. 14331-34] 2178

CHRONOLOGICAL SYNOPSIS 1033

August 28, 1974

Senate continued consideration of H.R. 15657 [51 Cong. Rec. 14363-78] 2186

    Debate on the committee amendment to section 18 was resumed. Sen. Culberson proposed an amendment to the committee amendment, changing "antitrust laws" to "any law of the United States," which was agreed to, as was the committee amendment as thus amended [51 Cong. Rec. 14364-67] 2186

    Minor committee amendment to section 19 was agreed to without debate [51 Cong. Rec. 14367] 2193

    Senate debated the interaction of sections 19, 20, and 22 and the right to a jury trial in contempt cases [51 Cong. Rec. 14367-76] 2193

    Minor committee amendments to section 20 (procedure in contempt cases) were agreed to without debate [51 Cong. Rec. 14377] 2215

    Thomas amendment adding a separability provision as new section 24 was agreed to [51 Cong. Rec. 14377] 2216

    Sen. Borah proposed an amendment to section 22, striking the exemption for contempts arising from court orders in government suits from the Act's contempt provisions [51 Cong. Rec. 14377] 2216

August 29, 1914

Senate continued consideration of H.R. 15657 [51 Cong. Rec. 14412-21] 2219

    Pending Borah amendment (introduced Aug. 28) was debated and rejected [51 Cong. Rec. 14412-17] 2219

    Sterling substitute contempt provisions for sections 19 and 20 were rejected [51 Cong. Rec. 14417-18] 2228

    Chilton amendment to section 9a, to add a sentence specifying that the section did not impair state court jurisdiction and that a state court judgment would be res judicata, was agreed to [51 Cong. Rec. 14418] 2231

    Section 8 was debated and several minor amendments adopted [51 Cong. Rec. 14418-20] 2231

August 31, 1914

Senate continued consideration of H.R. 15657 [51 Cong. Rec. 14451-79] 2236

    Unanimous-consent agreement limiting debate was agreed to [51 Cong. Rec. 14452] 2238

    Debate on section 8 was resumed [51 Cong. Rec. 14452-76] 2238

        Reed substitute for the first paragraph was rejected [51 Cong. Rec. 14452-59] 2238

        Walsh amendment to strike language at the end of the first paragraph, thereby making the sole test of illegality of a stock acquisition whether the effect was substantially to lessen competition between the acquired and acquiring corporations, was rejected [51 Cong. Rec. 14462] 2257

        Walsh amendment to the second paragraph, making holding companies *per se* unlawful, was rejected [51 Cong. Rec. 14462] 2257

        Walsh amendment to strike the words "eliminate or" from the second paragraph was agreed to; his amendment to delete the words "or to create a monopoly of any line of commerce" from the same paragraph was rejected [51 Cong. Rec. 14463] 2260

        Reed amendment to change the word "is" to the words "may be" in the first and second paragraphs, making the test for illegality for stock acquisitions "where the effect of such acquisition *may be* to substantially lessen competition," was agreed to without debate [51 Cong. Rec. 14464] 2261

        Shield amendments to strike the word "substantially" from the first and second paragraphs, thereby making the test of violation "where the effect . . . may be to lessen competition," were adopted [51 Cong. Rec. 14464] 2262

        Poindexter substitute for section 8, strictly prohibiting acquisition by one corporation of the stock of a competing corporation and imposing criminal penalties, was rejected [51 Cong. Rec. 14468] 2270

        Reed amendment to delete the clause making the section inapplicable to the formation of subsidiary corporations and branches thereof was rejected [51 Cong. Rec. 14473] 2281

August 31, 1914 — Cont.

    Conforming amendments, to strike the words "eliminate or" and "substantially" from several sentences in the section, were adopted [51 Cong. Rec. 14473] 2281

    Walsh amendment adding language specifying that the section was not intended to exempt any person from the penal provisions of the antitrust laws was accepted [51 Cong. Rec. 14473] 2281

    Cummins substitute for section 8 was rejected [51 Cong. Rec. 14476] 2287

Reed amendment to add a new section authorizing state attorneys general to bring antitrust suits was debated [51 Cong. Rec. 14476-79] 2287

    Sen. Kenyon offered an amendment to the Reed amendment, requiring the state attorney general to request the U.S. Attorney General to bring suit 60 days in advance of the state suit and disallowing state suits if a government suit is brought [51 Cong. Rec. 14478] 2293

September 1, 1914

Senate continued consideration of H.R. 15657 [51 Cong. Rec. 14513-47] 2294

    Pending Reed amendment (proposed Aug. 31), as modified to require 90-days notice to the U.S. Attorney General, to provide that a state suit may not be brought if the government brings suit, and to allow the U.S. Attorney General to participate in or control the state suit, was rejected [51 Cong. Rec. 14526] 2323

    Reed amendment to add a new section prohibiting corporations (other than common carriers) with capital and surplus exceeding $100 million from engaging in interstate commerce was rejected [51 Cong. Rec. 14527] 2324

    Reed amendment to add a new section providing for the dissolution of corporations that acquire assets from another corporation, partnership or individual so as to become a monopoly or a combination in restraint of trade was accepted [51 Cong. Rec. 14527] 2325

    Reed amendment to add a new section providing that a corporation convicted of an antitrust violation be fined at least 10% of the value of its assets plus the costs of suit was rejected [51 Cong. Rec. 14528] 2326

    Norris amendment to section 14, providing that private suits could be brought in any district in which one of the defendants resided, was agreed to [51 Cong. Rec. 14528] 2327

    Gallinger substitute for section 7 was rejected [51 Cong. Rec. 14530] 2331

    White technical amendment to section 9 was agreed to [51 Cong. Rec. 14530] 2332

    Pomerene amendment to section 9, allowing common carriers to make purchases from a corporation with an interlocking directorate without competitive bidding in emergency situations, was rejected [51 Cong. Rec. 14532] 2335

    Several technical amendments to section 9 were agreed to without debate [51 Cong. Rec. 14532] 2336

    Pomerene amendment to section 18, making injunctive relief available in labor disputes when necessary to prevent irreparable injury "to the party making the application" but not "to property, or to a property right, of the party making the application," was rejected [51 Cong. Rec. 14534] 2340

    Cummins amendment to section 9, removing the limitation that the prohibitions against interlocking directors only applied where at least one of the corporations had capital, surplus, and undivided profits exceeding $1 million, was rejected [51 Cong. Rec. 14543] 2358

    Cummins amendment to add a new section prohibiting corporations from engaging in commerce "if the amount of capital employed is so great as to destroy or prevent substantially competitive conditions in the general field of industry to which the business carried on belongs" and authorizing the FTC to enforce the prohibition was rejected [51 Cong. Rec. 14543] 2359

    Gallinger amendment to section 7, deleting agricultural and horticultural organizations from the antitrust exemption, was rejected [51 Cong. Rec. 14543] 2359

    Gallinger amendment to section 7, limiting the antitrust exemption to *"lawfully conducted"* labor, agricultural or horticultural organizations, was rejected [51 Cong. Rec. 14544] 2360

CHRONOLOGICAL SYNOPSIS   1035

Gallinger amendments to section 18, disallowing injunctive relief against "peaceful *and lawful*" persuasion of others to work or to abstain from working, were rejected [51 Cong. Rec. 14544]...2360

Poindexter amendment to section 8, prohibiting common carriers from holding or acquiring stock in mining and manufacturing corporations, was rejected [51 Cong. Rec. 14546]........2365

Sen. Cummins offered a substitute for section 7 [51 Cong. Rec. 14546-47]................2365

September 2, 1914

Senate concluded debate and passed H.R. 15657 with amendments [51 Cong. Rec. 14585-610].....2366

Pending Cummins amendment (introduced Sept. 1) was debated and rejected [51 Cong. Rec. 14585-90]..2366

Culberson amendment to section 7, to add the sentence "That the labor of a human being is not a commodity or article of commerce," was agreed to [51 Cong. Rec. 14591]...............2379

Cummins amendment to section 18, adding to the acts which cannot be enjoined that of "attending at any place where any such person or persons may lawfully be for the purpose of peacefully obtaining or communicating information," was agreed to [51 Cong. Rec. 14591]..2380

Lane amendment to section 12, proposing a limited informer's award, was rejected [51 Cong. Rec. 14596]..2389

Chilton amendment to add a new section declaring it unlawful for a corporation to do any business in a state contrary to the laws of that state or contrary to the laws of the state of incorporation was agreed to [51 Cong. Rec. 14596]...2390

Norris amendments to section 10, specifying that suits could be brought by stockholders of a corporation against the corporate officers, were agreed to. Norris amendment to section 14 (adopted Sept. 1) was then reconsidered and withdrawn [51 Cong. Rec. 14596]............2390

Senate agreed to further amend section 18 by striking the words "person or persons" and inserting the words "individual or individuals" [51 Cong. Rec. 14597]..................2392

H.R. 15657 as amended was reported from the Committee of the Whole to the Senate [51 Cong. Rec. 14597]...2392

Amendments other than those upon which a separate vote had been reserved were concurred in [51 Cong. Rec. 14597]..2392

Amendment to section 7, striking the word "consumers" (adopted Aug. 19), was concurred in [51 Cong. Rec. 14597]..2392

Clapp substitute for section 2 (stricken from the bill by the Committee of the Whole Aug. 17), prohibiting price discrimination between geographical areas, was rejected. The Committee's action in striking the section was then concurred in [51 Cong. Rec. 14597-99]..........2393

Section 4 as amended in the Committee of the Whole was debated and concurred in, with one additional, minor amendment. Senate rejected an amendment proposed by Sen. White rewording the section and an amendment by Sen. Newlands substituting for the entire section a provision for an FTC investigation of tying arrangements [51 Cong. Rec. 14599-606]......2396

Section 9a as agreed to in the Committee of the Whole was considered [51 Cong. Rec. 14606-07]...2413

Kenyon amendment to add the words "or intentionally or negligently permits or suffers to be misapplied" was rejected [51 Cong. Rec. 14606]....................................2413

Reed amendment to add the words "or willfully permits to be misapplied" was accepted [51 Cong. Rec. 14606]...2414

Section 9a as amended was concurred in [51 Cong. Rec. 14607].....................2415

Poindexter amendment to section 8 (rejected by the Committee of the Whole Sept. 1) was again rejected, and section 8 as amended by the Committee of the Whole was then concurred in [51 Cong. Rec. 14607]..2415

H.R. 15657 as amended was passed by the Senate by a vote of 46-16 [51 Cong. Rec. 14609-10]..2421

[Bill print]..2423

September 3, 1914

H.R. 15657 ordered to be printed with the amendments of the Senate numbered.
[Bill print] 2438

September 4, 1914

House disagreed to Senate amendments, asked for a conference, and appointed conferees [51 Cong. Rec. 14737] 2454

Senate insisted on its amendments, agreed to a conference, and appointed conferees [51 Cong. Rec. 14718] 2454

September 23, 1914

Conference report on H.R. 15657 (S. Doc. No. 583) was submitted in the Senate [51 Cong. Rec. 15588-91] 2455

September 24, 1914

Conference report on H.R. 15657 (S. Doc. No. 585) was reissued with corrections and presented to the Senate [51 Cong. Rec. 15637-40] 2456

September 25, 1914

Conference report on H.R. 15657 was submitted in the House.
[House Report No. 1168] 2456

Senate delayed consideration of the conference report on H.R. 15657 [51 Cong. Rec. 15663-64] ... 2470

September 26, 1914

Conference report on H.R. 15657 made the pending business in the Senate [51 Cong. Rec. 15774, 15789-93] 2472

September 28, 1914

Senate began debate on the conference report [51 Cong. Rec. 15818-31] 2474

September 29, 1914

Senate continued debate on the conference report [51 Cong. Rec. 15854-68] 2504

September 30, 1914

Senate continued debate on the conference report [51 Cong. Rec. 15934-58] 2533

October 1, 1914

Senate continued debate on the conference report [51 Cong. Rec. 15983-6008] 2586

October 2, 1914

Senate continued debate on the conference report [51 Cong. Rec. 16042-61] 2642

October 3, 1914

Senate continued debate on the conference report [51 Cong. Rec. 16105-18] 2683

October 5, 1914

Senate concluded debate and approved the conference report on H.R. 15657 [51 Cong. Rec. 16142-70] 2695

  Sen. Reed's motion to recommit the bill to the conference committee was rejected [51 Cong. Rec. 16170] 2756

  Conference report agreed to [51 Cong. Rec. 16170] 2757

October 6, 1914

House agreed to consider the conference report on H.R. 15657 [51 Cong. Rec. 16212-13] 2758

October 7, 1914

House began debate on the conference report [51 Cong. Rec. 16264-84] 2760

October 8, 1914

House concluded debate and agreed to the conference report on H.R. 15657 [51 Cong. Rec. 16316-45] 2789

October 15, 1914

H.R. 15657 signed into law by President Wilson.
 [*Statutes at Large* print] 1061

October 17, 1914

President Wilson commented on the statute in a letter to Rep. Underwood [51 Cong. Rec. A1187-88] 2837

Table of Reprinted Documents

CLAYTON ACT OF 1914

Statutory Materials

Clayton Act, ch. 323, 38 Stat. 730 (Oct. 15, 1914) 1061

Clayton Act as amended, 15 U.S.C. §§ 12, 13, 14-21, 22-27 (1976), 29 U.S.C. §§ 52-53 (1976)... 1043

Legislative Materials

Bills

Tentative antitrust bills ordered printed by Rep. Clayton (Tentative Nos. 1-4), 63d Cong., 2d Sess. (1914) 1074

H.R. 15657 (Clayton), 63d Cong., 2d Sess. (April 14, 1914) 1080

H.R. 15657 as reported by House Judiciary Committee, 63d Cong., 2d Sess. (May 6, 1914) 1163

H.R. 15657 as agreed upon in Committee of the Whole House, 63d Cong., 2d Sess. (June 2, 1914) 1728

H.R. 15657 as reported by Senate Judiciary Committee, 63d Cong., 2d Sess. (July 22, 1914) 1753

H.R. 15657 as amended and passed by Senate, 63d Cong., 2d Sess. (Sept. 2 [legislative day, Aug. 25], 1914) 2423

H.R. 15657 with Senate amendments numbered, 63d Cong., 2d Sess. (Sept. 3, 1914) ...2438

Hearings

Hearings Pursuant to S. Res. 98 Before the Senate Comm. on Interstate Commerce, 62d Cong., 3d Sess. 2184-88 (1913) (exhibit) 1071

Hearings on Trust Legislation Before the House Comm. on the Judiciary, 63d Cong., 2d Sess. 1567-83 (1914) (Tentative Bill Nos. 1-4) 1074

Reports

H.R. Rep. No. 627 (on H.R. 15657), 63d Cong., 2d Sess.

    Pt. 1 (May 6, 1914) reprinting H.R. Rep. Nos. 612 and 613 (majority views), 62d Cong., 2d Sess. (1912) 1089

    Pt. 2 (minority views) (May 12, 1914) reprinting H.R. Rep. Nos. 612 and 613 (minority views), 62d Cong., 2d Sess. (1912) 1125

    Pt. 3 (minority views) (May 13, 1914) 1152

    Pt. 4 (minority views) (May 13, 1914) 1160

S. Rep. No. 698 (on H.R. 15657), 63d Cong., 2d Sess. (July 22, 1914) 1744

H.R. Rep. No. 1168 (conference report on H.R. 15657), 63d Cong., 2d Sess. (Sept. 25, 1914) 2456

Congressional Record

Volume 51 – 63d Congress, 2d Session

Date	Pages	
May 6, 1914	8200-01	1181
May 22, 1914	9068-91	1182
May 23, 1914	9153-90	1233
May 25, 1914	9195-202	1317
May 26, 1914	9245-73	1330
May 28, 1914	9388-417	1390
May 29, 1914	9466-96	1448
June 1, 1914	9538-611	1506
June 2, 1914	9652-98	1661
June 5, 1914	9909-12	1738
June 6, 1914	9929	1743
July 22, 1914	12468	1743
Aug. 5, 1914	13319	1767
Aug. 12, 1914	13633	1768
Aug. 13, 1914	13658-70	1768
Aug. 17, 1914	13844-59	1791
Aug. 18, 1914	13897-925	1823
Aug. 19, 1914	13963-83	1877
Aug. 20, 1914	14010-42	1925
Aug. 21, 1914	14087-100	1985
Aug. 25, 1914	14200-29	2011
Aug. 26, 1914	14249-76	2078
Aug. 27, 1914	14312-34	2136
Aug. 28, 1914	14363-78	2186
Aug. 29, 1914	14412-21	2219
Aug. 31, 1914	14451-79	2236
Sept. 1, 1914	14513-47	2294
Sept. 2, 1914	14585-610	2366
Sept. 4, 1914	14718	2454
Sept. 4, 1914	14737	2454
Sept. 23, 1914	15588-89	2455
Sept. 24, 1914	15637	2456
Sept. 25, 1914	15663-64	2470
Sept. 26, 1914	15774, 15789-93	2472
Sept. 28, 1914	15818-31	2474
Sept. 29, 1914	15854-68	2504
Sept. 30, 1914	15934-58	2533
Oct. 1, 1914	15983-16009	2586
Oct. 2, 1914	16042-61	2642
Oct. 3, 1914	16105-18	2683
Oct. 5, 1914	16142-70	2695
Oct. 6, 1914	16212-13	2758
Oct. 7, 1914	16264-84	2760
Oct. 8, 1914	16316-45	2789
Oct. 17, 1914	A1187-88	2837

Presidential Document

Letter from President Woodrow Wilson to Rep. Oscar W. Underwood, 51 Cong. Rec. A1187-A1188 (Oct. 17, 1914) 2837

Case Reports

Citizen Publishing Co. v. United States, 394 U.S. 131, 89 S. Ct. 927, 22 L. Ed. 2d 148 (1969) 2885

Emich Motors Corp. v. General Motors Corp., 340 U.S. 558, 71 S. Ct. 408, 95 L. Ed. 534 (1951) 2865

Northern Pacific Railway Co. v. United States, 356 U.S. 1, 78 S. Ct. 514, 2 L. Ed. 2d 545 (1958)..2874

Standard Oil Co. of California v. United States, 337 U.S. 293, 69 S. Ct. 1051, 93 L. Ed. 1371 (1949)..2857

Tampa Electric Co. v. Nashville Coal Co., 365 U.S. 320, 81 S. Ct. 623, 5 L. Ed. 2d 580 (1961)...2879

United States v. E. I. du Pont de Nemours & Co., 353 U.S. 586, 77 S. Ct. 872, 1 L. Ed. 2d 1057 (1957)...2868

Miscellaneous

Representative lease and license agreement of the United Shoe Machinery Co. 1071

Current Version

CLAYTON ANTITRUST ACT AS AMENDED

15 U.S.C. §§ 12, 13, 14-21, 22-27 (1976)
29 U.S.C. §§ 52-53 (1976)

§ 12. Words defined; short title.

(a) "Antitrust laws," as used herein, includes the Act entitled "An Act to protect trade and commerce against unlawful restraints and monopolies," approved July second, eighteen hundred and ninety; sections seventy-three to seventy-seven, inclusive, of an Act entitled "An Act to reduce taxation, to provide revenue for the Government, and for other purposes," of August twenty-seventh, eighteen hundred and ninety-four; an Act entitled "An Act to amend sections seventy-three and seventy-six of the Act of August twenty-seventh, eighteen hundred and ninety-four, entitled 'An Act to reduce taxation, to provide revenue for the Government, and for other purposes,' " approved February twelfth, nineteen hundred and thirteen; and also this Act.

"Commerce," as used herein, means trade or commerce among the several States and with foreign nations, or between the District of Columbia or any Territory of the United States and any State, Territory, or foreign nation, or between any insular possessions or other places under the jurisdiction of the United States, or between any such possession or place and any State or Territory of the United States or the District of Columbia or any foreign nation, or within the District of Columbia or any Territory or any insular possession or other place under the jurisdiction of the United States: *Provided,* That nothing in this Act contained shall apply to the Philippine Islands.

The word "person" or "persons" wherever used in this Act shall be deemed to include corporations and associations existing under or authorized by the laws of either the United States, the laws of any of the Territories, the laws of any State, or the laws of any foreign country.

(b) Sections 61 to 66 of this title may be cited as the "Clayton Act". (Oct. 15, 1914, ch. 323, § 1, 38 Stat. 730; Sept. 30, 1976, Pub. L. 94-435, title III, § 305(b), 90 Stat. 1397.)

§ 13. Discrimination in price, services, or facilities.

(a) Price; selection of customers.

It shall be unlawful for any person engaged in commerce, in the course of such commerce, either directly or indirectly, to discriminate in price between different purchasers of commodities of like grade and quality, where either or any of the purchases involved in such discrimination are in commerce, where such commodities are sold for use, consumption, or resale within the United States or any Territory thereof or the District of Columbia or any insular possession or other place under the jurisdiction of the United States, and where the effect of such discrimination may be substantially to lessen competition or tend to create a monopoly in any line of commerce, or to injure, destroy, or prevent competition with any person who either grants or knowingly receives the benefit of such discrimination, or with customers of either of them: *Provided,* That nothing herein contained shall prevent differentials which make only due allowance for differences in the cost of manufacture, sale, or delivery resulting from the differing methods or quantities in which such commodities are to such purchasers sold or delivered: *Provided, however*, That the Federal Trade Commission may, after due investigation and hearing to all interested parties, fix and establish quantity limits, and revise the same as it finds necessary, as to particular commodities or classes of commodities, where it finds that available purchasers in greater quantities are so few as to render differentials on account thereof unjustly discriminatory or promotive of monopoly in any line of commerce; and the foregoing shall then not be construed to permit differentials based on differences in quantities greater than those so fixed and established: *And provided further*, That nothing herein contained shall prevent persons engaged in selling goods, wares, or merchandise in commerce from selecting their own customers in bona fide transactions and not in restraint of trade: *And provided further*, That nothing herein contained shall prevent price changes from time to time where in response to changing conditions affecting the market for or the marketability of the goods concerned, such as but not limited to actual or imminent deterioration of perishable goods, obsolescence of seasonal goods, distress sales under court process, or sales in good faith in discontinuance of business in the goods concerned.

(b) Burden of rebutting prima-facie case of discrimination.

Upon proof being made, at any hearing on a complaint under this section, that there has been discrimination in price or services or facilities furnished, the burden of rebutting the prima-facie case thus made by showing justification shall be upon the person charged with a violation of this section, and unless justification shall be affirmatively shown, the Commission is authorized to issue an order terminating the discrimination: *Provided, however*, That nothing herein contained shall prevent a seller rebutting the prima-facie case thus made by showing that his lower price or the furnishing of services or facilities to any purchaser or purchasers was made in good faith to meet an equally low price of a competitor, or the services or facilities furnished by a competitor.

(c) Payment or acceptance of commission, brokerage or other compensation.

It shall be unlawful for any person engaged in commerce, in the course of such commerce, to pay or grant, or to receive or accept, anything of value as a commission, brokerage, or other compensation, or any allowance or discount in lieu thereof, except for services rendered in connection with the sale or purchase of goods, wares, or merchandise, either to the other party to such transaction or to an agent, representative, or other intermediary therein where such intermediary is acting in fact for or in behalf, or is subject to the direct or indirect control, of any party to such transaction other than the person by whom such compensation is so granted or paid.

(d) Payment for services or facilities for processing or sale.

It shall be unlawful for any person engaged in commerce to pay or contract for the payment of anything of value to or for the benefit of a customer of such person in the course of such commerce as compensation or in consideration for any services or facilities furnished by or through such customer in connection with the processing, handling, sale, or offering for sale of any products or commodities manufactured, sold, or offered for sale by such person, unless such payment or consideration is available on proportionally equal terms to all other customers competing in the distribution of such products or commodites.

(e) Furnishing services or facilities for processing, handling, etc.

It shall be unlawful for any person to discriminate in favor of one purchaser against another purchaser or purchasers of a commodity bought for resale, with or without processing, by contracting to furnish or furnishing, or by contributing to the furnishing of, any services or facilities connected with the processing, handling, sale, or offering for sale of such commodity so purchased upon terms not accorded to all purchasers on proportionally equal terms.

(f) Knowingly inducing or receiving discriminatory price.

It shall be unlawful for any person engaged in commerce, in the course of such commerce, knowingly to induce or receive a discrimination in price which is prohibited by this section. (Oct. 15, 1914, ch. 323, § 2, 38 Stat. 730; June 19, 1936, ch. 592, § 1, 49 Stat. 1526.)

§ 14. Sale, etc., on agreement not to use goods of competitor.

It shall be unlawful for any person engaged in commerce, in the course of such commerce, to lease or make a sale or contract for sale of goods, wares, merchandise, machinery, supplies, or other commodities, whether patented or unpatented, for use, consumption, or resale within the United States or any Territory thereof or the District of Columbia or any insular possession or other place under the jurisdiction of the United States, or fix a price charged therefor, or discount from, or rebate upon, such price, on the condition, agreement, or understanding that the lessee or purchaser thereof shall not use or deal in the goods, wares, merchandise, machinery, supplies, or other commodities of a competitor or competitors of the lessor or seller, where the effect of such lease, sale, or contract for sale or such condition, agreement, or understanding may be to substantially lessen competition or tend to create a monopoly in any line of commerce. (Oct. 15, 1914, ch. 323, § 3, 38 Stat. 731.)

§ 15. Suits by persons injured; amount of recovery.

Any person who shall be injured in his business or property by reason of anything forbidden in the antitrust laws may sue therefor in any district court of the United States in the district in which the defendant resides or is found or has an agent, without respect to the amount in controversy, and shall recover threefold the damages by him sustained, and the cost of suit, including a reasonable attorney's fee. (Oct. 15, 1914, ch. 323, § 4, 38 Stat. 731.)

§ 15a. Suits by United States; amount of recovery.

Whenever the United States is hereafter injured in its business or property by reason of anything forbidden in the antitrust laws it may sue therefor in the United States district court for the district in which the defendant resides or is found or has an agent, without respect to the amount in controversy, and shall recover actual damages by it sustained and the cost of suit. (Oct. 15, 1914, ch. 323, § 4A, as added July 7, 1955, ch. 283, § 1, 69 Stat. 282.)

§ 15b. Limitation of actions.

Any action to enforce any cause of action under sections 15, 15a, or 15c of this title shall be forever barred unless commenced within four years after the cause of action accrued. No cause of action barred under existing law on the effective date of this section and sections 15a and 16 of this title shall be revived by said sections. (Oct. 15, 1914, ch. 323, § 4B, as added July 7, 1955, ch. 283, § 1, 69 Stat. 283; Sept. 30, 1976, Pub. L. 94-435, title III, § 302(1), 90 Stat. 1396.)

§ 15c. Actions by State attorneys general.

(a) Parens patriae.

(1) Any attorney general of a State may bring a civil action in the name of such State, as parens patriae on behalf of natural persons residing in such State, in any district court of the United States having jurisdiction of the defendant, to secure monetary relief as provided in this section for injury sustained by such natural persons to their property by reason of any violation of Sections 1 to 7 of this title. The court shall exclude from the amount of monetary relief awarded in such action any amount of monetary relief (A) which duplicates amounts which have been awarded for the same injury, or (B) which is properly allocable to (i) natural persons who have excluded their claims pursuant to subsection (b)(2) of this section, and (ii) any business entity.

(2) The court shall award the State as monetary relief threefold the total damage sustained as described in paragraph (1) of this subsection, and the cost of suit, including a reasonable attorney's fee.

(b) Notice; exclusion election; final judgment.

(1) In any action brought under subsection (a)(1) of this section, the State attorney general shall, at such times, in such manner, and with such content as the court may direct, cause notice thereof to be given by publication. If the court finds that notice given solely by publication would deny due process of law to any person or persons, the court may direct further notice to such person or persons according to the circumstances of the case.

(2) Any person on whose behalf an action is brought under subsection (a)(1) of this section may elect to exclude from adjudication the portion of the State claim for monetary relief attributable to him by filing notice of such election with the court within such time as specified in the notice given pursuant to paragraph (1) of this subsection.

(3) The final judgment in an action under subsection (a)(1) of this section shall be res judicata as to any claim under section 5 of this title by any person on behalf of whom such action was brought and who fails to give such notice within the period specified in the notice given pursuant to paragraph (1) of this subsection.

(c) Dismissal or compromise of action.

An action under subsection (a)(1) of this section shall not be dismissed or compromised without the approval of the court, and notice of any proposed dismissal or compromise shall be given in such manner as the court directs.

(d) Attorneys' fees.

In any action under subsection (a) of this section—

(1) the amount of the plaintiffs' attorney's fee, if any, shall be determined by the court; and

(2) the court may, in its discretion, award a reasonable attorney's fee to a prevailing defendant upon a finding that the State attorney general has acted in bad faith, vexatiously, wantonly, or for oppressive reasons.

(Oct. 15, 1914, ch. 323, § 4C, as added Sept. 30, 1976, Pub. L. 94–435, title III, § 301, 90 Stat. 1394.)

§ 15d. Measurement of damages.

In any action under section 15c(a)(1) of this title, in which there has been a determination that a defendant agreed to fix prices in violation of the sections 1 to 7 of this title, damages may be proved and assessed in the aggregate by statistical or sampling methods, by the computation of illegal overcharges, or by such other reasonable system of estimating aggregate damages as the court in its discretion may permit without the necessity of separately proving the individual claim of, or amount of damage to, persons on whose behalf the suit was brought. (Oct. 15, 1914, ch. 323, § 4D, as added Sept. 30, 1976, Pub. L. 94–435, title III, § 301, 90 Stat. 1395.)

§ 15e. Distribution of damages.

Monetary relief recovered in an action under section 15c(a)(1) of this title shall—

(1) be distributed in such manner as the district court in its discretion may authorize; or

(2) be deemed a civil penalty by the court and deposited with the State as general revenues;

subject in either case to the requirement that any distribution procedure adopted afford each person a reasonable opportunity to secure his appropriate portion of the net monetary relief. (Oct. 15, 1914, ch. 323. § 4E, as added Sept. 30, 1976, Pub. L. 94–435, title III, § 301, 90 Stat. 1395.)

§ 15f. Actions by Attorney General.

(a) Whenever the Attorney General of the United States has brought an action under the antitrust laws, and he has reason to believe that any State attorney general would be entitled to bring an action under sections 12 to 27 of this title based substantially on the same alleged violation of the antitrust laws, he shall promptly give written notification thereof to such State attorney general.

(b) To assist a State attorney general in evaluating the notice or in bringing any action under sections 12 to 27 of this title, the Attorney General of the United States shall, upon request by such State attorney general, make available to him, to the extent permitted by law, any investigative files or other materials which are or may be relevant or material to the actual or potential cause of action under sections 12 to 27 of this title. (Oct. 15, 1914, ch. 323, § 4F, as added Sept. 30, 1976, Pub. L. 94–435, title III, § 301, 90 Stat. 1395.)

§ 15g. Definitions.

For the purposes of sections 15c, 15d, 15e and 15f of this title:

(1) The term "State attorney general" means the chief legal officer of a State, or any other person authorized by State law to bring actions under section 15c of this title, and includes the Corporation Counsel of the District of Columbia, except that such term does not include any person employed or retained on—
  (A) a contingency fee based on a percentage of the monetary relief awarded under this section; or
  (B) any other contingency fee basis, unless the amount of the award of a reasonable attorney's fee to a prevailing plaintiff is determined by the court under section 15c(d)(1) of this title.
(2) The term "State" means a State, the District of Columbia, the Commonwealth of Puerto Rico, and any other territory or possession of the United States.
(3) The term "natural persons" does not include proprietorships or partnerships.

(Oct. 15, 1914, ch. 323, § 4G, as added Sept. 30, 1976, Pub. L. 94-435, title III, § 301, 90 Stat. 1396.)

§ 15h. Applicability of parens patriae actions.

Sections 15c, 15d, 15e, 15f, and 15g of this title shall apply in any State, unless such State provides by law for its nonapplicability in such State. (Oct. 15, 1914, ch. 323, § 4H, as added Sept. 30, 1976, Pub. L. 94-435, title III, § 301, 90 Stat. 1396.)

§ 16. Judgments.

(a) Prima facie evidence.

A final judgment or decree heretofore or hereafter rendered in any civil or criminal proceeding brought by or on behalf of the United States under the antitrust laws to the effect that a defendant has violated said laws shall be prima facie evidence against such defendant in any action or proceeding brought by any other party against such defendant under said laws or by the United States under section 15a of this title, as to all matters respecting which said judgment or decree would be an estoppel as between the parties thereto: *Provided*, That this section shall not apply to consent judgments or decrees entered before any testimony has been taken or to judgments or decrees entered in actions under section 15a of this title.

(b) Consent judgments and competitive impact statements; publication in Federal Register; availability of copies to the public.

Any proposal for a consent judgment submitted by the United States for entry in any civil proceeding brought by or on behalf of the United States under the antitrust laws shall be filed with the district court before which such proceeding is pending and published by the United States in the Federal Register at least 60 days prior to the effective date of such judgment. Any written comments relating to such proposal and any responses by the United States thereto, shall also be filed with such district court and published by the United States in the Federal Register within such sixty-day period. Copies of such proposal and any other materials and documents which the United States considered determinative in formulating such proposal, shall also be made available to the public at the district court and in such other districts as the court may subsequently direct. Simultaneously with the filing of such proposal, unless otherwise instructed by the court, the United States shall file with the district court, publish in the Federal Register, and thereafter furnish to any person upon request, a competitive impact statement which shall recite—

(1) the nature and purpose of the proceeding;
(2) a description of the practices or events giving rise to the alleged violation of the antitrust laws;
(3) an explanation of the proposal for a consent judgment, including an explanation of any unusual circumstances giving rise to such proposal or any provision contained therein, relief to be obtained thereby, and the anticipated effects on competition of such relief;
(4) the remedies available to potential private plaintiffs damaged by the

alleged violation in the event that such proposal for the consent judgment is entered in such proceeding;

(5) a description of the procedures available for modification of such proposal; and

(6) a description and evaluation of alternatives to such proposal actually considered by the United States.

(c) Publication of summaries in newspapers.

The United States shall also cause to be published, commencing at least 60 days prior to the effective date of the judgment described in subsection (b) of this section, for 7 days over a period of 2 weeks in newspapers of general circulation of the district in which the case has been filed, in the District of Columbia, and in such other districts as the court may direct—

(i) a summary of the terms of the proposal for the consent judgment,

(ii) a summary of the competitive impact statement filed under subsection (b) of this section,

(iii) and a list of the materials and documents under subsection (b) of this section which the United States shall make available for purposes of meaningful public comment, and the place where such materials and documents are available for public inspection.

(d) Consideration of public comments by Attorney General and publication of response.

During the 60-day period as specified in subsection (b) of this section, and such additional time as the United States may request and the court may grant, the United States shall receive and consider any written comments relating to the proposal for the consent judgment submitted under subsection (b) of this section. The Attorney General or his designee shall establish procedures to carry out the provisions of this subsection, but such 60-day time period shall not be shortened except by order of the district court upon a showing that (1) extraordinary circumstances require such shortening and (2) such shortening is not adverse to the public interest. At the close of the period during which such comments may be received, the United States shall file with the district court and cause to be published in the Federal Register a response to such comments.

(e) Public interest determination.

Before entering any consent judgment proposed by the United States under this section, the court shall determine that the entry of such judgment is in the public interest. For the purpose of such determination, the court may consider—

(1) the competitive impact of such judgment, including termination of alleged violations, provisions for enforcement and modification, duration or relief sought, anticipated effects of alternative remedies actually considered, and any other considerations bearing upon the adequacy of such judgment;

(2) the impact of entry of such judgment upon the public generally and individuals alleging specific injury from the violations set forth in the complaint including consideration of the public benefit, if any, to be derived from a determination of the issues at trial.

(f) Procedure for public interest determination.

In making its determination under subsection (e) of this section, the court may—

(1) take testimony of Government officials or experts or such other expert witnesses, upon motion of any party or participant or upon its own motion, as the court may deem appropriate;

(2) appoint a special master and such outside consultants or expert witnesses as the court may deem appropriate; and request and obtain the views, evaluations, or advice of any individual, group or agency of government with respect to any aspects of the proposed judgment or the effect of such judgment, in such manner as the court deems appropriate;

(3) authorize full or limited participation in proceedings before the court by interested persons or agencies, including appearance amicus curiae, intervention as a party pursuant to the Federal Rules of Civil Procedure, examination of witnesses or documentary materials, or participation in any other manner and extent which serves the public interest as the court may deem appropriate;

(4) review any comments including any objections filed with the United States under subsection (d) of this section concerning the proposed judgment and the responses of the United States to such comments and objections; and

(5) take such other action in the public interest as the court may deem appropriate.

(g) Filing of written or oral communications with the district court.

Not later than 10 days following the date of the filing of any proposal for a consent judgment under subsection (b) of this section, each defendant shall file with the district court a description of any and all written or oral communications by or on behalf of such defendant, including any and all written or oral communications on behalf of such defendant, or other person, with any officer or employee of the United States concerning or relevant to such proposal, except that any such communications made by counsel of record alone with the Attorney General or the employees of the Department of Justice alone shall be excluded from the requirements of this subsection. Prior to the entry of any consent judgment pursuant to the antitrust laws, each defendant shall certify to the district court that the requirements of this subsection have been complied with and that such filing is a true and complete description of such communications known to the defendant or which the defendant reasonably should have known.

(h) Inadmissibility as evidence of proceedings before the district court and the competitive impact statement.

Proceedings before the district court under subsections (e) and (f) of this section, and the competitive impact statement filed under subsection (b) of this section, shall not be admissible against any defendant in any action or proceeding brought by any other party against such defendant under the antitrust laws or by the United States under section 15a of this title nor constitute a basis for the introduction of the consent judgment as prima facie evidence against such defendant in any such action or proceeding.

(i) Suspension of limitations.

Whenever any civil or criminal proceeding is instituted by the United States to prevent, restrain, or punish violations of any of the antitrust laws, but not including an action under section 15a of this title, the running of the statute of limitations in respect of every private or State right of action arising under said laws and based in whole or in part on any matter complained of in said proceeding shall be suspended during the pendency thereof and for one year thereafter: *Provided, however,* That whenever the running of the statute of limitations in respect of a cause of action arising under section 15 or 15c of this title is suspended hereunder, any action to enforce such cause of action shall be forever barred unless commenced either within the period of suspension or within four years after the cause of action accrued. (Oct. 15, 1914, ch. 323, § 5, 38 Stat. 731; July 7, 1955, ch. 283, § 2, 69 Stat. 283; Dec. 21, 1974, Pub. L. 93-528, § 2, 88 Stat. 1706; Sept. 30, 1976, Pub. L. 94-435, title III, § 302(2), 90 Stat. 1396.)

§ 17. Antitrust laws not applicable to labor organizations.

The labor of a human being is not a commodity or article of commerce. Nothing contained in the antitrust laws shall be construed to forbid the existence and operation of labor, agricultural, or horticultural organizations, instituted for the purposes of mutual help, and not having capital stock or conducted for profit, or to forbid or restrain individual members of such organizations from lawfully carrying out the legitimate objects thereof; nor shall such organizations, or the members thereof, be held or construed to be illegal combinations or conspiracies in restraint of trade, under the antitrust laws. (Oct. 15, 1914, ch. 323 § 6, 38 Stat. 731.)

§ 18. Acquisition by one corporation of stock of another.

No corporation engaged in commerce shall acquire, directly or indirectly, the whole or any part of the stock or other share capital and no corporation subject to the jurisdiction of the Federal Trade Commission shall acquire the whole or any part of the assets of another corporation engaged also in commerce, where in any line of commerce in any section of the country, the effect of such acquisition may be substantially to lessen competition, or to tend to create a monopoly.

No corporation shall acquire, directly or indirectly, the whole or any part of the stock or other share capital and no corporation subject to the jurisdiction of the Federal Trade Commission shall acquire the whole or any part of the assets of one or more corporations engaged in commerce, where in any line of commerce in any section of the country, the effect of such acquisition, of such stocks or assets, or of the use of such stock by the voting or granting of proxies or otherwise, may be substantially to lessen competition, or to tend to create a monopoly.

This section shall not apply to corporations purchasing such stock solely for investment and not using the same by voting or otherwise to bring about, or in attempting to bring about, the substantial lessening of competition. Nor shall anything contained in this section prevent a corporation engaged in commerce from causing the formation of subsidiary corporations for the actual carrying on of their immediate lawful business, or the natural and legitimate branches or extensions thereof, or from owning and holding all or a part of the stock of such subsidiary corporations, when the effect of such formation is not to substantially lessen competition.

Nor shall anything herein contained be construed to prohibit any common carrier subject to the laws to regulate commerce from aiding in the construction of branches or short lines so located as to become feeders to the main line of the company so aiding in such construction or from acquiring or owning all or any part of the stock of such branch lines, nor to prevent any such common carrier from acquiring and owning all or any part of the stock of a branch or short line constructed by an independent company where there is no substantial competition between the company owning the branch line so constructed and the company owning the main line acquiring the property or an interest therein, nor to prevent such common carrier from extending any of its lines through the medium of the acquisition of stock or otherwise of any other common carrier where there is no substantial competition between the company extending its lines and the company whose stock, property, or an interest therein is so acquired.

Nothing contained in this section shall be held to affect or impair any right heretofore legally acquired: *Provided,* That nothing in this section shall be held or construed to authorize or make lawful anything heretofore prohibited or made illegal by the antitrust laws, nor to exempt any person from the penal provisions thereof or the civil remedies therein provided.

Nothing contained in this section shall apply to transactions duly consummated pursuant to authority given by the Civil Aeronautics Board, Federal Communications Commission, Federal Power Commission, Interstate Commerce Commission, the Securities and Exchange Commission in the exercise of its jurisdiction under section 79j of this title, the United States Maritime Commission, or the Secretary of Agriculture under any statutory provision vesting such power in such Commission, Secretary, or Board. (Oct. 15, 1914, ch. 323, § 7, 38 Stat. 731; Dec. 29, 1950, ch. 1184, 64 Stat. 1125.)

§ 18a. Premerger notification and waiting period.

(a) Filing.

Except as exempted pursuant to subsection (c) of this section, no person shall acquire, directly or indirectly, any voting securities or assets of any other person, unless both persons (or in the case of a tender offer, the acquiring person) file notification pursuant to rules under subsection (d)(1) of this section and the waiting period described in subsection (b)(1) of this section has expired, if—

>(1) the acquiring person, or the person whose voting securities or assets are being acquired, is engaged in commerce or in any activity affecting commerce;

>(2)(A) any voting securities or assets of a person engaged in manufacturing which has annual net sales or total assets of $10,000,000 or more are being acquired by any person which has total assets or annual net sales of $100,000,000 or more;

>(B) any voting securities or assets of a person not engaged in

manufacturing which has total assets of $10,000,000 or more are being acquired by any person which has total assets or annual net sales of $100,000,000 or more; or

    (C) any voting securities or assets of a person with annual net sales or total assets of $100,000,000 or more are being acquired by any person with total assets or annual net sales of $10,000,000 or more; and

    (3) as a result of such acquisition, the acquiring person would hold—

        (A) 15 per centum or more of the voting securities or assets of the acquired person, or

        (B) an aggregate total amount of the voting securities and assets of the acquired person in excess of $15,000,000.

In the case of a tender offer, the person whose voting securities are sought to be acquired by a person required to file notification under this subsection shall file notification pursuant to rules under subsection (d) of this section.

(b) Waiting period; publication; voting securities.

    (1) The waiting period required under subsection (a) of this section shall—

        (A) begin on the date of the receipt by the Federal Trade Commission and the Assistant Attorney General in charge of the Antitrust Division of the Department of Justice (hereinafter referred to in this section as the "Assistant Attorney General") of—

            (i) the completed notification required under subsection (a) of this section, or

            (ii) if such notification is not completed, the notification to the extent completed and a statement of the reasons for such noncompliance,

from both persons, or, in the case of a tender offer, the acquiring person; and

        (B) end on the thirtieth day after the date of such receipt (or in the case of a cash tender offer, the fifteenth day), or on such later date as may be set under subsections (e)(2) or (g)(2) of this section.

    (2) The Federal Trade Commission and the Assistant Attorney General may, in individual cases, terminate the waiting period specified in paragraph (1) and allow any person to proceed with any acquisition subject to this section, and promptly shall cause to be published in the Federal Register a notice that neither intends to take any action within such period with respect to such acquisition.

    (3) As used in this section—

        (A) The term "voting securities" means any securities which at present or upon conversion entitle the owner or holder thereof to vote for the election of directors of the issuer or, with respect to unincorporated issuers, persons exercising similar functions.

        (B) The amount or percentage of voting securities or assets of a person which are acquired or held by another person shall be determined by aggregating the amount or percentage of such voting securities or assets held or acquired by such other person and each affiliate thereof.

(c) Exempt transactions.

The following classes of transactions are exempt from the requirements of this section—

    (1) acquisitions of goods or realty transferred in the ordinary course of business;

    (2) acquisitions of bonds, mortgages, deeds of trust, or other obligations which are not voting securities;

    (3) acquisitions of voting securities of an issuer at least 50 per centum of the voting securities of which are owned by the acquiring person prior to such acquisition;

    (4) transfers to or from a Federal agency or a State or political subdivision thereof;

    (5) transactions specifically exempted from the antitrust laws by Federal statute;

    (6) transactions specifically exempted from the antitrust laws by Federal statute if approved by a Federal agency, if copies of all information and

documentary material filed with such agency are contemporaneously filed with the Federal Trade Commission and the Assistant Attorney General;

(7) transactions which require agency approval under section 1828(c) of Title 12, or section 1842 of Title 12;

(8) transactions which require agency approval under section 1843 of Title 12, section 1726 or 1730a(e) of Title 12, or section 1464 of Title 12, if copies of all information and documentary material filed with any such agency are contemporaneously filed with the Federal Trade Commission and the Assistant Attorney General at least 30 days prior to consummation of the proposed transaction;

(9) acquisitions, solely for the purpose of investment, of voting securities, if, as a result of such acquisition, the securities acquired or held do not exceed 10 per centum of the outstanding voting securities of the issuer;

(10) acquisitions of voting securities, if, as a result of such acquisition, the voting securities acquired do not increase, directly or indirectly, the acquiring person's per centum share of outstanding voting securities of the issuer;

(11) acquisitions, solely for the purpose of investment, by any bank, banking association, trust company, investment company, or insurance company, of (A) voting securities pursuant to a plan of reorganization or dissolution; or (B) assets in the ordinary course of its business; and

(12) such other acquisitions, transfers, or transactions, as may be exempted under subsection (d)(2)(B) of this section.

(d) Commission rules.

The Federal Trade Commission, with the concurrence of the Assistant Attorney General and by rule in accordance with section 553 of Title 5, consistent with the purposes of this section—

(1) shall require that the notification required under subsection (a) of this section be in such form and contain such documentary material and information relevant to a proposed acquisition as is necessary and appropriate to enable the Federal Trade Commission and the Assistant Attorney General to determine whether such acquisition may, if consummated, violate the antitrust laws; and

(2) may—

(A) define the terms used in this section;

(B) exempt, from the requirements of this section, classes of persons, acquisitions, transfers, or transactions which are not likely to violate the antitrust laws; and

(C) prescribe such other rules as may be necessary and appropriate to carry out the purposes of this section.

(e) Additional information; waiting period extensions.

(1) The Federal Trade Commission or the Assistant Attorney General may, prior to the expiration of the 30-day waiting period (or in the case of a cash tender offer, the 15-day waiting period) specified in subsection (b)(1) of this section, require the submission of additional information or documentary material relevant to the proposed acquisition, from a person required to file notification with respect to such acquisition under subsection (a) of this section prior to the expiration of the waiting period specified in subsection (b)(1) of this section, or from any officer, director, partner, agent, or employee of such person.

(2) The Federal Trade Commission or the Assistant Attorney General, in its or his discretion, may extend the 30-day waiting period (or in the case of a cash tender offer, the 15-day waiting period) specified in subsection (b)(1) of this section for an additional period of not more than 20 days (or in the case of a cash tender offer, 10 days) after the date on which the Federal Trade Commission or the Assistant Attorney General, as the case may be, receives from any person to whom a request is made under paragraph (1), or in the case of tender offers, the acquiring person, (A) all the information and documentary material required to be submitted pursuant to such a request, or (B) if such request is not fully complied with, the information and documentary material submitted and a statement of the reasons for such noncompliance.

Such additional period may be further extended only by the United States district court, upon an application by the Federal Trade Commission or the Assistant Attorney General pursuant to subsection (g)(2) of this section.

(f) Preliminary injunctions; hearings.

If a proceeding is instituted or an action is filed by the Federal Trade Commission, alleging that a proposed acquisition violates section 18 of this title or section 45 of this title, or an action is filed by the United States, alleging that a proposed acquisition violates such section 18 of this title or section 1 or 2 of this title, and the Federal Trade Commission or the Assistant Attorney General (1) files a motion for a preliminary injunction against consummation of such acquisition pendente lite, and (2) certifies to the United States district court for the judicial district within which the respondent resides or carries on business, or in which the action is brought, that it or he believes that the public interest requires relief pendente lite pursuant to this subsection—

(A) upon the filing of such motion and certification, the chief judge of such district court shall immediately notify the chief judge of the United States court of appeals for the circuit in which such district court is located, who shall designate a United States district judge to whom such action shall be assigned for all purposes; and

(B) the motion for a preliminary injunction shall be set down for hearing by the district judge so designated at the earliest practicable time, shall take precedence over all matters except older matters of the same character and trials pursuant to section 3161 of Title 18, and shall be in every way expedited.

(g) Civil penalty; compliance; power of court.

(1) Any person, or any officer, director, or partner thereof, who fails to comply with any provision of this section shall be liable to the United States for a civil penalty of not more than $10,000 for each day during which such person is in violation of this section. Such penalty may be recovered in a civil action brought by the United States.

(2) If any person, or any officer, director, partner, agent, or employee thereof, fails substantially to comply with the notification requirement under subsection (a) of this section or any request for the submission of additional information or documentary material under subsection (e)(1) of this section within the waiting period specified in subsection (b)(1) of this section and as may be extended under subsection (e)(2) of this section, the United States district court—

(A) may order compliance;

(B) shall extend the waiting period specified in subsection (b)(1) and as may have been extended under subsection (e)(2) until there has been substantial compliance, except that, in the case of a tender offer, the court may not extend such waiting period on the basis of a failure, by the person whose stock is sought to be acquired, to comply substantially with such notification requirement or any such request; and

(C) may grant such other equitable relief as the court in its discretion determines necessary or appropriate,

upon application of the Federal Trade Commission or the Assistant Attorney General.

(h) Disclosure exemption.

Any information or documentary material filed with the Assistant Attorney General or the Federal Trade Commission pursuant to this section shall be exempt from disclosure under section 552 of Title 5, and no such information or documentary material may be made public, except as may be relevant to any administrative or judicial action or proceeding. Nothing in this section is intended to prevent disclosure to either body of Congress or to any duly authorized committee or subcommittee of the Congress.

(i) Construction with other laws.

(1) Any action taken by the Federal Trade Commission or the Assistant Attorney General or any failure of the Federal Trade Commission or the Assistant Attorney General to take any action under this section shall not bar any proceeding or any

action with respect to such acquisition at any time under sections 12 to 27 of this title or any other provision of law.

(2) Nothing contained in this section shall limit the authority of the Assistant Attorney General or the Federal Trade Commission to secure at any time from any person documentary material, oral testimony, or other information under the Antitrust Civil Process Act, the Federal Trade Commission Act, or any other provision of law.

(j) Report to Congress; legislative recommendations.

Beginning not later than January 1, 1978, the Federal Trade Commission, with the concurrence of the Assistant Attorney General, shall annually report to the Congress on the operation of this section. Such report shall include an assessment of the effects of this section, of the effects, purpose, and need for any rules promulgated pursuant thereto, and any recommendations for revisions of this section. (Oct. 15, 1914, ch. 323, § 7A, as added Sept. 30, 1976, Pub. L. 94-435, title II, § 201, 90 Stat. 1390.)

§ 19. Interlocking directorates and officers.

No private banker or director, officer, or employee of any member bank of the Federal Reserve System or any branch thereof shall be at the same time a director, officer, or employee of any other bank, banking association, savings bank, or trust company organized under the National Bank Act or organized under the laws of any State or of the District of Columbia, or any branch thereof, except that the Board of Governors of the Federal Reserve System may by regulation permit such service as a director, officer, or employee of not more than one other such institution or branch thereof; but the foregoing prohibition shall not apply in the case of any one or more of the following or any branch thereof:

(1) A bank, banking association, savings bank, or trust company, more than 90 per centum of the stock of which is owned directly or indirectly by the United States or by any corporation of which the United States directly or indirectly owns more than 90 per centum of the stock.

(2) A bank, banking association, savings bank, or trust company which has been placed formally in liquidation or which is in the hands of a receiver, conservator, or other official exercising similar functions.

(3) A corporation, principally engaged in international or foreign banking or banking in a dependency or insular possession of the United States which has entered into an agreement with the Board of Governors of the Federal Reserve System pursuant to section 601 to 604a of Title 12.

(4) A bank, banking association, savings bank, or trust company, more than 50 per centum of the common stock of which is owned directly or indirectly by persons who own directly or indirectly more than 50 per centum of the common stock of such member bank.

(5) A bank, banking association, savings bank, or trust company not located and having no branch in the same city, town, or village as that in which such member bank or any branch thereof is located, or in any city, town, or village contiguous or adjacent thereto.

(6) A bank, banking association, savings bank, or trust company not engaged in a class or classes of business in which such member bank is engaged.

(7) A mutual savings bank having no capital stock.

Until February 1, 1939, nothing in this section shall prohibit any director, officer, or employee of any member bank of the Federal Reserve System, or any branch thereof, who is lawfully serving at the same time as a private banker or as a director, officer, or employee of any other bank, banking association, savings bank, or trust company, or any branch thereof, on August 23, 1935, from continuing such service.

The Board of Governors of the Federal Reserve System is authorized and directed to enforce compliance with this section, and to prescribe such rules and regulations as it deems necessary for that purpose.

No person at the same time shall be a director in any two or more corporations, any one of which has capital, surplus, and undivided profits aggregating more than $1,000,000, engaged in whole or in part in commerce, other than banks, banking associations, trust companies, and common carriers subject to the Act to regulate commerce, approved February fourth, eighteen hundred and eighty-seven, if such corporations are or shall have been theretofore, by virtue of their business and location of operation, competitors, so that the elimination of competition by agreement between them would constitute a violation of any of the provisions of any of the antitrust laws. The eligibility of a director under the foregoing provision shall be determined by the aggregate amount of the capital, surplus, and undivided profits, exclusive of dividends declared but not paid to stockholders, at the end of the fiscal year of said corporation next preceding the election of directors, and when a director has been elected in accordance with the provisions of this Act it shall be lawful for him to continue as such for one year thereafter.

When any person elected or chosen as a director or officer or selected as an employee of any bank or other corporation subject to the provisions of this Act is eligible at the time of his election or selection to act for such bank or other corporation in such capacity his eligibility to act in such capacity shall not be affected and he shall not become or be deemed amenable to any of the provisions hereof by reason of any change in the affairs of such bank or other corporation from whatsoever cause, whether specifically excepted by any of the provisions hereof or not, until the expiration of one year from the date of his election or employment. (Oct. 15, 1914, ch. 323, § 8, 38 Stat. 732; May 15, 1916, ch. 120, 39 Stat. 121; May 26, 1920, ch. 206, 41 Stat. 626; Mar. 9, 1928, ch. 165, 45 Stat. 253; Mar. 2, 1929, ch. 581, 45 Stat. 1536; Aug. 23, 1935, ch. 614, § 329, 49 Stat. 717.)

§ 19a. Repealed.   Aug. 23, 1935, ch. 614, § 329, 49 Stat. 717.

§ 20. Purchases by common carriers in case of interlocking directorates, etc.

No common carrier engaged in commerce shall have any dealings in securities, supplies, or other articles of commerce, or shall make or have any contracts for construction or maintenance or any kind, to the amount of more than $50,000, in the aggregate, in any one year, with another corporation, firm, partnership, or association when the said common carrier shall have upon its board of directors or as its president, manager, or as its purchasing or selling officer, or agent in the particular transaction, any person who is at the same time a director, manager, or purchasing or selling officer of, or who has any substantial interest in, such other corporation, firm, partnership, or association, unless and except such purchases shall be made from, or such dealings shall be with, the bidder whose bid is the most favorable to such common carrier, to be ascertained by competitive bidding under regulations to be prescribed by rule or otherwise by the Interstate Commerce Commission. No bid shall be received unless the name and address of the bidder or the names and addresses of the officers, directors, and general managers thereof, if the bidder be a corporation, or of the members, if it be a partnership or firm, be given with the bid.

Any person who shall, directly or indirectly, do or attempt to do anything to prevent anyone from bidding, or shall do any act to prevent free and fair competition among the bidders or those desiring to bid, shall be punished as prescribed in this section in the case of an officer or director.

Every such common carrier having any such transactions or making any such purchases shall, within thirty days after making the same, file with the Interstate Commerce Commission a full and detailed statement of the transaction showing the manner of the competitive bidding, who were the bidders, and the names and addresses of the directors and officers of the corporations and the members of the firm or partnership bidding; and whenever the said commission shall, after investigation or hearing, have reason to believe that the law has been violated in and about the said purchases or transactions, it shall transmit all papers and documents and its own views or findings regarding the transaction to the Attorney General.

If any common carrier shall violate this section, it shall be fined not exceeding $25,000; and every such director, agent, manager, or officer thereof who shall have knowingly voted for or directed the act constituting such violation, or who shall have aided or abetted in such violation, shall be deemed guilty of a misdemeanor and shall be fined not exceeding $5,000 or confined in jail not exceeding one year, or both, in the discretion of the court. (Oct. 15, 1914, ch. 323, § 10, 38 Stat. 734.)

§ 21. Enforcement provisions.

(a) Commissions and Boards authorized to enforce compliance.

Authority to enforce compliance with sections 13, 14, 18, and 19 of this title by the persons respectively subject thereto is vested in the Interstate Commerce Commission where applicable to common carriers subject to the Interstate Commerce Act, as amended; in the Federal Communications Commission where applicable to common carriers engaged in wire or radio communication or radio transmission of energy; in the Civil Aeronautics Board where applicable to air carriers and foreign air carriers subject to the Civil Aeronautics Act of 1938; in the Federal Reserve Board where applicable to banks, banking associations, and trust companies; and in the Federal Trade Commission where applicable to all other character of commerce to be exercised as follows:

(b) Issuance of complaints for violations; hearing; intervention; filing of testimony; report; cease and desist orders; reopening and alteration of reports or orders.

Whenever the Commission or Board vested with jurisdiction thereof shall have reason to believe that any person is violating or has violated any of the provisions of sections 13, 14, 18, and 19 of this title, it shall issue and serve upon such person and the Attorney General a complaint stating its charges in that respect, and containing a notice of a hearing upon a day and at a place therein fixed at least thirty days after the service of said complaint. The person so complained of shall have the right to appear at the place and time so fixed and show cause why an order should not be entered by the Commission or Board requiring such person to cease and desist from the violation of the law so charged in said complaint. The Attorney General shall have the right to intervene and appear in said proceeding and any person may make application, and upon good cause shown may be allowed by the Commission or Board, to intervene and appear in said proceeding by counsel or in person. The testimony in any such proceeding shall be reduced to writing and filed in the office of the Commission or Board. If upon such hearing the Commission or Board, as the case may be, shall be of the opinion that any of the provisions of said sections have been or are being violated, it shall make a report in writing, in which it shall state its findings as to the facts, and shall issue and cause to be served on such person an order requiring such person to cease and desist from such violations, and divest itself of the stock, or other share capital, or assets, held or rid itself of the directors chosen contrary to the provisions of sections 18 and 19 of this title, if any there be, in the manner and within the time fixed by said order. Until the expiration of the time allowed for filing a petition for review, if no such petition has been duly filed within such time, or, if a petition for review has been filed within such time then until the record in the proceeding has been filed in a court of appeals of the United States, as hereinafter provided, the Commission or Board may at any time, upon such notice and in such manner as it shall deem proper, modify or set aside, in whole or in part, any report or any order made or issued by it under this section. After the expiration of the time allowed for filing a petition for review, if no such petition has been duly filed within such time, the Commission or Board may at any time, after notice and opportunity for hearing, reopen and alter, modify, or set aside, in whole or in part, any report or order made or issued by it under this section, whenever in the opinion of the Commission or Board conditions of fact or of law have so changed as to require such action or if the public interest shall so require: *Provided, however*, That the said person may, within sixty days after service upon him or it of said report or order entered after such a reopening, obtain a review thereof in the appropriate court of appeals of the United States, in the manner provided in subsection (c) of this section.

(c) Review of orders; jurisdiction; filing of petition and record of proceeding; conclusiveness of findings; additional evidence; modification of findings; finality of judgment and decree.

Any person required by such order of the commission or board to cease and desist from any such violation may obtain a review of such order in the court of appeals of the United States for any circuit within which such violation occurred or within which such person resides or carries on business, by filing in the court, within sixty days after the date of the service of such order, a written petition praying that the order of the commission or board be set aside. A copy of such petition shall be forthwith transmitted by the clerk of the court to the commission or board, and thereupon the commission or board shall file in the court the record in the proceeding, as provided in section 2112 of Title 28. Upon such filing of the petition the court shall have jurisdiction of the proceeding and of the question determined therein concurrently with the commission or board until the filing of the record, and shall have power to make and enter a decree affirming, modifying, or setting aside the order of the commission or board, and enforcing the same to the extent that such order is affirmed, and to issue such writs as are ancillary to its jurisdiction or are necessary in its judgment to prevent injury to the public or to competitors pendente lite. The findings of the commission or board as to the facts, if supported by substantial evidence, shall be conclusive. To the extent that the order of the commission or board is affirmed, the court shall issue its own order commanding obedience to the terms of such order of the commission or board. If either party shall apply to the court for leave to adduce additional evidence, and shall show to the satisfaction of the court that such additional evidence is material and that there were reasonable grounds for the failure to adduce such evidence in the proceeding before the commission or board, the court may order such additional evidence to be taken before the commission or board, and to be adduced upon the hearing in such manner and upon such terms and conditions as to[1] the court may see proper. The commission or board may modify its findings as to the facts, or make new findings, by reason of the additional evidence so taken, and shall file such modified or new findings, which if supported by substantial evidence, shall be conclusive, and its recommedation, if any, for the modification or setting aside of its original order, with the return of such additional evidence. The judgment and decree of the court shall be final, except that the same shall be subject to review by the Supreme Court upon certiorari, as provided in section 1254 of Title 28.

(d) Exclusive jurisdiction of Court of Appeals.

Upon the filing of the record with its jurisdiction of the court of appeals to affirm, enforce, modify, or set aside orders of the commission or board shall be exclusive.

(e) Preference; liability under antitrust laws.

Such proceedings in the court of appeals shall be given precedence over other cases pending therein, and shall be in every way expedited. No order of the commission or board or judgment of the court to enforce the same shall in anywise relieve or absolve any person from any liability under the antitrust laws.

(f) Service of complaints, orders and other processes.

Complaints, orders, and other processes of the commission or board under this section may be served by anyone duly authorized by the commission or board, either (1) by delivering a copy thereof to the person to be served, or to a member of the partnership to be served, or to the president, secretary, or other executive officer or a director of the corporation to be served; or (2) by leaving a copy thereof at the residence or the principal office or place of business of such person; or (3) by mailing by registered or certified mail a copy thereof addressed to such person at his or its residence or principal office or place of business. The verified return by the person so serving said complaint, order, or other process setting forth the manner of said service shall be proof of the same, and the return post office receipt for said complaint, order, or other process mailed by registered or certified mail as aforesaid shall be proof of the service of the same.

(g) Finality of orders generally.

Any order issued under subsection (b) of this section shall become final—
> (1) upon the expiration of the time allowed for filing a petition for review, if no such petition has been duly filed within such time; but the commission or board may thereafter modify or set aside its order to the extent provided in the last sentence of subsection (b) of this section; or
> (2) upon the expiration of the time allowed for filing a petition for certiorari, if the order of the commission or board has been affirmed, or the

---

[1] So in original.

petition for review has been dismissed by the court of appeals, and no petition for certiorari has been duly filed; or

(3) upon the denial of a petition for certiorari, if the order of the commission or board has been affirmed or the petition for review has been dismissed by the court of appeals; or

(4) upon the expiration of thirty days from the date of issuance of the mandate of the Supreme Court, if such Court directs that the order of the commission or board be affirmed or the petition for review be dismissed.

(h) Finality of orders modified by Supreme Court.

If the Supreme Court directs that the order of the commission or board be modified or set aside, the order of the commission or board rendered in accordance with the mandate of the Supreme Court shall become final upon the expiration of thirty days from the time it was rendered, unless within such thirty days either party has instituted proceedings to have such order corrected to accord with the mandate, in which event the order of the commission or board shall become final when so corrected.

(i) Finality of orders modified by Court of Appeals.

If the order of the commission or board is modified or set aside by the court of appeals, and if (1) the time allowed for filing a petition for certiorari has expired and no such petition has been duly filed, or (2) the petition for certiorari has been denied, or (3) the decision of the court has been affirmed by the Supreme Court then the order of the commission or board rendered in accordance with the mandate of the court of appeals shall become final on the expiration of thirty days from the time such order of the commission or board was rendered, unless within such thirty days either party has instituted proceedings to have such order corrected so that it will accord with the mandate, in which event the order of the commission or board shall become final when so corrected.

(j) Finality of orders issued on rehearing ordered by Court of Appeals or Supreme Court.

If the Supreme Court orders a rehearing; or if the case is remanded by the court of appeals to the commission or toward [sic] for a rehearing, and if (1) the time allowed for filing a petition for certiorari has expired, and no such petition has been duly filed, or (2) the petition for certiorari has been denied, or (3) the decision of the court has been affirmed by the Supreme Court, then the order of the commission or board rendered upon such rehearing shall become final in the same manner as though no prior order of the commission or board had been rendered.

(k) Definition of mandate.

As used in this section the term "mandate", in case a mandate has been recalled prior to the expiration of thirty days from the date of issuance thereof, means the final mandate.

(*l*) Penalties.

Any person who violates any order issued by the commission or board under subsection (b) of this section after such order has become final, and while such order is in effect, shall forfeit and pay to the United States a civil penalty of not more than $5,000 for each violation, which shall accrue to the United States and may be recovered in a civil action brought by the United States. Each separate violation of any such order shall be a separate offense, except that in the case of a violation through continuing failure or neglect to obey a final order of the commission or board each day of continuance of such failure or neglect shall be deemed a separate offense. (Oct. 15, 1914, ch. 323, § 11, 38 Stat. 734; Feb. 13, 1925, ch. 229, § 2, 43 Stat. 939; June 19, 1934, ch. 652, § 602 (d), 48 Stat. 1102; Aug. 23, 1935, ch. 614, § 203 (a), 49 Stat. 704; June 23, 1938, ch. 601, § 1107 (g), 52 Stat. 1028; June 25, 1948, ch. 646, § 32 (a), 62 Stat. 991; May 24, 1949, ch. 139, § 127, 63 Stat. 107; Dec. 29, 1950, ch. 1184, 64 Stat. 1125; Aug. 28, 1958, Pub. L. 85-791, § 4, 72 Stat. 943; July 23, 1959, Pub. L. 86-107, § 1, 73 Stat. 243.)

§ 22. District in which to sue corporation.

Any suit, action, or proceeding under the antitrust laws against a corporation may be brought not only in the judicial district whereof it is an inhabitant, but also in any district wherein it may be found or transacts business; and all process in such cases may be served in the district of which it is an inhabitant, or wherever it may be found. (Oct. 15, 1914, ch. 323, § 12, 38 Stat. 736.)

§ 23. Suits by United States; subpoenas for witnesses.

In any suit, action, or proceeding brought by or on behalf of the United States subpoenas for witnesses who are required to attend a court of the United States in any judicial district in any case, civil or criminal, arising under the antitrust laws may run into any other district: *Provided*, That in civil cases no writ of subpoena shall issue for witnesses living out of the district in which the court is held at a greater distance than one hundred miles from the place of holding the same without the permission of the trial court being first had upon proper application and cause shown. (Oct. 15, 1914, ch. 323, § 13, 38 Stat. 736.)

§ 24. Liability of directors and agents of corporation.

Whenever a corporation shall violate any of the penal provisions of the antitrust laws, such violation shall be deemed to be also that of the individual directors, officers, or agents of such corporation who shall have authorized, ordered, or done any of the acts constituting in whole or in part such violation, and such violation shall be deemed a misdemeanor, and upon conviction therefor of any such director, officer, or agent he shall be punished by a fine of not exceeding $5,000 or by imprisonment for not exceeding one year, or by both, in the discretion of the court. (Oct. 15, 1914, ch. 323, § 14, 38 Stat. 736.)

§ 25. Restraining violations; procedure.

The several district courts of the United States are invested with jurisdiction to prevent and restrain violations of this Act, and it shall be the duty of the several United States attorneys, in their respective districts, under the direction of the Attorney General, to institute proceedings in equity to prevent and restrain such violations. Such proceedings may be by way of petition setting forth the case and praying that such violation shall be enjoined or otherwise prohibited. When the parties complained of shall have been duly notified of such petition, the court shall proceed, as soon as may be, to the hearing and determination of the case; and pending such petition, and before final decree, the court may at any time make such temporary restraining order or prohibition as shall be deemed just in the premises. Whenever it shall appear to the court before which any such proceeding may be pending that the ends of justice require that other parties should be brought before the court, the court may cause them to be summoned whether they reside in the district in which the court is held or not, and subpoenas to that end may be served in any district by the marshal thereof. (Oct. 15, 1914, ch. 323, § 15, 38 Stat. 736; June 25, 1948, ch. 646, § 1, 62 Stat. 909.)

§ 26. Injunctive relief for private parties; exception; costs.

Any person, firm, corporation, or association shall be entitled to sue for and have injunctive relief, in any court of the United States having jurisdiction over the parties, against threatened loss or damage by a violation of the antitrust laws, including sections 13, 14, 18, and 19 of this title, when and under the same conditions and principles as injunctive relief against threatened conduct that will cause loss or damage is granted by courts of equity, under the rules governing such proceedings, and upon the execution of proper bond against damages for an injunction improvidently granted and a showing that the danger of irreparable loss or damage is immediate, a preliminary injunction may issue: *Provided*, That nothing herein contained shall be construed to entitle any person, firm, corporation, or association, except the United States, to bring suit in equity for injunctive relief against any common carrier subject to the provisions of the Act to regulate commerce, approved February fourth, eighteen hundred and eighty-seven, in respect of any matter subject to the regulation, supervision, or other jurisdiction of the Interstate Commerce Commission. In any action under this section in which the plaintiff substantially prevails, the court shall award the cost of suit, including a reasonable attorney's fee, to such plaintiff. (Oct. 15, 1914, ch. 323, § 16, 38 Stat. 737; Sept. 30, 1976, Pub. L. 94-435, title III, § 302(3), 90 Stat. 1936.)

§ 27. Effect of partial invalidity.

If any clause, sentence, paragraph, or part of this Act shall, for any reason, be adjudged by any court of competent jurisdiction to be invalid, such judgment shall not affect, impair, or invalidate the remainder thereof, but shall be confined in its operation to the clause, sentence, paragraph, or part thereof directly involved in the controversy in which such judgment shall have been rendered. (Oct. 15, 1914, ch. 323, § 26, 38 Stat. 740.)

29 U.S.C. §§ 52-53 (1976)

§ 52. Statutory restriction of injunctive relief.

No restraining order or injunction shall be granted by any court of the United States, or a judge or the judges thereof, in any case between an employer and employees, or between employers and employees, or between employees, or between persons employed and persons seeking employment, involving, or growing out of, a dispute concerning terms or conditions of employment, unless necessary to prevent irreparable injury to property, or to a property right, of the party making the application, for which injury there is no adequate remedy at law, and such property or property right must be described with particularity in the application, which must be in writing and sworn to by the applicant or by his agent or attorney.

And no such restraining order or injunction shall prohibit any person or persons, whether singly or in concert, from terminating any relation of employment, or from ceasing to perform any work or labor, or from recommending, advising, or persuading others by peaceful means so to do; or from attending at any place where any such person or persons may lawfully be, for the purpose of peacefully obtaining or communicating information, or from peacefully persuading any person to work or to abstain from working; or from ceasing to patronize or to employ any party to such dispute, or from recommending, advising, or persuading others by peaceful and lawful means so to do; or from paying or giving to, or withholding from, any person engaged in such dispute, any strike benefits or other moneys or things of value; or from peaceably assembling in a lawful manner, and for lawful purposes; or from doing any act or thing which might lawfully be done in the absence of such dispute by any party thereto; or shall any of the acts specified in this paragraph be considered or held to be violations of any law of the United States. (Oct. 15, 1914, ch. 323, § 20, 38 Stat. 738.)

§ 53. "Person" or "persons" defined.

The word "person" or "persons" wherever used in section 52 of this title shall be deemed to include corporations and associations existing under or authorized by the laws of either the United States, the laws of any of the Territories, the laws of any State, or the laws of any foreign country. (Oct. 15, 1914, ch. 323, § 1, 38 Stat. 730.)

Original Version

CLAYTON ANTITRUST ACT
October 15, 1914

Ch. 323, 38 Stat. 730

An Act To supplement existing laws against unlawful restraints and monopolies, and for other purposes.

Be it enacted by the Senate and House of Representatives of the United States of America in Congress assembled, That "antitrust laws," as used herein, includes the Act entitled "An Act to protect trade and commerce against unlawful restraints and monopolies," approved July second, eighteen hundred and ninety; sections seventy-three to seventy-seven, inclusive, of an Act entitled "An Act to reduce taxation, to provide revenue for the Government, and for other purposes," of August twenty-seventh, eighteen hundred and ninety-four; an Act entitled "An Act to amend sections seventy-three and seventy-six of the Act of August twenty-seventh, eighteen hundred and ninety-four, entitled 'An Act to reduce taxation, to provide revenue for the Government, and for other purposes,'" approved February twelfth, nineteen hundred and thirteen; and also this Act.

"Commerce," as used herein, means trade or commerce among the several States and with foreign nations, or between the District of Columbia or any Territory of the United States and any State, Territory, or foreign nation, or between any insular possessions or other places under the jurisdiction of the United States, or between any such possession or place and any State or Territory of the United States or the District of Columbia or any foreign nation, or within the District of Columbia or any Territory or any insular possession or other place under the jurisdiction of the United States: *Provided,* That nothing in this Act contained shall apply to the Philippine Islands.

The word "person" or "persons" wherever used in this Act shall be deemed to include corporations and associations existing under or authorized by the laws of either the United States, the laws of any of the Territories, the laws of any State, or the laws of any foreign country.[5.302a]

SEC. 2.[5.303] That it shall be unlawful for any person engaged in commerce, in the course of such commerce, either directly or indirectly to discriminate in price between different purchasers of commodities, which commodities are sold for use, consumption, or resale within the United States or any Territory thereof or the District of Columbia or any insular possession or other place under the jurisdiction of the United States, where the effect of such discrimination may be to substantially lessen competition or tend to create a monopoly in any line of commerce: *Provided,* That nothing herein contained shall prevent discrimination in price between purchasers of commodities on

---

[5.302a] Section 1 (definitions) was designated subsection (a) and a new subsection (b) providing a short title (the "Clayton Act") was added by the Hart-Scott-Rodino Antitrust Improvements Act of 1976, Pub. L. No. 94–435, tit. III, § 305(b), 90 Stat. 1397, the legislative history of which is set forth in part II of this set. For the current version see 15 U.S.C. § 12 (1976), reprinted *supra.*

[5.303] Section 2 was substantially amended by the Robinson-Patman Act of 1936, ch. 592, § 1, 49 Stat. 1526, the legislative history of which appears *infra* at chapter 6.

account of differences in the grade, quality, or quantity of the commodity sold, or that makes only due allowance for difference in the cost of selling or transportation, or discrimination in price in the same or different communities made in good faith to meet competition: *And provided further*, That nothing herein contained shall prevent persons engaged in selling goods, wares, or merchandise in ⊥ commerce from selecting their own customers in bona fide transactions and not in restraint of trade.

SEC. 3. That it shall be unlawful for any person engaged in commerce, in the course of such commerce, to lease or make a sale or contract for sale of goods, wares, merchandise, machinery, supplies or other commodities, whether patented or unpatented, for use, consumption or resale within the United States or any Territory thereof or the District of Columbia or any insular possession or other place under the jurisdiction of the United States, or fix a price charged therefor, or discount from, or rebate upon, such price, on the condition, agreement or understanding that the lessee or purchaser thereof shall not use or deal in the goods, wares, merchandise, machinery, supplies or other commodities of a competitor or competitors of the lessor or seller, where the effect of such lease, sale, or contract for sale or such condition, agreement or understanding may be to substantially lessen competition or tend to create a monopoly in any line of commerce.

SEC. 4. That any person who shall be injured in his business or property by reason of anything forbidden in the antitrust laws may sue therefor in any district court of the United States in the district in which the defendant resides or is found or has an agent, without respect to the amount in controversy, and shall recover threefold the damages by him sustained, and the cost of suit, including a reasonable attorney's fee.[5.304]

SEC. 5.[5.305] That a final judgment or decree hereafter rendered in any criminal prosecution or in any suit or proceeding in equity brought by or on behalf of the United States under the antitrust laws to the effect that a defendant has violated said laws shall be prima facie evidence against such defendant in any suit or proceeding brought by any other party against such defendant under said laws as to all matters respecting which said judgment or decree would be an estoppel as between the parties thereto: *Provided*, This section shall not apply to consent judgments or decrees entered before any testimony has been taken: *Provided further*, This section shall not apply to consent judgments or decrees rendered in criminal proceedings or suits in equity, now pending, in which the taking of testimony has been commenced but has not been concluded, provided such judgments or decrees are rendered before any further testimony is taken.

Whenever any suit or proceeding in equity or criminal prosecution is instituted by the United States to prevent, restrain or punish violations of any of the antitrust laws, the running of the statute of limitations in respect of each and every private right of action arising under said laws and based in whole or in part on any matter complained of in said suit or proceeding shall be suspended during the pendency thereof.

SEC. 6. That the labor of a human being is not a commodity or article of commerce. Nothing contained in the antitrust laws shall be construed to forbid the existence and operation of labor, agricultural, or horticultural organizations, instituted for the purposes of mutual help, and not having capital stock or conducted for profit, or to forbid or restrain individual members of such organizations from lawfully

---

[5.304] Section 4A (suits by the United States in its proprietary capacity) was added by the Act of July 7, 1955, ch. 283, § 1, 69 Stat. 282 (codified at 15 U.S.C. § 15a (1976), reprinted *supra* under "Current Version".

Section 4B (statute of limitations) was added by the Act of July 7, 1955, ch. 283, § 1, 69 Stat. 283, and a minor, conforming amendment made by the Hart-Scott-Rodino Act of 1976, Pub. L. No. 94–435, tit. III, § 302(1), 90 Stat. 1396 (current version at 15 U.S.C. § 15b (1976), reprinted *supra*).

Sections 4C–4H (*parens patriae* actions by state attorneys general) were added by the Hart-Scott-Rodino Act of 1976, Pub. L. No. 94–435, tit. III, § 301, 90 Stat. 1396 (codified at 15 U.S.C. §§ 15c–15h (1976), reprinted *supra* under "Current Version").

[5.305] Section 5 was amended and designated subsections 5(a) and 5(b) by the Act of July 7, 1955, ch. 283, § 2, 69 Stat. 283.

Subsection 5(b) was redesignated subsection 5(i) and new subsections 5(b)–5(h) were added by the Antitrust Procedures and Penalties Act of 1974, Pub. L. No. 93–528, § 2, 88 Stat. 1706, the legislative history of which appears *infra* at chapter 19.

A minor, conforming amendment was made in subsection 5(i) by the Hart-Scott-Rodino Act of 1976, Pub. L. No. 94–435, tit. III, § 302(2), 90 Stat. 1396.

For the current version see 15 U.S.C. § 16 (1976), reprinted *supra*.

carrying out the legitimate objects thereof; nor shall such organizations, or the members thereof, be held or construed to be illegal combinations or conspiracies in restraint of trade, under the antitrust laws.

SEC. 7.[5.306] That no corporation engaged in commerce shall acquire, directly or indirectly, the whole or any part of the stock or other share capital of another corporation engaged also in commerce, where the effect of such acquisition may be to substantially lessen competition between the corporation whose stock is so acquired and the corporation making the acquisition, or to restrain such commerce in any section or community, or tend to create a monopoly of any line of commerce.

No corporation shall acquire, directly or indirectly, the whole or any part of the stock or other share capital of two or more corporations engaged in commerce where the effect of such acquisition, or the use of such stock by the voting or granting of proxies or otherwise, may be to substantially lessen competition between such corporations, or any of them, whose stock or other share capital is so acquired, or to restrain such commerce in any section or community, or tend to create a monopoly of any line of commerce.

This section shall not apply to corporations purchasing such stock solely for investment and not using the same by voting or otherwise to bring about, or in attempting to bring about, the substantial lessening of competition. Nor shall anything contained in this section prevent a corporation engaged in commerce from causing the formation of subsidiary corporations for the actual carrying on of their immediate lawful business, or the natural and legitimate branches or extensions thereof, or from owning and holding all or a part of the stock of such subsidiary corporations, when the effect of such formation is not to substantially lessen competition.

Nor shall anything herein contained be construed to prohibit any common carrier subject to the laws to regulate commerce from aiding in the construction of branches or short lines so located as to become feeders to the main line of the company so aiding in such construction or from acquiring or owning all or any part of the stock of such branch lines, nor to prevent any such common carrier from acquiring and owning all or any part of the stock of a branch or short line constructed by an independent company where there is no substantial competition between the company owning the branch line so constructed and the company owning the main line acquiring the property or an interest therein, nor to prevent such common carrier from extending any of its lines through the medium of the acquisition of stock or otherwise of any other such common carrier where there is no substantial competition between the company extending its lines and the company whose stock, property, or an interest therein is so acquired.

Nothing contained in this section shall be held to affect or impair any right heretofore legally acquired: *Provided,* That nothing in this section shall be held or construed to authorize or make lawful anything heretofore prohibited or made illegal by the antitrust laws, nor to exempt any person from the penal provisions thereof or the civil remedies therein provided.

SEC. 8.[5.307] That from and after two years from the date of the approval of this Act no person shall at the same time be a director or other officer or employee of more than one bank, banking association or trust company, organized or operating under the laws of the United States, either of which has deposits, capital, surplus, and undivided profits aggregating more than $5,000,000; and no private banker or person who is a director in any bank or trust company, organized and operating under the laws of a State, having deposits, capital, surplus, and undivided profits aggregating more than $5,000,000, shall be eligible to be a director in any bank or banking association organized or operating under the laws of the United States. The eligibility of a director,

---

[5.306] Section 7 (current version at 15 U.S.C. § 18 (1976), reprinted *supra*) was substantially amended by the Celler-Kefauver Act of 1950, ch. 1184, 64 Stat. 1125, the legislative history of which appears *infra* at chapter 7.

Section 7A (premerger notification and waiting period) was added by the Hart-Scott-Rodino Act of 1976, Pub. L. No. 94–435, tit. II, § 201, 90 Stat. 1390 (codified at 15 U.S.C. § 18a (1976), reprinted *supra* under "Current Version").

[5.307] Section 8 has been amended on numerous occasions (current version at 15 U.S.C. § 19 (1976), reprinted *supra*).

officer, or employee under the foregoing provisions shall be determined by the average amount of deposits, capital, surplus, and undivided profits as shown in the official statements of such bank, banking association, or trust company filed as provided by law during the fiscal year next preceding the date set for the annual election of directors, and when a director, officer, or employee has been elected or selected in accordance with the provisions of this Act it shall be ⊥ lawful for him to continue as such for one year thereafter under said election or employment.

No bank, banking association or trust company, organized or operating under the laws of the United States, in any city or incorporated town or village of more than two hundred thousand inhabitants, as shown by the last preceding decennial census of the United States, shall have as a director or other officer or employee any private banker or any director or other officer or employee of any other bank, banking association or trust company located in the same place: *Provided*, That nothing in this section shall apply to mutual savings banks not having a capital stock represented by shares: *Provided further*, That a director or other officer or employee of such bank, banking association, or trust company may be a director or other officer or employee of not more than one other bank or trust company organized under the laws of the United States or any State where the entire capital stock of one is owned by stockholders in the other: *And provided further*, That nothing contained in this section shall forbid a director of class A of a Federal reserve bank, as defined in the Federal Reserve Act, from being an officer or director or both an officer and director in one member bank.

That from and after two years from the date of the approval of this Act no person at the same time shall be a director in any two or more corporations, any one of which has capital, surplus, and undivided profits aggregating more than $1,000,000, engaged in whole or in part in commerce, other than banks, banking associations, trust companies and common carriers subject to the Act to regulate commerce, approved February fourth, eighteen hundred and eighty-seven, if such corporations are or shall have been theretofore, by virtue of their business and location of operation, competitors, so that the elimination of competition by agreement between them would constitute a violation of any of the provisions of any of the antitrust laws. The eligibility of a director under the foregoing provision shall be determined by the aggregate amount of the capital, surplus, and undivided profits, exclusive of dividends declared but not paid to stockholders, at the end of the fiscal year of said corporation next preceding the election of directors, and when a director has been elected in accordance with the provisions of this Act it shall be lawful for him to continue as such for one year thereafter.

When any person elected or chosen as a director or officer or selected as an employee of any bank or other corporation subject to the provisions of this Act is eligible at the time of his election or selection to act for such bank or other corporation in such capacity his eligibility to act in such capacity shall not be affected and he shall not become or be deemed amenable to any of the provisions hereof by reason of any change in the affairs of such bank or other corporation from whatsoever cause, whether specifically excepted by any of the provisions hereof or not, until the expiration of one year from the date of his election or employment.[5.308]

SEC. 9.[5.309] Every president, director, officer or manager of any firm, association or corporation engaged in commerce as a common carrier, who embezzles, steals, abstracts or willfully misapplies, or willfully permits to be misapplied, any of the moneys, funds, credits, securities, property or assests of such firm, association or corporation, arising or accruing from, or used in, such commerce, in whole or in part, or willfully or knowingly converts the same to his own use or to the use of another, shall be deemed guilty of a felony and upon conviction shall be fined not less than $500 or confined in the penitentiary not less than one year nor more than ten years, or both, in the discretion of the court.

[5.308] Section 8A, dealing with interlocking corporations or partnerships making loans on securities, was added to the Clayton Act by the Act of June 16, 1933, ch. 89, § 33, 48 Stat. 194; it was repealed two years later by the Act of Aug. 23, 1935, ch. 614, § 329, 49 Stat. 717.

[5.309] Section 9 was repealed by the Act of June 25, 1948, ch. 645, § 21, 62 Stat. 862. This provision is now covered by 18 U.S.C. § 660 (1976).

Prosecutions hereunder may be in the district court of the United States for the district wherein the offense may have been committed.

That nothing in this section shall be held to take away or impair the jurisdiction of the courts of the several States under the laws thereof; and a judgment of conviction or acquittal on the merits under the laws of any State shall be a bar to any prosecution hereunder for the same act or acts.

SEC. 10. That after two years from the approval of this Act no common carrier engaged in commerce shall have any dealings in securities, supplies or other articles of commerce, or shall make or have any contracts for construction or maintenance of any kind, to the amount of more than $50,000, in the aggregate, in any one year, with another corporation, firm, partnership or association when the said common carrier shall have upon its board of directors or as its president, manager or as its purchasing or selling officer, or agent in the particular transaction, any person who is at the same time a director, manager, or purchasing or selling officer of, or who has any substantial interest in, such other corporation, firm, partnership or association, unless and except such purchases shall be made from, or such dealings shall be with, the bidder whose bid is the most favorable to such common carrier, to be ascertained by competitive bidding under regulations to be prescribed by rule or otherwise by the Interstate Commerce Commission. No bid shall be received unless the name and address of the bidder or the names and addresses of the officers, directors and general managers thereof, if the bidder be a corporation, or of the members, if it be a partnership or firm, be given with the bid.

Any person who shall, directly or indirectly, do or attempt to do anything to prevent anyone from bidding or shall do any act to prevent free and fair competition among the bidders or those desiring to bid shall be punished as prescribed in this section in the case of an officer or director.

Every such common carrier having any such transactions or making any such purchases shall within thirty days after making the same file with the Interstate Commerce Commission a full and detailed statement of the transaction showing the manner of the competitive bidding, who were the bidders, and the names and addresses of the directors and officers of the corporations and the members of the firm or partnership bidding; and whenever the said commission shall, after investigation or hearing, have reason to believe that the law has been violated in and about the said purchases or transactions it shall transmit all papers and documents and its own views or findings regarding the transaction to the Attorney General.

If any common carrier shall violate this section it shall be fined not exceeding $25,000; and every such director, agent, manager or officer thereof who shall have knowingly voted for or directed the act constituting such violation or who shall have aided or abetted in such violation shall be deemed guilty of a misdemeanor and shall be fined not exceeding $5,000, or confined in jail not exceeding one year, or both, in the discretion of the court.

SEC. 11.[5.309a] That authority to enforce compliance with sections two, three, seven and eight of this Act by the persons respectively subject thereto is hereby vested: in the Interstate Commerce Commission where applicable to common carriers, in the Federal Reserve Board where applicable to banks, banking associations and trust companies, and in the Federal Trade Commission where applicable to all other character of commerce, to be exercised as follows:

Whenever the commission or board vested with jurisdiction thereof shall have reason to believe that any person is violating or has violated any of the provisions of sections two, three, seven and eight of this Act, it shall issue and serve upon such person a complaint stating its charges in that respect, and containing a notice of a hearing upon a day and at a place therein fixed at least thirty days after the service of said complaint. The person so complained of shall have the right to appear at the place and time so fixed and show cause why an order should not be entered by the commission or board requiring such person to cease and desist from the violation of

---

[5.309a] Section 11 (current version at 15 U.S.C. § 21 (1976), reprinted *supra*) has been amended on numerous occasions including the Celler-Kefauver Amendments of 1950, ch. 1184, 64 Stat. 1125, the legislative history of which appears *infra* at chapter 7.

the law so charged in said complaint. Any person may make application, and upon good cause shown may be allowed by the commission or board, to intervene and appear in said proceeding by counsel or in person. The testimony in any such proceeding shall be reduced to writing and filed in the office of the commission or board. If upon such hearing the commission or board, as the case may be, shall be of the opinion that any of the provisions of said sections have been or are being violated, it shall make a report in writing in which it shall state its findings as to the facts, and shall issue and cause to be served on such person an order requiring such person to cease and desist from such violations, and divest itself of the stock held or rid itself of the directors chosen contrary to the provisions of sections seven and eight of this Act, if any there be, in the manner and within the time fixed by said order. Until a transcript of the record in such hearing shall have been filed in a circuit court of appeals of the United States, as hereinafter provided, the commission or board may at any time, upon such notice and in such manner as it shall deem proper, modify or set aside, in whole or in part, any report or any order made or issued by it under this section.

If such person fails or neglects to obey such order of the commission or board while the same is in effect, the commission or board may apply to the circuit court of appeals of the United States, within any circuit where the violation complained of was or is being committed or where such person resides or carries on business, for the enforcement of its order, and shall certify and file with its application a transcript of the entire record in the proceeding, including all the testimony taken and the report and order of the commission or board. Upon such filing of the application and transcript the court shall cause notice thereof to be served upon such person and thereupon shall have jurisdiction of the proceeding and of the question determined therein, and shall have power to make and enter upon the pleadings, testimony, and proceedings set forth in such transcript a decree affirming, modifying, or setting aside the order of the commission or board. The findings of the commission or board as to the facts, if supported by testimony, shall be conclusive. If either party shall apply to the court for leave to adduce additional evidence, and shall show to the satisfaction of the court that such additional evidence is material and that there were reasonable grounds for the failure to adduce such evidence in the proceeding before the commission or board, the court may order such additional evidence to be taken before the commission or board and to be adduced upon the hearing in such manner and upon such terms and conditions as to the court may seem proper. The commission or board may modify its findings as to the facts, or make new findings, by reason of the additional evidence so taken, and it shall file such modified or new findings, which, if supported by testimony, shall be conclusive, and its recommendation, if any, for the modification or setting aside of its original order, with the return of such additional evidence. The judgment and decree of the court shall be final, except that the same shall be subject to review of the Supreme Court upon certiorari as provided in section two hundred and forty of the Judicial Code.

Any party required by such order of the commission or board to cease and desist from a violation charged may obtain a review of such order in said circuit court of appeals by filing in the court a written petition praying that the order of the commission or board be set aside. A copy of such petition shall be forthwith served upon the commission or board, and thereupon the commission or board forthwith shall certify and file in the court a transcript of the record as hereinbefore provided. Upon the filing of the transcript the court shall have the same jurisdiction to affirm, set aside, or modify the order of the commission or board as in the case of an application by the commission or board for the enforcement of its order, and the findings of the commission or board as to the facts, if supported by testimony, shall in like manner be conclusive.

The jurisdiction of the circuit court of appeals of the United States to enforce, set aside, or modify orders of the commission or board shall be exclusive.

Such proceedings in the circuit court of appeals shall be given precedence over other cases pending therein, and shall be in every way expedited. No order of the commission or board or the judgment of the court to enforce the same shall in any wise relieve or absolve any person from any liability under the antitrust Acts.

Complaints, orders, and other processes of the commission or board under this section may be served by anyone duly authorized by the commission or board, either (a) by delivering a copy thereof to the person to be served, or to a member of the partnership to be served, or to the president, secretary, or other executive officer or a director of the corporation to be served; or (b) by leaving a copy thereof at the principal office or place of business of such person; or (c) by registering and mailing a copy thereof addressed to such person at his principal office or place of business. The verified return by the person so serving said complaint, order, or other process setting forth the manner of said service shall be proof of the same, and the return post-office receipt for said complaint, order, or other process registered and mailed as aforesaid shall be proof of the service of the same.

SEC. 12. That any suit, action, or proceeding under the antitrust laws against a corporation may be brought not only in the judicial district whereof it is an inhabitant, but also in any district wherein it may be found or transacts business; and all process in such cases may be served in the district of which it is an inhabitant, or wherever it may be found.

SEC. 13. That in any suit, action, or proceeding brought by or on behalf of the United States subpoenas for witnesses who are required to attend a court of the United States in any judicial district in any case, civil or criminal, arising under the antitrust laws may run into any other district: *Provided*, That in civil cases no writ of subpoena shall issue for witnesses living out of the district in which the court is held at a greater distance than one hundred miles from the place of holding the same without the permission of the trial court being first had upon proper application and cause shown.

SEC. 14. That whenever a corporation shall violate any of the penal provisions of the antitrust laws, such violation shall be deemed to be also that of the individual directors, officers, or agents of such corporation who shall have authorized, ordered, or done any of the acts constituting in whole or in part such violation, and such violation shall be deemed a misdemeanor, and upon conviction therefor of any such director, officer, or agent he shall be punished by a fine of not exceeding $5,000 or by imprisonment for not exceeding one year, or by both, in the discretion of the court.

SEC. 15. That the several district courts of the United States are hereby invested with jurisdiction to prevent and restrain violations of this Act, and it shall be the duty of the several district attorneys of the United States,[5.310] in their respective districts, under the direction of the Attorney General, to institute proceedings in equity to prevent and restrain such violations. Such proceedings may be by way of petition setting forth the case and praying that such violation shall be enjoined or otherwise prohibited. When the parties complained of shall have been duly notified of such petition, the court shall proceed, as soon as may be, to the hearing and determination of the case; and pending such petition, and before final decree, the court may at any time make such temporary restraining order or prohibition as shall be deemed just in the premises. Whenever it shall appear to the court before which any such proceeding may be pending that the ends of justice require that other parties should be brought before the court, the court may cause them to be summoned, whether they reside in the district in which the court is held or not, and subpoenas to that end may be served in any district by the marshal thereof.

SEC. 16. That any person, firm, corporation, or association shall be entitled to sue for and have injunctive relief, in any court of the United States having jurisdiction over the parties, against threatened loss or damage by a violation of the antitrust laws, including sections two, three, seven and eight of this Act, when and under the same conditions and principles as injunctive relief against threatened conduct that will cause loss or damage is granted by courts of equity, under the rules governing such proceedings, and upon the execution of proper bond against damages for an injunction improvidently granted and a showing that the danger of irreparable loss or damage is immediate, a preliminary injunction may issue: *Provided*, That nothing herein contained shall be construed to entitle any person, firm, corporation, or association, except the United States, to bring suit in equity for injunctive relief against any common carrier

---

[5.310] "District attorneys of the United States" was changed to "United States Attorneys" by the Act of June 25, 1948, ch. 646, § 1, 62 Stat. 909.

subject to the provisions of the Act to regulate commerce, approved February fourth, eighteen hundred and eighty-seven, in respect of any matter subject to the regulation, supervision, or other jurisdiction of the Interstate Commerce Commission.[5.310a]

SEC. 17.[5.311] That no preliminary injunction shall be issued without notice to the opposite party.

No temporary restraining order shall be granted without notice to the opposite party unless it shall clearly appear from specific facts shown by affidavit or by the verified bill that immediate and irreparable injury, loss, or damage will result to the applicant before notice can be served and a hearing had thereon. Every such temporary restraining order shall be indorsed with the date and hour of issuance, shall be forthwith filed in the clerk's office and entered of record, shall define the injury and state why it is irreparable and why the order was granted without notice, and shall by its terms expire within such time after entry, not to exceed ten days, as the court or judge may fix, unless within the time so fixed the order is extended for a like period for good cause shown, and the reasons for such extension shall be entered of record. In case a temporary restraining order shall be granted without notice in the contingency specified, the matter of the issuance of a preliminary injunction shall be set down for a hearing at the earliest possible time and shall take precedence of all matters except older matters of the same character; and when the same comes up for hearing the party obtaining the temporary restraining order shall proceed with the application for a preliminary injunction, and if he does not do so the court shall dissolve the temporary restraining order. Upon two days' notice to the party obtaining such temporary restraining order the opposite party may appear and move the dissolution or modification of the order, and in that event the court or judge shall proceed to hear and determine the motion as expeditiously as the ends of justice may require.

Section two hundred and sixty-three of an Act entitled "An Act to codify, revise, and amend the laws relating to the judiciary," approved March third, nineteen hundred and eleven, is hereby repealed.

Nothing in this section contained shall be deemed to alter, repeal, or amend section two hundred and sixty-six of an Act entitled "An Act to codify, revise, and amend the laws relating to the judiciary," approved March third, nineteen hundred and eleven.

SEC. 18. That, except as otherwise provided in section 16 of this Act, no restraining order or interlocutory order of injunction shall issue, except upon the giving of security by the applicant in such sum as the court or judge may deem proper, conditioned upon the payment of such costs and damages as may be incurred or suffered by any party who may be found to have been wrongfully enjoined or restrained thereby.

SEC. 19. That every order of injunction or restraining order shall set forth the reasons for the issuance of the same, shall be specific in terms, and shall describe in reasonable detail, and not by reference to the bill of complaint or other document, the act or acts sought to be restrained, and shall be binding only upon the parties to the suit, their officers, agents, servants, employees, and attorneys, or those in active concert or participating with them, and who shall, by personal service or otherwise, have received actual notice of the same.

SEC. 20. That no restraining order or injunction shall be granted by any court of the United States, or a judge or the judges thereof, in any case between an employer and employees, or between employers and employees, or between employees, or between persons employed and persons seeking employment, involving, or growing out of, a dispute concerning terms or conditions of employment, unless necessary to prevent irreparable injury to property, or to a property right, of the party making the application, for which injury there is no adequate remedy at law, and such property or property right must be described with particularity in the application, which must be in writing and sworn to by the applicant or by his agent or attorney.

[5.310a] Provision for attorney's fees to plaintiffs who "substantially prevail" in section 16 actions was added by the Hart-Scott-Rodino Act of 1976, Pub. L. No. 94–435, tit. III, § 302(3), 90 Stat. 1396 (current version at 15 U.S.C. § 26 (1976), reprinted *supra*).

[5.311] Sections 17–19 were repealed by the Act of June 25, 1948, ch. 646, § 39, 62 Stat. 992. The provisions of these sections are now covered by rule 65 of the Federal Rules of Civil Procedure.

ORIGINAL VERSION 1069

And no such restraining order or injunction shall prohibit any person or persons, whether singly or in concert, from terminating any relation of employment, or from ceasing to perform any work or labor, or from recommending, advising, or persuading others by peaceful means so to do; or from attending at any place where any such person or persons may lawfully be, for the purpose of peacefully obtaining or communicating information, or from peacefully persuading any person to work or to abstain from working; or from ceasing to patronize or to employ any party to such dispute, or from recommending, advising, or persuading others by peaceful and lawful means so to do; or from paying or giving to, or withholding from, any person engaged in such dispute, any strike benefits or other moneys or things of value; or from peaceably assembling in a lawful manner, and for lawful purposes; or from doing any act or thing which might lawfully be done in the absence of such dispute by any party thereto; nor shall any of the acts specified in this paragraph be considered or held to be violations of any law of the United States.

SEC. 21.[5.312] That any person who shall willfully disobey any lawful writ, process, order, rule, decree, or command of any district court of the United States or any court of the District of Columbia by doing any act or thing therein, or thereby forbidden to be done by him, if the act or thing so done by him be of such character as to constitute also a criminal offense under any statute of the United States, or under the laws of any State in which the act was committed, shall be proceeded against for his said contempt as hereinafter provided.

SEC. 22. That whenever it shall be made to appear to any district court or judge thereof, or to any judge therein sitting, by the return of a proper officer on lawful process, or upon the affidavit of some credible person, or by information filed by any district attorney, that there is reasonable ground to believe that any person has been guilty of such contempt, the court or judge thereof, or any judge therein sitting, may issue a rule requiring the said person so charged to ⊥ show cause upon a day certain ⊥739 why he should not be punished therefor, which rule, together with a copy of the affidavit or information, shall be served upon the person charged, with sufficient promptness to enable him to prepare for and make return to the order at the time fixed therein. If upon or by such return, in the judgment of the court, the alleged contempt be not sufficiently purged, a trial shall be directed at a time and place fixed by the court: *Provided, however*, That if the accused, being a natural person, fail or refuse to make return to the rule to show cause, an attachment may issue against his person to compel an answer, and in case of his continued failure or refusal, or if for any reason it be impracticable to dispose of the matter on the return day, he may be required to give reasonable bail for his attendance at the trial and his submission to the final judgment of the court. Where the accused is a body corporate, an attachment for the sequestration of its property may be issued upon like refusal or failure to answer.

In all cases within the purview of this Act such trial may be by the court, or, upon demand of the accused, by a jury; in which latter event the court may impanel a jury from the jurors then in attendance, or the court or the judge thereof in chambers may cause a sufficient number of jurors to be selected and summoned, as provided by law, to attend at the time and place of trial, at which time a jury shall be selected and impaneled as upon a trial for misdemeanor; and such trial shall conform, as near as may be, to the practice in criminal cases prosecuted by indictment or upon information.

If the accused be found guilty, judgment shall be entered accordingly, prescribing the punishment, either by fine or imprisonment, or both, in the discretion of the court. Such fine shall be paid to the United States or to the complainant or other party injured by the act constituting the contempt, or may, where more than one is so damaged, be divided or apportioned among them as the court may direct, but in no case shall the fine to be paid to the United States exceed, in case the accused is a natural person, the sum of $1,000, nor shall such imprisonment exceed the term of six months: *Provided*, That in any case the court or a judge thereof may, for good cause

---

[5.312] Sections 21–25 were repealed by the Act of June 25, 1948, ch. 645, § 21, 62 Stat. 862. Provisions of sections 21, 22, 24, and 25 are now covered by 18 U.S.C. §§ 402, 3285, 3691 (1976). Section 23 is obsolete and not now covered.

shown, by affidavit or proof taken in open court or before such judge and filed with the papers in the case, dispense with the rule to show cause, and may issue an attachment for the arrest of the person charged with contempt; in which event such person, when arrested, shall be brought before such court or a judge thereof without unnecessary delay and shall be admitted to bail in a reasonable penalty for his appearance to answer to the charge or for trial for the contempt; and thereafter the proceedings shall be the same as provided herein in case the rule had issued in the first instance.

SEC. 23. That the evidence taken upon the trial of any persons so accused may be preserved by bill of exceptions, and any judgment of conviction may be reviewed upon writ of error in all respects as now provided by law in criminal cases, and may be affirmed, reversed, or modified as justice may require. Upon the granting of such writ of error, execution of judgment shall be stayed, and the accused, if thereby sentenced to imprisonment, shall be admitted to bail in such reasonable sum as may be required by the court, or by any justice, or any judge of any district court of the United States or any court of the District of Columbia.

SEC. 24. That nothing herein contained shall be construed to relate to contempts committed in the presence of the court, or so near thereto as to obstruct the administration of justice, nor to contempts committed in disobedience of any lawful writ, process, order, rule, decree, or command entered in any suit or action brought or prosecuted in the name of, or on behalf of, the United States, but the ⊥ same, and all other cases of contempt not specifically embraced within section twenty-one of this Act, may be punished in conformity to the usages at law and in equity now prevailing.

SEC. 25. That no proceeding for contempt shall be instituted against any person unless begun within one year from the date of the act complained of; nor shall any such proceeding be a bar to any criminal prosecution for the same act or acts; but nothing herein contained shall affect any proceedings in contempt pending at the time of the passage of this Act.

SEC. 26. If any clause, sentence, paragraph, or part of this Act shall, for any reason, be adjudged by any court of competent jurisdiction to be invalid, such judgment shall not affect, impair, or invalidate the remainder thereof, but shall be confined in its operation to the clause, sentence, paragraph, or part thereof directly involved in the controversy in which such judgment shall have been rendered.

THE ORIGINS

REPRESENTATIVE LEASE AND LICENSE AGREEMENT OF THE UNITED SHOE MACHINERY CO.[5.313]

EXHIBIT 5.

Goodyear Department [Form M. G. J., 6-806.]

LEASE AND LICENSE AGREEMENT NUMBER ———.

SEWING AND STITCHING MACHINES.

This agreement made at Boston, in the State of Massachusetts, this ——— day of ———, 19———, between the United Shoe Machinery Company, a corporation organized under the laws of the State of Maine, having an office in said Boston, hereinafter referred to as the lessor of the one part, and ———, of ———, in the State of ———, hereinafter referred to as the lessee, of the other part:

Witnesseth that the lessor, in consideration of the covenants and agreements on the part of the lessee herein contained, does hereby lease to and license the lessee under any letters patent belonging to the lessor or under which the lessor has the right to grant such license affecting any inventions which are now or hereafter shall be embodied therein or employed in the operation thereof, to use the machine or machines of the "Goodyear Department" of the lessor designated by number or numbers in the following shedule [sic], viz:

SCHEDULE OF MACHINES.

Goodyear Welt and Turn Shoe Machine, No.
Goodyear Universal Inseam Sewing Machine, No.
Goodyear Outsole Rapid Lockstitch Machine, No.
Extension Edge Attachment (A), No.
Extension Edge Attachment (B), No.
Welt Bevelling Attachment, No.

and any duplicate parts, extras, mechanisms, and devices relating thereto, or used in connection therewith, now attached to or delivered with the said designated machine or machines, or which may at any time hereafter be obtained from the lessor or be added thereto, by or with the consent of the lessor (the whole of which machine or machines, duplicate parts, extras, mechanisms; and devices held by the lessee under these presents, whether now or hereafter delivered to or in the possession of the lessee, is hereinafter referred to as the "leased machinery"), subject to the conditions hereinafter contained; and the lessor hereby grants to the lessee a license to use, in connection with welted boots, shoes, or other footwear made by the lessee, the welts of which have been sewed to their uppers wholly by Goodyear Welt and Turn Shoe Machines or by Goodyear Universal Inseam Sewing Machines, hereby leased or now held by the lessee under lease from the lessor heretofore executed, and the outsoles of which have been stitched

---

[5.313] This exhibit has been reproduced from *Hearings Pursuant to S. Res. 98 Before the Senate Comm. on Interstate Commerce*, 62d Cong., 3d Sess. 2184-88 (1913).

to their welts wholly by Goodyear Outsole Rapid Lock-Stitch Machines, hereby leased or now held by the lessee under lease from the lessor heretofore executed, the trade name or trademark "Goodyear Welt," and to use, in connection with turned boots, shoes, or other footwear made by the lessee the soles of which have been attached to their uppers wholly by the use of Goodyear Welt and Turn Shoe Machines or Goodyear Universal Inseam Sewing Machines, hereby leased or now held by the lessee under lease from the lessor heretofore executed, the trade name or trade-mark "Goodyear Turn."

And that the following are agreed to as conditions of this agreement, all of which the lessee convenants and agrees to keep and perform: . . .

5. The leased machinery shall be used only in the manufacture of boots, shoes, and other footwear made by the lessee known in the trade as "Goodyear Welts," which have been or are to be welted wholly by Goodyear Welt and Turn Shoe Machines or Goodyear Universal Inseam Sewing Machines held by the lessee under lease from the lessor, and the soles of which have been or are to be attached to their welts wholly by Goodyear Outsole Rapid Lock-Stitch Machines held by the lessee under lease from the lessor, or in the manufacture of boots, shoes, or other footwear made by the lessee known in the trade as "Goodyear Turns," the soles of which have been or are to be attached to the uppers wholly by Goodyear Welt and Turn Shoe Machines or Goodyear Universal Inseam Sewing Machines held by the lessee under lease from the lessor. The lessee shall not represent or sell as "Goodyear Welts" any boots, shoes, or other footwear which are not welted wholly by the use of Goodyear Welt and Turn Shoe Machines or Goodyear Universal Inseam Sewing Machines held under lease from the lessor, or the soles of which are not attached to their welts wholly by the use of Goodyear outsole rapid lock-stitch machines held under lease from the lessor or as "Goodyear Turns" any boots, shoes, or other footwear the soles of which are not attached to their uppers wholly by the use of Goodyear Welt and Turn Shoe Machines or Goodyear Universal Inseam Sewing Machines held under lease from the lessor. The lessee shall use the leased machinery to its full capacity in the manufacture of "Goodyear Welts" and "Goodyear Turns," limited only by the number of welted and turned boots, shoes, and other footwear made by or for him.

6. The lessee shall pay to the lessor throughout the full term of this agreement the respective amounts set forth in the following schedule in respect to each pair of welted boots, shoes, or other footwear, or portions thereof, manufactured or prepared by or for the lessee, which shall have been welted in whole or in part or the soles of which shall have been in whole or in part attached to welts by the use of any welting or stitching or sewing machinery, and in respect to each pair of "turned" boots, shoes, or other footwear, or portions thereof, manufactured or prepared by or for the lessee, the soles of which shall have been sewed or attached to their uppers in whole or in part by the use of any sewing or stitching machinery, viz:

Schedule of payments per pair.

	Sizes		Welts.	Turns.
	Form [sic] No.—	To No.—		
Children's	1	10½, inclusive	3 cents	1 cent.
Misses'	11	2, "	4 cents	1½ cents.
Women's	2½	and over	6 cents	1½ cents.
Youths'	9	13½, inclusive	4 cents	1½ cents.
Boys'	1	5, "	6 cents	1½ cents.
Men's	5½	and over	8 cents	1½ cents.

Such payments shall be made on the last day of each calendar month in respect to all such boots, shoes, and other footwear manufactured or prepared by or for the lessee during the next preceding calendar month: *Provided, however,* That in all cases when the lessee shall pay to the lessor on or before the fifteenth day of the calendar month the amount due pursuant to the schedule in this article hereof contained for the next preceding calendar month, the lessor will, in consideration of such prompt payment, grant a discount of fifty per cent from the amount so due for such preceding calendar month. The lessee, however, guarantees that the payments made in accordance with the foregoing schedule of payments under this agreement in respect to boots, shoes, or other footwear operated upon by the welting, stitching, or sewing machines hereby leased (after deducting all abatements) shall amount in each calendar year to at least fifteen dollars ($15) for each calendar month for each welting or stitching or sewing machine hereby leased, and at the end of each calendar year the lessee shall pay to the lessor the amount, if any, by which the total of such payments for said year is less than such guaranteed amount. All payments and the guarantee in this agreement provided for are independent of and in addition to all payments and guarantees provided for in any other leases or licenses or agreements between the lessor and the lessee: *Provided, however,* That (excepting in so far as is required by the guarantees herein contained or contained in other lease and license agreements between the lessor and the lessee), in case under any other "Goodyear Department" lease and license agreement between the lessor and the lessee covering one or more Goodyear Welt and Turn Shoe Machines, Goodyear Universal Inseam Sewing-Machines, or Goodyear Outsole Rapid Lock-Stitch Machines, the lessee shall have paid to the lessor the amount set forth in the schedule of payments in such lease and license agreement contained in respect to any pair of boots, shoes, or other footwear, then the lessee shall be relieved from said payment hereunder in respect to that pair of boots, shoes, or other footwear. . . .

And that the following stipulations and provisions are agreed to:

8. If at any time the lessee shall fail or cease to use exclusively welt-sewing and outsole stitching machinery held by him under lease from the lessor in the manufacture of all welted boots, shoes, or other footwear made by or for him, the welts or soles of which are sewed, stitched, or attached by the aid of machinery, or shall fail or cease to use exclusively turn-sewing machinery held by him under lease from the lessor in the manufacture of all turned boots, shoes, or other footwear made by or for him, the soles of which are sewed or attached by the aid of machinery, the lessor, although it may have waived or ignored prior instances of such failure or cessation, may at its option terminate forthwith by notice in writing any or all leases of or licenses to use machinery then existing between the lessor and the lessee, whether as the result of assignment to the lessor or otherwise, the possession of and full right to and control of all machinery the lease or license of which is so terminated, shall thereupon revest in the lessor free from all claims and demands whatsoever.

9. The term of this agreement shall be seventeen years from the date hereof. . . .

10. Upon the expiration of this agreement, or any extension thereof, or the termination of the lease and license hereby granted, the lessee, in addition to all other payments in this agreement provided for and without prejudice to any other rights or remedies of the lessor, shall pay to the lessor in respect to each welting or stitching or sewing machine hereby leased the sum of one hundred and fifty (150) dollars as partial reimbursement to the lessor for deterioration of the leased machinery, expenses in connection with the installation thereof, and instruction of operators.

TENTATIVE ANTITRUST BILLS ORDERED PRINTED BY REP. HENRY D. CLAYTON[5.314]
63d Cong., 2d Sess.
1914

[NO. 1.—COMMITTEE PRINT. TENTATIVE BILL.]

BY MR. CLAYTON.

63D CONGRESS,
2D SESSION.

H.R.

IN THE HOUSE OF REPRESENTATIVES

JANUARY —, 1914.

Mr. CLAYTON introduced the following bill; which was referred to the Committee on the Judiciary and ordered to be printed.

A BILL

To supplement an Act entitled "An Act to protect trade and commerce against unlawful restraints and monopolies," approved July second, eighteen hundred and ninety.

Be it enacted by the Senate and House of Representatives of the United States of America in Congress assembled, That the Act approved July second, eighteen hundred and ninety, entitled "An Act to protect trade and commerce against unlawful restraints and monopolies," is hereby supplemented and amended by adding thereto the following:

"SEC. 9. That it shall be deemed an attempt to monopolize trade or commerce among the several States, or with foreign nations or a part thereof, for any person in interstate or foreign commerce to discriminate in price between different purchasers of commodities in the same or different sections or communities, with the purpose or intent to thereby injure or destroy a competitor, either of such purchaser or of the seller: *Provided,* That nothing herein contained shall prevent discrimination in price between purchasers of commodities on account of differences in the grade, quality, or quantity of the commodity sold, or that makes only due allowance for difference in the cost of transportation: *And provided further,* That nothing herein contained shall prevent persons engaged in selling goods, wares, or merchandise in interstate or foreign commerce from selecting their own customers, but this provision shall not authorize the owner or operator of any mine engaged in selling its product in

---

[5.314] These bills were never introduced. They were ordered printed by the House Committee on the Judiciary, which was chaired by Congressman Clayton, and were reprinted in *Hearings on Trust Legislation Before the House Comm. on the Judiciary,* 63d Cong., 2d Sess. 1567-83 (1914).

interstate or foreign commerce to refuse arbitrarily to sell the same to a responsible person, firm, or corporation who applies to purchase.

"SEC. 10. That it shall be deemed an attempt to monopolize trade or commerce among the several States, or with foreign nations or a part thereof, for any person in interstate or foreign commerce to make a sale of goods, wares, or merchandise or fix a price charged therefor or discount from or rebate upon such price, on the condition or understanding that the purchaser thereof shall not deal in the goods, wares, or merchandise of a competitor or competitors of the seller.

"SEC. 11. That nothing contained in section nine or section ten hereof shall be taken or held to limit or in any way curtail the meaning and effect of the provisions of section two of this Act.

"SEC. 12. That whenever in any suit or proceeding, civil or criminal, brought by or on behalf of the Government under the provisions of this Act, a final judgment or decree shall have been rendered to the effect that a defendant, in violation of the provisions of this Act, has entered into a contract, combination in form of trust or otherwise, or conspiracy in restraint of trade, or commerce among the several States or with foreign nations, or has monopolized or attempted to monopolize, or combined with any person or persons to monopolize, any part of the trade or commerce among the several States or with foreign nations, the existence of such illegal contract, combination, or conspiracy in restraint of trade, or of such attempt or conspiracy to monopolize, shall, to the full extent to which such judgment or decree would constitute in any other proceeding an estoppel as between the Government and such person, constitute as against such defendant conclusive evidence of the same facts and be conclusive as to the same issues of law in favor of any other party in any other proceeding brought under or involving the provisions of this Act. In all cases where any person who shall have been injured in his business or property by any person or corporation by reason of anything forbidden or declared to be unlawful under the provisions of the Act entitled 'an Act to protect trade and commerce against unlawful restraints and monopolies,' approved July second, eighteen hundred and ninety, and who at the time or previous to the institution of any such suit by the United States as aforesaid has a cause of action under section seven of said Act or under section thirteen of this Act against any defendant in a suit wherein a decree or judgment has been obtained as aforesaid, the statutes of limitations applicable to such cases shall be suspended during the pendency of such suit and shall not again become operative until after the date of the final decree of judgment in such cause.

"SEC. 13. That any person, firm, corporation, or association shall be entitled to sue for and have injunctive relief, in any court of the United States having jurisdiction over the

20 parties, against threatened loss or damage by a violation of
21 this Act when and under the same conditions and principles
22 as injunctive relief against threatened conduct that will cause
23 loss or damage is granted by courts of equity, under the
24 rules governing such proceedings, and upon the execution of
1 proper bond against damages for an injunction improvidently
2 granted and a showing that the danger of irreparable loss or
3 damage is immediate a preliminary injunction may issue.

[NO. 2.–COMMITTEE PRINT. TENTATIVE BILL.]

BY MR. CLAYTON.

63D CONGRESS,
2D SESSION.

H.R.

IN THE HOUSE OF REPRESENTATIVES.

JANUARY —, 1914.

Mr. CLAYTON introduced the following bill; which was referred to the Committee on the Judiciary and ordered to be printed.

A BILL

To include within the meaning of every contract, combination in the form of trust or otherwise, conspiracy in restraint of trade or commerce among the several States or with foreign nations, and within the meaning of the word "monopolize," certain definite offenses, and to prohibit the same.

1 *Be it enacted by the Senate and House of Representa-*
2 *tives of the United States of America in Congress assembled,*
3 That the words "every contract," "combination in the form
4 of trust or otherwise," and "conspiracy in restraint of trade
5 or commerce," and the word "monopolize," as used in the
6 Act entitled "An act to protect trade and commerce against
7 unlawful restraints and monopolies," approved July second,
8 eighteen hundred and ninety, and in any Acts supplementary
9 thereto or amendatory thereof, shall be deemed to include
1 any combination or agreement between corporations, firms,
2 or persons, or any two or more of them engaged in trade or
3 business carried on in the United States between the States,
4 or between any State or Territory and the District of Co-
5 lumbia, or between the District of Columbia and any Ter-
6 ritory, or between any State, Territory, or the District of
7 Columbia and our insular possessions, or with foreign
8 countries for the following purposes:
9 First. To create or carry out restrictions in trade or to
10 acquire a monopoly in any interstate trade, business, or
11 commerce.
12 Second. To limit or reduce the production or increase
13 the price of merchandise or of any commodity.
14 Third. To prevent competition in manufacturing, mak-

15 ing, transporting, selling, or purchasing of merchandise,
16 produce, or any commodity.
17   Fourth. To make any agreement, enter into any ar-
18 rangement, or arrive at any understanding by which they,
19 directly or indirectly, undertake to prevent a free and unre-
20 stricted competition among themselves or among any pur-
21 chasers or consumers in the sale, production, or transporta-
22 tion of any product, article, or commodity.
23   SEC. 2. That any such contract, combination in the
24 form of trust or otherwise, conspiracy in restraint of trade or
25 commerce, or monopoly, is hereby declared to be unlawful.
1   SEC. 3. That any person, firm, or corporation violating
2 any of the provisions of this Act shall upon conviction be
3 adjudged guilty of a misdemeanor and be punished by a
4 fine not exceeding $5,000 or imprisonment not exceeding
5 one year, or by both, said punishment in the discretion of
6 the court.
7   SEC. 4. That whenever a corporation shall be guilty
8 of the violation of any of the provisions of this Act the
9 offense shall be deemed to be also that of the individual
10 directors, officers, and agents of such corporation authorizing
11 ordering, or doing any of such prohibited acts, and upon
12 conviction thereof they shall be deemed guilty of a misde-
13 meanor and punished as provided in the preceding section.
14   SEC. 5. That nothing contained in this Act shall be
15 taken or held to limit or in any way curtail the meaning and
16 effect of the provisions of the Act approved July second,
17 eighteen hundred and ninety, entitled "An Act to protect
18 trade and commerce against unlawful restraints and mo-
19 nopolies."

MEMO.—Paragraph relating to holding companies to be added

[NO. 3—COMMITTEE PRINT—TENTATIVE BILL.]

By MR. CLAYTON

63D CONGRESS,
2D SESSION.

H.R.

IN THE HOUSE OF REPRESENTATIVES.

JANUARY ——, 1914.

Mr. CLAYTON introduced the following bill; which was referred to the Committee on the Judiciary and ordered to be printed.

A BILL

To prohibit certain persons from being or becoming directors, officers, or employees of national banks, or of certain corporations.

1 *Be it enacted by the Senate and House of Representa-*
2 *tives of the United States of America in Congress assembled,*

That from and after two years from the date of approval of this Act no person who is engaged as an individual, or as a member of a partnership, or as a director or other officer of a corporation in the business, in whole or in part, of manufacturing or selling railroad cars or locomotives, or railroad rails, or structural steel, or mining or selling coal, or the conduct of a bank or trust company, shall act as a director or other officer or employee of any railroad or other public service corporation which conducts an interstate business.

SEC. 2. That from and after two years from the date of approval of this Act, no person shall at the same time be a director or other officer or employee in two or more Federal reserve banks, national banks, or banking associations, or other banks or trust companies, which are members of any reserve bank, and are operating under the provisions of the Act approved December twenty-third, nineteen hundred and thirteen, entitled "An Act providing for the establishment of Federal reserve banks, to furnish an elastic currency, to afford means of rediscounting commercial paper, to establish a more effective supervision of banking in the United States, and for other purposes," and a private banker, and a person who is a director in any State bank or trust company, not operating under the provisions of the said Act, shall not be eligible to be a director in any bank or banking association or trust company operating under the provisions of the aforesaid Act.

SEC. 3. That any person who shall violate section one or section two hereof shall be guilty of a misdemeanor, and shall be punished by a fine of $100 a day for each day of the continuance of such violation or by imprisonment for such period as the court may designate, not exceeding one year, or by both, in the discretion of the court.

SEC. 4. That if, after two years from the date of the approval of this Act, any two or more corporations, engaged in whole or in part in interstate or foreign commerce, have a common director or directors, the fact of such common director or directors shall be conclusive evidence that there exists no real competition between such corporations; and if such corporations shall have been theretofore, or are, or shall have been, by virtue of their business and location of operation, natural competitors, such elimination of competition thus conclusively presumed shall constitute a combination between the said corporations in restraint of interstate or foreign commerce under the provisions of and subject to all the remedies and penalties provided in an Act approved July second, eighteen hundred and ninety, entitled "An Act to protect trade and commerce against unlawful restraints and monopolies."

[NO. 4.—COMMITTEE PRINT. TENTATIVE BILL.]
BY MR. CLAYTON.

63D CONGRESS, 2D SESSION.

H.R.

IN THE HOUSE OF REPRESENTATIVES.

A BILL

To prohibit unlawful restraint of trade or monopolies in interstate or foreign commerce by corporations through the device of intercorporate stockholding.

Be it enacted by the Senate and House of Representatives of the United States of America in Congress assembled,

SECTION 1. That it shall be unlawful for one corporation engaged in interstate or foreign commerce to acquire directly or indirectly, the whole, or any part, of the stock or other share capital of another corporation engaged also in interstate or foreign commerce, where the effect of such acquisition is to eliminate or lessen competition between the corporation whose stock is so acquired and the corporation making the acquisition, or to create a monopoly of any line of trade in any section or community.

SEC. 2. That it shall be unlawful for one corporation to acquire, directly or indirectly, the whole, or any part, of the stock or other share capital of two or more corporations engaged in interstate or foreign commerce, where the effect of such acquisition, or the use of such stock by the voting or granting of proxies, or otherwise, is to eliminate or lessen competition between such corporations, or any of them, whose stock or other share capital is so acquired, or to create a monopoly of any line of trade in any section or community.

SEC. 3. That this Act shall not apply to corporations purchasing such stock solely for investment, and not using the same by voting, or otherwise, to bring about, or in attempting to bring about, the lessening of competition.

SEC. 4. That every violation of this Act shall constitute a misdemeanor punishable by a fine not exceeding $5,000, or imprisonment not exceeding one year, or both, such fine and imprisonment in the discretion of the court; and any individual, who as officer or director of a corporation, or otherwise, orders, takes action, or participates in carrying out any transaction herein forbidden, shall be held and deemed guilty of a misdemeanor under this section.

SEC. 5. That nothing contained in this Act shall prevent a corporation engaged in inserstate [sic] or foreign commerce from causing the formation of subsidiary corporations for the actual carrying on of their immediate lawful business, or the natural and legitimate branches thereof, or from owning and holding all, or a part, of the stock of such subsidiary corporations, when the effect of such formation is not to eliminate or lessen a preexisting competition.

SEC. 6. That nothing contained in this Act shall be held to affect or impair any right heretofore legally acquired: *Provided,* That nothing in this section shall make legal stockholding relations between corporations when, and under such circumstances that, such relations constitute violations of the Act approved July second, eighteen hundred and ninety, entitled "An Act to protect trade and commerce against unlawful restraint and monopolies."

H.R. 15657
63d Cong., 2d Sess.
April 14, 1914

Mr. CLAYTON introduced the following bill; which was referred to the Committee on the Judiciary and ordered to be printed.

A BILL

To supplement existing laws against unlawful restraints and monopolies, and for other purposes.

Be it enacted by the Senate and House of Representatives of the United States of America in Congress assembled, That "antitrust laws," as used herein, includes the Act entitled "An Act to protect trade and commerce against unlawful restraints and monopolies," approved July second, eighteen hundred and ninety; section seventy-three to seventy-seven, inclusive, of an Act entitled "An Act to reduce taxation, to provide revenue for the Government, and for other purposes," of August twenty-seventh, eighteen hundred and ninety-four; an Act entitled "An Act to amend sections seventy-three and seventy-six of the Act of August twenty-seventh, eighteen hundred and ninety-four, entitled "An Act to reduce taxation, to provide revenue for the Government, and for other purposes," approved February twelfth, ninteen [sic] hundred and thirteen; and also this Act.

"Commerce," as used herein, means trade or commerce among the several States and with foreign nations, or between the District of Columbia or any Territory of the United States and any State, Territory, or foreign nation, or within the District of Columbia or any Territory of the United States.

SEC. 2. That any person engaged in commerce who shall discriminate in price between different purchasers of commodities in the same or different sections or communities, with the purpose or intent to thereby injure or destroy the business of a competitor, either of such purchaser or the seller, shall be deemed guilty of a misdemeanor, and upon conviction thereof, shall be punished by a fine not exceeding $5,000, or imprisonment not exceeding one year, or both, in the discretion of the court. Corporations shall be deemed persons within the meaning of this section, and when any corporation shall be guilty of a violation of this section, the offense shall be deemed to be also that of the individual directors or other officers or employees of such corporation ordering or doing the prohibited act, and upon conviction they shall be punished as provided in this section: *Provided,* That nothing herein contained shall prevent discrimination in price between purchasers of commodities on account of differences in the grade, quality, or quantity of the commodity sold, or that makes only due allowance for difference in the cost of transportation: *And provided further,* That nothing herein contained shall prevent persons engaged in selling goods, wares, or merchandise in commerce from selecting their own customers. It shall be unlawful for the owner or operator of any mine engaged in selling its product in commerce to refuse arbitrarily to sell the same to a responsible person, firm, or corporation who applies to purchase.

SEC. 3. That any person engaged in commerce, who shall lease or make a sale of goods, wares, merchandise, machinery, supplies, or other commodites, or fix a price charged therefor, or discount from, or rebate upon such price, on the condition or understanding that the lessee or purchaser thereof shall not use or deal in the goods, wares, merchandise, machinery, supplies, or other commodities, of a competitor or competitors of the lessor or seller, shall be deemed guilty of a misdemeanor, and upon conviction thereof shall be punished by a fine not exceeding $5,000, or by imprisonment not exceeding one year, or both, in the discretion of the court. Corporations shall be deemed persons within the meaning of this section, and when any corporation shall be guilty of a violation of this section, the offense shall be deemed to be also that of the individual directors or other officers or employees of such corporation ordering or doing the prohibited acts, and upon conviction they shall be punished as provided in this section.

SEC. 4. That any person, copartnership, association, or corporation, which shall be injured in his or its business or partnership by any person, copartnership, association, or corporation, by reason of anything forbidden by section two or section three of this Act, may sue therefor in any district court of the United States in the district in which the defendant resides or is found, without respect to the amount in controversy, and shall recover threefold the damages by him or it sustained, and the cost of suit, including a reasonable attorney's fee.

SEC. 5. That whenever in any suit or proceeding in equity, brought by or on behalf of the United States under any of the antitrust laws, there shall have been rendered a final judgment or decree to the effect that a defendant has or has not entered into a contract, combination in the form of trust or otherwise, or conspiracy, in restraint of trade or commerce, or has or has not monopolized, or attempted to

monopolize, or combined with any person or persons to
monopolize, any part of commerce, in violation of any of
the antitrust laws, said judgment or decree shall to the full
extent to which such judgment or decree would constitute
in any other proceeding an estoppel as between the Government and such defendant, constitute in favor of or against
such defendant, conclusive evidence of the same facts, and
be conclusive as to the same issues of law in favor of or
against any other party in any action or proceeding brought
under or involving the provisions of any of the antitrust
laws. Whenever any suit or proceeding in equity is brought
by or on behalf of the United States, under any of the antitrust laws, the statute of limitations in respect of each and
every private right of action, arising under such antitrust
laws, and based, in whole or in part, on any matter complained of in said suit or proceeding in equity, shall be suspended during the pendency of such suit or proceeding in
equity.

SEC. 6. That nothing contained in the antitrust laws
shall be construed to forbid the existence and operation of
fraternal, labor, consumers, agricultural or horticultural organizations, orders or associations operating under the lodge
system, instituted for the purposes of mutual help, and not
having capital stock or conducted for profit, or to forbid or
restrain individual members of such orders or associations
from carrying out the legitimate objects of such associations.

SEC. 7. That no corporation engaged in commerce
shall acquire, directly on [sic] indirectly, the whole, or any part, of
the stock or other share capital of another corporation engaged also in commerce, where the effect of such acquisition
is to eliminate or lessen competition between the corporation
whose stock is so acquired and the corporation making the
acquisition, or to create a monopoly of any line of trade in
any section or community.

No corporation shall acquire, directly or indirectly, the
whole or any part of the stock or other share capital of two
or more corporations engaged in commerce where the effect
of such acquisition, or the use of such stock by the voting or
granting of proxies or otherwise, is to eliminate or lessen
competition between such corporations, or any of them,
whose stock or other share capital is so acquired, or to create
a monopoly of any line of trade in any section or community.

This section shall not apply to corporations purchasing
such stock solely for investment, and not using the same by
voting or otherwise to bring about, or in attempting to bring
about, the lessening of competition. Nor shall anything
contained in this section prevent a corporation engaged in
commerce from causing the formation of subsidiary corporations for the actual carrying on of their immediate lawful
business, or the natural and legitimate branches thereof, or
from owning and holding all, or a part of, the stock of such
subsidiary corporations, when the effect of such formation
is not to eliminate or lessen competition.

Nothing contained in this section shall be held to affect

or impair any right heretofore legally acquired: *Provided,* That nothing in this paragraph shall make legal stockholding relations between corporations when, and under such circumstances that, such relations constitute violations of the antitrust laws.

Nor shall anything herein contained be construed to prohibit any railroad corporation from aiding in the construction of branch or short line railroads so located as to become feeders to the main line of the company so aiding in such construction or from acquiring or owning all or any part of the stock of such branch line, nor to prevent any railroad corporation from acquiring and owning all or any part of the stock of a branch or short line railroad constructed by an independent company where there is no substantial competition between the company owning the branch line so constructed and the company owning the main line acquiring the property or an interest therein, nor to prevent any railroad company from extending any of its lines.

A violation of this section shall be deemed a misdemeanor, and shall be punishable by a fine not exceeding $5,000, or by imprisonment, not exceeding one year, or both, in the discretion of the court, and any violation by a corporation shall be deemed to be also the offense of its individual officers or directors, ordering, doing, or participating in, the prohibited act, and upon conviction, they shall be punished as herein provided.

SEC. 8. That from and after two years from the date of the approval of this Act, no person who is engaged as an individual, or who is a member of a partnership, or is a director or other officer of a corporation that is engaged in the business, in whole or in part, of producing or selling equipment, materials, or supplies to, or in the construction or maintenance of, railroads, or other common carriers engaged in commerce, shall act as a director or other officer or employee of any common carrier engaged in commerce, to which he, or such partnership or corporation, sells or leases, directly or indirectly, equipment, materials, or supplies, or for which he, or such partnership or corporation, directly or indirectly, engages in the work of construction or maintenance; and, after the expiration of said period, no person who is engaged as an individual, or who is a member of a partnership, or is a director or other officer of a corporation which is engaged in the conduct of a bank or trust company, shall act as a director, or other officer or employee, or any such common carrier, for which he, or such partnership, or bank, or trust company, acts, either separately or in connection with others, as agent in the disposal of, or is interested in the underwriting of, or from which he or such partnership, or bank, or trust company, purchases, either separately, or in connection with others, issues or parts of issues of securities of such common carrier.

That from and after two years from the date of the approval of this Act no person shall at the same time be a director or other officer or employee of more than one bank, banking association, or trust company organized and operating under the laws of the United States, either of which has deposits, capital, surplus, and undivided profits aggregating more than $2,500,000; and no private banker, or person who is a director in any bank or trust company, organized and operating under the laws of a State, having deposits, capital, surplus, and undivided profits aggregating more than $2,500,000, shall be eligible to be a director in any bank or banking association organized and operating under the laws of the United States.

No bank, banking association, or trust company organized and doing business under the laws of the United States in any city or town or [sic] more than one hundred thousand inhabitants shall have as a director or other officer or employee any private banker or any director or other officer or employee of any other bank, banking association, or trust company located in the same place.

That from and after two years from the date of the approval of this Act no person at the same time shall be a director in any two or more corporations engaged in whole or in part in commerce, other than common carriers, subject to the Act to regulate commerce, approved February fourth, eighteen hundred and eighty-seven, if such corporations are, or shall have been theretofore, by virtue of their business and location of operation, competitors, so that an elimination of competition by agreement between them would constitute a violation of any of the provisions of any of the antitrust laws.

That any person who shall violate any of the provisions of this section shall be guilty of a misdemeanor, and shall be punished by a fine of $100 a day for each day of the continuance of such violation, or by imprisonment for such period as the court may designate, not exceeding one year, or by both, in the discretion of the court.

SEC. 9. That any suit, action or proceeding under the antitrust laws, against a corporation, may be brought not only in the judicial district whereof it is an inhabitant, but also in any district wherein it may be found.

SEC. 10. That subpoenas for witnesses who are required to attend a court of the United States in any judicial district in any case, civil or criminal, arising under the Federal antitrust laws, may run into any other district.

SEC. 11. That whenever a corporation shall be guilty of the violation of any of the provisions of the antitrust laws, the offense shall be deemed to be also that of the individual directors, officers, and agents of such corporation authorizing, ordering, or doing any of such prohibited acts, and upon conviction thereof they shall be deemed guilty of a misdemeanor, and punished by a fine not exceeding $5,000, or imprisonment not exceeding one year, or by both said punishments in the discretion of the court.

SEC. 12. That the several district courts of the United States are hereby invested with jurisdiction to prevent and restrain violations of this Act; and it shall be the duty of the several district attorneys of the United States, in their respective districts, under the direction of the Attorney General, to institute proceedings in equity to prevent and restrain such violations. Such proceedings may be by way of petition, setting forth the case and praying that such violation shall be enjoined or otherwise prohibited. When the parties complained of shall have been duly notified of such petition, the court shall proceed, as soon as may be, to the hearing and determination of the case; and pending such petition, and before final decree, the court may at any time make such temporary restraining order or prohibition as shall be deemed just in the premises. Whenever it shall appear to the court before which any such proceeding may be pending that the ends of justice require that other parties should be brought before the court, the court may cause them to be summoned, whether they reside in the district in which the court is held or not, and subpoenas to that end may be served in any district by the marshal thereof.

SEC. 13. That any person, firm, corporation, or association shall be entitled to sue for and have injunctive relief, in any court of the United States having jurisdiction over the parties, against threatened loss or damage by a violation of the antitrust laws, when and under the same conditions and principles as injunctive relief against threatened conduct that will cause loss or damage is granted by courts of equity, under the rules governing such proceedings, and upon the execution of proper bond against damages for an injunction improvidently granted and a showing that the danger of irreparable loss or damage is immediate, a preliminary injunction may issue: *Provided,* That nothing herein contained shall be construed to entitle any person, firm, corporation, or association, except the United States, to bring suit in equity for injunctive relief against any common carrier, subject to the provisions of the Act to regulate commerce, approved February fourth, eighteen hundred and eighty-seven, in respect of any matter subject to the regulation, supervision, or other jurisdiction of the Interstate Commerce Commission.

SEC. 14. That no injunction, whether interlocutory or permanent, in cases other than those described in section two hundred and sixty-six of an Act entitled "An Act to codify, revise, and amend the laws relating to the judiciary," approved March third, nineteen hundred and eleven, shall be issued without previous notice and an opportunity to be heard on behalf of the parties to be enjoined, which notice, together with a copy of the bill of complaint or other pleading upon which the application for such injunction will be based, shall be served upon the parties sought to be enjoined a reasonable time in advance of such application. But if it shall appear to the satisfaction of the court or judge that immediate and irreparable injury is likely to ensue to property or a property right of the complainant, and that the giving of notice of the application or the delay incident thereto would probably permit the doing of the act sought to be restrained before notice could be served or hearing had thereon, the court or judge may, in his discretion, issue a temporary restraining order without notice. Every such order shall be endorsed with the date and hour of issuance, shall be forthwith entered of record, shall define the injury and state why it is irreparable and why the order was granted without notice, and shall by its terms expire within such time after entry, not to exceed ten days, as the court or judge may fix, unless within the time so fixed the order is extended or renewed for a like period, after notice to those previously served, if any, and for good cause shown, and the reasons for such extension shall be entered of record, and section two hundred and sixty-three of the Act entitled "An Act to codify, revise, and amend the laws relating to the judiciary," approved March third, nineteen hundred and eleven, is hereby repealed.

SEC. 15. That no restraining order or interlocutory order of injunction shall issue, except upon the giving of security by the applicant in such sum as the court or judge may deem proper, conditioned upon the payment of such costs and damages as may be incurred or suffered by any party who may be found to have been wrongfully enjoined or restrained thereby.

SEC. 16. That every order of injunction or restraining order shall set forth the reasons for the issuance of the same, shall be specific in terms, and shall describe in reasonable detail, and not by reference to the bill of complaint or other document, the act or acts sought to be restrained; and shall be binding only upon the parties to the suit, their agents, servants, employees, and attorneys, or those in active concert with them, and who shall, by personal service or otherwise, have received actual notice of the same.

SEC. 17. That no restraining order or injunction shall be granted by any court of the United States, or a judge or the judges thereof, in any case between an employer and employees, or between employers and employees, or between employees, or between persons employed and persons seeking employment, involving, or growing out of, a dispute concerning terms or conditions of employment, unless necessary to prevent irreparable injury to property, or to a property right, of the party making the application, for which injury there is no adequate remedy at law, and such property or property right must be described with particularity in the application, which must be in writing and sworn to by the applicant or by his agent or attorney.

And no such restraining order or injunction shall prohibit any person or persons from terminating any relation of employment, or from ceasing to perform any work or labor, or from recommending, advising, or persuading others by peaceful means so to do; or from attending at or near a house or place where any person resides or works, or carries on business, or happens to be for the purpose of peacefully obtaining or communicating information, or of peacefully persuading any person to work or to abstain from working; or from ceasing to patronize or to employ any party to such

dispute; or from recommending, advising, or persuading
others by peaceful means so to do; or from paying or giving
to, or withholding from, any person engaged in such dispute,
any strike benefits or other moneys or things of value; or
from peaceably assembling at any place in a lawful manner,
and for lawful purposes; or from doing any act or thing
which might lawfully be done in the absence of such dispute
by any party thereto.

SEC. 18. That any person who shall willfully disobey
any lawful writ, process, order, rule, decree, or command of
any district court of the United States by doing any act or
thing therein, or thereby forbidden to be done by him, if the
act or thing so done by him be of such character as to constitute also a criminal offense under any statute of the United
States, or at common law, shall be proceeded against for his
said contempt as hereinafter provided.

SEC. 19. That whenever it shall be made to appear to
any district court or judge thereof, or to any judge therein
sitting, by the return of a proper officer on lawful process,
or upon the affidavit of some credible person, or by information filed by any district attorney, that there is reasonable
ground to believe that any person has been guilty of such
contempt, the court or judge thereof, or any judge therein
sitting, may issue a rule requiring the said person so charged
to show cause upon a day certain why he should not be
punished therefor, which rule, together with a copy of the
affidavit or information, shall be served upon the person
charged with sufficient promptness to enable him to prepare
for and make return to the order at the time fixed therein.
If upon or by such return, in the judgment of the court, the
alleged contempt be not sufficiently purged, a trial shall be
directed at a time and place fixed by the court: *Provided,
however,* That if the accused, being a natural person, fail or
refuse to make return to the rule to show cause, an attachment may issue against his person to compel an answer,
and in case of his continued failure or refusal, or if, for any
reason, it be impracticable to dispose of the matter on the
return day, he may be required to give reasonable bail for
his attendance at the trial and his submission to the final
judgment of the court. Where the accused person is a body
corporate, an attachment for the sequestration of its property
may be issued upon like refusal or failure to answer.

In all cases within the purview of this Act such trial
may be by the court, or, upon demand of the accused, by a
jury; in which latter event the court may impanel a jury
from the jurors then in attendance, or the court or the judge
thereof in chambers may cause a sufficient number of jurors
to be selected and summoned, as provided by law, to attend
at the time and place of trial, at which time a jury shall be
selected and impaneled as upon a trial for misdemeanor;
and such trial shall conform, as near as may be, to the
practice in criminal cases prosecuted by indictment or upon
information.

If the accused be found guilty, judgment shall be entered

accordingly, prescribing the punishment, either by fine or imprisonment, or both, in the discretion of the court. Such fine shall be paid to the United States or to the complainant or other party injured by the act constituting the contempt, or may, where more than one is so damaged, be divided or apportioned among them as the court may direct; but in no case shall the fine to be paid to the United States exceed, in case the accused is a natural person, the sum of $1,000, nor shall such imprisonment exceed the term of six months.

SEC. 20. That the evidence taken upon the trial of any person so accused may be preserved by bill of exceptions, and any judgment of conviction may be reviewed upon writ of error in all respects as now provided by law in criminal cases, and may be affirmed, reversed, or modified as justice may require. Upon the granting of such writ of error, execution of judgment shall be stayed, and the accused, if thereby sentenced to imprisonment, shall be admitted to bail in such reasonable sum as may be required by the court, or by any justice, or any judge, of any district court of the United States.

SEC. 21. That nothing herein contained shall be construed to relate to contempts committed in the presence of the court, or so near thereto as to obstruct the administration of justice, nor to contempts committed in disobedience of any lawful writ, process, order, rule, decree, or command entered in any suit or action brought or prosecuted in the name of, or on behalf of, the United States, but the same, and all other cases of contempt not specifically embraced within section eighteen of this Act, may be punished in conformity to the usages at law and in equity now prevailing.

SEC. 22. That no proceeding for contempt shall be instituted against any person unless begun within one year from the date of the act complained of; nor shall any such proceeding be a bar to any criminal prosecution for the same act or acts; but nothing herein contained shall affect any proceedings in contempt pending at the time of the passage of this Act.

HOUSE CONSIDERATION

REPORT OF THE HOUSE COMMITTEE ON THE JUDICIARY
H.R. Rep. No. 627, Pt. 1
63d Cong., 2d Sess.
May 6, 1914

⊥ Mr. CLAYTON, from the Committee on the Judiciary, submitted the following ⊥1

REPORT.
[To accompany H. R. 15657.]

The Committee on the Judiciary, having had under consideration the bill (H.R. 15657) to supplement existing laws against unlawful restraints and monopolies, and for other purposes, report the same back with the recommendation that the bill be amended as follows, and that, as amended, it do pass.

Amendment: Strike out all after the enacting clause and insert in lieu of the language stricken out the following: . . .[5.315]

⊥ Your committee, after the delivery of a message by the President of the United ⊥7 States, on January 20 last, to the Congress, making certain recommendations relating to the matter of trusts and monopolies, immediately prepared and published tentative bills which were designed to give legislative expression to the views contained in the President's message, and in order that the country might be given ample time to discuss them, the committee conducted public hearings until April 4, at which time they were concluded. This method of dealing with so large a question, though new, met with general response from the business interests of the country, large and small; and though these hearings imposed upon the committee months of tedious labor they were exceedingly helpful to all concerned. The salient principle of the tentative bills as finally agreed upon with additional provisions have been embodied in the one comprehensive bill now reported.

The atmosphere of antagonism which such legislation might ordinarily be expected to encounter has not always been present and the entire question has consequently been approached with dispassionate fairness. There has been a liberal exchange of views between the committee and those who, from a business standpoint, must first adjust themselves to new conditions, and prudent, thoughtful, patriotic men seem to be agreed that the bill as proposed will go far to bring about business readjustment with as few, as slight, as easy, and simple changes as the object sought will admit of. "Nothing essential has been disturbed, nothing torn up by the roots, no parts rent asunder which can be left in wholesome combination."

The bill is not designed to destroy or hinder business, but on the contrary, to help business and the whole people of the country who are related to or affected by it. The able and patriotic message of the President has been ever before us and the program

---

[5.315] H.R. 15657 as reported by the House Committee on the Judiciary appears *infra* at 1163-81. This is the only deletion the editors have made in reprinting this report; other skips in pagination are accounted for by blank pages in the original print.

which he proposed is contained in the provisions of the bill, and if enacted into law will in truth be "additional articles in our constitution of peace—the peace which is honor and freedom and prosperity."

Analysis of the Bill.

I.

Definitions of Terms.

Section 1 of the bill defines technically for the purposes of this bill certain words, phrases, and terms used in the body of the bill. The definitions thus given are designed merely for convenient reference and to avoid repetition. The definition of commerce, it will be observed, is broadened so as to include trade and commerce between any insular possessions or other places under the jurisdiction of the United States, which at present do not come within the scope of the Sherman antitrust law or other laws relating to trusts. The act approved July 2, 1890, and commonly referred to as the Sherman law, and supplementary legislation pertaining to the same subject, are restricted in application to commerce among the several States and ⊥ Territories, the District of Columbia, and with foreign nations. Your committee can conceive of no good reason why the insular possessions or other places now under the jurisdiction of the United States should not be included within the provisions of our antitrust laws, and with this idea in view we have accordingly in this bill broadened the scope of these laws so as to make them applicable to all places under the jurisdiction of the United States.

II.

Price Discriminations.

Section 2 of the bill is intended to prevent unfair discriminations. It is expressly designed with the view of correcting and forbidding a common and widespread unfair trade practice whereby certain great corporations and also certain smaller concerns which seek to secure a monopoly in trade and commerce by aping the methods of the great corporations, have heretofore endeavored to destroy competition and render unprofitable the business of competitors by selling their goods, wares, and merchandise at a less price in the particular communities where their rivals are engaged in business than at other places throughout the country. This section expressly forbids discrimination in price between different dealers of commodities that are sold for use, consumption, or resale within the United States or any place within its jurisdiction, when such discrimination is made with the purpose or intent to thereby destroy or wrongfully injure the business of a competitor, either of such dealer or seller. It will be observed that the language used makes this section applicable only to domestic commerce, or, in other words, its application is restricted to commerce carried on in the United States, or in places under the jurisdiction thereof, and has no reference to commodities sold either in this country or abroad which are intended solely for our export trade. The violation of any of the provisions of this section is made a misdemeanor, and is made punishable by fine or imprisonment, or both. There are two provisos in this section which are important. The first proviso permits discrimination in prices of commodities on account of differences in grade, quality, and quantity of the commodity sold, or that makes only due allowance for difference in the cost of transportation. The second proviso permits persons selling goods, wares, and merchandise in commerce to select their own customers, except as provided in section 3, which will be considered later. The necessity for legislation to prevent unfair discriminations in prices with a view of destroying competition needs little argument to sustain the wisdom of it. In the past it has been a most common practice of great and powerful combinations engaged in commerce—notably the Standard Oil Co., and the American Tobacco Co., and others of less notoriety, but of great influence—to lower prices of their commodities, oftentimes below the cost of production in certain communities and sections where they had competition, with the intent to destroy and make unprofitable the business of their competitors, and with the ultimate purpose in view of thereby acquiring a monopoly in the particular locality or section in which the discriminating price is made. Every concern that engages in this evil practice must of necessity recoup its losses in the particular communities or sections where their commodities are sold below cost or without a fair profit by raising the price of this same class of commodities above their fair market value in other sections or communities. Such a system or practice is so manifestly unfair and unjust, not only to competitors who are directly injured thereby but to the general public, that your committee is strongly of the opinion that the present antitrust laws ought to be supplemented by making this particular form of discrimination a specific offense under the law when practiced by those engaged in commerce.

The necessity for such legislation is shown by the fact that 19 States have enacted laws forbidding this particular form of discrimination within their borders. These State statutes have practically all been enacted in the last few years, the most of them in the years 1911, 1912, and 1913. It is important that these State statutes be supplemented by additional legislation by Congress, for it is now possible for one of these great corporations doing business in not only the 48 States but throughout the world to lower the prices of its commodities in a particular State and sell within that State at a uniform price in compliance with State laws, and thereby destroy the business of all independent concerns and competitors operating within the State. The loss incurred by such gigantic effort in destroying competition can be more than regained by general increase in the prices of their commodities in other sections. In fact, complaint has been made to your committee that efforts have been made by certain great corporations engaged in commerce in some of the States which have enacted statutes forbidding such discrimination to circumvent the State laws by the methods above described. In seeking to enact section 2 into law we are not dealing with an imaginary evil or against ancient practices long since abandoned, but are attempting to deal with a real, existing, widespread, unfair and unjust trade practice that ought at once to be prohibited in so far as it is within the power of Congress to deal with the subject. This we think is accomplished by section 2 of this bill. As further showing the necessity for such legislation, we call attention to the States which have heretofore adopted statutes varying in form but for the purpose of preventing unfair discriminations in price, as follows:

1. Arkansas, act 1905, as amended March 12, 1913.
2. Idaho, antitrust act of 1911.
3. Iowa, Revised Statutes.
4. Louisiana, act of 1908.
5. Missouri, Revised Statutes.
6. Nebraska, act of 1913.
7. New Jersey, act 1913.
8. North Carolina, act 1913.
9. Oklahoma, act 1913.
10. South Carolina, act 1902.
11. Utah, act 1913.
12. Wisconsin, act 1913.
13. Wyoming, Revised Statutes, 1911.
14. Kansas, act 1905.
15. Michigan, act 1913.
16. Massachusetts, act 1912.
17. Montana, act 1913.
18. North Dakota, act of 1913.
19. California, act 1913.

III.

MINE PRODUCTS.

Section 3 of the bill makes it unlawful for the owner or operator of a mine, or the person controlling the sale of the product thereof in commerce, to arbitrarily refuse to sell such product to a responsible person who applies to purchase the same. This section, like section 2, is limited in its application to the United States and to places under the jurisdiction thereof, and has no reference to persons desiring to purchase such a product for export sale. In that case the seller is permitted to arbitrarily refuse to sell to a responsible bidder, for otherwise a foreign dealer being responsible might purchase the entire output of a mine, to the detriment of manufacturers and dealers in the United States and the owner be powerless to prevent it. The section is based on the broad conservation idea that natural products such as iron, coal, and other minerals stored in the earth as the result of nature's laws should not be monopolized by the mere acquisition of the title to the lands which contain such resources. The design is to prevent those who have acquired or may acquire a monopoly or partial monopoly of mines from discriminating against certain manufacturers, railroads, or other persons who need the products of the mines in carrying on their industries where the commodity is used in its crude state, as coal, and, further, to prevent arbitrary discrimination against responsible purchasers who desire to obtain such products for use or consumption or for resale to persons who desire to purchase same for use or consumption.

This provision is new, but in view of the fact that many railroad corporations, the United States Steel Corporation, and other corporations have acquired and own, either directly or indirectly, through the medium of subsidiary corporations, vast areas of land containing coal, iron, and copper and other minerals in common use, we feel that this legislation is needed and fully justified. By its enactment into law we make it impossible for mere ownership of mines to enable the owners or those disposing of the products thereof to direct the disposal of such products into monopolistic channels of trade. It will liberate from the power of the trust every small manufacturer who is compelled to go into the open market for his raw material and every person who desires to purchase coal for use or for resale to those who desire to purchase for use or consumption, and will afford to every such manufacturer an opportunity to purchase same for cash wherever offered for sale in commerce. The section expressly forbids the mine owner or person controlling the sale of the product of the mine to arbitrarily refuse to sell such product to any responsible purchaser, and thereby prevents the mine owner or operator from giving the preference to another and rival dealer in the disposal of such product.

IV.

EXCLUSIVE AND "TYING" CONTRACTS.

Section 4 of this bill has apparently been much misunderstood, and great confusion seems to have arisen in regard to its provisions. Whether designedly or from a misunderstanding of its purport, we know not, but it has been contended very earnestly that its provisions prevent exclusive or sole agencies. It not only does not prohibit or forbid exclusive agencies, but on the contrary it in no way whatever relates to agencies properly so termed. Let us therefore consider what this section really accomplishes. It prohibits the exclusive or "tying" contract made between the manufacturer and the dealer by purchase or lease, whereby the latter agrees, as a condition of his contract, not to use or deal in the commodities of the competitor or rival of the seller or lessor. It is designed merely to prevent this unfair trade practice now so common throughout the country, and which is generally regarded by everyone who has given the subject any serious consideration as unjust to the local dealer and to the community and as monopolistic in its effects. The section provides that any person engaged in commerce who either leases or makes a sale of goods, wares, and merchandise in the United States or in any places under its jurisdiction on the condition or understanding that the lessee or purchaser thereof shall not use or deal in the goods, wares, merchandise, machinery, supplies, or other commodities of a competitor of either the lessor or seller shall be deemed guilty of a misdemeanor and punished as provided in the section. The words "or fix a price charged therefor or discount therefrom or rebate upon such price" are merely descriptive of the different methods used by the manufacturers to induce the dealer or local merchant to enter into this exclusive or "tying" contract, which obligates him to surrender a right which every dealer should enjoy, namely, to handle any manufacturer's goods, wares, or merchandise he sees fit to handle. Of course, the manufacturer must offer some very flattering and extraordinary inducements on his part, for otherwise no dealer would be foolish enough to enter into any such contract. The first inducement in every case must of necessity relate to price.

By fixing the price so high that the retail dealer will make an extraordinary or unusual profit on the commodities actually sold, the manufacturer is enabled to induce him to enter into an arrangement whereby the local dealer can actually increase his profits for the time being at least by giving up his entire trade in competitive commodities which he is compelled to handle on a small margin. But, rest assured that when the local dealer enters into such a contract and gives up a portion of his trade to rivals, he at once attempts by the aid of the manufacturer to establish a monopoly in the trade of the commodity handled under the exclusive contract and sold at a higher profit. If the transaction results in completely driving out competitive articles from the community as the contract by its terms takes them out of the business of the local dealer, there can be little room to question the contention of the advocates of this system that both the manufacturer and the dealer are benefited by the transaction. If on the contrary the local merchant who has tied his hands by an exclusive contract can not drive out of the community competitive articles and thereby secure a monopoly of the trade in his immediate locality, it is manifest that he has been seriously hampered and injured in his business by the restrictions placed upon him by his contract. But, the advocates of this system and practice of monopoly, in dealing with this question never look beyond the manufacturer or the local dealer to the millions of American consumers who are compelled to purchase daily the necessary food, raiment, and all the necessities of life through the ordinary channels of trade in their respective communities. What about the interest of consumers—the general public—the American people, as a whole? How do they fare under this unnatural arbitrary system and trade practice devised by American manufacturers and put in operation by great and powerful combinations in trade for their own enrichment and with the ultimate view of obtaining a complete monopoly in their special line of industry? Undoubtedly, the system results in higher prices to consumers. Great department stores, and mail-order houses flourish under it. Local customers can not purchase or obtain at their local stores particular commodities desired and often necessary and hence are compelled to send their money abroad in order to secure the desired commodity which ought under any fair system to be procurable in their local community through their local dealer. On account of this very condition, the temptation to the local merchant is very strong to break away from his contract and to deal in the commodities of others. The needs of his customers demand constantly that he should do so.

The customer having once gone to another dealer or procured the desired commodity through a mail-order house may not return to his local dealer and the goods purchased under an exclusive or "tying" contract may remain on the shelves of the local merchant unsold. The local dealer has invested his money in them; he has paid for them; they belong to him. But the manufacturer has a contract that binds him not to deal in other like commodities. So every such contract provides for a discount from or rebate upon such price as a further inducement for the local merchant or retailer to enter into a discriminating contract which ties his hands. What is the result? Let us see. What is the motive and purpose of the manufacturer in making or entering into such exclusive contract? It is undoubtedly his purpose to drive out competition and to establish a monopoly in the sale of his commodities in that particular community or locality. His contract by its express terms completely shuts out competition in the business of the local dealer with whom he makes it. The dealer bound by this exclusive contract not to handle the goods, wares, and merchandise of another becomes the ally of the manufacturer in his effort and purpose to drive out competition in the locality or community in which such commodities are sold. This is done by means of extensive advertising, and let it be borne in mind also that this advertising is added in the price of the commodities and paid for by the consumer. If by the combined efforts of the manufacturer and the local dealer and the glowing and overdrawn and oftentimes false advertisements competitors are compelled to retire from the field, a monopoly in the particular community or locality is the invariable result. In this connection it is important to state that to-day in every village and locality where there is only a single store and this exclusive or "tying" contract is entered into between the manufacturer and the local dealer concerning any commodity, the exclusive or "tying" contract gives both the manufacturer and the local dealer a complete monopoly of that particular commodity in the locality or community. That the effect of such a system is detrimental to the consumers and to the general public can not be questioned for a moment.

The public is compelled to pay a higher price and local customers are put to the inconvenience of securing many commodities in other ⊥ communities or through mail-order houses that can not be procured at their local stores. The price is raised as an inducement. This is the local effect. Where the concern making these contracts is already great and powerful, such as the United Shoe Machinery Co., the American Tobacco Co., and the General Film Co., the exclusive or "tying" contract made with local dealers becomes one of the greatest agencies and instrumentalities of monopoly ever devised by the brain of man. It completely shuts out competitors, not only from trade in which they are already engaged, but from the opportunities to build up trade in any community where these great and powerful combinations are operating under this system and practice. By this method and practice the Shoe Machinery Co. has built up a monopoly that owns and controls the entire machinery now being used by all great shoe-manufacturing houses of the United States. No independent manufacturer of shoe machines has the slightest opportunity to build up any considerable trade in this country while this condition obtains. If a manufacturer who is using machines of the Shoe Machinery Co. were to purchase and place a machine manufactured by any independent company in his establishment, the Shoe Machinery Co. could under its contracts withdraw all their machinery from the establishment of the shoe manufacturer and thereby wreck the business of the manufacturer. The General Film Co., by the same method practiced by the Shoe Machinery Co. under the lease system, has practically destroyed all competition and acquired a virtual monopoly of all films manufactured and sold in the United States. When we consider contracts of sales made under this system, the result to the consumer, the general public, and the local dealer and his business is even worse than under the lease system.

The local dealer is required under the contract system to purchase and pay for each article secured for his business. He is required to contract for purchase on condition that he will not deal in like articles manufactured by competitors. If he can not sell the commodities so purchased, he must go out of business. It was shown in testimony before the committee during the recent hearings that a certain automobile manufacturing company, with a capital of only $2,000,000, had made a profit of $25,000,000 net on their investment in a single year. Was that a profit on the $2,000,000 actually invested by the manufacturing company? Not at all. It was the profit on that $2,000,000 supplemented by many times that many millions actually invested by local dealers in the machines of that company by so-called selling agencies throughout the country. The selling agencies are not in reality agencies at all, but are purchasers and owners of machines who have paid the full price therefor under contracts conditioned that these same dealers will not deal in the machines of any competitor or rival company. These extraordinary profits have been made largely on money actually invested in machines by customers, hundreds of which remain unsold in the possession of the local dealer. This illustration alone is sufficient to show the absolute unfairness of any such practice or system. The system is wholly bad for consumers and the general public, and in its last analysis detrimental to the interests of local dealers generally. We have penalized this practice under the provisions of section 4 and made it a misdemeanor punishable as prescribed in the section.

⊥ V.

SUPPLEMENT SECTION 7 OF SHERMAN ACT.

Section 5 is supplementary to the existing laws, and extends the remedy under section 7 of the Sherman Act to persons injured in their business or property by the wrongful acts of persons or combinations violating any of the antitrust laws, and allows the recovery of threefold damages therefor.

VI.

DECREE ADMISSIBLE IN OTHER SUIT.

Section 6 provides that a final decree obtained by the United States in a suit to dissolve a corporation or unlawful combination may be offered in evidence in a suit brought by a private suitor for damages under the antitrust laws by reason of the unlawful acts of the defendant corporation, and that when such decree or judgment is so offered it shall be conclusive evidence of the same facts and be conclusive as to the same questions of law as between the parties in the original suit or proceeding. This section also provides that the statutes of limitations shall be suspended in favor of private litigants who have sustained damage to their property or business by the wrongful acts of the defendant during the pendency of the suit or proceeding instituted by or on behalf of the United States. The entire provision is intended to help persons of small means who are injured in their property or business by combinations or corporations violating the antitrust laws.

It is in keeping with a recommendation made by the President in his message to Congress on the general subject of trusts and monopolies.

VII.

FRATERNAL, LABOR, AND OTHER ORGANIZATIONS.

The object of section 7 is to make clear certain questions about which doubt has arisen as to whether or not fraternal, labor, consumers, agricultural, or horticultural organizations, orders, or associations organized for mutual help, not having capital stock or conducted for profit, come within the scope and purview of the Sherman antitrust law in such way as to warrant the courts under interpretations heretofore given to that law to enter a decree for the dissolution of such organizations, orders, or associations upon a proper showing, as may be done in regard to industrial corporations and combinations which have been found to be guilty of violation of its provisions.

A second paragraph is inserted in this section to remove a question of doubt as to whether associations of traffic, operating, accounting, or other officers of common carriers for the purpose of conferring among themselves or of making any lawful agreement as to any matter which is subject to the regulating or supervisory jurisdiction of the Interstate Commerce Commission, come within the prohibitions of the antitrust laws.

It was contended before your committee by Mr. Gompers, president of the American Federation of Labor, that under the interpretations of the Sherman law as construed by the courts, the labor organizations as they exist to-day might, under certain conditions, be deemed and held illegal combinations in restraint of trade and be dissolved by a decree of the court under section 4 of the act of July 2, 1890, and that the American Federation of Labor and all organizations affiliated with it exist and operate to-day at the sufferance of the administration in power. Mr. Gompers, among other things in his address before the committee, said:

> Gentlemen, under the interpretation placed upon the Sherman antitrust law by the courts, it is within the province and within the power of any administration at any time to begin proceedings to dissolve any organization of labor in the United States and to take charge of and receive whatever funds any worker or organization may have wanted to contribute or felt that it is his duty to contribute to the organization.

Mr. WEBB. Are there any suits pending in the courts now looking to this end, Mr. Gompers?

Mr. GOMPERS. There are no suits now pending, but an organization of workingmen, the window-glass workers, was dissolved by order of the court under the provisions of the Sherman antitrust law, charged with conspiracy as an illegal combination in restraint of trade. And while that organization was dissolved by action of the court, yet it created no furor, for this reason: I have no desire to reflect upon the men who are in charge of that organization as its officers and representatives, but it was, in my judgment, supine cowardness for them not to resist an attempt of the dissolution of their associated effort as a voluntary organization of men to protect the only thing they possessed—the power to labor.

Mr. WEBB. Have you any case where a labor organization has been dissolved simply because they themselves united in asking or fixing a certain wage and went no further in uniting with the manufacturers?

Mr. GOMPERS. I can not tell you, sir, about that. But that is the very essence of the life of the organization. What I want to convey is this, that there are probably, of these 30,000 or more local associations of workingmen, what we call local unions of working men and working women, probably more than two-thirds of whom have agreements with employers. As a matter of fact, I think that every observer and every humanitarian who knows greeted with the greatest satisfaction the creation of the protocol in the sweated industries of New York City and vicinity which abolished sweatshops and long hours of labor, and the burdensome, miserable toil prevailing, and established the combination of employers and of work men and work women by which certain standards are to be enforced, and no employer can become a member of the manufacturers' association in that trade unless he is willing to undersign an agreement by which the conditions prevailing in the protocol will be inaugurated by him. Yet, under the provisions of the Sherman antitrust law that association of manufacturers has been sued, I think, for something like $250,000, because it is a conspiracy in restraint of trade.

What I mean to say is this: I am perfectly satisfied in my own mind that the Attorney General of this administration, the Attorney General of the United States under the present administration, is not going to dissolve or make any attempt to dissolve the organizations of the working people of this country. I firmly believe that if there should be any of them, any individual or an aggregation of individuals, guilty of any crime, that the present administration would proceed against them just as readily, and perhaps more so, as any other; I am speaking of the procedure against the organizations themselves and the dissolution of them. But who can tell whether this administration is going to continue very long, or whether the same policy is going to be pursued; that is, the policy of permitting these associations to exist without interference or attempts to isolate them? Who can tell? What may come; what may not the future hold in store for us working people who are engaged in an effort for the protection of men and women who toil to make life better worth living? We do not want to exist as a matter of sufferance, subject to the whims or to the chances or to the vindictiveness of any administration or of an administration officer. Our existence is justified not only by our history, but our existence is legally the best concept of what constitutes law. It is an outrage; it is an outrage of not only the conscience; it is not only an outrage upon justice; it is an outrage upon our language to attempt to place in the same category a combination of men engaged in the speculation and the control of the products of labor and the products of the soil on the one hand and the associations of men and women who own nothing but themselves and undertake to control nothing but themselves and their power to work.

Mr. FLOYD. I want to see if I understand your position. If I understand your position under the existing status of the law as determined by the Federal courts, if ⊥ the Attorney General should proceed to dissolve any of your labor organizations they could be dissolved. Is that your proposition?

Mr. GOMPERS. Yes, sir.

Mr. FLOYD. And that your existence, therefore, depends upon the sufferance of the administration which happens to be in power for the time being?

Mr. GOMPERS. Yes, sir.

Mr. FLOYD. What you desire is for us to give you a legal status under the law?

Mr. GOMPERS. Yes, sir.

Mr. FLOYD. So you can carry on this cooperative work on behalf of the laborers of the country and of the different organizations without being under the ban of the existing law?

Mr. GOMPERS. Yes, sir.

In the light of previous decisions of the courts and in view of a possible interpretation of the law which would empower the courts to order the dissolution of such organizations and associations, your committee feels that all doubt should be removed as to the legality of the existence and operations of these organizations and associations, and that the law should not be construed in such a way as to authorize their dissolution by the courts under the antitrust laws or to forbid the individual members of such associations from carrying out the legitimate and lawful objects of their associations. This will be accomplished by the provisions of section 7 of this bill, which recognize as legal the existence and operations of fraternal, labor, consumers, agricultural, or horticultural organizations, orders, or associations organized for purposes of mutual help, and not having capital stock or conducted for profit, and forbids the danger and possibility of the dissolution of such organizations, orders, or associations by a decree of the courts as unlawful combinations in restraint of trade or commerce under the provisions of the antitrust laws. It also guarantees to individual members of such organizations, orders, or associations, the right to pursue without molestation or legal restraint the legitimate objects of such association. This section should be construed in connection with sections 15 to 22, inclusive, which regulate the issuance of injunctions and provide for jury trials in certain cases of contempts in Federal courts. The sections relating to injunctions and contempts constitute for labor a complete bill of rights in equitable proceedings in United States courts.

This section further provides that nothing contained in the antitrust laws shall be construed to forbid associations of traffic, operating, accounting, or other officers of common carriers for the purpose of conferring among themselves or of making any lawful agreement as to any matter which is subject to the regulating or supervisory jurisdiction of the Interstate Commerce Commission. In actual practice the officers of common carriers in the interest of the public and to avoid complications must necessarily confer with the officers of other railroad companies, but as all agreements or arrangements made between them are subject to the jurisdiction of the Interstate Commerce Commission, your committee consider it but just to make clear that such associations are not in violation of the Sherman Act. When the desirability of this provision was brought to the attention of the committee, the question was referred to the Interstate Commerce Commission by the chairman of the committee for its opinion in regard to the proposed legislation, and this provision as drawn is in keeping with the views of the Interstate Commerce Commission.

VIII.
HOLDING COMPANIES.

Section 8 deals with what is commonly known as the "holding company," which is a common and favorite method of promoting monopoly. "Holding company" is a term, generally understood to mean a company that holds the stock of another company or companies, but as we understand the term a "holding company" is a company whose *primary* purpose is to hold stocks of other companies. It has usually issued its own shares in exchange for these stocks, and is a means of holding under one control the competing companies whose stocks it has thus acquired. As thus defined a "holding company" is an abomination and in our judgment is a mere incorporated form of the old-fashioned trust. Most of the corporations engaged in interstate commerce are organized under the laws of one or the other of the States. It is right that this should be so, and it is right that the various States, each of which has the right to exclude corporations of any other State from its borders, should exhibit comity to these other States, and that the Federal Government, which perhaps has the right to exclude corporations of any State from interstate commerce, should exhibit comity to all the States.

At common law a corporation had no right to own stock in another corporation, but from time to time the various States have, by special statutes, permitted it, until now certainly more than a majority of all the States permit corporate stockholding either generally or of certain kinds and under certain conditions. This legislation in its early operation may have served a useful, economic purpose. Trade and commerce could do as well without steam and electricity as without the idea of the commercial unit which is embodied in the word "corporation." Hence there are certain corporations which may properly be interested with individuals other than its own stockholders, but experience has taught us that the "holding company" as above described no longer serves any purpose that is helpful to either business or the community at large when it is operated purely as a "holding company." Section 8 is intended to eliminate this evil so far as it is possible to do so, making such exceptions from the law as seem to be wise, which exceptions have been found necessary by business experience and conditions, and the exceptions herein made are those which are not deemed monopolistic and do not tend to restrain trade.

IX.

INTERLOCKING DIRECTORATES.

Section 9 of the bill deals with the general subject of interlocking directorates. The President, in his message delivered before Congress on January 20, 1914, on the subject of trusts and monopolies, among other things, said:

We are all agreed that "private monopoly is indefensible and intolerable," and our program is founded upon that conviction. It will be a comprehensive but not a radical or unacceptable program, and these are its items, the changes which opinion deliberately sanctions and for which business waits:

It waits with acquiescence, in the first place, for laws which will effectually prohibit and prevent such interlockings of the *personnel* of the directorates of great corporations—banks and railroads, industrial, commercial, and public-service bodies—as in effect result in making those who borrow and those who lend practically one and the same, those who sell and those who buy but the same persons trading with one another under different names and in different combinations, and those who affect to compete in fact partners and masters of some whole field of business. Sufficient time should be allowed, of course, in which to effect these changes of organization without inconvenience or confusion.

Such a prohibition will work much more than a mere negative good by correcting the serious evils which have arisen because, for example, the men who have been the directing spirits of the great investment banks have usurped the place which belongs to independent industrial management working in its own behoof. It will bring new men, new energies, a new spirit of initiative, new blood, into the management of our great business enterprises. It will open the field of industrial development and origination to scores of men who have been obliged to serve when their abilities entitled them to direct. It will immensely hearten the young men coming on and will greatly enrich the business activities of the whole country.

In drafting the provisions of section 9 your committee has endeavored to carry out the recommendations of the President. In order that the corporations affected may have ample time in which to readjust their boards of directors in keeping with the requirements of this act, it is expressly provided that the provisions of this section shall not become effective until two years after the date of the approval of the act. This section is divided into three paragraphs, each of which relates to the particular class of corporations described, and the provisions of each paragraph are limited in their application to the corporations belonging to the class named herein.

The first paragraph deals with the eligibility of directors in interstate-railroad corporations, and provides that no person who is engaged as an individual or who is a member of a partnership or is a director or other officer of a corporation engaged in the business of producing or selling equipment, materials, or supplies, or in the construction or maintenance of railroads or other common carriers engaged in commerce, shall act as a director or other officer or employee of any other corporation or common carrier engaged in commerce to which he or such partnership or corporation sells or leases, directly or indirectly, equipment, material, or supplies, or for which he or such partnership or corporation, directly or indirectly, engages in the work of construction or maintenance. It is further provided in this paragraph that no person who is engaged as an individual or who is a member of a partnership, or is a director or other officer of a corporation which is engaged in the conduct of a bank or trust company, shall act as a director or other officer or employee of any common carrier for which he or such partnership, or bank, or trust company, acts, either separately or in connection with others, as agent for or underwriter of the sale or disposal by such common carrier of issues or parts of issues of its securities, or from which he or such partnership or bank or trust company purchases, either separately or in connection with others, issues or parts of issues of securities of such common carriers. The provisions of this paragraph prevent absolutely common directors or interlocking directors between corporations occupying relations to each other described therein, without any reference to the capital, surplus, and undivided profits of the corporations dealing with each other.

The second paragraph of the bill deals with the eligibility of directors, officers, and employees of banks, banking associations, and trust companies organized or operating under the laws of the United States, either of which has deposits, capital, surplus, or undivided profits aggregating more than $2,500,000, and provides that no private banker or person who is a director in any bank or trust company organized and operating under the laws of a State having such aggregate amount of deposits, capital, surplus, and undivided profits shall be eligible to be a director in any bank or banking association organized or operating under the laws of the United States. The purpose of this provision, which relates exclusively to banks and banking associations, is to prevent as far as possible control of great aggregations of money and capital through the medium of common directors between banks and banking associations, the object being to prevent the concentration of money or its distribution through a system of interlocking directorates. Your committee have not deemed it necessary or wise, therefore, to include within the provisions of this paragraph the smaller banks throughout the country, except where located in cities and towns of more than 100,000 inhabitants. There are three provisos relating to this paragraph. The first proviso excepts from its provisions mutual savings banks not having capital stock represented by shares. The second proviso permits a director, officer, or employee of a bank or banking association or trust company to be a director, officer, or or [sic] employee in another bank or trust company organized under the laws of the United States or any State where the entire capital stock of one is owned by stockholders in the other. And the third proviso allows a director of class A of a federal reserve bank, as defined in the Tederal [sic] reserve act, to be a director or officer, or both a director and officer, in one member bank. This is permitted by the provisions of the Federal reserve act, and this proviso is inserted to avoid repealing that provision.

The third paragraph of section 9 deals with the eligibility of directors in industrial corporations engaged in commerce, and provides that no person at the same time shall be a director in any two or more corporations, either of which has capital, surplus, and undivided profits aggregating more than $1,000,000, other than common carriers which are subject to the act to regulate commerce, if such corporations are or shall have been theretofore, by virtue of their business and location of operation, competitors, so that an elimination of competition by agreement between them would constitute a violation of any of the provisions of the antitrust laws. In this, as in the preceding paragraph relating to banks, it was not deemed necessary or advisable that interlocking directorates should be prohibited between the smaller industrial corporations. The importance of the legislation embodied in section 9 of this bill can not be overestimated. The concentration of wealth, money, and property in the United States under the control and in the hands of a few individuals or great corporations has grown to such an enormous extent that unless checked it will ultimately threaten the perpetuity of our institutions. The idea that there are only a few men in any of our great corporations and industries who are capable of handling the affairs of the same is contrary to the spirit of our institutions. From an economic point of view, it is not possible that one individual, however capable, acting as a director in fifty corporations, can render as effi⊥cient and valuable service in directing the affairs of the several corporations under his control as can fifty capable men acting as single directors and devoting their entire time to directing the affairs of one of such corporations. The truth is that the only real service the same director in a great number of corporations renders is in maintaining uniform policies throughout the entire system for which he acts, which usually results to the advantage of the greater corporations and to the disadvantage of the smaller corporations which he dominates by reason of his prestige as a director and to the detriment of the public generally.

As the President has well said in his message, the adoption of the provisions of this section will bring new men, new energies, new spirit of initiative, and new blood into the management of our business enterprises. It will open the field of industrial development and origination to scores of men who have been obliged to serve when their abilities entitled them to direct. It will immensely hearten the young men coming on and will greatly enrich the business activities of the whole country.

X.

VENUE.

Section 10 relates to procedure and provides that any suit, action, or proceeding under the antitrust laws against a corporation may be brought not only in the judicial district whereof it is an inhabitant but also in any district wherein it may be found. Under the law as it now exists, a suit against a corporation must be brought in the district whereof it is an inhabitant.

XI.

SUBPOENAS RUN INTO OTHER DISTRICTS.

Section 11 provides that in any suit, action, or proceeding brought by or on behalf of the United States, subpoenas for witnesses who are required to attend a court of the United States in any judicial district in any case, civil or criminal, arising under the antitrust laws, may run into any other district. Under the existing law, subpoenas for witnesses in such suits may run only in the district in which they are issued.

XII.

PERSONAL GUILT.

Section 12 is the personal guilt provision of the bill. It provides that whenever a corporation shall be guilty of a violation of any of the provisions of the antitrust laws the offense shall be deemed to be also that of the individual officers or agents of such corporation, and upon the conviction of the corporation, any director, officer, or agent who shall have authorized, ordered, or done any of such prohibited acts shall be deemed guilty of a misdemeanor and upon conviction therefor shall be punished as prescribed in the section.

XIII.

SAME AS SECTION 4 OF SHERMAN ACT.

Section 13 is a reenactment of section 4 of the act of July 2, 1890, so as to enable the United States to proceed against corporations for the violation of any of the provisions of this act as it is now authorized by law to proceed against corporations for violations of the Sherman Act.

XIV.

INJUNCTIVE RELIEF AUTHORIZED.

Section 14 authorizes a person, firm, or corporation or association to sue for and have injunctive relief against threatened loss or damage by a violation of the antitrust laws, when and under the same conditions and principles as injunctive relief against threatened conduct that will cause loss or damage is granted by courts of equity under the rules governing such proceedings. Under section 7 of the act of July 2, 1890, a person injured in his business and property by corporations or combinations acting in violation of the Sherman antitrust law, may recover loss and damage for such wrongful act. There is, however, no provision in the existing law authorizing a person, firm, corporation, or association to enjoin threatened loss or damage to his business or property by the commission of such unlawful acts, and the purpose of this section is to remedy such defect in the law. This provision is in keeping with the recommendation made by the President in his message to Congress on the subject of trusts and monopolies.

INJUNCTIONS AND CONTEMPTS.

The remaining sections of the bill, 15 to 23, inclusive, are substantially the same as the provisions of the two separate bills (H. R. 23635 and H. R. 22591, 62d Cong.), known as the Clayton injunction and contempt bills, which were considered and passed by the House of Representatives at the last Congress, but failed of passage in the Senate. They deal entirely with questions of Federal procedure relating to injunctions and contempts committed without the presence of the court. The reports upon these bills made to the House in the last Congress are comprehensive and explain in detail their purpose, and for convenience are adopted as a part of this report. They follow in order:

REGULATION OF INJUNCTIONS.[5.316]

APRIL 26, 1912.—Referred to the House Calendar and ordered to be printed.

Mr. CLAYTON, from the Committee on the Judiciary, submitted the following

REPORT.
[To accompany H. R. 23635.]

The Committee on the Judiciary, having had under consideration H. R. 23635, to amend an act entitled "An act to codify, revise, and amend the laws relating to the judiciary," approved March 3, 1911, report the same back with the recommendation that the bill do pass.

The too ready issuance of injunctions or the issuance without proper precautions or safeguards has been called to the attention of the Congress session after session for many years. The bill now reported seeks to remedy the evils complained of by legislation directed to those specific matters which have given rise to most criticism. These matters are so segregated in various sections of the bill that they may be separately discussed.

I.

The first section of the bill amends section 263 of the judicial code which relates to two distinct steps in the procedure, namely, notice and security. But the amended section relates only to the notice, leaving the matter of security to be dealt with by a new section 266a.

FORMER STATUTES.

In order to fully understand the subject of notice in injunction cases it is necessary to give an historical résumé of the subject. In the judiciary act of 1789 which was passed during the first session of that year, Congress having created the different courts according to the scheme outlined by Chief Justice Ellsworth, conferred upon the courts power to issue all writs, including writs of ne exeat (a form of injunction), according to legal usages and practice. In 1793, however, there was a revision of that statute, and among other things the same powers, substantially, were conferred upon the judges as before; but at the end of the section authorizing the issuance of injunctions, was this language: "No injunction shall be issued in any case without reasonable previous notice to the adverse party or his attorney."

The law stood thus until the general revision of 1873, during which period the law expressly required reasonable notice to be given in all cases. But the will of Congress as thus expressed was completely thwarted and the statute nullified by the peculiar construction placed upon it by the courts. The question frequently arose. The courts got

---

[5.316] H.R. REP. NO. 612, 62d Cong., 2d Sess. (1912). In 1912, Congressman Clayton introduced H.R. 23635 and H.R. 22591, regulating the use of injunctions and the procedures to be followed in contempt cases, respectively. Both bills were reported out of the Judiciary Committee by Congressman Clayton and were passed by the House, but died in the Senate. Since the language of the 1912 legislation was incorporated into H.R. 15657 in substantially unchanged form, both the majority and minority members of the 1914 Judiciary Committee omitted any further explanation of injunctive relief and the use of the contempt power, instead adopting the extensive discussions of the 1912 reports, reprinted herein.

around it in various ways, but usually by holding that it did not apply to a case of threatened irreparable injury, notwithstanding that its language was broad and sweeping, plainly covering all cases. Another form of expression often used is found in Ex parte Poultney (4 [sic] Peters C. C. C., 472):

> Every court of equity possesses the power to mold its rules in relation to the time of appearing and answering so as to prevent the rule from working injustice, and it is not only in the power of the court, but it is its duty to exercise a sound discretion upon this subject.[5.317]

The court found a similar method of evading the sweeping prohibition of the revision of 1793, with respect to notice in Lawrence v. Bowman (1 U. S. C. C., Alester, 230).[5.318]

But the earliest provision requiring notice came before the Supreme Court in 1799, in New York v. Connecticut (4. Dall., 1).[5.319] Its constitutionality was not questioned. The only issue was as to the sufficiency of the notice, Chief Justice Ellsworth, for the court, saying: "The prohibition contained in the statute that writs of injunction shall not be granted without reasonable notice to the adverse party or his attorney, extends to injunctions granted by the Supreme Court or the circuit court as well as to those that may be granted by a single judge. The design and effect, however, of injunctions must render a shorter notice, reasonable notice, in the case of an application to a court than would be so construed in most cases of an application to a single judge, and until a general rule shall be settled the particular circumstances of each case must also be regarded."[5.320]

Here was a case in which, although no point was made by counsel on any question of constitutionality, the Supreme Court accepted the comprehensive requirement of the act of 1793 as binding on all the Federal courts.

Now we come to the present law, found in section 263 of the Judicial Code, and reading thus:

> Whenever notice is given of a motion for an injunction out of a district court, the court or judge thereof may, if there appears to be danger of irreparable injury from delay, grant an order restraining the act sought to be enjoined until the decision upon the motion; and such order may be granted with or without security, in the discretion of the court or judge.

This was the law as contained in section 718 of the Revised Statutes, said section having been enacted in 1872. It simply embodies the practice of the courts with respect to notice, a practice established notwithstanding the nonconformity of the practice to the positive requirement of the act of 1793.

PROPOSED CHANGES.

But it will be seen that the giving of notice and requiring security, left by the present law to the discretion of the court, is by this bill a positive duty, except where irreparable and immediate injury might result from the giving of a notice or the delay incident thereto, in which case the court or judge may issue a temporary restraining order pending the giving of the notice. The concluding part of the amended section has an effect to safeguard parties from the reckless and inconsiderate issuance of restraining orders. Injuries compensable in damages recoverable in an action at law are not treated or considered by the courts as irreparable in any proper legal sense, and parties attempting to show why the injury sought to be restrained is irreparable would often disclose an adequate legal remedy. This provision requires the reason to appear in the order, but it should be read in connection with the new section 266b, requiring the order to be made by the court or judge to be likewise specific in other essentials, and section 266c, requiring that every complaint filed for the purpose of obtaining the

---

[5.317] The correct citation is *Ex parte* Poultney v. City of La Fayette, 37 U.S. (12 Pet.) 472, 475, 9 L. Ed. 1161, 1162 (1838).

[5.318] 15 F. Cas. 21 (No. 8134) (C.C.N.D. Cal. 1858).

[5.319] 4 U.S. (4 Dall.) 1, 1 L. Ed. 715 (1799).

[5.320] 4 U.S. (4 Dall.) at 2.

order, in the cases there specified, shall contain a particular description of the property or property right for which the prohibitive power of the court is sought, and that such complaint shall be verified.

A valuable provision of the amendment is one that a restraining order issued without notice "shall by its terms expire within such time after entry, not to exceed seven days, as the court or judge may fix, unless within the time so fixed the order is extended or renewed for a like period, after notice to those previously served, if any, and for good cause shown, and the reasons for such extension shall be entered of record."

A legislative precedent for such legislation is found in the act of 1807, wherein it was provided that injunctions granted by the district courts "shall not, unless so ordered by the circuit court, continue longer than to the circuit court next ensuing, nor shall an injunction be issued by a district judge in any case where a party has had a reasonable time to apply to the circuit court for the writ." (U. S. Stat. L., vol. 2, p. 418.)

If the views of President Taft on this subject have not changed, he will welcome an opportunity to approve a bill containing such provisions as those in the amendment governing notice, because in his message of December 7, 1909, to the regular session of the Sixty-first Congress, after a quotation from the Republican platform of 1908, he said:

I recommend that in compliance with the promise thus made appropriate legislation be adopted. The ends of justice will best be met and the chief cause of complaint against ill-considered injunctions without notice will be removed by the enactment of a statute forbidding hereafter the issuing of any injunction or restraining order, whether temporary or permanent, by any Federal court without previous notice and a reasonable opportunity to be heard on behalf of the parties to be enjoined: unless it shall appear to the satisfaction of the court that the delay necessary to give such notice and hearing would result in irreparable injury to the complainant, and unless, also, the court shall from the evidence make a written finding, which shall be spread upon the court minutes, that immediate and irreparable injury is likely to ensue to the complainant, and shall define the injury, state why it is irreparable, and shall also indorse on the order issued the date and the hour of the issuance of the order. Moreover, every such injunction or restraining order issued without ⊥ previous notice and opportunity by the defendant to be heard should by force of the statute expire and be of no effect after seven days from the issuance thereof or within any time less than that period which the court may fix, unless within such seven days or such less period the injunction or order is extended or renewed after previous notice and opportunity to be heard.

My judgment is that the passage of such an act, which really embodies the best practice in equity and is very likely the rule now in force in some courts, will prevent the issuing of ill-advised orders or injunction without notice and will render such orders, when issued, much less objectionable by the short time in which they may remain effective.

II.

Section 266a simply requires security for costs and damages in all cases, leaving it no longer within the discretion of the courts whether any such security or none shall be given.

Prior to the said act of 1872 (contained in the revision of 1873) there appears to have been no legislation on the matter of security in injunction cases; but that security was usually required is a fact well known to the legal profession. It seems clearly just and salutary that the extraordinary writ of injunction should not issue in any case until the party seeking it and for whose benefit it issues has provided the other party with all the protection which security for damages affords.

It appears by the authorities, both English and American, to have been always within the range of judicial discretion, in the absence of a statute, to waive security, though better practice has been to require security as a condition to issuing restraining orders and injunctions.

The new section, 266a, takes the matter of requiring security out of the category of discretionary matters, where it was found by the Committee on Revision and permitted to remain.

For a discussion of the existing law on the question of security, we refer to Russell v. Farley (105 U. S., 433).[5.321]

III.

Section 266b is of general application. Defendants should never be left to guess at what they are forbidden to do, but the order "shall describe in reasonable detail, and not by reference to the bill of complaint or other document, the act or acts sought to be restrained." It also contains a safeguard against what have been heretofore known as dragnet or blanket injunctions, by which large numbers may be accused, and eventually punished, for violating injunctions in cases in which they were not made parties in the legal sense and of which they had only constructive notice, equivalent in most cases to none at all. Moreover, no person shall be bound by any such order without actual personal notice.

EXISTING LAW AND PRACTICE.

There was heretofore no Federal statute to govern either the matter of making or form and contents of orders for injunctions. Of course, where a restraining order is granted that performs the functions of order, process, and notice. But the writ of injunction, where ⊥ temporary, is preceded by the entry of an order, and where permanent by the entry of a decree.

The whole matter appears to have been left, both by the States and the Federal Government, to the courts, which have mostly conformed to established principles.

The most important of these was that the order should be sufficiently clear and certain in its terms that the defendants could by an inspection of it readily know what they were forbidden to do.

See Arthur v. Oakes, 63 Fed. Rep., 310, 25 L. R. An., 414;[5.322] St. Louis Min., etc., Co. v. Co. c. Montana Min. Co., 58 Fed. Rep., 129;[5.323] Sweet v. Mangham, 4 Jur., 479; 9 L. J. Ch., 323, 34 Eng. Ch., 51; Cother v. Midland R. Co., 22 Eng. Ch., 469.

It should also be in accordance with the terms of the prayer of the bill. (State v. Rush County [sic], 35 Kan., 150;[5.324] McEldowney v. Lowther, 49 W. Va., 348.[5.325]) It should not impose a greater restraint than is asked or is necessary[.] (Shubert v. Angeles, 80 N. Y. App. Div., 625;[5.326] New York Fire Dept. v. Baudet [sic], 4 N. Y. Supp., 206[5.327]), and should be specific and certain. (Orris [sic] v. National Commercial Bank, 81 N. Y. App. Div., 631;[5.328] St. Rege's [sic] Paper Co. v. Santa Clara Lumber Co., 55 N. Y. App. Div., 225;[5.329] Norris v. Cable [sic], 8 Rich[.] (S. C.), 58;[5.330] Parker v. First Ave. Hotel Co., 24 Ch. Div., 282; Hackett v. Baiss, L. R., 20 Eq., 494; Dover Harbour v. London, etc., R. Co., 3 De. G. F. & J., 559; Low v. Innes, 4 De[.] G. J. & S., 286.)

So it appears that section 266b really does not change the best practice with respect to orders, but imposes the duty upon the courts, in mandatory form, to conform to correct rules, as already established by judicial precedent.

That such provision is necessary and timely will appear upon an inspection of some orders which have issued.

For instance, take the case of Kansas & Texas Coal Co. v. Denney, decided in the

---

[5.321] 105 U.S. 433, 26 L. Ed. 1060 (1882).

[5.322] 63 F. 310 (7th Cir. 1894).

[5.323] St. Louis Mining & Milling Co. v. Montana Mining Co., 58 F. 129 (C.C.D. Mont. 1893).

[5.324] The correct citation is State ex rel. Bradford v. Board of Comm'rs, 35 Kan. 150, 10 P. 535 (1886).

[5.325] 49 W. Va. 348, 38 S.E. 644 (1901).

[5.326] 80 App. Div. 625, 80 N.Y.S. 146 (Sup. Ct. 1903).

[5.327] The correct citation is Fire Dep't v. Beaudet, 4 N.Y.S. 206 (Sup. Ct. 1888).

[5.328] The correct citation is Orvis v. National Commercial Bank, 81 App. Div. 631, 80 N.Y.S. 1029 (1903).

[5.329] The correct citation is St. Regis Paper Co. v. Santa Clara Lumber Co., 55 App. Div. 225, 67 N.Y.S. 149 (Sup. Ct. 1900).

[5.330] The correct citation is Norris v. Cobb, 8 Richardson 58 (S.C. Sup. Ct. 1854).

district court for Arkansas in 1899. And here, as in most of such cases, no full official report of the case can be obtained, but a mere memorandum. In this case the defendants (strikers) were ordered to be and were enjoined from "congregating at or near or on the premises of the property of the Kansas & Texas Coal Co. in, about, or near the town of Huntington, Ark., or elsewhere, for the purpose of intimidating its employees or preventing said employees from rendering service to the Kansas & Texas Coal Co. from inducing or coercing by threats, intimidation, force, or violence any of said employees to leave the employment of the said Kansas & Texas Coal Co., or from in any manner interfering with or molesting any person or persons who may be employed or seek employment by and of the Kansas & Texas Coal Co. in the operation of its coal mines at or near said town of Huntington, or elsewhere."

It will be observed that a defendant in that suit would render himself liable to punishment for contempt if he met a man seeking employment by the company in a foreign country and persuaded him not to enter its service.

The bill further provides that it shall be "binding only upon parties to the suit, their agents, servants, employees, and attorneys, or those in active concert with them, and who shall by personal service or otherwise have received actual notice of the same." Unquestionably this is the true rule, but unfortunately the courts have not uniformly observed it. Much of the criticism which arose from the Debs case (64 Fed. Rep., 724)[5.331] was due to the fact that the court undertook to make the order effective not only upon the parties to the suit and those in concert with them, but upon all other persons whomsoever. In Scott v. Donald (165 U. S., 117),[5.332] the court rebuked a violation by the lower court in the following language:

> The decree is also objectionable because it enjoins persons not parties to the suit. This is not a case where the defendants named represent those not named. Nor is there alleged any conspiracy between the parties defendant and other unknown parties. The acts complained of are tortious and do not grow out of any common action or agreement between constables and sheriffs of the State of South Carolina. We have indeed a right to presume that such officers, though not named in this suit, will, when advised that certain provisions of the act in question have been pronounced unconstitutional by the court to which the Constitution of the United States refers such questions, voluntarily refrain from enforcing such provisions; but we do not think it comports with well-settled principles of equity procedure to include them in an injunction in a suit in which they were not heard or represented or to subject them to penalties for contempt in disregarding such an injunction. (Fellows v. Fellows, 4 John. Chan., 25, citing Iveson v. Harris, 7 Ves., 257.)
>
> The decree of the court below should therefore be amended by being restricted to the parties named as plaintiff and defendants in the bill, and this is directed to be done, and it is otherwise.[5.333]

IV.

Section 266c is concerned with cases between "employer and employees, or between employers and employees, or between employees, or between persons employed and persons seeking employment, involving or growing out of a dispute concerning terms or conditions of employment."

The first clause of the new section 266c relates to the contents and form of the complaint. It must disclose a threatened irreparable injury to property or to a property right of the party making the application for which there is no adequate remedy at law. And the property or property right must be described "with particularity."

These requirements are merely those of good pleading and correct practice in such cases established by a long line of precedents, well understood by the profession and which should be but perhaps have not been uniformly applied. To show this it is only necessary to briefly state the applicable rules, citing some of the numerous authorities.

As the granting of an injunction rests in some degree in the discretion of the chancellor, allegations in the complaint should show candor and frankness. (Moffatt [sic]

[5.331] United States v. Debs, 64 F. 724 (C.C.N.D. Ill. 1894).

[5.332] 165 U.S. 107, 17 S. Ct. 262, 41 L. Ed. 648 (1897).

[5.333] 165 U.S. at 117.

v. Calvert County Comm'rs, 97 Md., 266;[5.334] Johnston v. Glenn, 40 Md., 200;[5.335] Edison Storage Battery Co. v. Edison Automobile Co., 67 N. J. Eq., 44;[5.336] Sharp v. Ashton, 3 Ves. & B., 144.)

The omission of material facts which, in the nature of the case, must be known to the plaintiff will preclude the granting of the relief. (Sprigg v. Western Tel. Co., 46 Md., 67;[5.337] Walker v. Burks, 48 Tex., 206.[5.338])

An injunction may be refused if the allegations are argumentative and inferential. (Battle v. Stevens [sic], 32 Ga., 25;[5.339] Warsop v. Hastings, 22 Minn., 437.[5.340])

The allegations of the complaint must be definite and certain. (St. Louis v. Knapp Co., 104 U. S., 658.[5.341])

⊥ The complaint must set forth the facts with particularity and minuteness (Minor v. Terry, Code Rep. N. S. (N. S.), 384), and no material fact should be left to inference. (Warsop v. Hastings, 22 Minn., 437; Philphower [sic] v. Todd, 11 N. J. Eq., 54;[5.342] Perkins v. Collins, 3 N. J. Eq., 482.[5.343])

Facts, and not the conclusions or opinions of the pleader, must be stated. (McBride v. Ross (D. C.), 13 App. Cas., 576.[5.344])

An injunction should not ordinarily be granted when the material allegations are made upon information and belief. (Brooks v. O'Hara, 8 Fed. Rep., 529;[5.345] In re Holmes, 3 Fed. Rep. Cases No. 1, 562.[5.346])

The complaint must clearly show the threats or acts of defendant which cause him to apprehend future injury. (Mendelson v. McCabe, 144 Cal., 230;[5.347] Ryan v. Fulghurn [sic], 96 Ga., 234.[5.348]) And it is not sufficient to allege that the defendant claims the right to do an act which plaintiff believes illegal and injurious to him, since the intention to exercise the right must be alleged. (Lutman v. Lake Shore, etc., R. Co., 56 Ohio St., 433;[5.349] Attorney General v. Eau Claire, 37 Wis., 400.[5.350])

The bill must allege facts which clearly show that the plaintiff will sustain substantial injury because of the acts complained of. (Home Electric Light, etc., Co. v. Gobe [sic] Tissue Paper Co., 146 Ind., 673;[5.351] Boston, etc., Ry. Co. v. Sullivan, 177 Mass., 230;[5.352] McGovern v. Loder (N. J. Ch., 1890), 20 Atl. Rep., 209;[5.353] Smith v. Lockwood, 13 Barb., 209;[5.354] Jones v. Stewart (Tenn. Ch. App., 1900), 61 Sev., 105;[5.355] Spokane St. R. Co. v. Spokane, 5 Wash., 634;[5.356]) State v. Eau Claire, 40

[5.334] The correct citation is Moffat v. County Comm'rs, 97 Md. 266, 54 A. 960 (1903).

[5.335] Decided in 1874.

[5.336] 67 N.J. Eq. 44, 56 A. 861 (Ch. 1904).

[5.337] Decided in 1877.

[5.338] Decided in 1877.

[5.339] The correct citation is Battle v. Stephens, 32 Ga. 25 (1861).

[5.340] Warsop v. City of Hastings, 22 Minn. 437 (1876).

[5.341] City of St. Louis v. Knapp, Stout & Co., 104 U.S. 658, 26 L. Ed. 883 (1882).

[5.342] The correct citation is Philhower v. Todd, 11 N.J. Eq. 54 (Ch. 1855).

[5.343] 3 N.J. Eq. 482 (Ch. 1836).

[5.344] 13 App. D.C. 576 (Ct. App. 1898).

[5.345] Brooks v. Hardy & O'Hara Bros., 8 F. 529 (C.C.D. Iowa 1881).

[5.346] The reference is probably to In re Bloss, 3 F. Cas. 733 (No. 1562) (C.C.D. Mich. 1870).

[5.347] 144 Cal. 230, 77 P. 915 (1904).

[5.348] The correct citation is Ryan v. Fulghum, 96 Ga. 234, 22 S.E. 940 (1895).

[5.349] Lutman v. Lake Shore & M.S. Ry., 56 Ohio St. 433, 47 N.E. 248 (1897).

[5.350] Attorney Gen. v. City of Eau Claire, 37 Wis. 400 (1875).

[5.351] The correct citation is Home Elec. Light & Power Co. v. Globe Tissue-Paper Co., 146 Ind. 673, 45 N.E. 1108 (1897).

[5.352] Boston & M.R.R. v. Sullivan, 177 Mass. 230, 58 N.E. 689 (1900).

[5.353] 20 A. 209 (N.J. Ch. 1890), rev'd, 48 N.J. Eq. 275, 22 A. 199 (Ct. Err. & App. 1891).

[5.354] 13 Barb. 209 (N.Y. Sup. Ct. 1852).

[5.355] 61 S.W. 105 (Tenn. Ch. App. 1900).

[5.356] 5 Wash. 634, 32 P. 456 (1893).

Wis., 533.[5.357] And it is not sufficient to merely allege injury without stating the facts. Giffing [sic] v. Gibb, 2 Black, 519;[5.358] Spooner v. McConnell, 22 Fed. Cases No. 13245;[5.359] Bowling [sic] v. Crook, 104 Ala., 130;[5.360] Grant v. Cooke, 7 D. C., 165;[5.361] Coast Line R. Co. v. Caben [sic], 50 Ga., 451;[5.362] Dinwiddie v. Roberts, 1 Greene 363;[5.363] Wabaska Electric Co. v. Wymore Co. [sic], Nebr., 199;[5.364] Lubrs [sic] v. Sturtevant, 10 Or., 170;[5.365] Farland v. Wood, 35 W. Va., 458.[5.366])

Since the jurisdiction in equity depends on the lack of an adequate remedy at law, a bill for an injunction must state facts from which the court can determine that the remedy at law is inadequate. (Pollock v. Farmers' Loan & Tr. Co., 157 U. S., 429;[5.367] Safe-Deposit[,] etc., Co. v. Anniston, 96 Fed. Rep., 661.[5.368])

If the inadequacy of the legal remedy depends upon the defendant's insolvency the fact of insolvency must be positively alleged. (Fullington v. Kyle Lumber Co., 139 Ala., 242;[5.369] Graham v. Tankersley, 15 Ala., 634.[5.370])

An injunction will not be granted unless the complaint shows that a refusal to grant the writ will work irreparable injury. (California Nav. Co. v. Union Transp. Co., 122 Cal., 641;[5.371] Cook County Brick Co., 92 Ill. App., 526;[5.372] Manufacturers' Gas. Co. v. Indiana Nat. Gas, etc., Co., 156 Ind., 679.[5.373]) And it is not sufficient simply to allege that the injury will be irreparable, but the facts must be stated so that the court may see that the apprehension of irreparable injury is well founded. (California Nav. Co. v. Union Transp. Co., 122 Cal., 641; Empire Transp. Co. v. Johnson, 76 Conn., 79;[5.374] Orange City v. Thayer, 45 Fla., 502.[5.375])

The plaintiff must allege that he has done or is willing to do everything which is necessary to entitle him to the relief sought. (Stanley v. Gadsley [sic], 10 Pet. (U. S.), 521;[5.376] Elliott v. Sihley, 101 Ala., ⊥ 344;[5.377] Burham [sic] v. San Francisco Fuse Mfg. Co., 76 Cal., 26;[5.378] Sloan v. Coolbaugh, 10 Iowa, 31;[5.379] Lewis v. Wilson, 17 N. Y. Supp., 128;[5.380] Spann v. Sterns [sic], 18 Tex., 556.[5.381])

The second paragraph of section 266c is concerned with specific acts which the best opinion of the courts holds to be within the right of parties involved upon one side or the other of a trades dispute. The necessity for legislation concerning them

---

[5.357] 40 Wis. 533 (1876).

[5.358] The correct citation is Griffing v. Gibb, 67 U.S. (2 Black) 519, 17 L. Ed. 353 (1863).

[5.359] 22 F. Cas. 939 (No. 13,245) (C.C.D. Ohio 1838).

[5.360] The correct citation is Bolling v. Crook, 104 Ala. 130, 16 So. 131 (1894).

[5.361] 7 D.C. 165 (Sup. Ct. 1871).

[5.362] The correct citation is Coast Line R.R. v. Cohen, 50 Ga. 451 (1873).

[5.363] 1 Greene 363 (Iowa 1848).

[5.364] The correct citation is Wabaska Elec. Co. v. City of Wymore, 60 Neb. 199, 82 N.W. 626 (1900).

[5.365] The correct citation is Luhrs v. Sturtevant, 10 Ore. 170 (1882).

[5.366] 35 W. Va. 458, 14 S.E. 140 (1891).

[5.367] 157 U.S. 429, 15 S. Ct. 673, 39 L. Ed. 759 (1895).

[5.368] Safe-Deposit & Trust Co. v. City of Anniston, 96 F. 661 (C.C.N.D. Ala. 1899).

[5.369] 139 Ala. 242, 35 So. 852 (1904).

[5.370] Decided in 1849.

[5.371] 122 Cal. 641, 55 P. 591 (1898).

[5.372] Cook County Brick Co. v. Labahn Brick Co., 92 Ill. App. 526 (1900).

[5.373] Manufacturers' Gas & Oil Co. v. Indiana Natural Gas & Oil Co., 156 Ind. 679, 59 N.E. 169, *rehearing denied*, 156 Ind. 681, 60 N.E. 169 (1901).

[5.374] 76 Conn. 79, 55 A. 587 (1903).

[5.375] Town of Orange City v. Thayer, 45 Fla. 502, 34 So. 573 (1903).

[5.376] The correct citation is Stanley v. Gadsby, 35 U.S. (10 Pet.) 521, 9 L. Ed. 518 (1836).

[5.377] 101 Ala. 344, 13 So. 500 (1893).

[5.378] The correct citation is Burnham v. San Francisco Fuse Mfg. Co., 76 Cal. 26, 17 P. 939 (1888).

[5.379] Decided in 1859.

[5.380] 17 N.Y.S. 128 (Sup. Ct. 1901).

[5.381] The correct citation is Spann v. Stearns' Adm'rs, 18 Tex. 556 (1857).

arises out of the divergent views which the courts have expressed on the subject and the difference between courts in the application of recognized rules. It may be proper to notice, in passing, that the State courts furnish precedents frequently for action by the Federal courts, and vice versa, so that a pernicious rule or an error in one jurisdiction is quickly adopted by the other. It is not contended that either the Federal or the State courts have stood alone in any of the precedents which are disapproved. The provisions of this section of the bill are self-explanatory, and in justification of the language used we content ourselves with submitting quotations from recognized authorities. We classify these authorities by quoting first the clauses of the bill to which they have particular reference.

The first clause:

And no such restraining order or injunction shall prohibit any person or persons from terminating any relation of employment, or from ceasing to perform any work or labor, or from recommending, advising, or persuading others by peaceful means so to do.

In Allis Chalmers Co. v. Iron Molders' Union (C. C., 150 Fed. R., 155), Judge Sanborn said:

The conclusion to be drawn from the cases, as applicable to this controversy, is, I think, that the combination of the defendant unions, their members, and the defendant O'Leary, to strike, and to further enforce the strike, and if possible to bring the employers to terms by preventing them from obtaining other workmen to replace the strikers, was not unlawful, because grounded on just cause or excuse, being the economic advancement of the union molders, and the competition of labor against capital.[5.382]

In Arthur v. Oakes (63 Fed. R., 310, 317) Justice Harlan, for the court, said:

If an employee quits without cause, and in violation of an express contract to serve for a stated time, then his quitting would not be of right, and he would be liable for any damages resulting from a breach of his agreement, and perhaps, in some states of case, to criminal prosecution for loss of life or limb by passengers or others, directly resulting from his abandoning his post at a time when care and watchfulness were required upon his part in the discharge of a duty he had undertaken to perform. And it may be assumed for the purposes of this discussion that he would be liable in like manner where the contract of service, by necessary implication arising out of the nature or the circumstances of the employment, required him not to quit the service of his employer suddenly, and without reasonable notice of his intention to do so. But the vital question remains whether a court of equity will, under any circumstances, by injunction, prevent one individual from quitting the personal service of another? An affirmative answer to this question is not, we think, justified by any authority to which our attention has been called or of which we are aware. It would be an invasion of one's natural liberty to compel him to work for or to remain in the personal service of another. One who is placed under such constraint is in a condition of involuntary servitude—a condition which the supreme law of the land declares shall not exist within the United States, or in any place subject to their jurisdiction. Courts of equity have sometimes sought to sustain a contract for services requiring special knowledge or skill by enjoining acts or conduct that would constitute a breach of such contract.

The rule, we think, is without exception that equity will not compel the actual, affirmative performance by an employee of merely personal services, any more than it will compel an employer to retain in his personal service one who, no matter for what cause, is not acceptable to him for service of that character. The right of an employee engaged to perform personal service to quit that service rests upon the same basis as the right of his employer to discharge him from further personal service. If the quitting in the one case or the discharging in the other is in violation of the contract between the parties, the one injured by the breach has his action for damages; and a court of equity will not, indirectly or negatively, by means of an injunction restraining the violation of the contract, compel the affirmative performance from day to day or the affirmative acceptance of merely personal services. Relief of that character has always been regarded as impracticable.[5.383]

Sitting with Justice Harlan at circuit in that case were other learned jurists, but there was no dissent from these views.

[5.382] 150 F. 155, 179 (C.C.E.D. Wis. 1906).

[5.383] 63 F. 310, 317-18 (7th Cir. 1894).

In this connection we cite from the luminous opinion by Judge Loring delivering the opinion in Pickett *v.* Walsh (192 Mass., 572),[5.384] a clear exposition of our views here expressed. We regret the necessity of limiting the quotation, because the whole opinion could be studied with profit.

The case is one of competition between the defendant unions and the individual plaintiffs for the work of pointing. The work of pointing for which these two sets of workmen are competing is work which the contractors are obliged to have. One peculiarity of the case, therefore, is that the fight here is necessarily a triangular one. It necessarily involves the two sets of competing workmen and the contractor, and is not confined to the two parties to the contract, as is the case where workmen strike to get better wages from their employer or other conditions which are better for them. In this respect the case is like Mogul Steamship Co. *v.* McGregor (23 Q. B. D., 598; S. C., on appeal (1892); A. C., 25).

The right which the defendant unions claim to exercise in carrying their point in the course of this competition is a trade advantage, namely, that they have labor which the contractors want, or, if you please, can not get elsewhere; and they insist upon using this trade advantage to get additional work, namely, the work of pointing the bricks and stone which they lay. It is somewhat like the advantage which the owner of back land has when he has bought the front lot. He is not bound to sell them separately. To be sure, the right of an individual owner to sell both or none is not decisive of the right of a labor union to combine to refuse to lay bricks or stone unless they are given the job of pointing the bricks laid by them. There are things which an individual can do which a combination of individuals can not do. But having regard to the right on which the defendants' organization as a labor union rests, the correlative duty owed by it to others, and the limitation of the defendants' rights coming from the increased power of organization, we are of opinion that it was within the rights of these unions to compete for the work of doing the pointing and, in the exercise of their right of competition, to refuse to lay bricks and set stone unless they were given the work of pointing them when laid. (See in this connection Plant *v.* Woods, 176 Mass., 492, 502; Berry *v.* Donovan, 188 Mass., 353, 357.)

The result to which that conclusion brings us in the case at bar ought not to be passed without consideration.

The result is harsh on the contractors, who prefer to give the work to the pointers, because (1) the pointers do it by contract (in which case the contractors escape the liability incident to the relation of employer and employee); because (2) the contractors think that the pointers do the work better, and if not well done the buildings may be permanently injured by acid; and, finally, (3) because they get from the pointers better work with less liability at a smaller cost. Again, so far as the pointers (who can not lay brick or stone) are concerned, the result is disastrous. But all that the labor unions have done is to say you must employ us for all the work or none of it. They have not said that if you employ the pointers you must pay us a fine, as they did in Carew *v.* Rutherford (106 Mass., 1). They have not undertaken to forbid the contractors employing pointers, as they did in Plant *v.* Woods (176 Mass., 492). So far as the labor unions are concerned, the contractors can employ pointers if they choose, but if the contractors choose to give the work of pointing the ⊥ bricks and stones to others the unions take the stand that the contractors will have to get some one else to lay them. The effect of this in the case at bar appears to be that the contractors are forced against their will to give the work of pointing to the masons and bricklayers. But the fact that the contractors are forced to do what they do not want to do is not decisive of the legality of the labor union's acts. That is true wherever a strike is successful. The contractors doubtless would have liked it better if there had been no competition between the bricklayers' and masons' unions on the one hand and the individual pointers on the other hand. But there is competition. There being competition, they prefer the course they have taken. They prefer to give all the work to the unions rather than get nonunion men to lay bricks and stone to be pointed by the plaintiffs.

Further, the effect of complying with the labor unions' demands apparently will be the destruction of the plaintiff's business. But the fact that the business of a plaintiff is destroyed by the acts of the defendants done in pursuance of their right of competition is not decisive of the illegality of the acts. It was well said by Hammond, J., in Martell *v.* White (185 Mass., 255, 260) in regard to the right of a citizen to pursue his business without interference by a combination to destroy it: "Speaking generally, however, competition in business is permitted, although frequently disastrous to those engaged in it. It is always selfish, often sharp, and sometimes deadly."[5.385]

[5.384] 192 Mass. 572, 78 N.E. 753 (1906).

[5.385] 192 Mass. at 583–85.

* * * * * * *

The application of the right of the defendant unions, who are composed of bricklayers and stonemasons, to compete with the individual plaintiffs, who can do nothing but pointing (as we have said) is in the case at bar disastrous to the pointers and hard on the contractors. But this is not the first case where the exercise of the right of competition ends in such a result. The case at bar is an instance where the evils which are or may be incident to competition bear very harshly on those interested, but in spite of such evils competition is necessary to the welfare of the community.[5.386]

To the same effect is Allis-Chalmers Co. v. Iron Molders' Union (C. C.) (150 Fed. Rep., 155), per Sanborn, J.

The consensus of judicial view, as expressed in these cases and others which might be cited, is that workingmen may lawfully combine to further their material interests without limit or constraint, and may for that purpose adopt any means or methods which are lawful. It is the enjoyment and exercise of that right and none other that this bill forbids the courts to interfere with.

The second clause:

Or from attending at or near a house or place where any person resides or works or carries on business, or happens to be for the purpose of peacefully obtaining or communicating information, or of peacefully persuading any person to work or to abstain from working.

This language is taken from the British trades dispute act of 1906, the second section of which is as follows:

It shall be lawful for one or more persons acting on their own behalf or on behalf of an individual, corporation, or firm in contemplation or furtherance of a trade dispute to attend at or near a house or place where a person resides or works or carries on business or happens to be if they so attend merely for the purpose of peacefully obtaining or communicating information or of peacefully persuading any person to work or abstain from work.

This, it has been said, "might well be termed a codification of the law relating to peaceful picketing as laid down by a majority of the American courts." (Martin's Law of Labor Unions, sec. 173.) Upon the general subject the same author says:

There are some decisions which hold that all picketing is unlawful, and it has been said that from the very nature of things peaceful picketing is of rare occurrence and "very much of an illusion," yet the view taken by the majority of decisions and which is best supported by reason is that picketing, if not conducted in such numbers as will of itself amount to intimidation, and when confined to the seeking of information such as the number and names and places of residence of those at work or seeking work on the premises against which the strike is in operation, and to the use of peaceful argument and entreaty for the purpose of procuring such workmen to support the strike by quitting work or by not accepting work, is not unlawful, and will furnish no ground for injunction or an action at law for damages. * * * That the views set forth in this section are correct does not admit of doubt. Indeed, it may readily be seen that the right almost universally conceded to striking workmen to use peaceable argument and persuasion to induce other workmen to aid them in their strike might, and very probably would be, most seriously hampered if the right of picketing were denied. "The right to persuade new men to quit or decline employment is of little worth unless the strikers may ascertain who are the men that their late employer has persuaded or is attempting to persuade to accept employment." While it is true that in the guise of picketing strikers may obstruct and annoy the new men, and by insult and menacing attitude intimidate them as effectually as by physical assault, yet it can always be determined from the evidence whether the efforts of the pickets are limited to getting into communication with the new men for the purpose of presenting arguments and appeals to their free judgment. (Martin's Modern Law of Labor Unions, sec. 169, pp. 233, 234, and 235.)

The third clause:

Or from ceasing to patronize or to employ any party to such dispute; or from recommending, advising, or persuading others by peaceful means so to do.

The best opinion to be gathered from the conflicting opinions on this matter have been well summarized in the most recent textbook on the subject as follows:

[5.386] *Id.* at 585–86.

It is lawful for members of a union, acting by agreement among themselves, to cease to patronize a person against whom the concert of action is directed when they regard it for their interest to do so. This is the so-called "primary boycott," and in furtherance thereof it is lawful to circulate notices among the members of the union to cease patronizing one with whom they have a trade dispute and to announce their intention to carry their agreement into effect. For instance, if an employer of labor refuses to employ union men the union has a right to say that its members will not patronize him. A combination between persons merely to regulate their own conduct and affairs is allowable, and a lawful combination though others may be indirectly affected thereby. And the fact that the execution of the agreement may tend to diminish the profits of the party against whom such act is aimed does not render the participants liable to a prosecution for a criminal conspiracy or to a suit for injunction. Even though he sustain financial loss, he will be without remedy, either in a court of law or a court of equity. So long as the primary object of the combination is to advance its own interests and not to inflict harm on the person against whom it is directed, it is not possible to see how any claim of illegality could be sustained. (Martin's Modern Law of Labor Unions, pp. 107, 108, and 109.)

It is not unlawful for members of a union or their sympathizers to use, in aid of a justifiable strike, peaceable argument and persuasion to induce customers of the person against whom the strike is in operation to withhold their patronage from him, although their purpose in so doing is to injure the business of their former employer and constrain him to yield to their demands, and the same rule applies where the employer has locked out his employees. These acts may be consummated by direct communication or through the medium of the press, and it is only when the combination becomes a conspiracy to injure, by threats and coercion, the property rights of another that the power of the courts can be invoked. The vital distinction between combinations of this character and boycotts is that here no coercion is present, while, as was heretofore shown, coercion is a necessary element of a boycott. In applying the principles stated it has been held that the issuance of circulars by members of a labor union notifying persons engaged in the trade of controversies existing between such members and their employer and requesting such persons not to deal with the employer is not unlawful and will not be enjoined where no intimidation or violence is used. (Martin's Modern Law of Labor Unions, pp. 109 and 110.)

Said Mr. Justice Van Orsdel in his concurring opinion in Court of Appeals of the District of Columbia (the American Federation of ⊥ Labor et al., appellants, v. the Buck's Stove & Range Co.,[5.387] No. 1910, Decided Mar. 11, 1909):

* * * * * * *

Applying the same principle, I conceive it to be the privilege of one man, or a number of men, to individually conclude not to patronize a certain person or corporation. It is also the right of these men to agree together, and to advise others, not to extend such patronage. That advice may be given by direct communication or through the medium of the press, so long as it is neither in the nature of coercion or a threat.

As long as the actions of this combination of individuals are lawful, to this point it is not clear how they can become unlawful because of their subsequent acts directed against the same person or corporation. To this point there is no conspiracy—no boycott. The word "boycott" is here used as referring to what is usually understood as "the secondary boycott," and when used in this opinion it is intended to be applied exclusively in that sense. It is, therefore, only when the combination becomes a conspiracy to injure by threats and coercion the property rights of another that the power of the courts can be invoked. This point must be passed before the unlawful and unwarranted acts which the courts will punish and restrain are committed.

The definition of a boycott given by Judge Taft in Toledo Co. v. Penna. Co. (54 Fed., 730) is as follows: "As usually understood, a boycott is a combination of many to cause a loss to one person by coercing others against their will to withdraw from him their beneficial business intercourse through threats that, unless those others do so, the many will cause similar loss to them." In Gray v. Building Trades Council (91 Minn., 171) the word "boycott" is defined as follows: "A boycott may be defined to be a combination of several persons to cause a loss to a third person by causing others against their will to withdraw from him their beneficial business intercourse through threats that unless a compliance with their demands be made the persons forming the combination will cause loss or injury to him, or an organization formed to exclude a person from business relations with others by persuasion, intimidation, and other acts which tend to violence, and thereby cause him through fear of resulting injury to submit to dictation in the management of his affairs. Such acts constitute a conspiracy and may be restrained by injunction." In Brace Brothers v. Evans (3 R. & Corp. L. J., 561) it is said: "The word itself implies a threat. In popular acceptation it is an organized effort to exclude a person from

---

[5.387] 33 App. D.C. 83 (D.C. Cir. 1909).

business relations with others by persuasion, intimidation, and other acts which tend to violence, and they coerce him, through fear of resulting injury, to submit to dictation in the management of his affairs."

It will be observed that the above definitions are in direct conflict with the earlier English decisions and indicate a distinct departure by our courts. This undoubtedly is in recognition of the right of a number of individuals to combine for the purpose of improving their condition. The rule of the English common law, from which we have so far departed, is expressed in Bowen v. Hall (6 Q. B. Div., 333) as follows: "If the persuasion be used for the indirect purpose or [sic] injuring the plaintiff, or of benefiting the defendant at the expense of the plaintiff, it is a malicious act, which is in law and in fact a wrong act, and therefore a wrongful act, and therefore an actionable act if injury ensues from it."

From this clear distinction it will be observed that there is no boycott until the members of the organization have passed the point of refusing to patronize the person or corporation themselves and have entered the field where, by coercion or threats, they prevent others from dealing with such persons or corporation. I fully agree with this distinction.

So long, then, as the American Federation of Labor and those acting under its advice refused to patronize complainant, the combination had not arisen to the dignity of an unlawful conspiracy or a boycott.[5.388]

In Hopkins v. Oxley Stave Co. (83 Fed. R., 912), Judge Caldwell, in a dissenting opinion, said:

While laborers, by the application to them of the doctrine we are considering, are reduced to individual action, it is not so with the forces arrayed against them. A corporation is an association of individuals for combined action; trusts are corporations combined together for the very purpose of collective action and boycotting; and capital, which is the product of labor, is in itself a powerful collective force. Indeed, according to this supposed rule, every ⊥ corporation and trust in the country is an unlawful combination, for while its business may be of a kind that its individual members, each acting for himself, might lawfully conduct, the moment they enter into a combination to do that same thing by their combined effort, the combination becomes an unlawful conspiracy. But the rule is never so applied.

Corporations and trusts and other combinations of individuals and aggregations of capital extend themselves right and left through the entire community, boycotting and inflicting irreparable damage upon and crushing out all small dealers and producers, stifling competition, establishing monopolies, reducing the wages of the laborer, raising the price of food on every man's table, and of the clothes on his back and of the house that shelters him, and inflicting on the wage earners the pains and penalties of the lockout and the black list, and denying to them the right of association and combined action by refusing employment to those who are members of labor organizations; and all these things are justified as a legitimate result of the evolution of industries resulting from new social and economic conditions, and of the right of every man to carry on his business as he sees fit, and of lawful competition. On the other hand, when laborers combine to maintain or raise their wages or otherwise to better their condition or to protect themselves from oppression or to attempt to overcome competition with their labor or the products of their labor in order that they may continue to have employment and live, their action, however open, peaceful, and orderly, is branded as a "conspiracy." What is "competition" when done by capital is "conspiracy" when done by laborers. No amount of verbal dexterity can conceal or justify this glaring discrimination. If the vast aggregation and collective action of capital is not accompanied by a corresponding organization and collective action of labor, capital will speedily become proprietor of the wage earners as well as the recipient of the profits of their labor. This result can only be averted by some sort of organization that will secure the collective action of wage earners. This is demanded, not in the interest of wage earners alone, but by the highest considerations of public policy.[5.389]

In Vegelahn v. Gunter [sic] (167 Mass., 92)[5.390] Justice Holmes, now of the Supreme Court of the United States, delivering the opinion, said:

It is plain from the slightest consideration of practical affairs, or the most superficial reading of industrial history, that free competition means combination, and that the organization of the world, now going on so fast, means an ever-increasing might and scope of combination. It seems to me futile to set our faces against this tendency. Whether beneficial on the whole, as I

[5.388] *Id.* at 116–17 (concurring opinion).

[5.389] 83 F. 912, 932–33 (8th Cir. 1897).

[5.390] The correct citation is Vegelahn v. Guntner, 167 Mass. 92, 44 N.E. 1077 (1896).

think it is, or detrimental, it is inevitable, unless the fundamental axioms of society and even the fundamental conditions of life are to be changed. One of the eternal conflicts out of which life is made up is that between the effort of every man to get the most he can for his services and that of society, disguised under the name of capital, to get his services for the least possible return. Combination on the one side is potent and powerful. Combination on the other is a fair and equal way. * * * If it be true that the workingmen may combine with a view, among other things, to getting as much as they can for their labor, just as capital may combine with a view to getting the greatest possible return, it must be true that when combined they have the same liberty that combined capital has, to support their interest by argument, persuasion, and the bestowal or refusal of those advantages which they otherwise lawfully control.[5.391]

The logic of Justice Sherwood, of the Supreme Court of Missouri, in Marx & Haas Co. v. Watson (56 L. R. A., 951),[5.392] appears unanswerable. He discussed the question from a constitutional standpoint, taking for his text the Missouri bill of rights, substantially the same as the first amendment to the Federal Constitution, saying (p. 956):

> The evident idea of that section is penalty or punishment, and not prevention, because if prevention exists, then no opportunity can possibly arise for one becoming responsible by saying, writing, or publishing "whatever he will on any subject." The two ideas—the one absolute freedom "to say, write, or publish whatever he will on any subject," coupled with responsibility therefor, and the other idea of preventing any such free speech, free writing, or free publication—can not coexist.[5.393]

The opinion continues, after citing authorities, Federal and State, as follows:

> Section 14, supra, makes no distinction and authorizes no difference to be made by courts or legislatures between a proceeding set on foot to enjoin the publication of a libel and one to enjoin the publication of any other sort or nature, however injurious it may be, or to prohibit the use of free speech or free writing on any subject whatever, because wherever the authority of injunction begins there the right of free speech, free writing, or free publication ends. No halfway house stands on the highway between absolute prevention and absolute freedom.[5.394]

The fourth clause:

> Or from paying or giving to or withholding from any person engaged in such dispute any strike benefits or other moneys or things of value.

In at least two instances State courts (Reynolds v. Davis, 198 Mass., 294,[5.395] and A. S.. [sic] Barnes & Co. v. Chicago Typographical Union, 232 Ill., 424[5.396]) have held that if the purpose of a strike was unlawful the officers and members of unions should be enjoined from giving financial aid in the form of strike benefits in furtherance thereof. But in the only case of the kind disposed of by a Federal court an entirely different conclusion was reached. In A. S.. [sic] Barnes & Co. v. Berry (157 Fed. R., 883)[5.397] it was held without exception or qualification that an employer against whom a strike was in operation could not have enjoined the officers of a union from giving its striking members strike benefits. The reason assigned was that—

> the strike benefit fund is created by moneys deposited by the men with the general officers for the support of themselves and families in times of strike, and the court has no more control of it than it would have over deposits made by them in the banks.[5.398]

[5.391] 167 Mass. at 108 (Holmes, J., dissenting).

[5.392] Marx & Haas Jeans Clothing Co. v. Watson, 168 Mo. 133, 67 S.W. 391 (1902).

[5.393] 168 Mo. at 144.

[5.394] *Id.* at 149.

[5.395] 198 Mass. 294, 84 N.E. 457 (1908).

[5.396] The correct citation is A.R. Barnes & Co. v. Chicago Typographical Union No. 16, 232 Ill. 424, 83 N.E. 940 (1908).

[5.397] The correct citation is A.R. Barnes & Co. v. Berry, 157 F. 883 (C.C.S.D. Ohio 1908), *aff'd*, 169 F. 225 (6th Cir. 1909).

[5.398] 157 F. at 889.

This decision is in harmony with two recent English decisions—Denabey, etc., Collieries v. Yorkshire Miners' Assn. (75 L. J. K. B., 384); Lyons v. Wilkins (67 L. J., ch. 383).

The fifth and sixth clauses:

Or from peaceably assembling at any place in a lawful manner and for lawful purposes; or from doing any act or thing which might lawfully be done in the absence of such dispute by any party thereto.

After all that can be asserted against the provisions of section 266c, or any provision of the bill elsewhere found has been said, we can truly say that it does not transcend or contravene the clear and conclusive statement of the law as stated in National Fireproofing Co. v. Mason Builders Assn. (169 Fed. Rep., 260 [sic]).[5.399] Delivering the opinion of the court in that case, Judge Noyes said (p. 265):

As a general rule it may be stated, that when the chief objective of a combination is to injure or oppress third persons, it is a conspiracy; but that when such injury or oppression is merely incidental to the carrying out of a lawful purpose, it is not a conspiracy. Stated in another way: A combination, entered into for the real malicious purpose of injuring a third person in his business or property, may amount to a conspiracy and furnish a ground of action for damages sustained or call for an injunction, even though formed for the ostensible purpose of benefiting its members, and actually operating to some extent to their advantage. But a combination without such ulterior oppressive object entered into merely for the purpose of promoting by lawful means the common interests of its members, is not a conspiracy. A laborer, as well as a builder, trader, or manufacturer, has the right to conduct his affairs in any lawful manner, even though he may thereby injure others. So several laborers and builders may combine for mutual advantage, and so long as the motive is not malicious, the object not unlawful nor oppressive, and the means neither deceitful nor fraudulent, the result is not a conspiracy, although it may necessarily work injury to other persons. The damage to such persons may ⊥ be serious—it may even extend to their ruin—but if it is inflicted by a combination in the legitimate pursuit of its own affairs, is a damnum absque injuria. The damage is present, but the unlawful object is absent. And so the essential question must always be, whether the object of a combination is to do harm to others or to exercise the rights of the parties for their own benefit.[5.400]

Any attack upon the policy of this section of the bill must be directed at its specific prohibitions; nor will any mere general criticism, or any attack which does not particularize herein, be worthy of serious attention. The ready and perfect defense to all such is at hand, and imposes no difficult task. Is there any reason why the complainant, seeking an injunction against workingmen, should not describe with particularity in his cause of complaint the nature of the threatened injury, and the property or property right involved, as in other cases? Is there any reason why an injunction should issue at all involving or growing out of the relation created between employer and employee to prevent the termination of the relation, or advising and persuading others to do so, or to prevent the unrestricted communication and exchange of information between persons, or the giving of aid by financial contributions in any labor affair or dispute? Is there any reason, after a labor dispute has arisen and a socially hostile attitude has been created, for an injunction to prevent abstinence in patronizing or service by one party for the other's benefit, or the exercise of the right of free speech in advising or inducing such abstinence on the part of others? Is there, in short, any good reason why, after a dispute has arisen and the parties are "at arms length," a court of equity should interpose its strong arm merely because such dispute has arisen?

At its hearings the committee had the benefit of learned and illuminating arguments against the several bills. Counsel in opposition were patiently and respectfully heard, and the committee profited largely by having heard them, as is shown by the results of its labors. The bill does not interfere with the Sherman Antitrust Act at all; it leaves the law of conspiracy untouched, and is not open to effective criticism on any constitutional ground. The subject of the constitutionality of such legislation was exhausted at the hearings on the contempt bill (H. R. 22591),

---

[5.399] The correct citation is 169 F. 259 (2d Cir. 1909).
[5.400] Id. at 265.

returned to the House with a separate report in which all constitutional objections are fully met.

NO QUESTION OF CONSTITUTIONALITY INVOLVED.

This bill does not, any more than does the contempt bill, invade the jurisdiction of the courts or attempt legislatively to exercise a judicial function. It merely limits and circumscribes the remedy and procedure. While we here enter into no elaborate discussion of the authorities on this topic, yet, for convenience of reference, we insert a synopsis. On point of inconsistency between our theory of government and exercise of arbitrary power see Yick Wo v. Hopkins (118 U. S. Rep., 369 [sic]).[5.401] For a case in which Congress was held to have constitutionally exercised power to take away all remedy see Finck v. O'Neill [sic] (106 U. S., 272);[5.402] and for a case where a statute taking away the power to issue an injunction in a certain case wherein the jurisdiction had been previously held and exercised was recognized without question as of binding force see Sharon v. Terry (36 Fed. Rep., 365 [sic]).[5.403] For a general statement of the proposition that ⊥ the inferior courts of the United States are all limited in their nature and constitutions and have not the powers inherent in courts existing by prescription or by the common law see Cary v. Curtiss [sic] (3 How. (U. S.), 236, 254).[5.404] The same principle still more elaborately stated and applied, Ex parte Robinson (19 Wall. (U. S.), 505).[5.405]

Many decisions on the question of injunctive process and jurisdiction in labor cases are greatly influenced by, and, indeed, sometimes founded upon, precedents established when to be a wage earner was to be a servant whose social and legal status was little above that of slavery. But even England has preceded us in new views and policies herein. The English act of 1906, set forth at length in the hearings, goes farther than it has yet been deemed possible to go in this country in relieving labor, and especially organized labor, of legal burdens and discriminations. The Supreme Court has more than once protested against attempts by any branch of the Government to exercise arbitrary power, and the courts should, and probably will, welcome the definite limitations contained in this bill if it should be enacted.

The idea has been advanced, and ably supported in argument, by one of the proponents of this legislation that liberty, and more of it, is safe in the hands of the workingmen of the country. We are convinced of the merit and truth of that contention. The tendency toward freedom and liberation from legal trammels and impediments to progress and to a great social advance is seen in nearly all civilized nations. It is an unpropitious time to oppose a reform like that embodied in this bill, in view of the fact that the abuses of power which it seeks to terminate have been, admittedly, numerous and flagrant.

[H. R.. 23635, Sixty-second Congress, second session.]

IN THE HOUSE OF REPRESENTATIVES, APRIL 22, 1912.

Mr. Clayton introduced the following bill; which was referred to the Committee on the Judiciary and ordered to be printed.

A BILL To amend an act entitled "An act to codify, revise, and amend the laws relating to the judiciary," approved March third, nineteen hundred and eleven.

Be it enacted by the Senate and House of Representatives of the United States of America in Congress assembled, That section 263 of the act entitled "An act to codify, revise, and amend the laws relating to the judiciary," approved March third, nineteen hundred and eleven, be, and the same is hereby, amended so as to read as follows, and that said act be further amended by inserting after section 266 thereof three new sections, to be numbered, respectively, 266a, 266b, 266c, reading as follows:

"SEC. 263. That no injunction, whether interlocutory or permanent, in cases other than those

---

[5.401] The correct citation is 118 U.S. 356, 6 S. Ct. 1064, 30 L. Ed. 220 (1886).

[5.402] The correct citation is Fink v. O'Neil, 106 U.S. 272, 1 S. Ct. 325, 27 L. Ed. 196 (1882).

[5.403] The correct citation is 36 F. 337 (C.C.N.D. Cal. 1888).

[5.404] The correct citation is Cary v. Curtis, 44 U.S. (3 How.) 236, 11 L. Ed. 576 (1845).

[5.405] 86 U.S. (19 Wall.) 505, 22 L. Ed. 205 (1873).

described in section 266 of this title, shall be issued without previous notice and an opportunity to be heard on behalf of the parties to be enjoined, which notice, together with a copy of the bill of complaint or other pleading upon which the application for such injunction will be based, shall be served upon the parties sought to be enjoined a reasonable time in advance of such application. But if it shall appear to the satisfaction of the court or judge that immediate and irreparable injury is likely to ensue to the complainant, and that the giving of notice of the application or the delay incident thereto would probably permit the doing of the act sought to be restrained before notice could be served or hearing had thereon, the court or judge may, in his discretion, issue a temporary restraining order without notice. Every such order ⊥ shall be indorsed with the date and hour of issuance, shall be forthwith entered of record, shall define the injury and state why it is irreparable and why the order was granted without notice, and shall by its terms expire within such time after entry, not to exceed seven days, as the court or judge may fix, unless within the time so fixed the order is extended or renewed for a like period, after notice to those previously served, if any, and for good cause shown, and the reasons for such extension shall be entered of record.

"SEC. 266a. That no restraining order or interlocutory order of injunction shall issue except upon the giving of security by the applicant in such sum as the court or judge may deem proper, conditioned upon the payment of such costs and damages as may be incurred or suffered by any party who may be found to have been wrongfully enjoined or restrained thereby.

"SEC. 266b. That every order of injunction or restraining order shall set forth the reasons for the issuance of the same, shall be specific in terms, and shall describe in reasonable detail, and not by reference to the bill of complaint or other document, the act or acts sought to be restrained; and shall be binding only upon the parties to the suit, their agents, servants, employees, and attorneys, or those in active concert with them, and who shall by personal service or otherwise have received actual notice of the same.

"SEC. 266c. That no restraining order or injunction shall be granted by any court of the United States, or a judge or the judges thereof, in any case between an employer and employees, or between employers and employees, or between employees, or between persons employed and persons seeking employment, involving or growing out of a dispute concerning terms or conditions of employment, unless necessary to prevent irreparable injury to property or to a property right of the party making the application, for which injury there is no adequate remedy at law, and such property or property right must be described with particularity in the application, which must be in writing and sworn to by the applicant or by his agent or attorney.

"And no such restraining order or injunction shall prohibit any person or persons from terminating any relation of employment, or from ceasing to perform any work or labor, or from recommending, advising, or persuading others by peaceful means so to do; or from attending at or near a house or place where any person resides or works, or carries on business, or happens to be for the purpose of peacefully obtaining or communicating information, or of peacefully persuading any person to work or to abstain from working; or from ceasing to patronize or to employ any party to such dispute; or from recommending, advising, or persuading others by peaceful means so to do; or from paying or giving to or withholding from any person engaged in such dispute any strike benefits or other moneys or things of value; or from peaceably assembling at any place in a lawful manner and for lawful purposes; or from doing any act or thing which might lawfully be done in the absence of such dispute by any party thereto."

⊥ PROCEDURE IN CONTEMPT CASES.[5.406]

APRIL 26 (calendar day, APRIL 27), 1912.—Referred to the House Calendar and ordered to be printed.

Mr. CLAYTON, from the Committee on the Judiciary, submitted the following

REPORT.

[To accompany H. R. 22591.]

The Committee on the Judiciary, having had under consideration H. R. 22591, to amend an act entitled "An act to codify, revise, and amend the laws relating to the

---

[5.406] H.R. REP. NO. 613, 62d Cong., 2d Sess. (1912); see note 5.316 supra.

judiciary," approved March 3, 1911, report the same back with the recommendation that the bill do pass.

The bill leaves section 268 of the judicial code, formerly section 725 of the Revised Statutes, in full force and inserts five new sections, none of whose provisions conflict with said section 268.

ANALYSIS OF BILL.

By section 268a, in such cases of contempt specified in section 268 as constitute a criminal offense under any statute of the United States or at common law, the proceedings against the accused party shall be "as hereinafter provided"; that is, in the subsequent section of the bill.

Most of the important provisions of the bill are contained in section 268b. Before action by the court, except in the cases excepted from the operation of the bill, there must be presented a formal charge showing reasonable ground; and before the party is put upon trial he must be afforded an opportunity to purge himself of any actual or technical contempt which he may have committed. He can not be arrested until he has opportunity to either purge himself or make answer and has refused to do either. If arrested, or in case the matter can not be disposed of on the return day, he may be required to give bail.

The trial is by the court (1) in case no jury be demanded by the accused, (2) if the contempt be in the presence of the court or so near thereto as to obstruct the administration of justice, or (3) if ⊥ the contempt be charged to be in disobedience of any lawful writ, process, order, rule, decree, or command entered in any suit or action brought or prosecuted in the name or on behalf of the United States. In other cases the trial is to be by jury.

Section 268c provides for the preservation of bills of exception, for review upon writ of error, for stay of execution pending proceeding, for review, and for bail in case the accused shall have been sentenced to imprisonment.

Section 268d excepts from the operation of the act contempts in the presence of the court, or so near thereto as to obstruct the administration of justice, and contempts committed in disobedience of any lawful writ, process, order, rule, decree, or command entered in any suit or action brought or prosecuted in the name of or on behalf of the United States, and provides that in the excepted cases as well as in all other cases not specifically embraced within section 268a, the punishment shall be in conformity to the usages at law and in equity now prevailing.

Section 268e bars proceedings for contempt unless begun within one year from the date of the act complained of, and preserves the right of criminal prosecution, notwithstanding any proceeding and punishment for the contempts covered by the bill. It also excepts from the provisions of the bill any proceedings for contempt pending at the time of its passage.

Thus it is seen that the bill applies and gives a jury trial, with the exception noted, in all proceedings for contempt wherein the acts alleged to have been committed constitute a criminal offense, either under any Federal statute or at common law. The trial where a jury is had, is governed (sec. 268b), as near as is practicable, by the practice in criminal cases prosecuted by indictment or upon information.

Before calling further attention to the provisions of the bill now reported it is appropriate to review some of the contentions of those who have opposed every form of legislation whatever on this subject.

OBJECTIONS ANSWERED.

All the grounds of objection are reducible to two heads:

First. That any legislation whatever materially limiting or curtailing the power of the courts in the trial of contempts is unconstitutional.

Second. That any interference with the full and complete dominion or discretion of the judge in contempt cases tends to disorganization and a weakening of judicial efficiency.

Let us consider first the constitutional objections.

It is said that although the courts inferior to the Supreme Court owe their existence and jurisdiction to congressional action, yet a distinction should be made between the jurisdiction and judicial power, for instance, in the citation, trial, and punishment of a party charged with contempt of court.

The controversy goes back over 60 years. In 1831 Congress passed an act limiting the power of the courts subjectively; that is to say, it lopped off some of the jurisdiction which the court had assumed and exercised—a jurisdiction, or power, if the latter term be preferred, which Congress believed, and by its legislation asserted, was a usurpation. Never, until within a very recent period, was the authority of Congress to do that questioned, either by the courts or by any respectable authority. The particular circumstance or event, instigating the act of 1831, was the punishment by Judge Peck in Missouri, as for a contempt of court, of a party who had criticized one of his decisions in the columns of a newspaper.

The law before the act of 1831 read thus:

The said courts shall have power to impose and administer all necessary oaths, and to punish, by fine or imprisonment, at the discretion of the court, contempts of their authority.

The act of 1831 consisted in the addition of a proviso, reading as follows:

Provided, That such power to punish contempt shall not be construed to extend to any cases except the misbehavior of any person in their presence, or so near thereto as to obstruct the administration of justice, the misbehavior of any of the officers of said court in their official transactions, and the disobedience or resistance by any officer, or by any party, juror, witness, or other person, to any lawful writ, process, order, rule, decree, or command of the said court.

The extensive scope of this amendatory statute has been generally overlooked. The Federal courts were assuming and exercising the unlimited and unchecked powers resorted to by common-law courts, of deciding for themselves, not only the mode of procedure and degree and amount of punishment, but of selecting for themselves particular acts of alleged misconduct which should be placed in the category of contempts. Congress treated the term "power" as synonymous with "jurisdiction," circumscribed the field of jurisdiction, specified the acts which should constitute contempts, and said that such power or jurisdiction shall not extend beyond these specified acts.

It has been suggested that Congress might have refused to create the inferior courts, or even the Supreme Court, and have thus caused the failure of the Government.

But it is said that when Congress has acted and established a Federal court the common-law and equity powers of the courts immediately flow into these judicial receptacles out of the Constitution. It is only necessary to examine this new doctrine to know to what absurdities it would lead. The common-law courts of England, with the King's bench at their head, in addition to administering statutory law and the common law proper, exercised certain parliamentary powers. In the English system the legislative and judicial departments were, and are, entirely independent of each other. It is true that the courts were bound by acts of Parliament as construed by them, but outside the statutes their powers were as free from limitation as those of Parliament itself. They were the exponents and final arbiters of public policy for the Kingdom.

Though it is often said that the three departments of our Government are separate and independent, which is true in the sense that they must not invade each other's constitutional domain, and thus destroy each other, yet it is also true that arbitrary unchecked power does not abide with either of them. As the Supreme Court has well expressed it, in Yick Wo v. Hopkins (118 U. S. Rep., 369):

When we consider the nature and the theory of our institutions of government, the principles upon which they are supposed to rest, and review the history of their development, we are constrained to conclude that they do not mean to leave room for the play and action of purely personal and arbitrary power.[5.407]

[5.407] 118 U.S. at 369–70.

To concede that the courts might, even with the limits fixed in the act of 1831, exclusively decide when a contempt has been committed, and the amount or degree of punishment, with no power in Congress to set a limit thereto, would be to concede to the courts the power to annul every act of Congress, to paralyze the Executive arm, to confiscate all property, and destroy all liberty. Of course, few, if any, believe that the courts would ever proceed to such extremes, but it is sufficient to say that, according to our interpretation, the framers of the Constitution took care to safeguard the people against the possibilities of all such calamitous tendencies.

Referring to this bill, and comparing its provisions with the proviso added in 1831, it is seen that the bill only changes the procedure in contempt cases, while, as before stated, that proviso limited the jurisdiction subjectively.

The opposition was represented before the committee by able counsel and many authorities were cited, few of which, however, in our opinion, had any direct bearing on the question from a constitutional point of view. In fact, the power of Congress, as exhibited in the act of 1831, was so generally and uniformly conceded that not a single case has been found which ever questioned or doubted it. A few cases which, though not directly bearing upon the point of constitutionality, yet shed more or less light upon it will now be noticed.

It is argued that Congress can not require a court of equity to try issues of fact by jury. That is unquestionably sound doctrine, and the case of Brown v. Kalamazoo, Circuit Judge (87 Mich., 274),[5.408] is sound law. But it is wholly inapplicable here. No one has thus far ever insisted that contempt is of equitable cognizance, or other than what the textbooks designated, namely, a special proceeding, criminal in its nature, not necessarily connected with any particular suit or action pending in the court.

Numerous State cases were cited in argument. They may all be answered as a class. The relation between Congress and Federal courts is not the same as that between State legislature and the State courts. The constitutions of the various States themselves provide for and establish the court, partition the powers of government between the legislative, executive, and judicial departments, prescribing safeguards, and defining their powers in detail; whereas the Federal Constitution has delegated full and complete control of the matter to Congress. Nor should the fact be overlooked that the State decisions on the subject are often based upon precedents of the common law, which is no part of the Federal system. Thus, in Ex parte McCowan [sic] (139 N. Car., 95),[5.409] that being typical of many such cases relied upon, it was said:

> We are satisfied that at common law the acts and conduct of the petitioner, as set out in the case, constitute a contempt of court, and if the statute does not embrace this case and in terms repeal the common law applicable to it, we would not hesitate to declare the statute in that respect unconstitutional and void for reasons which we will now state.[5.410]

In Finck v. O'Neill [sic] (106 U. S. Rep., 272) it appeared that Congress has [sic] taken from the court all power to enforce its judgment, and the act of Congress was upheld by the Supreme Court of the United States. In that case (p. 280) the court said:

> The United States can not enforce the collection of a debt from an unwilling debtor, except by judicial process. They must bring a suit and obtain a judgment. To reap the fruit of that judgment they must cause an execution to issue. The courts have no inherent authority to take any one of these steps, except as it may have been conferred by the legislative department; for they can exercise no jurisdiction except as the law confers and limits it.

And in Cary v. Curtiss [sic] (3 How., 236, 254) the same court said:

> The courts of the United States are all limited in their nature and constitutions, and have not the powers inherent in courts existing by prescription, or by the common law.[5.411]

But in section 720, of the Revised Statutes, we have a statute of Congress

---

[5.408] The reference is apparently to Brown v. Buck, 75 Mich. 274, 42 N.W. 827 (1889).

[5.409] The correct citation is *Ex parte* McCown, 139 N.C. 95, 51 S.E. 957 (1905).

[5.410] 139 N.C. at 99–100.

[5.411] 44 U.S. (3 How.) at 245.

prohibiting the Federal courts from issuing injunctions in certain cases, and the constitutional validity of that statute was declared in Sharon v. Terry (36 Fed. R., 365 [sic]). Now, the writ of injunction is the arm of the Federal courts in the exercise of their equitable powers, which it has been urged enjoy complete immunity from congressional action. And here a Federal circuit court sustained an act of Congress which substracted [sic] an important part of equitable jurisdiction. Anyone taking the trouble to examine the judiciary act of 1789, with or without subsequent additions and amendments, will observe that it consists, in large part, of regulations of and limitations upon jurisdiction.

We close this head with the quotation from Ex parte Robinson (19 Wall., 505), cited with approval in the case of Bessette v. Conkey (194 U. S., 327 [sic]),[5.412] which is so clearly and obviously applicable and conclusive that no comment appears to be necessary:

> The power to punish for contempts is inherent in all courts. The moment the courts of the United States were called into existence and invested with jurisdiction over any subject they became possessed of this power, but the power has been limited and defined by the act of Congress of March 3, 1831. The act, in terms, applies to all courts. Whether it can be held to limit the authority of the Supreme Court, which derives its existence and power from the Constitution, may, perhaps, be a matter of doubt; but that it applies to the circuit and district courts there can be no question. These courts were created by act of Congress. Their powers and duties depend upon the act calling them into existence, or subsequent acts extending or limiting their jurisdiction. The act of 1831 is, therefore, to them the law specifying the cases in which summary punishment for contempts may be inflicted. It limits the power of these courts in this respect to three classes of cases.
> (1) Where there has been misbehavior of a person in the presence of the courts, or so near thereto as to obstruct the administration of justice.
> (2) Where there has been misbehavior of any officer of the courts in his official transaction.
> (3) Where there has been disobedience or resistance by an officer, party, juror, witness, or other person, to any lawful writ, process, order, rule, decree, or command of the courts. The law happily prescribes the punishment which the courts can impose for contempts. The seventeenth section of the judiciary act of 1789 (1 Stat. L., 73), declares that the court shall have power to punish of their authority in any cause or hearing before them by fine or imprisonment, at their discretion. The enactment is a limitation upon the manner in which the power shall be exercised, and must be held to be a negation of all other modes of punishment. The judgment of the court debarring the petitioner, treated as a punishment for contempt, was therefore unauthorized and void.[5.413]

As to the other ground of objection urged—that is, that any interference with the full and complete dominion and discretion of the courts tends to disorganization and to the weakening of judicial authority—judging by the course of previous discussion on this measure, it is not anticipated that the policy of the provision placing a limitation upon the punishment which can be inflicted will be strenuously criticized, and, therefore, we will make no further comment on that.

TRIAL BY JURY.

The feature of the bill against which the most strenuous argument has been directed is that providing for jury trials. But no one has shown that such provision amounts to anything more than a change of procedure. So that the question comes down to this, Has Congress or not the power to prescribe procedure? The courts will still, if this bill passes, have all the substantive power left in their hands by the act of 1831. Not one of the acts there catalogued will have been eliminated. The method of ascertaining the facts in certain cases is changed, but their ascertainment is still under supervision of the court, and ample safeguards are provided against evasions and miscarriages of justice.

A contemnor, from the moment the facts are judicially ascertained, is, by uniform

---

[5.412] The correct citation is Bessette v. W.B. Conkey Co., 194 U.S. 324, 24 S. Ct. 665, 48 L. Ed. 997 (1904).
[5.413] 86 U.S. (19 Wall.) at 509-12.

practice, either placed in durance or required to give bail. The result of an adverse judgment is always penal, both in form and effect, though the fine be sometimes turned over to a private litigant.

The manner of disposing of the fine does not alter, in any respect, the form and effect of the procedure, or change it from criminal to civil.

SUCH LEGISLATION LONG DEMANDED.

The bill is an evolution from prolonged and varied discussion, by no means limited to a recent date or to the present Congress. Every feature and provision of it has been subjected to attack and defense, but the whole controversy appears to have at length converged upon the issue of whether or not the policy and practice of jury trial in contempt cases shall be admitted in the Federal jurisprudence at all.

That complaints have been made and irritation has arisen out of the trial of persons charged with contempt in the Federal courts is a matter of general and common knowledge. The charge most commonly made is that the courts, under the equity power, have invaded the criminal domain, and under the guise of trials for contempt have really convicted persons of substantive crimes for which, if indicted, they would have had a constitutional right to be tried by jury. It has been the purpose of your committee in this bill to meet this complaint, believing it to be a sound public policy so to adjust the processes of the courts as to disarm any legitimate criticism; and your committee confidently believes that, so far from weakening the power and effectiveness of Federal courts, this bill will remove a cause of just complaint and promote that popular affection and respect which is in the last resolve the true support of every form of governmental activity.

ACTS OF CONGRESS RELATING TO CONTEMPTS.

Statutes at Large, vol. 1, First Congress, first session, chapter 20:

AN ACT To establish the Judicial Courts of the United States, approved September 24, 1789.

SEC. 17. *And be it further enacted*, That all the said courts of the United States shall have power to grant new trials, in cases where there has been a trial by jury for reasons for which new trials have usually been granted in the courts of law; (*a*) and shall have power to impose and administer all necessary oaths or affirmations, and to punish by fine or imprisonment, at the discretion of said courts, all contempts of authority in any cause or hearing before the same; (*b*) and to make and establish all necessary rules for the orderly conducting of business in the said courts, provided such rules are not repugnant to the laws of the United States. (This section at page 83; letters in parentheses refer to notes at the bottom of the page.)

Act of March 2, 1831, upon which sections 725, 5399, 5404, 5405, and 5406, Revised Statutes, above quoted, is based, was as follows:

Be it enacted by the Senate and House of Representatives of the United States of America in Congress assembled, That the power of the several courts of the United States to issue attachments and inflict summary punishment for contempts of court shall not be construed to extend to any cases except the misbehavior of any person or persons in the presence of the said courts, or so near thereto as to obstruct the administration of justice, the misbehavior of any of the officers of the said courts in their official transactions, and the disobedience or resistance by any officer of the said courts, party, juror, witness, or any other person or persons, to any lawful writ, process, order, rule, decree, or command of the said courts.

SEC. 2. *And be it further enacted*, That if any person or persons shall, corruptly, or by threats or force, endeavor to influence, intimidate, or impede any juror, witness, or officer, in any court of the United States, in the discharge of his duty, or shall, corruptly, or by threats or force, obstruct, impede, or endeavor to obstruct or impede, the due administration of justice therein, every person or persons so offending shall be liable to prosecution therefor by indictment, and shall, on conviction thereof, be punished by fine not exceeding five hundred dollars, or by imprisonment not exceeding three months, or both, according to the nature and aggravation of the offense.

Approved, March 2, 1831.

Section 725 Revised Statutes United States (1878):

SEC. 725. The said courts shall have power to impose and administer all necessary oaths and to punish, by fine or imprisonment, at the discretion of the court, contempts of their authority: *Provided*, That such power to punish contempts shall not be construed to extend to any case except the misbehavior of any person in their presence, or so near thereto as to obstruct the administration of justice, the misbehavior of any of the officers of said courts in their official transactions, and the disobedience or resistance by any such officer, or by any party, juror, witness, or other person, to any lawful writ, process, order, rule, decree, or command of said courts. (Stat. L., vol. 4, p. 487, 21st Cong., 2d sess., chap. 99, "An act declaratory of the law concerning contempts of court," approved Mar. 2, 1831.)

NOTE.—Section 725 of the Revised Statutes is reenacted by section 268 of the Judicial Code, effective January 1, 1912, and section 725 is repealed by section 297 of the same code.

⊥ Section 268 of the Judicial Code (1912):

SEC. 268. The said courts shall have power to impose and administer all necessary oaths, and to punish, by fine or imprisonment, at the discretion of the court, contempts of their authority: *Provided*, That such power to punish contempts shall not be construed to extend to any cases except the misbehavior of any person in their presence, or so near thereto as to obstruct the administration of justice, the misbehavior of any of the officers of said courts, in their official transactions, and the disobedience or resistance by any such officer, or by any party, juror, witness, or other person to any lawful writ, process, order, rule, decree, or command of the said courts. (Rev. Stats., sec. 725, 1878.)

Section 5399, Revised Statutes United States (1878):

SEC. 5399. Every person who corruptly, or by threats or force, endeavors to influence, intimidate, or impede any witness, or officer, in any court of the United States, in the discharge of his duty, or corruptly, or by threats or force, obstructs or impedes, or endeavors to obstruct or impede, the due administration of justice therein, shall be punished by a fine of not more than five hundred dollars, or by imprisonment not more than three months, or both. (Stat. L., vol. 4, p. 488; act approved Mar. 2, 1831.)

Section 5404, Revised Statutes United States (1878):

SEC. 5404. Every person who corruptly, or by threats or force, or by threatening letters, or any threatening communications, endeavors to influence, intimidate, or impede any grand or petit juror of any court of the United States in the discharge of his duty, or who corruptly, or by threats or force, or by threatening letters, or any threatening communications, influences, obstructs, or impedes, or endeavors to influence, obstruct, or impede, the due administration of justice therein, shall be punishable by a fine of not more than one thousand dollars, or by imprisonment not more than one year, or by both such fine and imprisonment. (Stat. L., chap. 420, vol. 17, p. 378; act of June 10, 1872.)

Section 5405, Revised Statutes United States (1878):

SEC. 5405. Every person who attempts to influence the action or decision of any grand or petit juror upon any issue or matter pending before such juror or before the jury of which he is a member, or pertaining to his duties, by writing or sending to him any letter or any communication in print or writing in relation to such issue or matter, without the order previously obtained of the court before which the juror is summoned, shall be punishable by a fine of not more than one thousand dollars or by imprisonment not more than six months, or by both such fine and imprisonment. (Stat. L., vol. 17, p. 378, chap. 420, act of June 10, 1872.)

Section 5406, Revised Statutes United States (1878):

SEC. 5406. If two or more persons in any State or Territory conspire to deter by force, intimidation, or threat any party or witness in any court of the United States from attending such court or from testifying to any matter pending therein freely, fully, and truthfully, or to injure such party or witness in his person or property on account of his having so attended or testified, or to influence the verdict, presentment, or indictment of any grand or petit juror in any such court, or to injure such juror in his person or property on account of any verdict, presentment, or indictment lawfully assented to by him, or of his being or having been such juror, each of such persons shall be punished by a fine of not less than five hundred, nor more than five thousand dollars, or by imprisonment with or without hard labor not less than six months nor more than six years, or by both such fine and imprisonment. (Stat. L., vol. 17, p. 13, Apr. 20, 1871.)

NOTE.—Sections 5399, 5404, 5405, and 5406 of the Revised Statutes are repealed by section 341 and reenacted by sections 135, 136, and 137 of the Criminal Code, effective January 1, 1910.

Section 135, Criminal Code (1910):

SEC. 135. Whoever corruptly, or by threats or force, or by any threatening letter or communication, shall endeavor to influence, intimidate, or impede any witness in any court of the United States, or before any United States commissioner or officer acting as such commissioner, or any grand or petit juror ⊥ or officer in or of any court of the United States, or officer who may be serving at any examination or other proceeding before any United States commissioner or officer acting as such commissioner, in the discharge of his duty, or who corruptly or by threats or force, or by any threatening letter or threatening communication, shall influence, obstruct, or impede, or endeavor to influence, obstruct, or impede the due administration of justice therein, shall be fined not more than one thousand dollars or imprisoned not more than one year, or both. (Rev. Stats., secs. 5399, 5404.)

Section 136, Criminal Code (1910):

SEC. 136. If two or more persons conspire to deter, by force, intimidation, or threat, any party or witness in any court of the United States, or in any examination before a United States commissioner or officer acting as such commissioner, from attending such court or examination, or from testifying to any matter pending therein, freely, fully, and truthfully, or injure such party or witness in his person or property on account of his having so attended or testified, or to influence the verdict, presentment, or indictment of any grand or petit juror in any such court, or to injure such juror in his person or property on account of any verdict, presentment, or indictment lawfully assented to by him, or on account of his being or having been such juror, each of such persons shall be fined not more than five thousand dollars or imprisoned not more than six years, or both. [(]Rev. Stats., sec. 5406.)

Section 137, Criminal Code (1910):

SEC. 137. Whoever shall attempt to influence the action or decision of any grand or petit juror of any court of the United States, upon any issue or matter pending before such juror, or before the jury of which he is a member, or pertaining to his duties, by writing or sending to him any letter or any communication, in print or writing, in relation to such issue or matter, shall be fined not more than one thousand dollars or imprisoned not more than six months, or both. (Rev. Stats., sec. 5405.)

⊥ THE BILL.

[H. R. 22591, Sixty-second Congress, second session.]

IN THE HOUSE OF REPRESENTATIVES, MARCH 29, 1912.

Mr. CLAYTON introduced the following bill; which was referred to the Committee on the Judiciary and ordered to be printed.

A BILL To amend an Act entitled "An Act to codify, revise, and amend the laws relating to the judiciary," approved March third, nineteen hundred and eleven.

Be it enacted by the Senate and House of Representatives of the United States of America in Congress assembled, That the act entitled "An act to codify, revise, and amend the laws relating to the judiciary," approved March third, nineteen hundred and eleven, be, and the same is hereby, amended by inserting after section 268 thereof five new sections, to be numbered, respectively, 268a, 268b, 268c, 268d, and 268e, reading as follows:

"SEC. 268a. That any person who shall willfully disobey any lawful writ, process, order, rule, decree, or command of any district court of the United States by doing any act or thing therein or thereby forbidden to be done by him, if the act or thing so done by him be of such character as to constitute also a criminal offense under any statute of the United States or at common law shall be proceeded against for his said contempt as hereinafter provided.

"SEC. 268b. That whenever it shall be made to appear to any district court or judge thereof, or to any judge therein sitting, by the return of a proper officer on lawful process, or upon the affidavit of some credible person, or by information filed by any district attorney, that there is reasonable ground to believe that any person has been guilty of such contempt, the court or judge thereof, or any judge therein sitting, may issue a rule requiring the said person so charged to show cause upon a day certain why he should not be punished therefor, which rule, together with a copy of the affidavit or information, shall be served upon the person charged with sufficient promptness to enable him to prepare for and make return to the order at the time fixed therein. If upon or by such return, in the judgment of the court, the alleged contempt be not sufficiently purged, a trial shall be directed at a time and place fixed by the court: *Provided, however*, That if the accused, being a natural person, fail or refuse to make return to the rule to show cause, an attachment may issue against his person to compel an answer, and in case of his continued failure or refusal, or if for any reason it be impracticable to dispose of the matter on the return day, he may be required to give reasonable bail for his attendance at the trial and his submission to the final judgment of the court. Where the accused person is a body corporate, an attachment for the sequestration of its property may be issued upon like refusal or failure to answer.

"In all cases within the purview of this act such trial may be by the court, or, upon demand of the accused, by a jury; in which latter event the court may impanel a jury from the jurors then in attendance, or the court or the judge thereof in chambers may cause a sufficient number of jurors to be selected and summoned, as provided by law, to attend at the time and place of trial, at which time a jury shall be selected and impaneled as upon a trial for misdemeanor; and such trial shall conform, as near as may be, to the practice in criminal cases prosecuted by indictment or upon information.

"If the accused be found guilty, judgment shall be entered accordingly, prescribing the punishment, either by fine or imprisonment, or both, in the discretion of the court. Such fine shall be paid to the United States or to the complainant or other party injured by the act constituting the contempt, or may, where more than one is so damaged, be divided or apportioned among them, as the court may direct; but in no case shall the fine to be paid to the United States exceed, in case the accused is a natural person, the sum of one thousand dollars, nor shall such imprisonment exceed the term of six months.

"SEC. 268c. That the evidence taken upon the trial of any person so accused may be preserved by bill of exceptions, and any judgment of conviction may be reviewed upon writ of error in all respects as now provided by law in criminal cases, and may be affirmed, reversed, or modified as justice may require. Upon the granting of such writ of error execution of judgment shall be stayed, and the accused, if thereby sentenced to imprisonment, shall be admitted to bail in such reasonable sum as may be required by the court or by any justice or any judge of any district court of the United States.

"SEC. 268d. That nothing herein contained shall be construed to relate to contempts committed in the presence of the court, or so near thereto as to obstruct the administration of justice, nor to contempts committed in disobedience of any lawful writ, process, order, rule, decree, or command entered in any suit or action brought or prosecuted in the name of or on behalf of the United States, but the same and all other cases of contempt not specifically embraced within section 268a of this act may be punished in conformity to the usages at law and in equity now prevailing.

"SEC. 268e. That no proceeding for contempt shall be instituted against any person unless begun within one year from the date of the act complained of; nor shall any such proceeding be a bar to any criminal prosecution for the same act or acts; but nothing herein contained shall affect any proceedings in contempt pending at the time of the passage of this act."

REPORT OF THE HOUSE COMMITTEE ON THE JUDICIARY (MINORITY VIEWS)
H.R. Rep. No. 627, Pt. 2
63d Cong., 2d Sess.
May 12, 1914

Mr. GRAHAM of Pennsylvania, from the Committee on the Judiciary, submitted the following

MINORITY VIEWS.

[To accompany H. R. 15657.]

We, the undersigned members of the Committee on the Judiciary, do not agree with the action of the committee on the bill (H. R. 15657) entitled "A bill to supplement existing laws against unlawful restraints and monopolies, and for other purposes."

The antitrust laws on the statute book at this time have been carefully considered by the Supreme Court and judicially interpreted through a period of 24 years, and if properly enforced are believed by us to strip corporations and trusts of any power to injure or oppress.

No possible good can come from constant interference with business. It is our belief that business should have a rest from further legislation and be given an opportunity to adjust itself to the environment created by the existing antitrust laws as the same have been interpreted and are now being administered.

The proposed legislation contains many new phrases and sets up new standards, all of which would require a period of years of interpretation by the courts before their full meaning can be definitely known by the business world.

It is very undesirable to bring about such a period of uncertainty and doubt to worry and harass the business of the country.

DISCRIMINATION IN PRICES.

The bill provides that any concern engaging in interstate commerce which shall discriminate in price between different persons or different localities (except on account of differences in grade, quality, or quantity of goods sold or differences in cost of transportation), with "the purpose or intent to thereby destroy or wrongfully injure the business of a competitor," shall be liable to a fine of $5,000 and to imprisonment for one year.

The phrase "with intent" to thereby destroy or wrongfully injure business is evidently relied upon to limit this prohibition to all such discriminations in price as would transgress the ethics of business competition.

Two things, however, make this view doubtful.

First. This section is intended to add something to the Sherman law; and an examination of the cases and decisions upon that law clearly shows that it already forbids all price discriminations that injure the business of a competitor in such a degree as to restrain trade.

It will probably be contended that this section forbids all price discriminations that wrongfully injure the business of a competitor, even though they fall short of "restraint of trade." This would introduce a new element and a new standard, and the meaning of the section would require judicial interpretation.

The ambiguous and uncertain language of this provision presents a difficult problem in judicial interpretation, and this would seem to us to be wholly unnecessary, in view of the fact that the law as it stands has already accomplished the object or purpose of this provision.

Second. The words "intent to wrongfully injure" present a modification of the bill as it was originally introduced, and relieves the section to some extent of the objections which could have been urged against it in its original form.

Nevertheless, it substitutes a new standard. In place of "monopoly" or "restraint of trade," the present standard, we will have to consider the "intent to wrongfully injure or destroy" the business of a competitor. This new standard must be construed in conjunction with the well-recognized presumption of law that a man always "intends" the natural consequences of his act. It would follow, therefore, that "intent to wrongfully injure" might be interpreted to cover every act by which one man obtains business from another in competition with him.

The word "wrongfully" has been introduced, evidently with the view of endeavoring to avoid this consequence; but it would seem to be inadequate for that purpose, because a jury might infer that any act which resulted in taking business from a competitor would necessarily be wrongful.

Price discriminations between different purchasers or different localities, adopted simply to avert business disaster by raising money to meet an exigency or to move unsalable goods, or adopted by a newcomer to get a foothold in a new territory—all of which might result in taking trade away from a competitor and thus "injure" his business—might be held to fall within the prohibition of this section.

It seems to us to be unwise to expose our business men to the peril of the interpretation of these new phrases when the law as it stands is definite and covers the subject matter of this section.

This section would seem to expose a manufacturer or jobber whose business extended over a wide area to a new and unjust risk. If confronted with competition at one point, and he lowers his price at such point merely and does so to meet the competitor's price in an endeavor (entirely within his legal rights) to keep the customers he has won in a successful business career, it would seem to require him to lower his ⊥ price all over the vaster area in which he sells his product. Otherwise he would be open to the accusation that his "intent" in lowering his price in the competitive territory was wrongful and might be made liable to fine and imprisonment.

A competitor who attacks at a single point and is in business only at that point might sell a small quantity of goods at lower prices, and to him this would be a negligible quantity, while the man whose business is assailed must, in order to avoid the appearance of evil and avoid the risk of litigation or prosecution, reduce his prices all over the country and thereby suffer a great loss.

If the section is intended to produce this result, then it is one that penalizes success in business. Mere size, although entirely lawful and not constituting a monopoly, would become a handicap. The business of such a manufacturer or jobber would be exposed to attacks savoring of blackmail; and yet, under the requirements of this section, he would have to sit supinely by and see his trade taken away; or, if he attempts to meet the attack—which would be his legal right—he must run the risk of appearing to wrongfully injure the business of the competitor or else, by reducing his price everywhere, meet with a great and destructive loss.

The policy of the antitrust laws is to foster competition, and is built upon the basis that that is the normal and desirable thing; but this law would tend to prevent competition, and put it in the power of an individual to manufacture prices instead of manufacturing products.

On the other hand, a concern trying to enter a new territory and seek new business would be equally cruelly dealt with. It could not make any reductions in the new territory without at the same time reducing its prices everywhere else.

An independent trying to acquire additional business would thus be dangerously handicapped; he would, in fact, be denied the right of competition.

Competition is a struggle for business between competitors. The law fosters it; the courts enforce the law; and yet this section would seriously interfere with, if not deny, competition, and take away from the general public the benefits which such competition might bring.

This section carefully recognizes the right to make different prices based upon grade, quality, and quantity of goods sold, and permits the taking into account of the cost of transportation; but it makes no provision whatever for the differences in local cost of distribution; nor does it make any provision covering differences in price due to differences in cost of production in different localities.

It is not a sound argument to say that within a few years 19 States have passed similar regulations. The answer to such an argument is that conditions in a locality might permit of such regulations, while in a great country like ours they would not.

Why should the conditions of cost of distribution and the cost of production be ignored?

The controlling fact, however, still remains that cutting prices, which transgresses business fair dealing, can now be adequately met and punished.

DUTIES OF MINE OWNERS.

This is a new and important invasion of business liberty. By this section a mine owner is deprived of a natural right to sell his product where and to whom he may. The mine owner is put upon the same basis as a public-service corporation.

The majority report says this is intended to meet cases where great corporations get control of mines and keep the raw materials to themselves. If such a thing were done by a great corporation, or by any corporation, so as to thereby create a monopoly or attempt to create one, or restrain trade, it can readily be dissolved and, if necessary, punished under the terms of the Sherman law. But if none of these things follow, the control of the raw material should not be condemned, for it would be a means of cheapening the cost of the product to the consumer.

The basis upon which public-service corporations are regulated does not exist with reference to mines. A great majority of mines are owned by small corporations and are entirely independent of all combinations. Upon each of these corporations this bill would impose all the conditions of a public-service corporation; yet how widely different are the circumstances and conditions affecting these two classes! The mine has a limited output; its capacity is limited; the demand for its product may extend to many places and localities; more customers may apply for its product than can be supplied. On the other hand, the public-service corporation will have no demands beyond the locality it serves. The product of a mine must decrease; the product of a public-service company would naturally increase to meet every possible demand of the growth of its business. Being limited in market and product, the mine operator can deal with only a few customers, and must pick and choose. Those who offer the best terms and the best prices and assure him steadfast and continued absorption of the product of the mine would naturally be chosen as customers. And why should they not be selected? Why should the freedom of the mine owner be invaded and destroyed? Why should he be subjected to a demand from a stranger for part of his product?

To extend to mine owners the duties of a public service company is to subject the most hazardous, most competitive, and least attractive business to duties which the law now imposes upon the least hazardous, most monopolistic, and probably the most attractive business under the new conditions.

Under this law, a mine owner is forbidden to select his own customers, although this right is carefully preserved with regard to every other business by the language of the proposed law.

EXCLUSIVE TRADE ARRANGEMENTS.

The bill provides that anyone engaged in interstate commerce who shall lease or sell "goods, wares, merchandise, machinery, supplies, or other commodities, or fix a price charged therefor, or discount from, or rebate upon such price, on the condition or understanding that the lessee or purchaser thereof shall not use or deal in the goods, wares, merchandise, machinery, supplies, or other commodities of a competitor" shall be liable to a fine of $5,000, and to imprisonment for one year.

The Sherman Act already forbids anyone to do any of these things in such a degree as to restrain trade. This bill goes further and restrains them in every degree.

This forbids the owner of a machine to lease or sell it under any arrangement by which the licensee shall buy all his spare parts and supplies from the manufacturer.

It would forbid the manufacturer to sell to a dealer under any arrangement by which the dealer would take a year's supply exclusively from the manufacturer.

It would forbid a manufacturer who has given a dealer exclusive territory for the sale of his line to require that dealer for a specified period not to carry any competitive line.

It wipes out the long-established agency system of doing business, and brands as criminal the time-honored practice of rewarding loyal dealers.

It would seem to be contrary to the principles of sound, fair, and legitimate business to forbid a manufacturer who desires to introduce his line of goods into a particular territory to make an arrangement with the retailer to concentrate his efforts upon the manufacturer's goods and push the introduction of them to the exclusion of all rival brands, yet this section would forbid any such arrangement.

Unless a manufacturer can give some assurance of reward to a retailer who undertakes the introduction of his goods, he can not hope to find a market for them in territory already occupied by his rivals. The bill, however, forbids the manufacturer to make any such arrangement.

A manufacturer selling a delicate machine, the successful operation of which depends upon perfectly adapted substitute parts, supplies, and supplementary appliances, agrees to furnish purchasers with perfectly adapted parts, supplies, and appliances at a special price, upon the understanding that they shall not use parts, supplies, or appliances of other manufacturers. This is done in the interest of maintaining the high standing and character of his machine. Yet this is forbidden by the bill.

Again, the manufacturer, instead of agreeing to sell these perfectly adapted parts, supplies, or appliances at a special price, agrees to sell the original machine at a special price, with the understanding that the purchaser shall not use imperfectly adapted parts, supplies, or appliances of any other manufacturer. This also is forbidden by the bill.

Again, the manufacturer sells no machines at all, but only leases them, and because they are delicate and any injury to them is his own loss, he leases them only to lessees who agree not to use imperfectly adapted parts, supplies, or appliances of other manufacture. Or he leases them at a special rental, upon the understanding that the lessees shall not use imperfectly adapted parts, supplies or appliances of any other manufacture. Or he agrees to sell to the lessee perfectly adapted parts, supplies, or appliances, upon the understanding that the lessee shall not use imperfectly adapted ones of other manufacture. Each of these transactions—which good morals and honorable business conduct from time immemorial have always sanctioned—is forbidden by the bill. For doing any of these things the manufacturer may suffer a fine of $5,000 and a year's imprisonment.

HOLDING COMPANIES.

The bill provides that no corporation shall acquire stock of another corporation where the effect of such acquisition is to "eliminate or lessen competition" between the corporation whose stock is so acquired and the corporation making the acquisition, or to make a monopoly of any line of trade in any section or community.

It also provides that no corporation shall acquire stock of two or more corporations engaged in commerce, where the effect of such acquisition, by the voting or granting of proxies or otherwise, would eliminate or substantially lessen competition between such corporations or any of them whose stock of share capital is so acquired, or to create a monopoly of any line of trade in any section or community.

There are various exceptions mentioned in the bill, such as the acquisition of stock solely for investment; the holding of stock of subsidiaries formed for carrying out the lawful business of the corporation or legitimate branches thereof; excepting also the acquisition by railroads of stock in an independent railroad where there is no substantial competition.

This provision goes further than the Sherman Act of 1890 with relation to holding companies. Under that act the doing of any of these things with intent to create or actually creating a monopoly or restraint of trade is forbidden; and the law in this respect is fully ample and competent to take care of all such offenses and the offenders. This act, however, goes beyond and leads us into a most dangerous realm, for it makes "elimination or lessening of competition" the test of illegality; while the Sherman Act makes "monopoly" or "restraint of trade" the test of illegality.

The only possible excuse and justification for legislation against holding companies lies in the fact that the holding company intended to be reached by the law creates a monopoly, or attempts to do so, or restrains interstate trade.

This proposed law, however, would make the acquisition of stock by one corporation in another in the same line of business, and although the two corporations taken together would form in their united business an infinitesimal fragment of the business of the locality in that particular line, a crime punishable by fine and imprisonment.

The existing law is sufficient to reach all malefactors who would monopolize or restrain trade. The new law introduces new phrases which would necessarily be the subject of judicial interpretation for years to come. It introduces new and uncalled-for risks and penalties. It exposes every business man who would by a holding company unite his control of two or more small corporations, so as to be able to manage them under one management, to the risk and peril of indictment and imprisonment, although his act in effect neither creates a monopoly nor restrains trade.

The courts have expressly held that "restraint of interstate trade" and "restraint of competition in interstate trade" are not interchangeable terms.

There may be, under the antitrust act, restraint of competition that does not amount to restraint of interstate trade. (U. S. v. E. I. du Pont de Nemours & Co., 188 Fed., 127, 151,[5.414] and the Supreme Court cases cited.)

Why new, untried, and indefinite phraseology which has been judicially declared to be inconsistent with the language of the Sherman law should now be substituted for phraseology which has obtained definite meaning in the Sherman Act through 24 years of judicial interpretation, and which has been held to be so "comprehensive and thorough" as "to prevent evasion of its policy by resort to any disguise or subterfuge in form," or "the escape of its prohibitions by any indirection" (Standard Sanitary Mfg. Co. v. United States, 226 U. S., 20, 49),[5.415] and to embrace "every conceivable act which could possibly come within the spirit or purpose of the prohibition of the law, without regard to the garb in which such acts were clothed," is hard to understand (U. S. v. American Tobacco Co., 221 U. S., 106, 181).[5.416]

This section is not calculated to affect larger corporations so much as it will harass and annoy smaller ones. Where a few people are interested in two or three corporations of minor importance which they desire—not being able to merge or unite them in one, for legal reasons—to control under a single management, they are denied this right by the terms of this section, although if they could merge and unite them they would be guilty of no violation of the law. If such persons were to attempt to exercise this natural business privilege and method of managing their own property, they would render themselves liable to fine and imprisonment.

INTERLOCKING DIRECTORATES.

The bill provides against interlocking directorates—(1) To exclude from directorates of every interstate common carrier everyone who, directly or indirectly, has any individual interest in any transaction with such common carrier; (2) to prevent, so far as possible, with certain exceptions as to size and location, everybody engaged in any capacity in any branch of the banking business from engaging at the same time in any capacity in any other branch of the banking business; (3) to exclude from the

---

[5.414] 188 F. 127, 151 (C.C.D. Del. 1911).

[5.415] 226 U.S. 20, 33 S. Ct. 9, 57 L. Ed. 107 (1912).

[5.416] 221 U.S. 106, 31 S. Ct. 632, 55 L. Ed. 663 (1911), portions of which are reprinted *supra* at chapter 1.

directorates of every industrial corporation engaged in interstate commerce everyone who is a director in any competitive corporation.

With the principle underlying the first, no one can quarrel. The only question is, whether the existing laws punishing directors who directly or indirectly profit individually by transactions with their corporations need any reenforcement, and whether this need is so extreme as to justify eliminating as directors industrial and financial leaders whose advice within the wide field of their experience is almost invaluable, and whose reputation for judgment and integrity, fortified by the strict duties which the law already lays upon them, insures the confidence of the entire business community in the corporations which they serve.

As to the provisions relating to banks, or the second purpose above named, it is hard to find an adequate reason for the language of the bill. The law arbitrarily dissects the whole field of banking into innumerable small compartments, and creates uncrossable boundaries for each of these, determined, not upon the basis of a monopoly or a trust in monetary affairs, or the attempt to create either, but according to the character of the institution, whether national bank, State ⊥ bank, trust company, or private bank, and according to the size of the institution, whether having more or less than $2,500,000 resources, and according to the population of the place in which the institution or bank is located, whether more or less than 100,000 inhabitants. Peculation or mismanagement in a community of more than 100,000 population would seem to be just as criminal as peculation or mismanagement in a community of less than 100,000 population. Mismanagement of or larceny from an institution of less than $2,500,000 resources would seem to be just as wicked, and perhaps more so, than larceny from or mismanagement of an institution of more than $2,500,000 resources. Why should legality or illegality depend upon such figures?

The arbitrariness of these figures emphasizes the unscientific character of the proposed legislation and the lack of principle in the entire proposal.

The third, or the provision relating to corporations engaged in interstate commerce (excepting common carriers), comes measurably closer to the principle of the Sherman Act than any of the preceding provisions relating to interlocking directorates. This provision, however, makes the bare possibility of "elimination of competition" the test of illegality, instead of the actuality of "eliminating or lessening of competition," which is the test adopted in the provision relating to holding companies; and instead of "restraint of trade," which is the test of illegality in the Sherman Act, this new standard of the "eliminating or lessening of competition" is substituted.

The phrase "so that an elimination of competition by agreement between them would constitute a violation of any of the provisions of any of the antitrust laws" affords no protection, but exposes all directors in more than one corporation engaged in interstate commerce to the peril of violating the law, because the proposed bill will be a part of the antitrust laws of the United States, and in it the "elimination of competition," or the liability to eliminate or lessen competition, instead of the creation of a monopoly or a restraint of trade, would become the governing test by which the directors would be judged.

Under existing laws, wherever interlocking directorates exist this fact can be shown, and if the interlocking tends to establish a monopoly or creates a monopoly or a restraint of trade, it can readily be reached and corrected and the evil removed. Neither the possibilities nor the actualities of "elimination of competition" ought to be substituted for "monopoly" or "restraint of trade" as the test of illegality.

This section will be full of difficulty and peril for small corporations, and will affect them in far greater degree than it will larger ones, against which the legislation is presumed to be aimed.

The use of interlocking directorates serves many useful purposes, and because in some instances it has been used to foster monopoly or create a restraint of trade, does not furnish a good reason why the use of interlocking directorates generally should be forbidden.

It is provided that this provision shall not relate to corporations whose capital, surplus, and undivided profits do not exceed $1,000,000. There is no occasion for any such limitation or provision, but if one is to be made it ought to be much higher than this. The unscientific character of the proposed legislation rests upon the fact that an effort is made to take the detail by which monopoly or restraint of trade is effected, and erect these into separate and distinct crimes, whereas the law should aim only at the monopoly or restraint of trade, and leave the detail or incident by which either is effected to the court and jury under the circumstances of each particular case.

This view brings us back to the original question whether the Sherman Act, which already forbids such interlocking directorates in its general prohibition of monopoly and restraints of trade, needs any reenforcement, and whether this need is so extreme as to justify eliminating as directors industrial and financial leaders whose advice within the wide field of their experience is most valuable, and whose reputation for judgment and integrity insures the confidence of the business community in the corporations which they serve.

PRIVATE SUITS UNDER ANTITRUST LAW.

The bill provides that the final judgement or decree in any suit brought by the United States under the antitrust laws shall "constitute in favor of or against such defendant conclusive evidence of the same facts, and be conclusive as to the same issues of law in favor of or against any other party" in any suit under the antitrust laws; that, while the United States is prosecuting any suit under the antitrust laws, the time within which any individual may sue on account of the same matter shall be suspended; that suits for treble damages and for costs of suit and for a reasonable attorney's fee may be brought by anyone injured by reason of any discriminations in prices or exclusive trade arrangements forbidden by the bill; that subpoenas for the attendance of witnesses may run into any other district; and that, subject to the rules covering injunction proceedings, any individual may sue any concern (except a common carrier subject to the interstate-commerce act) for an injunction against threatened loss or damage by reason of any violation of the antitrust laws.

These are all extraordinary remedies added to the existing remedy which every individual has of suing for treble damages and costs of suit and a reasonable attorney's fee for any violation of the Sherman Act. The only justification for these additional remedies must lie in the supposition that the existing remedy is insufficient.

Recovery of treble damages and costs of suit and an attorney's fee would seem, in themselves, sufficient inducements to any aggrieved party or his counsel to sue under the existing law.

The number of suits officially reported which have been brought to enforce this remedy show that in a large number the plaintiffs have obtained substantial verdicts. In all the other cases the courts show a strong disposition in favor of the plaintiffs upon the questions raised by the pleadings, and the history of this litigation shows the effectiveness of the remedy now afforded by the existing law.

From the standpoint of the Government, the proposal to make Government decrees conclusive in private suits is open to serious objection. In various proceedings taken by the Government under the Sherman Act, parties have been persuaded to consent to decrees granting all the relief which the Government demanded. Such consent decrees have accomplished, without the consumption of the time and expense involved in conducting prosecutions, all the relief which could be obtained by successful litigation. No hindrance should be put in the way of the Department of Justice in respect of these negotiations.

If this proposal were enacted, it would deter any company from ever consenting to the entry of a decree in a Government suit under the antitrust laws; for such a decree would simply invite a flood of litigation that might bankrupt any company.

The enactment of this provision into law would create an unfair discrimination unless, instead of restricting its operation to any suit or proceedings in equity hereafter brought, it were restricted to any suit or proceeding in equity hereafter brought for or by reason of any act, matter, or thing hereafter committed or omitted in violation of the antitrust laws. In other words, all past offenders should be put upon the same basis. Those against whom suits have been brought and determined are placed outside of the effect of this provision. So ought also those who might hereafter be sued, because of things heretofore done or committed. In other words, if the section were confined to future offenders, this discrimination would not exist.

The extension of time in which individual suits may be brought, until after the Government's suit is terminated, is perhaps too broad an enlargement of the time, and should be limited by some definite period; otherwise a protracted litigation might last for such a number of years as would end in the loss of evidence, the inability to find or produce witnesses; in other words, it tends to an indefinite extension of the statutory period. It ought, in our judgment, to be fixed so that there would be a time when, notwithstanding the suspension of the suit during the pendency of the litigation, no suit could be begun.

Under the proposed bill a peculiar hardship is threatened to witnesses in Government suits. Subpoenas are permitted to run into every district in the United States, and witnesses may be summoned to New York or Washington from San Francisco or Seattle, or vice versa. This would tend to expose witnesses to loss and suffering, and perhaps the attendant ruin of their business. It is our opinion that the present law, which provides for the taking of the testimony in the district where the witness resides or where he may be found, is amply sufficient.

The provision giving to any individual the right to enjoin any threatened loss or damage by reason of any violation of the antitrust law is a very serious one. Suits at law for damages such as may now be brought under the Sherman Act relate to past instead of to present or future conduct, and do not have the same evil effects as a proceeding for an injunction. The beginning of an investigation by the Government on any complaint that a concern has violated the antitrust law, almost immediately to some extent affects his credit, but not as seriously as an application for an injunction, and perhaps a receivership, which might be brought by any individual. There should be a different policy in respect to the two classes of remedy, which should be analogous to that which has been recognized in respect of railroads under the interstate-commerce act.

If Congress should see fit to enact the law providing an interstate trade commission, it should have the power and authority of considering all requests of individuals to begin suits for an injunction under the antitrust laws and to provide that the commission should ⊥ begin such suits in its own name whenever such requests seem warranted by the facts as the commission, upon its own investigation, shall discover them to be.

The Interstate Commerce Commission has substantially this power and duty now in respect of requests by individuals for equitable relief against railroads for violations or threatened violations of the interstate-commerce act. A similar practice, therefore, would seem to be logical in the matter of procedure under the antitrust laws.

The advantages of such a course would seem to be considerable: (1) In every worthy case, the individual would be saved an enormous expense, and the proceeding would be begun with all the weight and authority of a branch of the Government; (2) in every unworthy case, or case of mistake or misapprehension on the part of the complaining individual, the determination by the commission not to begin suit would save both the complaining individual and the accused concern enormous expense, and would prevent anything like blackmail or willful harassing of legitimate business; (3) in those few and almost never-occurring cases of a really worthy case, which neither the Department of Justice nor the interstate trade commission would find deserving of prosecution, the complaining individual would still be able to begin an action at law for treble damages under the antitrust act.

INJUNCTIONS AND CONTEMPTS.

Following the method pursued in the majority report,[5.417] we would submit that it is true that the other sections of the bill are substantially the same as the provisions of the two separate bills (H. R. 23635 and H. R. 22591, 62d Cong.), known as the

---

[5.417] *See* note 5.316 *supra*.

Clayton injunction and contempt bills, which were considered and passed by the House of Representatives at the last Congress, but failed of passage in the Senate. They deal entirely with questions of Federal procedure relating to injunctions and contempts committed without the presence of the court.

The minority reports made upon these bills in the last Congress explain their purpose and present the criticisms against them which might be made, and are comprehensive and should be read in conjunction with what has been set forth in the majority report. For convenience, we would present them as addenda to this report. They follow in order and are entitled "Appendix A" and "Appendix B."

All of which is respectfully submitted.

George S. Graham.
Henry G. Danforth.
L. C. Dyer.

APPENDIX A.[5.418]

RELATING TO INJUNCTIONS.

House report 612, part 2, Sixty-second Congress, second session.

REGULATION OF INJUNCTIONS.

MAY 3, 1912.—Ordered to be printed.

Mr. MOON of Pennsylvania, from the Committee on the Judiciary, submitted the following as the

VIEWS OF THE MINORITY.

[To accompany H. R. 23635.]

The undersigned members of the Judiciary Committee, to whom was referred the bill (H. R. 23635) to amend an act entitled "An act to codify, revise, and amend the laws relating to the judiciary," etc., which bill has been reported favorably, beg leave to submit herewith their views in opposition to the enactment of said measure.

The first section of the bill is intended as a substitute for the existing law on the subject of injunctions as found in section 263 of the Judicial Code, and the subsequent sections are intended to be supplementary to section 266 of the code.

According to the report of the majority of this committee, this bill intends to correct "the too ready issuance of injunctions, or the issuance without proper precautions or safeguards." If the report is predicated upon the "too ready issuance of injunctions," it is singular that it does not disclose a single case upon which the opinion of the majority could be founded. We are well aware of the charges iterated and reiterated before congressional committees alleging abuses in the issuance of injunctions. We have not found any more evidence to support them in the past than we now find in the report of the committee. We thoroughly believe, with the Supreme Court of the United States, "that no injunction ought to be granted except in a case reasonably free from doubt. We think such rule is and will be followed by all the judges of the Federal courts."

The minority members have at all times been willing to assent to a rational proposal to further safeguard the issuance of injunctions against even the possibility of abuse, and have introduced a bill for that purpose; but we can not consent to proposals which would operate to deprive the writ of half its efficiency in all cases and to

---

[5.418] *See* note 5.316 *supra* for an explanation of the origin of these appendices to the Minority Views.

determine its application in many instances by the character of the parties to the controversy rather than the nature of the wrong which is to be remedied. We think, furthermore, that the majority report is founded upon a misconception of the course of judicial decision respecting statutes regulating the issuance of injunctions, and that the legislation proposed is impracticable, invalid, in the interests of a class rather than of the community, and proposes standards of legality without parallel or precedent in our legislation.

To make our position clearer, we consider the bill in the order pursued in Report No. 612:

I.

Preliminary to a discussion of the bill, the majority gives an historical résumé of legislation respecting notice in injunction cases. We believe essential elements of that history have not received the consideration deserved from the majority, and we must disagree with them respecting conclusions drawn from both the legislation and judicial decisions of the past respecting that legislation.

On the 2d of March, 1793, was enacted legislation of which the following was a part:

Nor shall any writ of injunction issue in any case without reasonable previous notice to the adverse party or his attorney of the time and place of moving the same. (Ch. 22, vol. 1, U. S. Stat. L., p. 534.)

The majority concludes:

The will of Congress as thus expressed was completely thwarted and the statute nullified by the peculiar construction placed upon it by the courts.

It appears to us the majority [,] and not the courts, have misconstrued the will of Congress. They overlook, as the court did not, the distinction described in all authoritative textbooks, familiar to every lawyer and pointed out with striking distinctness by the courts, between restraining orders intended to preserve the status quo to protect the subject matter of litigation and the preliminary and final injunctions which are issued, if at all, after hearing upon the application for the equitable remedy. That the statute in question should not be construed to prevent the issuance of restraining orders was natural and inevitable. It was a practice recognized by the English chancery from time immemorial. The early English textbooks speak of it as well understood and essential, as, for instance, Eden on Injunctions, 1821; Adams Equity, 1845.

Had the court construed the act of Congress to forbid the preservation of the subject matter of litigation until the respective rights of the litigants could be adjudicated, it would have obviously given a construction against the very essentials of justice. Indeed, the majority recognizes and admits this by its own proposal, for while it criticizes the construction which permits the issuance of restraining orders without notice under special circumstances it provides in section 263 of its own bill for the doing of the very thing which it criticizes the courts for having done.

We call attention to the English practice, because it was early held respecting the judicial power of the courts of the Union in equity that:

The usages of the high court of chancery in England whenever the jurisdiction is exercised govern the proceedings. This may be said to be the common law of chancery, and since the organization of the Government it has been observed. (Penn. v. Wheeling, etc., Bridge Co., 13 How., 563; Meade v. Beale, 1 Campbell's Reports, 339, C. C. M. D. Tawney, 1850; Loring et al. v. Marsh, 2 Clifford's Reports, 469.)

Thus, the courts did not "get around" the statute, as is suggested by the majority, but construed it in accordance with an immemorial practice of English jurisprudence which recognized the necessity of issuing restraining orders under special circumstances that the court might preserve the status quo, protect the subject matter of litigation, and preserve from destruction that upon which it was to pass judgment.

The report implies that the case of New York v. Connecticut (4 Dall., 1) upheld a construction which forbade the issuance of even restraining orders without notice. That issue is not presented in that case decided in 1799. The practice was first recognized four years before in the case of Schermerhorn [sic] v. L'Espenasse (2 Dall., 360).[5.419] In this case the defendants, merchants of Amsterdam, had executed to the complainant power of attorney to receive for his own use the interest due on $180,000 of certificates of the United States, bearing interest at 6 per cent from the 1st of January, 1788, to the 31st of December, 1790, amounting to $32,400. Notwithstanding this assignment, the defendants, on the 16th of June, 1792, received certificates for the interest and funded the amount at 3 per cent in their own names. The bill prayed relief according to the equity of the case and a restraining order to prevent the defendants from transferring the stock or receiving the principal or interest. On the bill exhibited of the power of attorney and affidavits to the effect that the stock was registered in the name of the defendants on the books of the Treasurer the restraining order was granted. No subpoena was served until Mr. Lewis, on behalf of the defendants, moved for a rule to show cause why the injunction should not be dissolved. The motion was refused. An examination of the record discloses that Mr. Lewis, counsel for the defendants, supported his motion for dissolution on two grounds:

That the injunction was issued irregularly, as there was no affidavit made of the truth of the allegations contained in the bill.

In supporting this he said:

He did not object because the injunction was issued before a subpoena was served, as there were various cases in which justice could not otherwise be obtained.

This proceeding was had two years after the passage of the statute of 1793 before a justice of the Supreme Court who had been a member of the Congress which had enacted the statute; the hearing was held in a building adjoining that in which the act was passed and in the same district where the Congress was sitting. It demonstrates as no other case can the well-recognized equity practice in relation to temporary restraining orders, and shows the construction placed upon the statute by the profession and the court. In the meantime the practice of issuing restraining orders without notice under special circumstances of necessity was approved through the exercise of the power by the highest authority, including various justices of the circuit and district courts and Chief Justice Marshall (who is observed to issue an ex parte restraining order to prevent moneys alleged to have been improperly allowed by an administrator from being taken out of the country). (Green et al. v. Hanberry's Executors, 2 Brockenbrough's Reports, 405, Nov., 1830;[5.420] Love v. Fendall's Trustees, 1 Cranch C. C., 34;[5.421] Marsh et al. v. Bennett, 5 McLean, 117;[5.422] Crane v. McCoy, 1 Bond's Reports, 422;[5.423] Mowrey v. Indianapolis & C. R. Co., 17 Fed. Cas., 930.[5.424])

Too much space would be taken by the enumeration of cases of this character, and those cited are merely offered as examples.

Finally, during the debate upon the act of 1872, now section 263 of the Judicial Code, we find two of the most distinguished lawyers of the Senate expressing the recognized practice as follows:

Mr. CARPENTER. I understand if any judge having the jurisdiction by law to grant an injunction has presented to him a bill in equity, fortified with proofs which entitle the party by the acknowledged and usual practice of a court of equity to have an injunction, the judge has no discretion to deny it.

Mr. FRELINGHUYSEN. I think that elementary provision of the law even I may have been presumed to have heard and known of.

[5.419] The correct citation is Schermehorn v. L'Espenasse, 2 U.S. (2 Dall.) 360, 1 L. Ed. 415 (1796).

[5.420] 10 F. Cas. 1110 (No. 5759) (C.C.D. Va. 1830). The proper citation to Brockenbrough's is 2 Brock. 403 (1830).

[5.421] 15 F. Cas. 993 (No. 8547) (C.C.D.C. 1801).

[5.422] 16 F. Cas. 793 (No. 9110) (C.C.D. Mich. 1850).

[5.423] 6 F. Cas. 753 (No. 3354) (C.C.S.D. Ohio 1860).

[5.424] 17 F. Cas. 930 (No. 9891) (C.C.D. Ind. 1866).

Mr. CARPENTER. Therefore I was astonished to hear the Senator deny it.
Mr. FRELINGHUYSEN. I did not deny it. (46 Congressional Globe, p. 2492.)

Thus we find the practice respecting restraining orders recognized by Congress, by the courts, and the profession throughout the history of our Government and its necessity appreciated by the majority from its incorporation in this bill. Indeed, we believe the right to issue a restraining order upon a proper showing of its necessity to protect a right of a pecuniary nature against irreparable damage is an essential part of the judicial power in equity. If a suitor over whom a court has jurisdiction by a bill in that court discloses a state of facts where irreparable harm is threatened and where, if notice were given, irreparable damage would be done before hearing could be had or decree entered, were deprived by the legislature of the right to such a remedy, we believe it would be equivalent to a legislative determination in advance that under no circumstances can a plaintiff disclose a threatened irreparable injury without adequate remedy at law demanding immediate equitable intervention. If the Congress undertakes arbitrarily to determine in advance what a suitor would otherwise be entitled to as due process of law in a court of equity, we believe he would be deprived of a guaranteed constitutional right.

The first section of the bill, with one material exception, is almost an exact copy of a bill introduced in the Sixty-first Congress, known as the Moon bill. This bill was reintroduced in the present Congress, and was supported by the entire Republican membership of the Judiciary Committee.

The exception referred to has reference to the provision for the expiration of a restraining order granted by the court without notice. The Moon bill provided that the order should expire "within such time after service is made or notice given, which shall be made or given as speedily as possible, not to exceed seven days, as the judge or court shall fix." The proposed bill provides that "it shall expire at such time after entry as the court or judge shall fix, not to exceed seven days," etc.

A restraining order is of no effect until served, and under such a provision it would be only necessary for those having knowledge of the application to avoid service for seven days after the issuance of the order to defeat its purpose. We can conceive circumstances in which a few who might be served would notify other defendants to avoid it and on failure to make the order effective by service within seven days it would be necessary to give notice to all previously served before an extension of further time could be had. We can conceive of no more certain method of depriving a suitor of essential equitable protection. Many judicial districts of our country administer justice over vast areas in which the material circumstances of life must be taken into consideration. The proposal of this section is general. It applies to all forms of litigation, and in view of the physical as well as the personal difficulties attending the service of restraining orders under some circumstances we can not but believe that not only would many individual suitors suffer grievous injury, but we can from our public service and professional experience conceive many circumstances in which the public interest would be seriously jeopardized. All of these difficulties would be overcome if the restraining order should date from the time of service instead of the time of its entry.

II.

Section 266A provides that no restraining or interlocutory order shall issue except upon the giving of security against cost or damage.

Under the present practice this is within the discretion of the court, and while we should not be disposed to disagree with such a suggestion, we must again note that no reason is given for the suggested change which implies a failure upon the part of the courts to properly exercise this discretion. No evidence to this effect has been at any time submitted to the committee, nor do the majority offer any evidence to that effect as a reason for their action.

III.

Section 266B requires every restraining order or every injunctive order "to set forth the reasons for the issuance of the same to be specific in terms and describe in reasonable detail, and not by reference to the bill of complaint or other document the act or acts sought to be restrained;" it binds only the parties to the suit, "their agents, servants, employees, and attorneys or those in active concert with them, and who shall by personal services or otherwise have received actual notice of the same." This section is of general application. In support of this provision the majority point out that it is to be a safeguard against "dragnet or blanket injunctions," by which parties may be punished for contempt after "only constructive notice, equivalent in most cases to none at all."

Again, the majority asserts conditions as a basis for proposed legislation which are both unproven and unprovable. Nothing is clearer in the field of jurisprudence than the requirement that a respondent on a contempt charge must have actual notice of the existence of an order which he is accused of violating and that the order must have been unmistakably brought to his attention. (Bessette *v.* Conkey, 194 U. S.) All the Debbs [sic] cases, both in the circuit and district courts and on appeal, actually confirm this statement. The majority offer in proof of the necessity of their proposal merely an implication unwarrantedly reflecting upon the judiciary and without supporting proof of any character.

They have, moreover, properly provided in section 266 that every restraining order issued shall be accompanied by an entry stating the reasons for its issuance. It would be a useless waste of time to again set forth the reasons for the issuance of the order in the order itself, as is required by section 266B. Complaints are heard on every side against cumbersome and delaying procedure. This proposal multiplies the delays, difficulties, and inconveniences of procedure indefinitely. It requires every order to be a history, to repeat in irrelevant and cumbersome detail all the preliminary pleadings, and instead of enlightening the parties against whom it was issued the form suggested and the procedure prescribed would increase his confusion and doubt.

The majority point out that there is "no Federal statute to govern either the matter of making or form and contents of orders in injunctions," thereby inferring that this entire matter is left to the discretion or judgment of the judge granting the injunction. In this statement they entirely overlook the rules in equity of the Supreme Court of the United States binding upon all inferior Federal courts, prescribing with great minuteness and changed from time to time in accordance with the teaching of experience the forms of injunctive orders and forbidding the ceaseless repetition in decrees and orders of the contents of bills of complaint.

The effect of section 266B is to abolish the many rules in equity of the Supreme Court in conflict with it, representing the professional experience of a century, and amended from time to time to shorten procedure, increase the convenience, and protect the rights of litigants in the courts of the United States. The majority says section 266 does not change the best practice with respect to orders, but imposes the duty upon the courts in mandatory form to conform to correct rules as already established by judicial precedent. We respectfully submit that the equity rules of the Supreme Court express correct judicial precedents and that the majority have apparently overlooked this important fact.

The bill as reported would withdraw the application of the restraining order from parties not named in it and not in agreement with the parties named who may on their own initiative undertake its violation. Such cases are not uncommon. If the majority intend to exempt such violations of the order, they have created an unusual and remarkably privileged class of lawbreakers; if not, we are unable to discern the intention expressed in the limitation "in active concert with them."

IV.

The two paragraphs of section 266C must be read in connection with each other or their purpose and meaning are lost. The first paragraph provides that no judge or court of the United States shall issue any restraining order or injunction "in any case between an employer and employees, or between employers and employees, or between persons employed and persons seeking employment, involving or growing out of a dispute concerning the terms or conditions of employment, unless necessary to prevent irreparable injury to property or to a property right," etc. If this section is intended to withdraw civil rights from equitable protection in this class of cases, we must disapprove it as an evident effort to deny such protection as is given to civil rights in all other classes of cases, since it is axiomatic that it is the office of equity to protect by injunction, under proper circumstances, civil and even personal as well as property rights. We object to the implication contained in emphasizing controversies between employers and employees, or between employees or persons employed and seeking employment, and if the majority intends by ⊥ this to indicate that such rights are to have less or different protection from the same rights when involving controversies of another kind we must emphatically disagree with the principle implied, for in this country remedies are to be predicated at all times upon the character of the rights which are threatened, and not upon the class or nature of the persons involved in the controversy.

We do not comment upon the many cases cited by the learned members of the majority in support of their views upon equity pleadings in this connection. We quite agree with the correctness of such decisions, but we draw from them quite a different conclusion from that implied by the majority. We think they prove what the majority evidently adduces them to disprove. To us they are evidence that the pleadings required with such particularity in the special class of cases involved in section 266C are required generally in all applications for equitable intervention. The majority are thus seen to be offering as proof of the need of special legislation for pleadings in a particular class of cases the fact that the courts have substantially required such conditions and pleadings in all classes of cases of which the kind enumerated are a part.

The second paragraph of section 266C contains to our mind the most vicious proposal of the whole bill. It enumerates certain specific acts and provides that no restraining order or injunction shall prohibit the doing of them. Most of the acts thus recited are in themselves not amenable to the injunction process under existing law and practice. No court does or would enjoin them, but to declare by law that these acts should under no circumstances be restrained, we do not hesitate to say is a proposal without precedent in the legislative history of this country. No legislature has ever proposed that any act however innocent itself should be sanctified irrespective of the motive or purpose of the actor. "No conduct," says Mr. Justice Holmes in Aiken [sic] v. Wisconsin (195 U. S., 194),[5.425] "has such an absolute privilege as to justify all possible schemes of which it may be a part. The most innocent and constitutionally protected of acts or omissions may be made a step in a criminal plot, and if it is a step in a plot, neither its innocence nor the Constitution is sufficient to prevent the punishment of the plot by law."[5.426]

The majority have quoted various decisions in which particular acts under the pleadings presented to the court were held lawful and their prohibition denied. The same acts under other circumstances have been held unlawful and enjoined by the very courts, and in the course of the very decisions which the majority cites. Thus, in Arthur v. Oakes (63 Fed. Rep., 310), Mr. Justice Harlan is quoted to sustain the proposition that no man can by injunction be required to perform personal service for another, and in that decision Justice Harlan eliminated from the injunction the words "and from so quitting the service of the said receivers with or without notice as to cripple the property or prevent or hinder the operation of said railroad." The majority must observe, however, that Mr. Justice Harlan likewise held, "But different considerations must control in respect to the words in the same paragraph of the writs of injunction, and from combining and conspiring to quit with or without notice the service of said receivers with the object and intention of crippling the property in their custody or embarrassing the operation of said railroad."[5.427] Thus, the same act of quitting is lawful under one set of circumstances and unlawful under another, because the concerted ⊥ action in the first instance, in the opinion of Mr. Justice Harlan, "is a very different matter from a combination and conspiracy among employees with the object and intent, not simply of quitting the service of the receivers because of the reduction

---

[5.425] The correct citation is Aikens v. Wisconsin, 195 U.S. 194, 25 S. Ct. 3, 49 L. Ed. 154 (1904).

[5.426] 195 U.S. at 206.

[5.427] 63 F. at 319.

of wages, but of crippling the property in their hands and embarrassing the operation of the railroad."[5.428]

The majority undertakes to prescribe a set rule forbidding under any circumstances the enjoining of certain acts which may or may not be actuated by a malicious motive or be done for the purpose of working an unlawful injury or interfering with constitutional rights of employer or employee. In the same opinion Mr. Justice Harlan points out the impossibility of prescribing a set rule of this character and says,[5.429] "The authorities all agree that a court of equity should not hesitate to use its power when the circumstances of the particular case in hand require it to be done in order to protect rights of property against irreparable damage by wrong doers. It is as Justice Story said, 'because of the varying circumstances of cases that courts of equity constantly decline to lay down any rule which shall limit their power and discretion as to the particular cases in which such injunction shall be granted or withheld,'" and the authority proceeds, "there is wisdom in this course, for it is impossible to foresee all the exigencies of society which may require their aid and assistance to protect rights or redress wrongs. The jurisdiction of these courts thus operating by special injunction is manifestly indispensable for the purposes of social justice in a great variety of cases and therefore should be fostered and upheld by a steady confidence." (Story, Equity Jurisprudence, sec. 959B; Arthur v. Oakes, 63 Fed., 328.)

Among the acts which the second paragraph of section 266C declares shall not be restrained is to prohibit any person or persons to terminate any relation of employemnt [sic], or from ceasing to perform any work or labor or from recommending or persuading others by peaceful means so to do; of peacefully persuading any person to work or to abstain from working, or from ceasing to patronize or ["]employ any party to such dispute or from recommending, advising, or persuading others by peaceful means so to do"; etc.

While many of these acts are in themselves entirely harmless and would never be enjoined by any court, yet under certain circumstances the same acts might become a weapon of lawless and destructive industrial warfare demanding the protection of the courts, this section would prevent the issuance of the injunction in the Debs case (In re Debs, 158 U. S., 564);[5.430] it would prevent the issuance of the injunction in Toledo & Ann Arbor v. Pennsylvania Co. (54 Fed., 730);[5.431] it would prevent the issuance of any injunction to restrain either workmen or employers who were the objects of the most vicious form of boycott that has been passed upon by the courts, or can be devised by the ingenuity of boycotters. It changes the remedies by which the Sherman Act may be enforced, inasmuch as if any of these acts enumerated in section 266C were the means employed to enforce the restraint of trade or to damage the interstate business of any individual or corporation no injunction could be obtained either by a private individual or by the Government against such acts.

In the Debs case, a combination sought to paralyze the railroads of the United States and prevent the carrying of the mail until the railroad companies would agree not to haul Pullman cars because of a controversy between the Pullman Co. and certain of its employees who were not in the employ nor in any way related to the railroad companies. It is true there were acts of violence, but the general scheme was one of persuading all employees of the railroad companies to quit until the demands of the boycotters and strikers had been complied with. In the Toledo & Ann Arbor case the famous rule 12 of the brotherhood provided that none of its members should handle the cars of any carrier with which members of the brotherhood were in a dispute. In that case the brotherhood employees of the Pennsylvania refused to handle cars of the Toledo & Ann Arbor because of a dispute between that road and some of the brotherhood, and they threatened to quit the service of the Pennsylvania road unless it agreed to violate the provisions of the interstate-commerce act by not affording equal facilities to the cars of another road. No violence was threatened. The brotherhood

---

[5.428] *Id.* at 320.

[5.429] *Id.* at 328.

[5.430] 158 U.S. 564, 15 S. Ct. 900, 39 L. Ed. 1092 (1895).

[5.431] Toledo, A.A. & N.M. Ry. v. Pennsylvania Co., 54 F. 730 (C.C.N.D. Ohio 1893).

merely undertook to "peacefully persuade" the Pennsylvania Co. not to handle the cars of the other road under a threat of leaving their service—a thing which they had a perfect right to do to better their own condition, but not for the purpose of compelling the Pennsylvania Railroad Co. to violate the law.

The majority report quotes at length from the case of Pickett v. Walsh (192 Mass., 572), "and regret the necessity of limiting the quotations, because the whole opinion could be studied with profit." We agree with the majority that the whole opinion could have been studied with profit, since it condemns forms of "peaceful persuasion" from which the majority would withdraw equitable intervention. Speaking of the case before it, it says:[5.432] "It is a refusal to work for A, with whom the strikers have no dispute, because A works for B, with whom the strikers have a dispute, for the purpose of forcing A to force B to yield to the strikers' demands. * * * It is a combination by the union to obtain a decision in their favor by forcing other persons who have no interest in the dispute to force the employer to decide the dispute in their favor. Such a strike is an interference with the right of the plaintiffs to pursue their calling as they think best. In our opinion organized labor's right to coercion or compulsion is limited to strikes against the persons with whom the person has a trade dispute; or, to put it in another way, we are of the opinion that a strike against A, with whom the strikers have no trade dispute, to compel A to force B to the strikers' demands is unjustifiable interference with the right of A to carry on his calling as he thinks best. Only two cases to the contrary have come to our attention, namely, Bohn Manufacturing Co. v. Hollis (54 Minn., 223)[5.433] and Jeans Clothing Co. v. Watson (168 Mo., 133)."[5.434]

This case which the majority believe could be "studied with profit" is squarely against the proposal of their bill, and the two cases alluded to as being the only ones known to the court contrary to such view, for both have been overruled. Bohm [sic] Manufacturing Co. (54 Minn., 223) was overruled in Gray v. Building Trades Council (91 Minn., 171).[5.435] The second case is alluded to by the majority of the committee in support of its contentions and the majority declare the logic of the court in that case "appears unanswerable." This "unanswerable" logic was overruled by the Supreme Court of Missouri in Lohse Patent Door Co. v. Fuel [sic] (215 Mo., 421).[5.436]

The majority report also quotes in support of their contention from Vagelahm v. Gunter [sic] (167 Mass., 92), saying, "Justice Holmes, now of the Supreme Court of the United States, delivered the opinion." The opinion was delivered by Mr. Justice Allen and is squarely against ⊥ the contention of the majority, Mr. Justice Holmes having delivered a dissenting opinion in which he stood alone. The majority have been driven to the necessity of quoting from other dissenting opinions in support of their opposition, and to these we do not deem it necessary to give attention.

It is said by the majority that no question of constitutionality is involved. We submit that if the measure is to be construed, as it evidently is, to prevent the application of injunctive relief to certain acts in disputes between employer and employee which may be part of a scheme or plan to work irreparable injury, which acts could be enjoined in any other department of litigation, it is obvious that the parties affected would be denied the equal protection of the law and due process of law, coming well within the rule laid down in Connelly v. The Union Sewer Pipe Co. (184 U. S., 540);[5.437] Goldberg v. Stablemen's Union (149 Cal., 429);[5.438] Pierce v. Stablemen's Union (156 Cal., 70);[5.439] and Niagara Fire Insurance Co. v. Cornell (110 Fed. 816).[5.440]

[5.432] 192 Mass. at 587–88.

[5.433] 54 Minn. 223, 55 N.W. 1119 (1893).

[5.434] Marx & Haas Jeans Clothing Co. v. Watson, 168 Mo. 133, 67 S.W. 391 (1902).

[5.435] 91 Minn. 171, 97 N.W. 663 (1903).

[5.436] The correct citation is Lohse Patent Door Co. v. Fuelle, 215 Mo. 421, 114 S.W. 997 (1908).

[5.437] 184 U.S. 540, 22 S. Ct. 431, 46 L. Ed. 679 (1902).

[5.438] Goldberg, Bowen & Co. v. Stablemen's Local 8760, 149 Cal. 429, 86 P. 806 (1906).

[5.439] 156 Cal. 70, 103 P. 324 (1909).

[5.440] 110 F. 816 (C.C.D. Neb. 1901).

We do not consider the English act of 1906, which is quoted by the majority as a precedent for some of its proposals. There is no parallel whatever between the conditions at which the English act is aimed and the fundamental restrictions of the organic law of this country having no similitude in the constitution of the British Empire. The peculiar privileges conferred upon trades-unions by the English act of 1906 are accompanied by disabilities and criminal provisions of so drastic a nature that if they were offered as any part of the legislation of this country we should deem it our duty to oppose them in the interest of all workingmen.

We agree with the majority that "liberty and more of it is safe in the hands of the workingmen of the country." We are convinced of the merit and truth of that contention. We do not, however, believe that liberty is advanced in the person of any citizen by stripping him of remedial protection through processes which have received the deliberate and mature approval of the English-speaking race during all the centuries of its history. We can not believe that the due protection of person and property under constitutional guaranties and by remedies tested by time is "an impediment to progress," or that the destruction of the essential remedies by which person and property receive protection is "a great social advance." We believe with the President of the United States, in a famous statement made by him many years since to the American Bar Association, "It will not be surprising if the storm of abuse heaped upon the Federal courts and the political strength of Federal groups, whose plans of social reforms have met obstructions in these tribunals, shall lead to serious efforts, through legislation, to cut down their jurisdiction and cripple their efficiency. If this comes, then the responsibility for its effects, whether good or bad, must be not only with those who urge the change, but also with those who do not strive to resist its coming." (Address to American Bar Association at Detroit, 1895.)

John A. Sterling.
R. O. Moon.
Edwin W. Higgins.
Paul Howland.
Frank M. Nye.
Francis H. Dodds.

APPENDIX B.

RELATING TO CONTEMPTS.

House report 613, part 2, Sixty-second Congress, second session.

PROCEDURE IN CONTEMPT CASES.

April 29, 1912.—Referred to the House Calendar and ordered to be printed.

Mr. Sterling, from the Committee on the Judiciary, submitted the following as the

VIEWS OF THE MINORITY.

[To accompany H. R. 22591.]

We, the undersigned, members of the Committee on the Judiciary, do not agree with the action of the committee on the bill (H. R. 21100) entitled "An act to amend an act to codify, revise, and amend the laws relating to the judiciary," approved March 3, 1911.

The effect of the bill is to take from the courts the right to determine the guilt or innocence of one charged with contempt in certain cases and submit that question to a jury. If its provisions were put into actual practice it would greatly impair and might in some instances, we fear, totally destroy the power of the court to enforce its orders and decrees and maintain the peace of society.

We know of no necessity for the erratic and radical legislation provided for in this bill. He who would depart from long-established principles and usages should be able to give some reason therefor. He should be able to offer something better or show wherein abuses would be corrected or evils avoided by the departure. The proponents of this bill have failed to do either.

The committee has had extended hearings on this bill. Nowhere has it been made to appear to the committee that there has been any general abuse of the power of the courts to punish for contempt, nor has [sic] specific instances been shown where persons were wronged by the exercise of that power which this bill seeks to take from the court and lodge in another tribunal.

We desire to view this bill in three aspects: First, as to some of its provisions in detail; second, as to its constitutionality; and, third, as to whether it is desirable legislation on the ground of public policy.

Even though it were desirable to try any questions of contempt by a jury there can be no possible reason why those cases set apart by this bill to be dealt with in that way should be so distinguished from all others. It is important that all contempts should be punished with certainty and as summarily as possible consistent with justice. This is necessary in order to maintain the authority of the court and to secure to it that respect to which it is entitled. This is especially true where the acts constituting the contempt are acts of violence or where they constitute a crime. It is this class of contempts which this bill precludes from certain and summary punishment and no others. It provides that any act of disobedience to the law constituting contempt shall be tried by the jury if the act of disobedience also amounts to a crime, but it leaves the lesser offense of contempt not constituting crime to be punished summarily by the court. Punishment for violence in any form should be as certain and swift as is possible consistent with justice, and particularly so when that violence resists the execution of the processes and orders of the courts and the due course of justice. What reason can one assign for giving to the man who commits a crime in resistance to an order or process of court the right of trial by jury and denying it to the man who resists it by peaceful methods? The proponents of this bill have never here or elsewhere assigned any reason for the unjust and unfair distinction. As a concrete illustration of the working of such a law let us suppose a case. An officer of the law in the performance of his sworn duty seeks to serve one with a summons to attend court as a witness or juror, but is prevented from doing so by being assaulted and beaten. That offender is guilty of contempt by the commission of violence on an officer amounting to a crime, and under the provisions of this bill he is entitled to have his case of contempt taken away from the court whose authority he has violated and submitted to a jury, with all the delays and uncertainties incident to such practice.

In another case the officer serves one with a summons to attend as a witness or juror without molestation and makes due return to the court. But this man simply disobeys the order of the court by failure or refusal to attend, and he is denied the right of trial by jury and must submit to the summary determination of his contempt by the court whose order he disobeys. Thus, the graver offender, the one who defies the court and resists its authority by violence and crime, is given the right of trial by jury, if he demands it, while the lesser offender who simply fails or refuses to obey the order of the court is denied that right.

But even a graver injustice must inevitably flow from this invidious classification of contempts than that. The bill provides that trial by jury for contempt shall conform as nearly as may be to the practice in criminal cases prosecuted by indictment or upon information. Under that clause the court must apply the rules of evidence in criminal cases to that class of contempt cases which are submitted to a jury by this bill. It requires the court to instruct the jury that unless they believe from the evidence beyond all reasonable doubt that the accused is guilty of contempt he must be acquitted; and that if the acts of the accused can be explained on any other reasonable hypnothesis [sic] than that of guilt he must be found not guilty. But this favorable rule of evidence will only apply in the case of the graver offender who has defied the court by violence and intimidation and resisted its authority by the commission of crime. He, of all persons charged with contempt, is selected out to receive the benefit of any doubt, while the lesser offender, he who has passively disobeyed the order of the court, shall be convicted on a mere preponderance of the evidence. We believe in those rules of evidence which require strict proof, when liberty is at stake; but if they are made to apply to grave offenses in contempt cases, they should also be made to apply to slight offenses. We insist that if any distinction is to be made in this class of cases and in the degree of proof required, then the slight offender and not the grave offender should be favored in that distinction. This bill does the reverse.

Under this bill, prosecution for contempt would be subject to the delays and uncertainties incident to jury trials. This would be true in a measure even in law courts, of which the jury is a component part. Much of the time even these courts have no jury at hand. Under such conditions a jury must be drawn from the whole body of the people of the district, which would result in delay. The bill takes no account of a disagreement of the jury, or a failure to reach a verdict, and this would require the impaneling of another jury; and thus it will be seen that the authority of the court will be greatly weakened by delay and uncertainty, and the administration of justice greatly impeded by reason thereof.

It is very clear, however, that this bill is not intended, in its application, for contempt cases in the law courts. It aims at the courts of equity and seeks to impair their judicial power, by the intervention of a jury, to enforce their orders and decrees. This intervention of a jury in courts of equity, to determine questions of law and fact, is an innovation in practice unknown in the whole history of equity jurisprudence, and he who espouses it assumes the burden of showing it is a real reform and not a mere political exigency. Courts of equity have no jury nor the means of securing one. These courts grew up by reason of the very fact that they apply principles of justice and equity to the affairs of men which may be better administered by the chancellor than by a jury. They came as a necessity, to do justice in those cases where the rigid rules of law either wrought or permitted a hardship. This bill proposes to strip these courts of their true character as courts of equity and thus tie the hands of the chancellor in the administration of justice by the introduction of rules of practice which belong only to the courts of law.

It does violence to the experience of the centuries, that equity principles are best administered through the conscience of the chancellor. It is inconsistent, indeed it is folly, to confer upon courts of equity the judicial power to try and determine causes in equity and to then intervene between that court and the enforcement of its decrees another tribunal unknown to equity practice.

This bill contains one very remarkable exception. It makes a distinction between actions brought by or in the name of the United States and actions brought by persons. No reason has been assigned for this distinction, and we know of none. Section 268*d* provides:

> That nothing herein contained shall be construed to relate to contempts committed in disobedience of any lawful writ, process, order, rule, decree, or command entered in any suit or action brought or prosecuted in the name of or on behalf of the United States.

It leaves contempts arising in this class of cases to be dealt with as they are now. If this bill provides good practice in contempts arising in suits between persons, why is it not good practice in suits to which the Government is a party? If it would be bad practice in cases where the Government is a party, it would be bad in cases between persons. There is no escape from this conclusion. There is no rational or sensible reason for eliminating Government suits from the operation of the law, except that it would interfere with the proper administration of justice by hampering the courts in the enforcement of their orders and decrees and maintaining their authority and their complete integrity as courts. We fully agree that this is a conclusive reason for not applying the bill to such cases. It is just as conclusive a reason why it should not apply to other cases. It condemns the whole bill. The exception suggests the thought that it is desired to do as little harm as possible to the proper administration of justice, but to do only such harm as the political exigencies of the situation require. We respectfully submit that this is not the true and proper basis on which legislation should be predicated.

We are of the opinion that the proposed law is in violation of the Constitution. Congress can not take from the courts those inherent powers necessary to their existence or so regulate the exercise of them as to seriously impair them.

The judicial power of the United States is conferred upon the Supreme Court and such inferior courts as Congress may ordain and establish, by the Constitution, and not by any act of Congress. The language of the Constitution is as follows:

> The judicial power of the United States shall be vested in one Supreme Court and in such inferior courts as Congress may from time to time ordain and establish.

The Constitution made it the duty of Congress to create such courts as it deemed necessary, and the instant Congress had acted in the performance of its duty the judicial power vested in the courts thus created, by virtue of the Constitution.

Judicial power is the power to hear and determine causes in law and equity and to enforce the processes, orders, judgments, and decrees of the court. The power, too, to enforce its judgments and decrees are equally important as the power to hear and decide cases. A court without the power to enforce its orders would be a nullity and utterly powerless to administer justice. In the case of Kansas v. Colorado (206 U. S., p. 31 [sic]),[5.441] Mr. Justice Brewer discussed the constitutional grant of power to Congress and the courts as follows:

> In the Constitution are provisions in separate articles for the three great departments of Government—legislative, executive, and judicial. But there is this significant difference in the grants of powers to these departments: The first article, treating of legislative powers, does not make a general grant of legislative power. It reads:
>
> "All legislative powers herein granted shall be vested in a Congress," etc.
>
> And then, in Article VIII, it mentions and defines the legislative powers that are granted. By reason of the fact that there is no general grant of legislative power, it has become an accepted constitutional rule that this is a government of enumerated powers.
>
> In McCulloch v. Maryland (4 Wheat., 405, 4 L. ed., 601) Chief Justice Marshall said:
>
> "This Government is acknowledged by all to be one of enumerated powers. The principle that it can exercise only the powers granted to it would seem too apparent to have required to be enforced by all those arguments which its enlightened friends, while it was depending before the people, found it necessary to urge. That principle is now universally admitted."
>
> On the other hand, in Article III, which treats of the judicial department—and this is important for our present consideration—we find that section 1 reads that "the judicial power of the United States shall be vested in one Supreme Court and in such inferior courts as the Congress may from time to time ordain and establish." By this is granted the entire judicial power of the Nation. Section 2, which provides that "the judicial power shall extend to all cases, in law and equity, arising under this Constitution, the laws of the United States," etc., is not a limitation nor an enumeration. It is a definite declaration—a provision that the judicial power shall extend to—that is, shall include—the several matters particularly mentioned, leaving unrestricted the general grant of the entire judicial power. There may be, of course, limitations on that grant of power, but, if there are any, they must be expressed, for otherwise the general grant would vest in the courts all the judicial power which the new Nation was capable of exercising. Construing this article in the early case of Chisholm v. Georgia (2 Dall., 419, 1 L. ed., 440) the court held that the judicial power of the Supreme Court extended to a suit brought against a State by a citizen of another State. In announcing his opinion in the case, Mr. Justice Wilson said (p. 453; L. ed., p. 454):
>
> "This question, important in itself, will depend on others more important still, and may, perhaps, be ultimately resolved into one no less radical than this: Do the people of the United States form a nation?"
>
> In reference to this question attention may, however, properly be called to Hans v. Louisiana (134 U. S., 1, 33 L. ed., 842, 10 Sup. Ct. Rep., 504).
>
> The decision in Chisholm v. Georgia led to the adoption of the eleventh amendment to the constitution, withdrawing from the judicial power of the United States every suit in law or equity commenced or prosecuted against one of the United States by citizens of another State or citizens or subjects of a foreign State. This amendment refers only to suits and actions by individuals, leaving undisturbed the jurisdiction over suits or actions by one State against another. As said by Chief Justice Marshall in Cohen v. Virginia (6 Wheat., 264, 407; 5 L. ed.,

---

[5.441] The correct citation is 206 U.S. 46, 27 S. Ct. 655, 51 L. Ed. 956 (1907).

257, 291): "The amendment, therefore, extended to suits commenced or prosecuted by individuals, but not to those brought by States." See also South Dakota v. North Carolina (192 U. S., 286; 48 L. ed., 448; 24 Sup. Ct. Rep., 269).

Speaking generally, it may be observed that the judicial powers of a nation extends [sic] to all controversies justiciable in their nature, and the parties to which or the property involved in which may be reached by judicial process, and when the judicial power of the United States was vested in the Supreme and other courts, all the judicial power which the Nation was capable of exercising was vested in those tribunals; and unless there be some limitations expressed in the Constitution it must be held to embrace all controversies of a justiciable nature arising within the territorial limits of the Nation, no matter who may be the parties thereto. This general truth is not inconsistent with the decisions that no suit or action can be maintained against the Nation in any of its courts without its consent, for they only recognize the obvious truth that a nation is not, without its consent, subject to the controlling action of any of its instrumentalities or agencies. The creature can not rule the creator. (Kawananakoa v. Polyblank, 205 U. S., 349, ante, 834; 27 Sup. Ct. Rep., 526.) Nor is it inconsistent with the ruling in Wisconsin v. Pelican Insurance Co. (127 U. S., 265; 32 L. ed., 239; 8 Sup. Ct. Rep., 1370), that an original action can not be maintained in this court by one State to enforce its penal laws against a citizen of another State. That was no denial of the jurisdiction of the court, but a decision upon the merits of the claim of the State.

These considerations lead to the proposition that when a legislative power is claimed for the National Government the question is whether that power is one of those granted by the Constitution, either in terms or by necessary implication; whereas, in respect to judicial functions, the question is whether there be any limitations expressed in the Constitution on the general grant of national power.[5.442]

We believe that all the courts, where the question has arisen, have held that the power to punish for disobedience of the court's orders and decrees and for resistance to its authority is an inherent power which may not be taken away or impaired by legislative enactment. In the case of Middlebrook v. State (43 Conn., p. 257),[5.443] the court said:

The statute is not to be regarded as conferring the power to punish for contempts but merely as regulating an existing power. The power is inherent in all courts.[5.444]

But independently of the statute, we think the power is inherent in all courts. The court of justice must of necessity have the power to preserve its own dignity and to protect itself.[5.445]

The Legislature of Virginia passed an act very similar to the one proposed here, giving one accused of contempt of court a right of trial by jury. The courts of that State refused to recognize the power of the legislature to so regulate the powers of the court in contempt cases. In the Carter case[5.446] in the 96 Virginia reports the court say:

Being of opinion that the defendant was guilty of contempt, we shall not attempt any classification of it as a direct or indirect contempt. If it were a direct contempt, then its punishment was without doubt to be ascertained and fixed by the court without the intervention of a jury by the terms of the law.[5.447]

It is incumbent upon us to consider whether it was within the power of the legislature to deprive the court of jurisdiction to punish it without the intervention of a jury.[5.448]

In the courts created by the Constitution there is an inherent power of self-defense and self-preservation; that this power can be regulated, but can not be destroyed, or so far diminished as to be rendered ineffectual by legislative enactment; that it is a power necessarily resident in and to be exercised by the court itself, and that the vice of an act which seeks to deprive the court of this inherent power is not cured by providing for its exercise by a jury.[5.449]

[5.442] 206 U.S. at 81–84.
[5.443] 43 Conn. 257 (1876).
[5.444] *Id*. The quoted material is a headnote.
[5.445] *Id*. at 268.
[5.446] Carter v. Commonwealth, 96 Va. 791, 32 S.E. 780 (1899).
[5.447] 96 Va. at 805.
[5.448] *Id*.
[5.449] *Id*. at 816.

The Supreme Court of Michigan held the same doctrine in the case of Nichols v. Judge of Superior Court (130 Mich., 192),[5.450] decided in 1902. The Constitution confers judicial power on the courts of that State in much the same language as that used in the Federal Constitution. In that case the court used this language:

> The question, therefore, is again presented to this court, Have the circuit courts of this State the inherent power to punish for contempts, or are they subject to the control of the legislature? The question is an important one in the administration of the law. If the legislature can determine what acts shall constitute contempts in the circuit courts, it can abolish the power of such courts to punish for the contempts. There is no middle ground; either the courts have the absolute control, under the constitution, over contempt proceedings, or they have only such as the legislature may see fit to confer.[5.451]

In Hale v. The State (55 Ohio St. Rep., 210),[5.452] is another case in point:

> In this case the inherent power to punish contempts and enforce orders of court by summary proceedings is fully sustained, and it is said of sections 6906 and 6907 of the Revised Statutes, which make certain acts formerly punishable as contempts now punishable by indictment as offenses against public justice, that if it is to be interpreted to take away from a constitutional court its inherent right to punish offenses of this character when they are contempts of court, the statute will be invalidated.[5.453]

In Ex parte McCown (139 N. C.), decided in 1905, sections 648 to 657 of legislative act [sic] of 1871 were pleaded to prevent punishment for contempt. The court said:

> We are satisfied that at common law the acts and conduct of the petitioner, as set out in the case, constitute a contempt of court, and if the statute does not embrace this case and in terms repeals the common law applicable to it, we would not hesitate to declare the statute in that respect unconstitutional and void for reasons which we will now state.[5.454]

The case of Callahan v. Judd (23 Wis., 343),[5.455] has been cited often on the question as to whether the legislature has the power under the constitution to require courts of equity to employ a jury in their administration of the law. It is a well-considered case, and we quote from the opinion:

> I think the act invalid, and my reasons are, briefly, as follows: The power to decide questions of fact in equity cases belonged to the chancellor just as much as the power to decide questions of law. It was an inherent part and one of the constituent elements of equitable jurisdiction. If, therefore, it shall appear that by the constitution the equitable jurisdiction existing in this State is vested in the courts, I think it will necessarily follow that it would not be competent for the legislature to divest him of any part of it and confer it upon juries. If they can do so as to a part, I do not see why they may not as to the whole. If they can say that in an equity case no court shall render any judgment except upon the verdict of a jury upon questions of fact, I can see no reason why they may not say that a jury shall also be allowed to decide questions of law.
>
> But the constitution (sec. 2, art. 7) provides that "the judicial power of this State, both as to matters of law and equity, shall be vested in a supreme court, circuit courts, courts of probate, and justices of the peace. The legislature may also vest such jurisdiction as shall be deemed necessary in municipal courts. * * *"
>
> In order to determine the meaning of the phrase "judicial power as to matters of law and equity," it is only necessary to refer to the system of jurisprudence established in this country and derived from England, in which the court had certain well-defined powers in those two classes of cases. In actions of law they had the power of determining questions of law, and were required to submit questions of fact to a jury. When the constitution, therefore, vested in certain courts judicial power in matters at law, this would be construed as vesting such power

---

[5.450] 130 Mich. 187, 89 N.W. 691 (1902).

[5.451] 130 Mich. at 192-93.

[5.452] 55 Ohio St. 210, 45 N.E. 199 (1896).

[5.453] This language does not appear in the case report.

[5.454] 139 N.C. at 99-100.

[5.455] The correct citation is Callanan v. Judd, 23 Wis. 343 (1868).

as the court, under the English and American systems of jurisprudence, had always exercised in that class of actions. It would not import that they were to decide questions of fact, because such was not the judicial power in such actions. And the constitution does not attempt to define judicial power in these matters, but speaks of it as a thing existing and understood. But, to remove all doubt in actions at law, the right of a trial by jury is expressly preserved by another provision.

But, as already stated, the power of a court of chancery to determine questions of fact as well as of law was equally well established and understood. And when the constitution vested in certain courts judicial power as to matters in equity, it clothed them with this power as one of the established elements of judicial power in equity, so that the legislature can not withdraw it and confer it upon juries. * * *

The plain object of this provision was to enable the legislature to distribute the jurisdiction in both matters at law and in equity as between the circuit courts and the other courts in the State, giving the circuit courts such original jurisdiction and such appellate jurisdiction as it might see fit. But the jurisdiction there intended was jurisdiction of the suit.

It may well be that the legislature may deprive the circuit courts of original jurisdiction in actions for the foreclosure of mortgages. It is unnecessary to determine whether it could or not. But it is quite certain that this clause contains no authority for it, while leaving those courts jurisdiction of this class of action, to attempt to withdraw from them an acknowledged part of the judicial power and vest it in the jury.[5.456]

The Supreme Court of Oklahoma held an act of the legislature unconstitutional which required the courts to submit indirect contempts to a trial by jury. The following is the opinion of that court in the case of Smith v. Speed (11 Okla., 95):[5.457]

If it now should be found that the judge had no power to enforce his order at all or to punish for contempt, and that the court had no power to punish beyond a fine of $50 and imprisonment not exceeding a longer period than 10 days in the county jail, and that a change of judge may be had and a change of venue from the county, and that a trial by jury may be had to determine whether the recalcitrant party is in contempt at all or not, it will be admitted by the bar, acquainted with the law's delays, that the power to punish for contempt, either direct or indirect, being destroyed in the judge, will be to a great extent destroyed also in the court and rendered valueless.

If the contention now sought for by the plaintiff in error should be sustained, it would go to the extent that the court, in equitable proceedings, after a full hearing and a final determination and judgment upon the merits, is without the power to enforce its judgments by the imposition of a pecuniary penalty or imprisonment, and that in the endeavor to enforce its judgment by proceedings in contempt it would be subject to have its final judgment brought into review in the contempt proceedings upon a change of judge, or of venue, to a completely new jurisdiction and to a trial by jury, in which the merits of the final order, which has been made by the court, in the proceeding, should again be reviewed, including the question whether there was any merit, right, or authority of the court in the equitable proceedings in which the judgment had been rendered or the order made, and the equitable jurisdiction of the district court upon matters finally determined would thus be subject to be again brought in question by another judge in another venture and by a jury, a thing unheard of in the chancery jurisdiction. If such a state of things could be, it could but result in the degradation of courts and to make them truly the subjects of contempt.[5.458]

If the power to punish for contempt is inherent in the courts it can not be taken away or impaired by Congress or the State legislatures. If it is inherent then the courts can not exist without it. As to whether such power is inherent is well stated by the Supreme Court of Mississippi in the case of Watson v. Williams (36 Miss., 331),[5.459] as follows:

The power to fine and imprison for contempt, from the earliest history of jurisprudence, has been regarded as a necessary incident and attribute of a court, without which it could no more exist than without a judge. It is a power inherent in all courts of record and coexisting with them by the wise provisions of the common law. A court without the power effectually to

---

[5.456] *Id.* at 348–50.

[5.457] 11 Okla. 95, 66 P. 511 (1901).

[5.458] 11 Okla. at 104–05.

[5.459] Decided in 1858.

protect itself against the assaults of the lawless, or to enforce its orders, judgments, or decrees against the recusant parties before it, would be a disgrace to the legislation and a stigma upon the age which invented it.[5.460]

In Kalamazoo v. Superior Court Judge, in 75 Michigan, 274, the court argues the question in this way:

It is within the power of a legislature to change the formalities of legal procedure, but it is not competent to make such changes as to impair the enforcement of rights. * * * The functions of judges in equity cases in dealing with them is as well settled a part of the judicial power and as necessary to its administration as the functions of juries in common-law cases. Our constitutions are framed to protect all rights. When they vest judicial power they do so in accordance with all of its essentials, and when they vest it in any court they vest it as efficient for the protection of rights, and not subject to be distorted or made inadequate. The right to have equity controversies dealt with by equitable methods is as sacred as the right of trial by jury. Whatever may be the machinery for gathering testimony or enforcing decrees, the facts and the law must be decided together; and when a chancellor desires to have the aid of a jury to find out how the facts appear to such unprofessional men, it can only be done by submitting single issues of pure fact, and they can not foreclose him in his conclusions unless they convince his judgment. [. . .]

In all ages and in all countries this distinction by nature, which was never called "equitable" except in English jurisprudence, where it was first so called from an idea that the rights were imperfect because unknown in the rude ages, when property was scanty and business almost unheard of in the regions outside of great cities, has been recognized and provided for by suitable methods substantially similar in character. * * * The system of chancery jurisprudence has been developed as carefully and as judiciously as any part of the legal system, and the judicial power includes it, and always must include it. Any change which transfers the power that belongs to a judge to a jury, or to any other person or body, is as plain a violation of the Constitution as one which should give the courts executive or legislative power vested elsewhere. The cognizance of equitable questions belongs to the judiciary as a part of the judicial power and under our Constitution must remain vested where it always has been vested heretofore.[5.461]

The following cases and many others lay down the same doctrine: Ex parte Terry (128 U. S.);[5.462] Eilenbecker v. Plymouth Court (134 U. S.);[5.463] Ex parte [sic] Debs (158 U. S.).[5.464]

In conclusion, we call attention to the most recent utterance of the United States Supreme Court on this point in the case of Gompers v. Bucks Stove & Range Co. (221 U. S., 492 [sic])[5.465] and the cases therein cited.

Judge Lamar says:

For while it is sparingly to be used, yet the power of courts to punish for contempts is a necessary and integral part of the independence of the judiciary, and is absolutely essential to the performance of the duties imposed on them by law. Without it they are mere boards of arbitration, whose judgments and decrees would be only advisory.

If a party can make himself a judge of the validity of orders which have been issued, and by his own act of disobedience set them aside, then are the courts impotent, and what the Constitution now fittingly calls "judicial power of the United States" would be a mere mockery.

This power "has been uniformly held to be necessary to the protection of the court from insults and oppression while in the ordinary exercise of its duty, and to enable it to enforce its judgments and orders necessary to the due administration of law and the protection of the rights of citizens." (Bessette v. W. B. Conkey Co., 194 U. S., 333, 48 L. ed., 1004; 24 Sup. Ct. Rep., 665.)

There has been general recognition of the fact that the courts are clothed with this power, and must be authorized to exercise it without referring the issues of fact or law to another tribunal or to a jury in the same tribunal. For, if there was no such authority in the first instance, there would be no power to enforce its orders if they were disregarded in such

---

[5.460] 36 Miss. at 341.

[5.461] 75 Mich. at 283-85.

[5.462] 128 U.S. 289, 9 S. Ct. 77, 32 L. Ed. 405 (1888).

[5.463] Eilenbecker v. District Court, 134 U.S. 31, 10 S. Ct. 424, 33 L. Ed. 801 (1890).

[5.464] The correct citation is In re Debs, 158 U.S. 564 (1895).

[5.465] The correct citation is 221 U.S. 418, 31 S. Ct. 492, 55 L. Ed. 797 (1911).

independent investigation. Without authority to act promptly and independently the courts could not administer public justice or enforce the rights of private litigants. (Bessette *v.* W. B. Conkey Co., 194 U. S., 337, 48 L. ed., 1005; 24 Sup. Ct. Rep., 665.)[5.466]

What good can come from this legislation? What evils will be remedied and what rights will be more secure? If you can point to nothing it will accomplish in the way of enlightened progress then this bill should be defeated. If our present system of punishing contempts has worked well is it the part of wisdom for Congress, even if it has the power, to change it? Is is wise public policy to do so?

In this day of carping critics we hear much of criticism of our American institutions and especially of our courts. Criticism of some of the courts may be just, but that does not justify a radical change in the method of procedure that will hinder and embarrass our whole judiciary in the administration of justice. If in some instances, yet none have been cited, the judges have abused the power to punish for contempt, is it a wise policy to take from or seriously impair the power of all the judges to administer justice and maintain the dignity and authority of the courts of the land?

It has been urged that this legislation is needed to relieve the courts of the criticism that the judges are biased in their decisions as to whether their own orders have been violated and their authority defied.

They say that whether this criticism be just or not, they should be removed from the possibility of this charge. Even if this amounts to an argument it is not necessary to impair the power of the courts in the performance of their judicial functions to reach that end. If one accused of contempt feels that he can not have a fair trial before the judge "whose authority he has defied," it is not necessary to resort to the slow, uncertain, and cumbersome plan provided by this bill to remedy that evil, if it were possible under the Constitution to do so. The possibility of prejudice on the part of the judge may be eliminated by another plan much surer and more expeditious than this, and a plan that does no violence to the Constitution. Let the accused have the right to have another judge designated to try and determine whether he is guilty of the charge. A judge is qualified to know and understand the force and purpose of a decree and the importance to the litigants and to the people, of having it duly observed. This would avoid all the uncertainties and delays incident to the jury system. It would wholly remove the possibility of the accused being the victim of bias or prejudice and fully answers the charge that judges should be protected from the criticism that prejudice influences their decisions in such cases.

President Taft very ably discusses these two plans in his letter of acceptance:

DANGEROUS ATTACK ON POWER OF COURTS.

This provision in the [Democratic] platform of 1896 was regarded then as a most dangerous attack upon the power of the courts to enforce their orders and decrees, and it was one of the chief reasons for the defeat of the Democratic Party in that contest, as it ought to have been. The extended operation of such a provision to weaken the power of the courts in the enforcement of their lawful orders can hardly be overstated.

EFFECT OF JURY TRIAL.

Under such a provision a recalcitrant witness who refuses to obey a subpoena may insist on a jury trial before the court can determine that he received the subpoena. A citizen summoned as a juror and refusing to obey the writ when brought into court must be tried by another jury to determine whether he got the summons. Such a provision applies not alone to injunctions, but to every order which the court issues against persons. A suit may be tried in the court of first instance and carried to the court of appeals and thence to the Supreme Court, and a judgment and decree entered and an order issued, and then if the decree involves the defendants' [sic] doing anything or not doing anything, and he disobeys it, the plaintiff, who has pursued his remedies in lawful course for years, must, to secure his rights, undergo the uncertainties and delays of a jury trial before he can enjoy that which is his right by the decision of the highest court of the land. I say without hesitation that such a change would greatly impair the indispensable power and authority of the courts. In securing to the public the benefits of the new statutes enacted in the present administration the ultimate instrumentality to be resorted to is the courts of the United States. If now their authority is to be weakened in a manner never known in the history of the jurisprudence of England or America, except in the

---

[5.466] 221 U.S. at 450.

constitution of Oklahoma, how can we expect that such statutes will have efficient enforcement. Those who advocate this intervention of a jury in such cases seem to suppose that this change in some way will inure only to the benefit of the poor working man. As a matter of fact, the person who will secure chief advantage from it is the wealthy and unscrupulous defendant, able to employ astute and cunning counsel and anxious to avoid justice.

I have been willing, in order to avoid a popular but unfounded impression that a judge, in punishing for contempt of his own order, may be affected by personal feeling, to approve a law which should enable the contemnor upon his application to have another judge sit to hear the charge of contempt, but this, with so many judges as there are available in the Federal courts would not constitute a delay in the enforcement of the process. The character and efficiency of the trial would be the same. It is the nature and the delay of a jury trial in such cases that those who would wish to defy the order of the court would rely upon as a reason for doing so.

MAINTENANCE OF FULL POWER OF COURTS NECESSARY TO AVOID ANARCHY.

The administration of justice lies at the foundation of government. The maintenance of the authority of the courts is essential unless we are prepared to embrace anarchy. Never in the history of the country has there been such an insidious attack upon the judicial system as the proposal to interject a jury trial between all orders of the court made after full hearing and the enforcement of such orders.

We present a bill (H. R. 21722), introduced by Mr. Sterling, which provides a plan of procedure in contempt cases, and which gives to one accused of indirect contempt the right to have another judge designated to try and determine the charge of contempt against him, and recommend that it do pass.

It is as follows:

[H. R. 21722, Sixty-second Congress, second session.]

A BILL To amend an act entitled "An Act to codify, revise, and amend the laws relating to the judiciary," approved March third, nineteen hundred and eleven

Be it enacted by the Senate and House of Representatives of the United States of America in Congress assembled, That the act entitled "An act to codify, revise, and amend the laws relating to the judiciary," approved March third, nineteen hundred and eleven, be, and the same is hereby, amended by inserting after section two hundred and sixty-eight thereof seven new sections, to be numbered, respectively, 268 a, 268 b, 268 c, 268 d, 268 e, 268 f, and 268 g, reading as follows:

"SEC. 268 a. That contempts of court are divided into two classes, direct contempts and indirect contempts, as hereinafter defined.

"SEC. 268 b. That contempts committed in the presence of the court or of a judge at chambers are direct contempts. All other contempts are indirect contempts.

"SEC. 268 c. A person charged with direct contempt of court, if found guilty, shall be punished summarily and judgment thereon shall be entered of record accordingly, which judgment shall contain a statement of the acts constituting the contempt and a statement, if any, of the accused relied on as a defense or made in extenuation of the offense and the sentence of the court in the case.

"SEC. 268 d. Any person charged with indirect contempt of court shall be given a written statement of the charge or charges against him specifically setting forth the acts on which the charge of contempt is predicated. Thereupon the accused shall be arraigned and his plea entered of record. If the accused should plead guilty to the charge the court shall enter judgment thereon and impose sentence in the case. If he pleads not guilty the court shall set the case for trial and admit the accused to bail until final determination of the case. The trial shall be by the court, and witnesses ⊥ called and examined for and against the accused as in criminal cases. If the accused shall be found guilty, judgment shall be entered accordingly and the punishment prescribed. Said punishment may be by fine or imprisonment, or both, in the discretion of the court: *Provided*, That in cases where the fine is payable to the United States the same shall not exceed the sum of one thousand dollars in any case; and in no case shall the term of imprisonment exceed six months.

"SEC. 268 e. If any person who has entered a plea of not guilty to a charge of indirect contempt shall make affidavit that the judge before whom the case is set for trial in the first instance is prejudiced against him and that on account of such prejudice he believes he can not have a fair and impartial trial such judge shall designate forthwith some other judge to hear and determine the case.

"SEC. 268 f. That the evidence taken on the trial of any person accused of indirect contempt shall be preserved by bill of exceptions and any judgment entered in such case may be reviewed on appeal or by writ of error as now provided by law in criminal cases and such judgment may be reversed or modified as justice may require. When an appeal is taken or a writ of error granted, execution of the judgment shall be stayed and the accused shall be admitted to bail in such sum as is fixed by the court.

"SEC. 268 g. That the provisions of this act shall apply to all proceedings for contempt in all courts of the United States except the Supreme Court: *Provided*, That this act shall not affect any contempt proceedings pending at the time of the passage of this act."

The fundamental distinction between this bill and H. R. 21100 is that the latter provides a trial by jury in cases where the acts constituting the contempt also constitute a criminal offense, while this bill provides that in indirect contempts the accused may have another judge to try the contempt.

We believe that it meets every criticism, just or unjust, and avoids every evil that may be charged against the present practice.

It divides contempts into two classes, direct and indirect, and gives to each class the usual and natural definition.

It defines direct contempts as those committed in the presence of the court or of a judge at chambers. Under it these contempts shall be punished summarily by the court. No one would change the practice in that regard, and neither of the bills would deprive the court of the power to deal with such contempts in that way. It further provides that the judgment in such case shall be entered of record and that the judgment shall contain a statement of the acts and a statement, if any, of the accused, relied on as a defense or as an extenuation of the offense.

It provides a specific plan of procedure in all cases which charge an indirect contempt of court. The accused may in such case, upon his own affidavit that the judge is prejudiced against him and that on account thereof he believes that he can not have a fair trial, have another judge designated to hear and determine his case.

The bill also provides for a review by the higher courts on appeal or by writ of error.

We repeat that the only charge made against the present practice is that judges who have issued orders or rendered judgments and decrees should not be permitted to pass upon the question as to whether a person has violated such order or decree or has defied or assailed the authority of the court over which that judge presides. It is said that a judge under such circumstances is prone to bias and that his decision might be tainted with prejudice against the accused. This bill eliminates such a possibility and it does it more effectually than does the bill reported by the majority. Under that bill the judge conducts the trial of the case before the jury, he passes upon the admissibility of the evidence, and delivers the charge to the jury, so that under the system provided by that bill there is still a possibility of the same criticism against him as in the present practice. The accused might still feel that he was the victim of judicial bias.

Such is not the case in the bill offered by the minority. Under its provisions the judge whose decree has been violated or whose authority has been defied is eliminated from the case and it is submitted to another judge who could have no possible prejudice against the accused, because he has no connection with the case. This bill meets all objection to the present practice without doing violence to the long-established principles of equity which forbids [sic] the intervention of a jury in equity proceedings. It accomplishes the desired end without taking away or impairing the judicial power of the court conferred upon it by the Constitution.

Respectfully submitted.

John A. Sterling.
R. O. Moon.
Edwin W. Higgins.
Paul Howland.
Frank M. Nye.
Francis H. Dodds.

REPORT OF THE HOUSE COMMITTEE ON THE JUDICIARY (MINORITY VIEWS)
H.R. Rep. No. 627, Pt. 3
63d Cong., 2d Sess.
May 13, 1914

Mr. NELSON, from the Committee on the Judiciary, submitted the following

MINORITY VIEWS.

[To accompany H. R. 15657.]

The undersigned, a member of the Committee on the Judiciary, having had under consideration H. R. 15657 and similar bills, being unable to agree with the majority of the committee, submits the following minority views:

The so-called antitrust bill reported by the committee is a distinct disappointment to those who sincerely desire to destroy private monopoly. The question of the suppression of trusts receives only incidental consideration. Instead of directly dealing with the trust problem, which was the original program, the committee has turned to side issues, such as discrimination in price, exclusive contracts, and the use of injunctions in labor disputes. These subjects are treated irrespective of the question of restraint of trade or of monopoly; such vague phraseology is employed, and so many exceptions are made that it becomes doubtful whether it is harm or benefit that results. In so far as this bill touches the problem of private monopoly at all, it legislates in an arbitrary way against the form of the evil and not against the substance. This bill as a whole will afford little relief to the people from the oppressions of the trusts.

After months of hearings before the Judiciary Committee upon certain tentative bills prepared by a partisan subcommittee, in consultation with the President, the outcome has been this compromise measure, which is clearly intended as an assurance to big business and a sop to public opinion. During the hearings no big trusts appeared to oppose the tentative bills, nor has the introduction of this final draft created any uneasiness or flurry in Wall Street. On the other hand the smaller business men of the country have been very much concerned because of the far-reaching interference with business affairs that may follow the enactment of this measure. Like a Don Quixote the committee sallied forth valiantly to overthrow the giant monopoly, but under the pressure of political expediency it turned aside to assail the windmills of little business. The spirit of compromise which runs through every section of this bill is something quite apart from the spirit of the brave declaration that "A private monopoly is indefensible and intolerable," but rather in it we detect the "atmosphere of accommodation and mutual understanding" between the Government and big business which the President advocated in his trust message.

ANALYSIS OF THE BILL.

Sections 2-4 of this bill are designed to check methods of unfair competition. This matter is dealt with entirely apart from the question whether these business methods restrain interstate commerce or tend to monopoly. Nor is it treated comprehensively or in a satisfactory manner. Out of all the unfair business methods whereby the trusts have been able to crush the independents two are selected, discrimination in price and the making of exclusive contracts. This bill apparently permits trusts arbitrarily to refuse to sell to persons whom they wish to crush, except in reference to the products of mines, and it does not deal at all with such familiar practices as selling below cost to destroy the business of a competitor, placing prohibitive prices upon raw materials which are needed in the production of other commodities, spying upon the business of competitors, the doing of business under a fictitious name, or with intimidating the customers of a competitor by unwarranted threats of suits for alleged infringement of patents. To single out two unfair business practices—discrimination in price and the making of exclusive contracts—may have the bad effect of creating the impression that the other methods used to crush the independents are not under the ban of the law. As to the two practices prohibited, such exceptions are made in this bill that it apparently permits the trusts to do the very acts it aims to prevent. On the other hand these ambiguous sections may prove harassing and burdensome to the small business man. These new provisions are as likely to weaken as to strengthen the Sherman Act.

PRICE DISCRIMINATION.

Section 2 prohibits discrimination "in price between different purchasers of commodities in the same or in different communities." It is directed against an undoubted evil. But does this bill afford adequate protection against the continuance of this evil?

It must be noted that only discrimination "in price" is prohibited. There certainly can be many discriminations of a most serious character which do not involve the price at which a commodity is sold. One customer may be favored as against another in the manner and time of delivery, in more lenient terms of credit, and in any number of other terms of sale. This section permits all discriminations between purchasers except those relating to price.

Again, it is doubtful whether this section has any application to discrimination in price in bids and offers for sale to proposing purchasers. It prohibits discrimination only as between "different purchasers of commodities."

Nor does this section apply when commodities are not "sold for use, consumption, or resale within the United States." This exception clearly sanctions the practice of trusts in selling their commodities cheaper abroad than at home. What discrimination in price could be more vicious? Yet this bill expressly permits such discriminations against our own people.

There is, also, the big loophole that the discrimination in price must be shown to have been made with the purpose or intent to destroy or wrongfully injure the business of a competitor. This is a very indefinite element, yet, whenever such intent can not be proven, prosecutions for discrimination must fail.

Then, too, what discriminations in price may not be covered up as due to the grade, quality, or quantity of the commodity sold permitted by the first proviso? To allow discriminations on account of the quantity sold is to favor the trusts against the independents, the big purchasers against the small fellows.

The second proviso similarly destroys the intent of this section. It provides that this section shall not be deemed to prevent persons engaged in interstate commerce "from selecting their own customers." If trusts are given the power to select their own customers, they may discriminate between proposing purchasers. They may impose any conditions which they choose before they will deal with any proposing customer. They may refuse to deal with more than one person in any community, or for that matter throughout the United States. As far at least as this section goes, this proviso would have sanctioned the arbitrary action of the Motion Picture Trust in refusing to lease films to anybody but the General Film Co. This will permit a trust which controls the supply of some raw material, other than the product of any mine, which is needed in the production of some other commodity to absolutely refuse to sell such raw material whenever it cares to branch out into the manufacture of such other commodity. This proviso, it is probable, will sanction the practice of manufacturers to refuse to sell to any middleman who will not agree to sell their commodities at a certain fixed price, although the Supreme Court has decided that such efforts to control the prices to consumers are illegal.

The merits of this section can best be understood when it is restated in such manner as to bring out the discriminations permitted:

"That any person engaged in commerce is permitted to discriminate in price and in any other terms of sale in bids or offers for sale made to proposing purchasers of commodities, and every such person engaged in commerce is permitted to discriminate between different purchasers of commodities in the same or different sections or communities in reference to any terms of sale other than the price of such commodities and is permitted to discriminate in price if he merely gives a lower price to purchasers in foreign countries or if such discrimination in price is made on account of differences in the grade, quality, or quantity of the commodity sold or because of differences in the cost of transportation or if such discrimination results from the selection of their own customers by persons engaged in selling goods, wares, or merchandise in commerce or if it can not be established that such discrimination in price is made with the purpose and intent to thereby destroy or wrongfully injure the business of a competitor, either of such purchaser or seller."

MINE PRODUCTS.

In section 3 an exception from the permission granted in section 2 that all corporations engaged in interstate commerce may select their own customers is made in reference to the products of mines. The owners and operators of mines and the persons "controlling" the product of any mine are prohibited from "arbitrarily" refusing to sell such product of any mine to any "responsible person, firm, or corporation." The persons controlling the supply of any other commodity, even if it is some raw material required in the production of other commodities, may select their own customers and may arbitrarily refuse, at their pleasure, to deal with any person, firm, or corporation. Why should the products of mines be thus singled out? If this is a sound principle, why should it not be applied generally as to all commodities, or at least as to all raw materials which are required in the production of other commodities?

This section is open to the further criticism that the language employed is vague and indefinite. To convict an owner or operator of any mine, or any person controlling the product of any mine under this section, it is necessary to prove that he "arbitrarily" refused to sell such product "to a responsible person, firm, or corporation." The use of the words "arbitrarily" and "responsible" affords loopholes which may make it difficult to prosecute anyone successfully.

EXCLUSIVE CONTRACTS.

Section 4 aims at another method of unfair competition. This is the practice of trusts to refuse to sell to anyone who will not agree to handle or use exclusively their products. Here, again, there is an undoubted evil. The only question is whether this section adequately deals with that evil. It applies only to the leasing and selling of commodities. Should it not include, also, the licensing of the use of commodities by others, and the furnishing of goods by bailors to bailees? The prohibitions of this section may be evaded if commodities are not sold outright or leased, but are handled through nominal agents or bailees.

Again, this section prohibits exclusive contracts only in reference to the commodities "of a competitor or competitors of the lessor or seller." It is not enough to prove that a trust has required exclusive contracts from its customers. It must also be proven that the person against whom the contracts were directed was a business competitor of the trust. If the trust made the exclusive contract for the benefit of some allied corporation, or for any reason other than that of business competition, it can escape prosecution under this section.

What will be the effect of this section upon the right of persons engaged in interstate commerce to select their own customers, which section 2 of this bill seems to be so solicitous to protect? When sections 2 and 4 are read together, it is clear that this bill intends to confer upon sellers the right to choose their own customers. This implies that the seller may impose any conditions upon the customer which he chooses to make. But in section 4 he is prohibited from entering into any agreement or understanding with his customer to the effect that the latter will not use the commodities of some competitor of the seller. Yet the seller may select his own customers, and may refuse to sell for any reason that he sees fit, including the fact that the proposing customer handles the products of some competitor. As long as the seller does not enter into a definite agreement or understanding with the customer that he shall not handle or use the commodities of some competitor, he can not be prosecuted although he may refuse to sell to anyone who will not handle his goods exclusively.

This bill affords opportunities for doing secretly and in a roundabout way what it prohibits to be done aboveboard.

MACHINERY FOR ENFORCEMENT OF ANTITRUST LAWS.

In seeking a solution of the trust problem no matter is more vitally important than that of providing means for the more vigorous enforcement of the antitrust laws. The Sherman Act has been upon the statute books for almost a quarter of a century; but the trusts have been constantly increasing both in number and in power. The fault has not been that the prohibitions of the Sherman law have not been broad enough; but that this act has not been vigorously enforced. A large number of most excellent proposals to strengthen the Sherman law so as to make it practically self-enforcing were presented to the Committee on the Judiciary. Most of these proposals have been ignored. This bill will not permit States or independents to intervene in dissolution suits against trusts to protect their rights. Nothing is done to hasten the disposition of antitrust cases in courts. Even the suggestion that the Federal courts should be prohibited from enforcing contracts involving violations of the antitrust laws was rejected.

Section 6 aims to afford means for parties injured by the unlawful conduct of trusts to recover threefold damages for the losses sustained as provided in the Sherman Act. Although the purpose of this section is good, it is open to severe criticism. It does not permit private parties to make use of the facts and finding [sic] in suits brought by the Government, in accordance with section 13 of this act, for violations of any of its provisions. The decrees which private parties may make use of in their suits for damages are described as being "to the effect that a defendant has or has not entered into a contract, combination in the form of trust or otherwise, or conspiracy in restraint of trade or commerce, or has or has not monopolized, or attempted to monopolize, or combined with any person or persons to monopolize, any part of commerce, in violation of any of the antitrust laws." In other words the decrees which private parties may plead in damage suits which they may bring against trusts as res adjudicata are decrees secured in Government suits brought under the Sherman law. Where the decree secured by the Government is to the effect that a trust has discriminated in price between different communities or individuals or that it has entered into exclusive contracts, private parties are not allowed to plead such findings as res adjudicata in any damage suits which they may bring under this act.

Another defect in this section is to be found in the second paragraph. This provides that the statute of limitations in reference to any private right of action shall be suspended during the pendency of the Government suit. This does not always permit independents ⊥ adequate time to bring their suits for damages against trusts after the decree in the Government suit is entered. They have only such time to begin their suits as had not expired under the statute of limitations when the Government suit was instituted—whether this be one week or five years. Inasmuch as the right of action of private parties was very largely merely theoretical before the decree in the Government suit was available, a much better provision would be to allow private parties one or two years after the entry of the decree in the Government suit to begin their suits for damages.

The most vital defect in section 6 remains to be noticed. This is contained in the provision that decrees and judgments secured in Government suits may be pleaded as res adjudicata in suits between trusts and private parties either "in favor or against such defendant." To allow the decrees and judgments in Government suits to be pleaded "in favor of" the trusts against private parties who may sue them is violative of all sense of justice. Under this provision whenever the Government suit miscarries or an Attorney General allows a feeble compromise decree to be entered, a trust may plead the decree secured to prevent private parties injured by its unlawful conduct from securing relief therefrom or damages therefor.

These private parties have never had their day in court. Though they may be able conclusively to prove that they have been injured by a trust they are denied all chance for relief whenever the Government is unsuccessful in its suit, or when it enters into compromises with trusts. Though the Government mishandled the case, they had no chance to intervene in the suit to protect their rights; yet, when the Government suit fails, the trust may plead the decree therein as a bar against any suit which these private parties might bring. This provision is not only a measure in the interests of the trusts, but apparently violates the fifth amendment to the Constitution, inasmuch as it will operate to deprive private parties in many cases, without due process of law, of rights of action held to be property within the meaning of that amendment. The provision that the decrees in Government suits may be pleaded as res adjudicata against trusts in suits brought by private citizens is on an entirely different plane from the provision that the trusts may plead the decrees in Government suits in their favor. The trusts have had their day in court, and despite their pleadings the court has entered a final decree or judgment against them. The private parties who sue trusts after the decree in the Government suit has been entered have not had their day in court; and yet this section would deprive them absolutely of redress in a court of justice.

Section 12 is intended to secure the more vigorous enforcement of the criminal law against monopolists and trust magnates. What does it do to secure this end? The first part of this section provides that the guilt of the corporation shall be deemed to be also that of the individual directors, officers, and agents of such corporation; but the second part provides that only those directors, officers, or agents "who shall have authorized, ordered, or done any of such prohibited acts," shall be punished. Under the Sherman law as it stands those who authorize, order, or do any act in violation thereof may be criminally prosecuted. It is extremely doubtful whether this section will make the penalties of the antitrust laws more personal than they now are.

Attention must be directed, also, to the fact that the maximum fine which is provided in this section and throughout this bill is $5,000. To fine a great trust a maximum of $5,000, when the loot it gained may have been many hundred times that sum, is most ridiculous. The maximum should be much greater in amount. Nor is there any provision in this measure to the effect that punishments for violations of the antitrust laws shall not be omitted by suspension or other judicial action. Any judge may still suspend sentence in the case of trust officials found guilty of having violated the Sherman law.

Section 14 deals with another method of providing better machinery for the enforcement of the antitrust laws. This section would permit private parties who are being injured by the unlawful actions of trusts to secure injunctive relief. This is a most desirable provision, but the language of this section is such as to make it as difficult as possible for injured parties to secure relief. To do so it is not enough that they establish that they have suffered loss because of the action of some trust, but they must also show that a continuance of these acts is "threatened." This makes rigid a principle that is wholly proper in most equity cases, but which will often operate to deny a remedy to independents. Nothing is more difficult to prove than that acts of discrimination and other unfair practices of trusts are likely to be repeated. Again, there is a provision that no injunction shall be granted for the relief of a party injured by a trust except upon "the execution of a proper bond against damages for an injunction improvidently granted." To require an independent to give a bond sufficiently large to compensate a trust against possible damages will often prevent him from securing relief from the unfair tactics of the trust. Without this provision the matter of the bond would be left at the discretion of the court, in accordance with the provisions of the judiciary act.

HOLDING COMPANIES.

This measure deals, also, with two manifestations of the trust evil—the holding company and interlocking directorates. Both of these means have been employed by trusts to secure a stranglehold upon the industries of the country; but they represent only two of many forms of the evil of private monopoly. The possibility that holding companies and interlocking directorates may be used as a means to subject industry to Wall Street's dominance should be guarded against in every manner possible; but it is not enough to deal with these two manifestations of the trust evil, while the real and fundamental source of the evil exists through common-stock ownership or other forms of interlocking control.

Section 8 deals with the evil of the holding company. It does so in a most unsatisfactory manner. Nothing in this section applies to holding companies already organized. As for the organization of future holding companies, Mr. Samuel Untermyer, the attorney of the Pujo money-trust committee, has stated that this section will probably impair "the existing threadbare remedies" of minority stockholders. It prohibits one corporation from holding the stock of another corporation where the "effect" of such acquisition is to eliminate or substantially lessen competition. In the Northern Securities case the criterion when the holding by one corporation of the stock of another is unlawful under the Sherman antitrust law was laid down as being, not that the holding of the stock of such other corporation must be shown to have had the effect of lessening competition, but that it confers a potential power to lessen competition, whether that power has been exercised or not. Had this section of the bill been law, the Northern Securities case[5.467] would have been decided against the Government. Under this bill a corporation may acquire stock in any competing corporation, even to the point where it controls such other corporation, if it can not be shown to have exercised that control with the effect of lessening competition. If this section were genuinely intended to strengthen the Sherman Act in dealing with the evil of the holding company, why did it not simply declare that no corporation shall acquire any of the stock of another corporation where the acquisition of the whole of the stock of such other corporation would constitute a violation of the Sherman Antitrust Act? Instead of thus strengthening the Sherman law by preventing one competing corporation from edging toward the control of another, it provides that the potential power to lessen competition shall no longer be the criterion to determine the legality of a holding company's operations, but whether it has exercised that power with the effect of lessening competition.

REGULATION OF INTERLOCKING DIRECTORATES.

Section 9 deals with the evil of interlocking directorates. Such interlocking directorates have been one of the means employed for the building up of a powerful money trust, dominating many great industries. But interlocking directorates are but one of many manifestations of the real evil—the interlocking control of corporations in the same or allied fields of business. The interlocking control of such corporations must be prevented or there will be no real competition between them. Interlocking control of competing corporations may be evidenced by identity of stock holdings, voting trusts, and dummy directors as well as by interlocking directorates. The interlocking control is the vice, and it should be prevented, no matter how it may be manifested. There may be some doubtful advantage in forcing big business to substitute dummy directors for interlocking directorates; but certainly this does not solve the great evil of the Money Trust. There may be interlocking control although there are no interlocking directorates, and while it continues there will be no real competition.

Every paragraph in this section has the vice of striking at a form of the evil and not at the root of the evil itself. The first paragraph prohibits any person who is a director, officer, or employee of a cormon [sic] carrier from being also at the same time a director, officer, or employee of a corporation which sells materials to that carrier, or which does construction work for it, or of a bank or trust company which acts as a fiscal agent of such carrier. This paragraph is directed against the vice of having a set of men who control one corporation deal with themselves through another corporation which they also control, at the expense of the minority stockholders. This is one of the evils which the interlocking control of corporations makes possible. Dealings between two corporations in each of which the same set of men have a controlling interest are likely to result in the robbery of the minority stockholders. Such transactions should be prohibited, no matter how the interlocking control may have been secured. This paragraph does not apply at all to industrial corporations; nor does it directly prohibit such transactions as related to common carriers. It says only that the directors, officers, and employees of a common carrier shall not at the same time be directors, officers, or employees of banks, supply and construction companies with which such carriers have

---

[5.467] Northern Sec. Co. v. United States, 193 U.S. 197, 24 S. Ct. 436, 48 L. Ed. 679 (1904).

business relations; but they may own all of the stock of such other companies. Dealings which rob the minority stockholders may continue, although interlocking directorates are prohibited.

The other provisions of this section similarly aim at a form of the evil of interlocking control and not at the evil itself. Persons are prohibited from acting at the same time as directors, officers, or employees of two corporations of certain classes. Yet it permits these corporations to be controlled by the same man or the same set of men, if they but exercise their control through some other manner than that of interlocking directors. They may exercise their control through voting trusts, through dummy directors, or in any other manner, save that they must not themselves act as interlocking directors. One man or one set of men may control every bank and trust company in a city of above 100,000 population, or all the great banks of the country, but they must not act as directors of any two of the banks. This section permits identity of stock holdings in the corporations in which it prohibits interlocking directorates. While identity in stock holdings is permitted to continue it is idle to speak about restoring competition between these corporations. There will be interlocking control even when interlocking directorates are prohibited. A form of the evil only is prohibited; but the evil itself may still prevail.

THE EXEMPTION OF CERTAIN ORGANIZATIONS FROM THE ANTITRUST LAWS.

The apparent object aimed at in section 7 is to relieve certain classes of organizations which are generally recognized to be beneficial from the penalties of the Sherman antitrust law in carrying on their normal and proper activities. This is a most laudable object. The antitrust laws should place no restrictions upon the activities which the organizations enumerated in the first paragraph of this section normally carry on. They are beneficial, should be encouraged, and not discouraged.

None of the classes of organizations enumerated in this first paragraph have ever been held subject to the Sherman Antitrust Act or asked for exemption other than labor and farmer organizations. Labor and farmer organizations should not be treated as trusts. If labor is a commodity, it is certainly entirely different from every other commodity, inasmuch as the commodity labor can never be divorced from the human being—the laborer. And organizations of farmers at most aim merely to control the product of their own labor and not, like the great trusts, to engross the products of other men's labor. These organizations serve to protect the people against the evils of monopoly, not to enhance those evils.

The weakness of this first paragraph of section 7 is that it leaves the status of labor organizations under the antitrust laws uncertain and forbids in effect the cooperative efforts of farmers in buying commodities or selling their products. It is provided that nothing in the antitrust laws shall be construed to forbid the "existence or operation" of labor organizations or to forbid individual members of such organizations from carrying out "the legitimate objects thereof." What is meant by the "operation" of labor organizations and by "the legitimate objects" of such organizations is most vague. The majority of the committee, in its report, explains the purpose of this paragraph to be to make certain that the Sherman Antitrust Act does not "warrant the courts under interpretations heretofore given to that law to enter a decree for the dissolution of such organizations." If this is the correct interpretation of this paragraph, it will merely prevent suits for the dissolution of labor organizations, but will permit the taking out of injunctions under the Sherman Antitrust Act against labor organizations to restrain them from carrying out their purposes, and the bringing of suits for triple damages against them under that act.

This paragraph applies only to organizations "instituted for the purposes of mutual help, and not having capital stock or conducted for profit." We can not be entirely certain that all labor unions will be held to be conducted "for the purposes of mutual help" and as being not "conducted for profit." There can be no doubt that as to "consumers, agricultural, or horticultural" organizations this limitation is a fatal defect. Every organization of farmers which aims to cooperatively bargain as to the products of its members is "conducted for profit," and many of them have "capital stock." The only sort of farmer organization which this section sanctions is one which does nothing more than to discuss better agricultural methods. As soon as farmers combine to get better prices for their products, or to sell directly to consumers, this paragraph affords them no relief from the antitrust laws. In fact, this section is likely to bring down upon them the Sherman Act with all its penalties. When legislation is enacted specifically exempting certain classes of organizations, district attorneys and courts are likely to construe the antitrust laws as rendering unlawful the activities of the classes of organizations not exempted. This paragraph may sound the death knell to cooperation among farmers to better their conditions of life. The Department of Agriculture is constantly issuing literature urging the farmers to cooperate. Only recently a special commission which we sent to Europe to get suggestions upon how to encourage cooperation among the farmers has made its report. Yet this bill will not legalize farmer organizations if they are "conducted for profit" or have "capital stock."

The second paragraph of section 7 was inserted at a very late stage in the preparation of this bill. In the hearings before the committee there was no claim made by anyone that such legislation was either needed or desired. Nor is it clear what sort of agreements among common carriers are sanctioned by this paragraph. Associations of common carriers are authorized to make "any lawful agreement as to any matter which is subject to the regulating or supervisory jurisdiction of the Interstate Commerce Commission," but this is not to authorize "joint agreements by common carriers to maintain rates." Does this mean that carriers may agree to change rates but may not agree to "maintain" such rates? What sort of agreements among common carriers does this paragraph authorize, and what possible benefit do the people derive therefrom? Why insert an exemption from the antitrust laws which nobody asked for and which is of uncertain meaning?

THE INJUNCTION AND CONTEMPT PROVISIONS.

The last part of this measure deals with a matter which has no direct relation to the trust question—that of the use of injunctions in connection with labor disputes. In section 7 the exemption of labor unions from the operations of the antitrust laws is dealt with; but sections 15–23 have no reference to this question. They relate generally to procedure in injunction cases and to trials for contempt. Only one of these sections—section 18—applies to injunctions in labor disputes alone. In the Sixty-second Congress these sections were presented as two separate bills—the Clayton injunction limitation bill and the Clayton contempt bill.

Whatever divergent views Members may hold as to the desirability of these sections, there can be no question that they have no proper place in an antitrust bill. To combine these propositions with an antitrust bill, which throughout represents a minimum of what might be done to strengthen the existing law, has no merit other than that of political expediency.

John M. Nelson.

The foregoing views are concurred in.

A. J. Volstead.

REPORT OF THE HOUSE COMMITTEE ON THE JUDICIARY (MINORITY VIEWS)
H.R. Rep. No. 627, Pt. 4
63d Cong., 2d Sess.
May 13, 1914

Mr. MORGAN of Oklahoma, from the Committee on the Judiciary, submitted the following

MINORITY VIEWS.

[To accompany H. R. 15657.]

I am in hearty sympathy with the object and purpose of the legislation proposed in this bill, but I do not believe that all the provisions in the proposed measure are wise. In my opinion some are dangerous to the business and commercial interests of the country and will do more harm than good. On the whole the bill if enacted into law would be a great disappointment to the country. It certainly can not be regarded as a broad, comprehensive, carefully prepared measure which will protect the general public from the evils of big business and at the same time open to the legitimate business interests of the country a highway upon which to travel with safety and certainty. While in all so-called antitrust legislation we must keep in mind the welfare of the people generally, we must not ignore the fact that any material injury to the business of the country reacts and injures the people, whose interests it is our first duty to serve.

Taking the antitrust provisions of the bill as a whole, if they were all enacted into law, they would not destroy a single trust, abolish a single monopoly or add materially to the competition now existing. The provisions of the bill, if placed on the statute books, will not reduce the size of our great corporations, or materially lessen the power they now possess to arbitrarily control prices. Enact this bill into law, and big business will go on and on with no adequate restraint, either in the way of broad, comprehensive statutory enactments, or in the way of a properly empowered administrative, or semijudicial commission, which I regard as absolutely necessary for the protection of the people, as well as for the substantial and permanent prosperity of our industrial and business interests, both at home and abroad. It is true that there are some provisions of this bill which strike at existing evils in our interstate commerce, which will tend to prevent some unfair practices and business methods now resorted to, but great corporations, controlled and managed by vicious and unscrupulous directors, while desisting from the few practices prohibited in this bill, will invent other methods equally reprehensible, and equally effective to enable them to accomplish their ends. We can not assume that evil-disposed business men have exhausted their ingenuity in the invention of obnoxious business methods. So next Congress we will have something new to prohibit, and so on from year to year, but in the meantime nothing is settled, and no real relief is afforded the people. To illustrate: Section 2 of this bill makes it unlawful to discriminate in price with the intent or purpose to destroy or wrongfully injure a competitor. The only discrimination here prohibited is discrimination in price. But there are thousands of ways by which we may discriminate. This section easily could be made more comprehensive in its scope by making it unlawful to discriminate in price, terms, or otherwise. We would then make all kinds of discrimination unlawful—not only the kind of discrimination with which we are now familiar, but the prohibition would include all acts, practices, and methods which may be used in the future in perpetrating discrimination.

Again, section 2 prohibits only discrimination with the intent or purpose to destroy a competitor. Here is another illustration of the extreme narrow application of the provisions of the bill. It may be that Congress should seek to protect one competitor from another, but the great primary, fundamental purpose of this legislation should be to protect the masses of the people, to safeguard the public welfare against a well-known evil. If discrimination should be prohibited, we should prohibit discrimination done with the intent and purpose to establish and maintain the evil, which we wish to eradicate. This evil is monopoly. The one thing we are seeking to maintain in our business and industrial world is healthy, effective competition. It follows, therefore, that we should prohibit not only discrimination done with intent to destroy or injure a competitor, but above all we should prohibit discrimination perpetrated with the intent to establish monopolistic conditions or to materially or substantially lessen competition. I know that it may be said that the Sherman law now prohibits an attempt to monopolize. But the same argument is made by those who oppose all antitrust legislation. They assert that the Sherman law is all sufficient to prevent monopoly, and maintain competition. If it is necessary to enact a special law to prohibit discrimination we should prohibit all kinds of discrimination, done with the purpose or intent to establish a monopoly, to destroy or substantially lessen competition, or with the intent to accomplish any purpose that is inconsistent with good business ethics, or that is inimical to the public interests.

I think no one will deny this proposition: Business should have the greatest freedom consistent with the public good. Like individual freedom, liberty in business should be limited, restricted, and circumscribed only when necessary for the public good. Even our State governments should assume control of private business only when the private business becomes impressed with a public use. For greater reasons, the Federal Government should interfere with private business only when the private business becomes of public consequence from a national viewpoint. And I thoroughly believe there are many private business concerns engaged in industrial commerce which have become of public consequence, which from a national viewpoint have become impressed with a public use, and in the interests of the people of the Nation should be placed under strict Federal supervision and control. But I think it is very unwise to enact laws which will place almost an innumerable number of small business concerns under Federal laws, which will be a source of annoyance to owners of such concerns, hamper and hinder them in the management, development, extension of their business, multiply lawsuits, crowd our Federal courts with litigation, without materially benefiting the people, or substantially contributing to the solution of the real business problems confronting us as a Nation. Would it not be a better policy to limit Federal enactments which restrict the freedom of private business to those concerns which have clearly become impressed with a public use and which are of public consequence from a national viewpoint?

The National Government is entering upon dangerous ground when it enters upon the policy of enforcing uniformity in prices to all persons and all sections. The policy of the Government is to maintain competition. That was the object of the Sherman antitrust law. That is the object of the proposed legislation. Monopoly neans [sic] the absence of competition. Competition means a contest for business, for customers. The object of competition is to insure purchasers reasonable prices for articles purchased. Reduction of price has been universally regarded as a legitimate method of securing business. Merchants, manufacturers, and dealers have been left to fix their own prices. Is the National Government ready to enact a law that will tend to compel uniformity of prices—that will not permit a merchant or manufacturer to lower his prices to secure customers, to obtain business? Is not competition which reduces prices the kind of competition that will benefit the people? Here is the difficulty with the competition that now exists. The big concerns do not compete in price. The so-called independent concerns follow the prices fixed by the trusts. This tendency appeared in the testimony of one witness who testified before the committee in behalf of the independent oil dealers. He frankly admitted that the independent dealers sold at the price fixed by the Standard Oil Co.

Section 7 authorizes the existence and operation of labor, agricultural, and other organizations instituted for mutual help and not having capital stock and not conducted for profit. The provisions of this section certainly can not be satisfactory to labor organizations, to farmers, or even to the organization of business men who oppose any modification of the Sherman law which will exclude labor organizations from its provisions. It would hardly seem necessary in this day and age of the world to enact a law which merely permits the existence of labor organizations. If labor and farmer organizations are not to be given some substantial recognition by statutory enactment, it would seem unwise to place a new provision in the law, which can be of no material benefit to labor organizations, but which is bound to bring doubt and uncertainty as to what, if any, additional rights labor and farmers' organizations and the members thereof have under the new statute. If the provisions of our antitrust laws should not apply to labor organizations Congress should in plain and clear language so declare. We should not speak ⊥ in the doubtful, uncertain, indefinite terms which characterize the provisions of section 7 of this bill.

One of the elements of the high cost of living is the expensive system of the sale and distribution of the products of the farm and the factory. The producer and consumer must be brought closer together. The provisions of this bill would not permit consumers to organize if the associations had capital stock, or were organized for profit. Under the provisions of section 7 of this bill farmers' organizations with capital stock, organized for profit, would be left sub-subject [sic] to the provisions of the Sherman antitrust law. The law not only should not prohibit but should encourage farmers to organize with a view to purchasing implements, machinery, and other farm supplies at less cost and with the view to collective bargaining in the sale of their products and in the purchase of supplies. In France, Germany, and other European countries farmers' organizations are authorized by law. The line along which these organizations can act is definitely defined. Governmental aid, direction, and assistance is given. Such organizations are encouraged to engage in a wide field of purely business transactions. These organizations have contributed immensely to the expansion of the agricultural interests of these countries. It would be exceedingly unfortunate at this time, when we are about to enter upon the important task of providing our farmers with better credit facilities, to enact a law which may be construed to make all farmers' organizations unlawful except such as are organized for the mutual benefit of members along literary, insurance, and social lines.

I do not care to express my objections to all the provisions of this bill. I agree in the main with criticisms made by other members of the minority on the Judiciary Committee.

It has been nearly 24 years since the enactment of the Sherman antitrust law. Its meaning was long in doubt and obscurity. It is now better understood. The business world knows, in a way at least, its meaning. The law was not a success in preventing the concentration of business into large industrial units. We have large business organizations to-day, and there is no indication that through the enforcement of the Sherman law, or the enactments and enforcement of any new laws, our industrial units are to be materially lessened. The Sherman law has failed through the absence of proper administrative machinery to enforce its provisions. It is folly to enact more laws, when existing laws are not effective for lack of adequate enforcing agencies. What the country needs now is a law that will define and promulgate a well-defined national policy toward the great business interests of the country which will be just to our industrial forces, and which will be fair to the people, and fully protect them from exactions of business concerns possessed of monopolistic power.

Practically every other business is highly organized but the business of farming. There are about 6,500,000 farmers. Something like 12,000,000 persons over 10 years of age toil on the farm. The farmers are at a great disadvantage. Labor is organized. Business is organized. Concentration, combination, cooperation everywhere except among the farmers. With the most intelligent farmers of the world, in business cooperation our farmers are far behind the less intelligent farmers of other countries. To aid our farmers in ⊥ the line of greater cooperation has now become a national duty, and it would be hardly short of a public calamity to enact a statute which on its face restricts and limits to a narrow sphere the purposes for which agricultural associations may be formed.

In my judgment it is unfortunate that one committee should not have had exclusive jurisdiction over the proposed legislation to create a Federal trade commission and all antitrust legislation. The creation of a Federal commission with certain jurisdiction over industrial corporations engaged in interstate trade will mark an epoch in our national policy in Federal control of private business. Manifestly all legislation for the supervision, regulation, and control of private business engaged in interstate commerce will and should center in and around the national commission, whether its jurisdiction and power be great or small. So it seems to me, if the Sherman law is to be amended, the new statutory provisions should be drawn with the trade commission and its power in view. Because we are entering upon a new field of Federal activity in the control of private business; all our enactments should be suited to our new enforcing agency—the proposed Federal commission. But over this proposed legislation the Judiciary Committee has no jurisdiction, and it is not proper for me to discuss any of the provisions relative thereto.

Dick T. Morgan.

H.R. 15657 AS REPORTED BY THE HOUSE COMMITTEE ON THE JUDICIARY
63d Cong., 2d Sess.
May 6, 1914

⊥ Reported with amendments, referred to the House Calendar, and ordered to be printed.

[Strike out all after the enacting clause and insert the part printed in italic.]

A BILL

To supplement existing laws against unlawful restraints and monopolies, and for other purposes.

1 *Be it enacted by the Senate and House of Representa-*
2 *tives of the United States of America in Congress assembled,*
3 That "antitrust laws," as used herein, includes the Act
4 entitled "An Act to protect trade and commerce against
5 unlawful restraints and monopolies," approved July second,
6 eighteen hundred and ninety, section seventy-three to
7 seventy-seven, inclusive, of an Act entitled "An Act to
8 reduce taxation, to provide revenue for the Government, and
9 for other purposes," of August twenty-seventh, eighteen hun-
10 dred and ninety-four; an Act entitled "An Act to amend
11 sections seventy-three and seventy-six of the Act of August
2 twenty-seventh, eighteen hundred and ninety-four, entitled
3 "An Act to reduce taxation, to provide revenue for the
4 Government, and for other purposes," approved February
5 twelfth, nineteen hundred and thirteen; and also this Act.
6 "Commerce," as used herein, means trade or com-
7 merce among the several States and with foreign nations,
8 or between the District of Columbia or any Territory of the
9 United States and any State, Territory, or foreign nation,
10 or within the District of Columbia or any Territory of the
11 United States.
12 SEC. 2. That any person engaged in commerce who shall
13 discriminate in price between different purchasers of com-
14 modities in the same or different sections or communities,

15 with the purpose or intent to thereby injure or destroy the
16 business of a competitor, either of such purchaser or the
17 seller, shall be deemed guilty of a misdemeanor, and upon
18 conviction thereof, shall be punished by a fine not exceeding
19 $5,000, or imprisonment not exceeding one year, or both,
20 in the discretion of the court. Corporations shall be deemed
21 persons within the meaning of this section, and when any
22 corporation shall be guilty of a violation of this section, the
23 offense shall be deemed to be also that of the individual
24 directors or other officers or employees of such corporation
25 ordering or doing the prohibited act, and upon conviction
1 they shall be punished as provided in this section: *Provided*,
2 That nothing herein contained shall prevent discrimination
3 in price between purchasers of commodities on account of
4 differences in the grade, quality, or quantity of the com-
5 modity sold, or that makes only due allowance for difference
6 in the cost of transportation: *And provided further*, That
7 nothing herein contained shall prevent persons engaged in
8 selling goods, wares, or merchandise in commerce from
9 selecting their own customers. It shall be unlawful for the
10 owner or operator of any mine engaged in selling its product
11 in commerce to refuse arbitrarily to sell the same to a
12 responsible person, firm, or corporation who applies to
13 purchase.
14 Sec. 3. That any person engaged in commerce, who
15 shall lease or make a sale of goods, wares, merchandise, ma-
16 chinery, supplies, or other commodities, or fix a price charged
17 therefor, or discount from, or rebate upon such price, on the
18 condition or understanding that the lessee or purchaser
19 thereof shall not use or deal in the goods, wares, merchan-
20 dise, machinery, supplies, or other commodities, of a com-
21 petitor or competitors of the lessor or seller, shall be deemed
22 guilty of a misdemeanor, and upon conviction thereof shall
23 be punished by a fine not exceeding $5,000, or by imprison-
24 ment not exceeding one year, or both, in the discretion of
25 the court. Corporations shall be deemed persons within
1 the meaning of this section, and when any corporation shall
2 be guilty of a violation of this section, the offense shall be
3 deemed to be also that of the individual directors or other
4 officers or employees of such corporation ordering or doing
5 the prohibited acts, and upon conviction they shall be pun-
6 ished as provided in this section.
7 Sec. 4. That any person, copartnership, association, or
8 corporation, which shall be injured in his or its business or
9 partnership by any person, copartnership, association, or
10 corporation, by reason of anything forbidden by section two
11 or section three of this Act, may sue therefor in any district
12 court of the United States in the district in which the de-
13 fendant resides or is found, without respect to the amount in
14 controversy, and shall recover threefold the damages by him
15 or it sustained, and the cost of suit, including a reasonable
16 attorney's fee.
17 Sec. 5. That whenever in any suit or proceeding in
18 equity, brought by or on behalf of the United States under

~~19 any of the antitrust laws, there shall have been rendered a~~
~~20 final judgment or decree to the effect that a defendant has~~
~~21 or has not entered into a contract, combination in the form~~
~~22 of trust or otherwise, or conspiracy, in restraint of trade or~~
~~23 commerce, or has or has not monopolized, or attempted to~~
~~24 monopolize, or combined with any person or persons to~~
~~25 monopolize, any part of commerce, in violation of any of~~
~~1 the antitrust laws, said judgment or decree shall to the full~~
~~2 extent to which such judgment or decree would constitute~~
~~3 in any other proceeding an estoppel as between the Govern-~~
~~4 ment and such defendant, constitute in favor of or against~~
~~5 such defendant, conclusive evidence of the same facts, and~~
~~6 be conclusive as to the same issues of law in favor of or~~
~~7 against any other party in any action or proceeding brought~~
~~8 under or involving the provisions of any of the antitrust~~
~~9 laws. Whenever any suit or proceeding in equity is brought~~
~~10 by or on behalf of the United States, under any of the anti-~~
~~11 trust laws, the statute of limitations in respect of each and~~
~~12 every private right of action, arising under such antitrust~~
~~13 laws, and based, in whole or in part, on any matter com-~~
~~14 plained of in said suit or proceeding in equity, shall be sus-~~
~~15 pended during the pendency of such suit or proceeding in~~
~~16 equity.~~
~~17 SEC. 6. That nothing contained in the antitrust laws~~
~~18 shall be construed to forbid the existence and operation of~~
~~19 fraternal, labor, consumers, agricultural or horticultural organ-~~
~~20 izations, orders or associations operating under the lodge~~
~~21 system, instituted for the purposes of mutual help, and not~~
~~22 having capital stock or conducted for profit, or to forbid or~~
~~23 restrain individual members of such orders or associations~~
~~24 from carrying out the legitimate objects of such associations.~~
~~1 SEC. 7. That no corporation engaged in commerce~~
~~2 shall acquire, directly or indirectly, the whole, or any part, of~~
~~3 the stock or other share capital of another corporation en-~~
~~4 gaged also in commerce, where the effect of such acquisition~~
~~5 is to eliminate or lessen competition between the corporation~~
~~6 whose stock is so acquired and the corporation making the~~
~~7 acquisition, or to create a monopoly of any line of trade in~~
~~8 any section or community.~~
~~9 No corporation shall acquire, directly or indirectly, the~~
~~10 whole or any part of the stock or other share capital of two~~
~~11 or more corporations engaged in commerce where the effect~~
~~12 of such acquisition, or the use of such stock by the voting or~~
~~13 granting of proxies or otherwise, is to eliminate or lessen~~
~~14 competition between such corporations, or any of them,~~
~~15 whose stock or other share capital is so acquired, or to create~~
~~16 a monopoly of any line of trade in any section or community.~~
~~17 This section shall not apply to corporations purchasing~~
~~18 such stock solely for investment, and not using the same by~~
~~19 voting or otherwise to bring about, or in attempting to bring~~
~~20 about, the lessening of competition. Nor shall anything~~
~~21 contained in this section prevent a corporation engaged in~~
~~22 commerce from causing the formation of subsidiary corpora-~~
~~23 tions for the actual carrying on of their immediate lawful~~

business, or the natural and legitimate branches thereof, or from owning and holding all, or a part of, the stock of such subsidiary corporations, when the effect of such formation is not to eliminate or lessen competition.

Nothing contained in this section shall be held to affect or impair any right heretofore legally acquired: *Provided,* That nothing in this paragraph shall make legal stockholding relations between corporations when, and under such circumstances that, such relations constitute violations of the antitrust laws.

Nor shall anything herein contained be construed to prohibit any railroad corporation from aiding in the construction of branch or short line railroads so located as to become feeders to the main line of the company so aiding in such construction or from acquiring or owning all or any part of the stock of such branch line, nor to prevent any railroad corporation from acquiring and owning all or any part of the stock of a branch or short line railroad constructed by an independent company where there is no substantial competition between the company owning the branch line so constructed and the company owning the main line acquiring the property or an interest therein, nor to prevent any railroad company from extending any of its lines.

A violation of this section shall be deemed a misdemeanor, and shall be punishable by a fine not exceeding $5,000, or by imprisonment, not exceeding one year, or both, in the discretion of the court, and any violation by a corporation shall be deemed to be also the offense of its individual officers or directors, ordering, doing, or participating in, the prohibited act, and upon conviction, they shall be punished as herein provided.

SEC. 8. That from and after two years from the date of the approval of this Act, no person who is engaged as an individual, or who is a member of a partnership, or is a director or other officer of a corporation that is engaged in the business, in whole or in part, of producing or selling equipment, materials, or supplies to, or in the construction or maintenance of, railroads, or other common carriers engaged in commerce, shall act as a director or other officer or employee of any common carrier engaged in commerce, to which he, or such partnership or corporation, sells or leases, directly or indirectly, equipment, materials, or supplies, or for which he, or such partnership or corporation, directly or indirectly, engages in the work of construction or maintenance; and, after the expiration of said period, no person who is engaged as an individual, or who is a member of a partnership, or is a director or other officer of a corporation which is engaged in the conduct of a bank or trust company, shall act as a director, or other officer or employee, of any such common carrier, for which he, or such partnership, or bank, or trust company, acts, either separately or in connection with others, as agent in the disposal of, or is interested in the underwriting of, or from which he or such partnership, or bank, or trust company, purchases, either separately, or in

3 ~~connection with others, issues or parts of issues of securities~~
4 ~~of such common carrier.~~
5 ~~That from and after two years from the date of the~~
6 ~~approval of this Act no person shall at the same time be a~~
7 ~~director or other officer or employee of more than one bank,~~
8 ~~banking association, or trust company organized and operat-~~
9 ~~ing under the laws of the United States, either of which~~
10 ~~has deposits, capital, surplus, and undivided profits aggre-~~
11 ~~gating more than $2,500,000; and no private banker, or~~
12 ~~person who is a director in any bank or trust company,~~
13 ~~organized and operating under the laws of a State, having~~
14 ~~deposits, capital, surplus, and undivided profits aggregating~~
15 ~~more than $2,500,000, shall be eligible to be a director in~~
16 ~~any bank or banking association organized and operating~~
17 ~~under the laws of the United States.~~
18 ~~No bank, banking association, or trust company organ-~~
19 ~~ized and doing business under the laws of the United States~~
20 ~~in any city or town or [sic] more than one hundred thousand~~
21 ~~inhabitants shall have as a director or other officer or em-~~
22 ~~ployee any private banker or any director or other officer~~
23 ~~or employee of any other bank, banking association, or~~
24 ~~trust company located in the same place.~~
⊥1 ~~That from and after two years from the date of the~~ ⊥10
2 ~~approval of this Act no person at the same time shall be a~~
3 ~~director in any two or more corporations engaged in whole~~
4 ~~or in part in commerce, other than common carriers, subject~~
5 ~~to the Act to regulate commerce, approved February fourth,~~
6 ~~eighteen hundred and eighty-seven, if such corporations are,~~
7 ~~or shall have been theretofore, by virtue of their business and~~
8 ~~location of operation, competitors, so that an elimination of~~
9 ~~competition by agreement between them would constitute a~~
10 ~~violation of any of the provisions of any of the antitrust laws.~~
11 ~~That any person who shall violate any of the provisions~~
12 ~~of this section shall be guilty of a misdemeanor, and shall be~~
13 ~~punished by a fine of $100 a day for each day of the con-~~
14 ~~tinuance of such violation, or by imprisonment for such~~
15 ~~period as the court may designate, not exceeding one year, or~~
16 ~~by both, in the discretion of the court.~~
17 ~~SEC. 9. That any suit, action or proceeding under the~~
18 ~~antitrust laws, against a corporation, may be brought not~~
19 ~~only in the judicial district whereof it is an inhabitant, but~~
20 ~~also in any district wherein it may be found.~~
21 ~~SEC. 10. That subpoenas for witnesses who are required~~
22 ~~to attend a court of the United States in any judicial district~~
23 ~~in any case, civil or criminal, arising under the Federal anti-~~
24 ~~trust laws, may run into any other district.~~
⊥1 ~~SEC. 11. That whenever a corporation shall be guilty of~~ ⊥11
2 ~~the violation of any of the provisions of the antitrust laws,~~
3 ~~the offense shall be deemed to be also that of the individual~~
4 ~~directors, officers, and agents of such corporation authorizing,~~
5 ~~ordering, or doing any of such prohibited acts, and upon con-~~
6 ~~viction thereof they shall be deemed guilty of a misdemeanor,~~
7 ~~and punished by a fine not exceeding $5,000, or imprison-~~
8 ~~ment not exceeding one year, or by both said punishments in~~

the discretion of the court.

SEC. 12. That the several district courts of the United States are hereby invested with jurisdiction to prevent and restrain violations of this Act; and it shall be the duty of the several district attorneys of the United States, in their respective districts, under the direction of the Attorney-General, to institute proceedings in equity to prevent and restrain such violations. Such proceedings may be by way of petition, setting forth the case and praying that such violation shall be enjoined or otherwise prohibited. When the parties complained of shall have been duly notified of such petition, the court shall proceed, as soon as may be, to the hearing and determination of the case; and pending such petition, and before final decree, the court may at any time make such temporary restraining order or prohibition as shall be deemed just in the premises. Whenever it shall appear to the court before which any such proceeding may be pending that the ends of justice require that other parties should be brought before the court, the court may cause them to be summoned, whether they reside in the district in which the court is held or not, and subpoenas to that end may be served in any district by the marshal thereof.

SEC. 13. That any person, firm, corporation, or association shall be entitled to sue for and have injunctive relief, in any court of the United States having jurisdiction over the parties, against threatened loss or damage by a violation of the antitrust laws, when and under the same conditions and principles as injunctive relief against threatened conduct that will cause loss or damage is granted by courts of equity, under the rules governing such proceedings, and upon the execution of proper bond against damages for an injunction improvidently granted and a showing that the danger of irreparable loss or damage is immediate, a preliminary injunction may issue: *Provided*, That nothing herein contained shall be construed to entitle any person, firm, corporation, or association, except the United States, to bring suit in equity for injunctive relief against any common carrier, subject to the provisions of the Act to regulate commerce, approved February fourth, eighteen hundred and eighty-seven, in respect of any matter subject to the regulation, supervision, or other jurisdiction of the Interstate Commerce Commission.

SEC. 14. That no injunction, whether interlocutory or permanent, in cases other than those described in section two hundred and sixty-six of an Act entitled "An Act to codify, revise, and amend the laws relating to the judiciary," approved March third, nineteen hundred and eleven, shall be issued without previous notice and an opportunity to be heard on behalf of the parties to be enjoined, which notice, together with a copy of the bill of complaint or other pleading upon which the application for such injunction will be based, shall be served upon the parties sought to be enjoined a reasonable time in advance of such application. But if it shall appear to the satisfaction of the court or judge that

13 ~~immediate and irreparable injury is likely to en-~~
14 ~~sue to property or a property right of the com-~~
15 ~~plainant, and that the giving of notice of the appli-~~
16 ~~cation or the delay incident thereto would probably~~
17 ~~permit the doing of the act sought to be restrained before~~
18 ~~notice could be served or hearing had thereon, the court or~~
19 ~~judge may, in his discretion, issue a temporary restraining~~
20 ~~order without notice. Every such order shall be endorsed~~
21 ~~with the date and hour of issuance, shall be forthwith entered~~
22 ~~of record, shall define the injury and state why it is irrepar-~~
23 ~~able and why the order was granted without notice, and~~
24 ~~shall by its terms expire within such time after entry, not to~~
25 ~~exceed ten days, as the court or judge may fix, unless within~~
1 ~~the time so fixed the order is extended or renewed for a like~~
2 ~~period, after notice to those previously served, if any, and~~
3 ~~for good cause shown, and the reasons for such extension~~
4 ~~shall be entered of record, and section two hundred and~~
5 ~~sixty-three of the Act entitled "An Act to codify, revise, and~~
6 ~~amend the laws relating to the judiciary," approved March~~
7 ~~third, nineteen hundred and eleven, is hereby repealed.~~
8 ~~SEC. 15. That no restraining order or interlocutory~~
9 ~~order of injunction shall issue, except upon the giving of~~
10 ~~security by the applicant in such sum as the court or judge~~
11 ~~may deem proper, conditioned upon the payment of such~~
12 ~~costs and damages as may be incurred or suffered by any~~
13 ~~party who may be found to have been wrongfully enjoined~~
14 ~~or restrained thereby.~~
15 ~~SEC. 16. That every order of injunction or restraining~~
16 ~~order shall set forth the reasons for the issuance of the same,~~
17 ~~shall be specific in terms, and shall describe in reasonable~~
18 ~~detail, and not by reference to the bill of complaint or other~~
19 ~~document, the act or acts sought to be restrained; and shall~~
20 ~~be binding only upon the parties to the suit, their agents,~~
21 ~~servants, employees, and attorneys, or those in active concert~~
22 ~~with them, and who shall, by personal service or other-~~
23 ~~wise, have received actual notice of the same.~~
24 ~~SEC. 17. That no restraining order or injunction shall~~
25 ~~be granted by any court of the United States, or a judge or~~
1 ~~the judges thereof, in any case between an employer and em-~~
2 ~~ployees, or between employers and employees, or between~~
3 ~~employees, or between persons employed and persons seek-~~
4 ~~ing employment, involving, or growing out of, a dispute~~
5 ~~concerning terms or conditions of employment, unless neces-~~
6 ~~sary to prevent irreparable injury to property, or to a prop-~~
7 ~~erty right, of the party making the application, for which~~
8 ~~injury there is no adequate remedy at law, and such property~~
9 ~~or property right must be described with particularity in~~
10 ~~the application, which must be in writing and sworn to~~
11 ~~by the applicant or by his agent or attorney.~~
12 ~~And no such restraining order or injunction shall prohibit~~
13 ~~any person or persons from terminating any relation of~~
14 ~~employment, or from ceasing to perform any work or labor,~~
15 ~~or from recommending, advising, or persuading others by~~
16 ~~peaceful means so to do; or from attending at or near a~~

house or place where any person resides or works, or carries on business, or happens to be for the purpose of peacefully obtaining or communicating information, or of peacefully persuading any person to work or to abstain from working; or from ceasing to patronize or to employ any party to such dispute; or from recommending, advising, or persuading others by peaceful means so to do; or from paying or giving to, or withholding from, any person engaged in such dispute, any strike benefits or other moneys or things of value; or from peaceably assembling at any place in a lawful manner, and for lawful purposes; or from doing any act or thing which might lawfully be done in the absence of such dispute by any party thereto.

SEC. 18. That any person who shall willfully disobey any lawful writ, process, order, rule, decree, or command of any district court of the United States by doing any act or thing therein, or thereby forbidden to be done by him, if the act or thing so done by him be of such character as to constitute also a criminal offense under any statute of the United States, or at common law, shall be proceeded against for his said contempt as hereinafter provided.

SEC. 19. That whenever it shall be made to appear to any district court or judge thereof, or to any judge therein sitting, by the return of a proper officer on lawful process, or upon the affidavit of some credible person, or by information filed by any district attorney, that there is reasonable ground to believe that any person has been guilty of such contempt, the court or judge thereof, or any judge therein sitting, may issue a rule requiring the said person so charged to show cause upon a day certain why he should not be punished therefor, which rule, together with a copy of the affidavit or information, shall be served upon the person charged with sufficient promptness to enable him to prepare for and make return to the order at the time fixed therein. If upon or by such return, in the judgment of the court, the alleged contempt be not sufficiently purged, a trial shall be directed at a time and place fixed by the court: *Provided, however,* That if the accused, being a natural person, fail or refuse to make return to the rule to show cause, an attachment may issue against his person to compel an answer, and in case of his continued failure or refusal, or if, for any reason, it be impracticable to dispose of the matter on the return day, he may be required to give reasonable bail for his attendance at the trial and his submission to the final judgment of the court. Where the accused person is a body corporate, an attachment for the sequestration of its property may be issued upon like refusal or failure to answer.

In all cases within the purview of this Act such trial may be by the court, or, upon demand of the accused, by a jury; in which latter event the court may impanel a jury from the jurors then in attendance, or the court or the judge thereof in chambers may cause a sufficient number of jurors to be selected and summoned, as provided by law, to attend at the time and place of trial, at which time a jury shall be

~~selected and impaneled as upon a trial for misdemeanor;
and such trial shall conform, as near as may be, to the
practice in criminal cases prosecuted by indictment or upon
information.~~
  ~~If the accused be found guilty, judgment shall be entered
accordingly, prescribing the punishment, either by fine or
imprisonment, or both, in the discretion of the court. Such
fine shall be paid to the United States or to the complainant or other party injured by the act constituting the contempt, or may, where more than one is so damaged, be
divided or apportioned among them as the court may direct;
but in no case shall the fine to be paid to the United States
exceed, in case the accused is a natural person, the sum of
$1,000, nor shall such imprisonment exceed the term of six
months.~~
  ~~SEC. 20. That the evidence taken upon the trial of any
person so accused may be preserved by bill of exceptions, and
any judgment of conviction may be reviewed upon writ of
error in all respects as now provided by law in criminal cases,
and may be affirmed, reversed, or modified as justice may require. Upon the granting of such writ of error, execution
of judgment shall be stayed, and the accused, if thereby sentenced to imprisonment, shall be admitted to bail in such
reasonable sum as may be required by the court, or by any
justice, or any judge, of any district court of the United
States.~~
  ~~SEC. 21. That nothing herein contained shall be construed to relate to contempts committed in the presence of
the court, or so near thereto as to obstruct the administration of justice, nor to contempts committed in disobedience
of any lawful writ, process, order, rule, decree, or command
entered in any suit or action brought or prosecuted in the
name of, or on behalf of, the United States, but the same,
and all other cases of contempt not specifically embraced
within section eighteen of this Act, may be punished in conformity to the usages at law and in equity now prevailing.~~
  ~~SEC. 22. That no proceeding for contempt shall be
instituted against any person unless begun within one year
from the date of the act complained of; nor shall any such
proceeding be a bar to any criminal prosecution for the same
act or acts; but nothing herein contained shall affect any
proceedings in contempt pending at the time of the passage
of this Act.~~

*That "antitrust laws," as used herein, includes the Act
entitled "An Act to protect trade and commerce against
unlawful restraints and monopolies," approved July second,
eighteen hundred and ninety; sections seventy-three to
seventy-seven, inclusive, of an Act entitled "An Act to
reduce taxation, to provide revenue for the Government,
and for other purposes," of August twenty-seventh, eighteen
hundred and ninety-four; an Act entitled "An Act to amend
sections seventy-three and seventy-six of the Act of August
twenty-seventh, eighteen hundred and ninety-four, entitled
'An Act to reduce taxation, to provide revenue for the Gov-*

ernment, and for other purposes,' " approved February twelfth, nineteen hundred and thirteen; and also this Act.

"Commerce," as used herein, means trade or commerce among the several States and with foreign nations, or between the District of Columbia or any Territory of the United States and any State, Territory, or foreign nation, or between any insular possessions or other places under the jurisdiction of the United States, or between any such possession or place and any State or Territory of the United States or the District of Columbia or any foreign nation, or within the District of Columbia or any Territory or any insular possession or other place under the jurisdiction of the United States.

The word "person" or "persons" wherever used in this Act shall be deemed to include corporations and associations existing under or authorized by the laws of either the United States, the laws of any of the Territories, the laws of any State, or the laws of any foreign country.

SEC. 2. That any person engaged in commerce who shall either directly or indirectly discriminate in price between different purchasers of commodities in the same or different sections or communities, which commodities are sold for use, consumption, or resale within the United States or any Territory thereof or the District of Columbia or any insular possession or other place under the jurisdiction of the United States, with the purpose or intent to thereby destroy or wrongfully injure the business of a competitor, of either such purchaser or seller, shall be deemed guilty of a misdemeanor, and upon conviction thereof shall be punished by a fine not exceeding $5,000, or by imprisonment not exceeding one year, or by both, in the discretion of the court: Provided, That nothing herein contained shall prevent discrimination in price between purchasers of commodities on account of differences in the grade, quality, or quantity of the commodity sold, or that makes only due allowance for difference in the cost of transportation: And provided further, That nothing herein contained shall prevent persons engaged in selling goods, wares, or merchandise in commerce from selecting their own customers, except as provided in section three of this Act.

SEC. 3. That it shall be unlawful for the owner or operator of any mine or for any person controlling the product of any mine engaged in selling its product in commerce to refuse arbitrarily to sell such product to a responsible person, firm, or corporation who applies to purchase such product for use, consumption, or resale within the United States or any Territory thereof or the District of Columbia or any insular possession or other place under the jurisdiction of the United States, and any person violating this section shall be deemed guilty of a misdemeanor and shall be punished as provided in the preceding section.

SEC. 4. That any person engaged in commerce who shall lease or make a sale of goods, wares, merchandise, machinery, supplies, or other commodities for use, consumption, or resale within the United States, or any Territory thereof or the District of Columbia or any insular possession or other place under the jurisdiction of the United States, or fix a price charged therefor, or discount from, or rebate upon such price, on the condition or understanding that the lessee or purchaser thereof shall not use or deal in the goods, wares, merchandise, machinery, supplies, or other commodities of a competitor or competitors of the lessor or seller shall be deemed guilty of a misdemeanor, and upon conviction thereof shall be punished by a fine not exceeding $5,000, or by imprisonment not exceeding one year, or by both, in the discretion of the court.

SEC. 5. That any person who shall be injured in his business or property by reason of anything forbidden in the antitrust laws, may sue therefor in any district court of the United States in the district in which the defendant resides or is found, without respect to the amount in controversy, and shall recover threefold the damages by him sustained, and the cost of suit, including a reasonable attorney's fee.

SEC. 6. That whenever in any suit or proceeding in equity hereafter brought by or on behalf of the United States under any of the antitrust laws there shall have been rendered a final judgment or decree to the effect that a defendant has or has not entered into a contract, combination in the form of trust or otherwise, or conspiracy, in restraint of trade or commerce, or has or has not monopolized, or attempted to monopolize or combined with any person or persons to monopolize, any part of commerce, in violation of any of the antitrust laws, said judgment or decree shall, to the full extent to which such judgment or decree would constitute in any other proceeding an estoppel as between the United States and such defendant, constitute in favor of or against such defendant conclusive evidence of the same facts, and be conclusive as to the same questions of law in favor of or against any other party in any action or proceeding brought under or involving the provisions of any of the antitrust laws.

Whenever any suit or proceeding in equity is hereafter brought by or on behalf of the United Staes [sic], under any of the antitrust laws, the statute of limitations in respect of each and every private right of action, arising under such antitrust laws, and based, in whole or in part, on any matter complained of in said suit or proceeding in equity, shall be suspended during the pendency of such suit or proceeding in equity.

SEC. 7. That nothing contained in the antitrust laws shall be construed to forbid the existence and operation of fraternal, labor, consumers, agricultural, or horticultural organizations, orders, or associations instituted for the purposes of mutual help, and not having capital stock or conducted for profit, or to forbid or restrain individual members of such organizations, orders, or associations from carrying out the legitimate objects thereof.

Nothing contained in the antitrust laws shall be construed to forbid associations of traffic, operating, accounting, or other officers of common carriers for the purpose of conferring among themselves or of making any lawful agreement as to any matter which is subject to the regulating or supervisory jurisdiction of the Interstate Commerce Commission, but all such matters shall continue to be subject to such jurisdiction of the commission, and all such agreements shall be entered and kept of record by the carriers, parties thereto, and shall at all times be open to inspection by the commission: Provided, That nothing in this Act shall be construed as modifying existing laws prohibiting the pooling of earnings or traffic, or existing laws against joint agreements by common carriers to maintain rates.

SEC. 8. *That no corporation engaged in commerce shall acquire, directly or indirectly, the whole or any part of the stock or other share capital of another corporation engaged also in commerce, where the effect of such acquisition is to eliminate or substantially lessen competition between the corporation whose stock is so acquired and the corporation making the acquisition, or to create a monopoly of any line of trade in any section or community.*

No corporation shall acquire, directly or indirectly, the whole or any part of the stock or other share capital of two or more corporations engaged in commerce where the effect of such acquisition, or the use of such stock by the voting or granting of proxies or otherwise, is to eliminate or substantially lessen competition between such corporations, or any of them, whose stock or other share capital is so acquired, or to create a monopoly of any line of trade in any section or community.

This section shall not apply to corporations purchasing such stock solely for investment and not using the same by voting or otherwise to bring about, or in attempting to bring about, the substantial lessening of competition. Nor shall anything contained in this section prevent a corporation engaged in commerce from causing the formation of subsidiary corporations for the actual carrying on of their immediate lawful business, or the natural and legitimate branches or extensions thereof, or from owning and holding all or a part of the stock of such subsidiary corporations, when the effect of such formation is not to eliminate or substantially lessen competition.

Nothing contained in this section shall be held to affect or impair any right heretofore legally acquired: Provided, That nothing in this paragraph shall make stockholding relations between corporations legal when such relations constitute violations of the antitrust laws.

Nor shall anything herein contained be construed to prohibit any railroad corporation from aiding in the construction of branch or short line railroads so located as to become feeders to the main line of the company so aiding in such construction or from acquiring or owning all or any part of the stock of such branch line, nor to prevent any railroad corporation from acquiring and owning all or any part of the stock of a branch or short line railroad constructed by an independent company where there is no substantial competition between the company owning the branch line so constructed and the company owning the main line acquiring the property or an interest therein, nor to prevent any railroad company from extending any of its lines through the medium of the acquisition of stock or otherwise of any other railroad company where there is no substantial competition between the company extending its lines and the company whose stock, property, or an interest therein is so acquired.

A violation of any of the provisions of this section shall be deemed a misdemeanor, and shall be punishable by a fine not exceeding $5,000, or by imprisonment not exceeding one year, or by both, in the discretion of the court.

SEC. 9. That from and after two years from the date of the approval of this Act no person who is engaged as an individual, or who is a member of a partnership, or is a director or other officer of a corporation that is engaged in the business, in whole or in part, of producing or selling equipment, materials, or supplies to, or in the construction or maintenance of, railroads or other common carriers engaged in commerce, shall act as a director or other officer or employee of any other corporation or common carrier engaged in commerce to which he, or such partnership or corporation, sells or leases, directly or indirectly, equipment materials, or supplies, or for which he or such partnership or corporation, directly or indirectly, engages in the work of construction or maintenance; and after the expiration of said period no person who is engaged as an individual or who is a member of a partnership or is a director or other officer of a corporation which is engaged in the conduct of a bank or trust company shall act as a director or other officer or employee of any such common carrier for which he or such partnership or bank or trust company acts, either separately or in connection with others, as agent for or underwriter of the sale or disposal by such common carrier of issues or parts of issues of its securities, or from which he or such partnership or bank or trust company purchases, either separately or in connection with others, issues or parts of issues of securities of such common carrier.

That from and after two years from the date of the approval of this Act no person shall at the same time be a director or other officer or employee of more than one bank, banking association, or trust company organized or operating under the laws of the United States either of which has deposits, capital, surplus, and undivided profits aggregating more than $2,500,000; and no private banker or person who is a director in any bank or trust company, organized and operating under the laws of a State, having deposits, capital, surplus, and undivided profits aggregating more than $2,500,000, shall be eligible to be a director in any bank or banking association organized or operating under the laws of the United States. The eligibility of a director under the *foregoing provisions shall be determined by the average amount of deposits, capital, surplus, and undivided profits as shown in the official statements of such bank, banking association, or trust company filed as provided by law during the fiscal year next preceding the date set for the annual election of directors, and when a director has been elected in accordance with the provisions of this Act it shall be lawful for him to continue as such for one year thereafter under said election.*

No bank, banking association, or trust company organized or operating under the laws of the United States in any city or incorporated town or village of more than one hundred thousand inhabitants, as shown by the last preceding decennial census of the United States, shall have as a director or other officer or employee any private banker or any director or other officer or employee of any other bank, banking association, or trust company located in the same place: Provided, That nothing in this section shall apply to mutual savings banks not having a capital stock represented by shares: Provided further, That a director or other officer or employee of such bank, banking association, or trust company may be a director or other officer or employee of not more than one other bank or trust company organized under the laws of the United States or any State where the entire capital stock of one is owned by stockholders in the other: And provided further, That nothing contained in this section shall forbid a director of class A of a Federal reserve bank, as defined in the Federal Reserve Act, from being an officer or director or both an officer and director in one member bank.

That from and after two years from the date of the approval of this Act no person at the same time shall be a director in any two or more corporations, either of which has capital, surplus, and undivided profits aggregating more than $1,000,000, engaged in whole or in part in commerce, other than common carriers subject to the Act to regulate commerce, approved February fourth, eighteen hundred and eighty-seven, if such corporations are or shall have been theretofore, by virtue of their business and location of operation, competitors, so that an elimination of competition by agreement between them would constitute a violation of any of the provisions of any of the antitrust laws. The eligibility of a director under the foregoing provision shall be determined by the aggregate amount of the capital, surplus, and undivided profits, exclusive of dividends declared but not paid to stockholders, at the end of the fiscal year of said corporation next preceding the election of directors, and when a director has been elected in accordance with the provisions of this Act it shall be lawful for him to continue as such for one year thereafter.

That any person who shall violate any of the provisions of this section shall be guilty of a misdemeanor and shall be punished by a fine of $100 a day for each day of the continuance of such violation, or by imprisonment for such period as the court may designate, not exceeding one year, or by both, in the discretion of the court.

SEC. 10. That any suit, action, or proceeding under the antitrust laws against a corporation may be brought not only in the judicial district whereof it is an inhabitant, but also in any district wherein it may be found.

SEC. 11. That in any suit, action, or proceeding brought by or on behalf of the United States subpoenas for witnesses who are required to attend a court of the United States in any judicial district in any case, civil or criminal, arising under the antitrust laws may run into any other district.

SEC. 12. That whenever a corporation shall be guilty of the violation of any of the provisions of the antitrust laws, the offense shall be deemed to be also that of the individual directors, officers, or agents of such corporation; and upon the conviction of the corporation any director, officer, or agent who shall have authorized, ordered, or done any of such prohibited acts shall be deemed guilty of a misdemeanor, and upon conviction therefor shall be punished by a fine not exceeding $5,000, or by imprisonment not exceeding one year, or by both, in the discretion of the court.

SEC. 13. That the several district courts of the United States are hereby invested with jurisdiction to prevent and restrain violations of this Act, and it shall be the duty of the several district attorneys of the United States, in their respective districts, under the direction of the Attorney General, to institute proceedings in equity to prevent and restrain such violations. Such proceedings may be by way of petition setting forth the case and praying that such violation shall be enjoined or otherwise prohibited. When the parties complained of shall have been duly notified of such petition, the court shall proceed, as soon as may be, to the hearing and determination of the case; and pending such petition, and before final decree, the court may at any time make such temporary restraining order or prohibition as shall be deemed just in the premises. Whenever it shall appear to the court before which any such proceeding may be pending that the ends of justice require that other parties should be brought before the court, the court may cause them to be summoned, whether they reside in the district in which the court is held or not, and subpoenas to that end may be served in any district by the marshal thereof.

SEC. 14. That any person, firm, corporation, or association shall be entitled to sue for and have injunctive relief, in any court of the United States having jurisdiction over the parties, against threatened loss or damage by a violation of the antitrust laws, when and under the same conditions and principles as injunctive relief against threatened conduct that will cause loss or damage is granted by courts of equity, under the rules governing such proceedings, and upon the execution of proper bond against damages for an injunction improvidently granted and a showing that the danger of irreparable loss or damage is immediate, a preliminary injunction may issue: Provided, That nothing herein contained shall be construed to entitle any person, firm, corporation, or association, except the United States, to bring suit in equity for injunctive relief against any common carrier subject to the provisions of the Act to regulate commerce, approved February fourth, eighteen hundred and eighty-seven, in respect of any matter subject to the regulation, supervision, or other jurisdiction of the Interstate Commerce Commission.

SEC. 15. That no preliminary injunction shall be issued without notice to the opposite party.

No temporary restraining order shall be granted without notice to the opposite party unless it shall clearly appear from specific facts shown by affidavit or by the verified bill that immediate and irreparable injury, loss, or damage will result to property or a property right of the applicant before notice could be served or hearing had thereon. Every such temporary restraining order shall be indorsed with the date and hour of issuance, shall be forthwith filed in the clerk's office and entered of record, shall define the injury and state why it is irreparable and why the order was granted without notice, and shall by its terms expire within such time after entry, not to exceed ten days, as the court or judge may fix. In case a temporary restraining order shall be granted without notice in the contingency specified, the matter of the issuance of a preliminary injunction shall be set down for a hearing at the earliest possible time and shall take precedence of all matters except older matters of the same character; and when the same comes up for hearing the party obtaining the temporary restraining order shall proceed with his application for a preliminary injunction, and if he does not do so the court shall dissolve his temporary restraining order. Upon two days' notice to the party obtaining such temporary restraining order the opposite party may appear and move the dissolution or modification of the order, and in that event the court or judge shall proceed to hear and determine the motion as expeditiously as the ends of justice may require.

Section two hundred and sixty-three of an Act entitled "An Act to codify, revise, and amend the laws relating to the judiciary." approved March third, nineteen hundred and eleven, is hereby repealed.

Nothing in this section contained shall be deemed to alter, repeal, or amend section two hundred and sixty-six of an Act entitled "An Act to codify, revise, and amend the laws relating to the judiciary," approved March third, nineteen hundred and eleven.

SEC. 16. That, except as otherwise provided in section fourteen of this Act, no restraining order or interlocutory order of injunction shall issue, except upon the giving of security by the applicant in such sum as the court or judge may deem proper, conditioned upon the payment of such costs and damages as may be incurred or suffered by any party who may be found to have been wrongfully enjoined or restrained thereby.

SEC. 17. That every order of injunction or restraining order shall set forth the reasons for the issuance of the same, shall be specific in terms, and shall describe in reasonable detail, and not by reference to the bill of complaint or other document, the act or acts sought to be restrained, and shall be binding only upon the parties to the suit, their agents, servants, employees, and attorneys, or those in active concert with them, and who shall, by personal service or otherwise, have received actual notice of the same.

SEC. 18. That no restraining order or injunction shall be granted by any court of the United States, or a judge or the judges thereof, in any case between an employer and employees, or between employers and employees, or between employees, or between persons employed and persons seeking employment, involving, or growing out of, a dispute concerning terms or conditions of employment, unless necessary to prevent irreparable injury to property, or to a property right, of the party making the application, for which injury there is no adequate remedy at law, and such property or property right must be described with particularity in the application, which must be in writing and sworn to by the applicant or by his agent or attorney.

And no such restraining order or injunction shall prohibit any person or persons from terminating any relation of employment, or from ceasing to perform any work or labor, or from recommending, advising, or persuading others by peaceful means so to do; or from attending at or near a house or place where any person resides or works, or carries on business or happens to be, for the purpose of peacefully obtaining or communicating information, or of peacefully persuading any person to work or to abstain from working; or from ceasing to patronize or to employ any party to such dispute, or from recommending, advising, or persuading others by peaceful means so to do; or from paying or giving to, or withholding from, any person engaged in such dispute, any strike benefits or other moneys or things of value; or from peaceably assembling at any place in a lawful manner, and for lawful purposes; or from doing any act or thing which might lawfully be done in the absence of such dispute by any party thereto.

SEC. 19. That any person who shall willfully disobey any lawful writ, process, order, rule, decree, or command of any district court of the United States or any court of the District of Columbia by doing any act or thing therein, or thereby forbidden to be done by him, if the act or thing so done by him be of such character as to constitute also a criminal offense under any statute of the United States, or at common law, shall be proceeded against for his said contempt as hereinafter provided.

SEC. 20. That whenever it shall be made to appear to any district court or judge thereof, or to any judge therein sitting, by the return of a proper officer on lawful process, or upon the affidavit of some credible person, or by information filed by any district attorney, that there is reasonable ground to believe that any person has been guilty of such contempt, the court or judge thereof, or any judge therein sitting, may issue a rule requiring the said person so charged to show cause upon a day certain why he should not be punished therefor, which rule, together with a copy of the affidavit or information, shall be served upon the person charged with sufficient promptness to enable him to prepare for and make return to the order at the time fixed therein. If upon or by such return, in the judgment of the court, the alleged contempt be not sufficiently purged, a trial shall be directed at a time and place fixed by the court: Provided, however, That if the accused, being a natural person, fail or refuse to make return to the rule to show cause, an attachment may issue against his person to compel an answer, and in case of his continued failure or refusal, or if for any reason it be impracticable to dispose of the matter on the return day, he may be required to give reasonable bail for his attendance at the trial and his submission to the final judgment of the court. Where the accused person is a body corporate, an attachment for the sequestration of its property may be issued upon like refusal or failure to answer.

In all cases within the purview of this Act such trial may be by the court, or, upon demand of the accused, by a jury; in which latter event the court may impanel a jury from the jurors then in attendance, or the court or the judge thereof in chambers may cause a sufficient number of jurors to be selected and summoned, as provided by law, to attend at the time and place of trial, at which time a jury shall be selected and impaneled as upon a trial for misdemeanor; and such trial shall conform, as near as may be, to the practice in criminal cases prosecuted by indictment or upon information.

If the accused be found guilty, judgment shall be entered accordingly, prescribing the punishment, either by fine or imprisonment, or both, in the discretion of the court. Such fine shall be paid to the United States or to the complainant or other party injured by the act constituting the contempt, or may, where more than one is so damaged, be divided or apportioned among them as the court may direct, but in no case shall the fine to be paid to the United States exceed, in case the accused is a natural person, the sum of $1,000, nor shall such imprisonment exceed the term of six months.

SEC. 21. That the evidence taken upon the trial of any person so accused may be preserved by bill of exceptions, and any judgment of conviction may be reviewed upon writ of error in all respects as now provided by law in criminal cases, and may be affirmed, reversed, or modified as justice may require. Upon the granting of such writ of error, execution of judgment shall be stayed, and the accused, if thereby sentenced to imprisonment, shall be admitted to bail in such reasonable sum as may be required by the court, or by any justice, or any judge of any district court of the United States or any court of the District of Columbia.

SEC. 22. That nothing herein contained shall be construed to relate to contempts committed in the presence of

```
18    the court, or so near thereto as to obstruct the administra-
19    tion of justice, nor to contempts committed in disobedience
20    of any lawful writ, process, order, rule, decree, or command
21    entered in any suit or action brought or prosecuted in the
22    name of, or on behalf of, the United States, but the same,
23    and all other cases of contempt not specifically embraced
24    within section nineteen of this Act, may be punished in con-
25    formity to the usages at law and in equity now prevailing.
 1       SEC. 23. That no proceeding for contempt shall be
 2    instituted against any person unless begun within one year
 3    from the date of the act complained of; nor shall any such
 4    proceeding be a bar to any criminal prosecution for the same
 5    act or acts; but nothing herein contained shall affect any
 6    proceedings in contempt pending at the time of the passage
 7    of this Act.
```

HOUSE DEBATE
63d Cong., 2d Sess.
May 6, 1914

51 CONG. REC. 8206

SUPPLEMENTING EXISTING LAWS AGAINST UNLAWFUL RESTRAINTS AND MONOPOLIES

The SPEAKER. The Chair recognizes the gentleman from Alabama [Mr. CLAYTON]. [Applause.]

Mr. [HENRY D.] CLAYTON [D., Ala.]. Mr. Speaker, I desire to call the attention of the House to the fact that I have this day made a report on the bill H. R. 15657, a bill which is entitled "To supplement existing laws against unlawful restraints and monopolies, and for other purposes."

Mr. [VICTOR] MURDOCK [Prog., Kan.]. Mr. Speaker, will the gentleman yield?

Mr. CLAYTON. Certainly.

Mr. MURDOCK. Does that now complete the bills on trust matters that the gentleman will report?

Mr. CLAYTON. I think it does. I think I may say that this bill is comprehensive and embraces the subject matter which was contained in the several tentative bills which the committee had under consideration and with which the gentleman from Kansas is familiar.

Mr. [CHARLES L.] BARTLETT [D., Ga.]. Does it include the bond-issue proposition?

Mr. CLAYTON. No. The Committee on the Judiciary did not have jurisdiction of that subject. That belongs to the Committee on Interstate and Foreign Commerce.

Mr. [WILLIAM H.] STAFFORD [R., Wis.]. Will the gentleman yield?

Mr. CLAYTON. With pleasure.

Mr. STAFFORD. Can the gentleman inform the House as to his plans for early consideration of the bill?

Mr. CLAYTON. I have asked the Committee on Rules to bring in a special rule for its early consideration.

Mr. STAFFORD. What is the form of the rule as expressed in the request of the gentleman?

Mr. CLAYTON. Well, it is in the usual form in like cases.

Mr. STAFFORD. How much time for debate?

Mr. CLAYTON. It was suggested by this rule that general debate should be had for 16 hours and 4 hours under the five-minute rule. It has since been suggested that perhaps it would be wise for the Committee on Rules to amend the latter proposition so as to make the time for debate under the five-minute rule longer than 4 hours. . . .

⊥8201   ⊥ REPORTS OF COMMITTEES ON PUBLIC BILLS AND RESOLUTIONS.

Under clause 2 of Rule XIII, bills and resolutions were severally reported from committees, delivered to the Clerk, and referred to the several calendars therein named, as follows: . . .

Mr. CLAYTON, from the Committee on the Judiciary, to which was referred the bill (H. R. 15657) to supplement existing laws against unlawful restraints and monopolies, and for other purposes, reported the same with amendment, accompanied by a report (No. 627), which said bill and report were referred to the House Calendar.

HOUSE DEBATE
63d Cong., 2d Sess.
May 22, 1914

51 CONG. REC. 9068

The CHAIRMAN. Under the special order of the House, the bill (H. R. 15657) to supplement existing laws against unlawful restraints and monopolies, and for other purposes, is now before the committee for its consideration. Under the further terms of the special order the first reading of the bill will be dispensed with, and the Clerk will report the bill by title.

The Clerk read as follows:

A bill (H. R. 15657) to supplement existing laws against unlawful restraints and monopolies, and for other purposes. . . .

Mr. [EDWIN Y.] WEBB [D., N.C.]. Mr. Chairman, I would like to have the Chair notify me when I have used one hour.

Mr. Chairman, the Democratic Party in their convention in 1912, among other things, declared in favor of supplemental legislation to the now existing antitrust laws, such as prevention of holding companies, interlocking directorates, discrimination in price, and so forth. The Judiciary Committee in obedience to that plank in the platform, for the last four or five months have sat patiently and diligently in an effort to present to this House some bill which would carry out the reasonable demand found in that platform. It is proper to say, gentlemen, that the committee has dealt with this question faithfully, conscientiously, and studiously. For nearly four months the entire membership of that committee, or as many as could attend, sat and listened to witnesses from all parts of the United States on proposed or tentative bills. The subcommittee spent much time and great patience in trying to present a bill which would remedy the evils that are almost universally complained of and at the same time unfetter and unshackle legitimate business in the United States.

At least the majority of that committee feel that we have presented a bill which to a great extent does that very thing. The minority members of the committee are not satisfied among themselves about the provisions of the bill H. R. 15657, which is now under consideration. Mr. GRAHAM of Pennsylvania, Mr. DYER, and Mr. DANFORTH, if you will read their minority report, are very insistent that we have gone entirely too far; that we have put entirely too many teeth in this bill; that it is even radical; and that the Sherman antitrust law, as it now stands, is ample to root out all monopoly and

⊥9069   destroy all unfair restraints of trade and trade practices. On the other hand, ⊥ Messrs. NELSON and VOLSTEAD say that it is a distinct disappointment in that we have not gone far enough; that it is a mild makeshift; that it has not teeth enough; that it is not radical at all; and that it is a sop thrown out to business. And still another minority report is filled by our good friend Mr. MORGAN of Oklahoma, and he does not exactly agree with either one of the other factions of the minority, and it is understood by the majority of the committee, although he does not agree with the majority entirely or the minority or the minority of the minority, that he proposes to vote for this bill.

I say again, gentlemen, that the committee has labored patiently and honestly. And before I proceed to discuss the bill section by section, I want to be permitted to say one word in reply to the gentleman from Iowa [Mr. TOWNER], who a moment ago read an extract from the Washington Times, suggesting that the President had dictated and dominated the construction of this entire bill.[5.468] I want to tell my friend that that is absolutely unfair and untrue. The President has never at any time suggested or demanded that no amendment should be added to this bill; he has never at any time suggested that this bill should be put through as it is presented here to-day.

He has acted as any other great Executive should act who is anxious about the good of his country, about the unshackling and protection of honest business, and about the restraint and punishment of unscrupulous business. [Applause on the Democratic side.]

If, as my friend insinuates, the President has so much arbitrary power with the Democratic Members of Congress, pray tell us why the most liberal rule ever presented by the House of Representatives on any bill is before you now? The President might well have gone further if he had been dictatorial, as my friend intimates, and asked the Committee on Rules to put this bill through just as it is written, and not to allow an amendment to be offered or considered.

Mr. [JOHN N.] GARNER [D., Tex.]. And still be in entire keeping with what the Republican Party had been doing for 16 years?

Mr. WEBB. Yes. Many a time have I sat here under Republican rule and seen bills passed where no one was allowed to even offer an amendment or vote for one. But we

---

[5.468] Congressman Webb's reference is to the immediately preceding debate of the same day concerning the interstate trade commission (FTC) bill. The following excerpt from the debate is Congressman Horace M. Towner's (R., Iowa) statement appearing at 51 CONG. REC. 9066 (1914).

> Mr. TOWNER. Mr. Chairman, I desire to call the attention of the committee to an article that was published in the Washington Times day before yesterday. It is headed "Want more teeth in Wilson antitrust bills."
> I will read it for the enlightenment of the committee, and especially for the gentlemen having charge of this bill:
> "WANT MORE 'TEETH' IN WILSON ANTITRUST BILLS.
> "Efforts were made to-day by Congressman STEVENS of New Hampshire and Louis D. Brandeis, former counsel to the Interstate Commerce Commission, to persuade President Wilson to permit more 'teeth' to be placed in the administration antitrust bills. The callers presented their views to the President and urged him to consent to amendments to the bills after they have reached the Senate.
> "The President did not commit himself. It is not thought likely he will permit any changes at this time."
> During the debate on this bill in the House there have been many amendments presented, some of them substantive, some of them merely to correct the text of the bill, and some to correct both grammatical and other errors; but the committee would not allow a single one of these amendments to be adopted. They have all been voted down by the committee having charge of this bill. Now, we know the reason. It is not the House of Representatives that is legislating; it is the President of the United States, who says that these bills must not be changed from the form in which they have received his approval. These gentlemen sit here and pretend to legislate for the people, pretend to represent their constituencies, pretend to act upon the merits of the case; but they are merely recording the declared instructions of the President of the United States in regard to these trust bills. What a farce it is to call it by the name of legislation. These gentlemen are not doing what they want to do. They are intelligent men; they are not doing what they think best, although their judgment is good. They would be perfectly willing to accept amendments that appeal to their reason if they dared; but evidently they do not dare to do so. They are here under instructions. This bill, and I presume the other bills, are to be forced through under whip and spur, just as they have been written, and then sent to the Senate, and it is exceedingly doubtful whether the President will allow any amendments to be made there. This is not legislating for the people. It is no wonder that there are no teeth in this bill. It is no wonder that they are not to be considered on their merits. Evidently the President has determined that he will not allow the great interests of this country to even think they will be injured in any possible way by his trust bills. The trust bills are not even to scare any of the great industries of the country. The President now evidently intends to conciliate them. So, Mr. Chairman, we have been going through the farce of a pretended consideration of this bill and not a real one. I presume we will go through the farce of a pretended consideration of the other bills. But the result is all determined—all declared. These gentlemen have received their instructions and obediently they will obey.

give you 16 hours of general debate, and after the general debate is over we give you unlimited time, both on the Republican and on the Democratic side, to debate every line and section of this bill under the five-minute rule.

Mr. GARNER. And to offer any amendment which anyone wishes to offer?

Mr. WEBB. Yes. Any amendment can be offered and adopted if the House chooses. The President has not said that no amendment shall be offered or adopted to this bill. He has simply said that the general provisions of this bill meet his approval. But as to a hard-and-fast suggestion that he does not want the language of this bill added to or taken from, he has never uttered a syllable to any member of the committee who has seen him during the progress of the construction of this act to this effect.

Now, Mr. Chairman, having said that much, I am going to take it upon myself to give a running outline of the meaning and meat of each provision in this bill. I know how busy Members are, and it is no reflection upon a busy Member of this House when I say that probably not more than 10 per cent of the Members have read this bill; certainly have not read it carefully. It has only recently been reported, and Members are so busy that they can not, in the nature of things, read every bill that comes into the House; and at the risk of tiring the Members of the House, I am going to give a synopsis of the entire bill.

I anticipate that there are some Members of the House who hardly know that there is anything in this bill except the provision about labor. Now, there is a great deal more, gentlemen, as you will see, as I go along, section by section. I believe that a simple, straightforward, nontechnical statement as to its meaning may be helpful not only to the Members of the House, but to laymen who may care to know what the bill is and what it means.

Section 1, Mr. Chairman, is devoted entirely to terminology, as you will see. Section 2 provides—and let me call the attention of my friend from Iowa [Mr. TOWNER], if he is here, and that of my friend from Wisconsin [Mr. NELSON], if he is here, to the fact that Messrs. GRAHAM and DANFORTH and DYER think there are too many teeth in section 2. We start right here with the teeth they object to.

Section 2 forbids any person to discriminate in price between different purchasers of commodities in the same or different sections, if such commodities are sold for use within the United States or within any place under the jurisdiction of the United States, and if such discriminating sale is made with the purpose or intent to destroy or wrongfully injure the business of a competitor of either such purchaser or seller. The violation of this provision subjects a person to a fine of not exceeding $5,000 or to imprisonment not exceeding one year, or both.

This section does not apply when the discrimination in price is made on account of a difference in the grade, quality, or quantity of the commodity, or when the discrimination is only due to a difference in the cost of transportation. Nothing in this section prevents a person from selecting his own customers. The necessity for legislation of this character is apparent. Discriminating in price is a bludgeon which the trusts have often used to put competitors "out of business." For the last 20 years this practice has been one of the handmaids of monopoly, the advance guard of an army of arbitrary methods, which has injured and destroyed the business of thousands of smaller concerns.

The violation of this section subjects the person violating it to a fine of not exceeding $5,000 or a punishment not exceeding one year's imprisonment. But we provide—

> That nothing herein contained shall prevent discrimination in price between purchasers of commodities on account of differences in the grade, quality, or quantity of the commodity sold, or that makes only due allowance for difference in the cost of transportation: *And provided further*, That nothing herein contained shall prevent persons engaged in selling goods, wares, or merchandise in commerce from selecting their own customers, except as provided in section 3 of this act.

Section 3 forbids the owner or operator of any mine— . . .

Mr. [FINIS J.] GARRETT [D., Tenn.]. Do I understand that section 2 would prevent a retail merchant from discriminating in prices?

Mr. WEBB. No, sir. The retail merchant sells not in interstate commerce.

Mr. GARRETT of Tennessee. He might, of course, sell in interstate commerce, but it does not affect the general retail business?

Mr. WEBB. No, sir. That is generally intrastate, and we are dealing with interstate practices. . . .

Mr. [HENRY A.] COOPER [R., Wis.]. I would like to ask the gentleman from North Carolina why the trade commission was not given specific power to enforce a provision like that of section 2, which the gentleman has just read?

Mr. WEBB. One answer to that, Mr. Chairman, is that the Committee on the Judiciary did not have the consideration of the trade commission bill. That was in the Interstate Commerce Committee. Another reason is that in this section we make it a crime punishable by a fine not exceeding $5,000 and imprisonment not exceeding one year to violate any of the provisions of that section. . . .

Mr. [RAYMOND B.] STEVENS [D., N.H.]. Does the gentleman know that amendments to the trade-commission bill were ruled out of order on the ground that the Committee on Interstate and Foreign Commerce did not have jurisdiction of that subject, and that an amendment would clearly enlarge and change the scope of the bill? Apparently nobody has any jurisdiction over this sort of business. One committee has denied it, and the other committee says they could not do it because the other committee has it.

Mr. WEBB. We have exercised that jurisdiction, Mr. Chairman, in the second section of the bill. . . .

Mr. STAFFORD. As I understand it, the purpose here is to provide a uniform price for all persons and customers for the same quality of goods?

Mr. WEBB. And under like conditions.

Mr. STAFFORD. About which there can not be any competition at all, so far as the seller is concerned, in meeting the competition of some other competitor?

Mr. WEBB. Oh, yes; if he meets the competition of some other person, he is not meeting that competition for the purpose of destroying or wrongfully injuring his competitor. . . .

⊥ Mr. [WILLIAM L.] IGOE [D., Mo.]. Does this extend to the point of forbidding ⊥9070 the giving of discounts on payments or discounts on goods bought in large quantities?

Mr. WEBB. Discounts are not mentioned in this section.

Mr. IGOE. Would it include discounts for payments upon a certain day?

Mr. WEBB. I can not answer that positively, but if such amounts to discrimination, directly or indirectly, the section covers it.

Mr. IGOE. It ought to.

Mr. GARNER. Not if all customers are treated exactly alike.

Mr. IGOE. A merchant might make his customer pay for that time.

Mr. WEBB. I think the seller who gives a discount to one person and not to another ought to be included within the provisions of this section, and is, in my opinion.

Mr. GARNER. He ought to be.

Mr. [ALBEN W.] BARKLEY [D., Ky.]. But the purpose and object must be evil?

Mr. WEBB. Yes; the object must be evil, and to destroy the competitor or wrongfully injure him. . . .

Mr. [DANIEL E.] GARRETT [D., Tex.]. It is the only question I expect to ask concerning the bill. I think the whole thing is wrapped up in this language, in line 12, page 21:

> That nothing herein contained shall prevent persons engaged in selling goods, wares, and merchandise in commerce from selecting their own customers, except as provided in section 3 of this act.

And section 3 refers to other matters. Now, the question I want to ask is, if a monopoly in fact has the right under this law to go out over the country and select the persons to whom it will sell, then how can you have competition when that exclusive privilege is granted to a monopoly by law?

Mr. WEBB. In the first place, the gentleman assumes that a monopoly will be permitted to operate at will in the United States. We assume that if such monopoly does exist, it will be broken up under the provisions of the Sherman antitrust law, and we allow a person to select his own customer, because it is very doubtful whether you can forbid him doing that very thing.

But just one further suggestion. You will find that the evil in selecting customers is not in the mere selection of customers, but in the selection of a customer on condition that that customer will not sell a competitive article. We destroy the right to do that and make a person guilty of crime if a trust undertakes to sell an article to a merchant on condition that that merchant shall sell no competitive article.

Mr. GARRETT of Texas. Perhaps I should not have used the word "trust"; but here is what I had in mind—I will strike out the word "trust." Suppose an individual desires to go to the Harvester Co., which is a combination of all the manufacturers of harvesters in the United States, and offers that company the price at which it is selling binders and mowers and hayrakes to another person in his town. Can he do that under this bill? Would not the manufacturer have the right to say, "No; I will not accept your money, although you offer me the same price and the same terms which I am receiving from another citizen in your town"?

Mr. WEBB. That is undoubtedly true, and that is the law to-day. We have not changed the right of a man to select his own customer; but we have changed his right to select his customer on condition that that customer will not sell any competitive goods, and that is where the evil is most widespread in this country do-day and has been for 15 years.

Mr. BARTLETT. May I ask the gentleman a question on this section?

Mr. WEBB. Yes, indeed.

Mr. BARTLETT. In what way does this section which you are now discussing change the law as it now is, as construed by the Supreme Court in the Tobacco case?[5.469] Is it not a fact that one of the practices condemned by the Supreme Court in that case was the very thing that you now propose to prohibit?

Mr. WEBB. The difference between this section and the Tobacco case is this: Under this section there may be a hundred different offenses which are condemned, whereas under the Tobacco case it took all of those offenses combined to make them guilty of a restraint of interstate trade under the Sherman law. We condemn the individual acts which lead to a restraint of interstate trade, whereas at present you must show a sufficient number of such acts of restraint to make such a restraint as the Supreme Court will declare illegal under the trust laws.

Mr. BARTLETT. That is an answer to my question. . . .

Mr. [WOODSON R.] OGLESBY [D., N.Y.]. With regard to this particular section and the question asked by the gentleman from Texas [Mr. GARRETT], I understand that to mean—and I am asking the question to be corrected if I am in error—that if there were two merchants in a village, town, or city who wanted the agency for some article, and both of them applied to the manufacturer asking to handle that article, the manufacturer under this section would have the right to decide which one of those two men he would deal with, and which one should have the agency in that town.

Mr. WEBB. That is true.

Mr. OGLESBY. That has nothing whatever to do with the question of price.

Mr. WEBB. Not at all.

Section 3 forbids the owner or operator of any mine or any person controlling the product of any mine to arbitrarily refuse to sell such product for use within the United States. The violation of this section subjects a person to the same punishment as is described in section 2.

This section is based upon the idea that the products of mines are naturally God given, and no person ought to have the right to arbitrarily refuse to sell such products of necessity to responsible persons who wish to buy them. Often in the chill of winter the products of a few mines have been monopolized by a few dealers, and the price of coal has been advanced arbitrarily, ofttimes taking advantage of those who are too poor to resist and too weak to protest against such outrages.

Mr. GARNER. Is there much difference in principle between the mining industry and the lumber industry? Lumber is a God-given product. It gives a house to shelter

---

[5.469] United States v. American Tobacco Co. 221 U.S. 106, 31 S. Ct. 632, 55 L. Ed. 663 (1911), portions of which are reprinted *supra* at chapter 1.

people in the winter. In the way in which that industry is carried on in this country today, the manufacturers refuse to sell to certain lumber dealers who do not comply with the conditions of the wholesaler. I do not see much difference in the principle that you apply to the mining industry and the principle that ought to apply to the lumber industry.

Mr. WEBB. There is some force to that suggestion. In fact, there is force in the suggestion that the section be made to apply to all raw material; but I beg the House to remember that in framing antitrust laws or amendments thereto you find more difficulty than you do in the performance of any other duty in this House. If you do not believe it, try it. It is easy to rise here and talk in generalities, but when you come to write your suggestions into the mandates of law you get into great difficulty and wade in much deep water.

Mr. GARNER. I do not intend this as a criticism.

Mr. WEBB. I understand.

Mr. GARNER. I am simply directing the attention of the committee to this matter because the gentleman has said that he and his committee and the President would welcome any amendment to this bill that sought to make it a better law. I have simply made this suggestion in response to that statement.

Mr. WEBB. I answered my friend with absolute frankness. . . .

Mr. GARRETT of Tennessee. Is the Committee on the Judiciary clear in its judgment that this section is constitutional and enforcible?

Mr. WEBB. We are as reasonably clear on that as we can be, considering the decisions in reference to our interstate-commerce powers. It does announce a new principle, but we thought it was vital and important enough to base it upon many decisions which indicate that Congress has that power. We have undoubtedly the right to exclude coal companies from using interstate instrumentalities who do not obey the law.

Mr. GARRETT of Tennessee. Undoubtedly as a negative proposition, but when you undertake to lay down an affirmative proposition, have you any precedents for that?

Mr. WEBB. As I said a moment ago, it is a new principle. Now I will yield to the gentleman from Oklahoma.

Mr. [SCOTT] FERRIS [D., Okla.]. I am keenly interested in section 3, and I am aware of the fact that we are all hoping for a decision from the Supreme Court soon on the common-carrier proposition of pipe lines.

Mr. WEBB. The oil case?[5.470]

Mr. FERRIS. Yes. I wonder if the committee has given consideration to the proposition of divorcing the production of mines from the transportation. There is the real nucleus of the trouble. For instance, in the oil proposition the Standard Oil ⊥ pipe ⊥9071 lines and the Oil Trust, who have total control of carriage and transportation, go in and get alternative wells among the independent producers and refuse to take the oil of others because they are not common carriers. They will drain the land of oil by controlling these alternate wells. So it seems to me that two things might be considered in this section, one the bolstering up of the law of the common carrier and the other divorcing the production from transportation in any case.

Mr. WEBB. The committee did consider all that, but we felt that the control and regulation of common carriers was entirely within the jurisdiction and field of the Interstate Commerce Commission, and we had a hesitancy in stepping over on their territory.

Mr. FERRIS. But your section 3 is closely allied to that.

Mr. WEBB. Section 3 takes care of the mines, and that means gas, oil, and coal. We did not go further and try to control those things that belong to the control of the Interstate Commerce Commission.

Mr. FERRIS. But those who suffer from faulty and inefficient laws should not fall between stools. They should not be compelled to suffer. The committee should deal effectively with it.

Mr. WEBB. We went as far as the jurisdiction of our committee would warrant us

---

[5.470] See notes 5.552, 5.553, & 5.554 *infra* and accompanying House debate.

in going in providing what we have in that section, and we thought it would be encroaching on the Interstate Commerce Commission's field if we undertook to go further. . . .

Mr. GARNER. The gentleman speaks of the definition of the word "mine" as including oil and gas. Does the gentleman believe that that would include oil and gas wells?

Mr. WEBB. That was our interpretation.

Mr. FERRIS. I might say that that comes under a different branch of the mineral law. Oil and gas come under the placer mining laws and coal comes under the other laws. . . .

Mr. [SAMUEL B.] AVIS [R., W. Va.]. In asking the gentleman the question I expect to ask him, I want to say that I do not ask it in any partisan spirit. I come from a State that has 826 coal mines. The bituminous coal industry employs 73,000 men. I have received letters from hundreds of coal operators, irrespective of politics, who say to me that if this section is adopted it means the destruction of the small coal producer in the State of West Virginia. With that statement I want to add further, Did this committee in reporting on this measure consider the fact—

Mr. WEBB. I hope the gentleman from West Virginia will ask his question, as I want to get through. I do not mean any discourtesy to the gentleman.

Mr. AVIS. I was trying to lead up to the point that I wanted to get at. You provide in this section that—

It shall be unlawful for the owner or operator of any mine or for any person controlling the product of any mine engaged in selling its product in commerce to refuse arbitrarily to sell such product to a responsible person—

And so forth.

Now, I have taken the trouble to find out whether that word "arbitrarily" has ever been judicially defined, and I only find two decisions. One is an English decision and one a decision from the State of West Virginia. In the English decision they held that the word "arbitrary" means "not supported by fair, solid, and substantial cause, and without reason given." The West Virginia definition says "without any reason therefor." Now, if these definitions are to apply, what, then, does the committee consider would be the meaning of "arbitrarily refused"? That is the question I am leading up to.

Mr. WEBB. Mr. Chairman, I will say to the gentleman that it is a word ordinarily used. It means to act without justification, without cause, without reason, without just excuse. I think all of those are synonyms for the word "arbitrarily."

Mr. AVIS. Then that leaves it to the court to say what is a sufficient excuse, and the committee does not attempt to do so?

Mr. WEBB. Oh, we can not define it. That is for the court to define. You can not define fraud; you can not define a great many things. You have to leave that to the court.

Mr. AVIS. Mr. Chairman, will the gentleman yield further?

Mr. WEBB. I hope the gentleman will pardon me, but I think the decisions of the courts ought to be read in the gentleman's own time. . . .

Mr. BARKLEY. Mr. Chairman, I notice the committee permits manufacturers and dealers in products to select their customers in different portions of the country, and under section 3 certain industrial corporations are forbidden from doing that same thing. Has the committee considered whether or not that might be regarded as in a sense class legislation—permitting one class of people to do a certain thing and forbidding another class to do the same thing?

Mr. WEBB. Yes; we have gone all through that. There is quite a difference, in the first place, from the moral side on the question of policy. One is the product as it naturally lies in the bowels of the earth, placed there by God Almighty, and we think that a man who happens to own it, no matter how he happened to get title to it, ought not to have the right arbitrarily to close his fist and say that he will not sell except to a favored few, especially when the products of mines are put there for the benefit of God's creatures. . . .

Mr. [SILAS R.] BARTON [R., Neb.]. Mr. Chairman, I understood the gentleman to say to the gentleman from Texas [Mr. GARNER] that a distinction was made in this respect, that the man who sold the coal from the mine could not select his customers, but that the man who owned the vast forests and lumber could do it. Do I understand that statement correctly?

Mr. WEBB. We have not applied it to lumber. We have applied it to the products of the mines, and, as I frankly stated to the gentleman from Texas [Mr. GARNER], there may be some good reason why it should also be applied to all raw materials, but we have not done it. Further, it may seem as if this provision is class legislation to some extent, but the Federal Constitution does not clearly forbid this kind of legislation when based on the commerce power vested in Congress. There are sections in the Constitution of the United States which forbid class legislation by the States, but these sections do not restrict Congress, though undoubtedly glaring class legislation would be repugnant to the spirit of our Constitution and the genius of our institutions. . . .

Mr. [WARREN W.] BAILEY [D., Pa.]. There is nothing in this section or in the bill which makes it unlawful for a mine to be shut down and prices thus to be controlled.

Mr. WEBB. No. . . .

Mr. FERRIS. I want to inquire of the gentleman, if he will yield further, if he considered the advisability of inserting in section 3 the same regulation as to water power that he has as to the products of the mines. There is nothing on earth so susceptible of monopoly as falling water. It is not here to-day or to-morrow, but it is here for all time, and it brings light and heat and all of the multitudinous advantages that go into the home and into the city. I wondered why in the bill that the God-given commodities, the gentleman having referred to them in that term, ought not to include water. What could be more necessary than to include water power in that class?

Mr. WEBB. Mr. Chairman, I will make the same answer to my friend from Oklahoma that I made to the gentleman from Texas [Mr. GARNER]. There may be some reason for including that in this section, and it all shows the difficulty of framing a bill of this character, the difficulties that we run against when we consider it, for one man wants water power, another man wants lumber, another wants oil, another coal, and another iron included. We thought we were making a good beginning by including in it all of the products of the mine, and if that works well in the future it may be that we can include the other products which the gentlemen have suggested this afternoon.

Mr. FERRIS. The question of water power is so intensely important—

Mr. WEBB. I agree it is.

Mr. FERRIS. Because falling water is so susceptible of monopoly, its use is so universal by everyone that if there is any place on earth where it would take hold it seems to me it is right there. Of course, I am not making this in any criticism. . . .

Mr. [MARTIN B.] MADDEN [R., Ill.]. Under the provisions of this section 3, would the adoption of this into law prevent a man who is losing money as a mine operator from closing down his mine?

Mr. WEBB. I think not; that would not be "arbitrary," as I think my friend knows, although he is not a lawyer, but he is a man of fine sense, and he would at once answer that question in the negative.

Mr. MADDEN. It looks to me as if it would.

⊥ Mr. COOPER. Will the gentleman permit me to ask him one question about ⊥9072 section 2 which contains the so-called prohibition against discrimination?

Mr. WEBB. Yes, sir.

Mr. COOPER. I want to preface my question by saying that the bill seems to me expressly to permit discriminations, and on that point I will ask the gentleman how he interprets the proviso beginning on line 7:

> *Provided*, That nothing herein contained shall prevent discrimination in price between purchasers of commodities on account of differences in the grade, quality, or quantity of the commodity sold, or that makes only due allowance for difference in the cost of transportation.

Observe that the proviso expressly allows discrimination on account of "quantity of commodity sold" and "difference in cost of transportation."

Now, the gentleman knows, that if a retailer buys in carload lots he pays less for goods and less for transporting them than does his small competitor who buys exactly similar goods in less-than-carload lots. This proviso specifically permits the big retailer to buy goods from a wholesaler at a less cost than his little competitor must pay to the same wholesaler, and it also permits the big man to have cheaper transportation than his little competitor can secure, and therefore the proviso gives the big man an opportunity to become bigger and bigger and more and more able to drive the little man to the wall. By this difference in the cost of exactly similar goods, bought from the same vendor, and by this difference in the cost of transportation authorized by this proviso, there is a direct permission of discrimination such as the bill was said to prohibit.

Mr. WEBB. I will say to my friend if we did not take into consideration the cost of transportation we would be accused by that side, and possibly by ours, of making the most arbitrary rule ever sought to be enacted into law. That is a business method and practice you can not get away from, and, in addition, it has been the practice from time immemorial that a man buying wholesale lots necessarily is entitled to a little more consideration or a cheaper rate than the man who buys, to use an old expression, in "dribs" and "drabs," or by retail. That is a business necessity that the committee did not feel warranted in trying to disturb; and I am informed that this very provision, practically the same provision, exists in 17 or 19 of the States of the Union, and exists in the State of my friend from Wisconsin who now addresses this question to me.

Mr. COOPER. I am not attempting to argue nor make any statement as to the merits of the proposition.

The gentleman said "necessarily." Perhaps the word "customary" would be more accurate.

Mr. WEBB. I accept the gentleman's amendment.

Mr. COOPER. It is a germane amendment; entirely so. Another thing: This would allow great mail-order houses that buy in enormous quantities to retain the great advantage they have always had.

Mr. WEBB. Will the gentleman draw a section that corrects the evil he mentions and present it at the proper time?

Mr. COOPER. I am simply asking about the bill, which the gentleman defends as a measure that will prevent discriminations in business.

Mr. WEBB. I think we have very high authority for this section, and one of the authorities is the State of Wisconsin, from which the gentleman comes. . . .

Mr. Chairman, section 4 provides against any person making a sale of any commodities for use in the United States, or fix a price charged therefor, or discount from, or rebate upon any such price, on condition or understanding that the lessee or purchaser thereof shall not use or deal in the goods, wares, and so forth, of a competitor. A violation of this section subjects the person violating it to a fine of $5,000 or imprisonment not exceeding one year, or both, in the discretion of the court. This section strikes at another fruitful source of monopoly or restraint of trade. I contend, Mr. Chairman, that no one has the right to sell goods to a purchaser and receive his money for them and at the same time compel such purchaser to refuse to sell a competitive article. Such contract in itself is in restraint of trade and tends directly to monopoly. This practice has been in vogue in the United States for 20 years, and there is scarcely a retail merchant throughout this broad land who has not suffered from such practice, because our country has been literally plastered with these exclusive-sale contracts. And yet our friends tell us that there are no teeth in this section of the bill. . . .

Mr. [FRANK B.] WILLIS [R., Ohio]. I wanted to ask the gentleman whether his committee considered the effect that this would have on the small producer? Now, I am asking that question because there have come to me a number of protests from small concerns. For example, I have in mind a case of a manufacturer of machine tools in my home town, a small concern that employs 40 or 50 men. They take this position, that the only way that they have been able to sell their product is by making exclusive trade agreements with agents in different cities of the United States and that if this bill be enacted into law it will permit an outsider to come in and sell the product under the name in which the product has been worked up in that town, and that will destroy their agency, and therefore will play directly into the hands of their monopolistic competitor. They are up against very severe competition, with a strong organization back of it. Now, what does the gentleman say to that?

Mr. WEBB. I think the small concern which the gentleman mentions has been compelled to adopt that method by the very trusts that first adopted it. He is compelled to adopt it as a matter of self-defense. It is one of the trust's greatest weapons to destroy the little business, which we in this section are trying to protect. The small concern can make a careful selection of a good man to push and introduce its goods, and at the same time have the advantage of not permitting the trust to go to a neighborhood and monopolize on a certain article. As it is to-day, the trust goes to a crossroads merchant and there binds the merchant to sell no article except an article controlled by the trust. Now, what chance has a little fellow to get in with that merchant? He can not do it. He has no place in which to sell his goods. But this section will give your independent concern a right to go to the small merchant and tell him that he is not bound to refuse to sell a competitive article. The law gives him the right to sell that trust-made article and his, too, and the little man can tell him that he would like to have his article put in stock with the other. That would be better for the independent and better for the merchant.

Mr. WILLIS. They make this further objection, that the trust, by its great wealth, is able to maintain its own distributing agencies, but that if this right which they now enjoy is taken away from them, they will have no means whatever of maintaining these agencies, not having the great wealth with which to do it. What is the gentleman's opinion of that objection?

Mr. WEBB. Well, there may be some force in that suggestion, but it is a situation that Congress can not remedy. It is just a condition that we face when we see one strong man, weighing 180 pounds, in a contest with a man who weighs 65 or 100 pounds. It is a condition we meet with—a man worth a million dollars in a contest against a fellow who has only $500. If my friend can tell us a remedy for that, we will be glad to have it. We desire to unfetter both the merchant and the man who sells to the merchant and give him a fair field, and tell him, "You can buy from whom you please and sell wherever you please." . . .

Mr. AVIS. The gentleman has stated that the purpose here is to prevent the big fellow swallowing up the little fellow. Take, for instance, the coal business. I am a small operator. I have built up a trade by years of work, and what is to prevent the big fellow from coming over and taking my whole output and destroying my trade for that particular year?

Mr. WEBB. I suppose the gentleman would not want me to say he ought to be allowed to get it "vi et armis."

Mr. AVIS. You have coal mentioned there—that you can not refuse to sell to the first responsible bidder. Suppose I am a small coal dealer, and some big man comes along and lays down his certified check—a man representing a monopoly—and says, "I bid for your entire product of coal." What is to prevent him from destroying the trade that I have been for years building up?

Mr. WEBB. You would have the right to supply your customers and continue to sell to them.

Mr. AVIS. Does not the gentleman think I would have the right to prefer one customer over another—to prefer my old customers? Yet your bill forbids that.

Mr. WEBB. You can supply one customer and not meet the demands of monopoly.

Mr. AVIS. I thought the gentleman's statement as to section 3 was to the effect that it was intended to prevent discrimination between customers who sold coal and oil and minerals.

Mr. WEBB. It is so intended, and the object of that is to prevent you from selling your entire product to a monopoly when the little man wants to buy from you.

Mr. AVIS. I can not refuse to sell my product to any responsible bidder. That is the objection I have pointed out. I do not point this out in any partisan spirit. I really and sincerely think it would destroy nearly 700 independent coal people in my country, because the big fellows would come along and say, "I am willing to take your entire product, the whole of it, or a part of it"; and yet I, as a coal dealer, may have been building up my trade for years, and the section says I must not sell my whole product to the trust.

Mr. WEBB. You have other customers in whom you have confidence, and you can sell to them.

Mr. AVIS. Evidently the gentleman does not understand me. I said that under this particular language the trust might destroy my trade.

Mr. WEBB. "Sufficient unto the day is the evil thereof," I will say to the gentleman; and I think he should quiet his fears, for the danger he fears does not lie in this section. . . .

Mr. COOPER. In connection with section 4 I would like to ask the gentleman from North Carolina if there is a provision in the bill which prohibits a man selling to a purchaser on the condition that he does not buy from any other seller? Is there any provision here that would require a trust or a big manufacturer who makes a fine article to sell to the little man?

Mr. WEBB. No, sir.

Mr. COOPER. Why should there not be? That is exactly what goes on now. Suppose there are two little concerns in a given village. One of them is already engaged in selling certain articles that are useful and which have a large sale. There is a demand for another article of the same general description, but the maker of that other article will sell it to only one of those two stores in the village. Why should he not be compelled to sell to the customer, a bona fide, responsible customer, just the same as you propose to provide that the mine owner shall sell his products?

Mr. WEBB. We took this view of it: The man who, with his own industry and with his own money, manufactures or transforms the raw material into some useful object ought to have the right to select his purchaser; but we did not think that ought to apply to the man who takes products from the bowels of the earth as God deposited them.

Mr. COOPER. How would that be with a brand of flour?

Mr. WEBB. Well, there is more advancement in the manufacture of flour from the wheat than on the production of coal and oil that are simply taken from the bowels of the earth.

Mr. COOPER. We are trying to pass a law that will promote fair and square dealing and legitimate competition, are we not?

Mr. WEBB. Yes; but there are thousands of things that can not be covered by a bill of this class.

Mr. COOPER. I would like to have the gentleman assign a reason why he has not done in this bill what I have suggested. Does not the gentleman want to, or can he not do it?

Mr. WEBB. It is a question of policy. We think we ought not. . . .

Mr. [JOSEPH A.] GOULDEN [D., N.Y.]. I hope that my friend the new chairman of the committee will pardon a suggestion. In common with many others I am very much interested in the gentleman's statement, and if these interruptions are permitted—and the gentleman is too courteous to decline—I fear we shall not hear the gentleman complete his speech. I therefore suggest that hereafter the gentleman decline further interruptions until he can complete his able and satisfactory statement. [Applause.]

Mr. WEBB. Mr. Chairman, section 5 gives any person who may be injured in his business, by reason of anything forbidden in the antitrust laws, the right to sue for such injury in any district court where the defendant resides, or is found without respect to the amount in controversy and shall recover three-fold the damages sustained, together with the cost of the suit, including a reasonable attorney's fee. This section opens the door of justice to every man, whenever he may be injured by those who violate the antitrust laws, and gives the injured party ample damages for the wrong suffered.

Section 6 provides that when the Government brings a suit in equity against an alleged trust, and the final judgment is rendered in such suit to the effect that the defendant has or has not entered into a contract or conspiracy in the form of a trust or restraint of trade or commerce, that said final judgment may be used as evidence in any other proceeding brought by an individual against the same defendant, and shall be conclusive evidence of the same facts and the same questions of law, in favor of or against any party in any suit brought under the provisions of the antitrust laws. . . .

This section also suspends the running of the statute of limitations against individuals whenever the Government brings an equity suit against any person charged with violating the antitrust laws.

Section 7 provides that the antitrust laws shall not be construed to forbid the existence and operation of fraternal, labor, consumers, agricultural or horticultural organizations, orders or associations instituted for mutual help and having no capital stock and not conducted for profit; neither shall the antitrust laws be construed to forbid or restrain individual members of such organizations from carrying out the legitimate objects of such organizations. This section also permits the operation of traffic associations which are under the supervision of the Interstate Commerce Commission.

Section 8 forbids any corporation to acquire the capital stock of another corporation when both are engaged in commerce, if the effect of such acquisition is to eliminate or substantially lessen competition between such corporations or to create a monopoly of any line of trade anywhere. Nor shall any corporation acquire the capital stock of two or more corporations engaged in commerce if the effect of such acquisition or the use of such stock, by voting or otherwise, is to eliminate or substantially lessen such competition between corporations or to create a monopoly in any line of trade anywhere.

This section exempts purchases of stock for investment solely, and where same is not used by voting or bringing about or lessening competition.

This section permits one corporation to form subsidiary corporations for the actual carrying on of their immediate lawful business, and such parent corporation may own or hold the stock of such subsidiary corporations when this does not eliminate or substantially lessen competition.

This section does not apply to stock transactions heretofore legally made.

Under this section a railroad corporation may construct branch lines, so located as to become feeders, and the parent corporation may own all of or any part of the stock of such branch lines, and a railroad corporation may acquire the stock of a branch line constructed by an independent company where there is no substantial competition between the two. A railroad company under this section is permitted to extend its lines by buying the stock of other railroad companies where there is no substantial competition between the two.

A violation of the provision of this act subjects a person to a fine of not exceeding $5,000 or to imprisonment not exceeding one year, or both.

The common law never allowed one corporation to own the stock of another, but by degrees some of the States have relaxed this rule until the country has become burdened with pools and holding companies which are direct supports of trusts or monopolies. Pooling is practically a partnership of corporations, and their contracts have become nonenforceable, which gives them a fatal weakness. When the pool became a failure on account of this weakness the trust was formed by each corporation transferring its stock to common trustees. Thus, all of the stock of the component corporations was held by trustees, who completely controlled the business of all the corporations in the trust. Each constituent company retained its officers and continued its business, but the amount and price of its product was controlled by the trustees. This form of trust was clearly a partnership of corporations, with the business of all controlled by one head, and we are not surprised to find that this form of trust was declared illegal in the early nineties.

So the next stage of corporation partnership was the holding company, where the stock of each company is transferred to the holding corporation, and this corporation actually owns the stock of the constituent companies, making the constituent corporations subsidiary instead of independent; but in holding corporations the company controls the policy and price of commodities of constituent or subsidiary corporations.

The first State to repeal the common-law principle that any corporation could own the stock of another corporation was New Jersey. The States of Delaware, West Virginia, and Maine soon followed the lead of New Jersey.

After the holding companies came the complete merger, where the stock of the constituent companies is actually bought in and canceled, the only stock being that of the master com⊥pany. This act does not prohibit all holding companies, but only those which substantially lessen competition.

Section 9 provides that after two years from the approval of the act no person who is a member of a partnership or is a director or officer of a corporation engaged in producing or selling materials or supplies or in the construction of railroads shall act as director or officer of any other corporation or common carrier to which such person sells or leases equipment or supplies, and that no officer or director of a bank shall act as director or officer of any such common carrier for which he or such bank acts as agent for or underwriter of the sale or disposal by such common carrier of its securities or from which he or such bank purchases the securities of such common carriers. That two years from the passage of this act no person shall be a director, officer, and so forth, of more than one bank or trust company at the same time if either of such banks or trust companies has deposits, capital, surplus, and undivided profits aggregating more than $2,500,000, and no private bank or person who is director in a bank or trust company organized under the laws of a State having deposits, capital, surplus, and undivided profits aggregating more than $2,500,000 shall be a director in any bank organized under the laws of the United States. The eligibility of a director is determined by the average amount of deposits, capital, surplus, and undivided profits, as shown by a statement of such bank filed under the law during the fiscal year preceding the date set for the annual election of directors, and when a director has been elected according to the provisions of this act it shall be lawful for him to remain such director for one year.

This section further provides that no United States banking company in a city of more than 100,000 population shall have as a director, officer, or employee any private banker or director of any other bank or trust company located in the same place.

This section does not apply to mutual savings banks without capital stock, nor does it apply to the directors of one bank or one trust company when the entire capital stock of either is owned by the stockholders of the other. Nor does it repeal the provisions of the Federal reserve act which permits a director in class A of said act to be a director of one member bank.

This section further provides that after two years from the approval of the act no person shall at the same time be a director in two or more corporations either of which has a capital, surplus, and undivided profits aggregating more than $1,000,000 if such corporations shall have been theretofore competitors to such an extent that an elimination of competition by agreement between them would be a violation of any provision of the antitrust laws. Eligibility of stockholders under this section is determined by the aggregate capital, surplus, and undivided profits, exclusive of dividends declared but not paid, at the end of the fiscal year next preceding the election of directors, and a director who is elected under the provisions of this act may continue as such for at least one year.

Violation of the provisions of this act subjects a person to a fine of $100 a day during the continuance of such violation, or to imprisonment not exceeding one year, or both.

Section 10 allows suit, under the antitrust law, to be brought in any district where the defendant is an inhabitant or may be found.

Section 11 provides that in suits brought by the United States subpoenas for witnesses may run into any district.

Section 12 provides that when a corporation is found guilty of violating the antitrust laws the offense shall be deemed to be also that of the individual directors, officers, and agents of such corporation who shall have authorized, ordered, or done any of the prohibited acts, and such directors or officers are deemed guilty of a misdemeanor and shall be subjected to a fine of not more than $5,000, or to imprisonment not exceeding one year, or both. In this section we have attempted to make guilt personal, and we believe we have succeeded in doing so.

The President, in his message of January 20, 1914, on this subject, said:

> We ought to see to it, and the judgment of practical and sagacious men of affairs everywhere would applaud us if we do see to it, that penalties and punishments should fall not upon business itself, to its confusion and interruption, but upon the individuals who use the

instrumentalities of business to do things which public policy and sound business practice condemn. Every act of business is done at the command or upon the initiative of some ascertainable person or group of persons. These should be held individually responsible, and the punishment should fall upon them, not upon the business organization of which they make illegal use.

Section 13 gives the district courts jurisdiction to restrain and prevent violations of this act and makes it the duty of the district attorneys, under the direction of the Attorney General, to bring suits to prevent and restrain such violations. Such suits may be brought by way of petition, and after the parties complained of shall have been duly notified, the court shall proceed to hear and determine the case. During the pendency of the suit the court may issue temporary restraining orders, and the court may require other parties to be brought before the court, whether they reside in the district or not, and subpoenas to that end may be served in any district.

Section 14 gives any person the right to sue for injunctive relief against threatened loss or damage by a violation of the antitrust laws when and under the same conditions as injunctive relief is granted under the rules governing such proceedings; and upon giving proper bond and showing that the danger of irreparable loss or damage is immediate, then a preliminary injunction may issue, but no one shall bring suit in equity for injunctive relief against a common carrier except the United States.

Section 15 regulates the issuance of injunctions and conforms largely to the rules of the United States Supreme Court.

Section 16 provides that, except as provided in section 14, a restraining or interlocutory order of injunction shall not issue, unless security is given in such manner as the court may deem proper.

Section 17 requires that all orders of injunction or restraining orders shall set forth the reasons for issuance of same, be specific in terms, and describe in reasonable detail the act sought to be restrained, and shall bind only the parties to the suit, their agents, servants, employees, attorneys, or those in actual concert with them, and who shall, by personal service or otherwise, have received actual notice of the same.

Section 18 provides that no restraining order or injunction shall be granted in a case between employer and employee or between persons seeking employment, involving or growing out of a dispute concerning terms or conditions of employment, unless necessary to prevent irreparable injury to property or to a property right of the applicant, for which injury there is no adequate remedy at law, and such property right must be described with particularity in the application, which must be in writing and sworn to by the applicant or by his agent or attorney, and, further, that no restraining order or injunction shall prohibit any person from terminating any relation of employment, or from ceasing to perform any work, or from recommending or persuading others by peaceful means so to do, or from attending at or near a house or place where any person resides or works or happens to be for the purpose of peacefully obtaining or communicating information, or of peacefully persuading any person to work or quit work, or from ceasing to patronize or to employ any party to such dispute, or from advising others by peaceful means to do so, or by paying or giving to or withholding from any strike benefits, or from peaceably assembling at any place in a lawful manner and for lawful purposes, or from doing any act or thing which might lawfully be done in the absence of such dispute by any party thereto.

Mr. Chairman, when you read section 7, together with sections 17 and 18, the members of the Judiciary Committee declare unto this House, unto the country, and unto the laboring people that we have given them a bill of rights. We have given them a magna charta. We have given them what they have been demanding from this Congress for 20 long years, and I therefore express the hope that the sections in this bill which seem to be unsatisfactory to the trusts, monopolies, and unscrupulous business of the country—because we know that they are not particularly anxious to look after the laboring class of people—may be adopted by this committee and this House. We hear, on the other hand, that there may be some criticism from some quarter that we have not gone far enough in the interest of labor; but I appeal to the sensible men, the patriotic men on both sides of this floor, to agree that in these various sections of this bill we have given labor a bill of rights and a new charter. I trust that those who represent laboring men as I do—and in this connection I want to say that never in 11 years' service here have I voted against labor on the floor of this House or in the committee—will tell them, as I tell them as their friend, that they have a great charter in this bill, and that they ought to be thankful that it is here and be satisfied with it. I appeal to the men who represent labor directly. I have not a labor union in my district, and yet I have stood by labor and am standing by them now, because we have given them something that the head of the American Federation of Labor and other labor organizations of the United States have been clamoring for lo these many years; and, having gotten it, I believe they should sing a pean of joy and accept it as it is written in this bill.

Mr. [JAMES W.] BRYAN [Prog., Wash.]. Will the gentleman state what definite and particular objections he has to the amendments that the laboring men ask for—why he objects to granting them?

Mr. WEBB. I do not care to discuss that at this time for good reasons, but we shall discuss it fully later. . . .

Mr. [ROBERT M.] SWITZER [R., Ohio]. Will the gentleman please state how many members of this committee that considered this bill have coal mines in their districts?

Mr. WEBB. I have not made a poll of the committee, and do not know.

Now, Mr. Chairman, the next section of the bill is designed to give laboring men the right of trial by jury in indirect contempt cases where the contempt also involves the commission of a criminal offense either under statute or common law. That is another demand labor has made on Congress for many years. They now have it within their grasp. . . .

Mr. J. M. C. SMITH [R., Mich.]. In explaining the right to peaceably ask another person to work or to refrain from working you use the language "at or near a person's residence or home."

Mr. WEBB. I beg the gentleman's pardon. Not residence or home, but at any place, in a lawful manner.

Mr. J. M. C. SMITH. I would like to know if that would not allow a person to go into a man's residence for the purpose of persuading a workingman—peacefully, of course—to work or not to work?

Mr. WEBB. I think if he goes peacefully, if permitted to go in by the owner of the house, he could do so. If the owner of a house shuts his door, a person could not go in. There is no objection to a man going to my home or yours if he is permitted to do so by the owner of the castle.

Mr. J. M. C. SMITH. The gentleman thinks the owner of the house could keep him out?

Mr. WEBB. Oh, of course; that is his castle. Mr. Chairman, how much time have I occupied?

The CHAIRMAN. The gentleman has occupied one hour and nine minutes.

Mr. WEBB. Mr. Chairman, sections 19, 20, 21, 22, and 23 provide for a trial by jury of indirect contempts.

Section 19 provides that any person disobeying a writ, order, or decree of a district court, or of the District of Columbia, by doing any act or thing therein forbidden to be done, if the act or thing done by him be of such character as to constitute also a criminal offense, either by statute or common law, shall be proceeded against in the following manner—section 20, that is—when it appears to the court, by the return of an officer or upon affidavit of some person or upon information filed by the district attorney, that there is reasonable ground to believe that any person has been guilty of such contempt, the judge may issue a rule requiring such person to show cause, upon a certain day, why he should not be punished therefor, which rule, with a copy of the affidavit or information, shall be served upon the person charged, giving him time to prepare for and make return to the order. If his return does not sufficiently purge himself, in the opinion of the court, a trial shall be directed at a time and place fixed by the court. If the person fail or refuse to make return to the rule to show cause, an attachment may issue against his person to compel an answer.

In all cases arising under this section such trial may be held by the court, or if accused demand same, by jury, in which latter event the court may impanel a jury from the jurors in attendance, or the judge in chambers may cause a sufficient number to be selected and summoned to attend at the time and place of trial, at which time a jury shall be selected and impaneled, as upon a trial for misdemeanor, and shall proceed as in criminal cases prosecuted by indictment. If the accused shall be found guilty, judgment shall be entered describing the punishment, either by fine or imprisonment, or both. The fine shall be paid to the United States or to the complainant or other person injured by the act constituting the contempt, but in no case shall the fine to be paid to the United States by a natural person exceed the sum of $1,000, nor shall imprisonment exceed a term of six months.

Section 21 provides that evidence in such cases may be preserved and prescribes the method of appeal, and when a writ of error is granted execution of judgment shall be stayed and the accused admitted to bail.

Section 22 provides that nothing contained in this bill shall be construed to relate to contempts committed in the presence of the court, or so near thereto as to obstruct the administration of justice, nor to contempts committed in disobedience of any lawful writ, process, order, rule, decree, or command entered in any suit or action brought or prosecuted in the name of or on behalf of the United States.

Section 23 provides that no action for contempt shall be brought against a person after one year from the date of the act complained of, nor shall any such proceeding bar a criminal prosecution for the same act, and nothing herein shall affect pending cases at the time of the approval of this act.

Mr. Speaker, there is a general demand among lawyers and laymen throughout the United States for some check or limitation upon the power of Federal judges, who both try and punish for contempt. I believe that it is almost universally agreed that cases arising under section 19 of this act should be tried by a jury if the accused demands it. There are some who believe that a jury trial should be allowed in all indirect contempt cases.

The time may come before a great while when all indirect contempt cases will be tried by jury.

On the increasing growth of the power of the Federal courts I wish to read the following extract from an acticle written by Judge Henry Clay Caldwell, who was appointed Federal judge in 1864 by Abraham Lincoln, and who served as a Federal judge for 39 years:

> The modern writ of injunction is used for purposes which bear no more resemblance to the uses of the ancient writ of that name than the milky way bears to the sun. Formerly it was used to conserve the property in dispute between private litigants, but in modern times it has taken the place of the police powers of the State and Nation. It enforces and restrains with equal facility the criminal laws of the State and Nation. * * * In proceedings for contempt for an alleged violation of the injunction the judge is the lawmaker, the injured party, the prosecutor, the judge, and the jury. It is not surprising that, uniting in himself all these characters, he is commonly able to obtain a conviction. While the penalty which the judge can inflict by direct sentence for a violation of his code is fine or imprisonment, limited only by his discretion, capital punishment may be inflicted by indirection. All that seems to be necessary to this end is to issue a writ to the marshal or sheriff commanding him to prevent a violation of the judge's code, and then the men, with injunction nooses around their necks, may be quickly dispatched if they attempt to march across this injunction deadline. It is said the judge does not punish for a violation of the statutory offense, but only for a violation of his order prohibiting the commission of the statutory offense. Such reasoning as this is what Carlyle calls "logical cobwebbery." The web is not strong enough to deprive the smallest insect of its liberty, much less an American citizen. * * * A jurisdiction that is not required to stop somewhere will stop nowhere.
>
> Prof. Baird says fish have no maturity, but continue to grow until they die. This curious characteristic of fish is a very intensified form in the equitable octopus called injunction, for that has no maturity and never dies, and its jurisdiction grows and extends perpetually and unceasingly.

Mr. Chairman, this bill does not deprive the court of the power to punish for contempt in certain cases, but gives the accused the right to have the issue of his guilt or innocence tried by 12 men before punishment can be inflicted by the judge. It is wise to allow juries to try questions of fact, although there are some who are assaulting the jury system and declare it is a failure, but, in my opinion, it is the most perfect system ever devised by man to determine a controversy between man and man.

The Star Chamber in England tried to abolish the jury system and brought about a revolution. Our country's jurisprudence will never decline, and our country will always remain strong and great so long as the jury system is preserved inviolate and incorrupt.

It has been strenuously argued that Congress has no power to limit inferior courts in the exercise of their power to punish for contempt. The Constitution does say the judicial power of the United States shall be vested or shall rest in one Supreme Court and in such inferior courts as Congress shall from time to time establish. I take it that if you run down the decisions from 1709 to the present time you will not find a decision of any court but what says that these inferior courts are absolutely and entirely the creatures of Congress, and surely the power that can create can also limit the power of the creature. Inherent powers! There are no inherent powers in any inferior court. The only power that a district court possesses is that prescribed by Congress—the body that creates it—otherwise we could bring into being a power that would be superior to the creator.

On the question of the power of Congress to limit the courts in their punishment for indirect contempts, I wish to cite a few authorities.

The first authority I wish to cite in this connection was written in 1799 in the case of Turner against The Bank of North America,[5.471] in Fourth Dallas. Counsel said:

It is, then, to be remarked that the judicial power is the grant of the Constitution, and Congress can no more limit than enlarge the constitutional grant.[5.472]

Then Judge Ellsworth, Chief Justice at that time, interrupted this argument and said:

How far is it meant to carry this argument? Will it be affirmed that in every case to which the judicial power of the United States extends the Federal courts may exercise the jurisdiction, without the intervention of the legislature, to distribute and regulate the power?[5.473]

Justice Chase said:

The notion has frequently been entertained that the Federal courts derive their judicial power immediately from the Constitution, but the political truth is that the disposal of the judicial power (except in a few specified instances) belongs to Congress. If Congress has given the power to this court, we possess it, not otherwise; and if Congress has not given the power to us or to any other court, it still remains at the legislative disposal. Besides, Congress is not bound, and it would perhaps be inexpedient, to enlarge the jurisdiction of the Federal courts to every subject in every form which the Constitution might warrant.[5.474]

That was in 1799, and, gentlemen, from that good hour to this the suggestions of Chief Justice Chase and Judge Ellsworth have been followed.

Now, in United States v. Hudson (7 Cranch, p. 31[sic]):

Of all the courts which the United States may, under their general powers, constitute, one only—the Supreme Court—possesses jurisdiction derived immediately from the Constitution and of which the legislative power can not deprive it. All other courts created by the General Government possess no jurisdiction but what is given them by the power that creates them, and can be vested with none but what the power ceded to the General Government will authorize them to confer. * * * For the power which Congress possesses to create courts of inferior jurisdiction necessarily implies the power to limit the jurisdictions of those courts to particular objects; and when a court is created and its operations confined to certain specific objects, with what propriety can it assume to itself a jurisdiction much more extended, in its very nature very indefinite, applicable to a great variety of subjects, varying in every State in the Union, and with regard to which there exists no definite criterion of distribution between the district and circuit courts of the same district?[5.475]

[5.471] 4 U.S. (4 Dall.) 8, 1 L. Ed. 718 (1799).

[5.472] 4 U.S. (4 Dall.) at 10.

[5.473] Id.

[5.474] Id.

[5.475] The correct citation is 11 U.S. (7 Cranch) 32, 33, 3 L. Ed. 259, 260 (1812).

We next come to Third Howard, on page 245, Cary against Curtis,[5.476] and I may say that this decision was affirmed in Fink against O'Neil, in One hundred and sixth United States.[5.477]

Says the court:

Secondly, the doctrine so often ruled in this court, that the judicial power of the United States, although it has its origin in the Constitution, is (except in enumerated instances applicable exclusively to this court) dependent for its distribution and organization, and for the modes of its exercise, entirely upon the action of Congress, who possess the sole power of creating the tribunals (inferior to the Supreme Court) for the exercise of the judicial power and of investing them with jurisdiction, either limited, concurrent, or exclusive, and of withholding jurisdiction from them in the exact degrees and character which to Congress may seem proper for the public good. To deny this position would be to elevate the judicial over the legislative branch of the Government and to give to the former powers limited by its own discretion merely. It follows, then, that the courts created by statute must look to the statute as the warrant for their authority; certainly they can not go beyond the statute and assert an authority with which they may not be invested by it or which may be clearly denied to them.

* * * The existence of the judicial act itself, with its several supplements, furnishes proof unanswerable on this point. The courts of the United States are all limited in their nature and constitution, and have not the powers, inherent in courts existing by prescription or by the common law.[5.478]

What can be stronger, gentlemen, than that decision rendered in Third Howard and reaffirmed in One hundred and sixth United States in the case of Fink against O'Neil, at page 280?

Now, here is still another authority to which I wish to call the attention of the Members of the House, found in Forty-ninth United States, or Eighth Howard—Sheldon against Sill, page 441:

Courts created by statute can have no jurisdiction but such as the statute confers.[5.479]

It is absurd, it seems to me, to hold that the creator can create a thing which, after it is created, becomes bigger and more powerful than its creator. It was never so intended by the founders of the Government, and it is opposed to the genius of our institutions to suppose a thing created can become more powerful than the people who created it. Now, in this decision Judge Grier, rendering it, says:

It must be admitted that if the Constitution had ordained or established the inferior courts, and distributed to them their respective powers, they could not be restricted or divested by Congress.[5.480]

Nobody undertakes to say that we can restrict or divest the power of the Supreme Court of the United States, because that court was created by the Constitution, and that is the distinction this judge draws here:

But as it had made no such distribution, one of two consequences must result—either that each inferior court created by Congress must exercise all the judicial powers not given to the Supreme Court, or that Congress, having the power to establish the courts, must define their respective jurisdictions. The first of these inferences has never been asserted, and could not be defended with any show of reason, and, if not, the latter would seem to follow as a necessary consequence, and it would seem to follow also that, having a right to prescribe, Congress may withhold from any court of its creation jurisdiction of any of the enumerated controversies. Courts created by statute can have no jurisdiction but such as the statute confers. No one of them can assert a just claim to jurisdiction exclusively conferred on another or withheld from all.

The Constitution has defined the limits of the judicial power of the United States, but has not prescribed how much of it shall be exercised by the circuit court; consequently the statute

---

[5.476] 44 U.S. (3 How.) 236 (1845).

[5.477] 106 U.S. 272, 27 L. Ed. 196 (1882).

[5.478] 44 U.S. (3 How.) at 245.

[5.479] 49 U.S. (8 How.) 441, 449, 12 L. Ed. 1147, 1150 (1850).

[5.480] 49 U.S. (8 How.) at 448.

which does prescribe the limits of their jurisdiction can not be in conflict with the Constitution, unless it confers powers not enumerated therein.

Such has been the doctrine held by this court since its first establishment. To enumerate all the cases in which it has been either directly advanced or tacitly assumed would be tedious and unnecessary.[5.481]

I cite still another authority, Mr. Chairman. It is in Eighteenth Wallace, page 577, and is known as the case of the sewing machine companies. It bears out the decision which I have just read. It is as follows:

Circuit courts do not derive their judicial power immediately from the Constitution, as appears with sufficient explicitness from the Constitution itself, as the first section of the third article provides that "the judicial power of the United States shall be vested in one Supreme Court and in such inferior courts as the Congress may from time to time ordain and establish." Consequently the jurisdiction of the circuit court in every case must depend upon some act of Congress, as it is clear that Congress, inasmuch as it possesses the power to ordain and establish all courts inferior to the Supreme Court, may also define their jurisdiction. Courts created by statute can have no jurisdiction in controversies but such as the statute confers. Congress, it may be conceded, may confer such jurisdiction upon the circuit courts as it may see fit within the scope of the judicial power of the Constitution not vested in the Supreme Court, but as such tribunals are neither created by the Constitution nor is their jurisdiction defined by that instrument, it follows that inasmuch as they are created by an act of Congress it is necessary in every attempt to define their power to look to that source as the means of accomplishing that end. Federal judicial power, beyond all doubt, has its origin in the Constitution, but the organization of the system and the distribution of the subjects of jurisdiction among such inferior courts as Congress may from time to time ordain and establish within the scope of the judicial power always have been and of right must be the work of the Congress.[5.482]

Now, Mr. Chairman, in Nineteenth Wallace, Robinson's case, at pages 510 and 511, we have a contempt case. The syllabus says:

The act of March 2, 1831, entitled "An act declaratory of the law concerning contempts of court," provides in its first section:

"That the power of the several courts of the United States to issue attachments and inflict summary punishment for contempts of court shall not be construed to extend to any cases except the misbehavior of any person or persons in the presence of the said courts, or so near thereto as to obstruct the administration of justice, the misbehavior of any officers of the said courts in their official transactions, and the disobedience or resistance by any officer of the said courts, party, juror, witness, or any other person or persons, to any lawful writ, process, order, rule, decree, or command of the said courts."[5.483]

Mr. Justice Field in that case, after stating the facts, delivered the opinion of the court, as follows:

The power to punish for contempts is inherent in all courts; its existence is essential to the preservation of order in judicial proceedings and to the enforcement of the judgments, orders, and writs of the courts, and consequently to the due administration of justice. The moment the courts of the United States were called into existence and invested with jurisdiction over any subject they became possessed of this power. But the power has been limited and defined by the act of Congress of March 2, 1831. The act, in terms, applies to all courts. Whether it can be held to limit the authority of the Supreme Court, which derives its existence and powers from the Constitution, may perhaps be a matter of doubt; but that it applies to the circuit and district courts there can be no question. These courts were created by act of Congress. Their powers and duties depend upon the act calling them into existence or subsequent acts extending or limiting their jurisdiction. The act of 1831 is therefore to them the law specifying the cases in which summary punishment for contempts may be inflicted. It limits the power of these courts in this respect to three classes of cases: First, where there has been misbehavior of a person in the presence of the courts or so near thereto as to obstruct the administration of justice; second, where there has been misbehavior of any officer of the courts in his official

---

[5.481] *Id.* at 448–49.

[5.482] Grover & Baker Sewing-Mach. Co. v. Florence Sewing-Mach. Co., 85 U.S. (18 Wall.) 553, 577–78, 21 L. Ed. 914, 919 (1874).

[5.483] *Ex parte* Robinson, 86 U.S. (19 Wall.) 505, 510, 22 L. Ed. 205, 207 (1873) (part of the *Lawyers' Edition* "opinion" is actually part of the "statement of the case").

transactions; and, third, where there has been disobedience or resistance by any officer, party, juror, witness, or other person to any lawful writ, process, order, rule, decree, or command of the courts.[5.484]

There is no inherent power suggested there, because the Supreme Court says that Congress has the right to limit the power of the courts of this country to punish for contempt to three classes of cases. Now, if Congress can reduce them to three, it can reduce them to one, and if they can reduce them to one, Congress can destroy contempt cases altogether, and if Congress destroys them altogether, why can not it say that in certain cases a jury must intervene and determine whether or not the party is guilty before the judge shall inflict punishment?

"But," says the court, "the power is limited." What power? The power to punish for contempt. By whom is it limited? Nobody but the law-making power. Justice Field says:

> The act, in terms, applies to all courts. Whether it can be held to limit the authority of the Supreme Court, which derives its existence and powers from the Constitution, may perhaps be a matter of doubt.[5.485]

We find in this case, Nineteenth Wallace, Eighty-sixth United States, that we can limit the power over contempt in the circuit and district courts. These courts were created by act of Congress. Their powers and duties depend upon the act calling them into existence or subsequent acts extending or limiting their jurisdiction. The act of 1831 is, therefore, to them the law specifying the cases in which summary punishment for contempts may be inflicted. It limits the power of these courts in three classes of cases.

This is a direct decision in point, gentlemen of the House, which declares that the Congress has the power to limit the punishment to three classes of cases; and if it has the power to limit the punishment to three classes of cases, we can limit that power to one class or abolish it altogether. I contend that if Congress desires to take away from the inferior courts all power to punish for contempt it can do it.

We could abolish the circuit courts of the United States—which we have done—and the Commerce Court, the district courts, and all the courts, except the Supreme Court; and, therefore, it is absurd to argue that while we have the power to destroy we have not the power to regulate the thing we create.

I can not see how any lawyer can read these authorities from 1799 to the present and then contend that the people who create these courts through their Representatives in Congress have no right to provide that before a man shall be convicted of a crime by a judge there shall be flung between him and the judge's arbitrary power a jury of 12 men—one of the most sacred institutions in all the world, and especially to the people of the United States—simply to pass upon the facts and say whether he is guilty. If the man is guilty, the judge has all the power he needs to punish, provided it does not exceed six months' imprisonment or a fine of $1,000. [Loud applause.]

Mr. Chairman, I move that the committee do now rise.

The motion was agreed to. . . .

ANTITRUST LEGISLATION

The SPEAKER pro tempore. The House will resolve itself automatically into the Committee of the Whole House on the state of the Union for the consideration of the bill (H. R. 15657) to supplement existing laws against unlawful restraints and monopolies, and for other purposes, and other bills under the special order. . . .

Mr. [ANDREW J.] VOLSTEAD [R., Minn.]. Mr. Chairman, it is not my intention to enter into an extended discussion of this bill. I have been too busy with other matters to prepare anything like a speech, still there are some features to which I desire to call attention. When this session met it was generally understood that it would be devoted largely to trust legislation. A great many promises were made, a great many assurances were given as to what was going to be accomplished at this session. One thing that I remember which was especially emphasized was the necessity of erasing

---

[5.484] 86 U.S. (19 Wall.) at 510–11.

[5.485] *Id.* at 510.

from the Sherman antitrust act the word "reasonable," said to have been inserted in it by the Supreme Court in the Standard Oil Co. decision.[5.486] It was also urged that in many other respects the act needed to be strengthened.

Early in the session we commenced hearings in the Committee on the Judiciary, and somewhere along during the last of January or the first of February, four bills made their appearance as committee bills. Upon one of these there was an indorsement to the effect that another bill would be later introduced—one on holding companies. Those bills became known familiarly as the "Five Brothers."

The bill now under consideration embodies some features from all of those bills, except one—the so-called definitions bill.

That bill was designed to restore the Sherman Act to its former vigor and add some additional teeth. That bill has entirely disappeared in the shuffle. It is known that the President has been repeatedly consulted, but the Republican Members only know of these consultations through the newspapers or from some occasional remark dropped by those in the secret. In the years past the Democrats have loudly condemned this secret method of framing legislation. No one can tell just what sort of influences write bills when written in this fashion. Section 8 of this bill is the section that most directly affects the trusts. This is the one that deals with holding companies and the right of one company to acquire the capital stock of another company. The overshadowing importance of this section can not be doubted when it is remembered that nearly every trust has been formed by the purchase of the capital stock of one corporation by another corporation. If such purchases are permitted, the formation of trusts is permitted. The English common law condemns the practice of one corporation purchasing the capital stock of another corporation, upon the ground that it tends to monopoly. Our courts supported this view until different States, eager to profit by a tax on corporate franchises, removed this restriction to encourage the formation of corporations. Congress has not legalized the practice. Do we legalize it in this bill? If we do, the effect is to practically repeal the Sherman Antitrust Act.

If this section is enacted it will become a definite legislative declaration by Congress of its policy in regard to the formation of trusts, a policy that courts will necessarily apply not only to future but also to present trusts. The policy in this bill differs radically from that under present law. Under the law as it ⊥ stands, it is not necessary to show that a combination actually restrains or monopolizes trade or commerce in order to bring them within the language of the law. It is enough that the necessary effect of the combination is to give it the power to do those things. The decisive question is whether the power exists, not whether it has been exercised. In the Northern Securities Co. case,[5.487] the Trans-Missouri,[5.488] Joint Traffic,[5.489] Pearsal [sic],[5.490] and Addyston cases,[5.491] the United States Supreme Court held that it was immaterial that trade or commerce had not actually been restrained; that it made no difference, even, that rates and prices had been lowered, it being enough to bring the combination within the condemnation of the act that it had the power to restrain trade or commerce. But under the two first paragraphs of this section the existence of this power is not sufficient to make the combination illegal; it is necessary to show, in addition, that the consolidation of two competing corporations effected an elimination or substantial lessening of competition or that it has created a monopoly in any line of trade in any section or community. In paragraph 3 it is necessary to go still further; it there requires a showing that competition has been lessened by voting the stock that has been consolidated. In other words, the vice in this section is that it permits the

---

[5.486] Standard Oil Co. v. United States, 221 U.S. 1, 31 S. Ct. 502, 55 L. Ed. 619 (1911), portions of which are reprinted *supra* at chapter 1.

[5.487] Northern Sec. Co. v. United States, 193 U.S. 197, 24 S. Ct. 436, 48 L. Ed. 679 (1904).

[5.488] United States v. Trans-Missouri Freight Ass'n, 166 U.S. 290, 17 S. Ct. 540, 41 L. Ed. 1007 (1897).

[5.489] United States v. Joint Traffic Ass'n, 171 U.S. 505, 19 S. Ct. 25, 43 L. Ed. 259 (1898), portions of which are reprinted *supra* at chapter 1.

[5.490] The correct citation is Pearsall v. Great N. Ry., 161 U.S. 646, 16 S. Ct. 705, 40 L. Ed. 838 (1896).

[5.491] Addyston Pipe & Steel Co. v. United States, 175 U.S. 211, 20 S. Ct. 96, 44 L. Ed. 136 (1899).

formation of a trust and in effect declares this trust legal until it eliminates or substantially lessens competition or creates a monopoly, while under the present law the combination is declared illegal if it possesses the power to restrain commerce, whether it has that effect or not. If this section 8 had been in force when the Northern Securities Co. case was tried, the Government would have lost it, as no restraint of trade was shown in that case. There had been no substantial lessening of competition at the time when that suit was instituted that could be established. A combination can easily conduct its business so that it will be impossible to show that competition has been entirely eliminated or to show that a monopoly has been created as the word "monopoly" is construed by our courts. To prove that the consolidation has substantially lessened competition will be almost as difficult. No one can tell how the word "substantial" will be construed. As used in this section it may mean that the competition must be largely lessened. This word "substantial" is so indefinite that it affords the courts no guide. As applied to the facts in any ordinary case of conflicting testimony it will give them a license to hold that anything short of almost entire elimination of competition is legal.

To illustrate the vicious effect of the requirement that the combinations to be illegal must destroy or substantially lessen competition, let me suggest that if a corporation is formed to erect a factory to produce an article in competition with some other corporation, this section will permit the consolidation of these companies at any time before actual competition commences. Until then there can be no elimination or lessening of competition. Or if a company now engaged in business desires to enter new territory it can first purchase the capital stock of the corporation that would become its competitor; by doing so it has not lessened competition, because until it enters the new field there is no competition to lessen. To prevent and not to lessen competition a corporation may, under this section, purchase the capital stock of another corporation to prevent the latter from increasing its output of competitive goods. This need not lessen; it may even increase competition, though in effect it restrains trade as the law is now construed. The most astonishing proposition is that contained the third paragraph of this section. The purpose of that paragraph is to permit a corporation to purchase the stock of other corporations solely for investment purposes. The only limitation upon this right is that the corporation making the purchase must not use the stock by voting or otherwise to bring about or attempt to bring about the substantial lessening of competition. It may make this purchase even though it create an absolute monopoly. How anyone with any knowledge of trust methods could propose such a provision as in aid of the Sherman Antitrust Act is difficult to understand. The Northern Securities Co. was an investment company pure and simple. It had no power to run a railroad; its only function, as it insisted on the trial, was that of an investment company. The Supreme Court was not deceived by so thin a disguise. It saw clearly what every man in his senses saw, that competition between two roads that were in fact owned by the same party—the Northern Securities Co.—would be a sham. No incentive for competition remained. Every expenditure for the purpose of taking trade from each other would be a loss to the stockholders. In this provision the same vice that I have already called attention to appears. It is not sufficient that the combination created by these investments may result in the lessening of competition. It is necessary to show in addition that this lessening is caused by voting or other like use of the stock to bring it about.

The inevitable consequences of the combination is not enough, nor is the elimination of competition enough; there must, in addition, be proof that the stock has been used to accomplish the elimination of competition. How the Government is ever going to prove that is more than I can imagine. This provision will legalize every trust and practically wipe the Sherman law off the statute books. If any existing trust does not consider itself quite safe under the first two paragraphs of this section, it can put on the armor furnished for its use in the third paragraph and laugh at the Attorney General and all his assistants. It may be argued that the Sherman antitrust law will still remain in force and that the acts I have mentioned would be forbidden by that law. This can not be claimed with any show of reason. If this bill becomes a law, it will become a legislative construction of the Sherman Act, and to the extent that the present law is inconsistent with this section 8 that law will be modified. It is true that repeals by implication are not favored, but the rule is that an act that covers in a comprehensive way any prior law repeals such prior law. Section 8 is clearly intended to lay down fully the law in regard to stock consolidations of corporations. It would be labor lost to argue to a court that things Congress took pains not to prohibit by express exemption in the act are prohibited by some other law covering this subject in general terms. Paragraph 4 of this section may be cited as showing that section 8 does not apply to existing trusts; but a careful reading of that paragraph will show that its object is only to exempt the trusts from compliance with this section, so far as they may have any legal rights that this section may interfere with, but it is careful not to say that section 8 shall not legalize violations of the present law. What it does say is that if any legal rights that are reserved to it by this paragraph shall be held in violation of the Sherman Antitrust Act such reservation shall not legalize this illegality. . . .

Mr. WEBB. I suppose that the gentleman has read the bill, on page 26, line 8—

That nothing in this paragraph shall make stockholding relations between corporations legal when such relations constitute violations of the antitrust laws.

Mr. VOLSTEAD. I will come to that in a moment.
Mr. WEBB. So it could not repeal the antitrust law?
Mr. VOLSTEAD. I think the gentleman will find that does not accomplish the purpose he imagines it will. I think when you come to read it carefully you will find that it is one of the most adroit things that was ever placed in any bill.

I want to call the gentleman's especial attention to the language of that section, because that is one of the things that surprised me when I came to read it. I read:

Nothing contained in this section shall be held to affect or impair any right heretofore legally acquired: *Provided,* That nothing in this paragraph—

Note that it says paragraph, not section—

Provided, That nothing in this paragraph shall make stockholding relations between corporations legal when such relations constitute violations of the antitrust laws.

This is the whole paragraph.

In other words, this paragraph reserves to the trusts any rights which might be threatened by the passage of this act, but it says that this reservation shall not be construed to legalize a trust, but it does not say that section 8 shall not legalize the trust. It does not take these corporations out of the operation of this act at all. On the other hand it expressly recognizes that this section applies to existing trusts. This paragraph only exempts our present trusts from its operation so far as it may be to their advantage to be exempted. I do not know who is responsible for this attack upon our antitrust laws. If my construction of this section is correct, this is certainly as smooth a piece of work as can well be imagined. I want to call your especial attention to the fact that though practically every other provision in this bill has met bitter hostility in the committee, not one voice has yet been raised against this provision. Why is it? Do you believe that the men interested in the trusts, sharp and shrewd as they are, would not have objected strenuously to this provision if it does not mean just what I claim that it means? [Applause.] This means immunity, and that is why they want it; that is why they are silent. The real object of these combinations is to lessen or destroy competition. It is for that purpose that nearly every industry is to-day in the hands of some holding company, some trust. Instead of repressing this evil, trusts are to be legalized and declared to be good trusts so long as the Government is unable to prove a thing which it will be impossible to prove, and no matter though they rob the public by high prices.

I do not believe that any set of men, whether engaged in a trust or not, should be given monopolistic powers. No one can be safely trusted with such powers. Those who drew and the courts that have enforced the Sherman Antitrust Act struck directly at this evil, at the combination, the conspiracy, the trust. They sought to destroy, not to legalize. They sought to reach the root of the evil, not its symptoms. Passing from this section, I will briefly refer to some other sections; I shall not touch on all of them, because I do not want to take up too much time. Sections 2 and 4 of the bill attempt to define offenses. These sections may have some value, though it is true that the acts condemned are offenses under existing law; but they are made offenses standing alone. When the courts have held such acts offenses it has been in connection with other matters, and it may be an advantage to have these acts made separate offenses; but at the same time there is great danger that the use of specific language to define an offense may lead our courts to the conclusion that anything of a like nature, but not covered by the language of the new act, was not intended to be covered, and as such is eliminated from the prohibitions of the Sherman Antitrust Act.

Section 3 has been discussed somewhat upon this floor. It is my impression that section 3, which is the one to compel mining companies to sell generally to any responsible party, unless there is some good reason for refusing, might very properly be applied to any corporation. I do not believe that it should be applied to small corporations, but it seems to me that when a corporation gets so large that it handles a very large portion of the commerce of the country or the commerce of a section it might very properly be asked to deal equally and fairly without discrimination as between all the people. We ask this of common carriers. Why should not the same rule apply to any concern that is monopolistic in character?

Section 5 has been commented on by the chairman, and I think his comment is fair. I think that section may add quite a little to the remedy which private parties have in securing relief where they have been oppressed by unfair methods of competition. The same may be said of section 6, but that section is open to a very serious objection.

It makes the judgments that may be entered in suits brought by the Government to dissolve a trust, evidence not only in favor of but also against a person injured by a violation of the trust laws. In these days when judgments are entered by consent of parties without a public hearing, findings may not be of such a character as to serve a private party in recovering any claim he may have for injury to him. Upon what theory of justice a person who has never had his day in court to recover for injuries that may have ruined his business may be defeated by the action of an officer he can not control, and in a suit to which he is not a party is indeed strange. If this provision becomes a law, we shall have another sort of immunity bath and we may find the culprits seeking absolution at the hands of the Attorney General instead of dealing with their victims. Upon what theory a person can be deprived of his day in court I do not understand.

It seems to me when the Attorney General brings suit on behalf of all the people against a corporation and a judgment is recovered in favor of the Government against the trust, declaring that it is violating the law, it may very properly be used against that corporation if a suit is brought by a private party, but if for any reason the Attorney General fails to obtain a judgment, perhaps because he does not prosecute properly, it does not seem to me that a private party who may have been ruined by the conduct of some offending corporation should be debarred from ever suing that corporation for redress. We have a very conspicuous illustration as to how this may operate. The Government brought and lost a suit against the Sugar Trust.[5.492] Subsequently the injured party, the sugar refinery at Philadelphia, recovered, I believe, more than a million dollars. . . .

Mr. [CHARLES C.] CARLIN [D., Va.]. How could that statement be true when that provision applies only to decrees or judgments? If there be no decree or judgment why neither party would be bound, so that the statement that the Government would fail to prosecute would have no application. There would have to be a final determination of the court.

Mr. VOLSTEAD. I concede if no judgment was entered there would be no bar, but there may be a judgment of dismissal in the action, a judgment of no cause for action against the Government. If the judgment is entered against the Government it bars the suit of private parties who may even have commenced their actions years ago.

[5.492] United States v. E.C. Knight Co., 156 U.S. 1, 15 S. Ct. 249, 39 L. Ed. 325 (1895).

Mr. [WILLIAM] GORDON [D., Ohio]. Is not the degree of proof different in a suit for criminal action brought by the Government than in a suit brought by an individual?

Mr. VOLSTEAD. Oh, yes; but that does not make any difference so far as this section is concerned. A defendant convicted in a criminal action certainly could not complain that such a judgment should be binding upon him if binding in a civil suit, because more proof would be required in the criminal than in a civil suit.

Mr. GORDON. Exactly so; but a private individual who might want to bring the suit might complain, might he not?

Mr. VOLSTEAD. That is true. . . .

Mr. [JOHN C.] McKENZIE [R., Ill.]. Your judgment is, then, that this section should be stricken out entirely?

Mr. VOLSTEAD. No; my judgment is that the provision making the judgment in such a suit a bar against a suit brought by a private person should be stricken out.

Mr. McKENZIE. Would that be a fair proposition? Should not the rule, if it is applied at all, work both ways?

Mr. VOLSTEAD. No. One has been in court, and the other has not. The private party has not been in court at all. The trust has. He can not control the action of the Attorney General. He has no right to produce any evidence to sustain a decree. The Government may not have known about his evidence, or if it knew it, may not have produced it, and it may be, as in many instances it has been, simply a compromise judgment entered to settle some difficulty between the Government and the trust. It is not fair to make that sort of a judgment a bar to a private action. . . .

Mr. McKENZIE. If this section is left in the bill, do you not feel and believe that this decree that is mentioned in this section should be the decree of the court of last resort—the Supreme Court of the land?

Mr. VOLSTEAD. No.

Mr. McKENZIE. Should it not go that far?

Mr. VOLSTEAD. No; I can see no reason why.

Mr. McKENZIE. You think it would be good policy to leave a matter of such great importance in the hands of an inferior court?

Mr. VOLSTEAD. Yes. It looks to me like this: We have been trying to enforce the Sherman Antitrust Act for 20 years, and trusts have been growing and growing; and I do not think that we need fear that the trusts are likely to be injured. They can comply with the laws like other law-abiding persons, and they need have no fear of these decrees.

Mr. McKENZIE. If the gentleman will pardon me, I am not sympathizing with the trusts at all. That is not the point. But in legislating I believe we should be fair, even to the trusts.

Mr. VOLSTEAD. I think that is fair. The first paragraph of the seventh section is of no particular importance. The latter half, however, allows railroad companies to get together and fix rates and make all sorts of arrangements to stifle competition except in a few unimportant matters. And this may be done without asking the permission of the Interstate Commerce Commission and without even notifying the commission of the agreement.

The railroads have clamored for this right for many years, but I presume it is right that they should share in the "New Freedom" somewhat. [Laughter and applause on the Republican side.]

Section 12 is the section under which trust magnates are going to be sent to jail. It does not add a thing in the world to the present law. Guilt, so far as the law is concerned, has been personal ever since the statute was written. It does not add anything to the penalty. It does not add anything in any other respect. It is simply put in there for buncombe. People have made stump speeches all about the country, threatening to put these people in jail. Anybody who has ever followed the prosecutions had under the Sherman antitrust law knows that individuals who participate in forming any illegal combination, any illegal conspiracy, can be punished now, and a number of them have been punished, though not very severely.

The trouble has been this, not that the law has not been upon the statute book, but that there has always been strong sympathy, both on the part of the jury and on the part of the court, for the men who have been carrying on these gigantic operations. They have all felt a little as though there was some ⊥ virtue in these vast combinations, as though some of these men were a little bit too good to be put behind prison bars; and when they have been convicted the courts have shrunk from imposing a penalty which you men wrote into that law.

⊥9080

You have repeated it in this proposed statute. Do you think it will be any more effective now? Do you think anybody will have more respect for it now? I do not think so. When these same men appear before jurors and before courts there will be the same sympathy, there will be the same feeling, the same old plea, that these men did not know they had violated the law. They will say, "We guess we will let them go this time"; and they will be good hereafter. . . .

Mr. [SIMEON D.] FESS [R., Ohio]. I did not know that the Sherman antitrust law provided that if the corporation was found guilty of violating the law, that guilt would also be deemed to apply to the directors.

Mr. VOLSTEAD. This section does not say that or mean that. It simply says if they have been guilty of any of the acts defined in the Sherman Antitrust Act they shall be punished by a fine of $5,000.

Mr. FESS. The offense shall also be deemed to be that of the individual director of such a corporation?

Mr. VOLSTEAD. Read a little further.

Mr. FESS. I read:

And upon conviction of the corporation any director, officer, or agent who shall have authorized, ordered, or done any of such prohibited acts shall be deemed guilty of a misdemeanor.

Mr. VOLSTEAD. That is exactly what the present law provides for, only in slightly different language.

Mr. FESS. Does it mean that that law is simply to cover up something else?

Mr. VOLSTEAD. The fact that the corporation has been convicted does not prove that the particular individual is guilty. . . .

Mr. [WILLIAM R.] GREEN [R., Iowa]. The first part of the section is merely a catch phrase, which sounds well but has no effect whatever?

Mr. VOLSTEAD. That is true.

Mr. GREEN of Iowa. The binding part of it is in the latter part?

Mr. VOLSTEAD. Yes. There were submitted before the Committee on the Judiciary indictments for the purpose of showing how parties had been charged with the violation of the existing trust law. No one familiar with the drawing of indictments or who had any experience with prosecutions under criminal law can have any doubt that it is simply a repetition of the present statute. It is just couched in different language; that is all.

Now, let me say that while you may point with pride to this section 12 as the performance of a promise, let me remind my Democratic friends that there is very little in this trust program to carry out the promises so bravely made in the last Democratic platform.

How about holding companies? You have legalized them. In your platform you said that holding companies were "indefensible." You do not say that now.

You condemned interlocking directors. You have to some extent done that in this bill, but at the same time you have also legalized interlocking directors.

You also condemned watered stock. It is true you have a bill here for the purpose of preventing railroads from issuing watered stock, but other industrial corporations may float oceans of it. There is not a single scratch in any of these bills against the watered stock of a company like the United States Steel Corporation or any of the other larger combinations of capital. . . .

Mr. GORDON. Do you not recognize any difference between the public necessity for limiting the issues of stocks and bonds of railroad corporations and those of purely private corporations?

Mr. VOLSTEAD. There is some difference, but do you mean to say that it is proper to have watered stock to the extent found in the United States Steel Corporation?

Mr. GORDON. The people of the United States do not pay any dividends on the stock of private corporations. They do pay dividends on the stock of public corporations, like railroad corporations. There is the difference.

Mr. VOLSTEAD. One of the main objects in these consolidations has been to inject watered stock—

Mr. GORDON. Unquestionably.

Mr. VOLSTEAD. The very consolidations that your bill legalizes will invite it, and you will have more watered stock under this scheme as the years go by if you ever write it into law; but you will never dare to do it. . . .

Mr. GORDON. The point I sought to draw the gentleman out on was the legal relation of the railroad corporations to the public, to wit, that the railroads are entitled to a reasonable compensation for drawing the traffic of the country over public highways.

Mr. VOLSTEAD. Yes.

Mr. GORDON. Can not the gentleman see the public necessity for limiting and restricting the stock and bond issues of the railroad corporations, so as to enable the Interstate Commerce Commission to some extent to know how much money was actually invested in those corporations?

Mr. VOLSTEAD. I think I had the honor to introduce the first bill on that subject that was ever introduced into this House. It was introduced six or eight years ago. I called President Roosevelt's attention to it, and he promised to send a message to Congress asking for its passage. I think in every general message that he wrote after that time he called the attention of this House and of Congress to the need for legislation of that kind, and I am thoroughly in sympathy with the idea of preventing watered stock so far as railroad corporations are concerned, but it seems to me that some day we shall have to go further than that. It seems to me that these vast combinations that practically dominate whole industries must in some fashion be controlled; and it seems to me the financing of such institutions is one of the things we must control. An overcapitalized corporation must try to secure monopolistic powers or it can not compete with a competitor that is honestly financed. One of the reasons why this country is almost on the verge of ruin to-day is the fact that we have got all sorts of watered stock, all sorts of inflated capitalization which makes the conditions unsound and unsafe. If it were not for the effort to pay dividends upon such stocks there would not be the necessity for the high cost of living of which we are complaining. . . .

Mr. BAILEY. Upon what basis was this $700,000,000 of watered stock issued by the Steel Corporation?

Mr. VOLSTEAD. I have not been advised.

Mr. BAILEY. Was it not issued upon the tremendous power which was conferred upon that corporation by the United States Congress, when it gave that corporation an immense margin of profit through the protective tariff? Was it not a capitalization of the protective tariff law, which gave it that enormous opportunity for profit[?]

Mr. VOLSTEAD. I am not going to discuss the tariff at this time.

Mr. BAILEY. And is not the repeal of that protective tariff law the thing which has put down the common stock of the United States Steel Corporation?

Mr. VOLSTEAD. I do not know whether the tariff has affected this company or not, but I do know that a company trying to maintain any credit and pay dividends on the ocean of water that was put into capitalization is in sore straits.

Mr. BAILEY. It certainly brought it up to an artificial level.

Mr. VOLSTEAD. Gentlemen, I have spoken a good deal longer than I intended to speak. I wanted to call attention to these things because I think them important. . . .

Mr. FERRIS. I want to ask the gentleman if it is his opinion that this bill emasculates the Sherman antitrust law?

Mr. VOLSTEAD. I think it practically destroys it.

Mr. FERRIS. It is not sufficiently drastic; is that the gentleman's position?

Mr. VOLSTEAD. Yes. I think most of the provisions in the bill are of very doubtful value. There are some which I approve, but section 8, the one that deals with trusts, certainly does legalize trusts.

Mr. FERRIS. How does the gentleman stand on the labor amendment soon to be offered?

Mr. VOLSTEAD. I have not discussed the labor question, but I will tell the gentleman my position. I do not believe in exempting any class. I believe that before the law we ought all be equal. I do not think that we should exempt any special class. I may explain my views more fully on that at another time.

Allow me to thank the committee for its kind attention. [Applause.] . . .

Mr. MADDEN. Mr. Chairman, those accepting responsibility as Representatives should not treat lightly the duties which go with such responsibility. We can not afford, when acting the rôle of statesmanship, whether with great or small capacity, to proceed impulsively or rashly or hastily. True statesmanship consists in a large percentage of deliberation and a very small percentage of action.

What, then, shall be said of a measure reaching into the very vitals of every industrial and commercial enterprise in the Nation, from the railroad systems, whose lines extend thousands of miles, and the banks, whose affairs are the direct interest of all, down through all gradations to the smallest—a measure introduced in January, discussed in committee superficially and spasmodically, and reported the first week in May?

The pending bill not only regulates the managements of carriers and the directorates of 350,000 corporations, including banks, but touches the private affairs and contractual relations of every citizen. It prescribes new and untried methods of carrying on private business, breaking up and displacing those which, having stood the test of experience, are normal and acceptable to all. The sum total of the country's business transacted in conformity to existing rules and methods is incalculable. The billions representing bank clearances do not tell half the story.

Who are those who, after a few weeks consideration, with constant interruptions due to other important legislation coming up, have recommended to this body a voluminous code of business morality? Are our colleagues on the Judiciary Committee mechanical engineers or experts in finance, manufacturing, and transportation? Can they exhibit credentials or diplomas which justify our confidence in their familiarity with all science and all human affairs? Are they better fitted to build and equip railways, steamships, engines, and cars, or to operate them by the application of steam and electricity, than those now so employed? Should we now, after such a brief schooling, take their word for it that it is a crime if a man owns stock in two corporations or is a director in both, or as a producer sells to A at a certain profit, while selling to B at a greater or less profit, or sells a customer an article at a dollar and offers it to him at 90 cents on condition that he be given the customer's continuous orders? Even if I thought I could ever be convinced of the wisdom and justice of such changes by statute I would require better authority and more competent witnesses than the estimable gentlemen who have joined in a favorable report on this bill, for however sound their judgment in legal matters, however successful they have been as politicians, I can not believe they have been able in four short months to master the intricacies of the 10,000 branches of business affected by this legislation, or to give convincing sociological reasons for severing the close relations that men have built on mutual confidence in dealings running through the years, and decades of activity. We are no more justified in accepting their judgments, so contrary to common knowledge and experience, than the railroads of the country would be if they employed at a princely salary some brilliant theorist and doctrinaire who asserted that he could show them where and how to save a million dollars a day.

Before entering upon the separate provisions of the bill I wish to call attention to the short period of hopeful feeling and renewal of confidence in the business world between the presidential deliverance on the 19th of January and the publication of the so-called "tentative bills" early in February—or, rather, to the deliverance itself—in order to emphasize the wide divergence between promise and performance.

The President said in his message that—

Constructive legislation is always the embodiment of convincing experience and of the mature public opinion which finally springs out of that experience.

He further said:

What we are purposing to do, therefore, is happily not to hamper or interfere with business, as enlightened business men prefer to do it, or in any sense to put it under the ban. * * *

And fortunately no measures of sweeping or novel change are necessary; * * * what we have to do can be done in a new spirit, in thoughtful moderation, and without revolution of any untoward kind.

If it could be shown that there was a widespread or even any considerable demand for this legislation, still it would well become us, in view of its drastic character, to pause and consider until senseless clamor raised by the few mad and restless innovators who have prompted it had reduced their temperatures.

But, in sober truth, it has been concocted and sprung so unexpectedly, so suddenly, and demand or reason for it is so utterly wanting, that the action of the majority can only be accounted for upon the theory of supposed political advantage. If that theory be correct, then, however mistaken the Democratic opinion upon the political effect, no one will doubt the desperate nature of the emergency. The new tariff act has failed to reduce the cost of living, as was promised; the new currency act has not accelerated the wheels of industry, as was expected; hence this sudden tactical shift. The conciliatory message has been whispered into limbo in select presidential conclaves, and the dogs of war have been unleashed to tear and cripple the fabric of business and industrial life in its essence and structure to satisfy the clamor of the malcontents within the party. I again ask. Where and by whom and by how many is such legislation desired? It is a question that can not be answered, or if at all not satisfactorily, by naming shallow-pated doctrinaires and partisan opportunists.

Now, if I were seeking merely political advantage, my true interest would be to remain silent instead of giving such free expressions of my views as I propose giving. But the measure is so drastic, so immature, so untimely, so utterly ruinous, that, in order to save the country from the confusion and destruction it would produce, I am perfectly willing, if within my power, to persuade Democrats to refrain from supporting it in their own party interests, even if from no higher considerations. And although the practice of keeping party pledges has been recently obsoleted, I will first make a few comparisions between certain planks in the platform on which the President and Democratic Members of this Congress were elected and some of the provisions of this bill.

The most important declaration on the subject was in these words:

We regret that the Sherman antitrust law has received a judicial construction depriving it of much of its efficacy, and we favor the enactment of legislation which will restore to the statute the strength of which it has been deprived by such interpretation.

It will be noted that the uncertainty created by the decisions of the Supreme Court in the Standard Oil and Tobacco Co. cases was the inspiration for that declaration. Can anyone point out in this bill a line or word intended or calculated to change the interpretation of the law there given by the court? The challenge may stand throughout this debate, and no one will attempt to meet it. The eloquent gentleman from Kentucky [Mr. STANLEY] introduced a bill at the opening of this session which had the specific effect to change the law to mean what it meant, or was supposed to mean, prior to these decisions. He was accorded a hearing before the committee on his bill, but his bill went, along with his brilliant appeal, into the committee's capacious wastebasket. Nor is there even the vestige of anything in the bill embodying his idea, or any response whatever to the platform declaration and party pledge. I do not, of course, complain of this. I merely call attention to the fact.

I have already predicted confusion and uncertainty to result from this measure, if passed, and will presently discuss specific provisions in detail. But lest it be claimed that the various provisions of the bill have a combined effect to remove the uncertainty created by the court decisions, I call attention to the fact that the majority does not make any such claim, and no one will dare attempt, candidly and in good faith, to argue that any provision touches the subject matter of the court decisions or the party pledge based thereon.

I will now dispose of one or two items, as to which I make no complaint that the bill fulfills party pledges or interferes with the country's business; matters wherein the bill is merely a pretentious show of meeting platform pledges without substantial performance. The platform was profuse and explicit in its pledges to labor. It said:

RIGHTS OF LABOR.

We repeat our declarations of the platform of 1908, as follows:

* * * * * * *

"Questions of judicial practice have arisen, especially in connection with industrial disputes. We believe that the parties to all judicial proceedings should be treated with rigid impartiality, and that injunctions should not be issued in any case in which an injunction would not issue if no industrial dispute were involved."

I call attention to the fact that in no message or official deliverance from the White House is there a line or syllable ⊥ with reference to that pledge. I state emphatically, and propose making it so clear that even the blindest and most credulous partisan can not refuse to admit it, that the bill is an absolute failure, not only to accomplish what labor expected to be and claimed should be done, but accomplishes nothing whatever for labor's benefit.

First, as to what labor expected and had a right to expect. It will be noted that every word in the 1912 platform is a reiteration between quotation marks of the 1908 platform. In the 1908 campaign Mr. Gompers, president of the American Federation of Labor, was exceedingly active in support of Bryan, and positively asserted in his speeches, as doubtless did his associates, that the platform was an indorsement and approval of the Pearre bill. That bill had received the unanimous support of Democratic members of the Judiciary Committee of the House during two years prior to the 1908 convention. Mr. Gompers also claimed that his interpretation of the platform was in accord with the views of Mr. Bryan and other Democratic leaders. About 10 days before the election in 1908 President Roosevelt, in a public statement, called attention to Mr. Gompers's statements, and challenged Mr. Bryan to admit or deny them. But Mr. Bryan was silent until Gompers had answered reiterating his prior assertions. Then Bryan stated that Roosevelt had been already answered. That the 1912 platform pledged approval of the Pearre bill is shown by the fact that after this construction of the 1908 platform by both Gompers and Bryan its language was followed and quoted, word for word, in 1912. Moreover, Gompers strenuously urged that interpretation before the Judiciary Committee, both prior to and since the presidential election of 1912, and neither Bryan nor any member of the committee, nor President Wilson, nor any other Democratic officer, has thus far differed with him.

Now, compare the provisions of the Pearre bill and the sections of this bill treating of injunctions in labor cases. I am not, of course, understood as approving the Pearre bill; in fact, I still have great confidence in the courts. But here are the provisions of the Pearre bill:

A bill to regulate the issuance of restraining orders and injunctions and procedure thereon, and to limit the meaning of "conspiracy" in certain cases.

Be it enacted, etc. That no restraining order or injunction shall be granted by any court of the United States, or a judge or the judges thereof, in any case between an employer and an employee, or between employers and employees, or between employees, or between persons employed to labor and persons seeking employment as laborers, or between persons seeking employment as laborers, or involving or growing out of a dispute concerning terms or conditions of employment unless necessary to prevent irreparable injury to property or to a property right of the party making the application, for which injury there is no adequate remedy at law; and such property or property right must be particularly described in the application, which must be in writing and sworn to by the applicant or by his, her, or its agent or attorney. And for the purposes of this act no right to continue the relation of employer and employee or to assume or create such relation with any particular person or persons, or at all, or to carry on business of any particular kind or at any particular place, or at all, shall be construed, held, considered, or treated as property or as constituting a property right.

Sec. 2. That in cases arising in the courts of the United States or coming before said courts, or before any judge or the judges thereof, no agreement between two or more persons concerning the terms or conditions of employment of labor, or the assumption or creation or termination of any relation between employer and employee, or concerning any act or thing to be done or not to be done with reference to or involving or growing out of a labor dispute shall constitute a conspiracy or other criminal offense or be punished or prosecuted as such unless the act or thing agreed to be done or not to be done would be unlawful if done by a single individual, nor shall the entering into or the carrying out of any such agreement be restrained or enjoined unless such act or thing agreed to be done would be subject to be restrained or enjoined under the provisions, limitations, and definition contained in the first section of this act.

SEC. 3. That all acts and parts of acts in conflict with the provisions of this act are hereby repealed.

These provisions fully justified Mr. Gompers and his followers in their support of the Democratic ticket, according to their faith in the party pledges, if the subject of injunction in labor disputes was as important as claimed by them.

It will be observed that the Pearre bill entirely eliminates "the right to carry on business at any particular place or at all" from the category of property entitled to protection by injunction. You seek in vain for anything of that kind in this bill. The Pearre bill also had the effect to exempt labor from legal liability and from the injunctive process under the Sherman Antitrust Act in boycott cases. If the words of the second section, above quoted, do not mean that, then they mean nothing.

The claim in the committee's majority report that the so-called exemption clause for unions exempts anybody from any legal danger or interference is the rankest nonsense. It embodies a legal proposition never disputed by any court nor by any respectable authority.

And with respect to the so-called anti-injunction provisions of the bill, I start confidently with the assertion that if labor fully knows its rights and dares assert them, in keeping with its oft-expressed views of judicial power, it will be as much aroused in opposition to this bill as are all the intelligent business men of the Nation.

While having no fear that the courts would abuse the extensive new and arbitrary powers conferred by this bill, I am not deterred by that fact from calling attention to them. I am convinced, however, that our judges have not asked for and do not desire thrust upon them these arbitrary powers. I now quote from section 15 a sentence containing the gist of the whole section, which I deem it necessary to notice:

No temporary restraining order shall be granted without notice to the opposite party, unless it shall clearly appear from specific facts shown by affidavit or by the verified bill that immediate and irreparable injury, loss, or damage will result to property or a property right of the applicant before notice could be served or hearing had thereon.

If a statute said, "You shall not go into the street without your clothes on except to save some one from injury," I take it that such a statute would not deprive one of the privilege of wearing clothes on the street when not engaged in rescuing persons from injury. Surely no one would be so foolish as to insist that it did. Here the courts are forbidden to restrain parties without notice, except in the instance specified. Would it be possible to more clearly authorize them to issue restraining orders in any other cases they may see fit, and under all other circumstances which to them may appear to justify it, provided notice be given? I am no lawyer, and yet I would be ashamed to confess my inability to deduce from this language unlimited new authority to the courts to issue restraining orders at will upon notice.

The only limitation imposed is that, where no property or property right is involved, the ceremony of giving a notice, which may be one day's notice, must be observed. An examination of subsequent parts of the bill convinces me that this far-reaching effect of the language employed was not merely accidental, but had a definite purpose, which we discover when we read section 18.

Being a mere layman, I hesitated giving my own construction to section 18 until I had submitted it to legal Members of the House and found their views to accord with my own. The section is arranged in two paragraphs, possibly with a view to making it a little more difficult to discover how narrow and restricted the ground from which the courts are excluded. I find I can not make my points entirely clear without quoting the whole section. It reads as follows:

SEC. 18. That no restraining order or injunction shall be granted by any court of the United States, or a judge or the judges thereof, in any case between an employer and employees, or between employers and employees, or between employees, or between persons employed and persons seeking employment, involving, or growing out of, a dispute concerning terms or conditions of employment, unless necessary to prevent irreparable injury to property, or to a property right, of the party making the application, for which injury there is no adequate remedy at law, and such property or property right must be described with particularity in the application, which must be in writing and sworn to by the applicant or by his agent or attorney.

And no such restraining order or injunction shall prohibit any person or persons from terminating any relation of employment, or from ceasing to perform any work or labor, or from recommending, advising, or persuading others by peaceful means so to do; or from attending at or near a house or place where any person resides or works, or carries on business or happens to be, for the purpose of peacefully obtaining or communicating information, or of peacefully persuading any person to work or to abstain from working; or from ceasing to patronize or to employ any party to such dispute, or from recommending, advising, or persuading others by peaceful means so to do; or from paying or giving to, or withholding from, any person engaged in such dispute, any strike benefits or other moneys or things of value; or from peaceably assembling at any place in a lawful manner, and for lawful purposes; or from doing any act or thing which might lawfully be done in the absence of such dispute by any party thereto.

It will be observed that the section is inoperative until a case has been brought, and the case must be between persons holding certain relations; and not only so, it must be pending while the relation exists. It is important to note that property or a property right must be involved. Hence it would never apply in the rare event of an action between employees or between persons employed and those seeking employment. It is therefore limited to cases between employer and employees. But that relation terminates the moment a strike or lockout occurs. Would it ever apply in cases of strikes or boycotts? Do employees eat their cake and keep it, too? In other words, do they strike and yet keep right along at work? And is there an instance to be found of employees boycotting an employer while serving him? Such a thing may be possible but is unprecedented. Again, do persons employed and those seeking employment boycott or declare strikes against each other? Of course such a thing is inconceivable.

Now, when you have eliminated strike and boycott cases, I would like some one to point out any jurisdiction remaining for the operation of the prohibition worthy of mention. And to see that all in the second paragraph is brought within the narrow confines of the first, I call attention to the fact that it says, in the first line of the second paragraph, "and no such restraining order or injunction," and so forth. That obviously refers to those restricted with respect to relations and subject of litigation in the preceding paragraph. Any persuasion or withholding of patronage or assembling, however "peaceful" and "lawful," must, in order to come within the exemption, involve parties in a case standing in these relations, and the action must be one brought to protect property or property rights from irreparable injury. Suppose it be an action brought for a restraining order not involving property, but upon notice, as clearly it may be, under the provision of section 15, read in connection with the first paragraph of section 18. It is absurd to suppose the author of the bill and the committee intended that the courts should be bereft of jurisdiction in cases of violence, disorder, and trespass, in all that larger and more important class of cases where the relation of employer and employee never existed or has been severed by a strike. I do not accuse it of having done anything so foolish. And that is just where it misleads such of labor's representatives as believe that to have been done. If they believe the law is objectionable as it stands to-day, they will soon find that this act is much more amenable to the same grounds of objection.

Whether labor is entitled to have the jurisdiction of the courts regulated and limited is a question not before us, because if it were conceded that labor is entitled to legislation of that character, no bill containing it is before us, and the issue is not raised by this bill.

That some one representing labor is not satisfied with the bill in its present shape appears from the fact that marked copies have been laid upon the desks of Members by the American Federation of Labor. The suggested amendment to section 18 is a mere addition of these words, "nor shall any of the acts enumerated in this paragraph be considered unlawful in any court of the United States." It was stated in the New York World of May 2 that labor's representatives had been told at the White House that if that addition were made it would be clearly unconstitutional. Though the President may have missed the mark on other occasions, he is undoubtedly correct about this. I do not claim to know much constitutional law, but I know enough to know that, as Congress would here be attempting to direct the judicial department in the construction of statutes, which is a judicial and not a legislative function, it would be contrary to both the form and spirit of the Constitution.

I can not help marveling at the present subserviency of our friend Gompers and his associates. I have not forgotten his and their splendid show of courage and consistency at the first session of the Sixty-second Congress; how they took their stand for the Bacon-Bartlett bill, containing substantially the provisions of the Pearre bill, and even more; got it reported from the Labor Committee, whose chairman, W. B. Wilson, now officiates and luxuriates at the head of the Department of Labor; how the chairman of the Judiciary Committee found himself unable to control Mr. Wilson, but did succeed in controlling the gentleman from Texas [Mr. HENRY] so far as to prevent the report of a special rule for the consideration of the bill. Now, I shall be very much surprised if the American Federation of Labor and its friends on this floor so far stultify themselves and disappoint their followers as to accept so miserable a makeshift, so utterly ruinous a measure as that embodied in sections 15 and 18.

I would like to give some attention to the contempt provisions, which are, if possible, more objectionable than the other, but find so much of my time exhausted that I must devote the balance to the other provisions of the bill.

Section 2 of the pending bill reads as follows:

SEC. 2. That any person engaged in commerce who shall either directly or indirectly discriminate in price between different purchasers of commodities in the same or different sections or communities, which commodities are sold for use, consumption, or resale within the United States or any Territory thereof or the District of Columbia or any insular possession or other place under the jurisdiction of the United States, with the purpose or intent to thereby destroy or wrongfully injure the business of a competitor of either such purchaser or seller, shall be deemed guilty of a misdemeanor, and upon conviction thereof shall be punished by a fine not exceeding $5,000, or by imprisonment not exceeding one year, or by both, in the discretion of the court: *Provided,* That nothing herein contained shall prevent discrimination in price between purchasers of commodities on account of differences in the grade, quality, or quantity of the commodity sold, or that makes only due allowance for difference in the cost of transportation: *And provided further,* That nothing herein contained shall prevent persons engaged in selling goods, wares, or merchandise in commerce from selecting their own customers, except as provided in section 3 of this act.

The best that can be said for it is that from the moment of its passage and approval it would become and remain a dead letter and a mere encumbrance of the statute books. But it would at least cause doubts, fears, and uncertainty in the business mind. In a broad sense every sale that is made injures and is intended to injure a competitor, because the mere fact of a sale by A deprives B and other dealers of an opportunity to make a sale. But the prohibition is surrounded by so many loopholes for escape, provisos, and exceptions, practically covering some condition of every sale, that the jargon means very little. Its presence in the bill can only be accounted for upon the theory that persons are still living who were injured by evil practices of the Standard Oil Co. at a former period, and these have been sufficiently influential to have inserted in a bill affecting nearly all business this useless, confusing provision. The answer under any charge of a violation to the question of why the sale was made would be that the sale was made in order to make the sale. Or the accused party could say he got the business while in the act of getting it, or that he did the business in due course of doing business. He could answer in either of these meaningless ways and so put an end to any case brought under that section.

I pass now to section 4. In a general sense it forbids exclusive contracts.

If it were possible, I would like to ascertain just how much those who inspired or dictated that provision know about the established and normal course of the world's business of to-day. It is a fact well known to business men that the exclusive contracts here condemned and penalized characterize about three-fourths of the productive and mercantile business worth doing at all, and the balance would be done by the same methods if it were practicable.

Upon reading the hearings before the committee an impression is obtained that the only persons in the country who can possibly be injured by what the committee condemns as an exclusive contract is the small or crossroads merchant. Even if I admitted, which I do not, that his prosperity would be promoted by the elimination of exclusive contracts, still it would be just as absurd and unwise to do so as to burn a barn or sink a ship in order to get rid of rats.

Let me illustrate how the exclusive contract is operated. Mr. A, we will suppose, manufactures a special grade of men's underwear, from certain kinds of wool and cotton, taken in given proportions and combinations. Of course, there may be a dozen or hundred others making other brands which are better or just as good at the same price or slightly inferior at a much lower price. Now, at the beginning of the year A does not know whether his trade will amount to $50,000 or $100,000, so he goes to Smith & Co., wholesalers or jobbers, who are vast distributors, and arranges with them that they will take his entire output or surplus, after he has supplied his retail customers, off his hands at the end of each three months at a certain fixed price, provided he does not produce an annual excess of $100,000. They also bind themselves mutually that Smith & Co. shall not buy that class and grade of goods from anyone else, except to meet a demand in excess of A's supply, and that A shall not offer his surplus to anyone else.

Now, I am prepared to point out the advantages of that arrangement to the immediate parties. A knows for a year ahead just how much raw material to obtain, how many operatives to employ, how much the aggregate cost and the cost per unit, how much his profit on each unit of production, and, in the aggregate, just how much money to borrow and when to promise repayment. His employees are secure in their jobs for the entire year or during good behavior. Smith & Co. can calculate their profits per unit in advance, and can make similar exclusive contracts with retailers throughout the country and at a lower price than if all were left to chance, fancy, and the interference of competitors. And the same certainty, safety, and security is created in their establishment in the matter of employees, organization, expenses, and so forth, as in A's. All of which, as anyone can see, also makes for economy and lower prices.

How does it affect other producers and dealers? Using alphabetical representation, we have, say, makers of underwear down to J who are able to make these exclusive contracts, and they make them with as many different general distributors. They are in competition with each other up to the point of making the contracts and continuing in local competition, and their respective brands continue to compete with each other everywhere.

But below J are K, L, M, and so forth, in the same line of production, competing with all above and among themselves, but unable to arrange exclusive contracts. And there can be no doubt of ample competition between the distributors handling the various brands.

I now take up the case of the crossroads or village storekeeper, who is about the only party thought by the committee ⊥ to be worthy of consideration. His opportunities in the city's marts are indeed restricted; but that is the least of his disadvantages. His customers usually buy on credit, so that he is unable to turn over his capital more than once or twice a year. He has long seasons of depression and short seasons of excessive activity. But he always enjoys at least two options. He may enter into the exclusive contract, so limiting his commitment as to remain on the safe side, and then supply deficiencies from K, L, M, and so forth, or he may reject the exclusive contract and do all his business with the latter. If he and his customers must pay a little more than the denizens of the city or large town, that is only one of the inconveniences of rural life. In truth, however, the rural dweller enjoys to a large extent all the benefits of a world-wide competition.

I would like to portray some of the exclusive advantages of residence remote from the throngs, activities, and distractions of city life, but lack of time forbids. Instead of deploring the lot of such dwellers, I have always been inclined to envy them their normal, simple lives; their undisturbed sanity, serenity, and security.

The country merchant suffers more from the competition of mail-order houses than from the causes assigned by the committee. But what are you going to do about that? Will you take away from his customers their postal facilities? That would be just as nonsensical as to disintegrate for their benefit the delicate structure of the country's business, founded on years and decades of varied and shifting experience, thereby restoring waste, deceit, cheating, higher prices, bankruptcies, and other evils of unrestrained and unregulated competition. And from these evils by far the greater sufferers are residents in the country.

The section also strikes at leases, denying the manufacturers of special machines and patented articles the privilege of leasing and selling them on restrictive conditions. I will endeavor to illustrate with a great business institution against which no prejudice appears in the report. The two cases referred to by the committee appear to have been aggravated cases. But even there not the slightest injury to consumers or users was shown or even asserted. They were instances of disputes between rivals in business. Let us take for illustration a business in which a large number of men doing considerable business are interested. A great plant at West Orange, N. J., manufactures and sells or leases thousands of storage batteries used in autocars and autotrucks. The convenience and economy resulting to individuals from using these and dispensing with horses and wagons it would be difficult to estimate, to say nothing of the diminished wear and tear of vehicles and streets and interlocked wheels. Storage batteries require supervision, cleaning, and more or less scientific care. It would be a great loss both to the manufacturer and user to make outright sales and allow them to go beyond the control of the former. So, necessarily, in most cases that company uses the leasing form of agreement carrying with it a guaranty for a number of years, with the cost of all services to keep in perfect condition covered in the leasing price. But it would be impracticable to use the batteries without containers; and the expense of keeping in condition would be greatly enhanced if the batteries were used, as after a fashion they could be, with containers made by others than those who scientifically construct them for that company and nicely adjust them to the batteries. So when a battery is leased the lessee is required to purchase a container made by the company and must bind himself not to use any made by anyone else. The container is sold at actual cost and at a price no higher than that of others in the market, considering its superior excellence. Now, who will have the hardihood to question the right of that company to do business in that form which in the end makes for economy and profit to both parties? And that is but one of thousands of such illustrations that could be given.

But if this bill should pass with that fourth section retained in it, that company would hereafter have to make outright sales of the batteries, in which case they would soon get out of condition and be peddled about as secondhand articles or go into the junk heap, to the discredit and ruin of its business, because they could no longer couple their leases with conditions as to exclusive use of their containers, without which they must sell rather than lease the batteries.

The same condition is found in many branches of the automobile business. Handy mechanical contrivances which are not, as it is said, fool proof are leased and guaranteed. But the owners of such patents find that there is no profit in their manufacture and sale unless they can not only retain supervision through leases but also sell the lessees other parts that go with the patented part and place a prohibition upon the use of these other parts made by others.

It was shown before the Judiciary Committee at its hearings in 1912 that the business in this country which would be affected by such legislation amounts to the enormous annual sum of $25,000,000,000. A loss of even 1 per cent of that vast sum inflicted "by act of Congress" would be $250,000,000. How would that loss be compensated? Who would be the gainers? Suppose such great establishments as those manufacturing storage batteries and the great automobile factories were broken up and put out of business, who would profit by it? It would be found unprofitable for their successors, even if any would be found possessed of sufficient capital and brains to do the business in any other way and survive. In such institutions you must have cooperation and coordination of many departments and machines, and if only one company in the country has had the brains, enterprise, and foresight to assemble them into effective working relations, then that company will have a monopoly. The question is not at all whether a monopoly is desirable. If that were the question, no one would be readier with a negative answer than I. But the question is whether it is not better to endure a few monopolies, especially when it is not shown that their charges for service are unreasonable than make a disastrous attempt to put them out of business at the behest of disgruntled agitators and wreckers.

I have already noticed the first paragraph of section 7. I will now call attention to the second paragraph of the same section, which reads as follows:

Nothing contained in the antitrust laws shall be construed to forbid associations of traffic, operating, accounting, or other officers of common carriers for the purpose of conferring among themselves or of making any lawful agreement as to any matter which is subject to the regulating or supervisory jurisdiction of the Interstate Commerce Commission, but all such matters shall continue to be subject to such jurisdiction of the commission, and all such agreements shall be entered and kept of record by the carriers, parties thereto, and shall at all times be open to inspection by the commission: *Provided,* That nothing in this act shall be construed as modifying existing laws prohibiting the pooling of earnings or traffic, or existing laws against joint agreements by common carriers to maintain rates.

Need I emphasize the far-reaching effect of what I have just read?

Heretofore when such legislation was offered it did not extend to operating and accounting officers, nor did it authorize, as does this provision, the formation of permanent associations with memberships composed of the officers of rival railroad companies. It will be noted that this would enable the railroads to completely forestall all the activities and functions of the Interstate Commerce Commission. It would cover not only rates, but every form of service to the public and fiscal affairs. Skillfully the draftsman has left with the commission supervision not of the agreements, mind you, but of the matters forming the subject matters of the agreements. But care is taken not to confer on the commission any control over the terms of such agreements, nor of practices under them, those being here legalized. . . .

Such an enactment would thwart every effort of the commission and render its continued existence not worth while. If that were all, the public would be but slightly worse off than with the present slack-twisted pretense of rate regulation. But the prohibition of the antitrust act, the only barrier between the people and tyrannical, unrestrained monopolies of transportation, would be removed.

Many here will remember the persistent but heretofore unsuccessful efforts to have Congress exempt traffic agreements from the antitrust act. Here we have it in a more dangerous form than ever before presented. I trust that in this House, where on my motion, nearly four years ago, a much less dangerous form of the same exemption was stricken out of the amendatory act of 1910 by an overwhelming majority, it is only necessary to call attention to it. If I had thought there was the slightest probability of this Congress passing any such provision, I would have devoted most of the time allotted me to this clause of section 7. But surely the debates of four years ago, running through days and weeks, and the unanswerable reasons then urged against such legislation, have not been forgotten or lost their force.

Without intending to question the good faith of the committee, unless the facts constitute a reflection on it, I call attention to the bill as given to the public on Saturday, May 2. That bill contained no provision on the subject. Nor did the press of the country or the public have any hint that the bill would contain any such provision, until the committee made its report on May 6.

I was humbly born and I know what it is to toil; and I have always taken pride in being just on an equal plane of privilege with my fellow man, neither above nor below him, having no other feeling than scorn and contempt for any who would be above the law, while others are within it. I know of no more distinctive or important, nor any safer, American doctrine than ⊥ equality before the law. If a statute is not to stand ⊥9085 against all, let it be repealed; and if it is not to be enforced against all, let the officers of the law declare an intention to refuse its enforcement in any and every case.

I can not give time to a full discussion of section 8, containing, among others, several important provisions pertaining to railroad finance, including stock and bond deals. All of it would appear to be entirely far-fetched and out of place in a bill dealing with the antitrust laws. Within much cunning phraseology are embraced in it all the vices of the Townsend-Elkins bill of the Sixty-first Congress, a bill which was finally defeated—at least, as to all these provisions. Here again it bobs up serenely, occupying more than two pages of this bill, without discussion before the committee, without notice to or knowledge of anyone except those in the sacred inner circles of the committee room.

Notwithstanding the fact that the ownership by public-service corporations of the stocks of other public-service corporations was always denied when the issue was made before the courts, and notwithstanding that Congress has heretofore steadfastly refused to sanction it, the successive heads of the Department of Justice have winked at and condoned it and given effect to such acquisitions in actions under the antitrust act. I see in the provisions of section 8 an attempt to consummate in legislation the derelictions and evil practices of the Attorneys General. It is here attempted in the deceptive form of prohibitions with provisos and limitations. "Hereafter you shall not steal a sheep; provided, however, that nothing herein shall be construed to prevent your stealing a lamb." We are expected to close our minds to the fact that in a short time the lamb will become a sheep.

I feel so confident, with respect to the disposal by the House of section 8, that I will also refrain from discussing that section at length. But lest the brevity of my comment upon it mislead some one and make an impression that the closing paragraph of section 7 and all of section 8 are of comparatively slight importance, I appeal to every Member to give them careful and serious attention. Certain leading newspapers have been of late teeming with charges that the railroads have captured all the works at Washington under this administration. I make no such charge, but state the obvious truth that their power must be great, indeed, not only here in Congress, but also with the Chief Executive, if they are able to "put over" on the people any such legislation as is here proposed.

A vast conspiracy to promote railroad interests above all others in the conduct of this administration, intrigue, and the artificial creation of public opinion have been freely charged in some of the newspapers and elsewhere. Much evidence intended to establish the truth of these charges has become a matter of record in a coordinate body. In order to complete the record, I call attention to one or two additional facts: Double dealing on the part of the attorney chosen by the Interstate Commerce Commission, whose majority were appointed by President Wilson, was definitely and circumstantially charged last week by an attorney representing large associations of shippers and no less than seven sovereign States. An Associated Press news item appeared at the time reading as follows:

THORNE ASSAILS BRANDEIS—SAYS HIS OPINION ON RATE ADVANCE WAS NOT SUPPORTED BY FACTS.

Washington, May 7.

The Interstate Commerce Commission had before it to-day a supplementary brief filed by Clifford Thorne, representing the western railroad commissions before that body in the advanced-rate case, in which he bitterly arraigns Louis D. Brandeis, special counsel for the commission, who, in his closing argument in the case last Friday, stated that "on the whole, the net income, the net operating revenues, of the carriers in official classification territory are smaller than is consistent with their assured prosperity and the welfare of the community."

Mr. Thorne asserts that Mr. Brandeis commenced his argument before the commission "by conceding the position of the carriers." On behalf of those whom he represents Mr. Thorne says that he "repudiates in unqualified terms" the concession made by Mr. Brandeis in his closing argument. In so far as Mr. Brandeis's opinion is not supported by substantial reasons the commission should not give any weight to it.

Mr. Thorne then refers to the "unpardonable" attack of Mr. Brandeis on the surplus he [Mr. Thorne] had allowed.

"The surplus to which Mr. Brandeis applied the epithet 'niggardly,' " he says, "was precisely the surplus adopted, after careful and deliberate consideration, by the unanimous action of the commission in the former advanced-rate cases. Mr. Brandeis attempts to brand that surplus as 'niggardly' without giving the slightest argument, reason, or fact in support of his claim. Some of the companies are earning more than 20 percent after all other charges are paid. Not a word appears throughout the entire brief or in oral argument in favor of reducing their surplus earnings."

Mr. Thorne adds that the commission can not hold the revenues of the carriers affected inadequate unless it reverses the principles established in its former opinions.

I am merely availing myself of this opportunity to call the matter to the attention of the House. When so serious a charge is made by responsible authority, where so much is involved, so well calculated, if believed, to discredit that important executive branch, it is the duty of the legislative department, whose will it is the duty of the commission to faithfully interpret, to learn whether the charge be founded in fact or unfounded.

Section 8 and sections following it are of such considerable length that I shall not read them into the RECORD.

And I shall only discuss one other section, and that briefly. Section 9, filling four pages of the bill, contains provisions in detail concerning directorates in private corporations and the qualifications of directors. The principal reason assigned by the committee for embarking Congress upon this unexplored sea of legislation reads as follows:

> As the President has well said in his message, the adoption of the provisions of this section will bring new men, new energies, new spirit of initiative, and new blood into the management of our business enterprises. It will open the field of industrial development and origination to scores of men who have been obliged to serve when their abilities entitled them to direct. It will immensely hearten the young men coming on and will greatly enrich the business activities of the whole country.

In the days of Jackson the slogan of the party was, "To the victors belong the spoils." At a later period, a cardinal political theory was that there should be frequent rotations in public office. But never until the "New Freedom" was handed down to us did any one suggest that the Government should extend its powers to compelling rotation in places of private trust and confidence.

If the proposed regulation of directorates does not belong to the same category of political clap-trap as do other parts of the bill, at any rate in so far as it is not already covered by the Sherman Antitrust Act, when faithfully enforced, it is utterly abortive, because beyond Federal control. I need not elaborate this proposition, since others will be able to do so more clearly than I could, but it seems to me almost too obvious to require elucidation. Where the laws of a State have prescribed the qualifications for directors and defined the voting rights of stockholders in corporations of their own creation, what right has the Federal Government to interfere? But enormous wrong can be done and irreparable injury inflicted by an unconstitutional enactment before its invalidity can be established through a tedious course of litigation.

Probably a quarter million corporations, transacting the larger percentage of the country's business, would be affected by such legislation in their most vital parts—that is to say, at their heads. The rage for innovation and disruption is not satiated by tearing down and mutilating beyond all hope of repair the country's business fabric, but, giving free rein to the mania for capricious readjustment, the whole structure and system of corporate management is to be arbitrarily shifted. It is to be taken out of the hands of those who have been tried and found efficient and trustworthy; those who have invested their fortunes in the business and grown up with it. Those who were the choice of the stockholders are to be displaced and the business placed in new hands, intrusted to those who know nothing of corporate management, and are untested as to character and capacity. Nor is this new deal in directorates and business control limited to manufacturing and trading companies. Even banks of all kinds, including savings banks and trust companies, holding in trust the savings of the poor, are to be reorganized, from the ground up, and their funds intrusted to new hands, not by choice of stockholders but "by act of Congress."

It would be impossible to portray the full and ultimate effects of the program of legislation laid and to be laid before us to constitute the Democratic trust—or antitrust—program. To compare it to the effects, local and external, of the uprisings, revolutions, and counter-revolutions going on in Mexico during the past three years would be to unduly magnify the latter, and to draw comparisons between Villa and Carranza and Democratic leaders would be too intensely personal. But notwithstanding the respectable characters of those now in charge of the country's affairs, I warn them to pause before committing wrongs that can never be remedied, before they destroy the little of business prosperity which has survived their work thus far, and to forbear to break up the solid foundations upon which all prosperity may hereafter rest; to pause, to stay their ravages, to give time for investigation, and a kindlier reception than they have heretofore given to the voice of reason and justice. [Applause.] . . .

Mr. [M. CLYDE] KELLY [Prog., Pa.] . . .

Mr. Chairman, the gentleman from Illinois [Mr. MADDEN] has just stated that the demand for antitrust legislation at this time ⊥ comes from disgruntled agitators. He completely mistakes the temper and the will of the American people. The trusts and monopolies of this country are themselves responsible for the demand for remedial action, and their disregard of justice and every fundamental principle of this Republic has made the solution indispensable. Enterprises with great capital have deliberately sought not only industrial domination but political supremacy as well. They have entered the realm of government with insolent bearing and have attempted to name officials from the highest to the lowest.

Organized money, rioting ruthlessly in savage impulses, has forced this question upon us. We must decide whether wealth is to rule or manhood, whether this Nation is to be one of equal rights to all or special privileges to a few, whether honor and ability is to weigh in the selection of officials or cringing submission to corporate capital.

The conscience of the American people demands that action be taken, and any delay now will be a betrayal of their will. Great combinations of capital for many years have flaunted their power in the face of the citizenship, they have forced their corrupt way into politics and government, they have dictated the making of laws or scorned the laws they did not like, they have prevented the free and just administration of law. In doing this they have become a menace to free institutions, and must be dealt with in patriotic spirit, without fear or favor.

It is a common practice for standpatters to decry every forward step by denunciation of agitators. It would be well to pay some little attention to the fawning followers of crooked big business in the press, on the platform, and in public office. They sell themselves for price and place, and it would be well if they were dissected and their treason examined, while men are cataloguing the enemies of the Nation.

Mr. Chairman, I am in complete accord with the purpose and aim of this legislation, but I fear that its terms are such that if enacted into law it will only add more jests to the long list which has marked the antitrust legislation of America in the past. Trusts have been ordered dissolved in the past, and the only change effected was one in the methods of bookkeeping. It is time for straightforward action and an honest effort to protect the people from the powers that prey upon them.

GROWTH OF TRUST DOMINATION.

For 35 years combinations of capital have sought to form monopolies and profit from the community through the private taxing power which goes with the ability to control prices. In 1879 the Standard Alliance, composed of oil refiners, led the way, through a pooling system, and in a short time controlled 95 percent of the refining business of the country. The Western Exporters' Association, made up of whisky distillers, followed, and it soon was in absolute control of the business. Others followed in the same path, and this pooling system flourished for a time.

But it did not give the complete control desired. It did not concern itself with the management of individual plants, but simply apportioned out the pro rata share of production. Each member of the pool could withdraw without notice, and thus the agreement had no stability. In their anxiety for quick and large profits the producers broke the market by their very greediness. The Whisky Trust and the Wire-Nail Trust Association went so far as to raise prices 200 per cent in the midst of falling prices. Jealousy caused trouble also, and the Lackawanna Iron & Steel Co. once broke the steel-rail pool because it was allowed only 17 per cent of the production.

Such defects in the control of prices stirred the producers to find other schemes to secure their aim, that of throttling the public and forcing the highest possible prices for products.

The next plan was the trust agreement, through which trustees were assigned the majority stock in constituent refineries. They controlled the boards of directors and collected all dividends on stock and distributed them to the holders of trust certificates. It was a better plan than the pool, for the pool was an outlaw in the courts, while in the trust agreement the trustees had the law on their side and could enforce their contracts.

The injustices which followed such control of prices, however, stirred lawmaking bodies to action. In 1890 many State legislatures passed antitrust laws, and in the same year the Sherman antitrust law was enacted for the purpose of dealing with combinations doing an interstate business.

So, another plan was necessary, and legal sharps were set to work to discover some juggling trick which would enable great combinations to wring millions from helpless consumers. While they sought for this ideal plan, the producers, having tasted the sweets of despotic control, carried on their nefarious plans through a system known as "community of interest." By the knowledge gained through close association, officials of different companies were able to act together and to prevent competition, even without any formal agreement.

This plan was still weak, for disagreements and misunderstandings meant a return to competition at any time, and that was what the different companies were striving to prevent.

Then came the discovery of the ideal scheme—the "holding corporation." It provided for a corporation to own the stock of competing companies, and it was proved in a short time to be a method in which to legally violate both law and justice. It excelled other plans, because it was not necessary to purchase the companies outright. Buying up a majority of the stock of the companies served every purpose. It escaped the troubles of the trust agreement, which was declared illegal because it was a conspiracy of several individuals, and this plan meant having one person, in the form of a corporation, control all the individual companies.

The Sugar Trust was the first to put this plan into operation, but others followed thick and fast. In 1897 there were 63 "holding companies" in existence, and in 1898–99 there were formed 183 such companies with a capitalization of $4,000,000,000, representing one-twentieth of the entire wealth of the country and twice the amount of money in circulation.

From that time trusts have flourished until to-day a trust controls almost every commodity of daily life. This has been done in spite of all efforts to prevent restraint of trade. Suits have been entered against these vast combinations, but in most instances they have failed, and the victory won in the others was but a shadow victory. The decisions of the Supreme Court have involved legal somersaults and twistings and turnings, but the old issue still remains. It is to-day a muddle of 24 years' stirring, and the time for clearing is certainly here.

In clearing that muddle straightforward measures are necessary. It is not necessary to specifically describe every unfair trade practice, but it is necessary that some tribunal have the power to deal with every unfair trade practice which leads to monopoly. This measure mentions a few—and only a few—of these practices; and, even if they could be thus rooted out, others are sure to take their place, to remedy which other legislation will be needed.

Such an interstate trade commission as that proposed in the Progressive bill before this body would prevent confusion, delay, and injustice. It would prevent the evils mentioned in this measure, price discriminations, "tying" contracts, and so forth, and would be empowered to deal with every evasion as it might arise. Time will prove that only through a tribunal with proper powers can these unfair practices be prevented.

EXEMPTION OF LABOR UNIONS.

Section 7 of this measure, with the change necessary to clearly prevent application of antitrust laws to fraternal, labor, and other voluntary organizations, is a great step in advance. The section reads:

> That nothing contained in the antitrust laws shall be construed to forbid the existence and operation of fraternal, labor, consumers, agricultural, or horticultural organizations, orders, or associations instituted for the purpose of mutual help and not having capital stock or conducted for profit, or to forbid or restrain individual members of such organizations, orders, or associations from carrying out the legitimate objects thereof.

This section, properly amended, will help to write the gospel of humanity into law. It is a recognition of the fundamental difference between human labor and the products of labor. Legislation dealing with trusts which control the products of labor can not be justly applied to the association of workers for their own betterment and improvement. One deals with materials, the other with men; one with mines, the other with miners;

one with machines, the other with machinists; one with farms, the other with farmers; one with buildings, the other with builders; one with factories, the other with factory workers; one with tools, the other with toilers; one with property, the other with persons. You can not classify them together, for they are essentially different.

The free workers of America own themselves and their labor power. They may sell their labor power to others or they may withhold it. They may act together for the protection of their rights and interests, and it is a sham and a fraud to say that they may organize without the power to use means necessary to make organization a vital force in demanding and securing justice.

I stand for the right of labor to organize for its own advancement and to work for that purpose without being outlawed for it. This measure is right in purpose, and I hope it will be amended so that there shall be no shadow of doubt as to the right of the workers of this country to organize and exert themselves in legitimate activities without the danger of being prosecuted under antitrust laws. It is not a case of class legislation nor a demand for special privileges. It is simply a demand of humanity for freedom from restrictions and shackles that deny common justice.

The Sherman antitrust law has been made a potent force against organized labor, even while it proved unable to restrain marauding combinations of capital. In 1892 it was brought into action when some union men in New Orleans went on strike. Teamsters and workmen in many lines were concerned. Judge Billings, of the United States district court, declared that the strike was in restraint of interstate commerce and granted an injunction. The United States court of appeals agreed in his decision.[5.493]

Two years later the point was again reached in the Pullman strike in Chicago. Injunctions against the strikers were granted by the courts under the Sherman Act and a number of the strikers were jailed for several months for disobeying the injunction.[5.494]

Several years later another labor phase came into evidence. In Danbury, Conn., a small firm of hat manufacturers operated an open shop and was boycotted by labor unions. The court decided that the unions were acting as a combination in restraint of trade under the meaning of the Sherman antitrust law.[5.495]

Many other instances might be cited to show that the antitrust laws have been used as a club over voluntary organizations, which were never intended to come within their scope. When the Sherman antitrust law was passed in the Senate it was clearly and unequivocally stated that its provisions would not cover such organizations. But history shows that the victories won under it have been the suits against labor organizations, while great trusts and monopolies have grown and flourished. It is to remedy such a flagrant injustice that this provision is included in this measure; and after it is amended to clearly accomplish its purpose of exemption, it should have the support of every Member of this House.

INJUNCTIONS AND JURY TRIAL.

The provisions in this measure for the regulation of injunctions and the procedure in contempt cases, while somewhat beyond the scope of antitrust legislation, are reforms long demanded by the American people. The expression "government by injunction" has become current because in almost every labor controversy in recent years the courts have been used by powerful corporations in the carrying out of their plans to subjugate employees and to prevent the exercise of lawful rights. The abuse of the right of injunction in the past 10 years has been sufficient to arouse the public, and this legislation is demanded by every right-thinking American citizen to-day.

Similar to that demand is the determination that the constitutional provision that "no person shall be deprived of life, liberty, or property without due process of law and the judgment of his peers" shall be maintained. Freemen since the days of King John and Runnymede have demanded jury trial. It is a fundamental American doctrine.

[5.493] United States v. Workingmen's Amalgamated Council, 54 F. 994 (C.C.E.D. La. 1893), aff'd, 57 F. 85 (5th Cir. 1893).

[5.494] United States v. Debs, 64 F. 724 (C.C.N.D. Ill. 1894), *petition for writ of habeas corpus denied, In re* Debs, 158 U.S. 564 (1895).

[5.495] Loewe v. Lawlor, 208 U.S. 274, 28 S. Ct. 301, 52 L. Ed. 488 (1908) (the *Danbury Hatters* case).

If jurors are competent to judge the law and the fact in criminal cases, why are they not competent in matters of injunction and contempt? The judge is not more competent to judge of a litigant's rights when his life is not at stake than when it is, and the individual or corporation that is afraid to submit his case to a jury for trial has no right to dictate laws for the administration of justice.

THE INVISIBLE GOVERNMENT.

Mr. Chairman, the invisible government which has controlled the visible Government in this Nation for many years has been unscrupulous big business. We have been tracing some of its insidious, slimy ways in our lobby investigations of recent date. We have seen its arts of trickery and debauchery, its manipulations and its conspiracies. The time for forbearance is over and the time to strike has come. If this Nation is to be a government of the people by crooked big business, the doom of our free institutions is assured. I believe that firm and decisive action now will be for the best interest not only of the Nation at large but of business itself. Brazen defiance of the spirit of laws made to protect the public and cunning jugglery to evade them is in the final analysis the worst thing possible for business. Business protects itself against fires by vast expenditures for fire insurance, but there are other dangers worse than fires. One is the danger that the masses of the people will forget their patient endurance of injustice and long-suffering submission to wrong on the part of exploiting combinations and start a conflagration against which fire insurance will offer no protection.

Good business depends on the permanence of law and order. This Nation can not stand much more of fraud and plunder, savage impulses left unchecked, a controlled press, and misrepresentation of the truth and continue to have good business.

The real defenders of property to-day are not those who attempt to forestall every attempt at reform by denunciation and who put the blame for unrest not on those who pummel the people but on those who call attention to the black and blue spots. The real defenders of property are not the standpatters, who cry out against any change and shout, "let well enough alone," when the very worst thing that could happen would be to have things remain exactly as they are, no better and no worse.

No; the real defenders of property are the upholders of the rights of humanity, the Progressives, who believe that "new occasions teach new duties. Time makes ancient good uncouth. They must upward still and onward who would keep abreast of truth."

To-day, as always, there are men like Demetrius of Ephesus, who, when he saw that the preaching of Paul the apostle was harming his business of making silver idols, gathered his fellows together and raised a great hue and cry, shouting "Great is Diana of the Ephesians." Their fervid devotion to Diana was as false as that of monopolists and their defenders to-day who shout "Great is property," when the public conscience demands that justice be done.

The greatest security to property comes from the security of human rights, and the sooner business realizes that fact the better it will be for all concerned.

THE PERIL OF COMPROMISE.

Mr. Chairman, the American people have a right to expect a better measure than this weak, halting, halfway attempt at remedy of intolerable conditions. It does not go to the root of the evils which have brought concentration of wealth and diffusion of poverty. I sincerely hope that it may be amended so that its expressed purposes may be accomplished, for there is a deadly peril in compromise with the forces that prey. There is no golden mean between right and wrong, between courage and cowardice, between honor and dishonor, between patriotism and treason, between the people's rights and monopoly. I believe in industrial and commercial peace, but not the peace that is purchased at the expense of justice and human liberty. There can be no peace in America except with the destruction of the sordid social wrongs and the putrid political methods which have attended the growth of the great combinations and monopolies of this country. This is an irrepressible conflict and there is no middle ground. The Nation looks to its Congress to strike a fair and square blow at hoary wrongs, and thus better the living conditions of the people of America. Lawmakers can concern themselves with nothing greater than that, and it is the duty as well as privilege of every representative of the people to make that his chief end and aim in his decision upon every measure before this Congress. [Applause.] . . .

Mr. [JOHN J.] MITCHELL [D., Mass.]. Mr. Chairman, I think the Members of the House have been very much impressed particularly with the difference of opinion that appears to exist on the other side of the House. The senior member upon the Judiciary Committee on the Republican side of the House [Mr. VOLSTEAD] substantially said that this bill did not do anything. After he concluded his remarks, the distinguished and able gentleman from Illinois [Mr. MADDEN] stated that the bill was too drastic. Evidently it did something, and now we have just heard from the able representative of the Progressive Party, Mr. KELLY, that the bill does not do anything, and the only section of the bill that he has referred to in his eloquent address he proceeds to praise and to commend. I think, Mr. Chairman, that the condition made so manifest this evening on that side of the House is a condition that existed among our friends for the past 10 or 15 years, since these organizations have sought to come into existence and since they have been developed. One wing of the party wanted to regulate and to legislate. Another wing of the party, where these interests were so firmly intrenched, did not want to pass any legislation, so we have arrived at this situation, that there has been vouchsafed to the majority party of this House the responsibility of responding, I believe, to the wishes and to the hopes and the aspirations of 100,000,000 people and writing into the law this antitrust legislation. [Applause on the Democratic side.] Mr. Chairman, I do not think that the senior Representative of the Republican Party upon our committee did credit or justice to himself when he stated that this bill was conceived and perfected in secret session.

I have been a member of other legislative bodies, Mr. Chairman, in the days gone by, and I have never served upon any committee that sought, as this committee has sought, the light and the aid of counsel and the assistance of business men from every section of the country. Why, Mr. Chairman, we counseled with the minority Members upon the committee in the perfection of this bill. Why, Mr. Chairman, we prepared three tentative drafts of this bill, and I believe that every member of the committee, Republicans as well as Progressives, offered suggestions in connection with this legislation. All of the meetings, as far as my knowledge goes, were open, and I do not believe that the gentleman intended to say that the majority members of this committee did not give opportunity to every member of the committee to participate in this splendid legislation. . . .

Mr. [HOWARD] SUTHERLAND [D., W. Va.]. Will you kindly tell us what steps you took to get before your committee representatives of the coal mining interests in the perfection of section No. 3?

Mr. MITCHELL. Well, the committee gave announcement through the press of the country that they wanted the aid and the counsel and the assistance of business men in every line of business and in every line of effort. And I recall distinctly that the chairman of the committee, in the presence of the newspaper men, stated that there had been some misunderstanding on the part of some men who did not believe they had an opportunity to come in; and he said, "I want you to make this as plain as you possibly can, that we invite counsel and cooperation of business men in every line of effort." So it was spread broadcast, and, as a matter of fact, if the gentleman will examine the hearings which the committee held, you will find that very many business men in every line of effort appeared before that committee and submitted their testimony.

Mr. SUTHERLAND. Did, in fact, anybody who was familiar with the coal-mining business, with the production and sale of coal, appear before your committee and give information and advice with reference to the formulation of the ideas set forth in section No. 3?

Mr. MITCHELL. I think there was a brief filed. I do not recall any gentleman coming in and talking on that specific subject, but I think this committee had in mind the interests of these coal miners, and I am very sure that the members of the committee had in mind the interests of the coal consumers in this great country of ours.

Mr. [LOUIS] FITZHENRY [D., Ill.]. Just to refresh the recollection of my colleague, I will say that Mr. Beck, of Chicago, representing the coal dealers and handlers, was there and testified and filed a brief.

Mr. MITCHELL. I am quite sure that is true, Mr. Chairman.

For the third time in his administration the President of the United States, on the 20th of January, 1914, addressed the Congress. On this important occasion he pointed out the need and the necessity of enacting into law legislation "regarding the very intricate matter of trusts and monopolies."

Mr. SWITZER. I would like to ask the gentleman why these men were the ones selected as "goats" in this bill, and nothing was said about the lumber dealers? Why did you select somebody who was not in any of your districts?

Mr. MITCHELL. Mr. Chairman, I do not believe that the members of this committee selected the mine owners or anybody else to be "goats." I do believe, Mr. Chairman, that this committee in writing this new principle—and it is a new principle of law in this country—are carrying out and carrying into the law what millions of citizens believe should have been the law years ago. We believe that God placed these minerals in the bowels of the earth, and when these men obtain title to the lands we do not believe that the minerals in the earth should go with the lands; and we believe that these minerals were placed there in order that they might serve humanity in various ways. [Applause.]

Mr. SWITZER. I would like to ask if God had not anything to do with the growing of timber?

Mr. MITCHELL. I do not think my Christian friend requires an answer from me upon that question. [Applause.]

The President said, among other things:

> What we are purposing to do, therefore, is, happily, not to hamper or interfere with business as enlightened business men prefer to do it, or in any sense to put it under the ban. The antagonism between business and government is over. We are now about to give expression to the best business judgment of America, to what we know to be the business conscience and honor of the land. The Government and business men are ready to meet each other halfway in a common effort to square business methods with both public opinion and the law. The best-informed men of the business world condemn the methods and processes and consequences of monopoly as we condemn them, and the instinctive judgment of the vast majority of business men everywhere goes with them. We shall now be their spokesmen. That is the strength of our position and the sure prophecy of what will ensue when our reasonable work is done.

In pursuance of that notable message and in accord with its high purpose and courageous spirit the members of the Judiciary Committee have presented to the House for its consideration and determination this program of antitrust legislation. We confidently believe that its enactment into law will bring a new tone, a new spirit, a new independence, an initiative and a freedom to business that it has never known before. We believe that it will open the door of opportunity to those who have endeavored to enter the field of business free and untrammeled and that its manifold blessings will be more and more evident to all of our citizens as soon as business readjustments have taken place under its operation.

The committee has ever kept in mind and has endeavored to write into the law those things that will not hurt or hinder honestly conducted business, and it has kept before it the standard of justice, of equality, of opportunity, to all the people of the country.

This bill in its entirety is responsive to the best and most enlightened standards existing among men. The Sherman law, so called, passed in 1890, and was enacted to meet a condition that was becoming intolerable, indefensible, and oppressive. This bill supplements that act without changing its essential features. The speedy enactment of this bill into law will mark a new era in the business development of this Nation. Preceded in this administration by the tariff and currency legislation, it is the culminating feature of the program promised by our party platform, indorsed by the people of the Nation, urged by the President of the United States, and now to be enacted into law by the Congress of the United States. When the historian comes to write the story of the Wilson administration and this period of our national development, I think it will be referred to as the great constructive period of our history. We are, I believe, happily emerging from an era in which the standard of business morality has not been a credit to the country; from an era of criticism which laid bare the unfair and oppressive practices of business, but had in it only the germ of construction which is now finding its full fruition in this pending legislation.

No more earnest effort has ever been made by any body of men in any assemblage anywhere to readjust business enterprises, to develop and equalize opportunity, than by those who have been following the guidance of President Wilson in the tariff, currency, and antitrust legislation. [Applause.]

The all-important thing is to proceed sanely, fairly, and justly, in order that our people in this great land may share in the bounteous blessings that the Almighty has poured out with lavish hand in unstinted measure. The day of the man or the corporation or group of individuals who are a law unto themselves, who trample upon the laws of municipality, State, and Nation, who sweep aside every principle of equity and justice and fair dealing in their striving for unholy wealth, influence, and power by the enjoyment of some special privilege is, I believe, passing.

Their greatness and their power has neither awed nor influenced your committee, but, rather, has impressed it with the splendid opportunity which was afforded to legislate for that great unnumbered body of our citizens who are looking with their faces uplifted to this Congress to do justice to them and to give to them and their children the free and untrammeled right of doing business without bending the suppliant knee to any petty tyrant who heads some great industrial enterprise that wants the entire field for himself and all the citizens for his victims. [Applause.]

The policy of this legislation, the aim, the hopes, and the aspirations of the members of your committee are to build up, to construct, to develop, and to enlarge opportunity and to place business upon a footing so sound, so stable, so enduring, that countless millions of people will for years to come look back from the midst of their prosperity and their happiness to this great constructive piece of legislation in the trinity of measures passed by this administration.

Let us see what this antitrust measure seeks to accomplish.

DEFINITION OF COMMERCE.

The bill, in the first place, seeks to broaden the meaning of the word "commerce," as used in the Sherman Act of July 2, 1890, so as to make it include trade and commerce between any insular possessions or other places under the jurisdiction of the United States.

PREVENTION OF UNFAIR DISCRIMINATION.

One of the chief provisions of the bill, and one which should command the support and win the commendation of every Member of the House, is the provision of the bill seeking to prevent unfair discrimination. One of the greatest evils in business at the present time is this unfair trade practice. Certain great corporations, and even some of the lesser ones, have stifled and choked out competition by selling their products at a ⊥ lower price than their competitors in certain communities than in all other places where they have no competition. Invariably, when in any particular community they have vanquished their little competitor and put him out of business, they raise the price and rule the market with undisputed sway. This bill forbids such discrimination when it is made with purpose or intent to destroy or wrongfully injure the business of a competitor, either of such dealer or seller. The bill seeks only to prevent the unfair practice. It does not prevent discrimination in prices of commodities on account of differences in grade, quality, and quantity of the commodity sold, or on account of due allowance for the difference in the cost of transportation.

The chief offenders in this direction have been the Standard Oil Co. and the American Tobacco Co. Any fair-minded man can readily see that where in the community a corporation seeks to kill off competition by lowering the price of the commodity even below the cost of production or manufacture in many instances, this loss must be made up by charging more than the fair market price in other communities where there is no competition, but a free field to charge all that the consumer can possibly stand.

This evil practice has been one most widespread and one that has wrought great havoc with competitors and with the public. Different States of the Union, some 19 in number, have tried to cope with this evil, but their efforts have been weak and ineffectual. This is so because the method that proved disastrous and sent the prices soaring in the other sections of the same State to recoup the loss in a specific locality was carried out on the same plan, but on a larger scale. These gigantic organizations doing business in the 48 States of the Union were able, in States that prevented discrimination in different localities in the same State, to put their prices so uniformly low that they swept all competition from the State. Then, in order to recoup their losses in the State, they used the other States in the Union to make up their profits where they had no competition.

In the State which I have the honor to represent in part this evil practice was recognized and our legislature in 1912 passed an act, chapter 651, which I shall incorporate in my speech with some Massachusetts court decisions and illustrative cases on the evils of contracts which seek to restrain trade. I had urged and voted years ago for legislation of this character while a member of the Massachusetts House and Senate, and it is a great privilege to now be a member of an American Congress that will put through this splendid provision of law abolishing unfair discriminations. [Applause.]

Who can refuse to support a proposition of this character that has bound up in it the absolute breaking up of a great evil in business, the continuance of which will cost the American people millions of dollars and the ending of which will bring to business free and unrestrained competition and to the public an open market and reduced prices? This feature of the bill is one of the most praiseworthy and commendable in it. [Applause.]

DECISIONS AND ILLUSTRATIVE CASES ON THE EVILS OF CONTRACT IN RESTRAINT OF TRADE.

[Massachusetts Law, chap. 651, acts 1912.]

Any person, firm, association, or corporation, foreign or domestic, doing business in the Commonwealth and engaged in the production, manufacture, or distribution of any commodity in general use, that shall maliciously, or for the purpose of destroying the business of a competitor and of creating a monopoly in any locality, discriminate between different sections, communities, towns, or cities of this Commonwealth or between purchasers by selling such commodity at a lower rate for such purpose in one section, community, town, or city than is charged for such commodity by the vendor in another section, community, town, or city in the Commonwealth, after making due allowance for the difference, if any, in the grade or quality and in the cost of transportation, shall be deemed guilty of unfair discrimination, which is hereby prohibited and declared unlawful. (L. 1912. c. 651. sec. 1.)

It shall be unlawful for any person, firm, association, or corporation to combine with any other person, firm, association, or corporation for the purpose of destroying the trade or business of any person, firm, association, or corporation engaged in selling goods or commodities and of creating a monopoly within this Commonwealth, and any such combination is hereby prohibited and declared unlawful. (Id., sec. 2.)

Any person, firm, assocation, or corporation found guilty of violating any provision of this act, if an individual, shall be punished by a fine of not less than $500 or more than $5,000, or by imprisonment for not less than one month or more than one year, or by both such fine and imprisonment; and if the offender is a corporation, then by a fine as aforesaid. (Id., sec. 3.)

Whoever, in his individual capacity, or acting in behalf of any firm, association, or corporation, for the purpose of evading any provision of this act, shall appoint agents, secure or hold the control of corporate stock, or by agreement with any other person, firm, association, or corporation cause any of the commodities mentioned in section 1 to be sold for the purpose of such evasion or attempt to evade, shall be punished by imprisonment in the State prison for not less than six months or not more than five years, if an individual; and if any of the acts specified in this section are done by a corporation, then the directors, stockholders, or agents authorizing such evasion or discrimination shall each be held guilty thereof and shall be punished in the manner provided in this section for individuals. (Id., sec. 4.)

All contracts or agreements made in violation of any provision of this act shall be void. (Id., sec. 5.)

It shall be the duty of the district attorneys, in their districts, and of the attorney general to enforce the provisions of this act by appropriate actions in courts of competent jurisdiction, but nothing herein shall limit the right of any court to issue warrants and make commitments to await the action of the grand jury under this act in the case of crimes under the common law, and such power is hereby given to the courts of the Commonwealth. (Id., sec. 6.)

If complaint shall be made to the secretary of the Commonwealth that any person, firm, association, or corporation authorized to do business in this Commonwealth is guilty of any violation of this act, it shall be the duty of the secretary of the Commonwealth to refer the matter to the attorney general, who shall, if the facts justify it in his judgment, institute proceedings in the courts against such persons, firm, association, or corporation. (Id., sec. 7.)

If any corporation, foreign or domestic, authorized to do business in this Commonwealth is found guilty of any violation of this act, such finding shall cause a forfeiture of all the privileges and rights conferred upon the corporation by general or special law of this Commonwealth and shall bar its right to do business in this Commonwealth. (Id., sec. 8.)

If any corporation, after having been found guilty of any violation of this act, shall continue or attempt to do business in this Commonwealth, it shall be the duty of the attorney general, by a proper action in the name of the Commonwealth, to oust such corporation from all business of every kind and character in this Commonwealth. (Id., sec. 9.)

Nothing in this act shall be construed as repealing any other act, or part of an act, except such acts or parts of acts, if any there be, as are inconsistent herewith. (Id., sec. 10.)

[Chap. 709.]

An act to enlarge the powers and duties of the attorney general.

SECTION 1. It shall be the duty of the attorney general, and he is hereby authorized, to take cognizance of all violations of law or of orders of courts, tribunals, or commissions affecting the general welfare of the people, including combinations, agreements, and unlawful practices in restraint of trade or for the suppression of competition, or for the undue enhancement of the price of articles or commodities in common use, and to institute or cause to be instituted such criminal or civil proceedings before the appropriate State and Federal courts, tribunals, and commissions as the attorney general may deem to be for the interest of the public, and to investigate all matters in which he has reason to believe that there has been such violation. To carry out the purposes of this act he may appoint such assistant or assistants as he may deem necessary to act for him under his direction, and, with the approval of the governor and council, he shall fix their compensation. In all criminal proceedings instituted under this act the attorney general may require district attorneys to assist him and to act for him in their respective districts, and in all matters so referred to them the district attorneys shall be under the jurisdiction and direction of the attorney general.

SEC. 2. To carry out the provisions of this act the attorney general, with the consent of the governor and council, may expend a sum not exceeding $5,000 from the treasury of the Commonwealth.

SEC. 3. This act shall take effect upon its passage.

Approved, May 28, 1913.

COURT DECISIONS.

Gloucester Isinglass & Glue Co. *v.* Russia Cement Co. (154 Mass., 92).[5.496]
Opinion of the justices on the law of 1912 (211 Mass., 620).[5.497]
United Shoe Machinery Co. *v.* La Chapelle (212 Mass., 467).[5.498]

ILLUSTRATIVE CASES.

THE EVILS OF CONTRACTS IN RESTRAINT OF TRADE (MASSACHUSETTS, 1837).

The unreasonableness of contracts in restraint of trade and business is very apparent from several obvious considerations:

(1) Such contracts injure the parties making them, because they diminish their means of procuring livelihoods and a competency for their families. They tempt improvident persons, for the sake of present gain, to deprive themselves of the power to make future acquisitions, and they expose such persons to imposition and oppression.

(2) They tend to deprive the public of the services of men in the employments and capacities in which they may be most useful to the community as well as themselves.

(3) They discourage industry and enterprise and diminish the products of ingenuity and skill.

(4) They prevent competition and enhance prices.

(5) They expose the public to all the evils of monopoly; and this especially is applicable to wealthy companies and large corporations who have the means, unless restrained by law, to exclude rivalry, monopolize business, and engross the market. Against evils like these wise laws

---

[5.496] 154 Mass. 92, 27 N.E. 1005 (1891).

[5.497] 211 Mass. 620, 99 N.E. 294 (1912).

[5.498] 212 Mass. 467, 99 N.E. 289 (1912).

protect individuals and the public by declaring all such contracts void. (Alger *v.* Thacker, 19 Pick., Mass., 51.)[5.499]

AN AGREEMENT NOT TO MANUFACTURE FIRE ALARMS (MASSACHUSETTS, 1893).

An inventor and manufacturer of fire-alarm apparatus sold his machinery, stock, business, and patents to another person and agreed not to engage in such business and not to enter into competition with the purchaser, either directly or indirectly, for a period of 10 years. The court held the agreement good as regards the letters patent and the improvements which the inventor agreed to convey; but it was void in so far as it purported to bind the inventor not to manufacture or sell fire alarms under other patents or under no patents. (Gamewell Fire Alarm Tel. Co. *v.* Crane, 160 Mass., 50.)[5.500]

AGREEMENT OF BED-QUILT MANUFACTURER NOT TO SELL UNLIMITED AS TO SPACE (MASSACHUSETTS, 1888).

A manufacturer of bed quilts and comfortables conveyed to defendant his entire business and agreed not to engage in such business for five years. The court held that this was clearly illegal and void as being in restraint of trade, because not limited as to space. (Bishop *v.* Palmer, 146 Mass., 469.)[5.501]

CONTRACTS IN RESTRAINT OF TRADE AT COMMON LAW—AGREEMENT NOT TO RUN A STAGE ON A CERTAIN ROAD UNDER PENALTY (MASSACHUSETTS, 1811).

A man ran a stage on the road between Boston and Providence. A rival contemplated setting up a stage on the same road. The man who was running the stage sold his stagecoach and horse to his rival and entered into a bond not to run the stage on such road under a certain penalty. The court held the bond void, and said:

"If it does not appear whether the contract was or was not made on good consideration, so that the contract may be either good or bad, ⊥ it is the prima facie presumption of law that the contract is bad, because it is to the prejudice of trade and honest industry, because the mischief to one party is apparent, and the benefit only presumptive, and because the apparent mischief is not merely private but also public. Therefore all contracts barely in restraint of trade where no consideration is shown are bad. (Pierce *v.* Fuller, 8 Mass., 222.)[5.502]

THE RIGHT OF THE INDIVIDUAL TO THE DECREE OF THE GOVERNMENT SUIT.

A remarkable situation prevailed when the Government won its suits against the Standard Oil Co. and the Tobacco Trust. In these cases the Supreme Court of the United States found unanimously, without a dissenting voice, that acts had been committed which were not only illegal but immoral. These combinations had been effected, in large part, by the crushing out of rivals. At the end of these very long court proceedings a decree was finally entered, declaring that there should be a segregation. The lamentable fact, then, became patent that those who had been crushed and driven out of business, "the heroes," as one witness put it, "who had made it possible for the Government successfully to conduct its proceedings to a final decree," were left without a remedy, and no way could be found that would give them redress for the wrongs which they had suffered.

The situation was, indeed, intolerable and a travesty upon justice. Small wonder that men cried out in their hopelessness that there was no justice in the land for the poor. It was found that none of those who were injured could, under existing law, recover for the injuries that had been sustained by the illegal acts of these combinations. They could of course, institute entirely new proceedings, but they could not in any way benefit from the decree which had been entered. The further fact was presented that as these proceedings had covered a long period of time, even if the parties were alive and could proceed against the offending corporations, such proceedings would be barred by the statute of limitations.

These great proceedings signally failed, as far as those who had previously been injured were concerned. There was no way that most of them could recover damages

---

[5.499] 36 Mass. (19 Pick.) 51 (1837).
[5.500] 160 Mass. 50, 35 N.E. 98 (1893).
[5.501] 146 Mass. 469, 16 N.E. 299 (1888).
[5.502] 8 Mass. 222 (1811).

for the injuries sustained. President Wilson in his message specifically referred to this situation when he said:

> I hope that we shall agree in giving private individuals who claim to have been injured by these processes the right to found their suits for redress upon the facts and judgments proved and entered in suits by the Government where the Government has upon its own initiative sued the combinations complained of and won its suit, and that the statute of limitations shall be suffered to run against such litigants only from the date of the conclusion of the Government's action. It is not fair that the private litigant should be obliged to set up and establish again the facts which the Government has proved. He can not afford, he has not the power, to make use of such processes of inquiry as the Government has command of. Thus shall individual justice be done while the processes of business are rectified and squared with the general conscience.

This bill provides that a final decree obtained by the United States in a suit to dissolve a corporation or unlawful combination may be offered in evidence in a suit brought by any individual for damages sustained under antitrust laws, and that such decree of judgment shall be conclusive evidence of the same facts, and be conclusive as to the same questions of law as between the parties in the original suit or proceeding. It also further provides to meet the situation, and the President's suggestion, that the statute of limitations shall be suspended in favor of private litigants who have sustained damage during the pendency of the suit or proceeding instituted in behalf of the United States. It is a provision of the bill that is designed to help the man of small means who has been wrongfully injured, and places in his hands the result brought about by the legal machinery of the Government.

EXCLUSIVE AND TYING CONTRACTS.

During the past 10 or 15 years there has grown up in business an ingenious system of exclusive or "tying" contracts, which in operation is so completely monopolistic as to leave but a very narrow and restricted field for operation, constantly becoming smaller and smaller and only occupied with the greatest courage and perseverance. A gentleman testified before our committee that one company manufacturing shoe machinery now supplies about 99 per cent or perhaps 99 1/2 per cent of the machines that make welt shoes in this country. He was asked to put it the other way, and he said that 99 to 99 1/2 per cent of the welt shoes made in the country were made upon machinery of this company, and of all the other shoes perhaps in as great a proportion, but of all machine-made shoes at least 95 to 98 per cent. Another company has destroyed practically all competition and acquired a virtual monopoly of all kodak films manufactured and sold in the United States. It was shown before the committee that an automobile manufacturing company capitalized for $2,000,000 made a profit of $25,000,000, net, on their investment in a single year. This profit was the profit of that $2,000,000 supplemented by many times that many millions actually invested by local dealers in the machinery of that company by so-called selling agencies throughout the country. The system under which these monopolies have been able to dominate absolutely the field has been brought about by these so-called exclusive agencies and "tying" contracts.

A competitor who desires to place his goods upon the market against any of these companies is prevented from so doing because the leases or contracts of the other companies restrict him from so doing. It has been contended that the justification for leases which are so made is that the leases are upon patented articles. Thus they are granted the privilege of combining various companies. With these restricted contracts in which one machine is tied to another all other machines are excluded because their machines are subjects of patents.

This monopoly has been built up by these "tying" contracts so that in order to get one machine one must take all of the essential machines, or practically all. Independent companies who have sought to enter the field have found that the markets have been preempted. . . .

Mr. FESS. Is there danger in the fact that one company supplies all the machinery, or is it in the manner in which it reached that place, or is it in both?

Mr. MITCHELL. It is in the manner.

Mr. FESS. You would not object to the one company doing it if it could be done legitimately?

Mr. MITCHELL. Not if it could be done legitimately. They would be able to meet these great companies in competition, but there is no field for them. The manufacturers do not want to break their contracts with these giant monopolies, because, if they should attempt to install machinery, their business might be jeopardized and all the machinery now leased by these giant monopolies would be removed from their places of business. No situation cries more urgently for relief than does this situation, and this bill seeks to prevent exclusive "tying" contracts that have brought about a monopoly, alike injurious to the small dealers, to the manufacturers, and grossly unfair to those who seek to enter the field of competition and to the millions of consumers.

This system of monopolistic contract was recognized in the State of Massachusetts as far back as 1907, and a statute was passed, and the first of its kind, I believe, in the country, which sought to meet this evil. It was a brave effort on the part of the State, but it did not prove successful, as evil practices continue to an even greater degree. It was recognized as an evil as far as [sic] back as 1901, when a great shoe and leather journal said:

> The fact is the great strides made by American inventors and manufacturers of shoe machinery were made under competitive conditions. It has been so, and will be so again. As sure as day succeeds the night, the establishment of a virile opposition to the present machinery monopoly will bring to life new ideas and appliances in this field, as the showers and sunshine bring forth the flowers of the field.

It must be apparent that the sole object of these exclusive agencies, so called, is for the manufacturer to drive out competition and to establish a monopoly in the particular locality or community. This contract completely shuts out competition in the business of the local dealer with whom he makes it. The dealer, bound by the contract, becomes as anxious as the manufacturer to drive out competition in his locality. Vast sums of money are spent for advertising, and every means that it is possible to use is brought to the assistance of the local dealer to give him a complete monopoly of the commodity which he agrees to handle exclusively.

Who can question the damage and the detriment that such a system brings to the consumer and to the public generally?

This bill will stop that artificially created system of business and will open the competitive field where all may buy from whom and where they will, and the public shall have the benefit of this wholesome competition.

INTERLOCKING DIRECTORATES.

In recent years there has been a tremendous concentration of wealth in the hands of a few individuals and corporations, and this has developed and increased to such an extent as to challenge the imagination. It has been recognized by our party and by this Congress that one of the most effective ways to check this great evil, that such concentration may be further prevented, is to stop the interlocking of directorates of such corporations as banks and railroads, industrial, commercial, and public-service corporations.

It is inconceivable that any one man or any small, limited number of men are all who are qualified to serve upon boards of directors. This bill will prevent the interlocking of directorates. In the first instance, it provides that no person who is engaged as an individual or member of a partnership or as director or other officer of the corporation engaged in the business of producing or selling equipment, material, or supplies, or in the construction or maintenance of railroads or other common carriers shall be eligible to serve on the board of an interstate railroad corporation.

It is further provided in this paragraph that no person who is engaged as an individual or who is a member of a partnership, or is a director or other officer of a corporation which is engaged in the conduct of a bank or trust company shall act as a director or other officer or employee of any common carrier for which he or such partnership or bank or trust company acts, either separately or in connection with others, as agents for or underwriter of the sale or disposal by such common carrier of issues or parts of issues of its securities, or from which he or such partnership or bank or trust company purchases, either separately or in connection with others, issues or parts of issues of securities of such common carriers.

The next paragraph of the bill deals with the eligibility of directors, officers and employees of banks, banking associations, and trust companies organized or operating under the laws of the United States, either of which has deposits, capital, surplus, or undivided profits aggregating more than $2,500,000, and provides that no private banker or person who is a director in any bank or trust company organized and operating under the laws of a State having such aggregate amount of deposits, capital, surplus, and undivided profits shall be eligible to be a director in any bank or banking association organized or operating under the laws of the United States.

The last paragraph of the section deals with the eligibility of directors in industrial corporations engaged in commerce, and provides that no person at the same time shall be a director in any two or more corporations either of which has capital, surplus, and undivided profits aggregating more than $1,000,000, other than common carriers which are subject to the act to regulate commerce, if such corporations are or shall have been theretofore by virtue of their business and location of operation competitors, so that an elimination of competition by agreement between them would constitute a violation of any of the provisions of the antitrust laws. Mutual savings banks not having capital stock represented by shares are exempt from the provisions of this bill.

By means of the interlocking of directorates one man or group of men have been able to dominate and control a great number of corporations, to the advantage of those corporations and to the detriment of the small ones dependent upon them and to the injury of the public.

The evils of this system are so well known as to be commonly understood. This bill will wipe out these abuses, and, as has been well said, new men, new blood, new energy, and new enterprise will bring about an impetus to business that will redound to the benefit of the country. [Applause.]

DISTRIBUTION OF COAL AND OTHER MINE PRODUCTS.

There are various other provisions of great importance in this bill. I have not time on this floor at this time to dwell at length upon them. One provision of this bill makes it unlawful for the owner or operator of a mine or the controlling factor in the disposition of the product of the mine to refuse arbitrarily to sell such product to a responsible person who applies to purchase the same. God has placed the minerals, the coal, the iron, the copper in the bowels of the earth. They were placed there for the benefit of all mankind and not for the benefit and enrichment of those who have acquired title to the lands. This principle, new in the country, will free the dealer, manufacturer, and consumer from the monopolistic grip of the mine owner and give the great mass of our prople the benefit and the use upon equal terms of those things that were always believed to be until recent years for the good of all. Coal, particularly, which is so necessary, must be sold to all purchasers alike and not to a monopoly, which has been charging what it saw fit. No preference or discrimination will be allowed, and coal and other necessary mine products so useful to all our people will be at the disposal of all alike. I believe this provision of the bill will prove of inestimable and lasting benefit to the great consuming public.

RIGHTS OF LABOR.

Our party, in the passage of legislation, has given to the great laboring masses of the country and to organized labor already a fuller measure of service than has any Congress in a generation. Since the enactment of the Sherman antitrust law, it is contended by the laboring people of the country that their organizations were in constant jeopardy and danger of destruction. Labor should not stand upon such uncertain ground. The brawn and the brain and the sinews of the great body of the people of this country have always been its greatest asset in times of peace as well as in times of war. Labor brought forth the riches from the mines, has hewed the forests, has made the land to bloom and to blossom and bring forth its fruits; labor has manned the vessels, carried the products made by myriads of hands in factory, field, and forest to the marts of the world, and our party has ever recognized the country's greatest asset, the honest toiler and laborer. [Applause.] The right to organize and the legal recognition of such organizations should not be a debatable question.

In the last Congress a bill was passed through the House regulating the use of injunctions and also the procedure in contempt cases. These bills were incorporated in the bill now before the House for consideration, and I confidently believe that this Congress will write them into the law of the land.

CONCLUSION.

I believe that the country is quite familiar with the purpose and scope of the legislative program now about to be enacted. I have the disposition, but not the time, to discuss at length or to elaborate all of the beneficial features of this bill. I have taken occasion to refer to some of its most important provisions. Other provisions almost fully as important are embraced within it. Countless people are awaiting its passage and expect that under its operation a new era of industrial freedom will begin. That is the hope, the purpose, and the desire of those who stand sponsor for this legislation. Our party's record of achievement in the very brief time that it has been intrusted with power justifies the hope and confident expectation that the average man who only desires a free field and an equal opportunity will approve it as the greatest measure of industrial freedom that has been written on the statute books of our land; that the business man who desires an independence and a free field for his operations will find protection and ample opportunity here provided, and that the great public, the victims, helpless and unwilling as they have been, at the mercy of these extortionate organizations, will welcome and receive the bounteous blessings that I believe will flow freely through the land upon its passage. [Loud applause.]

Mr. WEBB. Mr. Chairman, I move that the committee do now rise.

The motion was agreed to.

HOUSE DEBATE
63d Cong., 2d Sess.
May 23, 1914

51 CONG. REC. 9153

The SPEAKER. The unfinished business is H. R. 15657. The House will resolve itself automatically into the Committee of the Whole House on the state of the Union, with the gentleman from Tennessee [Mr. HULL] in the chair.

The CHAIRMAN. The House is in Committee of the Whole House on the state of the Union for the further consideration of the bill (H. R. 15657) to supplement existing laws against unlawful restraints and monopolies, and for other purposes, and other bills embraced in the special order of the House. . . .

Mr. BAILEY. Mr. Chairman, the pending bill is one to which I intend to give my support. I am not going to undertake to discuss the trust question from the legal standpoint. I think the pending bill is a lawyer's bill, a lawyer's conception of the trust problem and methods of handling it. I am not a lawyer and have no technical knowledge whatever of the law. I have made some little study of this question from the economic standpoint, and in the brief time allotted to me I propose to discuss the trust question on a fundamental basis, on the basis of political economy. And I want to begin by saying that it was no mere jingle of words in which Oliver Goldsmith declared that—

> Ill fares the land, to hastening ills a prey,
> Where wealth accumulates and men decay.

The people of the United States during the last quarter of a century have witnessed a concentration of wealth and power so enormous as to be appalling, and this concentration still goes on with hardly a sign of abatement. The growth of the trust, so called, has been the phenomenon of the time. It has marked an industrial change more startling by far than any that has ever before been recorded in the history of the world, more startling, indeed, than that involved in the harnessing of steam and electricity. It has noted the rapid passing of the individual and the appearance upon the stage of a vast impersonal force which reduces the social unit from positions of independent initiative to a mere part in a huge machine. It is no longer easy for pluck and brains and energy to win in a struggle which involves relatively new and strange conditions. Pluck and brains and energy are still factors of success, but they no longer play the part they once enacted in the upbuilding of independence and the scoring of individual triumphs. They have become merchantable quantities, like common labor; they are bought in the open market by the highest bidder, and the highest bidder is that industrial creation of privilege which upsets the law of competition and by the forces of monopoly controls the field of production.

It is not my purpose here to detail the frightful process of concentration. To do so would be to burden my remarks with stupendous figures and to confuse the mind with facts that almost pass belief. Let me, rather, invite a consideration of the situation in its moral phase, casting aside all questions of expediency and of circumstance and looking only at the matter from the standpoint of right reason. Concentration in itself is not a bad thing. It is bad only when it involves something besides mere concentration. A thousand men working together can do more than a thousand times as much as one man working alone. It is only when men work together in large numbers that the enormous advantages of a division of labor are possible. And in like manner the concentration of capital is in the direction of economy. It is possible enormously to increase the efficiency of capital by massing it, as in a mighty steamship or a huge factory or a great mill. It must be borne in mind that money is not capital. Capital is wealth used in the production of more wealth; and money is not wealth, it is merely the representative of wealth, a tool employed for the facilitation of exchange. And it does not matter in the least what sort of money it may be so long as it passes current. The small open boat used in carrying goods is capital, but the small open boat is a less efficient means of transportation than a great steamship; and it is an advantage to the world when a hundred owners of small open boats get together and build a mighty leviathan of the deep into which thousands of tons of freight may be packed and safely carried across the multitudinous seas with an expenditure of labor far less relatively than was required in the hazardous ventures of the sloop and the schooner. The harm is therefore not in this massing of capital in noble ships and great factories and huge mills. It must be looked for elsewhere. And we shall find it, perhaps, in the special privileges with which certain aggregations of capital have surrounded and buttressed themselves. These special privileges appear in many forms, but they all possess a common character; they involve the use of a private taxing power, and whether they wield this in the shape of a tariff which enables them to avoid competition and sell their products at an arbitrary figure, as in the case of the Steel Trust, or whether they wield it in the shape of royalties exacted for the use of natural opportunities, as in the case of the Hard Coal Trust, which until lately was also shielded to an extent by tariff laws, the effect is the same.

They are enabled to command service without rendering service; they fix prices at what traffic will bear; their extortion is limited only by the ability of the people to sustain it. There may be pretenses of cheapening commodities, as in the case of oil; but commodities controlled by monopoly are cheapened in price only by their debasement in quality. Coal oil is cheaper per gallon, it is true; but it is also true that it is lower in standard; its illuminating power has been decreased. And the same is true throughout the whole list of trust articles. If prices have been nominally lowered, they have been relatively increased by the act of adulteration or debasement. The trust always takes everything it can get.

NO CORNERING OF THE NORTH WIND.

It should be observed that trusts do not attempt to corner the north wind. They seek to get control of things that are limited in quantity, and so every really effective trust in the long run must be one that in some form is a landlord. Take the Paper Trust. This trust for years was protected from foreign competition by a tariff on manufactured paper and by a tariff on wood pulp, which is the raw material of paper. But the Paper Trust would soon have gone to the wall had it been solely dependent upon the tariff. The tariff certainly aided it in victimizing the publishers; it enabled the trust for a time to increase prices by 33 1/3 per cent. Yet if the tariff had been its only bulwark, its career would have been as short lived and as disastrous as that of the famous Oatmeal Trust. It will be remembered that when the Oatmeal Trust put up the price of its commodity a hundred or possibly a thousand mills in all parts of the country awoke to the fact that they could grind oats as easily as wheat and corn, and just at the moment the trust was flushing with its success the independent manufacturers flooded the market with their product and the trust went to the wall. Its disaster taught other trust managers a lesson which they were not slow to learn, and now every trust which can hope to be more than temporarily effective as a taxing power is in control of something more than tools and machinery. Thus the Paper Trust set out to gain control of the sources of supply; it acquired practically all the spruce timber in the United States, and, in addition, it secured control of all the water power available to the timber supply. It was thus able to dominate the market until the tariff barrier against foreign paper was torn down by a Democratic Congress. Independent mills could get neither the wood nor the water, and they were thus utterly unable to enter into an effective competition. Yet had they then been permitted, as they are now permitted, to import spruce logs from Canada, where spruce abounds, they could have given the trust most serious trouble.

WHERE THE STRENGTH LIES.

The Steel Trust finds its strength in the ownership of ore beds. The same is true of the Copper Trust. The Hard Coal Trust is obviously a child of landlordism, fed and nursed until the passage of the Underwood bill by a tariff on soft coal. The Lead Trust, the Beef Trust, the Standard Oil Trust, the Sugar Trust, and, above all, the Railroad Trust, in the final analysis, are all founded upon the monopoly of certain limited natural opportunities. It is true that some trusts which own no natural opportunities flourish and would continue to flourish were the tariff repealed which protects them in greater or less degree even under the new schedules from foreign competition. But it will be found that in every such case the trust in question is a collateral or dependent of some trust which does control certain natural opportunities. The Beef Trust is largely the offshoot of the railways; it flourished on the discriminating freight rates which it was long able, and which it may still be able, to command; and this trust was not only able by its relations with the railways to extort tribute from the consumers of meat, but was also able in many cases to depress the prices of stock upon the hoof.

The strength of a monopoly is in its taxing power. Never in the service it may render. Always in that which it may withhold. Thus it happens that a monopoly which to-day can levy but a trifling tax upon the public is to-morrow able to impose a crushing burden of tribute. Take the gas monopoly of Chicago, for an example. There was a time years ago, at the time the monopoly was first granted, when the cost of service figured in the rates charged. Later, the charge was fixed entirely by what the comsumer would bear. Prof. Bemis was able to show beyond any possibility of dispute that the tribute exacted from the consumer in the good old days of unrestrained and unregulated monopoly was at least 50 per cent of the price charged. In other words, the consumer paid 50 cents for gas, including a fair profit on the investment, and 50 cents for tribute.

Can good citizenship tolerate the exercise of such private taxing powers? Is it not bound to protect itself and the public against all exactions save service for service? It is easy to say that monopoly gives service for service, but it is hard to prove. Monopoly may and often does exact royal tribute from industry without rendering any service at all in return. Examples of this might be multiplied, but one case from Michigan, cited by the commissioner of labor of that State in one of his reports, will suffice.

STORY OF THE COLBY MINE.

The illustration relates to the Colby mine, and the history of this mine is interesting and instructive. It will stand as an admirable type of a thousand other cases which enforce the point which I desire to make. This Colby mine cost the owners $1.25 an acre. They never spent a cent upon it for improvements, but they leased the privilege of taking out the ore on a royalty of 40 cents a ton to the Colbys, who in turn leased it to Morse & Co. for 52 1/2 cents per ton royalty. Morse & Co. contracted with a Capt. Selwood to take the ore out and deliver it on the cars for the sum of 87 1/2 cents per ton. Capt. Selwood in his turn got a capitalist who owned a steam shovel to dig the ore and put it on the cars—all that he had contracted with Morse & Co. to do—for the sum of 12 1/2 cents per ton. This was in the year 1885; and the ore, which was as easily dug as gravel from a gravel pit, brought loaded on the cars $2.80 a ton. Out of this $2.80 a ton the share of the mine owner was 40 cents a ton; Colby's, 12 1/2 cents; Capt. Selwood's share, after paying 12 1/2 cents, as above mentioned, for the work of production, was 75 cents; and the remainder, or $1.40 per ton, was at once the share and profit of Morse & Co. In the year in question there was mined 84,312 tons. At $2.80 a ton delivered on the cars ready for transportation it brought the sum of $236,073.60. Let me recapitulate:

84,312 tons, at $2.80 per ton	$236,073.60
Owners' royalty, at 40 cents per ton	33,724.80
Colby's profit, at 12 1/2 cents per ton	10,539.00
Morse & Co.'s profit, at $1.40 per ton	118,036.80
Selwood's profit, at 75 cents a ton	63,234.00
Capitalist's share for capital and labor in production	10,539.00
Total	236,073.60

•   •   •   •

Mr. BARTON. Will the gentleman state where that mine was located?

Mr. BAILEY. In Michigan. I copy this from the report of the labor commissioner of Michigan.

Up to the close of the period covered by the report from which I have quoted the total output of this mine was 1,116,418 tons. Since then the output has probably been increased, but the figures are not available. Nor do they matter for the purposes of this argument. What I wish to observe is that this mine has given something more than a comfortable living to each of four beneficiaries who performed absolutely no service in exchange for it. . . .

Mr. GORDON. I want to ask the gentleman what is the product of that mine?

Mr. BAILEY. Iron ore. The only person who did any work was the capitalist, and his share, for the capital and labor employed in mining and placing the ore on the cars, was less than 5 per cent of the total value of the product. In other words, monopoly claimed and got 95 per cent of the product and capital and labor divided between them 5 per cent. The difference represents the value of a private taxing power. It represents what privilege demands from the toiler for access to natural opportunities. It represents the difference between natural wages and the wages fixed by legal restrictions.

Now, I wish to inquire how we, as Democrats, can sustain so glaring a perversion of natural law? Under just conditions, ought not the product go to the producers? What possible title in morals can the men who get 95 per cent of the product of the Colby mine show to that product? They have performed no labor; they have rendered no service; they have expended no capital; they have done nothing whatever but stand between labor and capital and the natural opportunity. Did they make the iron ore? Did they create the demand for its use in the production of steel? Certainly not. They simply forestalled the opportunity and waited the time when labor and capital were so pressed by necessity that they would yield 95 per cent of their joint product for the bare privilege of access to the ore bed.

If this is true of ore mining, if monopoly taxes labor and capital 95 per cent for permission to produce, can we doubt that the same is true in coal mining, in silver mining, in lead mining, in lumbering, in quarrying, in all the various fields which have become subject to the forestaller? And if monopoly has learned the trick of levying a private tax upon capital and labor, compelling them to yield an enormous tribute for which no conceivable return is offered, can it be supposed that industry in general, that capital and labor in other lines, in manufacturing, in building, in commercial pursuits, in printing and merchandising and personal service, are exempt from exaction? If labor and capital in ore mining must pay 95 per cent of their product for bare opportunity, what do you suppose steel workers pay, what do you suppose clerks and small tradesmen pay, what do you think bricklayers and carpenters and blacksmiths and painters pay, what must teachers and musicians and preachers pay? Or to put it in another way, if labor and capital could freely engage in ore mining and retain their entire product undiminished by a private tax, how long would labor consent to work for the wages it is now glad to accept? For it should be remembered that this Colby mine is no isolated instance. It is typical. It illustrates the whole system of monopoly production under which we are working; and it is inconceivable that ore miners alone would consent to yield 95 per cent of their product as tribute while coal miners and lumbermen and steel workers were required to yield relatively less.

HOW WAGES ARE DETERMINED.

The truth is that on the average throughout all industry wages are determined, not by the product, as they should be, but by what monopoly leaves after it has taken its tribute. This any man may see who has eyes to see. And when you have been told, as we are often told, that wages of labor have advanced, the statement is made in clear defiance not only of the fact but of right reason, as one may readily perceive if one will but stop to consider that in the last analysis wages are governed by what may be obtained by the application of labor to the best free land in use. That the best free land in use must be very poor indeed is shown in the fact that in agriculture from a third to half the crop is willingly paid by tenants for the use of appropriated land; and since labor in the primary industry secures but half its product, less taxes, can you for a moment believe that labor in the secondary or more elaborate industries is relatively more fortunate? The reverse is probably if not demonstrably true, as must appear when we consider that in agriculture alone comparative freedom of opportunity is left. Farming is still free or largely free from trust control, yet even in farming the independent farm owner is fast disappearing, the tenant farmer is taking his place; and even the tenant farmer is giving away surely, if slowly, to the farm laborer.

It were supreme folly to attempt to destroy the trust, in so far as it marks a mere tendency to concentration. As was said before, there is no necessary harm in concentration. The evil grows out of concentration plus monopoly. And it has been asserted that no monopoly can long exist without some special grant of privilege. There are patent monopolies, but these can exist only for a limited period, and can therefore play no very serious part in the great economic drama. The tariff will enable its beneficiaries to rob the people up to the point where internal competition is invited, and this in turn invites combination. But suppose that every concern in the whole country engaged in the production of a certain commodity were to enter into a combination which would throttle competition and enable the producers of this commodity to sell up to the full tariff limit, what would hinder others from setting up in the same business? The combination would speedily break of its own weight unless it were the possessor of some valuable natural monopoly.

WHY RESTRICTION FAILS.

We have been dealing and we are proposing still further to deal with trusts by restrictive measures. These measures in the past have been abortive. Is there any reason to believe that new measures of restriction will afford better results? The proposition to license trusts is too grotesque to be seriously considered, but if we were to license trusts, as we do saloons, the trusts would go into politics then for sure, just as the saloons have done. The Sherman antitrust law has been as unavailing as it was probably intended to be by the able statesmen who sought to fool and did fool the people with it. And if a thousand other laws of restrictive character were piled upon the statute books the result would not be different. The trusts would continue business just the same.

This is no partisan question. It concerns every American. We can afford to divide on questions of policy, but we can not afford to divide on a question which involves the very essence of republicanism. Lincoln loved the plain people and often referred to them. He never ceased to trust them, and they never betrayed his trust. He said you could fool all of the people some of the time and some of the people all of the time, but you could not fool all the people all of the time. Apparently this wise yet homely saying is discredited by some of the leadership of to-day. It seems to be the governing thought that you can fool all the people all the time. But surely no one can be fooled by the pretense that our own rights are not in danger when the rights of others are abridged and denied. Nor can anyone of ordinary perception be fooled by the assumption that if the Government shall take care of the rich the rich will take care of the poor. Yet this assumption has been gravely made, and it has been too freely accepted, as the enormous monopolies which menace the land but too powerfully testify.

WHAT LINCOLN SAID.

Lincoln 50 years ago observed and denounced "the effort to place capital on an equal footing with labor in the structure of government." "It is assumed," he said, "that labor is available only in connection with capital, that nobody labors unless somebody else, owning capital, somehow by the use of it, induces him to labor." With an insight keener than that of any other statesman of his time, he saw the grotesque error of this assumption. He declared that there was no such relation between capital and labor. "Labor is prior to and independent of capital," he said in his first annual message to Congress. "Capital is only the fruit of labor and could never exist if labor had not first existed; labor is the superior of capital and deserves much the higher consideration." But he did not deny that capital had its rights, nor did he deny that there was and probably always would be a relation between capital and labor producing mutual benefits. He saw ahead of his time. He foresaw the growth of what some are pleased to call capitalism, but what he knew and we know as monopoly, but he did not make the sad mistake of imagining a war between capital and labor. He knew that these two partners in producing wealth could not quarrel—for how can a workman quarrel with his tools; how can the tools quarrel with the workman who uses them? But he understood that the man who could own another man could own and did own that other man's labor. And he saw that this was the fundamental economic fact—the real cause of that irrepressible conflict whose expression was found in rebellion and the open or covert attacks upon the people's right to govern themselves. He declared that no man was good enough to govern himself and another man. Freedom was his watchword, and he turns aside in a grave state paper, dealing with the perplexities of war and the mighty problems which rebellion thrust upon him, to felicitate the country on the fact that there was not of necessity any such thing as the free hired laborers being fixed to that condition of life.

Many independent men everywhere—

He observed—

a few years back in their lives were hired laborers. The prudent, penniless beginner in the world labors for wages a while, saves a surplus with which to buy tools or land for himself, then labors on his own account another while, and at length hires another new beginner to help him. This is the just and generous and prosperous system which opens the way to all, gives hope to all, and consequent energy and progress and improvement of condition to all. No men living are more worthy to be trusted than those who toil up from poverty; none less inclined to take or touch ought which they have not honestly earned. Let them beware of surrendering a political power which they already possess and which, if surrendered, will surely be used to close the door of advancement against such as they and to fix new disabilities and burdens upon them until all of liberty shall be lost.

These words were written over 50 years ago. What has become of that just and generous and prosperous system which then opened the way to all, gave hope to all, and consequent energy and progress and improvement of condition to all? Can it now be truly said that labor is not fixed to that condition of life? Lincoln said that labor was not so fixed in his day. Can you say as much in 1914? The prudent, penniless beginner of his time labored for wages a while, then he began working for himself, and then he became an employer. Has the beginner in my State of Pennsylvania any such spur to energy? Largely speaking, is there any hope for him ever to cease working for wages? Can he ever seriously aspire to rise much higher than to a petty foremanship? Is there one chance in a hundred thousand that he may become himself an employer?

THE GIANTS OF PRIVILEGE.

What has wrought this change? Chattel slavery has gone; invention has enormously increased the efficiency of human labor. It ought therefore to be easier for labor to win its way from penniless beginnings through the intermediate steps to a competency. But is it so? Does not the struggle grow harder and harder and the prospect less and less hopeful? And if the burden of industrial conditions even in that comparatively hopeful time rested upon the great soul of Lincoln, urging him to warn his countrymen against placing capital above labor, how much more it must devolve upon us to wave the danger signals. For capital has indeed been placed before labor. Legislation under 50 years of Republican rule has looked after the dollar and left the man to look after himself. Giants have been built up on privilege, and to-day we are facing those possibilities which Lincoln dreaded, when powers that the people have surrendered are being used to close the door of advancement and to fix new burdens and disabilities upon them. It is now but a matter of keeping on in the way we have been going until all liberty shall be lost, as he feared we should lose it.

Let us consider for a moment what privilege really means. There is nothing in itself in wearing a crown. Anyone could plait himself a crown of straw or of thorns if he pleased, and he might wear it without offense. He might even build a triple one of gold and have it set full of diamonds and precious stones, yet would it be but a bauble, a toy, the vanity of a fool, were that all. It is when there is something behind the crown, some power, some authority, some privilege, which it typifies. Thus a king with a hundred crowns and without a kingdom were as deviceless and as puny a monarch as that one who in a padded cell plaits his crown of straw and wields a broken reed for a scepter over the fantastic hosts trooping through his disordered mind. But let there be power, let privilege be vested, let authority be grasped and its exercise conceded, then, whether the man so clothed shall wear a crown and wield a scepter or not, whether he shall call himself a king or merely a "captain of industry," the effect upon those who must come when he says ⊥ come, must go when he says go, must render tribute when he demands it, must bow to his authority and acknowledge his privilege when he asserts them, is the same. And while we have no crowns in America and no titles of nobility, we still have a privileged class whose power over the lives and destinies of the rest is as absolute and as imperious as ever that imposed by czar or prince. Your Andrew Carnegie is a "triumphant Democrat," yet no monarch who ever bestrode a throne held sway more dominantly or wielded his imperial functions with a harder hand. For the essence of kingship is the taxing power. The Stuarts realized that in their bitter fight with the Parliament; and monarchy became a figurehead when that power was resumed by the people.

THE ROOT OF THE MATTER.

Then, surely here is the root of this matter. If we have principalities and powers in this free Government; if there be barons and dukes and princes; if there be underlords and overlords; if there be those that take who have the power and those that keep who can, what is the plain solution of the problem? Is it not to unhorse privilege by destroying its taxing powers? Let the kings and potentates continue if they please to wear their crowns; let them flaunt their robes of state and their insignia of royalty if that shall tickle their vanity; but let the people whom they have been taxing refuse to vote further supplies. Let the people keep what belongs to them, and let the kings and princes keep what is theirs. But what is it that belongs to the people? Is it not the product of their labor and all the product?

If the kings and the princes have produced anything, then surely that is theirs. The people will not chaim it. The people claim only what their labor has produced. And when our American royalty presents its demands for tribute, let the answer be refusal. And let this refusal be made effective, not by idle protests and by vain restrictive concessions, for every restriction is but a concession, but by the repeal of all laws which vest the taxing power in private hands. There is no other way. The trust which has no taxing power is a good trust. Every one which possesses the taxing power is a bad one.

And this is the distinguishing mark. Look into the nature of the trust. If it has the power of levying a tax, then it is bad and irredeemably bad. If it is not endowed by law with this special privilege or some form of it, then it is harmless if not beneficent.

THE WAR AGAINST ALL PRIVILEGE.

The war, then, is not against the trust per se; it is against privilege in general. The trust of which we complain is but an incident of privilege. Destroy the latter and the former falls as a limb falls when the tree is cut down. And since we have seen that the root of privilege is in the monopoly of natural opportunities, the first and the continuing assault should be directed to its extirpation. Attack the outposts and cut off the allies; reduce the outworks and destroy the guerrillas; yes; but press on toward the citadel. Until that has fallen, the robbers which have levied tribute upon labor, that have demanded service without returning it, that have compelled the people to make bricks without straw, will still be in command; they will still lay upon labor tasks and burdens; and its fighting and its sacrifices will have been in vain.

Repeal all tariffs.

Take over all natural monopolies.

Untax labor and the products of labor, and for all other taxes substitute a single tax on the value of land, irrespective of improvements.

And thus, and thus only, shall we destroy privilege and all its brood. [Applause.] . . .

Mr. [JOHN C.] FLOYD [D., Ark.]. Mr. Chairman, I desire to discuss some of the more important provisions of this trust legislation. In doing so I desire to go more into detail than has been done by those who have preceded me concerning certain provisions of the bill and the reasons therefor.

Before going into a discussion of the merits of the different propositions embodied in this proposed legislation I want to call attention briefly to some of the criticisms made against the bill. My colleague on the committee, Mr. VOLSTEAD, the senior member of the Judiciary Committee on the minority side, who filed a minority report, intimated last night in his speech, if he did not say it, that this bill had in some way been framed in secret. I desire to say that no bill that was ever brought into this House has been more openly considered, both by the committee and by the country at large and by everyone who desired to consider it, than has this bill. It is true that the Judiciary Committee assigned the work of framing the bill to a subcommittee composed of the chairman [Mr. CLAYTON], the gentleman from Virginia [Mr. CARLIN], and myself. We worked for hours, for days, and for weeks formulating the provisions of this measure when no one esle [sic] was present, but whenever we formulated a proposition we brought it into the spotlight, laid it not only before the members of the committee but before the country. This legislation was in response to the message of the President delivered January 20, 1914. . . .

Mr. [JAMES R.] MANN [R., Ill.]. Will the gentleman give us the names again of the subcommittee?

Mr. FLOYD of Arkansas. Chairman CLAYTON, the gentleman from Virginia [Mr. CARLIN], and myself.

Mr. MANN. There was no minority member on that subcommittee?

Mr. FLOYD of Arkansas. No; there was not. When the tentative bills were first prepared they were printed and notice was issued through the press to the country, inviting criticism, and people interested in the legislation came from all parts of the country and all sections of the country and criticized various provisions in the bills and suggested amendments. We had public hearings for weeks. I want to say that many of these criticisms proved valuable to the committee; many suggestions made were finally incorporated in the bill as it was finally submitted to the House.

But there is another class of critics to whom I want to pay my respects—the men that criticize the provisions of the bill who do not know what it contains. We get them from all sources and from all over the country. I have here a criticism of this kind; it came from my own State. It is from the Blytheville Courier, a newspaper published at Blytheville, Ark. It is a marked copy. It reads as follows:

A VICIOUS LAW.

Congressman CLAYTON has introduced in Congress an antitrust amendment to the law now operating which is vicious and should be defeated. It provides exemption for every known kind of organization not organized for profit except the retail associations. Under this law all corporations such as the retail corporations in Blytheville would be put out of business.

⊥ The measure was introduced April 14, and is brand-new. All retail associations or corporations should get busy with their Congressmen and Senators and have the bill killed. It is a case of act quickly, as the law is cleverly framed, and unless close attention is paid it might become a law.

⊥9157

And yet, as I will show you later, the provisions relating to the subjects he is discussing are, in the judgment of the committee, in favor of the smaller business men of the country, and are attempts to check the growth, power, and rapacity and the unfair methods of the great trusts and combinations.

Now, the editor of the Blytheville Courier is the editor of a small newspaper in Arkansas. I want now to read an editorial from another source, from the New York World of May 20, 1914:

[Editorial from the New York World of May 20, 1914.]

INOPPORTUNE.

The administration trust bills are not going to have any bed of roses to repose on during their consideration by Congress. Unscrupulous big business, against which they are aimed, is openly hostile to them. Scrupulous business, big and small, in whose behalf they are projected, is certainly not clamoring for them. And now labor is getting a large and heavy club ready for them.

Attacked by the special interests of capital and labor which they are deemed to antagonize, suspected by the honest business which they seek to befriend, there is left to these bills nothing but to petition the support of the general public which represents no special interest, good or bad, but solely the general welfare. And this general public has so far ignored them.

Why? Because, however inherently just these bills may be, they have committed the offense of being inopportune.

Those are the comments of the New York World, and it seems to me that the writer misconceives the purposes of the bill and misconceives the temper of the American people just as completely in other directions as did the editor of the Blytheville Courier. As a member of the Judiciary Committee of this House, I desire to take up and explain the provisions of this bill. No special interest is behind them but the general public, and the World seems to be impressed with the idea and to be of the opinion that there is nobody here to represent the general public. That is the function of the American Congress, and fortunate indeed will it be for the American people when the American Congress, in acting upon all measures of legislation, will stand not for any special interest but for the interest of the general public. [Applause.] I have an abiding confidence that this Congress, in the consideration of this great measure, will so act. . . .

While the Democratic Party in its platform for years has declared in favor of trust legislation, and other party platforms have declared in favor of trust legislation, while the Democratic President delivered to the Congress on January 20 last that able and patriotic message which sent a ring of joy into the hearts of the small business men all over this country, we bring this measure here, not as a party measure, not as a measure that the Democratic Party alone stands behind. It is not the result of any caucus action, and the questions involved in it, I will say frankly, are not party questions in a strict sense. This trust question is entirely different from the tariff question. There is a straight alignment between Democrats and Republicans, and there has been for years on the tariff question, but this trust evil is an evil recognized in Republican States as well as in Democratic States, and I think I will be able to show you that in so far as State legislatures are concerned, many Republican States have been more active in trying to curb these evils than some of our Democratic States. I make this statement in order that you may understand the attitude of this committee, the attitude of the President, and the attitude of the Democratic Party now in power. This bill is brought in under a rule, it is true, which limits general debate, but which is wide open when it comes to amendment and the time for debating those amendments; and in bringing this bill before you and before the House the members of the Judiciary Committee, who are intrusted with the grave responsibility of framing the legislation, must defend every line and every paragraph of it before the criticism and judgment of the Members of this House.

Mr. Chairman, this is a great question. The World says in its editorial that it is brought in at an inopportune time; but, so far as the Democratic Party is concerned, it has not written a platform since 1896 wherein it has not pledged to the American people if intrusted with power in national affairs to reform the evil of trusts; and now for the first time in power it ill becomes anyone to say that because the present Executive and the majority of the party in power have already finished two great tasks, the passage of the tariff law and the passage of the currency law, that their efforts are inopportune when they are endeavoring in good faith to live up to their pledges and promises to the American people and enact trust legislation. The criticism is unjust, even though to enact that legislation may be somewhat of a hardship on the individual Members of this Congress; but we are here to represent the public interests, and the public interests of this country demand legislation to further check and curb gigantic monopoly, corrupt monopoly—to use the language of the World, unscrupulous big business—in this country.

The first section of the bill deals simply with definitions, technical definitions for the purpose of convenient reference in the bill, and I do not care to take any further time about that provision.

I now desire to take up and discuss somewhat in detail section 2, one of the vital sections of the bill. It strikes at a great evil, strikes at a practice that has been exercised by great and powerful corporations in this country to drive out and destroy competitors. I refer to price discrimination. The States commenced years ago to deal with that important feature of this legislation, and I hold in my hand a compilation of the antitrust laws of the various States that have passed laws, similiar and identical in substance, somewhat varying in phraseology, to prevent the very wrong and injustice and unfair discrimination within the States which we now seek to protect the American people from in interstate commerce in section 2 of this bill.

I want to read you the list of the names of the States that have passed those laws, but of course I will not take the time to read any of these State laws. I want to get in the RECORD the names of the States that have adopted laws to prevent unfair discrimination, based upon the same principle that is embodied in this provision of the bill. They are Arkansas, California, Idaho, Iowa, Kansas, Louisiana, Massachusetts, Michigan, Missouri, Mississippi, Montana, Nebraska, New Jersey, North Carolina, North Dakota, Oklahoma, South Carolina, South Dakota, Utah, Wisconsin, Wyoming— 21 in number. We have been told by the critics of this provision of the bill that there is no necessity for it, that the States have adopted such laws, and that that is sufficient; but we have had before our committee testimony showing that both Wisconsin and Michigan have that kind of a statute on their books now, and that one of these great corporations engaged in selling its products in interstate commerce lowered the price of gasoline 1 cent lower in Michigan than in Wisconsin, in order to drive out all competitors from the State of Michigan. Should not the American Congress protect the States and the people of the States from any such unfair method of business? . . .

Mr. [JOHN M.] NELSON [R., Wis.]. Mr. Chairman, I dislike to interrupt the gentleman and will not indulge in it, but in preparing this list of States and in asserting that they have similar statutes the gentleman does not mean to infer that these statutes are like this provision in the bill, does he? For instance, in Wisconsin they are related to competition and restraint of trade, but the gentleman's provision has gone entirely out of that field. Is not that true?

Mr. FLOYD of Arkansas. I said for a similar purpose.

Mr. NELSON. But not identical in language?

Mr. FLOYD of Arkansas. Oh, no. I did not say that they were identical in language. The State statutes are more drastic than this provision. It is easier to convict a man under the State statutes than it will be under this bill if it becomes a law. We have thrown around this law certain technical requirements that are not present in most of the State statutes, in respect to conviction, and that is the criticism that our friend and our colleague on the committee, the gentleman from Wisconsin [Mr. NELSON], who has just interrupted me, makes of the bill—it is not drastic enough. The point I make is that we undertake in this provision to assert a principle and provide a law to prevent the unfair discrimination in sales in interstate commerce, and that that principle has been adopted in 21 States of the Union, and adopted because of the practice and unfair methods of these great and powerful corporations which are driving out competitors and destroying independent companies all over the country to such an extent that the people of those States in their sovereignty [sic] as States have asserted their authority, as far as it is within their power to assert it, and those are the people who represent no special interests, but who are represented by you and the membership of this House, and who are demanding legislation on the part of Congress. . . .

⊥ Mr. [DICK T.] MORGAN [R., Okla.]. This section provides, as the gentleman ⊥9158 knows, that this discrimination in price, in order to be unlawful, must be done with the intent or purpose to destroy or wrongfully injure a competitior [sic]. Is it not a fact that of all of these State statutes in the Union there is only one, the State of Louisiana, where that phrase is used, that in all of the other States this discrimination in price to be unlawful must be made to establish a monopoly, or to substantially lessen competition, or something of that kind, while there is only one—

Mr. FLOYD of Arkansas. No; I do not admit that, and I hope the gentleman will argue that proposition in his own time. I can not admit that. I am insisting upon this, not that this is a literal copy of the statutes of the States, or any of them, but that great abuses have grown up in this country by great and powerful corporations underselling in local communities in order to destroy competitors, to drive out competition, and to acquire monopolies; and if the gentleman will read the decisions of the courts in the great cases that have been already decided, like the American Tobacco Co. case and notably the Standard Oil case, he will find that this practice of discrimination is one of their favorite methods of suppressing competition and of building up these huge monopolies. The Standard Oil Co., incorporated in New Jersey, was given the right in its charter to operate not only in this country but throughout the world. . . .

Mr. COOPER. It is the same question I asked the gentleman from North Carolina [Mr. WEBB] yesterday and I would like to have the gentleman from Arkansas answer it. I make it without any desire to criticize, but simply for the purpose of obtaining information.

Mr. FLOYD of Arkansas. What is the question?

Mr. COOPER. In section 2, in the proviso beginning in line 7, page 21, there is an express authorization of discrimination, as I understand it—

Mr. FLOYD of Arkansas. I do not so understand it.

Mr. COOPER. I will ask the gentleman to read it with me, beginning with line 7 of the proviso—

Mr. FLOYD of Arkansas. I do not have to read it.

Mr. COOPER. Let me finish, please, my question, as it will take but a moment. This proviso says:

Provided. That nothing herein contained shall prevent discrimination in price between purchasers of commodities on account of differences in the grade, quality—

Now, here is the important thing—

or quantity of the commodity sold, or that makes only due allowance for difference in the cost of transportation.

Now, my question is this: Two dealers in a town buy from the same wholesaler. One retailer is a larger concern, and the other is a poor man with a small store. The large concern buys several carloads of a product. It gets the product for less than its small competitor, who buys only a half carload, and the large retailer pays less rates for transportation on the railroad than his small competitor pays who buys in less-than-carload lots. So the large retail concern, buying of the wholesaler and getting not only goods but transportation also at a less price than its smaller competitor, is permitted under this proviso an opportunity to practice unrestricted cutthroat competition and ruin the smaller dealer.

Mr. FLOYD of Arkansas. Now, I desire to answer the gentleman from Wisconsin frankly and fairly. That proviso authorizes nothing. Any man under the laws that exist to-day can do any of those things. It is a common business practice, practiced everywhere, and it has been practiced everywhere for ages. We simply leave the law as it is in that respect.

Mr. COOPER. If the gentleman will permit another interruption. I remind him that this proviso does not prohibit discrimination. It expressly authorizes it.

Mr. FLOYD of Arkansas. I desire to answer the gentleman's first question before I get to a second one. We leave the law as it is as to the things mentioned in the proviso. We are drafting a criminal statute, which some gentlemen who have discussed its provisions heretofore in this debate and many outside of this Chamber have regarded as exceedingly drastic. We make it a high crime under the law to discriminate in price by methods and evil practices described, but we have not attempted in this provision or anywhere in this bill to make it a crime for a man to carry on any legitimate and customary practice that the business world has recognized and followed for centuries, other than those methods and practices herein specifically condemned. The things mentioned in the provisos are authorized by existing law, and we do not forbid them. We did not intend to forbid them, and we do not believe they ought to be forbidden. The statutes of most States to which I have alluded make the same exceptions, and, if I am not badly mistaken, they occur in the statutes of the State of Wisconsin, from which the gentleman comes.

Mr. NELSON. Not as to the quantity, but on a different basis entirely. . . .

Mr. COOPER. The question I asked goes to the vitals of this whole question. We can not in this connection discuss anything more important.

Mr. FLOYD of Arkansas. What is the question? I agree to that.

Mr. COOPER. The gentleman says they did not intend to prohibit anything that the business world has authorized—

Mr. FLOYD of Arkansas. No; I did not say that; the gentleman misunderstood me. We did not intend to prohibit business methods which are mentioned in that exception, but we do prohibit other practices further on in this bill which we consider evils that the business world has recognized and practiced extensively, but, we believe, to the detriment of every small dealer in this country and to the detriment of the entire country.

Mr. COOPER. Then, will the gentleman answer this question? Does not this proviso expressly permit—

Mr. FLOYD of Arkansas. We leave the law as it is.

Mr. COOPER. But expressly permit a discrimination as between purchasers in large quantities who get their goods at a less price and transportation at a less price—a discrimination which will enable them in their discretion to crowd out the smaller man, as they do now.

Mr. FLOYD of Arkansas. I do not want the gentleman to put words in my mouth. It does no such thing. The provision is in plain language and seeks to prevent dealers from lowering the price of commodities in different sections and communities by unfair discrimination with the intent and purpose to destroy, ruin, or injure the business of a competitor. That is a recognized evil extensively practiced by great and powerful concerns to drive out competition and destroy competitors, which results to the serious detriment of the general public, and has been demonstrated to be a most effective means in acquiring a monopoly.

It does that and nothing more, and is not intended to do anything more. If there are other evil methods and practices that ought to be condemned and corrected, we leave it to the distinguished gentleman from Wisconsin [Mr. COOPER] and his colleague on the committee [Mr. NELSON], who has filed a minority report, to bring forward appropriate amendments here and debate them before this House, and we have left the bill open to amendment under the rule, so that anyone can tack on any amendment to it that can secure the necessary votes to sustain such amendment. . . .

Mr. [JAMES M.] GRAHAM [D., Ill.]. In regard to the question of the gentleman from Wisconsin [Mr. COOPER], he intimated or stated in the question that this dealt with the question of transportation in such a way as to make transportation cheaper when large quantities were transported than when smaller quantities were transported. Is there any such provision as that?

Mr. FLOYD of Arkansas. He is in error about that. If the quantity of goods should be larger, and if the railroad company should make a reduction there might be some remission of cost of freight there. But that is a matter concerning which we leave the law as it is. We have not undertaken to disturb that condition. We have left that to be determined by the Interstate Commerce Commission, and have not undertaken to deal with the particular question.

Now, gentlemen, we have been confronted with many questions, and—

Mr. [PATRICK H.] KELLEY [R., Mich.]. May I ask just a question before the gentleman leaves that?

Mr. FLOYD of Arkansas. Certainly.

Mr. KELLEY of Michigan. Now, as I understand you, if it can be proven that there is intent to destroy or injure a competitor, the person charged with the offense could not fall back on this proviso and say that he was saved because he was permitted to make a different price for different amounts of goods?

Mr. FLOYD of Arkansas. That would be a question for the jury. If you could prove the intent, and that he was discriminating for this specific purpose, he would be guilty.

Mr. KELLEY of Michigan. Although the proviso says—

Mr. FLOYD of Arkansas. If he were doing it merely in conformity with the purposes of the proviso, and not for the purpose of wrongfully injuring or destroying a competitor, he could not be guilty.

Mr. KELLEY of Michigan. There would be no presumption of the mere intent in the fact that he has shipped to one person at cheaper rates than to another? That leaves it wide open for discrimination.

Mr. FLOYD of Arkansas. We require the Government, in order to sustain conviction, to prove a specific case of wrongful intent and wrongful purpose. If by any circumstance the accused party can show that the lowering of the price was not unlawful discrimination, was not done for the specific purpose and with the wrongful intent of destroying or injuring a competitor, he would not be guilty under the provision of this section. . . .

Mr. [HATTON W.] SUMNERS [D., Tex.]. In drafting this bill, have not you merely recognized the fact that it costs less money for articles when sold in large quantities than when sold in small quantities, and in that sense it costs the man who is making the sale more money to sell in small quantities, and that he may receive a larger profit in the aggregate than by selling it in small quantities? Is not that the same principle recognized in fixing railroad rates? For instance, a man in shipping a carload of nails, the man who gets a carload gets a cheaper rate than the man who gets only one keg?

Mr. FLOYD of Arkansas. Mr. Chairman, I am attempting to make an outline of this bill under general debate. We will have unlimited debate under the five-minute rule, and I would consider it a courtesy if I might be permitted to proceed to give my views of several of the important provisions of this bill; and at the end of the time I will be glad to answer any questions, if I have any time left. If not, we will have the freest debate under the five-minute rule, and I can do so then. I do not mean by that to ask Members not to ask any questions, but I hope when it comes to discussing controverted matters and controverted points that you will leave those matters for consideration to a later period in the consideration of the bill.

Mr. FESS. As many of us are students trying to get at the truth of the matter, we would like to ask the questions from the man who has made a study of it, purely for information.

Mr. FLOYD of Arkansas. I shall be glad to answer such questions if I can.

Mr. FESS. I am beclouded yet on this point. I recognize it is an economic principle to allow a smaller price for large quantities. That is recognized the world over. But the question with me is whether you are curing the thing you want to cure by putting it on the basis of proving intent.

Mr. FLOYD of Arkansas. We are curing what is a recognized evil. You will bear in mind this is supplementary legislation to the Sherman antitrust law. You will bear in mind it is made an offense punishable by fine of not exceeding $5,000 and imprisonment not exceeding a year, or both. And your committee, following out the suggestions of the President in his message, intended not to disturb that which was not evil, not to disturb business any more than was necessary, in order to correct certain great evils and notorious practices that exist in this country to the detriment of the general public. . . .

Mr. [ELLSWORTH R.] BATHRICK [D., Ohio]. The Sherman antitrust law would not prevent discriminations in communities within the State, would it?

Mr. FLOYD of Arkansas. This provision, if enacted into law, will prevent discriminations in sales in interstate commerce.

Mr. BATHRICK. But not in communities wholly within the State?

Mr. FLOYD of Arkansas. No; not to discriminations wholly within the State.

Mr. BATHRICK. It will not?

Mr. FLOYD of Arkansas. Not at all.

Mr. [EDWARD L.] HAMILTON [R., Mich.]. I simply wish to ask the gentleman one question, and I will not interrupt him again. After all, does not this section perpetuate in law the scriptural proposition that—

For he that hath, to him shall be given; and he that hath not, from him shall be taken away even that which he hath.

It is just the same proposition we have been operating under for several years?

Mr. FLOYD of Arkansas. Not at all.

Mr. HAMILTON of Michigan. I would like to have the gentleman dwell on that.

Mr. FLOYD of Arkansas. I will answer that question most emphatically in the negative. This is to carry into transactions in interstate commerce prohibition of certain practices that have caused the utter ruin and destruction of hundreds and thousands of prosperous small business men by great and powerful corporations through unfair practices. The States have been more active than the Federal Government, but the fact is that in these 21 States that have adopted these laws most of them were enacted in 1911, 1912, and 1913. You have heard of a division in the great Republican Party between the insurgents—now called Progressives—and the Republicans, have you not? Let me tell you the origin of it. It is due to a difference in regard to this character of legislation. The Progressive Republican stands for regulation and curbing of these trusts and our old friends, the "standpatters," stood pat until all the popularity they ever had slipped away, and until in the last election they carried only two States. Their failure to enact legislation to curb and destroy monopolies and trusts was largely responsible for the division in their ranks which resulted in their defeat. . . .

Mr. McKENZIE. I will be very brief. Do I understand you to say that a corporation, for instance, in Illinois, engaged in selling goods all over the United States, would be subject to the provisions of this law for any violation of it, except in the State of Illinois?

Mr. FLOYD of Arkansas. No.

Mr. McKENZIE. I thought so.

Mr. FLOYD of Arkansas. Everywhere in the State of Illinois, if it is engaged in interstate commerce; but if it is not engaged in interstate commerce, then it would not be under the inhibitions of this statute.

Now, that brings me to the question of power, and I especially desire to consider this question in connection with the next section of the bill. I want to read from the Northern Securities case, 193 United States Reports, page 335:

By the express words of the Constitution Congress has power to "regulate commerce with foreign nations and among the several States, and with the Indian tribes." In view of the numerous decisions of this court there ought not at this day to be any doubt as to the general scope of such power. In some circumstances regulation may properly take the form and have the effect of prohibition. In re Rahrer, 140 U. S., 545;[5.503] Lottery case, 188 U. S., 321,

---

[5.503] 140 U.S. 545, 11 S. Ct. 865, 35 L. Ed. 572 (1891).

355,[5.504] and authorities there cited. Again and again this court has reaffirmed the doctrine announced in the great judgment rendered by Chief Justice Marshall for the court in Gibbons v. Ogden (9 Wheat., 1, 196, 197)[5.505] that the power of Congress to regulate commerce among the States and with foreign nations is the power "to prescribe the rule by which commerce is to be governed"; that such power "is complete in itself, may be exercised to its utmost extent, and acknowledges no limitations other than are prescribed in the Constitution"; that "if, as has always been understood, the sovereignty of Congress, though limited to specified objects, is plenary as to these objects, the power over commerce with foreign nations and among the several States, is vested in Congress as absolutely as it would be in a single government having in its constitution the same restrictions on the exercise of the power as are found in the Constitution of the United States"; that a sound construction of the Constitution allows to Congress a large discreion [sic], "with respect to the means by which the powers it confers are to be carried into execution, which enable that body to perform the high duties assigned to it, in the manner most beneficial to the people"; and that if the end to be accomplished is within the scope of the Constitution "all means which are appropriate, which are plainly adapted to that end, and which are not prohibited are constitutional."[5.506]

Again, in the case of the Northern Securities Co. v. United States (193 U. S., 237 and 238 [sic]), the court says:

Those who were stockholders of the Great Northern and Northern Pacific and became stockholders in the holding company are now interested in preventing all competition between the two lines, and as owners of stock or of certificates of stock in the holding company they will see to it that no competition is tolerated. They will take care that no persons are chosen directors of the holding company who will permit competitions between the constituent companies. The result of the combination is that all the earnings of the constituent companies make a common fund in the hands of the Northern Securities Co. to be distributed, not upon the basis of the earnings of the respective constituent companies, each acting exclusively in its own interest, but upon the basis of the certificates of stock issued to the holding company. No scheme or device could more certainly come within the words of the act—"combination in the form of a trust or otherwise * * * in restraint of commerce among the several States or with foreign nations"—or could more effectively and certainly suppress free competition between the constituent companies. This combination is, within the meaning of the act, a "trust," but if not, it is a combination in restraint of interstate and international commerce, and that is enough to bring it under the condemnation of the act. The mere existence of such a combination and the power acquired by the holding company as its trustee constitute a menace to and a restraint upon that freedom of commerce which Congress intended to recognize and protect and which the public is entitled to have protected. If such combination be not destroyed, all the advantages that would naturally come to the public under the operation of the general laws of competition, as between the Great Northern and Northern Pacific Railways Cos., will be lost and the entire commerce of the immense territory in the northern part of the United States between the Great Lakes and the Pacific at Puget Sound will be at the mercy of a single holding corporation, organized in a State distant from the people of that territory.[5.507]

The court in the case of Addyston Pipe & Steel Co. v. United States (175 U. S., pp. 228, 229) says:

In Gibbons v. Ogden (9 Wheat., 1) the power was declared to be complete in itself and to acknowledge no limitations other than are prescribed by the Constitution.

Under this grant of power to Congress that body, in our judgment, may enact such legislation as shall declare void and prohibit the performance of any contract between individuals or corporations where the natural and direct effect of such a contract will be, when carried out, to directly, and not as a mere incident to other and innocent purposes, regulate to any substantial extent interstate commerce—and when we speak of interstate, we also include in our meaning foreign commerce. We do not assent to the correctness of the proposition that the constitutional guaranty of liberty to the individual to enter into private contracts, limits the power of Congress and prevents it from legislating upon the subject of contracts of the class mentioned.

[5.504] Lottery Case (Champion v. Ames), 188 U.S. 321, 355, 23 S. Ct. 321, 326, 47 L. Ed. 492, 500-01 (1903).

[5.505] Gibbons v. Ogden, 22 U.S. (9 Wheat.) 1, 196-97, 6 L. Ed. 23, 70 (1824).

[5.506] 193 U.S. at 335-36.

[5.507] The correct citation is 193 U.S. at 327-28.

The power to regulate interstate commerce is, as stated by Chief Justice Marshall, full and complete in Congress, and there is no limitation in the grant of the power which excludes private contracts of the nature in question from the jurisdiction of that body. Nor is any such limitation contained in that other clause of the Constitution which provides that no person shall be deprived of life, liberty, or property without due process of law. It has been held that the word "liberty," as used in the Constitution, was not to be confined to the mere liberty of person, but included, among others, a right to enter into certain classes of contracts for the purpose of enabling the citizen to carry on his business. Allgeyer v. Louisiana (165 U. S., 578);[5.508] United States v. Joint Traffic Association (171 U. S., 505, 572). But it has never been, and in our opinion ought not to be, held that the word included the right of an individual to enter into private contracts upon all subjects, no matter what their nature and wholly irrespective, among other things, of the fact that they would, if performed, result in the regulation of interstate commerce and in the violation of an act of Congress upon that subject. The provision in the Constitution does not as we believe, exclude Congress from legislating with regard to contracts of the above nature while in the exercise of its constitutional right to regulate commerce among the States. On the contrary, we think the provision regarding the liberty of the citizen is, to some extent, limited by the commerce clause of the Constitution, and that the power of Congress to regulate interstate commerce comprises the right to enact a law prohibiting the citizen from entering into these private contracts which directly and substantially, and not merely indirectly, remotely, incidentally, and collaterally, regulate to a greater or less degree commerce among the States.

We can not so enlarge the scope of the language of the Constitution regarding the liberty of the citizen as to hold that it includes or that it was intended to include a right to make a contract which, in fact, restrained and regulated interstate commerce, notwithstanding Congress, proceeding under the constitutional provision giving to it the power to regulate.

Again, in same case, pages 230, 231, the court says:

In the Debs case (158 U. S., 564) it was said by Mr. Justice Brewer, speaking for the court: "It is curious to note the fact that in a large proportion of the cases in respect to interstate commerce brought to this court the question presented was of the validity of State legislation in its bearing upon interstate commerce, and the uniform course of decision has been to declare that it is not within the competency of a State to legislate in such a manner as to obstruct interstate commerce. If a State, with its recognized power of sovereignty, is impotent to obstruct interstate commerce, can it be that any mere voluntary association of individuals within the limits of that State has a power which the State itself does not possess?"

What sound reason can be given why Congress should have the power to interfere in the case of the State, and yet have none in the case of the individual? Commerce is the important subject of consideration, and anything which directly obstructs and thus regulates that commerce which is carried on among the States, whether it is State legislation or private contracts between individuals or corporations, should be subject to the power of Congress in the regulation of that commerce.

The power of Congress over this subject seems to us much more important and necessary than the liberty of the citizen to enter into contracts of the nature above mentioned, free from the control of Congress, because the direct results of such contracts might be the regulation of commerce among the States, possibly quite as effectually as if a State had passed a statute of like tenor as the contract.

The liberty of contract in such case would be nothing more than the liberty of doing that which would result in the regulation, to some extent, of a subject which from its general and great importance has been granted to Congress as the proper representative of the Nation at large. Regulation to any substantial extent, of such a subject by any other power than that of Congress, after Congress has itself acted thereon, even though such regulation is effected by means of private contracts between individuals or corporations, is illegal, and we are unaware of any reason why it is not as objectionable when attempted by individuals as by the State itself. In both cases it is an attempt to regulate a subject which for the purpose of regulation has been with some exceptions, such as are stated in Mobile County v. Kimball (102 U. S., 691, 697),[5.509] Morgan v. Louisiana (118 U. S., 455, 465),[5.510] Bowman v. Chicago & N. W. Railway (125 U. S., 465),[5.511] Western Union Telegraph Co. v. James (162 U. S., 650,

---

[5.508] 165 U.S. 578, 17 S. Ct. 427, 41 L. Ed. 832 (1897).

[5.509] 102 U.S. 691, 697, 26 L. Ed. 238, 239 (1881).

[5.510] Morgan's La. & Tex. R.R. & S.S. Co. v. Louisiana Bd. of Health, 118 U.S. 455, 465, 6 S. Ct. 1114, 1119, 30 L. Ed. 237, 242 (1886).

[5.511] 125 U.S. 465, 8 S. Ct. 689 & 1062 (concurring opinion), 31 L. Ed. 700 (1888).

655)[5.512] exclusively granted to Congress; and it is essential to the proper execution of that power that Congress should have jurisdiction as much in the one case as in the other.

It is indeed urged that to include private contracts of this description within the grant of this power to Congress is to take from the States their own power over the subject, and to interfere with the liberty of the individual in a manner and to an extent never contemplated by the framers of the Constitution and not fairly justified by any language used in that instrument. If Congress has not the power to legislate upon the subject of contracts of the kind mentioned, because the constitutional provision as to the liberty of the citizen limits, to that extent, its power to regulate interstate commerce, then it would seem to follow that the several States have that power, although such contracts relate to interstate commerce, and, more or less, regulate it. If neither Congress nor the State legislatures have such power, then we are brought to the somewhat extraordinary position that there is no authority, State or National, which can legislate upon the subject of or prohibit such contracts. This can not be the case.

The court, in same case, pages 233 to 235, further discussing the case, has this to say:

The remark in Railroad Co. *v.* Richmond, 19 Wall, 584,[5.513] that it was never intended that the power of Congress should be exercised so as to interfere with private contracts not designed at the time they were made to create impediments to interstate commerce, when read in connection with the facts stated in the reports, is entirely sound. * * *

There is no intimation in this remark that Congress has no power to legislate regarding those contracts which do directly regulate and restrain interstate commerce. The inference is quite the reverse, and it is plain that the case assumes if private contracts when entered into do directly interfere with and regulate interstate commerce, Congress had power to condemn them. If the necessary, direct, and immediate effect of the contract be to violate an act of Congress and also to restrain and regulate interstate commerce, it is manifestly immaterial whether the design to so regulate was or was not in existence when the contract was entered into. In such case the design does not constitute the material thing. The fact of a direct and substantial regulation is the important part of the contract, and that regulation existing, it is unimportant that it was not designed.

Where the contract affects interstate commerce only incidentally and not directly, the fact that it was not designed or intended to affect such commerce is simply an additional reason for holding the contract valid and not touched by the act of Congress. Otherwise the design prompting the execution of a contract pertaining to and directly affecting, and more or less regulating, interstate commerce is of no importance. We conclude that the plain language of the grant to Congress of power to regulate commerce among the several States includes power to legislate upon the subject of those contracts in respect to interstate or foreign commerce which directly affect and regulate that commerce, and we can find no reasonable ground for asserting that the constitutional provision as to the liberty of the individual limits the extent of that power as claimed by the appellants. We therefore think the appellants have failed in their contention upon this branch of subject.

The constitutionality of State statutes preventing these unfair discriminations has been upheld by the Supreme Court. Our contention is that the power of Congress, in the domain of interstate commerce, is as absolute as the power of the State over its intrastate commerce.

Now, I desire to take up next, in connection with this proposition, section 4 before I take up section 3, because it is more nearly related to this particular subject. Section 4 is the most misunderstood section of this bill, apparently. I hear every day of someone writing from somewhere to Members of Congress complaining that section 4 prohibits exclusive selling agencies. It not only does not do so, but it does not deal with that subject. It does not touch it. A man can establish an agency under the provisions of this bill and make any kind of a contract with his agents, on any terms upon which his agents shall sell his goods, that he sees proper to make. He is not affected by the provisions of this section. . . .

Mr. WILLIS. In the gentleman's opinion, how would this section affect the small producer who is not able to maintain independent agencies as the large combinations are? I ask that question because the objection has been brought to my attention by small manufacturers.

[5.512] 162 U.S. 650, 655, 16 S. Ct. 934, 936, 40 L. Ed. 1105, 1106–07 (1896).
[5.513] 86 U.S. (19 Wall.) 584, 22 L. Ed. 173 (1874).

Mr. FLOYD of Arkansas. Yes; and it has also been brought to our attention. The object of this section is to break up the power of giant monopoly and to liberate and free every small dealer in this land and put him in a position of independence in which he can do business in competition with any other business man in this country. This exclusive or tying contract is one of the most effective instrumentalities of monopoly that was ever devised or has ever existed. It can not be justified in morals, and the whole effect of it is monopolistic. I know we have had many arguments to the contrary, many suggestions that we should leave out this provision in order to protect the small man, and we have had many men high up in business to contend for that. But, gentlemen, it is a fallacy, and I think I can demonstrate to you that it is a fallacy. This provision is to the effect that it shall be unlawful for any person to sell in interstate commerce—to sell or lease in interstate commerce—goods, wares, or merchandise on the condition or understanding that the party purchasing or leasing shall not deal in the commodities of another who is a competitor.

Now, take the first person who makes that exclusive contract. So far as the merchant is concerned that he makes it with, he handles only the commodity of the contracting party. If it is in a city of 50,000 inhabitants or 300,000 inhabitants, there is only one place in that city where we can get that commodity, and you can not get at that store any competing article because, under the terms of this contract, he has agreed not to sell any competitive article. Now, I believe in giving every man the utmost liberty of contract concerning his own property. Hence we refuse to tie the hands of the man who is simply acting ⊥ as an agent. But when a manufacturer has sold his goods and has received the money, the full price therefor, what right has he in morals, what right ought he to have in law, to make it a condition of that contract that that particular merchant shall not deal in the commodities of another producer and competitor? . . .

Mr. [EDWARD W.] TOWNSEND [D., N.J.]. The gentleman is making a speech in which we are all interested. Inadvertently he allows his voice to fall to a colloquial tone.

Mr. FLOYD of Arkansas. I thank you. I will try to avoid that. . . .

Mr. [H. ROBERT] FOWLER [D., Ill.]. I am much interested in your able discussion, but I have a concrete example in my home town, wherein a wholesale merchant sold only to one retail merchant and would not sell to any other merchant in that town. Does this bill deal with that feature?

Mr. FLOYD of Arkansas. Absolutely; and section 4 is intended to prohibit that very thing, if it is made a condition of the contract that he will not deal in the commodities of a competitor.

Mr. FOWLER. Excuse me. The gentleman did not catch my point. I guess I did not make myself clear. For instance, the Douglas Shoe Co. manufactures a very good shoe. It sells to one firm only in each town where its goods are sold and refuses to allow any other man to handle them. I want to know if this bill covers that question.

Mr. FLOYD of Arkansas. If he refuses on the condition that a man who purchases the shoes will not deal in the goods of a competitor, this reaches him. But if he does not put any such condition in the contract, it does not reach him.

Mr. FOWLER. Suppose other merchants in the town wanted to handle the shoes. Would the Douglas Shoe Co. be justified in refusing to supply these merchants?

Mr. FLOYD of Arkansas. You will have to ask the Douglas Shoe Co. about that.

Mr. FOWLER. I am only referring to the Douglas Shoe Co. as an example. I am not picking it out.

Mr. FLOYD of Arkansas. They make what is called an exclusive or tying contract. That is, a manufacturer goes to a merchant in a town and agrees with him that if he will handle his goods exclusively and enter into a contract that he will not handle the goods of any other competitor in his line of business he will sell him the goods at a lower price and will give him a rebate at the end of a certain time or take back the remnant of the goods if he fails to sell them, exacting of the purchaser full payment for the goods, and then refusing to allow him to sell in that store the commodities of any competitor.

Now, the evil of this practice to the merchant is that it ties his hands. He can not supply his customers. He has one commodity, and perhaps his customers do not like that commodity, but would like something in the same line. Take breakfast food, for instance. He may make an exclusive contract with the local merchant to handle Corn Flakes on condition that he will not handle any other breakfast food. If a customer does not like Corn Flakes, he will have to do without other breakfast food or go to some other store. The result is that the retail merchants complain that the mail-order houses are destroying them by competition, and that the big department stores are doing likewise. It is true. Why? Because big business has tied the hands of the little merchant with exclusive contracts, and he can not supply his customers. Hence he loses his customers and fails. . . .

Mr. [RUFUS] HARDY [D., Tex.]. It seems to me the question of the gentleman from Illinois [Mr. FOWLER] propounds the reverse of the situation covered in section 4. In section 4, as I understand, the bill provides that no seller of an article shall prohibit the buyer from buying a competitive article; but there is another evil that grows up, that sometimes the large manufacturer sells to one individual and refuses to sell to any other. Now, section 3 seems to cover that condition as to mine products.

Mr. FLOYD of Arkansas. It does, but only as to mine products.

Mr. HARDY. And requires the seller of mine products to sell to anybody who wants to buy.

Mr. FLOYD of Arkansas. It does as to mine products only.

Mr. HARDY. Why not extend that provision to other products?

Mr. FLOYD of Arkansas. When I get to discussing section 3 I will be glad to answer that. I am discussing section 4 in connection with this proposition. . . .

Mr. GREEN of Iowa. Why does not the gentleman answer the gentleman from Illinois, when he asks whether a man may be permitted to sell to only one person, that in section 2, at the close of it, you have expressly authorized a party to select his own customer, excepting only coal dealers?

Mr. FLOYD of Arkansas. I told the gentleman that unless he makes this exclusive contract there is nothing to prevent a manufacturer dealing exclusively with one person or one person dealing exclusively with one manufacturer.

Mr. GREEN of Iowa. In fact, you expressly authorize it.

Mr. FLOYD of Arkansas. We have not prohibited it, and it is lawful now. I will not let the gentlemen who criticize this bill put me in any such attitude as that. There are in this country a vast number of recognized business practices and customs, and when we pick out one which we deem an evil practice the gentleman can not put me nor my committee in a false attitude by saying that we are authorizing what has existed from time immemorial. We are simply not prohibiting it. We are leaving it as it is. . . .

Mr. BARKLEY. Taking these two sections together, am I correct in interpreting the two together to mean this, that the Douglas Shoe Co., for instance, could select one shoe merchant in a given city and sell the Douglas shoe exclusively to that one merchant, provided their contract did not provide that that shoe merchant could not purchase shoes from the Robinson-Brown Shoe Co. or the Hamilton Shoe Co., or any other shoe company that might desire to sell him goods?

Mr. FLYOD [sic] of Arkansas. That is correct. If the gentleman will permit me to discuss this question without further interruption I shall be gratified, as I have some other matter here which I would like to discuss before I conclude. I think I can answer all these questions and give you the whole situation much more clearly if you will let me finish my remarks and ask your questions afterwards.

Mr. BARKLEY. That is perfectly agreeable to me.

Mr. FLOYD of Arkansas. Then I shall be glad to answer questions. Under the testimony introduced at the hearings it was shown that this tying or exclusive contract is one of the greatest means of monopoly, and it is a growing one. We have been told that it is forbidden by the Sherman law already, but in one of the decisions of the circuit court of appeals Judge Sanborn holds that it is not forbidden; and then we are told that you can not invade the right of contract; that it is an evil, but you can not prohibit it. But the Supreme Court of the United States has answered that question, and holds, in the Northern Securities case and also in the Addyston Pipe & Steel Co. case, already cited, that in exercising the power over interstate commerce we can forbid certain contracts, and that in doing so we are not interfering with or depriving either party to such contract of his constitutional rights as a citizen.

Mr. GREEN of Iowa. Will the gentleman please give the title of the case in which Judge Sanborn has held as the gentleman has stated?

Mr. FLOYD of Arkansas. I shall be pleased to do so. In the case of Whitwell against Continental Tobacco Co. et al.[5.514] Judge Sanborn held that the restriction of their own trade by defendants to those purchasers who declined to deal in the goods of their competitors is not a violation of the Sherman Antitrust Act. This case is reported in volume 125, Federal Reporter, page 454. . . .

I desire to show to the House some of the workings of this system. The shoe industry of this country is one of the greatest industries in America, and yet it is in evidence before our committee, and not controverted, that 98 or 99 per cent of all the shoe machinery used on uppers in the United States is not sold by the Shoe Machinery Company, but owned by it and leased to the shoe manufacturers in the United States on exclusive contracts, on condition that if the shoe manufacturer uses any piece of machinery of like kind, manufactured by any other concern in the United States, then, under the terms of the lease, the Shoe Machinery Company is given the right to take out of the factory every piece of their machinery, the effect of which would be to bankrupt the manufacturer and close his factory.

I am glad that last evening the gentleman from Massachusetts [Mr. MITCHELL], a Representative in this House from the State of Massachusetts, and a member of the Judiciary Committee, and who formerly served in the legislature of that State, spoke in support of this provision. What would be the liberty of the citizen if our business was all run upon that principle? No man would own his own shop. Go into some large shoe manufacturing establishment in St. Louis or Cincinnati. The machinery used there is leased from a trust and is not owned by the manufacturer. Although his business amounts to millions of dollars, yet the hands of the manufacturer are tied by an unsconscionable [sic] contract that if he patronizes a competitor by buying any piece of machinery used for a like purpose they will withdraw all of their leased machinery from his factory. Who can stand for such a contract as that? Congress has the power to make it unlawful. Let us do it.

Now, let us take another illustration which is most complete and interesting.

Mr. FESS. Before you leave this, may I ask a question?

Mr. FLOYD of Arkansas. Yes.

Mr. FESS. I wonder if this law does forbid the things we are trying to reach? Is there any danger that a concern like the Douglas shoe factory will establish its distributing points all over the country and not pass title to the shoes? Is there anything in that?

Mr. FLOYD of Arkansas. No; not a thing in the world, in my opinion. I have been through the shops and recognize the evil of this system. I walked through the shops in St. Louis and had the machines pointed out to me by a friend of mine, who stated that he was paying the worth of the machines as a royalty, but that he could not say a word, he could not buy a competitive article, he could not replace them with cheaper machinery because the company supplying them had some machines that were absolutely essential, and if he did they would take all the machines out under the terms of their contract and destroy his business and bankrupt him as they and other concerns who engage in this practice or system have destroyed hundreds and thousands of business men all over the country.

I call attention especially to the testimony of Mr. Rogers, an attorney who appeared before us in regard to the motion-picture business. I am not going to take your time to read you all that Mr. Rogers said, but I wish to call your attention to the testimony which begins on page 470 of the hearings. I quote, in part, as follows:

STATEMENT OF GUSTAVUS A. ROGERS, ESQ., OF NEW YORK, N. Y.

Mr. ROGERS. My reason for appearing before your committee is that I thought if I should recite to you some of the difficulties that my firm encountered as counsel for a concern in New York City which had been previously interferred with by the trust, so called, which is now being prosecuted under the Sherman Antitrust Act by the United States Government in an equity suit, in the eastern district of Pennsylvania, that the experience that my client had might give you a practical idea of some of the existing difficulties, and indicating strongly the necessity

---

[5.514] 125 F. 454 (8th Cir. 1903).

for adopting the provisions recommended or presented in the bills of Judge CLAYTON, supplemented, possibly, by several suggestions that I will make to you.

The suit that I refer to is the suit of the United States Government against the Motion Picture Patents Co.[5.515] and other defendants, generally the defendants in the suit are known as the Motion Picture Trust.

I think that the presentation of the situation and a recital of the circumstances under which that combination was effected, and its operations, will probably be as illustrative as anything else I could say to you of what is required in the way of an antimonopoly act. I think it is as illuminating as any case that will be called to your attention throughout your deliberations. I think I say that advisedly, because in this instance you not only have the presence of a combination of firms and corporations engaged in dealing in an important commodity, but you have the question presented of a combination of competing or correlated or interrelated or dependent patents into one holding company. You have a combination of manufacturers who, at the time of the creation of this combination, manufactured possibly 95 per cent of the entire commodity, and you have an organization created by this combination, by the manufacturers, as a selling agency for the combined output of all these manufacturers, and you have present a situation which shows that this combination, within a period of a few months after its organization, drove out of business, by means to which I shall call your attention presently, every one of the customers who had dealt with the manufacturers with the exception of my client, and how he was able to stay in business I shall show you in a few moments. They not only drove these customers out of business, but turned over to this sole selling agency company all the business in that particular industry.

I do not want to burden you with this matter, except as it is important to demonstrate how quickly a combination can do something that is utterly impossible for an individual ever to accomplish in a lifetime.

Up to the spring of 1908 the industry was absolutely open and without restriction. The motion picture films were made and manufactured and sold as unpatented articles. The dealer in the film—perhaps I ought to interpose here and speak for a moment about the film itself. The film itself which is commercially used is a celluloid film strip, consisting of a reel of approximately 1,000 feet in length. These different positives are printed from the negative taken with the camera; they are duplicate prints, in analogy representing positive photographs made from the negatives.

These reels of films were sold in the market. Anybody who wanted to purchase them would go to the manufacturer, make his bargain with him, and buy his film and do as he pleased with it. He might sell it or lease it for exhibition purposes. He could export it and do as he wanted with it. The projecting machine by which this film was projected on the screen was, prior to the spring of 1908, sold as an unpatented article, and there were thousands of them sold—several thousands, in any event.

In the spring of 1908 the Edison Co. at that time had already been defeated in the courts on a patent which was known as the Edison film patent, and under which Edison claimed that he was the inventor of motion pictures and consequently entitled under his patent to dominate the entire art. He had been defeated in that claim by the United States Circuit Court of Appeals for the Southern District of New York, and there was no mistake about the decision of that court. It declared his claim absolutely invalid in that respect.[5.516]

I was reciting the conditions as they existed in December, 1908, when the combination was first formed. These men were given the alternative of either taking the license agreement as it was drawn or going out of business entirely, because they could not get a supply of films anywhere else.

After some protest and considerable reluctance they finally concluded that they had no alternative except to sign the agreements, and the agreements were signed.

But, instead of permitting the business to be done by the entire 150 companies, that number was arbitrarily reduced to 100.

Mr. NELSON. There were 100 rental companies?

Mr. ROGERS. One hundred rental companies. Having gotten the field in that shape, the manufacturers then, within a very short time thereafter, about a year later, organized their own company, known as the General Film Co., and the avowed purpose of that company was to go into the rental business, and it was incorporated as a paper corporation, and the first thing that

---

[5.515] 225 F. 800 (E.D. Pa. 1915), *appeal dismissed,* 247 U.S. 524 (1918).

[5.516] Thomas Alva Edison was a party in many proceedings concerning patents. Edison v. American Mutoscope Co., 110 F. 660 (C.C.S.D.N.Y. 1901) (Edison patent held infringed upon), *rev'd,* 114 F. 926, 934 (2d Cir. 1902) (held not infringed); Edison v. American Mutoscope & Biograph Co., 144 F. 121 (C.C.S.D.N.Y. 1906) (Edison reissue patent not infringed upon), *rev'd,* 151 F. 767, 769 (2d Cir. 1907) (majority of claims infringed under special circumstances). The two appeals court opinions state, in dictum, that Edison was not the "inventor" of motion pictures.

company did was to begin a campaign, immediately after its creation, to drive out of business every one of these hundred companies then in existence, and they succeeded, because in November, 1911, every one of these rental companies had been driven out of business with the exception of my client, and my client to-day is the only one—my client is known as the Greater New York Film Record Co.—it is the only company in the United States, and when you say the United States you mean practically in the entire world, as I shall demonstrate—that gets the output of any of these 10 manufacturers, excepting their own selling company, the General Film Co.

From this brief and short extract from the testimony it will be observed that at the beginning of this trouble a few years ago there were 10 or 12 manufacturers engaged in making motion-picture films. There were 150 concerns selling throughout the United States. The films were not patented; they were merely a transformation and improvement on the old magic lantern of our boyhood days. Mr. Edison invented some kind of a device in regard to the films that enabled him to secure a patent at the United States Patent Office. That patent was held invalid. They got all the manufacturers together and formed a license company, known as the Licensed Manufacturers. All the manufacturers consolidated, and then they notified the 150 concerns that were purchasing and distributing the films throughout the country to gather together at a meeting. At this meeting they were notified that they must purchase all their supplies thereafter from this film company; that they must reduce the number of exchanges to 100. They protested, but the manufacturers were all in the combine. They had to agree to the arrangement because it was the only source of the films, so they had to yield, and 50 out of the 150 voluntarily went out of business. They ran for about one year under that arrangement. This new film company furnished or leased the entire films used by the 100 companies. Then they made a remarkable contract. They furnished the films on a contract of lease that required them to be returned at the end of seven months, but provided that in lieu of the return of the film they had issued to them under the lease they might return any old film on hand. Of course, if a dealer turned in an old film which he owned, he lost that, and after a time he was required to turn in the film that he had leased. At the end of the year the 100 distributors had nothing in their control except the leased films, having voluntarily surrendered the old films which they owned. When the film company got them in that condition they formed what they called the General Film Co., an exclusive leasing company, one consolidated company that distributed all the films manufactured by the Motion Picture Patents Co. . . .

Mr. NELSON. Under this law could not they have refused any but this one customer?

Mr. FLOYD of Arkansas. No; I think not. I do not like to be interrupted in the midst of my narrative.

Mr. NELSON. I simply wanted to ask the gentleman if they had not the right to select their customers.

Mr. FLOYD of Arkansas. That is not pertinent to what I am discussing. Now, at the end of the year they notified those that they were friendly with that they had better sell out, and they notified the others that on and after a certain date no more films would be furnished them under the terms of their contract. Thus arbitrarily they put out of business every concern save and except one, the one represented by Mr. Rogers.

One of these men had a theater in New York, costing him $75,000, and was doing a profitable business. He was notified that on and after a certain day his contract would be canceled. He went to the State courts. Now, bear in mind that the purchasing company was willing to pay the current uniform price. They refused to lease. He went into the State courts in 1907 or 1908 and secured an injunction against the film company. The case was finally carried to the court of appeals, which decided that the State court was without authority in the case. He then induced Attorney General Wickersham to bring a suit under the antitrust law, and the Attorney General induced the parties to make an agreement to furnish that one concern with films during the pendency of the lawsuit, and the suit is still pending.

That is the system and that is the way that it destroys competition. That is the way it builds up a monopoly. I ask you to read the story, for I have given only a brief outline of it. . . .

Mr. J. M. C. SMITH. If a person has a patented shoe-manufacturing machine, does not he have the right now to attach such conditions to the use of the machine, and has not the Supreme Court so held? Has it not held that they can make conditions as to the purchase of material necessary to use the machine? Does this law prevent them from making or leasing a patented machine with those conditions?

Mr. FLOYD of Arkansas. That is on a different proposition, if I understand it.

Mr. J. M. C. SMITH. Does this bill cover it?

Mr. FLOYD of Arkansas. No; we did not undertake to deal with the question of resale prices. This bill would prevent a tying or exclusive contract of every kind. This is intended to prevent contracts on condition that the purchaser or lessee will not deal in goods or wares of a competitor in the same line of business. I think this would prohibit a contract—if a machine was sold or leased—that attachments would have to come from that concern.

Mr. J. M. C. SMITH. Whether patented or not?

Mr. FLOYD of Arkansas. Whether patented or not. The patent law gives a man the right to the exclusive sale of a commodity in the first instance, and it is in the power of Congress to regulate the sale of patented articles when they pass out of the hands of the original owner into commerce, the same as of unpatented articles. There is no distinction, although the representatives of monopoly claim there is a difference, and appeared before our committee and endeavored to induce us to pass a law that would annul the decision of the Supreme Court in the O'Donnell case[5.517] and other like cases, wherein the court has held that a patentee has no right or control of the property after he had sold it, and that contracts to that effect are in violation of the Sherman Antitrust Act.

Mr. J. M. C. SMITH. After he has sold it, but in case he leased it he still has the right to fix the condition by which it shall be used.

Mr. FLOYD of Arkansas. Not if this becomes a law.

Mr. J. M. C. SMITH. I thank the gentleman. That is what I wanted to find out.

Mr. FLOYD of Arkansas. It is to prevent that very thing. The circuit court of appeals in this case holds that that is not in contravention of the Sherman law now, and that is very high authority, and we propose to write it in the statute and make it an unlawful contract. The Supreme Court, in the Northern Securities case, and in the case of Addyston Pipe & Steel Co. against United States, and in other cases, has held that wherever Congress in its wisdom sees fit to prohibit contracts that are deemed in restraint of trade in interstate commerce, it is within the power of Congress to do so. . . .

Mr. BRYAN. The gentleman referred to the unpatented film a moment ago, and called attention to the fact that the owner of an opera house in New York City was denied the use of this film, and that thereby his business was about to be taken away, and that the Attorney General under the present Sherman law succeeded in causing the film company to furnish films to this man until a certain suit was determined.

Mr. FLOYD of Arkansas. During the pendency of the suit.

Mr. BRYAN. Is it not a fact that if this law had been on the statute books the Attorney General's hands would have been tied by this provision in section 2:

And provided further, That nothing herein contained shall prevent persons engaged in selling goods, wares, or merchandise in commerce from selecting their own customers, except as provided in section 3 of this act.

And section 3 refers only to mines. Would not this law entirely validate the act of the company in refusing the gentleman in New York?

Mr. FLOYD of Arkansas. No; that law has no application to the case. If this law had been on the statute books, it would not have been in the power of the film company to destroy the business of 150 flourishing concerns.

Mr. BRYAN. Could not the film company, under the proviso I have just read, say to any man in New York City, "You can not buy my films"?

Mr. FLOYD of Arkansas. Absolutely they can say that now, and we do not

---

[5.517] Bauer & Cie v. O'Donnell, 229 U.S. 1, 33 S. Ct. 616, 57 L. Ed. 1041 (1913).

propose to prevent any manufacturing firm from saying that, except as to mines, and I will explain that later. But we do propose to say by this provision that men, by making unconscionable contracts, by making contracts affecting competitors, which they have no right in morals to make, and ought not to have in law, shall not longer build up a monopoly in this country by such nefarious practices and methods and destroy other worthy business men who are striving to build up their respective industries. As the President said in his admirable message on trusts and monopolies, we are not the enemies of business in proposing this legislation, but we are the friends of every honest man engaged in business. We do not propose by this legislation to destroy or injure business, but we are endeavoring as conscientious men, engaged in a great cause, to untie the hands of business men in this country that have been shackled for years by the greed of monopoly. [Applause.]

Mr. BRYAN. Mr. Chairman, I realize that, but the gentleman does not claim by his argument that this bill would help his man in New York?

Mr. FLOYD of Arkansas. I will be frank and say that I do not clearly understand the gentleman's point.

Mr. BRYAN. The gentleman in his argument does not mean to claim that this act would help this man in New York, referred to by him, who was in the unfortunate position of owning an opera house, and needing films, because this provision I have read says that the seller of the films shall have the right to select his own customer. Under the present law the gentleman has stated that the Attorney General was able to give relief, but I say, or at least it seems the way I read it, this law would tie the hands of the Attorney General, and he could not give relief, because the film company would say, "Your law says that I have the right to select my customer, and, Mr. New Yorker I do not select you." Under that what could the man in New York or the Attorney General do?

Mr. FLOYD of Arkansas. But if the film company had not by unfair and unjust and dishonest means and by this practice destroyed the business of 150 other film companies, that man would have had 150 exchanges to have purchased his films from, and could have been independent of the General Film Co. which refused to furnish films to him.

Mr. KELLEY of Michigan. The passage of this bill then presupposes the destruction of the film company, or the dissolution of it?

Mr. FLOYD of Arkansas. It presupposes the dissolution of monopoly, and to give the independents an opportunity to do business in this country upon fair and equal terms. That is the purpose of this provision. . . .

Mr. FESS. I understand that in the moving-picture business now 95 per cent of the films are distributed by three companies. They have exhibitors throughout the country, and they buy from whatever manufacturer they desire. The business, however, has largely gotten into the hands of the distributors. Will the gentleman's bill touch that situation at all?

Mr. FLOYD of Arkansas. Absolutely; it is intended to prevent that, and to prevent those exclusive monopolies that are built up by this system. If you destroy the power of monopoly any man can do business independently.

Mr. FESS. If they make their own exhibitions, I mean. The men who distribute the films and have control of them may have their own exhibition houses in every city. The gentleman is not touching that, is he?

Mr. FLOYD of Arkansas. The Sherman law will destroy them if those facts are established, and there is a suit pending. They will be dissolved by the Sherman law. This is to prevent that company or any other company by any such wrongful means putting out of business men who are engaged in legitimate enterprise, depriving them of their property by these unconscionable and damnable contracts that the people of the United States and the Congress of the United States ought to condemn everlastingly in this free country of ours. And it ought not to be a question of party. It ought not to make any difference whether a man is a Democrat, a Republican, or a Progressive when it comes to dealing with those powers of wealth and greed and monopoly that have wrecked hundreds of empires in the past. Men ought to rise to the high ground of patriotism and with courage do their duty. [Applause.]

Mr. FESS. The gentleman did not take it from my question that I asked him what I did in a partisan way. I simply wanted the facts.

Mr. NELSON. Then, why did not the gentleman permit some Republican to be upon the subcommittee? [Applause on the Republican side.]

Mr. FLOYD of Arkansas. I did not have the make-up of the subcommittee or the full committee. I am an humble member of the committee and perform as best I can whatever duties that are assigned to me.

Mr. NELSON. But the gentleman is a fair and honest member of the committee and can—

Mr. FLOYD of Arkansas. This suggestion—a little party quibble injected into the consideration of a great question—ought to be beneath the dignity of my able and distinguished friend from Wisconsin.

Mr. NELSON. Mr. Chairman, if I may interrupt the gentleman just at this point—

Mr. FLOYD of Arkansas. Not for that purpose. I say to the gentleman I am not responsible for the make-up of the committee and I can not explain that question. I state frankly the gentleman is not a member of the subcommittee. I state frankly that the chairman, Mr. CARLIN, and myself were the only members of the subcommittee. Why, I can not answer, because I do not know and never sought the position assigned to me as a member of the subcommittee. I have tried to do my duty in this as in every other position assigned to me by those in charge of great matters, both on the committee and in the House, and I am here upon this measure as much a representative of what I conceive to be for the best interests of the Progressives and Republicans as I am for what I conceive to be to the best interests of the Democracy; and I want every man in this House to understand my personal attitude. [Applause.] So much for No. 4. Now, just briefly I want to revert to section 3 simply to say that section 3 was inserted because we believed that in handling products of mines the owner or operator ought not be permitted to exercise that control or to secure a monopoly which might result in serious detriment to the general public. It is a concession in the interest of the public, so that we believe that the mine operator who handles coal should not be permitted to withhold his coal at his pleasure from customers.

The God of nature stored these great resources in the earth and we believe those who make the laws ought to deal with them in a different way from things like patented commodities or manufactured articles that are the work and product of men's hands. And this is in the interest of the manufacturers, too, because the evidence shows that many giant monopolies have been built up by owning both the manufacturing concerns and the mines and favoring the concern in which they were interested to the detriment and the ruin of the independent manufacturers who are struggling along for existence in the same kind of industry. . . .

Mr. AVIS. I only wanted to ask the gentleman with reference to section 3, and, as I said, I do not impugn to the gentleman any bad motives. I know the gentleman's motives are of the very best, and that the other members of the committee are actuated by the same motives, and the criticism embraced in the question I desire to propound, if at all, is a criticism of their judgment and not of their motives. Now, I come from a coal-producing section and knowing something of the coal business and knowing that there are 6,000 independent bituminous coal operators in that country. I want to ask the gentleman if the committee or any member thereof can point to one single abuse committed by any one of the bituminous coal operators of this country, or can the committee say to this House that they heard from any one of the 6,000 operators engaged in this industry before drawing this section?

Mr. FLOYD of Arkansas. I can not go into details to answer that question further than to say that the provision was inserted in this bill and generally met with the approval of men from all parts of the country who commented upon it.

Mr. AVIS. Does the gentleman know, or was the evidence before the committee, that instead of there being an underproduction of bituminous coal in this country there is an overproduction, and that the bituminous coal of this country is being sold and delivered, including freight, in New England at prices less than at the pit mouth at Cardiff, Wales?

Mr. FLOYD of Arkansas. I will state very frankly I do not recall whether any operators engaged in the mining of bituminous coal in West Virginia appeared before our committee or not, and I can not answer that question; but let me suggest to the gentleman, if he has facts that will tend to show this provision is wrong, let him secure time and present them. The bill is open to amendment. We have done the best we could with it, and we have brought it back to the House, and we submit it to you. We open wide the opportunity for amendment, and if it is wrong, and it can be demonstrated that it is wrong, we will not resist an amendment.

Mr. AVIS. If the gentleman will permit another short question, I will not trouble the gentleman any more—

Mr. FLOYD of Arkansas. I thought I answered the gentleman's question as to that particular locality.

Mr. AVIS. I thought perhaps the committee had in mind some abuse, and I want to ask the gentleman if his committee knew of a single abuse on the part of the bituminous operators of this country which whey had in mind in the preparation of this section?

Mr. FLOYD of Arkansas. The gentleman asks about bituminous coal?

Mr. AVIS. Yes; more particularly.

Mr. FLOYD of Arkansas. I will tell the gentleman what I said at the outset. I can not answer details of that sort; but we did have abundant evidence before our committee that those who control the production and mining of coal do so to the detriment of the public.

Now I desire to pass to section 5. Section 5 is simply a reenactment of the provisions of section 7 of the Sherman law, so as to make it applicable to the provisions of this bill. Section 6 provides—and I desire to discuss this section briefly—that where the United States institutes a suit and proceeds to final decree against an unlawful combination under the terms of section 4 of the Sherman Act that the final judgment or decree may be used as evidence in a suit by a private litigant against such corporation. . . .

Mr. HAMILTON of Michigan. Does this section 3, referring to mines, cover oil and gas?

Mr. FLOYD of Arkansas. We so understand it.

Mr. HAMILTON of Michigan. Are there decisions—

Mr. FLOYD of Arkansas. Yes; and if the gentleman desires to insert such an amendment he will have opportunity to do so. We understand that it does.

Mr. HAMILTON of Michigan. I assumed that the gentleman's committee had gone into that with very great care.

Mr. FLOYD of Arkansas. Now, I have made inquiries and I have heard very little objection to this provision, and will be glad if you would hear our position on that. Many combinations have been dissolved under the Sherman law by the decree of the United States courts. The proceedings were lengthened out for years, and at the end of the suits they were adjudged by the courts to be unlawful combinations, and yet parties who had been injured by the unlawful acts of those corporations were without redress. This proposes to suspend the statute of limitations during the continuation of such suits, and at the end of the suit, if the Government obtains a decree, or a decree is obtained, provides that that may be used in evidence in behalf of the private suitor in a suit for damages, under section 7 of the Sherman law and under the corresponding section of this bill. . . .

Mr. [GEORGE C.] SCOTT [R., Iowa]. I will be very brief. I notice that this section provides that in case of an adjudication in an antitrust suit to be brought by the United States, involving the Sherman law, that the judgment in the United States case shall be conclusive evidence either for or against the defendant in any subsequent suit brought under the antitrust law by individuals.

Mr. FLOYD of Arkansas. Against that particular corporation covering the period of that suit.

Mr. SCOTT. Yes. Now, what I want the gentleman to explain is this: Assuming that under section 5 here a corporation has been guilty of a violation of the antitrust law, entered into a great conspiracy, and has damaged me, we will say, in the sum of $10,000 or $20,000, and I bring suit against this corporation. After issue is joined I find I am confronted with this plea, that 60 days before, in a suit to which I had not been a party, a district judge sitting in equity had decided and rendered a decree to the effect that this corporation had not been guilty of a conspiracy.

Mr. FLOYD of Arkansas. I hope the gentleman will not take my time, but will ask the question.

Mr. SCOTT. This section says that that judgment or decree shall be conclusive evidence against me. Is that the gentleman's understanding?

Mr. FLOYD of Arkansas. Conclusive evidence in your favor if the judgment is against the corporation, but if the corporation has won its suit, conclusive evidence against you; yes, sir.

Mr. SCOTT. Then what becomes of my constitutional right, both of a trail by jury and of due process of law?

Mr. FLOYD of Arkansas. I do not think that interferes with your constitutional right. It simply relates to the decree and its admissibility as evidence. You can bring your suit. You can try it on the evidence adduced and before a jury. It affects nothing but the evidence in that suit and the law in that suit.

Mr. SCOTT. No. The fact is conclusive against me by that decree.

Mr. FLOYD of Arkansas. The fact in that suit.

Mr. SCOTT. Which was the conspiracy that was the cause of action.

Mr. FLOYD of Arkansas. It might be the state of facts proven had no relation to your cause of action.

Mr. SCOTT. But I am assuming this particular conspiracy is the one I am declaring upon.

Mr. FLOYD of Arkansas. Suppose the gentleman will pass that for the present. Take it up under the five-minute rule. I will be glad to debate it with him then. But I am trying to give you an outline of this bill for your information, and we have brought in a rule giving the greatest opportunity for debate under the five-minute rule. I hope the gentleman will permit me to proceed. That section simply provides—and it is based upon the broad ground of public policy—and these suits are brought in behalf of the whole people of the United States—that when a decree is obtained against an unlawful combination that the decree may be used in private suits brought against the defendant corporation. And I desire to state for the benefit of the Members of the House that very little objection has been urged to that provision before our committee. Some of the best constitutional lawyers that have been before that committee have never questioned for one moment its constitutionality.

Now, I must hurry along, and I desire to take up briefly section 7, which is the next section, in connection with sections from 15 to 23. These are the labor sections of this bill, and I want to detail to you briefly what is accomplished by them. Now, I will be glad to have your attention, gentleman, because I desire to discuss quite fully these labor sections of the bill.

There is a general impression among some, it seems, that section 7 is the labor section of the bill. That is only one of the labor sections of the bill. The sections from 15 to 23 relate exclusively to labor questions, and I desire to explain them, and then take up section 7 in conclusion and show you just what the labor provisions of this bill do, and explain the meaning and effect of section 7 and also its importance and scope.

During the Sixty-second Congress two bills relating to labor—what is known as the Clayton anti-injunction bill and what is known as the Clayton contempt bill—were passed in the House. Both passed the House, and I will give you the vote on each of the bills. Minority reports were filed against them by distinguished members of the committee, who were able lawyers, but when the injunction bill was voted on in the House only 31 votes were cast against it in the whole House, including Republicans, Progressives, and Democrats. When the bill giving right to trial by jury in contempt cases was voted on in the same Congress only 18 votes were cast against it in the whole House. We have placed those two bills, which passed the House, as stated, and which afterwards were indorsed at the Baltimore convention by the Democratic Party, bodily in this bill, with only slight amendment to section 15, to make it conform to equity rule 73 of the Supreme Court of the United States, since adopted by that court. What do we give labor in these several provisions? I will tell you what labor gets in the sections from 15 to 23.

United States courts are prohibited from issuing injunctions against persons on account of their ceasing to perform any work or labor—one of the things for which Federal courts in the past have issued injunctions in labor disputes.

Second. From issuing injunctions to prevent laborers from recommending, advising, or persuading others by peaceful means so to do.

Third. To enjoin laboring men from attending at or near a house or place where any person resides or works, or carries on business, or happens to be, for the purpose of peacefully obtaining or communicating information, or peacefully persuading any person to work or to abstain from work.

That is a thing for which laboring men from time to time have been enjoined by different Federal courts.

Fourth. Or from ceasing to patronize or to employ any party to such dispute.

This is another thing for which laboring men have been repeatedly enjoined, and which we regard as an abuse of the injunction writ.

Fifth. Or from recommending, advising, or persuading others by peaceful means so to do.

Another thing for which laboring men have been enjoined.

Sixth. Or from paying or giving to or withholding from any person engaged in such dispute any strike benefits or other moneys or things of value.

A monstrous thing to think of, but, according to the testimony of William B. Wilson, now Secretary of Labor, who testified before our committee at the last Congress that he, as secretary of one of these organizations, was enjoined during a strike from paying those sick benefits by the Federal courts. This prohibits for the future such outrageous injunctions being issued against any laboring man or labor associations.

Seventh. Or from peacefully assembling at any place in a lawful manner and for lawful purposes.

That is a thing that ought never to have been denied to any citizen in America—a guaranteed constitutional right—but a thing which the Federal courts, by the use of the injunctive process, have repeatedly enjoined laboring men from doing.

Eighth. Or from doing any act or thing which might lawfully be done in the absence of such dispute by any party thereto.

In other words, this puts laboring men upon the same equality under the law with every other citizen, and requires the same cause of action; requires an injunction in a case growing out of a labor dispute to be issued upon the same evidence as in any other case where a labor dispute is not involved. The injunction provisions of this bill give to labor a bill of rights on eight different propositions, in which, by the abusive practices of injunctions in the past, they have been harassed in numerous cases and often imprisoned.

Not only that, but it requires notice and forbids blanket injunctions. The provisions in the second bill give to laboring men the right of trial by jury in cases of indirect contempt, where the acts complained of would constitute criminal offenses under the law. And right here I want to call your attention to one significant thing. In the decision rendered by the Supreme Court in the Gompers case[5.518] a few days ago you will find a strong intimation given by the justice delivering the opinion that the trial of these cases by jury is more satisfactory than by courts.

Now, those are the labor provisions. We bring them to you. They have been specifically indorsed by this House. They have been specifically indorsed by our party. They have been adhered to and observed by many of the courts. But there is one additional provision which I will take up now, because it is new. It was not in the Clayton bill at the last Congress, and, so far as I know, it has never been in any other bill pending before this Congress. I refer to section 7 of the bill. I will explain to you briefly how that provision got into this bill.

The Democratic platform at Baltimore declared specifically in favor of the injunction bill passed in the Sixty-second Congress; declared for the right of trial by jury in contempt cases; and declared in favor of legislation that would differentiate and

---

[5.518] Gompers v. United States, 233 U.S. 604, 34 S. Ct. 693, 58 L. Ed. 1115 (1914), *rev'g Re Gompers*, 40 App. D.C. 293 (D.C. Cir. 1913). *See* note 5.522 *infra* for a more detailed explanation of the *Gompers* case.

distinguish labor and farmers' organizations from other organizations, saying, to use the language of the platform, that they should not be deemed or considered unlawful combinations in restraint of trade under the Sherman law. But it did not declare for any specific exemption from the Sherman law. Bear that in mind.

Now, on December 6, 1913, I believe it was, Mr. Gompers, the head of the American Federation of Labor, appeared before the Committee on the Judiciary of the House and made a plea for additional legislation in behalf of labor organizations. He read the Democratic platform; he read the Progressive platform; he alluded to the Republican platform, saying that its declarations for labor were nil. Then he made a speech, and I desire to quote from it and read it into the RECORD, because I think it is worthy of going into the RECORD. It is whispered now, since some people have become dissatisfied with this provision, that ⊥ there is nothing in his contention. I think there is. I quote from Mr. Gompers:

⊥9166

> Gentlemen, under the interpretation placed upon the Sherman antitrust law by the courts, It is within the province and within the power of any administration at any time to begin proceedings to dissolve any organization of labor in the United States and to take charge of and receive whatever funds any worker or organization may have wanted to contribute or felt that it is his duty to contribute to the organization.
>
> Mr. WEBB. Are there any suits pending in the courts now looking to this end, Mr. Gompers?
>
> Mr. GOMPERS. There are no suits now pending; but an organization of workingmen, the window-glass workers, was dissolved by order of the court under the provisions of the Sherman antitrust law, charged with conspiracy as an illegal combination in restraint of trade. And while that organization was dissolved by action of the court, yet it created no furor, for this reason: I have no desire to reflect upon the men who are in charge of that organization as its officers and representatives, but it was, in my judgment, supine cowardness for them not to resist an attempt of the dissolution of their associated effort as a voluntary organization of men to protect the only thing they possessed—the power to labor.
>
> Mr. WEBB. Have you any case where a labor organization has been dissolved simply because they themselves united in asking or fixing a certain wage and went no further in uniting with the manufacturers?
>
> Mr. GOMPERS. I can not tell you, sir, about that. But that is the very essence of the life of the organization. What I want to convey is this, that of these 30,000 or more local associations of workingmen, what we call local unions of workingmen and workingwomen, probably more than two-thirds have agreements with employers. As a matter of fact, I think that every observer and every humanitarian who knows greeted with the greatest satisfaction the creation of the protocol in the sweated industries of New York City and vicinity which abolished sweatshops and long hours of labor, and the burdensome, miserable toil prevailing, and established the combination of employers and of workmen and workwomen by which certain standards are to be enforced, and no employer can become a member of the manufacturers' association in that trade unless he is willing to undersign an agreement by which the conditions prevailing in the protocol will be inaugurated by him. Yet, under the provisions of the Sherman antitrust law that association of manufacturers has been sued, I think, for something like $250,000, because it is a conspiracy in restraint of trade.
>
> What I mean to say is this: I am perfectly satisfied in my own mind that the Attorney General of this administration, the Attorney General of the United States under the present administration, is not going to dissolve or make any attempt to dissolve the organizations of the working people of this country. I firmly believe that if there should be any of them, any individual or an aggregation of individuals, guilty of any crime, that the present administration would proceed against them just as readily, and perhaps more so, as any other; I am speaking of the procedure against the organizations themselves and the dissolution of them. But who can tell whether this administration is going to continue very long, or whether the same policy is going to be pursued; that is, the policy of permitting these associations to exist without interference or attempts to isolate them? Who can tell? What may come; what may not the future hold in store for us working people who are engaged in an effort for the protection of men and women who toil to make life better worth living? We do not want to exist as a matter of sufferance, subject to the whims or to the chances or to the vindictiveness of any administration or of an administration officer. Our existence is justified not only by our history, but our existence is legally the best concept of what constitutes law. It is an outrage; it is an outrage of not only the conscience; it is not only an outrage upon justice, it is an outrage upon our language to attempt to place in the same category a combination of men engaged in the speculation and the control of the products of labor and the products of the soil on the one hand and the associations of men and women who own nothing but themselves and undertake to control nothing but themselves and their power to work.

Mr. FLOYD. I want to see if I understand your position. If I understand your position under the existing status of the law as determined by the Federal courts, if the Attorney General should proceed to dissolve any of your labor organizations they could be dissolved. Is that your proposition?

Mr. GOMPERS. Yes, sir.

Mr. FLOYD. And that your existence, therefore, depends upon the sufferance of the administration which happens to be in power for the time being.

Mr. GOMPERS. Yes, sir.

Mr. FLOYD. What you desire is for us to give you a legal status under the law?

Mr. GOMPERS. Yes, sir.

Mr. FLOYD. So you can carry on this cooperative work on behalf of the laborers of the country and of the different organizations without being under the ban of the existing law?

Mr. GOMPERS. Yes, sir. . . .

Mr. HAMILTON of Michigan. Just at the beginning of Mr. Gomper's testimony did I understand he stated that there was an organization of employers in New York City who issued a protocol in relation to the employment of labor? I did not quite catch the meaning there.

Mr. FLOYD of Arkansas. No. That association was not dissolved, but a reference was made to the association of glassworkers that was dissolved.

Mr. HAMILTON of Michigan. The other was not?

Mr. FLOYD of Arkansas. No, sir. Mr. Gompers was speaking of the excellent work of the other organization, which was not dissolved.

Mr. HAMILTON of Michigan. He claimed that it could be dissolved?

Mr. FLOYD of Arkansas. Yes; he claimed that it could be dissolved. And anyone who has read carefully the decisions of the Supreme Court in the Standard Oil case and in the American Tobacco case and other leading cases decided by the Supreme Court, as a lawyer, must realize that Mr. Gompers's contention is correct.

If you find a court with the facts to sustain a conspiracy in restraint of trade and the courage to do it in a proper case, it is within the power of the court to enter a decree of dissolution. You can see what such a decree would do for labor organizations. When the Standard Oil Co. was dissolved there were millions of property which the equity court, under the rules of procedure, exercising its equity jurisdiction, was required to protect and conserve, and this property formed a nucleus around which a new organization was formed to take over the property and continue to operate, and the same with respect to the American Tobacco Co. But for what were those great combinations dissolved? For being combinations and conspiracies in restraint of trade. The inanimate thing known as "a combination" can do nothing. It acts through agencies, through living human agencies, that make the unlawful contracts, do the unlawful acts, perform the things that they are doing in violation of law; and if an industrial corporation and its agents have so violated the Sherman law, they can be dissolved. And who can gainsay the proposition that if individual members of labor organizations should do unlawful things and enter into unlawful contracts and enter into conspiracies in restraint of trade, the same power that dissolved the Standard Oil Co. and the same power that dissolved the American Tobacco Trust can dissolve the labor organizations, with this more disastrous effect—there being no nucleus of property around which to gather the fragments of the association, they would go to the four winds and be out of existence. And yet I am sorry to say that I have been told that there are those who contend that the committee has done nothing for labor by incorporating this provision in the bill. We are giving labor associations a legal existence and declaring their operations legal by this provision. We are taking them out from the ban of the present law to the extent that in the future they can not be dissolved as unlawful combinations. Their existence is made lawful and they are given a legal status.

In other words, recognizing and believing as a committee that the plea made by Samuel Gompers, the head of the great American Federation of Labor, was a just plea, well founded, in the light of past decisions, and that those great organizations of workingmen ought not to be considered and classed as unlawful combinations per se and ought not to be subjected to the same rule applied to industrial corporations or to be dissolved by court decree, we have incorporated section 7 in this bill, declaring legal labor and other organizations named therein. . . .

Gentlemen, I am sorry that my limited time has not permitted me to go into a discussion of other important features of this bill, but under the five-minute rule we will have ample opportunity to do so.

I should like to take up the question of interlocking directorates and the provision relating to holding companies. I should like to take up other provisions of the bill; but in the time allotted me I have only touched upon some of the more vital features of this great piece of legislation proposed in the interest of the American people generally, the labor provisions, constituting, as they do, a great bill of rights for labor, sections 2 and 4 furnishing a bill of rights and equity to every independent small dealer in this country. In conclusion, let me say we submit this bill as the result of an earnest effort on the part of the Judiciary Committee to carry out the will of the House in framing a bill which we trust will meet with the approval of the House, and we hope the approval of the country.

I thank you for your patient attention. [Applause.] . . .

Mr. NELSON. Mr. Chairman, with other minority Members, I shall support the first part of the present so-called antitrust program, the creation of an interstate trade commission. I do so with pleasure, because in its preparation the minority was granted recognition. It is a definite legislative measure, and, on the whole, this commission, with additional powers, may prove a beneficial agency for the final solution of the trust evil.

It is with a deep sense of disappointment that, for the same reasons reversed, I can not give my support to the bill now before us. It comes from the committee of which I have the honor of being a member. I have the highest personal esteem for the gentlemen of the subcommittee who framed the bill. ⊥ These gentlemen, but for a powerful restraining hand, have the ability and, I believe, the patriotic desire to construct a far better law: and I had hoped that we all could prepare and support a measure that would reflect credit upon the committee and redound greatly to the welfare of the country. . . .

Mr. [CHARLES H.] SLOAN [R., Neb.]. What restraining hand does the gentleman refer to? Is not this House free to do what it sees fit, and may not its Members exercise their own privileges and prerogatives?

Mr. NELSON. The gentleman has evidently not been reading the newspapers.

Mr. SLOAN. I recognize in the gentleman a greater authority, and I appeal to him.

Mr. NELSON. The gentleman must know from the discussion to-day that a subcommittee was appointed, consisting of three very able Democrats. No Republican was given any recognition on that subcommittee; and if we may rely on the newspapers they were constantly in consultation with the President on all details of the bill, and they are carrying out his instructions.

Much as I wish to act with my colleagues on the committee, I must truthfully state my views of this bill. It was conceived in the spirit of partisanship and molded in every detail by the motive of political expediency. It is not constructive legislation upon broad principles but by arbitrary selection, nor by positive and certain enactments but by vague and undefined exceptions, and does not bravely grapple with the giant evil of monopoly itself, but turns to its manifestations and unrelated side issues. Finally, it is doubtful whether the harm that will result from this bill will not outweigh the small amount of good some of its provisions might accomplish.

It will be a matter of extreme regret, I feel certain, to every American citizen, irrespective of politics, who takes a large and patriotic view of this whole subject that the party intrusted with power has failed so completely to measure up to the great opportunity and the sacred duty of the hour. Instead of devoting itself to the sincere solution of the problem of our day and generation, it has weakly yielded to the spirit of political expediency and truckling compromise, by way of inaction if not reaction. Before the last election the party pointed to the pathway of duty. It bravely asserted that "a private monopoly is indefensible and intolerable," and this was its platform pledge:

> We favor the vigorous enforcement of the criminal as well as the civil law against trusts and trust officials, and demand the enactment of such additional legislation as may be necessary to make it impossible for a private monopoly to exist in the United States.

There was a ring of genuine truth in that proclamation, and there was patriotism in that pledge, and it appealed to the American people. Private monopoly is intolerable, and competition must be restored as the working basis of our national life. Competition offers, in my opinion, the best environment for the advancement and the welfare of mankind in the individual initiative, the individual independence, and the individual responsibility.

We should now have the courage and foresight of statesmanship. We may yet be master of our country's future; but if we trifle, halt, or compromise too long competition, now greatly endangered, may never be restored, and then what—socialism?

No nation is so great that it can safely overlook the law of consequence. None are so blind as they who will not see. There are those who look upon socialism as a menacing evil, but what are the signs of the times? Is there no significance in the rapid progress that socialism is making both in the United States and abroad? Socialists sit in the cabinets of Italy, France, and Norway, and they are the strongest political party in Germany. In the United States Socialist gains have kept pace with the increase in the number and power of the trusts. For President of the United States in 1912, 1,000,000 American citizens voted for a radical Socialist. We can not safely ignore the principle of cause and effect. As surely and rapidly as the properties of all the people pass into the hands of a few trust magnates, public sentiment, rapidly forming, when once fully aroused, will multiply the socialistic vote as a protest against monopoly privilege. And the day when the people must choose between public ownership of trusts for the benefit of all and the private ownership of the trusts for the privilege of the few, will witness the final triumph of socialism in this country. Therefore we should act in our days of grace, while we are yet masters of our national destiny; but will this compromise measure before us now, this mere marking time, remove the cause, the special monopoly privilege of levying tribute manifested in the high cost of living, and thus prevent the much-dreaded social change in the conditions of our national life?

REGULATED MONOPOLY.

Some well-meaning theorists imagine they see a place of escape, a permanent middle ground, in a state of regulated monopoly. But they are merely deceiving themselves. They say that the trusts are more efficient and can produce more cheaply. They urge that the dangers of oppression may be removed by regulation and that the principle of concentration in industry under regulated monopoly will result in benefit to all the people. But these fond hopes and fancies are fallacious.

TRUSTS NOT EFFICIENT.

The trusts have not been efficient. The source of their success has been the unfair tactics employed against the independents and the monopoly privileges they have enjoyed. No trusts show cheaper cost of production than do the smaller independent plants. The explanation lies near at hand. When a concern grows so large that the men at the head can not possibly be familiar with every angle of the business, gross inefficiency results. The element of personal management so essential to business success disappears. In the interest, therefore, merely of cheaper production, it is desirable that the trusts should be destroyed.

PRICE FIXING.

Nor is regulation of monopolized industry practicable. In the pathway toward regulated monopoly there are many immovable rocks. The foremost is price fixing. With the specter of the cost of living before us we can not permit monopolies to charge prices at will. But in fixing prices the Government must do justice to all interests alike. It must take into consideration the values of these great properties, the rights of the owners, the needs of the consumers, the returns to the farmer for his raw materials, the wages of the laborer in the mills, and many other important matters. The problem is, as may be seen at a glance, a stupendous impossibility.

Fixing prices calls for commissions. How many—1 or 800? Able men who have given this point special study say that there would have to be a separate commission, at least, for each line of business. What a mire of bureaucratic government we would run into! Think of the arbitrary power of such commissions!

CORRUPTION.

Then, too, there are other accompanying evils. Big business to protect profits will go into politics; a small increase in prices will mean millions of extra profits; and in consequence we would always have present the grave danger of political and official corruption.

BUSINESS STAGNATION.

Regulated monopoly is likely to mean not only bad government but business stagnation. When commissions allow monopolies regular fixed profits, whether they be 6 per cent or 10 per cent, the keen incentive for making improvements in the processes of manufacture will disappear. Efficient or not, they will earn the same regular dividends.

PUBLIC OWNERSHIP.

The final consideration in regulating monopoly is that it will inevitably lead to socialism. Under regulation, if prices are high, candidates and parties will bid for votes on the plea of reducing the cost of living. Regulation may then lead to confiscation, and socialism is at hand. On the other hand, if prices are not reduced, there will be the increasing demand for public ownership. To compromise with monopoly is to end in socialism.

THE TEST OF LEGISLATION.

Difficult as the problem of restoring competition may seem, it presents no such insurmountable obstacles as lie in the pathway of regulated monopoly. As a Nation, with the Sherman law unrepealed, we are committed to competition. This bill, or any trust bill, must be measured by the standard of its efficiency to restore competition. There can be no satisfactory compromise. Monopoly in every form must be made impossible. Any measure which falls short of this is but a makeshift and not a thoroughgoing solution of this great evil.

THE CHANGE IN PROGRAM.

The President of the United States, a profound student of history, before his election saw plainly the duty of the hour, and I even now believe that he really desired to assail this evil with all the power of his great office, but after the tariff bill had been passed it became evident that the cost of living had not come down and that business was rapidly approaching a standstill. There were signs of panic in the air, and if not in the country there was a real panic among Democrats in Congress. There was a lively fear of a possible overturning of the political equilibrium. Thinking that readjustment of our currency system would restore public confidence, the party in power rushed through Congress its money bill, and still there was business paralysis.

It was evident to a close observer of current events that the party in power would not have the courage to grapple with the trust problem in dead earnest, but what was it to do? It had to steer between Scylla and Charybdis, betrayal of public confidence in deserting its trust program or so disturbing the big business interests that a panic might be precipitated in all its dreadful reality. Then it was that political expediency caused a sudden change in party program.

A PREDICTION.

Six months ago in magazine articles I pointed out just what would take place, and the expected has come to pass. Among other things this was said:

In this situation the easiest road is that of compromise—to pass some halfway measures and then try to make the people believe that the country has been relieved from the thraldom of the trusts. There is much talk of going slow. It is proposed to pass a few bills, such as making the penalties of the Sherman law personal and abolishing interlocking directorates, so as to make a showing of reform, but not seriously disturb Wall Street. It behooves the people to watch closely coming events. This is a time when words count for less than results.

At the same time the hope and sincere wish was expressed that the President would play the part of David and slay the Goliath of private monopoly.

ASSURING BIG BUSINESS.

But the President, yielding to the pressure of political expediency, in his trust address to Congress sounded the keynote of compromise when he told big business in honeyed words that "the antagonism between business and Government is over," that in its place "an atmosphere of accommodation and mutual understanding" has been ushered in. Vice President Marshall said, "What we need is much agitation and little legislation." Senator HOKE SMITH said, "Readjustments can be made peaceably and litigation will not be required." And Chairman CLAYTON assured big business interests that "nothing radical" would be done.

THE SUBCOMMITTEE.

To make certain of this, as chairman of the Committee on the Judiciary he appointed two Democratic members to act with himself as a subcommittee in the preparation of a trust program. This partisan subcommittee, in frequent consultation with the President, prepared three tentative bills. It was quite evident that Chairman CLAYTON'S promise was made good. These bills did not alarm the trusts; they did disturb small business men.

SUGGESTIONS OFFERED.

Extensive hearings were granted upon these tentative bills. Representatives of small business associations appeared to protest against the arbitrary manner in which their methods of doing business were interfered with. Thoughtful students of the trust problem—men like Louis D. Brandeis, Samuel Untermeyer, Albert H. Walker, and others—showed clearly that these bills would not be effective in restoring competition. Numerous excellent suggestions were offered to make them really effective means for destroying private monopoly.

PARTISANSHIP.

When hearings were concluded this partisan subcommittee presented a consolidated bill. It did not avail itself of the many helpful suggestions that had been made, dropped out the teeth in the defintions bill, and added some new provisions dealing with holding companies, farmer and labor organizations, and the use of injunctions in labor disputes. No Republican had any part whatever in the preparation of the bill. The partisan subcommittee worked behind closed doors. Not a change was made without its consent. The full committee reported the bill to the House by a strictly partisan majority. So evident, in fact, was the partisanship that no member of the minority cared to take any part in the final vote. From beginning to end, it may be said with perfect accuracy, this bill was conceived in a spirit of partisanship and molded in every detail by the motive of political expediency. [Applause on the Republican side.]

COMPROMISE.

The compromise character of this measure is apparent in every provision. It is a tight-rope performance with the fears of Wall Street balanced against the demands of the people. Hence its vagueness, its exceptions, and its side issues. Its various sections resemble certain signs which as you read them from the front say one thing, but when you read them from the side or the rear say something wholly different.

In the minority views I presented as a member of the Committee on the Judiciary a detailed analysis of this bill was made; here I shall point out only generally how it carries water on both shoulders in the effort to please plutocracy and at the same time placate the public.

TEETH IN SHERMAN LAW.

The first part deals with two unfair methods of competition—discrimination in price and the making of exclusive contracts. They are the remnant of the first attempt of the learned doctors on the subcommittee to equip the Sherman law with a full set of teeth, so as to repair the supposed ravages of the Supreme Court's rule of reason in the Oil and Tobacco cases. In the course of the hearings, however, the crude workmanship of the subcommittee was made so apparent that when the consolidated bill reappeared from the secret workroom of these conservative "trust busters" there were only two teeth left. These were not to be inserted in the Sherman Act, but were to constitute, so to speak, independent fangs, with which to threaten and to harass little business.

DISCRIMINATIONS.

The section dealing with price discrimination presents an interesting exhibit of the skill of these trust-law draftsmen in so writing the provision that it shall appear fair on its face to the public at large and yet shall not materially disturb the well-known practices of big business. To the public it apparently prohibits all discrimination between different individuals and communities, but upon examination we find various loopholes carefully provided for the benefit of the big fellows. Thus discrimination is not prohibited in bids and offers for sale.

Discrimination may be made in the time and manner of delivery of goods, in more lenient terms of credit, or in any other terms of sale except those of price. Even discrimination in price is permitted, unless it can be shown to have been made with the intent of wrongfully injuring or destroying the business of a competitor. The selling of goods cheaper at home than abroad is expressly authorized. Then there is the proviso that discrimination may be made on account of the "grade, quality, or quantity" of the commodity sold. Does anybody believe that a trust can be successfully prosecuted when it is allowed to discriminate on account of the quantity sold? Finally, the trusts are permitted to select their own customers. This means that they may altogether refuse to deal with anybody they wish to crush. No form of discrimination could be worse, but by this bill it is expressly legalized.

EXCLUSIVE CONTRACTS.

The section dealing with exclusive contracts has the same vice of uncertainty. It apparently prohibits exclusive contracts, but if they are made with nominal agents or bailees the trusts may readily evade the law. This bill says sellers shall not make exclusive contracts, but it also says that sellers may select their own customers. Interpreted in the most favorable light possible, the effect of this section will be to prohibit open and aboveboard contracts, but leaves open the means of accomplishing the same result through an undeclared and unexpressed understanding between the parties. . . .

Mr. HARDY. I want to see if I understand the gentleman. Does the gentleman mean by the remark he made a moment ago that if you give the Douglas Shoe Co. the right to sell its goods to only one person in a town you might thereby just as well give them the right to require that person to agree not to buy from anybody else except the Douglas Shoe Co.?

Mr. NELSON. Indeed, when I have the right to say to you that you can not be my customer, I can in my own mind prescribe the conditions under which I will refuse to make you my customer.

Mr. HARDY. In other words, if you agree that you will sell to me alone, it will be equivalent to my agreeing that I will buy from you alone.

Mr. NELSON. Yes; but the manufacturer must not make an outright contract with you. A man does not need to be hit on the head with a crowbar in order to grasp an idea or a suggestion.

Mr. HARDY. I do not think you need to make any further contract than that you will sell only to me, in order to induce me to buy only from you.

Mr. [JOHN A. M.] ADAIR [D., Ind.]. I want to ask the gentleman, does he believe that this law should go far enough to compel the Douglas Shoe Co.—as reference has been made to that company—to sell to everyone who would buy of that company in the same town? Do you not believe the company should have the right to make some particular firm or store its customer and give that customer the exclusive right to sell the Douglas product in that particular town?

Mr. NELSON. Answering the gentleman, I would say that I would be just to all. I would not discriminate. But we have here the gentleman saying to the mine owners, "You must sell ⊥ to all," and we have them saying to other than mine owners, "You may select your customer." I would make the rule either one way or the other. I would be fair, and not arbitrary.

Mr. [JACK] BEALL [D., Tex.]. How would the gentleman state the rule about that?

Mr. NELSON. If I had to state the rule about that I would be fair to all, and I think we are coming to that, when big business concerns have no right to say they will not sell to any customer who offers to pay cash.

Mr. ADAIR. You would be in favor, then, of a provision in this bill which would make it impossible for the manufacturer of any particular article to refuse to sell that product to anyone who wanted to buy it.

Mr. NELSON. If he offered cash for the commodity, I see no reason why the manufacturer should be permitted to refuse.

Mr. ADAIR. And on the same terms, and so forth.

Mr. NELSON. Now, on that question I want to say this, that having had no opportunity to participate in the preparation of this bill, so far as action of the subcommittee is concerned, and at any time only the merest pretense of opportunity, which amounted to listening to the hearings and seeing gentlemen on the other side offer some amendments to their bill, the Republicans and minority members have had nothing to do with it. Therefore we have not formulated a program, and we are not responsible for the program. If the gentleman wants to know what I would do, I would have taken, as the Committee on Interstate Commerce did, representatives of all parties, and then sought to legislate, along the lines of principle, for equal treatment for all, and not pick out the mine owner as the man who must sell to anybody, and then leave all the rest to have the right to select their own customers.

Mr. HARDY. Along that line, will the gentleman tell me whether there is any real difference in the situation of a mine owner, producing ore from the earth, and any other maker or producer as to any rights that the one should have and the other should not have to select his customers? In other words, why should section 3 apply to mine owners only?

Mr. NELSON. You heard what the eloquent and conscientious gentleman from Arkansas [Mr. FLOYD] said, and I wish to give him full credit, for he is an industrious, painstaking, and conscientious member of the Committee on the Judiciary. Yet I heard no such evidence before the committee that would cause me to say why they should select arbitrarily the mine owner. I see no reason at all for the discrimination.

Mr. ADAIR. I am interested in what the gentleman is saying and was trying to get information.

Mr. NELSON. I am very glad to give it to the gentleman if I have it.

Mr. ADAIR. Take an illustration. Here is a man who manufactures a certain kind of refrigerator that is his own idea of what is best. He goes through the country into the various cities and towns and establishes agencies for its sale with one merchant in a town, and that merchant probably spends more than his profits in one or two years in advertising that kind of a refrigerator, hoping to build up a business in that particular kind of a refrigerator that will make him some money in the future. Now, does not the gentleman think that a manufacturer should have the right to select his customer in the various towns to sell this particular kind of a refrigerator to, and does not the gentleman believe under such circumstances that it would be wrong to compel him to sell to any man in the town who sought to buy?

Mr. NELSON. The gentleman has asked me a controverted question as to which is the more for the public good, the right of the manufacturer to arbitrarily select his exclusive customer or to give the power to refuse to sell to a customer which tends toward monopoly. My own judgment is that in legislating on this question we ought first to destroy the monopoly before we go below and interfere with the everyday business practices. I would leave that open for the future.

Mr. ADAIR. It is a business practice?

Mr. NELSON. It is a business practice, and in many cases it works to the interest of the public to introduce a special article, but, of course, it may also be abused. That is a controverted question. . . .

Mr. HARDY. That is what this bill has done; it has left it open, has it not?

Mr. NELSON. I think not by leaving it in the power of the manufacturer to select the customer.

Mr. HARDY. You leave it as it is now. . . .

Mr. BRYAN. Under the present broad terms of the Sherman antitrust law persons engaged in selling goods, wares, merchandise in commerce are forbidden from selecting their own customers if such forbidding becomes a restriction in restraint of trade. Under this law persons engaged in selling goods, wares, and merchandise in commerce are absolutely protected in selecting their customers whether the agreement be in restraint of trade or not. . . .

MACHINERY.

The machinery provided by the bill for the enforcement of the antitrust law does really nothing to make certain that dissolutions of trusts shall be real and not merely nominal. A repetition is still possible of the sham dissolutions of the Oil and Tobacco Trusts, which boosted trust stocks enormously but did nothing to bring down prices. As in the Tobacco case, the independents and interested States are still denied the opportunity to intervene to protect their rights. Little is done to make the antitrust laws self-enforcing. There is no way to compel an unwilling Attorney General to act. The Sherman law, despite its excellent provisions, has failed to prevent the rapid increase of trusts, because Attorneys General, for reasons of political expediency, have not enforced it in all its effectiveness. This bill does the least possible to improve its machinery so as to make it self-enforcing and readily available for the adequate protection of the public welfare.

ESTOPPEL.

The committee points with much pride to the provision of this bill to make it easier for independents to recover damages for losses sustained through the unlawful actions of the trusts; but when this bill is read, it will be noted that not only may the decrees in Government suits be pleaded against trusts, but also in their favor. Although the independents have never had their day in court, they are absolutely bound by any feeble compromise the Attorney General may make. And can we be certain that no compromises will be made in the future? Only recently a compromise was arranged by the Attorney General with the American Telegraph & Telephone Co.,[5.519] under which it retained an almost complete monopoly of the telephone lines of the country. Other dissolutions by consent are reported to be in progress. Do these compromises and this bill, which allows trusts to plead these decrees in their favor, safeguard the rights of the independents? In thus dividing the loaf between them, which gets the bigger end—the independents or the trusts?

PENALTIES.

No part of this bill has been so much extolled by its authors as the section that pretends to make guilt personal. The people are told that, instead of fining corporations, hereafter the trust magnates will be put in jail. But trust magnates have no cause for alarm. This bill plainly says, in effect, that they shall be subject to fine and imprisonment only when they can be conclusively shown to have personally done any of the acts forbidden by the antitrust laws. This is now the law. Trust magnates heretofore have so rarely gone to jail, because Attorneys General, for reasons of political expediency, have not asked for prison penalties, or because judges have suspended sentence. Why is it that under this administration the Mellen indictment has been allowed to run along for 18 months, and is anybody ever to be brought to trial?[5.520] This bill still permits judges to suspend sentence. The prison penalties of the Sherman law are left as they were, and the maximum fine is still $5,000. Think of a $5,000 fine for the average American trust.

HOLDING COMPANIES.

This bill is represented to us as hereafter prohibiting holding companies; but big business knows that it expressly does not apply to holding companies already organized.

[5.519] United States v. American Tel. & Tel. Co., U.S. Dep't of Justice, 1 Decrees and Judgments in Federal Anti-Trust Cases 1890-1918, at 483 (1918) (D. Ore. 1914) (consent decree) [hereinafter cited as 1 D. & J.].

[5.520] A nolle prosequi was entered on March 30, 1920. See CCH, The Federal Antitrust Laws, with Summary of Cases Instituted by the United States 1890-1951, at 99 (1952) [hereinafter cited as Federal Antitrust Laws].

Moreover, this bill makes the test of a holding company's illegality not whether it has potential power to lessen competition, in substance held to be the law in the Northern Securities case, but instead it introduces a new element, and a dangerous one, whether the holding company actually uses that power with the effect of substantially lessening competition. Upon this test the Northern Securities case would probably have gone against the Government, and it will hereafter be exceedingly difficult to prove that a holding company is illegal.

We are told also that a great reform is accomplished by the prohibition of interlocking directorates. But this part of the bill has no great terrors for Wall Street. It is merely an annoyance. Instead of dealing with the real evil, the interlocking control of competing corporations, which grows out of common stock ownership, it deals only with one manifestation of this evil, the acting of the same men as directors of two or more corporations. The common stock ownership is allowed to continue. The interlocking control may still be exercised through dummy directors, voting trusts, or in any other manner than that of interlocking directorates. The trusts have not taken alarm at this bill, because they know that, though interlocking directors are prohibited, competition will not be restored while common stock ownership is undisturbed. To the legitimate, independent business men of the country, however, this section represents a needless and unjustifiable interference with business ability and freedom.

FOR LABORER AND FARMER.

This bill also contains a provision which is represented to the farmers and workingmen as righting a great wrong. It is pretended that the organizations of the toilers of the land formed to better their conditions of life are no longer to be treated as if they were trusts; but, again, upon closer examination of the bill we find the truth. The partisan subcommittee, in fact, rejected the demand of organized labor that its activities shall be exempted from the antitrust laws. Farmer organizations are legalized only when they do not have capital stock and are not conducted for profit. This makes impossible cooperative buying or selling by farmer organizations. Public-spirited men appeared before our committee to plead that nothing should be done to check the movement of cooperation among the farmers; but the partisan subcommittee, acting, no doubt, after consultation with the President, would not consider any proposition exempting from the antitrust laws farmer organizations that have capital stock or are conducted for profit. Congress sent a commission to Europe to study methods of encouraging cooperation among the farmers. The Department of Agriculture is constantly urging the farmers to cooperate; but this trust bill, claimed to be framed in the interest of the farmers, refuses to legalize such cooperative efforts to better their market conditions.

The farmers are waking up to it. Here is a telegram that I received from a farmers' organization in my State an hour ago:

Madison, Wis., May 22, 1914.

Hon. John M. Nelson,
House of Representatives, Washington, D. C.:

Our society, 12,000 strong, is counting on you at this time to champion the cause of agriculture in Wisconsin, which has already suffered from tariff legislation, by leading in enacting laws favorable to cooperation. Be sure to provide in impending antitrust legislation for free and unhampered cooperation in assembling, grading, standardizing, packing, storing, and marketing farm products. Agriculture must be permitted to do its business cooperatively; and business can not be done without capital. Would not a general provision permitting all cooperative business activities where all profits above operating expenses are returned to the patrons, producers, and consumers solve the problem? Anyway, it must be solved to save our greatest and most important industry in effecting economics in distributing and to protect consumers from unlimited exploitation.

Chas. A. Lyman,
M. Wes. Tubbs,
D. O. Mahoney,
Legislative Committee Wisconsin State Union
American Society for Equity.

Time will not permit me to discuss more fully the provisions of this compromise measure. Sufficient has been said to bring out its real character.

THE SMALL BUSINESS MAN.

Mr. Chairman, what will be the effect of the enactment of this legislation upon the life and happiness of the American people? Will the small business man, the merchant, and the independent manufacturer receive this act with joy? There are no such indications. The small merchant, with his back against the wall fighting for his very existence, came to the committee and through his representatives plead for relief against the crushing power of concentrated capital in the form of chain stores and department stores and big monopolies. What have you given him in this bill? Absolutely nothing. The independent manufacturer asked for larger business freedom. He may have mistaken his remedy, but what relief do you afford him in this measure? You arbitrarily place upon his business new restrictions that are vague, indefinite, and full of tempting loopholes. You burden, harass, and annoy needlessly independent, honest business. Surely the small business man, the merchant, and the manufacturer will not bless you for your efforts.

ORGANIZED LABOR.

Organized labor, representing millions of our countrymen who live by the toil of their hands in the sweat of their brows, have asked you to relieve them of being classified with capital. Their labor is part of their life, inseparable from them; and they have told you truly that it was not the intent of the framers of the Sherman law to classify their organizations with monopolies. It was organized labor that helped to put the administration into power. It asked for bread, but you gave it a bone. You pretend to exempt the workingmen from the law, but they know that your language is empty and meaningless, and that they are still subject to all its pains and penalties. Already their murmur of protest is being heard, but the President, so the press reports, will not allow you to give them relief.

THE FARMER.

The great army of farmers—will they thank you for this legislation? Not at all. They do not love you overly much now. You turned them over in your tariff bill to the tender mercies of competition with foreign countries. Through their representatives and organizations they joined labor in asking that the products of their toil be not classified with capital. Organizations of farmers are not trusts, no more than unions of laborers, and the Sherman law was not intended to apply to them. Farmers have acted separately and individually heretofore, and in consequence the return for their toil has been a pittance. Our progressive farmers everywhere are beginning to understand the value of acting together. Evidence was presented to the committee that East and West, North and South the farmers are cooperating to buy in larger quantities and to secure better prices through collective bargaining, but this bill puts this movement of the farmers under the ban of the law.

THE CONSUMER.

The consumers, your special protégés of the past, what of them? How they love you for reducing the high cost of living! You said it was due to the tariff; but has the cost of living come down? It was not the tariff, and you know it now. It was monopoly privilege; the power of the trusts to levy unjust tribute. Now, though you have the power, you weakly compromise. Will the consumers praise this measure? No; like lukewarm water they will spew it out of their mouths with disgust.

WALL STREET.

This bill is satisfactory only to Wall Street. You may have placated organized plutocracy temporarily. Big business appears to be satisfied, because you have done nothing. But you know that this bill will not stand the test of time. Many of you realize this, but you dare not run counter to the wishes of your master in the White House. You fear that the people will misunderstand your attitude if you go against the

President. Do you not realize that his power is due to the confidence of the people in the sincerity of his promise to destroy private monopoly? When the people learn that it is the truth—what the Wall Street bankers are saying—that "the President is the most conservative force in Washington," the party responsible for this craven compromise will reap the whirlwind. You were intrusted with the fullest power. You had an unequaled opportunity; but when the time came you lacked the courage for a thoroughgoing solution of the great monopoly problem. You have disturbed everything; you have settled nothing. As one who with others began the fight against monopoly privilege and special interests and for the rule of the people and the rights of all more than 20 years ago and has followed the fight up to this moment, I say to you your action will not meet with public approval. The people will come to understand your unpardonable temporizing policy. Men who will not compromise for the sake of political expediency will take your place of power. The great fight between the mass of the American people, seeking to restore competition, and the privileged class, still retaining monopoly control, will go on, and it will end only when it is indeed made "impossible for private monopoly to exist in the United States." [Applause.] . . .

Mr. [ISAAC R.] SHERWOOD [D., Ohio]. Mr. Chairman, the bill to supplement existing laws against unlawful monopolies reported by the distinguished chairman of the Judiciary Committee, Mr. CLAYTON, of Alabama, should command the support of every Member of the House. It is the mature product of the master minds of that great committee. It has received very careful consideration after a full hearing of all interests involved in our complex industrial system. It has both paternal and patriotic features. It is paternal in the guaranty of the civil rights of the great army of industrial workers, and the right to organize for mutual betterment and moral health. It is patriotic, because it involves the spirit of justice and a reverence for our Constitution and laws among the men and women who do the world's work. The impression has gone to the country that the proposed amendment to section 7, suggested by the representatives of organized labor, is too radical. This amendment is in harmony with the purpose explicitly stated when the so-called Sherman antitrust bill was under consideration, almost a quarter of a century ago.

The history of that very important legislation is needed to illuminate and instruct all persons and parties and organizations, because that record proves conclusively that it was the intention of the framers and proponents of this law to exclude organized labor from its provisions. This was well understood by the framers of the national Democratic platform adopted in Baltimore July 3, 1912. Here is the well-considered plank of the national platform touching this vital matter:

> The expanding organization of industry makes it essential that there should be no abridgement of the right of the wage earners and producers to organize for the protection of wages and the improvement of labor conditions, to the end that such labor organizations and their members shall not be regarded as illegal and combinations in restraint of trade.

The proposed amendment to section 7 is intended to carry out in letter and spirit the declaration of the Baltimore platform. Speaking as an individual, I desire to state that when this bill is under consideration during the five-minute rule an amendment will be offered which will probably allow section 7 in the bill to stand intact, with an improving sentence to make that section more lucid.

The claim is set up now by the opponents of this amendment that it is class legislation. This amendment is proposed as a protecting shield to about 30,000,000 of human beings in the United States who do the work of our ninety-five millions. If this is class legislation, how about the one hundred and forty millions appropriated this year for the Navy? How many of the 30,000,000 of wageworkers who are taxed on everything they wear and consume get any benefit out of this one hundred and forty millions? None worth mentioning, except the skilled workers in the navy yards. How many of the 30,000,000 of workers will get any benefit out of the two and a half millions of profit to the Armor Trust in the two-battleship program of 1914? How many skilled laborers will get any benefit out of the twenty-five millions voted for good roads? Is there anywhere concealed in this twenty-five millions of nebulous beneficence any benefit to any discouraged laborer out of a job? On the other hand, will he not find Jordan a harder road to travel?

How does this proposed amendment compare as class legislation with the $400,000 we recently voted out of the Federal Treasury for experiments in the eradication of cattle ticks? Have we reached a point in the evolution of our progressive civilization when the elimination of cattle ticks is more vital than the civil rights of the citizen?

We appropriated $200,000 this session of Congress to enable the Secretary of Agriculture, who is not a farmer, to give his views to the farmers on the marketing of farm products. And when this item was passed in a jiffy there was not an orator on this floor who would make an exclamation point that it was class legislation.

We appropriated this session $331,080 for the scientific investigation of insects and bugs and the Mediterranean fruit fly, and it went through the House in less than 10 minutes, with no question that insect legislation is class legislation. Yet, when the men and women who produce all the material wealth of the country ask for the protection of their civil rights, and do not ask for a dollar from the Federal Treasury, the claim is made that it is class legislation.

How does this proposed amendment compare as class legislation with the $500,000 voted slap-dab out of the Treasury for the eradication of hog cholera? Is it possible that we have statesmen on this floor who believe that the health of hogs is more precious than the health and betterment of the men and women whose labor and welfare are the dependable factor in the prosperity of the country?

Everywhere around the world where the benign doctrines of the Christian church find a lodgment in human hearts men and women believe that God created man for higher aims and a better destiny than the stupid and unthinking hog, whose head is always on a level with his belly. God made man erect, with head and heart above his belly, and the men of work, in brain and muscle, whose achievements and genius have made all there is of material value in this much vaunted and glorified Republic should have as much consideration in this historic Chamber as insects and hogs. [Applause.]

The preliminary history of this law is very valuable and illuminating. It proves that in the very conservative times of a quarter of a century ago, when the recognized leader of the conservatives in the Senate—John Sherman, of Ohio—was promoting this antitrust legislation, it was not even hinted, so far as I can learn, that the exemption of labor organizations from the provisions of the law was class legislation. Hence a review of this law is vital to this debate.

SHERMAN ANTITRUST LAW, 1890.

On February 28, 1890, Fifty-first Congress, Senator Sherman, of Ohio, introduced his antitrust bill in the Senate. It was referred to the Committee on Finance. On March 22, 1890, the Committee on Finance introduced a substitute for the Sherman bill. On March 25, 1890, Senator Morgan, of Alabama, moved to commit the bill to the Judiciary Committee; it failed to carry on a vote of 16 ayes to 28 nays. On March 25, 1890, Senator Sherman offered a proviso to be added at the end of the first section of the bill, as follows:

Provided, That this act shall not be construed to apply to any arrangements, agreements, or combinations between the laborers, made with a view of lessening the number of hours of labor or the increasing of their wages; nor to any arrangements, agreements, or combinations among persons engaged in horticulture or agriculture, made with a view of enhancing the price of agricultural or horticultural products.

The amendment was agreed to in the Senate without any opposing votes.

On March 26, 1890, Senator Stewart, of Nevada, made the following comprehensive statement:

The original bill has been very much improved, and one of the great objections has been removed from it by the amendment offered by Senator Sherman (for Senator George), which relieves the class of persons who would have been first prosecuted under the original bill without the amendment.

Senator Stewart then added:

The bill ought now in some respects to be satisfactory to every person who is opposed to the oppression of labor and desires to see it properly rewarded.

Labor was first prosecuted under the Sherman law, and that law has since been applied more generally to labor than against the monopolies it was intended originally to restrain.

I have in my hand a list of 101 cases where Federal judges have issued injunctions against labor organizations. This table has been carefully prepared, and I will print the same in connection with my remarks, showing the title and number of each case.

Mr. ADAIR. Were they all under the Sherman antitrust law?

Mr. SHERWOOD. All after the adoption of the Sherman antitrust law.

The amendment to the act above referred to was made while the Senate was sitting in Committee of the Whole. On March 27, 1890, discussion of the bill was resumed upon the proviso exempting farmers' organizations and trade-unions from the act. The debate that day on that subject is worth more than passing attention. Senators Hoar, Edmunds, George, Sherman, and many others participated. Finally Senator Walthall, of Mississippi, moved to refer the bill and the amendment to the Committee on the Judiciary with instructions to report to the Senate within 20 days. The motion carried by a vote of 31 ayes to 28 nays.

On April 2, 1890, the bill was reported to the Senate by the Committee on the Judiciary, but the Sherman-George amendment, which had been agreed to in Committee of the Whole on March 25, was not included in the bill. Nevertheless Senators in charge of the measure assured representatives of farmers' organizations and the trade-unions that under no possible construction would the judiciary include such organizations under the provisions of the act.

On April 8, 1890, the antitrust bill passed the Senate, as reported by the Committee on the Judiciary, by a vote of 52 ayes to 1 nay. It passed the House on June 21, 1890, and was approved July 2, 1890.

THE LITTLEFIELD ANTITRUST BILL.

On April 7, 1900, in the Fifty-sixth Congress, Representative Littlefield, of Maine, introduced bill H. R. 10539 for the purpose of amending the Sherman Antitrust Act, approved July 2, 1890. On June 2, 1900, while the bill was under discussion in the House of Representatives, the following exception by Representative Terry, of Arkansas, was added to the bill by a vote of 260 ayes, 8 noes, 76 not voting:

Nothing in this act shall be so construed as to apply to trade-unions or other labor organizations organized for the purpose of regulating wages, hours of labor, or other conditions under which labor is to be performed.

The bill was then passed with this amendment added by a vote of 274 ayes, 1 no, 70 not voting. The bill was sent to the Senate, but no action was taken by the Senate.

AMENDMENT TO SUNDRY CIVIL BILL.

On June 2, 1910, in the Sixty-first Congress, while the sundry civil appropriation bill was before the House of Representatives in Committee of the Whole, Representative Hughes, of New Jersey, offered the following amendment to the section making appropriations for the enforcement of the antitrust law:

Provided further, That no part of this money shall be spent in the prosecution of any organization or individual for entering into any combination or agreement having in view the increasing of wages, shortening of hours, or bettering the condition of labor, or for any act done in the furtherance thereof not in itself unlawful.

The amendment carried by a vote of 82 ayes to 52 noes.

On June 9, 1910, the Senate, by a vote of 34 ayes, 16 noes, decided to strike the Hughes amendment from the sundry civil bill.

On June 21, 1910, the conferees of the House were directed, on motion of Mr. Hughes, "that the House do further insist on its disagreement, and that the House conferees be instructed to refuse to agree with the Senate." It carried by a vote of 154 ayes to 105 noes, 12 answering "present," and 119 not voting.

On June 23, 1910, Chairman Tawney, of the conferees, moved "to recede and concur," which meant that the House agree with the Senate and strike the Hughes exemption proviso from the bill. A very animated debate followed, but the motion by Representative Tawney carried by a vote of 138 ayes to 130 nays, 16 answering "present," and 105 not voting. This vote was one of the most important ever taken in the House of Representatives. This action estranged organized labor from the Republican Party, then in control of the House of Representatives.

It is not pertinent to this debate to bring the record down to date. It is sufficient to know that the question has been before Congress for over 24 years, and is still unsettled, and that it is vital to settle it now and to settle it right.

This is supposed to be a Government of law, and a government guaranteeing the civil rights of the humblest of its citizens. Some magazine writer, a student of sociology, recently wrote:

> We have escaped from a despotic government by a king. We have realized, after many centuries, that a king is only a man. Are we going to permit the growing up a despotic government by the judges? Are they not only men?

It may be added that the despotism of a king, or one man, is of the same odious force and flavor as the despotism of a judge or a bench of judges.

The recent decision of the Supreme Court of the United States in dismissing the long-protracted case against Samuel Gompers and his associates of the American Federation of Labor has been cited on the claim that additional protective labor legislation is now unnecessary. But the Supreme Court did not decide any question vital to labor. As stated by a labor journal:

> This blessed week the celebrated case was taken by the ear, as it were, and gently led to a side door of the Supreme Court and let out into the street—and on a technicality. Not much was settled save that three very good men were not martyrized, for that dear old statute of limitations was invoked as a means of ridding the Supreme and other courts of a back-action situation, which was easy to dispose of with credit to the defendants, but which was full of embarrassments to the courts after the fellow Wright—now in limbo on impeachment charges—had put it up to the courts to sustain his Dogberry decision, or reverse the decision and make the courts ridiculous.

The Journal of Labor of May 15, 1914, published in Atlanta, Ga., gives in a few words all that this Supreme Court decision means. I quote from an editorial:

> The United States Supreme Court has without question dodged the great fundamental issues of whether (1) there shall be free speech in this country; (2) whether there shall be a free press in this country; (3) whether or not judges of the courts may usurp the functions of the legislative body and make law in their chambers by usurping power not authorized by statute and enjoining or restraining working people from the full exercise of their normal, personal, and inherent rights, thereby abusing and misusing the otherwise beneficent injunction writ.

As stated in the above paragraph, the Supreme Court has decided no fundamental question vital to labor.

The encroachments of the Federal judiciary, masquerading as the oracles of immutable law, upon time-honored rights guaranteed by organic law, is responsible for a large part of the popular agitation and unrest among the workers. In milder form these outrageous edicts of some of our Federal judges, notoriously Justice Wright, are patterned after the infamous Jeffreys, who voiced the aggressions of the Stuarts which led to the uprising of the Roundheads under Oliver Cromwell.

Call it evolution or revolution or what you will, a better and broader estimate of civil rights and duties has taken possession of the American people. It is the evolution of intelligence, based upon the assumption that they who toil and till should share in the harvest; that the workers in mines and mills, in steel and wool and cotton, should have a living wage and the right to organize, as all business and professional men and all religious and civic societies organize, in order to better their condition. All good men and good women are interested in improving the condition of the wageworkers. It is injustice and oppression that creates anarchy and fosters revolution. This is an ethical as well as an economic question. And now, in the presence of the anarchy and bloodshed in Colorado, in northern Michigan, and West Virginia, is the time to make a calm and diligent inquiry into the causes which provoked these deplorable conflicts. What do the records of the Federal courts disclose in injunction cases since the enactment of the Sherman antitrust law? I have here the record of 101 cases in which injunctions on labor cases have been granted. In the case of the Danbury Hatters the contention lasted for 10 years, commencing September 15, 1903, and ending January 24, 1913, resulting in a judgment with court costs against the hatters of $232,240.[5.521]

Let me cite another notorious case that has excited more criticism and aroused more antagonism among the industrial classes than any case in the entire history of the Federal jurisprudence of the United States. On December 23, 1908, Samuel Gompers, president of the American Federation of Labor; Frank Morrison, secretary; and John Mitchell, president of the Mine Workers' Union, were sentenced to imprisonment by Justice Wright, of the Supreme Court [sic] of the District of Columbia, for contempt of court,[5.522] upon the charge that they violated the terms of an injunction granted on petition of the Buck's Stove & Range Co., of St. Louis. As this case involves such rank injustice, I propose a brief review of some of the salient judicial atrocities. In pronouncing sentence upon these labor leaders Justice Wright exhibited such a malignant spirit and used such violent language and showed such alarming symptoms of pathognomonic hysteria that even as cautious and conservative a journal as the New York Evening Post referred to him editorially as exhibiting "an excess of heat and indulging in turbid rhetoric." [Laughter.]

This ill-tempered judicial harangue occupied 2 hours and 20 minutes, and only ceased when the judge had exhausted his vocabulary of invective. Then he emitted the following: "It is the judgment of the court that you, Frank Morrison, be imprisoned in the jail of the District of Columbia for a term of 6 months; you, John Mitchell, for a term of 9 months; you, Samuel Gompers, for a term of 12 months."

HONORED MEN JUDICIALLY PERSECUTED.

These three conservative officials of the industrial workers of the United States, all law abiding citizens, left the presence of this cruel judge in silence. For thirty-one times Samuel Gompers has been elected president of the American Federation of Labor, covering a period of 31 years. All this time he has been constantly in the limelight, and during all these years of his wearing work for the weary workers there has never been even a suspicion against his honesty or his fidelity among the workers. He has always stood for law and order. He has opposed strikes and has for the past decade favored peaceful arbitration. He has opposed arraying labor against capital. He has devoted the best part of his robust life to every humane movement for the moral and physical betterment of his fellow workers.

Did Judge Wright give the law and the facts in this case? No; he did neither.

The first amendment to the Constitution reads as follows:

> Congress shall make no law respecting an establishment of religion or prohibiting the free exercise thereof, or abridging the freedom of speech or of the press, or the rights of the people peacefully to assemble to petition the Government for redress of grievances.

Mr. [PERCY E.] QUIN [D., Miss.] Will the gentleman yield?

Mr. SHERWOOD. How much time have I got, Mr. Chairman?

The CHAIRMAN. The gentleman has 10 minutes remaining.

Mr. SHERWOOD. I will yield to the gentleman from Mississippi.

Mr. QUIN. Does not the gentleman think, to keep down judicial tyranny, we ought to stop the life tenure for judges—to elect them instead of appointing them for life?

Mr. SHERWOOD. I do not believe that in a Republic there should be any official, high or low, appointed for life. [Applause.]

⊥ THE JUDGE AND THE CONSTITUTION.

In commenting on this section Justice Wright said:

[5.521] Loewe v. Lawlor, 208 U.S. 274, 28 S. Ct. 301, 52 L. Ed. 488 (1908) (the *Danbury Hatters* case).

[5.522] Buck's Stove & Range Co. v. AFL, 36 WASH. L. REP. 822 (Sup. Ct. 1908) (no official reporter), *aff'd*, Gompers v. Buck's Stove & Range Co., 33 App. D.C. 516 (D.C. Cir. 1909) (jail sentences upheld), *dismissed without prejudice*, 221 U.S. 418, 31 S. Ct. 492, 55 L. Ed. 797 (1911); the Supreme Court of the District of Columbia again convicted the defendants and imposed jail sentences, *modified*, Re Gompers, 40 App. D.C. 293 (D.C. Cir. 1913) (Gompers' jail sentence upheld; Morrison and Mitchell received fines only), *rev'd*, 233 U.S. 604, 34 S. Ct. 693, 58 L. Ed. 1115 (1914) (convictions overturned). *See* note 5.567 *infra* and accompanying House debate.

So, with respect to the inhibition against abridging the freedom of speech and of the press, the Constitution nowhere confers a right to speak, to print, or to publish; it guarantees only that, in so far as the Federal Government is concerned, its Congress shall not abridge it, and leaves the subject to the regulation of the several States, where it belongs.[5.523]

In other words, this judge holds that a sacred right, guaranteed by the Constitution, that the supreme lawmaking power of the United States has no right to even abridge or modify, can be annulled by an inferior Federal judge. He asserts that the guaranteed rights of a citizen, that the supreme lawmaking power has no right to even abridge, "is subject to the regulation of the several States, where it belongs," and, further, this limber-minded Judicial pettifogger says "the Constitution nowhere confers a right to speak, to print, or to publish." It strikes me that any mature citizen with as much gray matter in his cerebrum as a gray goose will understand that when the Constitution inhibits the abridgment of free speech that, by clear implication, it confers a right to speak, to print, or to publish. Justice Wright held in this case that a judge may do by injunction what Congress is prohibited from doing by legislation. Can there be any doctrine more dangerous to individual rights and personal liberty than this? It is an infamous doctrine, and a Federal judge holding such views is unfit to hold any judicial office.

SOME VALUABLE OPINIONS.

I am glad I am not alone in sounding a danger signal on the many and glaring usurpations of our Federal judges. These numerous and drastic injunctions against the workers have aroused much popular indignation and called forth severe criticisms from lawyers, jurists, and students of sociology. I quote a few specimens. In October of 1907 Justice Moody, late of the Supreme Court of the United States, said:

> I believe in recent years the courts of the United States, as well as the courts of our own Commonwealth (Massachusetts), have gone to the very verge of danger in applying the process of the writ of injunction in disputes between labor and capital.

Hon. Thomas M. Cooley, president of the American Bar Association, said:

> Courts with their injunctions, if they heed the fundamental law of the land, can no more hold men to involuntary servitude for even a single hour than can overseers with a whip.

Judge M. F. Tuley, of the appellate court of Illinois, used these words:

> Such use of injunction by the courts is judicial tyranny, which endangers not only the right of trial by jury, but all the rights and liberties of the citizens.

Gov. Sadler, of Nevada, said:

> The tendency at present is to have the courts enforce law by injunction methods, which are subversive of good government and the liberties of the people.

Prof. F. J. Stimson, of Harvard University, one of the greatest legal authorities, in his new work on Federal and State Constitutions, after citing many authorities, says:

> These are sufficient to establish the general principle that the injunction process and contempt in chancery procedure, as well as chancery jurisdiction itself, is looked on with a logical jealousy in Anglo-Saxon countries as being in derogation of the common law, taking away the jurisdiction of the common-law courts and depriving the accused of his trial by jury.

Judge John Gibbons, of the circuit court of Illinois, declared that—

> In their efforts to regulate or restrain strikes by injunction they (the courts) are sowing dragons' teeth and blazing the path of revolution.

Why is it that far more consideration is given in England to the rights of the wageworkers than in the United States? Let me quote from a recent law of the British Parliament:

> *Be it enacted by the King's Most Excellent Majesty and with the consent of the Lords, spiritual and temporal, and the Commons in Parliament assembled, by the authority of the same:*

[5.523] 36 WASH. L. REP. at 841.

It shall be lawful for one or more persons, acting on their own behalf or in behalf of a trades union, in contemplation of a trade dispute, to attend peacefully and in a reasonable manner at or near a house or place where a person works or carries on business if he attend for the purpose of persuading any person to work or to abstain from working.

This is the land of King George, the hereditary successor of George III.

How do the descendants of the patriotic sires of the American Revolution like the comparison between the English "trades-dispute law" and the injunction record of our Federal courts, denying even the liberty of free speech to the American worker?

Shall the workers of the United States be compelled to turn for light and hope from democracy under an elective President across the Atlantic to the Government of a hereditary King?

Neither in England nor Germany nor France could the arrest and punishment of labor leaders of the type and conservative conduct of Samuel Gompers and his associates ever have been tolerated. Samuel Gompers is the ablest, most experienced, and most conservative labor leader around the world. Less radical than any of the labor group in the English Parliament or the German Reichstag or the Chamber of Deputies in France, he has for nearly half a century opposed strikes and boycotts and has given his best and most arduous efforts to prevent both and to reconcile the conflicts between capital and labor in order to promote the prosperity of both.

Labor demands and has the right to demand that laws be enacted making a fundamental difference between labor power and property. Labor power is not property, because it can not be separated from the laborer. It is personal. It lives only in the life of the worker and ends with his death. It can not be transferred like property. The Century Dictionary defines "labor" as follows:

Physical or mental effort, particularly for some useful or desired end. Exertion of power for some end other than recreation or sport.

Property is the product of labor applied to some substance of intrinsic value when perfected by labor. It is transferable, can be inherited, and does not die when the person who owns it or produced it dies.

What organized labor is now seeking is the assistance of Congresses and courts to restore the English common-law definition of property and restricting the jurisdiction of all courts of equity to its legitimate limitations, as it was universally recognized at the time of the adoption of the Constitution.

What recourse have any people, even under a Constitution guaranteeing civil rights to all alike, when they find themselves in the clutches of judges, appointed for life, who are deaf to popular appeals for justice, and whose official edicts, however cruel and unjust, can not even be modified by Congress, the supreme lawmaking power? [Applause.]

I submit as an appendix to my remarks the following—101—decisions of Federal courts on labor cases where injunctions have been issued, conspiracy charged, and alleging that the antitrust law was violated—all copied from the records of the Federal courts:

Allis-Chalmers Co. v. Reliable Lodge (111 Fed. Rep., 264; U. S. Labor Bul. 38, p. 183).
Allis-Chalmers Co. v. Iron Molders' Union No. 125 et al. (150 Fed. Rep., 155; U. S. Labor Bul. 70, p. 734; 166 Fed. Rep., 45; U. S. Labor Bul. 83, p. 157).
Aluminum Casting Co. v. Local 84 of International Molders' Union of North America et al. (197 Fed. Rep., 221).
American Steel & Wire Co. v. Wire, etc. (90 Fed. Rep., 608).
Armstrong Cork Co. v. Anheuser Busch Brewing Co. (1914).
Arthur v. Oakes (63 Fed. Rep., 301).
Atchison, Topeka & Santa Fe R. R. Co. v. Gee, Cir. Ct. Southern District Iowa (139 Fed. Rep., 582; 140 Fed. Rep., 153).
Bender v. Local Union 118, Bakers' Organization (34 Wash. Law Repr., 574; U. S. Labor Bul. 67, p. 894).
Barnes, A. R., & Co. v. Berry (156 Fed. Rep., 72; U. S. Labor Bul. 74, p. 259; 157 Fed. Rep., 833).
Beck et al. v. Railway Trainmen's Protective.

Besette *v.* Conkey & Co. (194 U. S., 324; 24 Sup. Ct. Repr., 665).
Blindell et al. *v.* Hogan et al. (54 Fed. Rep., 40).
Boutwell et al. *v.* Marr et al. (42 Atl. Repr., 607).
Bowels *v.* Indiana Railway Co. (62 N. E. Rep., 94).
Boyer et al. *v.* Western Union Telegraph Co., C. C. E. D., Missouri (124 Fed. Rep., 246).
Buck Stove & Range Co. *v.* American Federation of Labor (35 Wash. Law Rep., 797; U. S. Labor Bul. 74, p. 246).
Buck Stove & Range Co. *v.* American Federation of Labor (36 Wash. Law Rep., 822; U. S. Labor Bul. 90, p. 124, and No. 86, p. 355).
Buck Stove & Range Co. *v.* American Federation of Labor—Court of Appeals of District of Columbia (37 Wash. Law Rep., 154; U. S. Labor Bul. 33, p. 169; 31 Sup. Ct. Rep., 492; U. S. Labor Bul. 95, p. 323; 40 Wash. Law Rep., 412; U.S. Labor Bul. 112, p. 155).
Brewing & Malting Co. *v.* Hansen (Seattle) (144 Fed. Rep., 1011; U. S. Labor Bul. 68).
Barnes A. R., & Co. *v.* Chicago Typographical Union (83 N. E. Repr., 932; U. S. Labor Bul. 76, p. 1016).
Barnes, A. R., & Co. *v.* Berry (157 Fed. Rep., p. 883; U. S. Labor Bul. 76, p. 1019).
Boyer et al. *v.* Western Union Telegraph Co. (124 Fed. Rep., 246; U. S. Labor Bul. 50, p. 202).
Callan *v.* Wilson (127 U. S., 540–555).
Carter et al. *v.* Fortney et al. (170 Fed. Rep., 463; also 172 Fed. Rep., 722).
Central District & Printing Tel. Co. *v.* Kent (156 Fed. Rep., 173; U. S. Labor Bul. 74, p. 256).
Coeur d'Alene Con. Min. Co. *v.* Miners' Union of Wardner, Idaho (51 Fed. Rep., 260–267).
Commonwealth *v.* Hunt (4 Metcalf's Rep., 111).
Conkey (W. B.) Co. *v.* Russell et al. (111 Fed. Rep., 417).
Construction Co. *v.* Cameron et al. (80 N. S. Rep., 478).
Contempt—nature of proceedings, appeals, Gompers et al. *v.* Buck Stove & Range Co., Court of Appeals of the District of Columbia (37 Wash. Law. Rep., p. 708; U. S. Labor Bul. 86, p. 355).
Campbell et al. *v.* Johnson (167 Fed. Rep., p. 102; U. S. Labor Bul. 82, p. 682).
Carter et al. *v.* Fortney et al. (170 Fed. Rep., p. 463; U. S. Labor Bul. 86, p. 370).
Casey *v.* Typographical Union (45 Fed. Rep., 135).
Delaware, Lackawanna & Western Railroad Co. *v.* Switchmen's Union of North America (158 Fed. Rept., 541–690; U. S. Labor Bul. 77, p. 389).
Donovan et al. *v.* Penn Co. (26 Sup. Ct. Rept., 91; U. S. Labor Bul. 63).
Debs, In re Petitioner (158 U. S., 564).
⊥ Doolittle and United States (23 Fed. Rep. 544–547). ⊥9174
Doolittle and United States *v.* Kane, supra, re Higgins (27 Fed. Rep. 443).
Farmers' Loan & Trust Co. *v.* The Northern Pacific Railroad Co., C. C. E. D. Wisconsin (60 Fed. Rept., 803).
Frank et al. *v.* Herold et al. (52 Atl. Rep., 152).
Fordahl *v.* Hayde (82 Pac. Rep., 1079).
Garrigan *v.* United States (163 Fed. Rep., 16; U. S. Labor Bul. 79, p. 961).
George Jonas Glass Co. *v.* Glass Blowers' Association (54 Atl. Rep. 567; 79 Atl. Rep., p. 262; U. S. Labor Bul. 95).
Glass Co. *v.* Glass Bottle Blowers (66 Atl. Rep. 593; U. S. Labor Bul. 72, p. 629; 79 Atl. Rept., 262; U. S. Labor Bul. 95, p. 312).
Goldneid Consolidated Mines Co. *v.* Goldfield Miners' Union 220 et al. (159 Fed. Rep., 500; U. S. Labor Bul. 73, p. 586).
Gray *v.* Trades Council (97 No. W. Rep., 663).
Guaranty Trust Co. *v.* Haggarty (116 Fed. Rep., 510; U. S. Labor Bul. 43, p. 1291).
Hammond Lumber Co. *v.* Sailors' Union of the Pacific (149 Fed. Rep., 577).
Hitchman Coal & Co. *v.* Mitchell (172 Fed. Rep., 963; U. S. Labor Bul. 87, p. 686).
Hopkins *v.* Oxley Stave Co. (83 Fed. Rep., 152; 83 Fed Rep., 912).
Huttig, etc., Co., Fuette et al. (163 Fed. Rep., 363).
Illinois Central Railroad *v.* International Association of Machinists (190 Fed. Rep., 910; U. S. Labor Bul. 98, p. 495).
In re Debs, petitioner (158 U. S., 564).
In re Doolittle and United States (23 Fed. Rep., 544–547).
In re Doolittle and United States *v.* Kane, supra, re Higgins (27 Fed. Rep., 443).
In re Lennon (166 U. S., 548).
Irving *v.* Joint District Council, United Brotherhood of Carpenters, etc., United States Circuit Court of Southern District of New York (180 Fed. Rep., p. 896; U. S. Labor Bul. 92, p. 289).
Iron Molders' Union No. 125, of Milwaukee, *v.* Allis Chalmers Co. (166 Fed. Rep., 45; U. S. Labor Bul. 83, p. 157).

In re Reese (107 Fed. Rep. 942).
Jensen v. Cooke (81 Pac. Rep., 1069).
Jersey City Printing Co. v. Cassidy et al. (53, Atl. Rep., 230).
Jonas, George, Glass Co. v. Glass Blowers' Association of United States and Canada et al, court of chancery of New Jersey (54 Atl. Rep., p. 567; U. S. Labor Bul. 48, p. 1124).
Knudsen et al. v. Benn et al. (123 Fed. Rep., 636; U. S. Labor Bul. 50, p. 205).
Kargis Furniture Co. v. Local Union No. 131 (75 N. E. Rep., 877).
Keegan-Pope Motor Car Co. v. Keegan (150 Fed. Rep., 148; U. S. Labor Bul. 70, p. 757).
Kemmerer v. Haggerty (139 Fed. Rep., 693).
Kolley et al. v. Robinson et al. (187 Fed. Rep., 415).
Lawlor v. Loewe et al. (187 Fed. Rep., p. 522; U. S. Labor Bul. 96, p. 780; 148 Fed. Rep., 924; U. S. Labor Bul. 70).
Loewe v. Lawlor (28 Sup. Ct. Repr., 301; 130 Fed. Rep., 833; 142 Fed. Rep., 216; 148 Fed. Rep., 924; U. S. Labor Bul. 70, p. 710, and 75, p. 622).
Loewe et al. v. California Federation of Labor (139 Fed. Rep., 71, and 189 Fed. Rep., 714).
Loewe v. Lawlor (203 U. S. 274).
Lennon, In re (166 U. S., 548).
Lindsay & Co. v. Montana Federation of Labor et al. (96 Pac. Repr., p. 127; U. S. Labor Bul., 78).
Mackall v. Ratchford et al., C. C. D. W. Va. (82 Fed. Rep., 41).
March v. Bricklayers, etc. (63 Atl. Rep., 291).
Mobile & Ohio Railroad v. E. E. Clark et al. (May, 1903).
Montana Federation of Labor et al. v. Lindsay & Co. (96 Pac. Repr., p. 127; U. S. Labor Bul., 78).
National Telephone Co. of West Virginia v. Kent (156 Fed. Rep., 173; U. S. Labor Bul. 74, p. 256).
National Fireproofing Co. v. Mason Builders' Association (169 Fed. Rep., 259; U. S. Labor Bul. 84, p. 427).
Newport Iron & Brass Foundry v. Moulders' Union (1904).
O'Neil v. Behanna (37 Atl. Rep., 843).
Otis Steel Co. (Ltd.) v. Local Union No. 318, Cleveland, Ohio (110 Fed. Rep., 698; U. S. Labor Bul. 40, p. 638).
Oxley Stave Co. v. Coopers' International Union of North America (73 Fed. Rep., 695).
Pickett v. Walsh (78 N. E. Rep., 753).
Pope Motor Car Co. v. Keegan (150 Fed. Rep., 148; U. S. Labor Bul. 70, p. 757).
Pope Motor Car Co. v. J. H. Stitart or Stelert (June 9, 1906).
Rocky Mountain Bell Telephone Co. v. Montana Federation of Labor (156 Fed. Rep., 809; U. S. Labor Bul. 78, p. 804).
Reese, In re (107 Fed. Rep., 942).
Reinecke Coal Mining Co. v. Wood et al. (112 Fed. Rep., 477; U. S. Labor Bul. 41, p. 856).
Southern Railway Co. v. Machinists' Local, No. 14, et al. (111 Fed. Rep. 49; U. S. Labor Bul. 39, p. 496).
Shine v. Fox Bros. Manufacturing Co. (156 Fed. Rep., 357; U. S. Labor Bul. 74, p. 244).
Southern California Railway v. Rutherford et al., C. C. S. D. California (62 Fed. Rep., 796).
State v. Stockford (38 Atl. Rep., 769).
State v. Coyle, Oklahoma (130 Pac. Rep., 316).
Southern Railway Co. v. Machinists' Local (111 Fed. Rep., 49).
Thomas v. Cincinnati, New Orleans & Texas Pacific Railway Co., C. C. S. D. Ohio, N. D. (62 Fed. Rep., 669).
Thomas v. Cincinnati, New Orleans & Texas Pacific Railway Co., in re Phelan, C. C. S. D. Ohio, W. D. (62 Fed. Rep., 803).
Toledo, Ann Arbor Railroad v. Arthur and Railroad Companies (54 Fed. Rep., 730).
Toledo, Ann Arbor Railroad Co. and Northern Michigan Railway Co. v. Pennsylvania Railroad Co. (54 Fed. Rep., 738-746).
Union Pacific Railway Co. v. Ruef. United States Circuit Court for District of Nebraska (120 Fed. Rep., 102; U. S. Labor Bul. 47, p. 267).
Underhill v. Murphy, Typographical Journal of August 15, 1901 (174 —).
Union Pacific Railway Co. v. Ruef. (120 Fed. Rep., 102).
United States v. Agler (62 Fed. Rep., 82).
United States v. Cassidy (67 Fed. Rep., 698).
United States v. Debs et al. (64 Fed. Rep., 724).
United States v. Elliott (62 Fed. Rep., 801; 64 Fed. Rep., 27).

United States ex rel. Guaranty Trust Co. of New York v. Haggarty et al., C. C. N. D. W. Va. (116 Fed. Rep., 510).
United States v. Shipp, the Farmers' case (27 Sup. Ct. Repr., 165; 203 U. S. 563).
United States v. Kane (23 Fed. Rep., 748).
United States v. Patterson (53 Fed. Rep., 605-641).
United States v. Sweeney (95 Fed. Rep., 434).
United States v. Weber et al. (114 Fed. Rep., 950).
United States v. Workingmen's Amalgamated Council of New Orleans et al. (54 Fed. Rep., 994).
Vegalahn v. Guntner (167 Mass., 92).
Western Union Telegraph Co. v. Boyer et al. (124 Fed. Rep., 246; U. S. Labor Bul. 50, p. 202).
Wabash Railroad Co. v. Hannahan et al. (121 Fed. Rep., 563; U. S. Labor Bul. 49, p. 1374).
Weber et al. (114 Fed. Rep., 590; U. S. Labor Bul. 43, p. 1295).
Waterhouse et al. v. Comer (55 Fed. Rep., 149).

Mr. VOLSTEAD. Mr. Chairman, I yield 20 minutes to the gentleman from Missouri [Mr. DYER].

Mr. [L. C.] DYER [R., Mo.]. Mr. Chairman and gentlemen of the committee, it has been my desire and purpose to discuss this bill in detail. The Committee on the Judiciary, of which I am a member, has given a great deal of time, taken much testimony, and worked with much diligence in its preparation. There are some items in this bill that are worthy of commendation; but taking the bill as a whole and all sections covering it I am quite sure that it would be unwise to enact it into law. With the conditions as they exist in the business world as a result of legislation heretofore enacted, my judgment is that the consideration of this subject ought to be left to the next session of Congress, or, better yet, to a future Congress, before it is finally considered. At this time we ought to give every opportunity to business to revive, if possible, and to get on its feet—adjusting itself, if it can, to the legislation that this Congress and the last Congress enacted into law.

For the reasons stated, Mr. Chairman, I can not support this bill. I would like to do so because of the high regard I have for the members of the majority of the Judiciary Committee that reported this bill. The distinguished chairman who leaves us, the gentleman from Alabama, Mr. CLAYTON, has rendered to that committee distinguished service, and he has left it with the love and esteem of every member of it. Now, we have succeeding him one of our ablest and most spendid Members, the gentleman from North Carolina [Mr. WEBB]. With Judge CLAYTON and Chairman WEBB, the two members of the committee that have worked most assiduously, and perhaps had more to do with the actual writing of this bill, have been that splendid lawyer and statesman, the gentleman from Arkansas, Judge FLOYD, and the no less able and distinguished gentleman from Virginia, Mr. CARLIN. But regardless of my high regard for these colleagues of mine on this great committee, and of their sincerity of purpose, there is much in it that ought to be left out. I would like for an opportunity to discuss it in detail, but, as I said, I can not do so at this time because of being compelled to leave Washington this evening on account of sickness. I commend to the House the diligence of the Judiciary Committee, and especially of the subcommittee of the majority which wrote this bill. I can not commend the result of their work, this so-called antitrust bill, and my advise to the House is to defeat the bill for the best interests of the Nation.

Mr. Chairman, as a member of the Judiciary Committee, I gave long and diligent consideration and study to the antitrust laws upon the statute books, with due regard as to what the needs might be as to amending same at this time. My views are expressed in the minority views, part 2, of the Report 627, which in part says:

> The antitrust laws on the statute books at this time have been carefully considered by the Supreme Court and judicially interpreted through a period of 24 years, and if properly enforced are believed by us to strip corporations and trusts of any power to injure or oppress.
>
> No possible good can come from constant interference with business. It is our belief that business should have a rest from further legislation and be given an opportunity to adjust itself to the environment created by the existing antitrust laws as the same have been interpreted and are now being administered.

The proposed legislation contains many new phrases and sets up new standards, all of which would require a period of years of interpretation by the courts before their full meaning can be definitely known by the business world.

It is very undesirable to bring about such a period of uncertainty and doubt to worry and harass the business of the country.

Our industries and business are now in a turmoil and making every possible effort to get along under the existing Democratic tariff laws. Conditions are very bad almost everywhere. The results of the tariff law are apparent to all and can not be successfully denied.

Mr. Chairman, my judgment is that the American people have and will continue to suffer enough during this administration on account of laws it has already enacted. Let the antitrust laws remain as they are for proper enforcement and interpretation and do not let us add further trouble by enacting ⊥ this bill. It will do no good and will do much harm to honest and legitimate business, now sorely pressed.

Comparing business conditions for the period from October 1 to April 1 of the present year with a like period of last year, we find that the imports under Democratic tariff were $13,000,000 greater than under the Republican tariff. More work for the foreigners. Less work for Americans. But the cost of living is higher now than when we had America for Americans.

Take another instance—materials used by manufacturers. During the period mentioned we find that under the Democratic tariff we imported $48,000,000 less than we did under Republican tariff. This is due to the fact that the foreign manufacturers are making the finished articles now and sending them to this country, to the disadvantage of our American manufacturers. This makes less work for our people and more for the foreigners. What about the two tariff laws for the same period as revenue producers? We find that during the first six months of that law—from October 1, 1913, to April 1, 1914—the customs receipts were $140,000,000. During the same period last year they were $165,000,000. During the same period the excess of expenditures for this year over receipts was $37,000,000. During the same period last year the excess of receipts over expenditures was $7,500,000. These figures show conclusively that the protective tariff is not only better for the American manufacturers and the American wage earner, but is also a better producer of revenue. In other words, it makes plain to all who want to know the truth that the Democratic idea of the tariff is disastrous to this country. What are the figures as regard foreign-manufactured goods imported into this country? The increase in imports of November, 1913, over that of November, 1912, was $2,000,000. The increase of imports in December, 1913, over December, 1912, was $7,000,000. The increase in January, 1914, over January, 1913, was $4,000,000. The increase in February, 1914, over February, 1913, was $5,000,000. The increase in imports of March, this year, as compared with March of a year ago, amounts to $8,000,000 to the credit of the foreigners. Now, look at the figures for exports of the same month. The exports in March, 1914, were $133,000,000; the exports in March, 1913, were $183,000,000. What does this show? That the goods we sold in foreign markets for the month of March this year decreased $50,000,000, as compared with March of last year. The figures also show that the imports greatly increased for the same month. How can anyone truthfully say that this Democratic tariff law benefits this country in any particular?

Men engaged in the productive enterprises of our own country stand idle while others engaged in similar enterprises in foreign countries are supplying our markets. The farmers find the products of other countries in the market which they have supplied during the entire period of our country's history. It would be impossible to exaggerate the demoralized conditions into which you have thrown our domestic affairs.

Our conditions at home are discouraging and depressing to laboring men and business men in every section of our country. Conditions at home are bad, but you have humiliated and made us ridiculous in the face of the world by your foreign policy—or perhaps I should say by your want of a foreign policy.

You are surrendering our right to control our own affairs in Panama to England and other nations that may claim any rights there. You are giving to Colombia greater rights in the use of the Panama Canal than you assert for the people of our own country, and giving that country $25,000,000 as a gratuity, and, besides, making an abject apology for taking the steps that made the construction of the canal possible. You are simply incompetent to manage the affairs of a Nation as great as ours. Your policies, while attractive in theory, can not be made to work out in practice. There has not been such a deplorable condition in our country since you were in full power 16 years ago. Speed the day when you shall surrender the reins of government to more competent hands, when the sound doctrine of a Republican protective tariff shall again be put upon the statutes, and also when a firm foreign policy shall be again our honored boast.

The deplorable and humiliating conditions in which we now find our country is too bad. It shames our pride in our great United States, the "land of the free and the home of the brave." It also hurts us to see want and suffering in this "land of plenty." Everybody feels it—cities and country. Farmers lose $65,000,000 alone this year from free importation of corn. Free meat, free butter, and so forth, add to his loss. But no one gets these articles any cheaper, do they? Five hundred thousand dollars a day is the loss to textile workers. Disaster faces every business and industry in this country, with the exportation of merchandise falling off $7,434,586 in a single month, and the imports of merchandise increasing for the same month, as compared with that of one year ago for the same month, April, to the amount of $26,446,263. We are sending less of our goods abroad and buying more from foreigners, and we should also remember that the figures here given tell only the beginning of the workings of this Democratic tariff law. Here are some more figures with regard to the goods manufactured abroad and brought here ready for consumption:

Imports of merchandise ready for consumption in March, 1914, showing increase compared with imports in the same month in 1913.

Products.	1914 values.	1913 values.	Increase.	Per cent Increase.
Aluminum, manufactures of	$168,000	$60,767	$107,233	176.4
Watches, and parts of	317,329	205,280	112,049	54.5
Cotton cloths	1,402,071	721,902	680,169	94.2
Stockings	417,473	241,455	176,018	72.8
Other knit goods	366,251	44,675	321,576	719.8
Linen yarns	95,248	55,938	39,290	70.1
Fruit and nuts	4,012,244	3,088,108	924,136	29.9
Glassware	768,349	498,674	269,675	54
Cutlery	272,460	146,979	125,481	85.3
Tin plate	185,130	23,298	161,832	694.6
Leather and tanned skins	1,556,342	635,669	920,673	141.8
Gloves	990,977	755,242	235,735	31.2
Paper, and manufactures of	2,529,933	1,783,048	746,885	41.8
Manufactures of silk	3,695,975	2,604,608	1,001,367	37.1
Vegetables	1,423,939	960,857	463,082	48.1
Wool:				
Class 1	5,253,229	2,681,544	2,571,685	95.9
Class 2	616,845	383,638	233,207	60.7
Class 3	2,066,013	1,197,512	868,591	72.6
Woolen cloths	1,396,010	328,974	1,067,936	324
Dress goods	740,928	225,973	514,955	227
Wearing apparel	170,480	165,087	5,393	3.2
All other manufactures of wool	772,544	95,617	676,927	707
Total	29,218,670	16,994,865	12,223,805	71.9

Let me call attention to a few of the increases. For instance, on manufactures of aluminum the increase is 176.4 per cent. The increases on cotton cloths are 94.2 per cent. The increase on other knit goods is 719.8 per cent; on tinplate, 694.6 per cent.

On leather and tanned skins there is an increase of 144.8 per cent; on woolen cloths an increase of 324 per cent; on wearing apparel an increase of only 3.2 per cent; on dress goods an increase of 227 per cent; on all other manufactures of wool an increase of 707 per cent. The total average increase of goods ready for consumption during the month of March, this year, over the month of March, 1913, is 71.9 per cent. Then people wonder why so many of our mills are closed. People are asking why so many of our laboring men are out of employment. These figures tell the story. In the report of the Secretary of the Department of Commerce, just made, he states the value of the finished manufactures imported in six months. According to this report, there was imported in six months under the new tariff, from October 1 to April 1, of finished manufactures $228,000,000, against $215,000,000 in the same period last year, an increase of $13,000,000, which would represent a loss to American labor of more than $2,000,000 a month in wages.

The value of manufacturers' material imported in the first six months of the new Democratic tariff law is $469,000,000, against $517,000,000 last year. In other words, our labor worked with $50,000,000 less raw material during the last six months than last year.

The value of the manufactures exported in the first six months of the new tariff law decreased from $582,000,000 to $541,000,000, a loss in American trade of $41,000,000 in the last six months, or a little less than $8,000,000 a month to American labor.

These startling figures illustrate the unwisdom of recent tariff changes and call loudly for a reassertion of the historic policy of protection to American industry and labor. . . .

Mr. AVIS. Mr. Chairman and gentlemen of the committee, I want to confine my remarks to the probable effect of section 3 of the bill under consideration on one of the greatest industries of this country, namely, the bituminous-coal industry. In discussing this question I wish to say to you gentlemen that I do not approach the discussion from a partisan standpoint, but I approach it with the sincere belief that if section 3 becomes a law it will destroy the small mine owner and the small producer of the United States engaged in the bituminous-coal industry. Section 3 reads as follows:

> That it shall be unlawful for the owner or operator of any mine or for any person controlling the product of any mine engaged in selling its product in commerce to refuse arbitrarily to sell such product to a responsible person, firm, or corporation who applies to purchase such product for use, consumption, or resale.

You will note that I have emphasized the words "or resale." The presumable purpose of the Judiciary Committee, as expressed in its report, among other things, is to accomplish the following:

> The design is to prevent those who have acquired or may acquire a monopoly or partial monopoly of mines from discriminating against certain manufacturers, railroads, or other persons who need the products of the mines in carrying on their industry.

And in another part of the report is found the following language:

> By its enactment into law we make it impossible for mere ownership of mines to enable the owners or those disposing of the products thereof to direct the disposal of such products into monopolistic channels of trade. It will liberate from the power of the trust every small manufacturer who is compelled to go into the open market for his raw material and every person who desires to purchase coal for use or for resale to those who desire to purchase for use or consumption, and will afford to every such manufacturer an opportunity to purchase same for cash wherever offered for sale in commerce. The section expressly forbids the mine owner or person controlling the sale of the product of the mine to arbitrarily refuse to sell such product to any responsible purchaser, and thereby prevents the mine owner or operator from giving the preference to another and rival dealer in the disposal of such product.

Now, I am convinced, gentlemen, from what has been said here upon the floor, not meaning to impugn the motives or good faith of the committee, because I feel sure the committee is trying to do what it thinks is best for the people and the industries of our country, that section 3 was inserted in the bill without full knowledge or consideration of the past or present condition of the bituminous-coal industry.

In the first place, there is no such thing as a monopoly of the bituminous-coal industry of this country. The large number of persons and corporations engaged in mining bituminous coal prevents a monopoly of that industry. The only coal industry that I have ever heard mentioned as being in the class of monopolies is the anthracite-coal industry.

Do you know that, at this time, there are over 3,500 separate and distinct persons and concerns in this country operating over 6,000 bituminous and semibituminous coal mines? Not only is this true, but not much more than 50 per cent of the coal lands of this country are owned by the men who operate the mines thereon. As a matter of fact, the great majority of the small operators and producers, and a large number of the big operators and producers, lease the lands upon which their respective mines are established and pay royalties therefor on their respective productions.

The amount of capital invested in the soft-coal mines of this country in 1909 was $1,062,000,000. The number of miners engaged in this industry is nearly 600,000. The principal bituminous coal-producing States are Pennsylvania, West Virginia, Illinois, Ohio, Indiana, Alabama, Colorado, Kentucky, Iowa, Kansas Wyoming, Tennessee, Virginia, and Washington. The output of the mines is worth about $450,000,000 per annum. Of this amount, over $300,000,000 is paid out in wages and salaries each year.

No country in the world enjoys such cheap fuel as the United States. At this time we are shipping coal from West Virginia and placing it in the New England market, after paying the freight charges of more than $2.10 per ton, at a less price than it is sold at the pit mouth at Cardiff, Wales. There is an overproduction instead of an underproduction of bituminous coal, and, due to the present bad business conditions existing throughout the country and the great competition in this business, since the 1st of January of this year the coal mines of West Virginia have not run on an average of over two to two and one-half days a week. I am informed that conditions are similar in other States.

Competition is so great and has been so severe for the past five years that Mr. E. W. Parker, of the United States Geological Survey, in an address delivered before the American Mining Congress at Philadelphia last October stated that the profit on coal in the States of West Virginia, Illinois, Indiana, and Ohio for the year 1909 did not net 1 per cent on the capital actually invested in the plants in the four States. Business conditions in this country to-day are certainly much worse than they were in 1909. In the past 10 years railway freights, labor, and supplies used in the mines have advanced more than 50 per cent, taxes have about doubled, and other conditions pertaining to mining, brought about by State legislation, have gone toward increasing the cost of production; whereas the price of bituminous coal to-day is no higher than 8 or 10 years ago. In fact, coal is selling to-day at a lower price than at any time during the past 10 years.

Why, then, should coal be singled out for special legislation, conditions be made impossible, and the business be more demoralized? It would be far better for us to extend a helping hand to those engaged in and dependent upon this industry, so that the coal fields of the country could be conserved and profit enough be made to enable the mine owners to pay better wages to and to throw more safeguards around the men working in the mines.

You must remember that the price of coal at the mines is but a small part of the ultimate cost to the consumer, and experience has taught us that the public has suffered more because of the "middlemen" than from those engaged in mining coal.

Section 3 is vicious, drastic, and sweeping. In my humble opinion its operation will work greater hardships than those it professedly seeks to relieve, will prove detrimental to the mining interests of the country, and will upset and make worse existing conditions, now certainly bad enough.

The small coal producer can not afford to maintain selling agencies throughout the country. He may have a superior quality of coal that he is producing, and, as you gentlemen may know who live in mining sections, there are as many different qualities of bituminous coal and as many uses to which it may be put as there are grades of and uses to which timber or cotton may be put.

Assume that I am a small operator engaged in producing coal in the State of West Virginia.

In passing I might call your attention to the fact that there are nearly 900 coal mines in the State of West Virginia devoted to the production of coal and the making of coke, which give employment to 73,000 coal miners. West Virginia produces about one-sixth of all the bituminous coal produced in this country, and upon the coal industry of that State nearly one-third of its population depends for its livelihood. The great majority of the mines in West Virginia are owned by persons or companies whose capital is not large. This is true of the coal mines generally throughout the

United States. A majority of the mines in West Virginia will not average over 400 tons production per day.

Assume further that I have a superior quality of coal that I carefully mine and prepare for the market. I am trying to specialize, and my trade and business have been built up on the quality, preparation, and reputation of my coal. My output is limited. In securing my labor and in making my expenditures I am compelled to look to the future. I have four or five regular customers who have been dealing with me for years and of whose custom I am reasonably assured. Suppose that some competitor, a big corporation, with whose coal my coal is competing in some particular market, desires to injure my trade or the reputation of my coal or to deprive me of my regular customers. If this section becomes a law, I would be compelled to sell to him such portion of my output as he should apply for, I would be required, upon demand, to turn over my production to him, to work me or my coal such injury as he might elect. What is to prevent him, under this section, coming and saying to me, "I want to buy your entire output this year," and thus leave me without coal to supply any of my customers?

Mr. [CHARLES A.] TALCOTT [D., N.Y.]. Do you think that refusal would be an arbitrary refusal to sell to competitors?

Mr. AVIS. I think, in view of section 2 of this bill, it would be. Under the circumstances just detailed, I should certainly enjoy the freedom of contract and have the right to prefer the customers whose trade I have secured by years of work and the expenditure of large sums of money; but it is provided in section 2 of this bill—

That nothing herein contained shall prevent persons engaged in selling goods, wares, or merchandise in commerce from selecting their own customers, except as provided in section 3 of this act.

It is thus expressly provided that a mine owner can not and must not select his own customers.

What is meant by the words "refuse arbitrarily"? The extent of the evil of section 3 depends largely upon the words "refuse arbitrarily" and "responsible person, firm, or corporation." Yesterday, in asking questions of the gentleman from North Carolina [Mr. WEBB] relative to this section, I called his attention to the fact that the word "arbitrarily" had only been defined in one case—a West Virginia case. The court held that "arbitrarily" means "without any reason therefor." There is also an English decision that holds that the word "arbitrary" means "not supported by fair, solid, and substantial cause, and without reason given."

Any mine owner can give a reason for refusing to sell his product. If any reason is sufficient, then the section will only be useless and unavailing. If the section means that a mine owner must give a sufficient reason for his refusal to sell his product, the language of the section is uncertain, indefinite, and confusing, and the evil effects thereof can be appreciated at a glance, because of the uncertainty of the construction that may be placed thereon by the courts.

Just look at the dangers that a mine owner will be exposed to. Some dealer might make application to him for the purchase of his product. The dealer might be perfectly responsible financially, but at the same time might be unreliable in other ways, or might have some ulterior motive and might intend to treat his coal unfairly. The mine owner might be doubtful as to his purpose and refuse to sell him his product for a reason, that to the mine owner was a good one, but which was not satisfactory to the dealer. What will the dealer do? He might immediately institute a criminal prosecution against the mine owner and expose him to the danger of a year's imprisonment in jail, or a fine of $5,000, or both; and might also bring a civil suit against him for three times the amount of damages the dealer may claim to have sustained. . . .

Mr. FESS. One of the things that puzzles me in this section is that we all know there is a wide difference between purchasers. One may be just as responsible as the other, but he may be tardy in the payment of his bills. He may allow his paper to go to protest, and one of the quickest ways to bring that kind of a man to time is to refuse to sell him under the present law, but what would you do under this law?

Mr. AVIS. Undoubtedly, that is true. That is one of the difficulties here. The words "refuse arbitrarily" are not only dangerous, but the words that you refer to—"responsible person, firm, or corporation"—are almost as dangerous. Who is a "responsible person, firm, or corporation"? What is meant by "responsible"? "Financially responsible" is not sufficient. A person may be perfectly responsible financially, but he may be my competitor; he may be unprincipled; he may want my coal for some unfair purpose; he may want to control my output; he may want to sell it under an incorrect name or substitute it for other coals or other coals for it. In that sense he is not a "responsible" person. . . .

Mr. [CHARLES F.] BOOHER [D., Mo.]. I would like to ask the gentleman if he thinks it would be an arbitrary refusal to sell coal in circumstances such as detailed by the gentleman from Ohio [Mr. FESS] in the question that he just asked you?

Mr. AVIS. Hardly; but—

Mr. BOOHER. Now, here is a man, according to his statement, who is known to be slow in his settlements; he permits his paper to go to protest, and he comes to you to buy your property, but you say to him, "I can not sell to you; you are poor pay; your paper goes to protest." Is that an arbitrary refusal that would haul a man into any court on earth?

Mr. AVIS. I say frankly to the gentleman that in itself I do not believe it would be. But who is to determine as to the responsibility of the person who applies to purchase? What kind of responsibility is meant? . . .

Mr. FESS. Would not he be a responsible dealer, with plenty of ability to pay, and yet would not pay until he was forced to do so?

Mr. BOOHER. That would be one of the strongest reasons why it would not be arbitrary. If he had abundant resources and was abundantly able to pay and would let his paper go to protest, he ought not to be trusted by anybody. A man has to protect himself in business necessarily. I want to understand this section, because I think it is a very important one. Now, in the case you illustrated you mined your coal, you put it out and got it ready for sale, and you had your customers who took all your coal.

Now, you say, "Suppose a dealer comes to me and offers to buy all my coal. Under this section I am bound to sell to him. My refusal would be arbitrary." Do you think that that would be an arbitrary refusal?

Mr. AVIS. I think so, under the provisions of this section and section 2 of the bill. I can not escape that conclusion.

Mr. BOOHER. You have mined your coal for us, and you have said to the other gentleman who came, "My coal is all sold. I promised it to Mr. Smith and Mr. Jones and Mr. Brown." Now, tell me how it could possibly be considered an arbitrary refusal for you to sell your coal to us instead of to the man who came to buy that coal?

Mr. AVIS. I am glad the gentleman asked the question, and if his position is correct—and I assume that his question states his position—then section 3 is absolutely futile and unavailing in view of what the committee has stated that it seeks to accomplish. The committee has stated in reporting upon this section that the very purpose of it is to compel the mine operator to sell to the first responsible person, firm, or corporation who applies to purchase his product and not to discriminate against such person, firm, or corporation for some favorite customer that he may have. If you are aiming at an abuse, that abuse must be the abuse of discrimination. If you are aiming at, as suggested, the big corporations that control the output of certain mines and refuse to sell, say, copper to certain manufacturers, then the section will be unavailing if they are permitted to say, "We will reserve our product for Mr. Smith or Mr. Brown or Mr. Jones," as the case may be.

Mr. BOOHER. Is not the object of the committee here the prevention of monopoly? Or do you say you have to put your whole supply in the hands of some big dealer? Is not that the thing they are trying to avoid here?

Mr. AVIS. I think so; but this section will aid the big dealer, and instead of destroying monopoly—and I am with the gentleman on that score, for I am just as much opposed to a monopoly of the coal business as anybody else is in this House—I believe and prophesy in all sincerity that this section will destroy competition, produce bankruptcy, and in time create monopoly if it is enacted into law, with the knowledge that I have of the coal business. . . .

Mr. FESS. I would like to have the opinion of the gentleman as to the latitude of the word "arbitrary." If this particular deal or that particular deal is not arbitrary, who will say whether it is arbitrary or not?

Mr. AVIS. That is what I would like to know. As I said a few moments ago, I believe the evil effects of the section depend largely upon the construction which will be placed upon the words "refuse arbitrarily." It is a dangerous thing to leave the words open without any definition of their meaning. If we take the ordinary and common definition of "arbitrary" and the definition that has been given by the courts, the word means "without any reason"; and if it means without any reason, section 2 of the bill will be useless and will amount to nothing, because every mine owner can give some reason for refusal. . . .

Mr. FESS. Is it not true that the one feature of the Sherman antitrust law that has given most trouble is the feature of the "rule of reason"—the question of what is reasonable and what is not? It has been in litigation ever since the time the word was used.

Mr. AVIS. Yes. I think the majority of the Judiciary Committee is trying to overcome some alleged defect of the Shernan antitrust law; but in this instance, instead of overcoming any of the alleged defects of the Sherman antitrust law, it is my opinion and that of the coal producers from whom I have heard—and I have had letters from a large number of them who operate in West Virginia—that section 3 will eliminate or destroy every small coal producer and dealer in this country, and will ultimately build up a monopoly of the coal business.

There are three classes of coal companies. To the first class belong the large companies which have tonnage sufficient to place their product in the different markets which they can reach, and they have sales departments with branch offices located in all of the large distributing centers, and in this way are not forced to employ agents to sell their coal on commission, or brokers who do likewise. Such large companies, therefore, are in a position to accept orders from anybody who may come to them in the respective territory in which they are located.

To the second class belong the companies which sell part of their product to their own representatives in certain markets, and which may give to an agent or broker, who may sell on commission, territory in which they sell a certain number of thousands of tons during the year. The sales which this class of companies may make direct are not restricted in any way, excepting by tonnage to supply orders, or by reason of doubt as to the payment for the coal, but in such territory as they give over to an agent, similar to the territory in the New England States which it [sic] given over to agents, it is not within the power of such selling company, under present conditions, to accept orders from anybody else within that particular territory.

To the third class belong the companies whose tonnage is not large, and which are not able to establish offices and put their own salesmen on the road to make sales, which are entirely dependent upon what is known as the agent or broker to contract for their tonnage, which sell the same on commission; and the coal companies which have a few certain customers to whom they directly sell, and it is the third class which will likely ⊥ be destroyed by the provisions of section 3 of the bill, for agents or brokers will not make contracts with the mine owners unless they are given certain territory to sell in.

The great majority of those engaged in the mining of coal are men who have come from the ranks, men who secured their knowledge of coal mining by practical experience. A great number of these men have no knowledge of the sales end of the business.

There is a wide difference between the mining end and the sales end of the business. The people at the mines are not in touch with the peculiar and varying market conditions, and in the majority of cases when they have attempted to market their product they have not been successful. These mine owners are almost entirely dependent upon agents, brokers, or dealers, and these agents, brokers, and dealers are responsible for the expansion of the industry.

For instance, the jobber in Chicago, covering the West and Northwest, can sell West Virginia coal in that territory to much better advantage than the producer could. His traveling expenses are less; he is closer to his trade; and the trade itself prefers to buy nearer home. But if the jobber has to send men out all over his territory to work up a trade for any particular coal; if he has to advertise and circularize it, only to find, what would be possible under section 3 of this bill, that the consumer or a rival jobber or the operator himself could take that business away from him, then, indeed, there would be no incentive for him to push any particular grade of coal or to try to expand the market for the coal of any particular State.

The agents and brokers selling on commission, and particularly the small dealers throughout the country, could be driven out of business under this bill. Their customers could apply directly to the mine owners and compel them to sell to them, if responsible, and could thereby eliminate such dealers, agents, and brokers. This would be destructive to the coal dealers of the country who have given years of their lives to the upbuilding and development of their business and have large sums of money invested therein. . . .

Mr. AVIS. Now, what will this result in? Suppose that I am a small coal operator; that a dealer is representing my coal in a certain territory in which, at great expense of labor and money, he has built up a trade. What, under this section, will prevent the trade he has built up from coming directly to me, and thus deprive him of the fruits of his labor in that territory? In any event, what is to prevent a large competitor from eliminating me as a factor in that particular territory by buying up my entire output, either by himself or through some other person or agent? Those are some of the evils that are to be met if this section becomes the law.

Another thing I want to impress upon you is— . . .

Mr. HARDY. I suppose the gentleman would concede that if he could present to any court the facts that the purpose of this buyer to whom you refuse to sell was simply to eliminate you, your refusal would not be held to be arbitrary?

Mr. AVIS. Absolutely; but how can I show that? I can not look into the gentleman's breast and know what motives actuate him when he applies to purchase my coal. Again, the section will be unavailing if I am to have the right to question your motives when you offer to buy my coal. And there is no more reason why the coal industry—I am referring to the bituminous-coal industry—should be selected for such special legislation than the timber industry or any other industry. It is true that coal is a natural product, but no more so than timber, no more so than cotton and wheat. I will concede that if the industry were in the hands of a monopoly it would not only be our right but it would be our duty to pass laws to prevent a monopoly of that kind; but when the coal business is in the shape that it is in to-day, when very few, if any, of the men engaged in producing coal have made a dollar during the last year— and I doubt whether more than a very few of them have made anything in the past five years—why make it criminal for the small producer to endeavor to survive? Why force him into bankruptcy because he can not compete with his large competitor, who has selling agencies of his own to dispose of his product? You can readily see that if I am a small operator and my customers are likely to be taken away from me, and I can not prefer them this year over some other applicant, as has been expressly provided by this bill, I will not know what orders I will be assured of next year. If I am deprived of my customers this year by one man who buys my whole product or, say, by a half dozen men who in times of strikes or scarcity of coal are not regular customers, and who buy my entire product, what am I going to do next year for customers? I will have to go out into the market and scramble for new customers and if I am a small operator, with a small margin of capital upon which to work, and can not promptly secure orders, I will have to go to the wall, and there will be no redress for me.

Mr. HARDY. Would you not be in better shape if other business were placed in the same category with you? I take it that if you could present to the court the fact that you were necessarily required to refuse to sell to one customer because you had other customers whom you had agreed to supply, you could not be held to be arbitrarily refusing to sell. But would you not be in a little better shape if section 3 were amended so as to make it apply to all business?

Mr. AVIS. I do not know. I have not though of that. I know this, that section 2 provides that if I am engaged in interstate coal business I can not select my own customers.

Mr. HARDY. Except upon the theory that your business is already a monopoly.

Mr. AVIS. There is no one who charges a monopoly of the coal business. Living for 25 years, as I have, in a coal region, I have absolutely never heard of a single abuse that this section is stated to be aimed at. And I ask any gentleman within the sound of my voice to recall an instance when a responsible buyer or a responsible dealer could not purchase bituminous coal. The man who mines the coal and takes the risks must have the right, as long as he has no monopoly, to prefer and to discriminate in favor of his own customers, and to arbitrarily, in some instances, refuse to sell his coal to others.

Mr. [JOSEPH] TAGGART [D., Kan.]. How can a coal dealer be damaged if he is simply compelled to sell his product at the market price? You say there is an overproduction. Would it not help it out some if some one had a right to take your output and lay down the money for it?

Mr. AVIS. I will answer the gentleman's question by an illustration, if he will pardon me. Suppose the gentleman from Texas [Mr. HARDY] is a large coal operator. Suppose that I am a small mine owner and have a certain number of customers. What is to prevent the gentleman from Texas, whose coal is in competition with my coal, sending his agents to me and buying my coal for this year, and when my customers find that I can not supply them, what do they do? They will go to some operator or dealer who can supply them, and they will probably be lost to me for the future. . . .

Mr. TAGGART. Up to date we have said nothing about the price. I presume the gentleman had in mind the market price, as everyone else did. But if you had contracted to deliver your whole output to me, then you have a right to refuse the gentleman from Texas.

Mr. AVIS. The Constitution of the United States, in my opinion, would protect the obligation of such a contract. But I am talking of a case where the contract is not made and where I simply hope that the man who has been my customer for years will continue to give me his trade, and where he has been taken away from me by some person purchasing all of my coal and preventing me from supplying him. Now, will the gentleman permit me to answer him further by asking a question? The gentleman is a lawyer, is he not?

Mr. TAGGART. I have been charged with that.

Mr. AVIS. All right. Now, why should not the gentleman be required to furnish his services to the first responsible bidder? Why should the gentleman be permitted to select whom he will serve or not serve as an attorney any more than a coal operator, unless he has a monopoly of that business?

Mr. TAGGART. My services are not one of the products that nature has furnished, to begin with.

Mr. AVIS. I hope nature had something to do with it. [Laughter.]

Mr. TAGGART. Well, I have observed cases where nature seemed to have fallen short.

Mr. AVIS. That is doubtless true.

Mr. TAGGART. Anyhow, we will not bandy words over that. This section of the bill is intended—

Mr. AVIS. Will the gentleman please confine himself to a question, unless he can give me a little more time.

Mr. TAGGART. I will put it interrogatively. Is not this section intended to correct this particular abuse, to relieve persons who absolutely must have coal, and who have been arbitrarily refused by those who produce the coal?

Mr. AVIS. I think the answer to that question would come better from the gentleman. I know of no such abuse. Does the gentleman know of any such abuse?

Mr. TAGGART. I do not come from a coal region.

Mr. AVIS. But the gentleman comes from a coal-consuming region. Do you know of a single instance, or can any member of this committee point to a single instance where a responsible buyer could not get coal if he wanted it?

Mr. TAGGART. If that is the situation, there will never be a case under this section, if that happy condition continues.

Mr. AVIS. I am afraid the gentleman is not acquainted with the sharp competition that exists in the coal business in this country. And I want to say, in this connection, that a late report issued by the United States Government shows that the average selling price of soft coal at the mines in the United States is $1.15 a ton. On the other hand the same report shows that the Government is operating a mine in one of the Western States—I do not recall whether it is in one of the Dakotas or Nevada—and it is costing the Government $1.65 a ton to get out its coal.

The competition is so sharp and so severe that the mines have not for years been running full time. My remarks are directed to bituminous coal, for I know nothing about the anthracite coal region. I believe I did call attention to the fact that Mr. E. W. Parker, of the United States Geological Survey, stated that in 1909 the coal industries of Indiana, Illinois, Ohio, and West Virginia combined did not make but 1 per cent on the capital invested. I mention these things to show that there is no monopoly of the soft coal industry, and that the mine owners should be given the right to select their customers.

The coal business of the country is entitled to at least a little consideration. Let me call attention to one effect of the present tariff law. Prior to the acquisition of the Hawaiian Islands by the United States those engaged in commerce between Hawaii and the United States had the right to secure the cheapest transportation possible. The result was that they availed themselves of the cheapest transportation, and if a Japanese ship or a British ship or an American ship, or whichever ship offered them the cheapest transportation, they patronized that ship.

We have a law that requires that all commerce between the United States and Hawaii shall be carried in American bottoms.

Now, we had a protective duty on coal of 45 cents a ton. That permitted us to ship and sell coal to Hawaii. What has the Democratic majority done? By your taking off all the duty on coal and admittting it free we have absolutely lost the Hawaiian market to our coal, and it is now supplied by Austrailia in British bottoms. . . .

Mr. WEBB. The gentleman understands that the law of which he complains was made by the Republican Party, compelling passenger and freight traffic between the ports of the United States to be carried in American coastwise vessels. When we took over Hawaii a public official ruled that the Hawaiian Islands were a part of the coast of the United States, and did the very thing the gentleman complains of.

Mr. AVIS. Neither the Republican Party nor a Republican official ruled that the gentleman's party should take off the countervailing duty on coal so that American coal could not compete with Australian coal. That is what the gentleman's party did, and we can not now put a ton of coal in the Hawaiian market.

Now, I want to read, in connection with my remarks, portions of a letter received by me from a most distinguished gentleman of West Virginia, Mr. Edward W. Knight, who has given years of study to the coal business. I desire to call attention to the fact that he is one of the leading Democrats of that State. I wrote him about section 3, and he replied as follows:

> If it is the purpose of the bill to prohibit all preferences and discrimination by sellers of the products of mines as between customers or persons desiring to become customers, whether consumers or middle men, that purpose is both unfair and dangerous.
>
> Mining and selling of coal is not a business in the nature of public service; if it were, it would and should have, among other things, the right of eminent domain, which has always been denied by the courts, notwithstanding some legislative attempts to relieve hardships by undertaking to give rights of ingress and egress, drainage, etc., over the lands of others. Nor is mining monopolistic in its nature; certainly soft-coal mining is not.
>
> In the absence of a monopolistic character and of protection by a fixed schedule of prices binding sellers and buyers there is neither necessity for nor justice in such regulation of the business as is practiced with respect to carriers, telegraph companies, water companies, etc.
>
> The coal producer, like other merchants, has always discriminated, and I think must always be permitted to discriminate between customers or would-be customers. The best prices are given and should be given to the customer who buys the largest quantity or pays most promptly, or who buys at a time of year when business otherwise might be slack, or who makes a contract for a year or a term of years. Similarly in times of strikes or shortage of product from other causes the coal producer usually gives and should be permitted to give preference to his old customers and to customers whose business would be most hurt by shutting down or whose shutting down would cause public inconvenience, such as manufacturing industries requiring continuous operation and water works, lighting and traction companies. It would be most unfair to require a coal producer to sell coal to a person who has never before

been his customer, who is brought to him only by an emergency, and who will not be his customer again except under a similar emergency, when he knows or anticipates that the same coal is wanted by a concern that has been his customer for years and which he desires to continue to supply. It would be most unfair also to require a producer of coal to sell his coal to a competitor in order to enable the competitor to take a contract or to supply a contract already taken, which would perhaps prevent the seller from bidding on that particular contract or from taking other contracts for himself. An enterprising dealer might secure a contract and prevent the price being lowered by competition by taking the precaution to insist on buying the output of probable competitors for the contract for one or two months, preventing them from bidding on the contract and leaving them after losing the contract to look elsewhere for the disposing of their output for the remaining 10 or 11 months of the year.

I have known business men of ample financial responsibility, but whose reputations were such that a producer who valued his reputation and that of his coal would not want to have his coal sold by or through them; yet such a dealer under the proposed law might force such sale. A small amount of superior coal in the hands of an unscrupulous man habitually dealing in an inferior coal might seriously injure the reputation of the involuntary seller of the superior coal and aid in defrauding the customers of the unscrupulous dealer—

> How many men in this House can tell the difference between one kind of bituminous coal and another? And yet there is all the difference in the world—

Also such a law might lead to most reckless and harmful dealing in "futures." A man of small responsibility might take contracts with the intention of filling them by virtually condemning the necessary coal if prices during the time of performance should be low and of not filling the contract if prices should be high. It would result in a complete demoralization of market conditions and put a premium upon business immorality. And the law would inevitably be taken advantage of by speculators in times where high prices were anticipated to the disadvantage both of more conservative producers and merchants and of the consumers.

Finally such a law would practically prevent the maintenance of exclusive agencies. There is nothing else that is so vital a factor in the extension of a business to new markets as the establishing of exclusive agencies, whether they be middle men selling on commission or a branch office or agency of a producer or a principal selling agent. In either case the extension of a business in new territory means large expenses in the way of office rent, employment of salesmen, solicitors, clerks, etc., and advertising. It is the custom to protect the person incurring such expense by giving him the exclusive right of handling the product within his territory. And it would be most unfair to permit a coal dealer who is pushing the sale of one coal and who finds a customer who will not purchase his coal, but desires a coal handled through another dealer with an exclusive agency to insist upon a sale being made through him, depriving the exclusive agent of the other coal of the reward of his time, labor, and expense. In this aspect the bill would be paralyzing in its effect upon efforts to extend business and increase competition in any given territory.

If the reasons which I have above indicated as possibly dictating a refusal to make a sale, or a discrimination between customers, and other reasons which might be given if this letter were not already too long, which might appeal to the honest judgment of a fair-minded business man, would justify him in refusing to make a sale, then the bill is not so objectionable. But in such case, it seems to me, that the bill would be a useless one, since the existing antitrust act suffices to punish an attempt at monopoly or the restraint of trade or elevations of prices by corrupt agreement in respect to any article of interstate commerce, and gives any party thereby injured an ample right of action.

I have not considered the constitutionality of the section, which seems to me open to grave doubt, but for the practical reasons given the act seems an injustifiable attempt to interfere with a private business—a business which has none of the privileges or benefits enjoyed by public-service corporations, and either vicious or useless.

> I hope, under the circumstances, that the Members of the House will give this matter serious consideration before they further injure an industry which gives employment in my State alone to 73,000 coal miners and on which nearly one-third of the people of West Virginia depend, and an industry which is fraught with many financial risks to the mine owner and with many personal risks to the men who dig and mine the coal and face untold dangers underground.
>
> When you take into consideration the many perils and dangers which the men who dig and mine the coal daily face, they should be the best-paid laborers in the world; and nothing should be done by Congress which would even tend to injure or cripple the industry in which they are engaged or lessen their opportunity for better wages and living conditions.

I will be glad to furnish the gentlemen in charge of the bill with a great number of letters pointing out some of the evils of this section. The gentlemen from whom I have received such letters had not heard of this section until I called their attention thereto. I did not know that such a section was in the bill until I came across it a few days ago, and I immediately communicated with those who produce the coal in my district and asked their opinion thereon. Without exception, every man who has written to me about this section is bitterly opposed to its being made a law. . . .

Mr. [EDMUND] PLATT [R., N.Y.]. I have received one or two letters that lead me to think that some people have the idea that this section is aimed against the retail coal dealers, so that a customer who was not satisfied with their prices could go directly to the mine and purchase coal.

Mr. AVIS. Yes; this section will not only injure the mine operator, but the dealers as well. The coal dealer who has gone to great expense to acquire a yard and teams and the other necessary paraphernalia, and to work up a trade by personal solicitation and expensive advertising, can be eliminated either by the mine owner or his customers, because if this section becomes a law his customers can purchase directly from the mine owner and the mine owner will be compelled to sell directly to such customers.

For this further reason I think the gentlemen in charge of this bill should not insist upon the passage of this section, and if they are going to insist upon its passage and are going to leave the words "refuse arbitrarily" therein they should at least define them so that the mine owner will not be left to guess what may happen to him if he is prosecuted or sued in the courts for any refusal which he may in self-defense be compelled to make to sell his product upon demand.

And you can see why. As I stated before, if I were a mine owner every person to whom I might refuse to sell my coal, however good the reason might be to me, would have the right not only to institute a criminal prosecution against me, but he would have the right to bring a civil suit for what he claims to be threefold damages. Therefore you can see the dangers and perils to which a man who is engaged in the business of mining coal may be exposed. . . .

Mr. FESS. I am president of a college. We buy a great deal of coal. We always buy from dealers at home. Suppose I send to you directly for the amount of coal I want. Can you refuse to sell to me, although you do not know what my standing is?

Mr. AVIS. I do not know. That is what I want to know. Upon whom is placed the burden of determining whether the person who applies to purchase coal or other minerals is a responsible person or not? The seller? Is he to determine whether the person is responsible or not? Under this bill I can not determine.

Mr. FESS. I live in western Ohio, and the gentleman lives in West Virginia. I buy West Virginia coal, and I desire to buy it directly from the gentleman. I send you an order for it. What is your responsibility if you refuse to fill the order?

Mr. AVIS. I am subject to a possible $5,000 fine and to a year's imprisonment, or both, and I am subject to threefold damages if any ensue.

Mr. BARTLETT. Does the gentleman think it is the province of Congress, under the power to regulate commerce, to regulate these particular contracts which do not in effect impede commerce or create a monopoly?

Mr. AVIS. I do not.

Mr. BARTLETT. Is it not taking away from the citizen the right to make a contract to sell a product where he makes no effort either to monopolize or impede or interfere with commerce?

Mr. AVIS. I am glad the gentleman asked me that question.

Mr. BARTLETT. In other words, unless a man so uses his own property as to injure others the freedom of contract exists in this by reason of the constitutional guaranties. Now, to say arbitrarily that you can not, when you are not undertaking to have a monopoly and have not a monopoly, when you do not undertake to interfere with commerce but simply to make a contract for the sale of a product, does the gentleman think Congress, under what is known as the commerce clause of the Constitution, can limit and restrict that privilege of the citizens to contract?

Mr. AVIS. I do not think so. I think that the freedom and right of citizens to contract in regard to their property can only be limited or restricted by Congress in some instances. If the contract or contemplated contract is for an unlawful purpose, Congress can lawfully legislate; otherwise I think such legislation is unconstitutional. I have not attempted to discuss the constitutionality of the section. This section does not prevent one competitor from absorbing another competitor, or competitors, but in effect permits and legalizes such absorption. In the Northern Securities case the Supreme Court of the United States held that one competitor could not absorb another competitor, and that if he did he violated the provisions of the Sherman antitrust law.

Mr. BARTLETT. The purpose of that holding company, the Northern Securities Co., was for the purpose of interfering with commerce and destroying competition.

Mr. AVIS. Absolutely; and that is the point that I am making about this section, that it will permit one competitor to absorb another competitor, although the Supreme Court of the United States has held, not only in the Northern Securities case, but in the Standard Oil and Tobacco cases, that such absorption is unlawful.

Mr. BARTLETT. But unless we change the present antitrust law that law as construed by the Supreme Court would prevent that.

Mr. AVIS. But this will conflict with that and then where will we be?

Mr. BARTLETT. At sea.

Mr. AVIS. If this bill becomes a law, we will not know which is to apply to and govern sales to competitors of an entire output, the Sherman antitrust law or this law; and for that reason, and others already given, I believe that the small mine owners of this country, upon whom several hundred thousand of our laboring men depend, and from whom for every ton of coal mined labor receives an average of about 80 cents, will be left in uncertainty and doubt.

Mr. BARTLETT. I was not applying this solely to coal, I desire to say.

Mr. AVIS. My remark was addressed more particularly to coal because I know something about coal and I do not know so much about other minerals. . . .

Mr. TALCOTT of New York. I understand the gentleman to say that the prohibition of the Constitution against contracts applies to legislation by Congress—

Mr. AVIS. I do not understand the gentleman's question.

Mr. TALCOTT of New York. I understood the gentleman to say a moment ago that he did not think Congress had certain rights in regard to contracts.

Mr. AVIS. In regard to certain contracts.

Mr. TALCOTT of New York. The gentleman does not think the prohibition of the Constitution relates to legislation by Congress, does he?

Mr. AVIS. I do. As citizens we have certain inherent and vested rights, and under the fourteenth amendment of the Constitution, Congress can not deny the right or freedom of contract as to private property, unless such contract is against public policy or for some illegal or unlawful purpose.

Mr. BARTLETT. That is not under the fourteenth amendment, but under another provision of the Constitution.

Mr. AVIS. I said the fourteenth amendment. I am glad the gentleman corrected me. I meant the fifth amendment, which provides that no person shall be deprived of life, liberty, or property without due process of law, nor shall private property be taken for public use without just compensation. . . .

Mr. [JAMES F.] BYRNES [D., S.C.]. Mr. Chairman, when the currency bill was considered in the Democratic caucus I endeavored to have adopted an amendment prohibiting the interlocking of directorates in financial institutions. The caucus, in its wisdom, determined to refer this and similar amendments to the Democratic members of the Judiciary Committee with instructions to prepare and report a bill extending this prohibition to corporations engaged in interstate commerce, as well as financial institutions. Thereafter the President of the United States, in his message to Congress, urged the enactment of legislation along these lines, and in accordance with the direction of the caucus and the suggestion of the President, the Judiciary Committee has reported the bill now under consideration. In the time which I shall devote to the discussion of this measure I shall refer only to the provisions of section 9, the enactment of which into law will, in my opinion, do more than any other provision of the bill to destroy the concentration of credit which has hobble-skirted business and will restore competition and liberty of business in this country. This section is divided into three paragraphs. If I correctly understand the first paragraph, it is founded upon the old and well-established principle in equity that a trustee can not deal with himself. It provides that no person engaged as an individual or as an officer or director of a corporation in selling equipment, materials, or supplies to a railroad or other common carrier shall act as a ⊥ director or officer of such railroad or common carrier—in other words, that no man can deal with himself under different names. Certainly no one can question the righteousness of such a provision. No man should act as buyer and seller at one and the same time. If an individual acting as an officer of a railroad company is permitted also to act as an officer of a corporation selling supplies and equipments to that railroad, then the corporation in which he has the lesser interest is in danger of suffering at his hands. In the case of a private corporation, it can only result in loss to the stockholders; and in the case of a public-service corporation, it is certain to result in loss to the public in lessening improvements and restricting the service. No honest man wants to occupy this inconsistent relationship and no dishonest man should be permitted to do it.

The second paragraph provides that in any city of more than 100,000 inhabitants no bank shall have as a director or other officer or employee a person who is a private banker or director or officer or employee of another financial institution located in the same place. It also provides as to financial institutions not located in the same place that no person shall be a director, officer, or employee of two banks either of which has deposits, capital, surplus, and undivided profits aggregating more than $2,500,000. From the provisions of this paragraph mutual savings banks are exempted; and having in mind existing conditions, it also provides that a director, officer, or employee of a bank may be a director, officer, or employee of not more than one other financial institution, where the entire capital stock of one is owned by stockholders in the other.

The prohibition of this paragraph is founded upon the old and well-established principle that where their interests conflict no man can serve two masters. This system of interlocking directorates in financial institutions which has developed during the last 20 years, entirely indefensible as it is, has done more than all else to make possible the menacing concentration of credit in the hands of a few men. The man who controls the credit of the country can, if he desires to do so, control the country and the people who live in it. The control of financial power made possible by this system, together with the directorates held by the same men in the great insurance companies, common carriers, and industrial corporations, has resulted in the placing in the hands of a small group of men the power to say who shall and who shall not secure credit for the development of our great natural resources, and thus to decree the life or the death of business enterprises. . . .

Mr. [CYRUS] CLINE [D., Ind.]. Do I understand from that section that a man could not be director in a trust company and in a national bank and State bank?

Mr. BYRNES of South Carolina. The provision specifically exempts a banking corporation the entire stock of which is owned by the stockholders of another bank. My construction of it is that under the provision of this section a trust company operated in connection with a national bank, where the entire stock of the trust company is owned by stockholders of the national bank, would not be affected by this law.

Mr. CLINE. That goes directly to my inquiry.

Mr. BYRNES of South Carolina. It is especially exempted from it.

Because of this condition we have the third paragraph of this section, providing, substantially, that no person shall be a director in two corporations engaged in interstate commerce either of which has capital, surplus, and undivided profits aggregating more than $1,000,000, if such corporations are or have been competitors, so that the elimination of competition by agreement between them would constitute a violation of the antitrust law.

The effect of this last paragraph will be to minimize, if not actually destroy, monopoly and open the door of opportunity to the American of intelligence and energy who has until this time been obstructed and restricted in his endeavors to develop business enterprises against the opposition of monopolies. We are told that the so-called "unscrambling of eggs" which must result from the enforcement of this law will injure the industrial corporations, because there will not be a sufficient number of competent men to properly manage the industries of the country. Upon its face this criticism is not only unfounded but is a reflection upon the intelligence and ability of American business men. For every director who will be forced to resign a directorate in any one of the great corporations of the country there will be found ten men equally as well equipped to direct the affairs of the corporation in the interest of the stockholders; and, having an undivided interest in the particular corporation which he assumes to direct, the stockholders are sure to benefit.

The responsibility of directors will be increased, and the elevation to such a position of responsibility of a man whose activities have been heretofore restricted merely to carrying out the wishes of others must result in an impetus to business.

This contention that the banks will be injured by this legislation is not supported by the testimony of Mr. Reynolds, president of the Continental Commercial Bank of Chicago. When he was before the Pujo committee he stated:

Q. Do you approve of the identity of directors or interlocking directors in potentially competing institutions?

A. No, sir; personally I do not believe that is the best policy. That is the reason I am not a director or stockholder in any corporation that deals with us. There is not a day that I am not invited and do not have the opportunity to do it. It has been my theory of the proper method of banking to adhere to that policy.

Q. You have found that you could succeed in that way, too, have you not, Mr. Reynolds?

A. That is true as to whatever we have done. Some people would say that we have been successful. I am a little modest in that direction.

Q. Have you not the largest deposits in the country?

A. With one exception, at any rate; yes.

The enactment of this legislation, applying only to the larger banks, will result in the voluntary adoption by the smaller banks of the policy prescribed by law for the larger banks. . . .

Mr. COOPER. Would the section about which the gentleman is speaking prohibit, for example, a railroad company from hiring a construction company, the officers of which are also the railroad company's officers, to construct a line of railroad?

Mr. BYRNES of South Carolina. Of which its officers were members?

Mr. COOPER. Yes.

Mr. BYRNES of South Carolina. Where a director or officer of the company which contracts to sell supplies, material, or equipment to a railroad is an officer or director of such railroad it is a violation of this section.

Mr. COOPER. I have in mind an instance where four or five men sat on one side of a table as officers and directors of a railroad company and made a proposition for the building of a branch line of railroad, and then stepped around to the other side of the table, agreed to the proposition, and contracted with themselves as officers of a construction company.

Mr. BYRNES of South Carolina. I would say to the gentleman that under the provisions of this section that would be a violation of the law.

Mr. COOPER. That branch line of road was a little more than 100 miles long and was built for the Central Pacific Railroad Co. The Patterson Commission, appointed by President Cleveland, found that to build that branch line cost only about $3,200,000, but that the Central Pacific Co.'s officers paid the construction company more than $8,000,000 for the work—a difference and profit of $5,000,000 and more, which really came from the United States Treasury.

Mr. WEBB. This section would absolutely break that up.

Mr. BYRNES of South Carolina. It would make it a violation of the law.

Mr. COOPER. I refer to a contract of the Central Pacific Co., with the Pacific Construction Co.

Mr. BYRNES of South Carolina. This legislation, in my opinion, will also result in the reduction of the number of directors upon a board. As a result of the merger of many small corporations into a few large ones the number of directors have been increased in all of the great corporations. For instance, among the financial institutions, the National City Bank, of New York, has 24 directors and the National Bank of Commerce has 40. The consensus of opinion among financial leaders, testifying before the Pujo committee was that the smaller boards would be more effective, and certainly the rearrangement would leave no ground for the objection that as a result of this legislation it would be impossible to find a sufficient number of competent men to act as directors.

The minority members of the Judiciary Committee conclude their report with the suggestion that the Sherman Act now forbids interlocking directorates in its general provision against monopolies in restraint of trade, and, therefore, needs no reenforcement. These gentlemen can not possibly believe that the provisions of the present law could effectively destroy or lessen this concentration, else, in view of the fact that before the Pujo committee this concentration and control was admitted by those really responsible for it, the Department of Justice under the Republican administration would have taken steps to remedy the condition. They criticize the bill as being unscientific because of its arbitrary limitations of the application of the law to the large corporations, and at the same time they bewail the fact ⊥ that the enactment of this legislation will endanger the smaller corporations more than the larger ones. I agree that the elimination of competition between corporations doing business in a town of less than 100,000 inhabitants, or between industrial corporations having a capital stock of less than $1,000,000, is as wrong in principle as such conduct on the part of corporations in larger cities with larger capital; but this law is aimed at corporations which have been or are likely to do that which is hereby forbidden, and in the smaller cities and by the smaller corporations it is exceedingly unlikely that there will be formed any effective monopoly eliminating or lessening competition.

There may be isolated cases, but they will be exceptions and not the rule, and legislation must be enacted for the purpose of remedying the rule and not the exception. Again, we must recognize that in complying with the provisions of this section during the two years succeeding the passage of the bill many changes will have to be effected in the business world, and in the accomplishment of this legislation it should be our desire to restrict as far as possible the inconvenience to business. There is now no necessity to inconvenience the small corporation. Should it happen that those who spend their time seeking to evade the law hereafter devise some plan whereby the small corporation shall be effectively used to secure the same concentration of credit and control of business which has been effected by the present system in the larger corporations, then Congress can easily amend this bill so as to include in its provisions all corporations subject to its jurisdiction.

The minority of this committee, in the concluding paragraph of their report, express doubt as to whether the necessity for this legislation is so great as to justify the elimination of men of wide experience as directors. It would not have been surprising had they expressed this opinion two or three years ago, but in view of the testimony before the Pujo committee, not of muckrakers but of the so-called financial leaders themselves, it is difficult to conceive how any man can now doubt the extreme necessity for this legislation. So gradual has been the growth of this system of interlocking directorates, and so accustomed had we become to the control of our institutions being exercised by a few men, that when it was asserted there existed a concentration of credit amounting practically to a monopoly it was branded as demagoguery, and I am frank to say was received by me with little credence. But during my service as a member of the Pujo committee, I learned from the documentary evidence and from the testimony of financial leaders alleged to constitute the group in control of the credit of the country that 180 men hold 385 directorships in 41 banks and trust companies having total resources of $3,832,000,000 and total deposits of $2,834,000,000; 50 directorships in 11 insurance companies having total assets of $2,646,000,000; 155 directorships in 31 railroad systems having a total capitalization of $12,193,000,000 and a total mileage of 163,200; 6 directorships in 2 express companies and 4 directorships in 1 steamship company having a combined capitalization of $245,000,000 and a gross annual income of $97,000,000.

These same men hold 98 directorships in 28 producing and trading corporations having a total capitalization of $3,583,000,000 and total gross annual earnings in excess of $1,145,000,000; 48 directorships in 19 public-utilities corporations having a total capitalization of $2,826,000,000 and total gross annual earnings in excess of $470,000,000. In all, these 180 men hold 746 directorships in 134 corporations, having total resources or capitalization of $25,325,000,000.

We were told how private banking concerns, such as Morgan & Co. and some of the great trust companies, acted as the fiscal agents of the railroads, controlling the issue and sale of securities. In the case of the Southern Railway the Morgan interests, under a voting trust, name the trustees, who deal with Morgan & Co., bankers, as fiscal agents for the sale of the securities of that railroad. Thus for all purposes they are able to deal with themselves, and it is small wonder that within the last 20 years no dividends have been paid upon the common stock of this railroad. Indeed, holding in their hands as they have the power to deal with themselves in fixing the price at which the securities shall be sold and the commissions they will receive for such sale, it is a tribute to the self-restraint of these gentlemen that they have allowed so much of the earnings of this railroad to go to the development of its property. At the same time, information as to the manner as to which the railroad issues are handled should be of interest to State legislatures when in their efforts to regulate a railroad they are confronted with the argument that legislation would amount to confiscation because the stock of the railroad has for years paid no dividends.

The sincerity of such pleas should be tested by an investigation of the manner in which its securities are sold. The bankers controlling the railroads control its securities. As directors in the large insurance companies, they can direct the deposits of funds of the insurance companies in banks in which they are interested. With these funds they can purchase the securities of the railroads in which they are interested at prices fixed by them, and then they can turn around and sell the same securities as investments to the insurance companies controlled by them at their own prices.

Now, it is difficult to understand how any man can believe that this state of affairs should be permitted to continue if it be within the power of Congress to abolish it by legislation. It is true that the late Mr. Morgan in his testimony before our committee could not see anything wrong in this system, but many of his associates disagreed with him. Mr. George F. Baker, one of his partners, a man second only to Morgan in the power he has wielded in the financial world, stated to our committee that this concentration of credit had gone "far enough," because in the hands of the wrong man "it would be very bad." It is only natural that every man should be satisfied with his own control and believe that it is for the best interest of all concerned, especially when that control has resulted in the accumulation by him of a vast fortune; but in view of the recent disclosures before the Interstate Commerce Commission of the manner in which the assets of the New Haven Railroad Co. were dissipated while that railroad was under the guidance and domination of Morgan & Co., there may be justification for doubt on the part of some of the stockholders of that railroad and of the public as to whether or not this control is now in the hands of the right men. For my part I do not believe that it is right that such vast power, carrying with it the control of the happiness of men, should be concentrated in the hands of any one man. When Mr. Baker, interested as he is, can bring himself to say that it has gone far enough, we ought to be justified in saying that it has gone too far. Since the report of our Money Trust committee, recommending legislation similar to that contained in this bill, Mr. Morgan, who succeeded his father as director of many enterprises in which they were interested, has voluntarily resigned from a number of directorates, explaining that he did so because of the change of sentiment on the part of the public as to such dual and inconsistent relationships. He was mistaken in believing that the sentiment of the public had changed. It has only awakened to the existence of this condition of affairs.

In our investigation we could not ascertain that either in England, France, or in any other country has this system of interlocking directorates been found a necessity to insure the proper administration of the affairs of financial institutions. In fact, the law prohibits the participation of brokers and bankers in their councils on the theory that as those interests are likely to be dealing with the banks they should not be permitted to be represented on both sides of the bargain.

The laws on that subject are as follows:

Bank of England: Bankers, brokers, bill discounters, or directors of other banks operating in England are excluded as directors. (S. Doc. 405, p. 10.) Custom has enacted that the directors should never be chosen from the ranks of other banks. They are generally taken from the merchant firms and accepting houses. (S. Doc. 492, p. 67.)

Bank of France: Regents (directors) are chosen only from the commercial and industrial classes. The consulting discount committee is composed of 12 merchants and manufacturers. (S. Doc. 405, p. 190.)

National Bank of Belgium: The governers and directors can not be on the board of any other bank. (S. Doc. 400, p. 227.)

Russian banking law: No person is allowed to be a member of the board of management of more than one bank. (S. Doc. 586, p. 16.)

Union Bank of Scotland: No banker or stockholder is eligible as a director. (S. Doc. 405, p. 158.)

Commercial Bank of Scotland: Directors must not be directors of any other bank. (S. Doc. 405, p. 174.)

If instead of the continuance of this system, which in the opinion of Mr. Reynolds is "a menace," in the opinion of Mr. Baker has gone far enough, and in the opinion of the public has gone too far, we should return to the healthful rivalry prevailing in these countries, we will do much toward solving the business problems which confront us.

The Democratic Party has for years advocated the levying of tariff duties for revenue only, the enactment of a currency law, and such a revision of the antitrust laws as would destroy monopolies and restore competition. During this Congress we have given to the people a new tariff law, which has demonstrated the fallacy of the Republican argument that protection is necessary to the preservation of our industries. We have enacted a new currency law, which the Republicans promised to the people for years but failed to enact, and which is hailed by the country at large as the greatest constructive piece of legislation enacted in years, and now we propose to complete our program by the enactment of this antitrust legislation. So well considered that it will not disturb any corporation administered by men who believe in the fundamental principle of honesty in business and having in view the elimination of monopolies and the restoration of healthful competition, it is ⊥ certain to result in the promotion of the prosperity and happiness of the people. [Applause.] . . .

Mr. [RICHARD W.] AUSTIN [R., Tenn.]. Mr. Chairman, in connection with the bill now under consideration I desire to submit, for the thoughtful consideration of the Members of this House, two letters, which I will ask the Clerk to read, from Mr. John L. Boyd, of Knoxville, Tenn.

He is one of the large and successful coal operators of the eastern Tennessee field, is a man of high character, and any statement he makes is entitled to the respectful consideration of the Members of this House who desire the enactment of legislation which will be fair and just to the business interests of the country.

Mr. Boyd has always affiliated with the Democratic Party, and, I believe, voices the sentiment of the business people of the country in his objections to the pending measure.

I join him in protesting against the passage of this unwise, unjust, and unnecessary bill. Big as well as little business in this country should be given a rest.

The Clerk read the letters, as follows:

The Proctor Coal Co.,
Knoxville, Tenn., May 13, 1914.

Hon. R. W. Austin, M. C.,
Washington, D. C.

DEAR SIR: Many of your friends here, including myself, would like to know your attitude in respect to the proposed Clayton antitrust bill, which I understand is offered as a substitute for the Sherman antitrust law, and what are the prospects of its passage.

We look on it as a great menace to business generally, and we are very much in hopes it will not become a law.

Section 2 is in a sense almost confiscatory; at least it deprives the seller of any commodity of the exercise of his judgment in legitimate transactions, in that it provides that any person engaged in commerce who shall, either directly or indirectly, discriminate in prices between different purchasers of commodity in the same or different sections, shall be guilty of a misdemeanor and punishable by fine. This is giving to the purchaser of a small quantity the same price, rights, and privileges as a purchaser of large quantities, etc.

Section 3 makes it unlawful for the owner or operator of any mine to refuse to sell its product to a responsible person, firm, or corporation who applies to purchase such product, thus leaving the matter of responsibility subject to dispute.

These two sections, in my opinion, are productive of trouble and complication in business transactions, and will provoke no end of litigation. We may decline to sell a person, firm, or corporation on the grounds that from our viewpoint he or it is not responsible, and which at present would end the matter, but under the law as proposed he would have the right to bring suit against us, and if it should be proven that he is responsible, contrary to our investigation, then we would be guilty of a misdemeanor and subject to fine and imprisonment, etc., as provided for.

The main force of the bill, it appears, is against the business interests of the country and in favor of those who do not furnish employment to labor. The prohibition of interlocking directorates may be justified as attempting to curb vast monopolies and prevent the abuses that have resulted from such relationship, in respect to large concerns, but if applied generally and to small corporations, including banks of reasonable size outside of reserve centers, would disturb business generally and would involve a complete reorganization of a vast number of corporations, and in my opinion would work untold injury. The proposed bill is drastic and, as stated, is practically confiscatory.

Thanking you in advance for such attention as you may see fit to give this communication, I am,
    Yours, truly,

Jno. L. Boyd.

The Procter [sic] *Coal Co.,*
Knoxville, Tenn., May 21, 1914.

Hon. R. W. Austin, M. C.,
Washington, D. C.

DEAR SIR: I have read the proposed Clayton bill, and if I have not grossly misconstrued it, it is one of the most dangerous measures that has been offered, and so radical a departure from the customs and methods of business generally as would involve a complete reorganization in all lines and demoralize generally not only in my line of business, say, production of coal, but in all lines. For instance, certain sections provide that it shall be unlawful and subject to fine or imprisonment or both for a discrimination in price as between persons in the same community or different communities. This would require every wholesale and jobbing house to sell its goods to the consumer at as low price as it sells to the retail merchants. The factory or producer would violate the law for a refusal to sell its manufactured product to the consumer at the same price that it sells to the jobber or dealer. The coal companies, the iron producers, lumber manufacturers, and, in fact, all classes of commodities, supplies, etc., would have to be sold to the small consumer at the same price the large railroad companies pay for such goods in large quantities.

Another section provides that it shall be unlawful and subject the violator to fine or imprisonment or both, for a refusal to sell any person who is responsible who applies to purchase. The manufacturer or seller might not be able to determine exactly the responsibility, and the results would be a suit for damages, besides the part the Government would take in respect to the violation. In short, as I view it, the effect would be to eliminate the wholesale houses, jobbers, and dealers, and reduce the business through the country to transactions between producers and actual consumers.

I believe you appreciate the fact that if the producers through the country were reduced to transactions with consumers only that no calculation could be made as to the extent of operations, because no contracts could be made for quantities that would allow operations of mills, factories, etc. The prices would necessarily have to be advanced in order to cover the cost of doing business under such methods to the extent finally, I believe, the cost to the consumers would be equally as high, if not higher, than from the middleman or distributor.

The general plan seems altogether impracticable. The business of the country has been built up for the last century on a principle that allows the manufacturer and seller to select its customers, exercise its judgment in respect to responsible trade advantages, etc., that this proposed law will entirely overthrow.

There is practically an endless chain of valid objections and disadvantages that might be mentioned to the general plan of the Clayton bill, and if I have interpreted correctly the intent of the measure I confess that I am unable to see anything but disaster in its operations.
    Yours truly,

Jno. L. Boyd.

• • • •

Mr. [GUY T.] HELVERING [D., Kan.] Mr. Chairman, the specific work before us at the present time is to crystallize into legislation the last of the three most important pledges which we have made to the American people. In doing this we are at the same time offering to our friends in all parties the opportunity to show that their promises were made to be kept. We are practically all agreed as to the evils of trusts and of combinations; the people of the country are united in the determination that there must come a readjustment of conditions in the business world, and that this can be brought about only by a return to normal conditions and the elimination of the abnormal which have been brought into existence through the greed for gain and have continued to exist only by reason of legislative neglect.

The evils complained of have grown up quite often in a quasi-legal manner; special privilege had the power to have and to hold the best of legal advice and was able to live within the letter of the law while continually violating its spirit. It has taken time for us to realize by experience the loopholes in law which gave the opportunity for its violation, and we are now engaged in the work of legislating along the line which experience has demonstrated to be necessary.

In his address at the joint session of Congress, on January 20, President Wilson said:

> It will be understood that our object is not to unsettle business or anywhere seriously to break its established course athwart. On the contrary, we desire the laws we are now about to pass to be the bulwarks and safeguards of industry against the forces who have disturbed it. What we have to do can be done in a new spirit, in thoughtful moderation, without revolution of any untoward kind.

And that is exactly the spirit by which the Democratic Party is actuated. We would encourage every legitimate industry of the Nation and we can best do this by insuring to them fair play. We may, and undoubtedly will, harass the feelings of those who work illegitimately, but that is essential. Criminal laws are enacted, not because all men are criminals, but because honest men, and society in general, must be protected against the dishonest. Such laws are essential for the protection of society, and we believe that the legislation now under consideration is equally essential if we are to restore business to the plane of justice, throw down the bars which are keeping out the intelligent youth of the land from the field of opportunity, and give to the American people the protection which is essential if they are to be masters of their own destiny.

In closing the address before referred to, President Wilson said:

> I have laid the case before you, no doubt, as it lies in your own mind, as it lies in the thought of the country. What must every candid man say of the suggestions I have laid before you, of the plain obligations of which I have reminded you? That these are new things for which the country is not prepared? No; but that they are old things, now familiar, and must, of course, be undertaken if we are to square our laws with the thought and desire of the country. Until these things are done, conscientious business men the country over will be unsatisfied. They are in these things our mentors and our colleagues. We are now about to write the additional articles of our constitution of peace, the peace that is honor and freedom and prosperity.

In the desire "to square our laws with the thought and desire of the country" let us proceed to analyze the conditions which demand action on our part; be fair with those who differ with us on the questions involved and honestly and candidly discuss the legislation before us with a desire to have it so perfected that it will meet the necessities which have arisen and do so without danger to the business of the country or the bringing of undue hardship on legitimate industry.

There are those who profess to believe that the combinations called trusts are, in the main, good and are essential in the development of our resources.

They would have us believe that the present-day concentration of industry is in harmony with economic development and business efficiency; that by combination economy of production is secured and that the general public shares in the benefits accruing.

Also, that unrestrained competition is wasteful and destructive of human energy.

Theoretically, these propositions are correct; but in practice they fall down lamentably.

Once competition is crushed out, then the need of economic management and progressive methods is no longer so essential. The market for the inventor becomes one in which there is little, if any, competition, and as a natural result the incentive to spur on the inventor no longer exists.

Likewise, the destruction of competition leaves in the market but a single force or a minimum of forces actuated by a common and a selfish motive. Monopoly has the power to dictate to the producer of the raw material which it must buy, and it has the power to dictate to its labor the wage it will pay for the only commodity labor has to sell, and at the same time it is the absolute dictator of the price which the consumer must pay for the output of the monopolies. Such a centralization of power is a menace to the well-being of all, and, carried to its logical conclusions, it means the enslavement of the masses, the closing of the door of opportunity, and the centralization of all of the wealth earned by the brain and brawn of the American people in the hands of a few monopolists.

Let us see how monopoly is judged by those who can speak from experience of the evil which it has brought upon us.

The president of the Investors' Guild, in a memorial issued in November, 1911, has this to say:

> It is a well-known fact that modern trade combinations tend strongly toward constancy of process and products and by their very nature are opposed to new processes and new products originated by independent inventors, and hence tend to restrain competition in the development and sale of patents and patent rights and consequently tend to discourage independent inventive thought, to the great detriment of the Nation and with injustice to inventors, whom the Constitution especially intended to encourage and protect in their rights.

That is an arraignment which is based on known facts and can not be controverted. Monopoly is fatal to invention and ever stifles initiative. Whereas there was in the past every incentive for the young man who had a new idea, to-day his market is limited to a field in which there is no competition, and even when he does invent something of obvious value it may never see the light of day, for its purchaser may find it more profitable to put it away unused rather than to alter machinery and processes. The man with a monopoly does not need to encourage efficiency and improvement, for his profits are assured, even if he never makes progress.

In line with the foregoing, and to show to what extent monopoly prevents efficiency, I would quote the following from the Engineering News:

> We are to-day something like five years behind Germany in iron and steel metallurgy, and such innovations as are being introduced by our iron and steel manufacturers are most of them merely following the lead set by foreigners years ago.
>
> We do not believe this is because American engineers are any less ingenious or original than those of Europe, though they may, indeed, be deficient in training and scientific education compared with Germany. We believe the main cause is the wholesale consolidation which has taken place in American industry. A huge organization is too clumsy to take up the development of an original idea. With the market closely controlled and profits certainly following standard methods, those who control our trusts do not want the bother of developing anything new.
>
> We instance metallurgy only by way of illustration. There are plenty of other fields of industry where exactly the same condition exists. We are building the same machines and using the same methods as a dozen years ago, and the real advances in art are being made by European inventors and manufacturers.

How justifiable in the face of such testimony is the conclusion drawn by President Wilson:

> I am not saying that all invention has been stopped by the growth of trusts, but I think it is perfectly clear that invention in many fields has been discouraged, that inventors have been prevented from reaping the full fruits of their ingenuity and industry, and that mankind has been deprived of many comforts and conveniences, as well as the opportunity of buying at lower prices.

It is my firm belief that monopoly does not secure economy of production, and the authorities quoted would go to show that my contention is right. Contending, then, that monopoly is indefensible as an economic proposition, as well as an ethical and moral one, the question arises, What is the best method to be pursued to eliminate evils complained of and bring the business of the country back once more to a safe and sound basis?

THE RADICAL IDEA.

There are those who would have us take a radical stand, and that we are not prepared to do. Because evils have grown up coincident with the growth of the trusts, and often directly traceable to them, they would have us run amuck and destroy. They forget that in order to do this the punishment will fall upon more of the innocent than of the guilty, for those who have brought evil upon us were cunning enough to provide for their own future, and in many cases they have taken the kernel, leaving the responsibility and the empty shell in the possession of innocent investors.

We want to punish, where we can locate guilt, and we want to punish individuals rather than corporations. But it would be neither seemly nor wise for this great lawmaking body to permit itself to be carried to extremes and legislate along the line of revenge. I stand with the President, who has so well put it in this language:

Constructive legislation when successful is always the embodiment of convincing experience and of the mature public opinion which finally springs out of that experience. Legislation is a business of interpretation, not of origination; and it is now plain what the opinion is to which we must give effect in this matter. It is not of recent or hasty opinion. It springs out of the experience of a whole generation. It has clarified itself by long contest, and those who for a long time battled with it and sought to change it are now frankly and honorably yielding to it and seeking to conform their actions to it.

We will not go far astray if we follow the conclusions drawn by President Wilson in the paragraph quoted. The legislation before us interprets the experience of the generation. It presents a remedy for the economic evils which have sprung up as the result of the destruction of competition. This legislation would cure, while our radical friends propose a surgical operation which usually kills. We prefer to cure and utilize for the general good the life we save rather than to kill and put upon the people an extra burden of economic waste.

HONOR DEMANDS LEGISLATION.

A study of the foreign trade of the United States will convince that we are a world power to be reckoned with. The development of this trade means prosperity and permanent prosperity, for it means the continuous employment of our producers in shops and in factories. How essential, then, it is that we, as a Nation, should cultivate this field and permit nothing to mar the friendly relationship upon which international trade is founded.

Within the past two years this country has fallen in the estimation of the people of many foreign countries, and the cause of this is directly traceable to the greed of financiers who were more concerned with the acquirement of wealth than they were with the legitimacy of the means employed to secure it. The manipulation of the finances of the Frisco Railroad resulted in loss to many of the residents of France, who were inveigled into investing in it at the very time when those on the inside knew that failure could not be prevented. The manipulation of the properties of the Boston & Maine and the New York, New Haven & Hartford roads has intensified the bitterness engendered, and it is not without reason that foreigners look upon up with suspicion. In every national act we have shown to the world our desire to be fair and just in our dealings with nations and our wish to lead only in the paths of righteousness and enlightenment. But the acts of individuals whose only aim seems to be the acquisition of wealth, regardless of ethics or morality, can easily sweep away that which it has taken years of square dealing to build up. This we must legislate against. We must do so if we are to protect our own people, and we are obligated to do it if we wish to win and hold the respect of the world. I believe that House bill 16133 will go far in the direction of remedying the evils complained of, and, so believing, I shall take pleasure in voting for it.

ADVANTAGES OF PROPOSED LEGISLATION.

Regulation of the issuance of stocks and bonds under the authority of the Interstate Commerce Commission is a provision the necessity of which has been made manifest. It protects legitimate corporations, safeguards the investors and gives assurance as to the future financing of railroads so that dividends will be paid only on honest investment.

It provides for a trade commission, which will act as an active aid to the Department of Justice; will investigate and give publicity to the business of the various corporations; will see that the mandates of the courts are carried out and that there shall be actual observance of law, instead of an attempt to keep to the letter while violating the spirit.

It will prevent price discrimination in all of the territory of the United States, and thereby destroy one of the most effective methods ever used to break down competition. States have attempted such legislation, but their work could not reach the real evil, as big corporations could well afford to maintain a lower price within the jurisdiction of any State if by so doing a competitor could be driven out of business. With the passage of House bill 15657 this practice will be absolutely prohibited, for the same price will have to govern in every State, plus, of course, the difference in cost of transportation.

It will make it unlawful for the owner or operator of a mine or for a person controlling the sale of the product of a mine to refuse to sell to a responsible person who wishes to purchase. This eliminates the evils arising from the monopolization of coal and iron hands and lessens the powers which the monopolies now possess by the exclusive ownership or leasing privileges of such mines.

It prohibits exclusive and "tying" contracts, an evil which has contributed much to the cost of farming, as well as being ⊥ a heavy burden to those engaged in many other lines of business. "Tying" contracts help to create a monopoly in local markets, and by so doing they are instrumental in determining an excessive price which the consumer must pay to the exclusive agent. Under this system farming implements have long been marketed, not at a fair profit on cost but on a profit based on the needs of the consumer.

It provides for the punishment of personal guilt, and thereby will, to a great extent, be preventive of guilt. Time has demonstrated that the greatest weakness in our law comes from the punishment of corporations and the neglect to locate and punish personal guilt. By penalizing corporations it is often the case that innocent investors are the real sufferers, while the guilty parties are free to again violate the law, in the hope that they might escape detection. By enforcing penalities against responsible individuals we put at work an element which will aid in the enforcement of the law, for fear of a jail sentence is often effective where less drastic methods fail.

It puts an automatic force at work to aid in making the law effective by providing that on conviction of violation of its provisions a corporation can be sued by all who suffered damage by its illegal acts; that threefold damages can be collected, as well as the costs of the suits, and that the evidence secured by the Government to gain a conviction can be offered as conclusive evidence by the parties claiming damages. It must be plain that few corporations will care to run the risk of pursuing illegal methods knowing that they will make themselves liable, not merely to dissolution, but for the payment of damages to all parties injured.

It will abolish the evils of holding companies and put an end to interlocking directorates, twin evils which have been largely responsible for the power of monopoly and to which I shall refer later on.

And it will, to an appreciable extent, put an end to the abuse of the writ of injunction which has worked so much injustice in the past.

There is not one of the changes and reforms specified which has not been demanded by the people. There is not one of them which will work a hardship to legitimate business. We are here not to destroy but to build; not to harass, but to aid; not to impede, but to help in progress; and while here and there may be found those who will protest that the legislation will hamper them or interfere with personal rights or personal liberty, it will be found that in almost every case the complaint comes not from those who wish sane personal liberty, but rather from those who have profited by unbridled license and who desire no interference with their opportunities to exploit the American people.

NEED FOR REGULATING STOCK AND BOND ISSUES.

Seven years ago the Interstate Commerce Commission called attention to the advisability of having governmental regulation of stock and bond issues. No attention was paid to the recommendation. Last year, after concluding its investigation of the New Haven, the commission once more made recommendations as follows:

No student of the railroad problem can doubt that a most prolific source of financial disaster and complication to railroads in the past has been the desire and ability of railroad managers to engage in enterprises outside the legitimate operation of their railroads, especially by the acquisition of other railroads and securities. The evil which results, first, to the investing public, and finally to the general public, can not be corrected after the transaction has taken place; it can be easily and effectively prohibited. In our opinion the following propositions lie at the foundation of all adequate regulation of interstate railroads:

1. Every interstate railroad should be prohibited from spending money or incurring liability or acquiring property not used in the operation of its railroad or in the legitimate improvement, extension, or development of that railroad.

2. No interstate railroad should be permitted to lease or purchase any other railroad, nor to acquire the stocks or securities of any other railroad, nor to guarantee the same, directly or indirectly, without the approval of the Federal Government.

3. No stocks or bonds should be issued by an interstate railroad except for the purposes sanctioned in the two preceding paragraphs, and none should be issued without the approval of the Federal Government.

It may be unwise to attempt to specify the price at which and the manner in which railroad stocks and securities shall be disposed of; but it is easy and safe to define the purpose for which they may be issued, and to confine the expenditure of the money realized for that purpose.

I regret that while our committee had under consideration the amending of the law governing this commission it did not provide the legislation requested in the first and second recommendations quoted above. However, we go even further than the recommendation of the commission in providing for the supervision of the stock and bond issues. I firmly believe that it is the part of wisdom to do this; that it will give protection to investors, largely put an end to the flotation of water, and will be of benefit to every legitimate corporation, because the general public will have the assurance that a commission in which we all have faith has investigated the reason for such issue of stock or of bonds and gives its approval of the same. Further than that, the enforcement of such a provision will give us a better standing abroad with those who desire to put their money into American investments, for they will know that this great Government of ours is on guard and that there is a curb placed on the activities of those who would, if they could, market illegitimate securities.

OLD-FASHIONED HONESTY.

It is to be deplored that the rascality of men in positions of responsibility has wrecked so many of our best public utilities, but if we make full use of the lessons learned by bitter experience then can we gain by our loss and give protection to our people to-day and to the generations yet to come.

We have to some extent departed from old-fashioned ideals of common honesty and the justice upon which all of our actions should be based. In so far as we have done this, public confidence has been lost and suspicion holds sway. It would pay us to cultivate better ideals and learn a lesson from those who have placed personal integrity above aught else.

John M. Forbes, of Boston, conceived and built the Burlington Railroad. It was an honest road, built by an honest man, and one who used honest methods. In the modern world of finance Mr. Forbes would find no place. He would be classed as "old fashioned," "out of date," and an "old fogy." He had certain fixed rules by which he governed his personal conduct, and at an early date in his career he said:

I am unwilling to run the risk of having the reputation of buying from a company in which I am interested.

To-day we are discussing the necessity for legislation designed to vitalize the moral philosophy of Mr. Forbes and crystallize it into law. To-day men are eagerly anxious to run the risk of the imputation which Mr. Forbes resented, and we, with the knowledge that we are here to safeguard the rights of our people, are eager to put up barriers to prevent such iniquitous practices. We prevent public servants from dealing with themselves, prevent all Government employees from buying from companies in which they are interested, and in every way strive to remove all suspicion from those who hold a public trust. So it is that these men who are quasi public servants must be prevented from engaging in practices which are open to suspicion, even if they should be so morally blind as to desire to so engage. Mr. Forbes would not when he could, and we propose that representatives of high finance shall not if they would.

BAD FOR THE GENERAL PUBLIC.

We learn from the reports of the Stanley and of the Pujo committees that interlocking directorates practically control the bulk of the business of the country. That militates against efficiency, and the general public has to foot the bill.

In the first place, these men can not give the attention needed to the various branches of business which they are supposed to direct. Efficiency and success requires [sic] specialists, and yet here we are at the mercy of a ring of "Jacks of all trades" who subordinate everything to personal gain. The important contracts of the various companies are let to directors interested. Economy is supplanted by graft, and the gross earnings are often so manipulated that while the public is forced to pay for poor service and inefficiency, nevertheless the money so exacted never reaches the stockholders of the corporations, but is grabbed by directors who are in position to skim the cream so that none is ever distributed in the way of dividends. Read the history of the financial operations of the Frisco, the Rock Island, the Boston & Maine, and the New York, New Haven & Hartford lines and note how the stockholders have suffered in common with the communities served by the roads. Only the favored few on the inside were able to harvest a profit.

It is the stockholders and the general public who always suffer. Take the case of the New Haven road. For nearly six years the world of finance knew that ruin was inevitable, and those on the inside took to their cyclone cellars until the storm had passed. Of the New Haven stockholders, 10,474 are women and 10,222 hold only from 1 to 10 shares each. The directors, men high in banking circles, knew, but they never attempted to open the eyes of the stockholders. Many of them unloaded their own holdings in time and left the innocent purchasers to hold the sack, so that when the crash came it was mainly women in moderate circumstances and the estates of widows and orphans which had to bear the brunt of losses brought about by criminality, mismanagement, and high finance.

WORKING IN THE WRONG WAY.

The cause of failure of so many of the properties managed by banker directors can be easily traced. Such properties have been managed with an eye to present-day profits, present-day stock dividends, and selfish interest, rather than with an eye to the upbuilding of the properties and the safeguarding of the rights of the communities served by such corporations. As a result the shippers of the country are to-day paying interest on watered stocks and on investments which were pure graft. The business of the country is penalized because of the evil practices of the past, practices which law can not now reach and for which punishment can not be doled out. The railroads demand higher rates in order to be self-sustaining, when in many instances the money is needed to pay interest on fictitious or misapplied capitalization. If the increase is not granted, then business is paralyzed, and if it is given, then there is no hope of our country escaping similar demands in the future, unless we safeguard ourselves by enacting legislation along the lines suggested.

The men who have made fortunes by the indefensible practices complained of have long since "got out from under." The overissue of stocks are largely held by innocent investors—by the estates of the helpless innocent and in the hands of honest but misguided investors. We can not penalize them for the evils brought on by others, and while it may be said that we are by the proposed legislation locking the stable door after the horse has been stolen, we are in reality following the path of wisdom in locking the door, so that no more shall be stolen. By throwing safeguards around the present and the future we are taking the only possible step for the protection of the present and the future, and we harass no legitimate investment, but rather do we increase the faith of the investor, build up confidence which has been weakened or destroyed by vicious practices, and substitute healthy conditions in the business world instead of the diseased conditions which have brought to us decay and disaster.

INTERLOCKING DIRECTORATES.

The country is practically united in the belief that most of the evils complained of can be traced to the vicious source of interlocking directorates, and ever since the report of the Pujo committee focused the attention of the people upon the extent to which such community of interests controlled the business health—the very business life—of the Nation, the demand has been insistent that legislation be enacted to effect a cure.

As Louis D. Brandeis logically puts it:

The practice of interlocking directorates offends laws, human and divine. Applied to rival corporations, it tends to the suppression of competition and to violation of the Sherman law; applied to corporations which deal with each other, it tends to disloyalty and to violation of the fundamental law that no man can serve two masters. In either event it tends to inefficiency, for it removes incentive and destroys soundness of judgment. It is undemocratic, for it rejects the platform. "A fair field and no favors," substituting the pull of privilege for the push of manhood. It is the most potent instrument of the Money Trust. Break the control so exercised by the investment bankers over railroads, public-service and industrial corporations, over banks, life insurance and trust companies, and a long step will have been taken toward attainment of the New Freedom.

The deductions of Mr. Brandeis are strongly supported by the known facts. The report of the Stanley committee on the Steel Trust showed that the few men who control the Steel Trust are directors in 29 railroad systems, with 126,000 miles of line (more than half the railroad mileage of the country), and are also directors in many steamship companies. Through all these alliances the Steel Corporation controls transportation, not merely as carriers but as the largest customers of steel. These same men are directors in 12 steel-using street railway companies, including some of the largest in the world. They are directors in 40 machinery and other steel-using companies; in many gas, oil, and water companies, extensive users of iron products; and in the great wire-using telephone and telegraph companies. The aggregate assets of the companies controlled by these few men exceeds $16,000,000,000.

It can be plainly seen that by such control these men can catch the general public "a-comin' an' a-gwine." As producers of steel they sell to themselves as consumers, and are also in position to give to themselves, through their influence as railroad directors, special favors in transportation, when they can successfully hide from the scrutiny of the Interstate Commerce Commission. It needs no argument to convince that by the use of such power practical competition is made an absurdity. The Steel Trust is supreme in its sphere, and the legislation proposed is absolutely necessary if we are to look for relief.

It is to the report of the Pujo committee, however, that we must go if we are to get an insight into the wonderful ramifications of interlocking directorates. From this we find that two New York banks—the National City and the First National—with the Morgan firm, constitute the inner group of the Money Trust. George F. Stillman is the power in the National City and George F. Baker in the First National. The resources of the National City are about $300,000,000, those of the First National about $200,000,000, and while we do not know the resources of the Morgan firm, we have reason to believe that their deposits alone aggregate some $162,500,000.

Mr. Baker is, or was until recently when he saw the handwriting on the wall, a director in 22 corporations having, with their many subsidiaries, resources or capitalization of $7,272,000,000. Further than that, the directors of the bank which he dominates are directors in at least 27 other corporations, with resources of $4,270,000,000. So we see that this First National Bank has representation on the boards of 49 corporations, with aggregate resources of $11,542,000,000.

Here are a few of the companies in which Mr. Baker had influence, either as voting trustee, executive committeeman, or director; the list was prepared by Mr. Brandeis:

First. Banks, trust and life insurance companies: First National Bank of New York; National Bank of Commerce; Farmers' Loan & Trust Co.; Mutual Life Insurance Co.

Second. Railroad companies: New York Central lines; New Haven; Reading; Erie; Lackawanna; Lehigh Valley; Southern; Northern Pacific; Chicago, Burlington & Quincy.

Third. Public service corporations: American Telegraph & Telephone Co.; Adams Express Co.

Fourth. Industrial corporations: United States Steel Corporation; Pullman Co.

Mr. Stillman is a director in 7 corporations, with assets of $2,476,000,000, and the National City Bank, which he dominates, has directors in at least 41 other corporations which, with their subsidiaries, have an aggregate capitalization and resources of $10,564,000,000.

The members of J. P. Morgan & Co.'s firm hold 72 directorships in 47 of the largest companies of the country.

Here is what the Pujo committee found in regard to the members of the firm of J. P. Morgan & Co. and the directors of their controlled trust companies and of the First National and the National City Bank. They hold:

One hundred and eighteen directorships in 34 banks and trust companies having total resources of $2,679,000,000 and total deposits of $1,983,000,000.

Thirty directorships in 10 insurance companies having total assets of $2,293,000,000.

One hundred and five directorships in 32 transportation systems having a total capitalization of $11,784,000,000 and a total mileage—excluding express companies and steamship lines—of 150,200.

Sixty-three directorships in 24 producing and trading corporations having a total capitalization of $3,339,000,000.

Twenty-five directorships in 12 public-utility corporations having a total capitalization of $2,150,000,000.

In all, 341 directorships in 112 corporations having aggregate resources or capitalization of $22,245,000,000.

And, as Mr. Brandeis succinctly puts it, $22,000,000,000 is more than three times the assessed value of all the property, real and personal, in New England. It is nearly three times the assessed value of all the real estate in New York City. It is more than twice the assessed value of all the property in the 13 Southern States. It is more than the assessed value of all the property in the 22 States, north and south, lying west of the Missouri River.

And all of the power represented by this wealth is lodged in the hands of a few men. Can anyone doubt the danger which such concentration permits? Can we stop to inject partisanship into a discussion over methods proposed to wipe out such danger? It is useless to say that the power represented will never be used to the detriment of the American people. We could admit all that, even when we have had innumerable object lessons to show that the power has been so used; but even if it were in the hands of men in whom we all had implicit confidence, it is too great a power to be concentrated—it affords too great a temptation to frail humanity.

But the Money Trust is not content to operate within a limited field. Its tentacles reach out and grasp the activities and the resources of the Nation, wherever these activities and resources offer opportunity for gain. Take the case of Boston, and it is typical of practically every large city in the Union. The banking firms of Lee, Higginson & Co. and Kidder, Peabody & Co. practically control the National Shawmut Bank, the First National Bank, and the Old Colony Trust Co., with resources of $288,386,294, fully one-half of the banking resources of Boston. The directors of these banks are also directors in 21 other banks and trust companies, and all together they are practically in control of 90 per cent of the total banking resources of the city. In fact, 33 out of 42 banking institutions in Boston are interlocked, and these have aggregate resources of $590,516,239, which is about 92 1/2 per cent of the aggregate banking resources of Boston.

HOW THEY DO ABROAD.

Contrast the condition existing in New York, Boston, and, in fact, the entire country, with those in the older nations in Europe, and what do we find? The Bank of England, the Bank of France, the National Bank of Belgium, and the leading banks of Scotland all exclude from their boards persons who are directors in other banks. By law, in Russia no person is allowed to be on the board of management of more than one bank.

Such is the practice in countries where conservative methods rule. Here we have thrown conservatism to the winds, and a few men have by combination gained the power to make every activity of the people contribute to their selfish gains. The laborer is exploited; the farm owner has to pay an unnecessary toll all along the roads leading from his fields to the consumer; at every corner we are held up to pay a tax levied either by monopoly or vicious practice; and as a natural result the earnings of 99 per cent of the American people of the United States are subtracted from, to the end that the money reservoirs of less than 1 per cent may be filled with the proceeds of unjust tribute.

In the legislation now before us we offer to you the opportunity to cure the evils which bear so oppressively on your people and on mine. Will you join with us in legislating to the end that we shall travel along the road which the experience of other nations has demonstrated to be safe? We are not proposing to you any innovation; we bring forward no experiment and ask for your approval of it. Other countries have deemed it inadvisable to permit of combination which is a standing menace. You can see by the reports of the Stanley committee and of the Pujo committee to what extent such combinations are in effect to-day. Is it not better for you to join with us in curing while we can rather than to wait until the patient is dead and the people of our common country are industrial slaves?

NEED OF A TRADE COMMISSION.

In his recommendations in the message of last January President Wilson suggested the formation of a commission as an instrument of information and publicity and as a means of securing and disseminating the knowledge needed to correct evils in the business life of the Nation.

Such a commission is provided for in House bill 15613. The bill proposed lodges in this commission the authority now vested in the Bureau of Corporations, but at the same time it gives to this commission new powers, the need of which have been proved by experience. To a large extent this commission will have independent power and authority, and the bill removes entirely from the control of the President and the Secretary of Commerce the investigations conducted and the information secured. Hereafter this commission will have power to make investigations on its own initiative and make public such information as it deems best.

An abstract of the annual and special reports of each corporation, which reports are made obligatory by this legislation, must be made public by this commission. The faithful observance of such requirement can not but have a salutary effect. It gives to the investor an authentic guide as to the condition of corporations; shows to the public the physical condition, earning capacity, and expenses of all such corporations, and with this information available there is a protection given which can not help but be an important factor in eliminating unnecessary loss.

Speaking of the laws governing trusts, on January 1, 1896, Attorney General Harmon said:

If the Department of Justice is expected to consider investigations of alleged violations of the present law or of the law as it may be amended, it must be provided with a liberal appropriation and a force properly selected and organized. * * * But I respectfully submit that the general policy which has hitherto been pursued of confining this department very closely to court work is a wise one, and that the duty of detecting offenses and furnishing evidence thereof should be committed to some other department or bureau.

In this legislation we are striving to act upon the suggestion and recommendation made by Attorney General Harmon more than 18 years ago. Since that time we have had three Republican presidents, and for 14 of these years the Republicans have had absolute control of all branches of the Government, but it remained until the time when the Democrats secured full control before any attempt was made to provide constructive legislation to secure the things needed to make antitrust legislation effective.

It has been during the period from 1896 to 1910 that the trusts came to be a real force to reckon with in the United States. Under Republican rule they have waxed fat and have been encouraged by the party in power. They were looked to to finance Republican campaigns, were potent factors in fastening high protection upon us, and through their union with the banks and the insurance companies of the United States they have been able to hold all legitimate business of the country at their mercy. Today it is claimed that 50 men in the United States control 40 per cent of the wealth of the country. Such a condition of affairs is intolerable. It is a menace to the well-being of every man, woman, and child in the country. We clipped away part of the power of these combinations when we revised the tariff and put the industries of the Nation on a competitive basis; we further emancipated the people when we enacted currency legislation and took away from the trusts the opportunity to manipulate the earnings of the people for their own advantage and for the undoing of the real owners of the deposits. Now we have the opportunity, by the enactment of House bills 15613, 15657, and 16133, to remove the last of the obstacles which remain to prevent competition; and when we do this we will have kept our promises to the American people and made possible the return of an era in which there will be a fair field and no favors for either the big or the little fellow—a field on which special privilege will not be allowed to trespass.

THE DEMOCRATIC WAY.

Some there are who do not believe that we go far enough in the powers which we delegate to the proposed trade commission in the bill introduced. If they had their way, they tell us that they would insist upon clothing this commission with judicial powers— the power to not only hunt up evidence, but also the power to try, condemn, and inflict punishment.

It is somewhat strange, but in nearly every case we find that such suggestions and denunciations of the measure reported comes from those who are or have been affiliated with the party which was in power for 16 years, and who in all that time witnessed the rapid and steady increase of the pernicious practices complained of without making one effort to put an end to them.

For my part I am convinced that a danger even greater than that which we seek to guard against would menace the American people if we were to place in the hands of this commission the powers demanded. It would mean a centralization of authority such as this country has never seen. It would put into the hands of a few men power to hold up the industries of the country, and in the hands of the wrong men it could be used to hold in office any party in power which might be base enough to use the machinery provided.

Here we give to this commission ample power to investigate on its own authority or on request of the Government. It has the right to go into the accounts, business, and all activities of the combinations under its control, and when illegal acts are discovered then the Department of Justice is furnished the material on which to base action, and it would be compelled to take action on the behest of this commission or else be discredited before the country.

That surely furnishes ample power for the protection of the American people, while at the same time it safeguards the rights of legitimate business and protects it from the attacks of any partisan commission. It is the Democratic way. Out of power, we denounced centralization and fought every effort made to clothe bureaus or commissions with authority which could be used for partisan advantage. In power, we are consistent and we refuse to permit of a centralization of power which might inure to our advantage. It is our aim to protect legitimate business, not to harass it; to provide the means to run down illegitimate practices and to root them out. Under the authority granted by this legislation we have the power to gain the ends desired by our people. Anything less would be unsatisfactory; anything more would be dangerous.

WITH MALICE TOWARD NONE.

The Democratic Party has no quarrel with legitimate business, and never has had. The message of President Wilson in January was one of reassurance, and in that spirit it was accepted by the world of business. He voiced the opinion of the American people that competition must be restored; that indefensible methods had been employed by the combinations known as trusts, and that legislation was needed in order to safeguard the American people, as a whole, and the business of the Nation, little as well as big. The necessity for such legislation has been admitted by the platforms of all political parties. We were agreed as to the existing evils which required remedying; we disagreed only as to remedies. The President pointed out the things which, in his opinion, needed our attention, and the responses from all sources showed remarkable accord with his views. The plain citizen favored legislation suggested because he looked to see it put an end to practices which he had denounced; the small manufacturer and business man indorsed the message, for it gave to him hope for the future, and while the men who had profited by the evils complained of could not be expected to grow enthusiastic over prospective legislation which would do away with their illegitimate gains, nevertheless they realized that the ⊥ American people, long sorely tried, would not be content under further oppression.

It is in the spirit breathed by President Wilson that our committees have acted in preparing and presenting the bills before us. It is in that spirit that we, as Democrats, are considering the legislation. We have no quarrel with wealth honestly acquired, nor with profits legitimately secured. But we would be faithless as Representatives did we not demand that a stop shall be put to monopoly and that no business shall be so big that it shall be greater than our laws or superior to our control. Equal rights and equal privileges we are prepared to grant to all. To give less would mean that we are false to the teachings of the founders of our party; to give more would mean that we are embarking in a policy of giving special privileges from which we hoped to derive partisan advantage. Within our confines we have a market for the products of most of our American industries. By tariff legislation we have paved the way for the opening up of new markets which will give opportunities for the expansion of our industries. By currency legislation we provide for the legitimate circulation of money along natural lines; for the aiding of our foreign trade by means of branch banks abroad and by means of bank acceptances. Out of this legislation is bound to come vast benefit to American industries, and in the resulting benefit all of our people will share. Now, we lay down the command that business must be conducted fairly, legally, and in the open. The legitimate business man will welcome legislation which so provides, and with the illegitimate we can not afford to compromise. Our duty is to act equitably and in the best interests of our constituents. That I believe we are doing in supporting these measures, and with their enactment will result the fulfillment of three of our most important pledges to the people—revision of the tariff, reform of the currency system, and the elimination of trust evils. It is a wonderful program of legislation to be compressed within two years, and if we accomplish it, it will be because we have an administration which kept the faith and a Congress which has recognized but one master—the American people.

A WORTHY LEADER.

President Wilson has pointed out the road on which we are traveling to-day—the road to the new freedom. Keen in intellect, strong in his faith in the American people, and swayed only by an honest desire to be an instrument of service, his evident sincerity and honesty of purpose has broken down opposition and won for him a niche in the affections of all who admire honesty, courage, and truth. He realizes better than any man in modern public life the value of the victories of peace, and while he is militant in battling for the right, yet ever are his weapons those of light and truth. As I contemplate his career since he came into the arena of politics; as I analyze his career as governor of New Jersey and as President of the United States and note the patience, faith, and sublime courage always in evidence, there comes to my mind a poem by John Greenleaf Whittier, the lines of the last two verses of which well serve as a portrait of the man. They run:

> The truths ye urge are borne abroad
> By every wind and tide;
> The voice of nature and of God
> Speaks out upon your side.
>
> The weapons which your hands have forged
> Are those which heaven have wrought—
> Light, truth, and love; your battle ground
> The free, broad field of thought.

• • • •

Mr. SWITZER. Mr. Chairman, it is certainly remarkable that the majority of the great Judiciary Committee, bringing in this bill for the purpose of supplementing the Sherman antitrust law and strengthening it, and to suppress monopoly and to prevent unfair discrimination, have in the very first two sections of their bill been guilty of gross, rank, unfair discrimination against hundreds of men living in my district engaged in the bituminous-coal-mining industry. The only justification I have heard so far given for this act is that God put the mineral in the earth. That was the statement of the gentleman from North Carolina [Mr. WEBB], the gentleman from Massachusetts [Mr. MITCHELL], and the gentleman from Arkansas [Mr. FLOYD]. They said that it was unlike a product that came forth from the factory, that evolved from the brain and labor of some man in a manufacturing plant. I can not get the distinction in my mind. It seems to me that God also caused the timber to grow from the earth as much as putting the mineral into the earth. There has been more talk about the Lumber Trust in this country than there has been about any Coal Trust, I think, in the last 20 years, and I can not understand why this exemption or provision or, as you might call it, proviso in section 3 should not apply to the lumbermen. . . .

Mr. GARNER. Will the gentleman vote for the bill if amended so as to include the words "products of the forest"?

Mr. SWITZER. I will not say so now. [Laughter.] I am giving you my reasons for being against this bill.

Now, let us see about this matter. I do not know very much about the bituminous-coal-mining industry. I do not know very much about metalliferous mining. But on my short visit up into the State of Michigan last winter I found that it took a very bright, active brain and a great deal of labor to go away down into the earth and there drill and blast out the rock that contains the copper and take it to the surface and run it through those great crushing machines, and finally transport it to the lake, where there is abundance of water, and after recrushing and grinding it in the stamping mills, using 15 tons of water on every ton of rock, eliminate and separate the copper from the rock, and then put it through a smelting plant.

If that is not as much a manufactured product as the product of a man who, with an ax, cuts down a tree and then runs it through a sawmill and cuts it into lumber, then I do not know anything about the manufacturing business. Which requires the greater exercise of brain or the greater amount of labor—the product of the metalliferous mine in northern Michigan and in Montana or the product of the sawmill of the lumbermen in North Carolina, in Maine, or in Arkansas?

Now, I am not accusing these gentlemen of doing this deliberately, but you know we all work along the lines of least resistance, and I find that a Representative with a good many poor constituents can howl long and loud for a heavy tax on large incomes without having any fear of trouble with his constituency. [Laughter.] So it is with the gentlemen when they bring in a bill here that discriminates against the mine owner and operator. Having no mining industries in their own districts, except perhaps one or two instances, of course they know they will not have much trouble at home. If they put into this bill provisions affecting the lumbermen and the other people that ought, on the same theory, to be in here, there would be such a howl go up all over this country that you would not hear any more demands to enact antitrust legislation at this session.

Now, gentlemen, I happen to live in a district where one of the main industries is coal mining. I am not myself interested in the mining industry. I was interested in it at one time to my sorrow. That industry in my native county has not been very much developed. But I got interested in the industry in an adjoining county, as I say, to my sorrow; and as to the mine that I was interested in some years ago there is no danger of your hurting it. It has gone up the flume, and my investment has gone with it; and for that reason, of course, I have considerable sympathy for the small coal operator or mine operator in southeastern Ohio who is struggling at this time for an existence. I can corroborate the statement of the gentleman from West Virginia [Mr. AVIS] with the evidence of a great many mine operators, and I believe a majority of the small mine operators there have been carried along by bankers and have been in the last few years almost hopeless bankrupts. There are at least 50 independent mines in my district more or less engaged in interstate commerce, and hundreds of persons ⊥ are interested in those mines. There are two or three large companies, like the Sunday Creek Coal Co., that have mines in my district, and the Superior Coal Co., that has a large investment. The situation to-day is that the laborers, the coal miners, are out of employment. There are five or six thousand of them out in my district and about 45,000 of them out in the State of Ohio. I see by a newspaper that they are asking 5 cents per ton more on the run-of-mine basis under a law that has been enacted in Ohio than the operators will at this time agree to pay. They are probably entitled to it; at least they are certainly entitled to a living wage. The mine owners and operators say that under the business conditions at present prevailing in this country they can not pay it. The miners are out of employment—they are out on a strike and receiving strike benefits. I think one week's benefits to those miners in Ohio will exhaust their whole strike-benefit fund in their Local No. 5. It will require $150,000 or $200,000 every week to pay the benefits if these 45,000 remain out on strike, which will have to be borne by the labor organizations of this country.

Now, with this condition existing, with the families of these men suffering, and with the operators saying that they can not afford to pay a living wage, as demanded by these coal miners, I am asked here to vote for a measure that seems to me is bound to impose further burdens and greater hardships upon the coal operators and mine owners in my district and throughout the State of Ohio, and which will further embarrass them and possibly deter them from acceding to the demands of the miners and thereby greatly prolong the suffering of thousands of men, women, and children throughout my State.

And why this unjust discrimination?

Recollect, these men are not only subjected to all the prohibitions contained in section 2 of this bill, but by section 3 you say they must not arbitrarily refuse to sell their product to any responsible person who applies to purchase same. That proposition has been ably discussed by the gentleman from West Virginia [Mr. AVIS].

I think he has made a fair and thorough explanation of that. I will not undertake to go into details of the coal and copper industries, because I really do not know much about the details of either. But there is one thing stated here that I do not believe to be true. I do not believe that section 3 applies to the local coal dealers and distributors to the ultimate consumers in the various States. It reads in this way:

> That it shall be unlawful for the owner or operator of any mine or for any person controlling the product of any mine engaged in selling its product in commerce to refuse arbitrarily to sell such product to a responsible person, firm, or corporation who applies to purchase such product.

"For the owner or operator of any mine or for any person controlling the product of any mine." Therefore your law will not reach the coal dealer in the city or village unless that coal dealer happens to control the entire product of some mine. I do not think it is as far-reaching as some gentlemen here have suggested, and I think there is where gentlemen receive the impression that trust prices obtain in the coal trade. It is these local coal dealers in the large cities and towns who clique together and raise the price. [Applause.]

The copper content in the Michigan rock is usually only from 15 to 20 pounds to the ton, some of it running as high as 35 pounds. At the present prices the copper in a ton of rock yields from $2.25 to $5. This rock is drilled by compressed air and after it is blasted down it is hoisted thousands of feet to the surface of the earth by means of heavy cables and expensive machines.

Then it goes to the stamping mills and smelters, as I have just narrated, and all this involves a heavy expense. It can readily be seen that this rock is worked on a very narrow margin of profit, requiring hundreds of tons of rock to be taken daily out of the ordinary mine to pay the daily operating expenses. Many of these companies have been for years operating at a loss, but with the hope of striking a rock having a sufficient copper content to be worked at a profit.

It seems to me that the provisions of sections 2 and 3 of this bill will tend to discourage the operations of the exploration mines, and either drive out of business the mines now paying small dividends or compel their employees to take a very much less wage.

What is true of the copper industry is equally true of the bituminous-coal industry. If the small independent mine operator can barely exist and every few months witnesses some of them in bankruptcy at a time when they have the utmost freedom of contract, what will become of them when you impose the harassing and uncalled-for annoyances provided for in section 3 of this bill? Suppose you harness up in the same way the farmers, the manufacturers of the thousand and one things in this country, the lumbermen, and all those who are to some extent engaged in shipping commodities in interstate commerce, do any of you think you would be returned to Congress after such a law became effective?

With no mine owner or operator representing either metalliferous or coal mines heard before this committee, and it certainly would have been the part of wisdom to have had extensive hearings of both, and a committee absolutely ignorant of the conditions obtaining in metalliferous mining and the larger portion having no knowledge whatever of the coal-mine industry, we find them blindly imposing restrictions on the freedom of these persons to enter into contracts when they do not dare to impose like burdens on those engaged in industries which they do know something about.

Our Democratic friends go about enacting this sort of legislation just as if they were enacting a tariff law. I suppose it is force of habit and they can not help it. But I would think the results already being reaped by the Underwood tariff bill would cause them to at least want a little light as to the existing conditions of our metalliferous and coal mines before reporting the proposed legislation.

The copper mines of northern Michigan have natural ventilations and are not bothered with gas and dust to the extent of causing dangerous explosions.

These serious difficulties to some extent confront all bituminous coal miners, but some of them are confronted by greater difficulties of this character than others. The small, independent coal operator has also to compete with the large operator, frequently more favorably situated, with natural conditions respecting the mining of the coal in his favor, and advantaged by up-to-date electrical mining machinery, which would be too expensive an equipment for the small plant.

There are numerous lines of investigation in the production and marketing of coal that the committee could have pursued with great profit, and have given a vast amount of valuable information to this body in their report, and which would have enabled us to at least intelligently vote on this proposition.

But the various branches of the metalliferous mining industry should have been accorded a full hearing as well as the branches of the coal industry.

Sections 6 and 8 contain some objectionable provisions, ably pointed out by Mr. VOLSTEAD, of Minnesota, and it seems to me that he has clearly shown that the enactment of these sections as they now stand materially weakens the law it is so much desired to have strengthened.

There is a widespread desire throughout the country to have Congress adjourn, and I have no doubt but that this sentiment will be suddenly and greatly augmented if we pass this bill as it now stands. . . .

Mr. [CLEMENT C.] DICKINSON [D., Mo.]. Mr. Chairman, I am heartily in favor of this antitrust legislation and expect to give my support to the pending bill to supplement existing laws against unlawful restraints and monopolies, and for other purposes, and known as House bill 15657. I am inclined to believe that the bill as presented to the House by the Judiciary Committee, with an invitation for proper amendments, needs some amendment, at least in some sections. The law ought to be strong enough to cover every violation sought to be reached by this class of legislation.

The country is entitled to an efficient antitrust law to reach the evils complained of, and in addition thereto an intelligent and courageous court in every section of the land; not only a strong law, but an efficient court to sit in judgment upon the violations of the law. And besides the law and the court, in order to make the law effective, it must have honest, able, willing, and courageous officials desirous of and ambitious to enforce the law. The law and the courts may be without criticism, but there can be no enforcement of this law unless the violators thereof be brought to the bar of justice. The administration of the law is all important, and the people have often justly complained of the failure of its prosecuting officers to perform their full duty to the public and make effective the law of the land. But you may have the law and the courts and officers fully equipped, honest and anxious to discharge every duty, but it is important and necessary to bring the violator of the law within the process and jurisdiction of the court, and I want at this time to call attention especially to section 10 of the bill which provides—

That any suit, action, or proceeding under the antitrust laws against a corporation may be brought not only in the judicial district whereof it is an inhabitant, but also in any district wherein it may be found—

and especially to the last clause thereof.

It is possible that the committee has by its language, under the decisions of the courts, used words that are sufficient, but ⊥ I doubt it, and, in my judgment, this section ought to be amended. It provides that suit may be brought not only in the judicial district where the corporation is an inhabitant, but also in any district wherein it may be found. It seems to me the last clause ought to be amended. If so, the committee having charge of the bill should prepare and present a proper amendment thereto. Take, for instance, a New Jersey corporation or a corporation of any other State. It is an inhabitant of the State where it is incorporated. Its principal business may be done beyond the borders of that State or district of which it is an inhabitant. Its wrongs and violations of law for which it should be held amenable may have been committed in districts other than the judicial district whereof it is an inhabitant. . . .

To repeat, a corporation may be an inhabitant of one State or district, but its principal business may be outside thereof, and its wrongs and violations of law, for which it should be held amenable, may have been committed in districts other than and far removed from the judicial district whereof it is an inhabitant; and, in fact, it may do no business whatever in the State of its incorporation or the judicial district of which that State is a part. These great business concerns take out their incorporation papers and become inhabitants of the States desired or convenient to them because of more liberal laws to corporations and also because they do not desire to do business there, but elsewhere beyond its borders and possibly for the purpose of avoiding jurisdiction elsewhere.

But you say you give jurisdiction in any district where the corporation may be found. How are you going to find a corporation, for the purpose of jurisdiction, except by express words of statute law? I grant you may be able to find its officers, agents, or employees for the purpose of service of certain process, but is that a finding of the corporation so as to give jurisdiction as to the place of suit or trial? Jurisdiction is given by express statute. Why not at the end of the section, after the word "found," add other words, such as "doing business, or violating the provisions of this law, or wherever it may do business or where its agents, officers, or employees may be found," or other appropriate language. A dozen suggestions may be made in the way of amendment. Whenever the cause of action arises there should be jurisdiction provided for action and trial. I prefer that the committee in charge of the bill prepare and offer its own appropriate amendment. But the language ought to be extended sufficiently to reach every contingency, so that these concerns may be sued in that jurisdiction where they commit the wrong, where the acts complained of may be committed, where the officers, agents, or employees, acting for their master corporation, may be found setting aside the law, and where the witnesses are easily obtainable, and not leave the section so that those who have suffered damages at the hands of a corporation shall be compelled to bring suit in the remote State or district of which the corporation is an inhabitant by virtue of its incorporation therein, having selected that remote State for its home, while it goes forth in remote sections of the country, and where its greed for unlawful gain willfully disregards the rights of others and boldly sets aside the provisions of the law.

Immense fortunes are made by selfish interests in defiance of the law and because of the fact that they are beyond the law. Great combinations band together, and, conducting their business by unlawful means in restraint of trade, drive out all independent competition and then mercilessly rob the public.

Cruel monopoly has bid defiance to the law, the courts, and executive power. It has sought to restrain and to delay the enactment of appropriate and effective legislation. It has sought to control the courts by placing its own agents and attorneys in the seats of justice, so that its judgments and decrees be not unfriendly to them. It has sought to fill the executive places with minions of their own, so that the processes of the courts might be under their control. It has at times bid defiance to State and Federal authority and has played one against the other, in order that they may escape punishment for their ill deeds. They sometimes want the law to be weak and obscurely written and leave it for the courts to construe, so delay may come while they continue to pursue their own hard methods, and then would have friendly courts write decisions, wherever possible, along the lines of their own contention.

The time has come for action, for the enactment of law so clear and so plain that he who runs and reads may understand, a law so definite and certain that its meaning can not be misunderstood nor misconstrued. The conscience of the country is aroused; the demand for constructive law imperative; no delay will satisfy the public, and the people speak to-day through a determined Executive, who asks for a great antitrust law, that will be sufficient and strong enough to reach every violation of law, and so written that speedy justice may be dealt out to those who would violate it.

There is an unrest in the country. The many have toiled too long for the benefit of the few. Special interests have controlled the industries of the country and fattened thereon; corporate power born in remote States have seized the wealth in other States, bid defiance to State authority, crushed down labor, produced conditions of war, destruction of life, while the helpless have cried out in vain for justice. The people are reaching out for their rights, and will have them and will take no excuse for delay. They want promises made, to be fulfilled where possible.

It is true we have revised the tariff and taxed large incomes. We have given the country a great currency law, election of United States Senators by direct vote of the people, extended the powers of the Interstate Commerce Commission, provided for physical valuation of railroads, and passed many other wholesome laws desired by the people. But they want more; they want business unshackled and trust domination brought to an end; they want freedom of action in their struggle for better conditions; and they call upon Congress and the power of the Government to free them from the grasping and arrogant exercise of heretofore unrestrained power of greedy monopoly. I hope and believe that the Judiciary Committee will accept every reasonable amendment, that will strengthen the bill wherever needed, and that a real and effective antitrust law will be passed by Congress and become a law of the land. . . .

Mr. WEBB. Mr. Chairman, I move that the committee do now rise.

The motion was agreed to.

HOUSE DEBATE
63d Cong., 2d Sess.
May 25, 1914

51 Cong. Rec. 9195

The House met at 11 o'clock a. m. . . .

The SPEAKER. Under the rule the House resolves itself automatically into the Committee of the Whole House on the state of the Union for the further consideration of the bill H. R. 15657, and other bills. . . .

Mr. TAGGART. Mr. Chairman, it is not my purpose to make an extended speech on this bill. The bill has been under consideration for a long time and has been very ably and exhaustively presented to the committee. What I may say might not add to the light that has been thrown upon it, but I will occupy the time allotted to me in presenting at least some of the features of the bill.

I was deeply impressed by a speech made on this bill before the committee on Saturday by the gentleman from Wisconsin [Mr. NELSON], a member of the committee, and especially with what he said as to the growth of socialism and the reasons why socialism grows. It seems to me that the gentleman is deeply impressed with the fact, or, rather, with the fear, if American business becomes consolidated into the hands of great and ⊥ nation-wide business concerns, able to cater to the entire market in any line, that the greater the consolidation the easier it would be to take over those lines of business by the Government should socialism finally prevail.

[9196]

If each line of business is accumulated into one concern, there will be less resistance to the confiscation of it. If property is finally to be absorbed by the Government, it would add greatly to the convenience of those who hold that socialism is the solution of American industrial questions to have all business monopolized as much as possible before it is taken over.

There is a note of warning—of solemn warning—in what was said by the gentleman from Wisconsin. He has criticized this trust bill and has said that it will not prevent a further consolidation and monopoly of business, and therefore that it still remains as an encouragement to socialism. Strange as it may seem coming from a member of the Republican Party, and a distinguished and able one, the gentleman from Wisconsin has the sentiment of him who cried, "Lay on, Macduff!" He has criticized us for not being more drastic in our provisions for curbing big business in the United States. What has a party come to when one major general is shouting "Halt!" and the other major general is ordering us all to charge the breastworks? . . .

Mr. MANN. Is not that the situation on the Democratic side on this bill in reference to a number of things in it?

Mr. TAGGART. Well, now, I have not observed that there was any such disagreement as that on the Democratic side in reference to this bill.

Mr. MANN. If the gentleman will be here under the five-minute rule, he will observe that.

Mr. TAGGART. I observe that the distinguished gentleman from Illinois [Mr. MANN] is borrowing trouble.

Mr. MANN. Why, we were informed, if the gentleman will permit, by the gentleman who now holds the House in the hollow of his hand so far as business is concerned, the chairman of the Committee on Rules, that he proposes to strike out one of the most important provisions in this bill and insert something else in it.

Mr. TAGGART. I beg leave to say that the mysterious gentleman referred to by the gentleman from Illinois did not make such a statement as that or anything quite having that meaning, but he did say that a provision in section 7 of this bill would be submitted to this House for amendment under the five-minute rule, and that everybody in this House would have the free and full privilege of voting on it as he chooses.

Mr. MANN. Oh, he stated in a colloquy with me that they proposed to amend the bill and change it in that respect, and that they had the votes to do it.

Mr. TAGGART. Well, this is the House of Representatives, and the time has come when the House of Representatives is sufficiently reformed so that it will work out its will if it has the votes to do a certain thing. There was a day here when it had the votes to do things and was not permitted to do things.

Mr. MANN. That is the case now as to prohibition and woman suffrage.

Mr. TAGGART. Do you wish to express your enthusiasm for both of those great measures at this time? [Laughter.]

Mr. MANN. I am willing to vote upon them if you will give us the chance.

Mr. TAGGART. The gentleman from Illinois will have a golden opportunity when the time comes. [Laughter.]

Mr. MANN. I am afraid not.

Mr. TAGGART. Yes. There is something strange when there is a marshal commanding "Forward!" like Blucher on one side of the House, and on the same side of the House a Fabius who is willing to continue his retreat. You remember the lines that were written by Macaulay about the sack of Rome, where—

"Heaven help him!" quoth Lars Porsen, "and bring him safe to shore,
For such a gallant feat of arms was never seen before."

And there was a difference of opinion on a ground very much like that existing among you gentlemen now, for another shouted—

"Curse on him!" quoth false Sextus, "and let the villain drown;
But for this stay ere close of day we would have sacked the town."

This represents the difference here, at least on one side of the House, and if there is any difference on our side of the House that difference is represented by those who are willing to open this bill to the entire House, free from caucus action, free from all restraint, and call upon every Member of the House to vote upon every section of it as he sees fit—

Mr. GARNER. A thing you never had before under a Republican administration.

Mr. TAGGART. Yes; and I wish to say right here that in all the trust bills introduced in the whole history of this House such a privilege as that was never granted to the House of Representatives before. . . .

Mr. FESS. I wondered why it was necessary to have a caucus action on the currency question and on the tariff question, and not have it upon this question. Is there anything in this question that is less important than the other two?

Mr. TAGGART. I do not know that there is anything less important in this than in the other two, but there is less of a variety of opinion upon this than there was on the other two.

Mr. FESS. That means that caucus action is not to be held where there is not a variety of opinion?

Mr. TAGGART. The caucus action should be had in the discussion of those bills where the party is practically unanimous except as to details. With respect to those measures that are not party measures, like this one is not, but which is a national measure, part of it indorsed by practically the entire House of Representatives, there is no necessity for a caucus. There is a measure in this bill that had but 18 votes against it in a former Congress. There is another measure in this bill that had but 31 votes against it in a former House, and, in fact, the entire House of Representatives was practically unanimous with regard to the most important provisions of the bill in the Sixty-second Congress, and I dare say is practically unanimous now.

Why should any man's notions as to what should be placed in this bill, as if it were a commercial proposition like the tariff, be tied up by caucus action? The tariff is a commercial proposition—a proposition very much like bargaining over the counter of a store as to whether you will pay 35 cents or 40 cents for an article. Men would never agree about the tariff unless they first got together and discussed the matter fully.

In these matters that are rooted in the liberty of the American citizen I want to say that the Democratic Party is practically unanimous, and if there is anything that distinguishes a Democrat from his brother it is because he wants to extend more liberty to the American citizen.

Mr FESS. Then, you indorse the caucus action on certain kinds of bills and oppose it on other kinds of bills? Is that it?

Mr. TAGGART. I think caucus action is wise on certain kinds of bills, and I think that caucus action is unnecessary on other bills. It is not deciding between wisdom and unwisdom, but between what is necessary and what is unnecessary.

Mr. FESS. And the lack of diversity on this bill is the reason why you did not have caucus action on it? . . .

For the information of the gentleman from Connecticut. My point was—because the gentleman from Kansas [Mr. TAGGART] seems absolutely fair—why is it necessary to have caucus action on certain great measures and not on others? Is caucus action a necessary evil?

Mr. TAGGART. Now, the gentleman seems to throw the word "evil" in there gratuitously. It seems as though the gentleman regards a caucus as an evil, and is asking me what measure of evil there might be in caucus action on anything. Does the gentleman regard caucus action as an evil? If he does, I wish to say that the history of the gentleman's party is a compendium of the record of evil. [Laughter and applause on the Democratic side.]

Mr. FESS. I hope the gentleman will understand— . . .

That I am not holding a brief for any political party, past or present. I am trying to get light on this measure.

Mr. TAGGART. I am glad to say that no one rejoices in your conversion more than I. [Applause.] . . .

Mr. Chairman, this Government was founded to promote the liberty of the individual. The Constitution was drafted for the individual, not in his organized capacity but ⊥ in his individual capacity. The great American ideal is the free, untrammeled citizen, at perfect liberty under law to work out his own destiny and to succeed in that line of endeavor for which nature has fitted him best. The fathers who drafted the Constitution and who founded this Government lived on the verge and seashore of what Daniel Webster called "a fresh, untouched, unbounded, magnificent wilderness," practically unexplored, and uninhabited except by settlers in their little log houses, who tilled their farms and who lived in peace and comfort. There was then not a great manufacturer in the New World; perhaps there was not a manufacturing institution or a business house in which as many as a hundred persons were employed.

The Constitution, therefore, was not drafted as a law merchant, or primarily with the view of having business regulated. All the power that we have, and to which we are trying to give expression in this bill and other similar measures, is contained in 17 words in the Constitution:

The Congress shall have power to regulate commerce * * * among the several States and with the Indian tribes.

No other line or word in the Constitution adds to the power of Congress in dealing with the greatest concern of the American people at this hour, the greatest commercial people the world has ever known. But that Constitution had in it a bill of rights, a guaranty to every citizen of the same rights as every other citizen under the flag.

When this country grew to be the greatest of all commercial nations, and with the means of communication perfected, business began to fall into the hands of powerful combinations, and they, in the exercise of their power, denied and crushed out the rights of other citizens to do business in this country. Where a citizen started in to compete with them in the same line they spent their resources and sold goods at a loss, for the purpose of underselling him and compelling him to leave the business that was dear to his heart and in which he proposed to engage as a vocation during his whole life. The individual liberty to go where he pleased, to be a free man, to worship as he pleased, and all those other personal things that were mentioned in the Constitution remained to him; but he did not have what the nature of things gave him when the Constitution was adopted. He did not have the privilege and the right of working out his own destiny under his own flag as he thought he had the right to do.

The States were first to take these matters under consideration. I have the happiness here to say to-day that the State of Kansas was the first State in the Union to pass, in 1905, an act forbidding discrimination in price in different communities and localities within the confines of that great State, having 81,000 square miles. This was brought about through the operations of a great coal-oil company which had undertaken to monopolize the entire market for its product in that State, and which sent out its agents to follow up and waylay its rivals in business and destroy their business by underselling them and by selling its product at less than its product was worth. As a part of my remarks I will insert that portion of the Kansas statute which puts a penalty on discrimination in price in different localities in the State:

ACT OF 1905.

1. Any person, firm, or corporation, foreign or domestic, doing business in the State of Kansas and engaged in the production, manufacture, or distribution of any commodity in general use, that shall intentionally, for the purpose of destroying competition, discriminate between different sections, communities, or cities of this State by selling such commodity at a lower rate in one section, community, or city, or any portion thereof, than is charged for such commodity in another section, community, or city, after equalizing the distance from the point of production, manufacture, or distribution and freight rates therefrom, shall be deemed guilty of unfair discrimination. (L. 1905, ch. 2, sec. 1; G. S., sec. 5162.)

This statute has been followed substantially in as many as 18 States of the Union. Uniformity of price is required throughout the State, the cost of transportation being equalized and taken into consideration.

There was no statute of the United States dealing with this subject, and in section 2 of this bill we have provided what has been enacted in so many States of the Union. As a part of my remarks I insert the section:

SEC. 2. That any person engaged in commerce who shall either directly or indirectly discriminate in price between different purchasers of commodities in the same or different sections or communities, which commodities are sold for use, consumption, or resale within the United States or any Territory thereof or the District of Columbia or any insular possession or other place under the jurisdiction of the United States, with the purpose or intent to thereby destroy or wrongfully injure the business of a competitor, of either such purchaser or seller, shall be deemed guilty of a misdemeanor, and upon conviction thereof shall be punished by a fine not exceeding $5,000, or by imprisonment not exceeding one year, or by both, in the discretion of the court: *Provided*, That nothing herein contained shall prevent discrimination in price between purchasers of commodities on account of differences in the grade, quality, or quantity of the commodity sold, or that makes only due allowance for difference in the cost of transportation: *And provided further*, That nothing herein contained shall prevent persons engaged in selling goods, wares, or merchandise in commerce from selecting their own customers, except as provided in section 3 of this act.

Criticism was made here the other day by gentlemen who called attention to the proviso in the second section—

That nothing herein contained shall prevent discrimination in price between purchasers of commodities on account of differences in the grade, quality, or quantity of the commodity sold, or that makes only due allowance for difference in the cost of transportation.

Did any gentleman expect that we would make a statute that would require a uniform price regardless of the grade or quality of the thing sold? Even if it was within the power of Congress to enact a statute of that kind the statute would be worthless. It would be denying the fact that things have different values, and no legislative body can fix real value of any article or the relative value of different articles. The way to look at it is to consider what would be the case if we provided otherwise.

The criticism was made that inasmuch as quantity is mentioned here this bill will give liberty to sell large quantities at a lower relative price than small quantities, which will render the bill meaningless and incapable of enforcement. Suppose we enacted that a can of corn shall be sold at the same relative price as a carload of canned corn. Would you vote for a provision of that kind? If you did, you would then indeed destroy the meaning of the bill and render it absurd. The meaning of the bill is that if in one place in this country they sell a carload of any given commodity at a lower and discriminating price than they sell a carload of the same commodity at another place in this country, the cost of transportation being equalized and considered, then they are guilty under this law. That is the meaning of it. . . .

Mr. FESS. Suppose a small producer of canned corn, such as would be in my part of the State, wanted to open a market in Washington or in some city where he had no market. Would he be allowed to sell at a less price on the initiation of the contract, in order to get an opening, than in any other part of the United States where the cost of transportation would be the same?

Mr. TAGGART. There would be no exception made in a case of that kind. If he was making a superior article of canned corn, which of course they do in your district—

Mr. FESS. Certainly.

Mr. TAGGART. The corn would have to speak for itself. He would not be allowed to give it away for the purpose of taking the market away from somebody else.

Mr. FESS. Now, will not that be an advantage to the great producer, who has his agents everywhere, as against the small producer of the same article?

Mr. TAGGART. Why should it be?

Mr. FESS. Because he has advertising methods by which he can get his article before the community in a way in which my man can not.

Mr. TAGGART. The large producer has that advantage now, has he not? He has the same advertising methods now; and he not only has that advantage, but suppose there was some great canning company practically catering to the entire trade of the United States. If your friend in Ohio should undertake to initiate his trade in any community, he would perhaps find that he was followed up by an agent of this great company, who would give away canned corn until your man was forced out of business, and under the present law he could do it. If he had not established an agency in that State he could do it, under the present interstate-commerce laws of this country, even in a State where they require uniformity of price.

Mr. FESS. My point is this: Is there not a possibility under this section to favor the great producer as against the small producer, the thing you are trying to prevent?

Mr. TAGGART. I grasp just what the gentleman means, and it is this: That a small producer, who has some money and a great deal of enthusiasm, desires to go into the markets of the United States and by offering his wares at a cheap price introduce his product in certain neighborhoods.

Mr. FESS. Yes; that is the idea.

Mr. TAGGART. And give the people notice that after 60 or 90 days he will charge a higher price, but for the purpose of introducing it he will first sell it at cost or below cost. That has been a practice in the United States that has been engaged in ever since the interstate commerce began. What right has he to do that? [Applause.]

It would seem as though a well-meaning person or firm, desiring to introduce a new and superior article, ought to be ⊥ encouraged. Possibly a reasonable time for advertising an article, by selling it at a low price, ought to be provided in the bill. When the bill is submitted to the Committee of the Whole House a full opportunity will be given to amend this section.

Section 4 of the bill will afford relief to retail dealers, who are now required by wholesalers to handle certain articles exclusively and become sole agents for certain goods. These retailers have complained that they are injured by conditions imposed upon them by wholesale firms, and that their trade is limited and embarrassed. While the contracts that they are obliged to make to sell certain articles exclusively and refuse to sell competing articles of the same kind may be wholly void, the people engaged in big business, who sell to these retail dealers are able to enforce these contracts by refusing to supply the retail dealer any more of the same kind of goods if he should carry in his stock certain competing articles. This section does not prohibit sole agencies, as those who have not read it carefully have said that it does. A manufacturer of any article can employ a sole agent to sell that article wherever he pleases. A sole agent simply represents his principal. What it will prevent is compelling an independent dealer to become a sole agent for any article, by oppressing him commercially, if he chooses to buy and sell what he pleases. Abundant evidence was brought before the committee that great firms that lease machinery and supplies, and by the terms of the lease seek to compel, and do compel, the people who lease the supplies and machinery to patronize these firms exclusively. The manufacturer who is in the grip of this class of people has no liberty at all. This kind of oppression will be effectually prohibited by this bill.

Section 6 arms the Department of Justice and the courts of the United States with a new and formidable weapon to prevent and punish the crimes of destructive business. Under the provisions of this section when a suit is brought against a party by the United States and a final judgment is rendered against the defendant, showing that the defendant has violated the Sherman antitrust law, or any antitrust law, the record of that judgment can be put in evidence in a suit against the same defendant for damages that may be brought by any private individual, and the judgment so introduced will be considered conclusive evidence that the defendant had violated the antitrust laws, and the only question for the jury to decide will be the amount of damages that the plaintiff ought to recover.

A great many suits have been brought against trusts by the United States and many trusts have been dissolved. Some few have been punished, but the people whose business they destroyed have been practically without a remedy. When this bill becomes a law, the person who willfully destroys another person's business will do so at his peril. Damages can be recovered and the claim for damages will not be outlawed by the statute of limitations during the time that the United States is proceeding against the offending party. The Government can subpoena witnesses from any place in the Union and require their personal presence. Not alone will an offending corporation be punished, but any director, officer, or agent, who shall have authorized or shall have done any of the prohibited acts shall be held to be guilty.

The bill is framed for the purpose of liberating business and not for the purpose of injuring or destroying any business. Its great purpose is to protect small business from big business, and to compel all business to be conducted honestly.

In the Sixty-second Congress two bills relating to labor were passed in the House— the anti-injunction bill and the contempt bill. Although they were vigorously opposed by some of the Republican minority on the committee, there were but 31 votes against the anti-injunction bill and only 18 votes against the bill that provided for trial by jury in cases of indirect contempt. Both of these bills are included word for word in this bill, comprising sections 15 to 23, inclusive. Now, I do not propose to talk about the rights of labor. This would be, to my mind, a narrow view of the subject. We are not legislating for citizens simply because they belong to any organization or because they describe themselves or they may be described by any distinctive term or combination of words. I do not wish to appeal to men of a certain class or to convey the impression to them that I am pretending to represent them exclusively. This never was, and never ought to be, and I hope never will be, the position taken by any representative of the American people. We who are here represent them all. The whole people have particular respect for all classes of men who work earnestly and faithfully to bear the burden of modern civilization and the tremendous labor that is the glory of American life. In these nine sections are contained a charter of liberty and a bill of rights for the whole American people. The people of this country are not satisfied to have their sense of justice expressed wholly through the decisions and the decrees of a group of judges with a life tenure of office. While many of these men are of the highest character and interpret the law fearlessly as it has been provided for them, there are those among them who have made a different use of their tremendous power and who have earned the reputation of being the wisely selected and faithful guardians of big business. These provisions will come as a relief to the conscience of every wise and thoughtful Federal judge in the whole land. These sections will establish and make plain the simple rights that men have enjoyed for ages. The following are the rights that shall not be disturbed by the process of any Federal court when this bill becomes a law:

First. No injunction shall run against persons because they have ceased to perform any kind of work or labor.

Second. Courts are prohibited from issuing injunctions to prevent persons from recommending, advising, or persuading others to cease the work that they are doing.

Third. The right peaceably to assemble, guaranteed by the Constitution, must not be interfered with by any injunction to prevent persons from assembling peacefully at any place in a lawful manner and for lawful purposes, although the meeting may be had at or near a house or place where any person resides or works or carries on business or happens to be if the purpose of the meeting is peaceful and merely for the purpose of obtaining or communicating information or persuading any person in a peaceful manner, either to work or abstain from work.

Fourth. People will not, under this bill, be enjoined from ceasing to patronize or to employ any party to a dispute or controversy between employer and employee, or from giving to or withholding from any person engaged in such a controversy, any money or thing of value that they see fit to give.

Fifth. A controversy between employer and employee is shorn of its distinctive character by this bill. It has been treated in a class by itself in certain federal courts. Courts have issued process in a controversy when the same courts would hold that it would be unlawful to issue such process in a case which was not a controversy between employer and employee. In other words, the acts of men in the case of a dispute, although they may be peaceful, have been considered in a different light than their ordinary acts. Under the provisions of this bill no one shall be enjoined from doing any act or thing in the case of a dispute or while a controversy is pending which would be a lawful act if there were no controversy.

Sixth. The right of trial by jury for the offense called contempt of court, which is not committed in the presence of the court, is fully and effectually provided for in this bill. It is strange but true that courts and lawmakers have sharply distinguished between violations of positive law and violations of the orders and decrees of courts. In the case of one charged with a violation of the criminal law, especially a felony, a trial by jury has been the undisputed birthright of the English-speaking people of the world for more than a thousand years. But during all those centuries in the case of violating the order of the court, the offending person has been fined or imprisoned at the will and by the verdict of one man sitting on a bench. What reason has there been for this distinction? If there ever was any reason, the representatives of the American people are now ready and willing to declare, and do declare that that reason has ceased to exist.

This bill does not license destruction or interfere with the power of courts to prevent injury to persons or property. It simply provides that courts shall not unreasonably nor arbitrarily exercise that power. We are not so conservative as the English are, and yet a short time ago the British Parliament passed an act covering a phase of labor disputes that has been considered unlawful heretofore and has been the subject of particular attention in United States courts. The new British law is as follows:

> It shall be lawful for one or more persons, acting on their own behalf or in behalf of a trades-union, in contemplation of a trade dispute, to attend peacefully and in a reasonable manner at or near a house or place where a person works or carries on business, if he attend for the purpose of persuading any person to work or to abstain from working.

The bill we have prepared is a measure for the whole people. Under its provision no business will fail, except in so far as it is seeking by unfair and unlawful means to destroy a competing business. Honesty is encouraged and protected; dishonesty restrained and punished. Property and business are not abandoned to the mob and the rights of the citizen are not left solely in the hands of the autocrat of the bench. The Committee on the Judiciary, after a full and fair hearing of every person who chose to be present, took the middle course between these extremes, and with whatever measure of ability they had, pre⊥pared this bill, for the consideration of Congress and on behalf of all the people. Should its provisions fall short of justice they can be amended. Should they work injustice, they can soon be remedied, but ever and always let us keep before us that the humblest individual beneath the flag has an equal right to work out his destiny under the law in the way he chooses, and that the work of his life must be protected from those who from selfish motives would do him injury. . . .

Mr. GREEN of Iowa. Mr. Chairman, I trust that anything I may say in discussing this bill will not be treated as invidious criticism of the members of the committee who reported it. I have the highest opinion for the learning, the zeal, and the industry of these gentlemen. I have made a considerable study of this question, and my study has only forced upon me the sense of the enormous difficulties which confronted them when they prepared the bill. With all this, I will have to say that I have been considerably disappointed in the bill and the report which accompanied it. But perhaps I ought not to have been, when there was added not only to the natural difficulties with which the gentlemen were confronted the pressure of political necessity which required them to bring in a bill which would meet some partisan exigency, and in accordance with the direction of a particular person, I ought not to be surprised that the committee has failed, as I think they have, to bring in a proper bill.

The gentlemen who have spoken on the other side, and particularly the distinguished gentleman from Kansas [Mr. TAGGART] who has just taken his seat, have entirely misunderstood the trend of the criticisms upon this side. We do not object to this bill because it is too drastic; we object to the bill because it adds nothing to the law which precedes it and simply confuses and confounds men who are undertaking to do business under it. I am speaking now solely of the new provisions in the bill and not of the provisions which were already law by virtue of court decisions or statutes already enacted.

I object to this bill at this time, not because it adds too much power to the present law but because it detracts from and emasculates the Sherman law which is already on the statute books; not because it gives additional force and efficiency to the law we now have, but because it takes away in important respects the powers given to the Government in the law now on the statute books.

I object to it, further, because they have undertaken to add to a law which was clear and precise in its form provisions which are in some respects of doubtful constitutionality, and in one respect absolutely unconstitutional. They have done this by bringing in what I call a political bill, because members on this side have not been asked to assist in its preparation. In this respect they have done very differently from the framers of the original Sherman law. I suppose everyone is aware that the original Sherman law was not prepared by Senator Sherman.

Mr. BARTLETT. Only the title.

Mr. GREEN of Iowa. Only the title, as the gentleman from Georgia states. After Senator Sherman had prepared and introduced a bill in the Senate, a substitute was prepared by Senator Reagan, of Texas, which undertook, in something the same form as the bill now before us, to define specifically the offenses which might come under its provisions. After that bill had been considered the committee finally brought out a substitute for the Reagan bill. It is sometimes supposed that the bill known as the Sherman law was in fact prepared by Senator Edmunds; but the real fact, as now known, is that it was prepared by Senator Hoar. I never had an opportunity of listening to Senator Hoar, but those who have heard him speak and those who study his writings know that he possessed in a remarkable degree a faculty of clear, accurate, and comprehensive expression such as was probably possessed by no other man in public life of his day, and it is doubtful if his powers in this respect have ever been equaled in our legislative history.

The Sherman law is a model of clearness and of brevity and a marvel in comprehension. Somebody has said that it was like a universal joint in machinery—it can be pointed in any direction and will work in any manner the party using it sees fit. The trouble we have had with the growth and development of trusts under the Sherman law is not from any defect in the law itself, but from failure of its administration, which has arisen partly through an unwillingness to enforce the law from dread of the special interests, and partly because of defects in the administrative powers of the courts.

I have been surprised, upon consideration of the bill now before us and of the report of the committee, that neither here nor in the report accompanying the bill does anyone set forth how the Sherman law has failed to reach the evils which are claimed to exist under the present law. There are no citations to any cases; there are no particular facts pointed out as to which it is claimed that the Sherman law can not and does not reach any wrong which is alleged to prevail. . . .

Mr. BARTLETT. Has there been any case brought under the Sherman law, except one, where the present law as applied to the corporations, where the corporations have been convicted of violating the Sherman law, where the court has not upheld the law, except the Knight case,[5.524] which failed for want of jurisdiction?

Mr. GREEN of Iowa. I would say that the Knight case failed because it was not properly presented to the court.

Mr. BARTLETT. But it went off on a question of jurisdiction.

Mr. GREEN of Iowa. The gentleman is entirely correct. I wish to consider more particularly the provisions of this bill now before the House, and as I am now discussing it in an informal manner I will welcome any questions or interruptions. . . .

Mr. FESS. I think for the matter of the RECORD, to show that this was nonpartisan, the gentleman ought to state that it was unanimously adopted in the Senate and, I think, only one vote recorded against it in the House.

Mr. GREEN of Iowa. The gentleman is referring to the Sherman law?

Mr. FESS. Yes.

Mr. GREEN of Iowa. I had intended to mention that fact. It was discussed and adopted entirely in a nonpartisan way, and the vote upon it was almost unanimous, lacking only one vote, as the gentleman from Ohio has correctly stated.

I shall not have time to refer to all of the provisions of this bill to which I object, but I will call attention, first, to section 2, which provides, among other things, that any person engaged in commerce who shall discriminate in price between the purchasers of commodities with the intent and purpose thereby to destroy or wrongfully injure the business of a competitor, the purchaser and the seller shall be guilty of a misdemeanor. I would like to inquire what case there is that has ever held that actions of that kind are not punishable under the Sherman law as it now stands? An act such as is described in this section is clearly an attempt to monopolize business. . . .

Mr. BARTLETT. That species of monopoly and combination and trust, an effort to break down a competitor, is one of the earmarks of monopoly and violates the law and was pointed out in the celebrated Tobacco case[5.525] as being evidence of violation of the law.

Mr. GREEN of Iowa. The gentleman has expressed very forcibly a matter to which I intended to refer, and very correctly.

⊥ Mr. FLOYD of Arkansas. I am not able to point out to the gentleman where ⊥9200 that has ever been held not to be a violation of the law, but it has never been held to be a violation of the Sherman law, and, in my opinion, such act of discrimination is not within the purview of the Sherman law as it now exists. The gentleman can not cite a case in which it has been so held. It is an instrumentality which has been used by different corporations, referred to by the courts as evidence tending to show that the corporation has been guilty of a violation of the Sherman law; but the single transaction, the act of discrimination, taken alone, condemned in that section, has never been held by a court in any decision to be a violation of the Sherman law.

Mr. GREEN of Iowa. Mr. Chairman, the gentleman is quite correct as to the decisions, but at the same time it has been repeatedly held by the courts that such a transaction is one of the indicia and evidences of violations of the Sherman law. Section 2 of the Sherman law expressly states that every person who shall monopolize or attempt to monopolize or combine or conspire to monopolize any trade or commerce, and so forth, shall be subject to its provisions. If the gentleman means to say that these acts which he has described in section 2 of the bill are not done with intent to monopolize, and that he intends to make criminal acts which do not interfere with competition or tend to monopolize, then I will agree with him; but, otherwise, I am compelled to disagree.

Mr. FLOYD of Arkansas. Mr. Chairman, I will state to the gentleman that the object of that section is to strike down the practice that has been referred to by the courts in decisions in antitrust cases as one of the instrumentalities used in building up monopolies in this country, and I want to state further—

[5.524] United States v. E.C. Knight Co., 156 U.S. 1, 15 S. Ct. 249, 39 L. Ed. 325 (1895).

[5.525] United States v. American Tobacco Co., 221 U.S. 106, 31 S. Ct. 632, 55 L. Ed. 663 (1911), portions of which are reprinted *supra* at chapter 1.

Mr. GREEN of Iowa. I hope the gentleman will pardon me, but my time is slipping by, and I am not going to be able to reach some matters I want to speak of particularly.

After the provision making these matters subject to penalty it was found necessary to add a number of provisos. These exceptions necessarily afford an opportunity to evade the Sherman law, which reached everything covered by this section, in so far as it interfered with competition, without any provisos. The law as it stands is sufficient, and section 2 of the bill will merely weaken it through these provisos.

I wish also to speak of section 3, which provides in part as follows:

> That it shall be unlawful for the owner or operator of any mine or for any person controlling the product of any mine engaged in selling its product in commerce to refuse arbitrarily to sell such product to a responsible person, firm, or corporation who applies to purchase such product for use—

And so forth.

As has been observed, this applies simply to the owners of coal and other mines. It does not apply to persons who are operating in other natural products, such as lumber, timber, and articles of that kind. The fourteenth amendment to the Constitution provides that no State shall deprive any citizen of the equal protection of the law. Of course, this amendment applies only to the States, but it has never been held or contended, so far as I know, that the Constitution gives the Federal Government the right to deprive any citizen of the equal protection of its law. Of course, classifications can be made under the criminal law, where such classifications are not made arbitrarily: but what reason is given for selecting the coal miners or coal dealers under this provision? Why should not those who deal in lumber, those who own the forests, as well as those who control the mines, be subject to similar provisions, and what authority can gentlemen cite, giving Congress power to arbitrarily select certain individuals without any reason therefor and make them subject to penalty? . . .

Mr. [HERMAN A.] METZ [D., N.Y.]. While we are trying to get at monopoly here, and have in mind oil and coal, and so forth, does not section 2 practically put every business house, every dealer in any kind of goods, in the same category with those big corporations, with this exception, that he can choose his own customers?

Mr. GREEN of Iowa. Oh, no.

Mr. METZ. Oh, yes. It fixes the price.

Mr. GREEN of Iowa. I think I did not fully understand the remarks of the gentleman from New York. . . .

Mr. FESS. Does it not discriminate against the small producer rather than to put him on an equality with the large producer, who can send his men to represent his goods everywhere, while the small man can not, and therefore how is he going to get into the markets?

Mr. GREEN of Iowa. I think the gentleman has correctly stated an objection to the bill, and if the gentleman from New York [Mr. METZ] is correct, it would be an additional reason why this provision is of doubtful constitutionality.

Mr. METZ. I agree with the gentleman. I think it is of doubtful constitutionality.

Mr. GREEN of Iowa. Mr. Chairman, I see my time is passing rapidly, and I can only briefly refer to section 4. The distinguished gentleman from Arkansas [Mr. FLOYD] spoke of some decision which made necessary the enactment of this provision, but did not have the decision with him at the time he spoke, and I have not been able to find it since. In so far as acts covered by section 4—

Mr. FLOYD of Arkansas. If the gentleman will permit an interruption, the gentleman will find the decision in volume 125, Federal Reporter, page 454. It is the case of Whitwell against the Continental Tobacco Co. et al.

Mr. GREEN of Iowa. What kind of a case was it?

Mr. FLOYD of Arkansas. It was a case brought under the antitrust law, in which the court holds that kind of a contract is not in violation of the Sherman Act.

Mr. GREEN of Iowa. Well, I do not have time to discuss this matter fully, but if the framers of the bill wished to prevent the holders of a patent from putting restrictions upon the sale or lease of the patented article, we ought to have a separate and distinct bill for that purpose. Reference is made to a decision of a lower Federal court. If the decisions of the lower Federal courts stood, there would not be much left of the Sherman law. . . .

Mr. J. M. C. SMITH. I desire to ask the gentleman whether or not he thinks section 4 applies to patented articles at all. It says persons engaged in commerce. It does not make any difference, it does not say it should be a patented article that he is handling, but simply says it shall be a matter of commerce.

Mr. GREEN of Iowa. The gentleman calls attention to one of the vital defects of this provision. I am not prepared to say, and I doubt whether any gentleman is prepared to say definitely it would apply to such a case as the gentleman mentions. I now yield to the gentleman from Arkansas.

Mr. FLOYD of Arkansas. The gentleman refers to the decision cited by me as one rendered by a lower court? The decision rendered was in the United States circuit court of appeals by Judge Sanborn, in the case of Whitwell against the Continental Tobacco Co. et al., and can be found in volume 125, Federal Reporter, page 454.

Mr. GREEN of Iowa. The gentleman certainly is aware that that is not the highest Federal court.

Mr. FLOYD of Arkansas. It is a Federal court of very high authority, the highest next to the Supreme Court.

Mr. GREEN of Iowa. Mr. Chairman, before taking my seat I desire to refer to the provisions of section 6. There can be, as I said, no possible question but what the provisions of this section are unconstitutional. It provides that when a decree has been rendered in a suit commenced on behalf of the United States under the antitrust laws that—

said judgment or decree shall, to the full extent to which such judgment or decree would constitute in any other proceeding an estoppel as between the United States and such defendant, constitute in favor of or against such defendant conclusive evidence of the same facts, and be conclusive as to the same questions of law in favor of or against any other party in any action or proceeding brought under or involving the provisions of any of the antitrust laws.

The effect of this decision is such that if some third party should commence a suit for damages under the Sherman law he might find himself bound by a decree in an action brought by the United States against the same party, which holds that the Sherman law has not been violated. In such event, the party who wishes to commence his suit will find that he is estopped and precluded without having his day in court, without having any opportunity to be heard, without having any opportunity to present his evidence. The gentleman from Georgia has referred to the Knight case, in which the Sherman law was invoked, but where the case was dismissed with the findings of fact and conclusions of law that the Sherman law had not been violated. If the provisions of section 6 had then been in force and effect the parties who afterwards successfully maintained ⊥ a suit for damages against the Sugar Trust would have in all probability found the decree in the Knight case standing like a stone wall in their way. I have no hesitation in saying this provision is unconstitutional, and I feel confident that it will not be in this bill when it is finally enacted into law. . . .

Mr. BARTLETT. What effect does the gentleman think it would have simply to make it prima facie evidence? This bill makes it conclusive evidence, to which the gentleman has referred. Now, what effect would it have to say that the findings between the United States Government and the corporations should be affirmative evidence of a violation of the law to be rebutted by the evidence?

Mr. GREEN of Iowa. I will answer the gentleman by saying I think that the words "in favor of," which precede the word "defendant," ought to be stricken out. The defendant has had his day in court. He has had his opportunity to be heard. It is proper that the decree should constitute a final estoppel as against him, but not as against some third person who was not a party to the original action and has had no opportunity to present his case.

Now, I wish to speak briefly in reference to section 8. It is the provision with reference to holding companies. It states:

SEC. 8. That no corporation engaged in commerce shall acquire, directly or indirectly, the whole or any part of the stock or other share capital of another corporation engaged also in commerce, where the effect of such acquisition is to eliminate or substantially lessen competition between the corporation whose stock is so acquired and the corporation making the acquisition, or to create a monopoly of any line of trade in any section or community. . . .

Every gentleman in the House who has made a study of the law applicable to this subject is aware that the creation of a holding company for the purpose of eliminating competition has been held to be a violation of the Sherman law, but if this section is enacted we will have to go further than to secure a conviction under the law. It provides at the bottom of page 25—

This section shall not apply to corporations purchasing such stock solely for investment and not using the same by voting or otherwise to bring about, or in attempting to bring about, the substantial lessening of competition.

In the Northern Securities case it was held that the mere potential power to bring about a monopoly or effect a lessening of competition was sufficient to bring the contract under the provisions of the Sherman law, but under provisions that we have in this bill it will be necessary to show that some step was actually taken in the way of preventing or lessening competition before the law will apply. This section is another instance where the law as it now stands is not strengthened, but weakened.

In the few minutes I have remaining I wish to speak very briefly with reference to section 12. This is the so-called "personal guilt" section, in which the committee seemed to take a special pride, and yet I have no hesitation in saying that it adds to the burden imposed upon the prosecutor by the law as it now stands. In other words, it will be more difficult to convict or bring about the conviction of any person under this section than it is now under the Sherman law. The Sherman law is personal in its provisions; it applies to persons as well as corporations. There is no difficulty in making guilt personal under it. Section 12 provides—

That whenever a corporation shall be guilty of the violation of any of the provisions of the antitrust laws, the offense shall be deemed to be also that of the individual directors, officers, or agents of such corporation.

It does not provide and could not provide in any constitutional way that the mere fact that a corporation has been found guilty should also establish the guilt of some official or director. This probably was in the mind of the gentlemen who prepared this section, and they found it necessary to add thereto—

Any director, officer, or agent who shall have authorized, ordered, or done any of such prohibited act shall be deemed guilty of a misdemeanor.

It follows that, under the provision of this section, the corporation must first be convicted. After the corporation is convicted the individual must be convicted, and, finally, after two convictions, the guilt is made personal.

Mr. GORDON. Do you claim that you can not prosecute the individual in a separate indictment without first prosecuting the corporation under the language referred to?

Mr. GREEN of Iowa. So far as the provisions of this section are concerned, I do. If it does away with the provisions of the Sherman Act this would be necessary, because it expressly so states.

Mr. [PHILIP P.] CAMPBELL [R., Kan.]. I would like to ask in what way can the corporation violate the law except through its managing officer?

Mr. GREEN of Iowa. It can not; and the provisions of the Sherman law consequently apply to them where they have actually taken part in the violation of the law.

Mr. CAMPBELL. I was going to follow that and then ask if the Sherman law does not cover the case, if it is rigidly enforced, as it now stands upon the statutes?

Mr. GREEN of Iowa. If it is enforced at all, it covers it?

Mr. CAMPBELL. Yes.

Mr. GREEN of Iowa. This section only applies to a director, officer, or agent who shall have actually authorized, ordered, or done some of the prohibited acts, not of this section but of the antitrust laws. But whenever such facts are shown they become a crime under the Sherman law itself, and we have no need for this section whatever. . . .

Mr. SLOAN. Under that statute the officer who neglected to do the act he should have done and permitted the violation of the law is not covered in that statute, is he?

Mr. GREEN of Iowa. Very clearly not. . . .

I have not time to go over this bill as I would like; but I have shown, I think, with reference to these sections which are new, that instead of giving any additional force to the Sherman law they actually detract from its provisions and make it more difficult of enforcement. The criticisms we make upon this side are not because this law is not sufficiently drastic. We criticize because it adds little or nothing to the law as it now stands, because it confuses business and confounds business men by provisions that are indefinite, uncertain, and of doubtful legality or absolutely unconstitutional. Do gentlemen think they can make a decree stand against a person who was never a party to the original action? Do they think that they can single out one particular kind of merchants and leave out other kinds who stand in exactly the same position? Do they think it strengthens the law to enact definitions and then follow the definitions with a number of provisos? What we need, and what we ought to have—what we must have to stop the growth of monopoly in this country—is further provisions in reference to the effect which decrees shall have when enacted. I have introduced a bill which provides that in the case of a violation of the Sherman law the courts must impose a jail sentence. I think that would have some effect, but I do not think that that would accomplish the desired result by itself. The only way in which we can ever stop the growth of monopolies is by requiring all corporations engaged in interstate commerce to take out a Federal license, and then providing that when an action in equity is commenced and it is found that the defendants are violating the law an order shall first be issued restraining them from any further violation. It then should be provided that in event the order is violated not only that the officers of any offending corporation shall be in contempt of court, but also that the corporation itself shall forfeit its license to do interstate business.

Mr. J. M. C. SMITH. Is it not the idea of the gentleman that the bill is not drastic enough?

Mr. GREEN of Iowa. I do not want the present law weakened in any particular. The bill does reach the deficiencies in the present system.

Mr. J. M. C. SMITH. It was your idea that it is not drastic enough. I take it from what you said.

Mr. GREEN of Iowa. I do not know what the gentleman calls drastic. What I want is something that will make the present law more efficient; but I think this bill will weaken it in many respects.

MR. J. M. C. SMITH. If the gentleman would get some of the letters that I have, he would think it is murder in the first degree.

Mr. GREEN of Iowa. Well, business men are more excited about what this law will accomplish than they need to be. There is not anything in it except a general disturbance of business, as I view it. It will not go beyond the Sherman law in any of the respects that I have mentioned. . . .

⊥ Mr. TOWNER. As the gentleman has shown, in section 12 there is an absolute ⊥ 9202 reduction of the possibility of making guilt personal, is there not?

Mr. GREEN of Iowa. There is.

Mr. TOWNER. Because under the provisions of section 12, in order to prosecute an individual as an officer of the corporation who has authorized a violation of the law, it can only be done if the corporation has been indicted and convicted, and then must follow the indictment or conviction of the individual?

Mr. GREEN of Iowa. The gentleman is correct if you proceed under this section and not under the old Sherman law.

Mr. TOWNER. Is not this a later expression of the law?

Mr. GREEN of Iowa. It was so intended.

Mr. TOWNER. And if it passes, will it not be, in effect, a repeal of all of the other laws with regard to those matters?

Mr. GREEN of Iowa. The gentleman states one of the many points where it will introduce confusion with reference to law which is now well settled.

The CHAIRMAN. The time of the gentleman from Iowa [Mr. GREEN] has again expired.

Mr. FLOYD of Arkansas. Mr. Chairman, I move that the committee do now rise.

The motion was agreed to.

HOUSE DEBATE
63d Cong., 2d Sess.
May 26, 1914

51 CONG. REC. 9245

The House met at 11 o'clock a. m. . . .

ANTITRUST LEGISLATION.

The SPEAKER. The unfinished business is H. R. 15657. The House will resolve itself automatically into the Committee of the Whole House on the state of the Union, with the gentleman from Tennessee [BYRNS] in the chair. . . .

Mr. [WILLIAM J.] MACDONALD [Prog., Mich.]. Mr. Chairman, while I do not consider that this bill is framed to meet the trust problems at the proper angle, nor do I consider that the bill is provided with teeth to attack this enemy with the results designed to be accomplished by the Progressive bills, still, with what I consider certain necessary amendments, I am inclined to support this bill, because I believe it does take a step in the direction of accomplishing something toward settling our trust problems.

My Progressive colleagues who have spoken in this debate have ably pointed out the difference between the present Democratic program and the Progressive program, and I shall not dwell on that point. There are certain amendments that I think ought to be made to this bill. Some, I believe, will be made, and we shall probably hear them discussed at great length under the five-minute rule.

But the thing that impresses me particularly in this bill, and the thing that I find constantly coming up in every matter that vitally concerns us in our governmental problems, is the thing that overshadows everything else. That is the evidence found here of the immediate struggle that is going on between these great combinations of organized capital and the people. In this bill, try to conceal it as we may, we all know in our hearts that there is one important, great outstanding feature. That is the question as to whether this law shall be directed against the combinations of capital that it was designed to be directed against, or whether it shall be shifted, partially at least, and turned against the very people whom it was designed to protect. [Applause.]

A great deal of discussion has been going on pro and con for 24 years in regard to what class of people this antitrust legislation was directed against. The proposition is so simple that it seems absolutely ridiculous to think that there should be any doubt about it. The men who framed the first legislation of this kind that was put upon the statute books, the Sherman law, had no doubt as to whom this legislation was directed against, and they also, as shown by the debates at that time, were far-sighted enough to realize that these great combinations against whom this legislation was directed would be shrewd enough, as they always are, immediately to turn the legislative guns that were trained upon them against the very people themselves.

Senator Sherman, the nominal author of the so-called Sherman law, at least had no doubt as to this question, and in the debate in the Senate, on March 24, 1890, Senator Sherman said:

Now, let us look at it. The bill as reported contains three or four simple propositions which relate only to contracts, combinations, agreements made with a view and designed to carry out a certain purpose which the laws of all the States and of every civilized community declare to be unlawful. It does not interfere in the slightest degree with voluntary associations made to affect public opinion to advance the interests of a particular trade or occupation. It does not interfere with the Farmers' Alliance at all, because that is an association of farmers to advance their interests and to improve the growth and manner of production of their crops and to secure intelligent growth and to introduce new methods. No organizations in this country can be more beneficial in their character than farmers' alliances and farmers' associations. They are not business combinations. They do not deal with contracts, agreements, and so forth. They have no connection with them. And so the combinations of workingmen to promote their interests, promote their welfare, and increase their pay, if you please, to ⊥ get their fair share in the division of production, are not affected in the slightest degree, nor can they be included in the words or intent of the bill as now reported.

⊥9246

Notwithstanding the disclaimer on the part of Senator Sherman and many others in the Senate at that time as to the class of people designed to be reached by that legislation, Senator George introduced an amendment at that time providing:

> *Provided*, That this act shall not be construed to apply to any arrangements, agreements, or combinations between the laborers, made with a view of lessening the number of hours of labor or the increasing of their wages; nor to any arrangements, agreements, or combinations among persons engaged in horticulture or agriculture, made with a view of enhancing the price of agricultural or horticultural products.

Although Senator Sherman and many others at that time emphatically stated that the language of the bill was plain without such an amendment, the amendment was finally incorporated in the bill as it passed the Committee of the Whole in the Senate. The bill was thereupon sent to the Judiciary Committee, and when it returned from the Judiciary Committee it was passed without this amendment, which had been stricken out in the committee as unnecessary.

Mr. BARTLETT. May I ask the gentleman a question?

Mr. MACDONALD. Certainly.

Mr. BARTLETT. The original Sherman bill was considered and reported by the Finance Committee, but the last report upon the bill was from the Judiciary Committee.

Mr. MACDONALD. Yes.

Mr. BARTLETT. And upon that report Senator Hoar was heard, and he declared that the committee had considered that proposition and found it absolutely unnecessary to make any such amendment to the bill.

Mr. MACDONALD. I was about to say that and to quote what Senator Hoar said.

Mr. BARTLETT. I beg the gentleman's pardon; I did not mean to anticipate him.

Mr. MACDONALD. The bill introduced by Senator Sherman was considered in the Finance Committee. I have taken up the history of the matter after that report was made. . . .

Mr. SHERWOOD. The gentleman says that the amendment was stricken out in the committee; he means that it was not adopted by the Judiciary Committee.

Mr. MACDONALD. The amendment of Senator George, adopted in Committee of the Whole, was stricken out by the Judiciary Committee or was not adopted.

Mr. SHERWOOD. That is right.

Mr. MACDONALD. Senator Hoar, when the bill was being debated in the Senate, expressed the general attitude of the students of the question at that time in the following words, which leave no question possible as to the fact. Speaking in the Senate on March 27, 1890, Senator Hoar said:

> When you are speaking of providing to regulate the transactions of men who are making corners in wheat, or in iron, or in woolen or in cotton goods, speculating in them or lawfully dealing in them without speculation, you are aiming at a mere commercial transaction, the beginning and end of which is the making of money for the parties, and nothing else. That is the only relation that transaction has to the State. It is the creation or diffusion or change of ownership of the wealth of the community. But when a laborer is trying to raise his wages or is endeavoring to shorten the hours of his labor, he is dealing with something that touches closely, more closely than anything else, the Government and the character of the State itself.
>
> The maintenance of a certain standard of profit in dealing in large transactions in wheat or cotton or wool is a question whether a particular merchant or a particular class of merchants

shall make money or not; but the question whether the standard of the laborer's wages shall be maintained or advanced, or whether the leisure for instruction, for improvement shall be shortened or lengthened is a question which touches the very existence and character of government of the State itself. The laborer who is engaged lawfully and usefully and accomplishing his purpose in whole or in part in endeavoring to raise the standard of wages is engaged in an occupation the success of which makes republican government itself possible, and without which the Republic can not, in substance, however it may nominally do in form, continue to exist.

I hold, therefore, that as legislators we may constitutionally, properly, and wisely allow laborers to make associations, combinations, contracts, agreements for the sake of maintaining and advancing their wages, in regard to which, as a rule, their contracts are to be made with large corporations who are themselves but an association or combination or aggregation of capital on the other side. When we are permitting and even encouraging that, we are permitting and encouraging what is not only lawful, wise, and profitable, but absolutely essential to the existence of the Commonwealth itself.

When, on the other hand, we are dealing with one of the other classes, the combinations aimed at chiefly by this bill, we are dealing with a transaction the only purpose of which is to extort from the community, monopolize, segregate, and apply to individual use, for the purposes of individual greed, wealth which ought properly and lawfully and for the public interest to be generally diffused over the whole community.

These words are not the words of anyone especially interested in organized labor. They are not the words of anyone who, as I heard it characterized on this floor the other day by a Democratic Member in addressing especially the Democratic side of the House, was "carried away by socialistic doctrine." These are the words of the late Senator Hoar, a distinguished Senator from Massachusetts, to whom I believe no one will deny the virtue of conservatism. . . .

Mr. BARTLETT. May I make a suggestion to the gentleman?

Mr. MacDONALD. Certainly.

Mr. BARTLETT. That the members of the Judiciary Committee which made the report did not deny the statement of Senator Hoar. The members of that committee were such distinguished men as Senator Edmunds, Senator Vest, Senator George, and various other men who at that time were not only great Senators but great lawyers.

Mr. MacDONALD. I thank the gentleman for his suggestion. I have here a collection of short extracts from the speeches that were made by various Senators at that time, including some of those that the gentleman from Georgia has mentioned—Senator Edmunds, Senator Stewart, Senator Teller, Senator Reagan, Senator George, and some others—all without any question agreeing that the bill as it was presented to the Senate for final passage left no doubt as to the fact that it was not intended to include fraternal orders, labor organizations, or farmers' alliances. I will insert these views of Senators in the RECORD.

[Senate, page 2729, March 27, 1890. Mr. Hoar.]

I said the object of this bill was to prevent the speculation in and engrossing of wheat and similar commodities. I did not speak in that connection of corporations. I said, in speaking generally of the lawfulness and propriety of laborers combining in the matter of wages, that the persons with whom they were to contract were very largely the corporations which were themselves nothing but a combination or aggregation of capital for that purpose. I made no such suggestion as that corporations were the persons aimed at by this bill. That was in a different connection.

[Senate, page 2606, March 25, 1890. Mr. Stewart.]

Again, suppose that the employers, railroad companies, and manufacturing establishments should say that labor should be put down to two bits a day. Suppose that capital should combine against labor, as it is very much inclined to do, and there should be a combination among the laborers which would increase the cost of production and increase the cost of all articles consumed. Suppose there should be a combination among the laborers to protect themselves from grasping monopolies; they would all be criminals for doing it.

[Senate, page 2562, March 24, 1890. Mr. Teller.]

I know that nobody here proposes to interfere with the class of men I have mentioned. Nobody here intends that by any of these provisions, either in the original bill or in any amendment, and I have only called attention to it to see if the efforts of those who have undertaken to manage this subject can not in some way confine the bill to dealing with trusts, which we all admit are offensive to good morals.

[Senate, page 2562, March 24, 1890. Mr. Teller.]

I want to repeat that I am exceedingly anxious myself to join in anything that shall break up and destroy these unholy combinations, but I want to be careful that in doing that we do not do more damage than we do good. I know how these great trusts, these great corporations, these large moneyed institutions can escape the provisions of a penal statute, and I know how much more likely they are to escape than the men who have less influence and less money. Therefore I suggest that the Senators who have this subject in charge give it special attention, and by a little modification it may be possible to relieve the bill of any doubt on that point. . . .

Mr. BARTLETT. The Supreme Court in the Danbury Hat case, when they began to consider the question of the congressional history, referred to the history of this bill in the Senate, but said that Congress had not excepted them and therefore they included them in the decision; but the history which the gentleman has read and the action of Congress was referred to by the court in its decision of the Danbury Hat case[5.526] in 208 United States.

Mr. MACDONALD. There is no question about the legislative history of the matter. The construction that has been placed on the law, that has dragged these organizations into the purview of this matter, are court decisions and not legislation. The courts have legislated in this matter so far as putting into and bringing under the operation of this legislation classes of men that the legislators specifically did not intend to include and did not include in the bill.

In April, 1900, the Littlefield antitrust bill was introduced in Congress. An amendment there was again offered to the bill, exempting these organizations, as follows:

Nothing in this act shall be so construed as to apply to trades-unions, or other labor organizations, organized for the purpose of regulating wages, hours of labor, or other conditions under which labor is performed[.]

The bill was passed with this amendment by a vote of 274 yeas to 1 nay, 70 not voting. . . .

Mr. BARTLETT. Has the gentleman the vote on the amendment?

Mr. MACDONALD. Yes. The amendment was offered by Representative Terry, of Arkansas. . . .

Mr. BARTLETT. He was the minority Representative, the ranking Democratic Representative on the Judiciary Committee of the House, and he made the minority report, and recommended that amendment in the minority report, did he not?

Mr. MACDONALD. Yes. The amendment was added to the bill by a vote of 260 yeas, 8 nays, and 76 not voting. The bill then went to the Senate and incontinently died there; and it may be remarked in passing that the author of the bill, after this amendment was added to it, seemed to have lost interest in the matter.

On June 2, 1910, Representative HUGHES, of New Jersey, offered the following amendment to the sundry civil appropriation bill, which contained appropriations for the enforcement of the antitrust law:

Provided further, That no part of this money shall be spent in the prosecution of any organization or individual for entering into any combination or agreement having in view the increasing of wages, shortening of hours, or betterment of the condition of labor, or for any act done in furtherance thereof not in itself unlawful.

That amendment was agreed to by a vote of 82 yeas to 52 nays.

On June 9, 1910, the Senate, by a vote of 34 yeas to 16 noes, decided to strike the Hughes amendment from the bill. I ask especial attention of the committee to the history of this legislation, because it is not only vitally important as a matter of history,

---

[5.526] Loewe v. Lawlor, 208 U.S. 274 (1908).

but it may be vitally important to the Democratic side of the House as a matter concerning the future of the party. On June 21, 1910, the conferees of the House were directed, on motion of Mr. HUGHES of New Jersey—

That the House do further insist on its disagreement, and that the House conferees be instructed to refuse to concur with the Senate.

On this motion the vote was 154 yeas to 105 noes, 12 answering present, and 119 not voting.

On June 23, 1910, Chairman Tawney, of the conference committee, moved to recede and concur, which meant that the House agree with the Senate and strike the Hughes exemption proviso from the bill. Upon this motion the vote was 138 yeas to 130 nays, 16 answering present, and 105 not voting.

Mr. Chairman, it has been said that the vote upon this agreement was the main cause of the loss of the House of Representatives to the Republicans in the succeeding Congress. However that may be, there is no question as to the vital consequence to the party brought about by reason of that vote. No one can read the history of this legislation, the proceedings in the courts, and public events surrounding it without being impressed with the forces that are moving in this matter—that are arrayed in this battle that is being fought. The National Association of Manufacturers under various aliases has been for many, many years past directing its activities in legislative matters almost solely to legislation of this kind.

I think it can be safely said that the public sentiment that has been molded in regard to this legislation—much of it absolutely false, much of it specious—can be charged to the influence of this organization under the domination of officers and agents who were not scrupulous as to their methods, as I shall show a little later, and as is amply shown by the recent investigation of lobbying activities in this House. The acts of these powerful organizations and their secret machinations were sordidly corrupt and unbelievably offensive to the dignity of Congress. They have, by years of labor in obtaining publicity upon these matters succeeded in making current a sentiment that has deceived many honest men in regard to legislation of this character. It has been characterized as, and the fact has obtained belief in some quarters that this is, class legislation. It is not class legislation in any sense that is improper, because antitrust legislation itself is class legislation. It is legislation directed against a class of men and corporations of great wealth in this country who have engaged in criminal operations against the welfare of the people and no other. . . .

Mr. CLINE. Mr. Chairman, I notice in the history that the gentleman is giving of the vote on the Hughes amendment to the sundry civil appropriation bill and on the vote of the motion by Chairman Tawney to recede from the instructions that the House gave the conferees and agree with the Senate in striking out the amendment, that there was quite a radical change in the vote.

Mr. MACDONALD. Yes.

Mr. CLINE. Is the gentleman in possession of any information that would enlighten the House on the causes that led to that change?

Mr. MACDONALD. I will say to the gentleman from Indiana that I am in possession of a most remarkable piece of information on that point, and I will say further, before reading this, that if there is any Member of this House who has had any doubt in his mind about the existence, as a matter of fact, of the so-called "invisible government" in this country he needs only to read the hearings of your select committee on the investigation of lobbying activities to remove all doubt from his mind. Indeed, as a matter of fact, I think the letter that I am about to read, very comprehensive in its scope, practically tells almost the whole story itself, leaving very little to the imagination; but if you will take the trouble to read the hearings and the 4,000 letters that are published in connection therewith you will have no doubt left in your mind, not only as to the existence of that "invisible government" but as to its power, efficiency, and the actual results that it accomplished. Your mind will be changed, perhaps, in regard to some ideas you may have that lobbying activities mean mere petty corruption, individual venality on the part of Members of Congress. Indeed, you will probably find remarkably few cases of that kind, but you will find a great, gigantic system, that is almost inconceivable in the scope of its operations and its power to accomplish the things desired by those who father it. I ask the attention of the House particularly to the language of this letter, a letter that was written the day following the defeat of the Hughes amendment to the sundry civil appropriation bill, that being the amendment exempting labor organizations from the enforcement of the antitrust law, so far as the expenditure of the money appropriated in the sundry civil appropriation bill was concerned.

The letter was written by Mr. James A. Emery, then and now the chief lobbyist of the National Association of Manufacturers, operating in this particular case under the name of the National Council for Industrial Defense. The letter was written to Mr. John Kirby, jr., and bears date of June 24, 1910, and is found on page 2118 of Lobby Hearing Before House Committee, volume 3—

Mr. BARTLETT. Mr. Kirby at that time was president of the National Manufacturers' Association?

Mr. MacDONALD. Mr. Kirby at that time was president of the National Association of Manufacturers.

Mr. BARTLETT. I thought so.

Mr. MacDONALD. The letter is as follows:

June 24, 1910.

Mr. John Kirby, Jr.,
511 Reibold Building, Dayton, Ohio.

MY DEAR MR. KIRBY: I had the pleasure of wiring you last night the news of victory on the Hughes amendment after the closest and hardest struggle of the session.

Returning here Wednesday morning from our New York meeting, an interview with the Colonel, Mr. Dwight, and Senator Heybarn showed the Senate to be determined, the House exceedingly weak. Mr. Gompers made his headquarters in the office of Representative CARY, of Wisconsin, in the House Office Building, and had something in the neighborhood of 100 aids about him making a persistent office canvass, petitions and memorials being piled in from every union source. I called at the White House, and being unable to see the President because of engagements, took the matter up with his secretary, who showed the greatest interest and declared he believed the President would take personal part in the fight, and this the President did Wednesday night.

In the meantime, after an hour's conference with Mr. Dwight, the whip of the House—

Mr. BARTLETT. That is, he was the Republican whip?

Mr. MacDONALD. Yes. [Reading:]

at his office the program was outlined and carried out to the letter. To the colonel was given a list of 14 names, some Democrats, some Republicans, who voted with HUGHES. He accomplished his work so successfully that of the 14 but 1 failed to either absent himself or vote with us yesterday. I communicated with Mr. Bird, requesting certain telegraphic assistance through his office, and this was carried out, with extensions suggested by himself, with splendid success. In the meantime we hammered the South and West, and while we changed but 2 southern votes on the roll call, 28 Democrats who voted with HUGHES on the last roll call remained away and were as good as votes for us. This demonstration of what our southern friends can do is most encouraging. Especial thanks are due to Capt. Chamberlain, of Chattanooga, the Georgia Industrial Association, who influenced the Savannah, Atlanta, and Columbia and New Orleans members, who did likewise with their Representatives.

At Mr. Dwight's request I called Wednesday night on Judge Madison, the insurgent Representative from Kansas, who formerly sat on the bench. It was felt that if he could be induced to speak on the floor on this subject it would exert a great influence over insurgent Republicans. After a long discussion he agreed to speak and was supplied with all the data which this office could give, and made, as you will see from the RECORD, a most effective speech. Indeed, the language of the debate was bolder and nobler than I have ever heard on the floor, both Tawney and Madison declaring they would leave their seats in the House before they would support such a proposal.

I can not emphasize too strongly the confidence with which HUGHES and the labor people approached this vote. We know from newspaper men that they had telegrams and statements prepared for distribution through the press, and that it was felt that if the House retained its position the Senate, after this last vote, would recede from its position. While I have an assurance of two Senators that they would fight this issue to a finish, I have also the best of authority for believing that the Senate conferees would have recommended the abandonment of their position if the House by a large majority had continued to insist upon the amendment.

⊥ The motion, as presented to the House, was that the House recede from its amendment ⊥9248 and concur in the Senate amendment, striking out the Hughes proposal. On this motion the ayes were 138, noes 130, answered "present" 16, not voting 105. On Tuesday last the vote to insist on the Hughes amendment was 154 to 105. A majority of 49 was thus overcome, and we had 4 votes to spare, which were not used, the Speaker's vote and 3 Members who would have changed from not present to aye if necessary.

The debate on this subject is comparatively brief, but so instructive and educational, especially as the association was sharply criticized by Mr. HUGHES, the whole matter being presented as our fight, that I have ordered several thousand copies of the debate, as taken from the RECORD, for distribution. The number can be increased in accordance with any suggestion you may make. We can procure franks and distribute the matter as part of the CONGRESSIONAL RECORD free.

Adjournment is now expected Saturday, although a filibuster is under way in the Senate which may delay matters unexpectedly.

It might be well to consider this paragraph of the letter, in view of the urgent talk of immediate adjournment of this Congress:

Sore fears are also expressed that the President may be inclined to revive his injunction program if Congress is further delayed in adjournment, as he occupies a peculiarly powerful strategic position, the so-called "pork" bills being in his hands for signature, and, of course, no other subject is so dear to the Congressman as public buildings in his district, and he will do anything to get them. The best information at present is, however, that there is no danger in this matter unless Congress should be unduly and unexpectedly delayed in adjournment.
Very truly, yours,

James A. Em.

(Copies to Messrs. Jarvis, Hanch, Schwedtman, and Bird.)

Now, Mr. Chairman, in view of this exposure to the open gaze of the forces which have always been directing their attention to opposition to legislation such as contemplated in this amendment, it might be well at this particular time, when we are about in a short time to have another vote upon exactly this same proposition, to look about us, to scrutinize our surroundings, and see if the same forces are at work now. We have made an investigation of the lobby activities, that is true, and we will soon be able to celebrate the anniversary of the cause that led to the investigation; but do you doubt that the forces who are exposed by this investigation are still here and still at work? Do you doubt that some other individual is occupying the same position and writing the same kind of letters that Mr. Mulhall and the other active agents of these forces wrote at that time? You probably will hear speeches upon the floor of this House characterizing the exemption of these organizations as class legislation and vicious, and probably Mr. Emery or some other gentleman connected with the same forces will write a letter characterizing that speech as one of the "boldest and noblest" efforts he has heard upon the floor. Some men may even say that they would rather leave their seats upon the floor than take a part in such a proposal; but if the history of the past is any criterion, some of the gentlemen may have an opportunity to leave their seats, as did some gentlemen in the past who took that position.

Now, Mr. Chairman, I am going to ask leave to extend my remarks by inserting some correspondence which I will not take the time to read to the committee; but I wish to call the attention of the committee to this first letter as an example of the methods of this organization in the molding of public opinion, which is one of the most important activities that this class of men have at their command. I will read just the brief preliminary statement, signed by Mr. James W. Van Cleave, who was president of the National Association of Manufacturers, just as an example of how publicity is used to influence public opinion in these matters. This is from the hearings before the subcommittee of the Committee on the Judiciary, United States Senate, volume 4, page 3777, and is marked "Emery Exhibit No. 10."

EMERY EXHIBIT NO. 10.
THE NATIONAL COUNCIL FOR INDUSTRIAL DEFENSE.
An object lesson.

A most interesting illustration of the power of public opinion is furnished in the following items of a recent incident.

The large majority of our newspapers will be just and fair, providing they are well informed. It is our duty to keep them and through them the public at large informed regarding our work. What in this case was accomplished through the Citizens' Industrial Association of St. Louis can be accomplished in every case and in every place—providing of course that we are right and go about it properly.

Our success in every case, local or national, in which we have concentrated our power properly should be accepted by our membership in a spirit of solemn thanksgiving instead of exultation, and with a conviction that our efforts will continually bring employer and employee closer together, to the benefit of both and of the American public and country. Copy of Republic mailed to you for your full information.

Please read the following carefully and let me hear from you.

James W. Van Cleave,
Chairman.

[Extract from editorial of the St. Louis Republic, the leading Democratic morning paper of St. Louis.]

December 24.

The suit (Bucks Stove & Range Co. against the American Federation of Labor) was brought really at the instance of the Citizens' Industrial Association, which in respect of the employing forces represents even a greater degree of extremism and intolerance than does the leadership of organized labor.

[Mr. Van Cleave to the editor of the Republic.]

December 25.

Mr. Charles W. Knapp
President and Editor, St. Louis Republic, City.

MY DEAR SIR: I was very much surprised to read the following statement upon the editorial page of this morning's Republic. In discussing the sentence of labor leaders for contempt of court you say:

"The suit was brought really at the instance of the Citizens' Industrial Association, which in respect of the employing forces represents even a greater degree of extremism and intolerance than does the leadership of organized labor."

There is no foundation whatsoever for the statement that the suit in question was brought at the instance of the Citizens' Industrial Association. It was brought by the Bucks Stove & Range Co. in an endeavor to secure justice.

To say that the Citizens' Industrial Association represents intolerance and extremism is an attack upon every one of our 8,000 St. Louis members, which I, as president, can not let go unchallenged. Our organization consists of thousands of professional men, among them many ministers and lawyers, in addition to thousands of employers and employees. We have courted at all times and we are now courting the closest scrutiny of our work and of our principles. In justice to every member of this association I request that you give me the facts upon which you base your editorial expression. We invite the closest investigation, and after an impartial committee of one or two or three men has made such an investigation, if they can point out the slightest justice for calling us "intolerant" and "extremists," I shall resign as president of the association after advocating its disbandment.

It is your duty, as I see it to either make good your charge or to retract it. For your information I send you herewith a handbook of the Citizens' Industrial Association, and I quote from among hundreds of indorsements contained therein the following few:

The Most Rev. John J. Glennon, archbishop of St. Louis, states in a letter:

"I would like to say that there are many sound features in your organization and that the many irritations produced in the industrial world by the labor unions tend to induce many people to accept all your principles with all that they imply."

The Right Rev. Daniel L. Tuttle, presiding bishop of the Episcopal Church in America, writes us:

" * * * These duties also press so that I am precluded from ranging myself in membership with you as I would like to do, and so am shut up to the course of simply assuring you of my hearty sympathy with you in your earnest effort to stand by 'liberty, public and private,' and to try reasonable ways to explain classes to each other and remove friction between them."

The Rev. Brother Constantine, vice president Christian Brothers' College, writes:

"Needless to say that I enjoyed your course of lectures. You have adopted an excellent method of instructing the people on some of the vital questions of the day. No thinking man can underrate the value of such teachings, as well as the beneficial results obtained. * * * Hoping that you will continue your excellent propaganda of good sound principles and correct views of our great social questions."

The Rev. Henry Stiles Bradley, pastor St. John's Methodist Episcopal Church:

"Allow me to wish for the Citizens' Industrial Association the largest success in its efforts to secure the observance of law and order and bring about industrial peace and good fellowship."

Rabbi Samuel Sale says:

"I take it that this association represents the party of the third part, and it is to be hoped that its activity all over our land may grow so strong as to put an effective stop to this internecine warfare, this enemy of organized, civilized society."

The Rev. Dr. S. Parkes Cadman, of Brooklyn, said:

"You are acting here not only for St. Louis, but for the country at large; and not only for the country at large, but for the world beyond. There is not a statesman or a thinker in Europe or in the Farther East who does not watch your progress with the keenest anxiety."

I might go on quoting indefinitely from the statements of men whose unbiased judgment can not be questioned, but the letter has already grown longer than I wanted it to be. I shall send copy of this communication to every member of our association, and I respectfully request that you print it in full.

Truly, yours,

James W. Van Cleave,
President.

[Comments from the Republic of January 2.]

CITIZENS' INDUSTRIAL ASSOCIATION MEMBERS EXPLAIN PRINCIPLES—MEN AND FIRMS IN ORGANIZATION DENY THAT THEIR ANTAGONISM TO CLOSED SHOP AND OTHER RESTRICTIVE POLICIES OF ORGANIZED LABOR ARE EXTREME OR INTOLERABLE—SYMPOSIUM OF LETTERS TAKES EXCEPTION TO EDITORIAL COMMENT IN THE REPUBLIC—MEMBERS OF BODY ACCEDE TO REQUEST OF PRESIDENT VAN CLEAVE AND DISAVOW ASSUMPTION THAT ASSOCIATION INSTIGATED SUIT AGAINST UNION LEADERS—EXPOSITION OF PURPOSES.

Below will be found a number of letters addressed to the Republic by members of the Citizens' Industrial Association of St. Louis, at the request of Mr. J. W. Van Cleave, president of the association. A letter of similar tenor from Mr. Van Cleave himself was printed in the Republic of the day following the day on which the editorial appeared, to which these letters refer, but these additional letters contain such a full and complete exposition of the aims and purposes of the Citizens' Industrial Association, as they are understood by those who constitute the organization, that they will of found both interesting and timely. The declarations so positively made that the association was not in any way back of the proceedings against Gompers, Mitchell, and Morrison, instituted by the Buck's Stove & Range Co., must be accepted as statements of fact within the knowledge of the writers. The Republic cheerfully accepts, also, the earnest denials that the Citizens' Association in its antagonism of the closed shop and other restrictive policies of organized labor intends either extremism or intolerance.

Other letters than those printed to-day have been received by the Republic from members of the Citizens' Association, but, being marked personal, or request made that they be not published, they are withheld.

[Editorial.]

THE CITIZENS' INDUSTRIAL ASSOCIATION.

The Republic is indebted to members of the Citizens' Industrial Association of St. Louis for a most interesting symposium which is given place in its news columns to-day. Its readers will doubtless recognize a similar obligation for the full explanation they are given of the aims and purposes the members of this organization have in mind.

These letters, sent to the Republic at the request of Mr. J. W. Van Cleave, president of the association, quite positively correct the erroneous assumption of the Republic that the suit against Gompers, Mitchell, and Morrison was brought at the instance of the Citizens' Industrial Association. The Republic cheerfully gives publicity to this correction and welcomes the opportunity to present the complete exposition of the principles and objects of the organization which these letters embody.

What the association aspires to accomplish is more effectively set forth in these very interesting communications than it possibly can be in any formal platform, and the reader will find them an emphatic disavowal of any wish to encourage extremism or intolerance.

January 4, 1909.

Mr. *Charles W. Knapp,*
Editor *St. Louis Republic, City.*

MY DEAR SIR: I desire to thank you for the effort made in your issue of Saturday, January 2, to correct some of the erroneous statements of your editorials with reference to the Gompers,

Mitchell, and Morrison contempt proceedings, as well as to the Citizens' Industrial Association.

Your remarks regarding trial by jury for contempt are very illuminating in face of the statutes under the Constitution. You further say that—

"To bring Mitchell 'within the pale of the law,' for instance, the court quoted from Mitchell's book, 'Organized Labor,' to show that in it Mitchell counseled opposition to injunctions when they opposed anything lawful. The court also referred to the fact that Mitchell was the presiding officer at the miners' convention in January, 1906, when a resolution which made him in contempt of court was adopted. As that convention was held nearly a year before the injunction was applied for, and the book was written several years before, the pertinence of the allusions is not apparent, and only the utmost complacency would accept this part of the reasoning as sound."

It would seem that the reference to these matters was made only for the purpose of concealing and misstating them. Mitchell's views in his book were properly quoted as stated in 1903 and again in 1906, at a meeting of the Civic Federation in New York, to show his attitude and mind to all court orders.

The convention that you refer to was held in January, 1908, and the resolution which placed Mitchell in contempt of court was passed five weeks after the preliminary injunction had been granted, December 18, 1907.

However, as stated in the beginning, I feel well satisfied that you have made an honest effort to set the Citizens' Industrial Association right before the people of our city, and to correct the error contained in your editorial. The points referred to herein are not written for the purpose of continuing this discussion, but merely to call your personal attention to further errors in your editorial expression.

Very truly, yours,

J. W. Van Cleave,
President.

• • • •

Mr. MacDONALD. Now, Mr. Chairman, in conclusion, there is really existing no doubt as to the propriety of in express terms exempting associations of the character—fraternal orders, organizations of labor, and farmers' organizations—from the provisions of this legislation directed against the trusts, and that being so I have no doubt in some form or other such an amendment will be made, and that being so there ought to be no evasion possible after the adoption of that amendment.

The amendment ought to be couched in such terms as to leave absolutely no doubt as to the meaning. There ought not to be evasive or technical terms used that would enable the party seeking delay in these matters to plausibly urge the submitting it to the courts for construction. It ought to be plain and simple. Every one of these amendments I have read, offered in the history of this legislation, has been plain and simple. It has said in so many words that this legislation shall not apply to these organizations, and you can not make it any plainer or more complete than by saying these words. Human labor is not a commodity, and the right to organize in such bodies is inseparable from the right of the individual as a member of society, as a citizen. If you mean to exempt these associations from this bill, exempt them and say in so many words that this legislation is not intended to apply to these organizations. Do not attempt to leave any loophole for the claim that while the existence of these organizations is not prohibited yet the courts may still hold the exercise of their vital functions unlawful. No subterfuge, no evasion, is going to satisfactorily accomplish anything. If you intend to exempt these associations, exempt them, and the place to do it and the time to do it is here and now. [Applause.] . . .

Mr. GRAHAM of Illinois. Mr. Chairman, the Baltimore platform has in it this paragraph:

Experience has proved the necessity of a modification of the law relating to injunction, and we reiterate the pledges of our platforms of 1896 and 1904 in favor of a measure which passed the United States Senate in 1890, relating to contempt in Federal courts, and providing for trial by jury in cases of indirect contempt.

Questions of judicial practice have arisen, especially in connection with industrial disputes. We believe that the parties in all judicial proceedings should be treated with rigid impartiality, and that injunctions should not be issued in any case in which an injunction would not issue if no industrial disputes were involved.

The expanding organization of industry makes it essential that there should be no abridgment of the right of the wage earners and producers to organize for the protection of wages and the improvement of labor conditions, to the end that such labor organizations and their members should not be regarded as illegal combinations in restraint of trade.

In the time at my disposal I shall not attempt to discuss the bill as a whole, but shall confine myself to those portions of it which deal with questions of labor organizations and other organizations not having capital stock and not organized for profit, and more particularly with reference to the use of injunctions in such cases and to the question of indirect contempts growing out of them, and referred to in the portion of the platform I have quoted. Much of the trouble between capital and labor from which society has been and is suffering has resulted from the tremendous strides made during the last three-quarters of a century in the invention and perfection of labor-saving machinery. As a result, the relations which formerly existed between employer and employee have been completely changed. The personal relations which existed in the olden time exist no longer.

In the past the employer frequently worked side by side with the employee, and even though he did not do that, he still maintained personal relations with those who worked for him. He knew them individually. He knew their conditions, probably knew their families and more or less of their necessities. If there was sickness in their family he knew of it, and doubtless felt and manifested more or less sympathy and kindness toward them.

The invention of labor-saving machinery has changed all this. The purchase of necessary machines for any given industrial concern, the placing of them, the housing of them, and equipping them for service required an amount of capital greater than one man possessed, or, at least, greater than one man, if he possessed it, cared to risk in a single enterprise. Thus a number of men were required, acting together, to equip and run such an enterprise. In order to avoid personal responsibility for the debts of the concern, corporations were organized, stock was issued to represent the value of the property. Often the stock was "watered" by issues far beyond the value of the property it represented, and sold to persons who never saw the concern, but who were led to believe they would get dividends on their investment.

In this way the modern corporation was substituted for the individual as the employer of labor. The owners of the property ceased to have personal relations with those employed. Agents were selected to superintend and manage the business. Those who did the work and those for whom it was done were utter strangers to each other. Personal relations practically ceased, and all feeling of human sympathy between them ceased, too. About the only interest the stockholder had in the concern was to get dividends on his stock. It mattered little to him whether those who did the work were well or ill, whether their families were properly provided for or badly provided for. Indeed, he knew nothing about these things. Interest on his investment in the form of dividends was the thing that appealed to him, and if the superintendent or manager did not produce those dividends the stockholder would naturally want some one who could and would do that substituted for him.

Thus it might be said that the invention of labor-saving machinery not only caused but compelled the organization of capital into corporations, and now many of these corporations have drifted together—have been combined into great, giant organizations of capital, thus removing the employers of labor further and further away from those who do the labor. In the fierce struggle for dividends the employer and the employed have drifted so far apart that now a condition of antagonism has too frequently taken the place of those former friendly relations,

I have said that what the stockholder in an industrial enterprise looks for is dividends and in the struggle for dividends experience has demonstrated in the past that one of the easiest and most certain ways to get the dividends was by wage reductions, but a wage reduction in one industrial concern logically, if not necessarily, leads to a wage reduction in competing concerns, so that to keep his place in the market the one who began ⊥ reducing wages would, after his competitors had done likewise, be compelled to make a further reduction.

In the matter of coal mining in my own State within my recollection I have known these conditions to actually prevail. A mine with poor natural advantages, with poor equipments, with inferior management, would find itself unable to compete in the market with mines far superior to it in all those respects. It could only continue to do business by reducing the price of mining, but when it did that its competitors, using that reduction as a lever, forced a similar reduction upon their employees.

The former was then driven to the necessity of a further reduction, which was followed by further reductions on the part of competitors, and thus the process continued until the price for mining coal in Illinois reached so low a level that those who followed that occupation could barely keep soul and body together. It reached a price as low as 30 cents for each ton which passed over a screen with openings large enough to let one-third or more of the coal pass through, the miners getting paid only for that which escaped across the screen.

There were but three courses left for them to pursue—they could starve, quit the business, or organize. They followed the example of capital, they massed their forces, they organized. Instead of moving and acting as individuals, they moved and acted as phalanxes. They had learned by bitter experience the wisdom of Franklin's advice to the colonists, "We must all hang together, or assuredly we shall hang separately." The necessity for union was absolutely forced upon them. They had no other recourse. They acted sensibly and accepted the situation.

The movement to organize unions, to substitute collective strength for individual strength in dealing with their employers at first met serious opposition, indeed, stiff resistance, not always so violent and disgraceful, however, as it is meeting to-day in Colorado and in Michigan.

In many parts of the country the movement was quite successful, and every candid man now admits that the ameliorated conditions of labor are almost entirely traceable to the effectiveness of those labor unions. But the end is not yet. The men who constitute the unions can not for a moment relax their efforts or break their lines.

I do not say that this is the best possible condition. I am not sure that the relations of employers and employees have taken the most fortunate direction. I think it were possibly better if industrial development had taken a different course; but it did not. It developed and is developing in such fashion that wealth—great wealth—and the power that goes with it are on the one side and great numbers and the strength that goes with numbers when they are united are on the other side. So long as these forces are free and nearly equally balanced it will probably work out all right. The struggle has been a bitter one, and in many sections of the country it is still a bitter one. It is, however, but a repetition of history, and when the struggle ceases in this form it will be renewed and waged along some other line. At least that seems to be the teaching of history.

At one time in the history of our race the war lord reigned supreme over the multitude. They were compelled to follow him and to fight for him and even to die for him. Whether his object was to rob his neighbor baron or to keep his neighbor baron from robbing him was a matter of no consequence to them. In either case it was their duty to submit to their superior's will.

After ages of conflict the many succeeded in depriving the few of this supreme power over their lives. But the scene only shifted; the war lord became transformed into the landlord, and those who formerly had fought for him now merely worked for him. He was the absolute owner of the one thing most necessary to their existence—the land. He permitted them to get a bare living as the result of their toil. The rest was for him. And all this he accomplished through control of the machinery that made, determined, and enforced the law.

For centuries the many struggled for a nearer approach to justice, for a more liberal reward for their toil, and little by little they succeeded. They wrung from their masters the right to own the soil they cultivated, so that now, even in Ireland, where this system existed in its most malignant form, landlordism is rapidly disappearing, and it will soon have entirely disappeared in the Old World. We should be careful that it does not reappear in the new. But the disappearance of the war lord and the landlord is no sort of guaranty that like things may not happen again. Indeed, I might say that once more the scene has only shifted, and that in our modern life the industrial lord is their descendant or successor, and that he is now dominating society and exploiting the multitude as surely as the war lord and the landlord did in their day. Nor will the struggle ever cease so long as man inhabits the earth; in some form or other it will probably go on. The selfish men, endowed with superior ability, will seek and will gain advantage over their fellows, and such advantage can only be met and offset by concerted action on the part of those whom they would exploit.

No wiser or more practical aphorism has been spoken by anyone than was uttered by Wendell Phillips when he said, "Eternal vigilance is the price of liberty." I wish men would take it more to heart. The time will never come when those who love equal liberty, who believe in equal opportunity, can rest on their oars, feeling that the battle is won.

This struggle between organized wealth and organized labor has now reached a stage where more than merely industrial affairs are at issue. The liberties of the American people are now seriously involved in it. Liberty with us is an orderly thing. It does not mean license. Indeed, mere license is the fatal enemy of liberty. As Dr. Brownson said:

> True liberty secures at once the authority of the State and the freedom of the individual; the sovereignty of the people without social despotism and individual freedom without anarchy.

This is the kind of liberty we want—orderly, regulated liberty, never forgetting that in the great charter of liberty—the Declaration of Independence—the order of importance runs, "life, liberty, and the pursuit of happiness," or, more briefly, property.

Life is the primary right; without it we can not enjoy the others. Liberty—that is, the right to be free from unlawful restraint—stands second, and properly so. The right of property occupies only third place. Have we not been transposing this enumeration, and putting property too near the first place?

Under our scheme of government, in the last analysis questions in dispute have to go to the courts for settlement. They are the final arbiters between disputants. Their decisions give trend and direction to our affairs, and the machinery which we have adopted for administering distributive justice has in it an ingredient which is invaluable in a political way as it is in a judicial sense. I refer to the jury system.

The acute struggle between organized wealth and organized labor has found its way to the courts, and there is some reason for believing that the courts, and more especially the Federal courts, consciously or unconsciously, have leaned too much to the side of organized wealth, to the side of property. In no other way is this more apparent than in the use—might I not say the abuse—of the writ of injunction and the use of the court's power to punish for contempt of its orders when the alleged contempts were committed out of its presence. The writ of injunction, which was originally intended and used to preserve and protect property and property rights, has of late been extended beyond its original purpose, and, in my judgment, beyond its legitimate purpose and has been invading the field of the criminal law as well as of the common law.

The history of the world proves that the possessors of great wealth constantly strive for special privileges, and too often get them. Having obtained them, the possessors naturally object to dividing the advantage thus secured.

A certain gentleman whose wealth is so great that his laudable desire to die poor seems impossible of realization made a great deal of that wealth by exploiting labor. But when labor asked for an additional pittance out of the great tidal wave of dollars which swept into his coffers the request was contemptuously spurned and the Homestead strike which followed has helped to make history.

He was able to avoid the force of the law which should have hampered his action, and the law which favored his side of the controversy was not only availed of but stretched beyond its proper limitations. The same thing is happening to-day.

Hired thugs and assassins who should be in strict confinement, and hired private detectives who are most dangerous and unscrupulous fellows, at the suggestion of organized wealth are designated as officers of the law and necessarily given the discretionary power an officer of the law must have in performing his duty. Federal courts are appealed to for restraining orders to prevent the exercise of fundamental rights, and such orders are granted, at first with some reluctance and caution, but later with almost profuse liberality. Many of these restraining orders, in my judgment, are not within proper limits. They involve the principle that the right to labor is a property right, and can be dealt with in the courts as such, and therefore can be reached by the writ of injunction. In this, as I hope to show, lies an invasion of the rights of every citizen which, if followed and applied, would lead to the gravest and most dangerous form of tyranny. I do not believe this condition could ever have happened in this country, or would have been tolerated for a single moment but for some peculiar circumstances which are often overlooked. I think they are worth recalling at this time.

When these labor troubles first became serious a custom developed among employers of sending agents to those portions of Europe where unskilled labor was most plentiful and most easily obtained, where many of the people would be glad to emigrate if they only had money enough to pay their passage. These agents not only offered to pay their way to America, but to furnish them steady employment when they got here. Glad of the opportunity to get to this modern land of Canaan these people cheerfully entered into labor contracts covering periods of years, and thus bound up they were imported to the United States to take the places of striking workmen.

When their contracts expired, sometimes before, these people had learned that in America men had rights, and in their way they began to exercise those rights, and soon they passed from the stage of strike breakers to that of strikers.

As strike breakers they were kept together as much as possible; they were given little opportunity to associate with others or to learn the ways or the language of the country. They did not become a real part of the population among which they lived. They received no sympathy; they were the objects of contempt and even hatred, and so even when they passed to the stage of strikers there was little sympathetic feeling toward them. People generally remembered only what they had been, and when their employers succeeded in getting the courts to strain the law, to substitute equity law for criminal law in dealing with them, to strain the Constitution to fit what seemed an unconstitutional case, many people, I say, remembering only what these people had been and what they had done to others, thought, "Oh, well, they are only a bunch of foreigners who a little while ago were strike breakers, and it serves them about right." Few cared about an invasion of their rights, and so the precedent was easily established. Once established, it soon grew strong and lusty. Similar conditions are today paralyzing the governmental machinery of a great State to such an extent that it voluntarily abdicates its functions and surrenders the temporary exercise of them to the Federal Government. We can now see that it was a grave mistake to permit the sacrifice of the rights of those unfortunate immigrants, and that it would not be only a grave mistake but a crime to ignore the rights of these Colorado strikers of to-day because they are Greeks or Armenians or other foreigners who are alien to our ways and probably can not speak our language. When the rights of any man in America are invaded or sacrificed the rights of every man in America are endangered. Those who supinely look on while their neighbors' rights are being violated can not hope to long preserve their own.

The outrages which resulted from the importation of contract laborers brought about a salutary change in the law and resulted in the absolute prohibition of such immigration. But the change in the immigration laws did not change the practice as to the improper issuance of injunctions or improper punishments for alleged contempts. The camel had succeeded in getting his nose under the tent. Fortunately, perhaps, the evil kept on growing until public attention was riveted upon it and until the necessity for action became apparent to all right-minded, right-thinking people. Under this far-reaching injunctive power the Federal judge was wielding dangerous power; he was the law and the gospel and the prophets as well. He issued his ukase and then punished as for contempt anyone who, according to his view of the evidence, was guilty of violating it. Consitutional guaranties were brushed aside, trial by jury was ignored, and the same man whose order was supposed to be violated and whose dignity was thus invaded became both judge and jury. He heard the evidence; he determined the fact; he fixed the punishment; he spoke the first word and the last word, and from his conclusion there was no right of appeal.

Now, I lay down the proposition that there is no single factor in our system of Government more vital, more important to the people's liberties, than the jury system—than the right of trial by jury. . . .

Mr. FESS. In referring to the abuse of the injunction principle that the gentleman is addressing himself to, does he regard the Debs case[5.527] specifically speaking, as a concrete example of the abuse of the system?

Mr. GRAHAM of Illinois. There are some things in the Debs case that illustrate the point I am making. The whole case would not illustrate it. But I do not care to discuss that, if the gentleman will pardon me. I can not afford to do it at this time.

Mr. FESS. Does this law correct that feature?

Mr. GRAHAM of Illinois. Well, it will not be very difficult, in my judgment, to add to it in such a way as to reach that feature, and I hope the addition will be made. . . .

The jury system, I said, is the anchor of our liberties. From the earliest time nations that enjoyed a real system of jurisprudence separated the decision of questions of fact from the decision of questions of law.

Many a time in the history of the past have brave liberty-loving jurors stood between the people and judges who were venal or vicious and saved a victim from the vengeance of the Crown.

Under our system the courts are the sheet anchors of our liberties. If confidence in the integrity and impartiality of the law was lost the Republic could not long survive. But nothing tends more to preserve that confidence than the jury system. It is not a very difficult matter to apply the law to a given state of facts, but it is often difficult to ascertain what the real facts are.

Every wise system of jurisprudence recognized that it were better to have one set of men determine what the facts in a case are and another set of men to apply the law to those facts. The ancient Romans, who first gave the world a real system of jurisprudence, realized and adopted such a plan. They usually submitted questions of fact to laymen for decision, and that practice runs like a thread through the history of all English-speaking people. A great English jurist, Lord Camden, said:

> Trial by jury is the foundation of the British constitution; take that away and the whole fabric will soon molder into dust.

And this is even truer with us. The jury is even more necessary in popular governments than in constitutional monarchies.

The part which the jury takes in the administration of justice is a most important one. It brings the administration of justice home to the people themselves, and thus inspires confidence in the administration of the law. The jurors are chosen from the body of the people. Their neighbors know them personally and have confidence in their integrity. If they do happen to decide contrary to the judgment of their neighbors, it is called an error of judgment, and does not diminish public confidence in the honesty and integrity of the courts. Should a judge whom the people did not know render a similar decision it might, and probably would, be attributed to partiality or an even worse motive, and if repeated often would soon destroy that confidence in the administration of justice which is so essential to the stability of our Government. Those thoughtless or selfish persons who cry out against the jury system probably fail to realize how absolutely necessary it is as a political institution to the stability and permanence of the Republic.

True, juries sometimes make mistakes. But that is not quite the question. The real question is to reduce such mistakes to a minimum and to make it clear that they are only mistakes. Human justice is comparative, not absolute; it aspires to perfection with no hope of reaching it, and it is the judgment of many of our wisest and most experienced jurists that fewer mistakes are made in ascertaining the truth about the facts that are in dispute by twelve men from the ordinary walks of life than by one or even by twelve experienced lawyers or judges. As an eminent jurist has said:

> Juries take a common-sense view of every question according to the peculiar circumstances, whereas a judge generalizes and reduces everything to an artificial system formed by study.

Another of even greater experience says that judges are apt to acquire a habit of forcing cases into rigid forms and arbitrary classes.

[5.527] United States v. Debs, 64 F. 724 (C.C.N.D. Ill. 1894).

Justice Miller, late of the United States Supreme Court, said in a public address that—

Judges are not preeminently fitted over other men of good judgment in business affairs to decide upon mere questions of disputed fact.

Judge Dillon, a law writer of eminence and a jurist of more than national reputation, says:

Twelve good and lawful men are better judges of disputed facts than twelve learned judges.

Few judges had longer or more varied experience with juries than the late Judge Caldwell, of the eighth Federal judicial circuit. After 35 years of experience, he said:

It was because the people knew that judges were poor judges of the facts that they committed their decisions to a jury, and every day's experience confirms the wisdom of their action.

And Judge Cooley, whose writings illumine the Constitution and whose judicial decisions shed luster on the Supreme Court of Michigan, tells us that—

Juries are better calculated to judge of motives, weigh probabilities, and take what may be called a common-sense view of a set of circumstances involving both act and intent than any single man, however pure, wise, and eminent he may be.

In a recent case reported in the One hundred and thirty-fifth Federal Reporter, page 1, the court says:

The bench once accounted for familiar physical and mental conditions by witchcraft, and that, too, at the expense of the lives of innocent men and women. In that day it was said from the bench that to deny the existence of witchcraft was to deny the Christian religion. Juries would have done better. Then and now questions of fact were best tried by jury.[5.528]

The right of trial by jury is considered so fundamental, so very important that in my own State and in many other jurisdictions a defendant in a felony case will not be permitted to waive his constitutional right to trial by a jury and submit the evidence to a judge or, indeed, to any number of judges.

In Illinois a man over 60 years of age is disqualified under the law to serve as a juror, although he would have 11 others to assist him, and their joint verdict is subject to review by the judge, and under the Federal practice the same rule must be applied to jurors in the Federal courts in that State.

But a Federal judge who may be more than three score years and ten, sitting to hear a contempt case, hears the evidence alone, determines the facts alone, passes judgment, and inflicts whatever punishment he pleases, although in statutory cases of similar character, where the maximum punishment is not as severe, he could not qualify as even one-twelfth of the jury. And when we consider that the defendant has an absolute right to have the verdict of the jury reviewed in a higher court, whereas no such right of review exists in contempt cases passed upon by less than one-twelfth of a jury, the dangerous character of the proceeding becomes more apparent.

Instances illustrating this danger might be multiplied indefinitely. I will cite only one:

In a case before a certain New Jersey judge, the defendant, a clergyman, testified that he paid to the complainant, an old lady parishioner of his, $1,000 in bills for certain real estate she had deeded to him. She denied the payment. There were some other circumstances in evidence bearing on the issue of fact between them. After considering the evidence, the judge declared that the clergyman was untruthful, and decided the case against him. On the identical testimony the case was taken to the court of errors and appeals. It was there decided by a unanimous court of 12 judges that the clergyman had not sworn falsely and that the testimony of the old lady was glaringly false, and the judgment was reversed.

A little later the same judge wrote an elaborate opinion in a divorce case which he tried, exhaustively reviewed the evidence, declared the wife guilty of adultery, and

---

[5.528] Post v. United States, 135 F. 1, 11–12 (5th Cir. 1905).

granted the husband a divorce on that ground. The case was taken to the court of errors and appeals on the same evidence heard by him, and in a very able opinion written by Judge Vredenburg the judgment of the trial court was reversed and the wife's name saved from dishonor. Fifteen judges decided the case in the higher court, and in their opinion they say "her reputation under the proof is entirely without a stain or a blemish upon it."

The same judge, who was so absurdly wrong in these cases, afterwards tried, convicted, and sentenced some striking workmen for violating one of his own injunctions. Under the law the defendants had no right to appeal and had to abide by his decision. He alone heard the evidence, he alone decided the fact whether or not they were guilty of contempt of his order, and from his decision of the fact, whether right or wrong, the men had no appeal, no recourse. If his ability to weigh evidence and determining facts was no better in their case than in the others mentioned, what a gross outrage was probably perpetrated on these men in the name of the law; what a blow was given to popular confidence in the courts; what a wound was inflicted on the cause of real liberty!

How can a man subjected to such treatment feel that he stands equal before the law with those who obtained the order which was the foundation or the apology for his punishment?

How can he love such laws, and how can he love the country and the Government which tolerates them?

The Federal statutes contain a specific provision that any person who, by threats or force, obstructs or impedes the due administration of justice or endeavors to do so shall be fined not to exceed $500 or imprisoned not to exceed three months, or both. The defendant has a constitutional right to be tried by a jury under this law.

Such conduct, if proved, would only amount to contempt of court. But after a trial by a judge and jury of twelve men, three months is the longest punishment the court could inflict; but for violating an injunction order which forbade one to exercise the constitutional right of free speech or forbade him to walk on the public highway at a certain place, after a hearing before one man who is too old to be a juror, whose dignity is offended by a supposed violation of his order, and who for that reason alone would be subject to challenge as a juror, the accused might be—nay, has been—sent to prison for more than a year, and might in addition be fined thousands of dollars. Is it not monstrous?

Oh, but you say no judge would exercise such tyrannical power.

I answer, judges have closely approached it. And, besides, it is not enough to know that persons having such power have not used it; liberty-loving men want to know that no such power exists.

This bill secures that result. This bill provides for the determination of the facts in cases of indirect contempt by twelve competent jurors. This bill secures to the workingman equality before the law; it simply treats him as others are treated; under its provisions he ceases to become an outlaw because he protests against intolerable conditions by striking. It is a new bill of rights, a new charter of liberty, and marks the beginning of a new era in the emancipation of labor and in the practical application of the principles enunciated in the Declaration of Independence. . . .

Mr. [AUGUSTUS P.] GARDNER [R., Mass.]. It is my intention to vote for this Clayton antitrust measure in the hope that it will be remolded into proper shape in the Senate.

I am very much disappointed in the bill. It is loosely drawn and its meaning is so involved that useless lawsuits will be the result if it is not substantially changed in later stages. I had expected better results from the gentleman from Alabama, Mr. Clayton, the gentleman from Arkansas, Mr. FLOYD, and the gentleman from Virginia, Mr. CARLIN, the authors, as I am told, of this measure. I know that they are capable of far better work. I know that they intended to draw an effective bill. What we need are proper restraints on great combinations, not shackles on legitimate business. The authors of this bill have by no means presented a measure calculated to give us what we need.

The fact is that we have been in session continuously for 15 months. We have been trying to deal with an endless variety of subjects and our minds have become utterly flat, stale, and unprofitable. I confess that I am in that condition myself. My mental alertness, if I ever had any, has entirely lost its edge. If the first 15 months of Democratic rule has shown us nothing else, it has proved conclusively that it is better to have a short program thoroughly executed rather than to have a long program superficially polished off. [Applause.] . . .

Mr. [GEORGE S.] GRAHAM [R., Pa.]. Mr. Chairman, in the partial discussion of these bills there has come to the surface a peculiar condition at which I must express my surprise. I have the greatest respect for the gentleman [Mr. GARDNER] who has just addressed us; but when he says that he will vote for this measure as it is, hoping that the Senate will whip it into proper shape, it occasions in me much surprise.

The other day, when an amendment was offered to the bill for the creation of a trade commission, one of the gentleman in charge said:

> It is dangerous to amend a bill when it is on its passage in the House. Your amendment is well conceived and probably should be embodied in this bill, but we will let that be done when it goes over to the Senate.

Has this body lost all deliberative legislative power? Are we bound by the report of a committee so that we dare not touch the language of a bill to change or modify it? Must we simply be a recording machine to place in the RECORD by our votes the expression of the Chief Executive, made through a chosen committee? Must we simply yield everything up to the power of caucus rule, which shall tell us "You must pass this measure as it is: and, having received the imprimatur of the caucus, it is dangerous to meddle with it on the floor of the House, for we do not know where amendments will lead us to or what changes they may effect in the whole legislation"?

⊥ I am surprised to think that this House of Representatives is incapacitated from considering fairly and calmly and deliberately any measure and attempting to effectuate any amendment that might be thought proper and wise to incorporate in it. . . .

Mr. CARLIN. I just wanted to interrupt the gentleman to advise him that there has been no caucus, so far as this bill is concerned, or on either of the bills now included in the rule.

Mr. GRAHAM of Pennsylvania. The distinction may be real, and I do not question the veracity of the gentleman from Virginia when he makes his statement; not for a moment. But my understanding of the situation is that there was a caucus which decided upon a program. I do not mean that it went so far as to determine everything in connection with these bills, but there was a policy adopted, and that policy is being pushed through this House without any change. You could not amend the trade-commission bill, no matter what the reason might be that lay at the root of your amendment. . . .

And I fear you can not amend this bill for the same reason, although I am led to hope, from the language of my colleague on the committee, the gentleman from Arkansas [Mr. FLOYD], that perhaps with respect to this bill, fraught as it is with so many things of vital interest to the business community and the citizens of the country, there may be opportunity given to amend some of these provisions; and it is with the hope that that may be done that I take the time and try the patience of the House to speak at all upon the measure, for if I had not that glimmer of hope I would remain silent, having expressed my views, so far as I am able to do so, in the minority report which is now before the Members. . . .

Mr. BARTLETT. I will say to the gentleman that if he is laboring under the idea that there is any caucus action binding the Democratic Members to vote for this particular bill or to vote against all amendments, he is laboring under a mistaken idea; because there are some of us who intend to vote for some amendments that are to be proposed to this bill; that is, if they meet our judgment. [Applause.]

Mr. GRAHAM of Pennsylvania. That is a confirmation of the hope that is within me, and I am glad to have it confirmed from such a distinguished authority.

Mr. BARTLETT. I want to state to the gentleman that I am as loyal to the action of my party as any man in the House, and I do not understand that we are bound by anything except to vote to consider this bill as it is being considered and as it will be considered for amendment.

Mr. GRAHAM of Pennsylvania. For this information I am grateful, and I appreciate the fact that the gentlemen upon the other side are now free to vote for any amendment that may be offered to this measure; and there are many parts of it that require amendment before it shall be passed by this House. I hope to see this information fructify and be illustrated by the votes which will speak louder than protestations of freedom when the time comes to express yourselves by your votes.

What is the object of this present legislation? We are told in the report of the committee that it is to supplement existing laws against unlawful restraints and monopolies, and for other purposes. If it were limited to those things which have been well considered by the courts and are now understood by the business world, then the measure might commend itself to our judgment and our approval. But there are new standards set up in this measure that are unknown to the antitrust laws of the United States which will require new interpretations at the hands of our courts and will plunge business into a condition of uncertainty and doubt for probably 25 years more.

The majority report contains the following quotation—I presume it is taken from the address of his excellency, the President, to this Congress:

Additional articles in our constitution of peace, the peace which is honor and freedom and prosperity.

These provisions, expressed in this proposed bill, are thus denominated by the majority of our committee:

Additional articles in our constitution of peace.

I would that they were, for then they could be voted for without hesitation or objection. I would that the very thought which seemed to dominate the message of the President was really true, that he recognized that big business, as it is called, had seen the handwriting upon the wall, that it had taken note of the power of the Government to control our industries, and that it had bowed its head before the authority of statutes and courts. This was the message and proclamation of peace in which the President said:

We now understand each other, and will henceforth go forward, aiding to bring about the finest condition of prosperity of which the country is capable.

Does this measure which is now under consideration illustrate any such purpose?

We are told that this bill is not designed to hinder or destroy business, but to help it. When you examine the provisions of the bill separately and study their application to business, can you honestly reach such a conclusion as that? It were more true to say that this bill is designed to harass and annoy small business, small corporations, and invade the freedom of business to an extent hitherto unparalleled in the history of legislation in this country.

No one questions the importance of this subject. No one can but feel that this is really a measure that ought to have our best and most serious thought. This whole subject of the regulation of monopoly, regulation of interstate trade, or, as the Constitution puts it, regulation of commerce, is now perhaps the most important subject and topic that may engage our attention.

I wish to read the words of a distinguished lawyer and statesman, and one who, while he was on the bench, exemplified that he was a most learned and competent judge. I quote from the recent article of ex-President Taft:

The Federal antitrust law is one of the most important statutes ever passed in this country. It was a step taken by Congress to meet what the public had found to be a growing and intolerable evil in combinations between many who had capital employed in a branch of trade, industry, or transportation, to obtain control of it, regulate prices, and make unlimited profit. Whether Congress intended it or not—

I commend that portion of his remarks to the consideration of every Member of this House in connection with the question whether or not labor organizations should be exempted from the operation of this statute. There can be no doubt that the language of the statute on its face, by natural interpretation, must be applied as it stands to labor organizations and every other organization which by its combination may restrain trade or tend to create a monopoly.

Whether Congress intended it or not—

He says—

it used language that necessarily forbade the combinations of laborers to restrain and obstruct interstate trade.

The statute therefore qualified three important phases of what we include in the general term "individual liberty"—the right of property, freedom to contract, and freedom of labor.

In this law Congress used general expressions—"restraint of trade," "monopoly," "combinations," and "conspiracy."

And I interrupt the reading to comment that that is the true spirit and thought in legislation. Legislation is unscientific that attempts to deal with the details of every transaction that may come up. The purpose of legislation is to define in general and well-accepted terms something that is obnoxious to be a crime or illegal, and then leave it to the courts under the circumstances in every case to determine whether or not the law fits the facts. That is a question for the court and jury to answer, and the application of the law to the particular abuses that may be complained of, with its general definitions and terms, becomes a matter of ease and facility.

It was passed in a country that recognized as controlling that customary law handed down to us from England, and known as the common law. It was drafted by great lawyers who may be presumed to have used those expressions with the intention that they should be interpreted in the light of common law, just as it has been frequently decided that the terms used in our Federal Constitution are to be so construed. . . .

Mr. [WILLIAM A.] CULLOP [D., Ind.]. Does not the gentleman think that the reason that statutes are now made specific in regard to certain things such as the gentleman has enumerated there is because the courts in rendering decisions have attempted to legislate instead of construing the law as it has been enacted?

Mr. GRAHAM of Pennsylvania. On the contrary, my personal experience in connection with the administration of the law in our courts leads me to believe that there is no fairer and no safer method of administering the law than to leave the question in each specific case, under proof of the facts, to be determined by the court and the jury. All this talk about legislation on the part of the courts is justified only in a few exceptional instances. I know of nothing that is more unfair and untruthful than that which has become seemingly a shibboleth of the party in a political contest when they cry out that the Supreme Court of the United States wrought into the antitrust law the idea of reasonableness. Any man that understands the law, any man that practices the law, any man that follows the decisions of our courts, knows that the reasonable interpretation of the statutes is a part of the natural treatment that every court must give to it, and it is the only way in which human affairs can be administered with safety. [Applause.] And the writing of that was perfectly just, and it was not legislation; it was a proper interpretation of the statute. What else have we in the world, as Omar Khayyam says in his matchless verses, "but the light of reason" to guide us in our pathway through the mazes of this world? Reasonable interpretation! Why, that is law, logic, justice, and common sense. [Applause on the Republican side.]

Now, I wish in that connection to read a quotation from my very distinguished and able colleague on the committee, Mr. FLOYD, and I have read his argument in the RECORD with great interest, and do not hesitate to pronounce it as one showing great industry and great ability. I must, however, take exception to this:

The Progressive Republican stands for regulation and curbing of these trusts, and our old friends, the "standpatters," stood pat until all the popularity they ever had slipped away, and until in the last election they carried only two States. Their failure to enact legislation to curb and destroy monopolies and trusts was largely responsible for the division in their ranks which resulted in their defeat. . . .

Mr. GRAHAM of Pennsylvania. Mr. Chairman, I wish to remind gentlemen that the first law written upon the statute books of my country, this famous antitrust law, was conceived in the brain of Republican Senators, written on the statute books by the votes of a Republican majority and signed by a Republican President. [Applause on the Republican side.] The first legislation upon this subject came from us. The loss to which my learned brother refers was bred in the Chicago convention, and resulted from a split in the Republican lines which gave to the Democracy an accidental victory by which, though in the minority in the Nation, they possess the majority of votes in this House and have filled the place of the Chief Executive. . . .

Mr. [HORACE M.] TOWNER [R., Iowa]. Is it not further proof that the legislation in the States, which have brought about a reasonable control at least of the corporations of this country, was originated by Republicans and passed in Republican States before it was ever taken up or approved of by the Democrats in any way?

Mr. GRAHAM of Pennsylvania. I thank my colleague for calling attention to that. For if you take the 20 States that have passed antitrust legislation and read the record, you will find that it is largely Republican legislation that has written on the statute books these antitrust laws in reference to interstate-trade violations or the creation of monopolies. . . .

Mr. [CLEMENT] BRUMBAUGH [D., Ohio]. However that may be in other States, it is not true in the State of Ohio.

Mr. GRAHAM of Pennsylvania. Well, Ohio has always been somewhat exceptional in its political history. [Laughter.] . . .

Now, I am going to read a brief extract from the same distinguished statesman's address or lecture, because it is pertinent to what one is impressed with when one reads the debates in this House, and then I propose to refer to some speeches, not by the way of criticism but to make the suggestion as to how inappropriate much of the reasoning is and how inapplicable it is to the situation before us:

One difficulty in giving the public a clear understanding of the meaning and effect of the statute has been that it has been made a football of party politics, that shibboleths have been fabricated out of it without any clear understanding of the distinctions which the court has made, that results have been misrepresented and the superlatives of stump oratory have been substituted for a clear statement of the scope and operation of the law. Politicians have seized upon phrases that would attract the public eye, the meaning of which in the law they have not themselves understood, and have proposed amendments to accomplish purposes of a most indefinite character without knowing or caring how they were to operate, if only the pressing of the amendment gave them a ground for appeal for votes and for a claim to the gratitude of their constituents.

The statute dealt with a most difficult subject. The members of the Congress that passed it knew that it was a difficult subject. They made plain the object that they had in mind, and they used general expressions to accomplish it which they thought had had definition in existing law. The evil to be remedied was manifest, and they pursued the legislative course so often pursued before, or trusting to the learned, just, and equitable construction of the courts to effect their legislative intention.

I had purposed to review or refer to certain portions of the addresses which have been made on this measure, particularly by those supporting the report of the majority, but I shall not take the time. I cordially commend to my fellow Members the reading of the conclusion of the speech of the gentleman from Illinois [Mr. MADDEN] with reference to the effect that this bill is going to have on business. I noted the carefully prepared speech of the gentleman from Massachusetts [Mr. MITCHELL], and I wish to direct your attention for a moment to one or two thoughts in connection with his remarks. It was a quiet, dignified address. It was conservative, and such an address as one might expect from a gentleman of his knowledge and information. He says, however:

I have been a member of other legislative bodies, Mr. Chairman, in the days gone by, and I have never served upon any committee that sought, as this committee has sought, the light and the aid of counsel and the assistance of business men from every section of the country. Why, Mr. Chairman, we counseled with the minority Members upon the committee in the perfection of this bill. Why, Mr. Chairman, we prepared three tentative drafts of this bill, and I believe that every member of the committee, Republicans as well as Progressives, offered suggestions in connection with this legislation.

I respectfully dissent from the statement made by the gentleman with reference to the freedom that was given to the minority members to follow these bills as they were secretly prepared one after the other, and then flashed upon us as a whole; to the statement that we had an opportunity to make suggestions to them in order to reform what we thought was erroneous. On the contrary, three of our very distinguished and able Members framed these measures by and with the advice of the Executive of this Nation. Mr. Chairman, one of the things that grates harshly upon my sense of the proprieties in this legislative body is the intrusion of Executive suggestion and enforcement upon the acts of this deliberative body. [Applause on the Republican side.] I feel that the power of this House ought to be to originate and pass legislation.

The President may and ought to send us his suggestions from time to time in proper shape, or if he wishes to appear upon the rostrum and read them, then come and read them to us, but when that is done the power of legislation ought to be in the bosom or the heads of the men who are here on this floor representing their constituencies, and obligated by their oaths and by their duty to perform the legislative functions. But we have seen from the beginning to the end of this Congress the domination of the Executive power over this body, compelling legislation willy-nilly. Why, Mr. Chairman, men on this floor have said, when a measure was called to their attention, "Yes; I have not changed my mind upon it; when I voted for toll exemptions I agreed that it was right, it was not a subsidy, it was not a violation of the treaty." "Then, why do you not vote now against its repeal?" "Oh, I think I must follow the President—the President insists upon this."

I do not know how far the President insisted upon these several bills, but that they have come from him through this special committee, upon which there was not a single minority member, with his imprimatur thereon, I assert, and challenge contradiction. The gentleman from Massachusetts [Mr. MITCHELL] said further:

The President said, among other things:
"What we are purposing to do, therefore, is, happily, not to hamper or interfere with business as enlightened business men prefer to do it, or in any sense to put it under the ban. The antagonism between business and government is over."

Heaven save the mark! I have not yet seen in the proposed legislation any such truths declared or any such cessation realized. He then continues with the quotation from the President, as follows:

We are now about to give expression to the best business judgment of America, to what we know to be the business conscience and honor of the land. The Government and business men are ready to meet each other halfway in a common effort to square business methods with both public opinion and the law. The best-informed men of the business world condemn the methods and processes and consequences of monopoly as we condemn them, and the instinctive judgment of the vast majority of business men everywhere goes with them. We shall now be their spokesmen. That is the strength of our position and the sure prophecy of what will ensue when our reasonable work is done.

Mr. Chairman, are these measures the expression of the wishes of the great public? Out of a multitude of letters received let me read you two extracts. One is from the agent of a large number of cotton mills in the South, an important business man, whose word is veracity itself:

The attitude of the national administration, in my opinion, will result in greatly increased additions to the present bankrupt industrial enterprises of the recent past, and the result of this national legislation has certainly been to take away all inclination among business men and capitalists to do any more than routine transactions. Without an inclination to do business, I believe there can be no real prosperity in the country.

Further, I am firmly convinced that if the fundamental conditions of the generally abundant crops had not existed the discouragement and the depression into which the business world has been forced since the early commencement of the tariff discussion and the adverse national legislation there would have been, in effect, a practical panic, which I fear may still come upon us all unless business in general is given the rest which you advocate.

Among the cotton manufacturers in general, both North and South, with whom I come more fully in contact, the present question is not on what goods can we run our mills and make a profit, but how can we run our mills at the smallest possible loss and still not cause the operatives to be thrown out of employment. In the end, I believe, however, that a large proportion of the mills, both North and South, will have to shut down or else run only on part time, or else frankly tell their operatives that under the present conditions brought about through national legislation they will have to accept a largely decreased wage or else not work at all. . . .

Mr. [WILLIAM S.] HOWARD [D., Ga.]. I would like to ask the gentleman who the author of that letter is?

Mr. GRAHAM of Pennsylvania. I have no objection to giving it, for the letter, while addressed to me personally, I do not consider a confidential communication. It is Mr. Henry A. Haines, of Haines, Morehouse & Woodford, of New York City.

Mr. HOWARD. The statement was so inconsistent with the facts that I thought the gentleman might put it in the RECORD, because these mills are running full time all the time. . . .

Mr. GRAHAM of Pennsylvania. I believe the statement to be true, and from my own personal contact with business men I find more murmurings of what is coming than the people who shut their ears are willing to admit. I can point to a dozen instances where that idea of disinclination to do anything is holding back. I can point to a dozen manufacturers, one of whom only on Saturday afternoon told me, "I am only trying to keep my organization together and run my mill without suffering too much loss." The competition that is coming to him and others will have its effect; and that effect, unless it is checked, is going to write upon the business of this country in many departments the word "disaster." . . .

Mr. METZ. Does not the gentleman know that there are hundreds of corporations, dozens of them, running at a positive loss to-day just to keep their help together?

Mr. GRAHAM of Pennsylvania. That is absolutely true.

Mr. METZ. Just to keep their help going and nothing else? [Applause on the Republican side.]

Mr. GRAHAM of Pennsylvania. No one but him who will not understand it, who does not wish to understand it, will assert the contrary.

Now, with reference to that which concerns the banking interests of the country, I have a letter here, signed by the Philadelphia Clearing House Association, and to it are appended the names of some of our best citizens, men of the highest character and integrity.

The letter is too long for me to read, but I am going to ask permission at the close of my remarks to extend it in the RECORD. I believe I have that permission; but it sets forth how the entire banking interests in a city that has not been accused of maintaining Wall Street or sustaining a Morgan, but a conservative city, where capital has been handled fairly for business interests, how these men tremble at the prospect of legislation which you propose with reference to banks, and they plead that they—

Mr. CARLIN. Will the gentleman give the date of the letters?

Mr. GRAHAM of Pennsylvania. Yes. The first one I read was under date of May 16, 1914, and the one which I have not read, but placed in the RECORD, is under date of May 22, 1914, and is as follows:

May 22, 1914.

To the Committee on the Judiciary,
House of Representatives of the United States,
Washington, D. C.

GENTLEMEN: Representing the associated national banks of the city of Philadelphia, all of which have joined the new Federal reserve system and subscribed their proportion to the Federal reserve regional bank, we respectfully ask careful consideration by you of those provisions of the bill now before you [H. R. 15657] relating to interlocking directorates between national banks, State banks, trust companies, and certain other corporations, and the elimination thereby of certain existent corporate features in banking of the most vital import to this community and to the banks thereof, as well as to those of all cities and larger towns.

The motive prompting the introduction of the interlocking directorate feature into this new statute, as we understand it, seems to be the hoped for correction of certain abuses which it is alleged have crept into banking and more particularly into the extension of credit, and which it is further urged have curtailed competition.

In seeking to correct what has been claimed as an evil existing in one part of the country, a vital injury in the sum total may be done to the great mass of our banking institutions and to the community at large by the enactment of this law, and beyond that we believe irreparable harm will result to the regional bank system as a whole. This system should not be weighted down with unwise laws, but should be left to work out its problem untrammeled. By its merits it should attract the widest and strongest support—should draw to it through the advantages it offers every factor which makes for the larger success.

Here in Philadelphia through a long term of years we can not recall an instance in which interlocking directorates have prevented fair and reasonable competition or curtailed in any way the credit of any individual entitled to credit.

The act, as proposed, will affect many of our strongest boards of directors here in Philadelphia; in many instances it will practically destroy them. Many of these men are allied with vigorous trust companies and other important interests; these connections are not in competition in the proper sense of the word, but, on the contrary, are most helpful in promoting the general welfare of the banking community. A compulsory choice in these instances between a trust company and a bank will result in favor of the trust company, and thus weaken the management of many of the member banks of the regional system.

Can Congress afford to force this new legislation upon the country and lower the vigor and tone of the regional system at the start? This system has yet to be "tried out," and its success is not by any means beyond peradventure.

The national banks have with surprising unanimity entered this system, but neither you nor we should permit that fact to deceive us. Already there exists a feeling that later we may be disillusioned. Is it wise for Congress to add now any element which may increase the doubt and unrest which are in the thoughts of hundreds of bank managenents not now able to measure the results of the Federal reserve act, and which managements have assented with the purpose of trying out the plan in all fairness to it and to themselves?

Bankers in considerable numbers in various smaller towns are quietly expressing themselves in this way. They can make no forecast at this time of the advantages or disadvantages which will or will not accrue to their locality. They have elected to enter the system, knowing they can later go over to the State system if they prefer.

The State systems are growing with rapid strides in many sections of the country, outstripping the national banks in number and prestige, while it is worthy of note that our State banks and trust companies are not overstrenuous in their efforts to adopt the regional plan. Does it not therefore behoove Congress and all real friends of the regional system to move in a manner calculated to attract to that system strong banks and the strong, trained men of the country, rather than to repel, and by legislating drive these men out of the managements in which they are needed? Does it not seem the part of business acumen that in the first days of this new Federal system a confidence should be generated that would weld together a great mass of strong banks and strong men rather than that timidity and alarm should disintegrate it in whole or in part?

The ranks of well-equipped bank directors will never be overcrowded; these men are born of experience—they are not overnight products.

One of the hard problems confronting the bankers of to-day is to select new directors for their banks—men who have the training, the influence, and the analytical equipment to insure the safe extension of credit and proper care of depositors' money.

The causes for the collapse of a multitude of banks in this country reveal that the great majority have been wrecked through bad loans—loans permitted or recommended by directors thoroughly honest, but lacking the trained ability to judge credits. It takes years of experience to make a safe credit man.

We earnestly urge that Congress most carefully balance this whole problem, and that in trying to remedy one evil [possibly overestimated] a condition shall not be created which shall be far more harmful.

We respectfully submit that it is unwise to harass the country with too many new experiments, phases, and standards at one time. Let this new banking system, which has so much of merit in it, not be weakened by trying out too many theoretical problems; if this occur, in the end the unexpected may happen, and we may see the whole system thrown into financial discord.

This act prohibiting interlocking bank directorates, if enacted into law, will do more to tear down and lower the tone of bank management in this country than anything which has occurred in all the years gone by.

We beg to suggest it is but fair to the clean, straight bankers of this country, who probably represent nearly 100 per cent of the profession, and who have all through these years transacted a strictly uplifting, legitimate, honorable business, that they be not forced to replace tried, efficient directors of influence with men of inexperience during a period in which the acid tests are being applied to the new banking system.

Respectfully submitted.

The Philadelphia Clearing House Association,
Joseph Moore, jr., president;
Jno. C. Boyd, secretary;
L. L. Rue,
J. R. McAllister,
E. F. Shanbacker,
Chas. S. Calwell,
S. S. Sharp,
Effingham B. Morris,
W. G. Elliott,
Joseph Wayne, jr., committee.

Now, when my learned friend read that extract from the President, and I give you, by way of contrast, the plaintive appeal that comes up from business, I ask you, if this committee is carrying out the language, the intent, and purpose of the presidential message, are they giving peace and rest to the business world? The keynote that runs through all these speeches, without enumerating them, is that the President said thus and so. We are writing into the law what the President desired. Now, the illustration—and I refer to the gentleman from Massachusetts only as a type of the use being inapplicable. He quotes three cases from the courts of Massachusetts, each ⊥ one of which relates to an instance where clearly the facts as stated forces the conclusion that it was a violation of the common law against monopoly and restraint of trade. Not one of his illustrations fits the single issue raised by the bill that is before this House. I wish I had time to refer to them and analyze them. Now, along the same line comes an illustration from my friend and colleague from Pennsylvania, where he speaks of the Colby mines. I said to myself when reading his illustration, Is it possible that a gentleman on the floor of this House would use an illustration like that and then say that that is a picture of the mining industry of this country? How far from the facts. I do not know whether the Colby incident is true or false. I assume that he would not have uttered it unless he had some foundation in fact for it, but I do know these figures are inapplicable to any mining institution or corporation of which I have the slightest knowledge, and I have knowledge of a very great many. Take the soft-coal industry of West Virginia. The royalties there run from 8 to 10 cents a ton, which are reasonable, as any sane man must admit. The cost of labor is 65 to 70 cents, and when the mine owner is able to get 10 or 15 cents profit on a ton for all the capital he has invested and the risk he runs, that is all the compensation he receives.

Now, the picture of the Colby mine incident stands out in sharp contrast with the truth. Let me clear away in a sentence one other thing. A good deal of time has been given to discussion of monopoly. Men's voices were mellowed. I fancied as I read those speeches I could almost hear the tremble in the voices and see tears in the eyes as they pictured this monstrosity of monopoly and restraint of trade. What has that to do with the question that we are considering? We have all, in our platforms, in our actions, in our votes, condemned monopoly and restraint of trade, and so let us start on an even keel. We are just as full of energy to destroy monopoly and to restrain trade [sic] as you or any other persons who have anything to do with legislation or the formation of our laws. All these things should be swept aside in the forum of our reason and we should take the language of this law and ask ourselves this question: Does this law add anything to the Sherman antitrust law that will be beneficial to the community, or does it create doubts which will make the business world uncertain, or does it run the risk of inflicting conditions upon the men in the smaller businesses that will destroy their hopes and probably destroy their enterprises? That is the single question. I have not the time now to do it, but I hope to advert to some of these things under the five-minute rule when we come to consider the question of amendment. Discrimination in prices, tying up by contracts, holding companies, interlocking directorates, those are the things that the committee have aimed their shafts at instead of doing what I said in the beginning—take the scientific principle of legislation, which is to define crime, and not attempt to legislate upon individual instances. The law against interlocking directorates, while there have been evils under that system such as the ones that are pointed out in the Pujo investigation, yet there is not one but can be reached under the Sherman antitrust law and destroyed—not one. Every evil that is pictured as flowing from interlocking directorates can be reached under that law.

Now, then, our committee stands in this position. If a man— . . .

If a man took a spade and struck another man over the head with it, crushing his skull and killing him instantly, in a frenzy of reform our Judiciary Committee meets and it passes a law saying that henceforth no man shall ever carry or use a spade. That would be about as logical as it is to say that henceforth there shall be no interlocking directorates because of the fact that in some instances the money power has controlled through interlocking directorates. On the general definition that whatever creates a monopoly or tends to create it, whatever is in restraint of commerce, is within the grasp of the law, an energetic prosecution can produce results that will destroy all these things without this singular kind of detail legislation.

Now, I have only a word or two to say in the balance of my time. . . .

Take the case of discrimination in price, and I only want to say a few words about that. We ought as legislators to try as little as possible to invade the freedom of business. That is an axiomatic truth that ought to lie at the root of all legislation.

Some of us, I fear, are so eager to accomplish something that may look like being drastic reforms that we trample this primary principle under foot and pay no attention to it. It is a natural right of a man to fix prices for the commodities which he has to sell. It is a business liberty that ought not to be lightly taken from him, and I conceive of but two instances in which it ought to be regulated by law. One is when the exercise of a public right is concerned—a public-service corporation. The other is where a monopoly has been created and the welfare of the community is threatened by it. But this proposed legislation says that if he fixes a price here differing from the price he fixes yonder, and if it tends to injure or destroy a competitor, he is guilty of a crime. Competition, my friends, is war. Competition, if it means anything, is the taking from another what he has, through the avenue of trade. Your Supreme Court has said, the law as written has said, that competition is the normal and natural thing for which we must contend—it is the genius of our antitrust legislation. . . .

Compete? Why, when something is ordered to be sold at auction, there you have competition. If you are endeavoring to make a contract and you invite bids, there you have competition—one bids at so much, and another bids at so much, in order to reach a result. But this drastic legislation, in my judgment, would destroy the liberty of business, and it would make a condition that would involve business in serious trouble. Take the man of large business, and say that his business is assailed at one point—we will say Chicago—and under this law he must lower his price all over the United States. He dare not meet competition in Chicago, which is his lawful right to do, in the place where he is assailed, but you put a handicap and burden upon him because he is big. God has made big men, big measures, big mountains, and lots of big things, and never put a single stamp of disapproval upon them. As long as they are confined within legal limits and are not monopolistic and do not restrain trade they are often the result and complement of success and genius and power, and they ought to be respected. [Applause.] But you are going to place upon them the handicap of saying that they must keep their prices at such a point or pay $5,000 and be incarcerated in jail. God help the liberty of business under such discrimination. [Applause.]

I could give you a dozen illustrations. Suppose a man is short of money and must have it. In order to get it he must sell quickly. He goes out and makes a price at which he sells, below the price at which he sells in other places. Would you put upon him the duty of selling the article at the same price everywhere? And that is what this act would do, namely, make him sell everywhere at the same price. Yes; but the committee says this must be done with the intent to wrongfully injure or destroy. And that word "wrongfully" was carried into the last edition of that statute—I do not know when, how, or under what circumstances; but it is there, and I accept it. It is an axiomatic truth and the law that every man is intended, or is presumed to have intended, the natural consequence of his act. Now, the natural consequence of my act, if I sell at a lower price and take business from my neighbor, is to injure him pro tanto. I injure him. And yet this question is to be left to a jury as to whether it is a wrongful injury or not. The peril of a business man thus exposed is very, very great. There are a thousand other instances of the same kind.

Take the tying-up contract paragraph. You destroy agency, except where you have an exclusive agent that does nothing else—and I believe that is consistent with the language of this act—but you take away from the business man the right, if he has a new commodity, to go into a place and say, "I wish you, sir, to take this and handle it for me. I wish to gain a foothold in this business community, and I will sell to nobody else if you will only sell for me." But because that man deals in other articles you take away from him and the seller the liberty of making such a contract which honorable methods time out of mind have consistently approved of.

Take your holding-company provision, and the only people that it will hurt will be the small holding companies. Three or four men are engaged, for instance, in mining coal in West Virginia. They have leases. They can not consolidate their three companies, and yet the same group of men own every share of stock in these companies. It is their property. The whole three put together would not constitute a monopoly or restraint of trade, and no movement would be made against them. But you would forbid them from holding this stock in a holding company. You would forbid them from controlling it by interlocking directorates, and you leave them helpless, unless they put dummies in to look after their property. That is the position in which this bill places small business, and I tell you that the small business of the country runs up into hundreds of thousands of corporations, and every one of them would more or less be affected by this unscientific legislation.

I wish I could take up in detail the other provisions of this bill, but I have already consumed more time than I expected, and I will reserve what little individual criticism of specific sections I may have to make to the time when the bill itself is up for amendment. [Loud applause.] . . .

Mr. HOWARD. Mr. Chairman, I would not consume a moment of the time of the House were it not for the fact that I would like to reply in my own time to the contents of a letter read by the gentleman from Pennsylvania [Mr. GRAHAM]. The letter I have reference to is the Haines letter, in which are contained certain statements as to the condition of the cotton-mill industry in the South.

I simply want to state that from my own knowledge practically every mill in my State and in my district now is in full operation. Some of them are running "night shifts," as they are called, and none of them has been suspended by fear of intended legislation [applause on the Democratic side] or by the action of the tariff upon these industries.

But my main object in injecting myself into this debate at this time is this: The gentleman from Pennsylvania, after I had stated that the letter of Mr. Haines was inconsistent with the facts, severely criticized me for injecting that into the RECORD, I very promptly withdrew it, as the gentleman seemed to be so jealous of congressional ethics, and said that I had grossly violated the ethics of debate. I want to say now and reassert that I did not intend to offensively inject myself into the gentleman's debate, but I do want to reiterate that every word of the statement made in that letter about the cotton-mill industry in the South is absolutely unfounded in fact. It is another of those Republican bugaboos that they find on the side of the road every time we seek to control big business in this country, which has run rampant over the people for the last 16 years under Republican rule. [Applause on the Democratic side.] . . .

Mr. [WILLIAM E.] WILLIAMS [D., Ill.]. Mr. Chairman, I listened with a great deal of interest to the very remarkable speech of the gentleman from Pennsylvania [Mr. GRAHAM], and would not in the brief time of 15 minutes undertake to reply to the argument which he advanced. But, with the indulgence of the House, I do desire briefly to refer to some of the thoughts which he expressed.

I assume that the gentleman from Pennsylvania is the spokesman of the Republican side of the House on this bill, and that their whole argument and case may be judged by what he had to say. I assume this not only because of the liberal time awarded him, but also by reason of the fact that the minority report, and the objections urged against this bill, is filed in the name of the gentleman from Pennsylvania.

I was not amused nor was I surprised at the very remarkable plea made by the gentleman in behalf of big business. Just such pleas and arguments have brought the Republican Party to the desperate straits in which it finds itself to-day. The whole argument of the gentleman is summed up very briefly in a few paragraphs in the minority views which are filed with the majority report. In the minority report I find in two or three paragraphs the whole contention relied upon by gentlemen on that side and elaborated by the gentleman from Pennsylvania. Here is one:

The antitrust laws on the statute book at this time have been carefully considered by the Supreme Court and judicially interpreted through a period of 24 years, and if properly enforced are believed by us to strip corporations and trusts of any power to injure or oppress.

I want to tarry just here long enough to comment upon the thought expressed, that these laws have been in force 24 years, have been interpreted by the Supreme Court, and "if properly enforced are believed by us to strip corporations and trusts of any power to injure or oppress" I want to ask, and I wish some gentleman unfriendly to this bill, somebody on that side of this House, would answer this question: Why has not this law been properly enforced, and why do you now, after 24 years, have to come to the country and appeal for time in which to demonstrate its effectiveness and its force?

Now, it will not do to reply that the Democratic Party and the present administration have been charged with this responsibility. We will be now and in the future, I trust, for many years to come. What I charge is that for 16 years, at least, of the lifetime of the Sherman antitrust law there has been but very little effort, if any, made to enforce it upon the part of those who have been charged with responsibility and are to-day claiming credit for it and standing as its sponsors. Let me read further:

The proposed legislation contains many new phrases and sets up new standards, all of which would require a period of years of interpretation by the courts before their full meaning can be definitely known by the business world.

It is very undesirable to bring about such a period of uncertainty and doubt to worry and harass the business of the country.

Great solicitude for the business of the country, and it is in behalf of the business of the country that their plea for big business is heard. In that argument we find gentlemen seeking to delay or to defeat, if you please, the proposed bill.

Now, the gentleman criticized the fact that no amendments could be effected on the floor of the House. The gentleman from Pennsylvania [Mr. GRAHAM] went so far as to say that important amendments to this bill are necessary; but he and his colleagues filed a minority report without indicating or recommending a single amendment. The gentleman himself made a speech of one hour, and, except by general phrase, did not indicate nor propose a single amendment and afforded no light to this House as to wherein this bill is defective and requires amendment.

His whole argument is in keeping with the remark the other day by the distinguished gentleman from Illinois [Mr. MANN], the minority leader, when he said whether or not he would vote for the proposed amendment to section 7—the labor section—depended upon whether he could do more mischief to the Democratic Party by voting for or against the amendment. He used this language. I read from the RECORD of May 19:

The bill contains this provision:

"That nothing contained in the antitrust laws shall be construed to forbid the existence and operation of fraternal, labor, consumers, agricultural, or horticultural organizations"—

And so forth. Some gentlemen desire to change that to provide that nothing contained in the antitrust laws shall apply to these organizations.

When interrogated by the gentleman from Texas [Mr. HENRY] whether he would vote for such an amendment, he evaded the question in every possible way until pressed, when he replied: "How I stand now will depend very largely upon whether I can make more mischief on your side of the House by voting one way or the other."

Has it comes [sic] to this—that the old Republican Party, which boasts of its 50 years of splendid history, shall determine public questions solely from party expediency and its leader vote for or against an amendment vital to the interest of labor, and determine that vote by the effect it may have on the political situation? Has it come to this—that the Republican leader has ⊥ so far lost his sense of propriety and patriotism that he will sacrifice the interests of labor for party gain and party advantage?

The whole argument of the gentleman from Pennsylvania [Mr. GRAHAM] along the same line was to criticize and condemn, without suggesting a single remedy or a single amendment that might be of use or benefit.

Let me read further from the minority report:

> No possible good can come from constant interference with business. It is our belief that business should have a rest from further legislation and be given an opportunity to adjust itself to the environment created by the existing antitrust laws as the same have been interpreted and are now being administered.

Oh, what a plea! The Sherman Act has been on the statute books for a quarter of a century, during which time it has been ineffective or inoperative by reason of lax enforcement. I will not say that former administrations have been wholly void in their efforts to enforce the law, but I will say that the Department of Justice has not been very diligent in that direction. I will do the Republican Party the favor to say that the fault does not wholly lie in the failure to enforce the law. The law itself in many respects is weak and needs amendment. That is the very purpose of this bill, and I must contend that it does not come with good grace from those who have been responsible for the failure of the law in the past to oppose amendment on the pretext that it will disturb business. No one has any disposition to disturb honest industry or legitimate business, and such business can not and will not be disturbed by any effort to amend and render more effective the antitrust law. The kind of business that will take alarm and scamper to cover is the big offender, in behalf of whom appeals are made on this floor from that side of the Chamber, from which source such appeals have emanated since the birth of the Sherman antitrust law, and which appeals have done more than any other one thing to render the law ineffective and inoperative. We are now told, after this lapse of time, that business has just learned what the law means, and all that it asks is a further lease of time, a longer day of grace within which to conform and adjust itself to the law. I assume that it was immaterial what the law meant under the preceding administrations, and that business was not concerned to know what the law meant; but to the extent that the law is effective, it has become all at once very important, indeed, to business not only to know what the law means but to readily and properly conform and adjust itself to the law.

Mr. Chairman and gentlemen, I have heard much said in the course of this debate about the effect on business and business conditions throughout the country. You have heard letters read just now, by means of which the impression is sought to be left upon the House and the country that the Democratic Party has materially interfered with the business of the country. Now, I represent a State whose interests are largely agricultural. I represent in part the State of Illinois. I have seen much in the papers of late about the effect of our recent tariff legislation on prices, and to-day I procured from the Secretary of Agriculture some figures which I want to submit here in answer to the contention that the country is in need of a rest.

The argument which is urged here most strongly is that business needs a rest. Let me show you what Democratic legislation has done to disturb the business interests of the country. These figures speak louder than any language that I or others might employ.

I have here two columns of figures, one taken from the market reports of May 23, 1913, the other from the market reports of May 23, 1914, the corresponding date one year later. Here they are:

May 23, 1913, contract wheat for May in the Chicago market was 91 and 92 cents a bushel. In 1914, on the corresponding date, it was 97 5/8 to 98 cents a bushel.

Now, after the tariff bill has been in operation all these months wheat is 7 and 8 cents a bushel higher in the Chicago market than it was one year ago.

Contract corn, May 23, 1913, 57 1/4 to 58 1/2 cents per bushel. One year later, on the corresponding date of 1914, contract corn 69 5/8 to 70 cents per bushel; that is, corn to-day is 12 cents a bushel higher than it was a year ago, before the tariff bill became a law.

Of all the extravagant statements and wild-eyed clamor which has been indulged in for political effect within my recollection the most silly and ridiculous has been the statements and arguments advanced that the American farmer through the Central West is about to be ruined by the importation of Argentine corn. That contention is the most absurd and nonsensical clap-trap that I ever heard emanate from intelligent sources. Anyone who has seen a sample of Argentine corn will reach the prompt conclusion that no danger of competition or rivalry can ever result from its importation. Its use could only be occasioned by necessity arising from a famine or shortage at home which would compel its substitution and use. Men do not import corn for fun, and it will only be brought to our markets when the price at home, because of a shortage of our own crop, is so great as to attract or induce it. A trivial amount of such corn has been brought to our ports within the last few months, but it has not found any ready demand and has not in the least affected the market price of the domestic article. The 10,000,000 bushels which within a few months have been imported is but a drop in the bucket, and had about as much effect on the market price as an extra steer butchered in the Chicago stockyards would have on the price of beef for the day. Our production of corn amounts to over two and a half billion bushels per year, and it is utter nonsense for anyone to urge or contend that the pitiful amount of 10,000,000 bushels more or less could affect the market price of so large a yield and production. The price of corn above quoted is a complete answer and refutation of all contention and argument that Argentine corn is a source of competition, menace, or danger to the American farmer.

Rye, May 23, 1913, 63 1/2 cents per bushel; in May, 1914, 66 cents per bushel.

Cattle, May 23, 1913, beef steers, per hundredweight, $7.90 to $9.10; May, 1914, one year later, $8.40 to $9.50.

Sheep, in May, 1913, $5.25 to $8.25 per head; in May, 1914, $5.75 to $8.85 per head.

Live hogs, May 23, 1913, $8.15 to $8.75; May 23, 1914, $8.40 to $8.50.

These are some of the products of the American farm, and the price of every one of them is higher than it was one year ago.

I might here to advantage recall to the attention of gentlemen on the floor the argument urged in this Hall one year ago, when it was proclaimed with great force that we would ruin the wool industry in this country if we placed wool on the free list. We did not heed the warning, and are now gratified to bring to this House the assuring information that the industry is not ruined, and that not only sheep but wool is selling in the market to-day for a greater price than the same product sold for one year ago. Let some gentleman answer and explain this proposition in the light of the arguments advanced on that side of the Chamber last summer. . . .

Mr. McKENZIE. My colleague does not contend that the lowering of the duty on these various products has caused the price to go up to the American farmer, does he?

Mr. WILLIAMS. No; I do not contend that, but this I do contend: While the price of farm products has gone up in every particular, the price of the finished product and the essentials of every man's table have gone down. Do you doubt it? Let me call your attention to these figures: One year ago the price of pork per barrel was $20.37 1/2 to $20.50; to-day it is $19.90. While the price of hogs has gone up the price of pork, the finished product, has gone down. Lard was $11.10 a hundred pounds a year ago; to-day it is $9.95. Yet the price of hogs has gone up.

Short ribs were $11.50 to $12.12 1/2 one year ago, while to-day they are $11.20 to $11.22 1/2. While the price to the farmer has gone up, the price of the product for the poor man's table has gone down. . . .

Mr. MORGAN of Oklahoma. The gentleman said he would like to have some explanation of that fact.

Mr. WILLIAMS. Yes; but not in my time. If the gentleman has a question. I will answer it.

Mr. MORGAN of Oklahoma. May not that condition which the gentleman has explained be the result of the fact that the earning capacity of the great mass of the people is less now and they can not pay so much, and hence the price has gone down?

Mr. WILLIAMS. The gentleman's premises are false. The gentleman is assuming a thing that is not true. Wages to-day average higher than they did one year ago, and the facts and figures will prove it.

Mr. MORGAN of Oklahoma. One more question: Does the gentleman claim there are more people employed than there were one year ago, and does not that have some effect?

Mr. WILLIAMS. I can only speak for my own part of the country. There is no complaint there. Every man who wants work gets it. No men are seeking work, but employers are seeking help. That is true in the State of Illinois.

⊥ Now, let me call your attention to the prices of three or four more articles of table necessity in the New York market. Take sugar, for instance. There is reason for that. We took the tariff off sugar, and it is cheaper. May 21, 1913, it was 4.2 cents a pound, while to-day it is 4.1 cents a pound.

Coffee, Rio No. 7, May 21, 1913, was 11 1/2 cents and May 21, 1914, it was 8 3/4 cents.

Tea, Formosa, May 21, 1913, was 14 1/2 cents and May 21, 1914, 13 1/2 cents.

Rice, May 21, 1913, 4 1/8 cents; May 21, 1914, 4 cents.

These figures and articles can be indefinitely multiplied. Market prices to the American producer have increased; the average is higher than it was a year ago, and the prices of the necessities of life that must go to supply the table have decreased, and the general average is lower than it was a year ago. These are facts that I want somebody to answer. Until they are sufficiently answered no argument upon that side to the effect that we are disturbing business can affect the result or our duty with reference to this bill. [Applause on the Democratic side.] . . .

Mr. [DANIEL J.] McGILLICUDDY [D., Me.]. Mr. Chairman, if the Democratic Party, in addition to tariff reform as exemplified in the Underwood bill and currency and banking reform as exemplified in the banking and currency bill shall pass these antitrust bills at the present session of Congress, it will have created more constructive legislation in one session of Congress than any other political party in the history of our country.

I have listened with much pleasure and profit to the argument of the gentleman from Pennsylvania [Mr. GRAHAM]. The burden of his song is that the small interests in this country will suffer if this bill is passed. That is an old-time trust argument. Whenever you touch monopoly and the trusts, their cry immediately goes up that you are not hurting them, but the small business interests of the country. Whenever you hear this tender solicitude on the part of the trusts for small interests and small business you can be pretty sure you are getting the probe on the right spot. When I heard our friend from Pennsylvania he had a suspicious look in his eye that while he was talking about the small interests he was really interested in something bigger than the small interests of this country. It is akin to another complaint that I have heard in this House against this bill. I heard a gentleman say here the other day that the Democrats were bringing this forward as a matter of politics, because the tariff bill did not reduce the cost of living and high prices in this country as they promised to do.

Now, if our political opponents undertake to state the Democratic position, I hold that they ought to do it fairly. The Democratic Party never said that under present conditions the reduction of the tariff alone would accomplish the desired reduction in high prices in this country. The tariff is only one of the prime causes of high prices. Monopolistic power and trust control of production and prices the Democratic Party realized as most potent factors in high prices, and promised the country to reform and correct them. The tariff, of course, is intimately related. In fact, the trust itself in this country is the legitimate child of high tariff. It developed from the tariff as direct as the fruit from the blossom. In relation to high prices the two are interlocking, and both must be treated before relief is obtained.

It is well for us to see exactly what the Democratic Party did say about that, and I quote from the platform of 1912:

The high cost of living is a serious problem in every American home. The Republican Party, in its platform, attempts to escape from responsibility for present conditions by denying that they are due to a protective tariff. We take issue with them on this subject, and charge that *excessive prices result in a large measure from the high tariff laws* enacted and maintained by the Republican Party, *and from trusts and commercial conspiracies fostered and encouraged by such laws*, and we assert that no substantial relief can be secured for the people *without import duties on the necessaries of life are materially reduced and these criminal conspiracies broken up.*

A private monopoly is indefensible and intolerable. We therefore favor the vigorous enforcement of the criminal as well as the civil law against trusts and trust officials, and demand *the enactment of such additional legislation as may be necessary to make it impossible for a private monopoly to exist in the United States.*

The Democratic Party has revised the tariff downward in good faith with the people, precisely as that party promised that it would, and it is now on its way to fulfill its other great promise by the passage of this antitrust bill. It will fulfill it, and in the words of the Democratic platform, it will make it impossible for a private monopoly to exist in the United States.

I have listened to the attacks upon this bill from the Republican side of the Chamber. I find them in neither harmony nor agreement in the line of attack. If there was anything fundamentally wrong with the bill you can be assured that its opponents would have discovered it and united on a common ground of attack upon it.

If I felt there was any coherence in the Republican opposition to this bill I should have some fears about it, for I respect the arguments and I respect the integrity of our Republican friends; but I hear a portion of them, intelligent, patriotic men, telling us that this bill is too radical, that it goes too far, that it will be destructive, and I hear responding to it another portion of the same party, equally intelligent and patriotic, telling us that it is too neutral, too conservative, that it will not accomplish anything in the way of reform legislation. My belief is that if there was anything inherently wrong about the bill our opponents would be in substantial agreement in their grounds of opposition. They are not in harmony in opposition to the bill for the reason that they are unable to make common cause against it, and I am convinced that the bill as a whole is safe, practical, and rational, and that is precisely the kind of a bill the Democratic committee started out to frame.

No committee could construct a bill that would be satisfactory to everybody in the country. That is not to be expected. No group of men could write such a bill. It is not expected that this bill will correct every possible evil of trust conditions that oppress the people of this country. But that it is a long step in the right direction and will correct the great trust evils that oppress the people there can be no reasonable doubt in the mind of any fair and impartial men.

The Democratic Party should have a fair chance with reference to this legislation. You can not correct in a day the trust evils that have been steadily growing and gathering strength for the past 30 years. These evils in this country have become deep rooted, widespread, and are guarded by combinations of wealth and power unequaled on the face of the globe. They have not only controlled the business of the country, but its politics as well. Their giant forms have stalked into the legislatures of the States and even into the Congress of the Nation, compelling their will to be done. The executives of the States and Nation have not been free from their attacks, and it is even feared by the people that their sinister influence has made itself felt in the courts of the country. To right such wrongs, to correct such evils, is no holiday task.

I have said that the Democratic Party should have a fair chance with reference to this legislation. I believe the people of the country have confidence in President Wilson and his administration. That they will not only be fair and reasonable with the administration in the face of this stupendous task, but that they will be patient, knowing that efforts are being made in the best of good faith to bring back to the people that which was theirs but which they have lost. It would be easy, indeed, to draw a radical antitrust bill, regardless of its consequences. It would be equally easy to draw a neutral, meaningless measure that hurt nobody and accomplished nothing. But this was not the purpose of your Judiciary Committee nor the spirit in which they approached the task. To draw a bill that would be at once rational and practical, that would right the wrongs and correct the evils aimed at, and not injure or destroy any legitimate business in the country is our purpose. We believe it is safer to take one step less than to go one step too far.

It is easy to criticize but difficult to construct legislation. It certainly does not lie in the mouths of our Republican friends to criticize our legislation when for 16 years they had full power themselves to give the country relief by way of amendment to the Sherman law and never lifted a finger to do it. They not only failed to amend the law, but they failed to enforce it.

For 16 years prior to the inauguration of President Wilson's administration the Republican Party controlled the House, the Senate, and the Presidency. It could enact into law any legislation it saw fit. Yet during all that time it never added a single line of antitrust legislation to the statues of the country. The best possible proof that the Republican Party would do nothing to eradicate trust evils in this country is that it did not and would not do it when it had the chance.

Yet in that 16 years of uninterrupted and complete power there was a perfect saturnalia of trust expansion and development in the country, such as was never heard of in all its previous history.

GROWTH OF THE TRUSTS.

The climax of trust conditions and evils in this country was reached between the years 1897 and 1904. Previous to 1897 there were not more than 60 concerns in this entire country that ⊥ dominated the industries in which they were engaged. In the next three years following 1897 there were 183 gigantic combinations formed in this country under Republican administration, every one of them dominating the industry under which they were formed. In the one year of 1899 alone there were 79 of these combinations formed, with a capitalization of more than $4,000,000,000. It is estimated that these combinations comprised one-seventh of the entire manufacturing industry in our country and one-twentieth of all the wealth that existed in our country at that time, nearly twice the amount of money in circulation in the country, and more than four times the capitalization of all the manufacturing corporations that were organized from 1860 down to 1893.

This was the period in which the holding company was developed, an organization and scheme that trust attorneys conceived would absolutely defy the law. Now, I say that when that condition of things existed, one of two things ought to have been done—either the Sherman law, if it was adequate, as you now claim, should have been enforced and these gigantic trusts put out of existence, or, if it was found not to be sufficient, then it ought to have been amended so that it would be.

If you had enforced it and it was found not sufficient to prevent interlocking directors, holding companies, overcapitalization, discrimination, and control of prices, and other trust evils, it was within your power to amend it so that it would. If you had done either of these things, corporations and trusts in this country would have gotten down to a competitive basis, or else would have gone out of business as trusts, and free, natural competition would have been restored in the country.

FAILURE TO ENFORCE ANTITRUST LAWS.

As to the enforcement of the antitrust laws by Republican officials for the past 16 years, it is putting it mildly to say that they were at least indifferent. At times the Sherman antitrust law was deliberately ignored and practically considered a dead letter. Why this indifference on the part of public officials during this 16 years of trust development to the enforcement of this most important antitrust statute? It was because public officials whose sworn duty it was to enforce these laws were not selected from circles that were interested in antitrust enforcement. They were men not accustomed to breathe the ozone of an antitrust atmosphere.

Men are very largely influenced by their environments. With this fact in view, it is interesting to see from what circles men have been drawn to enforce the antitrust laws for the past 16 years. Under the present law the Attorney General practically has full control of the prosecutions of trusts. Hence it is a matter of the greatest concern not only to the trusts but to the public as to who fills this important office.

In the summer and fall of 1900 negotiations were under way between J. Pierpont

Morgan and his group on the one hand and Andrew Carnegie and his associates on the other, for the formation of the great United States Steel Corporation. By all means the most powerful and important constituent company in the proposed United States Steel Trust was the Carnegie Steel Co., of which Mr. Carnegie was the controlling owner. For years the attorneys of the great Carnegie Steel Co. were Knox & Reed, distinguished and able attorneys of Pittsburgh, Pa.

During that same summer and fall of 1900 William McKinley was the Republican candidate for President. Mr. McKinley was elected in November and inaugurated March 4, 1901. Philander C. Knox, of the firm of Knox & Reed, was made Attorney General in Mr. McKinley's cabinet, after receiving a very warm letter of recommendation for that position from Mr. Andrew Carnegie. Within 30 days after Mr. Knox was made Attorney General the great United States Steel Corporation, probably the most powerful trust in the world, was organized. Mr. Knox, under the provisions of the antitrust laws of that time, had complete control of antitrust prosecutions. At practically the same time Mr. Knox went into the Cabinet as Attorney General his partner, Judge Reed, was elected a director in the newly formed United States Steel Corporation.

Does anybody think it likely there would be any overwhelming zeal on the part of Attorney General Knox to prosecute the newly formed trust, composed in large and important part of his old client, the Carnegie Steel Co., or to prosecute his old partner, Mr. Reed, who was sitting on the newly formed board of directors of that corporation? If any such zeal ever seized him it was most successfully restrained.

During his entire term as Attorney General no prosecution was ever instituted against the Steel Trust, nor was any such prosecution instituted by his Republican successors until the year 1911, when this House became Democratic as the result of the elections of 1910. One of the first acts of that Democratic Congress of 1911 was to appoint a committee known as the Stanley Committee to investigate the organization, methods, and affairs of the Steel Trust. Within three months after that committee began its investigation and turned the light of publicity upon the organization, methods, and affairs of this company, the then Attorney General commenced prosecution of the Steel Trust under the provisions of the Sherman antitrust law. The Steel Trust was doing nothing in 1911 that it had not done continuously for the 10 preceding years.[5.529]

Why was prosecution delayed until a Democratic House aroused the public sentiment of the country by the disclosures of the Stanley Committee?

What is true of the Steel Trust in this regard is only typical of what is true all down the line with reference to trust prosecutions.

PROVISIONS OF THE BILL—DISCRIMINATION IN PRICES.

I now want to take up some of the provisions of the bill before the House.

The great ultimate purpose of a trust is to control prices. If it could not control prices, there would be very little object in forming a trust. Experience has shown to every student of the trust problem that one of the most vicious evils of trust domination is the practice of discrimination in prices. The power to discriminate in prices demonstrates the power to control prices.

The practice of discriminating in prices, making prices lower in one community than in another, is, of course, for the purpose of destroying competition. The trusts do not lower prices for the benefit of the public, but to destroy their competitors. As soon as competition is destroyed prices are immediately raised to the old level, or often higher, and thus the people themselves are made to pay the expense of killing competition, and competition is the very thing which under normal conditions would be for the people's benefit. It is a fact that to kill competition trusts have often reduced prices below the cost of production.

Under the bill which we propose this unfair system of price discrimination will be abolished.

Section 2 of the bill provides that any person who shall directly or indirectly discriminate in price between different purchasers of commodities in the same or

---

[5.529] At this time a Justice Department suit, filed in 1911, was pending against U.S. Steel. The district court ruled in favor of U.S. Steel, denying dissolution. United States v. United States Steel Co., 223 F. 55 (D.N.J. 1915), aff'd, 251 U.S. 417 (1920).

different sections or communities in the United States, or any place under its jurisdiction, for the purpose of destroying or wrongfully injuring the business of a competitor, shall be deemed guilty of a misdemeanor, and upon conviction shall be punished by a fine not exceeding $5,000 or by imprisonment not exceeding one year, or both, in the discretion of the court. With this rigid provision, no trust would ever dare to resort to the old practice of discriminating in prices in violation of this statute. Especially not when the guilt is made personal and those authorizing the discrimination are subject to the penalties of this bill. When you take the power to discriminate in prices out of the hands of the trusts you take from them one of the most powerful weapons to destroy competition, and consequently to control production and prices.

MINE PRODUCTS.

The next section of the bill, to wit, section 3, I regard as one of the most important in the whole program of antitrust legislation. All of the great trusts in this country, and especially those whose products form the great prime necessaries of life, foresaw the absolute necessity of controlling the raw material from which such products are made. For this reason they seized, in turn, upon the great natural resources of the country. They knew perfectly well whoever controlled these great natural resources controlled, of course, the products for use in daily life made therefrom.

This is particularly true of the great natural resources in the form of mines in the country. For instance, one of the first acts of the Steel Corporation was to get control of the iron ore in the ground, by purchase of the land. With that in its control it bid absolute defiance to competition. The same is true of copper, coal, and nearly all other great mine products. Having control of the mines, under the law as it now stands, they are absolute masters of the situation. They can sell the raw material from their mines to whomsoever they please, and refuse to sell when they please. For instance, if you or I, under the law, to-day go to the mine owners or operators controlling the hard coal in Pennsylvania, with the cash in our hands to purchase coal, the owner or operator can arbitrarily and without any reason absolutely refuse to let us have that great necessary of life. He coldly refers us back to our respective communities, with the information that he is selling coal to certain customers of his there, and we must buy our coal from them, and pay them, of course, the trust-regulated price.

If the bill now before the House becomes law, such practice can no longer be carried out. Under the terms of section 3 it is in substance provided that it shall be unlawful for the ⊥ owner or operator of any mine, or for any person controlling the product of any mine engaged in selling its product in commerce, to refuse arbitrarily to sell such product to a responsible firm or corporation that may apply for the purchase of the product for use, consumption, or resale within the United States or places under its jurisdiction, and any person violating this section shall be deemed guilty of a misdemeanor, and upon conviction be punished by a fine of $5,000 or by imprisonment not exceeding one year, or both, in the discretion of the court.

This provision of the bill is founded upon natural justice. Under it if you or I go to some mine owner or operator in Pennsylvania with the cash, or being financially responsible, we can demand that the mine owner sell and deliver to us coal, and he can not arbitrarily refuse to do so. He can no longer turn us back to our local coal dealer and his trust prices as at present. Furthermore, he must sell us coal at the same price he sells it to his other customers without favor or discrimination of any kind. This particular provision of this section will be of inestimable value to the people of my own State. Under the laws of the State of Maine, now held to be constitutional by our Supreme Court, municipalities are authorized, upon the vote of the people, to establish coal and wood yards and furnish fuel to the people at cost. Under the present conditions this law is of little value to our people. If the purchasing agent of such municipality now goes to the mine owner or operator of Pennsylvania he is refused coal and turned over to his local coal dealer for the purchase. Under this bill the purchasing agent of the municipality can go to the mine owner or operator and demand the sale of coal to him; the mine owner can not arbitrarily refuse to do it, and the result is that our municipalities under this bill will get their coal and get it at the same prices coal operators sell to their other customers. It will be readily seen that this operation will result in great and direct benefit to the people of the affected municipalities.

HOLDING COMPANIES.

Another trust evil with which the present bill deals is what is known as the holding company. Under modern trust development this so-called holding company, in the words of the report, is an "abomination." The holding company serves no good purpose. It employs no labor, neither does it produce anything. It adds nothing to the wealth or the welfare of the country. Its sole purpose is to hold the stock of subsidiary corporations in order that it may control the acts of those corporations, and is particularly for the purpose of dividing production among them and controlling and limiting competition. It is, in fact, an ingenious device for a combination of the combines, the product of the shrewdest and ablest trust lawyers to technically comply with the letter of the law while deliberately and flagrantly violating its spirit and intent.

Section 8 of the proposed bill limits the evil of the holding company, so far as it is possible to do so. Present business conditions and experience render it necessary to make certain exceptions; but the bill limits the holding company in its most objectionable feature, namely, its tendency to promote monopoly and restrict or destroy competition.

INTERLOCKING DIRECTORATES.

The next great trust evil to which I wish to refer is that of interlocking directorates.

By means of this vicious practice the business of the country has been practically absorbed by a select and limited coterie of powerful financial magnates. They absolutely control the transportation of the country through control of the railroads; they control the banking institutions of the country, and consequently its credits; and they have very largely succeeded in taking unto themselves the great industrial institutions of the country. They have manipulated stocks and securities, made themselves at once buyers and sellers, borrowers and lenders, between great corporations which they absolutely control. It is needless to elaborate the evil consequences of their deeds. It is particularly needless to us in New England, who are now in the midst of the disasters shown by the pitiable and far-reaching consequences in recent developments in connection with the management of the New Haven and other New England railroads. Interlocking directorates, with all the evil consequences of the system, will become things of the past when this measure becomes law. The shackles will be stricken from transportation, banking, and industrial developments, and an era of free development will follow. The President well stated the benefits of this provision when, in his message, he said the adoption of it will bring new men, new energies, new spirit of initiative, and new blood into the management of our business enterprises. It will open the field of industrial development and origination to scores of men who have been obliged to serve when their abilities entitled them to direct. It will immensely hearten the young men coming on, and will greatly enrich the business activities of the whole country. The President never spoke words more pregnant with true prophecy.

PERSONAL GUILT.

Section 12 of the bill deals with one of the most important of trust conditions, and provides one of the most necessary and important remedies in the whole measure. I refer to the personal-guilt provision of the bill. Under it directors, officers, agents of corporations who have authorized, ordered, or done anything prohibited by the antitrust laws shall be deemed personally guilty of a misdemeanor, and upon conviction shall be fined not exceeding $5,000 or by imprisonment not exceeding one year, or both, in the discretion of the court. This practically transfers the pains and penalties for violations of antitrust laws from the corporation to the individuals responsible for the acts, as it should be.

Fines upon corporations for violations of law are often borne by innocent stockholders, who had no hand or part in the violations; if not upon the stockholders, the amount of the fines is practically taken out of the purchasing public by raising prices to the extent of meeting the fines imposed. In this way the innocent stockholder, or the yet more innocent public, were made to bear the burden of the wrongful acts of the officials of the corporation. Under this bill not the corporation nor the innocent stockholder nor the innocent public are to suffer, but the pain will fall upon the guilty perpetrator where in justice it ought. With the doors of the penitentiary open before them, trust magnates will have a care as to what they do in violation of the antitrust laws.

INJUNCTIVE RELIEF AGAINST THREATENED DAMAGE.

Under the present law any person injured in his business or property by acts in violation of the Sherman antitrust law may recover his damage. In fact, under the provisions of the law he is entitled to recover threefold damage whenever he is able to prove his case. There is no provision under the present law, however, to prevent threatened loss or damage even though it be irreparable. The practical effect of this is that a man would have to sit by and see his business ruined before he could take advantage of his remedy. In what condition is such a man to take up a long and costly lawsuit to defend his rights?

The proposed bill solves this problem for the person, firm, or corporation threatened with loss or damage to property by providing injunctive relief against the threatened act that will cause such loss or damage. Under this most excellent provision a man does not have to wait until he is ruined in his business before he has his remedy. Thus the bill not only protects the individual from loss or damage, but it relieves him of the tremendous burden of long and expensive litigation, often intolerable.

LABOR AND FARMERS' ORGANIZATIONS.

The rights of labor and agricultural organizations are protected under the provisions of this bill as never before by any statute in the history of our country. At the time of the enactment of the Sherman antitrust law nobody dreamed that labor organizations, organized not for profit but solely for bettering conditions for laboring people, were included within its prohibitive provisions. By section 7 of this bill the status of labor organizations is made clear. The dangers of legal dissolution of labor organizations, which by reason of recent court decisions were threatened, cease to exist when this bill becomes law. The bill has been truly called "Labor's bill of rights."

The labor provisions of this bill have been severely criticized in certain quarters. It is my belief that these criticisms have been hasty, ill-considered, and unwarranted. Let us look at the provisions of the bill and see just what it does for labor and labor organizations.

First, it provides that in cases of indirect contempt where the acts complained of would constitute criminal offenses under the law, the defendant on demand may have the right to trial by jury to determine questions of fact.

How long is it since any fair-minded and impartial American citizen would object to a trial by jury on questions of fact? What is there radical or new about that provision? Trial by jury is one of the most sacred of American institutions. It is one of the highest safeguards of the rights and liberties of American citizenship. The right to punish for contempt is at best something of an arbitrary right, and in its exercise may be tyrannical.

In cases of indirect contempt the act or acts complained of take place outside of the presence of the court—it may be a hundred miles away. The judge has no personal knowledge of the conditions or facts. What harm can possibly result either to the citizen or to society by having a jury intervene in determining the questions of fact, and the actual guilt of the offender be established by a jury before he is deprived of his liberty. ⊥ This provision of the bill is in absolute accord with every spirit of Americanism and American institutions.

INJUNCTIONS.

Next, there is the provision with reference to issuing injunctions. The power to issue injunctions is a great one. It is far-reaching in its effect. The evidence unquestionably shows that it has frequently, in certain parts of the country, been abused. At times its abuse has verged upon scandal.

Under the provisions of this bill the injunctive power is simply limited in cases where experience has shown that it ought to be. Let us carefully examine the provisions of the bill in this regard and see just what they are.

First, the bill provides that no preliminary injunction shall be issued without notice to the opposite party. Is not this a reasonable and just provision?

Next, that no temporary restraining order shall be granted without notice to the opposite party, unless it shall clearly appear from specific facts shown by affidavit or by the verified bill that immediate and irreparable injury, loss, or damage will result to the property or property right of the applicant before notice could be served or hearing had thereon. Surely no reasonable or fair-minded man can object to this provision of the bill.

Next, except as provided in section 14, no restraining or interlocutory order of injunction shall issue, except upon the giving of security by the applicant in such sum as the court or judge may deem proper, conditioned upon the payment of such costs and damages as may be incurred or suffered by any party who may be found to have been wrongfully enjoined or restrained thereby. The requiring of security under such conditions for the payment of costs and damages is one of the ordinary courses of procedure, and is in every way in accord with American ideas of justice and legal procedure.

Next, that every order of injunction or restraining order shall set forth the reasons for the issuance of the same, and shall be specific in terms; shall describe in reasonable detail the act or acts sought to be restrained; and shall be binding only upon the parties to the suit, their agents, servants, employees, and attorneys, or those in active concert with them, and who shall by personal service or otherwise receive actual notice of the same.

What is there wrong, unfair, or unjust about this provision? Certainly orders of injunction should give the reasons for the issuance thereof, and should be specific in terms, so that the defendant may know exactly what he has to meet. This is in absolute accordance with legal principles and procedure. That the order should be binding only upon the parties to the suit, their agents, servants, employees, attorneys, and those in active concert with them, and who have received actual notice, is a most reasonable and just provision. To include in a blanket injunction other persons outside of the parties to the suit who have had no notice of the same or knowledge thereof is a most unjust proceeding, absolutely antagonistic to ordinary legal procedure, and almost certain to work great wrong and damage to absolutely innocent parties who have no connection with the matter in dispute.

It further provides that the Federal courts are prohibited from issuing injunctions against persons because of their ceasing to perform labor. It would seem almost unthinkable that under the power to issue injunctions Federal courts under this process would undertake to prevent a person from ceasing labor at his will. Yet it has been done, but can never be repeated if this bill passes.

It further prevents issuing injunctions to restrain laborers from recommending, advising, or persuading others to cease labor. Why should not laborers be unmolested in their right to advise with one another and to persuade one another when it is all done in a perfectly peaceful manner?

It further forbids the issuing of injunctions enjoining laboring men from attending meetings at or near places where persons reside or work or carry on business or happen to be for the purpose of peacefully obtaining or communicating information or peacefully persuading persons to work or to abstain from work.

Why should laboring men in cases of disputes between employer and employees be restrained by injunction from conferring together, advising with one another, informing and peacefully persuading their associates in regard to matters of vital importance to them? Do not employers of labor under such conditions and during such disputes meet together at their houses, offices, and places of business for the purpose of conferring together and communicating information to one another and reasoning with their associate employers, and even with employers who are not associated with them, and persuading them to join with them as employers of labor during the pendency of strikes or labor disputes? Why should laborers be denied the same rights under such conditions that are freely accorded to and exercised by employers?

The bill further forbids the issuance of injunctions restraining paying, or giving to or withholding from any person engaged in such disputes, any strike benefits, money, or things of value.

Again, I say, it would seem unthinkable to a free-born American citizen that when laboring people contribute together sums of money to be used for mutual benefit purposes in case of a labor dispute or strike, that the court should have the power by injunction process to prevent those laborers from distributing these benefits among their needy associates, who perhaps have been brought to actual want by the tyranny and injustice of their employers.

It further prevents the issuance of injunctions against any persons assembling at any place in a lawful manner and for lawful purposes.

The right to peacefully assemble in lawful manner and for lawful purposes was thundered from the cradle of liberty, old Fanuel Hall, in Boston, and was sealed by the blood of Revolutionary patriots. Their sculptured forms would move in shame from their pedestals if that right was to be denied by their descendants.

These are the provisions of the bill with respect to injunctions. They simply place the laboring man upon the same equality with every other citizen so long as he obeys the law.

It is simply an application of the old and sacred Democratic doctrine of equal rights to all. This is the bedrock of Democratic principles. The Democratic Party is the party of equal rights. It is not a rich man's party nor a poor man's party, not the party of big business or of little business, not the party of capital or of labor, not the party of employer or employee, but the party of the whole people pledged by its history, its traditions, and its eminent statesmen, living and dead, to the everlasting observation of the great principles of equal rights. To promote the "general welfare" was one of the first reasons set forth in the preamble to the Constitution. Mark you, the "general welfare" and not the special interests, or welfare of the favored or privileged few. In the mad race for wealth the general welfare has been forgotten, not only in business but in legislation. The Democratic Party intends to remove the dollar mark from legislation in this country and place in its stead the symbol of manhood. The days of privilege and plunder have gone, let us hope forever.

> Ill fares the land, to hastening ills a prey,
> Where wealth accumulates and men decay.

It is no exaggeration to say that the pending bills have to do with the most important economic and industrial problems in the history of the country. The questions involved not only essentially affect the business interests of the country, big and little, but vitally reach the welfare, comfort, and happiness of every man and family in the land. Aye, more, they reach the very groundwork of American free institutions and affect the stability of our governmental system as established by the fathers of this Republic.

In passing this antitrust legislation the Democratic Party is keeping absolutely good faith with the people. The Republican Party having utterly failed in the discharge of its mission, so far as antitrust legislation is concerned, the people of the country have turned to the Democratic Party for relief. If you pass these antitrust bills now before the House you will do much to inspire the people with confidence and hope in the assurance that "a government of the people, by the people, and for the people" is still with us. [Applause.] . . .

Mr. METZ. Mr. Chairman, I do not want to take up the time of the committee to make a speech, but only to point out some of the special features of the bill that appeal to me and to reply to a question asked while the gentleman from Pennsylvania [Mr. GRAHAM] was speaking. I was asked why it was that a great many of the textile and other mills were running without profit or at a loss while apparently being busy. I want to answer that question to begin with. Those of you who know how business is done in the textile industry, and, for that matter, in other industries also, will realize that when a mill starts on a season's goods—and everything depends upon seasons with us—they, or their selling agents, send out their salesmen or their stocks are open to buyers who come to look at them, either way, and the mill's production is sold up for that season as quickly as possible, and that means that they can lay out their ⊥ plans and run their looms on certain patterns, finish them up, and can then start new ones, and arrange to run for the season, according to the capacity of the mill, and the business for that season is arranged and the goods made up and shipped. To-day, and it has been so since the agitation of the tariff question began—and I want to say that the tariff is fair, and I think that it is the first scientific one we have had, and that it will work out all right if left alone and we are not bothered with other conditions; I am not afraid of the tariff even in the textile industry—but to-day no mill can sell and no buyer is buying ahead, and I refer to the big dry-goods stores, the department stores, and other large buyers. Salesmen in certain lines go out in two seasons—in May and June and November and December—and usually sell out the entire capacity of the mill for the season's output in those months. For the last year or so they have not sold their capacity in that time. The salesmen come home having sold, say, only one-third their quota.

The mill, therefore, only buys raw material in small lots, and pays more money, but the mill is running and labor is working, because they are making some goods, and during the balance of the season their orders may have come in just the same, so the total volume of business may not have decreased and we are not coming to a panic or failures; but the mill has been running in such an uncertain way because you could not foresee what was coming. Take, for instance, in the carpet business alone. A carpet is the last thing that a man is going to buy. He will put it off another year if he needs something else more and money is scarce. But even the carpet mills have run to full capacity, even if they had to run on dribs and drabs, by putting a pattern on the loom and then taking it off, and putting another pattern on and taking that off, and then changing back again, instead of running each one out. That means that the overhead expense has gone ahead and increased and that the mill has not made or has even lost money, while the help has been on the job right along, however, getting full pay, and have not suffered, and the fact that they have not suffered is the reason that makes business as good as it is to-day. The manufacturer, the stockholder, and the owner are the men who have suffered. The manufacturer does not dare go ahead, because he does not know when we are going to stop interfering or whether we are going to keep on interfering with him. That is the real situation in the manufacturing industries. I said that the stockholders in many mills have not received a dollar's worth of dividends in years, while the help has been working. The mill did not dare to shut down. In a small mill town you and I know what stopping means. The mill town is entirely helpless without the mill. It depends on the mill running. If it shuts down or there is a fire, the next day the mill help are scattered all over the country, and it is a hard thing to get back an organization. The manufacturer keeps on running to hold his organization and his market. The pay of the help has not been cut down; it has gone up. Rents have not gone up in those mill towns to any extent, and there have been no big revenues from the tenements to the owners. The help has gone on working, but the stockholders have not had any dividends, and I think the income tax is a good thing, if it simply shows these very people what they have not been making for some time past.

My friend from Georgia [Mr. HOWARD] talks about the cotton mills in the South. Mr. Chairman, I have seen more mill men from the South in the last four weeks who are engaged in the cotton-manufacturing business than he has in a year. They were up in New York at the cotton manufacturers' convention. They are not crowing about prosperity. They are in the same condition as manufacturers in other sections, even if they are Democrats; and they admit they have got to be Democrats in the South; but business men and manufacturers have not got to be Democrats in the North, and they are not going to be if you do not let them alone. The gentleman's statements about the cotton mills in the South are not based on facts. I know that. I am in close business touch with them, and the gentleman is not. So much for conditions and the reasons therefor.

As to the provisions of the bill, I first want to refer to section 2, in respect to discrimination. The bill says you have to show intent to injure or destroy a competitor. It may be true that that may eventually be held to be the case, but suppose I am doing business with A and B in the same town. A is a big buyer, has experts enployed, and he sends his buyer to New York and will not have me come near his plant at all. I am speaking now of consumers of mill supplies. B has a small plant, and he has not any expert chemist or expert of any kind, and I have to show him what to do. I have to send a trained man into his shop and show him how to use a product. It costs me more to sell to B than it does to sell to A. . . .

. . . The result is that though A comes to my place and makes his own terms, because he is better posted on competing products, and I have got to meet them, no matter how close my margin, or lose the order, under this section I have got to sell B at the same price as A, because the law says that I must not discriminate in price for same commodity. I am not injuring B's business, mind you, when I sell cheaper to A, but B finds out that I sell to A at a certain price, and then he refuses to pay his bills and sets up a defense that I have injured him by charging a higher price. I have got to go to court and defend his action, because he has not paid my bill. That is where you will hurt small business, because some large trusts may have held out on somebody else by refusing to sell or underselling to some one else for specific reasons of their own.

Section 4 refers to sale agents. The big concerns are the only ones who can afford to maintain agencies in every town and city. In many lines it is absolutely impossible. Take the machinery business. Nearly every machinery manufacturer does business in this way: He will appoint an agent for his machine, and that agent must bind himself to sell nothing in competition with that particular machine. There is not business enough to warrant his selling no other line of machines or similar products, so he makes similar contracts for exclusive sales of various kinds of machines, but only one of each type, and none competing with any of the others he carries. He sells products of various makers and he sells other machines, but he should not sell any competing with the manufacturer who supplies him with catalogues, supplies him with information, supplies him with facts, without which he would lack the experience to sell that or any other machine, and in supplying this the manufacturer uses the local exclusive agent instead of his own salesman, whom it would not pay to send out. This covers many other lines besides machinery, and if you wipe out the exclusive contracts and selling agencies you wipe out the business of a large percentage of the manufacturers in this country by checking their distribution, and that injures the working people and consumers of this country instead of helping them as you intend.

Mr. MADDEN. Seventy-five per cent?

Mr. METZ. Yes; 90 per cent; and you might say all, practically. The propositions are ridiculous. They are not fair, they are not right, and that is why the business and manufacturing interests of the country are praying and hoping that we will adjourn, go home, and let them alone. [Applause.] . . .

Mr. SLOAN. Mr. Chairman, the gentleman from Illinois [Mr. WILLIAMS] pursued a rather peculiar course in his speech in the numerous challenges which he submitted for answer to his supposed invulnerable argument as to prices and their causes, in order to convince this House that the change of administration and its resultant legislation had been beneficial to the farmer. He submitted a set of figures as to prices for 1913 and also for corresponding dates in 1914. I submit that it is not a fair basis of comparison. A fairer basis of comparison is where we have a set of figures based upon a time and a set of circumstances when the people of this country did not know that the blight of Democracy was to fall upon it. That was in May of that period in 1912, two years ago instead of one. One year ago the present administration was in power. One year ago the tariff policy of this country had been announced and a change determined upon.

The Underwood tariff bill, prior to the date given by the gentleman from Illinois, had passed this House. We knew what it was, and the business men of the country could readily predict and reason what it would do. It was the express purpose of the Underwood bill to lower the price of farm products and incidentally to injure the producers, and if this was not accomplished then it would be a confession of failure in its purpose.

Now, then, I shall submit for the RECORD a list of prices taken from a paper which did not oppose the present tariff law. I will read some of these figures and submit the rest in the RECORD under the rule. Wheat, average price in 1912 on May 1, was $1.22; in 1914 it was $1.03 1/2. If the gentleman's rule is to be applied it would indicate a loss of 18 1/2 cents in the period ⊥ influenced by the present administration, because it was not long after the 1st of May, 1912, when it became apparent to the people of this country that there was to be a change of policy in this country, and the legislation which we have was clearly foreshadowed in the tariff legislation of the Sixty-second Congress. Corn in 1914 was 75 cents; in 1912 it was 86 1/2 cents, a difference of 11 1/2 cents. Oats in 1912 were 63 cents, and in 1914; 43 1/2 cents. Flour in 1914 was $4.25, and in 1912, $5.10.

Mr. Chairman, I do not care to take up the time of this committee. I had not expected to discuss this question, but when any gentleman coming from an agricultural State, like the State of Illinois, pretends to tell the farmers of this country that following or caused by the tariff legislation of this administration there has been improvement in any respect in price in the products of the farm, he merits contradiction. A careful figuring and investigation of the subject must convince him, as it has already convinced 30,000,000 people of the United States interested in farming, that the tariff legislation of this administration is directed against their interests and they are feeling its effect every time they go to market. [Applause on the Republican side.]

The figures are as follows:

	May 1, 1914.	May 1, 1912.	Change.
Wheat, bushel	$1.03 1/2	$1.22	$0.18 1/2
Corn, bushel	.75	.86 1/2	.11 1/2
Oats, bushel	.43 1/2	.63	.19 1/2
Barley, bushel	.67	1.36	.69
Rye, bushel	.68 1/2	1.02	.33 1/2
Flour, barrel	4.25	5.10	.95
Beeves, live	9.40	9.00	.40
Sheep, live	5.85	8.25	2.40
Hogs, live	8.35	7.75	.60
Muttons, carcasses, pound	.12 1/2	.15	.02 1/2
Hogs, carcasses, pound	.11 3/4	.11	.00 3/4
Muttons, carcasses, pound	.12 1/2	.15	.00 1/2
Milk, quart	.04 1/2	.04 1/8	.02 1/4
Eggs, dozen	.22	.20	.02
Beef, barrel	19.00	16.50	2.50
Pork, barrel	22.25	20.75	1.50
Bacon, pound	.11 3/4	.11 1/4	.00 1/2
Hams, pound	.16	.13 1/2	.00 1/2
Rice, pound	.06 1/4	.05	.01
Butter, pound	.25 1/2	.36	.10 1/2
Cheese, pound	.14	.15 3/4	.01 3/4
Coffee, pound	.08 3/4	.14 5/8	.05 5/8
Hides, pound	.17	.15 1/2	.01 1/2
Oak leather, pound	.45	.10	.05
Cotton, pound	.13	.11 3/8	.01 5/8
Wool, O. & P., pound	.24 1/2	.26	.01 1/2
Wool, Australian, pound	.67	.85	.18
Flax, pound	.05 3/4	.05	.00 1/4
Print cloths, yard	.03 5/8	.03 7/8	.00 3/8
Ginghams, yard	.06 1/4	.06 1/4	—

•   •   •   •

Mr. PLATT. Mr. Chairman, I did not expect to have anything to say on this bill, but it seems to me perhaps there are one or two facts that ought to be set forth in some form. One is that anyone who has studied the events that led up to the passage of the act of July 2, 1890, the Sherman antitrust law, knows that the agitation which led to that legislation was not started in the interest of consumers, it was not started by consumers, and the antitrust agitation never has been in the interest of consumers, nor have the laws worked in the interest of consumers. The consumers have always been the goats, and in this bill they are made more than ever the goats.

This bill will create a lot of contention. It is a bill—omitting the part cut out by the committee in writing one amendment—of some 21 pages. The Sherman law is only about 2 pages—a very short act. It has taken some 24 years even to construe with something approaching definiteness what it means. How long will it take to find out what this bill means? It is unwise to pass it, because of the uncertainty it will create and because it is bound to cause disappointment among the people, since it will not do what the people expect. They expect it to lower prices, and it is not going to lower prices. In some respects it is distinctly against lower prices for the people.

In one of its sections—section 2—this bill is exactly and diametrically opposite to the purposes of a bill we have passed in this House at this session. We passed a bill not long ago known as the river and harbor bill, for the express purpose, in large part, of making the railroads discriminate in prices between localities. Section 2 of this bill apparently applies to railroads.

Yet gentlemen on that side of the House who have spoken in favor of this bill, and also in favor of the river and harbor bill, said that the reason for improving certain rivers was to make the railroads come down in their rates in certain neighborhoods. The majority report on this bill says:

> Every concern that engages in this evil practice must of necessity recoup its losses in the particular communities or sections where their commodities are sold below cost or without a fair profit by raising the price of this same class of commodities above their fair market value in other sections or communities.

Now, if that is true, it must be true, also, of the railroads. If they have to lower their prices to meet water competition in places where we have provided the water competition, at public expense, they must recoup their losses by making them up in other localities. . . .

Mr. [WILLIS J.] HULINGS [Prog., Pa.]. This bill permits discriminations to be made on account of the quantity of goods sold?

Mr. PLATT. It does.

Mr. HULINGS. Do you believe that is right and proper?

Mr. PLATT. I do not see why that is not right and proper. What you mean to say is that wholesale prices may be lower than retail prices?

Mr. HULINGS. It does not say wholesale or retail, but it says that on account of quantity discrimination can be made. Is that right?

Mr. PLATT. It is in accordance with the universal trade practice, and I would not want to say that it is wrong.

Mr. HULINGS. Now, if that kind of discrimination is permitted, do you not simply permit the big concern to grow great by what it feeds upon, because continually it would be handling larger and larger quantities?

Mr. PLATT. I think that is to some extent true.

Mr. HULINGS. Now, do you think the bill provides any remedy or prohibition of that sort of thing, and, if it does not, do you not think it should?

Mr. PLATT. Well, I doubt whether it should. I do not think it does. It leaves undone several things which might well be done and tries to do several things which should not be done. I think the chief thing the bill does is to raise a whole lot of new trouble and uncertainty, which will have to be settled by the courts in the end, and which, it seems to me, are unwise and unnecessary. As I have said, the bill is not in the interests of the consumers, and I can not see what its supporters expect it to accomplish of real value. . . .

Mr. [J. HAMPTON] MOORE [R., Pa.]. If this new antitrust law goes into effect, will it not give employment to a great many more lawyers?

Mr. PLATT. I think that perhaps is one of the purposes of it.

Mr. MOORE. And that is a very important matter so far as consumption is concerned?

Mr. PLATT. So far as the lawyers are consumers, do you mean?

Mr. MOORE. Yes. It will create business for antagonists at law?

Mr. PLATT. I am strongly of the opinion that it will.

Mr. MOORE. And for almost an indefinite period; that is, a man who goes into business with a capital of $50,000 will have to take a lawyer in with him whom he will have to keep for 20 years until the courts decide the case.

Mr. PLATT. I think perhaps that will be true. If it takes 20 years to find out what a 2-page law means, how long will it take to find out what a 20-page law means?

Mr. MOORE. Well, it means employment for somebody, anyhow?

Mr. PLATT. Yes; I admit that much cheerfully; but it does not mean benefit to the general public. . . .

⊥ [Mr. CALDER addressed the committee. See Appendix.] . . .[5.530]   ⊥9265

Mr. MORGAN of Oklahoma. Mr. Chairman, in closing the general debate for the minority, while I shall criticize the provisions of this bill, I shall at the same time sound a note of progress.

I believe that any Member of the minority, for a number of good and sufficient reasons, might vote against this bill. Certainly there are good reasons why any minority member of the Judiciary Committee or any Republican might vote against this bill. I have been asked whether I will vote for the bill. I have said that it was my intention to do so; not that I think many of the provisions are wise or will be beneficial or helpful to the country, but because in a way I believe the bill represents progress.

The Republican Party for nearly a quarter of a century in its platforms has declared that the Sherman antitrust law should be supplemented by other legislation. The Republican Party has at almost every national convention declared in favor of further regulation of the large industrial concerns, and in favor of a stricter control of their practices and business methods. My conception is that the Republican Party is not only not opposed to so-called antitrust legislation, but is positively in favor of such legislation. And I feel sure, Mr. Chairman, that if the majority party in this House that had control of this bill, that molded it and fashioned it and brought it into this House in its present shape, had presented a bill that really met the situation, that presented a wise, positive, constructive policy for the proper regulation and control of the great industrial corporations, the Republicans, as well as the Progressives, would have lined up solidly for the bill. But unless the bill shall be materially amended, certainly a Republican may vote against it consistently and perhaps wisely.

Mr. Chairman, I think that in all antitrust legislation we should follow a few general rules and principles. We should have these in mind in preparing the various provisions and sections of the bill: First, we should have in mind the fact that the one thing we wish to destroy is monopoly; the one thing that we wish to properly control and regulate and bring under proper subjection is the great industrial corporation that really has power—the power to arbitrarily control prices and thus exact unjust profits from the people. . . .

Mr. FESS. I wanted to know whether, in the gentleman's opinion, this bill does destroy monopoly or affects it injuriously in any way—that is, in the gentleman's opinion?

Mr. MORGAN of Oklahoma. In my opinion it does not, and that is what I propose to show. Second, we should have in mind this important fact, that the one thing we wish to maintain, and retain and sustain, is competition. We want to destroy monopoly and restore and maintain competition.

Third, in preparing this legislation, we should make the provisions in the bill comprehensive in the number of abuses which they prohibit, but restrict and narrow its scope in so far as the actual number of business concerns brought under its control. That is to say, we should not interfere with private business any more than is necessary for the protection of the public interests; and the Federal Government should not interfere with the control of private business within the States any more than is necessary to protect the public interests from a national viewpoint.

Small concerns, so far as is compatible with national interests, should be left to the control of the States. Through Federal laws we should seek to control only corporations which have such capital, such wealth, such business organizations, such control over natural resources that make their regulation and control necessary for the protection of the people of the entire Nation. We are entering a new field of legislation. We went along for a hundred years before we enacted the Sherman law. That was the first

---

[5.530] A diligent effort has been made to locate in the *Congressional Record* and to review all extensions of remarks indicated in these debates. In numerous instances no such extended remarks can, in fact, be located. Although none of the extensions that were found were deemed pertinent to the legislative history of the Clayton Act, the Appendix page references of these remarks are noted herein. In the many instances where the remarks found in the Appendix were not extended on one of the days Congress was debating the Clayton Act, no references appear herein to such extensions of remarks. Congressman Calder's remarks appear at 52 CONG. REC. A510–12 (1915).

attempt of the National Government to control what we usually term private business. The pure-food law may be regarded another instance. That was to protect the health of the people of the Nation. Excepting the Sherman law and the pure-food law, the National Government has gone 125 years without controlling private business. Shall the Federal Government now, in one act, assume control of every business concern in the Nation? Certainly not. The National Government has a plenty to do, has a sufficient problem to solve, if it will give its entire attention and all its great power to properly solving the problems that grow out of big business. The smaller concerns may be taken care of later. Let us first control the big concerns before we waste our thought and energy upon the ninety and nine that have not gone astray and need no control. Section 2 of the bill brings within its provisions not only all corporations, but it brings all persons and individuals engaged in interstate business.

To illustrate, the second congressional district of Oklahoma, in which I live, is situated along the northern part of the State. It extends for a distance of 400 miles along the Kansas border. There are four or five railroads crossing the Kansas line from my district. There are small cities all through that section of the country. Those people do more or less interstate business. There are no great monopolies there, yet under this bill every corporation, every concern, every person that does business across that line will come under section 2 of this act, and the prices at which they dispose of their products will be under the provision of the National Government. If a farmer takes eggs and butter and garden products across the line to a neighboring city and for some reason wants to cut the price thereon in order to get rid of his goods, he will be liable to be investigated by the Federal Government.

Section 2 is not comprehensive in the number of unfair discriminations which it prohibits, because it prohibits only one thing. It prohibits only discrimination in price, with the intent to destroy or wrongfully injure a competitor. That is very narrow. I would broaden the language by making it include all discrimination by saying "to discriminate in price, terms, or otherwise." Then, under section 2 of this act, no discrimination is unlawful unless done with the intent "to destroy or wrongfully injure a competitor." Why should not we prohibit discrimination done with the intent to establish a monopoly or to destroy or lessen competition?

Remember, it is monopoly that we want to destroy. Remember, it is competition we wish to maintain. Then, why did you make it an offense to discriminate in price with the intention of injuring a competitor, and leave it so that a man may have as his object in discrimination the establishment of a monopoly or the destruction of competition and be free from prohibitions of the law? To make this section broader and more comprehensive I suggest the following substitute:

SEC. 2. That any person engaged in commerce who shall discriminate in price, terms, or otherwise, as between persons, sections, or communities, with intent thereby to destroy or wrongfully injure a competitor or to establish a monopoly or to destroy or lessen competition in the production, manufacture, distribution, or sale of any such article, product, or commodity, shall be deemed guilty of a misdemeanor, and upon conviction thereof shall be punished by a fine not exceeding $5,000 or imprisonment not exceeding one year, or both. . . .

Mr. FESS. The large monopoly that we are trying to hit by this bill might be affected. What about the hundred small industries in the same business, like the shoe business, for example? What effect will this provision have upon them?

Mr. MORGAN of Oklahoma. The effect upon them will be to annoy them, to restrict and limit their business, and in that way injure, retard, and restrict trade, commerce, and industry. We ought to leave business free, so far as we can, so long as it is unnecessary to restrict it in the interest of the public.

Now, I think the gentleman from Arkansas [Mr. FLOYD] read a list of States that he said had statutes practically similar to the provisions of section 2 of this act. There are a number of States—15 or 18 of them—that have a somewhat similar statute. Apparently they have been copied one from another. Well, it does not follow that the problem we have to solve is the same problem that the States have to solve, and the mere fact that some of the States have similar statutes does not necessarily mean that we should copy those statutes into our national law.

I have here copies of 14 of those State statutes. Here is New Jersey, which has a similar statute. The laws of New Jersey ought to have weight with the other side of the House. The New Jersey statute makes it a crime to discriminate in price, not for the purpose or intent of injuring a competitor, but makes it a crime to discriminate in price "if the effect or intent thereof is to establish and maintain a virtual monopoly, hinder competition, or restrict trade."

That is the language of the New Jersey statute. The California statute makes discrimination in price a crime, if it is done "with the intent to destroy the competition of any regularly established dealer in such commodity, product, or service, or prevent competition." The language used in these various State statutes is as follows:

ARKANSAS–DISCRIMINATION IN PRICE.

With the intent and purpose of driving out competition or for the purpose of financially injuring competitors.

CALIFORNIA–DISCRIMINATION IN PRICE.

With the intent to destroy the competition of any regularly established dealer in such commodity, product, or service or to prevent the competition of any person, firm, private corporation, or municipal or other public corporation.

LOUISIANA–DISCRIMINATION IN PRICE.

Intentionally for the purpose of injuring or destroying the business of a competitor in any locality.

NEBRASKA–DISCRIMINATION IN PRICE.

Intentionally for the purpose of destroying the business of a competitor in any locality.

NEW JERSEY–DISCRIMINATION IN PRICE.

If the effect or intent thereof is to establish or maintain a virtual monopoly, hindering competition, or restricting trade.

NORTH DAKOTA–DISCRIMINATION IN PRICE.

Intentionally for the purpose of destroying or preventing competition.

OKLAHOMA–DISCRIMINATION IN PRICE.

Intentionally for the purpose of destroying the competition of any regularly established dealer in such commodity or to prevent the competition of any person who in good faith intends amd attempts to become such dealer.

SOUTH DAKOTA–DISCRIMINATION IN PRICE.

With intent and for the purpose of destroying competition by any regular established dealer in any such commodity or product.

UTAH–DISCRIMINATION IN PRICE.

Intentionally for the purpose of destroying the competition of any regular established dealer in such commodity or to prevent the competition of any person who in good faith intends and attempts to become such dealer.

WISCONSIN–DISCRIMINATION IN PRICE.

Intentionally for the purpose of destroying the competition of any regular established dealer in such commodity or to prevent competition of any person who in good faith intends or attempts to become such dealer.

IDAHO–DISCRIMINATION IN PRICE.

For the purpose of driving out of business any other person engaged therein.

MICHIGAN [APPLIES ONLY TO PETROLEUM PRODUCTS]–DISCRIMINATION IN PRICE.

Intentionally for the purpose of destroying the business of a competitor.

MISSOURI–DISCRIMINATION IN PRICE.

Intentionally for the purpose of destroying the competitor of any regular established dealer.

NORTH CAROLINA–DISCRIMINATION IN PRICE.

To willfully injure or destroy or undertake to injure or destroy the business of any rival or opponent.

Now, Mr. Chairman, out of all these 14 statutes which I have collected there is not one that exactly agrees with this bill, but the Nebraska and the Louisiana statutes use practically the same language used in this bill. Most of these State statutes make discriminations in price unlawful when done to establish monopoly or to destroy competition; and if we are to use the State statutes, we should follow the majority, unless there is some good reason why we should not do so.

It has been said here in this general debate that the minority Members criticize, but do not make any suggestions. But I shall do more than criticize. I shall present substitutes for the provisions which you have in this bill for a number of sections, as I have already presented a substitute for section 2.

In this bill there are but three or four things prohibited. First, it prohibits discrimination in price; second, it prohibits mine owners from arbitrarily refusing to sell the products of the mine; third, it prohibits a dealer from making any contract so as to prevent a purchaser from dealing in the goods, wares, and merchandise of others; fourth, it prohibits in a way holding companies; fifth, it prevents to a certain extent interlocking directors. Those are the only things prohibited. Do you believe that these include all the unfair practices? Do you believe that the enactment of this law prohibiting these four or five things will destroy a single trust, will obliterate a single monopoly, will bring any great business concern under the control of the Government or into effective competition so that it will not have arbitrary power to control the prices of its products? Certainly you do not.

Here is what I would suggest as a substitute for section 3:

SEC. 3. That it shall be unlawful for the owner or operator of any mine or for any person controlling the sale or distribution of the product of any mine engaged in commerce to discriminate in the sale or distribution of such product as between persons, corporations, or communities in the matter of price, terms, or otherwise, so as to give any undue or unreasonable preference or advantage to any particular person, firm, corporation, or community in any respect whatsoever, or so as to subject any particular person, firm, corporation, or community to any undue or unreasonable prejudice or disadvantage in any respect whatsoever, and any person violating the provisions of this section shall be deemed guilty of a misdemeanor and upon conviction thereof shall be punished by a fine not exceeding $5,000, or by imprisonment not exceeding one year, or by both, in the discretion of the court.

There is a provision that would make that section workable. It would be fair, because it would only prohibit those acts of a mine owner which will enable him to give any undue or unreasonable preference or advantage to any person, or to cause undue or unreasonable prejudice or disadvantage to any person or corporation. . . .

Mr. PLATT. The gentleman is a member of the committee and has given a great deal of study to this question. Can the gentleman say what the word "mine" means in section 3?

Mr. MORGAN of Oklahoma. No; I can not.

Mr. PLATT. Is a stone quarry or a sand bank a mine? I think the statistics of mining includes quarries.

Mr. MORGAN of Oklahoma. I went to the dictionary to reach a conclusion for myself, but I think the matter as it stands here will be of doubtful meaning. . . .

Mr. SLOAN. What was the particular purpose in drafting this bill that special attention was given to mines rather than to other industries; for instance, forestry or other products of the soil?

Mr. MORGAN of Oklahoma. I do not think any Member can explain it, and I do not think that any gentleman on the floor in debate has explained the purpose of simply placing the mine owners under that provision.

Mr. SLOAN. Is there any explanation known to any member of the committee?

Mr. MORGAN of Oklahoma. Not to me; and I can not answer as to the others.

Now, I believe I have prepared a section which will include all that is in sections 2, 3, and 4; absolutely includes every unfair practice or discrimination in those three sections and many others, too. I will read it:

SEC. —. That any person engaged in commerce who shall by the price or charge for any article, product, or commodity sold or leased, or by the terms granted or given to the purchaser or lessor of any article, product, or commodity, or by the contract, arrangement, or condition upon which any such article, product, or commodity shall be sold or leased, or by any other means discriminate as between persons, localities, or communities so as to give any undue or unreasonable preference or advantage to any particular person, firm, corporation, locality, or community in any respect whatsoever, or so as to subject any particular person, firm, corporation, community, or locality to any undue or unreasonable prejudice or disadvantage in any respect whatsoever, shall be deemed guilty of a misdemeanor, and upon conviction thereof shall be punished by a fine not exceeding $5,000, or by imprisonment not exceeding one year, or by both.

When the Federal Government enacted the act known as the interstate-commerce act, February 4, 1887, it placed in it a section which was intended to include all unfair practices by railway companies or common carriers. I have adopted the language largely used in the above draft, and the provision in the interstate-commerce act was taken from the English traffic act enacted in 1854.

I think, gentlemen, that in our enactment for the control of great industrial corporations and in providing our procedure we ought to follow as near as we can, so far as applicable, the legislation to control common carriers and public-utility companies. There are many reasons for that. In the first place, large business concerns in the greater part are similar to transportation companies, not only in the extent of business but in the effect upon the public in those practices that injure the general public or injure localities or injure individuals. Then we have a precedent to follow. Now, the language used in this amendment which I would suggest has been construed over and over again by the Interstate Commerce Commission, and it has been construed time and again by the Supreme Court of the United States.

There is much in the suggestion by my colleague from Pennsylvania that when we multiply our statutes here we introduce uncertainties, because every statute has to be construed and will be construed, and it will take years and years to determine just what a statute means. So that it is wisdom on our part to follow the language so far as we can of statutes which have been construed, and the meaning of which has been determined time and time again. Here you are introducing a large number of new statutory provisions to be construed by the courts, and as the Sherman law was written, it took the courts of our land 25 years for us to get any real conception of what it meant. So there would be wisdom in drafting a statute that is to cover unfair practices, that is to cover unfair discriminations, because that is what it means, by taking language that has been already construed. If a man varies his prices to injure another, that is unfair discrimination. If he establishes a monopoly by making the purchaser agree not to deal in goods of other dealers, that is an unfair practice. . . .

So here in this amendment I have placed it in the language of the interstate-commerce act that has been construed. If we adopt that, we would have some conception of what it meant, business interests would have some conception of what is meant, and it would not injure any business by new provisions which you have introduced.

Now, my greatest objection to this bill, so far as it represents proposed antitrust legislation, is that under it we will get no results.

If the real purpose and aim is to control the great business concerns, then we ought to provide some practical way, and I have prepared here a section, which I hope to offer as a new section, which I think would provide a practical way of actually controlling big corporations with power to dictate prices. It is as follows:

That whenever any United States attorney shall have reliable information that any corporation engaged in commerce in the manufacture, sale, or distribution of any necessity of life, or of any article, product, or commodity in common use, by reason of the nature, character, or extent of its business, the absence of effective competition, or for any other cause, possesses the power to control arbitrarily the price or prices of any necessity of life, or of any article, product, or commodity in common use, it shall be the duty of said United States attorney, under the direction of the Attorney General, to file a petition in the United States court against said corporation, alleging the aforesaid facts and praying that the said corporation shall be adjudged to be a quasi public corporation and subject to the control of the Commissioner of Corporations, or subject to the control of any commission that may at the passage of this act or thereafter be the successor of the Commissioner of Corporations, in all its practices, prices, and charges, in like manner and to the same extent that common carriers are now subject to the control of the Interstate Commerce Commission; and if the court shall find that the material facts alleged in the petition are true, it shall render a decree adjudging the said corporation to be a quasi public corporation, subject in all its practices, prices, and charges to the control of the Commissioner of Corporations, or the commission, as the case may be, as prayed for in the petition: *Provided*, That thereafter the practices of said corporation in conducting its business and the prices at which it shall sell its products shall be just, fair, and reasonable.

I propose a practical method. Of course, if we are not in earnest in this matter, if we expect these large corporations that do have monopolistic power to go on and on indefinitely, without any real control, without any real regulation, then the provisions which you have here are well enough, but I say here, and I have become thoroughly convinced of that, that a few prohibitions making three or four things unlawful will absolutely not change the condition that we have before us. If there exists monopoly in this country, if we have corporations that have the power to control the prices of the necessities of life, or of commodities in common use among the people, while we are trying to destroy them, let us at least control them, so as to save the people from harm. . . .

Mr. SLOAN. Did the gentleman submit his amendments to the committee on mediation with the administration in the construction of this bill, so that they had the benefit of his suggestions?

Mr. MORGAN of Oklahoma. Not this particular one, but some of them I did, and they do not appear to be incorporated in the bill. As I say, I believe the Republican Party stands for additional legislation. I believe the Republican Party, if placed in power, would enact additional legislation. I believe there are great concerns in this country that should be brought under stricter regulation and control. There may be large concerns that can not be dissolved under the Sherman antitrust law. Take, for instance, the Standard Oil Co.

I listened to testimony before the Committee on Interstate and Foreign Commerce, telling how one of the companies into which the Standard Oil Co. had been dissolved had, down in my State, absolute control of a great business interest of that country in the production, distribution, and sale of oil, and yet no law on the statute books to control it—an institution that had been dissolved under the Sherman antitrust law! Yet that corporation is in absolute power to control the price of the product and the distribution and the sale. Is this thing to go on? Will we act like schoolboys at play, or will we prepare some measure that will be effective, that will secure results? I have sometimes criticized some of the provisions of the constitution of my own State, and yet to-day there is not a State in the Union that has better laws for controlling business concerns with monopolistic power than Oklahoma, and if the majority in this House will model the legislation on the legislation of that State it would give to the interstate trade commission such power as our corporation commission holds, such jurisdiction as our commission has, and enact such laws as I suggest; then it will be progress; but the legislation which you propose here will be disappointing to the people; it will not bring results, and, in my judgment, you will have made no real progress in settling the great industrial problems which confront us, and the people will be disappointed in your works and place the Government in the hands of those who will solve these great problems correctly. . . .

Mr. WILLIS. Mr. Chairman, I do not know that I shall need all of the five minutes. I simply want to call the attention of the committee to one of the objections which is being made to this legislation. I have two or three times called the attention of Members who were speaking in favor of this bill to what seems to be a serious objection in section 4. I have no doubt the framers of the bill intended this measure should operate in the interest of the public and in the interest of the small producer, but as I understand this section, as the small producers that have written me understand the section, it will militate very severely against their interest. My attention has been called to this fact, and I am presenting it in order that it may be explained, if it can be explained. They called my attention to the fact that under the present arrangement the only way in which they can secure opportunity to sell their goods in the great trade centers is by making exclusive sale agreements. For example, my attention is called to this matter by one of my constituents, a small independent concern that has been fighting the trust independently all of these years, and fighting it rather successfully. This small concern employs 40 or 50 men. It has only very limited capital.

The only way in which it is able to sell its products, which in this particular case consists of shapers and planers, is to go into the industrial centers and make a contract with some man that he shall have the exclusive agency of their products, and that in turn he shall agree not to sell the products of any competitor. Under that arrangement there is an encouragement to the dealer to push this particular brand of goods. If we enact this section 4 into law in its present form, what will be the result? There will be no incentive whatever to the dealer in the various industrial centers to push this or that particular kind of goods. In other words, it will not be possible for the little fellow to maintain his selling agency. If he can not do so, his market is taken from him, and he is compelled to suffer great financial loss, his mill will be closed for lack of market for his product, and the workmen who have heretofore been busy at work manufacturing this product will be thrown out of employment or compelled to suffer great reductions in wages. Now, that will not affect the trusts. The big concern can do, under the terms of this bill, as it is doing now. It can maintain its own selling agency, because it has the money with which to do it; but the small concern can not maintain the selling agency; and by taking away the right which it is now enjoying of making these contracts with dealers it does seem to me that the law will operate, certainly not as it was intended by the committee, but it will nevertheless operate, not in favor of the small dealer, not in favor of the public, but in the long run this section, I believe, will play into the hands of the big producer who now has a practical monopoly of the market. Now, it may be that there can be an answer to that objection.

I have listened to a number of speeches which have been made and I have asked a number of questions, but I have not heard any answer given to that objection, and I present the matter here now in order that any gentleman who may discuss the bill will give some attention to this phase of the proposed legislation. We want legislation here that will operate in the interest of the public and will not operate to crush out of existence the small producer. So far as I am concerned, I believe in the principle of competition. I believe we ought to undertake here to legislate so as to encourage competition and to make it possible for the small producer to sell his wares in the markets. I am afraid if we pass this bill in its present form that we are so legislating, not purposely, I am sure, but we are nevertheless so legislating as to make it impossible for the small concern to carry on its business—the small concern employing 25, 30, 40, or 50 men, with a limited capital of $50,000, $60,000, or $100,000. I much fear this legislation, if enacted without amendment, would make it impossible for that sort of a concern to continue to do business, and therefore we would be playing unwittingly into the hands of the big corporations which have the wealth and the power to maintain their own selling agencies. I am sure gentlemen do not wish to do that. I shall ask consent to extend my remarks by printing one of the letters to which I have referred.

The letter is as follows:

Kenton, Ohio, May 15, 1914.

Hon. Frank B. Willis,
Washington, D. C.

DEAR SIR: We call your attention as our Representative in Congress to section 3 of House bill 15657, amending the Sherman law so as to make the practice of exclusive selling agreements between the manufacturer and middleman a misdemeanor. This section as it stands is in the interest of large combines and monopolies. These large companies do not need the middleman the same as the smaller competitors, because they can afford to establish their own selling organizations in the various market centers; in fact, most of them have their own selling organizations, and this section, prohibiting exclusive selling agreements, takes away the only means by which smaller competitors of these big combines are able to compete with them in selling.

This company, the Ohio Machine Tool Co., manufactures planers and shapers, which are classed as machine tools. We can not afford in any sense of the word to have our own selling organization in each trade center, and there are not enough of our machines sold, even in the larger cities, to warrant having an office at these points. This company employs about 50 men, and we depend entirely upon our dealers absolutely to sell our product. We have one dealer in each industrial center, who represents us exclusively. In other words, he has agreed to sell no other planers or shapers manufactured by our competitors, and we have agreed not to sell through any of his competitors in the same territory; he, having the exclusive agency thus created, offers our machines whenever he receives an inquiry, and he knows that all the work he puts in in trying to make a sale will not be lost, because if his customer purchases one of our machines he will receive the commission.

Kindly appreciate the state of affairs that would exist if we were obliged to sell our machines through any dealer who wishes to make the sale. If one of our dealers had worked up the business by talking our tools, for maybe a year or more, then another dealer would come in, and perhaps because he was the man on the ground at the time would obtain the order. That is not a fair proposition to any dealer, because all his work in advertising his product is lost when he lost his sale, and under these conditions we very shortly would have nobody pushing our tools, and this company would be obliged, in all probability, to shut down.

Our large competitors, who manufacture not only one or two different kinds of machine tools, but many different kinds, who happen to have their own offices in the different parts of the country, with their own salesmen, and by plugging uninterrupted on their own product, it wouldn't take long to drive the little fellow to the wall.

It seems to us that if our Congressmen have a clear idea of what this really means, that they will use their efforts to protect the smaller concerns, and hence our desire of writing you in detail. Under the present method of exclusive arrangement there is ample competition between the various dealers for the benefit of the customers; each dealer is fighting every other dealer in the interest of his exclusive line. If the exclusive agency agreement is abolished and the manufacturer must sell all dealers, who in turn must sell all competitive makes of the same article, then economic and efficient selling is destroyed and selling expenses greatly increased, due to the larger stocks, larger warehouses, and more salesmen required, it goes without saying that the increased expenses must ultimately be paid by the consumer.

We have explained the above matters to the foremen in our shop, advising them what this bill means to us and to other shops of similar character, with the idea of having them explain to the workmen what such a law would accomplish if passed by Congress.

We would be glad to receive a letter from you, stating that you will oppose this section of the bill.

Yours, very truly,

The Ohio Machine Tool Co.,
C. C. Swift, Secretary.

• • • •

Mr. CARLIN. Mr. Chairman, for nearly six months I have been intimately and closely associated with the bill which is now before this House for consideration and it is my purpose to-day to explain it in detail, from the standpoint of the majority membership; but before doing so I want to make reference to some irrelevant matter which has found its way into the RECORD. I say "irrelevant." Perhaps from a partisan political standpoint it may be considered, by those who gave utterance to the expressions to which I intend to refer, to be relevant, but I was surprised and almost astounded to hear the two gentlemen representing the minority, Mr. VOLSTEAD and Mr. NELSON, complain in this House, in the presence of the country, of secrecy and of partisanship in the preparation of this bill. Neither charge has any foundation in fact.

Never has legislation been proposed more in the open or considered more in the open, in every line and in every section, than the bill which is now before this House. This committee did an unusual and, so far as I know, unprecedented thing. Before entering into the consideration of this important subject it gave to this House and the country tentative bills, and when they were offered we invited the country to be heard upon the subject, giving them something about which to think and about which we might have earnest, honest, and intelligent discussion. The committee sat for over three months in hearing everyone who applied to be heard. Volumes of testimony have been taken. At every one of those hearings the minority Members were present and consumed, in my judgment, more time than the majority Members. It so happens that the record will bear me out in this statement. The first name which appears in the record is that of Mr. MORGAN, a minority member of the committee, and the very last name which appears in the record is that of the same gentleman. Mr. VOLSTEAD himself occupied, in my judgment, more time in interrogating witnesses than any other member of the committee. Mr. NELSON occupied as much time as he pleased, and was always present at the hearings. There was no partisanship that crept into this matter until the time arrived for a vote upon the bill, when the Republican minority absented itself from the committee, in my judgment and belief, for the purpose of breaking a quorum and to delay final consideration. [Applause on the Democratic side.] That is the first act of partisanship that made its appearance in connection with these bills, until now, when we come to the House for consideration, then what do we find?

We find that the Republican Party, a once harmonious body for forceful, efficient work and service, and capable of honest thought, has divided itself into fragments by disputes among its leaders that are impossible of being reconciled. The only cry made upon which they do unite, the only thing upon which they seem to be united, is the cry of "do nothing." The party that once boasted of its power of constructing legislation, the party that once prided itself upon its performances, now only in chorus can unite in asking and recommending that nothing be done. The old Know Nothing Party seems to have given away had been supplanted by the "Do-Nothing" Party.

Now, Mr. Chairman, the gentleman from Illinois [Mr. MADDEN] injected himself into this debate and read quite a lengthy argument against the bill, upholding the contention, as the gentleman from Pennsylvania [Mr. GRAHAM] has done, that the bills are too drastic. We find Mr. NELSON, who has given some consideration to the subject, stating with seeming seriousness to the country that the bills are worthless because they do not accomplish anything. And we find Mr. VOLSTEAD, the minority leader of the committee, telling the country that the only thing accomplished by the bill is practically to repeal the Sherman law, so far as holding companies are concerned. We have a unique enemy confronting us, going in three different directions. The speeches of Messrs. GRAHAM and MADDEN will be circulated in manufacturing sections of the country, thickly populated, with the intention of scaring business interests by telling them that we are destroying business; while the soft, milder, and sweeter tones of Brother NELSON'S speech will be circulated in the less thickly settled sections of the country, in the rural and agricultural districts, and will say to those people that we are doing nothing whatever. So their speeches have been carefully prepared to catch all sections of the country and all classes of the people in the next campaign, though upon conflicting statements. As delivered here in the House, from every viewpoint and every standpoint, as I said, they are irreconcilable, but, nevertheless, may make campaign material. But I want to point out, above all things, to the country that not a single member of the minority, not even Mr. MADDEN, the great statesman, who says that we are not engineers and we are not a great many things that we perhaps ought to be, has proposed a substitute bill. Not one man or a dozen men on that side of the House have taken the time or had the good conscience to tell the country in what respect and detail a better bill could be prepared and offered. [Applause on the Democratic side.]

If this proposed legislation is wrong, why not point it out? The gentleman from Pennsylvania [Mr. GRAHAM], a great lawyer and a good man, spent an hour this morning in railing against the Democratic Party and its attitude as reflected in this bill. He says that it ought to be amended. I ask him why he has never offered an amendment in committee to any section of the bill? If the bill needs amendment, why has he not pointed it out? [Applause on the Democratic side.] In his lengthy speech this morning he reminded me of a gentleman who sent his son out into the country some months ago to shoot a turkey. He said, "Son, when that turkey lights, you fire both barrels." The boy came back two hours afterwards without the turkey. The father said, "Why did you not kill that turkey?" The son replied, "Father, he never lit." And so with Mr. GRAHAM's speech; he never "lit," and discussed but one section of the 23 sections that this bill contains. He has neither told the House nor the country wherein this bill is destructive [applause on the Democratic side]; and, what is more, he can not. He has used every adjective in the English language to denounce it, but has not, with all of his great ability, pointed out one single desirable amendment which this House ought to adopt. But in his report he places himself where the Republican Party has been for the last 24 years, squarely upon the Sherman law, and says that it is good enough, and that we should let it alone. He takes exactly the position that has been taken on the stump in the last five months by former Attorney General Wickersham, namely, that the Sherman law is a sacred instrument and we ought not to disturb it. We have in part followed that policy. We have adopted the policy not of disturbing it but supplementing it with such legislation as is within the common knowledge of all people necessary now for the protection of the people. [Applause on the Democratic side.]

They criticize the President of the United States for his course on this bill. My countrymen, I do not belong to the "cuckoo" class. I was not a Baltimore general or even one of the privates. I preferred either of the two associates of mine in this House for the Presidency, and, if I could have accomplished it, one or the other would have been nominated. But since he has come to be President I have come to know the man, and I want to say to my fellow Democrats in this House to-day that if we follow his leadership in the future as we have within the past 12 months we will remain in power for the next quarter of a century. [Applause on the Democratic side.]

The gentleman from Pennsylvania says he resents Executive interference. Now, let me tell this House in frankness what Executive interference has consisted of in the preparation of this bill. First, the Executive came before the American Congress and surprised the country by his frankness in laying down a specific program. He said we should amend the antitrust laws, and he stated in what respects they should be amended. After that utterance your committee prepared the tentative bills. We discussed them with him, and I want to say that from that day to this, in the many conferences that it has been my privilege to enjoy with him, I never have observed a freer, franker, or more open mind than his has been in the discussion of this important matter. [Applause on the Democratic side.] And he has been not only willing and anxious to listen to gentlemen charged with the responsibility of the preparation of these bills, but has given us of his valuable time the greatest abundance. In spite of the fact that the country has been facing war with Mexico, with every kind of a public question that can be imposed on the human intellect bearing heavily upon his, there never has been a moment when he has not been willing to give counsel and advice to the gentlemen who have had charge of this bill. And when we came to bring it to the House in final shape, though it does reflect the best judgment of the committee and the judgment of the President, we have been willing to lay it before the Congress of the American people in order that in its last analysis it may reflect their judgment by amendment. Now it is thrown open for amendment in every direction. And I invite gentlemen on the other side of this House who rail against this bill to let the country know their views on trust legislation by offering them in the shape of amendment or another bill. But this will not be done. They will content themselves with finding fault with what the majority has done and think that they have escaped their responsibility to the country in crying against us. [Applause on the Democratic side.]

We have proven that we are not afraid of big business. We have, in the preparation of this bill, undertaken to say to the country that this is a big country and we want big business, but we want little business to have an opportunity to grow big. [Applause on the Democratic side.]

Gentlemen have railed on the other side, charging that we were injuring little business. My good friend from Pennsylvania [Mr. GRAHAM] was one of those who took that position. Everybody knows that from his very environment in that great manufacturing city of Philadelphia he is tender and solicitous about little business. O champions of little business on the other side of the House, are you afraid now to mention big business? Have you really got little business in your speeches while big business is in your mind? The truth is what this country wants; it is what this country is entitled to; and the Democratic Party speaks it as an encouragement to business, big and little alike. [Applause on the Democratic side.]

⊥9270 ⊥ There is not a line in this bill that has been drawn with any idea of injuring or destroying American enterprise or American capital. It has been drawn for the purpose of encouraging investment, encouraging intelligent action and opportunity, but with the old Democratic principle underlying it all—"Equal rights to all and special privileges to none." [Applause on the Democratic side.]

It has been complained of here that we have done nothing to destroy the "rule of reason." My countrymen, let me express the hope that the time will never come in this country when any party that wants to destroy any rule of reason will be large enough to impress itself upon our people. There is in the minds of everyone a little lamp that illuminates and points the way to intelligent action. That lamp is reason, and when reason ceases, all rules must fall.

We have not changed the "rule of reason" because we found upon investigation of every decision of the Supreme Court that the men who railed against reason had lost their bearings in the forest and were groping in the dark; because that court, in applying the "rule of reason," has applied it in the interest of the people, and there has never been a combination sought to be dissolved up to this moment that has not been dissolved by the application of the "rule of reason." When you have an active force acting along that line in behalf of the people it would be a crime to destroy it.

The Sherman law is not a new statute. It has been on our books for 24 years, and the party that now says, "Let it alone" is somewhat consistent, because it let it strictly alone for 20 years. No effort was made to enforce it; no effort was made to bring under its provisions the men who had been monopolizing and restraining the commerce of our country. It was not until by the lash of public sentiment you were whipped into active prosecution of the law that the real force of it was known and felt.

I believe Mr. Roosevelt claims the credit for the Northern Securities case. He certainly claims the credit for every other thing. Since I have mentioned his name, permit me to say I have heard that the gentlemen whom he led out of the party a year or two ago are soon to be led back again. He has marched them up the hill, and he has marched them down again; and when they are up they are up, and when they are down they are down, but they are only happy when in the middle, neither up nor down. [Laughter and applause.] . . .

Now, Mr. Chairman, to the bill itself. There is more, thank God, in our country than politics. Patriotism still lives in our land, and when we come now facing, as we do, the relationship of the Federal Government to industrial corporations and combinations which touch the very life blood, the arteries of life itself, we ought to be able to deal with these questions from a patriotic standpoint, at least from an economical standpoint.

Now, when we come to examine the political economies of the situation, what do we find? We find there are two schools of thought in the country, one school advocating the regulation and control of industrial combinations, the school to which I belong advocating dissolution of industrial combinations in order and to the end that the natural laws of competition may control in trade. [Applause on the Democratic side.] Upon one side much has been said in favor of regulation and control. They desire the same rule applied to industrial combinations that the country has applied to common carriers—regulation and control. But I think it is a dangerous school of thought, because in the last analysis it means Government monopoly or Government-sanctioned monopoly.

When we come to price fixing through a commission, or regulating by commission private trading between man and man, you have stepped into a socialistic atmosphere that has no place under the Stars and Stripes. Individuals will find themselves—the small business man, the business man that seems now to be the special care of my Republican friends, the little fellows—will find themselves in this shape: The Government could and would fix the price of the commodities produced by large manufacturers, the price of their articles, upon the basis of a reasonable profit. What little man can live in business upon the basis of an interest-bearing percentage profit? And as a consequence when the Government had once fixed the reasonable price at which those articles should be sold, the little fellow would disappear from business, and the big one alone could live. But, oh, what a short life his would be?

It has been a surprising fact that a great many of the large manufacturers of the country sought the aid of this committee and asked that it recommend a price-fixing commission. The answer to them is this: Gentlemen, while you may be able to stand it and desire the Government to fix your prices now, thinking that you would get a high price for your commodities, or a better price, the demand from the consumers would be greater in the last analysis than anything the manufacturer could hope to withstand, and his price would be reduced and reduced and reduced until finally business would be on crutches. [Applause on the Democratic side.]

Now, then, to the problem before us of "unscrambling the eggs." What have we done to carry out this economical theory? Mr. NELSON has said we have done nothing. Let us see what we have done in the way of new legislation, in the way of doing new things that had behind them the shadow of old and well-known vices that need correcting.

Let us see what we have done for the individual, who is, after all, the unit of American citizenship. When you have taken care of the individual you have builded a solid rock foundation upon which to erect your superstructure. So we have started with the individual, by giving him rights that he has never possessed under the law—not for the injury of another, but for the protection of himself.

First, we found that the Sherman law did not permit an injunction on petition of an individual. The Government could enjoin a combination or trust; and though an individual was standing face to face with destruction, though the monster of monopoly was knocking at his door, he would have to wait until destruction came, and then pursue his remedy at law for treble damages. So the Democratic Party, through its membership on the committee, proposed to place in this bill a law which allows the individual to sue for equitable relief and to enjoin monopoly when he is threatened with irreparable loss or damage. Is there anything in the Sherman law which gives that relief? I ask the gentleman from Pennsylvania [Mr. GRAHAM] to point to anything in the Sherman law which gives that relief.

But we did not stop there. We went further in our effort to help the individual. We said "When you have been damaged in your business by a combination operating in restraint of trade we are going to put you no longer to the expense of gathering the testimony and of combating the wealth of the world in order to recover your damages." When the Government has procured a decree against the combination, we say now by the proposed statute that that decree shall be used by the individual and shall be conclusive evidence for all that it purports to be. So the individual who had what was considered relief under the Sherman law by way of treble damages, but who, in reality, never could recover them because of his inability to prove his case, now has the benefit of the proof of the Government placed at his disposal and made conclusive evidence in his behalf. Is there anything in the Sherman law which gives this relief? If there is, I challenge you to point it out.

But yet we were fair. We saw that it would be unfair to allow the decree to be conclusive evidence as to one party unless it were conclusive as to the other; and so in a spirit of fairness, even to big business, we made that decree applicable to both.

In addition to this, what have we done? We have said that while suit is pending on behalf of the Government the statute of limitations shall be suspended for the benefit of individuals until suit is concluded. Was there anything in the Sherman law that does that? Then why do you say we do nothing? Why does the great lawyer from Pennsylvania [Mr. GRAHAM] say that the Sherman law covers everything that could possibly be done?

Let us see what else, my friends. Section 8 of the bill deals with a recognized evil of trust organization, "holding companies." We have had many speeches about the evils of holding companies, but we have never had anyone who was thoughtful enough to draw a bill on the subject, or kind enough even to furnish us with a form; speeches galore, but no bill. So the bill as drawn is original, and has that merit if no other.

But what does it do or attempt to do? At common law one corporation could not own the stock of another corporation, whether it was a competitor or not. They were confined to the ownership of their own stock. But under our statutes of various States corporations have sprung into existence empowered to own stock of other corporations. But it remained until within a quarter of a century for the real abuse of the system to be pointed out, and that came through the holding company, where gentlemen would organize one company and then put into that company 5 or 6 or 10 or 12 other companies, until the holding company had absorbed the stock of these other companies and issued its own stock in lieu thereof and become the real operating force of the half dozen corporations that had been combined into the one holding company. And so the Northern Securities case was brought. Now, my friend, the gentleman from Minnesota [Mr. VOLSTEAD], tells us that we would not have won a decision in that case if this proposed holding-company provision of ours had been written into the law. I am inclined to think that my friend fails under the rule of Blackstone, who says no man ought to attempt to write a new law unless he is familiar with the old one; and my friend ought not to have attempted to discuss this proposed statute with regard to the Northern Securities case until he had first familiarized himself with that case.

Now, what was that case? It was the case of one New Jersey corporation, formed as a holding company pure and simple, into which by purchase was poured the stock of the three railroad companies which were natural competitors, and when that case was decided the Supreme Court held that it had not only lessened competition but had eliminated competition, and thus restrained trade.

We have supplemented the language of the statute and taken a forward step. We have gone forward, not backward. The Sherman law in its operation is limited to three things: First, a contract or combination in the form of a trust or otherwise; second, a conspiracy in restraint of trade; third, an attempt to monopolize. There is nothing about competition in the Sherman law. There must be actual restraint of trade under the Sherman law to bring anyone under either its civil or criminal process.

Under this bill there has to be only a lessening of competition. Competition may be lessened without restraint of trade. Competition may be lessened without attempt to monopolize. Competition may be lessened without conspiracy. It may be the natural effect of the putting together in close relationship through a holding company of two corporations that are natural competitors, or ought to be. Yet there would not be restraint. So, instead of subtracting from the Sherman law, as the gentleman has told the country, we have added to the Sherman law a most effective rule, by which the actions of these combinations in the future may be determined; but still, with due regard to the gentlemen who have come to love the Sherman law, we have left it intact, and have said by an express provision of our bill that nothing in our bill shall be construed to alter, amend, or repeal the Sherman law. It is as effective now as it has ever been. . . .

Mr. VOLSTEAD. Does the gentleman refer to paragraph 4 of section 15?

Mr. CARLIN. I refer to the paragraph which contains the language I have just recited.

Mr. VOLSTEAD. I will read it, it is very short. Does the gentleman mean to say that that leaves the Sherman Antitrust Act in force?

Mr. CARLIN. I not only mean to say so, but every other man who understands the subject will say the same thing.

Mr. VOLSTEAD. It says "Nothing in this section contained shall be deemed to alter, repeal, or amend section 266 of an Act entitled 'An act to codify, revise,'" and so forth, approved March 3, 1911.

Mr. CARLIN. The gentleman has spoken on this matter for two hours. Now will he let me have a little time?

Mr. VOLSTEAD. The gentleman is mistaken; I only spoke about half an hour.

Mr. CARLIN. The gentleman from Pennsylvania [Mr. GRAHAM] says that this—the Sherman law—is a Republican law and has been a good, wholesome thing for the country, and that we owe it to the Republican Party. My friend, who is usually accurate in his statements, always beautiful in what he says, overlooked the history of the Sherman law, because if he will examine the record he will find that that law had its birth and origin in the State of Texas, that Senator Reagan, a Democrat, was the first man who ever undertook or attempted to control monopoly by statute in this country. [Applause on the Democratic side.]

He says furthermore—and I am paying a great deal of attention to what the gentleman said, not only because I want to pay him that compliment, but because he has frequently said—that we need nothing more than the Sherman law, claims credit for the Republican Party, and in the next breath rails against sections 2 and 4 of the bill, not realizing that he is criticizing his own party, because of the 21 States that have found it necessary to adopt that character of progressive legislation 14 are Republican States and 7 Democratic. . . .

Mr. GRAHAM of Pennsylvania. Does not the gentleman know that the basis or standard of these State laws is totally different from the standard you have introduced into this law? Here it is the lessening of competition and there it is restraining of trade and monopoly.

Mr. CARLIN. I know just the reverse. I was speaking with reference to discriminatory statutes, or statutes against discrimination, and the principle is the same. Every one of these States has tried to compel uniform prices within the borders of the State. The penalty and methods have been different, but the statutes have been aimed at that.

Now, to go back to holding companies. A holding company has been the device, as I have said, by which every trust combination has ever organized in our land, and yet we are told that we should leave the Sherman law alone. When we know that destruction of competition is not the goal sought, we ought to apply the rule of reason. We are engaged in an effort to bring about competition; that is the economics of this bill. [Applause on the Democratic side.] Unless you have taken the trouble to understand what we are driving at, of course you can not tell the direction in which we are going.

Now, let us see what else we do. As to interlocking directorates, the gentleman from Pennsylvania said there was nothing proposed in this bill that could not be prosecuted under the Sherman law. Can he point to a single prosecution of any individual because he has been a director in more than one competing company? . . .

Mr. GRAHAM of Pennsylvania. To be a director in more than one corporation was not a crime, but if a man was a director in more than one competing company creating a monopoly or a restraint of trade, it could be introduced in evidence that he was destroying that competition.

Mr. CARLIN. It was one of the things allowed to be introduced in evidence as a link in the chain, but not of itself was it ever considered an offense until it was proposed in this bill.

Let us see why it is proposed and what this bill means. After all, gentlemen, this is the provision in the bill that self-constituted champions of little business seem to be railing against. The fact is, when we analyze it, little business, if railing at the bill at all, is doing it at the bid of big business, because we do not strike at little business, but, on the contrary, specifically exclude it and exempt it from the bill.

Now, interlocking directorates has come to be an evil so well known that the men who have given that character of business an impetus by the loan of their names have come to see it. Mr. Morgan resigned at one time 47 directorships, and stated that he did it in response to public sentiment. He will do it in the future in response to a public statute. [Laughter and applause.]

There are two evils in interlocking directorates. My friend from Illinois [Mr. MADDEN] complained of the bill in that respect. He would not have done it if he had read the last bill, because his speech showed that he had read the tentative bill and not the bill as now proposed. Let us see the reasons for this statute. One man representing a great financial concern becomes a director in a great railroad. Then he becomes a director in a corporation that furnishes the railroad with supplies—oil, steel, coal—and by virtue of his trusteeship in the railroad directorship, what does he accomplish? If the railroad wants to borrow any money or sell its securities, he stays there, votes first that they need the extra money; secondly, that it shall be raised by the issue of bonds, and votes for that; third, he fixes the price at which these bonds shall be sold; fourth, he fixes the commission that the selling agent shall receive; and ⊥ then, last but not least, he elects himself both selling agent and purchaser, at his own price. [Applause.] . . .

Mr. MADDEN. Will the gentleman be kind enough to tell the House why it is that the committee, in writing this bill, thought it was necessary to exempt railroad companies from the provisions of the Sherman antitrust law?

Mr. CARLIN. That is exactly what we have not done. I said, and I said it kindly, that my friend had not read this bill. I challenge him to point out any such provision.

Mr. MADDEN. The second paragraph of section 7 gives them authority to enter into all sorts of traffic associations, operating and accounting associations, and the subject matters of contract which are authorized under this section to be entered into, subject only to the supervision of the Interstate Commerce Commission. And the contracts themselves are only necessary to be filed with the Interstate Commerce Commission, and over these contracts the Interstate Commerce Commission has no jurisdiction whatever.

Mr. CARLIN. Mr. Chairman, the gentleman makes a good speech, but he has made that speech once already.

Mr. MADDEN. I am making it again so that the gentleman will understand it.

Mr. CARLIN. But he ought not to inflict it on the House in my time.

Mr. MADDEN. Oh, the gentleman challenged me to tell him the location of it in the bill, and I have done it.

Mr. CARLIN. Yes; and I am going to answer the gentleman. That provision in the bill, like every other provision which affects common carriers, was drawn to prevent interference with the Interstate Commerce Commission, because, as I have said, this country has reached the economical doctrine, so far as common carriers are concerned, of regulation and control, and we propose to do nothing that will change that system for the present. The Interstate Commerce Commission recommended to us that we place that provision in the bill. [Applause on the Democratic Side.] That is there with their consent, with their advice, and in assistance of the doctrine of regulation and control. . . .

Mr. MADDEN. I simply wanted to say that the mere fact that the Interstate Commerce Commission recommended this proposition does not answer the question that I asked the gentleman.

Mr. CARLIN. Oh, but it answers this. To read that provision simply means that we have allowed them to meet, which they might not now have the right to do, and to enter into lawful agreements, and the word "lawful" is used, and they are subject to the supervision of the Interstate Commerce Commission, and before that provision was put in the bill we sent it to the Interstate Commerce Commission, and they sent it back with their approval. [Applause on the Democratic side.]

Mr. MADDEN. Does the gentleman contend that the Interstate Commerce Commission has any jurisdiction whatever over the agreements into which these railroads are authorized to enter?

Mr. CARLIN. I think they have, absolutely.

Mr. MADDEN. Absolutely they have not.

Mr. CARLIN. If they have not, then I suggest to the gentleman that he submit a plan and propose an amendment that will make it plain.

Mr. MADDEN. That is what I propose to do.

Mr. CARLIN. I hope the gentleman will, but I hope he will take time enough to read the section before he undertakes to amend it.

As to interlocking directorates, I have pointed out one evil that comes from them. That is not all. The director sits on the great railroad corporation directorate and buys supplies from himself. He is a fiduciary, for that is what a director is. He sits on the one board and buys supplies for himself from the other corporation upon whose board he sits, until we find him buying and selling to himself, and we are big enough not to object to that, if it were not for the fact that he is doing it with other people's money, and so we put a provision covering that evil into the bill. We divided this interlocking directorate bill into three subdivisions—first, the railroads and the common carriers, over which Congress has undisputed jurisdiction; second, national banks, over which we have undisputed jurisdiction; and, third, industrial corporations and combinations. We have exempted the little fellow, the mutual savings bank, and we have gone to the limit of two and a half million dollars in other banks. When a bank gets to be the size of two and a half million dollars it is pretty well grown, and, when you get them into a combination, the opportunity for evil is very great. . . .

Mr. GRAHAM of Pennsylvania. The gentleman does not mean that the two million and a half exemption has any application to the industrial corporations?

Mr. CARLIN. Oh, no; we apply an entirely different rule to the industrial corporations. A man can be a director in as many industrial corporations as he pleases under our bill, unless those corporations would of themselves constitute by combination a violation of the Sherman law. . . .

Mr. GRAHAM of Pennsylvania. If the language in the bill were plain that it must constitute a violation of the Sherman law, I might have no objection to it, but you have introduced a new standard, to lessen competition, and you say wherever an agreement between two companies will lessen competition it shall be declared to be illegal. You can not get two corporations pursuing the same business having interlocking directorates without violating that principle.

Mr. CARLIN. My friend, it is true that you and I are not as young as we used to be, but I hope that we have not yet gotten too old to be willing to do a new thing once in a while. I have been contending that we are doing a new thing. It is the purpose of this bill to do new things, but we are doing them in supplement to existing law, and not by way of disturbing existing law.

What else have we done that is new? For 20 years organized labor has knocked at the doors of American Congresses, asking relief from certain things of which it complained. There was no response until the Democratic House undertook to give relief, and so we passed a bill called the Clayton injunction bill, and another called the Clayton contempt bill, through the Democratic House, and sent these bills to a Republican Senate. I mean no disrespect to the Senate when I say that there was, while its membership was Republican, a morgue concealed somewhere around the premises, and that it seemed that whenever legislation that had the merit of being new was attempted it found its way to that morgue, and these two bills went there, and so it has remained until now for a Democratic Congress, in both of its branches, to let labor understand whether we propose to carry out our platform pledges or whether we do not. As an evidence of what our intentions are, we have written them into this bill. I want to say that I yield to no one in my regard for the man who earns his living by the sweat of his brow. I have known what it means to labor. I have known what it means to be poor. I have worn the badge of poverty, and I have suffered the distresses which come from need, and every fiber of my nature responds to the demand of the wage earner whenever it is possible under our form of constitutional government to yield to his rightful demand.

For years the courts of our country have thrown out drag net injunctions, issued them in blank, the marshal having the right to fill in a multitude of names, and the names were filled in from time to time as he passed them on the street, peaceful or violent, it mattered not, if they were in line of his march. They were brought into court and fined for contempt of court, for violating an injunction they had never seen and of which they had never heard, a system and a practice that is most pernicious, everyone will so admit. This bill proposes that in contempts committed without the presence of the court to require a rule to be issued and a process to be served and the individual brought into court, and then when brought there not to be subjected to the whim or caprice of the court but to be tried by 12 of his countrymen to determine whether he had been guilty of a crime or not. [Applause on the Democratic side.] We were told this was an attack upon the courts. My friends, if you commit murder, arson, or any other crime you are entitled to a trial by jury, but if you commit the crime of being ignorant of an injunction that was issued by a Federal judge you are not entitled to a trial by a jury, but only by the judge himself. And we have concluded in this great country of ours, where every man is equal before the law, that he shall have an opportunity to be heard and tried by his countrymen when his life and liberty are at stake. [Applause on the Democratic side.] But in our desire to do right by the citizen we have done no wrong to the court, because we have carefully reserved the right of the court to maintain its dignity and its power for contempts that are committed in its presence. So again we have adhered to part of the old, which was right, and had the courage to take a step forward to the new, which is likewise right. [Applause on the Democratic side.] Now, my friends, to reply finally to the demagogue who is present everywhere, and whom we know find in chorus saying, "Do not disturb the business of the country by any more legislation; stop where you are, you have done well enough," and so say the letters which were read from New York to-day, "go no further, you will disturb the business interests of the country," and the press in certain sections of the country have taken up the siren song.

I will tell you now, my colleagues, why we do not stop. I will tell you why we are going forward with this legislation; and if we must commercialize it I will tell you why from the standpoint of business. First, the business world has a right to know what we are going to do, and if it is disturbed at all it is disturbed by reason of uncertainty, and the sooner we pass this bill and let them know under what rule business is to be controlled the sooner business prosperity will be accentuated. [Applause on the Democratic side.] We say to business not to stop, but to go on. Secondly, we promised this legislation to the country in our platform. Should we stop now, what would be said? I can imagine my friend from Illinois and my friend from Pennsylvania saying, with burning eloquence, "If we would only stop; oh, if we would only do it," and turning to the country and saying, "They were afraid to go on." [Laughter and applause on the Democratic side.] "They have sold out to the trusts." [Applause on the Democratic side.] "They dare not go forward." But, no; the membership of this House is going to battle in November with the enemy. Do not go in with cold feet; and we must not go in with cold feet: and so now we are doing the thing which appeals to business. We are going to settle the question that for 20 years the Republican Party has been afraid to approach. [Applause on the Democratic side.] The same men who cry out now, "Do not go any further; these bills will ruin the country," told us the same thing about the currency bill. Now they say it is a splendid bill, and they were mistaken. [Applause.] And when this bill comes into operation, what will you find, not that we have destroyed the game of business, if it may be so designated, but we have simply changed the rules by which it is to be played. We have broken up the brutal center rush, the wedge play, and substituted in its stead the "forward pass." [Laughter and applause.] So that the game has become open and fair, and more people can play it with peace and with profit. [Applause on the Democratic side.]

Mr. PLATT. If the gentleman is a football player, he will admit that the forward pass is not so much easier.

Mr. CARLIN. But it is much fairer and less brutal [applause on the Democratic side], and so many more people can play it. And so it is, gentlemen of the House, that your committee has finished its labors; it has brought to you a bill which embodies the best intellect and thought of the country, political and economical. [Applause on the Democratic side.]

It has brought to you a bill that was born and has lived in the open, a bill that was drafted by the hands of your own colleagues. Not a line of that bill came from anybody's pocket or anybody's office, departmental or otherwise. [Applause on the Democratic side.] If we have made mistakes, we have made them in the effort to do the right thing by our party and by our country. [Applause on the Democratic side.] We have had before us the inspiration of a matchless leader [applause on the Democratic side], a man willing to do the right and the courage with which to do it. And so we confidently believe that this House will give its approval, and when you have done so and written it upon the statute books it is my confident belief that posterity will rise up and call you blessed. [Loud applause.] . . .

[Mr. FITZHENRY addressed the committee. See Appendix.*]

[Mr. REILLY of Wisconsin addressed the committee. See Appendix.*]

[Mr. BRYAN addressed the committee. See Appendix.*]

Mr. MADDEN. Mr. Chairman, I would like to ask, before the gentleman proceeds, whether it is the intention to go on with the consideration of the bill under the five-minute rule now until half past 5.

Mr. WEBB. It is my intention to have the first section of the bill read under the five-minute rule.

Mr. MADDEN. With the understanding that it is open to amendment when we meet again?

Mr. WEBB. You mean section 1?

Mr. MADDEN. Section 1.

Mr. WEBB. I have no objection to that.

The CHAIRMAN. The Chair will state to the gentleman that under the rule the bill originally introduced would have to be read, of course. Does the gentleman intend to read that or the amendment?

Mr. WEBB. I think the rule dispenses with the reading of the bill.

The CHAIRMAN. The gentleman did not understand the Chair. The amendment submitted by the committee proposes to strike out all the sections of the bill. Unless there is some agreement by unanimous consent, the original bill will have to be read first.

Mr. WEBB. I ask unanimous consent that the reading of the original bill, which was stricken out by amendment, be omitted, and that we begin to read the amendment.

Mr. MADDEN. I think the rule provides for it.

The CHAIRMAN. The Chair has not the rule before him.

Mr. WEBB. If there are any amendments, of course I do not wish to cut off any right to offer them.

The CHAIRMAN. The rule says that the substitute shall be read instead of the bill. The Clerk will read.

The Clerk read as follows:

---

* Not reprinted herein.

Be it enacted, etc., That "antitrust laws," as used herein, includes the act entitled "An act to protect trade and commerce against unlawful restraints and monopolies," approved July 2, 1890; sections 73 to 77, inclusive, of an act entitled "An act to reduce taxation, to provide revenue for the Government, and for other purposes," of August 27, 1894; an act entitled "An act to amend sections 73 and 76 of the act of August 27, 1894, entitled 'An act to reduce taxation, to provide revenue for the Government, and for other purposes,'" approved February 12, 1913; and also this act.

"Commerce," as used herein, means trade or commerce among the several States and with foreign nations, or between the District of Columbia or any Territory of the United States and any State, Territory, or foreign nation, or between any insular possessions or other places under the jurisdiction of the United States, or between any such possession or place and any State or Territory of the United States or the District of Columbia or any foreign nation, or within the District of Columbia or any Territory or any insular possesion [sic] or other place under the jurisdiction of the United States.

The word "person" or "persons" wherever used in this act shall be deemed to include corporations and associations existing under or authorized by the laws of either the United States, the laws of any of the Territories, the laws of any State, or the laws of any foreign country.

Mr. WEBB. Mr. Chairman—

Mr. MADDEN. Mr. Chairman, I would like to ask a question before the gentleman moves to rise. I have no amendment to any of these definitions, but I want to ask that this paragraph be not considered as closed to amendment, so if any person wants to offer an amendment at the next session of the committee I would like it be [sic] understood that such permission will be granted.

Mr. WEBB. I will ask the gentleman from Minnesota [Mr. VOLSTEAD] if he has an amendment to offer.

Mr. MADDEN. There may be some person that would like to offer an amendment.

Mr. VOLSTEAD. I have not, but I would like very much to have it deferred.

Mr. WEBB. Very well, Mr. Chairman, I will agree that it remain open for amendment when we next meet.

The CHAIRMAN. Under the agreement it will be left open for amendment.

Mr. WEBB. Mr. Chairman, I move that the committee do now rise.

The motion was agreed to.

HOUSE DEBATE
63d Cong., 2d Sess.
May 28, 1914

51 CONG. REC. 9388

The SPEAKER pro tempore. Under the rule the House resolves itself automatically into the Committee of the Whole House on the state of the Union for the further consideration of the antitrust bill, and the gentleman from Tennessee [Mr. BYRNS] will take the chair. . . .

The CHAIRMAN. When the committee rose on Tuesday the Clerk had read section 1. If there are no amendments—

Mr. MORGAN of Oklahoma. Mr. Chairman, I wish to offer an amendment as a new section following section 1.

The CHAIRMAN. The gentleman from Oklahoma offers an amendment, which the Clerk will report.

The Clerk read as follows:

Amend by adding a new section, to be numbered section 1a, to follow immediately after section 1, page 20, as follows:

"SEC. 1a. That no firm, association, or corporation shall be subject to the provisions of sections 2, 4, and 8 of this act, unless by itself, or with one or more other corporations owned, operated, controlled, or organized in conjunction with it so as to constitute substantially a business unit, has an aggregate capital, including stocks and bonds issued and surplus owned, of not less than $5,000,000."

The CHAIRMAN. The question is on agreeing to the amendment.

Mr. MORGAN of Oklahoma. Mr. Chairman, one of the proper criticisms to sections 2, 4, and 8 is that it [sic] includes all small business concerns in its provisions. It is the contention of some of us on this side of the House that we should go to the full length and extent of our control over the large concerns, but should eliminate so far as we can any effort to annoy and burden and restrain the small concerns which possess no monopolistic power, and which, from a national viewpoint, do not affect the general interests of the country.

Now, that very proposition came up before the Committee on the Judiciary and it came up before the Interstate Commerce Committee as to what corporations should be brought under the control and regulation of the interstate trade commission. I think when the bill was first drawn and introduced by the chairman of the Judiciary Committee, the interstate trade bill, all concerns were brought under the control and regulation of that commission. And I for one, in speaking before the Interstate Commerce Committee, advocated that it should be amended so as not to include all concerns engaged in interstate commerce, and others advocated the same thing. And so when that bill was finally drawn it did not include all concerns or corporations engaged in interstate business. Therefore I have drawn this section, which in language practically corresponds with the language used in the Covington interstate trade bill.

I think it is wise that if we are entering upon a new policy in two directions, with two arms, interstate trade commission, and then the enactment of additional laws to bring these concerns under proper control, that they should go together, that these two sections should correspond in their jurisdiction over concerns exactly with those concerns that are brought under the interstate trade commission.

And so, having this conviction, having this conception, believing that especially at the start we ought to limit our restrictions of [sic] the larger concerns that possess monopolistic power, I have in good faith presented this amendment, bringing within these sections only the concerns that shall be brought under the interstate trade commisison. I think it is a wise amendment and I hope the committee will adopt it.

The CHAIRMAN. The question is on the adoption of the amendment of the gentleman from Oklahoma [Mr. MORGAN].

Mr. FLOYD of Arkansas. Mr. Chairman, I desire to oppose the amendment offered by the gentleman from Oklahoma, for the reason that we do not think that such amendment ought to be adopted. The fact is that our friend from Oklahoma has gotten the trade-commission idea in his head, and he seeks at every opportunity, and did in the committee, and I presume he will here, to inject some provision relating to the trade commission into this bill.

Now, in the first place, we do not think that there should be any limitation as to capitalization or surplus whatever as to sections 2, 3 [sic], or 8. We have provided limitations of this character in another section of the bill pertaining to interlocking directorates. Here he proposes to raise the limitation we have placed in that section and put a limitation of $5,000,000 in these particular sections. We have been endeavoring by these sections referred to to forbid certain wrongs that exist in our system, and we believe that any such amendment as that proposed by the gentleman from Oklahoma would tend largely to defeat the purposes of each of these sections. And therefore we oppose the amendment and hope the committee will vote it down.

The CHAIRMAN. The question is on the amendment offered by the gentleman from Oklahoma [Mr. MORGAN].

The question was taken, and the amendment was rejected.

The CHAIRMAN. The Clerk will read.

The Clerk read as follows:

SEC. 2. That any person engaged in commerce who shall, either directly or indirectly, discriminate in price between different purchasers of commodities in the same or different sections or communities, which commodities are sold for use, consumption, or resale within the

United States or any Territory thereof or the District of Columbia or any insular possession or other place under the jurisdiction of the United States, with the purpose or intent to thereby destroy or wrongfully injure the business of a competitor of either such purchaser or seller shall be deemed guilty of a misdemeanor, and upon conviction thereof shall be punished by a fine not exceeding $5,000, or by imprisonment not exceeding one year, or by both, in the discretion of the court: *Provided*, That nothing herein contained shall prevent discrimination in price between purchasers of commodities on account of differences in the grade, quality, or quantity of the commodity sold, or that makes only due allowance for difference in the cost of transportation: *And provided further*, That nothing herein contained shall prevent persons engaged in selling goods, wares, or merchandise in commerce from selecting their own customers, except as provided in section 3 of this act.

Mr. WEBB. Mr. Chairman, I should like to ask my friend from Minnesota [Mr. VOLSTEAD] if we may come to some agreement as to the time to be consumed in discussing this section and amendments thereto.

Mr. VOLSTEAD. I think it would be better to let the debate proceed for a little while.

Mr. MANN. It is a little early yet to shut off debate. There are a number of amendments which gentlemen on this side desire to propose.

Mr. WEBB. There is no desire to shut off amendment.

Mr. MANN. I understand that. There are a number of amendments to be offered to this section. We will try to help the gentleman expedite the bill.

Mr. WEBB. I thank the gentleman. I will make no request at this time, Mr. Chairman, as to limiting debate.

Mr. [JEFFERSON M.] LEVY [D., N.Y.]. Mr. Chairman, I have an amendment.

Mr. GRAHAM of Pennsylvania. Mr. Chairman, I desire to offer an amendment.

The CHAIRMAN. The Chair recognizes the gentleman from Pennsylvania [Mr. GRAHAM], a member of the committee. The Clerk will report the amendment proposed by the gentleman from Pennsylvania.

The Clerk read as follows:

Page 20, line 20, after the word "shall," insert the words "except in lawfully meeting competition."

Mr. BARTLETT. Mr. Chairman, I ask to have the amendment read again. We could not hear it.

The CHAIRMAN. The committee will be in order. If there be no objection, the Clerk will again report the amendment.

The amendment was again read.

Mr. GRAHAM of Pennsylvania. Mr. Chairman, on day [*sic*] before yesterday the gentlemen upon the other side invited us to present our views toward improving any of the terms or provisions of this bill. It is with that end in view that I offer this amendment, which, if adopted, would largely remove the objections to which this section of the proposed bill is now subject.

The great scope and purpose of our antitrust laws is to put down monopoly and restraint of trade and to foster and protect competition. As is pointed out in the minority report, this section as framed is calculated to limit and destroy competition. There certainly can be no objection, therefore, to writing the words of this amendment into this paragraph, so that no fetter or restraint will be put upon lawful competition.

It has been held in some of the cases that have been tried that wherever prices are cut below cost that is unfair trade practice; but where a man meets another's price in protecting his business in a district with a price it is his lawful right and privilege, and it is the object of competition that he should meet his price. The benefit of competition is supposed to flow to the public. That is the only way in which it can reach the consumer or the public. Now, if this clause is limited in this respect, it obviates many of these objections.

There is another difficulty, however, to which another amendment may be applied, and I will not speak of that at this time.

Mr. WEBB. Mr. Chairman, we hope this amendment will not be adopted, because in our opinion it adds nothing to the section. We think under the provisions of the section any man who honestly meets competition is not thereby "intending to destroy or wrongfully injure any other person." If that is his object, meeting honest competition, this section will not hurt him, and we consider it useless to write into this section the amendment of my friend from Pennsylvania [Mr. GRAHAM]. Therefore I hope it will be voted down. . . .

Mr. GRAHAM of Pennsylvania. Is not one of our objects to avoid subjecting business men to the possibility of lawsuits and litigation? If you say that making a price to meet lawful competition is not within the prohibition of the bill, then why not write it into the body of the bill?

Mr. WEBB. My friend is a good lawyer, and he would not advise any client he has or ever will have that this section would reach the cases that he wishes to exempt, because any person who honestly meets competition for that purpose is not thereby intending to destroy or wrongfully injure any other person. . . .

Mr. GRAHAM of Pennsylvania. I simply desire to bring out my exact purpose in offering this amendment. There is nothing latent or hidden in it. I am simply endeavoring to improve the language of the bill, so as to carry out its purpose. I would certainly advise any client or business man who consulted me about the present language of the bill that it is fraught with great peril to him if he in a particular district is met by competition and cuts his prices there, and does not cut his prices in every other district wherever he trades. I should advise him that if he fails to do that he is committing an offense under this section.

Now, again, if a man cuts the price to meet a competitor, is he not open to prosecution under this section, because every man is presumed to intend the natural consequences of his acts? That is a legal axiom. Now, the natural consequence of my act in cutting a price to retain my business is either to take business from a competitor or to hold my own business, and under this language the question is left to the jury to say whether it was wrongfully done. Now, why should the business community be subjected to trial upon that issue, whether or not the act is wrongfully done?

Mr. WEBB. The case which my friend cites will never arise under this section. Everybody is given the right of self-defense, and if a man cuts his price to meet competition, and without any intent or purpose to destroy or wrongfully injure a competitor somewhere else, my friend knows there is no tribunal that would undertake to indict him under this section, because he is not acting with a wrongful intent.

Mr. STAFFORD. Will the gentleman yield?

Mr. WEBB. Yes.

Mr. STAFFORD. When a jobber cuts his price, or gives a dating, for instance, or a discount which he does not give to the general public, in order to get business, does he not thereby intend to injure some other jobber, or some other dealer to whom he is not giving that preferential price?

Mr. WEBB. Oh, no; not necessarily.

Mr. STAFFORD. Why, necessarily. He is doing it for the purpose of not giving the same favor to the trade generally.

Mr. WEBB. If he gives that advantage to one jobber and not to another jobber under the same general conditions and thereby discriminates with intent to destroy, and so forth, he is liable to indictment under this act, and ought to be.

Mr. STAFFORD. That is the very purpose with which business is to-day carried on, and your view would make it a criminal offense, and every large wholesaler would be subjected to criminal prosecution under this present phraseology.

Mr. WEBB. He ought to be indicted if he cuts prices and discriminates therein for the purpose of destroying or wrongfully injuring a competitor.

Mr. STAFFORD. That is not the morale of the business public generally.

Mr. WEBB. It is good business morals to-day, and ought to be enforced by law. . . .

Mr. [WILLIAM] KENT [I., Cal.]. I would like to ask the gentleman if competition itself may not inherently be an injury?

Mr. WEBB. That depends upon the standpoint from which you view the matter. Some argue that it is and some argue to the contrary. Economists have not agreed on that question.

Mr. KENT. You intend to control a man's business, if you can, in order to prevent his injuring you.

Mr. WEBB. No; but this practice has been a favorite bludgeon used by the trusts—to go to a town and say I will sell these goods 20 or 30 per cent lower than our competitor sells them, and in that way put independents out of business in that community. I say if they do that they ought to be indicted. . . .

Mr. BARTON. We had an illustration recently where a big fire insurance company came into the State where local insurance companies have been doing business, not confined to the border of the State, and cut prices in that immediate locality until we had in three States 40 or 50 local companies put out of business, and then the price was put back where it was profitable to the company. Might not this same condition exist where we started a wholesale house in a State where their territory was confined to the State—might it not be a reduction of prices for putting that institution out of business?

Mr. WEBB. If the purpose is to wrongfully injure or destroy a competitor, this section will cover such practice; but insurance companies are not reached, as the Supreme Court has held that their contracts or policies are not interstate commerce.

Mr. BARTON. Is it not right that they should come within the law?

Mr. WEBB. Yes.

Mr. MOORE. Mr. Chairman, I wish to ask the chairman of the committee whether it is intended to reach mail-order houses by this paragraph.

Mr. WEBB. It means to embrace everybody who operates in interstate commerce and discriminates in price for the purpose of destroying or wantonly injuring a competitor.

Mr. MOORE. Suppose a large mail-order house in Chicago was circularizing the country and should enter into competition with the crossroads store in the gentleman's county, would the department store, the mail-order house in Chicago, be liable to prosecution under this act?

Mr. WEBB. If it discriminated in prices for the purpose of destroying or wrongfully injuring such crossroad store, it would be guilty.

Mr. MOORE. And that is the purpose of the act?

Mr. WEBB. Yes.

Mr. MOORE. Suppose one large department store in Washington in the ordinary competition with smaller stores should on certain days of the week advertise that shoes would be sold at a reduced price, a price far below that at which shoes were sold in hundreds of smaller stores, would the passage of this act enable the smaller stores to prosecute the department store?

Mr. WEBB. I think it would be very hard in that case to prosecute the department store under the terms of the law. It would sell the same shoes to everybody at the same price, and it would be difficult to prove that it was being done to put the small competitor out of business.

Mr. MOORE. In the case of the department store advertising that on a certain day it will reduce the price of certain articles which would put several competitors out of business, this act would not apply in the interest of the small business man, would it?

Mr. WEBB. That would be wholly within the State and would not be affected by this act. It would not affect the Philadelphia or the New York department store if they sold within the confines of their State.

Mr. MOORE. The effect of the act, then, would not be to relieve the small dealer, but to permit the large concern, with its great capital and its fine advertising facilities, to invite and attract the public in large numbers, and thus put out of business the small competitor in a perfectly natural way.

Mr. WEBB. The gentleman knows that the evil he is speaking of is within the State control. We can only handle transactions which affect interstate business.

Mr. MOORE. I grant that, if the business is wholly within the State, but you think your act would apply to the mail-order house that is circularizing the country and doing business in other States.

Mr. WEBB. It would.

Mr. MOORE. And houses in other States undertaking to do business in the gentleman's county.

Mr. WEBB. If it intended to destroy or wrongfully injure a competitor, it would.

Mr. MOORE. There would be no relief to the small dealer in the State jurisdiction, but there would be to the crossroads dealer in the gentleman's State, providing there was an interstate business. That is the gentleman's opinion?

Mr. WEBB. Certainly; and you would have to go to the States for relief in the other case. . . .

Mr. GARDNER. Would the adoption of the amendment offered by the gentleman from Pennsylvania [Mr. GRAHAM] open the door to the practices which you seek to prevent by section 2?

Mr. WEBB. It might be a suggestion to the parties that that could be done.

Mr. GARDNER. Is not the real reason for the gentleman's opposition to the amendment that you do not wish to have one line of the bill changed if you can help it?

Mr. WEBB. No sir; that is not the case at all. We invite helpful amendments. I oppose this amendment because, as I said, I think the amendment of the gentleman from Pennsylvania is useless and unnecessary. . . .

Mr. MANN. There are five amendments to be offered on this side, and, so far as I know, that is all that will be offered from this side to that section. Can we reach an agreement about debate?

Mr. WEBB. I hope that we may. I suggest a half an hour.

Mr. MANN. We want 25 minutes on this side.

Mr. MURDOCK. The gentleman had better take some time for himself, for he will need it.

Mr. WEBB. Then, Mr. Chairman, I ask unanimous consent that all debate on this section and amendments thereto be closed in 50 minutes, one half of the time to be controlled by the gentleman from Minnesota [Mr. VOLSTEAD] and the other half by myself.

The CHAIRMAN. The gentleman from North Carolina asks unanimous consent that debate on this section and all amendments thereto close in 50 minutes, one half of the time to be controlled by the gentleman from Minnesota [Mr. VOLSTEAD] and the other half by himself. Is there objection?

There was no objection.

Mr. LEVY. Mr. Chairman, I have an amendment which I desire to offer. Is it proper now?

The CHAIRMAN. There is an amendment pending. The question is on the amendment offered by the gentleman from Pennsylvania [Mr. GRAHAM].

The question was taken, and the amendment was rejected.

Mr. GRAHAM of Pennsylvania. Mr. Speaker, I offer the following amendment which I send to the desk and ask to have read.

⊥ Mr. LEVY. But, Mr. Chairman, the Chair said that he would recognize me. ⊥9391

The CHAIRMAN. But the gentleman from Pennsylvania is a member of the committee. The Chair understands the rule to be that members of the committee are entitled to preference. The Chair will recognize the gentleman from New York later. The Clerk will report the amendment of the gentleman from Pennsylvania.

The Clerk read as follows:

Page 21, line 11, after the word "for," insert the words "difference in cost of production in different localities and for."

The CHAIRMAN. The question is on agreeing to the amendment. . . .

Mr. GRAHAM of Pennsylvania. Mr. Chairman, I ask the very serious and impartial consideration of this amendment by the committee which has this bill in charge. This amendment covers one of the conditions that perhaps inadvertently has been left out of the bill, and I really think ought to be inserted in it as a matter of fairness and justice. Everyone in this House knows that the cost of production varies in different localities, so that a price based on a single cost of production can not be maintained as a universal price. I have simply asked here that in line 11, after the words "allowance for," the words "difference in cost of production in different localities and for" be inserted. To allow for that difference is just as fair and reasonable as to allow for the difference in transportation, and I have received communications from business men calling attention to this fact and showing how it would work injuriously to them and their business if they were obliged to charge a uniform price. They can not do it; and yet the language of the section compels them to. Unless the committee is wedded, as the gentleman from Massachusetts [Mr. GARDNER] suggested, to putting this bill through the House line for line and word for word, without change, then I appeal to the reason and fairness of gentlemen [sic] of the committee to insert this amendment in this section of the bill.

I yield back the remainder of my time. . . .

Mr. FLOYD of Arkansas. Mr. Chairman, I do not care to take up the five minutes yielded to me on this amendment. I desire to say only a word. The exceptions in this statute are the usual exceptions in the statutes of the several States that have enacted legislation on this question. . . .

Mr. GRAHAM of Pennsylvania. Does the gentleman mean to say to this body that because certain language has been adopted in some State legislatures it is therefore binding upon us when a question of an amendment appeals to our reasoning and sense of justice?

Mr. FLOYD of Arkansas. Why, not at all.

Mr. GRAHAM of Pennsylvania. Then why refer to State legislation?

Mr. FLOYD of Arkansas. And I am surprised at the gentleman asking such a question. I object to the amendment of the gentleman from Pennsylvania because there is no necessity for it and there is no good reason for it. The place of production will be the point from which the cost of transportation would be reckoned. . . .

Mr. GRAHAM of Pennsylvania. Does not the gentleman know that a great many producers have plants located in different localities and that at each one of those plants, owing to local and other causes, the cost of production is different, and that each of those plants is for the purpose of supplying its own section of the country? Is not that a reason for this amendment?

Mr. FLOYD of Arkansas. I understand that there is a difference in cost of production in different sections of the country, but we do not think that, in striking at the evil we are striking at, that element is serious enough to warrant us in putting in this exception. This provision is striking at a known evil, one of the worst evils that has ever been practiced in this country, to the detriment of manufacturers in different sections of the country, and we think when we have made the exceptions we have made here that we have gone far enough. We are striking at monopoly, at these powerful corporations that make a practice of discriminating in prices and in underselling in particular localities, and thereby absolutely destroying and putting out of business independent manufacturers all over the country. The object is to give opportunity to build up manufacturing industries in every section of the country and to enable men in different sections to build up new enterprises, and thus save communities and States and sections of the country the cost of transporting the same commodities from some central point in the United States to every part of the country.

Mr. GRAHAM of Pennsylvania. Will the gentleman answer me how the adoption of this amendment would prevent the purpose that the gentleman has in mind, that of preventing monopoly? Why has the committee recognized difference in cost of transportation and yet refused to recognize difference in cost of production in different localities?

Mr. FLOYD of Arkansas. I will explain to the gentleman that in drafting this bill we think we have placed in it all of the exceptions that are essential. This is a criminal statute. Certain elements must be proved and established beyond a reasonable doubt before any man can be convicted under its provisions. We are striking at a known stupendous evil, from which the people of every section of this country have suffered, and we do not desire to weaken the bill by placing additional exceptions into the provisions of the bill, and in that connection I desire to answer further suggestions made by the gentleman from Pennsylvania in the outset. There might be a thousand things, a hundred things, or twenty things not mentioned in these exceptions that would be a complete defense to a charge under this section, because in order to convict any man under the provisions of this section you must show two things: You must show that he is selling at discriminating prices in one locality, different from the prices at which he is selling in other localities, and you must show further that he is doing it with a wrongful purpose and intent to destroy or injure a competitor, either of the seller or of the purchaser. . . .

Mr. FLOYD of Arkansas. And there may be many things not mentioned in these exceptions that would completely exonerate the person charged with unlawful discrimination. In other words, no man could be convicted unless the criminal acts made necessary to constitute a crime in this provision are established. . . .

Mr. GRAHAM of Pennsylvania. There is no device in the amendment; it is apparent upon its face that it is perfectly fair. I would ask my learned colleague on the committee if this bill does not require from the producer to maintain a uniform price throughout the whole country wherever he operates? Now, is it fair, in relation to a commodity of such a kind, that it must be produced at different places and sold in the community adjacent thereto, and forming its environment, to put the burden on him of maintaining a uniform price everywhere when the cost of production in different localities varies? Now, you have allowed for the different cost of transportation, why do you not in equity and justice allow for this difference also?

Mr. FLOYD of Arkansas. I do not admit the gentleman's premise. The man might lower the price for any lawful purpose. It might be proper to meet the cost of transportation or any other purpose providing he did not have in his mind an evil purpose and intent of lowering the price to put out of business a competitor. That is my answer to the proposition. . . .

Mr. MOORE. A parliamentary inquiry.

The CHAIRMAN. The gentleman will state it.

Mr. MOORE. Is there any more time to discuss the amendment on this important matter?

The CHAIRMAN. The Chair states that the time to be devoted to this section and all amendments thereto is under the control of the gentleman from North Carolina and the gentleman from Minnesota by agreement in the committee.

Mr. MOORE. And we are restricted to such time as has been designated?

⊥ The CHAIRMAN. Those gentlemen have control of the time. ⊥9392

Mr. MOORE. I shall not consent to any further unanimous consents if there is to be such a limitation of time for debate on questions of this great importance to the people of this country. . . .

The CHAIRMAN. The question is upon the amendment offered by the gentleman from Pennsylvania.

The question was taken, and the Chairman announced the noes seemed to have it.

Mr. GRAHAM of Pennsylvania. Division, Mr. Chairman.

Mr. HULINGS. Mr. Chairman, I rise to a parliamentary inquiry.

The CHAIRMAN. The gentleman will state it.

Mr. HULINGS. I desire to know just what this amendment is, and I ask that it be again reported.

The CHAIRMAN. Without objection, the amendment will be again reported.

The amendment was again reported.

The committee divided; and there were—ayes 29, noes 46.

So the amendment was rejected.

Mr. LEVY. Mr. Chairman, I have two amendments which I desire to offer.

The CHAIRMAN. The Clerk will report the first amendment.

The Clerk read as follows:

On page 20, line 20, between the words "indirectly" and "discriminate," insert the word "unreasonably." . . .

Mr. LEVY. Mr. Chairman, the amendment offered by me is no more than fair and just. It has been decided by the Supreme Court of the United States, and if the Supreme Court of the United States had not put in the word "reasonable" in the Sherman law about one-half of the business of the United States would have been compelled to close up. I say, again, it is no more than fair that the word "unreasonably" should be put in the bill. That is my view of it, as well as the people's. I think it is a great mistake to rush this question to such rapid conclusion. It is a question that ought to be seriously considered, as I conceive it is one of the most important bills that has been before the House of Representatives this session, and will require many years for its construction by the courts.

The CHAIRMAN. The question is on the amendment offered by the gentleman from New York.

The question was taken, and the amendment was rejected.

The CHAIRMAN. The Clerk will report the second amendment.

The Clerk read as follows:

On page 21, strike out lines 5 and 6 and the word "court," in line 7, and insert in lieu thereof the following: "by a fine not exceeding $1,000 for the first offense, and for the second and each succeeding offense by imprisonment not exceeding one year, or by both fine and imprisonment, in the discretion of the court." . . .

Mr. LEVY. Mr. Chairman, we do not want to declare all our citizens criminals before they are given an opportunity to have the law construed. If it is decided that they have violated the law, they should be punished by a fine for the first offense, and for a second and each succeeding offense it should be imprisonment.

The question was taken, and the amendment was rejected.

Mr. GREEN of Iowa. Mr. Chairman, I offer the following amendment.

The CHAIRMAN. The Clerk will report the amendment.

The Clerk read as follows:

Page 21, lines 1, 2, and 3, after the word "thereby," strike out "destroy or wrongfully injure the business of a competitor of either such purchaser or seller" and insert in lieu thereof the following: "create a monopoly, hinder competition, or restrain trade." . . .

Mr. GREEN of Iowa. Mr. Chairman, the gentlemen in charge of the bill have stated in the report that in preparing this section they had simply followed the provisions of laws which had already been enacted in some 19 States. This statement, however, is an error. The laws of the States to which reference is made in this connection in the report, with the exception of two or three, are not drawn upon similar lines to this section. In fact, the only ones that correspond substantially are those of Louisiana and Nebraska. Michigan has a somewhat similar statute with reference to petroleum products. The statutes of the other States are aimed simply at the evil of destroying or preventing competition or restraining trade. The restriction which is made in this section will apply whether there is any attempt at monopoly, whether there is any attempt to restrain trade, or whether there is any attempt to prevent competition. In order to so frame the section that business might not be prevented, framers of the bill have inserted a number of provisos which would not be necessary if the section was in proper form.

Now, let me illustrate how this section will apply in actual business. There is in my own town a small canning factory. I have no interest in it whatever myself. It manufactures probably a couple of million of cans of corn a year. It sells some of the product in my own State, in my own town, but the larger portion of it in States farther west, principally Colorado, Utah, and California. Necessarily it must make a different price in my own State than that which it makes in the States of Utah and California. The bill says it may do this provided this discrimination is based simply and solely on the cost of transportation. But they can not regulate the price in that manner, for the grade of corn they make there is a fairly uniform price in the States of Utah and California, and they must compete there with canners from the State of my friend from Nebraska [Mr. BARTON], who have a less rate of freight than this canning factory in my town would be able to obtain. Then, according to the proviso in the bill, if we change the price at all in Utah and California we would be obliged to fix it strictly in accordance with the rates of freight. If this is done, the canning company could not sell its products at all in those States.

The distinguished gentleman from North Carolina and also the distinguished gentleman from Arkansas, defining the acts to which this section applies, have said it was cases where there was an attempt to drive out a competitor by means of fixing a lower price in some particular locality than was fixed in another State. If that is correct, why not so provide in that section instead of using words to which nobody can give a definition? What do the words "wrongfully injure" mean? One gentleman says one thing, and another says another thing. Nobody has undertaken to define the term beyond this mere statement that has been made by the gentleman from South Carolina [Mr. WEBB] and the gentleman from Arkansas [Mr. FLOYD]. If they use the terms I have provided for in this amendment, "to create a monopoly, to hinder competition, or restrain trade," then they will have words that have been passed upon judicially and which business men are ready to act under, and which will require no provisos which will permit of loopholes and evasions by which the whole act can be rendered nugatory.

Mr. Chairman, I think this amendment ought to be accepted and adopted. . . .

Mr. FLOYD of Arkansas. Mr. Chairman, in reply to the gentleman from Iowa [Mr. GREEN], I desire to state it is not contended that the verbiage of this section is the same as that included in all of the different State statutes; but our contention is that the principle, the wrong that we are attempting to correct by the provisions in section 2 of this bill, has become so notorious and so well known that 21 States have passed statutes preventing discrimination, following the same principle. Now, the gentleman proposes to weaken the effect of what we have written here by requiring it to apply only when the effort is made to create a monopoly.

We are dealing with interstate trade and commerce. If the purpose is to create a monopoly, the persons offending are violating the Sherman law; and at the risk of giving the court some trouble in construing the statute, and at the risk of giving a wrongdoer some trouble in construing the statute, we have proposed a statute here which we believe, if enacted into law, will be more effective than all the provisions of the Sherman law have ever been in suppressing one of the grossest and greatest wrongs in the business methods of the great and powerful corporations of this country. For that reason we hope that the House will not weaken this provision by adopting the amendment offered by the gentleman from Iowa, which has the exact wording of the provisions of some of the State statutes. . . .

Mr. GREEN of Iowa. Surely the gentleman did not want to misstate my amendment. It covers not merely an attempt to create a monopoly, but anything that had the purpose to injure competition or restrain trade. Now, can the gentleman state anything that will be covered by this section as it is worded now that is not covered by my amendment?

Mr. FLOYD of Arkansas. I think so. I think it is more specific and more definite. Gentlemen complain of the difficulties of the business world on account of these provisions. I believe that in drafting statutes, and especially in drafting a criminal statute, we should make them so plain and specific that any man who reads can understand. . . .

Mr. MURDOCK. I would like to ask the gentleman, in connection with what he has said, in line 11, page 21, what does the language of the bill mean by "difference in cost of transportation"? Do you mean the published rates, the rates filed with the Interstate Commerce Commission, or not? What do you mean by "transportation" there?

Mr. FLOYD of Arkansas. We mean the actual cost of transportation.

Mr. MURDOCK. Take the Standard Oil Co., and, as the gentleman knows, it owns great tank-line steamers and pipe lines which other people do not have the use of, and all manner of special means of transportation—are those included in this or not; or only the rates filed with the Interstate Commerce Commission, and no other rates, included in this line?

Mr. FLOYD of Arkansas. The rates of transportation, the cost of transportation, whatever it may be or by whatever means it may be incurred.

Mr. MURDOCK. The gentleman said he wanted to be specific in the statute, and I was trying to find out.

Mr. FLOYD of Arkansas. Well, that is the way I understand it. Of course if a company has a pipe line of its own, the situation might be different.

Now, since the gentleman has mentioned the Standard Oil Co., the testimony in the great trial against the Standard Oil Co. has developed the fact that one of the very worst offenders that has ever existed in this country in this evil practice of unfair discrimination is that same Standard Oil Co.

Mr. MURDOCK. Does the gentleman think he has reached them in that phrase?

Mr. FLOYD of Arkansas. We certainly do. We have reached the Standard Oil Co., and we have reached every other concern that comes within the purview of this particular provision. . . .

Mr. HULINGS. I see, in line 10, page 21, that one of the exceptions is that discrimination can be made when there is a difference in the cost of the commodity. Now, does not that provision specifically provide that the big man will always have that discrimination in his favor, and if you allow that do not you make just an open road for big business to avoid the law? . . .

The CHAIRMAN. The question is on the amendment offered by the gentleman from Iowa [Mr. GREEN].

The question was taken, and the Chair announced that the noes seemed to have it.

Mr. VOLSTEAD. Division, Mr. Chairman.

The committee divided, and there were—ayes 34, noes 42.

Accordingly the amendment was rejected.

Mr. GARDNER. Mr. Chairman, I desire to offer an amendment.

The CHAIRMAN. The gentleman from Massachusetts offers an amendment, which the Clerk will report.

The Clerk read as follows:

Page 21, line 1, transpose the word "thereby" and the word "to." . . .

Mr. GARDNER. Mr. Chairman, this is in order to avoid a split infinitive. The gentleman from Vermont [Mr. GREEN], who is much more of a rhetorician than I am, tells me that we could never be relected [sic] in New England if we allowed—

The CHAIRMAN. The time of the gentleman has expired.

Mr. WEBB. The gentleman is from Massachusetts, a State of scholars, and we owe a great deal to its scholars, orators, and statesmen. Therefore, in order to avoid the calamity of a split infinitive, which the gentleman seeks to prevent, we will accept the gentleman's amendment. [Applause and laughter.]

The amendment was agreed to.

Mr. TOWNER. Mr. Chairman, I offer an amendment.

The CHAIRMAN. The gentleman from Iowa offers an amendment, which the Clerk will report.

The Clerk read as follows:

Page 21, line 2, strike out the words "or wrongfully injure the business of a competitor, of either such purchaser or seller" and insert in lieu thereof the word "competition." . . .

Mr. TOWNER. Mr. Chairman, this is quite similar to the amendment offered by the gentleman from Iowa, my colleague, Mr. GREEN. However, I think it is more clearly evident that this will be an extension of the rule rather than a limitation. Certainly the evident purpose of the section is to prevent the destruction of competition. If this amendment is adopted, the statute will read:

That any person engaged in commerce who shall, either directly or indirectly, discriminate in price * * * with the purpose or intent thereby to destroy competition, shall be deemed guilty of a misdemeanor.

I submit to the gentleman from Arkansas that this language is much more comprehensive than the language in the bill, and very much less liable to meet with adverse construction by the courts.

The amendment was rejected.

Mr. AVIS. Mr. Chairman, I offer an amendment.

The CHAIRMAN. The gentleman from West Virginia offers an amendment, which the Clerk will report.

The Clerk read as follows:

Page 21, lines 13 to 15, inclusive, after the word "customers," in line 14, strike out the comma, and in lines 14 and 15 strike out the words "except as provided in section 3 of this act" and insert in lieu thereof the following: In line 13, after the word "wares," the words "bituminous or semibituminous coal," and insert a period after the word "customers," in line 14. . . .

Mr. AVIS. Mr. Chairman and gentlemen, I appeal particularly to the gentlemen who come from bituminous and semibituminous coal-producing States to consider carefully the amendment that I have just offered. The committee has stated that it is the purpose of section 2 to prevent one competitor from destroying or injuring another competitor. It has also been stated that its purpose is to control or prevent monopoly. I say to you gentlemen that, in my humble opinion, coming from a coal-producing State and knowing conditions in the bituminous coal fields, if this bill becomes a law as it is to-day, instead of destroying monopoly it will destroy competition and create monopoly.

You will notice that section 2 permits every man to prefer and select his own customers, except as provided in the last four lines:

That nothing herein contained shall prevent persons engaged in selling goods, wares, or merchandise in commerce from selecting their own customers, except as provided in section 3 of this act.

And in section 3 of this act it is provided that no operator or owner of a coal mine can "refuse arbitrarily" to sell, and ⊥ so forth, and those words are limited by the words of section 2, which prevent him from selecting his own customers. And I want to say to you gentlemen who come from the great coal-producing States of the Union—I am not referring to anthracite coal, but to bituminous coal—that there is no monopoly of the coal business; that the production now is greater than the demand therefor; and that, notwithstanding the fact that freight rates, labor, and mine supplies have doubled in price, bituminous coal is selling as cheaply to-day, if not more cheaply, than it sold 8 or 10 years ago, and we in West Virginia are putting coal into New England and paying $2.10 a ton freight on it and selling it more cheaply than it is sold at the pit mouth at Cardiff, Wales. . . .

Mr. FLOYD of Arkansas. Will the gentleman read the paragraph as it will read if amended? . . .

Mr. AVIS. As it is now the language is—

That nothing herein contained shall prevent persons engaged in selling goods, wares, or merchandise in commerce from selecting their own customers, except as provided in section 3 of this act.

As amended it will read:

That nothing herein contained shall prevent persons engaged in selling goods, wares, bituminous or semibituminous coal, or merchandise in commerce from selecting their own customers.

Gentlemen, there is no monopoly of the coal business, not nearly so much as there is of the timber and cotton business. As I say, competition is so great that in my State the mines are not running more than two and one-half days a week.

Mr. FLOYD of Arkansas. What does the gentleman do with the last clause?—

Except as provided in section 3 of this act.

Mr. AVIS. I propose to strike out the words—

Except as provided in section 3 of this act.

In other words, to-day the competition is so great in the bituminous coal industry—

Mr. FLOYD of Arkansas. Will the gentleman permit a suggestion there?

Mr. AVIS. Yes.

Mr. FLOYD of Arkansas. That relates to section 3. The language the gentleman complains of is in section 3.

Mr. AVIS. Yes; in sections 2 and 3.

Mr. FLOYD of Arkansas. It seems to me that the gentleman's exception ought to be in section 3.

Mr. AVIS. Except for this purpose, if the gentleman will permit me and give me a little further time to answer— . . .

I desire to answer the gentleman from Arkansas. The trouble with section 3 is that its purpose is to cover all minerals, even oil and gas. Now, by section 2 you prevent, or rather you limit or define the meaning of the words "refuse arbitrarily," in section 3, by saying, in effect, in section 2, that it is an arbitrary refusal to select one's own customers by a coal operator or a mine owner. Either that exception ought to be in section 2 or the words stricken out of that section that would cause any confusion if a question should be taken before the courts to decide what was intended. I hope that gentlemen who come from the great States of Illinois, Ohio, Pennsylvania, Indiana, Kentucky, West Virginia, Virginia, Alabama, Utah, Washington, and Wyoming and the other States engaged in the bituminous-coal industry will hesitate before they decline to adopt this amendment. . . .

Mr. FLOYD of Arkansas. Mr. Chairman, aside from whatever merits may be embodied in the amendment offered by the gentleman from West Virginia, I desire to call his attention to the fact that there is nothing in the section he proposes to amend that in any way deals with the subject matter about which he complains. That is in section 3, and the effect of his amendment incorporated in section 2 would completely destroy section 3, and it seems to me that in order to reach the purpose desired by the gentleman this language which he proposes to strike out should remain intact in section 2, and whatever amendment he desires to incorporate in regard to mine products ought to be offered to section 3.

Mr. AVIS. I will say to the gentleman that if I thought that was a fact I would not ask to have it adopted here, or if you put the exception in section 3 it might cover the point, but how do you know that the House is going to do so? If you leave the words "except as provided in section 3 of this act" in section 2, and incorporate the amendment I propose in section 3, you would have two sections apparently conflicting. You would have one section excepting bituminous coal, and then you would have another providing that nothing herein contained shall prevent a person selecting his own customers, except as provided in section 3.

Mr. FLOYD of Arkansas. I think I can make it clear that the gentleman's statement is not correct. It says that nothing herein contained shall prevent persons engaged in selling goods, wares, and merchandise in commerce from selecting their own customers, except as provided in section 3 of this act. Now, if section 3 of the act did not exist, and if reference to that section is stricken out of the language in section 2, there would be nothing to prevent bituminous-coal operators from selecting their customers in section 2. The limitations are in section 3, and I insist in perfect good faith that the gentleman ought to offer his amendment to section 3, which deals with the products of mines and contains the provisions complained of.

Mr. AVIS. I appreciate the courtesy of the gentleman from Arkansas, but what is confusing to me is that if you put my amendment into section 3 it will apparently conflict with this language, that—

nothing herein contained shall prevent persons * * * from selecting their own customers, except as provided in section 3 of this act.

Mr. FLOYD of Arkansas. If the gentleman's amendment is incorporated in section 3, it will relate back to section 2, and modify its provisions accordingly.

Mr. AVIS. The gentleman may be right, but I am afraid the meaning will be obscure. Will the gentleman accept my proposed amendment to section 3 [sic]?

Mr. FLOYD of Arkansas. No; I could not afford to accept the amendment; but I think if the gentleman offers it in section 3, as I suggest, he will accomplish his purpose without in any way affecting or displacing the purpose of section 3 as to other products of mines. It is unnecessary to make any amendment to section 2, providing you can secure an amendment in section 3 excepting bituminous-coal products from the provisions of that section.

Mr. AVIS. The gentleman may be right—and I am inclined to think that he is—but, at the same time, I think that the language might be obscure and cause confusion.

Mr. FLOYD of Arkansas. Well, Mr. Chairman, we oppose the amendment because we do not think it has any place in this section . . . .

Mr. SWITZER. Mr. Chairman, I desire to ask the chairman of the Judiciary Committee a question. Does the word "commodities" in this section include everything that can be shipped, like live stock, live poultry, horses, mules, and so forth?

Mr. WEBB. I think so; why should it not?

Mr. SWITZER. There has been some query about it on this side.

Mr. MADDEN. Does it include coal?

Mr. WEBB. It would include coal except for the provision in section 3.

Mr. SWITZER. Mr. Chairman, I desire in support of the amendment offered by the gentleman from West Virginia [Mr. AVIS] to read a few lines from a coal operator in my district—Mr. Edwin Jones, of Jackson, Ohio—relative to section 3. It is as follows:

> I find the bill states that an operator can not arbitrarily refuse to sell such product to persons, firms, or corporations. As you quite well understand, occurrences are common wherein business firms are responsible financially, but oftentimes their business methods are such that you would not be desirous of doing business with them. Oftentimes mine owners have arrangements that have been in force for years, wherein they have given exclusive sale to certain jobbers of coal, and frequently we find cases where a man, firm, or corporation will be justly at that time entitled to credit, but that you had good reason on account of the habits of the man or individual in charge to believe that he could not continue to be successful.

Mr. Chairman, I think the criticism of this bill respecting this industry is well timed and should be considered before voting on section 2.

The CHAIRMAN. The question is on the amendment offered by the gentleman from West Virginia.

The question was taken, and the amendment was rejected.

Mr. MORGAN of Oklahoma. Mr. Chairman, I offer the following amendment.

The Clerk read as follows:

> Amend by striking out section 2 on page 20 and inserting in lieu thereof the following:
> "SEC. 2. That any person engaged in commerce who shall discriminate in price, terms, or otherwise as between persons, sections, or communities, with intent thereby to destroy or wrongfully injure a competitor or to establish a monopoly or destroy or lessen competition in the production, manufacture, distribution, or sale of any such article, product, or commodity, shall be deemed guilty of a misdemeanor, and ⊥ upon conviction thereof shall be punished by a fine not exceeding $5,000 or imprisonment not exceeding one year, or both." . . .

⊥9395

Mr. MORGAN of Oklahoma. Mr. Chairman, I would like the attention of the other side to the provisions of this amendment. I want to call attention to the fact that section 2 prohibits but one thing—it prohibits simply discrimination in price. So far as this section is concerned, a man may be guilty of any other discrimination that would have the same effect in destroying competition, in injuring a competitor, or in injuring the public in any way, but yet it is not made unlawful under this section. . . .

Mr. MURDOCK. The gentleman knows that one of the great cereal food manufacturers of this country, when he sells a large amount of that cereal to one man, gives a certain number of boxes in addition as a premium. Is that practice reached in this section?

Mr. MORGAN of Oklahoma. Certainly not, and that is one fact I wish to impress on that side of the House. In my first amendment the distinguished gentleman from Arkansas [Mr. FLOYD] complained because I wanted to restrict the application of this section to the large concerns, and now I wonder what answer he will make to this amendment, which I have offered, because here I want to enlarge the language, and enlarge it so that it will comprehend and include practically all unfair discrimination. He will vote one down because it narrows and vote the other down because it broadens. In the end we get the same result. The language which I have inserted is so as to add to the words "discrimination in prices" the words "in terms or otherwise," so that it will include all unfair discrimination. Are you partial to one discrimination? . . .

Mr. WEBB. Does not the gentleman think his amendment is covered if this is done directly or indirectly? Does not that cover the very ground that the gentleman seeks to cover now?

Mr. MORGAN of Oklahoma. No; because "directly or indirectly" apply only to discrimination in price. Why should not it be unlawful for one to discriminate in terms? I hold here the report of the Commissioner of Corporations for 1913 upon the International Harvester Co. What does he show there? He shows that one of the most effective methods used in acquiring a monopolistic control in that great industry was by discrimination in terms. Notice what he says on page 35 of that report:

> In this connection there is large complaint that the company grants unusually long terms of

credit to purchasers of some of these newer lines. One of the competitors of a company said, "The International Harvester Co. sells terms, not harrows."

One of the most effective methods of the International Harvester Co. was to give better terms than the independent and smaller concern could give, and the report of the Commissioner of Corporations shows that these dealers complain that the International Harvester Co. sold "terms and not harrows," and yet when you are legislating for the purpose of controlling and making unlawful the methods of the great concerns of the country, you say to them, "Go ahead and use all kind [sic] of discrimination in terms, use all kinds of unfair practices, use all kinds of disreputable methods in the interest of the big corporations, and so long as you do not discriminate directly or indirectly in price, you shall be free and untrammeled to go and devour the small concern and exact undue profits from the people by your excessive prices." I want to know whether the Members of that side of the House will vote against enlarging this section, so that you shall make other things unlawful.

Take the second proviso. It provides that only discrimination in price "for the purpose or intent of destroying or wrongfully injuring a competitor" shall be unlawful. You can discriminate for all other purposes, so long as you do not discriminate with the purpose of destroying or injuring a competitor. . . .

Mr. GARDNER. I want to ask the gentleman whether his amendment does anything further, substantially, than to strike out the words "in price," because, as I heard it read, it strikes out the last two provisos of that section as well?

Mr. MORGAN of Oklahoma. Yes.

Mr. GARDNER. I am in sympathy with the gentleman striking out the words "in price."

Mr. MORGAN of Oklahoma. I do not strike out "in price," but I add "in terms or otherwise."

Mr. GARDNER. I am in sympathy with that, but what about striking out the two provisos?

Mr. MORGAN of Oklahoma. I had an object in that. I enlarged the section in this, because I make it unlawful not only to discriminate with the purpose of destroying a competitor, but with the purpose of establishing a monopoly or lessening or destroying competition. Why should you not enlarge it? It does not weaken the section if I leave the language which you use and add this other language. It does enlarge it. It may enable you to prosecute some large concern that you could not prosecute under this section as it is.

When I want to narrow one of these sections, you vote it down, because you do not want it narrowed; and when I want to broaden one so as to make it more comprehensive, you vote that down on that account.

I have left out that first proviso and also the second proviso, because when in one part of the section you prohibit the great concerns of this country from discriminating in price and then add a proviso that this shall not apply to any discrimination on account of grade, quality, or quantity, what have you done? You have opened the gates—not the eye of a needle, but the gates of a great highway—into which the trusts can enter. Why? Take the International Harvester Co. They have many brands of machinery, many kinds of harvesters, various classes of farm implements. The great concern may have one brand of goods to sell in Oklahoma and another to sell in Nebraska. They have the capital, they have the organization, and they have the financial backing. They can have all kinds of qualities and grades of goods. The small concern can not.

The CHAIRMAN. The time of the gentleman from Oklahoma has expired. The question is on the amendment offered by the gentleman from Oklahoma.

The question was taken; and on a division (demanded by Mr. MORGAN of Oklahoma) there were—ayes 30, noes 47.

So the amendment was rejected.

Mr. BRYAN. Mr. Chairman, I offer the following amendment which I send to the desk and ask to have read.

The Clerk read as follows:

Page 21, line 11, after the word "transportation," strike out the remainder of the paragraph. . . .

Mr. BRYAN. . . . Mr. Chairman, the present terms of the Sherman antitrust law are such that the seller of goods making an attempt to select his customers and refusing to sell to all others, if such selection or discrimination be in restraint of trade, it is a violation of the law. But under this provision the seller can select his customer to the exclusion of all others, and it is legal whether it is in restraint of trade or not. I think that the only effect of this proviso in the bill is to give all parties an opportunity to name their customers where they are prohibited from doing so under the present law. For instance, this says—

⊥ That nothing herein contained shall prevent persons engaged in selling goods, wares, or ⊥9396 merchandise in commerce from selecting their own customers.

What would prevent the paper manufacturers of this country from refusing to sell the Democratic Party publications paper? Suppose they would sell paper only to the Progressive and Republican papers. Suppose the shoe manufacturers of a particular locality would say they would not sell shoes to anybody except a certain set of people, the bakers refuse to sell bread to strikers, the butchers refuse to sell meat to members of the union. Under the present law that is absolutely prohibited if it is a selection or discrimination in restraint of trade, and in this bill such transactions are unconditionally protected. . . .

Mr. FLOYD of Arkansas. Now, as we understand the proposition, under the present law things that the law prohibited are not authorized by any proviso. We leave the present law as it is, and this proviso simply does not undertake to make it an offense or fix a penalty under this particular provision of the statute.

Mr. BRYAN. Is the gentleman quite sure the court, in interpreting this provision as a substitute for the former statute, will not take this proviso—

Mr. FLOYD of Arkansas. Absolutely sure.

Mr. BRYAN (continuing). And say that this proviso governs in that particular matter? That the proviso is a part of the whole section, and where the main provisions of the section apply the proviso must follow?

Mr. FLOYD of Arkansas. The proviso does not authorize anything. When we insert a proviso applying to certain things we leave the law as to those things exactly as it is. If it is a violation of the law now, it will be a violation of the law after the enactment of the provision into law.

Mr. BRYAN. Then, why not agree to my amendment and strike out the proviso and let the law stand as it is if we are going to depend upon the law as it is?

Mr. FLOYD of Arkansas. This provision if made a statute would then make them unlawful, and we would prohibit many things we do not desire to prohibit. We do not desire to disturb customs that are not wrong within themselves. We have said that throughout this debate. We are seeking to correct real wrongs; and where customs and practices appear to be proper and right, we do not propose to disturb them; and the effect of the gentleman's proviso would make the things mentioned in the exception unlawful that are not now unlawful under the Sherman law; and if any one of these things mentioned in the proviso are unlawful under the Sherman law, this does not repeal the Sherman law.

Mr. BRYAN. Yes; but you prohibit certain things provided the seller may select his own customers, and so forth. Now, it seems to me you can not enforce your prohibition except under the stated terms of your proviso.

The CHAIRMAN (Mr. HARRISON). The time of the gentleman has expired. The question is on the amendment offered by the gentleman from Washington.

The question was taken, and the amendment was rejected.

Mr. BRYAN. Mr. Chairman, I offer this amenedment [sic].

The CHAIRMAN. The Clerk will report the amendment.

The Clerk read as follows:

Page 21, line 14, after the word "customers," insert "except when such act tends to create monopoly, destroy competition, restrain trade, or."

Mr. BRYAN. Mr. Chairman, I do not care to debate the amendment.

The CHAIRMAN. The question is on the amendment offered by the gentleman from Washington.

The question was taken, and the amendment was rejected.

Mr. [JAMES W.] GOOD [R., Iowa]. Mr. Chairman, I offer an amendment on page 20, line 20, to strike out the words "in price."

The CHAIRMAN. The Clerk will report the amendment.

The Clerk read as follows:

Amend, page 20, in line 20, by striking out the words "in price."

The CHAIRMAN. The question is on the amendment.

The question was taken, and the Chairman announced the noes seemed to have it.

Mr. MURDOCK. Mr. Chairman, let us have a division on that.

The committee divided; and there were—ayes 35, noes 46.

So the amendment was rejected.

The Clerk read as follows:

SEC. 3. That it shall be unlawful for the owner or operator of any mine or for any person controlling the product of any mine engaged in selling its product in commerce to refuse arbitrarily to sell such product to a responsible person, firm, or corporation who applies to purchase such product for use, consumption, or resale within the United States or any Territory thereof or the District of Columbia or any insular possession or other place under the jurisdiction of the United States, and any person violating this section shall be deemed guilty of a misdemeanor and shall be punished as provided in the preceding section.

Mr. WEBB. Mr. Chairman, it was suggested the gentleman from West Virginia [Mr. AVIS] is very much interested in this section, and he desires to leave, and if there is no objection I will ask that this section be passed until to-morrow.

Mr. AVIS. And that it will be taken up the first thing to-morrow, or some time to-morrow.

Mr. WEBB. The request is that we pass it over until to-morrow.

Mr. BATHRICK. Mr. Chairman, I have got to go away to-morrow myself, and I desire very much to present an amendment to this section.

Mr. [PERL D.] DECKER [D., Mo.]. Offer it and let it be pending.

The CHAIRMAN. The gentleman from North Carolina asks unanimous consent to pass over this section until to-morrow. Is there objection?

Mr. BATHRICK. Now, Mr. Chairman, reserving the right to object, what disposition will you make affecting my amendment because of my being obliged to be absent to-morrow?

Mr. WEBB. So far as the committee can say, I will be glad to have you offer it now and have it pending.

Mr. MANN. Let me suggest to the gentleman that the section be read, and then the gentleman from Ohio offer his amendment, and let that be disposed of, and then the section be passed over.

Mr. BATHRICK. That is agreeable to me, Mr. Chairman. I offer the amendment.

Mr. WEBB. Mr. Chairman, I ask that all amendments be offered now.

Mr. MANN. I do not think it is desirable to have a half a dozen amendments offered at once.

The CHAIRMAN. Does the gentleman from North Carolina withdraw his request for unanimous consent?

Mr. WEBB. No, sir; but I postpone the request until the gentleman from Ohio [Mr. BATHRICK] offers his amendment and speaks on it.

The CHAIRMAN. The Clerk will report the amendment offered by the gentleman from Ohio [Mr. BATHRICK].

The Clerk read as follows:

After the word "mine," in lines 17 and 18, page 21, insert the words "or natural mineral deposit."

Mr. BATHRICK. Now, Mr. Chairman, as near as I can gather by any definition which I am able to find, the word "mine" does not cover an oil well. One of the most powerful means which the Standard Oil Co. has to carry on their monopoly is their power to refuse to sell the products of oil wells to independent refiners. Another means which they have to accomplish monopoly is to go into those oil sections where independent oil wells are located and temporarily, by very small sums on different occasions, overbid the price which independent refineries will pay for this oil. The result is that the independent oil companies are often thus encouraged to refuse to sell their oil to independent refineries. In this connection, reverting to section 2, I have thought that a discrimination in the price offered for a raw material could as well carry out an intent to destroy and wrongfully injure the business of a competitor as the discrimination in the price asked of purchasers. But that thought is aside from my amendment.

Now, this section as it is drawn, in my opinion, and with all respect to the committee for their careful and intelligent labors, to the purpose of preventing monopoly, leaves the door wide open for the Standard Oil Co. and others who own oil wells, which are not mines, to be exempt from this provision. And I say to the gentlemen of this House that if you intend to strike at the capsheaf monopoly of this country, the one which has formed the basis for most of the condemnation which has been directed toward monopoly, this section must be amended in some such respect as I have indicated.

As the Clerk has read, I propose to insert the words "or natural mineral deposit" after the word "mine," in lines 17 and 18 of section 3. Oil is a mineral, but an oil well is not a mine; and if we use the words "or natural mineral deposit" in the place that I have indicated I think there is no question whatever that we will cover the subject of oil. . . .

Mr. FERRIS. I am inclined to think that there is something to what the gentleman says, and I am wondering whether it will be better to also insert the word "placer" or "lode." Now, there is a question of whether washing sand on the surface is not mining. There is also a question as to whether producing oil from an oil well is mining. In either event, it ought to be made clear, and the clause ought to have the word "transporter" in there, as well as the word "owner" and the word "operator."

Mr. BATHRICK. I wish to say further that I offered this amendment as it stands, with the knowledge that what the gentleman from Oklahoma says about placer mines is correct. I will also direct the attention of the committee to the fact that there is a strange sameness of prices asked of consumers of fertilizer. This product relies largely upon phosphate mines, but there is a large supply of phosphate rock dredged from rivers, and I doubt that these deposits would come under the definition of the word "mine," although phosphate, I think, is a derivative of phosphorus, which is an inorganic substance coming from the earth, and would be construed as a "mineral" as well as oil.

These matters I ask the committee to take into consideration. I expect to be absent to-morrow, and I trust some of the gentlemen on the floor of this House will take the matter up and see that that section is taken care of in these respects, if it should happen that I can not be here and no vote under the agreement can be had to-day. . . .

Mr. FERRIS. Mr. Chairman, if I could have my preference, I would willingly let this matter go over until to-morrow; but as that course is not desired, I may as well say what I have to say now. I will offer the amendments I have in mind to-morrow.

This section of the bill should undoubtedly be amended. On page 21, line 16, after the word "owner," there should be inserted a comma and the words "transporter, transportation companies, including pipe lines," so that you will catch the pipe lines. That is, roughly, amendment No. 1.

The second amendment that should be offered is along the line of the amendment offered by the gentleman from Ohio, which I am perfectly willing to support; but I think a better amendment would be, in line 18, page 21, after the word "any," to insert the words "including the products from placer or lode mines," so that you will be sure to take in the sands of the sea or rivers that are washed on the surface, from which mineral is obtained, which may or may not be a mine, under the strict construction of the term. One thing is certain, it is never an effort in vain to make certain that which is at best uncertain.

I am not at all sure that placer mining, under which oil is removed from the surface of the earth, can be considered to be a mine at all. It may be, but it is doubtful. There is a question whether or not under the commodity clause the pipe lines that carry it can be reached. The Commerce Court held the law declaring them carriers void, and the matter is now pending in the Supreme Court;[5.531] and so far we can not get a decision out of the Supreme Court. We have been expecting it for a long time. This is the most important matter to the great oil industry of this country within my knowledge.

There should be another amendment to this section, which I will offer as soon as I get a chance, after the word "mine," in line 18, page 21, to insert the words "or hydroelectric water power or products produced by such power."

When the chairman of the committee explained this section in his initial speech he said that the well-grounded and competent reason for the adoption of a section similar to this with reference to mines was because the products of mines are a God-given treasure for all of us that should not be monopolized by any of us.

I thought his explanation, interpretation, and definition of it was a full, complete, and magnificent one; but can any living man on earth say that anything is so subject to monopoly as falling water? Can anybody say that one commodity over another is more God-given than falling water, which, dependent upon the topography of the country at a given point, is high and low at another point; and can anyone here or elsewhere justify the omission of water power from this section? No question is more important, few questions are more universal. It affects all of us. Water power lights American homes, streets, and cities. It runs our sewing machines, our automobiles, our vehicles, cooks our food, warms our homes, and every conceivable thing that electricity has been applied to in the last generation. Remember, gentlemen, that electricity is fairly in its infancy. Nobody knows what 50 years will bring to us in hydroelectric development, and no one can safeguard too well the water power of the country and prevent its getting into the hands of selfish monopoly that may torture all mankind as long as the human race exists. We ought to put in that restriction, and we ought to pass some other bills in relation to water power in this country. Approximately 12 per cent only of the water-power possibilities on the public lands of this country have been utilized so far. This House ought to make it possible to utilize the rest of that water power and put statutes onto the books which will enable us not only to lease water power for a short time but contain sufficient recapture clauses, so that we can bring it back and utilize it by the Government, or utilize it by local municipalities if they elect to take it over. Nothing is needed worse than cheap power and cheap illumination. This bill ought not to omit it. I hope the committee will be glad to accept it.

The committee has accomplished much good here, but this is too important to omit. It is not sufficient to leave out oil and water power. They are the two large questions of this day.

Mr. CAMPBELL. Has the gentleman from Oklahoma any plan whereby the remaining portion of this water power may be utilized?

Mr. FERRIS. I have. We have a bill on the calendar now. It is not reported yet, but it is authorized to be reported. The gentleman from Illinois [Mr. GRAHAM], of the Public Lands Committee, has been designated to write the report. It was introduced by me. It has the support of the conservative people of this country.

Mr. CAMPBELL. I take it some one will have to harness the water before it can be made use of.

Mr. FERRIS. Very true; and we have furnished ample provision for that. I hope the amendment of the gentleman from Ohio will be adopted.

Mr. WEBB. I want to say that when we drafted this section we intended that it should apply to oil. As there seems to be some doubt about it, the committee thinks the amendment of the gentleman from Ohio makes it more certain, and I am perfectly willing to accept the amendment, because it is our intention to include oil as one of the products of mines.

The CHAIRMAN. The time of the gentleman has expired. All time has expired. The question is on the adoption of the amendment of the gentleman from Ohio [Mr. BATHRICK].

Mr. BARKLEY. I ask unanimous consent to have the amendment again reported.

The Clerk read the amendment again, as follows:

[5.531] *See* notes 5.553 & 5.554 *infra* and the accompanying House debate.

After the word "mine," in line 17, and in 18, on page 21, insert the words "or natural mineral deposit."

The amendment was agreed to.

Mr. MURDOCK. Now get in your request for unanimous consent.

Mr. WEBB. Mr. Chairman, I renew my request.

The CHAIRMAN. The gentleman from North Carolina asks unanimous consent that this section be passed for amendment to-morrow.

Mr. AVIS. Reserving the right to object, may I ask the gentleman from North Carolina a question?

Mr. FLOYD of Arkansas. Were those words also inserted after the word "mine," in line 18?

The CHAIRMAN. Both amendments were read and adopted.

Mr. DECKER. Mr. Chairman, I should like to have the amendment read which I send to the Clerk's desk.

The CHAIRMAN. The request of the gentleman from North Carolina [Mr. WEBB] for unanimous consent is pending.

Mr. WEBB. I withdraw that request in view of the fact that the gentleman from Missouri [Mr. DECKER] says he can not be here to-morrow and would like to have his amendment offered and to speak five minutes on it.

The CHAIRMAN. The Clerk will report the amendment offered by the gentleman from Missouri [Mr. DECKER].

The Clerk read as follows:

On page 21, in line 19, after the word "arbitrarily," insert the following:
"With the purpose or intent thereby to destroy or wrongfully injure the business of any person."

[Mr. DECKER addressed the committee. See **Appendix.***]

Mr. WEBB. Mr. Chairman, I think this amendment is useless. What we really aim to punish under this section is the big operator who has millions of tons of coal and who arbitrarily refuses to sell to any but those he favors. Although I may go to him or you may go to him with the money and ask him to sell to us, he arbitrarily, capriciously, without any good reason whatever, refuses to sell his product, and we think he ought to be punished if he so refuses. . . .

Mr. MADDEN. Does the gentleman know of a case of that kind in the United States?

Mr. WEBB. I do not recall one at present.

Mr. MADDEN. Neither does anybody else. It is mere nonsense and ought to be stricken out.

Mr. WEBB. If the gentleman from Illinois knew the high authority and the great men who favor this provision he perhaps would not make that statement. . . .

Mr. MANN. What does it mean when it says "refuses arbitrarily to sell"? What does the word "arbitrarily" mean?

Mr. WEBB. It means without reason, without cause, capriciously.

Mr. MANN. The gentleman says "without cause." A man sells to one and he does not sell to another, because he does not like him, perhaps, and that is cause.

Mr. WEBB. That would be arbitrarily, I should say.

Mr. MANN. Does it mean sufficient cause, and if so, what is sufficient cause? Does the gentleman think that the courts would be able in 20 or 30 years to determine what this means?

Mr. WEBB. Yes; if they applied everyday common sense to it they would reach a conclusion very soon.

Mr. MANN. It would require more common sense than I possess or than is possessed by the gentleman from North Carolina, because he is not able to define it. What does "arbitrarily" mean? The definition the gentleman gave was "without cause."

Mr. WEBB. Yes; without reason or cause—capriciously. . . .

---

* Not reprinted herein.

Mr. BRYAN. The gentleman says that they are after the big operators; but suppose a man comes from Alaska with a big bag of gold dust or nuggets and some one offers to purchase it from him, by what right could he refuse to sell? He has it for sale for no other purpose whatever. This statute would compel him to sell it at the first proposition.

Mr. WEBB. If he got his price for it, he would be glad to be relieved of it, and if he did not get his price he need not sell, though I hardly think this section would apply to the case stated by the gentleman.

Mr. BRYAN. The statute does not say anything about big operators; it says "all operators."

Mr. WEBB. It is intended to apply to the monopolistic operators.

Mr. LEVY. Does this apply to the coal lands in Alaska?

Mr. WEBB. No; they are owned by the Government and are held for all the people. I hope that the amendment offered by the gentleman from Missouri will not be adopted.

The CHAIRMAN. The question is on the amendment offered by the gentleman from Missouri [Mr. DECKER].

The question was taken, and the amendment was rejected.

Mr. WEBB. Mr. Chairman, I ask unanimous consent that all discussion on this section and amendments thereto go over until to-morrow morning.

The CHAIRMAN. The gentleman from North Carolina asks unanimous consent that the remaining discussion on this section and amendments thereto go over until to-morrow morning. Is there objection?

Mr. FERRIS. Is it the arrangement to take this up the first thing in the morning?

Mr. WEBB. We probably will.

Mr. MANN. Unless something is pending.

Mr. FERRIS. The first thing you do on this bill will be to take up this section?

Mr. WEBB. Unless something is pending.

Mr. GARDNER. Mr. Chairman, I would like to ask the gentleman from North Carolina whether this unanimous consent implies that no new amendments will be offered?

Mr. WEBB. Oh, no; it does not.

Mr. GARDNER. I have no objection.

The CHAIRMAN. Is there objection to the request of the gentleman from North Carolina?

There was no objection.

The Clerk read as follows:

SEC. 4. That any person engaged in commerce who shall lease or make a sale of goods, wares, merchandise, machinery, supplies, or other commodities for use, consumption, or resale within the United States, or any Territory thereof or the District of Columbia or any insular possession or other place under the jurisdiction of the United States, or fix a price charged therefor, or discount from, or rebate upon such price, on the condition or understanding that the lessee or purchaser thereof shall not use or deal in the goods, wares, merchandise, machinery, supplies, or other commodities of a competitor or competitors of the lessor or seller shall be deemed guilty of a misdemeanor, and upon conviction thereof shall be punished by a fine not exceeding $5,000, or by imprisonment not exceeding one year, or by both, in the discretion of the court.

Mr. [WALTER I.] McCOY [D., N.J.]. Mr. Chairman, I offer the following amendment, which I send to the desk and ask to have read.

The Clerk read as follows:

Page 22, line 14, insert, after the word "seller," the following:

"With the intent of obtaining or establishing a monopoly or of destroying the business of a competitor." . . .

Mr. McCOY. Mr. Chairman, I notice in the report of the committee on this bill, on page 11, the following:

Section 4 of this bill has apparently been much misunderstood, and great confusion seems to have arisen in regard to its provisions. Whether designedly or from a misunderstanding of its purport we know not, but it has been contended very earnestly that its provisions prevent exclusive or sole agencies.

I do not know in whose mind any confusion has or ought to have existed in regard to the question of exactly what this section does mean. Before proceeding with what I have to say I want to ask the members of the committee, when those who are in opposition to this amendment are heard, not to allow any red herring to be drawn across the scent and not to permit the matter to become mixed with this question of leases, because if they do, then they will have argued before the committee not the amendment which I propose, but they will have to go all over the question of the United Shoe Machinery Co.'s tying leases. I am just as much opposed to those as anybody can be. I do not propose by this amendment to permit that thing to be done, and I ask the committee to keep their minds on just the one proposition.

Nobody has maintained in support of this section that it had for its purpose the prohibition of what is known as an agency; that is, a straightaway agency, where there is simply the question of principal on one side and agent on the other. The committee itself says that it is not intended to do away with that sort of thing, and the absurdity of their position in that respect I hope to be able to demonstrate. In other words, the committee says that anybody, any manufacturer or producer, no matter who he is, can have just as many strict agencies as he wants to have. They can be agents who have roofs over their heads, or they can be commercial travelers, traveling throughout the country—that they do not seek to prevent that in any way, but that what they do seek to prevent is the making of contracts to create what are known as sole selling agencies. I do not know how much explanation is necessary in order to show what a so-called sole selling agency is. It has come to have a sort of technical meaning. Of course the number of contracts which can be executed, and by which sole selling agencies, so called, are created, can be infinite in their variety, but the main gist of a sole selling agency contract—and that is the thing which the committee seeks to hit—is a contract by which the man who has a thing to sell undertakes to give an exclusive territory to an agent, and on the other hand undertakes to bind that agent not to sell in that territory any of the goods of a competitor. I want to call the attention of the committee to this fact. I presume they know this much of it, that the Committee on the Judiciary did have hearings in regard to these trust bills, tentative and otherwise. I do not know how many pages of testimony were taken, but a great many pages. I do not claim to have read all of the testimony. I have not, in fact, read it all, nor have I heard it all, but I have, so far as I have had the time, gone through the hearings, and have had in mind what was said when I was present at the hearings, and I believe, although I may be to some degree mistaken, that no member of the committee can point out any objection made by any man who appeared before our committee to these technical sole selling agencies. So far as I have been able to discover anything in the hearings, it will be found at page 140, and I call attention to the fact that it is the testimony of Mr. J. B. Moorehead, of Lexington, Mo., who was the national secretary of the Retail Merchants' Association of the United States.

It is obvious that if there is any harm to be remedied, if any harm has been done to the retail merchants of the country by permitting these sole selling agencies, the secretary of this association would have pointed it out. Let us take it up from the point of view of these retail merchants. I desire to call attention to the fact that the witness is now testifying about one of these so-called tentative bills, and I read from his testimony:

Mr. CARLIN. Do you not think that section 10 of bill No. 1 would give you some relief?
Mr. MOOREHEAD. I am not prepared to say.
Mr. CARLIN. I will read the language of that section to you:
"That it shall be deemed an attempt to monopolize trade or commerce among the several States or with foreign nations or a part thereof for any persons in interstate or foreign commerce to make a sale of goods, wares, or merchandise, or fix a price charged therefor or discount from or rebate upon such price, on the condition or understanding that the purchaser thereof shall not deal in goods, wares, or merchandise of a competitor or competitors of the seller."

Mr. MOOREHEAD. I am not up on forms of law. I do not know whether that would cover the case or not.

Mr. CARLIN. The intention is to liberate the retailer and give him a right to sell anybody's goods he wants to sell and to prevent a contract which would require him to sell exclusively a particular line of goods.

Mr. MOOREHEAD. That may be the difficulty of some lines of retailing, but that is only incidental to the great problem.

The business that is big enough, the aggregation of capital that is big enough to say to the manufacturer: "You sell us your product at such a price. If you do not do it, we will manufacture that product ourselves." That is the main thing. And what is the result?

Mr. CARLIN. You do not catch the idea of this section. The idea is that the manufacturer shall not say to any one man that he shall sell the particular line of goods of that particular manufacturer exclusively. It liberates the retailer. It liberates the retailer from that situation and allows him to buy goods of anybody he wants to and sell them in his store.

Mr. MOOREHEAD. I think that may be all right, but where that might be relevant to one case, there would be hundreds of cases that would not be on that line.

Mr. CARLIN. I am calling your attention to that one thing now, and ask you whether you do not think that would be helpful?

Mr. MOOREHEAD. I see no objection to it now.

That is not to be compared to the big question. Here is the proposition: As I started to say, the manufacturer may be intimidated to sell his goods to a large distributor by having it said to him, "You must sell us these goods at such a price, or we will make them ourselves." What is the result? The big buyer gets the goods at cost, and that gives him a tremendous advantage over the little fellow.

That is all my colleague on the committee could get out of the retailer. So apparently the retailer is not damaged in any way by the making of these sole selling agency contracts. . . .

Mr. GARDNER. In the report Mr. Clayton says in his report that this section "not only does not prohibit or forbid exclusive agencies," and so forth, and the gentleman uses the term "sole selling agencies." Many of us do not understand the difference.

Mr. McCOY. Mr. Chairman, as I stated in the beginning, this bill does not undertake to forbid contracts creating a strict agency, where the agent is a strict agent, and the man on the other side is a strict principal, and I see that I have failed to make the question of a sole selling agency clear. . . .

Mr. Chairman, the gentleman from Massachusetts, by his suggestion, reminds me that I did not complete the explanation of what a sole selling agency is. It involves not only this creation of an exclusive territory, in which the principal will sell only to one person and in which the so-called agent will deal only in the goods of that person, but the so-called agent buys the goods from the principal. That is what is technically known as a sole selling agency. . . .

Mr. MADDEN. It would not prevent the sole selling agent from having a sole selling agency for another class of goods that were not in competition?

Mr. McCOY. Not at all; but simply the one particular kind of goods that the principal is making.

Mr. MADDEN. He could have as many sole selling agencies as he could handle without any conflict with the other in competition.

Mr. McCOY. As many as he could possibly handle. It only relates to one thing or perhaps two or three other things that the principal is making.

Mr. GARDNER. Even yet I do not understand. Now, apparently section 4 forbids any person to make a sale of goods on condition that the lessee or purchaser thereof shall not use or deal in the goods of a competitor.

Mr. McCOY. Yes.

Mr. GARDNER. Now, the report says that this provision is not intended to prevent exclusive agencies. The gentleman, I take it, is contending, however, that the provision does, as a matter of fact, prevent sole selling agencies.

Mr. McCOY. Where the so-called agent buys the goods?

Mr. GARDNER. Where the so-called agent buys the goods; and the gentleman's amendment is intended to permit them—

Mr. McCOY. No; my amendment is aimed simply at—I will read the amendment. It is to leave the section as it stands and forbids that kind of thing. It is to amend the section so as to permit that sort of contract to be made where it is not made with the intent to obtain or establish a monopoly or to destroy the business of a competitor.

Mr. GARDNER. That is what I understand. What I was going to say was that the gentleman's amendment is designed to permit sole selling agencies where the agent buys the goods, provided the transaction is not engaged in for the purpose of restraining trade or creating a monopoly. Is that correct?

Mr. McCOY. That is correct.

Mr. GARDNER. May I ask the gentleman how he interprets these words: "or fix a price charged therefor, or discount from, or rebate upon such price"? What is the need of those words if you forbid the sale of goods.

Mr. McCOY. I do not think they add anything; but the committee itself says, at page 11 of the report, that the words "or fix a price charged therefor, or discount therefrom, or rebate upon such price," are merely descriptive of the different methods used by the manufacturers to induce the dealer or local merchant to enter into this exclusive or tying contract.

Mr. GARDNER. That is all very well; but the report goes on and explains that "the first inducement in every case must of necessity relate to price." Now, suppose it was found that one of these exclusive agents or exclusive purchasers had created a restraint of trade by some device other than the fixation of prices or rebates; might not a court hold that the very inclusion of those words, which the committee says are descriptive, had by implication legalized the use of other methods of discrimination?

Mr. McCOY. I would say to the gentleman from Massachusetts I would rather not discuss that proposition now. The gentleman may be right about it, but I would like simply to take up this question of my amendment.

Mr. GARDNER. I want to get it clear in my mind in connection with the other.

Mr. McCOY. I do not know but that the gentleman is right; but I have not considered that end of it. Now, the committee in its report says that the provision of section 4 "is designed merely to prevent this unfair trade practice, now so common throughout the country, and which is generally regarded by everyone who has given the subject any serious consideration as unjust to the local dealer and to the community and as monopolistic in its effect."

Now, I will call the attention of the committee to what are the facts in regard to the community at large, and who fail to say at any rate in regard to these hearings where they had an opportunity to do. Now, then, let us see what this does. For instance, we have a great many manufacturers of machine tools. Those are these big tools we see in the various machine shops in the country, and I do not need to describe them; I do not need to tell you how bulky they are. They look expensive and they are expensive. Now, these manufacturers of machine tools all make these exclusive selling agencies. They do it for this reason: They are not a trust; they are not combined together in any way to stifle competition. Some of them are not big. There is one in my district, a very small concern, comparatively. Now, if it had to carry a stock of these expensive machine tools all over the United States, wherever they naturally would be in the hands of the ordinary agent—that is, the principal retaining the title and simply turning them over to the agent for sale—do not you see, can not anybody see, that unless they have enormous resources they can not afford to do that sort of thing, and that is the very cause leading to these sole selling agents. . . .

Mr. MADDEN. The very thing the gentleman complains of would prevent anybody starting any new business.

Mr. McCOY. Surely; and I am coming to that. Now, what is the consideration which moves the so-called agent to go into this matter and put up his money? Why it is, of course, that he would get a better price for the machines than he could get otherwise, and it is perfectly natural, because he puts up the money, and he should have a better price than if the machines were sold outright to somebody who did not want to put up the money to carry these goods but wanted them for actual use. In other words, the manufacturer with a small capital goes substantially into a partnership with the agent who is to handle these goods. The manufacturers say, "I will not sell or allow anybody else to sell in that territory." The agent says, "On account of these prices which you have given to me, I will not sell the goods to anybody else." . . .

Mr. STAFFORD. Can the gentleman inform the committee whether these many business houses who have the exclusive selling contracts are protesting against the character of that form of business dealings?

Mr. McCOY. I have protests from everywhere about it.

Mr. STAFFORD. Are they protesting against the character of the contracts?

Mr. McCOY. You mean the people who make the contracts?

Mr. STAFFORD. The persons who make them and the business houses who are the recipients of the contracts.

Mr. McCOY. Not at all. I understand that all the automobile people carry on their business in that way. Let us suppose, for the sake of—

Mr. STAFFORD. And there is the office-furniture business—the Yawman & Erbe, the Shaw-Walker concerns, and any number of other manufacturers that have exclusive contracts for dispensing their wares. . . .

Mr. McCOY. The gentleman asks whether these agents, for whom the committee rather tries to arouse our sympathies, are taking these contracts by having them forced onto them by the manufacturers. I think a little imagination should answer that question. All the automobile concerns, I believe, have these sole selling agency contracts. Now, let us suppose that every one of these agents in the city of Washington should die to-morrow. Do you believe that the automobile manufacturers would have to chase to Washington to get agents? Detroit would be filled with Washingtonians wanting to get these contracts.

The argument made by one of the members of the committee, who principally supports this proposition, is this, that it is unfair that a man should first sell his goods and then exact from the man to whom he has sold them a contract that he will not sell anybody else's goods. Now, the proposition eats itself. One does not first sell the goods and then exact something from that man. He could not do it. If he sold the goods without any form of contract except as to sale and delivery, that would be the end of it. But the contract on the one hand to sell and the contract on the other hand not to sell is a mutual agreement which both of them are perfectly willing to enter into.

Now, the gentleman from Illinois [Mr. MADDEN] has suggested something about somebody going into business. Let us take a couple of young men who have some article for sale which they think is a pretty good article. They think that if it could be properly placed it would have a big sale. They have a small capital. What are they going to do? They can not hire agents, commercial travelers, and send them all over the country. They can not establish agencies all over the country. The only thing they can do, and I believe every lawyer here has known plenty of cases of that kind, is to get somebody who will take one of these sole selling agencies, and who will give his attention to their business and build up a trade for the little man. . . .

Mr. MURDOCK. Does not the argument the gentleman is making put upon the new corporation or new company the necessity of establishing a finely articulated retail business all over the United States, which is the very trouble the committee is trying to reach, thereby shutting out the new man from the retail trade by exclusive contracts?

Mr. McCOY. I do not quite understand the gentleman. Do you mean the committee is endeavoring to remedy by this provision the cessation of retail business?

Mr. MURDOCK. No. The committee is trying to give the new man a chance to get his wares out to the public through existing retail agencies. And does not the gentleman's proposition cut the new firm out of that opportunity?

Mr. McCOY. No. It does not cut them out of the opportunity. The bill cuts them out of the opportunity. It provides that the man who has, for instance, a small invention and wants to market it—it prevents a man who wants to get into any kind of business, without a great amount of capital, from being able to do that. Now, here is one thing the committee does claim, and it is along the line of a suggestion of the gentleman from Kansas. They claim that by creating an agency in a small place and making the so-called agent agree not to sell the goods it throws the community over into the hands of the mail-order houses. On the other hand, they argue that people go to the mail-order stores because of this sole selling agency there, and ⊥ the result of their going is to destroy this retailer who takes this sole order agency. Again, one argument eats the other.

Mr. MADDEN. How can you stop a mail-order man doing that, except by taking his postal privileges away from him?

Mr. McCOY. You can not. But here is what you can do: If a manufacturer has one of these sole selling agencies, he will not permit the mail-order house to sell in that district in competition with that dealer. As this provision stands, it simply means that concerns like the Standard Oil Co., the Tobacco Trust, and all other big concerns that have enough capital to enable them to establish strict agencies all over the United States, will proceed to do business in that way.

Mr. MADDEN. What the gentleman means by "strict agency" is the man who represents the concern and handles the commodity under contract?

Mr. McCOY. They go there and put in a store, and hire the agent, and have the money to do it. But the little fellow, the man you and I know in our districts, is in all kinds of business. He will not be able to compete with people in his line of business simply because he can not have these agencies. He can not carry the goods in these agencies.

Mr. GARDNER. May I see once more if I get the gentleman's idea correctly. Supposing a small manufacturer of automobiles up in Massachusetts, with limited capital, desires to sell his automobiles throughout the Union. If he desires to sell his wares through the kind of agency which this bill permits to exist, then he is obliged to supply all the capital and own all those automobiles?

Mr. McCOY. Absolutely.

Mr. GARDNER. Whereas if he can go to a smart young man in Washington, for instance, and say, "You have got a little capital; I am ready to sell you my automobiles at a low price, but I want to have somebody to hustle my automobiles on the market in preference to other automobiles." As I understand it, this bill says to that manufacturer who has not the capital to own the business himself, "You can not make any such trade in order to have your automobile boosted instead of the Packard automobile."

Mr. McCOY. Absolutely.

Mr. GARDNER. You say that the manufacturer who has a small capital ought to be able to sell his wares to some smart young man on an exclusive contract, so that he may compete with the manufacturer with large capital, provided that his agreement with the smart young man is not designed to create a monopoly in restraint of trade?

Mr. McCOY. Absolutely.

Mr. GARDNER. If I get the gentleman's idea—

Mr. McCOY. Absolutely. My amendment is in the interest of the small man, and the committee proposition is in the interest of the big man.

Mr. GARDNER. Precisely, if I understand the gentleman correctly.

Mr. McCOY. That is the exact situation.

Mr. STAFFORD. As I understand these contracts in the business world, they are for a limited period, and they do not place any hardship upon the contractee, the one who has the exclusive agency. He can terminate it under certain stipulations or at the termination of the contract, which is usually for one year or two years.

Mr. McCOY. The contract runs for a short period, and if an article is worth selling you can get hundreds of people who will seek these contracts.

Now, I want to say to the members of the committee that I would ask those who oppose my amendment to point out where in the hearings that sort of thing was complained of. And if they can not find it in the hearings then I ask proof from somewhere or other, except from mere statements that these things may happen, to justify this section without my amendment.

I yield the balance of my time.

Mr. MADDEN. Mr. Chairman, if section 4 of the bill is not amended along the line suggested by the gentleman from New Jersey [Mr. McCOY] it will restrict the opportunity of men who have never been in business before from going into any business at all. The bill purports to protect the small business man in his right to do business; but the truth is that it protects the man who needs no protection, and discriminates against the man who ought to be encouraged. A man can not go into business originally, under this provision of the bill, without taking somebody's customer away; and if he takes a man's customer away, under this section of the bill he commits a crime, because he does the man an injury. If we are not to permit men to go into business because they take the business of somebody else away from them, thereby injuring them in their business, and as a result of that commit a crime, we are not opening up competition in business; we are establishing a monopoly by this bill.

The agencies that must, as a matter of course, be permitted to be established in order to develop the growing business of the men engaged in the industrial affairs of America can not be restricted. We must have the right to establish these agencies or we can not expand. We have a convention being held in this city to-day, gathered from every quarter of America, for the purpose of devising means by which we can expand our foreign trade, and the men who are here are men who are versed in the commercial life of the world. You can not restrict the advance of commerce by any law. You can not change the trend of events by any language that you can write into any section of any bill. The development of the world can not be stopped by an attempt to limit monopoly and to extend the right of competition. It becomes apparent at once that the wise men who have tried for more than 2,000 years to regulate trade by law and to surround that trade with protection in every way, and to fix punishments for violations of the law, have not been improved upon much by the gentlemen who sit at the table of the Judiciary Committee of this House, and who have had the honor to prepare this bill. The business of the world will be done because of the activity of the men of the world— . . .

. . . To say that you can not establish an agency to put on the market the goods of the man who is starting in business for the first time, is to say that you restrict the opportunity for men to engage in business. A man with $10,000 capital, making a specialty, may have sufficient money to manufacture a small quantity of the specialty; but he has not a sufficient amount of money to expand the sale of this commodity throughout the country; and so he must, as a matter of course, engage some man who is willing to take an exclusive agency, and to that man he will sell his goods for delivery and sale within a given territory. The contract between those two men will provide that in consideration of the sale of a certain quantity of this specialty, a certain percentage will be delivered to the agent who has the contract, at a fixed price below the price at the factory. Automobile manufacturers engage agents everywhere to sell their automobiles exclusively, and they allow them 20 per cent, and out of that 20 per cent the agent pays his own expenses, his rent, his salesmen's salaries, and everything connected with the operation of the agency. . . .

Mr. McCOY. Is it not frequently a term of these contracts that the continuance of the contract depends upon the agent selling a certain number or a certain quantity of the goods?

Mr. MADDEN. Certainly.

Mr. McCOY. So that he is pushed in the competition.

Mr. MADDEN. I was just coming to that. The terms of the contracts themselves provide that the agency will not be allowed to remain in the man who has the contract unless he produces certain results, unless he is able to pay for a certain quantity of the commodity placed on the market. And so by the establishment of these agencies, by encouraging men of small means to enter business and push their trade into every section of the Nation, you not only encourage competition but you actually create the competition; whereas if you say to a man that he can not establish an agency, you immediately prevent competition and establish a monopoly.

In connection with this legislation I have heard a good deal said to the effect that a man ought not to be allowed to select his own customer, or that he may be permitted under certain circumstances to select his own customer. Anybody would imagine, from the reading of the bill, permitting a man to select his own customers, that the people of the United States are clamoring to buy the goods of the various manufacturers of the country. The fact is there is not a manufacturer anywhere in the United States, unless it be the Standard Oil Co. and the American Tobacco Co., that have not men all over the country ransacking every nook and corner in order to find customers to whom they may sell their goods. . . .

Mr. [HALVOR] STEENERSON [R., Minn.]. The gentleman stated that the usual commission was 20 per cent on automobiles. Is it not a fact that the system here referred to permits an exorbitant charge to the ultimate consumer, and is not there a larger commission ⊥ provided for the middleman than there is on the ordinary articles, like wagons, buggies, and so forth?

Mr. MADDEN. I do not know how much commission ought to be allowed for the sale of automobiles.

Mr. STEENERSON. Is it not a fact that automobiles are unreasonably high?

Mr. MADDEN. I do not know; I do not know what they cost.

Mr. STEENERSON. Do they not allow an exorbitant commission?

Mr. MADDEN. I do not think it is an exorbitant commission to a man who runs an agency, who has to sell exclusive machines, who has rent and taxes to pay, who pays in advance for the machines, invests his money, has to pay for advertising, employs salesmen, bookkeepers, and all those things that enter into the conduct of a business. I maintain that there is no business in the United States conducted by anybody, unless it is a business of a fabulous amount, that can be conducted for less than 15 per cent for the average business done. If that be true, it can not be said that 20 per cent is a high commission to pay, because out of the 20 per cent he must pay 15 per cent for expenses, and if he can retain 5 per cent he is not overpaid.

Mr. STEENERSON. But the cost of production—

Mr. MADDEN. I do not know anything about the cost of production. It may be that the manufacturer can build a machine for $1,000 that he sells for $2,000.

Mr. STEENERSON. Does not this system enable the manufacturer as well as the agent to dispose of his goods for three or four times the price that it costs to produce them?

Mr. MADDEN. Any argument that we might have on the floor would not settle that question. It takes scientific information, scientific organization properly assembled, properly conducted, to run a great business, and if anybody on this floor can tell me how a great business enterprise can be conducted successfully, and tell me what it ought to cost to conduct that enterprise, I would like to get his picture. [Laughter.]

Mr. FLOYD of Arkansas. Mr. Chairman, section 4 of this bill is intended for the benefit of the consumer. I am not going to controvert the contention that the tying or exclusive contract forbidden in this section is for the benefit of the manufacturer. I am not going to controvert that this system may be so used as to be beneficial to the retailer, but our friends who are opposed to this provision never look beyond the manufacturer or local dealer, never look to the interests and the rights of the consumers of this country. I desire to speak for the consumer, and to show you how this provision will be beneficial not only to the consumer but to every independent small manufacturer in this country.

The contention that under this system and by this kind of contract the small dealer can build up a trade is an absurdity. Here is the proposition. One of these big manufacturers carries a line of manufactured goods into your town and makes a contract to the effect that he will place the goods with a local dealer on condition that the merchant will not handle the goods, wares, or merchandise of his competitor in that line. What is the effect of it? They have commodities that are absolutely essential to the business of the merchant or small dealer, and in order that no other manufacturer may sell anything that that merchant uses to that merchant, he makes this exclusive or tying contract. If he is a manufacturer of shoes, he must be supplied with every implement, or otherwise the big manufacturer of shoe machinery would withdraw everything and cut off his supplies. The best illustration you can find of this evil practice is the leasing system of the United Shoe Machinery Co. They lease on condition that the man who takes their goods under the lease shall not deal in the commodities of any competitor. . . .

Mr. McCOY. Do they lease on condition that he will not deal in any other goods; is it not on condition that he will not use any other goods?

Mr. FLOYD of Arkansas. Well, will not use, because the shoe-machinery company will not sell, but lease their machines. The manufacturers of shoes do not own the machines, and yet the gentleman from New Jersey stands for that kind of a system in this country.

Mr. McCOY. I know the gentleman wants to be fair. He knows that I do not stand for the system of the United Shoe Machinery Co., does not he?

Mr. FLOYD of Arkansas. I have heard the gentleman from New Jersey repeatedly say that he did not; but he stands for a principle that has made the shoe machinery company a gigantic monopoly in this country, and if he stands for the system he stands for encouraging the building up of other like monopolies. What counts it to the American people for the gentleman to oppose the shoe machinery company if he stands for the principle that enables them to build up and enables them to maintain a great monopoly?

Mr. McCOY. Is not my amendment aimed at monopoly?

Mr. FLOYD of Arkansas. The gentleman's amendment is practically in the language of the Sherman law so far as monopoly is concerned, and yet the circuit court of appeals has held that this particular contract is not within the provisions of the Sherman law, and hence we insist that a change of the language shall be made so that it will be within the law.

What is the effect of it? The gentleman from Minnesota struck at the vital point of this whole controversy. It is the consumer. The gentleman from New Jersey seems not to understand that there is any testimony in the hearings bearing upon this question. If he will read the hearings, he will find an abundance of testimony condemning this system. . . .

One manufacturer of rim glasses was before our committee and he was a great advocate of this system. He made frames for $1.25, sold them to the dealer for $2, and required the dealer to sell them to the consumer for $5. The whole effect of this system and practice is to drive out competition locally and to enable the manufacturer to get higher prices. That is not the only evil of it. It discommodes the American people everywhere. Whenever a manufacturer comes along and makes one of these exclusive or tying contracts and gets the local merchant bound down to the proposition or agreement that he will handle this particular commodity, and will not handle any other commodity of like kind, manufactured or produced by a competitor, and then cuts out all other like commodities, the consumers must take that commodity or nothing, if they deal with that merchant. . . .

Mr. [ALFRED G.] ALLEN [D., Ohio]. Is not the case that the gentleman cited just now, the eyeglass case, one that involves the principle of resale, fixing the resale price, while the one that we have under consideration is one where the manufacturer has simply sold his machine or whatever it may be to the merchant or factor who represents him in the community?

Mr. FLOYD of Arkansas. True, and these same men who were before the committee opposing this provision spent days asking the committee to bring in a provision to annul the effect of the Supreme Court decision,[5.532] which denies them the right to fix the retail price. . . .

Mr. McCOY. Do I understand the gentleman to contend that the people who were opposing section 4 were there advocating the right to fix the retail price?

Mr. FLOYD of Arkansas. Not necessarily all of them.

Mr. McCOY. Were any of them?

Mr. FLOYD of Arkansas. I think so.

Mr. McCOY. I disagree with the gentleman. There was not anybody there who was advocating that.

Mr. FLOYD of Arkansas. The gentleman from New Jersey insists that under this system the small man can promote his business. Let us see. The very reverse is true. The big, the powerful manufacturer makes it impossible for the small man to get in; but suppose one does get in and gets an exclusive contract of some kind, then you have two monopolies, and you never get beyond monopoly. If you had three or four, they would all result in restricted monopolies, and in the meantime the American public are denied many conveniences, and denied them by means which are tending all the time to build up monopoly and to create higher prices. . . .

Mr. GARDNER. Does not the gentleman think that the fact that all of these automobile companies have been able to build themselves up from small organizations by this very system has resulted in a benefit to the consumer?

Mr. FLOYD of Arkansas. The gentleman takes an illustration in which I am not particularly concerned—the automobile.

Mr. GARDNER. But the gentleman has been using the United Shoe Machinery Co. as an illustration.

[5.532] Dr. Miles Medical Co. v. John D. Park & Sons Co., 220 U.S. 373, 31 S. Ct. 376, 55 L. Ed. 502 (1911).

Mr. FLOYD of Arkansas. It is the American consumer, the man who buys bread and meat and medicine, the man who ⊥ labors in the sweat of his brow and who toils in season and out in order to eke out an existence that I am referring to; and to allow a system that will permit these powerful monopolies to deny them the comforts of life and extort high prices from them under exclusive contracts is what I object to. . . .

The gentleman from Massachusetts has mentioned the automobile business. I am very glad that he did. Under this system, this favored system, this system that is going to build up the small man, it is in testimony before our committee that these contracts, exclusive contracts, have enabled one automobile company, with a capital of $2,000,000, to make a profit of $25,000,000 in one year, and they or their representative gave the testimony before your committee. . . .

How did they do it? How did they make it? Do you think that any business man in America with a capital of $2,000,000 can earn a profit of $25,000,000 in one year on that $2,000,000 alone? Not at all. . . .

I decline to yield at this time. I want to get through with this automobile business. I am not criticizing this automobile company, but I am describing the method they use, which I think is wrong and detrimental to the American public, one that makes automobiles higher than they should be and gives the manufacturers unusual and unjustifiable profits, not on their own investment, but upon the investment of men who deal with them, whose hands are tied and whose money is invested in property bound by an exclusive contract. . . .

I decline to yield until I get through answering the question of the gentleman from Massachusetts. How did they do it? They made contracts with agents throughout the country—exclusive agents—and they did not turn over their machines to these exclusive agents on their own money, but they made each agent take six machines and pay for them; and after he had taken six machines and paid the full price therefor they called him a sole selling agent and made him enter into a contract that he would not buy or handle or use the automobiles of any competitor. . . .

. . . I am not through with the automobile business. They made these local agents, so called, buy their machines and pay for six machines, and then they gave them enormous profits to sell them to the general public, to make them active, and the result was that they sold many of these automobiles at high prices and made enormous profits, and at the end of the year this automobile company in footing up its accounts found that with an investment of $2,000,000 they had earned $25,000,000 profit in one year, speculating on other men's money, and the consumer paid the bills and paid the profits.

The dealer's hands were tied. The man who dealt with that particular dealer had to purchase that particular class of automobiles and could not buy any other. . . .

Mr. McCOY. Is not the net result of the Ford operations that the Ford machines are now cheaper than baby carriages used to be?

Mr. FLOYD of Arkansas. I do not know how high baby carriages used to be [laughter], but the price of the Ford machine, if they are making a profit of $25,000,000 a year on a $2,000,000 investment, is certainly high enough for American customers and purchasers. . . .

⊥ Mr. ALLEN. Mr. Chairman, I have read this amendment carefully, and it seems to me that the gentleman in charge of the bill ought not to object to it, because I think it is reasonable, and should be adopted for the same reasons that impelled the committee to incorporate substantially the same language in section 2 of the bill, relating to price discrimination. While it is stated in the report that there is no objection to the establishment of exclusive agencies and no intention to prohibit same, yet, if the language is not amended as proposed by the gentleman from New Jersey [Mr. McCOY], all that a concern that wanted to evade the law would have to do would be to say to its agent, "If, after instructing you in the use of our machine, advertising it, and so forth, you sell the similar goods of some other concern we will decline to renew our contract with you," and thus evade the law. Now, we do not want to write the law in that way. What we want to do is to write a law that will promote competition by enabling the small manufacturer to maintain agencies throughout the country, where otherwise he could not do so. The great corporations are able to maintain their own selling organizations. Therefore this amendment appeals to me as being in the interest of the small manufacturers.

Now, I want to have read in my time a letter from the Business Men's Club of Cincinnati, Ohio, where this matter was thoroughly discussed, and also a letter and resolutions from the Chamber of Commerce of Cincinnati in reference to the same subject.

The CHAIRMAN. The Clerk will read.

The Clerk read as follows:

The Business Men's Club Co.,
Cincinnati, May 16, 1914.

Hon. Alfred G. Allen,
House of Representatives, Washington, D. C.

MY DEAR MR. ALLEN: At the regular monthly meeting of the board of directors of the Business Men's Club held last night a resolution was passed protesting against the passage of section 4 of H. R. 15657, and directing me to convey to you the protest of the Business Men's Club's directors and to ask you to see that it receives proper attention and is presented as soon as possible to the proper committee considering the bill.

The resolution passed is as follows:

"*Resolved*, That the board of directors of the Business Men's Club Co., of Cincinnati, strongly protests against the passage of section 4 of House bill 15657 because—

"This section as it stands is in the interest of the large combines and monopolies. They do not need the middleman as do their smaller competitors. They can afford to establish their own selling organization in the various market centers—in fact, most of them now have their own selling organizations—and this section, prohibiting exclusive selling agreements, takes away the only means by which the smaller competitors of these big combines are enabled to compete with them in selling. The smaller concerns, as a rule, can not afford to establish their own selling organizations, and therefore must have the aid of the middleman.

"This section would prohibit smaller concerns from selecting an exclusive middleman representative under an exclusive arrangement. They would have to sell to all middlemen, which would mean indifferent and inefficient representation in competition with the bigger concern with its direct selling organization. When all middlemen may handle identical products, then no middleman takes any special interest in it.

"Under the present method of exclusive selling arrangements there is ample competition between the various middlemen for the benefit of the consumer. Each middleman is fighting every other middleman in the interest of his exclusive line. If the exclusive agency arrangement is abolished and the manufacturer must sell all middlemen [*sic*], who in turn must sell all competing makes of the same article, then economy and efficiency in selling are destroyed and selling expenses greatly increased; for this would mean that the middleman must maintain larger stocks, larger warehouses, greater number of salesmen, etc. These increased expenses must ultimately be paid by the consumer.

"The 'exclusive agency agreement' method of sale is very widely employed to-day in all the various channels of business. Certain makes of shoes, hats, clothes, tobaccos, foods, manufacturing supplies, automobiles, etc., are handled exclusively by certain middlemen. A provision, therefore, which makes this arrangement a misdemeanor under the Sherman Act, if enacted in the law, would bring about a very wide disturbance of existing business methods. All of this seems unnecessary and unwise, inasmuch as the 'exclusive agency' method of sale as practiced to-day does not in any way act in restraint of trade or of full competition for the benefit of the consumer.

"*Be it further resolved*, That a copy of this resolution be sent to Congressmen ALFRED G. ALLEN and STANLEY BOWDLE, with the request that it be presented as soon as possible to the proper committee considering the bill."

Thanking you for the interest you may take in the matter, I am,

Respectfully, yours,

Rutherford H. Cox,
Civic Secretary, Business Men's Club.

Cincinnati Chamber of Commerce,
Cincinnati, May 20, 1914.

Hon. Alfred G. Allen,
House of Representatives, Washington, D. C.

MY DEAR MR. ALLEN: Inclosed please find copy of resolution adopted by the board of directors of the Cincinnati Chamber of Commerce at a meeting held May 19, 1914.

If consistent, the chamber of commerce would appreciate your support of this amendment, and believes you will find, upon investigation, ⊥ that this feature was included in the bill under

a misapprehension of business conditions and that its adoption would tend to stifle rather than promote competition.
Very truly, yours,

W. C. Culkins, Executive Secretary.

Whereas the Clayton bill, No. 15657, now pending in the House of Representatives, forbids the establishment of exclusive selling agreements between the manufacturer and the "middleman" and makes the same a misdemeanor under the Sherman law; and

Whereas the present method of establishing exclusive selling agreements is widespread and a common practice in business; and

Whereas it tends to promote competition by enabling the smaller producer to maintain agencies at many places where he would be unable to provide a selling organization, thereby leaving that territory under the exclusive control of the larger organizations, who maintain their own individual selling force: Therefore be it

Resolved by the board of directors of the chamber of commerce, That we are opposed to the inclusion in the Clayton bill of the provisions prohibiting such selling agreements and urge that they be stricken from the bill: and be it further

Resolved, That copies be sent to the Representatives of this county and to the Senators from Ohio. . . .

Mr. IGOE. Mr. Chairman, I desire to have read in my time a letter, which I send to the Clerk's desk. This letter is from probably the largest shoe manufacturing company in the world and is in favor of section 4 of the bill.

The CHAIRMAN. The Clerk will read the letter.

The Clerk read as follows:

St. Louis, Mo., May 20, 1914.

Hon. William L. Igoe,
House of Representatives, Washington, D. C.

MY DEAR SIR: The Clayton bill (H. R. 15657), introduced in the House on May 2, is of deep interest to shoe manufacturers.

Particularly is this true with regard to section 4 of said bill.

In shoe manufacturing there prevails to-day more keen, active competition than exists in any other great industry, but progress and development in shoe manufacturing is being retarded by the lack of competition in shoe machinery.

The present system of leasing shoe machinery, with stipulations that the machines so leased shall exclude the use of similar machines of another make, has reached a high degree of monopoly in shoe machinery.

It appears to the shoe manufacturer that more time has been spent in developing and perfecting the various and numerous clauses in the leases by the Shoe Machinery Co. than has been given to development and improvement of machines.

Under the lease system when a factory is once equipped with machines which pay a constant and high royalty to the machinery company, there is no incentive to the machinery company to put new and improved machines into such a factory, for by so doing the profit-paying machines then in operation will be made useless by the later models.

This strong incentive to stifle improvement in shoe machinery is one of if not the greatest evil of "exclusive use" at which the Clayton bill is directed.

Respectfully, yours,

International Shoe Co.,
By F. C. Rand.

• • • •

Mr. STEENERSON. Mr. Chairman. I am opposed to the amendment and I favor the provision as it stands. While the gentleman from Illinois [Mr. MADDEN] was discussing this amendment he referred particularly to the price of automobiles, and he admitted that the result of this system was to maintain the retail price—the price to the consumer of that article—no matter how much competition there might be in the actual supply. And that is the result of the operation of this system, namely, that it destroys competition in price. You might have a billion automobiles for sale, of one hundred thousand different varieties, and yet you would have to pay five or six or ten times more for them than it costs to produce them. . . .

Now, take this system, and it may be said as to certain lines it is all right. Now, I will illustrate it in a matter that affects the actual living expenses. Some years ago my attention was called to the fact that on a line of railroad running out of St. Paul, Minn., we had a number of towns located in a rich farming country where they raised live stock, and one of these farmers asked me why they could not sell a fat steer or even a corn-fed steer to the local butcher, but that the local butcher had to buy his meat from a refrigerator car sent out by the Beef Trust from St. Paul. I went to the butcher shops in several of those towns and was informed that in order to get fresh beef they had to buy it from that trust. If they bought from the farmer, then they could not get these other staple articles that every butcher shop has got to keep or get out of business, for instance, lard, ham, bacon, cheese, salt fish, pickles, and various other of these side lines.

Now, if they could not buy those articles they could not keep shop, and they would not sell them to them because they did not buy their fresh meat from them. If they bought one steer from a farmer, either dressed or killed it themselves, they could not buy these other articles, and the result was, that although a laboring man in one of those towns could have bought his meat for 10 or 15 cents a pound and still give the butcher a reasonable profit, if the butcher had been able to buy from the farmers, as a matter of fact he had to pay 25 to 30 cents a pound, an enormous profit to the Beef Trust.

Now, this proposition contained in this bill is the only proposition I have seen yet coming from the Democratic Party that will actually tend to reduce the cost of living. I have criticized their tariff bill as failing to reduce the cost of living, and I stand by every word I have said, but they have, either intentionally or accidentally, in this section hit upon a way by which the ultimate consumer will in a certain degree receive the benefit and have a little chance to get a lower cost of living. [Applause.] . . .

Mr. McCOY. Now, I would like to have the gentleman point out how section 4 of this bill meets that particular situation which he has described up in his State.

Mr. STEENERSON. I say that the man could not be supplied with these other articles unless he bought these articles.

Mr. McCOY. That has nothing to do with this section.

Mr. STEENERSON. Oh, yes; it has.

Mr. McCOY. Not with my amendment.

Mr. STEENERSON. The practice in some of those places has been destroyed by the State law, but, for instance, there are articles such as was read from the desk, in the letter presented by the gentleman from Ohio [Mr. ALLEN], articles of food, for instance, cereal food, that cost 1 cent a pound to produce, and they sell them for 15 cents a pound, and you exclude the right to sell any other competing article.

Mr. McCOY. There is no testimony before the committee to that effect.

Mr. STEENERSON. I know there is not, but we have got to go by our experience throughout the country. There is the article of stock food, for instance. It is a matter of common knowledge that one manufacturer of stock food in Minneapolis, who gets his screenings and his bark from the sawmill for only a fraction of a cent a pound, through this tying system excludes all other articles from his exclusive agencies and is enabled to charge an exorbitant price. Of course he spends a very large part of it for fraudulent advertising, such as is described in the report on this bill, and the result is that people pay three or four times as much for the article as it costs. There is the test. It is a system that does not tend to supply the public goods at a reasonable price or that tolerates competition in price. It does not tend to efficiency. The test of efficiency is cheapness to the consumer. Price is ordinarily governed by supply and demand, but this system nullifies that law and enables the manufacturer and middleman to exploit the consumer at will. It is a system that is indefensible from the public point of view. . . .

There is the test of the system: Will it produce a more economical distribution of the necessities of life? Will the abolition of this system tend to give to the consumer cheaper clothing, cheaper food, and cheaper vehicles? I asked the gentleman from Illinois about the comparative profit there was in selling other vehicles, like sleighs, wagons, and buggies. Does anybody suppose that the manufacturer of bobsleighs or of lumber wagons or of buggies would expect to give his agent 20 per cent commission, or that he could sell his buggy to his agent for two or three times what it cost to produce it? No. They are articles which enter into ordinary commerce, and the tendency is to produce them as cheaply as possible and to give the benefit of that cheaper production to the man who buys them, whereas no matter if you live in a land of plenty, no matter if the automobile is a vehicle that is as plentiful as the air you breathe, under this system you would have to pay three or four or five times more than it costs to produce them.

I am opposed to this amendment and am in favor of the provision of the bill. . . .

⊥ Mr. MURDOCK. Mr. Chairman, my intention is to go with the committee on this proposition, although I think anyone who has sat here for the last hour and listened to this discussion must in honesty confess that it is completely confusing. It has been proved here that a sales agency is, under certain circumstances, a good thing, and it undoubtedly has been proved here, on the contrary, that a sales agency can be a very bad thing, and both propositions are true. A monopoly, exercising the power which comes through a sales agency, can crush the retail trade down, and has crushed it down; can prey upon the ultimate consumer, and does prey upon him. Yet at the same time the instrument of a sales agency can be used, as in the beginning of a new business, for the benefit of the retail trade and for the benefit of the consumer. ⊥9406

This situation, which is so plainly exemplified in the contradictions of this discussion, is a natural result of trying to write into law statutory prohibitions against business forms by adopting definitions of changing business practices. Take, for instance, the actual practical application of this section 4. We are simply turning the matter over to the courts. For after Congress shall have passed it, made it law, the Attorney General will, with timidity and hesitation, attempt to enforce it. It will finally reach the courts for interpretation, and after the lapse of 8, 10, or 12 years the business world will reach some sort of a definite understanding about the actual meaning of the section. What will happen to business in the meantime? Advantage to the powerful and monopolistic, and harm and disadvantage to smaller business.

The Democratic Party had its chance this year to create an interstate trade commission with real power to differentiate between big business which is monopoly and big business which is not monopoly, between monopoly which is harmful and big business which is not. You did not embrace that opportunity, and you are going to pay your penalty in a good many different ways. You stand before the country to-day timid and hesitating. You have against you the great predatory powers, and they are using your very hesitant course of action here in this trust program to terrorize small business. I want to read to the gentleman from Arkansas [Mr. FLOYD] a letter which I have received. By the way, I am not antagonizing the position of the gentleman from Arkansas on this particular section in so doing. A merchant in my district has received a letter from the president of the Pictorial Review, a fashion publication in the city of New York. This letter, sent to me by William Allen White, of Emporia, Kans., is as follows:

New York, May 1, 1914.

DEAR SIR: We take the privilege of writing you on a subject of vital importance to yourself and the country at large. It is no doubt evident to you that prosperity has been lost somewhere in this country, owing to the mischievous activities of the politicians, as recognized by all men.

We inclose herewith draft of a letter which embraces the views of a majority of the thinking business people of our section of the country and which should be addressed to the President of the United States, the Congress, and members of the Interstate Commerce Commission, respectively. Might we suggest, if you agree with us, that you take the trouble of writing letters of a similar character to the President, the Members of the United States Senate and the House of Representatives from your State? If you prefer to use copies of the inclosed letter we will mail you as many copies as you can conveniently use. Just send us a postal card. It will be more effective, however, if you write them on your own letterheads. The sooner this appeal is made the greater effect it will have on the politicians who have caused the loss of prosperity.

Inclosed find a list of names and addresses to whom the letter should be sent, but we omit the names of the Representatives and Senators from your State, with whom you are no doubt familiar.

Yours, respectfully,

The Pictorial Review Co.
W. P. Almelt, President.

With this letter is a draft of another letter to be addressed to Members of Congress, the President of the United States, the Interstate Commerce Commissioners, the Speaker of the House, and others. This draft of a proposed letter is as follows:

Honored Sir:

We respectfully appeal to your sense of justice and ask in the name of the suffering American people, in the name of common sense, why wantonly harass business at this juncture when it is struggling for its very existence?

Why throw more thousands of men idle when so many families are already starving?

Why subject business to any experimental legislation now, when it is not prosperous? Postpone it. Drastic action on your part is a peril at this time. What we do need is a little building up—no more tearing down. We have had a sufficiency of experimental legislation for the present.

The granting of the petition of the eastern railroads for a 5 per cent freight increase will do more for the prosperity and development of the country than all legislation against unlawful restraint and monopolies. Such a determination will result in a movement forward, not backward, and any contrary determination by the Interstate Commerce Commission will emphasize the fact that Washington hostility is balking prosperity. The merchants of this country are vitally interested. Business must not be retarded, otherwise commercial failures will increase. The continual senseless attacks by governmental bodies upon merchants, by impending assaults upon railroad, industrial and mercantile corporations, revision of the tariff, and currency reform have resulted in sinking business to such an extent that it has thrown hundreds of thousands out of employment, reduced wages, and decreased values in railroad industries and mercantile corporations to the extent of at least $3,000,000,000.

The most serious situation that confronts the country to-day is the fact that unemployment is growing more acute. We need relief. We ask the Congress of the United States to halt before it is too late. Postpone all antibusiness legislation. Give the country a rest, and last but not least permit Congress to earn a well deserved early rest.

Yours, respectfully,

This letter from this New York concern is apparently sent to dry goods men all over the land, asking them to write to all these various officials in Washington to cease what the letter designates antibusiness legislation. It is part, apparently, of the plan of the great powers in New York City to terrorize small business and the effort is not fruitless, for that terror has reached the hearts of the Democratic leaders. You are putting through this body and expect to pass through the Senate halfway patch-work legislation that will not reach the sore spot in this country, but which will add to already deplorable business confusion. When you do that you are playing into the hands of the big interests who want no legislation at all, who want merely further confusion and delay. That is the truth of the matter. You had a chance on the Democratic side this year, and I was hoping that you would take advantage of it, to give to an interstate trade commission power to make the differentiations, which would clarify instead of befogging the business world. You did not take it. You passed the problem up to the courts, and we will wait 8 or 10 or 12 years for them to tell us what section 4 means. The country can not afford to wait. The larger interests are all the time growing larger and more powerful, and little business is growing more desperate. And all the time the monopoly pirates, fattening upon inadequate statutes or delay, are working to induce the smaller men out over the country to write to Congressmen protesting against any legislation at all. The country needs legislation, but it needs legislation that will bring quick remedies to business ills, and not put the matter over into the overcrowded courts, ill adapted for this work, while the honest business of the country is made to wait helplessly and hopelessly on through the years. [Applause.]

Mr. WEBB. Mr. Chairman, there may be some of the 23 sections of this bill that are open to criticism along the line the gentleman has just made, that they are of doubtful meaning, for it is sometimes very hard to make words in the English language express just exactly what you mean; but I believe this section 4 is the least open to that objection of any section in the bill, and I am rather surprised that my friend from Kansas [Mr. MURDOCK] should make that criticism of this particular section. Stripped of some of its verbiage, that section reads as follows:

SEC. 4. That any person * * * who shall lease or make a sale of goods, * * * or fix a price charged therefor, or discount from, or rebate upon such price, on the condition or understanding that the lessee or purchaser thereof shall not use or deal in the goods * * * of a competitor * * * shall be deemed guilty of a misdemeanor.

It means simply this, that if I am a manufacturer or a wholesaler, and go to a small town and pick out the most popular merchant in that town—I have advertised my goods well—and, of course, naturally he is anxious to buy them. I go to this most popular merchant and tell him that I will let him buy my goods, provided he will not sell or carry in stock any of my competitor's goods. Now, I do not know how other gentlemen may look at such a contract, but that contract, in my opinion, is in and of itself a contract in restraint of trade. Enough of those particular restraining contracts combined would make such manufacturer or wholesaler guilty of violating the Sherman antitrust law. One act, one contract, would not come within the meaning of the Sherman antitrust law, but a series of acts, each one of which we condemn in this section, would bring them within the terms of the Sherman antitrust law, and what we are trying to do is to forbid the various individual acts which irresistibly lend to monopoly....

Mr. [H. H.] SELDOMRIDGE [D., Colo.]. This provision, as I read it, seems to affect the seller of the goods and not the purchaser. Suppose there is a merchant in town who desires to purchase a line of goods handled by another dealer, made by some manufacturing concern, under this bill he could not compel the manufacturer to sell these goods to him.

Mr. WEBB. I do not quite understand the gentleman.

Mr. SELDOMRIDGE. I have in mind a manufacturer of a line of stock food. I am engaged in selling stock food. It is sold by my competitor, and I can not buy it because it is being handled by my competitor. Is there anything in the bill which would allow me to compel the manufacturer or producer to sell to me? As I read the bill I am prevented from buying it.

Mr. WEBB. Oh, no; not at all. You could not compel him to sell to you. He can choose his customers. All this section forbids is that when I sell goods to a purchaser and get my money for them I can not at the same time contract with him that he shall not sell anybody's goods which compete with mine....

Mr. MOORE. Suppose I am the manufacturer of a soap and I make a specialty of it. I have advertised it extensively, and I go into the town which the gentleman has referred to and try to make an arrangement with the local merchant that he will sell my soap. I have gone to great expense in advertising, but I do not say to him that I want him not to use the goods of my competitor. Am I violating the law?

Mr. WEBB. Not at all.

Mr. MOORE. If I build up a trade and establish a reputation for my goods, I can go into the gentleman's town and make an arrangement with the local dealer to sell my goods, provided I do not say that he must not sell the goods of my competitor?

Mr. WEBB. Yes; so long as you do not bind him not to sell your competitor's goods.

Mr. MOORE. Suppose I am the inventor and the manufacturer of a phonograph and I have devised certain records that produce sound more clearly than other phonographs, and I go into the gentleman's town and offer the local dealer my business, the exclusive right to sell my particular records, and another and inferior article is offered to that dealer, am I to be punished because by reason of my inventive genius, superior knowledge, and the superiority of my article, I say to the local dealer that I will give him my exclusive trade and that he is not to put on the shelves something that will be advertised as "just as good," thus faking the public?

Mr. WEBB. Yes; you are to be punished if you make a contract with him that will prevent him from selling a competitive article. He should be left free to sell such articles as he chooses to keep in stock.

Mr. MOORE. Suppose I have a proprietary medicine, a cough cure, selling at 25 cents a bottle, and some one has something not so good, but which can be produced a little cheaper, and I make an arrangement with the dealer as against the inferior article. Can I still be punished?

Mr. WEBB. If you make a contract with the merchant that he shall not sell any competing goods but yours, you are to be punished, and you ought to be punished. Let the public find out the inferior quality of the goods, but give the merchant freedom in his business. The public is more interested in preventing monopoly than in the quality of the goods. If we can prevent monopoly, the public will soon discover the fake or inferior goods. . . .

Mr. [HENRY T.] HELGESEN [R., N.D.]. Take the illustration used by the gentleman from Pennsylvania, where a manufacturer goes into the town and offers business to the dealer, but does not say to him that he must not handle the goods of any competitor, but says, "If you will handle mine I will give you 5 or 10 per cent extra discount," would he be punishable?

Mr. WEBB. Yes; he would be; he would come within the intent and meaning of this section if such agreement is to prevent the sale of competitive goods. . . .

Mr. TOWNER. Does not the gentleman think that this will result in a decrease of competition rather than an increase of competition, which of course we all desire? For instance, three dealers handling phonographs may each handle them all; would not there be more competition if each handled one than if all three dealers handled all of the phonographs? Is not there likely to be a decrease of competition?

Mr. WEBB. In answer to that I will say that it is barely possible, but not probable. Business should be left to take care of itself if not built on immoral or illegal contracts. I do not believe there is a man on either side of the House who will say that it is right or fair business for a manufacturer to make a contract with the merchant to sell only his goods and that he shall not sell goods that compete with his. It ought not to be allowed. . . .

Mr. ALLEN. This amendment offered by the gentleman from New Jersey does not affect the proposition, for the gentleman has stated "it shall be done with intent to establish a monopoly or destroy the business of a competitor."

Mr. WEBB. Yes; and there you have two things necessary to be proven. The amendment which my friend from New Jersey has offered sends us back to the Sherman law. You have got to prove both the illegal contract and the intent, and so forth. In the section as written you have only to prove the illegal contract. If the manufacturer makes a monopolistic contract, he ought to be punished for it without having to prove also that he intended to hurt some one thereby. He should not be allowed to make such contract, whether he actually intends to injure or not. . . .

Mr. STAFFORD. Would not the logic of the gentleman's position be that any jobber would not be permitted to select an agent or drummer to sell exclusively his wares?

Mr. WEBB. No; there he is the agent or the drummer, and he does not buy the goods from the manufacturer, but simply represents the jobber as agent.

Mr. STAFFORD. But he might sell them on certain commissions.

Mr. WEBB. He represents the manufacturer, and is the agent. . . .

Mr. [WILLIAM E.] HUMPHREY [R., Wash.]. I want to ask the gentleman this question: Suppose a dealer comes into a city, goes to the manufacturer and says to him, "I will handle your goods if you will not permit anyone else in town to do it," would that be legal?

Mr. WEBB. I think it would come within the spirit of the section if the manufacturer accepted such condition, and I think it ought to.

Mr. HUMPHREY of Washington. I think it ought to also; but it does not seem to me that it would. It seems to me that you cover it only in one way. Suppose the retailer says to the man, "I will handle your goods if you will not make a contract with anyone else to handle them."

Mr. WEBB. That might be done, but we are trying to unfetter the little business man and protect him and his customers from monopolistic contracts imposed by the big dealer.

Mr. HUMPHREY of Washington. If you do not stop that sort of procedure, will not the other be useless?

Mr. WEBB. Not at all.

Mr. HUMPHREY of Washington. Will they not simply change the manner of doing business?

Mr. WEBB. We want the little merchant to be able to buy all kinds of goods, keep a variety, and sell them to his customers, instead of being confined to one particular man's line.

Mr. HUMPHREY of Washington. Under the statement the gentleman has made, would it not still be a monopoly in any particular village, because they would select one particular man?

Mr. WEBB. It would be a monopolistic contract if the buyer and the seller agreed to such condition. . . .

Mr. ADAIR. There is nothing in this bill, as I understand it, that prevents a manufacturer from establishing an agency for his goods in any town, and giving that agent the exclusive right to sell the goods, provided he does not tie him up with a contract not to sell anybody else's goods?

Mr. WEBB. That is true.

Mr. ADAIR. I would not vote for this bill if it prevented a manufacturer from establishing an agency.

Mr. WEBB. It prevents the manufacturer from going to a little or big merchant and selling goods to him on condition that that merchant shall sell only his goods and not sell the goods of any competitor, and I ask both Republicans and Democrats on the floor of this House to give their support to that proposition, because it is good business morals, and it is a long step toward unfettering the little business man all over the country, and it will make the little country merchant feel that he can furnish supplies of all sorts and varieties to his customers instead of forcing them to go to the big mail-order houses to get what they want because they can not find the goods on the shelves of their local merchant.

Mr. MOORE. Mr. Chairman, is there anything to prevent a competitor from going into a country town and making the same deal that the person sought to be affected by this bill made? Why could not a competitor go into the country town and set up his business in his own way with another dealer?

Mr. ADAIR. He does; and he should.

Mr. MOORE. Is not that his remedy?

Mr. ADAIR. That is his remedy. Will the gentleman yield for one more question?

Mr. WEBB. Yes; just for one question.

Mr. ADAIR. I am engaged in the manufacturing business. We go out into the markets and establish agencies. We sell our line of goods to one man in a county, and to nobody else, but we do not bind him up in a contract to buy the goods of no one else.

Mr. WEBB. Then the gentleman is exempt from this section, and ought to be. If there are a dozen kinds of knives and razors, every merchant who buys them ought to have the right to buy all of them and sell them to anyone he pleases, and no one manufacturer ought to have the right to exclude him from the privilege of buying any razor or knife in competition with the one that he is selling him.

Mr. ADAIR. It is no part of monopoly for a manufacturer to establish an agency.

Mr. WEBB. No. Certainly not under this section. What we are striking at is the monopolistic contract.

Mr. McCOY. Does not the Standard Oil Co. have agencies all over the United States?

Mr. WEBB. Yes, I understand so.

Mr. McCOY. Is not that the biggest monoply [sic] there is?

Mr. WEBB. Yes. But we are not aiming at monopoly per se in this section, but at a contract or contracts which lead to monopoly. Monopoly is covered by the Sherman law, and we are trying to prevent those contracts which build up and lead to such monopoly. . . .

Mr. MANN. It being a common practice for people who invent something or who manufacture a specialty to place it in the hands of a local merchant and advertise it at the expense of the manufacturer or the seller, under this provision, if that should be done so as to build up a trade in this specialty in this store, the storekeeper would have a right to take in a competing article and get the benefit of the advertisement, as I understand it.

Mr. WEBB. Yes.

Mr. MANN. That looks moral, also.

Mr. WEBB. He has that right now, and exercises it every day under a decision of the Supreme Court.

Mr. ADAIR. You walk into a drug store down here in the city and ask for a bottle of Hood's sarsaparilla, and the druggist says, "Yes; I can give you that, if you want it, but here is one that is just as good," and he sells it to the customer at a cheaper price.

Mr. MANN. Not to me, not sarsaparilla. [Laughter.]

Mr. ADAIR. Since when did the gentleman quit drinking sarsaparilla?

Mr. MANN. I never quit, for I never commenced.

Mr. ADAIR. Oh, I beg the gentleman's pardon. I believe his beverage is Peruna?

Mr. MANN. Oh, that is the gentleman's specialty, not mine. [Laughter.]

Mr. WEBB. Briefly, Mr. Chairman, this section does not prohibit any manufacturer from establishing agencies, for when he establishes agencies he furnishes the goods to the agents, and the title to the property usually remains in the manufacturer, and the agent acts for him and sells his goods and returns the money when he sells them.

It does not forbid the manufacturer to go into a town and sell to one customer alone, provided he does not add to that sale the condition that that customer shall not sell competitive articles. It does not prevent that kind of sale, provided the illegal condition is not added to it. Now, I want to say this. Unscrupulous big business and the trusts are not in favor of this section, for it destroys one of their favorite weapons. They are trying to put forth the small business fellow to oppose this section, to make it appear that the little fellows are against this provision; but, as a matter of fact, those who are destroying competition in this country are the real opponents of this section. . . .

Mr. McCOY. Did one of these little fellows who were crowded out come before the committee?

Mr. WEBB. Every independent, as I remember, who spoke before the committee was in favor of section 4.

Mr. McCOY. I would like to have one name.

Mr. WEBB. If the gentleman will give me time to look the matter up in the volumes of hearings, I could find it, and my colleagues will bear out my statement. . . .

. . . This illegal, monopolistic contract system is what has built up the big mail-order houses and practically destroyed the little merchants all over this country, because the little merchant is ordinarily an honest man, and when an agent of a trust walks into his little store and says, "I will sell you these articles that have been splendidly advertised if you agree never to sell any of our competitors' articles." The little merchant agrees, and he feels bound to stand by it. His customers see that they can buy but one line of articles from him and turn to the mail-order house, where a variety of articles is found, and his customer sits down and orders from the mail-order house and soon the little merchant is destroyed, because he is fettered by the trust's exclusive contract. [Applause.]

Mr. MADDEN. Will the gentleman tell the House what gives the mail-order house a monopoly if it is not the Government of the United States by giving it the use of the mails?

Mr. WEBB. I am not talking about the monopoly given by the United States, but I am talking about the small merchant whose business we are trying to unfetter by this bill.

Mr. MADDEN. The gentleman said the mail-order house had a monopoly. What gives it a monopoly if it is not the Government of the United States, which gives it the use of its mails?

Mr. WEBB. I did not say the mail-order house was a monopoly; but that the exclusive contract we forbid has driven farmers to the mail-order house. We can destroy that condition somewhat with the unfettering of the little merchant from these exclusive contracts which compel him not to sell competing goods.

Mr. MADDEN. Can we take away the right of the people to use the mails if they want to send a letter to a mail-order house?

Mr. WEBB. No; but when the small merchant is permitted to handle all the articles he pleases the mail-order house will cease to get the business, because the small man will be permitted to carry all kinds of goods on his shelves and not be confined to one single line of goods.

Mr. [MICHAEL] DONOHOE [D., Pa.]. Does this measure propose to interfere with the relation between the manufacturer and his salesman who sells on commission?

Mr. WEBB. Not at all.

Mr. GARDNER. Do the mail-order houses undersell the local merchant?

Mr. WEBB. I do not know. They sometimes do by selling an inferior quality of goods, by attractive advertising, and they gull a good many people; but they find it out sooner or later, and will go back to their honest local merchant if he carries a variety of articles from which they can select what they want. . . .

Mr. [GEORGE J.] KINDEL [D., Colo.]. Is it not a fact the parcel-post rates [laughter] have more to do with that than any other thing?

Mr. WEBB. That may have something to do with it. Now, if gentlemen of the House wish to destroy this section 4 they will vote for the amendment of my friend Mr. McCoy. If they want to retain the tooth in it, then vote that amendment down, and we will force the United Shoe Machinery Co., which is one of the completest monopolies in shoe machinery in the world, to abolish their monopolistic contracts and give the shoe manufacturers of this country a chance to live and maintain their existence by buying and using or leasing such machinery as they choose. [Applause.] . . .

Mr. GARDNER. Mr. Chairman, the gentleman from Arkansas [Mr. FLOYD] tells us that in the interest of the consumer he is against the amendment offered by the gentleman from New Jersey, and the gentleman from North Carolina [Mr. WEBB] tells us that in the interest of the country merchant he is against the amendment of the gentleman from New Jersey because the country merchant is being put out of business by the mail-order house. Now, if the mail-order house puts out of business the country merchant, the mail-order house ⊥ puts him out of business by underselling him, which many people hold to be in the interest of the consumer.

In answer to an inquiry from the gentleman from Indiana [Mr. ADAIR], the gentleman from North Carolina says that section 4, as it stands—and I, for one, believe in section 4, although I favor the amendment of Mr. McCoy—does not prohibit exclusive agencies. It does not prohibit exclusive agencies for the man or corporation who has capital enough; but it does prohibit the kind of exclusive agency which the man with small capital is forced to contract with. For instance, if I were an automobile manufacturer with a small capital, I could not all over the country establish agencies such as would be permitted in section 4 as it is drawn at present. I could not afford to carry the enormous stock of automobiles which would be necessary in order to break into the market. If, however, the amendment offered by Mr. McCoy is adopted, I could pursue the present practice of the automobile trade, a practice by which a small man can avail himself of the capital of other small men. That is the way the automobile business has been built up. A man who has a new make of automobiles comes to some bright young man in Washington and says, "I can not afford to make you my agent, but I will sell this machine to you if you agree to sell my machines and my machines only. If you sell other machines, I can never establish a demand for mine, because of these great automobile concerns which are already competing for the market."

This amendment is distinctly in the interest of the small manufacturer. It is the men who began as small manufacturers who have built up the automobile trade. One of them is the person who made those vast amounts of money which the gentleman from Arkansas [Mr. FLOYD] has been telling us about. He did it by cutting down the cost and the price of an automobile, cutting it down and down. Apparently he can manufacture at half the cost of his competitors. Now, the gentleman from Arkansas says, "Yes; he has made such an enormous amount of money that we will build a wall around him and prevent him from having any competitor." That is what you are doing if you leave section 4 unamended. You are building a wall around these gigantically successful people, so that the next Mr. Ford who comes along will not be able to break into the business, because he will not have at his command enough capital to own automobiles all over the United States.

Neither the gentleman from Arkansas nor the gentleman from North Carolina has answered one word of what the gentleman from New Jersey [Mr. McCoy] has said. They have told you about practices, very reprehensible ones, in restraint of trade, practices which, as a matter of fact, do produce monopolies and which are intended to produce monopolies. They have cited those practices for the purpose of defeating the amendment of the gentleman from New Jersey, just as if his amendment were designed to permit those practices, or would permit them. On the contrary, the gentleman's amendment forbids those practices, inasmuch as it provides that these exclusive agencies shall not be permitted if they are to be used for the purpose of building up monopolies or for the purpose of restraint of trade. . . .

Mr. GRAHAM of Pennsylvania. Mr. Chairman, there is an old story that illustrates a good deal the present situation. It tells of a man passing along the street and noticing another man working with a crowbar at the side of a cellar wall that projected above the sidewalk. He said, "My friend, what are you trying to do?" "Well," he says, "that cellar is very dark, and I am trying to let some light into it." The first man went about his business for a couple of hours, and coming back he saw the other man still working and the aperture not very much larger than when he first saw it. He said to him, "Well, my friend, how have you succeeded?" The man replied, "I haven't let much light into it, but I have let a power of dark out." [Laughter.]

And it seems to me that in much of the discussion we are indulging in here we are letting a power of dark out about this question. But, all boiled down, it is a simple proposition, as I view it. Now, I may be letting more dark out.

There are two classes of transactions aimed at in this section 4. One is a lease and the other is a sale. It is quite true that there is nothing in this section which forbids the creation of agencies. That is to say, the manufacturer may have an agent who exclusively sells his goods, because employing an agent does not involve either a lease or a sale. Indeed, the manufacturer might go to a retail dealer in some village or city or town and say, "I wish to introduce my goods here; I want to have you as my special agent, and I want you not to handle the goods of any competitor of mine"; and so long as there is not a transaction in the nature of a lease or a purchase there, then that retailer can transact that business and do it lawfully, and there is no prohibition in section 4 against such a piece of conduct as that.

Now, so far as selling is concerned, a system or practice has grown up in the business world where a man has a limited capital, or where for the protection of the manufacturer contracts are made in the nature of an agency contract, but the goods are invoiced to the man that has to do the handling of the goods, and the price is paid to the manufacturer and the transaction amounts, perhaps, to a sale. That is the kind of thing that this section 4 does forbid. I know of nothing immoral in such a transaction as that. A man can not serve two masters. He must be loyal to one or the other when their interests conflict. Wherefore, if you make such an arrangement as that, and to conserve your capital or for your own protection make a conditional sale of the goods and engage this man to handle those goods exclusively for you, there is no element of immorality involved in such a transaction. And yet that is forbidden.

The amendment of the gentleman from New Jersey would cure the evil that is in this proposition created by the language of this section. You would leave business free to make any transaction that it pleases so long as it does not amount to what this amendment would cover, namely, a restriction of trade or the creation of a monopoly.

Now, let me ask in relation to the leasing question, whether it would not also cure that. In the minority report we have said:

> Again, the manufacturer sells no machines at all, but only leases them, and because they are delicate and any injury to them is his own loss, he leases them only to lessees who agree not to use imperfectly adapted parts, supplies, or appliances of other manufacture. Or he leases them at a special rental, upon the understanding that the lessees shall not use imperfectly adapted parts, supplies, or appliances of any other manufacture. Or he agrees to sell to the lessee perfectly adapted parts, supplies, or appliances, upon the understanding that the lessee shall not use imperfectly adapted ones of other manufacture. Each of these transactions—which good morals and honorable business conduct from time immemorial have always sanctioned—is forbidden by the bill.

The amendment of the gentleman from New Jersey [Mr. McCoy] would cure that evil, because unless these practices amount to a restriction of trade or creation of a monopoly, they ought not to be forbidden, and would not be forbidden. Therefore I favor the adoption of the amendment. . . .

Mr. GREEN of Iowa. Mr. Chairman, this section of the bill is like the rest of this proposed statute. It lays burdens upon the small manufacturer and the small dealer, but leaves the whole matter wide open for the large concern. It is perfectly easy for any large institution to evade the provisions of this section. All they have to do in the world to except themselves from its provisions is simply to establish a selling agency of their own, to have their own agent, to hire him in accordance with any terms that they see fit, and exempt themselves entirely from the provisions of this bill. On the other hand, burdens are laid upon the small manufacturer and dealer, as has been shown here.

The amendment offered by the gentleman from New Jersey [Mr. MCCOY], instead of taking away anything from the section actually adds to it by depriving the large manufacturer of the power to set up a monopoly through his selling agency in defiance or disregard of this section. It brings us back, really, to the Sherman law, it is true, but what harm is there in any of these trade agreements unless there is a monopoly or a restraint of trade or a hindrance of competition in some way? Who has been injured thereby? What evil is there that needs to be remedied, except something of that nature? Why should we undertake to hamper trade when that which is sought to be restricted or stopped is injuring no one and doing no damage to the business world?

The gentleman from Arkansas has said that this section was based upon a decision of the United States Circuit Court of Appeals rendered by Judge Sanborn;[5.533] but that case, in my judgment, is no authority for the position which the gentleman from Arkansas has taken. The suit was one for damages under the Sherman law.

It is true that Judge Sanborn did state in that case that contracts of sale which provided that the lessee or purchaser of the article sold should not use or deal in goods furnished by other parties was not an act inhibited by the Sherman law, for the reason that he considered it was not an act done in hindrance or suppression of competition or in creation of a monopoly. But this has nothing to do with the point upon which the case actually turned and upon which the decision was based. That point was that the plaintiff was not harmed in the least by the transaction which he complained of.

The Department of Justice has never taken the position that contracts of this character, made for the purpose of promoting a monopoly or for the purpose of hindering or restraining trade, was [sic] legal, but, on the contrary, has commenced several cases and prosecuted many individuals because of their entering upon just such transactions as this. No Attorney General that I know of under any administration has ever taken the position which is now taken by the majority of the committee as a reason for bringing forward this section. The real fact is that it adds nothing in proper form to the provisions of the Sherman law, but, as I have said, simply gives additional advantages to the large concerns and throws additional restrictions upon the small dealer. [Applause on the Republican side.].

Mr. MITCHELL. Mr. Chairman, I do not think there should be any mistake among the Members of the House with reference to the extreme importance of this section of this bill. There are some important provisions in this bill, but I do not believe that there is a more vital or more important provision in it than section 4. One of the evils that this section seeks to cure is the evil with reference to the "tying contracts," and I want to call attention to one specific condition which exists in this country which has been created by this system of tying contracts. A gentleman appeared before the Judiciary Committee, an independent shoe-machinery manufacturer, who stated that from 95 to 98 per cent of all of the machinery used in the manufacture of shoes in this country was manufactured by one company. He said that they absolutely controlled and dominated the field by this system of tying contracts. They have in the manufacture of shoes some of the best machines, essential machines, machines that it is absolutely necessary for every manufacturer to have in order to do business. Manufacturers who furnish some of the minor machines and who are in the field trying to get a foothold and a market for their machines can not commercialize their business, can not get the machines into these factories because this gigantic

---

[5.533] Whitwell v. Continental Tobacco Co., 125 F. 454 (8th Cir. 1903).

monopoly—and there is no monopoly more powerful—has this system of tying contracts with the manufacturers. The manufacturers, in order to get the essential machines, must sign a contract that they will also take these other minor machines where there is some competition. If they do not do that, then, according to the provisions of their contract, the shoe-machinery company is able to remove all the machinery from the factory. As a result of that system, they have practically the field to themselves.

Now, Mr. Chairman, the States of this Union have recognized that evil. In Massachusetts this corporation was organized by the consolidation of a number of independent machine companies in about 1899. The manufacturers began to protest in a feeble kind of way against the continuation of this trust. The shoe journals protested against its organization and its system of doing business. The protest became so strong that in 1907 the Massachusetts Legislature passed a law seeking to remedy this evil and to open the door to the inventive genius of the thousands of men who are engaged in the shoe-machine business and who want to put shoe machines on the market. The legislature passed a law in 1907, but the effect of it has been circumvented. We have had investigations, and the Attorney General is proceeding against the shoe machinery company, believing that it is in violation of the Sherman antitrust law. I do not believe that this Congress ought to speak in any uncertain terms. I think the Members on both sides of the House ought to give this provision of the bill their support. I am not quite as familiar as are some other Members with the exclusive contracts, but I know that they form one of the greatest instruments, one of the greatest means of creating a monopoly in this country, and we have an opportunity in this bill to stop that system and break it up where it is at the present time.

What is the inducement that is offered the small dealer or the small grocery man or small business man or the dealer in any community to take one of these exclusive agencies? . . .

Mr. GREEN of Iowa. Was I not correct in saying that these acts were in violation of the Sherman antitrust law?

Mr. WEBB. I will answer that. The Department of Justice has held that one individual act is not, but that a series of acts will bring him within the Sherman antitrust law.

Mr. MITCHELL. We want to make sure of our ground in this act. We want to give everyone a fair field and no favors. We want to give opportunity to the little fellow. We want the shoe workers, shoe manufacturers, machine manufacturers, and the great body of consumers to be freed from the grip and fetters of monopoly and special privilege. [Applause.]

The CHAIRMAN. The time of the gentleman has expired. All time has expired. The question is on the amendment offered by the gentleman from New Jersey [Mr. MCCOY].

The question was taken; and on a division (demanded by Mr. MCCOY) there were 28 ayes and 71 noes.

So the amendment was rejected.

Mr. MORGAN of Oklahoma. Mr. Chairman, I offer the following amendment.

The Clerk read as follows:

Amend, section 4, page 22, by inserting, in line 4, after the word "of," the words "or appoint an agent to sell," so that the section will read:

"SEC. 4. It shall be unlawful for any person engaged in commerce to lease or make a sale of, or appoint an agent to sell, goods, wares, merchandise, machinery, supplies, or other commodity [sic] on condition or with any understanding, agreement, or contract that the lessee or purchaser thereof shall not use or deal in the goods, wares, merchandise, machinery, supplies, or other commodities of a competitor or competitors of the lessor or seller; and any person violating the provision of this section shall be decreed guilty of a misdemeanor, and on conviction thereof shall be fined not to exceed $5,000 or by imprisonment not exceeding one year, or by both.["]

Mr. WEBB. The effect of that amendment would be that nobody could sell his goods except he sold them in person; he could not establish an agency; he could not send out men to sell goods for him. . . .

Mr. MORGAN of Oklahoma. Mr. Chairman, gentlemen will observe that in discussing the amendments to this section that the section applies only to the leasing and sale of goods. I voted against the amendment offered by the gentleman from New Jersey because I think there is some real merit in this section as it now stands. But, gentlemen, if we really desire to destroy monopoly, if we really desire to protect the people against monopoly, then we ought to broaden this section so that one who sells through agencies can not prohibit the agent from dealing in the goods of a competitor, because a corporation through agents can establish and maintain a monopoly with the same degree of success that it can by the selling or leasing of goods with the understanding that the purchaser will not deal in the goods of a competitor. Now, a large number of my constituents are farmers. They deal largely with the International Harvester Co., an institution or a corporation with $120,000,000 capital.

Unless you accept my amendment, this gigantic corporation not only has a monopoly in the sale, largely, of farm machinery through agents in Oklahoma, but throughout this great Nation—to all of the 6,500,000 farmers. Are you going to leave section 4 so that it will not protect the farmers of this country against this monopoly? It seems that you are. I am in favor of reducing the power of the shoe machinery company to maintain a monopoly by leasing machines, but I am also in favor of extending the section so that it will reach the International Harvester Co., that sells the farmers of this country perhaps two-thirds, if not three-fourths, of all of their harvesting machinery. Yet, again, the majority in this House is going back on the farmers of this Nation. You are still leaving in the hands of that gigantic corporation the power to establish exclusive agencies, with an agreement or contract that they shall not act as the agents of any other firm. How is an independent manufacturer to get his goods on sale throughout the Nation? He is handicapped by the fact that the great harvester company has monopolized the active, able agents throughout this great Nation. In the report of the Corporations Commissioner upon the methods used by the International Harvester Co. he cites that that is one of the methods they use to establish and maintain their monopoly. It has been said here frequently in this debate that the section as it stands, in a measure, controls the small concern ⊥ that must sell its goods ⊥9411 direct because it has not got the power to establish agencies, but the mammoth concern may establish local and exclusive agencies, and this law will not touch it.

The CHAIRMAN. The time of the gentleman from Oklahoma has expired. The question is on the amendment offered by the gentleman from Oklahoma.

The question was taken, and the amendment was rejected.

Mr. TOWNER. Mr. Chairman, I offer the following amendment, which I send to the desk and ask to have read. I will state that the amendments which I shall offer are merely to perfect the text, and I will ask careful attention of the committee to the amendments.

The CHAIRMAN. The Clerk will report the amendment.

The Clerk read as follows:

Page 22, line 3, strike out the words "engaged in commerce," and in line 4, after the word "sale," insert the words "in commerce.". . .

Mr. TOWNER. Mr. Chairman, that amendment, I will say, is more important, perhaps, than will appear at first blush. By the language used in the text you limit the prosecution of any person to persons who are engaged in commerce, which, under the definition of commerce, means those who are engaged in interstate commerce. That is not what you mean, certainly, because you do not mean that it shall be required to prove that any person who violates this act shall be engaged in interstate commerce. The language of all of these bills is that any person who violates or does the thing which the law prohibits shall be punished. The language, for instance, of the Federal antitrust law is that "every person who shall make any such contract or engage," and so forth. In section 2 of this bill the language is "every person who shall monopolize," and so forth. In section 3 the language is "every person who shall make any illegal contract," and so forth.

This is the difficulty with the language used. It is not as descriptive of the person that the phrase "in commerce" should be applied, but it is as descriptive of the act, and therefore the words "in commerce" should follow the word "sale" in section 4, so that it will read:

That any person—

No matter whom he may be, engaged in commerce or not—

That any person who shall lease or make a sale in commerce of goods, wares, merchandise—

And so forth.

Otherwise this section would be inoperative and perhaps unconstitutional, because it would apply in the form in which it is to sales made in intrastate commerce, which would be absolutely unconstitutional, as the gentleman knows, for Congress has not that power, so that the limitation placed here being upon the person is a limitation that ought not to exist, and the lack of that limitation on the sales would make it apply to all sales, even in intrastate commerce, and, therefore, for both reasons, the section ought to be amended, as I have suggested.

The CHAIRMAN. The question is on the amendment offered by the gentleman from Iowa.

The amendment was rejected.

Mr. TOWNER. Mr. Chairman, I yield back the balance of my time on that amendment and offer another amendment, which I send to the desk and ask to have read.

The CHAIRMAN. The gentleman yields back two minutes and offers an amendment, which the Clerk will report.

The Clerk read as follows:

Page 22, line 9, after the word "states," strike out the word "or" and insert in lieu thereof the words "and shall." . . .

Mr. TOWNER. Mr. Chairman, it would appear that that amendment ought to be adopted without any question whatever. The other amendment ought to have been adopted, but it is a habit that it is the requirement of gentlemen on the other side to vote down all amendments no matter whether the amendment affects the text and makes the bill stronger or not. The word "or" has no business here. It means nothing. What the gentleman means is:

Or any Territory thereof or the District of Columbia or any insular possession or other place under the jurisdiction of the United States, and shall fix a price charged therefor—

And so forth.

The word "or" certainly must have been unintentionally or carelessly used, or else it was used for the purpose of making the provision of the statute inoperative and of no effect.

The CHAIRMAN. The question is on the amendment offered by the gentleman from Iowa.

The question was taken, and the amendment was rejected. . . .

Mr. TOWNER. Mr. Chairman, I offer a third amendment.

The CHAIRMAN. The Clerk will report the amendment.

The Clerk read as follows:

Page 22, line 10, after the word "condition," insert a comma and the word "agreement." . . .

Mr. TOWNER. Mr. Chairman, it would seem also to the ordinary man—

Mr. WEBB. Does this amendment come after the word "understanding"?

Mr. TOWNER. No; after the word "condition." Of course it is better there—

Mr. WEBB. Mr. Chairman, I think the amendment is good; and, as far as the committee are concerned, we will accept it. [Applause.]

The CHAIRMAN. The question is on the adoption of the amendment.

The question was taken, and the amendment was agreed to. . . .

Mr. MOORE. Mr. Chairman, I move to strike out the last word. A little while ago I asked the gentleman from North Carolina [Mr. WEBB] as to the effect of this section upon those who undertake after advertising to place their wares by a special arrangement with a local dealer, and his answer was that unless the merchant or manufacturer who made the deal with the local dealer insisted that the exclusive right to sell should be granted apart from the question of competition that he would not be punished, but that if he in any way insisted that the competitor's goods should be eliminated, then he would be subject to the fine and imprisonment imposed by the section. And all this new and drastic legislation in the interest of the local dealer or the country merchant.

Now, Mr. Chairman, I have been looking at this matter from the viewpoint of the man who is struggling to build up a business in this local way. Say there are two merchants in the gentleman's town, each striving for business, and the manufacturer of a certain brand of soap or soup, it makes no difference, comes along and says to one of them, the one who is more energetic than the other, perhaps, that he may have the exclusive right to sell the product, a specialty that he has advertised well, and that is so popular that even "the children cry for it," as some advertisements read. The goods are salable, and have been made so by the genius of the inventor or manufacturer and because of the heavy promotion expenditure made upon them. . . .

. . . Now, after all this labor and energy and expense of advertising it appears that if the manufacturer or jobber undertakes to say to the local merchant, "I will give you the exclusive privilege and authority of selling my popular soup or soap," he has to go to jail. That is not a very great inducement either to the manufacturer, the inventor, or the local business man. It does not aid the local business and, so far as the question of morals is concerned, it seems to punish the industrious and progressive business man in favor of the faker or the manufacturer of spurious or inferior articles, who may thus derive advantage from the legitimate advertising and the scientific energy of those who created the business and paid dearly to advance it. In other words, Dr. COOK reaps the gate receipts while the real explorer, the real patentee, the real inventor, the real manufacturer, who did the work and filled the house, would suffer the penalty of fine and imprisonment. If this be the effect of the enactment, the man who has not expended any energy, time, or money in promoting or advancing trade could always play a waiting game and then come in and take advantage of all the facilities of the trade established by the man who had the enterprise and courage to spend his money to acquire it. This does not seem fair or moral.

And there is another side to it. I make the statement now, and I challenge anybody to contradict it, that the Government of the United States itself—that is to say, the present administration of the Government—is now encouraging the very kind of business that the gentleman from North Carolina assumes by this measure to stop.

It is advertising for supplies to be used in the Mexican emergency, particularly in the Navy Department, many of which ⊥ are specified, so that the manufacturer only who has made his goods popular can sell them to the Government. It is so in the case of soup, it is so in the case of soap, it is so in the case of tobacco, and a good many other articles. Specifications issued by this very administration, which is advancing and insisting upon this so-called antitrust legislation, call for supplies for our Mexican necessities which even specify certain brands of tobacco made by the Tobacco Trust; certain brands of soup, made exclusively by certain manufacturers; certain brands of soap, made exclusively by certain manufacturers of soap. This is what a trust-busting administration demands for itself. . . .

⊥9412

Mr. Chairman, I shall therefore avail myself of leave to extend, so that I may place in the RECORD several communications which relate to this bill. I believe they should have consideration, because they represent the sober judgment of some of the leading citizens of Philadelphia—citizens who have been deeply concerned over the recent trend of legislation and who know what they are talking about.

I submit letters from representatives of two of the oldest of our banks, presenting the views of experienced and conservative men with respect to section 9 (interlocking directors), and a memorial from the Philadelphia Board of Trade in general opposition to the bill:

The Central National Bank,
Philadelphia, March 25, 1914.

Hon. J. Hampton Moore,
House of Representatives, Washington, D. C.

DEAR SIR: An act has been introduced into the House with the intent of prohibiting interlocking directorates between certain corporations. This act has been drafted to correct certain abuses which it is alleged have crept into banking and the extension of credit on the part of certain groups of banks, presumably in New York.

In seeking to correct that which is claimed as an evil existing in the metropolis of the country far greater harm in the sum total will be done to the mass of our banking institutions and to the community at large by the enactment of this new law.

We can not recall a single instance here in Philadelphia in which the interlocking directorate feature has prevented competition or militated unjustifiably in any way against a single individual in the commercial community. In the history of this bank, through its long and honorable record of a half century, we do not know of an instance in which the members of its board of directors have been influenced in the extension of credit in any manner which has unduly favored or has disfavored any portion of the commercial community entitled to credit from this bank.

The bill as lined up will affect probably 10 of our directors, and in the end we may lose half of them—possibly more—men whose influence stands paramount, whose integrity has always stood for the best in this community, and whose influence will not unlikely go to some State trust company here, and thus this bank will thereby be materially weakened in the personnel of its management. These men will be hard to replace, owing to their trained minds, their discriminating and analytical judgment. We cite our own bank as a concrete case; the same conditions obtain among many others here in this city, as well as among a majority of the national banks in the larger towns and cities throughout the country.

It seems to us that Congress should very carefully balance this problem, and in trying to remedy one evil not create a condition which will be even more harmful. You are seeking to build up a great banking system for us, yet this act, if it shall become a law, will weaken many of the integral parts (its leading member banks) and strengthen the State banking systems as against the regional system. Can you afford to do this, particularly when we are trying to help you in every way possible? Do you think it the part of wisdom to force large groups of the most desirable and influential men in cities like Philadelphia out of the national system into State bank or trust company directorates, and thus build up the State system at the expense of the regional system? Is it fair to harass and unjustly punish the clean, straight bankers of this country, who are in the great majority, and who have through all these years transacted a strictly uplifting, legitimate business, in order to correct an alleged abuse in one particular city?

We respectfully submit the foregoing for your consideration, and we feel it our duty in the interest of our stockholders and in the interest of the new regional system which you are seeking to build up to enter our protest against the enactment of a law which we believe will prove not only harmful to the member banks of the regional system, but will weaken the system as a whole.

Very truly, yours,

Wm. T. Elliott, President.

The Girard National Bank,
Philadelphia, May 18, 1914.

Hon. J. Hampton Moore,
House of Representatives, Washington, D. C.

MY DEAR MR. MOORE: You have requested me to write you concerning the interlocking directorate feature of the trust bill now before Congress for consideration.

There is no real demand on the part of intelligent people for the enactment of any such legislation as is contemplated in the bill as it affects the directorships in national banks. Such unwise legislation will be of disastrous consequence to the banks really affected by its provisions, and as the bill is now constituted it grossly discriminates against national banks that are unfortunate enough to be operating in cities of over 100,000 population.

Interlocking directors of national banks in cities or towns of under 100,000 population could be of much more detriment to their respective communities than similar directors in larger cities, as the number and scope of the banks in smaller cities are much more concentrated, and as a consequence the possibility of a director's power greater than in the larger cities where there are a number of strong competing institutions. If so-called interlocking directors are permissible in and helpful to smaller communities, there is no line of logical reasoning that will show they are not of increasing usefulness to the cities of over 100,000 population.

We national banks in the larger cities are now to operate under the Federal reserve act, which will of necessity make a great change in the conduct of our business; in the reserve cities the banks are facing a large shrinkage of deposits on account of the reserve of other banks being transferred to the Federal reserve banks, and it is the banks in the reserve cities that will be vitally affected by the provisions of the new trust bill, and yet before we have had any opportunity to adjust ourselves to the changed conditions along comes more legislation that will deprive our banks of the services of the directors that are really the backbone of our institutions, not only on account of the value of their wide experience and the business they have been able to bring to us, but the feeling of confidence in the institution that is engendered by their association with us. What will be the effect?

The State banks and trust companies that are already getting a lion's share of the really desirable business will corral all the men of affairs and their business and their influence to the great detriment of the national banks, and the national banks will be greatly weakened by their loss, with no possible benefit to the very people the proposed legislation is supposed to benefit.

A bank can not prosper unless it gives its customers as good, if not better, treatment than its immediate competitors, and the bank with the strongest board, comprised of men of affairs interested in numerous enterprises, is usually the most alert, most aggressive, and accommodating and most useful to any community. It is against such a bank with a board that is of real benefit to its customers that this bill will discriminate; and to what good end?

Another thing that must not be overlooked—these very men that are being legislated out of directorships have in the majority of cases been invited to become associated with our financial institutions with which they are identified and have not bought their way in to control its affairs, as is so generally misrepresented, and have been, as a rule, the big factor in the success of the institution under consideration.

Take the banks in Philadelphia, for example—the important trust companies are large holders of the stocks of all the older national banks through the administration of trusts, not as actual owners, and are large depositors with our national banks. What exception can be taken to the fact that the officers of these trust companies are directors in our national banks? It is of importance to the trust companies that they are so represented, important to the trusts they represent, and of great value to the customers of the bank with which they may be identified, and of no possible harm to any interests.

Some of the most useful and conscientious national-bank directors are members of private banking firms. Why should they be eliminated by law from a directorship in a city bank? I can assure you they are of more use to any bank than the bank is to them.

You can go all along the line and take the men interested in million-dollar companies engaged in commerce and eliminate them from the directorships in national banks as provided in the act and you will take away the very men that are of the most importance, directly and indirectly, to the customers, large and small, of our national banks, and I ask who is to be benefited by their forced withdrawal? Absolutely no one, and a great business—that of national banking—disarranged and damaged.

In other words, don't drive out of national banking the very class of men that collectively are of inestimable value to the national banks, and through them to the multitude of bank customers and shareholders, and force these men into a position where they will naturally gravitate toward State banks and trust companies—with them will go their business and their influence. Instead of strengthening the national banking system you will impair its usefulness. The national banks have difficulty enough now holding their own with what are known as State banks and trust companies; the recent enormous increases in the latters' number and resources prove this.

The national banks have welcomed constructive legislation; destructive legislation along the lines contemplated is unwarranted and will be only a detriment to the country's development.

Yours, very truly,

J. Wayne, Jr.,
Vice President and Cashier.

Philadelphia Board of Trade,
Philadelphia.

To the honorable the Senate and House of Representatives of the United States in Congress assembled:

Your memorialist, the Philadelphia Board of Trade, respectfully represents:

That there has been introduced into the House of Representatives a bill (H. R. 15657) entitled "A bill to supplement existing laws against unlawful restraints, monopolies, and for other purposes."

Your memorialist submits the following reasons for its opposition to this proposed measure:

PRICE DISCRIMINATION.

In section 2 of the act it is declared to be a crime to discriminate in price between purchasers of commodities with the purpose or intent to injure the business of a competitor.

With the general moral purpose ascertainable in this provision no one would disagree. There is such a thing as an effort to wantonly destroy the business of a competitor by means other than those recognized as fair competition. The act, however, as drawn is, we believe, unsound and likely to do substantial harm.

Discriminations in price are essential to any freedom in trade. The manufacturer or dealer in goods who has a large supply in the West with a small demand must be at liberty to sell in the West at a lower price than he would in the East, if he had there a small supply and an active demand. He must sell at an advancing or declining scale of prices and on such market as may exist in different localities. Discrimination in price per se is a part of the life of trade, and contains no element of immorality.

Moreover, discrimination in price is an essential to competition. Competition means obtaining business formerly done by others, and this is accomplished by price cutting in the market where the competitor is operating. It would be mere hypocrisy to pretend that competition does not injure or destroy the business of the competitor. The avowed purpose of the competition is to take the competitor's business from him, as he is attempting to take your business from you. Competition is the settled policy of the law, and it would be manifest folly to pass an act requiring that the effects of competition must not exist. The direct effect of competition is "to injure or destroy."

It follows therefore that every person in a competitive business who cuts prices in order to obtain the business formerly held by some other competitor would come within the terms of the proposed act, since the direct effect of his price cutting is to injure the business of his opponent, and he is presumed to know the effect of his acts. The act as drawn should not therefore be passed. It would place everyone doing business in the United States in jeopardy of fine and imprisonment.

If we assume that there is such a thing as a willful and malicious attempt to injure or destroy the business of a competitor outside the scope of legitimate competition, legislation should be directed against such willful and malicious attempt, whether accomplished by price cutting, the spreading of false reports, or any other dishonest means or practices. What is a willful and malicious attempt should be left to the courts. The act ought not to be open to the construction that cutting prices in order to take away the competitor's business is a crime.

The Supreme Court has interpreted the Sherman Act to mean that where ruthless and destructive methods are employed with the "primary" intent to injure or destroy the business of a competitor, such acts bring the offender within the purview of the present law. Under these circumstances we do not believe that additional legislation is needed.

THE RIGHT TO SELL.

Your memorialist respectfully submits that no public necessity justifies the denial to the owners of mines or mining properties the right to sell or to withhold from sale the products of mines developed at their own risk and with their own capital. There can be no freedom unless the inherent rights of the individual are interfered with only when overpowering public necessity demands.

INTERLOCKING DIRECTORATES.

Your memorialist believes that it will be conceded by all that the achievements and prosperity of a nation are dependent upon the productivity of the individual. Unless the man of brains, resource, and energy has scope for the use of these gifts and qualities the whole country is the loser, at home and abroad. The provision against interlocking directorates prohibits the individual with the capacity which is most needed from doing his best service for the country. For such a restriction upon individual liberty and such a handicap placed upon the energy of the Nation it should be shown that there exists a great public necessity, to be met by this means and no other. Your memorialist believes that neither prerequisite for this enactment exists.

The reasons which have been advanced for an interference by Government with existing conditions are three in number:

1. That interlocking directorates, so called, may be used to create a combination in restraint of trade. Granting this possibility, there is nothing in it to justify curtailing the usefulness of the best abilities of the country. If several directors of one corporation are acting on the board of a competing corporation in such a way as to effect a combination in restraint of trade, the arrangement can be set aside by the courts under existing law. It is not the presence of the same individual on two boards of directors that is the evil; why, then, cut down our national effectiveness?

2. That they (interlocking directorates) may sometimes be made use of to effect dishonest schemes for individual profit. Here, again, it is entirely feasible to legislate against making secret or dishonest profits from official position without depriving the business of the country of its most efficient servants.

3. That sometimes a person of large means or abilities is elected to a number of directorates and thus may become too powerful in the world of business or finance.

This ground is untenable. No country can prosper unless the incentives for individual effort are great, unless the prizes for usefulness and success are position and power. To be afraid that position and power may be misused, to take away the incentive for a nation's efforts, because some one will perhaps abuse them, is cowardice and folly.

We respectfully submit, therefore, first, that there is no overpowering public necessity for the proposed act, and, second, that other means are available for meeting any wrongs in existing conditions without emasculating the energy of the people or curtailing the productivity of the genius of the country. Legislate against fraud, conspiracies to do unlawful acts, or abuse of official positions; do not legislate against the proper liberty of the individual.

STOCK OWNERSHIP.

The provisions of the proposed act relating to stock ownership are, in the opinion of your memorialist, unnecessary and unwise. It is hard to believe that anyone familiar with business conditions can honestly assert that competition without limit is for the best good of the people; the destructiveness of competition is too evident. The degree of competition which will work the best result for all can not be determined by legislation—it must be worked out by the slow process of evolution. The great period of consolidation through which the country has passed was due partly to the realization that unrestrained competition was wasteful and uneconomic; partly because the world trade has grown to a point where the countries which would lead must operate through larger and more powerful units of business. The result has been on the whole good. No one familiar with conditions at the beginning of the period of consolidation and expansion would return to them. The law as it stands prohibits consolidations which unduly restrain trade or create monopoly. Assuming that this restriction is necessary, upon what might perhaps otherwise develop into too great a degree of consolidation, it is evident that the growth of the units of business must go on, and if two or more weaker units find it of advantage to unite it would be bad policy to prevent the working out of their salvation in their own way. We have legislated fully against the danger of monopoly, we should not be afraid of the natural working out of economic laws lest we kill our own advancement.

PICKETING.

Your memorialist most earnestly objects to the provision of the bill relating to "picketing." This practice means in plain terms the surrounding of a place of employment by those who desire to stop work in such a way that those who desire to work may be prevented by persuasion if possible, or by force if necessary, from working. The individual who desires to work ought in a free country to be protected in that right. The owner of the factory who desires to run his factory ought to be protected from willful interference. For the Government to give its official sanction to a practice which would not have to be legalized, if it were not immoral and used for purposes of intimidation, would be altogether abhorrent to fair play and stable government.

CONCLUSION.

Your memorialist believes that the consensus of opinion of the business men of this country is against the passage of this or any other so-called antitrust bill, and that to pass such an act as is now proposed would do violence to the judgment of that portion of the community perhaps best able to judge of its effect upon the welfare of the country.

The fact that the act in question is described as an antitrust bill, when in reality it deals with the law of business relations generally, is persuasive proof that the time is not ripe for the passage of additional legislation of this character. It is evidence that the framers of the bill are thinking in terms of an attack upon some more or less mythical embodiment of evil called a trust. It is certain that the country must suffer, unless the laws affecting business are framed with a scientific accuracy to prohibit only the thing that is wrong, without interfering with the convenient machinery of business or limiting the initiative and effective energy of the people.

For which reasons, among others, we respectfully submit that this bill should not receive your favorable consideration.

And your memorialist will ever pray.
True copy.

Wm. M. Coates, President.

Attest:

Wm. R. Tucker, Secretary,

Malcolm Lloyd, Jr., Chairman,
Samuel T. Kerr,
S. B. Vrooman,
Chas. S. Walton,
S. Pemberton Hutchinson,
Nathan Hayward,
Joseph A. Janney, Jr.,
Committee on Legislation.

* * * *

Mr. TAGGART. Mr. Chairman, I am wholly unable to understand why the distinguished gentleman from Pennsylvania [Mr. MOORE] would seem to favor the first man that comes to town with a thoroughly advertised article and would claim the right to the exclusive market because he was the first one that came along. He grants no rights whatever to a man that might come the next day and who might have an article that he had patented, that he had thoroughly advertised, and that finally might become such a well-accepted article by the American public that even the United States Government would make choice of it for supplies for the Navy or Army. Why do you have a choice? Who is entitled to the American market? The man who simply has advertised? The man who appears first? Do you grant no right whatever to the man who comes in second or third or fourth? Suppose your favorite arrived after the merchants had been tied up with exclusive selling contracts? Would you be satisfied? Now, the first man that you seem to favor would never have gotten a start in the world, he never would have had an article thoroughly advertised and acceptable to the public if exclusive agencies were in complete operation when he began to put it on the market, because under your theory when he would come to town the merchants would all have been tied up by exclusive contracts, and perhaps the very one who is now your favorite would not have any chance at all. The idea is not only to liberate the man who has the right to purchase and sell anything and every lawful thing that he pleases to sell anywhere, but to liberate the second man or the third man or the fourth man who comes to visit the merchant, and who offers his wares to the merchants of the town and places them on the market. Give them all the same even chance. [Applause.] . . .

Mr. GARDNER. Mr. Chairman, I should like to ask the gentleman from North Carolina [Mr. WEBB], the chairman of the committee, if it would detract anything from his bill, page 22, lines 9 and 10, if we strike out the words "or fix a price charged therefor, or discount from, or rebate upon, such price"?

Mr. WEBB. Well, I will say to the gentleman I think it would. It would hurt the effect of the bill considerably and might license the doing of those very things to which we object.

Mr. GARDNER. But you have only specified three of the devices which are customary in the case of exclusive-sale contracts. Are you not afraid that a court might hold that you intended to permit the devices which you left out?

Mr. WEBB. To what devices does the gentleman refer?

Mr. GARDNER. Now, I call your attention to your report, in which you use the expression, "the first inducement in every case must of necessity relate to price." Take the case of the United Shoe Machinery Co., which is situated in my district. The United Shoe Machinery Co. obviously might make a contract under which they would say to the shoe manufacturers, "If you will use our machines exclusively, then we will keep all your machines in order." Now, as a matter of fact, one of the reasons why the United Shoe Machinery Co. has so many supporters among the small manufacturers in my district is because of the fact that they keep all their machinery in order. I have not any sympathy with their system of "tying" leases at all, but their system for promptly repairing machinery is remarkable.

Mr. WEBB. I think the words "discount from" or "rebate upon" would cover what the gentleman desires.

Mr. GARDNER. I doubt it.

⊥ Mr. WEBB. If there is any doubt, and the gentleman will offer an amendment to cure it, the committee will accept it.

Mr. GARDNER. I should prefer to have the gentleman from North Carolina do that. It is a rather embarrassing thing for me to do, seeing that the United Shoe Machinery Co. is situated in my district. The gentleman from Massachusetts [Mr. PHELAN] can give the gentleman from North Carolina [Mr. WEBB] full information as to the facts.

The CHAIRMAN. The time of the gentleman has expired. Without objection, the pro forma amendment will be withdrawn, and the Clerk will read.

Mr. DICKINSON. Mr. Chairman, I offer an amendment.

The CHAIRMAN. The gentleman from Missouri offers an amendment which the Clerk will report.

The Clerk read as follows:

Page 22, in line 22, after the word "found" strike out the comma and insert the words "doing business and the cause of action may accrue."

Mr. DICKINSON. Mr. Chairman, I have prepared this amendment to be inserted after the word "found" in section 6 [sic] — the words "doing business and the cause of action may accrue;" and I have also prepared an amendment to be inserted in section 10 after the word "found," using the same language. . . .

As I have only five minutes, I prefer to proceed for a few minutes, and then when I have made my statement I will ask for additional time, for the purpose of responding to any questions, if consent is given.

On last Saturday, during the general debate, I made some suggestions with reference to adding some language after the word "found" in section 10, which reads as follows:

SEC. 10. That any suit, action, or proceeding under the antitrust laws against a corporation may be brought not only in the judicial district whereof it is an inhabitant, but also in any district wherein it may be found.

Upon considering the bill, it seemed to me that the same amendment ought to be offered on page 22, in section 5, after the word "found," which says:

That any person who shall be injured in his business or property by reason of anything forbidden in the antitrust laws, may sue therefor in any district court of the United States in the district in which the defendant resides or is found.

You will note that on page 20, at the end of section 1, the following language is used:

The word "person" or "persons" wherever used in this act shall be deemed to include corporations and associations existing under or authorized by the laws of either the United States, the laws of any of the Territories, the laws of any State, or the laws of any foreign country.

I have been told that the language used in these sections is the same language as that used in the Sherman antitrust law. I am informed that the same suggestion I now offer has been made by a distinguished judge who is dealing with this class of legislation and prosecutions under the antitrust law. . . .

Mr. FLOYD of Arkansas. That last suggestion follows the words of the Sherman law, and I never heard any complaint about it:

The word "person" or "persons" wherever used in this act shall be deemed to include corporations and associations existing under or authorized by the laws of either the United States, the laws of any of the Territories, the laws of any State, or the laws of any foreign country.

Mr. DICKINSON. Yes.

Mr. FLOYD of Arkansas. We simply copied the language of the Sherman law.

Mr. DICKINSON. I understand that; but let me proceed further for a moment. I want to call the attention of members of the committee to the fact that this law seeks to provide for an action, suit, proceeding, or trial in the judicial district where the corporation, as mentioned specifically in section 10, is an inhabitant. I want to call attention to the fact that a corporation is an inhabitant of the State where it gets its incorporation, and which it selects as its place of residence. Speaking for a moment with reference to the corporation as distinguished from the person, in section 10, when you use the language—

And also in any district wherein it may be found—

How are you going to find a corporation for the purposes of jurisdiction, not for the purposes of mere service? Of course you can find it by serving certain processes upon its agents, officers, or employees.

Mr. CULLOP. I would suggest that to correct the very matter you are driving at—because this is an attempt to give jurisdiction wherever the cause of action arises—you strike out the words "is found" and insert the words "has an agent." That will give service wherever the cause of action arises. Otherwise, if you leave it in this way, you will have to go to the home of the corporation.

Mr. DICKINSON. Mr. Chairman, I do not agree with the gentleman from Indiana [Mr. CULLOP] in that suggestion. I have before me the amendment suggested by an eminent judge, using somewhat similar language; but I believe that these suits, actions, and proceedings ought to be brought, in the case of a corporation, not only where it is an inhabitant by virtue of its incorporation, and not only against a person who is an inhabitant of a certain State, not only where that corporation or that person may have some agent in a remote district, but it ought to be brought where the corporation or the person is doing business and where the cause of action accrues. . . .

For instance, take a corporation or a person, inhabitant of New Jersey. They may be doing a small business in the State wherein they are incorporated, or where the individual is a citizen, and the principal business may be done in West Virginia or Colorado or in Missouri. Wherever the cause of action accrues, wherever the damage is done, wherever the witnesses are, there is the place where it ought to be at least permitted to be sued and trial to be had.

A New Jersey corporation or a West Virginia corporation may transact business in Missouri or in Colorado or in far-away California. There is where the wrongs may be done, where the violations of the law may be committed, and there is the evidence of these things; and they should not be compelled for the purposes of a trial to have suit brought in some far-away State or district, of which they are the inhabitant by virtue of the incorporation therein or selection of a residence therein. I think, after the word "found," there ought to be additional language such as I have offered in this section. I will ask the Clerk to read the amendment.

The Clerk read as follows:

On page 22, line 22, after the word "found," strike out the comma and insert the words "doing business and the cause of action may accrue."

Mr. DICKINSON. Now, one more suggestion. The same amendment, it seems to me, ought to follow the word "found" in section 5 and in section 10. The same language ought to follow where it provides for the prosecution of a corporation and the prosecution of the person taking into consideration the definition of the word "person." I do not ask to strike out any language of the committee, but simply to add to it, to make clear and definite and certain so that any person and any corporation may be sued not only where it has its residence as a corporation or individual, but that it can be sued wherever it is found doing business and the cause of action may arise.

Mr. [JOHN H.] STEPHENS [D., Tex.]. I desire to ask the gentleman if he will not change the point at which he has offered his amendment. I thoroughly agree with him, but I think it ought to come in after the word "resides," line 22, page 22, so that it will read, "in which the defendant resides, does business, or is found."

Mr. DICKINSON. Mr. Chairman, I much prefer that the amendment finally agreed upon should come from the committee. I have no disposition to inject any amendment of my own or my personality into this bill, but I want such appropriate language as will make it certain and definite. . . .

⊥ Mr. Chairman, I have before me a suggestion of an amendment which came from a distinguished representative of the Government, a distinguished judge, formerly a high official, in which he suggests the following words: It is to insert the words "in the district wherein the defendant may be doing business or have an agent, representative, or director." That does not seem to me to cover the situation entirely. The suit ought to be authorized to be brought against the corporation or person in the district of which he is an inhabitant or where the cause of action accrues and not merely where some agent or representative may be located remote from the point where the damage is done. . . .

Mr. SCOTT. What is the gentleman's understanding of the word "found"; what is its import as used in this section?

Mr. DICKINSON. I understand that there is some decision by some court that I am not very familiar with that may possibly cover the very thought suggested by my proposed amendment. I do not believe that it meets the situation, and if there be any doubt about it, in order that the Government may prosecute successfully and institute suits and actions and have trials the language ought to be clear and definite, and so plain that he who runs may read, so that there can not be two constructions.

Mr. FLOYD of Arkansas. Mr. Chairman, will the gentleman yield?

Mr. DICKINSON. Yes.

Mr. FLOYD of Arkansas. I desire to make an explanation of this provision. It is one of the administrative features of the bill which has the approval of the Attorney General, who has been connected with some of these great trust suits, and this language was used to make this section conform to the existing law and enable him to have greater liberty in bringing these suits. I want to call the gentleman's attention to the fact that that language has the approval of the Attorney General, and while of course that does not bind us, I think if we adopt any amendments to it, it should be after mature consideration.

Mr. DICKINSON. Mr. Chairman, in response to that, I want to say again, as I said before, that I have no disposition to press any amendment suggested by me, and I want to repeat that I prefer that the amendment come from the committee in appropriate language. For that reason I do not care to further press the amendment at this time.

Mr. CULLOP. Mr. Chairman, I desire to offer an amendment to the amendment, in line 22, after the word "or," to strike out the words "is found," and insert the words "has an agency."

The CHAIRMAN. The Clerk will report the amendment to the amendment.

The Clerk read as follows:

Page 22, line 22, strike out the words "is found" and insert in lieu thereof the words "has an agency."

Mr. CULLOP. Mr. Chairman, that will make it read:

In which the defendant resides or has an agency doing business, and the cause of action may accrue.

Mr. FLOYD of Arkansas. Why strike out the words "is found"?

Mr. CULLOP. Because the words "is found" will not avail anything in serving a process or getting jurisdiction of the defendant, except at the place where the corporation resides. The word "found" as used there is vague and indefinite, and means nothing, so far as acquiring jurisdiction is concerned. But I can see that it will do no harm to leave them, and I shall at the proper time ask to modify the amendment in this respect. . . .

Mr. FLOYD of Arkansas. This act applies to persons as well as to corporations?

Mr. CULLOP. Certainly.

Mr. FLOYD of Arkansas. And the words "is found" would certainly give you advantage in dealing with a person.

Mr. CULLOP. It may in such instance. But suppose a person lives in New Jersey, doing business there, how can jurisdiction of him be acquired in any Federal court in Colorado or Nevada? Suppose process is served on him, he will enter his appearance and move to quash the process, and answer that he was called into that jurisdiction by the process of some court. That defendant will never go into Colorado in such a way that he will be subject to a valid service, and if he was called there upon some public business he can quash the service, if it be made upon him, because when a man is compelled to go into a jurisdiction upon public business, you can not serve a process of the court on him and bring him into court and require him to answer a cause of action; but if he has an agency doing business there, then jurisdiction can be obtained over the corporation or the individual in the territory where the cause of action arises. But why insert the language "is found" in this without he has an agent? It may result, and more than likely will result, in a failure to acquire jurisdiction other than at the place where the corporation or individual resides. . . .

Mr. J. M. C. SMITH. Is it not true that in all the States foreign corporations are compelled to appoint a person at the capital for the very purpose of receiving service?

Mr. CULLOP. All that I know of. I thank the gentleman for the suggestion that he has made. In nearly every State there is a law, as the gentleman from Michigan suggests, requiring the corporation to appoint an agent for the purpose of serving process upon him, and if the corporation has no agent in my State the auditor of state is made the agent for that purpose; but now, if we undertake to limit the service of process upon the defendant to wherever it is found, we will never in all probability get jurisdiction in these cases except at the place of the home of the individual or the corporation. What objection could there be to inserting the language "or has an agent"? It will clarify the matter and make certain that which is now uncertain. The defendant can then be found to serve the process upon him; but if you do not do that, when and where will we find the defendant? In many instances only certain persons are delegated by the corporate acts or by-laws upon whom the legal service can be had. That person in such a case would never go into the territory where a cause of action arises, but he would send somebody else there, upon whom legal service could not be made. . . .

In such cases the defendant would always avoid sending the person in the territory upon whom process could be served, and get the defendant into court to answer any cause of action which might be brought, and the cause would go out of court on a plea in abatement. I am trying to have this made so jurisdiction can be secured by a service of process upon the agent, and when there is service upon the agent it will compel the corporation or individual to answer in court the cause of action, but by the amendment of the gentleman from Missouri I fear no one will ever get one of them into court to answer a cause of action or respond to one. He will never be found, he will avoid being found, he will be in hiding, and the injured party will never get service upon him. If he does find him, he will be in a position to quash service for some reason known to some statute in that jurisdiction. Hence I ask the gentleman from Missouri to let the amendment that I have offered be inserted, so it will be of some real purpose to the people who may have occasion to bring suit under this statute, and not be, as it is now, that they will have to travel probably from California to New Jersey or New York to bring suit.

Mr. DICKINSON. I would like to make the inquiry would not the same objection the gentleman makes now apply to the statute where the corporation is an inhabitant by virtue of it having been incorporated there?

Mr. CULLOP. No; clearly not. Let us make this so there will be no avenue for escape.

Mr. DICKINSON. I want to say I have no objection to any additional language. I want to add additional words after the word "found," but I care not whether it be the language I have suggested or the additional language suggested by the gentleman from Indiana, but I really prefer that the committee in charge of this bill offer its own amendment complete and perfect if for consideration. . . .

Mr. FLOYD of Arkansas. Mr. Chairman, I desire to state that the provision written into the bill has the approval of the Attorney General, who is engaged in prosecuting these suits, and the purpose of it is to broaden the language so as to give the Government the widest latitude in securing service, and the amendments suggested are limitations upon that authority. The very broadest language that can be used in a statute of this kind conferring jurisdiction is to give the jurisdiction where the corporation resides or is found. . . .

Mr. [JOSHUA W.] ALEXANDER [D., Mo.]. This is not new language. I think this is language, in haec verba, of section 7 of the Sherman antitrust law.

Mr. WEBB. This is absolutely taken from section 7 of the Sherman antitrust law.

Mr. CULLOP. Will the gentleman permit a question right there?

Mr. FLOYD of Arkansas. Let me read the language of section 7. It says "in the district in which the defendant resides or is found," and, this being supplemental, it was intended to make it read and give it the same effect as in the Sherman law.

Mr. CULLOP. But "is found." A corporation does not move around; it is a stationary affair, and its residence is some place fixed in its articles of incorporation. Now, then, it is stationary. It is the agent who moves around, and then either the law or the by-laws of the corporation provide who are the persons upon whom service can be made to bring them into court; but if you fix it "any agent," as I have suggested, then you have it that wherever there is an agency in any State or District in the Union you can get a valid service if they have any such agent, and then you get it by the law, as most of the States have a statute.

Mr. FLOYD of Arkansas. If the gentleman will permit, I desire again to call his attention to the fact that individuals may be guilty of violating this provision the same as corporations, and that individuals do not necessarily have agents, and it is necessary that we retain this provision in the bill as it is written, in order to give service upon individuals, and corporations are found wherever they are engaged in business and wherever they have agents.

Mr. CULLOP. But individuals doing an interstate business.

Mr. FLOYD of Arkansas. We have here a provision in reference to service that is incorporated in the original act which we are proposing to supplement, so why not follow the language of the Sherman Act in that regard, for that is all we do. . . .

Mr. GARNER. Has the Supreme Court ever passed on that language of the Sherman Act "is found"?

Mr. FLOYD of Arkansas. I do not think so. It is the language of the statute in my State and I think in many others.

Mr. GARNER. Does the gentleman know in investigating this matter or has he run across any decision of the Supreme Court construing that language in the Sherman antitrust law?

Mr. FLOYD of Arkansas. I never did. I never heard of any complaint in regard to it, and in this bill the provisions with reference to service follow the original Sherman law. It has the approval of the Attorney General's office, and there never has been any difficulty about the interpretation of the Sherman law as to service. And so in passing supplementary legislation we should, I think, content ourselves in that regard with the terms of the Sherman law.

Mr. CULLOP. May I suggest to the gentleman from Arkansas that every suit which has arisen under the Sherman antitrust law has been brought at the home of the corporation itself, or at its principal place of business, and therefore there was no occasion to construe this language, "is found," which is ambiguous and uncertain. If you are to construe "is found," you will have to construe that as the place of the residence of the corporation, because it is not migratory. You can not get service upon some person traveling throughout the country and hold your jurisdiction throughout that territory.

Mr. CARLIN. Why should not the suit be brought in the habitat of the corporation? We have been successful so far in that matter.

Mr. CULLOP. In this case for the very best reason, I think. The gentleman from Virginia [Mr. CARLIN] now has disclosed the purpose of this language, and that is why I am combating it, and for the best of reasons, I think. I do not want to make a resident of California come to Trenton, N. J., to bring a suit for violation of this law, but I want him to sue at home in the jurisdiction where the cause of action arose. . . .

Mr. DICKINSON. Mr. Chairman, merely for the purpose of a question, I want to ask the distinguished gentleman from Arkansas whether some similar amendment has not been suggested by a distinguished representative of the Government now engaged in prosecution under the Sherman antitrust law, extending the language, after the word "found," so as to make it clear and certain?

Mr. FLOYD of Arkansas. There has been such a suggestion made by Mr. Dickinson, who is now engaged in prosecuting the Steel Trust for the Government. But this language is broader than the language you contend for. I contend when you leave the words "is found" in the law you can get service on an individual anywhere within the jurisdiction in which he happens to be found and upon a corporation in any place where it is doing business or has an officer or agent upon whom service may be had; and the words of the proposed amendment are words of limitation.

As this is supplementary legislation to the Sherman law, I would ask some of these distinguished gentlemen to explain to me what reason or what policy would require or justify that we should provide one rule as to service under the original law, which we do not repeal nor modify in that regard, and a different rule for bringing suits under this supplementary law. The suggestion was made by the Attorney General, as I understand, so as to harmonize the provisions of the proposed law with those of the existing law and to give the Government the widest possible scope in getting service in these cases, and the provision is right as it is written and ought not to be changed. . . .

Mr. GARNER. The gentleman says this gives the broadest scope possible for the bringing of suits against agents and others. Can the gentleman point out under the Sherman antitrust law any suit that has been brought against a corporation outside of the jurisdiction of its home?

Mr. FLOYD of Arkansas. I can not.

Mr. GARNER. If there has been no suit in these 20 years—

Mr. FLOYD of Arkansas. I do not say there has not. I say that I have not investigated that point.

Mr. GARNER. I was going to assume that there were no suits brought against a corporation except in the jurisdiction of its home, and the prosecuting officers must have assumed that was the only place they had jurisdiction or else there would have been some suit somewhere brought outside of the jurisdiction of the home of that corporation.

Mr. FLOYD of Arkansas. I do not deny or affirm that. I have not investigated that question.

Mr. GARNER. The very fact that there have not been any suits brought in these 20 years—

Mr. FLOYD of Arkansas. I do not admit there have not. I do not concede the fact stated.

Mr. GARNER. I was asking the gentleman that question.

Mr. ALEXANDER. If the gentleman will yield. I think that there are two suits pending in New York against foreign shipping lines for violation of the Sherman antitrust law.

Mr. CULLOP. Now, will the gentleman yield to me for a question?

Mr. FLOYD of Arkansas. You see in this— . . .

Mr. CULLOP. Now, Mr. Chairman, I desire to ask this: You say it is provided in this that where the defendant is found—

Mr. FLOYD of Arkansas. Resides or is found.

Mr. CULLOP. Resides or is found?

Mr. FLOYD of Arkansas. Yes.

Mr. CULLOP. Now, under that language you could not get jurisdiction of the defendant by serving process on an agent, unless you have fixed in the law that service upon the agent will give jurisdiction of the corporation. So that you add nothing whatever to this in any respect, except, as I take it, to fix the place of the residence of the corporation. I ask the gentleman, is it legal to serve process on an agent, and is jurisdiction obtained by such service, unless the law makes him an agent upon whom service of process will confer jurisdiction against the corporation? . . .

Mr. FLOYD of Arkansas. Mr. Chairman, in answer to the gentleman from Indiana, I think it would be a very dangerous practice for us here, in the heat of debate, with differing opinions, to amend a provision relating to service of process, when the very language that is incorporated in this bill has been written in the existing law for 24 years, and there has never been any complaint from any source concerning it, nor any confusion about it; and when the Attorney General of the United States, who was heretofore connected with one of the most notable trust suits that has ever been brought and is now in control of all trust suits now pending, asks us to fix the service in this supplementary legislation in the exact words in which it is found in the existing law.

We followed his judgment. We believe we did right in following it, and we think this House will be wise in following his judgment, because we are not amending the Sherman law. We are merely supplementing it by additional legislation; and there it stands, just as it is written. We are proposing new and supplementary legislation, and in doing so you are proposing by these amendments offered to fix a different rule for service of process in this bill from that provided in the original act. Gentlemen talk about confusion. This would bring confusion. A person in bringing suit under the original Sherman law would obtain service wherever the person or corporation resides or is found, but in bringing suit under the supplementary legislation he would have to follow this new statute and the new rule relating to service injected into it. In the interest of harmony, and especially when there is no objection to the Sherman law in that regard, especially when the highest legal officer in this Government, charged with the enforcement of the law, has recommended it, we feel that we ought to bow to his judgment and reject the amendments proposed. We believe this House would do well to follow recommendations of your committee and leave the provisions relating to service as they are in the bill. The same language used here occurs in other sections further on in the bill. Why have two rules for service in the enforcement of the antitrust laws of this country? Why have one rule in the original Sherman law as it is written and another rule in the supplemental provisions thereto proposed in this bill, which are intended to broaden, and extend the provisions of the Sherman Act, without attempting to curtail or cut short in any respect the virtue, power, and efficacy of that law as it is written? . . .

Mr. GARNER. Would the gentleman favor a statute which would permit service on an agent?

Mr. FLOYD of Arkansas. I think you can get service on an agent under this provision. I do not know how you can sue a railroad corporation unless you get your service on an agent.

Mr. GARNER. If the gentleman finds, upon further investigation, that this provision would not permit it, then would the gentleman object to an amendment?

Mr. FLOYD of Arkansas. If, on mature investigation, we find that any provision of this bill is defective in any way and will not carry out the purpose for which it is intended, I assure the gentleman that nobody will be more willing to accept such an amendment than your committee; but I appeal to you not to change these provisions hastily, in the heat of debate. I think the provisions relating to service properly drafted as they appear in the bill, and that the proposed amendment and others suggested in the debate would narrow the scope of the provisions as drawn. I hope that the amendment will be rejected and that section 5 will not be amended, as the words objected to are a verbatim copy of language used in section 7 of the Sherman Act, proposed for reenactment here so as to make this supplementary legislation harmonize with the existing law.

Mr. SCOTT. Mr. Chairman, I believe the language both in the Sherman law and in this particular section was advisedly used. I think some of the gentlemen on the other side have forgotten some of the occasions when they found it necessary to look up the decisions on this question. It is not a new or unsettled question. The expression "found" as used in connection with Federal jurisdiction of corporations means where the corporation is doing business. A corporation must submit the [sic] jurisdiction of the Federal court either in the home of the corporation, which is the State that creates it, or in some other district or State where it is found doing business. And that does not mean merely where it has an agent or an agency, because many times corporations have an agent or an agency in a State and is [sic] not doing business within the jurisdiction clauses of the statutes. . . .

Mr. SUMNERS. Does it not occur to the gentleman that since this bill contemplates suits may be brought by private individuals, that they be permitted to bring suit where the wrong is done and follow the old rule of procedure?

Mr. SCOTT. You could not adopt any method that would introduce more confusion into the law than that, because the question as to where the cause of action accrued is very often one of great difficulty to decide. It is a matter over which State statutes have no control.

The statute, as suggested by the gentleman from Indiana, of his State could have no effect of conferring jurisdiction on the Federal courts. While I do not think it would harm the section to say "found doing business," because that is what the expression means, it would introduce confusion to use the expression "agent or agency," because that has no limitations in the Federal decisions up to the present time. The expression "found doing business" has become fairly well defined.

The gentleman from Indiana is again mistaken when he says that there have been no suits brought to enforce the Sherman antitrust law except at the home of the corporation. I hope he has not forgotten the great Beef Trust prosecutions[5.534]—a New Jersey corporation was a defendant—which were tried out in Chicago. . . .

Mr. SUMNERS. Does the gentleman believe that if a private individual in California, wronged by a corporation that has its domicile in New York, was forced to resort to the courts in New York you would practically deprive that man of an opportunity, if he was an ordinary citizen, of pursuing the remedy which the law provided?

Mr. SCOTT. You do not do that, because he could always bring suit in California if he can find anyone upon whom to serve process. He brings it in the State court, and the corporation at once takes it to the Federal court. That has been the history and procedure. . . .

Mr. DICKINSON. Take a New Jersey corporation doing business in Texas and doing business in Illinois. It may commit no violation of the law, no wrong, no damage in Texas; and if so, a suit ought not to be brought there. If this same corporation does some one an injury, does do damage in Illinois, ought not the suit to be brought there? I give the widest liberty of bringing suits where the damage is done and where the action arose. My amendment seeks to be fair both to the corporation and to the person and to the plaintiff.

Mr. SCOTT. I could not conceive that anything would deprive the plaintiff of his right to choose the place of trial if he so desired, either in the district where found or where the corporation resides.

Mr. LEVY. Mr. Chairman, this bill is full of ambiguities. The trouble with it is that it will take 20 years to decide what it means, as it did the Sherman antitrust law. The discussion of this bill here has proved conclusively how dangerous it is to interfere with the business relations and rights of citizens all over the country. I claim that these provisions in this bill at the present time are disastrous to the business of the United States. Let me read to you a resolution or petition made by three of the largest manufacturing associations in the world:

We, the undersigned, representing the National Implement and Vehicle Association, the Ohio Manufacturers' Association, and the Illinois Manufacturers' Association, in which States the manufacturing industry represents 33,164 factories, employing 1,084,000 employees, with an annual pay roll of $782,365,000, desire to cooperate with the Congress in legislation which will eliminate business abuses.

We favor an interstate trade commission properly regulated, but we are opposed to all legislation which is discriminatory, and we ask that all other business legislation be deferred until the business men of the United States can become acquainted with the proposed laws, of which they are now entirely ignorant.

Mr. WEBB. Mr. Chairman, I move that the committee do now rise.

The motion was agreed to.

HOUSE DEBATE
63d Cong., 2d Sess.
May 29, 1914

51 CONG. REC. 9466

The SPEAKER pro tempore. Under the rule the House resolves itself automatically into the Committee of the Whole House on the state of the Union for the further consideration of the antitrust bill, and the gentleman from Tennessee [Mr. BYRNS] will take the chair. . . .

[5.534] United States v. Swift & Co., 122 F. 529 (C.C.N.D. Ill. 1902), aff'd with modifications, 196 U.S. 375 (1905).

HOUSE CONSIDERATION 1449

The CHAIRMAN. When the committee rose on yesterday there was pending an amendment offered by the gentleman from Missouri [Mr. DICKINSON], to which an amendment had been offered by the gentleman from Indiana [Mr. CULLOP]. The question now is on the amendment to the amendment.

Mr. WEBB. Mr. Chairman, the committee has an amendment to this section which we think will satisfy the gentlemen who have offered amendments, and if they will withdraw their amendments we will now offer the committee amendment.

Mr. FLOYD of Arkansas. Mr. Chairman, I desire to suggest and offer as a substitute for the pending amendment the following:

Page 22, line 22, insert after the words "is found" the words "or has an agent."

The CHAIRMAN. The Clerk will report the amendment.
The Clerk read as follows:

Page 22, line 22, after the word "found," insert the words "or has an agent." . . .

Mr. DICKINSON. Mr. Chairman, I am contented to withdraw the amendment I offered, with the consent of the gentleman from Indiana [Mr. CULLOP] and of the House, so that it may not stand in the way of the substitute proposed by the committee.

Mr. CULLOP. Mr. Chairman—

Mr. DICKINSON. One second. I want to say this, that while I believe the additional words added would be a better amendment than the one proposed in the substitute, as far as I am concerned I will withdraw my amendment. But I want to give notice that when we reach section 10 I purpose [sic] to offer an amendment to that, using the words "or has an agent where the cause of action arose." . . .

Mr. BARTLETT. As I understand now, you propose to amend the proposition by inserting after the word "found" the words "or has an agent"?

Mr. FLOYD of Arkansas. Yes, sir.

Mr. BARTLETT. And that would apply equally to individuals as well as to corporations?

Mr. FLOYD of Arkansas. Certainly.

Mr. BARTLETT. So that if you could not find an individual against whom you desired to bring suit, but the agent of the individual, you could serve the agent of the individual. Is that true?

Mr. FLOYD of Arkansas. That is true.

Mr. BARTLETT. Ought not the gentleman to further define the agent as an agent who has to transact the business of the corporation? If the gentleman will permit me just a moment; I do not desire to take his time unnecessarily, but it is an important proposition.

Mr. FLOYD of Arkansas. Certainly.

Mr. BARTLETT. Mr. Chairman, I desire to call the attention of the committee to this state of facts. This is an important proposition, because upon the service thus obtained will rest this suit and all suits. If you inquire into the various statutes of the States providing for service upon corporations and upon their agents you will not find, or I have not found at least, any place where the agent of an individual is permitted to be served by a process and to bind the individual.

Mr. MANN. Will the gentleman yield for a question?

Mr. BARTLETT. One moment. Let me finish this sentence. But you can obtain jurisdiction of the individual in any State where he is found by serving upon the person a copy of the process or writ. Now I yield.

Mr. MANN. The gentleman will notice that this provision only relates to the district in which suit may be brought and has nothing to do with service on the defendant. In other words, if this language were inserted and suit might be brought in the district where one person had an agent in the form of another person, service on the agent would not be sufficient to bring the individual into court.

Mr. BARTLETT. Then if the purpose of the section is to give jurisdiction to the court in that particular locality, that court would serve its process upon those within its jurisdiction.

Mr. MANN. Well, it could not serve process upon an individual who was not within its jurisdiction?

Mr. BARTLETT. It could not. No.

Mr. MANN. So after all this provision apparently only fixes the district in which suit may be brought?

Mr. BARTLETT. Yes.

Mr. MANN. Now, it may be that you can serve the agent of a corporation and thereby get service upon the corporation, but you could not serve the agent of an individual and thereby get service upon the individual?

Mr. BARTLETT. Because there happens to be a provision in the Constitution that requires an individual to be sued in the district where he resides.

Mr. MANN. Oh, no. The gentleman is mistaken about that.

Mr. BARTLETT. I am not. At least I do not think I am.

Mr. MANN. The gentleman has in mind a provision about the criminal prosecution where the offense is committed.

Mr. BARTLETT. No; I have not. Anyhow, I will fortify my statement about that, if necessary. Anyhow, my judgment is this should be amended in order to make it safe. To give jurisdiction to a court in that district or that State or that locality over an individual who may have an agent not to transact this business about which you are suing him for, but to transact entirely some other kind of business, such as running a farm, would, in my judgment, be very fatal to it; and this provision with reference to the agency should be limited to the question of an agent of a corporation, because the statutes of the various States on that subject have been upheld. . . .

The CHAIRMAN. The gentleman from Missouri [Mr. DICKINSON] asks unanimous consent to withdraw his amendment, and the gentleman from Indiana [Mr. CULLOP] makes a like request with reference to the amendment to the amendment. Is there objection?

Mr. SCOTT. Reserving the right to object, Mr. Chairman, a parliamentary inquiry.

The CHAIRMAN. The gentleman will state it.

Mr. SCOTT. What would there be before the committee?

The CHAIRMAN. The gentleman from Arkansas [Mr. FLOYD] proposes to offer an amendment. Is there objection to the request made by the gentleman from Missouri and the request of the gentleman from Indiana to withdraw their amendments?

There was no objection.

Mr. FLOYD of Arkansas. Mr. Chairman, I offer the amendment which I have sent to the Clerk's desk, and ask to have the amendment reported again.

The CHAIRMAN. The Clerk will report the amendment.

The Clerk read as follows:

Amend, page 22, line 22, by inserting, after the word "found," the words "or his agent."

The CHAIRMAN. The question is on agreeing to the amendment offered by the gentleman from Arkansas.

⊥ Mr. FLOYD of Arkansas. Mr. Chairman, I understand that some gentlemen desire to speak upon it.

Mr. SCOTT. Mr. Chairman, the amendment to my mind would bring about an anomalous condition. As the section now stands, providing that suit may be brought in any district where the defendant is found, it means that it may be brought in any district—and I refer to corporations—where a corporation may be found transacting business permanently.

Mr. FLOYD of Arkansas. Undoubtedly that is what it means.

Mr. SCOTT. It would not include any agent. The amendment enlarges the present interpretation of the word "found" as applied to the corporate jurisdiction, and permits suit to be brought, with absolute discretion on the part of the plaintiff, in any district in which the defendant may have an agent, without defining the character of that agent.

Now, we all know that there is an almost infinite number of characters of agents. Corporations transacting interstate business have agents, we may say, in practically every State of the Union for some purpose. Surely it can not be possible that the gentleman would attempt to confer jurisdiction and venue upon the Federal court in every district in the United States where any agent can be found, regardless of the question whether the corporation is domiciled in that State or district, or whether it is doing business there.

I believe gentlemen will find themselves in serious difficulty and confusion when it comes to certain other sections of the Federal statutes—those sections pertaining to the removal of causes, for instance, and in many others—because we have a consistent code of procedure at the present time. We have many expressions which through a long series of years of use have crystallized to well-understood meanings and interpretation. If we are to open this venue or jurisdiction to any district in the United States where any agent may be found, we are going to have a great deal of confusion and great injustice is to be done. It is going to open the door wide for annoyances to business, if any man can go anywhere in the United States and institute his action, if he can obtain any colorable service and compel the business institutions of the country to follow him about.

That has been one of the reasons, if not the cardinal reason, why the courts have given the present construction to the word "found," interpreting it to mean the place where the corporation does business, and in giving that interpretation, further, only those suits can be brought there which grow out of the business which the corporation is doing in that State or district. In other words, you can not go into the district of Texas and maintain a suit against a corporation in Texas, with respect to a cause of action which did not pertain to its business in Texas, but which pertained to its business in the State of its domicile. You are going to adopt that line of business if you adopt this amendment, in my opinion. . . .

Mr. SUMNERS and Mr. SINNOTT rose.

The CHAIRMAN. The gentleman from Texas [Mr. SUMNERS] is recognized.

Mr. SUMNERS. Mr. Chairman, I believe this matter of venue is one of the most important connected with the whole subject of antitrust legislation.

As suggested by the gentleman who has just spoken [Mr. SCOTT], unless the venue be properly placed, on the one hand, you may subject the defendant to blackmail. We used to have a custom down in Texas under which suits would be brought in remote sections of the State and the defendants in humble positions would be compelled to pay the amounts demanded because they could not go to the expense of hiring lawyers, taking depositions, and so forth, to defend the causes of action far removed from their homes. The possibility of this sort of procedure ought to be guarded against. On the other hand, if the venue be not properly placed, the plaintiff in humble position may be deprived of the benefits of this bill. The philosophy of legislation with regard to this subject should give the venue at the place wherein the cause of action arises. The recognition of this right to parties injured runs through the whole system of American procedure. It has come down from the common law of England, in which Government it has stood the test of centuries. Why should you not bring a man before the court at the very place where the injury has been inflicted? Why drive a man who has a cause of action to a foreign jurisdiction in order to get his remedy?

I say to you gentlemen in charge of this bill that it ought to be amended so that a man who suffers in his goods or his business in a given locality may bring the man or the corporation that inflicts the injury before the court in that locality, and there have their differences adjudicated, instead of driving the man injured in Texas, for instance, to California or New York in order to procure a redress of the injury that has been inflicted upon him in Texas. It violates the philosophy of remedial legislation and is contrary to that system of procedure which will insure justice among the people and make this law effective. . . .

Mr. STEPHENS of Texas. Is it not a fact that in your city of Dallas, Tex., there are a great many distributing agencies of many manufacturing concerns all over the country, engaged in selling farm implements and farm equipment, and agencies for other purposes, and would it not be a great benefit to the people of our State who purchase machinery from those people to have the right to bring suit in Dallas, for instance, and serve the process upon the agent who has sold this machinery to our citizens? Would not that be a great advantage over the present law?

Mr. SUMNERS. That would be true; but if a corporation or individual, doing business in Texas, with an agent located in Dallas, should go into the Panhandle of

Texas and there inflict an injury on a citizen living in the Panhandle of Texas, that citizen ought to have the right to bring the man or the corporation to the court in the Panhandle, and there compel reparation for the injury inflicted.

Mr. BARKLEY. Is it the gentleman's construction of this amendment that if it is adopted an individual residing in Missouri, having a just complaint against a corporation residing in New York, may go down to Dallas, Tex., and bring a suit against that corporation in New York, and obtain service on an agent in Dallas, Tex., and that that service, under this amendment, would be valid?

Mr. SUMNERS. I am not talking about service. This confusion arises from not drawing the distinction between the individual upon whom service may be had and the place where suit may be brought. That is the confusion that arises under this bill. The service upon the agent is merely a technical method of procuring service upon the corporation; and the residence or nonresidence of the agent cuts no figure in the proceeding, save as it gives a means of getting service. It is all right, in so far as service is concerned, to provide in the bill that service may be had upon the agent and that service upon the agent is service upon the corporation. I am not criticizing that provision. What I am complaining of is that the provisions of this bill giving the right of recovery to the citizen injured by some act prohibited by the antitrust laws may become of no value to the humble citizen unable to go to a foreign jurisdiction to prosecute his suit. . . .

Mr. FLOYD of Arkansas. Mr. Chairman, I call for a vote.

The amendment was agreed to.

Mr. FERRIS. Mr. Chairman, can we not revert to section 3?

Mr. CARLIN. I think that was the agreement—that we should revert to section 3 this morning.

The CHAIRMAN. If there be no objection, the committee will revert to section 3.

There was no objection.

Mr. FERRIS. Mr. Chairman, I offer the following amendment.

The CHAIRMAN. The gentleman from Oklahoma offers an amendment, which the Clerk will report.

Mr. CULLOP. A parliamentary inquiry, Mr. Chairman.

The CHAIRMAN. The gentleman will state it.

Mr. CULLOP. Is not the amendment of the gentleman from West Virginia [Mr. AVIS] now pending and to be disposed of first? I understand it was introduced yesterday.

Mr. AVIS. I have not offered my amendment yet.

The CHAIRMAN. The Clerk will report the amendment of the gentleman from Oklahoma [Mr. FERRIS].

The Clerk read as follows:

Page 21, strike out lines 16, 17, and 18, down to and including the word "products," and insert in lieu thereof the following:

"That it shall be unlawful for the owner, operator, or transporter of the product or products of any mine, oil, or gas well, reduction works, refinery, or hydroelectric plant, producing coal, oil, gas, or hydroelectric energy, or for any person controlling the products thereof, engaged in selling such products"—

Mr. BARTLETT. It is unlawful to do what?

Mr. FERRIS. That is stated in the language of the bill to which this is an amendment.

Mr. STAFFORD. In line 18 the word "product" occurs twice. Which one is referred to on this amendment?

Mr. FERRIS. The second one.

Mr. Chairman, on yesterday the chairman of the Judiciary Committee indicated a willingness to accept and the committee adopted an amendment which included minerals in place. I have been fairly active last night and this morning to determine whether or not that amendment was sufficient, and I have become convinced that it is not sufficient to include oil, the products of oil, or give us any relief, and of course it does not include water power or hydroelectric energy at all. So, if the chairman of the

HOUSE CONSIDERATION 1453

Committee on the Judiciary or those gentlemen in charge of the bill will listen to this amendment, it does three things and no more.

It first prescribes the same sort of regulation for oil and water power that they propose in the bill for other minerals.

On yesterday the house adopted an amendment which I am to-day moving to strike out, with other language, and insert in lieu thereof the language just read by the Clerk. I do not know how the House will feel about it, for I know there is a strong disposition not to amend this bill; but when we come in here with an amendment or a section in this new bill which specifically regulates coal and other minerals, I can not for the life of me understand why we can not at the same time regulate the sale and handling of oil, gas, and water power. The oil question and the abuses that have grown up about it are so important, the appeals on every hand for some relief from it makes me feel a word on what the industry is would be of interest to this House. It follows, as developed in the recent hearings of the Oklahoma oil producers, and can be found on page 11 thereof:

PRODUCTION AND VALUE OF PETROLEUM IN THE UNITED STATES.

In the following exhibit will be found the production of petroleum in the United States since the birth of the industry in 1859 to the close of the year 1912, together with the daily average production and daily average value. Also the combined production and combined value through the series of years, from the records of the United States Geological Survey.

Calendar year.	Years.	Production.			Value.		
		Yearly production.	Daily average production.	Total production, series of years.	Yearly value.	Daily average value.	Total values, series of years.
1859	1	2,000	6	2,000	$32,000	$88	$32,000
1860	2	500,000	1,670	502,000	4,800,000	13,151	4,832,000
1861	3	2,113,609	5,791	2,615,609	1,035,668	2,138	5,867,668
1862	4	3,056,690	8,375	5,672,299	3,209,525	8,793	9,077,193
1863	5	2,611,309	6,332	8,283,608	8,225,663	22,536	17,302,856
1864	6	2,116,109	5,797	10,397,717	20,896,576	57,261	38,199,432
1865	7	2,497,700	6,843	12,897,417	16,459,853	45,095	54,659,285
1866	8	3,597,700	9,857	16,495,117	13,455,398	36,864	68,114,683
1867	9	3,347,300	9,170	19,842,417	8,066,993	22,101	76,181,676
1868	10	3,646,117	9,989	23,488,534	13,217,474	36,211	89,398,850
1869	11	4,215,000	11,548	27,703,534	23,730,450	65,015	113,129,300
1870	12	5,260,745	14,413	32,964,229	20,503,754	56,175	133,633,054
1871	13	5,205,234	14,261	38,169,513	22,591,180	61,804	156,224,234
1872	14	6,293,194	17,242	44,462,707	21,410,503	58,541	177,664,737
1873	15	9,893,786	27,106	54,356,493	18,100,464	49,590	195,765,201
1874	16	10,926,945	29,937	65,283,438	12,647,527	34,651	208,412,728
1875	17	8,787,514	24,075	74,070,952	7,368,133	20,187	215,780,861
1876	18	9,132,669	25,021	83,203,621	22,982,822	62,967	238,763,683
1877	19	13,350,363	36,576	96,553,984	31,788,566	87,092	270,552,249
1878	20	15,396,868	42,211	111,950,852	18,044,520	49,420	288,596,769
1879	21	19,914,148	54,560	131,864,998	17,210,708	47,153	305,807,477
1880	22	26,286,123	72,017	158,151,121	24,600,638	65,399	330,408,115
1881	23	27,661,238	75,784	185,812,359	23,512,051	64,417	353,920,166
1882	24	30,349,897	83,151	216,162,256	23,631,165	64,743	377,551,331
1883	25	23,449,633	64,246	239,611,889	25,740,252	79,521	403,291,583
1884	26	24,218,438	66,352	263,830,327	20,476,924	56,101	423,768,507
1885	27	21,858,785	59,887	285,689,112	19,193,694	52,585	442,962,201
1886	28	28,064,841	76,890	313,753,953	20,028,457	54,872	462,990,658
1887	29	28,283,483	77,490	342,037,436	18,856,606	51,662	481,847,264
1888	30	27,612,025	75,649	369,649,461	17,950,353	49,179	499,797,617
1889	31	35,103,513	96,330	404,812,974	26,963,340	73,872	526,760,957
1890	32	45,823,572	125,571	450,636,546	35,365,105	96,891	562,126,062
1891	33	54,292,657	148,747	504,929,201	30,526,553	83,634	576,652,615
1892	34	50,514,657	138,396	555,443,858	25,906,463	70,977	618,559,078
1893	35	48,431,066	132,688	603,874,924	28,932,326	79,267	647,491,404
1894	36	49,344,516	135,190	653,219,440	35,522,095	97,321	683,013,499
1895	37	52,892,276	144,910	706,111,716	57,691,279	158,058	704,704,778
1896	38	60,960,361	167,012	767,072,077	58,518,709	160,321	799,223,487
1897	39	60,475,516	165,686	827,547,593	40,929,611	112,136	840,153,098
1898	40	55,364,233	151,710	882,911,826	44,193,359	121,080	884,346,457
1899	41	57,070,850	156,358	939,982,676	64,603,904	176,997	948,950,361
1900	42	63,620,529	174,303	1,003,603,205	75,752,691	207,542	1,024,703,052
1901	43	69,389,194	190,107	1,072,992,399	66,417,335	181,965	1,091,120,387

Calendar year.	Years.	Production.			Value.		
(Continued)		Yearly production.	Daily average production.	Total production, series of years.	Yearly value.	Daily average value.	Total values, series of years.
1902	44	88,766,916	243,197	1,161,759,315	71,178,910	195,011	1,162,299,297
1903	45	100,461,337	275,236	1,262,220,652	94,694,050	259,436	1,256,993,347
1904	46	117,080,960	320,770	1,379,301,613	101,175,455	277,193	1,358,168,802
1905	47	134,717,580	360,081	1,514,019,192	84,157,399	230,568	1,442,326,201
1906	48	126,498,936	346,556	1,640,513,128	92,444,735	253,273	1,534,770,936
1907	49	166,095,335	455,056	1,806,608,463	120,106,749	329,060	1,654,877,685
1908	50	178,527,355	489,116	1,985,135,818	129,079,184	353,642	1,783,956,869
1909	51	183,170,874	501,838	2,168,306,692	128,328,487	351,585	1,912,285,356
1910	52	209,557,248	574,129	2,377,863,940	127,899,688	350,410	2,040,185,044
1911	53	220,449,391	603,971	2,598,313,331	134,044,752	367,246	2,174,229,796
1912	54	222,538,604	609,695	2,820,851,935	164,087,342	449,554	2,338,317,138
Total	—	2,820,851,935	—	—	2,338,317,138	—	—

(Supplement to the Oil and Gas Journal, Tulsa, Okla., Oct. 2, 1913.)

⊥9469 ⊥ The shocking growth of this mammoth monopoly, which is now paying 50 cents per barrel for oil in Oklahoma oil fields and selling the same oil at Port Arthur to the Federal Government for $1.39 per barrel, and its profits and dividends are so amazing that it is worth while to pause and observe them. Its dividends, exclusive of other profits, since its organization are as follows:

Standard Oil Co. of New Jersey—Dividends paid since organization.

		Total production, United States, barrels.	Total value.
1882 to 1901, inclusive	$351,833,000	887,180,070	$726,700,123
1902, rate, 45 per cent	43,851,956	88,766,916	71,178,910
1903, rate, 44 per cent	42,877,478	100,461,337	94,694,050
1904, rate, 36 per cent	85,188,266	117,080,960	101,175,455
1905, rate, 40 per cent	39,335,320	134,717,580	84,157,399
1906, rate, 40 per cent	39,335,320	126,493,836	92,444,735
1907, rate, 40 per cent[1]	39,335,320	166,095,335	120,106,749
1908, rate, 40 per cent[1]	30,335,320	178,527,355	129,079,184
1909, rate, 40 per cent[1]	39,335,320	183,170,874	128,328,487
1910, rate, 40 per cent[1]	39,335,320	209,556,048	127,896,328
Total	709,762,620	2,192,050,411	1,675,761,300

[1] Estimated.

Dividends by rates paid from organization to 1901, inclusive, were as follows: 1882, 4 1/2 per cent; 1883 and 1884, 6 per cent; 1885, 10 1/2 per cent; 1886 and 1887, 10 per cent; 1888, 11 1/2 per cent; 1889-1891, 12 per cent; 1892, 12.21 per cent; 1893 and 1894, 12 per cent; 1895, 17 per cent; 1896, 31 per cent; 1897, 33 per cent; 1898, 30 per cent; 1899, 33 per cent; 1900 and 1901, 48 per cent.

At the recent hearings before the Interstate Commerce Committee on this matter Mr. J. J. Maroney, an independent producer of Oklahoma, introduced into the record a comment on those figures that are as true and forceful as they are illuminating and instructive.

His remarks are as follows:

Magnificent though the figures above given are as representing the profits actually taken down by the monopoly during the years of its growth, they really present but the most trivial portion of the wonderful potentialities of the concern to extract profit from the business. There is no possible accounting of the extent of properties bought up by this company itself and by its numerous subsidiaries, side companies, and sometimes professed opponents, and much-advertised "independents." These properties were bought up at prices fixed by the conditions which it was in the power of the monopoly to make, having the power to fix and to manipulate the quoted prices of the crude article. The limitless power of the monopoly, in other words, has been but partially seen and exposed in the record of dividends actually paid. The relentless use of that power is seen in the conditions in the fields where the choicest properties are constantly gravitating to the possession of the interests in which the power vests. That the condition has not changed with the so-called dissolution is as plain as the virility of the exercise of the same power during the halcyon days of the open avowal of the monopoly and its purposes. The thoughtful will see in this plain lesson that unregulated transportation in the article is the thing that is to be dissolved if the prevailing conditions are to be changed, and not the monopoly, which is the inevitable fruition of that power which private control of transportation gives. While the fact continues that the article is transported by agencies which are subservient to private interests and not, as in all other commercial articles, to public interests, the private interests in control will naturally, inevitably, and always continue to soak up the profits in the business. Men are not rascals for doing this. By all rules of business, which has its resemblance to piracy in some of its aspects and always will have, those men are "shrewd"; and shrewdness is a relative term and trait. If all men were equally alert, each one just exactly the peer of every other, there would be none accorded the credit of being "shrewd." It is not innate perversity which guides men to take the limit of advantage which comes to them by the less than equal alertness of their fellows. The "general results" in part indicated by the table above spells more than anything else the lack of shrewdness which prevails in an industry where the burden of "hazard" falls apparently all to one side and the bounty of profit so largely to the other.

Our people have been robbed by pipe lines, by drilling offset wells, by refusing to carry the oil at all, by maltreatment until our patience is gone.

Oil from its character can only be carried through pipe lines, all of which are interstate, so they escape our State law, and it is up to Congress while legislating on trusts to relieve us from the most vicious of them all.

It can not await another session. It has waited too long now. We are on the subject of regulating trusts; our hands are to the plow; let us get some relief from such oppression to the people who produce, to the people who consume.

There is no more fertile field in which to work, and I think the committee should adopt this amendment. . . .

The abuses of the Standard Oil Co. in my State are enough to amaze not only the State of Oklahoma but the entire universe. We are second in the United States in the production of oil. The State of California is first in its production. Our State, however, produces 65 per cent of the refinable oil of the United States. This morning I have submitted my amendment to some departmental experts of the Geological Survey. I have submitted it to the Assistant Attorney General for the Interior Department, in whom I have confidence and from whom I have received help before, and they think my amendment will accomplish much good and, in short, do the business. I dislike very much to come in here and offer an amendment to the bill of the Judiciary Committee, but on yesterday the committee said with great frankness that they intended to include oil, and I have no doubt they would be glad to include water power. If the amendment is not what it should be, we can perfect it in the Senate or in conference, or later you can revert to it and perfect it here. This is not the last word on the subject. There is no chance to go wrong when proceeding in the right direction. Undoubtedly this Congress ought not to pretend to legislate on minerals without including oil, gas, and water power. The worst monopoly in the country to-day is the Standard Oil Co. What earthly reason can anyone assign why it should be omitted?

Mr. Chairman and gentlemen of the committee, in my haste I have omitted many of the things I feel duty bound to say with reference to the oil situation in my State and in the country. But for want of time I shall for the moment pass to a question so intricate, so monumental in importance, that I scarcely dare to try to say a word about it in this Hall of Congress. Up to a few months ago I might well and truthfuly [sic] say I knew little or nothing about water power or the many ramifications and intricate problems connected with it. I am again within the facts to say that I know now but little of it, its importance, or an intelligent handling of it. I must, however, in frankness say that during the last three months the Committee on the Public Lands have given the most patriotic attention and study to this monumental problem.

There developed in hearing much testimony brought to us by Secretary Franklin K. Lane, and, to my mind, he is the most efficient, the most capable Secretary of the Interior that the country has had in administering its affairs. The country is peculiarly fortunate in having a man at the helm who has first-hand information on these problems. The country is again fortunate to have a man who knows how to do and dares to do the things that should be done. Such a man is Hon. Franklin K. Lane, the present Secretary of the Interior.

His unbounded patriotism and industry made him willing to, and he did, turn over to the Committee on the Public Lands for their use, information, and edification two of his very best men, to wit, Dr. George Otis Smith, the head of the Geological Survey, whose industry, patience, and ability as a geologist and an engineer is worthy of the keenest commendation. Again, he afforded us and kept ever present in the committee during the sessions Mr. E. C. Finney, Assistant Attorney General for the Interior Department, whose efficiency and ability may well be acknowledged.

The Agricultural Department afforded us the services of the chief engineer of the Forest Service, Mr. Merrill, who gave us much valuable information that we needed to have in dealing with this intricate question. The chart which I have brought in before you and which now stands before you on the pedestal was prepared by the departments, pursuant to long, careful, and faithful work. It brings in a word what some would not have time to run down and shows clearly the interlocking situation with reference to water power and its various ramifications.

The hearings quite well disclosed that the control of the water powers of the country is coming more and more into a few hands. This was strikingly shown by the testimony given in the recent hearings before the Public Lands Committee and in the evidence there submitted. Not only is the complexity of interlocking directorates shown by the chart before you, but a statement discussing this control of water-power development in the Western States was incorporated in the hearings of our committee at the suggestion of my colleague on the committee, the gentleman from Illinois [Mr. GRAHAM]. The statement goes into the matter with considerable detail and forms about 60 printed pages, and was prepared by engineers of the United States Geological Survey. The information regarding the water power developed in the 11 Western States is largely taken from original data in the files of the Geological Survey and the Forest Service, while the affiliations of the corporations controlling the great bulk of this power were ascertained by the works of reference dealing with corporation matters, as well as the current files of financial journals.

This statement is valuable as a continuation of the 1912 report of the Commissioner of Corporations on the subject, and it is especially noteworthy that the short period which has elapsed between that report and the preparation of the present statement, although only two years, has witnessed marked changes ⊥ in the situation. In the first place, the increase in amount of development in these Western States has been large, while the tendency toward concentration into large financial units has been even more marked, so that the stage is already reached where the entire territory of these 11 Western States is practically divided among the larger companies. Thus 28 operating companies control 90 per cent of the developed power in the West, and 6 of these companies control over 100,000 horsepower each. Even more striking, however, is the increase in the number and importance of public-service securities holding companies during these recent years. While 3 of such companies were active in 1912 and were then noted as "general electric companies," these appear to have been but the forerunners of a horde of such corporations whose titles are characterized as simply "bewildering permutations of a few adjectives and nouns." It is because of the enormous capitalization of these companies and their large holdings of the securities of the operating companies I have just mentioned that the subject attains the utmost importance.

The system of stock holding through these holding companies is elaborate. While the stocks and bonds of the operating companies are offered to the public for investment, the controlling interest is usually retained by a holding company; in many cases the method of control exercised is publicly known, while in still other cases the holding companies confine their public reports of their activities to bare statements of the amount of securities held, concealing the identity of the operating companies over which control may be so exercised.

In the detailed statement submitted to the Public Lands Committee it is noted that while many of the holding companies, so far as public information indicates, have no relations with any particular operating companies, they do possess directors in common with other holding companies whose affiliations are more definitely known. Instances of interlocking directors, which of themselves might not be conclusive evidence that the same general financial interests are concerned, are repeated, however, to such an extent that a practically complete network of holding companies is established and thus the evidence of community of interest becomes very strong. The compiled list of the important companies operating in the West includes 24 holding companies, and it is to be noted that certain men are very conspicuous. In these 24 holding companies 50 men together hold 135 directors' positions, so that if the 24 companies were considered as together forming one large corporation in which each man had as many votes as he now has in the separate companies these 50 men would have little short of a majority. Further, 2 of the directors are each connected with 7 holding companies, 3 with 5, and 4 others with 4; all of these gentlemen are connected with the General Electric Co. and its acknowledged subsidiaries. The relations brought out by these lists of directors make it reasonable to assume that the General Electric Co. dominates the water-power situation. In some cases the companies are direct subsidiaries, in others they bear a subsidiary relation to the General Electric Co.; in the third class there is shown a predominant General Electric influence, while in the fourth class the companies are associated with the General Electric Co. through interlocking directors, and in a fifth class there is an apparent association through banking affiliations. The statement before our committee suggests that the harmonious relations between those who control the water-power situation of the West are to an important extent due to affiliation of interests of greater magnitude than may have been analyzed in this connection. It may be regarded as entirely probable that relations similar to those indicated in this statement and on this chart as existing between the operating and holding companies under discussion would be found to extend much further if the relations of the General Electric Co. and the American Telephone & Telegraph Co., the United States Steel Corporation, the Standard Oil Co., the Amalgamated Copper Co., and the large railroad companies to the great financial interests were studied.

The gist of the whole matter is that large and powerful financial interests of the East are strongly intrenched in their control of the water-power situation of the West as well as of the East. Future additions to their monopolistic holdings may be prevented by legislation now proposed by the various committees already mentioned, but that will not suffice. The present strangle hold by these big monopolies must be broken if the communities and industries of the West are to have freedom. Nor should we in our thoughts or in our legislative acts separate the mineral fuels and their monopolistic control from this subject of hydroelectric energy and its control; together the fuels and the water power constitute the great public utilities, which are not only of importance to present-day prosperity, but are coming more and more to be vitally essential to the civic and industrial life of the future. If trust legislation is to free the people, it should not neglect any one of these great natural resources—coal, oil and gas, and hydroelectric energy. The trusts have not neglected them.

We have had before us ex-Secretary of the Interior Walter Fisher. We have had before us Mr. Gifford Pinchot. We have had before us the head of the Geological Survey, Dr. George Otis Smith. We have had before us Secretary of the Interior Lane's most competent men to help us. We have had before us the best talent and the best information we could get on the subject. As a result of that we have reported a bill which the House may or may not reach this session. The parliamentary situation is such we can not, in all probability, reach it this session. In any event, we are at work on control and regulation of the abuses that have grown up in the mining and removal of coal and other minerals, and we should reach the other offenders, who are as bad or worse.

Mr. CAMPBELL. I did not get from the reading of the amendment at the Clerk's desk just what its purpose is. Its purpose is to include oil, gas, and water power, to give the same sort of regulation that the bill proposes to give to coal, minerals, and so forth; and if any live man on either side of this Chamber, inside or out of it, can assign one reason why it should not be done I would like to hear it. . . .

Mr. BRYAN. If your amendment carries, any concern that has water power to sell must sell it and can not arbitrarily refuse to sell it to any responsible person. The city of Seattle has a lot of current to sell, and if your amendment passes and the Stone-Webster people want to buy it, will we have to sell it them [*sic*]?

Mr. FERRIS. If they offer to pay the same price and you have it to sell. Remember this amendment or the original text has no application unless the commodity is being sold "arbitrarily."

Mr. BRYAN. Will not your amendment make every municipality in the country sell out?

Mr. FERRIS. No; you might as well say that every coal mine in the country would have to sell all their coal to a single concern. That was so stated here the other day, but no one could possibly be misled by that. The gentleman's trouble is not a real one, I am sure. It is purely fanciful.

Mr. BRYAN. How can the gentleman say that and say that Seattle must sell?

Mr. MANN. Look at the map.

Mr. BRYAN. I see the map.

Mr. FERRIS. This amendment, if agreed to, does precisely for water power and oil what the bill now does for coal.

Mr. GARNER. If it ought not to apply to coal, it ought not to apply to water power. . . .

Mr. BARTLETT. The gentleman speaks about water power. He means the current produced by water power?

Mr. FERRIS. Yes; my amendment says the current produced by hydroelectric plants. There is no difficulty about that; it will include them.

The CHAIRMAN. The time of the gentleman from Oklahoma has expired. . . .

Mr. [BYRON P.] HARRISON [D., Miss.]. The gentleman says operator or transporter. The question I desire is whether or not the word "transporter" carries with it the distribution of this electric current or the transmission of the electric current.

Mr. FERRIS. I think it would, and it would also include pipe lines, which is very much desired. The electricity and oil are only susceptible of one method of transmission; oil goes through the pipe line and the current of electricity is transmitted by wire. They ought to be included as common carriers and be subjected to the same regulation as common carriers. On yesterday the chairman of the Judiciary Committee expressed a willingness to take in oil, and I hope he will now consent to take in water power as well. . . .

Mr. STEPHENS of Texas. Does the gentleman believe that his amendment is sufficiently strong to include pipe lines carrying oil to market? I am very much interested in that, because the greatest oil field in the United States is in my district.

Mr. FERRIS. I think it is. Of course, if it is not strong enough, we can adopt this and then amend it. It ought to be drawn tight enough to accomplish it. . . .

Mr. [JOHN I.] NOLAN [Prog., Cal.]. If I remember aright, the Hetch Hetchy bill contains a provision that prohibits the city of San Francisco from distributing any electric energy from Hetch Hetchy to private corporations for resale. How would this provision affect that?

Mr. FERRIS. If the power they use themselves, this would not have any effect on it. As to the surplus power, it would decree that they should sell to those who applied on equal terms. It would at least prevent any arbitrary sale of it, and it ought to.

Mr. J. I. NOLAN. Would the Great Western Power Co. and the Pacific Electric Co. come in on equal terms with private municipalities?

Mr. FERRIS. Not at all; the city owns its own plant and can use it for its own purposes as it desires. That is a special act on a lot of conditions contained therein, and this does not meddle with that.

Mr. J. I. NOLAN. But I am speaking about cities along the right of way.

Mr. FERRIS. I do not think so: it would not apply any more than it does to the coal provision in the bill. You will recall that none of this section applies unless arbitrary methods are resorted to. There certainly can be no objection to that. The facts stated by the gentleman have no application here.

Mr. J. I. NOLAN. I understand that; but I want to know how this affects the Hetch Hetchy current.

Mr. FERRIS. I do not think it affects it in any way. That is a special grant and it would not affect it. . . .

Mr. DECKER. I would like to ask the gentleman, in a word, what the meaning of this language will be after he amends it and what it means now? Does this section mean that a man can not sell to one man and withhold selling from another, or refuse to sell to another? Is that what it means, or does it mean that if you have anything of this nature mentioned in the section to sell, you would have to sell it if any responsible person wants to buy it?

Mr. FERRIS. The gentleman reaches to the main fabric of the section which was more fully explained by the chairman of the committee yesterday than I could do in the short time allotted me.

Mr. DECKER. I did not understand that explanation.

Mr. FERRIS. Well, the chairman of the committee can state it more ably than I can. In a word, my amendment does for water power and oil precisely what the Judiciary Committee seeks in this bill to do for coal.

Mr. DECKER. What does the section mean now is what I want to know.

Mr. FERRIS. I refer the gentleman to the chairman of the Judiciary Committee.

Mr. DECKER. And then I want to know what it means after the gentleman has amended it by his language.

Mr. FERRIS. My own view is, and it is not the best or last word on the subject, it is intended as an antimonopoly amendment, and it seeks to keep the party producing from mines coal or other minerals from practicing extortion on one set of citizens to the exclusion of others. Its purpose is certainly a laudable one and I am sure it appeals to the gentleman.

Mr. DECKER. Does the gentleman think that that is what it does?

Mr. FERRIS. I think that is what it accomplishes. I am contending for the same regulation that they apply to coal to be applied to oil and water power.

Mr. [MARTIN D.] FOSTER [D., Ill.]. Will the gentleman allow me to suggest that the very energy produced by coal provided for in this bill is also produced by water power which you want to include.

Mr. FERRIS. The gentleman is correct about that. I thank him for the suggestion. It is true. . . .

Mr. BARKLEY. Before anybody will understand what this section means the court will have to pass upon it. Now, the definition of the word "arbitrarily" is the crux of the whole matter in this section.

Does the gentleman believe that this section as amended or as it now stands might be construed by the court to mean that any responsible purchaser might come and propose to purchase the entire output or product of any given corporation, and that corporation, notwithstanding the needs of various individuals in that community, could be compelled to sell its entire product to that responsible corporation if it offered the price demanded?

Mr. FERRIS. Mr. Chairman, the gentleman can have his distorted idea of what it means. My idea is not a distorted one, nor is the idea of the Judiciary Committee distorted but they are seeking to regulate the sale of the God-given treasures of the universe to all mankind alike, and the section, I think, accomplishes that. They might distort and force into it complicated constructions of it and try to make it mean something else, but I do not think so. I am willing to adopt in toto the views of the Committee on the Judiciary on the section and say that it is a good section, but I want to add to it two of the most notorious monopolies in the world and make it a better section.

Mr. BARKLEY. Is the gentleman able to suggest any further amendment that would relieve the section of the possibility of such construction? I am in sympathy with the gentleman's idea.

Mr. FERRIS. I will leave that to the Committee on the Judiciary. If the general tenor of the section is not pleasing to the gentleman or to the Members of the House, they can amend it. . . .

Mr. FLOYD of Arkansas. Mr. Chairman, the committee is not willing to accept the amendment offered by the gentleman from Oklahoma, and I desire to state very briefly the reasons why we oppose the amendment and why we think the question involved in it should not be incorporated in this measure. The gentleman from Oklahoma is the chairman of the Committee on the Public Lands, and the question involved in his proposition constitutes one of the greatest and one of the most controverted issues in this country to-day, and it is the province of the committee, of which the gentleman is the chairman, to deal with this great question, and we do not think this trust legislaton which is intended to deal with certain specific subjects and known evils ought to be loaded down with such issues as this. We think that the particular subject which he intends to embody here is worthy of a great and carefully considered bill, which I hope the gentleman's committee will bring into this House at an early date. He includes in his amendment questions and issues that are not embodied in the provision as it is written. In section 3 we deal with raw material, mineral, and mineral products, and your committee have stated heretofore that the language incorporated in the bill as originally presented was designed and intended to include oil and gas, but on account of doubts expressed as to that fact and as to the scope of the provision as written, we readily consented to the amendment which was adopted on yesterday, which expressly includes oil and gas, and when we have done that we think we have gone far enough. Gentlemen do not seem to realize in proposing this legislation we are not going along lines of easy resistance. Every proposition in this bill is controverted by terrific forces, and every gentleman who succeeds in getting a more drastic and far-reaching provision placed upon the bill is helping the enemies of the bill in addition to helping the proposition for which he stands. . . .

Mr. FERRIS. The gentleman says that the committee of which I am fortunate enough to be the chairman should deal with this.

Mr. FLOYD of Arkansas. Undoubtedly the gentleman's committee has jurisdiction to deal with it.

Mr. FERRIS. Oh, not at all. We have jurisdiction over the disposition of sites only, and have nothing whatever to do with the regulation of these matters. It is purely up to the gentleman's committee, and we have no jurisdiction over it. We have reported a bill with reference to the disposition of sites, but I know the gentleman from Arkansas on a moment's thought will recognize that we have nothing to do with the regulation of sites already existing.

Mr. FLOYD of Arkansas. Then I suggest that the gentleman should have appeared before the Committee on the Judiciary, if his contention is correct, and presented reasons and arguments in support of the amendment now proposed. I suggest the exceeding great danger not only to the ultimate fate of this bill but to its speedy consideration in bringing in propositions of such momentous importance as those suggested by the gentleman from Oklahoma, who asks us on a few moments' discussion to accept them. . . .

Mr. [JAMES S.] DAVENPORT [D., Okla.]. Mr. Chairman, I would like to ask the gentleman if his objections to the amendment are because of the fact that he fears it may endanger the passage of the pending bill, or because he thinks there is no merit in the amendment?

Mr. FLOYD of Arkansas. Not exactly either and partly both. In regard to the first suggestion, I think that whenever we interject a proposition of that kind, on which there is a division, we do encourage and aid the enemies of the bill, because we bring new recruits to aid in the future those who are against the bill; and in regard to the merits of the proposition, I submit we have had no opportunity to consider them; and the gentleman from Oklahoma has offered the amendment here on the floor of the House and yet never before suggested to the Judiciary Committee, and no one else ever suggested, that that particular phase of the water-power question was a thing to be dealt with in this trust bill; and I insist it is not fair for the gentleman from Oklahoma, who has been giving this question great study, and which is an issue almost as great in itself as the trust question, to bring it in in this way before us and insist upon its adoption at this time. . . .

Mr. DAVENPORT. Mr. Chairman, I wanted to say to the gentleman from Arkansas that I have not very much knowledge with reference to water power. Unfortunately or fortunately, I live in a country where we have very little water power, but I am especially interested in the provision relating to the transportation or sale of the crude oils and their refined products, which are produced to a large extent in my State. Does not the gentleman think we should have some relief?

Mr. FLOYD of Arkansas. That is an intrastate matter, and we have no jurisdiction over that. We can only deal with matters in interstate commerce.

Mr. DAVENPORT. I was asking from the point of view of interstate legislation and not intrastate, and because I took it that the consumption of oil by the entire people of the United States is an interstate question and not an intrastate question.

Mr. FLOYD of Arkansas. We have conceded an amendment as to oil and gas; we have allowed it to go into the bill. Now, there is another objection to putting this legislation in here. This, in so far as antitrust legislation is concerned, is a new provision, a new departure in legislation. Section 3 stands out alone, a new proposition, based upon certain conservation ideas in this country. The section as written limits its application to raw materials, the products of the mines producing iron, copper, coal, and other minerals, including oil and gas, but the gentleman proposes to extend its scope into the domain of manufactured products. . . .

And we draw the line in section 3 upon such products. It was insisted by some extremists that we ought to extend the provisions of section 3 so as to make them apply to manufactured products. It was not the purpose or the design of the committee to do anything of the kind, and the gentleman, on a much more difficult question, is seeking to depart from the original purpose of the bill and deal with manufactured products, such as electricity, when we refused to apply this section to any manufactured product of any kind whatsoever. . . .

Mr. FERRIS. Does the gentleman think that oil which comes out of the earth or power produced by falling water is a finished product? What could be more God-given than those two things? Why does the manufacture occupy any different status—

Mr. FLOYD of Arkansas. You will never pass any statute in this House or elsewhere that will control falling water that comes from the heavens. You are attempting an absurdity in such talk. You are endeavoring to control a product of manufacture as a result of water power. Electric currents sent by the hand and instrumentality of man by machinery into the current of interstate trade and commerce are manufactured and not natural products.

Mr. FERRIS. I will debate that with the gentleman if he so desires. . . .

Mr. HARRISON. Is the gentleman aware of the fact there is now a bill pending and on the calendar from the Committee on Interstate and Foreign Commerce dealing with the question of water power?

Mr. FLOYD of Arkansas. I am perfectly aware of that, and I think the Interstate Commerce Committee and the Committee on the Public Lands, of which the gentleman from Oklahoma is chairman, are the committees that ought to take up this great question and deal with it in a separate bill, matured and duly considered in all its phases; and for that reason, not saying anything against the merits of the proposition, I oppose the amendment. It may contain merit, but I advise the House never to accept an amendment of such magnitude and of such far-reaching consequences as are involved in this proposal in this way.

Mr. [CHARLES M.] THOMSON [Prog., Ill.]. Mr. Chairman, the argument of the gentleman from Arkansas to this amendment might apply to any amendment that might be offered on the floor of this House. Certainly he does not propose to say that the membership shall be precluded from offering amendments, important or not important, if they happen not to have appeared before the committee and urged them there. . . .

Mr. FLOYD of Arkansas. Not at all; but this amendment was brought in by the gentleman from Oklahoma [Mr. FERRIS], chairman of a committee having jurisdiction of this question, and if he proposes to legislate in this bill concerning one of the greatest questions before the American people, and one of the most controverted, and incorporate provisions in this bill relating to it, I think it is due the Committee on the Judiciary, under those circumstances, that he should have appeared and submitted the matter to the committee.

Mr. THOMSON of Illinois. The very facts that the gentleman recites are additional reasons why this amendment should be considered and adopted. It comes from the chairman of the committee that has jurisdiction over the subject matter with which this amendment has to do, but that committee does not have jurisdiction over the precise thing involved in this amendment. One of the reasons why I rose, Mr. Chairman, was to answer my friend from Washington [Mr. BRYAN], who says that the adoption of this amendment would necessitate—

Mr. BRYAN. Attempt to answer.

Mr. THOMSON of Illinois. I will attempt to answer—

Mr. BRYAN. The gentleman evidently did not expect to get recognition until I made my speech.

Mr. THOMSON of Illinois. Oh, I heard the speech, and sometimes the gentleman is heard without making a speech. [Laughter]. He contends that this amendment, or the adoption of the amendment, will force a municipality to sell out to a trust. I confess I do not like the substantive language of this section. It says it shall be unlawful for an owner or an operator of a mine or any person controlling its products to refuse arbitrarily to sell such product to anybody who applies for it. If somebody who controls a product, heat, let us say, or power, should apply under this section to a municipality for that product and the municipality should refuse to sell certainly no court would hold that that was an arbitrary refusal where the municipality went into court and showed, as they could do under such circumstances, that the applicant for the power was merely trying to get hold of it for the purpose of monopolizing it and using it as a trust. That would not be construed as an arbitrary refusal to sell. The court would not therefore compel the municipality to dispose of the product to the first person coming along providing that was the kind of person it was. This is an important amendment, and it is important that it should be adopted, and the fact that Mr. FERRIS, chairman of the Committee on Public Lands, which committee has jurisdiction of this subject matter, happens not to have appeared before the Committee on the Judiciary and urged the amendment is no reason why it should not be considered, and every reason cited by Mr. FERRIS why it should be adopted is in my opinion sound, and I hope the committee will adopt it. . . .

⊥ Mr. LEVY. Mr. Chairman, I offer the following amendment.

The CHAIRMAN. An amendment is pending.

Mr. LEVY. They say that all amendments have to be put in now. . . .

Mr. BARTLETT. Mr. Chairman, I am opposed to this amendment, because, in my judgment, if it is adopted and made a part of this bill and finally becomes a law, we will venture into a sea of confused conditions and ideas with reference to the administration of this law which would be more complicated and confused and crossed and obsure than the diagram of the wires that we see in front of us and to which the gentleman has referred. [Applause.]

Why, Mr. Chairman, the law which we propose to amend and which we have probably wisely proposed to amend, having passed one bill to give relief, known as the "trade-commission bill," is an advance along the lines of regulating and controlling interstate commerce and those who may engage in it. It took 20 years of consideration and adjudication of cases in the Supreme Court of the United States to finally reach a position where the present law is understood and can be enforced. It took 20 years in order to arrive at a point where sane and sound suggestions might be made and to propose sane and sound amendments to that law.

In 1910 this House passed an act putting oil pipe lines and things of that character under the control of the Interstate Commerce Commission, and it has taken the Supreme Court a long time in that case and in its consideration, and it has not yet been able to render a decision of whether Congress has the right to regulate or control the transmission of oil through pipe lines. Now, we propose to venture further upon the sea of law and say that not only pipe lines and gas lines, but lines that transmit power by electricity, because it is produced by the water power of the land, shall be regulated by Congress.

⊥ Mr. Chairman, I am ready at all times to advance along lines where we may render relief to the people against monopolies and restraints of trade in interstate commerce. I do not concede the doctrine that Congress has any right to control the water power of the land except in order to provide for navigation.

I do not concede the right of Congress to regulate in any way the prices of water power generated by the use of the streams. And, so far as that is concerned, I have heretofore expressed my views upon the question and filed them in this House. In connection with the very able Members of this House now connected with the Committee on Interstate and Foreign Commerce, I have given my views on that subject; and whatever may be the clamor or the demand that we proceed and destroy all business of every kind and take away from the States the rights that have been conceded to them, I am not ready to yield to that public clamor now, nor do I expect hereafter to yield to it. . . .

Mr. [J. A.] FALCONER [Prog., Wash.]. I wanted to ask the gentleman if he thinks the natural resources in the Western States, for instance, or any other State, ought to be used for the benefit of the people of the whole United States?

Mr. BARTLETT. Oh, I think the States have the right, where it is not public domain or land that belongs to the United States Government, to regulate the water power on that domain and the resources of it through State laws in the States in which those resources are situated, and the States should not be interfered with by Congress, and I believe that Congress has not the right to interfere. I do not say that with regard to the Western States simply because the Western States have asserted that doctrine of late and have maintained it. I have asserted it as my doctrine with reference to the rights of every State, and that is the position that every man who hopes to see the perpetuity of our system of Government ought to take and stand upon.

Mr. Chairman, I repeat that this Committee on the Judiciary, after months of careful inquiry and patient study, dealing with the laws and decisions in the past, has brought into this House a bill covering all the subjects that they have deemed it wise and proper to consider for the purpose of amending the Sherman antitrust law. . . .

My opinion is that in some phases we have gone too far; but this, I venture to say, is a venture upon a sea of uncertainty which you can not fathom and can not sail upon. . . .

Mr. KENT. Mr. Chairman and gentlemen, if there is any possible excuse for putting into this bill a clause providing for equitable distribution of coal these other sources of power and energy should without question be placed in equal position.

I do not know whether or not this bill will be of service to the public. I am not sure but that these matters can be equally well handled under the common law or the vague Sherman law, which has been made more or less definite by court decisions. But the bill is here before us, and if we are going to recognize the evils of monopoly in the anthracite coal fields, and possibly some of the other fields by this provision in section 3, we certainly should recognize the necessity of controlling other forms of energy. In a little while we shall clearly realize that the control of the mechanical energy of the Nation, either by the Nation or by the States on one side or by private and oftentimes greedy individuals on the other, means the welfare or the ruin of our prospects for greater equality of economic opportunity.

Gentlemen have talked about bills emanating from other committees. The bill from the Committee on Interstate and Foreign Commerce, referring to power on navigable waterways, is based necessarily upon a request for a concession from the Federal Government. To my mind, it is sadly inadequate. As conditions precedent to such grants there may be demanded, and should be demanded, regulation in the public interest. In the water-power bill, which the Committee on the Public Lands has reported, we have worked on that theory and have fully protected the public. We find that we can control the concession granted by and in the name of the Federal Government for the interest of the consumers. But those sources of supply and those bills do not by any means include sufficient remedies against abuse that are to be attempted by this bill. They are merely incidental to a present partial public ownership. In this bill we are legislating concerning property in private ownership in order to prevent trusts and monopolies, resultant in extortion by the improper use of so-called private property, all of which is only held by the power and the privilege granted by organized society; and if we are to control monopoly of anything and prevent extortion under any cloak, we are here and now forced to control this water-power product in the interest of the public, whether situate on public or private land.

If we are going to demand equality of treatment in the oil and in the coal and gas business and in the other resources that furnish energy, the proper and only place where we can define such control is right here and now in this bill. If this bill means anything looking toward trust and monopoly regulation it certainly must take into account the control of these most important items. [Applause.] . . .

Mr. BRYAN. Mr. Chairman, I am as heartily in favor of any law that will restrict the Water Power Trust, the General Electric Co., or whatever you call it, as any man on the floor of this House. I believe in the public ownership of these utilities. I believe in the cities and communities owning and operating them, and I believe in putting this Water Power Trust out of business and taking away its rights entirely.

But under the present conditions these two forces are struggling for supremacy all over this country—the Water Power Trust and the public—in the various municipalities. The cities and larger municipalities come here, like the city of San Francisco, and get a grant from Congress, such as the Hetch Hetchy, and then counties and States are going into that line of activity more or less, and there is a continual fight between those two contesting forces. To-day the trust is trying to absorb every water power that it can and prevent the municipalities from winning or from progressing along those lines. The municipalities have the right and power of eminent domain. They can demand and take away from the trust, and they can demand and take away from any private owner of these water-power grants their rights, and can appropriate them to the use of the municipalities and sell the current, sell the product of the water power at cost, without any profit whatever.

But now we come to a provision that requires any owner of such a water power—a municipality, for instance, after it does go through the condemnation proceedings and gets possession of it—to sell the product to any concern that comes along and wants to buy. We boast that our cities are able to sell this current cheap, and they are so able. They reduce the price continually. And so when the trust comes along and says, "I will pay you more than you are getting now for the current produced by this water right; I will pay you twice what you are getting"; and the city says, "No; I will not sell it to you." The Water Power Trust says, "By this bill of Congress you are compelled to sell it to me, and you can not refuse to sell it to me." Thus one of the effects of the bill would be to give the General Electric Co. and the Water Power Trust of this country that which is superior to the right of eminent domain against the municipalities of this land. It would be to give those people the right to take away from us, whenever they wanted to, those utilities by buying the entire product of the plant we had acquired.

I am willing to have a law of this kind passed if it provides that no such refusal to sell shall be permitted when in restraint of trade, and let it be determined whether or not each particular case is in restraint of trade. Let each case stand on its merits when the time comes; but I am opposed to putting into the law a provision that gives to any set of men the absolute, unequivocal right to buy in small or in wholesale quantities the rights that the cities of this land have acquired by all the toil and trouble incident to the acquirement of these utilities. These private individuals have the cash in bank. They can draw their checks for $500,000 or $1,000,000 and say, "Here is the money." The cities can not do that. The cities have to float bonds; they are hampered in every way about getting the money, so that the General Electric Co. could go to any city at any time and say, "Here, I want to buy your plant. You are competing, and we want your plant or the product of your plant. We have out there a competing plant. I will give you 25 per cent more than you are making now. Will you refuse?" The city would say, "Yes, indeed, we refuse." Then they will produce this law ⊥ which says that it shall be unlawful for the owner or operator of any such utility to refuse.

Mr. SUMNERS. Does the gentleman contend that a private corporation can exercise the right of eminent domain against a municipal corporation?

Mr. BRYAN. Of course I do not. It can not do it; but you put this law on the statute book, and any corporation, firm, individual, company, or concern can go and take the product of a public utility away from a city merely by offering to buy and tendering the cash, and the city can not refuse; it is absolutely prohibited. The trust could go and get a court order compelling the city to deliver, and if they did not deliver, the mayor and council would go to jail. The corporations will not get the right of eminent domain, but they will get a power superior to it. If the cities of this country could go to a private corporation and say, "Here, we want to buy your plant, and here is the money for it, you have got to sell it to us," that would be an easy way of getting it; but they can not do that. They have got to go into the courts and have long procedure, and the delays incident to the exercise of the power of eminent domain before they get it; but here you want to fix it so that the General Electric Co. can come and say. "Here, we want this. Here is the money, and you must sell it to us." The little city of Bremerton has just voted on the proposition of buying the electric lighting plant. I do not know how the election went, but I think they will buy it. But in the meantime, under such a law as this, a private concern could exercise the right of buying up the product of that light plant after the city acquired it, and then they could raise the rates on the people. Let the people alone in this country and in a few years cities and towns will not be pestered by Boston financiers who are attempting to monopolize all the traction companies and other public utilities.

Mr. DAVENPORT. Mr. Chairman and gentlemen of the committee, I confess I am not as much interested in that part of the amendment offered by my colleague from Oklahoma [Mr. FERRIS], which relates to water power, as I am in that part of the amendment which relates to oil and gas. The State which I have the honor to represent in part is one of the largest oil-producing States in the Union, and yet new oil fields in Oklahoma are being brought in every few months. The independent producers and refiners in Oklahoma are without the proper protection from the pipe-line companies, owned or controlled by the Standard Oil Co. or its subsidiaries, one of the greatest monopolies to-day in the United States. The provision of this amendment relating to oil and gas is not broad enough to furnish all the relief necessary to aid the independent producers in the oil fields in Oklahoma, but it will be a start in the right direction, and I am anxious to see the amendment adopted, or a similar amendment, that will require the sellers of oil and its by-products to treat all customers fairly and to sell to all alike. I want to see the law so drafted that the pipe-line companies may be prohibited from engaging in the production of oil. If we can so draft the law as to prevent owners of pipe lines from engaging in the production in competition with the other producers, then we will have accomplished what is necessary to prevent monopoly in the oil fields by the pipe-line owners. Without assigning any reason and with no visible condition to cause a reduction the Standard Oil Co. and its subsidiaries, the Prairie Oil & Gas Co., began to reduce the price of crude oil in the Oklahoma fields and reduce the price from $1.05 per barrel in the Healdton field to 50 cents per barrel, and in the other fields in Oklahoma from $1.05 to 75 cents per barrel. The situation in the Oklahoma field is anomalous and seems to be growing worse daily, and the question is, What remedy is the proper one to enact into law so as to give the people who are producing oil and gas in Oklahoma the protection that they are entitled to?

I do not think the amendment that was incorporated in this section on yesterday is sufficiently broad to control those engaged in the transportation and selling of both crude and refined oil. I am specially interested in the oil proposition, because my State produces one-third of the output of oil to-day in the United States and almost 65 per cent of the refinable oil in the United States, and we are in a very peculiar condition in Oklahoma with reference to the production, transportation, and sale of oil. The independent producers of Oklahoma are absolutely at the mercy of the pipe-line companies as the purchasers of their oil. It was suggested to me awhile ago by the gentleman from Arkansas [Mr. FLOYD] that it was an intrastate question. I say it is not an intrastate question. We can regulate the sale and control of the product as long as we can consign it to points in the State; but we can only handle it to the State line, and then when it comes to a question of getting a market and transporting the oil and selling it beyond the State line it becomes an interstate proposition, and the pipe-line companies are to-day trying and doing everything they can to choke out the independent oil producer in Oklahoma and compel him to sell his product for anything that they choose to give him. Three months ago crude oil was selling in the Oklahoma fields at $1.05 a barrel.

The statement I am including in my remarks will show the production of oil from 1850 down to and including 1912. It may be claimed by some that supply and demand regulate the price of crude oil and that the reason for reducing the oil to the price it had been reduced by the pipe-line companies in Oklahoma is because of the quantity of oil they have on hand and the market for the sale of the same and its products. I do not believe this contention to be correct, nor do I believe the facts surrounding the transactions in the mid-continent oil field will bear out such a theory. It is indisputable that the pipe-line companies and the Standard Oil Co. are not developers of oil fields, but that the oil field is developed by the independent producer, who seeks out a location where he believes oil is to be found and spends his hard-earned money in developing the field. It is true that the moment the independent producer develops oil in a locality the great oil monopoly or one of its branches immediately rush into the field, through its paid employees, and begin to take leases and will, if possible, give a higher bonus for a lease than the independent men can possibly pay. Not only that, it is the history of the oil monopoly, so far as I have been able to observe it, that it will raise the price of oil and encourage development until an oil field is well developed and until the independent producers have invested heavily in production and development, and then it has been the experience of indepedent [sic] producers that the oil monopoly will reduce the price of oil for the purpose of forcing out the independent producer and compelling him to sell his product to the controllers of the pipe lines or the oil monopolies operating in the field. Another condition that is very detrimental to the independent producer and the independent refiners of oil is the fact that the pipe-line companies, or those who control the pipe-line companies, as soon as a field is developed, immediately begin to secure leases and become producers in competition with the independent producers and will develop the property belonging to those who control the pipe line in such a way as to force the independent producer to expend great sums of money in development to protect his line; that is, the pipe-line company, or those who own the pipe-line stock, will secure a lease adjoining a lease belonging to an independent producer and will immediately develop their property by drilling wells along the line of the lease of the independent producer, and this forces the independent producer to drill his property or to permit the pipe-line company or the parties owning the lease with whom they are operating to drain his land through their wells. Such manipulation of oil leases in the oil field as I have just spoken of is largely responsible for the bankruptcy of many independent producers and works a hardship and disadvantage to all of the independent producers and damages them very materially in their properties.

The relief needed by the independent oil producers and the refiners in the way of legislation is a law that will beyond question make the pipe-line companies common carriers and prohibit a pipe-line company or anyone who is owner of the stock in a pipe-line company from engaging in or being interested in the production of crude oil in a field where the pipe-line company that he owns or is interested in enters the field for the purpose of transporting oil from one place in a State to another place in said State or from one State to another. No common carrier should be interested in the production of the product it is carrying to the extent that it should be permitted to discriminate against those who are producing, by carrying its own product and refuse to carry the product of others. I want to see the oil industry prosper and I want to see men who invest their money make a profit, but I do not desire to see one class of men engaged in an industry and manipulate it in a way as to rob another class of men who are in a legitimate business for legitimate profit.

If the wells in the Oklahoma fields were permitted to run their full capacity, it would be 225,000 barrels a day: the reduction of 30 cents per barrel amounts to $67,500 a day that is being taken from the people of Oklahoma: less than what they were receiving three months ago. . . .5.535

⊥ Mr. WEBB. I yield to the gentleman one minute more, in order to ask him a question. I wish to state to the gentleman from Oklahoma that the gentleman from Ohio [Mr. BATHRICK], who seems to be something of an expert on this oil question, and who is just as insistent that oil be included in this section as the gentleman from Oklahoma is, offered an amendment which the committee accepted, so that the section would read that it shall be unlawful for the owner or operator of any mine or natural mineral deposit to refuse arbitrarily to sell. The gentleman from Ohio [Mr. BATHRICK], with his expert knowledge, assured the committee that "natural mineral deposit" included oil.

5.535 At this point Congressman Davenport inserted in the *Record* a chart identical to that reprinted *supra* at 1453-54.

Mr. DAVENPORT. I hope the gentleman is correct. I have not run down the definition of "natural mineral deposit" sufficiently to say whether or not that is technically correct. I hope it is. I am in doubt, and I think the Geological Survey is in doubt upon that question. . . .

Mr. [JOHN E.] RAKER [D., Cal.]. Mr. Chairman and gentlemen of the committee, I am in favor of the Ferris amendment. Having determined that it shall be unlawful for one operator to dispose of the product of his mine to one and refuse it to another, which is intended unquestionably to mean coal, there can be no question why the operator of the oil well should not come under the same category as the mine owner. It is for the same purpose, used in the same way, and if one should be controlled the other should. There is no distinction to be made in regard to gas. The committee has fully and thoroughly gone into this subject and determined that this legislation is necessary in regard to coal mines. Now, it is not a question of going into the natural features as to oil and gas; it is only a question for the determination by the House whether or not they should apply the same rule to oil and gas as they apply to coal; and to the question of hydroelectric power, which is the fourth subject, it is the same as the other three.

The committee has determined that it should regulate the question of coal. The question of the conservation or the non-conservation, whether a man should have the right to build a reservoir on the public domain, what should be the rules of the Government in regard to it, how much he should pay, whether or not navigable or nonnavigable streams should be regulated, whether or not the bill as prepared by the Committee on Interstate and Foreign Commerce should be passed, whether or not the bill of the Public Lands Committee should be passed, has nothing to do with this question. Having once determined the right, having once entered into interstate trade, can there be any reason why you should regulate the man that handles the coal, and should not control the one that deals in oil or gas that covers all the various industries as coal, and the same way in regard to hydroelectric energy that is distributed?

It does not matter what the Government is going to do on navigable streams nor as to the method regulating it, nor does it apply to the nonnavigable streams on the public domain. All those things will be disposed of by proper legislation, and in due time—and that will be at this session of Congress. But the point is that having once determined the right, the man entering into business in distributing hydroelectric energy, in distributing oil and distributing gas, should be placed on the same basis, under the same rules and restrictions, as the man who is dealing in coal. The question suggested by one gentleman opposed to this amendment that a man can go out and buy out these dealers or distributors of gas and electric energy ⊥ is all moonshine of the worst kind, because this bill is intended only for the purpose, as I have stated—that when you have a supply of hydroelectric energy, if he is supplying it to any particular locality, then he must supply it to the adjoining city or the adjoining party who desires to have it for mining or milling purposes. You could not buy the whole plant. It is only a question of saying that A and B shall be equally treated; that they shall be permitted to buy at the same price; not that you can go in and say, "Mr. A, I want to buy you out, and you will be compelled to sell or else come under a penalty." I therefore trust that the committee will adopt the amendment offered by the gentleman from Oklahoma. . . .

Mr. BEALL of Texas. Mr. Chairman, the committee in framing this bill attempted to reach certain evil practices connected with the conduct of business in this country and at the same time sought just as few restrictions as possible consistent with reaching the recognized evils.

In the conduct of business in this country it has always been recognized that a man should have a right to select his own customers, and the committee in this bill specifically prescribe that that right shall remain with the man who is proposing to do business. But the question came up that with respect to certain natural products there had been abuses of such a character that some regulation was demanded. So the committee put into this bill the provision that the man who engaged in commerce who owned mines and handled the product of the mine should not have this right, ordinarily given a man who is engaged in business, to select his own customers, but that he should be compelled to sell that product to anyone who applied to him for purchase; in other words, that he should not have the arbitrary right to refuse to sell. . . .

Mr. RAKER. A man, on the one hand, operating a coal mine and the other a gas well—can there be any distinction between [the two?][5.536]

Mr. BEALL of Texas. As I understand it, the bill as it stands now has been broadened so that there is no question but that it includes not only the product of the mines, but also the product of the gas and oil wells. Those are great natural products. Now, gentlemen say because you include coal you ought to include gas and oil. Very well; we have done that. Now they say, having included the natural products, you must go a step further and include all the instrumentalities that are used for the distribution and use of the natural products. The gentleman from Oklahoma says you must include the pipe lines. If they are pipe lines operating wholly within the State of Oklahoma, they are within and under the control of the State of Oklahoma. If they are pipe lines operating in interstate business, they are all under the control of the Interstate Commerce Commission, placed there by Congress. Whatever regulation may be necessary for the control of pipe lines Congress has already authorized and empowered the Interstate Commerce Commission to provide.

Now, gentlemen go further and say that you ought to include not only these natural products but those things that are manufactured out of the natural products, the refined oil; you ought to include not only water power but electric energy that is developed from water power. You see that there is a progressive demand and that there is no end to it. If you ought to include electric lines because electricity is developed by water power, then you ought to include steam, because steam comes from coal.

Mr. FERRIS. They are already controlled.

Mr. BEALL of Texas. And you ought to include the manufactured products of the factory, because they are manufactured by a power which is generated by steam that comes from coal, that comes out of one of these mines, and so on and on. This committee, as I said in the beginning, attempted in this bill not to cover the whole universe, not to cover or attempt to correct every conceivable evil that might arise in connection with doing business in this country, but it sought to reach certain recognized, well-defined evils, to bring them under the inhibition of the law, to apply the corrective power of the law to these specific things, and it is my judgment that you will have a much more effective law, a much simpler law, a much better law, if you will limit the provisions of this bill to universally recognized evils, correcting them, and when you have done that I think the country will be willing to approve your efforts. . . .

Mr. [CHARLES D.] CARTER [D., Okla.]. Mr. Chairman, I am very glad to know that my friend from Texas [Mr. BEALL] wants to confine the operations of this bill to some specific injustice, for there is no business under heaven's canopy that has been the subject of such oppression and mistreatment as has fallen to the lot of the independent oil producers in Oklahoma. We have in that State five pipe-line companies, all owned or controlled, it is asserted, by the Standard Oil Co. These oil companies, it seems, in order to evade responsibilities as common carriers refuse to ship the oil of the independent producers, but buy it at their own price. They have the independent people completely at their mercy and can purchase oil at their own price, for they make of themselves exclusive purchasers when they refuse transportation of the product of any other person. Having a monopoly of transportation facilities they can and do fix the price of oil as best suits their convenience. This is not the worst. If the pipe-line companies would only take the oil production at their own price, the independent producers might be able to exist; but it is asserted by the independent producers—and I believe it to be a fact—that the pipe-line companies will not give independent producers a fair distribution in transportation.

The oil of the independent producers is flatly refused at any price until the

---

[5.536] The words "the two?" appear in the daily *Congressional Record* print, 51 CONG. REC. 10275 (daily ed. May 29, 1914), but not in the permanent edition.

production owned by the pipe-line companies is taken care of. This is the worst monopoly on the face of the earth. It is worse than monopoly; it is larceny, for the pipe-line companies themselves, mind you, are producers of oil and own leases and titles to land right adjacent to that of the independent producers. I say larceny, because when they refuse to take the product of the independent operator they simply draw the oil from his land beneath the surface and produce it from their own wells, so that within a few years the independent producer finds his profitable oil well converted into a "duster."

I want to call your attention to the Healdton field in my home county. This Healdton field was brought in about eight or nine months ago, and arrangements were made with pipe-line companies to take care of the production at $1.05 per barrel, and the pipe line companies continued to take this product at $1.05 per barrel until 60 or 90 days ago. Then within 30 days different cuts in price were made by pipe lines, who are the only purchasers, and who have a complete monopoly of the field, until oil today in this field is only worth 50 cents per barrel. The Healdton producers when they were induced to develop that field were first led to believe that they would have no difficulty in getting pipe lines to take all the oil they could produce. At different times restrictions in the amount transported have been made until now the pipe-line companies refuse to carry over 8,000 barrels per day, and I see by the papers that one of the many wells in this field is now producing 6,000 barrels per day. So that the pipe-line companies really will take only 2,000 barrels more than the production of the largest well. A cut in price within 30 days from $1.05 to 50 cents and a reduction of the amount purchased from perhaps 20,000 to 6,000 is the deplorable condition that the small operators in this field are up against.

Mr. BEALL of Texas. How can we reach that by this law? How can we compel a man to buy?

Mr. CARTER. Oh, Mr. Chairman, the gentleman had five minutes and I wanted to interrupt some of the statements made by him very badly, but I did not do it on account of the short time he had, and I hope he will now let me continue.

This amendment may not reach that specific point, and I believe it can be improved upon, but as has been said by the gentleman from Oklahoma [Mr. FERRIS] most of that can all be trashed [sic] out either by the Senate or in conference, so that our people will get some relief.

My friend from Texas [Mr. BEALL] asserted that pipe lines had all been taken care of by Congress. I would like to know when that was done. I also want to call the gentleman's attention to the fact that the decision of the Commerce Court held that pipe lines were not even common carriers, and for this reason our small operators in the past have been unable to get them to take any part of their product at any price, not even at 50 cents per barrel. If the Supreme Court of the United States should reverse the Commerce Court and declare these lines to be common carriers, that would give considerable relief, but what should be done is to divorce production from transportation. Pipe lines ought not to be permitted to own oil deposits, for whenever they do you will place all other operators completely at the mercy of the pipe lines and permit them to rob them of all their own oil, as I have already stated, by drawing it off through the wells of the pipe line company.

You have a bill here to supplement existing laws against unlawful restraints and monopolies and other purposes. You are providing for relief from monopolistic oppression along other lines. On what ground, then, do you refuse to assist the small independent oil operators in the State of Oklahoma and other oil-producing States? . . .

Mr. KELLY of Pennsylvania. Mr. Chairman, the logic of the gentleman from Texas [Mr. BEALL] seems to be that an evil must grow intolerable before it should be dealt with by legislation. That is hardly the end and aim of this legislation, if it is to protect the people against the evils of monopoly. I hope that this amendment of the gentleman from Oklahoma [Mr. FERRIS] will be adopted, because without it this bill will not touch one of the mightiest potential monopolies in this Nation. Charles Steinmetz, consulting engineer of the General Electric Co., made a statement recently in which he pointed out the possibilities of water-power development, and said that in a few years not a running stream of water would be found in the country but that the water would be stored in reservoirs and dams to furnish power to be used for every routine duty of the household, as well as for transportation.

The General Electric Co. at the present time owns 35 per cent of the developed water power of the Nation, and will become one of the main monopolists of the Nation if this monopoly is to be permitted to continue. Without such a provision as this amendment of the gentleman from Oklahoma, it seems to me, this antimonopoly measure would be as bad as the tragedy of Hamlet with Hamlet left out, because the railroad monopoly, the United States Steel Trust, and other monopolies will be as nothing compared to the menacing possibilities of the water-power monopoly of this Nation, unless action be taken in time.

We have heard from the gentleman from Georgia [Mr. BARTLETT] of the sanctity of State rights and that such sacred rights must not be desecrated. I want to say, Mr. Chairman, that the State rights theory has passed its day and we are not solving national problems by piecemeal and by fractions in this year of 1914. Here is a problem, national in scope, that touches the people of the United States, and this amendment should have the support of every Member of the House who believes that the people of the Nation make up an entity and that a State can not be expected to solve a national problem such as the water-power monopoly, which concerns every man and woman and child of the United States.

President Roosevelt in his message in 1908 called attention to the fact that the water monopoly threatened to become one which would interfere with the rights of every American citizen. In his message of February 26 of that year he said:

Among these monopolies, as the report of the commission points out, there is no other which threatens, or has ever threatened, such intolerable interference with the daily life of the people as the consolidation of companies controlling water power.

Must we wait until this "intolerable interference with the daily life of the people" becomes an accomplished fact before dealing with it? Surely we have seen enough of that kind of let-alone policy, which has resulted in a brood of marauding monopolies, to convince us that an ounce of prevention is worth a pound of cure.

I would call your attention, further, to the recent report of the Inland Waterways Commission, which contains the following statement:

Wherever water is now or will hereafter become the chief source of power, the monopolization of electricity produced from running streams involves monopoly of power for the transportation of freight and passengers, for manufacturing, and for supplying light, heat, and other domestic, agricultural, and municipal necessities, to such an extent that unless regulated it will entail monopolistic control of the daily life of our people in an unprecedented degree.

The Nation must act if we are to prevent special-privilege control of the sources of power and its production and distribution. Here is an opportunity to do something now, and I hope that this House will show its appreciation of the value of this great asset of the American people. If the section means anything, this amendment will reach the question of water power, the basis of the greatest monopoly possibility in the Nation. That is the demand of to-day—not to wait until intolerable evils have grown up, but to guard against conditions which may become intolerable in the future. [Applause.] . . .

Mr. [FRANK W.] MONDELL [R., Wyo.]. Mr. Chairman, I desire to offer a substitute for this amendment.

The CHAIRMAN. The Clerk will report the substitute.

The Clerk read as follows:

Page 21, line 17, strike out all after the word "mine," all of lines 18 and 19 down to and including the word "commerce," and insert in lieu thereof the following: "Oil or gas well or water-power plant, or anyone controlling the products of mines, oil or gas wells, or water-power plants to discriminate in price or otherwise as between persons or places for a like product delivered under similar terms and conditions, or." . . .

The CHAIRMAN. The question is on the substitute offered by the gentleman from Wyoming. . . .

Mr. MONDELL. Mr. Chairman, the committee, in reporting this bill, intended to compel miner operators, and those controlling mine products, to sell their products to whoever made a reasonable offer for them. That is undoubtedly the intent of the provision. Unfortunately it is not happily stated, and if the paragraph were adopted as it is in the bill it would take the courts the next 20 years to determine what constitutes an arbitrary refusal to sell a product. What we ought to do, if we are going to legislate on this matter of the sale of products at all, is to say that there shall be no discrimination as between persons and places in the sale of products delivered under similar terms and conditions. That sort of a provision will meet the evil we seek to meet, the evil under which the owners of mines, the owners of oil wells and gas wells, the owners of water-power plants sometimes refuse to sell to any except those with whom they have made contracts. It would take the courts a good long time to decide whether such a refusal was an arbitrary one if it were not an outright refusal, but an offer to sell at an impossible price and under conditions of delivery to which a person seeking to purchase could not accommodate himself. . . .

Mr. AUSTIN. Under the gentleman's amendment would a coal operator be compelled to sell 10 tons of coal at the same price as he sold 1,000 tons of coal?

Mr. MONDELL. The gentleman is a good judge of the English language, and he knows that under my amendment he would not be required to do it; he would be required to sell a like product under similar terms and conditions of delivery and in like quantities for the same price. In other words, he would be compelled to sell to Jones, if he had it for sale, the same amount of coal in the same quantity and under the same terms of delivery at the price at which he sold to Brown.

Mr. AUSTIN. How does the gentleman interpret the original provision of section 3 on that point?

Mr. MONDELL. It is impossible for anyone to interpret it. As a matter of fact, the point I am attempting to make is not directly treated in section 3. All that section 3 says is that there shall not be an arbitrary refusal to sell. What is an arbitrary refusal to sell? And is there a gentleman here who can venture, or will venture, a guess as to what the courts might say constituted an arbitrary refusal to sell? I have intended in my amendment to cover the ground covered by the amendment of the gentleman from Oklahoma, and in addition to that I have attempted to define what it is that we seek to prohibit; that is, the refusal to sell the same product under similar terms and conditions of delivery at the same price to all who may seek to buy. . . .

Mr. WEBB. We intended to cover that very proposition in section 2 of the bill. Section 3 goes a little further, because we are dealing with products of the mine. . . .

Mr. MONDELL. Mr. Chairman, my opinion is that there is a real evil that we must meet. There has been a great deal of complaint throughout the country of the high price of bituminous and anthracite coals in many localities. When you come to investigate that question in its relation to bituminous coals you find this to be the fact, that bituminous coals are sold at the pit mouth all over the country under the keenest competition and at low prices—at prices so low that it is difficult, owing to the competition, for the operator to make proper provision for safety in the mines. But before the coal reaches the consumer it has gone through processes of contract under which the consumer is compelled to pay in many instances an outrageous price. If we prohibit the refusal to sell to anyone who seeks to purchase, and do it in an equitable way, as provided by my amendment, we will, I believe, relieve a situation which is acute and intolerable in many parts of the country.

Gentlemen have referred to oil and water power. My motion is that, while the amendment would be useful and valuable with regard to oil and water power, it is of even more importance with regard to bituminous coal. It may be exceedingly important with regard to the sale and distribution of water power. While we are legislating on this subject we should make it very clear and definite what it is that we prohibit. My amendment, reading it with the balance of the section, is that it shall be unlawful for the owner or operator of any mine, oil or gas well, or water-power plant, or anyone controlling the products of these mines or wells or plants, to discriminate in price or otherwise between persons and places for a like product delivered under similar terms and conditions. And then it shall be unlawful for them to arbitrarily refuse to sell. My amendment definitely states what it is we prohibit, and the courts will then have no difficulty in determining what constitutes an arbitrary refusal to sell.

Mr. LEVY. Will my colleague allow me?

Mr. MONDELL. In just a moment. Without a provision of this kind it will be utterly impossible for the courts to determine. An operator may offer to sell at a price far above what he is receiving from others. He may offer to sell under impossible conditions of delivery. He may agree to sell quantities in excess of the needs of the purchaser, and the courts will have no sort of guide without some language such as I suggest as to what constitutes arbitrary refusal to sell. If my amendment is adopted, then we shall have prohibited discrimination as between persons and places for like quantities under similar terms and conditions, and the courts will be able to determine in each individual case whether the law has been violated.

I yield now to the gentleman from New York.

Mr. LEVY. I would like to ask the gentleman if he does not consider the United States acted arbitrarily in Alaska in refusing to sell coal lands or opening them up?

Mr. MONDELL. Oh, yes. But because some officials of the department may have done wrong, there is no reason why in legislating now on this matter we should not do our duty. I do not fear the effect upon legitimate operation of legislation of this character when it is properly drawn and clearly defines its purpose. Such a provision as this was contained in a bill for the leasing of coal lands in Alaska, which I introduced several years ago, and which should have become a law. Such a provision is contained in two bills which I have introduced at this session of Congress for the leasing of coal and oil and gas lands. . . .

Mr. HARRISON. Mr. Chairman, this amendment enlarges the present section of the bill by proposing to include in it coal, gas, oil, and hydroelectric energy. The amendment adopted to the section on yesterday, which was offered by the gentleman from Ohio [Mr. BATHRICK], included mineral deposits. It seems to be conceded that coal and oil and gas are included in the words "mine or mineral deposits," and I shall therefore confine my remarks to the question of hydroelectric power. In my opinion, there is no question before the American people that is quite so large and important as the regulation and control of water-power corporations and monopolies throughout the country, and I concede to no Member here a more progressive spirit in that direction than I entertain. I believe it is such a large question that more consideration should be given to it than the few minutes' discussion that we have had here in the House on this section. It is so large and important that three committees of this House have been working on it for many months. This amendment is carelessly drawn. There is even a variance of opinion between those Members of the House who advocate the amendment, not only in the meaning of it but the effect of it. You can not legislate intelligently on so important a matter in an hour and a half's consideration.

There is now on the calendar of this House a bill reported out of the Committee on Interstate and Foreign Commerce that deals with this question intelligently. I believe it will be called up for consideration and passage before the House adjourns. There has also been reported by a subcommittee to the full Committee on Foreign Affairs a bill dealing with the question of hydroelectric energy developed at Niagara Falls. That bill will be reported to the House shortly. There is now on the calendar a bill that deals with the question of hydroelectric energy generated from water power on the public lands of the country, reported out of the committee over which the author of this amendment, the distinguished gentleman from Oklahoma [Mr. FERRIS], presides. These bills deal with this question in all its phases, and will give all the Members of the House an opportunity to express their views, so that we can really get at the very milk in the coconut of this question. And it seems to me, Mr. Chairman, that we ought not now to pass this amendment that deals with it in a loose-shod kind of a way and does not give the relief that is really needed.

The question that actually confronts us is not, so far as respects hydroelectric energy, that water power companies will not sell their hydroelectric energy to other concerns or people, and thereby create a monopoly, but the important question, so far as concerns water power, is that these companies charge too much for their current and they are not answerable, so far as service is concerned, to the Interstate Commerce

Commission of the United States or the public service commissions of the various States . . .

That is quite a different proposition from that which would apply to coal and to mines, because the mines and mineral products of the country have been gobbled up and controlled by a few companies to that extent that the owners of them will not sell their products so that the people can be benefited. They are withheld from the market for various reasons. The greatest trouble with the water-power companies is service and rates. Let us wait and pass such water-power legislation as will deal with the question fully, completely, and intelligently. [Applause.]

The CHAIRMAN. The time of the gentleman from Mississippi has expired.

The question is on the amendment offered by the gentleman from Wyoming [Mr. MONDELL] as a substitute to the amendment offered by the gentleman from Oklahoma [Mr. FERRIS].

The question was taken, and the Chair announced that the noes seemed to have it.

Mr. MONDELL. Division, Mr. Chairman.

The committee divided, and there were—ayes 39, noes 45.

So the substitute was rejected.

The CHAIRMAN. The question recurs on the amendment offered by the gentleman from Oklahoma [Mr. FERRIS].

Mr. STEPHENS of Texas. Mr. Chairman, I desire to offer an amendment to the amendment. After the word "production" in the amendment I desire to add the word "transportation." I think the gentleman will accept the amendment.

Mr. FERRIS. I will vote for it. Go ahead and offer it.

The CHAIRMAN. Will the gentleman state the amendment again?

Mr. STEPHENS of Texas. The word "transportation" already comes in after the word "production"—hydroelectric plants, production, transportation, coal, oil, gas, and so forth. It only carries out the idea of placing pipe lines in this amendment. If the gentleman will not accept it, I will withdraw the amendment.

The CHAIRMAN. Without objection, the gentleman will be permitted to withdraw his amendment to the amendment. [After a pause.] The Chair hears none. The question is now on the amendment offered by the gentleman from Oklahoma [Mr. FERRIS].

The question was taken, and the Chairman announced that the ayes seemed to have it.

Mr. FLOYD of Arkansas. Division, Mr. Chairman.

The committee divided; and there were—ayes 58, noes 24.

Mr. WEBB. Mr. Chairman, I ask for tellers.

Tellers were ordered; and the Chairman appointed Mr. WEBB and Mr. FERRIS to act as tellers.

The committee again divided; and the tellers reported—ayes 65, noes 28.

So the amendment was agreed to.

Mr. AVIS. Mr. Chairman, I desire to offer the following amendment.

The CHAIRMAN. The gentleman from West Virginia [Mr. AVIS] offers an amendment, which the Clerk will report.

The Clerk read as follows:

Page 21, line 17, after the word "mine," insert the words "except bituminous and semibituminous coal mines," and on line 18, after the word "mine," insert the words "except as aforesaid." . . .

Mr. AVIS. Mr. Chairman, the purpose of this amendment is to except bituminous and semibituminous coal mines from the provisions of section 3.

I have already at great length discussed this subject, but feeling as I do, and, as I have said before, that if this section becomes a law it will promote and create monopoly rather than destroy it, I want, in the limited time that I have, to repeat some things that I have already said.

In the first place, there is no such thing as a monopoly of the soft-coal industry of the United States. There are at this time over 6,000 of these soft-coal mines throughout the United States, located in the great States of Illinois, Pennsylvania, Ohio, West Virginia, Kentucky, Virginia, Alabama, Washington, Utah, Wyoming, and a number of other States, and these mines are owned by over 3,500 separate and distinct owners.

Now, if this section becomes law, from the little knowledge that I have of the coal business—and I claim to have some knowledge of it, having lived in a coal-producing section for 25 years—I believe it will absolutely permit the large corporations, the very ones you are aiming this section at, to destroy the small corporations.

There are three classes of concerns engaged in the soft-coal production industry. There are the large corporations that have a tremendous output, that are enabled to place their agencies and storehouses over the United States and supply such demands as may be made upon them. These corporations maintain expensive sales agencies, and they have their own men to represent them. There is a second class of coal producers in this country who sell a portion of their output to certain dealers and employ agents and brokers to sell the balance. The third class—and the great majority of the mine owners in this country belong to that class—consists of those who have an output of about 400 tons a day, or less, who are unable to maintain their own sales agencies and who do not handle the sales end of their business. In order to dispose of their respective productions these concerns are compelled to employ agents and brokers to work up a trade for their coal upon commission, in such territory as may be assigned to them, and these operators compete with the big operators in such territory.

For instance, these small operators, on account of the good quality of their coal and on account of the extreme care they take in preparing it for the market, have customers who have been brought to them through the quality of their coal and the efforts of such agents and brokers in the respective territories that have been assigned to them, such as the lake section, the Northwest, or New England.

Now, what is the result? Under this section such small operators will be compelled to sell their coal, to the first responsible firm, person, or corporation who applies to purchase it—not alone for use or consumption but for the purpose of resale.

Now, what is to prevent me, if I am a big operator or big corporation, with whose coal the coal of the small operator is competing in that territory, from going to him, under this section, and saying, "I am a responsible bidder; I will buy your entire output for this year"? I might be buying it for some unfair purpose, and could destroy his trade in that territory, yet this section would require the small operator to sell to the large operator and would thereby enable the large operator to destroy the small operator, who is dependent upon that method of disposing of his product.

Now, if there were a monopoly in this business the situation would be different. I realize that this committee is trying to curb monopolies, and I am in favor of preventing monopoly; but, as I said before in this discussion, there is no such thing as monopoly of the soft-coal business of this country. Competition is so great to-day among the soft-coal mine operators of this country that they have scarcely made a dollar in the last five years, and none of them, with perhaps few exceptions, has made a dollar in the past year, and that is largely due to the fact that there is an overproduction of soft coal throughout this country. The competition is so great, as I said the other day—and the figures will bear me out—that we are selling coal to-day at about the same prices at which we sold it 8 or 10 years ago, notwithstanding the fact that freight rates, wages, and mine supplies have doubled in cost. Therefore, if this section becomes a law you will be playing into the hands of the big fellow.

In the limited time that I have let me also invite your attention to the fact that this is a tremendous industry, and a great many States are engaged in it. In 1909 there were nearly $1,100,000,000 invested in this industry. The value of the soft-coal output of this country at the mine is about $450,000,000 a year. Of that amount over $300,000,000 goes directly to labor, and the number of miners engaged in this industry exceeds 500,000 and many hundred thousands more people are directly dependent upon it.

Now, you should not do anything to cripple or injure an industry of this magnitude, so as to lessen the opportunity of those engaged in it to provide the safeguards that the miners of this country are entitled to, so that the men who daily face the dangers and hazards underground in mining may be better protected in the future. If this bill becomes a law I honestly believe that you will put out of business a great number of the soft-coal producers of the country. I insist that there is no monopoly of the bituminous-coal industry, and that you are aiming this section at something that does not exist. You should not attempt to cripple the soft-coal industry of this country and stop the development of my State—in which State over one-third of the people are dependent upon the soft-coal industry—without great care and consideration. . . .

Mr. RAKER. Taking the statement that the gentleman made, that concerning the man who is producing 400 tons a day and has his regular customers and is selling at the regular price, without a monopoly, you contend that the large corporation could come in now and compel this man to set aside his regular customers and sell his coal to the corporation?

Mr. AVIS. Undoubtedly. Listen to the language of section 2. Section 2 provides— and you have adopted that section:

Nothing herein contained shall prevent persons engaged in selling goods, wares, or merchandise in commerce from selecting their own customers, except as provided in section 3 of this act.

Now, while you have provided that no mine owner shall refuse arbitrarily to sell his product to any responsible person, firm, or corporation who applies therefor, yet you have made this limitation by section 2, which qualifies the words "refuse arbitrarily." . . .

I should like to explain a little further, in reply to the gentleman. I imagine the evil that some gentlemen anticipate is that which might exist in a community where a consumer could not purchase coal from some dealer. Now, that is not the fault of the mine owner. The mine owner sells his coal in a certain territory, and if a dealer gets the control of his ⊥ output he can put up the price or refuse to sell, as he may please; and that is the very thing that, by this section, you are enabling the dealer to do, because the dealer may not be engaged in interstate commerce. You compel the mine owner, if he is engaged in interstate commerce, to sell not only for use and consumption, but to sell for the purpose of resale. Therefore, if some dealer wants to control the output in a certain section, he can go to the operator directly, if he is a responsible person, firm, or corporation, and buy his entire output, or a great part of it, in that way depriving the operator of his customers, and control that particular coal in his section, and therefore have a monopoly of it.

Mr. GREEN of Iowa. And that particular local transaction could not be reached by this bill, because the transaction between the dealer and the consumer would be entirely intrastate and beyond the reach of any interstate provision.

Mr. AVIS. Yes. That could not be reached at all.

Mr. GREEN of Iowa. And therefore the very evil that they are trying to reach will not be struck at all.

Mr. AVIS. That is absolutely true. Now, when this bill was being considered I knew nothing about the intention to incorporate this section. Had I known of it, I would have appeared before the committee, and I would have had others go also. As soon as I observed this section I communicated with the coal men in my district. As I said a moment ago, in my State we have nearly 900 coal mines. We produce one-sixth of all the bituminous coal produced in this country. The value of the product is over $60,000,000 a year. I communicated with these gentlemen as soon as I learned of this section, and every single one of them has pointed out some of the evils that I have attempted to point out to you—and they realize that they are in great danger. It does seem to me that it is manifestly wrong to attempt to legislate concerning an industry as if it were a monopoly, when it is just the reverse, and when severe competition is now hurting that industry so badly that nobody can make a dollar from it. I ask any gentleman on this floor, representing any bituminous coal producing district, to point out any small miner of soft coal in his section who is earning any money to-day. The big concerns may be earning some money, but not the small ones.

Mr. AUSTIN. I wish to say to the gentleman that the coal operators of my district have been consulted, and they take the same position as that taken by the operators of the gentleman's State.

Mr. AVIS. I am glad to hear the gentleman's statement. This provision will affect not only the operators, but also the dealers. Say I am a small operator having a mine in the State of Illinois and want to sell my coal in a certain town. I can not afford to establish a selling agency in that town. In order to get a dealer in that town to circularize and sell my coal there I have to give him that territory on commission, so that he can compete with the large dealers who are also engaged in selling coal in that town. He has procured a number of customers. This section will permit those customers to come to me directly, to come to the mine owner, and compels me, the mine owner, to sell directly to the customers whom the dealer has procured. Thereby it tends to eliminate the coal dealers of this country who have spent money and years of time in working up a trade in their respective sections. Now, is that fair to the mine owner? Is it fair to the dealer? Is it fair to anybody to put an industry in the class of monopolies when there is no monopoly of that industry—not nearly so much of a monopoly as there is of the lumber industry or of the cotton industry or of many other industries in this country? . . .

Mr. [WILLIAM H.] MURRAY [D., Okla.]. Mr. Chairman, a parliamentary inquiry.

The CHAIRMAN. The gentleman will state it.

Mr. MURRAY of Oklahoma. I understand that there is a limit to this debate on this section and all amendments thereto.

The CHAIRMAN (Mr. GARNER). That is correct.

Mr. MURRAY of Oklahoma. I want to offer an amendment to this section. . . .

The CHAIRMAN. The gentleman from Oklahoma may offer his amendment for information. It can only be read at this time for information. The Clerk will report the amendment of the gentleman from Oklahoma.

The Clerk read as follows:

Page 21, line 24, before the word "and," insert the words "or any cooperative association making purchases for distribution among its members." . . .

Mr. CULLOP. Mr. Chairman, to meet some of the evils at which this section strikes, on February 13, 1914, I introduced a bill which was referred to the Interstate and Foreign Commerce Committee. That bill (H. R. 13354) prohibiting common carriers from owning or leasing coal lands, is as follows:

Be it enacted, etc., That it shall be unlawful for any common carrier subject to the provisions of this act to acquire ownership of any lands underlain by coal or of any coal underlying any lands, except as may be necessary and intended for its use in the conduct of its business as a common carrier.

SEC. 2. That it shall be unlawful for any common carrier subject to the provisions of this act to lease or sell upon a royalty basis to any person or persons, firm or firms, corporation or corporations, any lands underlain by coal, or any coal underlying any lands, whether the ownership of such lands and coal or such land or coal has been heretofore or may be hereafter acquired by said common carrier.

SEC. 3. That from and after January 1, 1916, it shall be unlawful for any common carrier subject to the provisions of this act to transport from any State, Territory, or the District of Columbia, to any other State, Territory, or the District of Columbia, or to any foreign country any coal or products of coal or products from land underlain by coal manufactured, mined, or produced by it or under its authority, or by any person or persons, firm or firms, corporation or corporations, to whom or to which said common carrier may have or hereafter may have leased or sold upon a royalty basis any lands underlain by coal or any coal underlying any lands, except such coal or products of coal or products from land underlain by coal as may be necessary and intended for its use in the conduct of its business as a common carrier.

The committee in charge of the bill now under consideration state the objects of this section, as follows:

This provision is new, but in view of the fact that many railroad corporations, the United States Steel Corporation, and other corporations have acquired and own, either directly or indirectly, through the medium of subsidiary corporations, vast areas of land containing coal, iron, and copper and other minerals in common use, we feel that this legislation is needed and fully justified. By its enactment into law we make it impossible for mere ownership of mines to enable the owners or those disposing of the products thereof to direct the disposal of such products into monopolistic channels of trade. It will liberate from the power of the trust every small manufacturer who is compelled to go into the open market for his raw material and every person who desires to purchase coal for use or for resale to those who desire to purchase for use or consumption, and will afford to every such manufacturer an opportunity to purchase same for cash wherever offered for sale in commerce. The section expressly forbids the mine owner or person controlling the sale of the product of the mine to arbitrarily refuse to sell such product to any responsible purchaser, and thereby prevents the mine owner or operator from giving the preference to another and rival dealer in the disposal of such product.

The independent operators to-day are not in the position which the distinguished gentleman from West Virginia [Mr. AVIS] has supposed, but they are in the hands of a monopoly, and are being crushed by that monopoly; and it was the independent operators of Illinois and Indiana who came before the Interstate and Foreign Commerce Committee and demanded legislation upon this subject which would relieve them from the grasp of that monopoly which was destroying their existence and blighting their opportunities. If in their monopolistic greed they should succeed, then they would control the coal production and the price and reap a golden harvest. Aware of this situation and gravity of the condition, the independent operators appealed to Congress for protection from the injuries with which they were threatened, and to relieve that unfortunate situation I introduced the measure which I have read; and as this section will afford them additional relief, I hope it will stand and the amendment of the gentleman from West Virginia [Mr. AVIS] will not prevail. The facts in those two States justify their alarm, and I call the attention of the committee to them. The conditions existing in two States—Indiana and Illinois—from the statistics are shown to be as follows:

There are approximately 3,000,000 acres of coal lands in Indiana and Illinois, about 1,000,000 of which are presently available for coal operation from a commercial standpoint; the other 2,000,000 acres will not become available until the further passage of time, with improved methods, additional railroad facilities, and higher prices.

Of the 1,000,000 acres of coal available at present, it is estimated that about 160,000 acres are in Indiana and the other 840,000 acres in Illinois. It has come about that of the Indiana available coal lands, 60 per cent have come into the ownership of the railroads operating in Indiana either directly or indirectly through stock ownership in other companies or by bond holding in other companies or by financial backing by any one of various methods.

In Illinois the proportion is a little more than 60 per cent—about 66 2/3 per cent. In other words, of the 840,000 acres of available coal lands in Illinois at present, approximately 541,000 acres are in the hands of railroads, besides 75,000 acres in the hands of large holders who are believed to hold the same for the railroads, a total of 616,000 acres.

Here is the way the available coal lands are distributed in Illinois: The C. & E. I. Railroad Co. has 35,000 acres of coal lands; the Illinois Central 25,000 acres; the Rock Island has 5,000; the St. Paul has 25,000; the Missouri Pacific has 10,000; the Wabash has 25,000; the Union Pacific, which does not run in Illinois at all, as I understand, has 45,000 acres in that State. But the Union Pacific, as you will remember, owns the stock control of the Chicago & Alton; and to protect the Chicago & Alton the Union Pacific has 45,000 acres in Illinois.

The Big Four lines have 90,000 acres in Illinois; the United States Steel Corporation has 75,000 acres in Illinois; the Clover Leaf has 15,000 acres; the Litchfield & Madison has 15,000; the St. Louis, Troy & Eastern has 4,000; the St. Louis & O'Fallon has 15,000; and Messrs. Corey and others, the Steel Corporation officials, have 20,000 acres. This makes a total of 541,000 acres of Illinois property out of the 840,000 available for present coal production; in other words, 64 per cent. Adding the 75,000 acres above referred to, and the total becomes 616,000 acres out of 840,000 acres; in other words, 73 per cent.

This is the real condition of the coal situation in these two States, and it warrants substantial treatment.

It is this ownership in these two States, and doubtless in the State of West Virginia the same thing exists, that is putting the independent coal operator out of commission and monopolizing the bituminous coal trade and regulating the price. When they get them once in their clutches they can control not only the output but the price as they please to fix it; and they have and will continue to do so, as all experience has demonstrated. . . .

That is the condition of the independent coal operator to-day in the States of

Indiana and Illinois; and in the State of Ohio it is, I am informed, practically the same. I have no doubt it exists in the State of West Virginia and in the district from which the distinguished gentleman comes.

If there is no legislation such as is proposed here to control the sale and output of these mines, the railroads will dominate the whole production, the price, and have a complete monopoly; crowd out the independent producer and the people will be made to suffer. Regulation is demanded, and should be speedily had in order that monopoly may not punish and plunder the public.

True, as the gentleman says, the independent operator has been running at a loss not only this year but last year as well, and the cause of this will be found in the fact that the railroads are attempting to drive them out of business, and are about to succeed in doing so, and when once success has crowned their efforts in this respect, then they will remain complete masters of the situation, and the public will pay dearly for fuel. We should handle this question so as to prevent them from carrying their purpose into effect. Public good requires treatment of this matter, and, if need be, heroic, drastic treatment. Railroads buy coal lands in the States I have named, open and equip mines ready for operation, then lease them to some person, sometimes no doubt a dummy, at a royalty of 8 or 9 cents a ton. He produces, the roads haul the product to market; there may be no profit in the sale of the product; the price is beaten down, but the railroads make money out of the freight charges for transportation, and hence can afford this method of reducing prices. They do not suffer because of what they earn in hauling the product to market. But the employment of the method is crushing the independent operator, and the low price thus produced is causing him in order to compete to operate at a loss, and soon he must abandon the business and leave the field to the railroad companies. With the independent operator out of business, competition has vanished, and they have complete control of the situation; can dictate the quantity of the production and the price at which the same shall be sold. They then become the masters of the situation of this great necessity, and can dominate both our domestic and industrial consumption of fuel. This condition, for truly it is a serious condition, requires serious consideration for the adoption of some real remedy that may relieve the people from its disastrous effects, if once attempted to be carried out. This is the solution of the unfortunate condition of the independent coal operators now, and from it they need and require relief.

Once our great fuel supply passes entirely under the control of monopoly, the people will suffer as never before from the exactions of its greed as they fall prey to its insatiable avarice. [Applause.] This provision as it now stands will afford some, if not complete, protection, and I hope it will be permitted to remain as it is in order that the independent operator may have some assistance in his great effort to sustain competition, and that the whole of this great industry may not entirely pass under the control of the great railroads of the country. . . .

Now, this provision of the bill seeks to remedy, in part, at least, this evil, a remedy that the independent coal miners are demanding in at least two of these States and I understand likewise in the State of Ohio—something that will relieve them of the grip of these monopolies that are grabbing up these coal lands, that now have two-thirds of them in three of the greatest coal-producing States in the Union, enabling them to conduct the operation of the mines and the disposal of the product as they please. The independent coal operator will be put out of business at the behest of these great monopolies, controlling the product as they do, unless we pass this or some other remedial legislation. [Applause.] . . .

Mr. HULINGS. Mr. Chairman, I would like to ask some member of the committee whether Congress has the right to legislate upon a matter of this nature. The oil producer produces his oil in the State of Oklahoma or Pennsylvania. He sells his product at the well; invariably almost it is purchased by the Standard Oil Co. I want to know whether the committee holds that that transaction, entirely within the State, is covered by this legislation?

Mr. FLOYD of Arkansas. It would not and could not be affected by this legislation. This legislation would only reach those transactions in interstate commerce.

Mr. HULINGS. I wish to say that, so far as I know the oil business, the producer of the oil sells his product at the well and the transaction is completed there.

Mr. FLOYD of Arkansas. In cases where that is true this legislation would not affect it.

Mr. HULINGS. It is almost invariably true of the oil business. When the pipe-line company, the buyer, gets the oil, it may transport it out of the State, and that would make its transaction interstate commerce and be under the jurisdiction of Congress, but the oil producer would not be within the jurisdiction of Congress and only liable to State regulation.

Mr. FLOYD of Arkansas. Undoubtedly; and the second clause of the provision provides for those in control of the product, which would reach the second man referred to provided he was engaged in interstate commerce.

Mr. HULINGS. This section applies to the owner or operator of oil wells, and it is very rare indeed that the operator of an oil well ever engages in interstate commerce.

Mr. FLOYD of Arkansas. Then I want to say to the gentleman that in that case this legislation would in nowise affect him.

Mr. HULINGS. That is what I supposed. Now, Mr. Chairman, it seems to me that the amendment offered by the gentleman from Wyoming [Mr. MONDELL], which would define what an "arbitrary refusal" is, ought to have been adopted. But since that was cast out I propose the following amendment, which I send to the desk that it may be read for information.

The Clerk read as follows:

Page 21, line 24, after the word "States," insert the following: "where the effect of such refusal shall be to restrain trade or to secure to such owner or operator monopolistic control of such products."

Mr. HULINGS. Mr. Chairman, I think there should be something of that sort in this bill. On the question of "arbitrary refusal," suppose it is arbitrary and does not restrain trade or does not give monopolistic control of the products. There is nothing in the refusal itself, unless it does these things, and I want to suggest to the committee that the amendment which I have proposed, I believe, carefully defines and carries out the purpose of the section. . . .

Mr. BARKLEY. Mr. Chairman, I offer the following amendment, which I send to the desk and ask to have read for information.

The CHAIRMAN. The gentleman offers an amendment to be read for information, which the Clerk will report.

The Clerk read as follows:

Page 21, line 19, after the word "products," insert the following: "in reasonable quantities."

Mr. BARKLEY. Mr. Chairman, I offer this amendment because I am somewhat in doubt about the effect of the section as it is written in the bill. In the report of the committee—and I desire to call the attention of the committee to this report—the following language is used referring to setcion [sic] 3 of the bill:

This section, like section 2, is limited in its application to the United States and to places under the jurisdiction thereof, and has no reference to persons desiring to purchase such a product for export sale. In that case the seller is permitted to arbitrarily refuse to sell to a responsible bidder, for otherwise a foreign dealer being responsible might purchase the entire output of a mine to the detriment of manufacturers and dealers in the United States and the owner be powerless to prevent it.

If that provision as applied to coal that had been intended for foreign trade would have permitted a foreign dealer to purchase the entire output of a miner, and the latter could not, by reason of this provision in the bill, refuse to sell the whole output, then the same thing would apply to a local purchaser who undertook to purchase the entire output of the mine. The same reason that would apply to the foreign dealer who undertook to purchase the entire output of the American miner would apply to a domestic transaction, because the owner could not prevent it by reason of this section, would apply equally and with the same force to a monopolist in the United States who was a responsible purchaser, and who went to a mine owner and offered to take the entire output of the mine. . . .

Mr. FLOYD of Arkansas. In the first place, as I have already explained a moment ago, this has no reference to the local dealer who is selling his product within his own State. He can sell it in any way he sees proper to any person to whom he desires.

Mr. BARKLEY. I realize that.

Mr. FLOYD of Arkansas. It applies only to persons who are selling such products in commerce, and it only applies to those who arbitrarily refuse to sell to a responsible person applying to purchase. I am unable to conceive how such a provision would result to the detriment of the small dealer. The object and purpose of the section is to prevent those who have obtained a monopoly upon vast areas of lands containing these minerals to arbitrarily refuse to furnish the products to consumers for use and consumption or to manufacturers who are engaged in competitive business with those producing or handling the products who at the same time are using such products themselves, or selling them to other and favored manufacturers engaged in a similar line of business. That is the object of it, and I do not think the small dealer could be detrimentally affected by it.

Mr. BARKLEY. Mr. Chairman, I realize the object of the bill as written is to prevent monopolists from refusing to sell to independent dealers or bona fide purchasers who want to use the article, either for the manufacture of other products or for resale; but the bill as it is written does not limit it to those men, but is universal in its scope, and takes in the little dealer as well as the big dealer. I realize that Congress can not regulate a transaction that occurs wholly within a State; but suppose the Standard Oil Co. of New Jersey should go into a community in another State— . . .

. . . Suppose the Standard Oil Co. or some other corporation which is a monopoly should go to an independent oil well or an independent mine owner in Oklahoma and some other State and see piled up a great quantity of coal or see stored a great quantity of oil and should say, "We will offer you the market price for this whole quantity"; and suppose the mine owner or the well owner should say, "I do not want to sell it to you," and the Standard Oil Co. should reply, "But here is a provision that says you can not arbitrarily refuse to sell it to me, for I am a responsible purchaser." Then the well owner might say, "I want this to use in this community to supply my customers," but the Standard Oil Co. would reply, "You have more oil in your well and you have more coal in your mine and you can get it out; but I want this which is lying here, and you are not using it, and you have no right to refuse to sell it to me." Then the court must pass on whether that is an arbitrary refusal. . . .

Mr. FLOYD of Arkansas. I desire to suggest that in my judgment and opinion, if he had any good reason for refusing, it would not be an arbitrary refusal. . . .

Mr. Chairman, my suggestion is that if a mine owner has any good reason, such as that he desires to sell to his customers or that he has contracts outstanding to be filled or any other legitimate good reason, no court would ever hold that such act would constitute an arbitrary refusal under the provisions of this section as drawn.

Mr. BARKLEY. I want to say this to the gentleman. I realize the force of his argument and the value of this section, but if this amendment which I propose is adopted, then the question of the power to refuse to sell the entire output can never arise, because then the owner can say, "We will sell you a reasonable amount of this product, but we want the balance of it for the supply of our own customers," and if this amendment were adopted it would be impossible to raise the question in any court as to the power of the local miner to refuse to sell his entire output.

Mr. CARLIN. Would you not in the last analysis have to submit to the court the determination of what is a reasonable quantity?

Mr. BARKLEY. Yes; but it would be no more harmful to have to pass on what would be a reasonable quantity than to have to interpret the meaning of the word "arbitrary."

Mr. CARLIN. The difficulty is twofold.

Mr. BARKLEY. Not at all. It would be easier for the court to pass on the question of whether or not a definite refusal to sell a given quantity of coal or oil was a reasonable quantity or within the discretion of the local well or mine owner than it would to go into all the facts that would make it necessary to give a different interpretation to the word "arbitrary" in every transaction. I now yield to the gentleman from West Virginia.

HOUSE CONSIDERATION

Mr. AVIS. In connection with what the gentleman has just stated, and in connection with the reply made by the gentleman from Arkansas [Mr. FLOYD], in which he stated, as I understood him, that section 3 would have no effect on sales within a State, where the mine owner operated in such State, under the terms of this bill, would not mine owners, if they were engaged in interstate commerce—and practically all of the mine owners are—be compelled to sell their product outside of the State to the first person who applied therefor, if he were a responsible person, firm, or corporation, to the exclusion of the people within such State?

Mr. BARKLEY. The responsible purchaser applies to the mine owner or operator anywhere in the United States or any Territory under the jurisdiction of the United States; and if the responsible purchaser from one State goes into another State and offers to purchase the entire output of a given mine or oil well, I am afraid of this section as it is written, because it leaves the possibility of prosecution in a court of justice if he refused to sell the entire output of any mine or any well, and I believe the language that I have offered will take away that possibility or that doubt. . . .

Mr. LEVY. Mr. Chairman, I offer the following amendment.

The CHAIRMAN. The gentleman from New York offers an amendment for information, which the Clerk will report.

Mr. LEVY. In my limited time I can hardly explain it.

The Clerk read as follows:

Page 21, line 16, after the word "owner," insert "the United States Government in Alaska."

Mr. LEVY. Mr. Chairman, my object is to throw open the coal lands of Alaska. This is the greatest monopoly in the United States to-day. The cause of business depression throughout the United States at the present time is due to too much legislation. Every time we legislate to centralize power in the hands of the Federal Government it seems the citizens of the United States have to pay more for their products. When the Hepburn bill was enacted into law coal advanced, and it has never come down in price since; and so it will be with this bill—the people will be obliged to pay increased prices. The question is solely one of supply and demand, and so it is with oil and other products. I regret exceedingly that such propositions as this should come before the Congress, because it will only increase the burdens of the people. [Applause.] . . .

⊥ Mr. MURRAY of Oklahoma. Mr. Chairman, the clear intention of this section ⊥9484 is to compel the producer of mine products to sell to the dealer. It would hardly be construed that any consumer or any individual citizen could buy whenever he got ready. Now to make a concrete example, my amendment provides that every "cooperative association that makes purchases for distribution among its members" shall also be included in the class which shall have the right to buy under this provision. I remember such an association in western Oklahoma attempted to buy coal and they refused them because they were not a "commercial concern," because they were not selling for profit, and they had to buy coal from West Virginia. This amendment which I offer is to permit "cooperative concerns" or societies to buy as well as dealers, and that is all there is to the amendment. I regret I am allowed no more time to urge its adoption. . . .

Mr. [CALEB] POWERS [R., Ky.]. Mr. Chairman, we have in southeastern Kentucky over 10,000 square miles of bituminous coal territory. The western coal field of Kentucky has over 6,000 square miles, making in all in the State of Kentucky over 16,000 square miles of bituminous coal territory. There are only 14,000 square miles in the entire State of Pennsylvania—I mean of bituminous coal territory—so it can be readily seen that the State of Kentucky is vitally concerned in section 3 of this bill. Under its provisions I see nothing to prevent any of the great moneyed interests of this country from buying up under compulsion the entire coal output of southeastern Kentucky or of any other section of this great country. Section 3 says:

That it shall be unlawful for the owner or operator of any mine or for any person controlling the product of any mine engaged in selling its product in commerce to refuse arbitrarily to sell such product to a responsible person, firm, or corporation who applies to purchase such product for use.

The amendment offered by the gentleman from Kentucky [Mr. BARKLEY] to the effect that the amount of coal to be sold ought to be limited to a reasonable amount, it seems to me, ought to prevail. When we absolutely throw open and give the great moneyed interests of this country the power to buy up, without any power to refuse, the entire coal output, it looks to me that instead of taking it out of the hands of monopolies of this great country that you are putting it into the hands of the monopolies and giving them power to control absolutely the entire coal output of the country.

Mr. AVIS. Mr. Chairman, my attention has been called to the fact that my amendment as drawn would not read connectedly with the present section as adopted a moment ago, and I therefore desire to modify it.

The CHAIRMAN. The gentleman from West Virginia asks unanimous consent to modify his amendment. Is there objection? The gentleman offers his amendment after what?

Mr. AVIS. I have sent it to the Clerk to be reported.

The CHAIRMAN. The Clerk will report the amendment as modified by the gentleman from West Virginia.

The Clerk read as follows:

Page 21, amend the Ferris amendment by inserting after the word "energy" in the amendment the following: "except bituminous and semibituminous coal mines."

The CHAIRMAN. The question is on the amendment offered by the gentleman from West Virginia— . . .

Mr. GARDNER. Mr. Chairman, a parliamentary inquiry.

The CHAIRMAN. The gentleman will state it.

Mr. GARDNER. The question now is upon the amendment offered by the gentleman from Kentucky [Mr. BARKLEY] to the amendment of the gentleman from West Virginia, is it not?

Mr. BARKLEY. My amendment is not offered as an amendment to his, but as an independent amendment.

The CHAIRMAN. The amendment of the gentleman from Kentucky is an independent amendment. The Chair recognizes the gentleman from Tennessee for seven minutes.

Mr. AUSTIN. Mr. Chairman, early in the consideration of this measure, on the 23d day of the present month, I had read from the Clerk's desk two letters from Mr. John L. Boyd, manager of the Proctor Coal Co., of Knoxville, Tenn., urging the same objections which have been so well stated by the gentleman from West Virginia [Mr. AVIS].

In my opinion, Mr. Boyd voices the sentiment of all of the operators of that eastern coal field of Tennessee. There is no combination in the coal fields of Tennessee among the operators, and I know of no ownership of coal lands by any of the railroad corporations of that State. The coal business has not been a profitable one, as the records will show, and to-day there is a decrease, and has been a constant decrease, in the coal output and the sale of coal in the country and in the Tennessee coal fields since the Underwood tariff bill went into operation.

The State of Tennessee has employed in its mines from 800 to 1,000 convicts digging coal, and for the first time since the State engaged in that industry they have been unable to dispose of the output from the State mines, unable to find a market, and hence have required the closing down of the mines in which the State convicts have been employed. This bill will not aid the coal industry. It will not aid any legitimate industry in this country. It is not offered for that purpose. Those who are in charge of legislation here are not seeking to develop or promote the business interests of this country. They were not elected upon a platform of that kind, and they would be untrue to the traditions of their party if they sought by legislation to promote or advance the business interests of the country. [Applause on the Republican side.]

The Underwood tariff bill did not increase the number of pay envelopes, but it did furnish an army of 2,000,000 unemployed workingmen that had constant employment before the enactment of that bill. We were told in the consideration of that measure that it would promote American industry and extend trade, and when it failed we were then told that a currency reform was needed, and not a tariff for revenue only, to improve the condition of the working people and to promote the business of the country. We were told that same identical thing 20 years ago, when the Wilson bill was tried.

Mr. Bryan and the leaders of the Democratic Party stated that it was not the tariff, but that it was the reform of the currency—16 to 1—that was needed in order to stop depression and promote business. And having failed to carry out the promises made in the platform at Baltimore by the Underwood tariff bill, we were then given a nostrum in the shape of the currency bill. And when that failed, along with the Underwood tariff bill, we are handed the so-called antitrust legislation as a remedy for the closing of mills and for the idle mechanics, all of whom were employed before the Underwood tariff bill became a law.

And so, Mr. Chairman, in the interest of the American people, in the interest of business, and in the name of the idle, honest, deserving workingmen, I protest against this bill, which will not help, but which will depress, retard, and injure, along with the Underwood tariff bill and the currency bill, the business condition of affairs in this fair land of ours. [Applause on the Republican side.] . . .

Mr. WEBB. Mr. Chairman, I sincerely trust that the amendment of the gentleman from West Virginia [Mr. AVIS], exempting bituminous-coal operators from the provision of this section, will not be accepted. The complaint which he makes that it will be possible for one operator to buy the product of four or five or more of the independent operators and thus monopolize the output is answered by saying that those who so buy for purposes of monopoly would be guilty of violating the Sherman antitrust law. I do not think it is fair to assume that that would be done, in order to get my friend's operators and constituents exempted from this just law, which would apply to all coal-mine operators alike.

And in addition to that, I doubt very much the right or power of Congress to exempt one set of coal operators from the operation of the law and putting another set of coal-mine operators within the law. I do not think Democrats or Republicans believe in that kind of class legislation, as it is contrary to the very spirit and genius of our institutions.

The CHAIRMAN. . . .

The question is on the amendment offered by the gentleman from West Virginia [Mr. AVIS].

The question was taken, and the Chairman announced that the noes appeared to have it.

Mr. AVIS. Division, Mr. Chairman.

The committee divided; and there were—ayes 32, noes 81.

So the amendment was rejected.

The CHAIRMAN. The Clerk will report the amendment offered by the gentleman from Oklahoma [Mr. MURRAY].

The Clerk read as follows:

Page 21, line 24, before the word "and," insert:
"Or to any cooperative association making purchases for distribution among its members."

The CHAIRMAN. The question is on agreeing to the amendment.

The amendment was rejected.

⊥ The CHAIRMAN. The Clerk will report the amendment offered by the gentleman from Pennsylvania [Mr. HULINGS]. ⊥9485

The Clerk read as follows:

Page 21, line 24, after the word "States," insert the following:
"Shall be where the effect of such refusal shall be to restrain trade or to secure to such owner or operator monopolistic control of such products."

The CHAIRMAN. The question is on agreeing to the amendment.

The question was taken, and the Chairman announced that the noes seemed to have it.

Mr. HULINGS. Division, Mr. Chairman.

The committee divided; and there were—ayes 43, noes 68.

So the amendment was rejected.

The CHAIRMAN. The Clerk will report the amendment offered by the gentleman from Kentucky [Mr. BARKLEY].

The Clerk read as follows:

Page 21, line 19, after the word "product," insert the following: "in reasonable quantities."

The CHAIRMAN. The question is on agreeing to the amendment.

The question was taken, and the amendment was rejected.

The CHAIRMAN. The Clerk will report the amendment offered by the gentleman from New York [Mr. LEVY].

Mr. LEVY. It is to modify the amendment.

The CHAIRMAN. The gentleman from New York [Mr. LEVY] asks unanimous consent to modify his amendment. Is there objection? [After a pause.] The Chair hears none. What is the modification?

Mr. LEVY. The modification is only to apply to the amendment that has been passed—the amendment of the gentleman from Oklahoma [Mr. FERRIS].

Mr. MANN. I object.

Mr. LEVY. Then I offer it as I offered it before.

The CHAIRMAN. The question is on the amendment offered by the gentleman from New York [Mr. LEVY].

The question was taken, and the amendment was rejected.

Mr. MORGAN of Oklahoma. Mr. Chairman, I desire to offer an amendment.

The CHAIRMAN. The gentleman from Oklahoma offers an amendment, which the Clerk will report. . . .

Mr. MORGAN of Oklahoma. I offer an amendment to follow section 3. . . .

Mr. FLOYD of Arkansas. Mr. Chairman, I desire to make a point of order against the amendment offered by the gentleman from Oklahoma [Mr. MORGAN], on the ground that it is not to section 3.

Mr. MORGAN of Oklahoma. Mr. Chairman, I withdraw the amendment.

The CHAIRMAN. The gentleman from Oklahoma [Mr. MORGAN] withdraws the amendment.

Mr. BRYAN. Mr. Chairman, I move to amend by striking out the section.

The CHAIRMAN. The gentleman from Washington [Mr. BRYAN] offers an amendment, which the Clerk will report.

The Clerk read as follows:

Strike out all of section 3.

The CHAIRMAN. The question is on agreeing to the amendment.

The amendment was rejected.

Mr. MONDELL. Mr. Chairman, I offer an amendment.

The CHAIRMAN. The gentleman from Wyoming [Mr. MONDELL] offers an amendment, which the Clerk will report.

Mr. MONDELL. The amendment I offer comes in at the beginning of line 19.

The CHAIRMAN. The Clerk will report the amendment offered by the gentleman from Wyoming [Mr. MONDELL].

The Clerk read as follows:

Amend, page 21, line 19, after the word "commerce," by inserting the words "to discriminate in price or otherwise as between persons or places for a like product delivered under similar terms and conditions."

The CHAIRMAN. The question is upon agreeing to the amendment.

The question was taken, and the Chairman announced that the noes seemed to have it.

Mr. MONDELL. A division, Mr. Chairman.

The CHAIRMAN. A division is demanded.

The committee divided; and there were—ayes 40, noes 63.

So the amendment was rejected.

The CHAIRMAN. The Clerk will read.

Mr. MORGAN of Oklahoma. Mr. Chairman, I now offer my new section.

The CHAIRMAN. The gentleman from Oklahoma [Mr. MORGAN] offers an amendment, which the Clerk will report.

The Clerk read as follows:

Mr. MORGAN of Oklahoma moves to amend by adding a new section, to be numbered section 3a, to follow section 3, as follows:

"SEC. 3a. That any person or corporation engaged in commerce who shall by the price charged for any article, product, or commodity sold or leased, or by the terms granted or given to the purchaser or lessor of any article, product, or commodity, or by the contract, arrangement, or condition upon which any such article, product, or commodity shall be sold or leased, or by any other means, discriminate as between persons, localities, or communities, so as to give any undue or unreasonable preference or advantage to any particular person, firm, corporation, locality, or community in any respect whatsoever, or so as to subject any particular person, firm, corporation, community, or locality to any undue or unreasonable prejudice or disadvantage in any respect whatsoever, shall be deemed guilty of a misdemeanor, and upon conviction thereof shall be punished by a fine not exceeding $5,000, or by imprisonment not exceeding one year, or by both."

The CHAIRMAN. The question is on agreeing to the amendment.

Mr. MORGAN of Oklahoma. Mr. Chairman, sections 2, 3, and 4— . . .

The CHAIRMAN. The Chair understands that the amendment is offered as a new section to the bill.

Mr. MORGAN of Oklahoma. Yes; as a new section. I would like to explain to the Members of this House the purposes of the section. We have under section 2 prohibited discriminations in price. We have in section 3 prohibited the arbitrary refusal to sell coal, and so forth. We have in section 4 prohibited a man from selling goods, and— . . .

The object of the section I have offered is to put in a general section that will include unfair discriminations that are not included in sections 2, 3, and 4. In fact, if sections 2, 3, and 4 were stricken out and this section placed in the bill, it would cover, comprehend, and include all that is included in sections 2, 3, and 4. That is the kind of language we should use; that is, language that will comprehend not simply a single unfair practice, but, if possible, all unfair practices. There is not in this bill any section that includes generally unfair practices. . . .

Mr. WEBB. Did the gentleman offer this amendment to the trade-commission bill the other day?

Mr. MORGAN of Oklahoma. I think not. I want to read section 3 of the act to regulate commerce, because this section is fashioned after that.

The first paragraph of section 3 of the act to regulate commerce provides—

That it shall be unlawful for any common carrier subject to the provisions of this act to make or give any undue or unreasonable preference or advantage to any particular person, company, firm, corporation, or locality, or any particular description of traffic, in any respect whatsoever; or to subject any particular person, company, firm, corporation, or locality, or any particular description of traffic, to any undue or unreasonable prejudice or disadvantage in any respect whatsoever.

Now, that section has been construed many times by the Interstate Commerce Commission, many times by the Supreme Court of the United States; and, more than that, it was taken from the English traffic act which was enacted in 1854, and it has been construed by the English courts. Under that section the Interstate Commerce Commission have been able to prevent many unfair discriminations and practices by the common carrier—discriminations and practices that could not have been foreseen and prohibited specifically. So, if you are in earnest in trying to control unfair practices, in trying to prevent unjust discriminations, why not insert in this bill a general provision of law that will prevent discrimination in price, in terms, by contract arrangements or agreements or otherwise, so as to give one person or locality an undue or unreasonable advantage over another, or so as to subject any person or locality to undue or unreasonable prejudice or disadvantage.

With such a section as this in this act, as time shall go on, it will suppress many unfair practices and unjust discriminations which can not now be named. The language has been construed. The provision has been found useful in preventing unfair discriminations by common carriers. It would be useful and effective in controlling the large industrial concerns, which in the monopolistic power they possess rank with our railways. This bill prohibits only a few things. Big concerns may desist from things prohibited herein. But they may resort to other practices just as reprehensible, just as dangerous, and yet just as effective in driving out competition. To my mind it would be exceedingly unwise to pass this bill without one section that is drawn so as to make all business practices which are unjust and unreasonable unlawful. It is useless to close a few of the avenues which lead to monopolistic control of business without an attempt to close all. For as long as there is one way open those seeking undue advantage over others will find it. No legitimate objection can be urged against this section which I have proposed. It makes it unlawful for any person through the price charged or the terms given or the contract entered into to discriminate so as to give any person, locality, or community any undue or unreasonable advantage over any other person or community, or so as to subject any other person or community to any undue prejudice or disadvantage. Can there be any objection to this? Is not this just the sum and substance, the very heart of what you are attempting to do? Is it not the practice or method that gives one an undue advantage over another that you want to prevent? This is my understanding of what you are attempting. If I am correct, then the new section which I have offered should be adopted.

Mr. WEBB. It strikes me that the gentleman's amendment ought not to have been offered as section 3a, but as a substitute for sections 2, 3, and 4.

Mr. MORGAN of Oklahoma. That is the way I intended it, but I could not get it in that way. If this is adopted, I shall move to strike out sections 2, 3, and 4.

Mr. WEBB. The gentleman's amendment is a sort of omnium gatherum in which he undertakes to cover the practices condemned in sections 2, 3, and 4. I believe the House is fairly well satisfied with these three sections as we have adopted them, and that it will prefer them to the amendment of my friend from Oklahoma, and I therefore hope his amendment will be voted down.

The CHAIRMAN. The question is on the amendment of the gentleman from Oklahoma.

The amendment was rejected.

Mr. TOWNER. Mr. Chairman, I offer an amendment to section 5.

The CHAIRMAN. The Clerk will report the amendment.

The Clerk read as follows:

Page 22, line 19, after the word "forbidden," insert the words "or declared to be unlawful."

Mr. CARLIN. In order to get the matter straightened out, I make the point of order that section 5 has been passed and that therefore the amendment is not in order.

The CHAIRMAN. The Chair will state to the gentleman from Iowa that section 5 was completed yesterday, and that the next section to be considered is section 6. After section 5 had been completed the chairman of the committee requested that we return to section 3. Therefore the Chair thinks that the amendment offered by the gentleman comes too late.

Mr. TOWNER. If the Chair will pardon me just a moment, I think the Chair is entirely right in his statement; but there was an agreement stated by the gentleman from Illinois [Mr. MANN] yesterday that we should return to section 3 after we had disposed of any pending amendments that we had under consideration last evening. This morning we did dispose of the pending amendments to section 5, and then—

Mr. MANN. Under the circumstances I ask unanimous consent that the gentleman have the privilege of offering his amendment. There was a misunderstanding.

The CHAIRMAN. The gentleman from Illinois asks unanimous consent that the gentleman from Iowa be permitted to offer the amendment which has been read from the Clerk's desk. Is there objection?

There was no objection.

Mr. TOWNER. I call the attention of the committee to this amendment. I think they ought to accept it. I move to add the words "or declared to be unlawful" for the reason that in some of the sections of this bill certain things are forbidden and in others they are declared unlawful. If the gentleman will turn, for instance, to section 8, he will find that in that section certain things are forbidden. The language of section 3 is that it shall be unlawful for the owners, and so forth. I offer this amendment for the purpose of perfecting the language of the text, because certain things are forbidden and certain things are declared to be unlawful, and this section ought to be made to apply to both.

Mr. WEBB. Does not the gentleman think anything that is forbidden in law is unlawful?

Mr. TOWNER. I do not know whether the courts would so hold or not.

Mr. WEBB. I do not think there is any doubt about it.

Mr. TOWNER. But that is not the customary language, and it certainly ought not to be left in doubt. Why do you hesitate to accept an amendment which will remove all possibility of doubt? Do you want the doubt to continue?

Mr. WEBB. The committee think that anything which is forbidden is declared to be unlawful.

Mr. TOWNER. I think the committee never thought about it at all.

Mr. WEBB. I am stating it now.

Mr. TOWNER. They have not given it any consideration. There are certain things in this law that are forbidden, and there are certain other things that are declared to be unlawful. You want this section to apply to both. Why do you not say so?

Mr. WEBB. Everything that is declared to be unlawful in this bill or in the antitrust law is forbidden by law.

Mr. TOWNER. Very well, if that is the gentleman's attitude.

The CHAIRMAN. The question is on the amendment of the gentleman from Iowa [Mr. TOWNER].

The amendment was rejected.

The Clerk read as follows:

SEC. 6. That whenever in any suit or proceeding in equity hereafter brought by or on behalf of the United States under any of the antitrust laws there shall have been rendered a final judgment or decree to the effect that a defendant has or has not entered into a contract, combination in the form of trust or otherwise, or conspiracy, in restraint of trade or commerce, or has or has not monopolized, or attempted to monopolize or combined with any person or persons to monopolize, any part of commerce, in violation of any of the antitrust laws, said judgment or decree shall, to the full extent to which such judgment or decree would constitute in any other proceeding an estoppel as between the United States and such defendant, constitute in favor of or against such defendant conclusive evidence of the same facts, and be conclusive as to the same questions of law in favor of or against any other party in any action or proceeding brought under or involving the provisions of any of the antitrust laws.

Whenever any suit or proceeding in equity is hereafter brought by or on behalf of the United States, under any of the antitrust laws, the statute of limitations in respect of each and every private right of action, arising under such antitrust laws, and based, in whole or in part, on any matter complained of in said suit or proceeding in equity, shall be suspended during the pendency of such suit or proceeding in equity. . . .

Mr. VOLSTEAD. . . . Mr. Chairman, I offer the following amendment, which I send to the desk.

The Clerk read as follows:

Page 23, line 5, strike out the words "or has not"; in line 7, same page, strike out the words "or has not"; in line 14, same page, strike out the words "or against"; in line 16, same page, strike out the words "or against."

Mr. VOLSTEAD. Mr. Chairman, this amendment would change the section so that the decree or judgment would only be binding on any combination that may be found to be in restraint of trade and not in its favor. This section in effect provides that in the event a judgment is entered it can be pleaded by the offending party not only against but also in its favor. I think that is entirely unjust, and it seems to me that it is clearly unconstitutional. It does not seem to me that there can be any argument in favor of such a proposition. . . .

Mr. BARTLETT. What effect does the gentleman's amendment have on the proposition that the judgment shall be conclusive as to the violation of the law as to all parties?

Mr. VOLSTEAD. Under the amendment the decree would still be conclusive against an illegal combination, but it would not be conclusive in its favor. It seems to me that it should not be evidence in an action brought by a private party that has never been in court. To illustrate: The Government brings a suit, and it is prosecuted to judgment. If the judgment is against the Government, it absolutely relieves the corporation from any suit by a private party for damages, though this private suitor may never have known of the action nor have had any opportunity to introduce evidence or be heard.

Mr. BARTLETT. Provided the judgment is in favor of the corporation?

Mr. VOLSTEAD. Yes. It can not possibly be legal to deprive a person of his rights in this way. To illustrate: I was told that in Philadelphia a refinery was wrecked by illegal acts in restraint of trade committed by the Sugar Trust. The Sugar Trust was sued by the Government, but the Government lost the suit.[5.537] If this section had been in force the refinery which had been wrecked, completely ruined by this trust, would not have been able to recover at all. The refinery brought a suit, which was settled out of court for something like $2,000,000.

Now, it seems to me that there is no sense or justice in the position assumed by the committee in this instance. It is doubtful whether you can make the judgment conclusive against an illegal combination or in favor of a party that has not been in court, but you certainly can not bind parties who have had no opportunity to litigate a question.

Mr. BARTLETT. If I understand the purport and effect of the gentleman's amendment, it is that the judgment in favor of the alleged violator of the law shall not be considered conclusive in a suit between him and some other party; in other words, that it shall not take a man's property without due process of law or denying him equal protection of the law.

Mr. VOLSTEAD. It would confiscate every claim that a private party had in case there was a judgment in favor of the corporation.

Mr. BARTLETT. This is in the interest of the individual and not in the interest of the corporation.

Mr. VOLSTEAD. Exactly.

Mr. GREEN of Iowa. Mr. Chairman, I want to call the attention of the gentleman from Minnesota to a clerical error in his amendment. . . .

The gentleman wishes a judgment to stand as against the defendant in the case. Now, in line 14, therefore, he does not wish the word "against" stricken out, but, as the Clerk has it, the word "against" is stricken out.

I have examined the copy. In line 14 the words which I am satisfied the gentleman wishes to have stricken out are the words "in favor of or."

Mr. VOLSTEAD. Mr. Chairman, I admit the error, and I ask to be permitted to amend it by changing line 14.

Mr. GREEN of Iowa. Mr. Chairman, I will read it, if the House will permit and the gentleman yields, as it should be:

Line 14, strike out the words "in favor of or."

The CHAIRMAN. The gentleman from Minnesota asks unanimous consent to modify his amendment as indicated. Is there objection?

There was no objection.

Mr. SCOTT. Mr. Chairman, will the gentleman from Minnesota yield for a question?

Mr. VOLSTEAD. Certainly.

Mr. SCOTT. Mr. Chairman, I ask the gentleman whether in the case of a suit brought at law against a corporation for damages under the antitrust law, as it exists to-day, such defendant corporation would have the constitutional right to demand a jury trial in the law action?

Mr. VOLSTEAD. Certainly; it would.

Mr. SCOTT. Then how can we, by legislation, make a decree in equity conclusive evidence against that corporation?

[5.537] United States v. E.C. Knight Co., 156 U.S. 1, 15 S. Ct. 249, 39 L. Ed. 325 (1895).

Mr. VOLSTEAD. I do not think we can.

Mr. SCOTT. Does not the gentleman's amendment seek to do that very thing?

Mr. VOLSTEAD. I do not think so. My amendment seeks to avoid making a judgment conclusive against a private party.

Mr. SCOTT. But as against a corporation. Having tried the case before a court in equity, it is deprived of the right to jury trial in the law action for damages which the Constitution guarantees. The gentleman has substituted a court of equity for the constitutional jury.

Mr. VOLSTEAD. Mr. Chairman, personally I will be perfectly willing to have this section stricken out, because I do believe that this section, instead of being an advantage, is going to be a disadvantage in many ways. I believe that rather than make a provision of this kind we ought to permit the evidence introduced in a Government suit to be admissible in any private suit, because then the two suits could proceed at the same time, and they could proceed while the witnesses were living, while there would be some interest in the prosecution, rather than years afterwards, when perhaps many of the parties who might be used as witnesses would be dead. . . .

Mr. MURDOCK. There is some doubt as to what the amendment does. What is it designed to do?

Mr. VOLSTEAD. The design is to change this section so that a judgment in favor of a corporation declared to be an unlawful monopoly shall not bar a private suit by an individual that may be injured by that monopoly.

The CHAIRMAN. The question is on the amendment offered by the gentleman from Minnesota. . . .

Mr. FLOYD of Arkansas. Mr. Chairman, I desire to explain to the House this particular section, as there will probably be other amendments offered to it. The President in his message delivered to the House on January 20, 1914, among other recommendations, had this to say:

> There is another matter in which imperative considerations of justice and fair play suggest thoughtful remedial action. Not only do many of the combinations effected or sought to be effected in the industrial world work an injustice upon the public in general; they also directly and seriously injure the individuals who are put out of business in one unfair way or another by the many dislodging and exterminating forces of combination. I hope that we shall agree in giving private individuals who claim to have been injured by these processes the right to found their suits for redress upon the facts and judgments proved and entered in suits by the Government where the Government has upon its own initiative sued the combinations complained of and won its suit, and that the statute of limitations shall be suffered to run against such litigants only from the date of the conclusion of the Government's action. It is not fair that the private litigant should be obliged to set up and establish again the facts which the Government has proved. He can not afford, he has not the power, to make use of such processes of inquiry as the Government has command of. Thus shall individual justice be done while the processes of business are rectified and squared with the general conscience.

That is the recommendation made by the President. The Committee on the Judiciary in considering this question did not depend alone on the recommendation of the Executive, but we sought information from different sources. We examined bills introduced in Congress pertaining to this subject, and among other bills we found one introduced in the House by the gentleman from Wisconsin [Mr. LENROOT], and one in the Senate by Senator LA FOLLETTE, in which we found this language:

> SEC. 12. That whenever in any suit or proceeding, civil or criminal, brought by or on behalf of the Government under the provisions of this act a final judgment or decree shall have been rendered to the effect that a defendant, in violation of the provisions of this act, has entered into a contract, combination in form of trust or otherwise, or conspiracy in restraint of trade or commerce among the several States or with foreign nations, or has monopolized or attempted to monopolize or combined with any person or persons to monopolize any part of the trade or commerce among the several States or with foreign nations, the existence of such illegal contract, combination, or conspiracy in restraint of trade or of such attempt or conspiracy to monopolize, shall to the full extent to which the facts and issues of fact or law were litigated and to the full extent to which such fact, judgment, or decree would constitute in any other proceeding an estoppel as between the Government and such person, constitute as against such defendant conclusive evidence of the same facts and be conclusive as to the same issues of law in favor of any other party in any other proceeding brought under or involving the provisions of this act.

The amendment incorporated in the bill is that provision modified, but not substantially affected, except in the one particular to which the amendment of the gentleman from Minnesota pertains. . . .

Mr. [S. F.] PROUTY [R., Iowa]. In the bill that the gentleman has just read, and also in the recommendation of the President, it only anticipates that the defendant in that suit would be estopped. Has the gentleman any authority or advice on how that estoppel could be made binding as against a man who was not a party to a suit or privy to it?

Mr. FLOYD of Arkansas. I desire to be heard on that question.

Mr. PROUTY. Has the gentleman any authority on that question?

Mr. FLOYD of Arkansas. I have no direct authorities on the proposition, because this is a new proposition, but I desire to be heard upon it. The purpose was set forth in the President's recommendation. In endeavoring to follow out that recommendation, which your committee deemed a good one, and in searching for information from different sources, we found the ideas embodied in the President's message incorporated in a proposed bill by the gentleman from Wisconsin, Mr. LENROOT, and we did not hesitate to use that provision in our bill. In our tentative bill we used it practically as it was written in the bill introduced by the gentleman from Wisconsin, but we found, after we had placed the bill in the limelight, that the one criticism that was made against that provision was that it was unfair to permit the judgment to be used in favor of one of the parties to the suit and to refuse to permit the judgment to be used as to the same facts and upon the same questions of law in favor of the other party. And in the interest of justice and common fairness, believing that it was a sound proposition of law and justice to do so, we modified it so as to make the decree conclusive as to both parties. . . .

Mr. PROUTY. Do I understand the gentleman to say that the provisions of this bill are the same as those of the gentleman from Wisconsin, Mr. LENROOT?

Mr. FLOYD of Arkansas. I said that the general proposition was the same, and I read the provision of the bill introduced by the gentleman from Wisconsin, showing that the original proposition in our tentative bill was substantially the same, but we modified it when we made it applicable to both the parties.

Mr. PROUTY. Well, in Mr. LENROOT's bill it would only be binding on one party to the suit.

Mr. FLOYD of Arkansas. The President in his message only suggested and recommended that it be made binding upon the corporation and in Mr. LENROOT's bill he provided that it should be only binding upon the corporation, but your committee, after having hearings on the subject, after listening to criticisms of that provision, found that it was subject to criticism if we made the decree applicable in favor of one party and not applicable against him in case the decision was adverse to the Government, and in the interest of what we believe to be justice and fair play ⊥ we modified it accordingly, and neither Mr. LENROOT nor the President is responsible for that modification, but your committee is responsible for it.

Mr. PROUTY. What I really desired to ask the gentleman was whether he has any authority that would show under any circumstances—

Mr. FLOYD of Arkansas. If the gentleman will permit me, I will explain, and I expect to submit not a specific authority, for never in the history of legislation, in my knowledge, has this particular proposal been submitted to us. We are dealing with a new question—

Mr. PROUTY. I agree with the gentleman in that.

Mr. FLOYD of Arkansas. My purpose is to justify it not only in morals but in law. Now, what are the facts; what is the situation? You take the case of the Standard Oil Co. and the American Tobacco Co. case. After years of litigation they were terminated, and there were volumes of proof showing that they committed acts which were held by the court to be unlawful, and it was shown in the testimony that by such unlawful means those great combinations had destroyed the business of hundreds of competitors. If the statute of limitation— . . .

Mr. SCOTT. Will the gentleman yield at this time?

Mr. FLOYD of Arkansas. Not at this time. I desire to make a general statement, and if I have time then I will yield. These combinations were declared to be unlawful and being unlawful were liable in treble damages under section 7 of the Sherman law, and yet private persons injured were absolutely without remedy because their causes of action were barred by the statute of limitation. The second provision of this section saves the statute of limitation to these litigants. Now, upon what principle can this lgeislation [sic] be justified? I desire to say that the only principle upon which the antitrust legislation, the Sherman Act, the supplemental acts thereto, and this act can be justified is upon the broad ground of public policy. The only authority, the only reason, that justifies the Government in interfering in the affairs of private citizens or in the affairs of corporations incorporated under laws of the several States is based upon the principle of public policy or for the general good, the general welfare. When one of these suits is brought against a combination alleged to be an unlawful combination the public money is expended in large sums in order to maintain that suit. For what purpose? For the general good, for the good of all the citizens, for the good of the entire people of the United States, based upon the broad principle of public policy. The courts have upheld this character of legislation which has been assailed from every quarter, bitterly contested. The highest court of this land has upheld the Sherman law, and has upheld the statutes of the States adopted to accomplish the same purpose in the States, always upon the ground that the Government has the right to inquire into and to deal with and prohibit and regulate the affairs of individuals and of corporations upon the ground of public policy. . . .

. . . Now, if that be true, then, when one of these suits is instituted, carried on by the Government at the public expense, it is carried on in the interest of the American people and of every citizen. It is true those directly concerned, affected, or injured by the corporation, may have a greater interest than other citizens, but it is in the interest of the people generally, the whole people, the Government representing the people, representing all the citizens; and, so far as that decree as between the Government and the corporation is concerned, I do not believe that anyone can question the justice or the right of making it conclusive. Such decree imports absolute verity, binding upon the Government and the party to the suit, both as to findings of fact and questions of law determined in the suit. Does anybody question that? That is the common rule of law applied to all judgments and decrees of all courts of record. That is an old doctrine of the law. Then what do we propose in this case? The word "conclusive" seems to have created confusion in the minds of a great many persons. What are we seeking to do? We are not giving to that decree any element or quality except such as attaches to every other decree. A decree or judgment of a court of record imports upon its face absolute verity. Such decree is binding upon all parties to the suit, and can not be attacked collaterally. What we are attempting to do in this case is to apply that decree, with its usual effect, with its usual force, in another suit wherein one of the parties was not a party to the original suit. . . .

Mr. ALEXANDER. I would like to get an answer right at that point. Does the gentleman mean against that defendant, or against anybody else? The gentleman certainly does not want that decree to estop parties to enter suit where the defendant is not a party, does he?

Mr. FLOYD of Arkansas. I do not know that I understand the gentleman's question.

Mr. ALEXANDER. I can very well understand why if it is a suit against the United States Steel Corporation,[5.538] where the corporation in a suit by the United States has been decreed to be in a trust in violation of the terms of the antitrust laws should be excluded in another suit by another party against that corporation, but I can not understand where a party can be estopped if they are different parties to the controversy.

Mr. FLOYD of Arkansas. Well, I will try to explain that to the gentleman. I must decline to yield now, because I have not the time. I am endeavoring to state my position. This is a new question, based upon new principles, and I am endeavoring to justify it, and I will be glad to permit interruptions after I have stated the proposition.

Now, is there any objection to using it against a convicted corporation when a

---

[5.538] See note 5.529 supra.

private litigant brings a suit against such corporation? Is there any valid objection to making that decree binding upon the defendant corporation although this private individual seeking redress was not a party to the suit brought by the Government against the corporation for violations of the Sherman Act, in which the corporation is adjudged guilty by final decree of the court?

Mr. ALEXANDER. I would say, none whatever. So far, so good. . . .

Mr. VOLSTEAD. I want to call your attention to a provision in the Constitution that provides that in a suit at common law, where the value in controversy shall exceed $20, the right of trial by jury shall be preserved.

Mr. FLOYD of Arkansas. I have that marked, and I shall discuss it later. I hope the gentleman will not insist upon my going into that question now.

Mr. VOLSTEAD. I wanted to call your attention to that in connection with an equity suit.

Mr. FLOYD of Arkansas. Then I assume, in response to my last question, that there is no serious, at least no legal, objection to making that decree binding upon the defendant corporation found guilty of violations of the antitrust laws, although in the new suit a private litigant, who was not a party to the Government suit, is the complainant in an action for damages against the convicted corporation. Now, that is what was recommended by the President, that is what was provided in Mr. LENROOT'S bill, that is what was provided by your committee in its tentative bill on the subject, and the amendment of the gentleman from Minnesota [Mr. VOLSTEAD] seeks to restore the bill in that respect to the form in which it was originally drafted. The only serious criticism that we ever had from any source as to this particular section proposed was the criticism that it was made binding in favor of a private litigant against the corporation, but not in favor of the corporation when the facts and law were found to be in favor of the corporation. It was argued that in that case to refuse to make it binding also against the individual was unjust, unjustifiable in law, and grossly unfair. . . .

Mr. CULLOP. My question is this: Supposing a collusive suit was brought and the defendant won on the issue, then is every outsider barred from any further suit? According to this language he is.

Mr. FLOYD of Arkansas. I understand the question, and I will answer it. But I hope the gentleman will not interrupt me until I state my position fully.

The gentleman from Indiana asks as to the effect of this provision if a collusive suit is brought. My answer to that proposition is that if the time ever comes in this Government when any Attorney General will enter into collusive suits with corporations and combinations engaged in unlawful acts, it will be an evil day for our Republic, a day when every statute will become useless and justice will become a mockery. I am not prepared to believe that any such condition will arise or can exist, or has existed, under any administration in the past, or will exist under any administration in the future. I have too much faith in the integrity of our institutions to be alarmed by any such suggestion as that.

Now, what do we propose, then? We propose, in the first place, in one of the sections of this bill, to give every private suitor who has a cause of action against a combination acting in violation of law triple damages under this bill, as he is given triple damages under section 7 of the Sherman Act against the offending corporation. But the remedy given in section 7 of the Sherman Act has been of little value and practically useless in the past, because the individual, the small man, and the small concern, were utterly helpless in their efforts to confront in the courts these great and powerful corporations, and the result was that the remedy provided in the Sherman Act has been of little efficiency, and the remedy provided in this bill for similar offenses, for violation of its provisions, may be of little efficiency unless we supplement it and lend to private litigants the aid of this great Government, that has the means, the opportunity, and the force, and the machinery to cope with the greatest and most powerful corporations and combinations in the country. . . .

Mr. SUMNERS. It is not clear to my mind how an individual claiming to be injured by a corporation could profit by the judgment already rendered in favor of the Government.

Mr. FLOYD of Arkansas. I will endeavor to make that clear. Not only do we allow the judgment to be offered in evidence in such suits, but we provide that from the day that the Government institutes its suit until the termination of that suit the statutes of limitations are suspended in favor of the party injured by the wrongful acts of the corporation. After the termination of that suit, if by the judgment of a Federal court the defendant corporation is found to be guilty of an unlawful combination, the party injured, with the proofs furnished by the Government in that suit of wrongful acts—it may be pertaining to this very litigant—can institute a suit, offer the judgment or decree against the corporation in obtaining his judgment, and the court will then assess threefold damages. It is as simple as can be. . . .

Mr. SUMNERS. Now, section 5 provides that triple damages may be rendered in favor of the person who has been injured by an act, not by a trust, but by an act done in violation of the antitrust law. Now, when he comes to bring his suit, I do not see how he could avail himself of the judgment already rendered declaring the defendant to be a trust, unless the facts in the case in which the defendant was found to be a trust involved the particular individual suing.

Mr. FLOYD of Arkansas. The gentleman from Texas is mistaken, badly mistaken.

Mr. SUMNERS. I am asking for information; that is all.

Mr. FLOYD of Arkansas. If no fact in the Government suit related in any way to the party's case, there would still be this advantage: It is a condemned corporation under the law, and he would not have to prove it was acting unlawfully in restraint of trade. The Government has already established that fact, and it is conclusive against defendant corporation. All that the private litigant is required to do under that section as proposed in the bill is to introduce his decree, which is conclusive against the corporation, showing that that corporation has been condemned as an unlawful combination acting in restraint of trade, and then produce the facts to show that he has been damaged by it and to what extent. What better advantage could you afford a litigant than to enable him to avail himself of the benefit of the Government's decree in that way? Now, this has been criticized, and the amendment offered by the gentleman from Minnesota [Mr. VOLSTEAD] is responsive to that criticism, on the ground that we have no right to make it binding upon the individual or litigant not a party to the Government suit, and also a constitutional question has been raised to the effect that to make the decree binding against the private litigant not a party to such original suit is tantamount to denying him the right of a trial by jury.

Now, I want to answer the arguments on each of those propositions. In the first place, as a matter of practical effect, the legislation is largely against the offending corporation and chiefly in favor of the injured litigant who is complaining of the wrongful acts of the corporation. And even if in some few cases the litigant might be deprived of a portion of his rights or of a portion of his evidence by a decree in favor of a corporation, how few would be the number of cases and what an infinite advantage is given to litigants in general upon the broad proposition that the Government suit was brought by the Government for the benefit of all of its citizens, and that when a decree has been obtained enables all of its citizens to take advantage of the work and of the decree of the Government in private suits. But as a matter of practical effect, assuming as I do that the men in high position in this Government will act honestly, will not go into collusion with any unlawful combination, I can see no great danger to private litigants in providing that the decree shall be conclusive against private litigants in cases wherein corporations have been charged with being unlawful combinations in restraint of trade and have been adjudged not guilty.

What possibility would there be for any individual to maintain a suit when this great Government of ours, the greatest in the world, has exhausted its resources to prove that a combination is unlawful and has failed to do it? Do you think there is much in their argument? What private litigant could undertake it after the Government, with its resources, its money, its detectives, its Secret Service men, its opportunities for gaining information, its bureaus—with all those things at its command had exhausted its resources and failed? What private individual would stand any chance or have any opportunity to accomplish more than the Government did, and in consequence lose anything by this provision? . . .

Now, it has been contended that this provision as drawn interferes with due process of law and with the right to trial by jury. I have been asked to give my authority. I can not cite any decisions directly in point, because it is a new proposition; and, besides, I have not had any opportunity to run down decisions on other questions that may have a bearing on this subject. But I have the Constitution here; I have the provisions in the Constitution; and I confidently assert that there is no principle in the Federal Constitution that is violated by this provision.

Now, I want to read you the fifth amendment to the Constitution. It reads:

Article V.

No person shall be held to answer for a capital or otherwise infamous crime unless on a presentment or indictment of a grand jury, except in cases arising in the land or naval forces or in the Militia, when in actual service in time of war or public danger; nor shall any person be subject for the same offense to be twice put in jeopardy of life or limb, nor shall be compelled in any criminal case to be a witness against himself, nor be deprived of life, liberty, or property without due process of law; nor shall private property be taken for public use without just compensation.

Is that provision in the Constitution violated by what we propose? The corporation is not proceeding against an individual. An individual is proceeding against a corporation. Get that distinction clearly in mind. In what we propose a corporation is not proceeding against an individual for the purpose of depriving him of either life, liberty, or property, but the individual is asserting his legal rights against the corporation; and that principle would be applicable to the corporation sued, but not to the individual that is instituting a suit and asserting a right against the corporation for torts committed by it.

Now, in maintaining or trying suits what is the rule? The legislative body makes the rules of evidence, prescribes what may be evidence, and the things that may be legally admitted in evidence in a trial by the courts; and there is nothing in this amendment violative of the right of trial by jury, and no provision of the Constitution is violated by what we propose in this provision. . . .

[Mr. BEALL of Texas addressed the committee. See Appendix.*] . . .

Mr. GREEN of Iowa. Mr. Chairman, the first paragraph of section 6 is so clearly unconstitutional as it stands that there ought to be no discussion or argument about it in a body composed largely of lawyers, as is this House. This section provides that a third party may be estopped by a decree or judgment rendered in a case in which he was not a party and had no opportunity of appearing nor any notice served upon him whatever. If there is any proposition of law that is well settled, it is that no person can be estopped or concluded by a decree or judgment which is rendered in a case to which he is not a party, or where he has not had his day in court, or of which he has not had notice. And yet all of these three propositions are controverted by section 6 as it now stands. It gives the third party no day in court, no opportunity to be heard, and it provides for no notice upon him whatever. It is not strange that the gentleman from Arkansas has said that this is entirely new. It certainly is new to jurisprudence in this country.

Mr. BARTLETT. It is new to assert such a proposition, but the other proposition is old enough that a man can not be deprived of his property without due process of law or giving him a day in court.

Mr. GREEN of Iowa. That proposition is as old as the law in this country. The provision of the Constitution that forbids it is found in the fifth amendment, which provides that no man shall be deprived of his property or rights without due process of law, and yet they seek to provide in this section that he shall be deprived of his property without any due process of law, without even notice of hearing or any day in court. So far as that particular matter is concerned there need be no discussion. When it comes to the question of fairness and justice in the matter I think it is fair that the defendant corporation, who has had its day in court, should be estopped, while the third party, who has had no opportunity to be heard, ought not to be estopped or concluded.

---

* Not reprinted herein.

It can be reasonably said that the defendant had introduced all of the evidence he had on the subject; that he has had every opportunity that could be given him in another case; that it would not change the result or the decree if the case were heard over again as to him, but the third party, the private corporation or individual, as it might be, which was not a party to the original case, has never had any opportunity whatever. The gentleman from Arkansas [Mr. FLOYD] said, as I understood him, that there had been no case where the Government had failed, and that no other corporation or private individual has succeeded in a suit on the same facts or a similar case.

Mr. FLOYD of Arkansas. Oh, I think the gentleman misunderstood me.

Mr. GREEN of Iowa. I would be glad to have the gentleman correct me if I have misstated what he said.

Mr. FLOYD of Arkansas. I said the cases were rare.

Mr. GREEN of Iowa. I was about to say that in the well-known Knight case against the Sugar Trust the Government did fail because of incompetence or carelessness on the part of the Government attorney. There was no other reason. The suit ought to have been won. Subsequently another party or corporation, I forget which, did obtain judgment for something like $2,000,000 against the Sugar Trust for violation of the Sherman antitrust law, and it was stated by the gentleman from Texas [Mr. BEALL], who just preceded me and who made as able an argument as could be made for this provision, that the third party would not be estopped unless the facts were similar. Unfortunately we have a provision in this section that makes the estoppel as complete as it would be against the Government, and that provision is:

> Said judgment or decree shall, to the full extent to which such judgment or decree would constitute in any other proceeding an estoppel as between the United States and such defendant, constitute in favor of or against such defendant conclusive evidence of the same facts, and be conclusive as to the same questions of law in favor of or against any other party in any action or proceeding brought under or involving the provisions of any of the antitrust laws.

The rules of estoppel apply in the same way if the Government failed to make out its case, because it did not produce sufficient evidence when it had it; then the third party would be estopped as conclusively as the Government, and that is exactly what the section says.

I wish to speak for a moment with reference to the objection raised by my colleague, Mr. SCOTT. I am not entirely clear as to whether this section is constitutional even as against the defendant corporation, but I am inclined to think that the provision might stand in that respect. It is true that the original decree in favor of the Government might have been rendered in an equity suit. The suit commenced by a third party might be a suit for damages commenced in a case at law, in which either party is entitled to a trial by jury. But the trial by jury will still go on as to the extent of the damages, as to the amount of the judgment which might be rendered, and this decree is only rendered conclusive as to the findings of fact, and the conclusions of law with reference to the existence of a trust and the violation of the Sherman law. But I agree with the gentleman from Texas [Mr. BEALL] in saying that even as to that matter the section is of doubtful constitutionality, and I have some doubt as to whether it will be of very much benefit to the private individual in any event. He can always avail himself of the search which the Government has made in order to obtain the evidence. He can use, presumably, and obtain the same evidence which the Government has used, even though the decree be not made conclusive in his favor; but if it is possible, if it can constitutionally be made conclusive in his favor, I would be in favor of having it done. In any event, the amendment of the gentleman from Minnesota [Mr. VOLSTEAD] ought to be agreed to. . . .

Mr. PROUTY. Mr. Chairman, the question here involved is a very simple one, if carefully analyzed. Article V of the amendment to the Constitution which binds the Federal Government expressly provides that no man shall be deprived of life, liberty, or property without due process of law. Every court that has ever passed upon that provision of the Constitution—and there are some 60 or 70 cases in the United States Supreme Court—has held that no one can be deprived of his property unless he has had his day in court. "Due process of law" has been held again and again to mean that he must have his day in court, by notice and otherwise.

The second proposition I presume no one will question—that the rights involved in a suit at law or claim for damages against anyone is property within the meaning of the Constitution. Therefore we can safely say that the Constitution provides that no one shall be deprived of his rights in a lawsuit except by due process of law. Keeping this in mind, just see where this section as it now stands would lead us. Suppose I had a case against the Standard Oil Co., as I did at one time, in which I alleged conspiracy to defraud, conspiracy in restraint of trade, under the Sherman antitrust law. Suppose, now, when I got that case ready to be submitted to the jury, and the Standard Oil Co. should come into court with a case that had been tried down in New Jersey, in an equity proceeding, and should say, "You can not recover anything from us, because that question was adjudicated in an equity proceeding down in New Jersey." I would say, "Why, I never heard of that case; I do not know anything about it; and how can I be estopped, how can I be deprived of my rights against the Standard Oil Co. in a proceeding to which I never was a party and of which I knew nothing?"

If the theory of these gentlemen is correct, a man can be absolutely deprived of his right to property without any knowledge of it whatever. There is the second provision that is just as clear when carefully analyzed, and that is the sixth article of the amendment to the Constitution, which provides, in substance, that a man shall be entitled to trial by jury in all cases in which the amount involved is more than $20. Just take the case I have now named. Suppose I had started suit against the Standard Oil Co. in the city of Des Moines and was asking a trial by jury upon the question of facts, the prime central fact of all those cases, and that is whether there was a conspiracy, whether there is a contract in restraint of trade. Suppose I were ready to try that case before a jury in the city of Des Moines. The Standard Oil Co. would say, "Why, that identical question was determined in an equity case down in New Jersey three years ago." I would reply, "It can not be possible that I am going to be deprived of the right of trial ⊥ by jury on a question of fact when I am guaranteed that right by the Constitution of the United States." But the judge on the bench would reply to me and say, "Why, Congress has passed a law saying that the decree in equity shall be conclusive evidence"—not, as the gentleman from Texas said, presumptive evidence, but conclusive evidence, and conclusive evidence of the law as well. . . .

Mr. [THOMAS U.] SISSON [D., Miss.]. I notice the last paragraph of section 4, in line 19, provides that in the event the gentleman should bring suit believing he had been injured by some combination in violation of law and thereafter the Federal Government, by the Attorney General, should institute a suit, instantly the gentleman's right of action would be suspended until the Federal court had decided the suit of the Federal Government, would it not?

Mr. PROUTY. Yes; I think so, under the terms of this act.

Mr. SISSON. The only thing reserved to the gentleman would be his right of action, because the statute of limitations would not run against that right in the event the Government recovered.

Mr. PROUTY. That part of the section, I think, is all right and is not subject to criticism.

Mr. SISSON. That part is all right, but does the gentleman believe that his rights in the court should be determined upon the questions raised by the Attorney General of the United States?

Mr. PROUTY. Why, certainly not; the Constitution expressly prohibits it. In other words, the Attorney General could go in and prevent my having a trial before a jury.

Mr. SISSON. That is the point I had in mind.

Mr. PROUTY. By instituting a proceeding in equity and having the case tried.

Mr. SISSON. That is the point I had in mind, that the Attorney General, if he was disposed to do so—we would not charge that of any particular Attorney General—might cook up a case which would directly defeat the rights of every individual if he had been injured.

Mr. PROUTY. While I do not say that, but there was a purpose on the part of the men who adopted this constitutional provision that every man should have the right of a trial by jury. It is well known and everybody knows who has read jurisprudence that there is a tendency in the courts to act along certain lines dangerous to popular rights; and one thing that all countries, not alone the United States, have had to do was to assert their rights in order to protect themselves against the courts by having the right to appeal to a jury of their peers; and we put into the first amendments we adopted to the Constitution a provision that no man could be deprived of the right of a trial by jury; yet, if this law passes, that provision has been made absolutely nugatory. The question of fact and of law both have been determined in a proceeding in equity. Now, is there any doubt about that? Starting with the section—

> That whenever in any suit or proceeding in equity hereafter brought by or on behalf of the United States under any of the antitrust laws there shall have been rendered a final judgment—

And so forth.

Then it ends by saying that it shall be binding both for and against the defendant and be conclusive as to the same questions of law and conclusive as to the same questions of fact. Now, if that does not violate the sixth article of the Constitution, which requires trial by jury, then I do not read correctly. Now, you can not say any more than this. When I stood up here and asked the gentleman—who is an able lawyer, as I know he is—whether he had found any precedents in any decisions of the United States courts that had held that a man could be absolutely barred and stopped by a lawsuit to which he was not a party, he said that he had not found one, and I was not surprised, and I listened to his speech, first for 10 minutes and then for 20 minutes and then an extension, and he has not called our attention to a single decision, and I venture the assertion that he can not find one. Now, the recommendation of the President does not correspond with this bill. He only asked Congress to pass a bill that will bind the defendant in the equity suit. While I have some doubt on that phase, as has been suggested here, yet there is a reason why a defendant corporation might be bound by a determination of a case in which it was a defendant, but there is no court who has ever held that a man was bound by a case to which he was not a party. . . .

Mr. LEVY. Mr. Chairman, I desire to offer an amendment.

The CHAIRMAN. There is an amendment already pending offered by the gentleman from Minnesota. . . .

Mr. SCOTT. Mr. Chairman, I endeavored to be permitted to ask the chairman of the committee a question in reference to the report of the committee. I find on page 14 of the report this language:

> And that when such decree or judgment is so offered it shall be conclusive evidence of the same facts and be conclusive as to the same questions of law as between the parties in the original suit or proceeding.

It is therefore quite evident that the gentlemen who prepared the report on this bill had not carefully examined the bill which they were reporting. They have reported that judgments and questions should be conclusive only as between the parties to the original suit, but they have reported a bill so framed as to be conclusive between not only the parties to the original litigation, but conclusive as to the whole world. Now, it is probably unnecessary for me, following the able arguments which have been presented upon this constitutional question, to repeat in any measure what has already been said. I think that nearly everyone here now recognizes that it would be a constitutional impossibility to enact a law which would deprive persons who were not parties to an original suit of their right to their day in court. The chairman of the committee suggested as a reason for this provision that after the United States, with all of its powers and all of its machinery, had litigated the question and failed, that it would be improbable that anyone would be so bold as to institute a suit against the corporation for damages. That was the purport of his question. I suggest that a man might be so bold as to go before a jury of American citizens and ask for justice when the United States had failed before a United States district judge.

It is also suggested by the chairman of the committee that in considering this bill the committee had thought it unfair to so frame it as to be conclusive only as against the corporation defendant in the original suit. It seems to me rather inconsistent to say that it would be unfair to conclude the corporation charged with conspiracy by a decree of a court of equity and then say it would be fair to conclude an individual who brings a suit for damages by a decree of a court, and in a suit to which he was not a party. But apparently the committee have sought to even up this question. They have said that they thought it unfair merely to conclude a party to a suit by a decree in equity, but they believed it would be perfectly fair to conclude the other individual without any day in court at all. I think there is a grave question also as to the constitutionality of the statute, even if changed to conform to the amendment offered by the gentleman from Minnesota. However, I am not clear upon that question. I am satisfied, however, that the matter never will be settled until it reaches the Supreme Court of the United States. When you enact into this statute a provision which deprives a corporation of the right to a hearing before a jury as provided by the Constitution you will find that statute challenged and you will never know what the law is upon the question until the court of last resort speaks the last word. Personally I am inclined to the opinion that the statute so amended would be constitutional. I am inclined to the opinion that if the corporation is brought into a court of equity upon a proper bill and by a proper service, and with subject matter over which the court has jurisdiction, that probably the findings of fact would be conclusive upon the corporation and would be binding, leaving open only the matter of damages to be submitted to the jury.

However, upon no course of reasoning could it be held that this statute in its present form would be constitutional, and, therefore, I believe that the amendment of the gentleman from Minnesota should prevail. But if it is thought best to take the chances of the decision of the Supreme Court as it may come in the future upon the statute as it will be when amended that way, that is a matter for this House to decide.

The CHAIRMAN. The question is on the amendment offered by the gentleman from Minnesota [Mr. VOLSTEAD].

Mr. [HORACE W.] VAUGHN [D., Tex.]. Mr. Chairman, I ask unanimous consent that the amendment be again read.

The CHAIRMAN. Without objection, the amendment will be again read.

The amendment was again reported. . . .

Mr. [IRVING L.] LENROOT [R., Wis.]. Mr. Chairman, with the general purpose of the committee with reference to this section I am heartily in sympathy. Without this section both the provision of the ⊥ Sherman law and section 5 of this bill, relating to damages, are absolutely ineffectual so far as affording any real relief or remedy to a litigant is concerned. Take the case of the Standard Oil Co., as already mentioned. It was absolutely impossible for any private individual, no matter how great his injury may have been, to have instituted a case against the Standard Oil Co. and secure a judgment for damages. But Mr. Chairman, in the effort of the committee to equalize this question of estoppel I am not in sympathy, and I regret exceedingly that the committee has taken the position it has.

I am aware that in the tentative bill that the committee framed that objection was made to the provision relating to estoppel, claiming that it was one-sided and unfair and unjust, and there was some argument made that for that reason it was unconstitutional. At that time, Mr. Chairman, I had made somewhat careful examination and investigation of the authorities with reference to this question, and I became satisfied that the provision as it stood in the tentative bill was constitutional. But, Mr. Chairman, if there was doubt as to the provision in their tentative bill the doubt has been doubled in the bill now before the committee, for originally the estoppel worked only against the defendant, a defendant who had had his day in court, who had had an opportunity to litigate every question that was involved, but now they create an estoppel against a third party, who has never had a day in court, never an opportunity to be heard, and you say that he shall be estopped in the same manner and to the same degree as the defendant, who has had an opportunity to litigate every question that is involved.

Now, Mr. Chairman, what is the right of a defendant in this case or in any kind of a case? It is the right to an opportunity to be heard and a judicial determination upon the facts involved, before his property can be taken from him, and when he has had that opportunity, whether it be in a case between the Government and the defendant or between other parties, the legislative body has a right to say that once that question has been determined it shall be determined for all time, so far as the party is concerned who has had his day in court. . . .

Mr. FLOYD of Arkansas. I will ask the gentleman from Wisconsin whether in his judgment the decision, if made applicable only to the defendant who had his day in court, is subject to the criticism that it violates any provision of the Constitution?

Mr. LENROOT. I do not think it is, and I will state my reason.

Mr. FLOYD of Arkansas. I will be glad to hear you.

Mr. LENROOT. Now, the question of right of trial by jury is subject to limitation. For instance, two private individuals, the plaintiff and defendant, in an equity suit, litigate certain questions, and afterwards a case between the same parties at law arises. They are entitled to a trial by jury at law under the Constitution, but they are not entitled to a trial by jury of every fact or every issue that may be set up in that action of law. If any of those questions have been tried and settled in an action in equity between the same parties, their determination becomes conclusive in an action at law, and an estoppel, as well as in an action at equity. There is the distinction. The defendant here is a party in equity. He and the Government are two parties in equity. Now, when it comes to an action at law between the third party and this defendant who has been one of the parties in the equity suit, it is entirely proper, and not open to any constitutional objection, to say that that judgment that has been rendered between those parties, one of them the defendant, shall be an estoppel against the defendant who was a party to the suit in equity. But it is quite a different thing to say that it shall be an estoppel as against the party who never had a day in court, who was never a party to the equity proceeding.

Now, it has been said by the gentleman from Texas [Mr. BEALL] that this right of action given the private individual is only a privilege given by the statute and therefore we may make such conditions as we choose. That is true, Mr. Chairman, so far as treble damages are concerned, but no further. It does not require any statutory provision to give a private individual the right to sue for simple damages any corporation or any individual for violation of the antitrust law. He has that right the same as he has the right against any individual for damages for violation of law. But as this bill now stands it would cut him off and work an estoppel against him in an action that he has regardless of any statute—a right that he has regardless of any statute. And therefore, Mr. Chairman, if this section shall be of any value, it seems to me that the amendment proposed by the gentleman from Minnesota should be adopted, and, if adopted, I believe that the section will be sustained and affirmed by the Supreme Court of the United States. If the section shall stand as it is, I have very grave doubt whether any portion of it will stand, and I am rather inclined to think that the Supreme Court will hold that by reason of this attempted estoppel of third parties who had never had their day in court the entire section will be held invalid. . . .

Mr. CULLOP. Mr. Chairman, I am opposed to this provision in the bill as it stands, and am in favor of the amendment of the gentleman from Minnesota [Mr. VOLSTEAD]. If this proposition as contained in the bill stands, it would furnish a great advantage to the combinations and trusts of this country, and would enable them to carry on their nefarious business more successfully than heretofore. This provision as it comes from the committee into this House, if adopted, would fortify every combination in restraint of trade, every trust and organization created to suppress competition. Under it they would thrive and flourish as never before. This section if enacted would revolutionize the doctrine of estoppel, as it is a complete innovation in the practice and procedure of now well-established rules. It creates by statute an estoppel which can be invoked against parties who were not connected with litigation, who were strangers to it, who had no knowledge of it, and who had no opportunity to be heard. To my mind it is a most dangerous step, one fraught with evil consequences, and will be productive of much injury in the end. So dangerous do I for one consider it that I can not under any circumstances give it my support. The doctrine of estoppel is a wholesome one, and its employment under existing well-established rules, familiar to all lawyers, serves a valuable purpose in our judicial system. But give it the force and application proposed in this provision and it is made an instrument of danger, to be employed to defeat the ends of justice in meritorious cases. Every illegal combination in restraint of trade, every trust in the country would be gratified with its passage.

Suppose some corporation or individual doing business in New Jersey in violation of this law, in order, under it, to become immune from its provisions, would enter into a collusion with some scoundrel to have a suit brought for the purpose of securing a judgment in its or his favor, in order to plead an estoppel in some other jurisdiction. Application would be made to the district attorney to file the action. He would do so. He would make the charge cover every phase of the law, and then, upon the trial, fail, because of want of a preponderance of the evidence. Testimony would be produced tending to support every material charge necessary to warrant a recovery, but this would be overcome by the defendant either by number of witnesses or intelligence of witnesses or character of witnesses, or for any reason, and judgment on the issues and evidence would be rendered for the defendant. That judgment under this provision would be a complete bar when pleaded in estoppel in any other suit growing out of the same cause of action, it would not matter by whom or where brought. This is a concrete illustration of how injuriously it could be invoked. What a weapon of danger it places in the hands of the law violators, of those who have by their indefensible methods been preying upon the public. Can we adopt such a provision? Others may do as they like—the responsibility is theirs; but, for myself, I should not support it, but do what I can to have it amended so as to escape this pitfall for the engulfment of the people's rights.

I do not care to discuss its constitutionality; others may assail it for that reason. But I do not believe the courts would permit it to stand if it remains as it now is, for the reason it is destructive of the right of the citizen to have his case tried in the courts of the country on its merit and not on the merits of some one else.

Let me take the case that I gave to the gentleman from Texas, involving the same facts. Supposing the Government should bring an action and when it came to trial have only one witness to prove its cause of action, and the defendant came in with three or four witnesses equally as credible and denied the charge. Under the well-settled rules of evidence the defendant would obtain a judgment in the case exonerating it from the charge. This judgment could be pleaded as an estoppel in all subsequent suits involving the same cause of action, it matters not where nor by whom brought. Such a doctrine, in my conception of the administration of justice, is wrong and productive of harm. I can not support such a proposition.

Supposing the same violation of the law should occur in some other State or jurisdiction, and suit was instituted by some other person, and five witnesses were produced to prove the same facts alleged as a violation of the law, and would come into court and establish the facts by an overwhelming preponderance of the evidence, but the defendant would answer that the same facts were litigated in the former trial in some other court between other parties, where the plaintiff had only one witness and the defendant had five or six witnesses, and judgment was rendered for the defendant in that trial. That judgment would be an estoppel against the complainant in the subsequent action. Does any man on this committee think that provision ought to stand? Every man knows, it matters not how strong the evidence would be of the breach of the law, charging the same facts as in the former cause of action, would be forever barred and could not recover.

Furthermore, this provision seems to suppose that these combinations will always do business and use the same methods as they have been using, and yet we all know they are changing their plans of operation every year. But the violations of the same over the same subject matter would constantly be going on and no remedy to prevent it. Does any man in this committee think that kind of a law would be fair to the citizen? He has surely suffered enough. It matters not how strong the evidence would be. Because there was not sufficient evidence in the first case tried or because of collusion, parties are forever estopped from prosecuting suits successfully. The facts are the same. Does any man believe that legislation of that kind would be right? Would it be in aid of the trusts or would it be in the suppression of their unlawful business? Better have no legislation than permit this provision to remain in the measure. It will sorely vex us if we do.

I read that paragraph of the President's message to which the distinguished gentleman from Arkansas [Mr. FLOYD] alluded. I do not agree with him in his construction of what the President says in that paragraph in reference to this matter. . . .

Mr. FLOYD of Arkansas. If the gentleman had paid particular attention to what I said he would know that I stated expressly that the President only recommended that it should be binding as against the corporation, and that the committee had put in this other provision.

Mr. CULLOP. Yes; I agree with the President in his recommendation in that respect and assert he goes no further on that subject, but I do not agree with the committee in their proposed legislation in this particular matter. I regret the committee insists upon it remaining in the bill. I hope it changes its position in this regard. . . .

Now, in answer to the statement of the gentleman from Arkansas about litigation in these cases, if we were to leave this open so that every individual could go into court if he desires, the gentleman says it would be too costly upon the litigants. I say to the gentleman that that matter concerns the litigants alone and not the Members of Congress. That is none of their affair. We are not to become the guardians of the individual, to determine how the private individual shall expend his money. That is his business and not ours.

The courthouse doors ought to swing inwardly, and do to every citizen of this country. Yet if we enact this provision as the committee has brought it in here we have closed the doors of the courthouse to the citizens of this country. That is a matter of the highest concern to them. We will have denied to the citizen by the enactment of this provision the right to go into court and recover damages for wrongs inflicted. Why? Forsooth, because a collusive suit has been brought in some place, or had been tried without preparation, or had been tried without sufficient evidence; and yet a stranger, an innocent person, is bound by that decree. He had no say; he took no part in it; and yet by this proposed legislation the door would be shut against him and his cause of action. We are adopting antitrust legislation for relief to a suffering public, furnishing a remedy for wrongs long perpetrated, but I fear if provisions of this kind are incorporated in the measure we will not accomplish our purpose or perform the duty as well as the people desire it should be done. I hope that the amendment of the gentleman from Minnesota will be adopted. . . .

Mr. VOLSTEAD. Mr. Chairman, I offer another amendment which I desire to call to the attention of the committee, and I ask to have it read.

The CHAIRMAN. An amendment is pending.

Mr. VOLSTEAD. I offer another amendment at the end of this section, and ask to have it read at this time for the information of the committee.

The CHAIRMAN. The Clerk will report the amendment.

The Clerk read as follows:

At the end of section 6, page 23, after the word "laws," on line 18, add "and any evidence or a transcript of any evidence taken at or before the trial of any such suit or proceeding to establish any such determinations shall at any time be admissible in evidence in any action or proceeding brought by any other party than the United States. . . .

Mr. MURDOCK. Suppose that the Associated Press, a news agency, should be attacked by the Government, and the courts should hold that it was not a trust, not a combination in restraint of trade. Under the provisions of this bill as it now stands, would all publishers be estopped from bringing suit against the Associated Press?

Mr. VOLSTEAD. Yes; they would be estopped so far as suing for any damages under the antitrust laws.

Mr. MURDOCK. Either simple damages or damages in treble the amount?

Mr. VOLSTEAD. Yes.

Mr. MURDOCK. Is there any question about that?

Mr. VOLSTEAD. There is not.

Mr. MURDOCK. The gentleman's amendment which he offered previous to the last amendment would remedy a difficulty of that kind?

Mr. VOLSTEAD. Yes; that is the object.

Mr. Chairman, I call attention to the amendment that has just been read. During the hearings our attention was called to the fact that something of this kind ought to be written into the law. A suit may be pending and may drag along in the courts. The Government may not prosecute it. During that time, of course, no advantage can be secured from any proceeding on behalf of the Government. Now, it seems to me that if a suit has been brought by an individual and the evidence necessary to establish that suit has been introduced in an action brought on behalf of the Government that evidence might properly be used in the private suit, as well as in the suit in which it was originally taken.

I do not believe any harm would come. It certainly seems to me that if the decree itself can be used as evidence, no real objection can be urged against using the testimony that has been introduced to secure that decree. A defendant charged with being a trust would have the right to introduce testimony in opposition to this evidence, and would otherwise have the right to dispute it. It would be very much fairer than to introduce the decree itself, and it seems to me that if the committee is willing to go as far as they do in this section—that is, to make the decree binding—they ought to be willing to allow that testimony to be used. It would save a great deal of cost and expense to the private litigant if he could take a transcript of the testimony in a suit brought by the Government and use it in his case; take, for instance, depositions or evidence taken before a master in such a suit. . . .

Mr. SCOTT. I was going to ask whether the amendment would permit the use of these depositions and the testimony before the submission of the suit in which such testimony was taken?

Mr. VOLSTEAD. Yes; I tried to draw the amendment so as to permit that.

Mr. SCOTT. Would not that be open to this objection, that until it was received in evidence no ruling would be made upon its competency?

Mr. VOLSTEAD. No; but the ruling would be made when it was offered. If it was not competent testimony, it could not ⊥ be introduced in the suit, but if it was competent, it seems to me it would be perfectly proper to admit it.

Mr. SCOTT. I understood that the amendment went so far as to make it admissible.

Mr. VOLSTEAD. It makes it admissible upon the particular issue that is to be determined. That is the object of it. I had a letter a day or two ago from the attorney general of the State of Louisiana, asking for this very thing others asked for before our committee, and it seems to me it would be a proper amendment. It is an amendment to accomplish the purpose sought by this section. If we are honestly striving to help the private litigant, we ought to give him this additional assistance. . . .

Mr. WEBB. I call the attention of the gentleman to his last amendment, which, it seems to me, does the very thing he is striving not to do in his first amendment. The amendment reads as follows:

And any evidence, or a transcript of any evidence, taken at or before the trial of any such suit or proceeding to establish any such determinations—

I think that ought to be "issues"—

Mr. VOLSTEAD. The word I used was "determinations."

Mr. WEBB. The amendment continues—

shall at any time be admissible in evidence in any action or proceeding brought by any other party than the United States.

That gives both the plaintiff and the defendant the right to use the transcript of evidence.

Mr. VOLSTEAD. It is not conclusive; it is only evidence.

Mr. WEBB. But you permit either the plaintiff or the defendant to use it.

Mr. VOLSTEAD. It would be evidence in favor of the private party.

Mr. WEBB. It would be evidence in favor of either party who cared to use it.

Mr. SCOTT. I would like to ask the gentleman if it would be objectionable to modify his amendment by saying "competent and material evidence."

Mr. VOLSTEAD. No; but I do not think the court would admit anything not competent and material.

Mr. SCOTT. The amendment as framed makes it admissible, and it strikes me that it would be rather a strong word unless you add the words "competent and material."

Mr. VOLSTEAD. It would not be evidence unless it was competent and material. The court would exclude it if it was not competent or material.

Mr. SCOTT. But your amendment uses the word "testimony."

HOUSE CONSIDERATION

Mr. LEVY. Mr. Chairman, I ask unanimous consent to offer an amendment and have it pending.

The CHAIRMAN. The gentleman from New York offers an amendment.

The Clerk read as follows:

Page 23, after the word "laws," in line 18, insert "That nothing herein contained shall interfere with legitimate business or commercial enterprises, and no citizen shall be deprived of his liberty or happiness while pursuing the same." . . .

Mr. FLOYD of Arkansas. Mr. Chairman, I am opposed to the last amendment offered by the gentleman from Minnesota. I want to say a few words further in regard to his first amendment. I do not think that the section as drawn is subject to the constitutional objections made to it, or that it denies the right of trial by jury. It relates to evidence, it does not cut off jury trials. I desire to explain again, as I explained in the outset, that the recommendation for this legislation in the President's message was to the effect that the judgment might be used against the corporation adjudged guilty of violations of the Sherman Act in suits by private litigants, and that in the bill introduced by the gentleman from Wisconsin [Mr. LENROOT], from which we took substantially the wording of the provision, the proposition was to make the judgment binding only upon the defendant corporation. I desire to state further that in the tentative bill prepared by the committee and submitted to the House and to the country for consideration we incorporated substantially the language of the provision in the Lenroot bill, providing alone for the introduction of such decree as evidence against the defendant corporation. In the hearings and during the consideration of this section practically all the criticism that was made against it, which provision we regard as one of the most excellent provisions in the bill, was to the effect that to make it apply to only one of the parties litigant was unfair, unjust, and would render the proposition unconstitutional. In view of such criticism we modified it and made it apply equally to both parties.

As I stated, the amendment or modification was made by the Judiciary Committee of the House. Now, speaking for myself and associates on the subcommittee, who had in charge the preparation of the bill, after conference and after this debate, I desire to state that we withdraw our resistance to the first amendment offered by the gentleman from Minnesota, but we still ask the House not to adopt the second amendment offered by the gentleman.

Mr. WEBB. Mr. Chairman, may we have the first amendment reported?

The Clerk read as follows:

Page 23, line 5, strike out the words "or has not." In line 7, strike out the words "or has not." In line 14, strike out the words "in favor of or." In line 16, strike out the words "or against."

The CHAIRMAN. The question is on the amendment.

The question was taken, and the amendment was agreed to.

The CHAIRMAN. The Clerk will read the second amendment.

The Clerk again reported the second amendment offered by Mr. VOLSTEAD.

Mr. VOLSTEAD. Mr. Chairman, I ask unanimous consent to withdraw that amendment. While I believe that there ought to be legislation along that line, it is not in just the form that I think it ought to be, and I ask unanimous consent to withdraw it.

The CHAIRMAN. The gentleman from Minnesota asks unanimous consent to withdraw his amendment. Is there objection?

There was no objection.

The CHAIRMAN. The Clerk will now read the next amendment offered by the gentleman from New York [Mr. LEVY].

The Clerk read as follows:

Page 33 [sic], after the word "laws," in line 18, insert "that nothing herein contained shall interfere with legitimate business or commercial enterprises, and no citizen shall be deprived of his liberty or happiness while pursuing the same."

The CHAIRMAN. The question is on the amendment offered by the gentleman from New York.

The question was taken, and the amendment was rejected.

The Clerk read as follows:

SEC. 7. That nothing contained in the antitrust laws shall be construed to forbid the existence and operation of fraternal, labor, consumers, agricultural, or horticultural organizations, orders, or associations instituted for the purposes of mutual help, and not having capital stock or conducted for profit, or to forbid or restrain individual members of such organizations, orders, or associations from carrying out the legitimate objects thereof.

Nothing contained in the antitrust laws shall be construed to forbid associations of traffic, operating, accounting, or other officers of common carriers for the purpose of conferring among themselves or of making any lawful agreement as to any matter which is subject to the regulating or supervisory jurisdiction of the Interstate Commerce Commission, but all such matters shall continue to be subject to such jurisdiction of the commission, and all such agreements shall be entered and kept of record by the carriers, parties thereto, and shall at all times be open to inspection by the commission: *Provided*, That nothing in this act shall be construed as modifying existing laws prohibiting the pooling of earnings or traffic, or existing laws against joint agreements by common carriers to maintain rates.

Mr. WEBB. Mr. Chairman, I give notice that on Monday morning at 11 o'clock the committee will offer an amendment to this section, and I reserve the right now to offer it.

Mr. MADDEN. Mr. Chairman, I desire to offer an amendment. I shall not be here on Monday, and I would like to have my amendment pending.

Mr. WEBB. I have no objection to the gentleman from Illinois offering an amendment.

Mr. MADDEN. Mr. Chairman, I move to strike out the second paragraph of section 7.

The CHAIRMAN. The gentleman from Illinois offers an amendment which the Clerk will report.

The Clerk read as follows:

Page 24: Strike out the second paragraph of section 7, being lines 11 to 24, inclusive.

Mr. MADDEN. Mr. Chairman, I want to say in this connection, if I may be permitted for just a moment to do so, that I believe this second paragraph of section 7 exempts the railroads of the United States from the provisions of the Sherman antitrust law, that it is more drastic in its provisions in that respect than was section 7 in a bill to regulate the railroads passed by the House in 1910. This not only gives traffic associations connected with railroads the opportunity for organizing, but it gives also the operating, accounting, and other officers of common carriers the same privilege. It grants to the officers of one railroad, the traffic officers, the executive officers, and all other officers connected with the railroad, the privilege of entering into a combination with similar officers of any other railroad, permits them to enter into any traffic arrangements they choose, giving to the Interstate Commerce Commission the ⊥ right to supervise the matters which are the subjects of traffic agreements, but does not give the Interstate Commerce Commission any right whatever over the agreements themselves. All the Interstate Commerce Commission would have the right to do under this provision would be to accept the contracts entered into by the combination permitted to the railroad companies under this second paragraph of section 7, for filing purposes.

I protest against the passage of this paragraph, and I wish to give notice to the country that the committee in recommending it for adoption have simply recommended the relief of the railroad companies of the country from prosecution under the provisions of the Sherman antitrust law, whereas all the way through the bill they seek to restrict all other branches of business from entering into trade agreements of any kind and provide for the imposition of fines and imprisonment for those who enter into such agreements. It seems strange that in the same bill the committee should recommend the exemption of railroads from the provisions of the Sherman law while imposing greater restrictions on all other business organizations. I see no justification for such action. All should be treated alike; all should be exempt or none should be. This bill creates monopolies on the one hand and destroys legitimate business on the other, gives to those who have and takes away from those who have not.

The wish of the Democratic leaders seems to be to satisfy the railroads, and in the next to fool the labor leaders. No one should close his eyes to the deal with the railroads evidenced in section 7. The railroads would be worse hurt by a real exemption than any other interest, and the second paragraph of section 7 was smuggled in at the last minute. But not one word of objection comes from that source, nor will there be any organized opposition to the compromise amendments, so called. Before taking them up, I call attention to an excerpt from the New York Sun, which is ever on the alert for any menace to capital:

> President Wilson, on the other hand, takes the stand that the amendment he has approved will not preclude the prosecution of labor unions for acts in violation of the antitrust laws. His supporters in the House, who had aided in drafting the amendment, have advised him that the language to be added to the Clayton bill will merely clarify that section which deals with labor organizations, and that it will not, in fact, exempt them from prosecution.

It is proposed to add at the end of the first paragraph this sentence:

> Nor shall such organizations, orders, or associations, or members thereof, be held or construed to be illegal combinations in restraint of trade under the antitrust laws.

The addition is superfluous and merely senseless repetition in its purport of what precedes.

If the antitrust laws are not to be construed "to forbid," and so forth, or "to forbid or restrain individual members," and so forth, what need to say that they shall not "be held or construed to be illegal combinations or conspiracies in restraint of trade under the antitrust laws"? Laws such as the antitrust act do not apply to any individuals or classes, whether acting together or singly as such, nor has any court ever said that they do. The law applies not to any persons, natural or artificial, as persons or as organizations, but solely to their acts or conduct. If members of an organization should in fact restrain trade, according to the judgment of a court, section 7 neither as it stands nor as it is proposed to amend it would protect them. They would not restrain trade in their organized capacity. They would not if they tried, because not within the legal purposes of the organization. The courts would simply ignore their relation to the labor organization, as they did in the case of Loewe against Lawler [sic].[5.539] Section 7 is simply abortive. The purpose that labor would accomplish by it should not be attempted in the exercise of congressional power under the interstate-commerce clause, but under the power to create courts and regulate their jurisdiction.

Section 7 therefore, whether considered as it stands or as it is proposed to "amend" it, is merely innocuous and abortive.

But sections 15 and 18 are not mere "gold bricks." They are gold bricks containing dynamite. Democratic Party pledges have been profuse and explicit, but the alleged performance is not merely a mockery. It is a betrayal and death thrust. Those who pretend to represent labor and yet cast their fortunes in with the Democrats on sections 15 and 18, believing that exposure will not be swift and complete, have another guess coming.

Now, what is the revamped "amendment" to section 18? At the end of the second paragraph of section 18 it is proposed to add the words, "Nor shall any of the acts specified in this paragraph be considered or held unlawful." I would like you to take the matter up for yourself and answer for yourself this question. Does that meet any criticism that has been offered to the section?

The amendment directs the courts to take the view as to certain acts which, upon reading the paragraph, they must take anyhow.

None of the acts specified ever were held unlawful per se; and after the care taken to annex to them the qualifying words "peacefully" and "lawfully," or "peaceful" and "lawful," how would it be possible for a court to now hold them unlawful per se? And that is all that the new amendment purports to require of them.

The vice of section 18 is the fact that it gives with one hand and takes away with the other, as is shown in some of the speeches on the floor, and that sections 15 and

---

[5.539] The correct citation is Loewe v. Lawlor, 208 U.S. 274, 28 S. Ct. 301, 52 L. Ed. 488 (1908) (the *Danbury Hatters* case).

18, in combination, confer a new jurisdiction, or, at any rate, confirm a jurisdiction, which, it was claimed, was usurped and heretofore exercised destructively.

No one has attempted to answer this criticism, and no one can answer it; so I need not dwell upon it. I will, however, add just a few words. Some one may say that the section will be given a liberal construction. On the contrary, having the form of an exemption from ordinary course of procedure, it must be construed strictly. And when anyone argues that the words "employer and employees" will be held to mean those previously holding the relation, the courts will refuse to so radically change and extend the meaning.

In conclusion I call attention to this from the New York World:

> A decision not to wait for the House to act on the trust legislation was reached to-day by the Senate Interstate Commerce Committee, which has been considering an omnibus trust bill. This measure, it was decided, should be reported out as soon as possible, regardless of what the House might do in the meanwhile.

Let the significance of that be noted. The President has evidently studied Capt. Cuttle, and is "devilish sly." After labor has been betrayed by its friends in the House, their work will be nullified in the Senate. But they will have taken the gag from the Democrats and won popular support for Democracy's candidates, unless their exposure be complete and prompt. The World is the administration's mouthpiece.

Mr. WEBB. Mr. Chairman, a parliamentary inquiry.

The CHAIRMAN. The gentleman will state it.

Mr. WEBB. Mr. Chairman, it is understood that if the committee rise at this time other amendments may be in order on next Monday morning when the House reconvenes at 11 o'clock?

The CHAIRMAN. Certainly.

Mr. WEBB. Mr. Chairman, I move that the committee do now rise.

The motion was agreed to.

HOUSE DEBATE
63d Cong., 2d Sess.
June 1, 1914

51 CONG. REC. 9538

The SPEAKER. The regular order is that the House resolve itself automatically into the Committee of the Whole House on the state of the Union for the further consideration of the bill H. R. 15657 and other bills embraced within the special rule. In the absence of Mr. HULL, the gentleman from Tennessee, Mr. BYRNS, will take the chair. . . .

Mr. WEBB. Mr. Chairman, I wish to offer an amendment to section 7.

Mr. GARNER. Mr. Chairman, there is one amendment now pending, offered by the gentleman from Illinois [Mr. MADDEN] immediately before the committee rose on Friday last. Shall we not have to vote first on that amendment?

The CHAIRMAN. The chairman of the Committee on the Judiciary has an amendment in addition to that offered by the gentleman from Illinois.

Mr. MANN. Mr. Chairman, if we have to dispose of the first paragraph before we take up the second paragraph of that section, I suggest that the gentleman from North Carolina ask unanimous consent that the first paragraph of the section be taken up before the second paragraph, and that they be considered separately; that the two paragraphs be considered as entirely separate.

Mr. WEBB. My idea was, Mr. Chairman, to let all amendments to the section be disposed of, as has been the practice in the past.

Mr. MANN. It is immaterial to me. I thought perhaps the gentleman would like to take up the labor proposition first.

Mr. WEBB. Then, Mr. Chairman. I ask unanimous consent that the amendments to the first paragraph of section 7 be disposed of before we take up the second paragraph of that section.

The CHAIRMAN. The gentleman from North Carolina asks unanimous consent that the first paragraph of section 7 be first considered. Is there objection? . . .

There was no objection.

The CHAIRMAN. The Clerk will report the amendment offered by the gentleman from North Carolina [Mr. WEBB].

The Clerk read as follows:

On page 24, at the end of line 10, amend by striking out the period and inserting a semicolon and by adding the following: "Nor shall such organizations, orders, or associations, or members thereof, be held or construed to be illegal combinations or conspiracies in restraint of trade under the antitrust laws."

The CHAIRMAN. The question is on agreeing to the amendment offered by the gentleman from North Carolina.

Mr. [ROBERT Y.] THOMAS [JR.] [D., Ky.]. Mr. Chairman, I wish to offer an amendment to the amendment offered by the gentleman from North Carolina.

The CHAIRMAN. The Clerk will report the amendment offered by the gentleman from Kentucky [Mr. THOMAS] to the amendment of the gentleman from North Carolina [Mr. WEBB].

The Clerk read as follows:

Strike out all of section 7 down to and including the word "thereof," in line 10, and insert the following: "The provisions of the antitrust laws shall not apply to agricultural, labor, consumers, fraternal, or horticultural organizations, orders, or associations."

Mr. WEBB. Mr. Chairman, I desire to make a parliamentary inquiry.

The CHAIRMAN. The gentleman will state it.

Mr. WEBB. That is, to know whether the amendment just presented by the gentleman from Kentucky is in order. From its construction it seems to be an amendment to an amendment to an amendment. I make a point of order on it.

Mr. MANN. I make the point of order, Mr. Chairman, anyhow, just to preserve the record straight and conform to the rules of the House. As a matter of fact, Mr. Chairman, we have treated the existing committee bill, which is an amendment in itself, as though it were an original bill, and all through the discussion and consideration so far we have allowed amendments to amendments to the committee amendment, although I think that was a little irregular; but nobody has said anything about it, because it is usual when you bring in such a thing to treat a committee substitute as though it were an original bill.

Mr. MURDOCK. The committee substitute is the one which was reported under the rule.

The CHAIRMAN. That would be in keeping with the rule in Committee of the Whole, to permit an amendment to an amendment.

Mr. MANN. But this is not an amendment to the amendment offered by the gentleman.

The CHAIRMAN. The Chair thinks it should not be treated as an amendment. Does the gentleman from North Carolina insist on his point of order?

Mr. WEBB. I withdraw it. We are going to have a vote on it anyhow.

Mr. MACDONALD. Mr. Chairman, I offer an amendment.

The CHAIRMAN. The gentleman from Michigan [Mr. MACDONALD] offers an amendment, which the Clerk will report.

Mr. NELSON. Mr. Chairman, as a member of the committee, I think I have the privilege of offering an amendment before the other gentleman.

The CHAIRMAN. The gentleman is correct. The Clerk will report the amendment offered by the gentleman from Wisconsin.

Mr. NELSON. I offer it as a substitute.

The Clerk read as follows:

Insert after the word "profit" and before the words "or to forbid," in line 8, page 24, the following: "Or of cooperative associations formed by farmers for the purpose of buying more cheaply and of marketing their products to better advantage." so as to make the first paragraph of this section read: "That nothing contained in the antitrust laws shall be construed to forbid the existence and operation of fraternal, labor, consumers', agricultural, or horticultural organizations, orders, or associations instituted for the purposes of mutual help, and not having capital stock, or conducted for profit; or of cooperative associations formed by farmers for the purpose of buying more cheaply and marketing their products to better advantage; or to forbid or restrain individual members of such organizations, orders, or associations from carrying out the legitimate objects thereof; nor shall such organizations, orders, or associations, or the members thereof, be held or construed to be illegal combinations or conspiracies in restraint of trade under the antitrust laws."

Mr. MANN. Mr. Chairman, I shall have to make a point of order that that is not a substitute, on the face of it. We shall get all confused and mixed up in this section unless we treat the amendments as separate amendments.

Mr. MURDOCK. Let us have them all offered as amendments.

Mr. MANN. The gentleman from Wisconsin will have the opportunity to offer the amendment that he desires to offer at the proper time, without question.

Mr. NELSON. I have no objection to taking them up in order.

The CHAIRMAN. The Chair will state that there is an amendment and substitute pending now.

Mr. GARNER. Mr. Chairman, my understanding was that the gentleman from North Carolina [Mr. WEBB] offered his amendment for the purpose of allowing all gentlemen to offer amendments thereto at this time for purposes of information and to have them considered as pending.

Mr. MANN. He can not do that. I made the point of order before that the amendment of the gentleman from Kentucky was not an amendment to the amendment of the gentleman from North Carolina. It plainly is not.

The CHAIRMAN. The Chair thinks the point of order raised by the gentleman is well taken.

Mr. FERRIS. Mr. Chairman, let me inquire of the chairman if the gentleman does not think the reading of so many amendments would tend to confuse rather than to help us? I can not hold in my head five or six different amendments, all relating to different phases of the subject.

Mr. MURDOCK. They will be reported before we come to vote on them.

Mr. GARNER. The gentleman from Oklahoma realizes that we ought to get a limit of debate, if possible, on this paragraph. Now, the object of the chairman of the committee, as I understand it, is to have all amendments offered at this time for information, and as the different amendments are discussed, they will be reported from the desk, and the committee in that way will be able to understand the merits of each one of the amendments.

Mr. FERRIS. The trouble about that is that we do not have the amendments printed, and we will have to go to the desk to see what they are, and it will be confusing.

Mr. MANN. I shall have to make a point of order against the offering of these amendments in this way. Nobody will know where we are in a few minutes.

The CHAIRMAN. The point of order is sustained.

Mr. MANN. Mr. Chairman, a parliamentary inquiry. What is now pending?

The CHAIRMAN. The Chair will state to the gentleman that the amendment offered by the gentleman from North Carolina [Mr. WEBB] and the substitute offered by the gentleman from Kentucky [Mr. THOMAS] are pending.

Mr. MANN. What became of the point of order which I made on the amendment offered by the gentleman from Kentucky that it was not an amendment to the amendment?

The CHAIRMAN. The Chair understands the gentleman from Kentucky offers it as a substitute for the amendment offered by the gentleman from North Carolina.

Mr. MANN. Yes: but I make the point of order that it is not a substitute. It is offered to a different part of the section. They have no relation to each other.

Mr. THOMAS. It is offered to the first part of the section. It is either a substitute or a separate amendment to the first paragraph of the section.

Mr. MANN. That would be in order; but the amendment of the gentleman from North Carolina [Mr. WEBB] comes in at the end of the paragraph, and the amendment proposed by the gentleman from Kentucky comes in at the beginning of the paragraph. They might both be agreed to by the committee. One is not a substitute for the other in any sense.

Mr. GARNER. It makes no difference, just so you get a vote.

The CHAIRMAN. Does the gentleman from Kentucky [Mr. THOMAS] desire to be heard on the point of order?

Mr. THOMAS. I will say this much, may it please the Chair, that the amendment or the substitute, as the case may be, which I have offered, is to the first paragraph of section 7. I understand that the amendment offered by the gentleman from North Carolina [Mr. WEBB] is to the last part of this paragraph. That is what I understood the gentleman from Illinois to claim.

Mr. MANN. If the gentleman will pardon me, the amendment offered by the gentleman from North Carolina is to add something at the end of the paragraph.

Mr. THOMAS. Yes.

Mr. MANN. The amendment proposed by the gentleman from Kentucky is practically to change the language of the paragraph. Now, Mr. Chairman, if it is to be held as an amendment to the amendment, and if the amendment of the gentleman from Kentucky is agreed to, there will be no chance of getting a vote upon the amendment of the gentleman from North Carolina; and although the committee might want to agree to both amendments, it could not possibly do it, if it is held to be an amendment to the amendment, because it would not be in order, I take it, to offer this amendment over again after we had substituted something for it.

Mr. [ROBERT L.] HENRY [D., Tex.]. I suggest to the gentleman from Kentucky that he offer his amendment later.

Mr. MANN. The amendment of the gentleman from Kentucky will be in order after the amendment of the gentleman from North Carolina is disposed of.

Mr. THOMAS. My amendment is certainly an amendment to the first part of the paragraph.

Mr. MANN. Oh, undoubtedly.

The CHAIRMAN. The Chair thinks that, strictly speaking, the amendment of the gentleman from North Carolina [Mr. WEBB] should be considered as an amendment to perfect the text of the bill. The amendment offered by the gentleman from Kentucky strikes out the paragraph and proposes to insert new matter. For that reason the Chair feels constrained to sustain the point of order. Of course, the gentleman from Kentucky will have an opportunity to offer his amendment later. The question is on the amendment offered by the gentleman from North Carolina. . . .

⊥ Mr. WEBB. Mr. Chairman, the amendment which is under consideration is, in the opinion of the committee, in keeping with the declaration of the Democratic platform—to the effect that labor organizations and farmers' organizations organized for mutual help shall not be considered or construed to be illegal combinations or conspiracies in restraint of trade under the antitrust laws. ⊥9540

It is needless to say that we have had much diversity of opinion in adopting and agreeing on this particular section, but after all, Mr. Chairman, we have embodied in this amendment what we understand to be the best legal interpretation of the best judges in the United States. Personally I have never had any idea that the existence and operation of labor organizations, of farmers' unions, or fraternal orders were ever intended to come within the provisions of the antitrust law. However, some labor leaders have contended for many years that labor organizations have their existence as a matter of sufferance and at the whim of the Attorney General, and if suit should be brought, if they were not dissolved entirely, much trouble could be given them. We are therefore writing into the statutes of the United States the concensus of opinion of the best judges of the country on this troublesome question. I have not had an opportunity of reading the opinion, but only last Friday the circuit court of appeals of the fourth circuit at Richmond, Va., held that a labor organization was not a conspiracy or combination in restraint of trade.[5.540] Therefore we say that we have embodied in this section as set forth in the first part of section 7 and as expressed in the latter part of this amendment which I now offer what is generally understood to be the law and should be the law in the United States with reference to labor organizations, as well as fraternal and farmers' organizations. [Applause.]

I now yield 15 minutes to the gentleman from Texas [Mr. HENRY].

Mr. HENRY. Mr. Chairman, there has been so much controversy about what was intended when the original Sherman antitrust law was passed that I think we should make clear just what we intend by this law. Some of us did not believe section 7 as originally written by the Committee on the Judiciary expressed exactly what should be in this bill. Therefore we took exception to the language of the first part of the paragraph in section 7 and insisted there should be additional language. Among those who agreed that the language was not plain enough were the gentleman from North Carolina, Mr. KITCHIN, the gentleman from Illinois, Mr. HINEBAUGH, the gentleman from Illinois, Mr. GRAHAM, the gentleman from Iowa, Mr. TOWNER, the gentleman from Maryland, Mr. LEWIS, and myself. We met to confer, and concluded that we ought to make the language more explicit. In that conference held in the committee room of the Committee of Rules, on the evening of May 21, 1914, we agreed that this language should be added at the end of the first paragraph of section 7, to wit, after the word "thereof":

Nor shall such organizations, orders, or associations or the members thereof be held or construed to be illegal combinations or conspiracies in restraint of trade under the antitrust laws.

This language I have read is exactly the verbiage used by the gentleman from North Carolina [Mr. WEBB] in the amendment offered by him and is the amendment agreed upon by Mr. KITCHIN and our conferees in my office. The Committee on the Judiciary courteously accepted the language as prepared by the gentlemen in the conference, believing, I assume, that we were correct and that the original language used by them was not quite explicit. So we came to a satisfactory agreement with the House Judiciary Committee about this addition to the first part of section 7, and, as far as I am concerned, we are standing squarely with the committee for that paragraph with our added language. We called into the conference with us the heads of the American Federation of Labor, and submitted this amendment to them, and said to them that we believed its adoption as an addition to section 7 would clearly exempt labor organizations and farmers' organizations from the provisions of the antitrust laws.

They agreed with us; they called their counsel into conference with them and with us, and we all concurred that this amendment added to the paragraph of section 7 would give these organizations what they have desired so long, and all they have been struggling for since the original enactment of the Sherman antitrust law.

In my judgment, when Congress was dealing with "combinations in restraint of trade" it never intended that the law should apply to labor organizations or farmers' organizations without capital and not for profit. The courts took a different view of it and construed the act as it was never intended that it should be interpreted. The time has come when we can correct that error and write the language in the law as those gentlemen insist that it should be and should have been.

I am glad of the opportunity of espousing their cause to-day and standing with them in accord and agreement. The Judiciary Committee has acceded to their position to the extent indicated by me, and so has the President. This is entirely a satisfactory solution of the question. [Applause.]

Mr. Chairman, unfortunately there are many men in this country who hesitate to espouse the cause of organized labor or the farmers for fear they will be called "demagogues." That has kept many a man from advocating on the floor of this House what he believed in his heart, because he dreaded adverse criticism. We have come up to the proposition to-day and we propose to meet it and say that these men are entitled to what they have been demanding, and we shall write it in the antitrust laws. Let us review the history of that matter for a little while. When the original Sherman law was

---

[5.540] Mitchell v. Hitchman Coal & Coke Co., 214 F. 685 (4th Cir. 1914). *See* notes 5.545 & 5.546 *infra* and accompanying debate.

proposed in the Senate, Senator George, of Mississippi, not a demagogue, but a great lawyer and a great statesman, offered this amendment:

> *Provided*, That this act shall not be construed to apply to any arrangements, agreements, or combinations between the laborers made with a view of lessening the number of hours of labor or the increasing of their wages; nor to any arrangements, agreements, or combinations among persons engaged in horticulture or agriculture made with a view of enhancing the price of agricultural or horticultural products.

The amendment was agreed to without opposition. A little later in the proceedings the bill with amendments was referred to the Committee on the Judiciary, and when the committee reported it back to the Senate the George amendment was left out, because all agreed that the act as written without that language in it meant exactly what was contained in the George amendment. . . .

Mr. GARNER. The gentleman contends that it never was the intention to prohibit farmers' unions, for instance, from organizing to get better prices for their products?

Mr. HENRY. Yes.

Mr. GARNER. Will the gentleman contend that his proposed amendment will permit farmers' organizations to warehouse their cotton and agree among themselves that they will not sell it except at a certain price?

Mr. HENRY. Beyond the peradventure of a doubt it allows that very thing, and if it did not I would not vote for the amendment.

Mr. GARNER. There is where the gentleman differs from me with reference to the effect of his amendment.

Mr. HENRY. If it did not, I would not support it a single instant. It is as broad and strong as the George amendment and ought to be written into this law. Let us trace the history a little further. Later on, in 1900, when the Littlefield antitrust bill was before the House—and I happened to be a Member of that Congress—Mr. Terry, of Arkansas, offered an amendment which was agreed to in the House by a vote of 260 yeas to 8 nays. That amendment was offered on June 2, 1900, and is as follows:

> Nothing in this act shall be so construed as to apply to trade-unions or other labor organizations, organized for the purpose of regulating wages, hours of labor, or other conditions under which labor is to be performed.

So it was written into the antitrust bill as it passed this body and went to the Senate. After we put that exemption in the bill Mr. Littlefield lost all interest in it, and it was not heard of again in the Senate of the United States.

Next, on June 21, 1910, Mr. HUGHES, of New Jersey, offered an amendment to the sundry civil appropriation bill to this effect:

> *Provided further*, That no part of this money shall be spent in the prosecution of any organization or individual for entering into any combination or agreement having in view the increasing of wages, shortening of hours, or bettering the condition of labor, or for any act done in furtherance thereof not in itself unlawful.

By a vote of 82 to 52 that amendment was inserted in the sundry civil appropriation bill, and on June 23, 1910, when the bill came back from the Senate, Mr. Tawney, chairman of the Committee on Appropriations, moved to recede and concur—which meant that the House agreed to the Senate amendment—striking the Hughes exemption from the bill. That motion was agreed to by a vote of 138 to 130, and then it was that the disintegration of the standpat Republican Party began. No matter what gentlemen may say or think, when the Republican Party made it manifest that they were not willing to write this exemption in the antitrust laws the great labor organizations lost confidence in them and turned to another party. They came to the Democratic convention at Denver, and we wrote a promise in our platform. And then they came to Baltimore in 1912, and we wrote a pledge in that platform. We are here to redeem our word, just as we made it, and put the promised exemption in the antitrust legislation and send it to the Senate of the United States. [Applause.]

The amendment which has been offered by the Judiciary Committee, and has been prepared by Messrs. KITCHIN, LEWIS of Maryland, TOWNER, GRAHAM of Illinois, HINEBAUGH, and myself, in connection with them, is in the exact language of the Baltimore platform, to this effect:

The expanding organization of industry makes it essential that there should be no abridgment of the right of wage earners and producers to organize for the protection of wages and the improvement of labor conditions *to the end that such labor organizations and their members should not be regarded as illegal combinations in restraint of trade.*

This language construes itself. It is the Baltimore platform in exact words. It is the spirit, the substance, the verbiage, and the promise of the Democratic platform, and Democrats will do no less than carry out their pledges to the people on this question. [Applause on the Democratic side.]

Mr. Chairman, again, on February 26, 1913, when the sundry civil appropriation bill was under consideration, this amendment was offered by Representatives HAMILL and Roddenbery:

Provided, however, That no part of this money shall be expended in the prosecution of any organization or individual for entering into any combination or agreement having in view the increasing of wages, the shortening of hours, or bettering the conditions of labor, or for any act done in furtherance thereof, not in itself unlawful; *Provided further,* That no part of this appropriation shall be expended for the prosecution of producers of farm products or associations of farmers who cooperate or organize in the effort to obtain and maintain a fair and reasonable price for their products.

The House agreed to that amendment, and on March 4, 1913, President Taft vetoed the bill because it contained that exemption. We passed it over his veto by the overwhelming vote of 264 yeas to 48 nays, and it went to the Senate, where the fight was waged on the question of exemption, and there in the Senate the bill failed.

Then the Democratic administration came into power, and again the Hamill-Roddenbery amendment was inserted in the sundry civil appropriation bill, which was passed through the Sixty-third Congress and signed by Woodrow Wilson. For these identical exemptions I have fought, and continue to fight. Our amendment, offered by Mr. WEBB, chairman of the Judiciary Committee, is as strong, salutary, and far-reaching as the twice-approved Hamill-Roddenbery amendment.

Now, gentlemen, organized labor has never asked that they be permitted under the law to commit crimes or to do unlawful things. They have never come to this Government and pleaded for special privilege. They have never asked for anything to which they are not entitled at our hands. They have said that when we are dealing with *conspiracies in restraint of trade and combinations and trusts* it was never intended that the man who sells his labor—his God-given right—should be classed as conspiring against trade or in unlawful combinations against the antitrust laws. We are now about to correct that error, and make it plain and specific, by clear-cut and direct language, that the antitrust laws against conspiracies in trade shall not be applied to labor organizations and farmers' unions.

When, as chairman of the Committee on Rules, I had the honor to present the resolution bringing up for consideration this bill and the Democratic administration antitrust program, it was my privilege to announce that section 7 of this antitrust bill was not satisfactory to labor, and that I heartily concurred in that view; and that a plain provision clearly exempting them from the antitrust laws would be presented and adopted by the House. We have prepared such provision, and the gentleman from North Carolina [Mr. WEBB] has presented it for us as labor and the farmers wish it. In the beginning of my remarks it is set out as approved by labor, the Committee on the Judiciary, the Democratic President, and skilled legal counsel for the wage earners. It is apparent that in a few brief moments it will be adopted by an overwhelming vote of the House. This executes the meritorious and just contract the Democratic Party has made with labor; and I rejoice that I am here to witness and participate in the triumph of the honorable men who win their bread by the sweat of their brow.

RECOMMENDATIONS OF THE PUJO MONEY TRUST COMMITTEE.

It is gratifying to state that not only has this important bill satisfied the laborer and the farmer, but it contains many other salutary and strong provisions, including some of the best recommendation [sic] of the Pujo Money Trust committee, which, as chairman of the Committee on Rules, I had the proud privilege of originating and putting on foot in the House a little over two years ago.

INTERLOCKING DIRECTORATES.

In dealing with banking corporations, interstate railways, and industrial corporations and trusts, the measure contains strong and effective provisions against interlocking directorates and all their attendant evils. It carries out the substantial provisions of the magnificent Money Trust and Steel Trust reports. Adequate penalties are provided. The plighted faith of the Democratic platform at Baltimore is kept and written into law. It makes guilt personal and consigns to prison flagrant violators of the law.

GOVERNMENT BY INJUNCTION ABOLISHED.

In several sections "government by injunction," through the usurpation of petty judicial tyrants, is destroyed and forever discontinued. No longer through the writ of injunction and the equity processes of the court can the unjust and tyrannical judge imprison and outrage honorable citizens without the right of trial by jury. The "midnight injunction" is banished and the citizen must have due and reasonable notice before he is deprived of his liberty and rights. He will have his day in court and not be outraged by secret judicial decree while his back is turned and the temples of justice shut against him. This is a great triumph for labor and justice, written in the very heart of this bill.

THE NEW FREEDOM FOR LABOR.

In section 18 a bill of rights, establishing a "new freedom" for labor, is written into solemn law to endure as a Magna Charta for those who toil and produce for the balance of mankind. I am happy to witness this day and to assist in passing this section that dedicates in our statutes a permanent command to the courts of equity and law to respect the rights of labor and cease outraging their inherent and God-given privileges. It reads:

SEC. 18. That no restraining order or injunction shall be granted by any court of the United States, or a judge or the judges thereof, in any case between an employer and employees, or between employers and employees, or between employees, or between persons employed and persons seeking employment, involving, or growing out of, a dispute concerning terms or conditions of employment, unless necessary to prevent irreparable injury to property, or to a property right, of the party making the application, for which injury there is no adequate remedy at law, and such property or property right must be described with particularity in the application, which must be in writing and sworn to by the applicant or by his agent or attorney.

And no such restraining order or injunction shall prohibit any person or persons from terminating any relation of employment, or from ceasing to perform any work or labor, or from recommending, advising, or persuading others by peaceful means so to do; or from attending at or near a house or place where any person resides or works, or carries on business or happens to be, for the purpose of peacefully obtaining or communicating information, or of peacefully persuading any person to work or to abstain from working; or from ceasing to patronize or to employ any party to such dispute, or from recommending, advising, or persuading others by peaceful means so to do; or from paying or giving to, or withholding from, any person engaged is such dispute, any strike benefits or other moneys or things of value; or from peaceably assembling at any place in a lawful manner, and for lawful purposes; or from doing any act or thing which might lawfully be done in the absence of such dispute by any party thereto.

Then to make sure that no court shall ever attempt to pervert and nullify the law we are going to add at the end of section 18 this broad and explicit language:

Nor shall any of the acts specified in this paragraph be considered or held unlawful.

Is this not indeed a notable and triumphant victory for the laboring forces after their long and severe struggle for justice? My heart swells with pride when I ascribe this act of justice to the master hand of Democracy.

JURY TRIAL IN CASES OF CONSTRUCTIVE CONTEMPT.

Then follows ample provision for jury trials in cases of indirect contempt. Such is our platform promise, and thus by this strong language and act have we redeemed it. It satisfies labor and they have accepted it as a solemn redemption of our tendered pledge. What more could be asked? What more could be accomplished? In this bill labor has secured more rights and just privileges than all the legislation accorded them in a hundred years of Federal enactments! A great achievement for them and a wonderful record for Democracy!

THE STOCK-AND-BOND LAW.

The next bill coming up for consideration under the special rule is the Rayburn stock-and-bond law. This is another important recommendation of the Pujo Money Trust report. It prohibits the fraudulent and fictitious issuance of stocks and bonds by interstate railway corporations. It is patterned after and based upon the Hogg stock-and-bond law of Texas. It places these roads under the strong and dominating hand of the Government, and, wisely administered, will prevent the recurrence of the New Haven frauds and similar corrupt transactions. And so in a series of bills Democracy has come to the rescue of the people and honest men. We are doing those things we have promised the voters we would accomplish.

And having struggled through my public career for many years to bring about these reforms, I crave pardon for exulting with just pride that I have been instrumental as a member of the Rules Committee and Representative in helping to advance all these measures to the point of consummation. Let us hope that never again will special privilege be enthroned in high governmental places and the people plundered, despoiled, and robbed by those ever seeking unwarranted advantage. [Applause.] . . .

Mr. MURDOCK. Mr. Chairman, if the amendment which the Committee on the Judiciary offered is amended, as proposed by the gentleman from North Carolina, and it will be, and that perfected paragraph satisfies those who have contended for years for the right of organized labor to exemption from the provisions of the Sherman antitrust law, this is the end of one of the most notable battles in the history of our country; but if this amended paragraph does not satisfy them, then the American Congress this morning is enacting a legislative tragedy—

Mr. GARNER. Will the gentleman yield?

Mr. MURDOCK. I would like to get started, if the gentleman will permit me. For over a period of 10 years this particular battle, which many presume is now about to close, has been one of the chief activities here. The men who have headed the American Federation of Labor, Mr. Gompers and those associated with him, have left no stone unturned, they have worked day and night, year in and year out, to accomplish this exemption. They not only have plead [sic] with every great national convention for party platform pledges for the enactment of this exemption into law, but they have worked here in Washington in season and out of season to accomplish this. And they have accomplished upon occasion in this body within my experience political revolution. They have upset party regularity and party majority. They have overriden the veto of a President. They stood here face to face for years against the powerful National Association of Manufacturers, which attempted in every way to block the avenues to public service and to keep back this legislation. The old Republican stand-pat leadership for years had as one of its chief activities the defeat of this proposition. They locked and doubled [sic] locked this proposition in the pigeonholes of committees; but the leaders of labor who were fighting for it never repined; they never lost heart. They kept on fighting for it. Why? Because they believed in it. When this Government made the first attack upon monopoly, labor had already begun to combine itself into organization. Why? For self-preservation and for self-protection; and when labor combined in this, my friends, it soon awoke to the benefactions and blessings of cooperation.

Now, I am one of those who are sometimes designated as the gentleman from Texas says some men here are designated. For there are those who have persistently called me a demagogue because from the very start of my career I have stood for all amendments which went to the exemption of organized labor from the provisions of the Sherman antitrust law. Why did I vote for them? Because I believe with all my heart and soul that the leaven that is working to the perfection of our Democracy is the aspirations and ideals of labor. [Applause.] I am in favor of giving to labor an exemption from the hindrances to progress that the courts have put upon it. Now, when we first passed the Sherman antitrust law labor believed it was exempted, and it went to the courts and the courts after long litigation told organized labor that under the terms of the Sherman antitrust law it was not exempt. That is, the courts sent organized labor back to Congress. It came here and prayed at the doors of your committees for exemption. If fought the most powerful lobby that has ever flourished in this country. It met rebuff and defeat. But it fought on and, finally, by the help of organized labor, the Democratic Party came into power. That party had given a pledge of exemption in the Baltimore platform which had been in the Democratic platform of 1908, and in response to the platform pledge the Bacon-Bartlett bills were introduced. They were direct and explicit in their terms.

Mr. BARTLETT. Will the gentleman permit me to interrupt him?

Mr. MURDOCK. I wish they had come out of the committee—

Mr. BARTLETT. Permit me to say—

Mr. MURDOCK. The gentleman realizes I have but a few moments—

Mr. BARTLETT. But they did come out of the committee and went on the calendar and an effort was made to get a rule from the Committee on Rules over which the gentleman from Texas presided and it could not be done.

Mr. MURDOCK. Yes; the Bacon-Bartlett bill has been smothered. Now, the Bacon-Bartlett bill was in plain, specific terms. It would have met the situation. But in place of its provisions the Democratic leadership placed upon this bill an amendment which did not exempt labor, which was unsatisfactory to a number of gentlemen on the Democratic side—

Mr. GARNER. Will the gentleman yield?

Mr. MURDOCK. If the gentleman will just let me go on with this narrative—those who protested against the original amendment in this bill as it was reported out of the committee succeeded in making themselves heard, and after a discussion pro and con there was added to the original amendment the phrase which we have offered to the bill to-day in the way of an amendment by the gentleman from North Carolina. Now, what does that amendment mean?

Mr. GARNER. That is what I wanted to ask the gentleman.

Mr. MURDOCK. What does it mean? Some of the friends of labor say that that amendment does exempt organized labor from the provisions of the Sherman antitrust law, but its enemies say that it does not exempt organized labor. Who knows? No man on the floor of this House. Who will determine? The courts.

Now, the tragedy of this transaction, my friends, is this: That after labor went to the courts and after the courts had sent it back to Congress, Congress sends labor back to the courts again. Eight or ten or twelve years hence the courts will decide what the amendment which we are about to adopt means. . . .

Now, Mr. Chairman, I am going to vote for this amendment. I voted originally for the Hughes amendment—in which I believe; which was explicit. I voted for the Hamill amendment. I have voted every time this matter came up in the House for plain, direct, specific language in favor of exemption. Had I been a Member of Congress 14 years ago I should have voted for the Terry amendment. I want the House to listen again to the language of the Terry amendment. Listen:

> Nothing in this act shall be so construed as to apply to trade-unions or other labor organizations organized for the purpose of regulating wages, hours of labor, or other conditions under which labor is to be performed.

How certain that is, how direct, how sweeping, compared with the amendment which has been offered!

Now, I will yield to the gentleman from Texas [Mr. HENRY].

Mr. HENRY. When the amendment says that these organizations shall not be regarded as conspiracies or illegal combinations in restraint of trade under the antitrust laws, how can you make it plainer?

Mr. MURDOCK. Ah, you could make it a good deal plainer. . . .

I want to say to the gentleman from Texas [Mr. HENRY] that the gentleman from Michigan [Mr. MACDONALD] will offer an amendment which is direct, and which will make it plain, and will not be a subject of doubt in the courts, but will give the exemption to which labor is entitled under the law. . . .

Mr. BARTLETT. Mr. Chairman, I shall support the Webb amendment, but in the time allotted to me I can not say what I desire to say on this subject, because for years I have ⊥ devoted much attention to it and have frequently voted for the principle embodied in it and endeavored to have legislation of this character enacted. I did hope that I might have opportunity to speak more at length on the proposition and not simply confine myself to a synopsis of the history of this matter or to mere statement of my reasons for insisting that labor organizations and farmers' associations should not fall under the antitrust law, but I have but a few minutes. Whatever may be the result of this amendment to the antitrust bill, I claim no special credit for it, but I do insist that I have endeavored, in season and out of season, at all times, to have the injustice of the Sherman Antitrust Act, as construed by the Supreme Court, which held such associations subject to that act, corrected by proper legislation.

In the last Congress I introduced a bill which has become known as the Bartlett-Bacon bill, or the Bacon-Bartlett bill, and which was reported to this House from the Committee on Labor and went on the calendar at an early day of that Congress, and the report of the committee on that bill I hold in my hand, which is as follows:

Be it enacted, etc., That it shall not be unlawful for persons employed or seeking employment to enter into any arrangements, agreements, or combinations with the view of lessening the hours of labor, or of increasing their wages, or of bettering their condition; nor shall any arrangements, agreements, or combinations be unlawful among persons engaged in horticulture or agriculture when made with the view of enhancing the price of agricultural or horticultural products; and no restraining order or injunction shall be granted by any court of the United States, or by any judge thereof, in any case between an employer and employee, or between employers and employees, or between persons employed and persons seeking employment, or involving or growing out of a dispute concerning terms or conditions of employment in any case, or concerning any agreement, arrangement, or combination of persons engaged in horticulture or agriculture with the view of enhancing prices as aforesaid, or any act or acts done in pursuance thereof, unless in either case said injunction be necessary to prevent irreparable injury to property or to a property right of the party making the application for which there is no adequate remedy at law; and such property or property right must be particularly described in the application, which must be sworn to by the applicant or by his agent or attorney.

In construing this act the right to enter into the relation of employer and employee, to change that relation and to assume and creat [sic] a new relation of employer and employee, and to perform and carry on business in such relation with any person in any place or do work and labor as an employee shall be held and construed to be a personal and not a property right. In all cases involving the violation of the contract of employment by either the employee or employer where no irreparable damage is about to be committed upon the property or property right of either no injunction shall be granted, but the parties shall be left to their remedy at law.

SEC. 2. That no person or persons who are employed or seeking employment or other labor shall be indicted, prosecuted, or tried in any court of the United States for entering into any arrangements, agreements, or combinations between themselves as such employees or laborers, made with a view of lessening the number of hours of labor or increasing their wages or bettering their condition, or for any act done in pursuance thereof, unless said act is in itself unlawful; nor shall any person or persons who may enter into any arrangements or agreements or combinations among themselves for the purpose of engaging in horticulture or agriculture with a view of enchancing the price of agricultural or horticultural products, be indicted, prosecuted, or tried in any court of the United States on account of making or entering into such arrangements, agreements, or combinations, or any act done in pursuance thereof, unless said act is in itself unlawful.

The purpose of this bill was to make arrangements, agreements, or combinations of wageworkers or farmers lawful, which the courts in interpreting the Sherman antitrust law have held to be illegal combinations in restraint of trade, and to restrict the injunctive power exercised by the courts over personal relations between individuals where no real property right is endangered or involved, and relegating causes in such personal relations to the adjudication of the law courts.

There has been some doubt expressed as to whether or not the Sherman antitrust law was ever intended to apply to organizations of workingmen and farmers when dealing with their own labor or the products of their own labor; but whether or not it was intended to apply to organizations of that character, the fact remains that it has been applied to them. An examination of the debates in the Senate discloses the fact that the author of the law, Senator Sherman, did not intend it to be and did not believe that it would be applied to organizations of workingmen or farmers. In the debate on the bill in the Senate on March 21 and March 24, 1890, Senators Hiscock and Teller called attention to the possibility of the measure applying to organizations of that character. Replying, Senator Sherman said:

> The bill as reported contains three or four simple propositions which relate only to contracts, combinations, agreements made with a view and designed to carry out a certain purpose which the laws of all the States and of every civilized community declare to be unlawful. It does not interfere in the slightest degree with voluntary associations made to affect public opinion to advance the interests of a particular trade or occupation. It does not interfere with the Farmers' Alliance at all, because that is an association of farmers to advance their interests and to improve the growth and manner of production of their crops and to secure intelligent growth and to introduce new methods. No organizations in this country can be more beneficial in their character than farmers' alliances and farmers' associations. They are not business combinations. They do not deal with contracts, agreements, etc. They have no connection with them. And so the combinations of workingmen to promote their interests, promote their welfare, and increase their pay if you please, to get their fair share in the division of production are not affected in the slightest degree, nor can they be included in the words or intent of the bill as now reported.

Efforts were made time and time again to have that bill considered. A resolution was introduced by me, which went to the Committee on Rules, over which the gentleman from Texas [Mr. HENRY] presides, asking for a rule making the bill privileged, so it could be considered. This resolution was pressed in a hearing had before that committee, and the committee was urged to give us an opportunity to have the bill considered by the House, because it was known whenever the House could have an opportunity to vote upon this measure it would pass it, having on several occasions supported a like measure in no uncertain terms and by no uncertain majorities. But we could not persuade the Committee on Rules to report the bill. Again, when this Congress met, the first bill I introduced was this same bill, a copy of which I will make a part of my remarks. The principle of my bill is now incorporated into this bill reported by the Committee on the Judiciary and as contained in the amendment offered by the gentleman from North Carolina [Mr. WEBB].

I congratulate the Committee on the Judiciary; I congratulate the country that the hour is now at hand when the shackles placed by a misconstruction of the Sherman antitrust law upon labor and like organizations shall be stricken from them, and when they shall stand before the country free to exercise their right to perform and do those acts as organizations that they are entitled to do and those things which no one should ever construe they were forbidden to do by the Sherman antitrust law. [Applause.]

In pursuance of that, I wish to put into the RECORD as to the right to do them the statement of that great lawyer and learned Senator, Mr. HOAR, who made it on the 27th day of March, 1890, when this original proposition was before the Senate, and when the right of Congress to pass it was challenged by other great lawyers, among them Mr. Edmunds, of Vermont. Senator Hoar then made that statement, clear and forcible, which assured the Members of the Senate that, in his opinion, we had the right to enact such legislation. It was not enacted. It was put upon the bill as an amendment, and it was referred to the Committee on the Judiciary in the Senate, and the bill came back without it; and those same Senators, Senator George and Senator Vest, stated to the Senate that that amendment had not been incorporated because no one could construe that the Sherman antitrust law would in any way affect labor organizations.

I quote from the CONGRESSIONAL RECORD of March 27, 1890:

> The PRESIDING OFFICER. The question is upon the amendment last reported.
> Mr. EDMUNDS. Let it be read again.
> The CHIEF CLERK. On page 4, line 66, section 1, after the word "action," the Senate, as in Committee of the Whole, inserted the following clause:
> "*Provided*, That this act shall not be construed to apply to any arrangements, agreements, or combinations between laborers made with a view of lessening the number of hours of their

labor or of increasing their wages; nor to any arrangements, agreements, associations, or combinations among persons engaged in horticulture or agriculture made with the view of enhancing the price of their own agricultural or horticultural products."

Mr. HOAR. Mr. President, I wish to state in one single sentence my opinion in regard to this particular provision. If I correctly understood the Senator from Vermont—I did not hear him fully, and very likely, hearing only a part of what he said, I did not apprehend it—he thought that the applying to laborers in this respect a principle which was not applied to persons engaged in the large commercial transactions which are chiefly aimed at by this bill was indefensible in principle. Now, it seems to me there is a very broad distinction which, if bourne in mind, will warrant not only this exception to the general provision of the bill, but a great deal of other legislation which we enact, or attempt to enact, relating to the matter of labor.

When you are speaking of providing to regulate the transactions of men who are making corners in wheat, or in iron, or in woolen or in cotton goods, speculating in them or lawfully dealing in them without speculation, you are aiming at a mere commercial transaction, the beginning and end of which is the making of money for the parties, and nothing else. That is the only relation that transaction has to the State. It is the creation or diffusion or change of ownership of the wealth of the community. But when a laborer is trying to raise his wages or is endeavoring to shorten the hours of his labor, he is dealing with something that touches closely, more closely than anything else, the government and the character of the State itself.

The maintenance of a certain standard of profit in dealing in large transactions on wheat or cotton or wool is a question whether a particular merchant or a particular class of merchants shall make money or not, or shall deal lawfully or not, shall affect the State injuriously or not; but the question whether the standard of the laborer's wages shall be maintained or advanced or whether the leisure for instruction, for improvement, shall be shortened or lengthened is a question which touches the very existence and character of government of the State itself. The laborer who is engaged lawfully and usefully and accomplishing his purpose in whole or in part in endeavoring to raise the standard of wages is engaged in an occupation the success of which makes republican government itself possible and without which the Republic can not in substance, however it may nominally do in form, continue to exist.

I hold, therefore, that as legislators we may constitutionally, properly, and wisely allow laborers to make associations, combinations, contracts, agreements, for the sake of maintaining and advancing their wages in regard to which, as a rule, their contracts are to be made with large corporations who are themselves but an association or combination or aggregation of capital on the other side. When we are permitting and even encouraging that, we are permitting and encouraging what is not only lawful, wise, and profitable, but absolutely essential to the existence of the Commonwealth itself.

It is true that in the Danbury Hat case, in Two hundred and eighth United States, the Supreme Court decided that the action of the labor union involved in that case was a violation of the Sherman antitrust law. It is also true that no longer ago than Friday last another circuit court of appeals of the United States decided in a like case that such action of a labor organization was not in violation of the Sherman antitrust law. Therefore, to make the thing clear, in order to do that which Congress has the right to do, to make the statute so clear that "he that runs may read," to make the way so plain that "the wayfaring man, though a fool, can not err therein," we propose to put the proposition in this bill in compliance with the universal demand of the labor organizations, in compliance with the Democratic platforms in 1908 and 1912, and, above all, in compliance with the demands of right and justice and civilization. [Applause.] . . .

Availing myself of the privilege of extending my remarks, the Democratic national convention of 1908 declared in its platform:

The expanding organization of industry makes it essential that there should be no abridgement of the right of wage earners and producers to organize for the protection of wages and the improvement of labor conditions, to the end that such labor organizations and their members should not be regarded as illegal combinations in restraint of trade.

The Democratic national convention of 1912 also declared:

The expanding organization of industry makes it essential that there should be no abridgement of the right of the wage earners and producers to organize for the protection of wages and the improvement of labor conditions, to the end that such labor organizations and their members should not be regarded as illegal combinations in restraint of trade.

At the first session of this Congress I introduced the bill I have just referred to, which reads as follows:

A bill (H. R. 1873) to make lawful certain agreements between employees and laborers, and persons engaged in agriculture or horticulture, and to limit the issuing of injunctions in certain cases, and for other purposes.

Be it enacted, etc., That it shall not be unlawful for persons employed or seeking employment to enter into any arrangements, agreements, or combinations with the view of lessening the hours of labor, or of increasing their wages, or of bettering their condition; nor shall any arrangements, agreements, or combinations be unlawful among persons engaged in horticulture or agriculture when made with the view of enhancing the price of agricultural or horticultural products; and no restraining order or injunction shall be granted by any court of the United States, or by any judge thereof, in any case between an employer and employee, or between employers and employees, or between persons employed and persons seeking employment, or involving or growing out of a dispute concerning terms or conditions of employment in any case, or concerning any agreement, arrangement, or combination of persons engaged in horticulture or agriculture with the view of enhancing prices as aforesaid, or any act or acts done in pursuance thereof, unless in either case said injunction be necessary to prevent irreparable injury to property or to a property right of the party making the application for which there is no adequate remedy at law; and such property or property right must be particularly described in the application, which must be sworn to by the applicant or by his agent or attorney.

In construing this act the right to enter into the relation of employer and employee, to change that relation and to assume and create a new relation of employer and employee and to perform and carry on business in such relation with any person in any place or do work and labor as an employee shall be held and construed to be a personal and not a property right. In all cases involving the violation of the contract of employment by either the employee or employer where no irreparable damage is about to be committed upon the property or property right of either no injunction shall be granted, but the parties shall be left to their remedy at law.

SEC. 2. That no person or persons who are employed or seeking employment or other labor shall be indicted, prosecuted, or tried in any court of the United States for entering into any arrangements, agreements, or combinations between themselves as such employees or laborers, made with a view of lessening the number of hours of labor or increasing their wages or bettering their condition, or for any act done in pursuance thereof, unless said act is in itself unlawful; nor shall any person or persons who may enter into any arrangements or agreements or combinations among themselves for the purpose of engaging in horticulture or agriculture with a view of enhancing the price of agricultural or horticultural products, be indicted, prosecuted, or tried in any court of the United States on account of making or entering into such arrangements, agreements, or combinations, or any act done in pursuance thereof, unless said act is in itself unlawful. . . .

Mr. THOMAS. Mr. Chairman, to say the least of this amendment, it is as ambiguous as the prophecy of a Roman oracle. As a matter of fact it means nothing. It is a mere declaration of that which is now the law. To make the statement that this law shall not be construed so as to hold certain organizations to be illegal is simply to state that those organizations per se shall not be declared illegal by this law. You might insert a paragraph declaring that under this law the Baptist Church or the Masonic Order should not be construed to be an illegal combination in restraint of trade. They are not illegal, even, in the absence of that declaration. Agricultural organizations and labor organizations under this law are not illegal combinations, even without that declaration; and notwithstanding that declaration the very moment that an agricultural association or a laborers' organization violates any provision of this law it is applicable to such association, and they can and will be punished under the law. Any man knows that. For instance, should these associations have in their by-laws or charters articles which allowed them to form conspiracies, to form monopolies in restraint of trade, does any man contend that the very moment they attempted to carry out such declaration of the organization they would not fall under this law? To be sure they would. If you are going to exempt these organizations, exempt them. If you are not going to exempt them, say so. The amendment which I shall offer after this amendment has been voted on simply declares that the provisions of the antitrust laws shall not apply to any of these organizations. There you have a clear-cut exemption. I understood from the gentleman— . . .

Mr. HENRY. The question is this: This amendment provides that these organizations shall not be held to be conspiracies or illegal combinations in restraint of trade under the antitrust laws. Now, what else would you allow them to do?

Mr. THOMAS. I would exempt them from the operations of this law. Notwithstanding the amendment which you are supporting, the very moment they violated any of the provisions of this law they would be punishable under the law.

Mr. HENRY. Would the gentleman allow them to commit violence under his amendment?

Mr. THOMAS. No, sir; they would not be allowed to commit violence under my amendment, because there are laws in this country to punish any man who commits violence or who destroys property. There are laws outside of the antitrust laws for the punishment of crime. . . .

Mr. Chairman, the amendment which I shall offer after the committee amendment has been voted on is simply to the effect that the provisions of this law shall not apply to these organizations. Mr. Chairman, there are some Members of this House who want to talk all the time and do not want anybody else to talk.

The CHAIRMAN. The committee will be in order.

Mr. THOMAS. As I had started to state, I believe when we go a-catting we ought to go a-catting; and I believe that if we are going to take these organizations out from under this law we ought to do it in such a way that there can be no mistake about it and no reason for any court decisions upon the question hereafter. [Applause.] My amendment simply says that these antitrust laws shall not apply to these organizations. If any man thinks he can make an amendment plainer than that, I would like to hear from that gentleman, even the gentleman from Texas [Mr. HENRY].

Now, these organizations ought to be exempt. These antitrust laws are intended for the suppression of monopolies and trusts. Who ever heard of an agricultural trust? Who ever heard of a laborers' trust? They are not the men who have the wealth of this country. Yet under these antitrust laws as they have been construed by the courts if a number of farmers pool their tobacco or their wool or any other agricultural product and employ an agent to sell it for them in order to get the best obtainable prices they commit an act for which they are subject to punishment under these antitrust laws, as the tobacco farmers of the State of Kentucky were. You have heard of that case. A number of farmers pooled their tobacco. One of them went out of the pool, took his tobacco to the depot, and got a bill of lading for it to Cincinnati. His neighbors met and sent a committee to him and asked him to stand with them and not ship his tobacco to Cincinnati. He said, "Well, he had had the trouble of hauling it to the depot, and that it was all right if they would haul it back." They hauled it back. For their action they were indicted and fined $3,500.[5.541] President Taft finally pardoned them of the fine,[5.542] but he never would do it until the prosecution of the Beef Trust under these antitrust laws failed in Chicago.[5.543] So I say, gentlemen, that if you are going to take them out of the provisions of these laws, take them out. If you are going to keep them in, why, keep them in, and do not go to beating the devil around the bush about it. Come out plainly and let us keep them in or take them out, one of the two. The gentleman from Texas [Mr. HENRY] tells you that when the Sherman law was passed it was intended to exempt farmers' and laborers' organizations. . . .

Mr. MACDONALD. Mr. Chairman, I am very much in favor of the principle of exempting these organizations from the operation of the antitrust laws. I expect to vote for the Webb amendment, if for no other reason, for the moral effect that the adoption of that amendment will have; but I am not given to self-deception, and in voting for that amendment I am not deceiving myself as to the effect of that amendment. That amendment may have some beneficial effect for the organizations mentioned therein,

---

[5.541] United States v. Steers, 1 D. & J. 739-44, aff'd, 192 F. 1 (6th Cir. 1911).

[5.542] Fines remitted by President Taft upon payment of costs, as the tobacco trust had been dissolved, 1 D. & J. 745-46.

[5.543] United States v. Swift, 1 D. & J. 752 (N.D. Ill. 1912) (jury verdict for defendants doing approximately 80% of the meatpacking business in the nation).

but it will not exempt those organizations from the operation of the antitrust laws. Now, the Supreme Court in the case of Loewe against Lawlor, commonly known as the Danbury Hat case, put this matter up to Congress in no uncertain terms. They say, on page 279 of volume 208 of the United States Reports:

> After the Sherman law was enacted bills were introduced in the Fifty-second Congress—

And then they enumerate all the bills that have been introduced to amend the Sherman antitrust law, making it inapplicable to labor and these other organizations. And then they say:

> Congress therefore has refused to exempt labor unions from the comprehensive provisions of the Sherman law against combinations in restraint of trade, and this refusal is the more significant, as it followed the recognition by the courts that the Sherman antitrust law applied to labor organizations.[5.544]

Now, the amendment that has been offered by the gentleman from North Carolina makes by implication these organizations subject to the terms of the law. It defines certain acts which are said in general terms to be permissible, and therefore by implication it leaves forbidden other acts which are not permissible, and makes by implication these organizations subject expressly to the terms of the Sherman law if they should violate any of the provisions of the law.

Another point is this: The amendment provides that they shall be liable only within certain limits and those limits are confined to this—where they exercise their powers only for mutual help and not for profit. They are limited absolutely to that field in their operations, and who, forsooth, will decide whether their operations fall within the restrictions of mutual help and not for profit? Why, the courts, of course; and you will have the same old battle for definite construction over and over again. Therefore you have for certain purposes and as to certain acts brought these organizations where the courts may hold them expressly within the operation of the Sherman law.

Now, every gentleman who gives this matter any consideration instinctively realizes that this is true. The gentleman from Texas [Mr. HENRY] realizes it as well as anybody else, because in his speech this morning he said, "Gentlemen, we are going to make this law not to apply to these organizations." He said in this speech "not apply"; why does he not say so in the amendment? There is no way of making it any plainer or simpler or doing what you want to do than to use the language that the gentleman used in his speech, but which is not used in the amendment.

Mr. MURDOCK. Will the gentleman yield?

Mr. MACDONALD. Certainly.

Mr. MURDOCK. And are not the words "shall not apply" the words used in the Terry amendment, in the Hamill amendment, and in the Hughes amendment?

Mr. MACDONALD. Yes; every amendment proposed to this law have [sic] used the words, and that was in the amendment that the Supreme Court in the Danbury Hat case said if Congress had done those things there would be no question about the operation of the law. [Applause.] . . .

Mr. [THOMAS F.] KONOP [D., Wis.]. Mr. Chairman, I am in favor of the amendment exempting labor, farm, and other like organizations from the operations of antitrust laws. Section 7 of this bill, which provides that the existence and operations of such organizations shall be construed not to be forbidden, means very little and provides no exemption whatever. I am in favor of exempting these organizations because in this bill we are not dealing with associations of men but associations of dollars for profit. We are aiming at the gigantic trusts and combinations of capital and not at associations of men for the betterment of their condition. We are aiming at the dollars and not at men. We do aim to put an end to association of men's dollars which unlawfully restrain trade, destroy competition, and create monopoly. Let us put the man above the dollar and exempt all associations of men organized for the betterment of their condition. [Applause.]

[5.544] 208 U.S. at 280 (both this quote and the quote immediately preceding are from the "Argument for Plaintiffs in Error" in the Court's syllabus, not from the text of the opinion).

Mr. Chairman, we are a great country. We have been blessed with wonderful natural resources. We have a great Government. We have great farms and great industries. And what is it that makes our country so great? Not the idler, not the men who sit amidst downy bolsters and costly appliances, but the men who work with hand and brain. These are the men who contribute to our country's greatness. These are the men who produce the wealth of this country. It is true that both capital and labor are essential in our industrial progress, both are entitled to consideration, but the men who labor are entitled to higher consideration, because they are the producers of all wealth and capital. The men who labor in the field and factory are the men who make our country great.

The almighty dollar needs no protector. The idle rich, whose money is invested in great, oppressive trusts and combinations, have always been able to take care of themselves and then yet some. But the laboring man has struggled through the ages for emancipation. The struggle is still on. Slavery, peonage, feudalism, and oppression of every kind has been the lot of the producers of wealth. But a new era has come. Labor is now organized. The farmers are now organized. And because of those organizations much has been done to elevate the toiler to a higher plane. Much is being done toward a complete emancipation of the man who works. Better, sanitary, and safer places and conditions are provided for labor to work. The hours of labor are being shortened and a better living wage is being paid, not because of the philanthropy of capital, but because through organization labor is able to obtain these reforms. Where would parcels post be had it not been for the organized demand of the farmers of the country? What we should do is not to hamper these great organizations of laborers and farmers of the land, but to encourage them in the conservation of the health and welfare of the great masses. [Applause.]

Some say that this amendment is class legislation, and hence unconstitutional. Mr. Chairman, way back in March 25, 1890, nearly a quarter of a century ago, when the Sherman antitrust bill was under consideration in the Senate as in Committee of the Whole, Senator Sherman offered an amendment to the bill, as follows:

Provided, That this act shall not be construed to apply to any arrangements, agreements, or combinations between laborers, made with a view of lessening the number of hours of their labor or of increasing their wages; nor to any arrangements, agreements, associations, or combinations among persons engaged in horticulture or agriculture, made with a view of enhancing the price of their own agricultural or horticultural products.

This amendment was adopted on that day. On March 27, when the bill was before the Senate, some discussion arose as to the constitutionality of the amendment, and Senator Hoar, of Massachusetts, used these words, in which I entirely concur:

I hold, therefore, that as legislators we may constitutionally, properly, and wisely allow laborers to make associations, combinations, contracts, agreements for the sake of maintaining and advancing their wages, in regard to which, as a rule, their contracts are to be made with large corporations who are themselves but an association or combination or aggregation of capital on the other side. When we are permitting and even encouraging that we are permitting and encouraging what is not only lawful, wise, and profitable, but absolutely essential to the existence of the Commonwealth itself.

When, on the other hand, we are dealing with one of the other classes, the combinations aimed at chiefly by this bill, we are dealing with a transaction the only purpose of which is to extort from the community, monopolize, segregate, and apply to individual use, for the purposes of individual greed, wealth which ought properly and lawfully and for the public interest to be generally diffused over the whole community.

Mr. Chairman, the Sherman antitrust law was passed in 1890. It was aimed at trusts and combinations of capital; and in spite of that law the trusts and combinations have grown. Its author at that time hoped that it would solve the trust problem, but the trusts and combines grew with impunity, and we are to-day hoping that we have a cure for the trust evils. I shall vote for these three trust bills because I believe it is a step in the right direction. My only hope and wish is that the trust evil can be curbed. But in the discussion of the different sections of these bills we hear that we can not go further than interstate commerce goes in curbing these great combinations. I think the trust problem could better be handled if constitutionally we had power to regulate all commerce, and I think the time will come when an amendment to the Constitution of the United States giving Congress power to regulate commerce, intrastate as well as interstate, will be given serious consideration.

Now, Mr. Chairman, in conclusion, I hope that the amendment exempting these organizations will prevail. Let us give encouragement to the toilers and farmers of the land. These men are the very bulwarks of our prosperity and greatness. . . .

Mr. QUIN. Mr. Chairman, I understand they are about to slip a little amendment in here that the courts and the country can easily handle. Now, I want to put something in that has guts in it. This amendment talks about the courts "construing" and "holding." My friend from Texas talks about what Gen. George did. I have the honor to come from the same State that James G. George came from. If Senator George were here, he would be an advocate for this amendment. He was recognized as one of the greatest lawyers in the whole Union, and if he were living to-day he would throw up his hands in holy horror at the forward steps taken by the Federal courts of this country. In his day, gentlemen, the courts did not undertake to legislate away the rights of the people; but now it has come to the point that the people can not get their rights except through Congress, and when we come here some Members want to put a little easy stuff in that the courts can construe against the farmers' unions and the labor unions. Let us put language in here that they can not misconstrue; let us put in language that nothing in this antitrust law shall apply to farmers' unions and labor unions. We know that these organizations and farmers' unions are not any criminal trusts. The great trusts and monopolies of this country that with greedy hands grind profits out of human blood want such measly language as you are proposing to put into this antitrust law. They do not want the strong, virile language, the Anglo-Saxon words that every schoolboy, much less a Supreme Court judge, will understand; and for that reason I hope that the House will adopt the Thomas amendment into this antitrust law. [Applause.]

The great and powerful influence of monopolistic corporations has been growing and overriding the United States Congress and the courts. Many on this floor claim that the Sherman law is good enough. If that law is good enough, I ask in the name of the people why it is that ever since this law has been on the statute books the trusts and monopolies have organized, grown, multiplied, and prospered to such an extent that the people have been robbed and the courts of the country openly defied? If the Sherman antitrust law is good enough, there is something radically wrong with the Federal courts and the Federal district attorneys. I am induced to believe that there is something the matter with both. The Republican Party never did want to enforce the law against big money.

Virtually all of the Federal judges and the United States district attorneys are the appointees of the Republican Presidents. Some of them try to enforce all the law.

When these district judges and attorneys endeavored to put the big criminals, the head men in these gigantic trusts, behind the bars, these conscientious officials have been handicapped in every possible manner. Many judges have endeavored to enforce the Sherman antitrust law, but have you heard of one of these trust nabobs being sent to the penitentiary? The only effective way that it has been enforced is against the poor people. It has never yet hurt a rich man. The poor men who compose farmers' unions and labor unions have felt the heavy hand of the Sherman antitrust law.

My friend from Texas [Mr. HENRY] says Senator George never thought the law would apply to such beneficent organizations. The whole record shows that the great lawyers of that Congress never dreamed of such an outrage as the Sherman antitrust law being construed by the courts so as to affect the farmers and labor organizations of this country. The only way on earth to keep the eagle eye of the Federal courts off the farmers' unions and the labor unions is to make this antitrust law so plain that they are not included in its scope that any child in the United States can understand it. If there is the slightest ambiguity in the language, you will hear of some Federal Judge in "Possum Hollow" announcing a decision that the farmers' union is a trust in restraint of trade and that the individual members are subject to indictment if by concert of action they hold their cotton or other farm products for a higher price. I am going to vote for the Webb amendment, and on top of that I shall support the Thomas amendment. The Webb amendment leaves too much for the courts to construe; but if you will follow it up by adopting the Thomas amendment, we all know the farmers' unions and the labor organizations will be in the "clear" for all time.

The great capitalists of the United States have been busy for many years organizing powerful trusts, and, as an incident to their business, they have oppressed labor, destroyed honest competitors, robbed and plundered the people. Their activities have not been confined to any special lines, but these financial freebooters have operated in every nook and corner of every field of all commerce. Every household necessity is now under the control of some trust. They did not even think enough of the poor to let meat remain free from their greedy, monopolistic hands. Can any man in this House think of an organization of thieves equal to that gigantic aggregation of capitalists who form the Beef Trust? Why is it that none of these men are wearing stripes in the penitentiary? It is either the fault of the law or it is the fault of the Federal judges and district attorneys where they operate. I believe this bill we are passing now will be so plain that no judge can construe it so as to release the trust magnates.

The public-service corporations in many instances have been operated in a highhanded way by trust officials. Right now you have under your observation in the Department of Justice an investigation of one of the biggest railroad "steals" that ever disgraced this country. I refer to the New York, New Haven & Hartford Railroad episode. The ex-president of that system, Mr. Mellen, under oath, admits that Mr. Morgan and other capitalists who held positions as directors openly robbed the stockholders out of many millions of dollars. In 1903 that railroad system had liabilities of $94,000,000, and more than 22,000 people put their savings into it in the form of stock at $240 a share, which paid annual dividends of 8 and 10 per cent every year. These trust magnates began to plunder it, and after raking in fabulous fortunes through methods that ought to lead them direct into the northeast corner of a penitentiary, the railroad system in 1913 had the enormous liability of $415,000,000, and its stock pays no dividend at all; but the once splendid system is now a financial wreck, a sad monument to the rascality of big business. This is just one little case I am calling to mind.

Nearly all of the great railroad systems of this country have been robbed in the same way. It is made possible through the interlocking directorate. If the big bankers who have the handling of other people's money are permitted to own and control the directors of railroads and steamship lines, as well as other public utilities, the people are going to suffer. Many of these big bankers have demonstrated that they will do shady tricks to get a few extra millions of dollars. The men who compose the many trusts seem to think all the people of the United States are mere slaves, to work to add increased millions to the greedy coffers of the avaricious money kings. Right now these railroad corporations are before the Interstate Commerce Commission endeavoring to be allowed to raise their freight rates. The captains of industry have been quite successful under the Sherman antitrust law in robbing these railroads, and they now have the gall to come up to the Capitol and ask that the servants of the people give them legal permission to rob the people through high freight rates. The American people are not going to stand this much longer. They have demanded relief through legislation, and this Congress must give it to them. The men who toil with their hands—the farmers and the artisans and tradesmen—have turned their eyes toward this Capitol and they are going to watch till relief comes or they will place men in these seats who will transmute their sentiments into law. The people know that no man could get to be worth $800,000,000 in 50 years if the laws were not so fixed that the few can prey on the many. They demand that we correct that evil, and unless I am badly fooled I believe this Congress has done much to correct ⊥ it. If we pass these antitrust laws properly, I am certain that many millions of our population will see the dawn of a brighter day. If the money power were to continue to dominate this Government as it did before the Democracy came into power, the signs of a revolution would soon be seen on our national horizon, and it would not be a bloodless one, either. The great amalgamation of capital and the greed that seems to animate the powerful men in control of the great wealth of this Republic is a reason for the foundations of our Government to begin to shake. How have these financial kings, many of them common thieves, filling high places, operated for the last few years?

Here is what one of them testified to in Washington City on the 23d day of May, 1914, just one week ago last Saturday: Mr. Charles S. Mellen, ex-president of the New York, New Haven & Hartford Railroad, being on the witness stand, said Prof. Weyman, of Harvard, got $10,000 a year from the New Haven Railroad for "fanning" fires of sentiment in the railroad's favor; his brother $25 a day and his father $50 a day. Lawyer Wardell got $12,000 and Lawyer Innes $15,000. Many other names were mentioned in this connection. Gentlemen, the idea of such a proposition—the officers of that railroad stealing the stockholders' money to hire a college professor and a few lawyers to fool the people. Listen. Mr. Mellen swore that more than 1,000 newpapers received various sums from the railroad. That is not all. One E. D. Robbins, a lawyer of Hartford, got $100,000 "for the purpose of molding public sentiment in Connecticut in 1907 over a charter." Gentlemen, that is the kind of business many of the captains of industry have been engaged in in all branches of big business. Immense fortunes are spent in spreading propaganda to fool the people, and then the people are robbed threefold to pay it back with big profits. These same henchmen of big money have contributed $50,000 and $100,000 to campaign funds with the nonchalance of a drummer buying a cigar. They did not give that money away, but they gave it with the intention of having a "friend at court," and it seems they never failed to have a friend at court till Democracy put a President in the White House. Do you believe that any honest business man in this country would object to this bill if he understood what it means? We are trying to help the honest and legitimate business of this country, and this law will help. I want to put the criminals in business in the penitentiary and free the American people from the shackles they have been forced to wear all these years. The law ought to give the little man in business the same show that it gives the big, strong financial magnate. The law we are fixing to pass will land the big fellow behind the bars if he wrongfully destroys the business of his little competitor. The powerful trusts of this country have not only held up the public and forced them to pay an exorbitant price for all the necessities of life, but they have been able to hold the produce of the farm down to the minimum price. They have forced the farmers to pay big prices for what they buy and compelled them to accept small prices for what they raise on their farms. This greed of organized wealth has held the wages of the poor men, women, and children in factories and mines down to the lowest scale, and the tills of the powerful have been filled with dollars coined out of this poor, human labor.

Gentlemen, can any man who has a heart that throbs with sympathy and justice oppose the amendments to protect the farmers and the laboring people? I am going to stand by them on every vote. [Applause.] . . .

Mr. TOWNER. Mr. Chairman, I was not satisfied with the original language used in the paragraph, neither am I satisfied with the amendment proposed; nevertheless, I will support the amendment. I will do this because it is the best that can be obtained, and I believe will assist, as least in some degree, to make clear the object and purpose of the provision.

That object and purpose is, Mr. Chairman, to definitely state that the provisions of the antitrust laws shall not be so interpreted as to forbid the existence or operation of labor or farmers' organizations instituted for mutual help. With that object and purpose I am in entire sympathy.

I presume there has been no proposition discussed in recent years which has absolutely no valid objection to it that has been more misrepresented and abused. It has been termed a proposal to exempt certain classes from the operation of the law, while others are included; to punish one and release another for the same act; to say that all are not equal before the law. It is none of these things.

Any association of the classes mentioned, or any member who violates the antitrust laws will be liable to their penalties the same as any other association or person. It is merely provided that the organization or legitimate operation of such associations shall not be held to be within the prohibitions of the statute.

NOT WITHIN PURPOSE OF SHERMAN ANTITRUST ACT.

Nothing is better established than the fact that such associations were not intended to be included in the Sherman antitrust law. In February, 1890, Senator Sherman introduced his bill making associations or agreements in restraint of trade or to monopolize trade illegal. A month later, and while his bill was pending, the question was raised as to whether under any circumstances it would apply to labor or farmers' organizations. In order to settle this, Senator Sherman himself proposed the following amendment to his bill:

Provided, That this act shall not be construed to apply to any arrangements, agreements, or combinations between the laborers, made with a view of lessening the number of hours of labor or increasing their wages; nor to any arrangements, agreements, or combinations among persons engaged in horticulture or agriculture made with a view of enhancing the price of agricultural or horticultural products.

This amendment was agreed to by the Senate without a division.

The bill and amendment went to the Senate Judiciary Committee, and was sent back to the Senate without the amendment. When the reason for the omission of the amendment was demanded, Senators George and Vest stated that the amendment had not been included because it was unnecessary; that no one could construe the act so as to include such associations.

Referring to the claim that such organizations might be affected, Senator Sherman said:

It does not interfere in the slightest degree with voluntary associations made to advance the interests of a particular trade or occupation. It does not interfere with the Farmers' Alliance at all, because that is an association of farmers to advance their interests and to improve the growth and manner of production of their crops and to secure intelligent growth and to introduce new methods. No organizations in this country can be more beneficial in their character than farmers' alliances and farmers' associations. And so the combinations of workingmen to promote their interests, promote their welfare, and increase their pay, if you please, to get their fair share in the division of production, are not affected in the slightest degree, nor can they be included in the words or intent of the bill as now reported.

Senator Hoar, who had a large part in the framing of the act, defended the exclusion of labor organizations from the operation of the bill on the broadest grounds. He said:

When you are speaking to regulate the transactions of men who are making corners in wheat or in iron or in woolen and cotton goods, you are aiming at a mere commercial transaction, the beginning and end of which is the making of money for the parties, and nothing else. * * * But when a laborer is trying to raise his wages, or is endeavoring to shorten the hours of his labor, he is dealing with something that touches closely, more closely than anything else, the government and the character of the State itself. * * * I hold therefore that as legislators we may constitutionally, properly, and wisely allow laborers to make associations, combinations, contracts, agreements, for the sake of maintaining and advancing their wages, in regard to which, as a rule, their contracts are to be made with large corporations, who are themselves but an association or combination or aggregation of capital on the other side. When we are permitting or even encouraging that, we are permitting and encouraging what it [sic] not only lawful, wise, and profitable, but absolutely essential to the existence of the Commonwealth itself.

The circumstances attending the adoption of the Sherman Antitrust Act are thus referred to that it may be thoroughly understood that the law was not intended to apply to farmers' or labor organizations. The great men who took part in formulating that law did not desire, and did not intend, that under any circumstances any such organizations should be prohibited or punished. The bill could not have had the support of its own sponsors if it has been so interpreted. It could not have passed had it been so understood. There has never been a time since that a law having such interpretation could have passed either House or Congress. What an assumption of superior virtue it is that condemns as unjust and unmoral efforts to make the law in form and substance what was from the first the intention of Congress, and ever has been, and is now, its purpose!

An unfortunate interpretation by the courts has given the act a meaning not intended and not desired. Now we propose to make clear what was intended and what is desired. That is all. To do so is neither novel nor strange. It is being done everywhere in cases where an act is found not to have the intended purpose. If the objects sought to be reached are not secured, the act is enlarged to include the intended objects. If persons or objects not intended to be included or affected are found to be within the terms of the act, it is amended so as to exclude them. And that is what we propose to do here.

It is a strange thing that gentlemen will endeavor to hold included within the prohibition of the statute those things not intended to be included, and thus to compel a submission to penalties on the part of those whom they would not venture even to propose to punish as an independent proposition. Imagine anyone here proposing to make a labor organization ⊥ illegal, and to punish the efforts of its members to obtain better wages, shorter hours, or better conditions by fine and imprisonment! Who would dare on the floor of this House to introduce and defend a bill making farmers' cooperative associations, designed to obtain better prices, greater market facilities, or cheaper transportation rates unlawful? And yet certain persons affect to see in an effort to avoid such calamitous result something questionable and unworthy. I never would have supported a proposition to punish the organization or operation of such associations, and I do not hesitate now to support any legislation necessary to prevent such punishment; and I do so without apology, because I believe it is right and justifiable from every possible standpoint.

⊥9548

THE PROVISION AS AMENDED.

It may be well to state the provision as it will stand if this amendment is adopted:

SEC. 7. That nothing contained in the antitrust laws shall be construed to forbid the existence and operation of fraternal, labor, consumers', agricultural, or horticultural organizations, orders, or associations instituted for the purposes of mutual help and not having capital stock or conducted for profit, or to forbid or restrain individual members of such organizations, orders, or associations from carrying out the legitimate objects thereof, nor shall such organizations, orders, or associations, or the members thereof, be held or construed to be illegal combinations or conspiracies in restraint of trade under the antitrust laws.

I am sorry the language used is not clearer. I regret that it contains limitations which may obscure its meaning. The first limitation, that such associations shall be instituted for the purpose of mutual help, is not important, for it would be easy to prove that such was their purpose.

The next limitation, that such associations must not have capital stock, is of more importance, for many strictly cooperative associations issue capital stock to their members as an incident to corporate organization and operation. It is a needless requirement and should have been omitted.

The next requisite, that such associations to be within the benefits of the exclusion must not be conducted for profit, is unnecessary and dangerous. It should have been omitted. Still, I do not give it the broad interpretation given it by some Members. It is true that any association, social, scientific, or literary, may be conducted with profit to its members. But the word "profit" as used in the bill has no such broad meaning. It means, and will doubtless be interpreted to mean, conducted for the purpose of obtaining profits as an organization to distribute dividends to its stockholders. Most farmers' cooperative associations would not fall within its terms. Indeed, it is reasonably clear that no cooperative association where the receipts above salaries and operating expenses are returned to the patrons, producers, or consumers of the association would be within the excluded classes. Neither would labor organizations which succeeded in raising wages, although of undoubted "profit" to their members, be within the terms of the statute. "Profit" in a general sense and "profit" in a business transaction are entirely distinct and separate in meaning and application, and it is the latter meaning which is intended in the provision. Still, it would have been better to have omitted language subject to possible misinterpretation. The paragraph should have been entirely recast and its meaning made clear.

But I do not believe Members will be justified in voting against the provision because its language is not all that could be desired. The matter is too important to allow minor imperfections to bring about its defeat. It may secure all we desire. It must better existing conditions. At least it is something gained, a distinct step in advance.

The general purpose is clear. It is to be hoped that in its interpretation the courts will be governed by the larger view. That such is the present trend of decisions is a hopeful sign. As Senator Sherman said in the debate on the great and beneficial act of which he was the author, "It is difficult to define in legal language the precise line between lawful and unlawful combinations."

"Trade" has a broad meaning, and "restraint of trade" is a phrase of wide scope. Many things may result in a restraint of trade entirely innocent and even praiseworthy. Thousands of the agreements of everyday life might be interpreted as a restraint of trade if an absolute meaning is given the term. It is not the purpose of the law to prevent or punish these. The restraint of trade meant in the act is that which is intended to destroy competition, to establish monopoly, to drive out of business an honest competitor. As Senator Sherman said:

> It is the unlawful combination, tested by the rules of common law and human experience, that is aimed at by this bill, and not the useful and lawful combination.

It needs no argument to prove that labor organizations to better the conditions of the workingmen and that farmers' organizations to better transport and market the food products of the country ought not to be considered or made by statute unlawful. It is to prevent such result that this provision is inserted in the bill, and for the reasons stated it should receive the support of every just and fair-minded man.

LABOR ORGANIZATIONS.

It is altogether too common to condemn labor unions because of the violence of some frenzied striker. It is quite likely that the outrages of those who represent the employers in labor troubles are at least equal in number and enormity to those chargeable to the strikers. All who really wish for the betterment of conditions and the good order of society hope for a method by which the peaceful settlement of these unfortunate conflicts can be secured. But it is wrong and altogether unjust to condemn all labor organizations because of the violence or crimes of some of their members.

Labor unions have accomplished a great good and are absolutely necessary to protect labor against the exactions and impositions of capital. They have brought about better wages, shorter hours, and better conditions of labor, and such results are not only a blessing to those immediately affected, but they are a blessing to society and the State. It ought to be our desire and effort as legislators to encourage and foster such organizations, and not to discredit and punish them. Manhood and not money is here involved. The welfare and happiness of men, women, and children are here affected, not mere property rights. We are dealing with things vital and sacred, and should not touch them lightly or with selfish or sordid aim.

There are in the United States more than 30,000 local labor associations. Many, perhaps most, of these have agreements with their employers. These agreements relate not only to wages but to many things beneficial alike to employer and employees. If these agreements should be held as restraint of trade, if the organizations should be dissolved and the members sent to jail, the Nation would be shocked and its sense of justice outraged. Yet that is what may occur at any time a Government prosecutor sees fit to institute proceedings. It is to prevent this that the provision under discussion is incorporated in this bill.

It is objected that this legislation is class legislation. If by that is meant that it will not apply to all our population it must be admitted. It does not apply to all of our 100,000,000; it only applies to about 30,000,000. But that is rather a large proportion. It constitutes a considerable interest. Most of our legislation is class legislation if this is class legislation. Nine-tenths of the items of every appropriation are class legislation in this sense. There is no merit in this objection.

The English act of 1875 specifically relieved combinations of wage earners, concerned with questions of wages, working hours, and labor conditions, from the condemnation which the common law applied to combinations in restraint of trade. We are now at this late date only doing what a sense of justice and of sound policy led England to do nearly 40 years ago. It is a reproach, which we should hasten to remove, that our regard for the rights of labor and the welfare of our workingmen is not so great, nor our humanitarian standards so high as that of Great Britain.

FARMERS' ASSOCIATIONS.

The benefits of farmers' organizations designed to induce a larger production, better quality, cheaper transportation rates, better prices, and better market facilities are generally recognized. Trusts among the farmers or monopolies in farm products by the producers are impossible. Local cooperative association is perhaps the most effective means by which conditions in regard to the matters stated can be improved, and such improvement will result in benefit for the consumer as well as the producer. To restrain such associations would be absurd. To declare them unlawful would be the very height of folly. To allow them to remain subject to possible prosecution and their members liable to indictment as criminals is indefensible from every possible standpoint.

Discussing the fact that the farmer and producer does not receive a fair proportion of the price paid by the consumer the Secretary of Agriculture, in his last annual report, says:

It is clear that before the problems of marketing the individual farmer standing alone is helpless. Nothing less than concerted action will suffice. Cooperation is essential. * * * All the successful attempts in the marketing of any product anywhere in the world have come through organized effort. * * * The aim should be an economic arrangement which shall facilitate production, lead the producer to standardize and prepare his product for the market and to find the readiest and best market for his product. Such action will result in gain to the producer as well as to the consumer. Furthermore, it is desirable that such concerted action shall proceed from below upward. * * * Experience shows that the best results are secured only when the members of such a cooperative society are those who are bona fide producers.

Already is the wisdom and, indeed, the necessity of such cooperation becoming evident to the farmers. There are now ⊥ established and in operation in the United States cooperative associations of creameries, 2,165; of cheese factories, 336; elevators, 2,020; besides many hundreds of fruit, cotton, tobacco, and other associations regarding which accurate statistics are not available. This is but the beginning of a movement which is bound to develop to immense magnitude as its necessity shall be understood and its merits recognized.

⊥9549

The food problem of a nation is ever a vital one. The high price of food products paid by the consumer and the small price received by the producer is becoming understood and is a condition that must be remedied. That one half of the price finally paid by the user of food products is absorbed by transportation and middlemen is a condition everyone must see ought not to exist. It is the concensus [sic] of opinion of those who have most carefully and dispassionately studies the question that the remedy lies in associated effort, in cooperative associations of the producers. As the Secretary of Agriculture says:

All successful attempts in the marketing of any produce anywhere in the world have come through organized effort.

It is to protect such associations from assault by those who will profit by their absence that this provision is inserted in this bill. It is to prevent the possibility that efforts which are so manifestly for the benefit of all the people should be discredited and punished that we are now urging the adoption of the pending legislation. . . .

Mr. [ALBERT] JOHNSON [R., Wash.]. Mr. Chairman, I am proud to say that I am and have been for a long time an active member of the International Typographical Union. And for a great many years it has occurred to me that it has been a mistake on the part of those in high places, while admitting that the differences between capital and labor constitute a great problem, to invariably put it up to labor itself to solve that problem—the knottiest one of all. Why should labor—tired with tedious hours and strenuous effort—be always asked to find for itself the solution?

This section 7 of this antitrust bill is a case in point. Not so long ago it was discovered that the Sherman antitrust law does what its framers did not intend it to do—that is, it catches by the throat and would throttle organized labor.

Thereupon organized labor must solve another problem. This section 7 of this new antitrust bill was written. Labor accepted the section. Then the discovery was made that section 7 would not serve the purpose—that it is like the hollow log lying under the wire fence through which the pig undertook to go from one field to another. The pig went through the hollow log all right, but the log was curved, and the pig landed right back in the same field. That is your section 7. Labor figured it out, and asked for the amendment which is now offered by Chairman WEBB, and which I support. My regret is that section 7 and the amendment are made a part of an antitrust bill which I fear can not stand up when it comes under the close criticism of another lawmaking body.

It is not a partisan question, as some have tried to make it appear here to-day. The flaw in section 7 was, I understand, pointed out by one of the Nation's leading Republicans. I am glad that organized labor accepted that tip.

Does anyone contend that the Sherman antitrust law ever was meant to prevent the organization of labor? Few—very few—make that declaration. Some men who unfortunately can not see that those who pay wages to labor need the upgrading, contract-making, legitimate American labor organizations, manned by leaders who would mean well to all labor—be it union or otherwise—would hang on to these decisions, and would gladly see skilled labor deprived of its right to organize.

Some who deal with labor consider the whole proposition with alarm. But they need not. On the one hand is labor, organized under competent leaders, willing to give a fair day's work for a fair day's pay; willing to make contracts and live up to them; willing to have peace—in fact, urging peace.

On the other hand, if you strike down organized labor, choke it to death, you will add to the ranks of those so-called revolutionists, who will not have peace, who are in the hands of agitators, who go from one strike into another, and who do not and can not help those who toil.

Let those who pay wages choose with whom they prefer to deal. I have heard the prediction made by the gentleman from Iowa [Mr. TOWNER]. I will go a step further and predict that the time will come—let us hope that it is far distant—when the people of the United States will thank God they have organized and ready the American Federation of Labor, which lays the flag of the United States on its altar, which respects the rights of property, and which is eternally opposed to revolution; firmly opposed to direct action; an organization which helps workingmen instead of destroying them, and which stands against those aggregations which make contracts only to break them; against those organizations which teach "No God, no master"; against those un-American agitators who pledge men to disregard their oaths and urge them to perjure themselves whenever necessary, who advocate the destruction of property secretly, and who do all in their power to stop the wheels of progress. Oh, if these be dilemmas, which will you have? One is American, the other is not. One leads on to peace, the other leads to strife. Which will you have? [Applause.] . . .

Mr. GRAHAM of Pennsylvania. Mr. Chairman, I do not agree with the suggestion of the gentleman from Washington [Mr. JOHNSON] with reference to the language incorporated in this bill by the Committee on the Judiciary. I think their intention by that language was to accomplish precisely what is being accomplished by the insertion of this amendment. Evidently it satisfied everybody for a while, with the exception of a few, and as a result of the objection raised by them this new amendment is proposed.

I must take exception to the remark of the gentleman from Texas [Mr. HENRY] when he said this amendment was submitted to the Judiciary Committee and comes before the House approved by that committee. It was not submitted to the Committee on the Judiciary in any form that I ever heard or knew of, but is presented here as an amendment on the floor of the House. . . .

Mr. THOMAS. I would suggest to the gentleman from Pennsylvania that probably there is a new Judiciary Committee, and that the gentleman from Texas [Mr. HENRY] is the chairman of it. [Laughter.]

Mr. GRAHAM of Pennsylvania. Mr. Chairman, I accept the suggestion of the gentleman from Kentucky. It may be true. I regret exceedingly that this bill comes before this House involving three separate subjects of legislation. One is the regulation of business, another is the regulation of judicial procedure, and another is the regulation of labor and other organizations. If these matters were prepared and presented to us in separate bills, then they could receive their distinct support or opposition as men might feel toward them.

So far as the Webb amendment now proposed is concerned, it seems to me that it effectuates what the committee proposed in the original section 7, only in broader and clearer language. It provides that a certain class of organizations and their members shall not be held liable as conspiracies in restraint of trade or monopolies under the language of the antitrust law. As I understand it, it does not exempt them if they are guilty of aggressive, malicious, and criminal acts. If these are committed, then they are as much liable as any other class or set of citizens, and that is as it should be, for in matters of crime there ought to be no classification of the citizens of our country. . . .

Mr. GARNER. Mr. Chairman, I proposed an inquiry to my colleague, Mr. HENRY, of Texas, when he was discussing this amendment, and I desire to now propound the same inquiry to the gentleman from Pennsylvania, because I have a great deal of respect for his opinion concerning the legal constructions of this amendment. That is this: If cotton raisers should warehouse their cotton, a number of them, we will say 10,000 farmers, representing, say, a million bales of cotton, and determine that they would not sell until they got a certain price, would not that be a violation of this law?

Mr. GRAHAM of Pennsylvania. Mr. Chairman, I will answer that directly, first, by saying that in my judgment it would, for the simple reason that that would be creating a corner in cotton, and a conspiracy to raise or depress the price of any commodity has been a crime in all the history of the Anglo-Saxon people. I will answer it in another way. The Webb amendment provides that certain organizations shall not be held to be conspiracies or organizations in restraint of trade, and that refers us back to the language of section 7 to ascertain what class of associations are covered by this exemption. When we refer to section 7 we read:

> Associations instituted for the purpose of mutual help and not having capital stock or conducted for profit. . . .

9550 These are the organizations that are intended to be exempt as organizations from the operations of these antitrust laws. I was very much impressed with the argument of my young friend, the Progressive in Pennsylvania, Mr. William Draper Lewis, the dean of our law school, when he said before the Judiciary Committee that the same law ought not to operate and regulate wares and merchandise and things that operated to regulate labor; and these bills ought to be divorced; the three portions ought to be divorced and separated from each other. For I am in this embarrassing position: I am going to vote to sustain the Webb amendment to this bill and incorporate it in the bill, and upon other grounds in which the bill is damaging and injurious to the business interests of this country I must vote against it as a whole. The Webb amendment will be adopted and the bill will be triumphantly passed in this House by the Democratic majority, so the absence of my vote on its final approval will not be missed, whereas I shall have expressed by willingness to exempt from the operations and effect of this statute the existence of these corporations but not any unlawful acts. [Applause.] . . .

Mr. LENROOT. Mr. Chairman, I shall vote for this Webb amendment, because it does accomplish a purpose that there ought not to be any difference of opinion about. Whether it goes as far as it ought to is a question that we need not discuss now; and I wish just for a moment, Mr. Chairman, to give my opinion of what will be accomplished by the adoption of this amendment. In the first place, I must disagree with the gentleman from Pennsylvania [Mr. GRAHAM] that the original section 7 accomplished the same purpose. . . .

Mr. GRAHAM of Pennsylvania. I meant to say—and if I did not I did not express myself fully—that it was intended by the gentlemen of the committee to accomplish the same purpose. That was my understanding; that is all.

Mr. LENROOT. With that statement I have nothing further to say, but it is entirely clear to me that the original section accomplished absolutely nothing so far as the exemption of these organizations are concerned from prosecution under the antitrust laws; but with this amendment it does just this—that whatever opinion may be entertained as to the acts of individual members of these organizations, with this amendment adopted the organization itself can not be dissolved, the organization itself can not be pursued as having violated the law, and therefore it is a step forward regardless of the question of whether it goes far enough or not. But now, Mr.

Chairman, I want to direct myself for just a moment to another proposition, a legal proposition, that runs all through section 7, and that is the use of the words "shall be construed," and so forth. It is most unfortunate, Mr. Chairman, that the committee has used this language.

It is of course within the province of this Congress to construe any act of its own; but, Mr. Chairman, it is not within the province of this Congress to attempt to construe any act of a previous Congress. But by this language it is attempted to construe all of the antitrust laws. Now, it is entirely clear to every lawyer that it is the province of the legislature to make the law and it is a judicial function to construe it. This Congress has no power to say to the court how it shall construe a law heretofore made; and the effect of all of it is, if the courts specifically uphold it, as I believe they will, they will entirely throw out of consideration the words "shall be construed" and say that it was the intention of Congress to change the law, as unquestionably it is. Now, this language has been criticized time after time by the courts. For instance, in a case in the Supreme Court of the United States, speaking of identical language, it said:

But for the unfortunate and unnecessary use of the word "construed" in this sentence we apprehend that none of the resistance to this class of taxes now under consideration would have been thought of.

And all the way through the cases the courts have struggled to uphold the acts of Congress and legislatures, but only by saying that, while the legislature used the words "shall be construed," the real purpose was not to construe the law but to change it. . . .

Now, Mr. Chairman, I am satisfied the courts will in interpreting this law say that the words "shall be construed" shall be thrown aside, and that it was the intention of this Congress to modify the existing antitrust laws; but this Congress has no power to modify the existing antitrust laws as to acts committed under them prior to the passage of this act; and if there is any idea that by using this language we are changing the law with respect to existing cases, we have no power to do it, and we have utterly failed. . . .

Mr. HULINGS. Mr. Chairman, I have always believed that the organization of labor is the only defense the workingman has against the inevitable tendency under the competitive system to reduce wages to the lowest point of subsistence. I therefore am in favor of legalizing and recognizing to the fullest extent these organizations; but it seems to me that the committee in proposing this legislation did not accomplish anything in that direction. If you will permit me to paraphrase this seventh section, it will read something like this:

That nothing contained in the antitrust laws shall be construed to forbid the existence and operation of a railroad company or a steamboat company or to forbid or restrain individual members of such organizations from carrying out the legitimate objects thereof.

And adding the Webb amendment:

Nor shall such organizations or members thereof be held to be unlawful combinations or conspiracies in restraint of trade.

Of course a railroad company is not an unlawful combination, and of course a labor organization is not an illegal organization, and if that be true what does the section mean? It seems to me that there is a concealed purpose here to throw to the laboring men of the country something that means nothing; in fact, something that gives them nothing that they do not now have. Of course these organizations are not now illegal and in restraint of trade and conspiracies, and they never were. Take out of the section "labor organizations" and put in instead "railroad organizations," and nobody will pretend that under the antitrust laws the section would exempt the railroad organization from dissolution by the courts for violation of the antitrust law. How, then, can it be maintained that if the language of the section so paraphrased would make a railroad organization liable to dissolution that the section as it stands would not make a labor organization liable to dissolution?

But what you ought to do—and I suppose this is the real meat in the coconut—is to do something which will meet the real question. If members of such an organization commit an illegal act, that will be sufficient under the antitrust laws to warrant the dissolution of that organization.

Now, that, as I understand, is the real thing, Nobody, I suppose, wants to exempt people in this country from the consequences of illegal acts. Nobody asks Congress to do that. A railroad, a trust organization, if it commits illegal acts, may be dissolved by the courts; the whole institution may be dissolved. The purpose of the laboring man, as I understand it here, is that if they commit illegal acts, the court may go after the individual members responsible for the illegal acts; but the labor organization of which the lawbreakers may be members itself can not be dissolved. But the section under consideration does not do this at all, and I fear it does not give labor and farm organizations any real exemption. . . .

Mr. MURDOCK. It is a question as to what is illegal. The gentleman has read the bill. Does he believe, under this bill, that in case of a strike, where the strikers assemble peaceably, remote from the place of the strike, an injunction would lie against them for peacefully assembling?

Mr. HULINGS. I do not think it ought to; and I think the power of injunction has been greatly abused by the courts, especially in labor disputes.

Mr. MURDOCK. It look to me, under this bill, as if it will.

Mr. HULINGS. That would be a matter for the court when the act should be brought before it for adjudication. I fear the act itself is not clear. . . .

⊥ Mr. [WALTER L.] HENSLEY [D., Mo.]. Mr. Chairman, I am in hearty accord with the purpose sought to be obtained by the amendment offered by the gentleman from North Carolina [Mr. WEBB], chairman of the Committee on the Judiciary. I am in favor of exempting labor organizations, farm organizations, and fraternal organizations from the operations of the antitrust laws. I have never been able to understand the process of reasoning on the part of the courts of our country which has brought these organizations within the purview of the Sherman antitrust law. One has but to review the speeches made by Senator Sherman, author of the antitrust act; Senator Vest, of Missouri—than whom there were no greater—and many other noted lawyers and statesmen then serving in the Senate of the United States to see and to understand to a certainty that Congress had no thought of including these organizations within the operation of the law; but nevertheless, in some instances, the courts have construed the law to apply to these organizations, which has resulted in great harassment to the laboring people everywhere. ⊥9551

The laboring people, through their representatives, for many years have put up a gallant fight, insisting upon this law being construed as the lawmakers intended it to be and as common humanity and even-handed justice demand. The representatives of labor on the part of the farmers of this Nation and those representing the men who toil in the factories and toil in the mines, the men who produce the wealth of the Nation and who fight the battles of our country, have pressed upon Congress to write an exemption into the law which would indicate the intention of Congress to not bring these people within the operations of the antitrust act; but the party heretofore in power has at all times turned a deaf ear to these appeals and have failed and refused to do that which, it seems to me, to have been their plain duty to this great body of toilers. So finally the Democratic Party, in convention assembled at Baltimore in 1912, declared in favor of this exemption, and so it remains for this Congress, this Democratic Congress, to write into this antitrust legislation an exemption which will be so clearly and unmistakably put that none can be deceived by the language employed, that none of the organizations heretofore mentioned shall be affected by this antitrust legislation or the Sherman antitrust law. It is written in this amendment just as the people most affected by it asked that it be written. So that, Mr. Chairman, to-day by this piece of legislation we are crowning the efforts of the laboring people, covering many years, with the success that is only their just deserts: and I rejoice in this triumph, because it is not only for the good of these organizations mentioned in the amendment, but for the common good of all mankind. . . .

Mr. RAKER. Mr. Chairman, I shall support the amendment to section 7, proposed and presented by the gentleman from North Carolina [Mr. WEBB], the chairman of the committee. I believe that it will add to the efficiency of the section and will carry out the desires of labor.

I understand that those organizations, those interested, have gone over the proposed amendment, and are satisfied with the amendment as it is now proposed by the committee instead of the proposed amendment that was presented by them and sent to each Congressman some days ago, where they proposed to amend section 7 by striking out certain language and using the words "shall not apply."

Gentlemen have discussed here the language "shall construe." You will find here that there is an additional word—"the court shall not hold" or will not be permitted to hold that these organizations are acting in restraint of trade.

Section 7, with the addition of the Webb amendment, will then read as follows:

SEC. 7. That nothing contained in the antitrust laws shall be construed to forbid the existence and operation of fraternal, labor, consumers, agricultural, or horticultural organizations, orders, or associations instituted for the purposes of mutual help, and not having capital stock or conducted for profit, or to forbid or restrain individual members of such organizations, orders, or associations from carrying out the legitimate objects thereof; nor shall such organizations, orders, or associations, or the members thereof, be held or construed to be illegal combinations or conspiracies in restraint of trade under the antitrust laws.

The section as thus amended has been agreed upon and is satisfactory to the American Federation of Labor, the Farmers' National Organization, and the Brotherhood of Locomotive Engineers and Firemen of the United States. This will bring about the legislation that labor has been working for for over 25 years, and it now becomes the privilege of a Democratic Congress and a Democratic President to see that such legislation is enacted. The executive council of the American Federation of Labor has been actively and earnestly engaged in bringing about this legislation. In the American Federation of Labor Weekly News Letter, published at Washington, D. C., on Saturday, May 23, 1914, they have given a history of the legislation that is now being considered as contained in section 7 of this bill, which is as follows:

AMERICAN FEDERATION OF LABOR EXECUTIVE COUNCIL ACTS ON TRADE-UNION EXEMPTION CLAUSE.

Washington, May 23.

The American Federation of Labor executive council takes exception to the trade-union exemption clause of the Clayton antitrust bill which, it is claimed, is intended to cover those demands of organized labor embodied in the Bartlett-Bacon bills. At the council's session last week, the following resolutions were adopted:

Whereas the American Congress, in its wisdom, enacted a law on July 2, 1890, known as the Sherman antitrust law, which was intended by them to apply exclusively to large combinations of wealth—so-called trusts of property—for the avowed and specific purpose of preventing monopoly and exploitation of special privileges.

It was undoubtedly the intention of Congress to enact a law that would be effective in the prevention of huge combinations of wealth from crushing their competitors in the business world; it was also the avowed and openly expressed opinion of the statesmen who wrote that law that it should not apply to farmers' or laborers' organizations established for the betterment of producers of wealth.

The United States Senate, in Committee of the Whole, on March 26, 1890, while considering the Sherman bill, almost unanimously agreed to a provision exempting the organizations of working people from the proposed act.

On June 2, 1900, in the Fifty-sixth Congress, the House of Representatives, by a vote of 260 to 8, adopted a similar declaration in a supplementary amendment to the Sherman Act.

On June 2 and June 21, 1910, the House of Representatives again declared that the Sherman Act should not apply to the voluntary association of working people.

On February 20, 1913, in the Sixty-second Congress, the House of Representatives again made a similar declaration.

On February 28, 1913, the Senate accepted those provisions.

On March 4, 1913, after President Taft had vetoed the declaration, the House of Representatives, by a vote of 364 to 48, passed the bill over the veto of President Taft with the declarations intact.

On April 14, 1913, in the Sixty-third Congress, the House of Representatives, by a vote of 198 to 47, again declared itself in favor of the above-stated declarations.

On May 7, 1913, the United States Senate, by a vote of 41 to 32, agreed to the House declaration, and on June 23, 1913, President Woodrow Wilson signed the sundry civil appropriation bill, approving the Hamill-Roddenbery provisos exempting labor and farmers' organizations from the antitrust appropriation section of that act.

At the Denver convention of the Democratic Party in 1908, and at the Baltimore convention of the Democratic Party is 1912, emphatic declarations were unanimously adopted by those conventions pledging the Democratic Party, if elected to power, to enact legislation so that the organizations of labor and producers "should not be regarded as illegal combinations in restraint of trade."

Hon. Woodrow Wilson, the candidate for the Presidency, in his speech of acceptance, emphatically pledged himself to support that specific plant in the platform of his party.

The above historical facts can neither be disputed nor denied: and

Whereas the antitrust bill, H. R. 15657, now being considered by the House of Representatives, is the administration measure and is intended to cover supplementary trust legislation, with the avowed purpose to meet the Democratic platform declarations in reference to its labor planks.

I here insert an article from Organized Labor in its issue of May 23, 1914. Speaking upon this question, the following pertinent and applicable language is used:

[From Organized Labor, Saturday, May 23, 1914.]

LABOR'S POSITION ON THE ANTITRUST LAW.

President Wilson is said to be in favor of subjecting trades-unions to the provisions of the Sherman law against combination in restraint of trade. It is proposed that the unions shall not be subject to injunction for such action as may restrain trade. A strike or a boycott may be punished just as the organization of a trust in business. This proposal is supported by the contention that the law should bear upon all people alike, upon the labor striker as upon the engrosser and forestaller of commodities or the railroad combiner. To exempt the unions would be, it is said, to grant them a special privilege. All of which sounds and looks good; but is it?

A labor union has no special privilege bestowed by the State. It hasn't even a charter. Corporations have advantages as such. They are creatures of the State and subject to regulation. Labor unions are not formed to make profits. They are formed to prevent the lowering of wages even more than to further the raising of wages. That the unions seek a labor monopoly in restraint of trade is not true. Their end is not a monopoly of work, but proper pay for the work the workers perform. And it must not be forgotten that back of the labor union is the laboring man. That man has a right to himself. He has a right to work or not work, as he pleases, and if he withholds his work he is not restraining anybody's trade or commerce. If he prevents another man from working, that is something more than an offense against the Sherman Act, if it is anything. He can be punished for it as a crime or misdemeanor under other laws, but he should not be punished ⊥ by penalties for ignoring injunctions ex parte. The contention of union-labor leaders that unions should be exempt from the operation of the injunction provisions of the Sherman Act is a sound one, says Reedy's Mirror. It is a contention based upon the workingman's right to his own labor. The inclusion of labor unions under the new act is not necessary. If they violate that law, they usually lay themselves open to prosecution for more serious violations of law.

Clearly the Sherman antitrust law was not meant to apply to combinations of labor. That law was and is directed against combinations of corporations. There is no question of equality under that law as between privileged corporations and united workers. Surely no sane person wants the Sherman Act used to force a man to work for some one he doesn't want to work for. That's what the application of the Sherman Act to union labor would amount to. Union labor hasn't anything belonging to all the people entitling the Government to regulate it beyond compelling it to keep the peace. But the big corporations have governmental privileges, special favors, and Government rightly regulates them. A labor organization that might be subject to action under the proposed law would be subject to more drastic action for grosser offenses first. And this consideration alone makes it plain that the Sherman Act was never intended to apply to union labor. The exemption of organized labor would be no privilege at all. What labor organization aims at and what combinations and trusts aim at are entirely different things. The one seeks only to see that the laborer gets his proper hire. The other seeks to gough labor of its share of what it produces. The President should favor the labor exemption, because if he does not the Sherman Act will be made the means to prevent the workingman from bettering his pay or the conditions under which he shall earn that pay.

In speaking upon this same subject the following appears in the American Federation of Labor, published at Washington, D. C., in its issue of Saturday, May 30, 1914:

VICTORY IS IN SIGHT—LABOR TO BE FREED FROM ANTITRUST LAWS, INJUNCTION ABUSE, AND UNJUST CONTEMPTS.

Washington, May 28.

The parliamentary situation of the Clayton antitrust bill in Congress, in which labor is vitally affected, has reached a satisfactory stage. For years the American Federation of Labor contended that the Sherman antitrust law was never intended to apply and should not have been applied to the voluntary organizations of the working people. By reason of the decision of the Supreme Court in the Hatters' case, and of several courts in other cases, that law was made to apply to organizations of workers. It is unnecessary at this time to recount the various phases and developments of the efforts to secure remedial legislation which the working people of the country have so long and so justly demanded. There was an apparent disposition on the part of those in control of legislation to enact a bill adequate to meet the needs of the working people. But upon close study and scrutiny the representatives of the American Federation of Labor soon learned that the labor sections of the tentative drafts of the Clayton antitrust bill were ineffective, and insisted upon changes to conform to declarations of the Democratic and the Progressive Parties. For a time it appeared that divergent opinions would result in a permanent cleavage. Representatives of the American Federation of Labor insisted upon good faith being observed. After many changes the representatives of all parties and the American Federation of Labor reached a general agreement. The American Federation of Labor has had the hearty cooperation of the labor group in Congress and the representatives of the railroad brotherhoods and of the farmers' organizations.

In the Clayton bill dealing with supplementary legislation on the Sherman antitrust law is incorporated the following agreed-upon section:

"SEC. 7. That nothing contained in the antitrust laws shall be construed to forbid the existence and operation of fraternal, labor, consumers, agricultural, or horticultural organizations, orders, or associations instituted for the purposes of mutual help and not having capital stock or conducted for profit, or to forbid or restrain individual members of such organizations, orders, or associations from carrying out the legitimate objects thereof, nor shall such organizations, orders, or associations, or the members thereof, be held or construed to be illegal combinations or conspiracies in restraint of trade under the antitrust laws."

There are other sections of the Clayton bill which deal with the regulation and limitation of the issuance of injunctions. There are sections dealing with the subject of the regulation of contempt proceedings and providing for jury trials in alleged indirect contempts. The section dealing with injunctions, in which labor is primarily interested, is as follows:

"SEC. 18. That no restraining order or injunction shall be granted by any court of the United States, or a judge or the judges thereof, in any case between an employer and employee, or between employers and employees, or between employees, or between persons employed and persons seeking employment, involving or growing out of a dispute concerning terms or conditions of employment, unless necessary to prevent irreparable injury to property, or to a property right, of the party making the application, for which injury there is no adequate remedy at law, and such property or property right must be described with particularity in the application, which must be in writing and sworn to by the applicant or by his agent or attorney.

"And no such restraining order or injunction shall prohibit any person or persons from terminating any relation of employment, or from ceasing to perform any work or labor, or from recommending, advising, or persuading others by peaceful means so to do; or from attending at or near a house or place where any person resides or works or carries on business or happens to be for the purpose of peacefully obtaining or communicating information, or of peacefully persuading any person to work or to abstain from working, or from ceasing to patronize or to employ any party to such dispute, or from recommending, advising, or persuading others by peaceful means so to do; or from paying or giving to or withholding from any person engaged in such dispute any strike benefits or other moneys or things of value; or from peacefully assembling at any place in a lawful manner and for lawful purposes, or from doing any act or thing which might lawfully be done in absence of such dispute by any party thereto, nor shall any of the acts specified in this paragraph be considered or held unlawful."

The sections dealing with the contempt proceedings and jury trials are as follows:

"SEC. 19. That any person who shall willfully disobey any lawful writ, process, order, rule, decree, or command of any district court of the United States or any court of the District of Columbia by doing any act or thing therein, or thereby forbidden to be done by him, if the act or thing so done by him be of such character as to constitute also a criminal offense under any statute of the United States or at common law shall be proceeded against for his said contempt as hereinafter provided.

"SEC. 20. That whenever it shall be made to appear to any district court or judge thereof, or to any judge therein sitting, by the return of a proper officer on lawful process, or upon the affidavit of some credible person, or by information filed by any district attorney that there is reasonable ground to believe that any person has been guilty of such contempt, the court or judge thereof, or any judge therein sitting, may issue a rule requiring the said person so charged to show cause upon a day certain why he should not be punished therefor, which rule, together with a copy of the affidavit or information, shall be served upon the person charged with sufficient promptness to enable him to prepare for and make return to the order at the time fixed therein. If upon or by such return, in the judgment of the court, the alleged contempt be not sufficiently purged, a trial shall be directed at a time and placed fixed by the court: *Provided, however,* That if the accused, being a natural person, fail or refuse to make return to the rule to show cause, an attachment may issue against his person to compel an answer, and in case of his continued failure or refusal, or if for any reason it be impracticable to dispose of the matter on the return day, he may be required to give reasonable bail for his attendance at the trial and his submission to the final judgment of the court. Where the accused person is a body corporate, an attachment for the sequestration of its property may be issued upon like refusal or failure to answer.

"In all cases within the purview of this act such trial may be by the court or, upon demand of the accused, by a jury, in which latter event the court may impanel a jury from the jurors then in attendance or the court or the judge thereof in chambers may cause a sufficient number of jurors to be selected and summoned, as provided by law, to attend at the time and place of trial, at which time a jury shall be selected and impaneled as upon a trial for misdemeanor, and such trial shall conform as near as may be to the practice in criminal cases prosecuted by indictment or upon information.

"If the accused be found guilty, judgment shall be entered accordingly, prescribing the punishment either by fine or imprisonment, or both, in the discretion of the court. Such fine shall be paid to the United States or to the complainant or other party injured by the act constituting the contempt or may, where more than one is so damaged, be divided or apportioned among them as the court may direct, but in no case shall the fine to be paid to the United States exceed, in case the accused is a natural person, the sum of $1,000, nor shall such imprisonment exceed the term of six months.

"SEC. 21. That the evidence taken upon the trial of any person so accused may be preserved by bill of exceptions, and any judgment of conviction may be reviewed upon writ of error in all respects as now provided by law in criminal cases, and may be affirmed, reversed, or modified as justice may require. Upon the granting of such writ of error execution of judgment shall be stayed and the accused, if thereby sentenced to imprisonment, shall be admitted to bail in such reasonable sum as may be required by the court or by any justice or any judge of any district court of the United States or any court of the District of Columbia.

"SEC. 22. That nothing herein contained shall be construed to relate to contempts committed in the presence of the court, or so near thereto, as to obstruct the administration of justice, nor to contempts committed in disobedience of any lawful writ, process, order, rule, decree, or command entered in any suit or action brought or prosecuted in the name of or on behalf of the United States, but the same and all other cases of contempt not specifically embraced within section 19 of this act may be punished in conformity to the usages at law and in equity now prevailing.

"SEC. 23. That no proceeding for contempt shall be instituted against any person unless begun within one year from the date of the act complained of; nor shall any such proceeding be a bar to any criminal prosecution for the same act or acts; but nothing herein contained shall affect any proceedings in contempt pending at the time of the passage of this act."

It is confidently predicted, justified by the parliamentary situation, that the bill, with the above sections, will be passed by the House within the next few days. . . .

Mr. BARKLEY. Mr. Chairman, for a number of years there has been much discussion and agitation in this country on the subject of trusts and monopolies. In 1890 Congress passed what is known as the Sherman antitrust law in an effort to curb, prevent, or restrain unlawful combinations in restraint of trade and insure lawful and wholesome competition in the commerce of the United States. Notwithstanding that law has been in force for 24 years, combinations, trusts, and monopolies have increased at a marvelous rate and have grown so enormous in size as almost to stagger with bewilderment and confusion the mind that undertakes to contemplate or unravel them. So successful have these great combinations of wealth been in the past, not only in their organization but also in their operation, that we are now compelled to buy much that we buy from a trust, and to sell to a trust much that we have to sell. This condition in the past has enabled the trust and monopoly to fix the price of the thing it bought from us and the thing it sold to us, the result being that the real producer and the real consumer have both been at the mercy of these great aggregations of wealth.

It would be interesting, if time permitted, to go somewhat into detail in undertaking to show the methods these corporations have adopted and practiced in stifling competition and controlling the markets of trade. But this is a familiar story. We have seen them force out of the market independent concerns by the most destructive and unfair methods and practices. We have seen them, by threats and by intimidation, ⊥ force a competitor to sell out to them or be financially ruined. We have seen them go into communities and in order to drive out a legitimate competitor reduce the price of their own article below the cost of production, and then, after the competitor had gone to the wall or sold out his business, the trust would raise the price of its own article far above the cost of production and a reasonable profit. Why could it do this? Because, after driving its competitor out of business, it had control of the field. Who paid in the end for this method of transacting business? The consumer, who was compelled to buy from them, because there was no one else left from whom to purchase.

This method of big business has been very largely practiced in the manufacturing industry. It was this method which enabled great corporations like the Standard Oil Co., the American Tobacco Co., the International Harvester Co., and many others of like size and purpose to obtain absolute control of the manufacture and sale of the commodities which they manufactured and sold.

This condition has been recognized by all parties in the United States for the past 15 or 20 years. Real competition in trade has been gradually growing less and less as monopoly has increased. Notwithstanding there has been an insistent and persistent demand from the people of every class and creed for relief from these burdensome conditions, no administration and no party has made any honest effort to correct these manifest evils until the Democratic Party came into power on March 4, 1913. It is true the Republican administration "prosecuted" a few corporations, and possibly "fined" the "corporation"; and it is true that they "dissolved" the Standard Oil Co. and the American Tobacco Co. But the small fines assessed against the corporation as such resulted in no real benefit to the people, and the dissolution of the Standard Oil Co. and the American Tobacco Co. was soon followed by a rise in the value of their shares of stock, which greatly enriched their owners without corresponding benefit to the people. No officer of either company was ever prosecuted.

In the campaign of 1912 the Democratic Party, at its convention at Baltimore, adopted the following plank in its platform, upon which it went before the people and asked their votes:

A private monopoly is indefensible and intolerable. We therefore favor the vigorous enforcement of the criminal as well as the civil law against trusts and trust officials, and demand the enactment of such additional legislation as may be necessary to make it impossible for a private monopoly to exist in the United States.

We favor the declaration by law of the conditions upon which corporations shall be permitted to engage in interstate trade, including among others the prevention of holding companies, of interlocking directors, of stock watering, of discrimination in price, and the control by any one corporation of so large a proportion of any industry as to make it a menace to competitive conditions.

We condemn the action of the Republican administration in compromising with the Standard Oil Co. and the Tobacco Trust and its failure to invoke the criminal provisions of the antitrust law against the officers of those corporations after the court had declared that from the undisputed facts in the record they had violated the criminal provisions of the law.

We regret that the Sherman antitrust law has received a judicial construction depriving it of much of its efficacy, and we favor the enactment of legislation which will restore to the statute the strength of which it has been deprived by such interpretation.

There is, Mr. Speaker, no evasion or equivocation about the language of that platform. There is nothing in it that the simplest mind can not understand. It demands the enforcement of the criminal laws against those who have violated the antitrust laws, and it demands the enactment of further laws prescribing the conditions upon which corporations may engage in trade between the States, among them being the prevention of holding companies, interlocking directors, unfair discrimination in price, and the control by any one corporation of so large a proportion of any given industry as practically to wipe out competition.

We, the Democratic Party and the Democratic administration, are now engaged in undertaking to enact a law in compliance with the pledges of that platform. We are seeking at this time to do what no other party has attempted to do, either for lack of courage or intelligence, namely, to write into the statute laws of the United States provisions designed to protect legitimate business against the unfair methods of monopoly and to protect the people themselves against the encroachments of those who in the past have sought to hinder and obstruct the freedom of competition in everything necessary to the prosperity and happiness of the people.

The provisions of the bill now under consideration are intended to prevent unfair discrimination, in so far as that end may be accomplished by legislation. Section 2 of the bill is designed to correct a widespread and common unfair trade practice whereby certain great corporations have heretofore endeavored to destroy competition and render unprofitable the business of competitors by selling their goods and merchandise at a lower price in the community of their rivals than at other places throughout the country, hoping that after the rival in business had been driven from the field the corporation would then enhance the price sufficiently to regain the loss made necessary in driving out the competitor. This section expressly forbids such practices when intended to injure or destroy the business of a competitor. This bill is not designed nor intended to prevent the lowering of prices in a legitimate way, for we are all interested in seeing that the cost of those things which are necessary to human progress and happiness shall not be above their reasonable value. But our experience in the past has demonstrated the fact that when a great corporation which has or is seeking a monopoly of the products of human labor goes into the field and by its unfair methods drives out a competitor in business, the people have usually been compelled to pay increased prices for the article controlled by such corporation after it has obtained a monopoly and driven out competition. It is an old axiom that competition is the life of trade, and the measure now before the House is designed to restore as far as possible healthy competition, so that the people may receive the benefit of the natural flow of trade in every legitimate channel.

The necessity for such legislation is shown by the fact that within the last few years 19 States of this Union have enacted laws forbidding such unfair discrimination and unfair practices, and it is important that Congress should supplement these State laws with similar legislation, as Congress alone has the power to regulate interstate commerce and the conditions upon which it may be engaged in.

In like manner, section 3 of the bill is intended to prevent owners or operators of mines, oil or gas wells, or other mineral products to refuse arbitrarily to sell his product, or any part of it, to a responsible purchaser. It is now recognized that the great mineral deposits which God has placed in the earth were placed there for the benefit of mankind. The coal, the oil, the gas, the copper, the gold and silver, the iron and steel, and other forms of mineral wealth are absolutely indispensable to human development and comfort in these modern days. In the past it has frequently happened that legitimate enterprises have been made to suffer because the coal barons and the oil kings refused to sell to them the necessary coal or the necessary oil with which to carry on their business. Such refusal has sometimes resulted in the closing of manufacturing plants and the throwing out of employment of men, simply because the owner of the coal or of the oil or other product of the mine practiced favoritism and discrimination as between purchasers, with the intention of building up one concern and destroying the other. Recognizing that these great natural sources of mineral wealth belong in truth to all the people and were created for all the people, it is sought in this measure to prevent their monopolization for the benefit of a few and to the injury of the great masses of those who depend upon them for the comforts and necessities of life.

Section 4 of the bill is designed to prevent what is known as "tying contracts." A great manufacturing company will go into a community and make a contract to let one certain person, firm, or corporation handle its products, provided such person, firm, or corporation will agree not to handle the goods of any other manufacturer who is a competitor. The very essence of such a transaction is monopoly. The local concern is not always nor usually to blame, because it desires to handle the particular articles in question, and perhaps it would like to handle similar articles manufactured by other concerns. But he frequently can not obtain the articles made by one manufacturer without agreeing not to handle the competitive articles made by another manufacturer, and so a monopoly of the given articles is created and an unlawful and unwholesome restraint of trade is the result, and the people are frequently unable to obtain the benefits of competition because the manufacturer ties the local merchant with a contract not to sell the products of a like or similar character made by a competing manufacturer. This bill will not prevent a manufacturer from selecting his customer or from making one person, firm, or corporation in any community his sole agent for the distribution of his products, because such a provision would be impracticable and perhaps work injury to legitimate business. But while it is true that he can designate a given concern to whom he will sell the products of his factory, he can not compel that concern to agree not to handle also the products of other manufacturers if he wants to do it. The merchant is not required to handle the products of others, unless he wants to do it. But this bill is intended to give the local merchant the right to handle as many competitive articles of the same kind as he may wish to handle, without tying his hands to one and only one concern under penalty of being refused or denied the right to handle such concern's products. The object and intention of this section of the bill is to create and sustain competition in trade and give the people the right of choice as to what articles of merchandise they will use.

Suppose, for instance, a manufacturer of plows should go to a local merchant in some agricultural community and propose to allow the merchant to handle his particular brand of plows. Or suppose the merchant himself should seek the handling of those plows in that community. The manufacturer might say, "I will let you handle my plows, provided you agree not to handle the plows made by any other concern." But the merchant would say in reply, "Many people in my community use other brands of plows, and I would like to handle other plows, so that I can furnish them to those who may desire them." The manufacturer, under the present law, would have the right to say, "You can not handle my plows unless you agree not to handle any other plow on the market." The result would be that the merchant would have to agree to that or be denied the right to handle the plows in question. In that event the merchant suffers because he is in the power of the trust or monopoly of a given brand of plows, and the community suffers because of a lack of competition and because of a frequent inability to secure the article they desire. All such conditions operate to restrain the freedom of trade and to build up monopoly at the expense of the people. It is hoped that this provision of the pending bill will go far to relieve trade of such handicaps and to restore and maintain the proper sort of competition.

Other sections of the bill forbid one corporation from acquiring the stock or shares of another corporation where the effect of such acquisition and control would be to eliminate or substantially lessen competition. This provision is intended to prevent what is commonly known as "holding companies." A "holding company" is a company that holds the stock of another company or companies, and one whose primary object is to "hold" the stock of other companies, which is a common and favorite method of promoting monopoly.

Under this method one corporation may buy up all the stock of several competing corporations engaged in commerce, or enough of their stock to give the "holding company" control of them all, and thereafter all the different corporations whose stock has been thus bought up are under the same control and are operated as though it were one concern. As thus defined, a "holding company" is created for the sole purpose of fostering monopoly and stifling competition, and is simply an incorporated likeness of the old-fashioned trust. For instance, a great corporation located in the city of New York or Chicago, under that system, might purchase the stock of 25 or 50 different smaller corporations in different States engaged in manufacturing similar and competitive products. These smaller corporations would remain separate corporations as organized under the laws of the different States, but their stock would be owned and they would be controlled by the corporation in New York or Chicago which owned their stock; and whereas previously they had all been competitors in the markets of the world, they would now, for all practical purposes, operate as parts of one great "holding" corporation, and competition would be at an end. This measure is designed to prevent that, where the primary purpose or the necessary consequence is to destroy of substantially lessen competition in trade.

Another great evil in the conduct of business, which is denounced by the Democratic platform, is what is commonly called "interlocking directors." By this term we mean the condition where the same men are directors and officers of many different corporations, some of them supposedly competitors, but all of them actuated by a community of interest which in many instances in the past has resulted in disaster. Recently one man in New York resigned from the board of directors of 50 different corporations. His published reason for so doing was that he recognized the changed condition of public sentiment regarding this manifest evil, and desired to adjust himself to the new ideals now permeating the business world. Whether this action was brought about by the dictates of conscience or the exercise of a prudent foresight we need not now stop to inquire.

The same conditions exist with reference to many others who have not yet adjusted themselves to the new conditions and demands of modern business thought, but who are as intricately "interlocked" in the boards of directors of naturally competing corporations as was he to whom I have just referred. There can be no real competition between companies engaged in commerce where the same persons control the policy of the different companies. It would be contrary to the weakness of human nature if they did not manipulate all of such companies for their selfish ends regardless of the interests of the public. Many examples could be called to mind where the directors of railroads, banks, coal companies, steamship companies, and various manufacturing concerns have been and are now so linked and "interlocked" that there is no competition in management and therefore none in operation. The whole design of the bill now under discussion in so far as it affects business is to secure and maintain fair and free competition among concerns and products naturally competitive, and therefore, in accordance with the declaration of our platform, it is provided in this measure that such conditions are to be remedied in so far as legislation may make this possible and practicable.

I desire, Mr. Chairman, to discuss briefly at this point the provisions of this bill which affect the rights of labor and of those who labor.

In searching the sacred pages of the Holy Scriptures for inspiration and guidance through this earthly journey we call life we find nowhere a command that we shall form a monopoly or that we shall become vastly rich or that we shall oppress our fellowman. Nowhere within the covers of that wonderful book are we admonished to "toil not, nor spin." But we are commanded to labor. Out of the voiceless silence of the ages past comes the command that "in the sweat of our faces" shall we eat bread. Thus in this, as in many other passages of the Bible, labor is not only sanctioned, but is sanctified; and we read each time with renewed consolation the invitation of the Son of man to "Come unto me, all ye that labor and are heavy laden, and I will give you rest."

Mr. Speaker, there is nothing more ennobling than honest toil, and none more noble than the honest toiler. In every age, in every clime, in every condition of human progress, he has borne more than his share of the burdens of the fight. In every battle for human liberty he has been in the forefront, willing to give his life, if necessary, that others might have life and have it more abundantly. When home and country have been in need of defense, he has harkened to the voice of duty and gone forth from those he loved to return no more. In religion, in patriotism, in service to humanity, in the drudging hardships of camp and quarry, of field and factory, the man who works and the woman who works have contributed more to the welfare of the world than all the hosts combined whose claim to our remembrance is bolstered chiefly through the "boasts of heraldry or the pomp of power." And some day, somewhere, I hope to see erected to those who toil and have toiled, or shall ever toil, a monument more beautiful, more imposing, and more lasting than any that has been erected in the name of cruel war or selfish greed. [Applause.]

Imbued deeply with the sentiments I have sought feebly to express, it is not strange that I place myself upon the side of those who favor the amendment to this bill, which exempts labor organizations and farmers' organizations from the operation of the antitrust law.

In support of that amendment, I submit that it was never the intention of Congress to apply the antitrust laws to such organizations, and if they had intended it such intention would have been wrong. The object in view in passing the antitrust laws was to strike at and destroy an evil, to curb monopoly, and punish combinations and conspiracies in restraint of trade. No one will contend, in the light of history, that labor unions or farmers' organizations are an evil; but, on the contrary, they have been greatly beneficial to those who labor in factory, field, or shop, and the blessings flowing therefrom have been shared by many indirectly who were not members of such organizations.

The offense denounced by the Sherman antitrust law is that of combining or conspiring in restraint of trade. Can it be said that an organization of men who work with their hands, who have organized for mutual help, for improving the conditions of labor, or advancing the wages which they receive is a combination or conspiracy in restraint of trade? Manifestly such an interpretation of the law would be an injustice to labor. Can it be said that an organization of farmers, who have organized for mutual protection and in order to insure an adequate price for the products which they have dug from the soil, is an illegal combination in restraint of trade? Such a construction of the law would be unjust and unwarranted. The great trusts and monopolies are offensive organizations. They are organized for profit and exploitation. Laboring men and farmers have been compelled to organize in self-defense in order to protect themselves against the rapacity of those whose acts are denounced by the Sherman antitrust law.

So that we may in truth say that this amendment exempting such organizations from the operation of the antitrust law gives to labor and to agriculture what it asks and is entitled to. It recognizes the difference between the man whose only asset is his power to work and the man who seeks to use labor and the products of labor for monopolistic purposes. It recognizes the self-evident truth that all real wealth in the final analysis is produced by those who toil, and that therefore the man who toils and eats his bread in the sweat of his brow has a moral and legal right to cooperate with others of his fellow men in the same condition for the purpose of mutual help, protection, and improvement not only of the conditions of labor, but for the advancement of the compensation which he receives therefor.

This principle was recognized in the Democratic platforms of 1908 and 1912, when a plank was incorporated therein advocating the thing we are now about to write into this law. It is gratifying to be able at this time, when the Democratic Party is engaged in writing into the statutes new laws for the reestablishment of legitimate conditions of business, to place in the law a provision giving to labor a legal status. And as business under the provisions of this bill will be eventually liberated from the unwholesome conditions which have crippled and shackled it in the past, so will the man who with his hands makes business and prosperity possible receive that share of legal recognition to which he is entitled. And I hope and believe that the provision under discussion will be overwhelmingly adopted. [Applause.]

In conclusion, Mr. Speaker, I desire to call attention briefly to the great work which has been accomplished by the present Democratic administration in carrying out the platform pledges and enacting laws for the benefit of the whole people of the United States.

On the 4th day of March, 1913, the Democrats obtained control of every branch of the National Government. President Woodrow Wilson came into office as the first Democratic President in 16 years, having behind him the loyal support of a Democratic Senate and House of Representatives. He called Congress into extraordinary session on April 7, 1913, and since that date it has been in continuous session. During that length of time it has revised the tariff downward, in accordance with the mandate of the people and the doctrines of the Democratic Party. Our party has always advanced and fought for the principle that the taxing power of the Government should not be used except for the collection of public revenue sufficient to carry on the Government economically administered, and that it ought not to be exercised to enrich a few at the expense of the masses. The Democratic tariff of 1913 recognized that principle in every detail.

During the period since the Democratic Party came into power it has placed upon the statutes an income tax, which has been demanded by the American people for nearly a generation. Under this law the swollen wealth of the country will contribute its just proportion toward the expenses of Government, whereas heretofore it has enjoyed the benefits of this Government without contributing to its support in proportion to the benefits received and the ability to pay. The Democratic Party has for many years, in and out of season, without ceasing, and without shadow of turning, advocated the passage of an income-tax law, and we are now able to see the result of its efforts crystallized into a law which all men now recognize as just and equitable.

During that period the Democratic administration has passed a law reforming and reorganizing the banking and currency laws of the United States, a task which had been ignored by the Republican Party for 50 years. The passage of that law meant the death knell of the Money Trust; the impossibility of Nation-wide financial panics; makes it impossible for a few high financiers to concentrate the money of this country in Wall Street; extends a strong, helping hand to the farmer, while fully protecting the interests of the business man and the banker; provides for the establishment of foreign branches to take care of our foreign commerce; provides for the issuance of elastic currency, which will meet the demands of trade in every season and in every part of the United States; and takes from the hands of a few money manipulators the power to control the financial policy of this Government and places it with the people through their constituted authorities, where it ought to be. When this new system has been fully organized and put in operation it is the belief of all classes of our people that it will prove itself to be one of the greatest pieces of constructive legislation ever enacted by Congress.

In addition to these things, the administration of President Wilson has been instrumental in eliminating from Washington a lobby which in former times has exercised a baneful influence upon legislation. It has secured the repeal of that provision of the Panama Canal act which gave to a shipping monopoly a subsidy of nearly $2,000,000 per annum out of the pockets of the people. It has caused to be signed treaties with more than half the nations of the world providing for the arbitration of international disputes, thus hastening the day when peace may dwell among the peoples of the world and the staggering expenditures for war and its horrors may be greatly reduced.

It has passed the industrial employees' arbitration act, providing for mediation, conciliation, and arbitration in controversies between employers and employees.

It has developed and extended the Parcel Post System to a high degree of perfection, resulting in a reduction of rates and an increase in the size of packages, making home life for the city man and for the farmer easier and cheaper.

It has inaugurated in the Department of Agriculture a system of markets whereby scientific and modern business methods will be applied toward the elimination of waste in transporting and distributing farm products.

It has passed the Lever bill providing for farm-extension work, which is designed to increase greatly the productiveness of American farms and thereby add to the general wealth of the Nation. It is intended to carry directly to the farm all the scientific discoveries of the Department of Agriculture and the State agricultural colleges. When it is remembered that during last year the farmers of the United States created nine billions of wealth, the importance of the passage of such a bill can be easily understood.

It has passed through the House of Representatives and hopes to pass through the Senate a bill granting Government aid to the different States and their subdivisions for the construction and maintenance of good roads, thus making more easy the transportation of farm products and adding to the prosperity and happiness of the people.

Many other important matters of legislation and administration for the benefit of the people have been inaugurated, to which I can not call attention for lack of time. And now Congress is engaged in the passage of these bills to supplement the antitrust laws, to prevent overcapitalization of railroads engaged in interstate commerce, to curb and restrain and, as far as possible, destroy monopoly and restore honest and practical competition in trade. And in addition to this it has under course of preparation bills for the establishment of a practical and effective system of rural credits, which will afford to those engaged in farming facilities for obtaining credit on long time and at lower rates of interest than are at present available, which we hope to enact into law in the near future, and which we hope will result in permanent good to those who need credit, that they may establish homes and finance their agricultural enterprises with greater chances of success than is possible under conditions as they exist at present. [Applause.]

Such a record, Mr. Speaker, is sufficient to cause any party or any administration to feel that its labors have not been in vain. Such a record is sufficient to demonstrate to the country that the Democratic Party knows how to serve the people, and that it has the courage and the intelligence to go forward instead of backward; that it has the patience to tire not in well-doing; and that it has the foresight to strive for the accomplishment of those things which shall in the end make for industrial peace at home and international peace abroad, and set a new mark in the advancement of the ages which shall reflect honor upon our efforts and glory upon our flag. [Applause.] . . .

Mr. [ROBERT] CROSSER [D., Ohio]. Mr. Chairman, there is no economic problem which engages the attention of the people so much as the trust or monopoly evil. The iron hand of monopoly is felt by every person in the United States, and indeed by the people throughout the world. It is well that the public mind is aroused, because failure to check the growth of monopolies and failure to prevent the ravages of those already in existence will result in industrial slavery.

What is a monopoly and what is its source of power to oppress? It is created by welding together all of the industries which produce any article and placing this combination under one control. There is then no one to offer at a lower price articles similar to those produced by the monopoly. In other words there is no competition. The monopolist can then demand and receive all the public can and will pay rather than be without the article in question. The monopoly being the only employer of the kind of labor required in the production of the article which it alone produces, can and does say what such labor will be paid as wages. The customer must pay what the monopoly or trust demands for its product, or do without, as no other can offer the same for sale. The workman skilled only in making the thing sold by the monopoly must accept the wages it offers or do without and try to learn some other business.

It does not require much thought to enable any man to understand the danger to free men from the tyrannical power which monopolies can wield. Every earnest man who thinks for a moment of others agrees that something should be done to limit the power if not destroy monopolies. As a remedy we have now before this House a measure called "A bill to supplement existing laws against unlawful restraints and monopolies." I intend to vote for this bill, for while I do not believe that we shall get complete relief from it, I am ready and anxious to support any measure which will do something toward breaking the power of monopoly. But will this proposed law accomplish the desired result? I am anxious that it should strip monopoly of its power, and yet I can only feel that it will do much better in the way of regulation than the present law.

I believe that this bill is the most perfect development thus far of the plan to solve the problem of monopoly by control and regulation. But the job of controlling and regulating a monopoly is much the same as if you were to give a man your farm and then try to order when he should plow, where he should sow, at what price he should sell his crops, and to say that he should not talk to his neighboring farmer across the fence about the price of what they have to sell. You lost the right and power to control effectively when you gave away the farm, and so the people of the country are unable to control and regulate monopolies because they have given them the natural resources of the country. It makes little difference whether the grant was originally made to one person or to a number of persons. The true remedy and, in fact, the only real cure for the evils of monopoly is to restore to the public as far as possible these natural resources. If a tax sufficient to absorb economic rent were levied upon the real value of oil land, coal land, ore land, and other sources of raw material, we would find the strangle hold of monopoly soon loosened. No man or men could then afford to withhold from use the natural resources which they have gotten into their possession. In order to pay such a tax they would be compelled to make use of the land or resources under their control; and if they should do this, they would turn out their products in such quantities as to make it necessary to sell at a reasonable price in order to dispose of their output. The customers would then be able to buy the products more freely. Labor would receive higher wages, because of the increased demand for labor resulting from the using of resources heretofore held out of use by monopoly. Of course increased demand for anything, including labor, means that more must be paid to get it. Why have we not applied this simple remedy? Why do we give the earth to a few and then try to regulate them?

The explanation, it seems to me, is that men's minds usually accept, as an explanation for any difficulty, the cause which is most apparent and nearest to the trouble. So when we see a few men getting immense fortunes in a very short time, we begin to blame the men and try to regulate their actions. Restore to the people their rights in the natural resources of the country and the trust question will solve itself. This, as I have already suggested, can be done by taxation. But, answer some, this would not be fair to those who have paid for these privileges in the natural resources. Let me call your attention to the fact that the taxing of such resources at a rate about equal to its natural rent would simply prevent the monopoly from playing the dog-in-the-manger game of withholding the natural resources from use, but would still leave them the title and possession and a reasonable profit if they will but use them. The profit which has come to monopoly merely from the privilege of controlling the natural resources would of course be much reduced under the plan which I have suggested, but you who support the pending bill can not offer that as an objection to the plan. The very purpose of the bill before this House is to prevent the trusts or monopolies from getting an unfair profit. The plan of the bill reported by the committee is to leave the trusts in possession of their special privileges in the natural resources, but to tell them how to sell their product and to whom they must sell it, so that they will be fairer to the people. But if by taxation we compel the holders of the natural resources to use them or to let others use them, the natural law of supply and demand will reduce prices and raise wages, and this would mean prosperity for all.

There has been a great deal said during the debate on this bill about the proposal that labor unions shall not be subject to the terms of the antitrust law. We have observed the tearful anxiety of those who shudder at the very thought of class legislation when it appears to favor the cause of labor. Keeping in mind the purpose of this bill, does the so-called exception in favor of labor constitute class legislation? I claim that it does not.

The evil that the bill is intended to correct is the monopoly of the natural resources—to prevent a few persons from getting control of such portions of the earth as contain the raw material or means of production of the necessities and comforts of life. We have a natural and moral right to prevent a monopoly of the earth, the storehouse provided by God for the human family. We have a right and duty to destroy special privilege in the earth which was provided by the Creator, not for one or a few but for all His people. To permit anything else, to permit one or a few to own and absolutely control the earth, is to put the rest of mankind at the mercy of these few, because they can only live and labor on the terms made by the few.

But no man has any natural or moral right of ownership in another man's body or his power to labor, and therefore no man has any right to say that another shall or shall not work or to say that he shall not consult with his fellows about working or refusing to work or in regard to the terms of employment so long as the conference is free from violence. The same right as to his labor, whether manual or mental, must be conceded to the individual employer or if a corporation be the employer, then the officials of such corporation have the right to consult with one another or with like officials of some or all other corporations in regard to the terms upon which they will do their work. This, however, is an entirely different thing from permitting a monopoly of the resources of the earth.

It is the old, old story of the struggle of the millions of human beings for the fruits of their toil, on the one hand, and by the holders of special privileges for the fruits of other men's toil on the other hand. And yet, all this is permitted in the name of justice. Millions of men and women toil wearily from day to day and drag out only a miserable existence. Countless children are without food enough to fully nourish them, and know not how to laugh. Mr. Chairman, we can not much longer tolerate such conditions. We must soon stop trying the time-worn plan of permitting a few men to monopolize the earth, and then trying to compel them by law to be kind enough to give others their just share of its fruits. We must go to the root of the evil. We must remove the cause by abolishing special privilege itself. . . .

Mr. [COURTNEY W.] HAMLIN [D., Mo.]. Mr. Chairman, I can not hope to say much within the time allotted me. I will say, however, that I am heartily in favor of the amendment offered by the chairman of the committee to section 7 of the bill. I do not believe that it would be right to place labor organizations, farmers' organizations, and fraternal organizations in the same category with organizations formed for the express and sole purpose of making money. One organizes for the purpose of uplifting humanity, the other for the purpose of exploiting humanity.

The present method of business is to put the brawn and muscles of human beings in one end of the scale and dollars in the other end and weigh it out, just as the grocer weighs out his sugar to a customer. This is revolting to any man who loves his fellow man. Involved on one side of the balance are the cold, unsympathetic dollars; on the other side are the lives, the happiness, and existence of human beings.

Surely the law ought to make a distinction between the two. Human happiness and human welfare ought not to be put on the auction block and knocked off to the highest bidder as a chattel may be. The only reason why trusts and combinations are declared illegal is because they are organized and operated for the express purpose of the more effectively exploiting the people by taking advantage of their necessities and controlling the price of these necessities to the consumers, as well as the purchase price which they have to pay for the raw material. They do this by consolidating or controlling all business in their line and thereby shutting out competition. Combinations of capital seek to control both the selling and purchasing price of all articles of necessity.

Labor seeks only to protect the selling price of one article, to wit, his brawn and muscle. This amendment protects the labor organizations, farmers' organizations, and fraternal organizations from the operation of the Sherman antitrust law, and in that the Democratic Party fulfills another pledge made in its platform.

I am truly glad to see our Republican friends lining up for this amendment; true some of us remember that for 16 long years of Republican rule they never found it convenient to protect the laborers of this country from the effects of the Sherman antitrust law, still we welcome them over to our standard and say we will gladly accept your votes even though you had to be forced to do it by a Democratic Congress.

I think that every Member here recognizes that one of the big questions before us it [sic] to deal fairly and right with labor and capital. For a long time I have felt that capital is largely responsible for the struggle that is on between the employer and the employee. Capital has been too domineering and selfish. I once heard the president of a large operating coal company, ⊥ in dealing with the demand of their employees for better wages, say, "What right have these d—n fellows to make demands on us and attempt to tell us how we shall run our business? We have thousands invested and they haven't a penny." I said to him, "That is where you are radically wrong. These laborers have infinitely more invested in the business than you have. You have only a portion of your money invested and these laborers have their very existence and the existence of their wives and children invested, and who can measure the love of a parent for his child, or who will attempt to do so in cold dollars and cents?" Mr. Chairman, let us not deal with the comfort and happiness of human beings as we deal with steel rails, oil, and other commodities.

I repeat what I said in the beginning, that labor organizations and farmers' organizations ought not to be placed in the same category with organizations formed for the express purpose of making money. I hope this amendment will be adopted. . . .

Mr. [JOHN J.] CASEY [D., Pa.]. Mr. Chairman, it was with considerable interest I took up the study of this very important measure. The more I delved into it the more and more I became impressed with the absolute need of an amendment such as has been offered by the gentleman from North Carolina [Mr. WEBB]. I realize and appreciate the importance of this bill, because I believe it is one of the most important that has or will come before this House for consideration.

ORIGINAL CLAUSE UNSATISFACTORY.

When it was reported by the Judiciary Committee I, as well as a number of my colleagues, went over it with careful deliberation, section by section, and when we reached section 7 it was apparent that it did not and could not meet expectations.

We asked the committee to change the phraseology so as to give labor organizations and farmers' organizations and beneficial societies the recognition promised in the Democratic platform. After some consideration the committee agreed to do so.

I desire to say to the Members who are hesitating about voting for the amendment that it is my sincere belief that the Webb amendment gives labor, gives the farmers, and gives the beneficial organizations the relief they are seeking. And I want to add that by following the recommendations of the Judiciary Committee we are doing that which the members of the great American Federation of Labor, what the members of the great Brotherhoods of Railroad Trainmen, the Railroad Conductors, the Railroad Firemen, the Railroad Engineers, and the farmers' organizations, that are directly and vitally interested in this legislation, desire we should do.

DISTINCT LINE DRAWN.

In consideration of their wishes, in consideration of the great moral issue involved, and in consideration of the world desire to draw the line between labor and its product, and in consideration of the desire to give the farmer as well as the laborer a greater scope, so that they may develop, so that they may live with a greater degree of comfort, so that they may prosper; and when these great forces are content the leaven of a greater and better mankind will dominate in this country; and I ask you, in consideration of all these things, to adopt the amendment offered by the gentleman from North Carolina [Mr. WEBB], chairman of the Judiciary Committee.

Mr. Chairman, wherever the working people have made progress some form of organization has been the agency that has transformed individual impotency into collective strength—fraternities, lodges, merchant guilds, craft guilds have been helpful; but the labor unions—trades-unions—have been the most potent factors in the forward movement.

HIGHER STANDARD OF LIFE.

The demand for higher wages represents the conviction that a constantly greater share of increased social wealth should go to those who create it. The progress of humanity results from the elimination of poverty. Poverty means degrading environment and influence that result in intellectual and moral degeneration. Permanent amelioration of the human lot must have as its basis material resources. The next step is to distribute these products so that the greatest number may fairly benefit thereby. As an element in the forces determining distribution, the trade-union has been most potent. A comparison of conditions prevailing among the unorganized with those that have employed collective bargaining reveals unmistakable proofs of the beneficent results due to trade-unionism. Higher wages mean better homes, better clothing, better food, better bodies and minds, recreation, a higher standard of life.

The aim for a higher standard of life is the incentive for the demand for a shorter workday. The verdicts of modern scientists are confirming the fundamental importance of this demand which the trade-union has so long been pressing. These scientists are warning us against the danger to the race from the continuous industrial strain and concentration of energy in modern industry. Commerce and industry can be allowed to exploit the leisure of the workers only at the expense of national well-being. The shorter workday means increased efficiency of the worker in the shop, better, longer, and happier living, and development of the higher emotions and feelings. It increases the productive period of the worker, lengthens his life, and enables him longer to provide for those dependent upon him, that the children may have an opportunity to taste of the pleasures of child life before assuming the burdens of the human "struggle for existence."

CONSERVE HUMAN RESOURCES.

This more efficient, more human worker demands better working conditions, the aim being to conserve human resources. Much has been done to let pure air and sunshine into working places, to exclude conditions breeding organisms injurious to life, but ever-increasing knowledge and the widening of our conception forbid us to stop or stay in the crusade for human welfare. Among all the organizations on the American continent working upon the various phases of this great problem, in my opinion, the great American Federation of Labor is the leader, and has often been the pioneer blazing the way.

These three demands of organized labor are comprehended in this larger and ultimate ideal—to enrich, enlarge, and magnify humanity. The influence and the potency of the American labor movement are so well appreciated by the thinkers and leaders in our Nation's affairs that almost every considerable movement for humanitarian, economic, or political reform has endeavored to enlist their approval and support. Men of labor play an honorable and important part in the affairs of this great Nation. They are daily helping to determine its destiny.

For years the laboring people have contended that the Sherman antitrust law was never intended to apply and should not have been applied to the voluntary organizations of the working people. By reason of the decision of the Supreme Court in the Hatters' case, and of several courts in other cases, that law was made to apply to organizations of workers. It is unnecessary at this time to recount the various phases and the developments of the efforts to secure remedial legislation which the working people of the country have so long and so justly demanded.

THE SEVENTH SECTION.

In this bill, dealing with supplementary legislation on the Sherman antitrust law, is incorporated the following section as amended:

"Section 7. That nothing contained in the antitrust laws shall be construed to forbid the existence and operation of fraternal, labor, consumers', agricultural, or horticultural organizations, orders or associations instituted for the purpose of mutual help and not having capital stock or conducted for profit, or to forbid or restrain individual members of such organizations, orders, or associations from carrying out the legitimate objects thereof, nor shall such organizations, orders, or associations, or the members thereof be held or construed to be illegal combinations or conspiracies in restraint of trade under the antitrust laws."

There are other sections of this bill which deal with the regulation and limitation of the issuance of injunctions. There are sections dealing with the subject of the regulation of contempt proceedings and providing for jury trials in alleged indirect contempts. The section dealing with injunctions as amended, in which labor is primarily interested, is as follows:

"SEC. 18. That no restraining order or injunction shall be granted by any court of the United States, or a judge or the judges thereof, in any case between an employer and employee, or between employers and employees, or between employees, or between persons employed and persons seeking employment, involving or growing out of a dispute concerning terms or conditions of employment, unless necessary to prevent irreparable injury to property, or to a property right, of the party making the application, for which injury there is no adequate remedy at law, and such property or property right must be described with particularity in the application, which must be in writing and sworn to by the applicant or by his agent or attorney.

THE RESTRAINING HAND.

"And no such restraining order or injunction shall prohibit any person or persons from terminating any relation of employment or from ceasing to perform any work or labor, or from recommending, advising, or persuading others by peaceful means so to do, or from attending at or near a house or place where any ⊥ person resides or works or carries on business or happens to be, for the purpose of peacefully obtaining or communicating information, or of peacefully persuading any person to work or to abstain from working; or from ceasing to patronize or to employ any party to such dispute, or from recommending, advising, or persuading others by peaceful means so to do; or from paying or giving to or withholding from any person engaged in such dispute, any strike benefits or other moneys or things of value; or from peacefully assembling at any place in a lawful manner, and for lawful purposes; or from doing any act or thing which might lawfully be done in absence of such dispute by any party thereto, nor shall any of the acts specified in this paragraph be considered or held unlawful.

CONTEMPT CASES; JURY TRIALS.

"SEC. 19. That any person who shall willfully disobey any lawful writ, process, order, rule, decree, or command of any district court of the United States or any court of the District of Columbia by doing any act or thing therein, or thereby forbidden to be done by him, if the act or thing so done by him be of such character as to constitute also a criminal offense under any statute of the United States or at common law shall be proceeded against for his said contempt as hereinafter provided.

"SEC. 20. That whenever it shall be made to appear to any district court or judge thereof or to any judge therein sitting, by the return of a proper officer on lawful process, or upon the affidavit of some credible person, or by information filed by any district attorney, that there is reasonable ground to believe that any person has been guilty of such contempt, the court or judge thereof, or any judge therein sitting, may issue a rule requiring the said person so charged to show cause upon a day certain why he should not be punished therefor; which rule, together with a copy of the affidavit or information, shall be served upon the person charged with sufficient promptness to enable him to prepare for and make return to the order at the time fixed therein. If upon or by such return, in the judgment of the court the alleged contempt be not sufficiently purged, a trial shall be directed at a time and place fixed by the court: *Provided, however,* That if the accused, being a natural person, fail or refuse to make return to the rule to show cause, an attachment may issue against his person to compel an answer, and in case of his continued failure or refusal, or if for any reason it be impracticable to dispose of the matter on the return day, he may be required to give reasonable bail for his attendance at the trial and his submission to the final judgment of the court. Where the accused person is a body corporate, an attachment for the sequestration of its property may be issued upon like refusal or failure to answer.

"In all cases within the purview of this act such trial may be by the court or, upon demand of the accused, by a jury, in which latter event the court may impanel a jury from the jurors then in attendance, or the court or the judge thereof in chambers may cause a sufficient number of jurors to be selected and summoned, as provided by law, to attend at the time and place of trial, at which time a jury shall be selected and impaneled as upon a trial for misdemeanor; and such trial shall conform, as near as may be, to the practice in criminal cases prosecuted by indictment or upon information.

THE PUNISHMENT PRESCRIBED.

"SEC. 21. That the evidence taken upon the trial of any person so accused may be preserved by bill of exceptions, and any judgment of conviction may be reviewed upon writ of error in all respects as now provided by law in criminal cases, and may be affirmed, reversed, or modified, as justice may require. Upon the granting of such writ of error, execution of judgment shall be stayed and the accused, if thereby sentenced to imprisonment, shall be admitted to bail in such reasonable sum as may be required by the court, or by any justice, or any judge of any district court of the United States or any court of the District of Columbia.

"SEC. 22. That nothing herein contained shall be construed to relate to contempts committed in the presence of the court, or so near thereto as to obstruct the administration of justice, nor to contempts committed in disobedience of any lawful writ, process, order, rule, decree, or command entered in any suit or action brought or prosecuted in the name of or on behalf of the United States, but the same and all other cases of contempt not specifically embraced within section 19 of this act may be punished in conformity to the usages at law and in equity now prevailing.

"SEC. 23. That no proceeding for contempt shall be instituted against any person unless begun within one year from the date of the act complained of; nor shall any such proceeding be a bar to any criminal prosecution for the same act or acts; but nothing herein contained shall affect any proceedings in contempt pending at the time of the passage of this act."

SOCIETY AND JUSTICE.

The foregoing paragraphs, as amended by the Judiciary Committee, indicate plainly that justice is the purpose toward which society is groping slowly—uncertainly yet ultimately. The ideal may change and shift, but justice ever remains the goal. The law of the land embodies concepts of rights that must be granted individuals to secure them freedom of self-development and action. Justice exists when these rights are accorded to all individuals.

To the courts of our country belongs the duty of making justice a forceful reality in the lives of men. The courts are the guardians of the rights and ideals of the Nation. They are the agencies by which justice is brought into the lives of people. If they do justice, they create respect for governmental authority. If they deny justice, they create contempt for law and rebellion against governmental authority.

American courts have an unusually grave responsibility, for their power has become practically unlimited. Their power to interpret law and to pass upon its constitutionality makes them superior to the legislatures. Judges are the least responsible of all our governmental agents.

An independent judiciary is necessary for purity of justice. Yet this very independence constitutes a menace, for judges are human, and may allow practices and concepts to become established which pervert justice. Such perversions of justice have been the reason for all the great legal reforms. Such perversions of equity courts now demand reform.

POWER OF EQUITY COURTS.

Equity courts were established in England to infuse into legalism a morality which was precluded by the strict letter of the law. Practically all equity law has resulted from judicial legislation. The judge makes the law, determines whether or not his law is violated, and determines the penalty for any violations of his law. Therefore equity proceedings reflect the personal attitude of mind, convictions, and animus of the individual judge.

The power built up by equity courts in the United States is unlimited. Like all arbitrary power, it has been abused. The particular class of abuses that has caused the greatest injustice and has aroused most bitter discontent is the use of the injunctive process in industrial disputes to regulate personal relations and to assume the functions of the law courts.

The writ of injunction was intended to protect property against injury from which the law afforded no protection. Under the influences of judges who had no personal knowledge of industrial affairs, no sympathy with workers in industry, and no understanding of the difference between property rights and personal rights, injunctions have been issued for the purposes which transform the agencies of justice into engines of injustice and oppression.

BURDENS OF INDUSTRY.

Those who bear the burdens of industry and the brunt of whatever injustice prevails have for years, in protest, called attention to grievous wrongs that have been inflicted upon them by the courts.

The effort to secure decent working conditions, a fair wage, and reasonable hours of work has involved the workers in a struggle with all the forces of greed and intrenched power, whose aim is to deny the growing economic and social demands of the workers.

The struggle has not infrequently degenerated into a conscienceless war to hold the workers in subordination and in the domination of every political agent to accomplish this purpose. Judges have been induced to serve this purpose—some consciously and some unconsciously. Injunctions have been issued that deny workers rights guaranteed them by constitutional and statutory laws; that deny workers freedom of speech, press, and normal action.

Judges have sentenced workers for doing that which they have a lawful right to do; have sentenced them for violations of the injunctions when the injunctions themselves were issued in direct contravention of specific inhibitions of law. Let us present the basic principles which determine the jurisdiction of equity courts and limit their powers.

INJUNCTIONS AND THEIR IMPORT.

The writ of injunction should be exercised exclusively for the protection of property and property rights.

To secure the aid of equity courts by the injunction process the petitioner must have no other remedy at law.

He who seeks equity must come into court with clean hands.

The injunction writ must never be used to regulate personal relations or to curtail personal rights.

⊥ Equity power—injunctions—must never be used in an effort to punish crime. This is the function of the law courts.

The equity courts must not be used as a means to set aside trial by jury.

In all America there is not a man learned in the law who will dispute that the principles just stated are the fundamental bases for equity procedure in the issuance of injunctions.

DEMANDS FOR JUSTICE.

Mr. Chairman, though courts have jailed workers, they have not silenced indignant protest or stifled or jailed love and demand for justice. Though they have jailed workers for contempt of unwarranted judicial orders, they have not been able to jail their contempt for arbitrary abuse and usurpation of authority. With defiant challenge of wrong, the workers demand that the courts of justice be restored to their rightful purposes; that they be made the courts of all the people, and not the courts of a privileged class—the employing class. There are those who believe that American workers exaggerate the need for legislation to prevent abuses of the injunctive process. There are others who wish to create that impression in order to retain the special privileges and advantages these abuses afford them. All the forces of prejudice and greed are lined up to prevent legislation which shall free the workers from restrictions upon normal efforts to protect and further their own material interests.

GOVERNMENT BY INJUNCTION.

What is "government by injunction" or, in other words, the misuse of the equity power? It is the modern use of the writ of injunction, especially in labor disputes, which is revolutionary and destructive of popular government.

Our Government was designed to be a government by law, said law to be enacted by the legislative branch, construed by the judiciary, and administered by the executive.

An injunction is "an extraordinary writ issued out of equity enjoining a threatened injury to property or property rights where there is not a plain, adequate, and complete remedy at law."

The definition of equity is: "The application of right and justice to the legal adjustment of differences where the law, by reason of its universality is deficient" or "that system of jurisprudence which comprehends every matter of law for which the common law provides no remedy * * * springing originally from the royal prerogative, moderating the harshness of the common law according to good conscience." In other words, it is the exercise of power according to the judgment and conscience of one man.

PROPERTY RIGHTS.

It was for this reason that in Great Britain, whence the United States derives its system of equity, as well as of law, the equity power was limited to the protection of property or property rights, and in such cases only where there was no remedy at law; the words adequate and complete have been added here.

When the courts of equity take jurisdiction over and issue injunctions in labor disputes they do so to protect business, which, under late rulings by several courts, is held to be property. These rulings are disputed and condemned by other courts, which hold that relations between employers and employees—between buyer and seller—are personal relations, and as such, if regulated at all, are regulated by statute or common law only. If the latter contention be right, and of this we believe there can be no question, the ruling that makes business property or the right to carry on or continue in business a property right is revolutionary and must lead to a complete change, not only in our industrial, but in our political life. If the court of equity be permitted to regulate personal relations, it will gradually draw to itself all legislative power. If it be permitted to set aside or to enforce law, it will ultimately arrogate to itself jurisdiction now held by the law courts and abolish trial by jury.

LAW AND EQUITY.

The Constitution confers equity power upon the courts by stating that they shall have jurisdiction in law and in equity in the same way that it makes it their duty to issue the writ of habeas corpus and in substantially the same way as it provides for trial by jury. Equity power came to us as it existed in England at the time of the adoption of our Constitution, and it was so limited and defined by English authorities that our courts could not obtain jurisdiction in labor disputes except by the adoption of a ruling that business is property.

If business be property in the case of a strike or boycott, and can therefore be protected by the equity court against diminution of its usual income, caused by a strike or boycott conducted by the working people, then it necessarily must be property at other times and therefore entitled to be protected against loss of income caused by competition from other manufacturers or business men. Business and the income from business would become territorial and would be in the same position as land and the income from land. The result would be to make all competition in trade unlawful; it would prevent anyone from engaging in trade or manufacture unless he comply with the whims and fancies of those who have their trade or means of production already established.

No one could enter into business except through inheritance, bequest, or sale.

DEFINITION OF PROPERTY.

In order to show the fallacy of this new definition of property we here state the accepted legal definitions of property, business, and labor.

Definition of property: Property means the dominion of indefinite right of user and disposition which one lawfully exercises over particular things or subjects and generally to the exclusion of all others. Property is ownership, the exclusive right of any person freely to use, enjoy, and dispose of any determinate object, whether real or personal. (English and American Encyclopedia of Law.)

Property is the exclusive right of possessing, enjoying, and disposing of a thing. (Century Dictionary.)

A right imparting to the owner a power of indefinite user, capable of being transmitted to universal successors by way of descent, and imparting to the owner the power of disposition from himself and his successors. (Austin, Jurisprudence.)

SOLE DESPOTIC DOMINION.

The sole and despotic dominion which one claims and exercises over the external things of the world in total exclusion of the right of any other individual in the world. (Blackstone.)

It will be seen that property is the products of nature or of labor, and the essential element is that it may be disposed of by sale, be given away, or in any other way transferred to another.

There is no distinction in law between property and property rights.

From these definitions it is plain that labor power or patronage can not be property, but aside from this we have the thirteenth amendment to the Constitution prohibiting slavery and involuntary servitude.

LABOR AND PROPERTY.

Labor power can not be property, because it can not be separated from the laborer. It is personal. It grows with health, diminished in sickness, and ceases at death. It is an attribute of life.

The ruling of certain courts makes of the laborer a serf, of patronage an evidence of servitude, by assuming that one may have a property right in the labor or patronage of another.

Definition of business: That which occupies the time, attention, and labor of men for the purpose of livelihood or profit; that which occupies the time, attention, and labor of man for the purpose of profit and improvement. (American and English Encycl. of Law.)

That which busies or that which occupies the time, attention, or labor of one as his principal concern, whether for a longer or shorter time. (Webster's Dictionary.)

Definition of labor: Physical or mental effort, particularly for some useful or desired end. Exertion of the powers for some end other than recreation or sport. (Century Dictionary.)

It will be seen from the definitions that while there is a fundamental difference between property and business there is none at all between business and labor, so that if business be property, so is labor, and if the earning power of business can be protected by equity power through injunction, so can the earning power of labor; in other words, the laborer may obtain an injunction against a reduction of his wages or against a discharge, which would stop the wages entirely.

If this new definition of property, by including therein business and labor, be accepted, then the judge sitting in equity becomes the irresponsible master of all men who do business or who labor.

DISCRETIONARY GOVERNMENT.

We contend that equity power and jurisdiction—discretionary government by the judiciary—for well-defined purposes and within specific limitations granted to the courts by the Constitution, has been so extended that it is invading the field of government by law and endangering constitutional liberty; that is, the personal liberty of the individual citizen.

As government by equity—personal government—advances, republican government—government by law—recedes.

We have escaped from the despotic government of the king. We realized that, after all, he was but a man. Are we going to permit the growing up of a despotic government by the judges? Are not they also men?

⊥ PRESERVATION OF LIBERTY.   ⊥9560

The despotism of one can, in this sense, be no better than the despotism of another. If we are to preserve "government of the people, by the people, and for the people," any usurpation by the judiciary must be as sternly resisted as usurpation by the executive.

What labor is now seeking is the assistance of all liberty-loving men in restoring the common-law definitions of property, and in restricting the jurisdiction of the equity courts in that connection to what it was at the time of the adoption of the Constitution.

To those who ask proof of the justice of labor's demands for correction of abuses of the injunctive process there is no better proof than can be found in the injunctions of Judge Dayton, of the Federal District Court for the Northern District of West Virginia. No injunctions have been more persistent, arbitrary, flagrant abuses of judicial power than those issued by that court.

CONDITIONS IN WEST VIRGINIA.

Conditions in that district are conducive to such abuses—West Virginia is a corporation-ridden State. The coal companies own vast tracts of territory over which they exercise practically absolute control. Their great industrial power has created the false impression that profits for the companies are tantamount to prosperity for the State. The companies have been allowed to interpret what constitutes prosperity and how it shall be maintained. Company managers are held responsible for profits.

Naturally they condemn anything that decreases profits or "interferes" with business. That human rights may conflict with property rights is to them of no consequence, for they think property rights only concern profits. As what could not be accomplished in "other ways" was done through injunctions—the coal fields of West Virginia have been an injunction-governed district.

WORKERS DENIED CERTAIN RIGHTS.

The injunction rule that Judge Jackson inaugurated Judge Dayton has maintained with great "efficiency." The purpose of that rule is to deny free workers the right to organize in order to better their working conditions. Every agent of Government and force has been used to maintain the mines nonunion—to maintain the same "freedom" that the Colorado Fuel & Iron Co. is trying to force upon the miners of Colorado. The serious injustice that has resulted is most conclusively demonstrated by the injunctions issued by Judge Dayton against the coal miners during the strike of 1912–13.[5.545]

The West Virginia-Pittsburgh Coal Co., incorporated under the laws of West Virginia, and operating large coal mines in the northern Panhandle district of West Virginia, petitioned for and obtained from Judge Dayton, on September 29, 1913, a temporary restraining order. The restraining order forbade the officers of the United Mine Workers, "their committees, agents, servants, confederates, and associates, and all persons who now are, or hereafter may be, members of said United Mine Workers of America, and all persons combining and conspiring with the said designated persons, and all other persons whomsoever, and each and every one of them" from organizing the company's mines, from "conspiring" to inaugurate a strike against the company, or from doing anything to aid in any strike against the company. The restraining order with slight modifications was made a preliminary injunction December 2, 1913.

OUTRAGE AGAINST RIGHTS.

Mr. Chairman, the injunction is so preposterous, such an outrage against the rights of the workers, such an arrogant usurpation of power, that the specific inhibitions are given in full. In reading the injunction and considering the things which the miners are forbidden to do, the extensive land holdings of the company should be held in mind. The miners lived in the company's houses, built upon the company's property. It was impossible for them to move outside their own dwellings without "trespassing" upon the company's land.

The wording of the injunction is also significant. The words are so chosen as to convey the idea that normal, lawful activities are "conspiracies." The injunction assumes the lawful right of the company to whatever relations with its employees will produce greatest profits, and to regard those relations as part of the right to do business. The "right to continue service" from employees is the basis for several prohibitions. Judge Dayton assumed that a strike is unlawful, that labor organizations and their purposes are illegal.

SPECIFIC PROHIBITIONS IN JUDGE DAYTON'S INJUNCTION.

The officers and the present and future members of the United Mine Workers, their associates, and all other persons are enjoined and restrained:

"1. From interfering and from combining, conspiring, or attempting to interfere with employees of the plaintiff for the purpose of unionizing plaintiff's mine, without plaintiff's permission and consent, and in aid of such purpose knowingly and willfully bringing about in any manner the breaking by plaintiff's employees of contracts of service known to them at the time to exist which plaintiff now has with his employees, and from knowingly and willfully bringing about in any manner the breaking by plaintiff's employees of contracts of service which may hereafter be entered into by persons with plaintiff and be known to them, while the relationship of the employer and employee as to such employee so brought to break his contract exists, and especially from knowingly and willfully enticing plaintiff's employees, present or future,

---

[5.545] Hitchman Coal & Coke Co. v. Mitchell, 202 F. 512 (N.D. W. Va. 1912), *rev'd*, 214 F. 685 (4th Cir. 1914), *rev'd*, 245 U.S. 229 (1917) (decree of district court modified, and, as modified, affirmed).

knowing such relationship, while the relationship of the employer and employee, as to such employee enticed, exists, to leave plaintiff's service, giving or assigning directly or indirectly as a reason for any such act so brought about, or enticing and leaving the plaintiff's service, that plaintiff does not recognize the United Mine Workers of America, or that plaintiff runs a nonunion mine, or that the interests of the United Mine Workers of America require that plaintiff shall not be permitted to run a nonunion mine, or that the interests of the union will be best promoted thereby.

"2. From interfering and combining, conspiring, or attempting to interfere with the employees of plaintiff so as knowingly and willfully to bring about in any manner the breaking by the plaintiff's employees of contracts of service known to them at the time to exist, which plaintiff has with its employees, and from knowingly and willfully bringing about in any manner the breaking by plaintiff's employees of contracts of service which may hereafter be entered into by persons with plaintiff, and be known to them, while the relationship of employer and employee, as to such employee so brought to break his contract exists, and especially from knowingly and willfully enticing plaintiff's employees, present or future, knowing such relationship of employer and employee as to such employee so enticed exists, to leave plaintiff's service without plaintiff's consent, against plaintiff's will, and to plaintiff's injury.

SOME STARTLING SPECIFICATIONS.

"3. From interfering with, hindering, or obstructing the business of plaintiff, or its agents, servants, or employees, in the discharge of their duties as such, at and about plaintiff's mines or elsewhere, by trespassing on or entering upon the grounds and premises of the plaintiff, or within its mines for the purpose of interfering therewith, or hindering or obstructing its business in any manner whatsoever, or with the purpose of compelling or inducing, by threats, or force, intimidation, violence, violent or abusive language, or persuasion, any of the employees of plaintiff to refuse or fail to perform their duties as such employees.

"4. From compelling or inducing, or attempting to compel or induce, by threats, intimidation, force, or violence, or abusive or violent language, any of the employees of plaintiff to leave its service or fail or refuse to perform their duties as such employees, or to compel or attempt to compel by threats, intimidation, force, violent or abusive language, any person desiring to seek employment in or about the plaintiff's mine and works from so accepting employment therein.

"5. From entering upon or establishing a picket or pickets of men on or patrolling railroads or highways, public or private, passing through or adjacent to the plaintiff's property for the purpose of inducing or compelling by threats, intimidation, violence, violent or abusive language, or persuasion, any employee of plaintiff to fail or refuse to perform his duties as such, or for the purpose of interviewing or talking to any person or persons on said railroad or highways coming to plaintiff's mines to accept employment with plaintiff, for the purpose and with the intention of inducing and compelling them, by threats, violence, intimidation, violent or abusive language, persuasion, or in any other manner whatsoever, to refuse or fail to accept service with plaintiff.

REGULATING THE EMPLOYEE.

"6. From compelling or inducing or attempting to compel or induce by threats, force, intimidation, or violent or abusive language any employee of said plaintiff to refuse or fail to perform his duties as such employee; and from compelling or attempting to compel, induce by threats, intimidation, force, or violence, or abusive or violent language, any such employee to leave the service of plaintiff; and by like methods to prevent or attempt to prevent any person desiring to accept employment with plaintiff in or about its mines or works or elsewhere from doing so by threats, violence, intimidation, or violent or abusive language.

"7. From interfering in any manner whatsoever, either by threats, violence, intimidation, persuasion, or entreaty with any person in the employment of plaintiff who has contracted with ⊥ and is in the actual service of plaintiff, to entice or induce him to quit the service of plaintiff or fail or refuse to perform his duties under this contract of employment, and from ordering, aiding, directing, assisting, or abetting in any manner whatsoever any person or persons to commit any or either of the acts aforesaid.

"8. From congregating at or near the premises of plaintiff, and from picketing or patrolling said premises for the purpose of intimidating plaintiff's employees or coercing them by threats, intimidation, violence, abusive or violent language, or preventing them, in the manner aforesaid, from rendering their service to the plaintiff; and in like manner from inducing or coercing them to leave the employment of plaintiff; and from in any manner so interfering with the plaintiff in carrying on its business in its usual and ordinary way; and from interfering by threats, intimidation, violence, violent or abusive language, with any person or persons who may be employed or seek employment by plaintiff in the operation of the plaintiff's mines or works.

RIGHTS OF LABOR QUESTIONED.

"9. From either singly or in combination with others collecting in and about the approaches to plaintiff's mines and works for the purpose of picketing or patrolling or guarding the highway and approaches to the property of the plaintiff for the purpose of intimidating, threatening, or coercing any of plaintiff's employees from working in its said mines or works, or any person seeking employment therein, from entering into such employment, and from interfering with said employees in going to and from their daily work in and about the mines and works of plaintiff.

"10. And from either singly or collectively going to the homes and boarding homes of plaintiff's employees, or any of them, for the purpose of intimidating or coercing any or all of them to leave plaintiff's employment."

The injunction then enjoins the miners from "conspiring" to strike, from even using "persuasion" to "induce" employees to strike, from "trespassing," that is, going outside their homes for the purpose of "enticing" employees to leave the company's service. Can these workers be free if they do not have the right to stop work? If they have that right, how can they be restrained from "conspiring" to exercise it?

WHAT FREEDOM MEANS.

Mr. Chairman, have free workers a right to organize to promote their own welfare and happiness? How can they be restrained from conspiring to achieve that purpose, even without the permission of the company? In organization workers exercise personal rights. Note the skillful twist of this injunction specialist in the phrase "unionizing plaintiff's mine," which is intended to give the impression that property rights were endangered.

Note in section 3 another touch of the expert—"elsewhere"—limitless, boundless "elsewhere." And again "in any manner whatsoever." Can any judge be justified in forbidding the United Mine Workers from obstructing the business of the West Virginia-Pittsburgh Coal Co. "in any manner whatsoever"? Think of the manifold activities, perfectly legal, normal activities, covered by the phrase "in any manner whatsoever."

DESPOTIC LEGISLATION.

How can justice exist when a judge is permitted to issue injunctions which amount to despotic legislation? If even one judge may under existing conditions deprive even one worker of rights necessary to his freedom, then those existing conditions must be changed without delay. One human being is more valuable than a mine. But Judge Dayton ruthlessly trampled upon the rights of many workers, and by precedent all workers.

In section 5 the miners are forbidden to use railroads, private or public highways "passing through or adjacent to the plaintiff's property" for the purpose of "interviewing" or "talking to any person" or "in any manner whatsoever" to explain working conditions in the mines to enlist support for the cause of the strikers. Think of it—freedom of speech denied by an injunction in order to help the mine operators to keep their employees or "prospective employees" ignorant of their opposition to organized labor, higher wages, and better conditions of work.

The prohibitions of section 6 are not for the purpose of protecting mine property, but are for the very obvious purpose of helping the operators to fasten their grip upon their unorganized, impoverished employees. What property right has the West Virginia-Pittsburgh Coal Co. in the labor power of its employees? It has no property or property right in the labor of the mines. Then by what authority can any judge command workers not to induce fellow workers to refuse or fail to perform personal service—labor? If any of those conducting the strike should become too vehement in the manner of their inducement there is recourse at law for disturbance of the peace, and so forth. Assuming that the purpose of a judge in issuing an injunction may be good, yet by usurping authority, by establishing a precedent that constitutes a menace to free institutions, the issuance of that injunction is a greater and more far-reaching wrong than any act of violence by a worker overwrought from a sense of injustice.

ENTICE OR INDUCE ILLEGAL.

In section 7 members of organized labor and "all other persons whomsoever" are enjoined from interfering "in any manner" to "induce" the employees of the company to strike, or from ordering, aiding, directing, assisting, or abetting a strike "in any manner whatsoever." A strike is legal, yet this judge presumes to forbid free man [sic] to "entice or induce" free workers to "commit" legal acts.

What is the value of law if irresponsible judges may ignore it and substitute their own orders? How long can a constitutional government be maintained under judicial anarchy? How long can such a judiciary retain the respect of just, law-abiding citizens? Under section 7 of the injunction payment of strike benefits are prohibited: distribution of food and clothing to strikers and their families; every charitable impulse and every sympathetic desire to help those fighting for industrial justice are forbidden.

The prohibitions of section 8 are based upon the assumption that the right of the company to "carry on its business in its usual and ordinary way" is so sacred that the judicial authority of the United States may be exerted to protect that right and to prevent striking miners from securing higher wages and better working conditions.

Sections 9 and 10 prohibit the miners' officials and all persons whomsoever from singly or collectively using their influence with the company's employees or any seeking employment with the company to join the strikers' cause.

WRITTEN CONTRACTS BINDING.

The injunction contains several references to contracts of workers, implying that the company entered into written contracts with its employees equally binding upon both. Miners testified that they were hired from day to day under no formal contract; in fact, the only way the coal company could have had a contract with its employees was through the method it had rejected—collective bargaining with the representatives of its employees. Even had such a contract existed, it would give the employers no right to enforce performance of specific services.

The thirteenth amendment to the Constitution of the United States is a specific denial of such a right. It reads:

Neither slavery nor involuntary servitude, except as a punishment for crime whereof the party shall have been duly convicted, shall exist within the United States or any place subject to their jurisdiction.

Those who know the industrial world know the powerful, heartless force of greed which opposes betterment of working conditions in order to maintain high profits; they know the long, unending struggle of the workers from slavery up to greater freedom; they know that in law, philosophy, and even in common phrases of speech are incorporated principles or fragments of principles based upon the concept that workers are slaves. All these constitute barriers to the freedom and progress of the workers. Many eminent conscientious judges do not understand this struggle of labor in effort to establish distinctions between human rights and property rights and to secure legal recognition of human rights for those who labor.

TRADITION MOLDS SYMPATHIES.

This injunction issued by Judge Dayton is typical of the injustice done by those whose habit of thought and sympathies are molded by traditions of the sacredness of property. Government was first established to protect property, but its functions have been constantly widened until now they extend to the protection of individuals and their rights as human beings. Some judges have not yet sensed this development; such a one is Judge Dayton, another is Judge Taft, one of those who inaugurated the practice of using injunctions to help employers against their employees in industrial conflicts.

Perhaps some qualm of an unsuspected conscience moved Judge Dayton to add the following paragraph to the temporary injunction:

The plaintiff's employees who have signed and entered into contracts introduced in evidence in this suit have the right at any time to terminate the contract and to go to work elsewhere, and when they have done so they have a perfect right to join the union of the United Mine Workers of America or any other labor union, and nothing in this order shall be construed as in any manner limiting their said rights.

A vague suspicion seems to be stirring in the judge's intellect, causing him to think that even labor unions may be legal in some localities. Perhaps he may have yet another idea, and ⊥ wonder how, if labor unions be lawful, men may be legally restrained from joining them.

JUDGE DAYTON'S CONTEMPT DECISIONS.

On November 11, 1913, the West Virginia-Pittsburgh Coal Co. filed a petition and several affidavits asking that Van Bittner, president of the Pittsburgh district of the United Mine Workers, several employees of the coal company, and Meyer Schwartz, a local storekeeper who had leased to the United Mine Workers land upon which to hold meetings, be attached for contempt of alleged violation of the restraining order.

The injunctions and the suit brought, as we have already shown, were for the purpose of enabling the coal company to invoke the assistance of a Federal court in its controversy with its employees concerning wages and hours of employment. Is not this occasion sufficiently serious to cause thoughtful citizens to ponder upon the effect that such interference will have upon the attitude of the workers toward governmental authority and their respect for law and the judiciary? Injustice ever begets discontent and demands for reform. A wise and generous nation will give heed to these demands, however crude their expression. Sea captains might as well scuttle their ship as to ignore signs of approaching storms. The workers will not always patiently endure both burdens and injustice.

In March, 1914, some thirteen or fourteen of the employees of the company and three or four organizers of the United Mine Workers were tried at Philippi, W. Va., a town situated at a distance of about 150 miles from the company's mines, although the original chancery suit had been docketed as Wheeling, only a few miles from the mines.

JUDGE DAYTON'S METHODS.

Judge Dayton tried the cases, of course, without a jury. Particularly significant of his judicial attitude is the fact that he permitted hearsay and all kinds of evidence to be introduced before him, declaring that he would later determine for himself what part of the evidence was legally admissible and what part should be excluded.

The court rested its decision upon the supposition that the United Mine Workers is an illegal conspiracy and took "judicial notice" that in the chancery cause of the Hitchman Coal & Coke Co. v. John Mitchell et al.,[5.546] an entirely separate and distinct case now pending in the United States Circuit Court of Appeals for the Fourth Circuit, the court had found and determined the United Mine Workers of America to be an unlawful organization, "an unlawful and criminal conspiracy both under common law and the Federal Sherman Trust Act."

It follows that if a Federal judge can "take judicial notice" that the United Mine Workers of America has been determined an illegal conspiracy in another case, now

---

[5.546] *Id.*

pending before the court, any finding of a court may be regarded as established for any other case, and any Federal judge may "take judicial notice" that any other voluntary association of working people is "at common law and under the Federal Sherman Act" likewise an illegal conspiracy. If this precedent be established, any injustice may thus be perpetuated to the lasting injury of the working people, and, regardless of evidence in particular cases before a court, that court will be able to act upon "judicial notice" of what has happened in other cases.

ARGUMENT FOR REVISION.

These new abuses introduced by Judge Dayton constitute one more pressing argument for revision of the law and the practice regulating injunctions as well as the Sherman antitrust law. The application of the Sherman antitrust law to organizations of workers and the issuance of injunctions to regulate personal relations are based upon the same fundamental principle—that labor power is property. The workers demand that they be recognized as freemen, that the rights be restored to them which were theirs before the courts applied law and legal principles in a manner that robs them of personal rights of freemen.

In announcing his findings in the case, Judge Dayton called attention to a number of acts "committed" by the defendants as evidence of violations of the restraining order. Among them are these:[5.547]

A few days after, on Sunday, Van Bittner and Oates appeared at the mine at Collier with a brass band of about 35 men, followed by a procession of some 125 organization men and sympathizers, from Steubenville, Ohio, largely, who marched across the company's property and held a meeting on the public road, which meeting was addressed by Bittner.

Shortly afterwards Oates rented from Myer Schwarz a small angle of unoccupied ground, possibly an eighth of an acre, surrounded on two or three sides by the company's property and an old road, about 1,000 feet from the company's pit mouth, and erected two tents there over which was placed a large sign, "Headquarters of the United Mine Workers of America." For the rental of this ground for six months Oates paid Schwarz $200, as he admitted, out of the organization funds, although the true rental value did not exceed for this six months $10 or $12 at most.

STRUGGLING TO ESTABLISH.

All acts of the miners struggling to establish better conditions of life and work in West Virginia should be considered in their relation to the power of the mine operators. That power was made practically supreme by ownership of the property and land upon which the miners must live and move. It was maintained by supervision of post offices, by control over stores and supplies, by ownership and control over schools and churches, by the company's mine guards, agents of detection and compulsion. These miners did not have one square foot of ground on which to exercise their guaranteed rights to life, liberty, and the pursuit of happiness; not one square foot for freedom of speech and the promotion of their own welfare and interest. Yet under the vague all-inclusive terms of a judicial order, a Federal agent of justice assumes the power to punish free men for renting a strip of ground upon which to live, to organize a union, and to carry out the normal and lawful purposes of that union. Under that restraining order the officials of the Mine Workers' Union are forbidden to give that organization friendly advice as to how to promote their interests or to aid them in efforts in any manner whatsoever. The purpose of this restraining order was to prevent organization among the workers, to prevent all methods by which the miners could make their protests effective, and to use the Federal courts as a strike-breaking agency in order to assist the mine operators to "control" their men to conduct their business in any manner that assured the highest dividends.

CONSPICUOUS ILLUSTRATION.

A funeral of a miner killed by the company's hired thugs was made conspicuous as an illustration of the company's method of dealing with men who retain a spark of independence. This the judge particularly notices in his findings.

[5.547] It should be noted that the remarks attributed to Judge Dayton here and below do not appear in the case text.

Judge Dayton points out that funds of the United Mine Workers were used to retain lawyers to defend the men before the courts; to pay the fines of men arrested, and to furnish bail bonds. Could any judicial situation be more intolerable? What manner of justice does injunctive rule establish when it becomes unlawful to pay moneys demanded by the law?

In considering the defendants individually and in sentencing them Judge Dayton said:

Now the eighth paragraph of this finding will be to the effect that, while I do not deem it necessary in law to show further the connection of these men than that they joined this organization and were part and parcel of it, yet it will be in effect the setting forth of the individual acts of these defendants, and I propose to find these facts.

VERY QUEER VERDICT.

Frank Ledvinka was called before the court and declared guilty of the following:

This court will find that you are an organizer of the United Mine Workers, and have been for the last seven years a national organizer; that you come from Ohio for the purpose of organizing and carrying on this strike after the decision in the Hitchman Coal Co. case was decided and determined; that the United Mine Workers was a conspiracy and an unlawful organization; that you divided with James Oates the authority and leadership in directing and controlling the activities of the strikers, made speeches in which you urged the inauguration and the prosecution of the strike; sent Harry Youshack to the home of one of the company's employees to threaten him; aided in defending strikers who were arrested for assaulting nonunion men; broke the promise you made to this court on December 2; advised the strikers that they must fight, must stop the company's employees from working, must beat and assault them for the purpose of preventing them from working; that you were authorized, as stated, by Frank M. Hayes, international vice president of the United Mine Workers of America, to make this attempt to unionize the mines of the Panhandle section of West Virginia, and did what was done in this strike in pursuance of that authority.

EARNEST GIRL REPRIMANDED.

Fannie Sellins, a faithful, earnest girl, struggling to aid and improve the toilers' working conditions, was called before the bar and was thus addressed:

This court finds from this evidence that you are a paid organizer of the United Mine Workers; that you have made the false pretense of being engaged in religious and charity work; that you frequented the camp at Collier, which was not a fit place for any decent woman; spent most of your time with James Oates and Secundo Coliffe, aiding and assisting them in directing the activities of the strikers in preventing the company's employees from working; made inflammatory speeches intended to incite the strikers to act of violence [sic]; incited and attempted assaults on the company's employees at the railroad bridge; aiding in providing supplies for the camp at Collier, using funds of the United Mine Workers; aided in the defense of the strikers arrested for assaulting the company's employees; participated in the attempt to make the Moore funeral a means of inciting the strikers to acts of violence; that you advised the strikers to beat up the nonunion men; that you advised the strikers to go to No. 3 mine and beat and assault nonunion men; that you led a mob of from 150 to 200 men to intercept the company's employees north of Wellsburg, paid their fares on the cars to the place where they divided into three several troops for the purpose of intercepting the company's men, whom you expected to come from work by one of the roads; that you advised the strikers to knock the heads off the nonunion men, whom you designated as "scabs"; preached to the strikers your defiance of the orders of this court and urged them to defy and disobey the court and its injunction; that you broke your promise made to this court on December 2, and, after promising to obey the injunction, made a speech in which your proclaimed your defiance and your intention to continue to disobey the injunction.

This being the evidence, the sentence of this court is that you be imprisoned in the Marion County jail for a period of six months.

EVIDENCE DECLARED FALSE.

Miss Sellins asked, "May I say one word?"
Judge Dayton replied, "Not one word."
Then Miss Sellins said, "That evidence is all false."
To Tom Smith Judge Dayton said:

This court finds from this evidence that you participated in the Moore funeral procession and assisted in the attempt to incite the strikers to violence by carrying banners with inflammatory inscriptions; that you aided in organizing and carrying on the strike at Collier and in many of the acts done there in violation of the injunctions; that you were a part of the time in charge and control of the camp at Collier and directed the picketing and other means of preventing nonunion men from going to work; that you did picket duty yourself for the purpose of preventing nonunion men from going to work; that you trespassed on the company's property after being warned not to do so.

This court sentences you to five months in the Wetzel County jail. Bond, $2,500.

The West Virginia mine operators have made efforts to induce immigrants to go to the State. Workers from countries where the standards of work and life are lower than in the United States, workers unacquainted with the American spirit of independence and self-protection, constitute, for a time at least, docile employees. For this reason the mine operators have sent agents abroad and to the port of New York to direct immigration toward their mines. Some of these miners acquired American views and joined the strike for greater freedom, and because of that are now said to be in danger of deportation as "undesirables." One of these "undesirable foreigners" tainted by American ideals, Ernest Ewald, was found guilty, as follows:

IMMIGRANTS INDUCED.

This court ascertains that you were an occupant of the tents at Collier from the time the camp was established and stayed there for the purpose of picketing the approach to the mine and preventing nonunion men from going to work there and of intimidating those who were working; that you did picket duty for the purpose of preventing nonunion men from going to work there; that you trespassed on the company's property and were fined by the local authorities for so doing; that you stopped men on their way to work at Collier and caused them to turn back and go away; that you patrolled as a picket at the camp at night armed with a gun. You are a foreigner. I have no doubt but what you were misled into this, but, nevertheless, it is clear that you came to this country, where you can make twice as much for a day's wage as you can at your home; yet you preferred to follow this unlawful organization instead of earning your living honestly in legitimate labor and the sweat of your brow. You preferred to take their hired pay of a few dollars a week and work against law and order and peace and sobriety and the rights of men and the rights of property; you preferred to do that. You will be sentenced to three months in the Monongalia County jail. Bond, $1,500.

Another foreigner was given this judicial interpretation of American liberty and justice:

This court finds from the evidence that you frequented the camp at Collier; that you did picket duty for the purpose of preventing the nonunion men from going to work, and trespassed on the company's property at the mouth of the mine frequently.

You are a foreigner, and came to this country for the purpose of improving your condition. You were making more money, twice over, than you could get in your own country, yet you preferred to join this unlawful organization and engage in these unlawful practices rather than to work and make the higher wages, honestly and upright and under the law. You still remained there after you quit work instead of going away and leaving this company to exercise its rights over its own property. I will sentence you to 30 days in the Hancock County jail. Bond, $500.

MENTAL BIAS AND PREJUDICE.

The language of Judge Dayton reflects mental bias and prejudice against the workers. He permitted to be laid before the court as evidence hearsay and other improper testimony. Witnesses for the prosecution were permitted to testify as to facts and occurrences not within their personal knowledge. Witnesses were permitted to testify in such a way that it was not possible to tell what statements were based on personal knowledge and what on information gained from others. Testimony of a prejudicial nature, not pertinent to the charges, was admitted in evidence. The court so ordered, saying that he would determine what should be accepted and what rejected. Yet, in announcing his findings, Judge Dayton said:

Now, gentlemen, touching the questions of these motions that have been made, I want to say I do not regard it as incumbent upon myself as a judge to go to the labor of setting forth in detail what part of this testimony is irrelevant, improper, and immaterial. There are 759 pages of it. I do regard it as my duty to file in these cases a finding of fact from the material and relevant testimony, rejecting the consideration of that which is immaterial and irrelevant.

Judge Dayton's methods destroy the definiteness of rights of law and undermine the foundations of justice.

An appeal was taken to the United States Circuit Court of Appeals, where the cases were argued during the first of May.

APPALLING PROOFS.

No more distressing, appalling proofs of need of reform of law relating to the injunctive process can be found than the injunctions issued by Judge Dayton. It is the abuses of judicial authority, jurisdiction, and power that beget bitter, burning indignation against the methods and agents of justice. If we would prevent our courts from being brought into contempt, we must see to it that they are really agents of justice. No court should be prostituted to the service of the private purpose of individuals. No court should be used as a strike-breaking agency.

The restraining order, the temporary injunction, the contempt proceedings in Judge Dayton's court show that the purpose for which the usurpatory power was invoked was not to prevent irreparable injury to property, but to rivet the fetters on the workers to defeat an industrial movement to secure better wages and conditions of work and to prevent any weakening of the autocratic rule and domination of the mine owners.

JUSTICE, TRUTH, AND EQUALITY.

Such "judicial proceedings" will solidify the great labor movement in West Virginia, and with the solidification will come the public awakening, now dormant, to the realization that an autocratic court can only temporarily trample upon the rights of its citizens, but in the end justice, truth, and equality must stand before the American courts as truth, justice, and equality stand before God.

While the period of transition is in progress, while certain courts are cleaning themselves of their present unwholesome associations; throwing off the cloak of selfish and sinister influence, labor will have to fight its battle, make the sacrifice, be punished, reprimanded, and made unhappy; yet so surely as the silver lining follows the cloud, so surely will it emerge from its present unfortunate condition in West Virginia, redeemed and triumphant. And with the redemption will come a clean court, with honor, justice and equality actuating its every movement; and with the same redemption the court will see about it a happy people, honoring and respecting it because of its strict adhesion to the American principles of justice.

THE RESTRAINING ORDER.

I desire to say a word on the "restraining order" and "temporary injunctions." These legal instruments forbid acts which may cause injury to property, and broadly prohibit any acts which would enable the workers individually or collectively to work in furtherance of their particular interests.

In violation of these intended sacred principles of equity the evident purpose of the West Virginia mine operators was, and in certain sections of the same State now is, to perpetuate anti-union policies for their own greed and aggrandizement, and forcing upon their employees working conditions little better than slavery.

I believe, and it is my sincere conviction, that the principle of justice is of incalculable importance to these miners of West Virginia and to the workers elsewhere in these cases.

I believe in the right of dissatisfied workmen and their sympathizers to organize; to conduct a strike for the purpose of securing better terms and conditions of employment; the right to furnish and receive strike benefits.

I do not believe in the practice of employers, under the guise of "sacredness" of contracts for personal services, preventing anyone from approaching their employees to ask them to quit work and to join with fellow workers for the protection and the promotion of the interests of all; I do not believe in the practice of a judge issuing orders restraining persons from doing that which they have a lawful right to do and the practice of a judge punishing them for violating such unlawful orders.

BETTERMENT OF HUMAN LIFE.

The House is now considering a bill for the reform of abuses of the injunctive process. Those abuses American workers have felt more keenly than all other citizens. In the name of justice they demand the speedy enactment of law adequate to prevent future perversions of justice. They demand not only that organizations of workers be deemed lawful, but that they be accorded the legal right to such normal and necessary activities as will make organizations real forces for the betterment of human life.

Associated effort for self-help is the only protection upon which the workers can rely. It has done more than any other force for the uplift of the masses of our country. It will do more as the way is opened to greater opportunities. The workers demand these opportunities in the name of justice and humanity. They demand legislation that shall exempt them from the provisions of the Sherman Antitrust Act and protect them from abuses of the injunctive process. [Applause.] . . .

⊥ Mr. MORGAN of Oklahoma. Mr. Chairman, evidently no argument is necessary before this House to secure the passage of this amendment. I wish, however, expressing my own personal views, to declare myself in favor of this amendment, not that I believe that this amendment contains all that should be added to this section, but because I understand the proposed amendment has the approval of the labor organizations of this country, and I assume the leaders of such organizations have carefully examined the amendment and are satisfied with its provisions. ⊥9564

Mr. Chairman, if there be a conflict between capital and labor—and, in a broad sense, there should not be—but if there be or is such a conflict, so far as I am concerned, after the most careful and deliberate consideration on my part, I propose to place myself on the side of labor. [Applause.]

Because, gentleman, I believe that on that side lie the interests of my country and of humanity. The great bulk of the citizens of this country are wage earners. The great bulk of the wealth produced in this country is distributed through the payment of wages. Labor organizations have their imperfections, no doubt. But, on the whole, I believe such organizations are beneficial to the country and helpful to all wage earners. Such organizations may be at times subject justly to criticism. But what organization of human beings is not subject to criticism? But with all their defects I believe it would be a calamity for this Nation if such organizations should cease to exist. In my judgment it would be a misfortune to the country if through our national laws our labor organizations should be hampered and hindered in all their legitimate work. So far as we can aid them by national legislation in their great purpose of shortening the hours of labor, increasing wages, and improving conditions under which labor is performed we should do so, and by so doing I believe we are rendering a patriotic service to our country. There are many who think legislation favorable to labor organizations means hostility to the great business interests of the country. This is not true. The intelligent wage earners of the United States know that, after all, their own welfare depends upon the prosperity of business. They know that business must prosper or labor will suffer. Employees know that any serious loss to employers will react unfavorably upon employees. So that, after all, I believe the business interests of this country are really safe in the hands of labor. We have in the United States the most intelligent workingmen in the world. They know that their share of wealth must come through wages paid; that good wages can not be paid by business concerns that are unprofitable. So that I can not think that our labor organizations are hostile to business or are dangerous to industrial peace. More than that, the very strength of this Nation, the perpetuity of this Republic, depend largely upon the attitude of the wage earners of this country toward our institutions and our flag. I believe the National Government should by its legislation indicate its friendliness toward the labor of this country, so that the great labor organizations of this country and the rank and file of the army of wage earners of this Nation who are not in organized labor will have a friendly attitude to our institutions, to our country, and to our flag; so that in time of war, in time of stress, in time of danger, the great body of wage earners, constituting the masses of this Nation, will remain true and loyal to the flag of our country. [Applause.] . . .

Mr. VOLSTEAD. . . .

I desire to call attention to a peculiar situation. This morning I read in one of the newspapers that labor claims for this proposed amendment one meaning while the administration claims an entirely different meaning. It seems to me that we ought to write the amendment so that it will not be open to dispute as to its meaning. If this amendment is intended to legalize the secondary boycott, this House ought to know it. If it is intended, as I believe it is claimed by those who present it on this floor, simply to legalize the existence of these organizations, I do not believe there is anyone here who would be opposed to it. It is very unfortunate that an amendment should be proposed to this bill which must of necessity go into the courts after it becomes a law before anybody will know definitely just what it means. It looks as though it has been drawn to deceive somebody. It is perfectly plain that if those who drew it intended to write a clear exemption of labor into this statute, they could easily have found the language. It is unfortunate, and it seems to me that before we close the discussion on this paragraph some proposition ought to be submitted that no one can dispute. We ought to know what we are voting for. [Applause.] . . .

Mr. GREEN of Iowa. Mr. Chairman, while I agree with the gentleman from North Carolina that this amendment only expresses the consensus of the best opinion as to what the law now is, I am still of the opinion that it is well to put in the statute an affirmative declaration which can not be misunderstood. Under the Sherman law as it now stands a labor organization is perfectly legal, and a peaceable strike or peaceable picketing is perfectly legal, under the decisions of a majority of the courts.

Mr. Chairman, I had occasion not long ago to advise a committee of a labor organization who waited upon me. They were engaged in a strike against the Harriman and Illinois Central lines. They represented a body of machinists. They told me they were threatened by the attorneys of those railroads with a prosecution under the Sherman law. I advised them that the Sherman law had no application to the situation as it existed under their strike, for their strike was a perfectly peaceable one. They had committed no violence. They had threatened no one with violence, but had simply expressed by their action their right as organized members of a fraternity to stop work peaceably. I told the men not to be alarmed; that no prosecution would be begun, and to tell the railroad attorneys to go ahead if they desired, but in the end they would meet an action for damages for malicious prosecution. But the men were not prosecuted. There was no action begun against them, nor was anything done under the Sherman law. Yet there is, as I think, some necessity for this provision, for the reason that there have been isolated decisions by the lower Federal courts holding that the mere organization of a body of laborers for the purpose of maintaining or raising wages is contrary to law. There have been some indictments under the Sherman law, and one is now pending, as I understand it, in Colorado. It is true that the reason has been given that in the particular instances to which the law has been so applied that violence had been committed or attempted. But there should be some definite standard, and the section as amended fixes one, and labor organizations which confine themselves to legitimate purposes need not fear the law. . . .

Mr. DECKER. Mr. Chairman, I shall support this amendment. It distinguishes between the man and the dollar, between the ore and the man who digs the ore, between the throttle and the man at the throttle. It distinguishes between labor and the products of labor. It is a just distinction, which was written before the formation of government upon the tablet of nature by Almighty God. [Applause.] . . .

Mr. [THOMAS L.] REILLY [D., Conn.]. Mr. Chairman, I am in favor of the plainest statement of the intention of the committee in regard to the amendment under consideration. If the committee intended to exempt labor and farmers' organizations from the operation of the Sherman antitrust law, why does it not say so?

I am not a lawyer; just a common layman, without ability to give a judicial opinion, but I do know what is meant when it is stated that the Sherman antitrust law shall not apply to certain organizations.

Let us state the case as plainly as possible, so there will be no doubt in the mind of anyone as to what it is intended to do. If these organizations are to be exempted, let us say so; if they are not, let us say that. Do not let us quibble nor leave it to courts to upset the intention of Congress in this matter. . . .

Mr. BRUMBAUGH. Mr. Chairman, I desire to state that personally I favor the plainest and most explicit declaration possible in behalf of the rights of labor. I think this is best for both sides concerned and interested in this matter. I shall vote for this amendment, because I understand it meets with the approval of labor organizations that have carefully examined it, and at the same time it is considered fair by those who employ labor. In fact, I am informed that the amendment is the result of mutual understanding between both labor leaders and employers of labor, and I have been advised and assured personally by labor leaders in whom I place every confidence that the ⊥ amendment is satisfactory to labor organizations and friends of labor everywhere.

Mr. Chairman, it is gratifying, indeed, to those of us who have been the friends and champions of labor and labor laws for years, both here and elsewhere, and who at the same time have wanted this great advance made in justice not only to labor but to honest employers of labor as well, to see this great question settled in this sensible, reasonable, amicable manner, in this spirit of fairness to all concerned, and thus see this tardy justice done to the great cause of labor, upon which the prosperity and happiness of the people as a whole and the growth and grandeur of our great Nation must ever rest. No nation can be or ought to be strong and great and secure that does not respect and honor its laboring men and women. The most honorable and dignified thing in all this world for any man or woman is honest labor, whether of hand or heart or brain; for did not the Nazarene Carpenter, the Christ Himself, give to honest labor a halo of honor and dignity that no rank of birth or wealth can equal or enjoy?

Extremely gratifying to me, indeed, is it to see this great Democratic Congress keep and redeem our promises made to labor and labor organizations; to see this Democratic Congress place the man above the dollar and to be able to hear the heartbeats of humanity above the clinking of the coin of commercialized wealth. [Applause.]

No other Congress in 50 years has done so much by law to assist and relieve labor. By our tariff law we take the hand of trust monopoly on the high prices of the necessaries of life out of the pockets of the laboring man. By our currency bill we protect his little saving in the banks from the panicky gambling heretofore pastime operations of the money power. By this amendment we take the hands of those who would oppress and tyrannize off of the throat of labor and let it breathe free.

Mr. Chairman, personally I want to say that I am proud to have come from the ranks of laboring people myself. I know by years of personal experience their life of toil, and I can sympathize with their struggles and needs. Laboring men seldom ask for aught but their just deserts, and the Good Book says that the laborer is worthy of his hire and condemns those who would oppress the laborer in his way.

I propose now, as I always have in the past, to stand for all just demands in labor's interests.

I congratulate my friends and fellows, the laborers, on this advance, which is the promise, I trust, of the dawning of a better day wherein labor shall receive its just recompense of reward, wherein life shall be sweeter, labor lighter, and the world for all a better place to live upon. [Applause.] . . .

Mr. [DAVID J.] LEWIS [D., Md.]. Mr. Chairman, I want to extend my sincere congratulations to the committee that has reported this bill and that has now proffered the amendment which will perfect section 7. It is not too much to say that by this single measure, with its complementary sections on injunctions and contempts, by one single stroke of the legislative hand more is being done in our country to rectify the judicial status of the great toiling masses than has ever been accomplished in our history before. [Applause.] Nor does this mean violent or radical treatment of the relations of labor and capital.

This section 7, taken with its complementary sections, places the American workman where the British workman was placed by Parliament in 1906. Their experience shows that property will be as safe, the rights of employers will be as secure, if this measure is enacted into a law, which I predict will become known as the great magna charta of American workmen. [Applause.]

Everybody understands that section 7 would have been written into the Sherman Act in 1890 had there been any thought of the application since made of that great act. Everybody knows that Congress at that time had no thought of legislating with regard to the relations of employers and employees. I challenge contradiction for that statement. If Congress had ever intended to legislate upon these relations and saw fit to do what the States may well do and are doing, for it is their subject matter and not a Federal subject matter—prescribing penalties for individual wrongs when committed—I challenge the gentlemen of this House to say that Congress would have ever said to the toiler: "If you overstep the line and commit a tort, you shall be subject to threefold damages." That was the natural sentence to have pronounced on the trust, an outlaw organization that sought to suck up all the commercial profit and power of the Republic. That is a sentence—the sentence of outlawry—that never can be pronounced, now or in the future, on a peaceful organization of workingmen. [Applause.]

I know there is some misapprehension. Some honest people are inclined to think that this section may mean a species of class legislation. They commit the error of considering labor as a commodity, a natural error inspired by the circumstances under which the price of labor, unfortunately, is sometimes determined by the iron laws of the market. But there is this distinction between labor and a barrel of oil, a commodity: Labor is never in truth a commodity; labor can never under our institutions be property, either before the court or before the legislature. Under our Constitution, property in human beings has forever ceased. While a barrel of oil is not only a commodity in the market, it is a commodity before the courts; it is a commodity before the legislature. The legal attribute of a commodity is property; but the legal attribute of the workingman is citizenship. A different principle of sociology and justice apply to these two subject matters when they are before Congress or before the courts. The rules that are rationally applicable to property can seldom be justly applied to the man. I thank you, gentlemen, for your attention. [Applause.] . . .

Mr. CARLIN. Mr. Chairman, I want to read into the RECORD two editorials, one from the Globe and Commercial Advertiser, of New York, of Thursday, May 28, and another from the Springfield Daily Republican, of Thursday, May 28.

They are as follows:

THE SO-CALLED LABOR EXEMPTION.

The Globe is pleased to note a subsidence of the determination to misrepresent and to appeal to prejudice against an explicit recognition by Congress of the right of labor organizations to exist. A year and two years ago, when the issue was up, the public was confused by untrue statements, oracularly made, that the labor unions were browbeating Congress into exempting them from prosecution under the Sherman law. A reading of the proposed amendment to the Sherman law revealed the misrepresentation, but few could be induced to read it. It became almost a truism in certain quarters that the wicked labor unions were asking the special privilege of committing crimes at pleasure.

But last night the Evening Post, which has been one of the worst offenders in the past, published in its Washington correspondence a fair summary of the proposed amendment. And this morning the Times, which has formerly raged against the black horror of authorizing the commission of crimes, acknowledges in its editorial that the law gives to the unions no greater rights than are already theirs under a reasonable reading of Chief Justice White's "rule of reason." Only the Sun remains to cry out in the old, lusty way against the alleged tyranny of Gompers and his associates.

If labor organizations now have the right to exist and to carry out the legitimate objects of the association, then the amendment is merely declaratory of the present law, and in the nature of surplusage. But in the Danbury hat case the Supreme Court used language that suggested that perhaps labor unions are per se illegal under the Sherman law—that it is an illegal restraint of trade for men to agree to work for similar wages or to quit work in a concerted way. Several Federal district attorneys have threatened and one or two have actually begun proceedings for the dissolution of labor unions as involving restraint of trade. Their right to exist being thus called in question, it is not strange that the labor organizations ask for an affirmative recognition.

There is no license to commit crime. Talk along this line is bosh. If a labor organization violates the Sherman law, it will be open to prosecution under the Sherman law. But its members may not be sent to jail for merely belonging. This may be the law now; but doubt has been thrown on the right of men to combine together for the joint selling of their labor, and it is worth while to have the doubt removed.

THE LABOR AMENDMENT.

Organized labor by no means gets what it demanded in the labor amendments to the Federal antitrust law now under consideration by the lower branch of Congress. But it has secured something from the majority party. Complete and unqualified exemption from the operation of the Sherman Act was asked for on the lines indicated by the bill introduced and championed by the late Senator Bacon, of Georgia, a conservative of the older school, it is interesting to note. Senator Bacon always stoutly maintained that no intention whatever existed on the part of the Congress that passed the Sherman Act in 1890 to bring labor organizations within its prohibitions, but the courts did what Congress did not do by interpretations of the law. Such is the strong belief of many of the students of that legislation. Yet none of the leading political parties has ventured to indorse fully the exemption demand. The Democrats in 1908 and 1912 inserted in their national platform:

"The expanding organization of industry makes it essential that there should be no abridgment of the right of wage earners and producers to organize for the protection of wages and the improvement of labor conditions to the end that such labor organizations and their members should not be regarded as illegal combinations in restraint of trade."

That idea, so far as it goes, if carried into effect, would insure exemption for labor organizations from the antitrust law, but it has to do only with the "restraint-of-trade" prohibition contained in the act. The exemption should surely go that far, if no further, and the Republican is glad to see that the amendment said to be agreed to by the House leaders and the radical labor representatives in the body reads as follows:

"That nothing contained in the antitrust laws shall be construed to forbid the existence and operation of fraternal, labor, consumers', agricultural, or horticultural organizations, orders, or associations instituted for the purpose of mutual help and not having capital stock or conducted for profit, or to forbid or restrain individual members of such organizations, orders, or associations from carrying out the legitimate objects thereof; and such organizations, orders, or associations, or the members thereof, shall not be construed or held to be illegal combinations in restraint of trade under the antitrust laws."

The reason why the amendment of the antitrust act, to that length at least, is desirable and even necessary is that section 1 of the act is so comprehensive in its scope that the courts are at liberty to regard anything in the form of a combination that has the effect of "restraining trade," as a criminal conspiracy. Logically speaking, there is no reason whatever why the Federal courts should not outlaw strikes of wage earners as conspiracies whenever those strikes, as they often do, have the effect of restraining trade or commerce among the States. It is well known that down until recent times the lawful right to strike, to quit work in concert, was not recognized. The right to withdraw labor power, not individually but collectively, is the very foundation of the modern labor movement. It corresponds to the churchman's constitutional right to the free exercise of his religion. The Sherman antitrust law menaces the right to strike, and therefore the demand for the amendment of the law is justified.

That labor's fears are well founded concerning the gradual extension of the scope of the law of 1890 to prohibits [sic] acts whose lawfulness had been recognized in England and America, after generations of struggle, as a necessary concession to labor's moral right to improve its economic condition under the wage system appears convincingly in the several suits brought under the statute in recent years against labor organizations. Suits of that character are now pending in the courts. One Federal judge in Louisiana ruled that a strike to force employers to enter into a joint agreement with union labor was in restraint of trade under the antitrust act.[5.548] Union labor in the West Virginia coal fields has been lately haled into the Federal courts accused of conspiracy under the same law. A clearer legal definition, a more specific legal understanding of labor's rights under Federal law in initiating and maintaining strikes and other acts of industrial warfare—so long as that sort of warfare is permitted and even legalized under our system—becomes most desirable. The extreme comprehensiveness of the Sherman Act, so much admired by those who imagine that it is the last word in legislation affecting monopoly, may become a danger the moment the law is permitted to run beyond those "unlawful restraints and monopolies" in interstate commerce which it was chiefly designed to curb.

Violent protests against these labor amendments to the antitrust law emanate from several quarters. It is urged most vehemently that they grossly violate the principle of equality of all people before the law. But the truth is that when wage earners won the right to quit work in concert they were necessarily conceded an exceptional status under the old conspiracy laws. "Inherent differences that exist" should be "recognized by the laws and the courts as well as by reason," says Samuel Gompers, and Samuel Gompers, for once at least, tells the truth with

---

[5.548] United States v. Workingmen's Amalgamated Council, 54 F. 994 (C.C.E.D. La. 1893), aff'd, 57 F. 85 (5th Cir. 1893).

much clearness and force. There are inherent differences between combinations of wage earners and combinations of corporations seeking to monopolize industries. So, too, there are inherent differences between industrial corporations and railroad corporations, which should be recognized by the laws. The Federal antitrust law is unsatisfactory; it will never be wholly successful in its working until it is confined to its proper field. Railroads should be exempt from it; so should labor. But that is not saying that railroads and labor should be exempt from all law. There will be law enough to go around, everyone should believe.

Mr. Chairman, I want to say just a word in concluding the debate on this great subject. The Democratic Party is now about to fulfill its promise made to the great labor organizations and the farmers' organizations of this country. [Applause.] We have decided that flesh and bone shall no longer be considered a commodity in the sense of manufactured products. We have decided that human beings shall be placed above things. We have decided that men with consciences and minds shall be recognized before the law as such, and that those that labor with their hands and hearts for wages shall be separated from the things which they produce. [Applause.]

We have gone as far as we can consistently and rightfully go under our Constitution. A step further, in my judgment, toward the amendment offered by the gentleman from Kentucky [Mr. THOMAS] and the gentleman representing the Progressives on this floor would be in the very teeth of the Constitution itself, and while they cry out that they want to do more for labor they know or ought to know that what they can do for labor organizations must be done under our Constitution and not in violation thereof. [Applause.]

The CHAIRMAN. The question is on the amendment offered by the gentleman from North Carolina.

The question was taken; and on a division (demanded by Mr. MURDOCK and Mr. THOMAS) there were 207 ayes and no noes.

So the amendment was agreed to.

The CHAIRMAN. The Clerk will read the amendment offered by the gentleman from Kentucky [Mr. THOMAS].

The Clerk reads [sic] as follows:

Strike out all of section 7 down to and including the word "thereof" in line 10 and insert the following:

"The provisions of the antitrust law shall not apply to agricultural, labor, consumers, fraternal, or horticultural orders or associations."

Mr. BARTLETT. Mr. Chairman, a parliamentary inquiry.

The CHAIRMAN. The gentleman will state it.

Mr. BARTLETT. If that amendment is adopted, it leaves the amendment by the gentleman from North Carolina that we have just adopted in the bill, does it not?

The CHAIRMAN. The amendment of the gentleman from Kentucky seems to strike out the paragraph as amended.

Mr. BARTLETT. It strikes it out down to and including the word "thereof," so it would not strike out the amendment just adopted.

Mr. THOMAS. Mr. Chairman, I move to strike out the first paragraph of section 7 as amended.

The CHAIRMAN. The gentleman from Kentucky asks unanimous consent to modify his amendment. Is there objection? [After a pause.] The Chair hears none.

Mr. BARTLETT. Mr. Chairman, a parliamentary inquiry.

The CHAIRMAN. The gentleman will state it.

Mr. BARTLETT. Mr. Chairman, as I understand it, this amendment of the gentleman from Kentucky [Mr. THOMAS], if adopted, does not affect the amendment that we have just adopted?

The CHAIRMAN. The Chair thinks that it strikes out the whole of the first paragraph of section 7 as amended.

Mr. BARTLETT. Then this amendment of the gentleman from Kentucky, if adopted, would take the place of the paragraph as it has been amended?

The CHAIRMAN. That is the opinion of the Chair. The Clerk will report the amendment as modified.

The Clerk read as follows:

Strike out the first paragraph of section 7 as amended and insert in lieu thereof the following:

"The provisions of the antitrust laws shall not apply to agricultural, labor, consumers', fraternal, or horticultural organizations, orders, or associations."

Mr. THOMAS. Mr. Chairman, it is well enough, as a distinguished gentleman from Georgia at one time said on the floor of this House, to stop and see just where we are at. Courts in construing laws always construe the law as a whole. Let us read and construe this section as amended, and see just where we are at. Section 7 provides that nothing contained in the antitrust laws shall be construed to forbid the existence and operation of fraternal, labor, consumers', agricultural, or horticultural organizations or associations instituted for the purpose of mutual help and not having capital stock or conducted for profit. As amended it will read:

Labor, fraternal, agricultural, or consumers' organizations shall not be held or construed to be illegal combinations in restraint of trade under the antitrust law.

What labor organization? What agricultural organization? Construing this law as a whole, only those organizations which do not have capital stock or are not conducted for profit. Those are the only two classes that this bill as amended applies to. If a labor organization is conducted for profit, this amendment does not apply to that organization; if a labor organization has capital stock, this amendment does not apply to such an organization, because, reading and construing the law as amended, in its entirety, only organizations which have no capital stock and which are not conducted for profit are exempt under this amendment.

What is the object, the very primary object of a labor organization? It is profit. Profit how? To advance and increase the wages of its members. That is a profit to them, and consequently that amendment can not apply to such organizations, because you have got to construe this law in its entirety, and no court will construe it piecemeal. What is the object of the farmers' organization? It is to obtain better prices for their products, and that is a profit to the farmer, and if that is a profit to the farmer then your amendment does not apply, because your amendment can apply only to those organizations which are named in the body of this bill. This bill limits it to those organizations which do not have capital stock and are not conducted for profit.

I voted for this amendment. I do not think there is anything in it. I do not believe that it changes in one iota the original text of the bill. Gentlemen have said that they desire above all things to exempt these organizations from the operations of the antitrust laws. If you do, why do you not do it? My amendment is plain. It is concise; it will not take any court to construe it, because it provides that these antitrust laws shall not apply to these associations, and that is what the farmers and the laborers of this country want; and if you want a clear, clean-cut exemption, vote for this amendment of mine and you will get it; otherwise you will not. . . .

Mr. MACDONALD. Mr. Chairman, I wish to offer an amendment, which I send to the desk, as an amendment to the amendment offered by the gentleman from Kentucky.

The CHAIRMAN. The Clerk will report the amendment to the amendment, offered by the gentleman from Michigan.

The Clerk read as follows:

Amend section 7 by striking out all of the first paragraph before the Webb amendment after the word "shall," in line 4, page 24, and insert the following in lieu thereof: "apply to trade-unions or other labor organizations organized for the purpose of regulating wages, hours of labor, or other conditions under which labor is to be performed, nor to any arrangements, agreements, or combinations among persons engaged in horticulture or agriculture, made with a view of enhancing the price of their own agricultural or horticultural products; nor to fraternal or consumers' organizations, orders, or associations, instituted for the purposes of mutual help and not having capital stock or conducted for profit."

Mr. MACDONALD. Mr. Chairman, this amendment will accomplish the purpose designed by the amendment of the gentleman from Kentucky [Mr. THOMAS], but it will also leave in the Webb amendment, so that those who are really interested in getting an exemption of these organizations in this law will have the benefit of both of those ideas. There are many gentlemen on this floor who are not in favor of this idea, and there are many gentlemen who are in favor of the idea of really exempting these organizations; and I say again that if you are in favor of exempting these organizations specifically from the operation of these laws, vote for this amendment. If you are not, do not vote for this amendment, because this makes it plain and unmistakable in its meaning.

Mr. WEBB. Mr. Chairman, I take it that the Committee of the Whole has perfected section 7 to its satisfaction when it adopted the amendment which was just adopted by a vote of 207 to nothing. These amendments offered in addition thereto have been discussed, and I understand that the sentiment of the House is that section 7 should be amended as it was amended a moment ago, and no further. . . .

Mr. MURDOCK. The gentleman has heard the amendment of the gentleman from Kentucky and that offered by the gentleman from Michigan, and we have just had a vote which shows a remarkable state of affairs, that every Member present is in favor of the exemption of organized labor from the provisions of the Sherman antitrust law. This is a matter which has been in controversy for 24 years, and what I want to ask the gentleman is this: In view of this remarkable unanimity, does not the amendment offered by the gentleman from Kentucky and that offered by the gentleman from Michigan go much further than the gentleman's amendment?

Mr. WEBB. I could not say it goes much further; but why should the gentleman from Kansas [Mr. MURDOCK] want a division on the floor of the House when there is no division as between labor and capital and the farmers. All of us are united on this.

Mr. MURDOCK. From the debate I will say to the gentleman that there is a great difference of opinion as to just what his amendment does. I do not think, and I do not think the gentleman thinks, that it goes as far as that amendment offered by the gentleman from Kentucky [Mr. THOMAS] and that amendment offered by the gentleman from Michigan [Mr. MACDONALD], and I would like to ask the gentleman from North Carolina this, and then I will take my seat: Did the Committee on the Judiciary intend the Webb amendment to exempt organized labor from the provisions of the Sherman antitrust law?

Mr. WEBB. It certainly does exempt their existence and operation if organized for mutual help and without profit.

Mr. MURDOCK. Does it say anything—

Mr. Webb. We wanted to make it plain that no labor organization or farmers' organization organized for mutual help without profit should be construed to be a combination in restraint of trade or a conspiracy under the antitrust laws. Now, I will say frankly to my friend that we never intended to make any organizations, regardless of what they might do, exempt in every respect from the law. I would not vote for any amendment that does do that. [Applause.]

Mr. MURDOCK. If the labor organization goes beyond the province of mutual help, then is it subject to the Sherman antitrust laws?

Mr. WEBB. If it violates the law, it is. Of course it is an organization subject to the law, and I ask if my friend from Kansas would vote to exempt it from all laws?

Mr. MURDOCK. I would vote to exempt it from being confined under the antitrust laws to mere inactive existence.

Mr. WEBB. But the gentleman would not vote to exempt it and nobody else from all laws?

Mr. MURDOCK. I understand that, but I would give strikers the right to peaceful assemblage.

Mr. WEBB. We give them that right in this bill.

Mr. MURDOCK. I doubt it very much.

Mr. CARLIN. The gentleman can not doubt it if he will read section 18.

Mr. MURDOCK. Section 18 of this bill confines its jurisdiction to employers and employees. Strikers are not employees. The relation of employer and employee ceases when employees strike.

Mr. WEBB. I do not know how my friend—

Mr. MURDOCK. That is the way I read section 18.

Mr. WEBB. The gentleman should read it like the lawyers of the labor unions of the country read it, and I believe they understand it. We expressly provide in section 18 that labor organizations can strike, that they can persuade others to strike, that they can pay strike benefits, that they can have peaceful assemblages, and a great many other things. That is their bill of rights and they are satisfied with it, and what is it that dissatisfies my friend from Kansas if the labor people of this country, if the farmers of the country, and the capitalists of the country are satisfied with it? [Applause.]

Mr. MURDOCK. I will tell the gentleman why I am not satisfied. The gentleman from North Carolina and the Judiciary Committee have left out the same words, "shall not apply to," which have been carried in all amendments for the last 24 years and put into the amendment language that must be construed by the courts and construed how heaven only knows and the gentleman from North Carolina does not know.

Mr. WEBB. That is what was said about "restraint of trade," "reasonable doubt," and a thousand expressions you can not exactly define, but you have got to leave something to the courts. This is what labor wants, and I think my friend from Kansas ought to be satisfied. . . .

Mr. [EDWARD] KEATING [D., Colo.]. I want to ask the gentleman from North Carolina if it was not the fact that the representatives of the organizations of labor in this city who represent the great national organizations and the representatives of the great national farmers' organizations had not gone over this amendment and if they did not state this is exactly what they wanted?

Mr. WEBB. That is my understanding, and of course everybody so understands it.

Mr. KEATING. And if the representatives of labor and the representatives of the great farmers' organizations have not some kick coming to them, what does the gentleman want us to do now? [Applause.]

Mr. MANN. That is my understanding.

Mr. NELSON. Mr. Chairman, the gentleman does not know—

The CHAIRMAN. The time of the gentleman has expired.

Mr. SCOTT. Mr. Chairman, I move to strike out the last word.

Mr. NELSON. Mr. Chairman, I move to strike out the last word, just to ask a question of the gentleman, because if these amendments are voted down, as possibly they may be, I wish to offer an amendment which I have carefully prepared on the question of farmers' organizations. The gentleman said that the representatives of the farmers' associations have agreed to this amendment. I ask him to name one representative of any farmers' association that agreed to this amendment. I have received telegrams from farmers' associations protesting most vehemently against them. Now, will the gentleman name one representative from these farmers' associations—

Mr. WEBB. I will say to my friend that I have never heard of a single farmer objecting to the provisions of this bill.

Mr. NELSON. Has the gentleman seen a single representative of the farmers' associations in reference to this amendment?

Mr. HENRY. If the gentleman will permit, I will try to answer that question.

Mr. MANN. The gentleman is not chairman of that committee.

Mr. WEBB. What is the question the gentleman wants to ask?

Mr. NELSON. Name a single representative of any farmers' association who agreed to this amendment.

Mr. WEBB. I can not name a single representative of farmers' associations who is against it.

Mr. HENRY. I submitted this proposed language to the Farmers' Union of Texas and asked if it would satisfy the farmers, and they wrote back it was entirely satisfactory.

Mr. NELSON. Did the gentleman point out the effect of the language, "and not conducted for profit"—

Mr. HENRY. Yes; and I pointed that out and asked for suggestions, and they said they had no suggestions to make, because it was as plain as the English language could make it.

Mr. NELSON. Did the gentleman point out that it exempted no organization except those who came together for mutual discussion of methods, and that farmers' organizations that were conducted for the purpose of marketing their product should not be exempted?

Mr. MANN. Will the gentleman permit? Do I understand that Congress has abdicated its province and right of legislation and has gone into a searching committee to find out what certain organizations want, without any regard to the merits of the proposition?

Mr. NELSON. I was speaking of the statement of the chairman that farmers' organizations were not opposed to it, whereas I have received a number of telegrams from farmers' organizations protesting against it.

As soon as this amendment is disposed of, I wish to offer an amendment that, I think, will meet the approval of farmers' organizations. . . .

Mr. WEBB. I have no protests filed with the committee. The committee received no protests against the provisions of this section which was put in the bill as section 7. I am reliably informed by gentlemen on the floor that the general counsel of the Farmers' Union very heartily indorses this amendment which the gentleman has just voted for and which seems to be acceptable to labor as well. . . .

Mr. NELSON. I want to say to the gentleman that in the committee I filed protests from organizations of farmers against the language that was then proposed to be inserted in the law and this new section, in effect, does the very same thing against which they protested at that time.

Mr. Chairman, I yield now, and shall offer an amendment and speak in my own time later on.

Mr. GARDNER. Mr. Chairman, I take the negative of the motion to strike out the last word for the purpose of asking a question of the gentleman from Kansas [Mr. MURDOCK].

Do I understand the gentleman from Kansas to portray the position of the Progressive Party in saying that he advocates the exemption of cotton planters' associations and woolgrowers' associations and associations gotten together for the purpose of enhancing the prices of the staples of life from the operation of the antitrust laws?

Mr. MURDOCK. I have made no statement about the growers of cotton or the growers of wool, and I have not spoken for anybody but myself this morning. But I will say to the gentleman from Massachusetts that I am in favor of a law here which will directly, in terms, exempt farmers' organizations and labor unions from the provisions of the Sherman antitrust law.

I do so because I believe, in the first instance, that labor is not a commodity, and because, in the second instance, I believe that agriculture is so highly individualized that it is in no sense a menace to society; and I believe that the Sherman antitrust law was passed not to reach the farmers' organizations, and not to reach the labor unions, but to reach monopoly, which thrives, by the way, more in the gentleman's district than it does in mine. [Laughter and applause.]

Mr. GARDNER. Possibly it is a fact that it does; but if you exempt cotton planters' associations and if you exempt woolgrowers' associations, and if you exempt these associations gotten together for the purpose of enhancing the cost of the necessaries of life, as is proposed by the Progressive Party in the proposition which has been brought forward by the gentleman from Michigan [Mr. MACDONALD], you will find that in the gentleman's district—have I the attention of the gentleman from Kansas?

Mr. MURDOCK. Yes.

Mr. GARDNER. You will find that in the gentleman's district in Kansas there will be more injury done to the people of the United States than in my district. . . .

Mr. MANN. Mr. Chairman, a parliamentary inquiry.

The CHAIRMAN. The gentleman will state it.

Mr. MANN. Is not debate exhausted on this amendment?

The CHAIRMAN. The Chair will state that it is. This debate is proceeding by unanimous consent.

Mr. MANN. I ask for a vote, Mr. Chairman.

The CHAIRMAN. The question is on agreeing to the amendment offered by the gentleman from Michigan [Mr. MACDONALD].

Mr. [A. W.] GREGG [D., Tex.]. Mr. Chairman, I move to strike out the last word.

Mr. MANN. Mr. Chairman, I make the point of order that that amendment is not in order. We have already that amendment in the third degree.

Mr. GREGG. I move, then, Mr. Chairman, to strike out the last two words.

Mr. MANN. That is an amendment in the fourth degree.

The CHAIRMAN. The debate is exhausted on the pending amendment.

Mr. GREGG. Mr. Chairman, I ask unanimous consent to talk for three minutes. . . .

There was no objection.

Mr. GREGG. Mr. Chairman, this provision, section 7 of the bill, even after the adoption of the Webb amendment, which was intended to improve the section, exempts from the operation of the antitrust laws only such labor, agricultural, and horticultural organizations, orders, or associations as have no capital stock or are not conducted for profit.

Now, if we are going to grant this exemption to the labor and agricultural orders and organizations, and everybody here seems willing to grant it, we should do it in such broad and unequivocal language as to give them the full benefit, which I am afraid this provision as written does not do.

Labor orders are organized not only to improve the hours and conditions of labor but also to increase their wages to the highest reasonable rate and to maintain them at that standard. This is right, and what I want them to have. I fear that under this section the courts will construe that the organization to increase and maintain their wages is for profit, and therefore that they are not exempt from the antitrust laws. Should the courts so hold, the labor organizations will not have received any benefit from this provision. I want to make it so plain that there can be no mistake that they are exempt.

Again, suppose that in the future it should become necessary for labor organizations in the conduct of their business to issue capital stock to raise money needed in their business; in that event they would at once become subject to the antitrust laws. We are not legislating only for the present and present conditions, but for the future and future conditions. We should not so hem them in that in the future they may not adopt such methods of conducting their business as may seem best to them.

What is the object of farmers' organizations? One of the main objects is by cooperation to secure the best market and price for their products. Should they agree not to sell their cotton, wheat, corn, or other products at less than a given price, I fear the courts would hold that they were an organization for profit, and under this provision as now worded they would not be exempt from prosecution and punishment under the antitrust laws. Thus would be destroyed one of their main objects for organization. I am not willing to subject them to any such danger.

Again, suppose an agricultural or horticultural organization in my county or anywhere else should, in addition to their other purposes, wish to organize for the purpose of erecting a warehouse and issue stock for that purpose, a thing which they have done in some cases, in order to have some place in which to store their products, while they are holding them for more favorable conditions in the market. Most of them are people of small means and not able by voluntary contributions to build warehouses, and if they should issue capital stock to build one, they at once, under the provisions of this section as worded, would become subject to the operations of the antitrust laws. Thus you force them either to expose their products to the weather or to rent warehouses possibly at exorbitant rent. For one I am not willing to to this, but want them to have the right by issuing stock or otherwise to build and own their own warehouses. If we are going to do anything for them, let us do it ungrudgingly.

The amendment offered by the gentleman from Kentucky [Mr. THOMAS] meets and obviates all the objections which I have pointed out, and I shall therefore vote for it.

Mr. THOMAS. Mr. Chairman—

The CHAIRMAN. All debate has expired.

Mr. THOMAS. Mr. Chairman, I ask unanimous consent to ask the gentleman from Colorado [Mr. KEATING], if he will yield to me, a question, in view of the statement he made a while ago. [Cries of "Vote!" "Vote!"]

The CHAIRMAN. The gentleman from Kentucky [Mr. THOMAS] asks unanimous consent to proceed for two minutes. Is there objection?

Mr. MURDOCK. The gentleman from Colorado [Mr. KEATING] is not here. What are you going to ask him?

Mr. THOMAS. Wait, and you will find out. He is here.

Mr. Chairman, the gentleman from Colorado [Mr. KEATING] a few moments ago, in interrogating the gentleman from North Carolina [Mr. WEBB], stated that this amendment is just what organized labor wanted. Is it not a fact that organized labor wanted to exempt organized labor entirely from the operation of the antitrust law, such as is not here offered, and was not this Webb amendment simply the result of a compromise?

Mr. KEATING. If I had the time, Mr. Chairman, I would be very glad to answer that question.

Mr. THOMAS. That could be answered by yes or no.

Mr. KEATING. The amendment proposed by the gentleman from Kentucky [Mr. THOMAS]—

Mr. THOMAS. Mr. Chairman, I object to the gentleman's making a speech in my time. I simply asked him a question.

Mr. KEATING. I have to answer the question clearly. The amendment offered by the gentleman from Kentucky [Mr. THOMAS] was considered by the representatives of organized labor, and they decided that the proposition submitted by Mr. WEBB, of North Carolina, was a stronger proposition and more beneficial to labor organizations than the proposition submitted by the gentleman from Kentucky. [Applause.]

Mr. THOMAS. Is it not a fact that the Webb amendment was accepted by organized labor only after they came to the conclusion that they could not get the amendment that I submitted?

Mr. KEATING. The statement which I made—and I made it very deliberately, because it was repeated to me since this House met, by a leader of organized labor, who is qualified and authorized to speak for organized labor—was that the amendment as submitted by the gentleman from North Carolina [Mr. WEBB] was better, from the viewpoint of organized labor, than the Thomas amendment, which had been previously considered by the labor leaders. [Applause.]

The CHAIRMAN. The question is on the amendment offered by the gentleman from Michigan [Mr. MACDONALD].

The question was taken, and the Chairman announced that the noes appeared to have it.

Mr. MURDOCK. Division, Mr. Chairman!

The committee divided; and there were—ayes 51, noes 98.

Accordingly the amendment was rejected.

The CHAIRMAN. The question now recurs on the amendment offered by the gentleman from Kentucky [Mr. THOMAS].

Mr. THOMAS. Mr. Chairman, I ask to have that amendment read for information.

The CHAIRMAN. If there be no objection, the amendment will be again reported.

The Clerk read as follows:

Strike out the first paragraph of section 7 as amended and insert in lieu thereof the following:

"The provisions of the antitrust laws shall not apply to agricultural, labor, consumers', fraternal, or horticultural organizations, orders, or associations."

The question being taken, the Chairman announced that the noes appeared to have it.

Mr. THOMAS. Let us have a division.

The committee divided; and there were—ayes 70, noes 79.

Mr. THOMAS. Mr. Chairman, I ask for tellers.

Tellers were ordered, and the Chairman appointed Mr. THOMAS and Mr. WEBB.

The committee again divided; and the tellers reported—ayes 69, noes 105.

Accordingly the amendment was rejected.

Mr. BRYAN. Mr. Chairman, I offer an amendment.

Mr. NELSON rose.

The CHAIRMAN. Will the gentleman from Washington withhold his amendment[?] The gentleman from Wisconsin [Mr. NELSON], a member of the committee, will first be recognized.

Mr. NELSON. I desire to offer an amendment.

The CHAIRMAN. The gentleman from Wisconsin offers an amendment, which the Clerk will report.

The Clerk read as follows:

Amend the paragraph as amended by inserting after the word "profit" and before the words "or to forbid," in line 8, page 24, the following "or of cooperative agricultural associations formed for the purpose of buying more cheaply, and of marketing their products to better advantage," so as to make the first paragraph of this section read:

"That nothing contained in the antitrust laws shall be construed to forbid the existence and operation of fraternal, labor, consumers', agricultural or horticultural organizations, orders or associations, instituted for the purpose of mutual help, and not having capital stock or conducted for profit, or of cooperative agricultural associations formed for the purpose of buying more cheaply and marketing their products to better advantage, or to forbid or restrain individual members of such organizations, orders, or associations from carrying out the legitimate objects thereof; nor shall such organizations, orders, or associations, or the members thereof, be held or construed to be illegal combinations or conspiracies in restraint of trade under the antitrust laws." . . .

Mr. NELSON. Mr. Chairman, this House has now done justice to labor organizations, and I am very glad of it. As a member of the committee I earnestly did all I could to secure this result in our report from the committee. I am not going into any argument on this feature of it. I discussed it fully in the report made from the committee and in the speech I made to the House.

I now want to appeal to the House to do justice to the farmers' associations of our country. I want to say to you that this section does nothing for the farmers except to permit them to come together to discuss better methods of farming. Of course, such organizations never were under the Sherman antitrust law; but the language of this section is carefully selected, and in defining the associations that are exempt it says that if they have capital stock or are conducted for profit, then it will not take them from under the ban of the law. This does not legalize organizations of farmers cooperatively buying supplies or selling their products, but may have the effect of clearly rendering them illegal.

Now, gentlemen, I want to impress upon you the importance of business cooperation on the part of farmers in this country and in foreign countries, and at the risk of tiring you a little I wish to call your attention to this voluminous report— . . .

Mr. LEWIS of Maryland. Would not the effect of the permission to organize cooperative associations be to repeal the word "profit" and the words "capital stock" in the clause as perfected up to this time?

Mr. NELSON. Let me say to the gentleman that as I drew this amendment first, to get at this difficulty I struck out the words "not having capital stock and not conducted for profit"; but those words may be necessary with reference to other organizations that might pretend that they were fraternal, or horticultural, or something of that kind. So I have amended this and made a separate classification, specifically exempting agricultural associations that are cooperative, but leaving in the limitation "not having capital stock and not conducted for profit" as to these other organizations.

Mr. LEWIS of Maryland. I will ask the gentleman whether the qualification he desires to make would not open the gate to commercial organizations that the antitrust laws were originally designed to prevent?

Mr. NELSON. I think not. They would have to be shown to be bona fide agricultural associations, and, of course, any sham would be exposed in court.

Now, I wish to call attention to this volume, Senate Document No. 214, Agricultural Cooperation and Rural Credit in Europe. It contains nearly 1,000 pages of testimony taken by a double commission, an American commission consisting of delegates from various States and from Canada, and a United States commission. On the American commission were men appointed from nearly all the States and from the Provinces of Canada, and there was a United States commission consisting of Members of this House and the Senate. Both commissions have made extensive reports which have been printed as public documents. I wish briefly to read a few extracts from the very excellent report of the American commission, which will show you what this movement is.

The person who goes among European farmers for the first time will be impressed with the fact that cooperation is the most important thing about European agriculture. It is, of course, not true that all the farmers band themselves together, and yet that is a very common way of doing farm business. Farmers buy together, sell together, borrow and lend together, insure together, own machinery together, and in some cases actually carry on a farm together. There are 25,000 cooperative societies of various kinds in Germany alone. It is really astonishing to see the extent to which the farmers, particularly the small farmers, have accomplished results which would have been impossible if each farmer had depended upon himself.

* * * * * *

The last sentence is the key to much of the success of the European farmer. He found that alone he could do nothing; together with his fellows he could do a great deal. He proved that one and one are more than two; at least, that two people who work together can accomplish a great deal more than two people who work separately. Hence was formed a habit of doing collectively what farmers had been doing singly and alone, and it was found that as the farmers became accustomed to doing business in this way it proved to be the better way. So gradually at first the method spread. It is important to know that there has been a greater development of cooperation in practically all the Eu⊥ropean countries in the last 10 years than in any previous period in the history of the movement.

As to the extent of cooperation in Europe, the commission said:

The commission visited a dozen countries, and in every one they found active agricultural cooperation. They were not able to visit some countries, as, for example, Bulgaria. But so far as could be learned, with the possible exception of Turkey, there is not a single country in Europe that has not developed a more or less complete system of agricultural cooperation.

There are many more interesting and striking paragraphs to which I would call your attention, showing the enthusiasm which farmers in Europe are showing for cooperative movement. Time will not permit me to read them.

Speaking of cooperation in the United States, it said:

There is in the United States as a whole considerable successful business cooperation in agriculture. The fruit growers of the West through their selling societies, the grain growers of the Central West in their cooperative elevators, the dairymen of the Northwest in their cooperative creameries, the vegetable growers of the eastern coast in their selling societies, the many mutual insurance societies, and the great numbers of cooperative country stores are doing a successful business and are increasing rapidly.

Again, under the head of "Cooperation and its application to the United States and Canada":

Nevertheless the American farmer should gradually, even if slowly, give up the individual method of doing his business and take up the collective method. Otherwise he can not hold his own except in the comparatively few cases of the very large and well-to-do farmers. The great masses of farmers will soon be perfectly helpless in their business relationships unless they can, by collective effort, place themselves on a par with other business men.

Under the head of "Cooperation and the consumers," the report of the commission says:

The immediate purpose of cooperation is a more effective and less expensive means of distributing the products which the farmer grows to the individuals who finally consume them. At present the farmer gets too little of what the consumer pays and probably the consumer pays more than he ought to. Cooperation between producers and cooperation between consumers ought to increase the price to producers and decrease the cost to consumers.

Now, I wish to call your attention to what some gentlemen said to the committee on this subject, and I am surprised to see that the committee has deliberately ignored their recommendation. . . .

Mr. [JOHN R.] FARR [Prog.-R., Pa.]. Will the Webb amendment prevent the cooperation which the gentleman desires?

Mr. NELSON. Unquestionably; it permits nothing except that the farmers can come together and discuss better methods. The moment that they cooperate they must have shares of stock, and it will be considered that they are conducting the organization for profit, and therefore this section does not apply to them. . . .

Mr. GARDNER. Would not it be possible to amend the gentleman's amendment in such a way as to permit a farmers' organization with capital stock, if it so desires, to purchase more cheaply, without opening the door to such an organization to market its products at a price indicative of a combination in restraint of trade?

Mr. NELSON. I think not. But answering that question, the gentleman is fearful of something of which there is no danger of at all to the country. The farmers handle perishable products, and they only hold it over so that it will not be sold when the market is glutted. In the fall they assist each other in reaching a better period of the year. Moreover, the farmers are all hard up, they must have money, they can not hold it over very long. Cooperative marketing merely enables them to find a better market. There is no danger that the farmers of the country could go to such an extent that they would practically monopolize any product. . . .

Mr. GARDNER. Did I understand the gentleman to say that cotton and wool are perishable products?

Mr. NELSON. I did not say so.

Mr. GARDNER. Or potatoes?

Mr. NELSON. Are not potatoes perishable products?

Mr. GARDNER. Not particularly.

Mr. MANN. What does the gentleman from Massachusetts know about potatoes?

Mr. NELSON. It shows what he knows about farming. Now, Mr. Chairman, I want to show you what you are doing. President Van Hise says— . . .

Mr. Chairman, President Van Hise, of the University of Wisconsin, in speaking about the Sherman law and other things before the Committee on the Judiciary, used this language:

The law that stands in the way of beneficent cooperation of this kind should be modified so as to permit that useful and beneficial cooperation. Now, this rising tide, this pressure, has come upon us so that we have increased our force in the department of economics very materially, and there are always farmers in 15 or 20 communities that want instruction along this line; and in this way the cooperation among farmers is increasing in Wisconsin, Nebraska, California, and in many of the States of the South, and in a few years it will sweep over the entire country and we shall have cooperation among the farmers along all lines in the handling of their products. They have now, in the handling of eggs, an association similar to that for the handling of cranberries in Wisconsin and the citrous-fruit [sic] growers of southern California, and under the circumstances it is questionable whether it will be quite so popular a political position to attack cooperation among the farmers.

And I may add that in Wisconsin not only do the cranberry growers cooperate in marketing their products, but the cheese producers, the tobacco raisers, and the potato growers as well.

President Seth Low, of the Civic Federation, an educator, came before the Committee on the Judiciary and, speaking of this very law, which was a ban upon the farmers, he said:

For the last seven years or more I have been carrying on a farm at Bedford Hills in New York. In doing that I very soon became aware of what, I think, is the fundamental problem of the farmer. I am speaking now of the small farmer; it does not affect me at all or other men with capital. But the fundamental problem of the farmer, certainly in the eastern part of the country, and, I suspect, more or less all over the Union, is this: That he buys at retail and sells at wholesale. He has to pay retail prices for everything he gets and then has to take wholesale prices for what he sells. I submit to the committee that there is not another business in the country that can do that. Imagine what would happen to any manufacturer, or any railroad, if they had to pay retail prices for coal and everything that they purchased, and then had to sell their product at the wholesale price of the day. That is the problem with which the farmer is confronted. That was the problem that confronted Denmark and all the European countries. In Europe, where the pressure has been greater, they have solved it through cooperation. They form cooperative societies which have two objects. In the first place, they want to buy together so as to get things at wholesale rates instead of at retail rates; then they want to sell together, so that they can get the benefit of businesslike care in the handling of their products.

Mr. CARLIN. How has that affected the consumer?

Mr. Low. The consumer does the same thing; he combines to buy direct and at wholesale. As I was going to say to you, however, these cooperative associations on the part of consumers would be absolutely ⊥ forbidden under this proposed law. The details of cooperation are a little different in almost every country. England is especially notable for these cooperative associations of consumers.

Further on he said:

I do not believe that the farmer ought to have rights that other Americans have not; but I do think they are entitled to form cooperative societies and to agree to give to them all their business for the purpose of purchasing more cheaply together and for the purpose of selling what they produce to better advantage.

* * * * * * *

I think you will recognize the propriety of cooperative associations of consumers as well as of producers: because they certainly have the right, or ought to have the right, to buy together for the purpose of getting things more cheaply, just as producers should have the right to combine together for the purpose of getting better prices for their products. It is very vital, of course, as far as the farmers are concerned and in its effect upon agriculture. You take these gentlemen in Kentucky who raise tobacco; they can not afford to raise tobacco unless they can get an adequate price; and it is the same way with every other producer. You must encourage generous production by enabling the producer to get all that his goods are worth. I come right back to what I said at the beginning, that the trouble with the farmer is that he has to buy at retail and sell at wholesale. That is not reasonable; and cooperative societies are formed to change that, so that under cooperation the small farmer can get his plow as cheaply as the man who has a bigger business. That must be encouraged. When cooperation is thoroughly well developed, a man who produces a small amount of tobacco can get as good a price as the man who raises a great deal of tobacco.

In answer to the argument that the legalization of cooperative organizations among farmers amounts to class legislation Seth Low said:

Now, what I want to point out is that those people do not combine, either the consumers or the farmers, for the purpose of monopoly. Not a single cooperative association aims at monopoly; it aims at something very different. What it wants to do is to enable the small farmer to buy his plow, to buy his fertilizer, and buy his seed at prices that a man with capital has to pay and at no higher prices.

Mr. Low offered the following suggestions to the committee, as to how the bill ought to be amended so as to legalize cooperative buying and selling by organizations of farmers:

I am not a lawyer; and, with all respect to the lawyers who have suggested this language, I think it would be better to change that phraseology so as to permit in terms the formation of such cooperative associations of producers and of consumers, because I think they have, and ought to have, the right to combine in order to buy more cheaply—to buy at wholesale and distribute economically what they produce.

* * * * * * *

Yes; that would be my suggestion; and I think in that way you would avoid a sort of criticism which I have seen aimed at this bill—that it is class legislation. It is not class legislation if you word it right. I do not think anybody can say it is class legislation to say that laboring men can have the same right to combine for collective bargaining as stockholders have. That is good sense; it is not class legislation. Neither is it class legislation to say that farmers and consumers can combine for the sake of buying more cheaply or selling to greater advantage. That is not class legislation; everybody ought to have that right.

Mr. Chairman, I use the language suggested by Seth Low in this amendment, specifically relieving these cooperative associations from the Sherman law; and that is the only effect the amendment will have.

I have nothing further to add but to repeat that there is a difference between organizations of farmers and monopolies. They are not only different, but are radically opposite. The farm organization is in existence to protect itself from the other. The farm organization is the only way possible for the farmer to protect himself against the oppressions of monopolies and trusts. The farmer deals with his own labor, the product of his life—it is inseparable from him—while the monopolist deals with the capital and credit of others. Monopoly is oppressive, and exacts tributes; but there is not a single case on record where a farm organization has ever practiced oppression upon the consumers, and it is impossible, as I have pointed out. We who have been brought up with farmers, and know what these associations are doing, know that they can not keep their goods; they can not organize so that they can practice oppression. . . .

Mr. WEBB. Does the gentleman think it would be right to allow the cotton farmers of the South or the corn raisers of the West to form corporations whereby they could hold, corner, or monopolize the entire cotton crop or corn crop of the season and compel the world to pay them 25 or 30 or 40 cents a pound for it, or $2 a bushel for corn, and clean up two or three hundred millions of dollars? Does the gentleman think that would be right? I want to get his opinion.

Mr. NELSON. Mr. Chairman, I want to say to the gentleman that I have had that query propounded to me by the gentleman before, and this is my candid judgment. The gentleman is conjuring up an imaginary evil.

Mr. WEBB. Oh, no.

Mr. NELSON. Wait one moment, until I answer the question. If these cotton growers are like the farmers of the Northwest, and I do not believe they are any more thrifty, they can not afford to hold their crops to any such extent. They must dispose of them within a reasonable time to meet the payments of interest and principal on mortgages, and their tenants oftentimes have the results of their toil to live on during the year. The gentleman takes one specific crop. He can make an exception, but the vast quantity of products of the farm are perishable, and there is not a particle of danger; and I will ask the gentleman if his question does not imply that he is not exempting the farmers from the operation of the Sherman law if they have shares of stock or are conducted for profit?

Mr. WEBB. I do. I do not think they ought to be exempted if they form great corporations for profit.

Mr. NELSON. And the gentleman has not exempted them.

Mr. WEBB. No; and I want to say further that when the farmers or any other class of men form a corporation for profit, to pay dividends, and undertake to monopolize any product in this country they ought to come within the Sherman antitrust law, and I would hate to live in a country where that sort of thing did not prevail, and the farmers in my district view this matter just as I do. They do not want to violate law or good morals. They want a fair deal and yield the same to others.

Mr. NELSON. If you have not taken them out, what sort of farm organizations have you taken out of the ban of the law?

Mr. WEBB. Mutual organizations, such as generally exist to-day among them.

Mr. NELSON. That have no capital?

Mr. WEBB. Certainly.

Mr. NELSON. But get together to discuss better methods?

Mr. WEBB. Yes. Has the gentleman any metaphysical scissors that will tell us the difference between the man who forms corporations for monopolistic purposes and the man who spins in the factory or the man who raises sheep?

Mr. NELSON. Can the gentleman name a single instance where any cooperative farm organization has practiced oppression upon the country?

Mr. WEBB. That is not the question.

Mr. NELSON. You have denied this right because you have conjured up an imaginary case with the cotton growers.

Mr. WEBB. Mr. Chairman, I want to say this: I have never had a farmer, whether he raises corn or wheat or oats, ask me to give him a right that he would not have given to every other man in the country. They are an honest set, and ask for no special privileges.

Mr. NELSON. That is what I am insisting upon—not special privilege, but equal rights. You permit capital in any quantity to avail itself of this cooperative principle. They can put their money together, and the money is represented by capital stock, but you deny the farmers of this land the right to do the same.

Mr. WEBB. Oh, we do not at all.

Mr. NELSON. The gentleman says that they can do it, but he knows that they can not very well. The farmer wants to keep his individual farm. He does not want to hold it under a corporation. He wants to be independent, but he wants to cooperate with other independent farmers in buying supplies and in marketing his products without being under the ban of the law—without being a criminal. This you do not permit him to do. . . .

Mr. [EDWARD E.] BROWNE [R., Wis.]. Mr. Chairman, I am in favor of the amendment offered by my colleague, Mr. NELSON, of Wisconsin, which provides that all cooperative agricultural associations formed for the purpose of buying more cheaply and marketing their products to better advantage shall not be construed to be illegal combinations in restraint of trade under the antitrust laws.

Section 7 of this bill, as it now stands, does not exempt any agricultural, horticultural, or cooperative association that is organized for profit or has capital stock.

A great many, I believe, that voted for the Webb amendment did so with the understanding that it exempted from the operation of the law the bulk of the farm organizations, but the gentleman from North Carolina, who drew the amendment, now admits that it was not so intended and does not exempt any farm organization which has capital stock or which is organized for profit.

So the issue at this time is well defined, and it means that if this law is passed without the Nelson amendment that all farmer organizations and cooperative associations that are organized for profit or have capital stock will be prevented from doing business.

At least 75 per cent of the farmer organizations in the United States are organized for profit and have capital stock.

WISCONSIN FARMERS HIT BY THE PROPOSED LAW.

In Wisconsin all our creameries are organized by farmers and our farmers' cooperative organizations are organized for profit, and have capital stock, and would be prohibited from doing business under this proposed law.

The Sherman antitrust law was never intended to apply to farm organizations, and it was not applied to them until it had been in operation many years.

In the famous Kentucky Tobacco case, where the farmers attempted to pool their tobacco so that they could get a fair price for it, a complaint was made, and they were indicted and fined $3,500.[5.549] The complaint was instigated by a combination that desired to distract the attention of the country from the Beef Trust and other prosecutions and make the Sherman law unpopular so it would be repealed.

PURPOSE OF ANTITRUST LAWS.

The antitrust laws were enacted for the protection of the people from monopoly; that is, to prevent speculators from cornering a product and exacting a profit from the consumer many times larger than the amount of labor they placed upon it.

Whoever heard of the farmers of the country getting a monopoly on wheat, potatoes, corn, oats, or dairy products? We all know that there is no danger of the producers scattered all over the United States getting a corner on farm products and selling them at exorbitant prices. We know that the farmer has not the capital; that he is not brought in close enough contact with his neighbor a thousand miles away to corner the market; and that the corn grower in Illinois and the corn grower in Iowa, the potato grower in Maine and the potato grower in Wisconsin could not cooperate so as to control the market.

Cooperation among farmers, with the greatest encouragement the different States and the United States can give, can never possibly be more than local cooperation extending over a few townships or counties.

The antitrust laws are enacted to prevent vast aggregates of capital handled by men in the great centers of population cornering the market, controlling the necessities of life, taking advantage of the producers' necessities and buying at a low figure, sometimes below the cost of production, and without changing the product simply by transporting it and storing it, exacting an outrageous profit from the consumer, a profit out of all proportion to the amount of labor expended, and in many instances amounting to more than the total amount received by the real producer.

[5.549] United States v. Steers, 1 D. & J. 739–44, *aff'd*, 192 F. 1 (6th Cir. 1911).

The Meat Trust is a conspicuous example of the monopoly the antitrust laws are aimed at.

COOPERATION OF FARMERS IN WISCONSIN.

The dairy farmer, through cooperation, is receiving no more than he ought to for his product, but is getting what the consumer is paying less the fair cost of making the butter and cheese and the handling and selling of it. With all other farm products from 35 to 45 per cent of what the consumer pays goes for transporting, handling, and distributing the article.

The cooperative cheese factories in Sheboygan County, one of the great cheese counties in Wisconsin, have an organization for the sale of their cheese, and they are receiving 3 or 4 cents per pound more than the cheese producers in the State of New York, and yet the consumer gets his product cheaper than he does in that State, showing that cooperation of the farmer not only helps him as a producer but also helps the consumer.

The Agricultural Department is expending large sums of money to very good advantage in showing the farmer how he can raise more bushels of grain per acre. In addition to this, it should assist him in marketing his farm products, encouraging him to cooperate, so that he can get a fair profit for the crops that he raises.

There should be no doubt about the law as to it allowing the farmer to cooperate to the fullest extent. It should be so plain that no one would question it, and the adoption of the Nelson amendment will make it so.

The legislative committee from the Society of Equity, of Wisconsin, representing 12,000 farmers, are not satisfied with the proposed law as it now is.

I offer a letter written by Charles A. Lyman, J. Wes. Tubbs, and D. O. Mahoney, legislative committee of the Society of Equity, regarding section 7 of this bill, a similar letter having been sent to the Hon. JOHN M. NELSON:

American Society of Equity,
Madison, Wis., May 23, 1914.

Hon. Edward E. Browne,
House of Representatives, Washington, D. C.

DEAR SIR: Our society, 12,000 strong, is counting on you at this time to champion the cause of agriculture in Wisconsin, which has already suffered from tariff legislation, by leading in enacting laws favorable to cooperation.

Be sure to provide in impending antitrust legislation for free and unhampered cooperative action in assembling, grading, standardizing, packing, storing, and marketing farm products.

Agriculture must be permitted to do its business cooperatively and business can not be done without capital.

Would not a general provision permitting all cooperative business activities where all profits above operating expenses are returned to the patrons—producers and consumers—solve the problem? Anyway it must be solved to save our greatest and most important industry, to effect economies in distribution, and to protect consumers from unlimited exploitation.

Charles A. Lyman,
M. Wes. Tubbs,
D. O. Mahoney,
Legislative Committee.

DEMOCRATIC PARTY CAN NOT AFFORD TO BE UNJUST TO THE FARMERS.

This Congress and the Democratic Party can not afford to strike a blow at the great agricultural interests of this country like the passage of this law will.

The Democratic Party in the solid South may be able to roll up its customary majority regardless of its attitude toward the farmers, but the citizenship of the great northern and western agricultural States do not inherit their political faith. They are not voting a party ticket because their fathers and grandfathers did, but are holding the party in power to a strict accountability.

THE DEMOCRATIC PARTY HAS NOT DEALT FAIRLY WITH THE FARMERS.

I charge the Democratic Party with not dealing fairly with the farmers of the North and West.

I ask, What have you done for the farmers who, during the last crop year, produced nearly $10,000,000 worth of wealth?

You have appropriated $141,000,000 for battleships. You have appropriated $100,000,000 for the Army, although you spent almost two weeks' time making speeches on the Winston Churchill peace resolution. You have appropriated $44,000,000 for rivers and harbors.

You have done all this after talking economy and accusing the former Republican administration of being extravagant.

The 12,000,000 farmers of this country have received very little consideration at your hands.

NOTHING FOR GOOD ROADS.

The $25,000,000 appropriation for wagon roads that passed this House in February is sleeping the peaceful sleep of death in one of the committees of the Senate.

RURAL CREDITS SHELVED.

The farmers of the country demanded and were promised by this administration a law that would enable them to borrow money at a lower rate of interest and on easier terms. This would help the farmer in moving his crops and enable the tenant farmer and the young man with small capital to become the owner of a farm with a fair chance of paying for it.

Many wanted rural-credit legislation to be written into the banking and currency law, where it could have been appropriately placed, but "the powers that be" said no, and it looks as though rural-credit legislation has been relegated with the other broken promises of the Democratic Party.

UNDERWOOD TARIFF DISCRIMINATES AGAINST THE FARMERS.

By taking off the tariff on farm products you have opened wide the doors of the great home market of the United States to the farmers of the world and invited them to dump their surplus.

Argentina, since the tariff bill went into effect, has sent millions of dollars' worth of butter, beef, and corn into the United States.

Canada, which has more acres of agricultural land than the United States, is already in competition with us.

Prof. Charles McCarthy, reference librarian at Madison, Wis., an authority upon the subject, says:

A year ago when I made the statement that the farmers would be in a bad way unless they organized to meet the low tariff some laughed at the statement. Verification of what I said then now comes from other sources.

The president of the Chamber of Commerce of Manchester, England, says:

In three short months all the surplus cattle of Canada have been sold to American buyers. Imports of chilled meats in New York quickly became an established trade. Canadian cream and milk has been sold to such a large extent that there is practically no Canadian butter for export and the quantity of cheese for this market will rapidly diminish. New Zealand butter is also finding an outlet to America.

Dr. McCarthy says:

My statement is borne out by these facts. The farmers should begin to organize for better marketing and production as their only hope to meet the increased competition. We now have what are practically summer prices for butter. I believe this also demonstrates that organization is necessary or our farm industries will eventually go to the wall.

OVERPRODUCTION.

Every farmer knows that we have a surplus crop of some farm product almost every year, which brings down the price of that product below the cost of production.

Overproduction will be a frequent occurrence with no tariff on farm products.

We sometimes think that the United States is the only agricultural country.

Germany raises on an average of from six to seven times the amount of potatoes raised by the whole United States.

Last year the United States raised 331,525,000 bushels of potatoes against Germany's 1,988,591,308 bushels of potatoes. Ireland raised 139,602,358 bushels of poratoes, Canada 78,544,000 bushels, and many other countries raised a large quantity of this product.

It should be remembered that potatoes can be shipped from these countries to our sea ports on the Atlantic sea coast and to our southern ports for from 6 to 8 cents a bushel, about as much as it costs the average farmer to haul his potatoes to the nearest railroad station.

In the year 1913 Russia raised 700,000,000 bushels of wheat; France, 350,000,000 bushels; British India, 280,000,000 bushels; Germany, 138,000,000 bushels; Canada, 170,000,000 bushels; and Argentina, 135,000,000 bushels.

They are shipping eggs to this country from far-away China. In the month of December, 1913, 1,514,296 dozen of eggs, valued at $343,315, were shipped to this country. Under the 5-cent duty on eggs no importations were made.

The importation of corn has increased from 25,819 bushels to 1,632,643 bushels in November, and from 638 bushels to 2,343,444 bushels in December, and in the case of fresh meats of various kinds the importations have advanced from nothing under the old tariff to a total of 16,029,189 pounds under the new.

This shows a surrender of our market to foreign importers.

THE CONSUMER HAS RECEIVED NO BENEFIT.

If anyone will send for Government Bulletin No. 138, issued by the United States Bureau of Labor Statistics, they can get the retail prices of the principal articles of food in each of the 40 important cities throughout the United States.

This bulletin shows that the retail price of the 15 staple articles of food were increased over the same months the year before the tariff went into effect.

I herewith attach statement from this Government bulletin:

Comparing retail prices on October 15, 1913, with prices on the same date 1912, 13 of the 15 articles for which quotations are given advanced and 2 declined in price. Potatoes advanced 42.3 per cent, eggs advanced 14.2 per cent, round steak advanced 12.9 per cent, ham advanced 10.6 per cent, rib roast advanced 8.8 per cent, sirloin steak advanced 8.3 per cent, bacon advanced 8.2 per cent, hens advanced 7.5 per cent, pork chops advanced 6.3 per cent, butter advanced 3.7 per cent, milk advanced 2.7 per cent, corn meal advanced 1.7 per cent, and lard advanced 1 per cent. Sugar declined 8.8 per cent, and flour declined 2.6 per cent.

When the price of each of the articles of food is weighted, according to average consumption in workingmen's families, retail prices were at a higher level on October 15, 1913, than at any other time during the last 23 years and 10 months. Retail prices of food on October 15, 1913, were 70.9 per cent above the average price for the 10-year period, 1890 to 1899; 7.9 per cent above the price on October 15, 1912, and 16.9 per cent above the price on October 15, 1911.

The cities for which actual prices are shown are Atlanta, Ga.; Baltimore, Md.; Birmingham, Ala.; Boston, Mass.; Buffalo, N. Y.; Charleston, S. C.; Chicago, Ill.; Cincinnati, Ohio; Cleveland, Ohio; Dallas, Tex.; Denver, Colo.; Detroit, Mich.; Fall River, Mass.; Indianapolis, Ind.; Jacksonville, Fla.; Kansas City, Mo.; Little Rock, Ark.; Los Angeles, Cal.; Louisville, Ky.; Manchester, N. H.; Memphis, Tenn,; Milwaukee, Wis.; Minneapolis, Minn.; Newark, N. J.; New Haven, Conn.; New Orleans, La.; New York, N. Y.; Omaha, Nebr.; Philadelphia, Pa.; Pittsburgh, Pa.; Portland, Oreg.; Providence, R. I.; Richmond, Va.; St. Louis, Mo.; St. Paul, Minn.; Salt Lake City, Utah; San Franciso, Cal.; Scranton, Pa.; Seattle, Wash.; and Washington, D. C.

STAGNATION IN BUSINESS.

President Wilson, when interviewed May 28, 1914, on the business depression throughout the United States, said:

That while he was aware of the present depression of business, there was abundant evidence that it was merely psychological; that there is no material condition or substantial reason why the business of the country should not be in a most prosperous and expanding condition.

The most conservative authorities upon the unemployed say that there are from one and one-half to two million men out of employment in the United States. These conditions seem due to something more than a state of mind, as indicated by the President.

When our laboring people are out of employment they cease to become consumers, and this injures the markets of the farmer.

Every man, woman, and child in the United States consumes 4.7 bushels of wheat a year, which is equivalent to a barrel of flour a year, while in Russia the consumption of wheat is 2.6 bushels, and in India seven-tenths of a bushel of wheat is consumed by the average inhabitant.

The American people are better clothed and better fed than any class of people in the world, and therefore the 100,000,000 inhabitants of America afford the best home market for the farmers of any country in the world.

FOREIGN CONVICT LABOR COMPETITION.

A recent investigation establishes the fact that there are 2,441,000 convicts in foreign prisons competing with our American workmen. This convict labor is being sold by the countries where the prisons are located at from 5 cents to 25 cents per day. The foreign manufacturer who buys this labor has no rent, storage, light, heat, or power to pay for in the majority of cases. These convicts are manufacturing practically every kind of article that is being manufactured abroad, and these convict-made goods are coming to the United States under the Underwood tariff law in unrestricted competition with goods manufactured by our American labor.

It is conservatively estimated that the annual output of foreign convict labor amounts to $560,000,000 per year.

No wonder our imports are steadily increasing and our exports are falling off.

EXPORTS FALLING OFF.

Official figures from the Department of Commerce show that under the heading of "Manufacturers for the further use in manufacturing" our exports have fallen off $5,100,000 in the single month of April, 1914, compared with the corresponding month of the previous year.

I voted against the passage of the Underwood tariff bill, and in doing so I said, in a speech I made against it, that the passage of that bill would be a reversal of a great industrial policy of the United States, an industrial policy which has brought us great prosperity.

If this prosperity continues under the new industrial policy of "tariff for revenue only," it will be the first time in our country's history.

The Underwood tariff bill has been in force less than nine months, but in that brief space of time it has proven such a failure that there is an overwhelming sentiment against it.

I can not vote for the so-called "Clayton antitrust bill" in its present form, with a discrimination against farmer organizations. I am disappointed in the bill in this and other particulars, and hope it may be amended by the adoption of the Nelson and other amendments. . . .

Mr. HULINGS. Mr. Chairman, if I am in order I desire to offer an amendment to the second paragraph—

The CHAIRMAN. The time has been fixed.

Mr. HULINGS. A parliamentary inquiry.

The CHAIRMAN. The gentleman will state it.

Mr. HULINGS. What is before the committee?

The CHAIRMAN. The committee is considering the first paragraph and debate has been fixed at 70 minutes. The gentleman can offer his amendment later. . . .

Mr. [WILLIAM L.] LA FOLLETTE [R., Wash.]. Mr. Chairman, I do not know as I desire to use five minutes on this question, but I do want to say that, in my opinion, the framers of the Sherman antitrust law never dreamed that at any time it would be used as an instrument to oppress either organized labor or farmers' associations. It would seem, at first thought, when you come down to the legal or ethical point, that farmers' organizations, if incorporated, should be controlled as any other corporation; but when we take into consideration the slight chance of controlling commodities of universal production it would seem to be impossible for the farmers as a class to organize and get their product in such shape they could so control it as to become a monopoly. They can cooperate to such an extent they can keep from becoming the prey of commission and unprincipled middle men. That has been the main object of farmers' societies and farmers' cooperative associations. It has been to try to get at least a fair share of the profit of their toil and a fair share of the money that the consumer pays. I have seen before the days of farmer's cooperative associations when they have had a hard time to make a living, and after they had established the cooperation that they had bettered their condition.

It seems to me that no one should desire to see them put at the mercy of either the commission men or the middle men who prey on them, and that is the reason I think that the farmer, who is the largest in number of any one class in our country, should have the benefit of some fair laws and some fair consideration. I do not think that the farmers as a class want any special legislation or any marked favor. Neither do they desire to be put in a class where, without any chance to form a monopoly, they can be accused of attempting to monopolize trade and be harassed, as they can be, if we leave this bill in its present form. That should not be done. They should not be harassed and forced out of business or forced back into the old ruts that they had to follow before they commenced to cooperate, and I think if you put this measure on the statute books in its present form that so far as the American farmer, the principal class in numbers in this country is concerned, you are taking a step backward and injuring him instead of benefiting him. [Applause.] . . .

Mr. SLOAN. Mr. Chairman, I desire to say in this behalf that I have consulted three Members of the Committee on the Judiciary and was informed that no representative of the farmers came before that committee and demanded this legislation or any part of it. The facts are that the farmers' part in this bill is simply to be used as a stalking horse to obtain other features of this legislation. Well was it said—I noticed the gentleman from Pennsylvania [Mr. CASEY] in his maiden speech said it—that that side of the House was redeeming its pledges, in that ancient and stately joke perpetrated and promulgated at Baltimore, to the farmers and laborers. I desire to speak about it, especially relating to the trust feature, and in support of the Nelson amendment, which seeks to give at least a measure of the favor professed in this bill but in fact withheld.

So far as the farmers are concerned, this is the second installment of the so-called favorable trust legislation. The first installment was presented in the Underwood tariff bill, the sponsors of which claimed it to be a fulfillment of the tariff plank of the Baltimore convention. That plank stated the general Democratic policy for tariff revision downward as follows:

> We favor the immediate downward revision of the existing high and, in many cases, prohibitive tariff duties, insisting that material reductions be speedily made upon the necessaries of life.

You will note that it stood for a reduction of duties rather than a removal of duties. The bill was said to be one for revenue only. In a subsequent clause it provided that certain articles should have the tariff removed absolutely and placed upon the free list, the following being the language used:

> Articles entering into competition with trust controlled products and articles which are sold abroad more cheaply than at home should be put upon the free list.

This is the only authority for expansion of the free list found in the Baltimore platform. In the Underwood bill there was a large expansion of the free list. Eighty per cent of the value of all the American products placed upon the free list and which were not on the free list under the Payne law were products of the farm, so that the majority of this House considered farm products as being in competition with trust-controlled products or were sold abroad more cheaply than at home.

Every farmer in the United States knows that neither one of those statements are true, so that in the name of antitrust legislation a most gigantic imposition was perpetrated upon the farmers of this country.

Two statements are surprising to the country. First, that the farmers' products are trust produced or in competition with trust-produced articles; second, that farmers' products are sold abroad cheaper than at home, and yet these two statements are the only basis for the free listing of nearly all the products of the Northwest.

And now they come in with their second installment of trust legislation for the farmers, and while the first installment was an imposition this one is a fraud. They first include the farmer organization with the laboring men in section 7. Here they pretend to preserve for the farmers, laboring men, and horticultural associations special privileges. But they are preserved only while in a state of repose so far as the farmers are concerned. When they come into action for the purpose of carrying out only those things that can be of value to them, they are prohibited, except where a further provision is provided in the act itself. Now, then, in section 7 the farmers and the labor organizations were placed upon a parity; but in section 18 we find the labor organizations are specially provided for. So that each and every act by which they can accomplish the legitimate purposes of their organization is permitted by the law. We find no corresponding section to section 18 to protect the farmers. Section 18 is as follows:

SEC. 18. That no restraining order or injunction shall be granted by any court of the United States, or a judge or the judges thereof, in any case between an employer and employees, or between employers and employees, or between employees, or between persons employed and persons seeking employment, involving, or growing out of, a dispute concerning terms or conditions of employment, unless necessary to prevent irreparable injury to property, or to a property right, of the party making the application, for which injury there is no adequate remedy at law, and such property or property right must be described with particularity in the application, which must be in writing and sworn to by the applicant or by his agent or attorney.

And no such restraining order or injunction shall prohibit any person or persons from terminating any relation of employment, or from ceasing to perform any work or labor, or from recommending, advising, or persuading others by peaceful means so to do; or from attending at or near a house or place where any person resides or works, or carries on business or happens to be, for the purpose of peacefully obtaining or communicating information, or of peacefully persuading any person to work or to abstain from working; or from ceasing to patronize or to employ any party to such dispute, or from recommending, advising, or persuading others by peaceful means so to do; or from paying or giving to, or withholding from any persons engaged in such dispute, any strike benefits or other moneys or things of value; or from peaceably assembling at any place in a lawful manner, and for lawful purposes; or from doing any act or thing which might lawfully be done in the absence of such dispute by any party thereto. Nor shall any of the acts specified in this paragraph be construed or held unlawful.

This matter, Mr. Chairman, as I say, was not asked for by the farmers of the United States. The farmers of the United States are in favor of equality before the law with the manufacturers, miners, laborers, and all others of this country. But when there is presented, as this bill presents, a motley mass of discriminations and favors to various industries denied to others, then in the general skirmish and scrimmage the farmers are entitled to have their share of that discrimination. For that reason the farmers of the United States do not want this meaningless sop thrown to them in this bill, which has no more substance or satisfaction in it than a Dead Sea apple, which would crumble to ashes upon touch; because there is no provision throughout the whole bill in any place that would protect them in carrying out any special course of action whereby they might forward their industry for the purpose of increasing the prices of their products or perhaps reducing the prices of those which they bought.

Perhaps the most exasperating feature of this legislation is the cheap estimate placed upon the farmers' intelligence and vigilance. The farmers of this country will see through this cheap attempt to placate them for the wrongs which have been inflicted upon them by this Congress and will resent the attempt to make them a stalking horse for other classes interested in legislation. This bill discriminates against the small dealer certainly; whether there is a discrimination against the large dealer is a problem. It has nets to catch small fishes, but none apparently strong enough to catch large ones. The discriminations in section 3 must operate in favor of the large mine owner and against the small.

Section 7 to the farmer must appear a fraud upon its face.

Section 8 grants to the railroads of the United States means of combination and agreement hitherto denied by Congress and until this committee acted which neither House of Congress ever dared to favor.

The Nelson amendment we are now discussing is a discrimination. But if you are in the discriminating business, it is important that you give 30,000,000 people of the United States interested in agriculture their share of the discrimination. But this you deny.

I can understand why this bill was drafted by three Members of the majority party in conjunction with the White House with the minority excluded, as was stated in the opening of this debate. It was so with the tariff bill, which discriminates against the farmer. It was drafted by the majority Members with the same aid, because it is a better means of keeping the real purpose of legislators in the dark. A great many people in the United States thought when the tariff bill was being drafted that trust articles and trust-controlled products, and those that were in competition with trust-controlled products, should be placed upon the free list; that that was intended for the manufacturing interests of the United States, and especially those of the East. But when it was unveiled it was found to strike to the extent of 80 per cent the products of the soil, and to the extent of only 20 per cent other products. [Applause on the Republican side.] . . .

Mr. [WOODA N.] CARR [D., Pa.]. Mr. Chairman, history and chronicle are full of the achievements of heroes, kings, and statesmen in war and politics, but slight insight is given us into the commercial customs or methods of business of ancient or even medieval times. And yet we know that mighty wars were fought whose obscure objects were really the extension of trade, the acquisition of land, the increase of wealth. Since the day when Joseph forced the people to pay him for his corn, first their money, then their flocks, their cattle, and their asses, and lastly their land and their freedom, the spirit of monopoly has pervaded trade. From the primitive practices of royal monopolies of brick and papyrus in Egypt, of mines and banking in Greece, of salt in Rome, and of many less extensive but more significant methods of trade control among merchants, factors, and shipowners, this genius of monopoly has grown through the years in strength and influence until recently one of the leading bankers of America, Mr. George F. Baker, was constrained to admit before the Pujo committee that the conditions prevailing in the United States has brought about a situation not entirely comfortable for a great country to be in. This grave situation is not a result of the natural growth of industry. On the contrary, it has been brought about through unfair trade practices, through the artificial elimination of competition, through the control of credit achieved by a small group of men over our banks and industries. This result has been attained by three principal methods: First, through the consolidation of banks and trust companies, the reservoirs of money, and their control and the control of the large funds of life insurance companies, through stock holdings, voting trusts, and interlocking directorates; second, through large combinations and consolidations of public-service corporations and the formation of huge industrial trusts, intertwined in interest through common directors, voting trusts, and stock holdings; and third, through banker management. The very immensity of these trusts and combinations made necessary their financing through bankers who had acquired the power to control the resources of the depositories of the people's money, and thereby enabled a few large banking houses to demand representation upon the directorates and to dictate the business policy of these large commercial units, the issue of stocks and bonds beyond the reasonable needs of business, the purchase of supplies from favored concerns at prices wholly arbitrary, and for the benefit of corporations in which the same group of men were largely interested.

In other words, through the power acquired by the bankers to grant or withhold credit they were not only able to decree the combination and consolidation of industrial units, thereby making necessary large issues of securities and stocks, determined in amount almost absolutely by the will of the bankers, but they were enabled to charge for their services as underwriters all that the traffic would bear. These huge commissions were only made possible through large consolidations, and therefore it became the interests of the bankers to control industrial organizations and to effect these combinations. With the consequent elimination of competition and the ability to fix prices and control markets they were enabled to earn their interest charges and to pay dividends upon fictitious valuations.

An interesting example of the "vicious circle of control through which our financial oligarchy now operates" is stated by Mr. Louis D. Brandeis in his book, Other People's Money, and How the Bankers Use It:

J. P. Morgan (or a partner), a director of the New York, New Haven & Hartford Railroads, causes that company to sell to J. P. Morgan & Co. an issue of bonds. J. P. Morgan & Co. borrow the money with which to pay for the bonds from the Guaranty Trust Co., of which Mr. Morgan (or a partner) is a director. J. P. Morgan & Co. sell the bonds to the Penn Mutual Life Insurance Co., of which Mr. Morgan (or a partner) is a director. The New Haven spends the proceeds of the bonds in purchasing steel rails from the United States Steel Corporation, of which Mr. Morgan (or a partner) is a director. The United States Steel Corporation spends the proceeds of the rails in purchasing electrical supplies from the General Electric Co., of which Mr. Morgan (or a partner) is a director. The General Electric sells supplies to the Western Union Telegraph Co., a subsidiary of the American Telephone & Telegraph Co., and in both Mr. Morgan (or a partner) is a director. The telegraph company has an exclusive wire contract with the Reading, of which Mr. Morgan (or a partner) is a director. The Reading buys its passenger cars from the Pullman Co., of which Mr. Morgan (or a partner) is a director. The Pullman Co. buys (for local use) locomotives from the Baldwin Locomotive Co., of which Mr. Morgan (or a partner) is a director. The Reading, The General Electric, the Steel Corporation, and the New Haven, like the Pullman, buy locomotives from the Baldwin Co. The Steel Corporation, the Telephone Co., the New Haven, the Reading, the Pullman, and the Baldwin Cos., like the Western Union, buy electrical supplies from the General Electric. The Baldwin, the Pullman, the Reading, the Telephone, the Telegraph, and the General Electric Cos., like the New Haven, buy steel products from the Steel Corporation. Each and every one of the companies last named markets its securities through J. P. Morgan & Co., each deposits its funds with J. P. Morgan & Co., and with these funds of each the firm enters upon further operations.

This specific illustration is in part supposititious, but it represents truthfully the operation of interlocking directorates. Only it must be multiplied many times, and with many permutations, to represent fully the extent to which the interests of a few men are intertwined. Instead of taking the New Haven as the railroad starting point in our example, the New York Central, the Santa Fe, the Southern, the Lehigh Valley, the Chicago & Great Western, the Erie, or the Pere Marquette night have been selected; instead of the Guaranty Trust Co. as the banking reservoir, any one of a dozen other important banks or trust companies; instead of the Penn Mutual as purchaser of the bonds, other insurance companies; instead of the General Electric, its qualified competitor, the Westinghouse Electric & Manufacturing Co. The chain is, indeed, endless, for each controlled corporation is entwined with many others.

Mr. Chairman, the Democratic Party is pledged not to the regulation of monopoly but to its absolute destruction by the enactment of specific legislation. The Baltimore platform declares:

A private monopoly is indefensible and intolerable. We, therefore, favor the rigorous enforcement of the criminal as well as the civil law against trusts and trust officials, and demand the enactment of such additional legislation as may be necessary to make it impossible for a private monopoly to exist in the United States. We favor the declaration by law of the conditions upon which corporations shall be permitted to engage in interstate trade, including, among others, the prevention of holding companies, of interlocking directorates, of stock watering, of discrimination in price, and the control by any one corporation of so large a proportion of any industry as to make it a menace to competitive conditions.

The series of trust bills presented to this Congress are designed to fulfill that pledge to the American people. The present bill embraces six important provisions exclusive of procedural rules, as follows:

First. It attempts to prevent unfair discrimination in price whereby great corporations, by selling their goods at a less price in the particular communities where their rivals are engaged in business than in other places throughout the country, endeavor to destroy competition and render unprofitable the business of competitors. The prohibition is comprehensive and permits of exception only on account of differences in grade, quality, and quantity of the commodity sold, and on account of differences in the cost of transportation. Although 19 or 20 States have, within the last few years, enacted such laws to correct such discriminatory practices within their borders it is very necessary that there should be national legislation on the subject, as it is now possible for a great corporation to lower the prices of its commodities throughout the borders of one State without violation of State laws, and thereby destroy the business of competitors within that State.

Second. It is made unlawful for the owner or operator of a mine or the selling agent thereof in commerce to refuse to sell such product to a responsible person who applies to purchase the same. Thereby it is made impossible that the bounty of the earth shall be monopolized.

Third. It is made unlawful for a manufacturer to contract with a dealer not to use or deal in the commodities of a competing manufacturer. Such practice results in driving out competitive articles from a community and tends to establish a monopoly in the trade of the commodity handled under the exclusive contract and generally results in sales at a higher profit. Very often, however, the merchant finds his shelves filled with articles he is unable to sell. It is unfair to the dealer, but it is more grievously unfair to the millions of American consumers who are compelled to purchase the necessaries of life through the ordinary channels of trade in their respective communities.

Fourth. It is made unlawful for a corporation engaged in commerce to acquire the whole or any part of the stock of another corporation engaged in commerce where the effect of such acquisition is to eliminate or substantially lessen competition between the corporation whose stock is so acquired and the corporation making the acquisition or create a monopoly of any line of trade in any section or community. The evil to be avoided by this prohibition is obvious. It goes much further than the Sherman antitrust law and defines with practical precision in what an undue restraint of trade consists.

Fifth. It is made unlawful after two years (a) for an individual, a member of a partnership, or a director or other officer of a corporation engaged in the business of producing or selling equipment, materials, or supplies to railroads or common carriers to act as a director, officer, or employee of another corporation or common carrier purchasing from such person or the partnership of which he is a member or the corporation of which he is a director or other officer; (b) for any banker, director, or other officer of a bank to be a director, officer, or employee of any common carrier for which such person or bank or trust company acts as underwriter or from which such person, banker, or trust company purchases securities; (c) for any person to be at the same time a director, officer, or employee of more than one bank, banking association, or trust company whose deposits, capital, surplus, and undivided profits aggregate more than $2,500,000; (d) for any person to be at the same time a director in any two or more commercial corporations either of which has capital, surplus, and undivided profits aggregating more than $1,000,000, except common carriers subject to the control of the Interstate Commerce Commission.

Sixth. It is provided that nothing contained in the antitrust law shall be construed to forbid the existence and operation of fraternal, labor, consumers', agricultural, or horticultural organizations or to restrain individual members of such organizations from carrying out the legitimate objects thereof.

The provisions of sections [sic] 9 against interlocking directorates is one of the important and far-reaching legal restraints in the whole history of corporate reform. It is one which, as the President has said, opinion deliberately sanctions and for which business waits. In his message of January 20, 1914, the President said:

It [business] awaits with acquiescence, in the first place, for laws which will effectually prohibit and prevent such interlockings of the personnel of the directorates of great corporations, banks, and railroads, industrial, commercial, and public-service bodies, as in effect result in making those who borrow and those who lend practically one and the same, those who sell and those who buy but the same persons trading with one another under different names and in different combinations, and those who affect to compete; in fact, partners and masters of some whole field of business.

It was developed by the Pujo committee that Mr. George F. Baker, chairman of the board of directors of the First National Bank of New York, is a director in 22 corporations having aggregate resources of $2,272,000,000, and that the directors of that bank are directors in not less than 27 other corporations whose aggregate resources are $4,270,000,000. Mr. James Stillman, chairman of the board of directors of the National City Bank, is a director in 7 corporations, with aggregate resources of $2,476,000,000, and that the directors of that bank are directors in no less than 41 other corporations which have aggregate resources of $10,564,000,000; that the members of the firm of J. P. Morgan & Co. are directors in 47 of the largest corporations in the country; and that these three groups, Messrs. J. P. Morgan & Co., the directors of the First National Bank, and the National City Bank, hold 118 directorships in 34 banks and trust companies having total resources of $2,679,000,000 and total deposits of $1,983,000,000; 30 directorships in 10 insurance companies having total assets of $2,293,000,000; 105 directorships in 32 transportation systems having a total capitalization of $11,784,000,000 and a total mileage of 150,200 miles; 63 directorships in 24 producing and trading corporations having a total capitalization of $3,339,000,000; 25 directorships in 12 public-utility corporations having a total capitalization of $2,150,000,000; in all, 341 directorships in 112 corporations having aggregate resources or capitalization of $22,245,000,000.

Such a condition is contrary to public policy, is violative of the spirit of business fairness, and is destructive of that freedom and democracy of individual opportunity which ought to characterize the institutions of a republic. It is offensive to that scriptural injunction that—

> No man can serve two masters, for either he will hate the one and love the other, or else he will hold to the one and despise the other.

It is in moral opposition to that relationship of trust which legally exists between a corporation and a director. It is a clear rule of law that directors of a corporation are trustees for the stockholders and that the corporate property is a trust fund to be administered by them in the utmost good faith. No contract in which a director is interested can be sustained against attack where the interested director is a necessary part of the quorum. In England they have a rule that whenever it appears that a director of a corporation is interested in corporate matters under consideration by the board of directors, such director is thereby removed from office. In an Ohio case it was said:

> A director whose personal interests are adverse to those of the corporation has no right to be or act as a director. As soon as he finds that he has personal interests which will conflict with those of the company he ought to resign.

Each corporation is interested in obtaining an advantageous bargain and each ought to have a sole claim upon the best endeavors of its agents. As the New York court said:

> The law permits no one to act in such inconsistent relations. It does not stop to inquire whether the contract or transaction was fair or unfair. It stops the inquiry when the relation is disclosed, and sets aside the transaction or refuses to enforce it, at the instance of the party whom the fiduciary undertook to represent, without undertaking to deal with the question of abstract justice in the particular case.

As long ago as 1880 Mr. Justice Field said:

> It is among the rudiments of the law that the same person can not act for himself and at the same time, with respect to the same matter, as the agent of another whose interests are conflicting. The two positions impose different obligations, and their union would at once raise a conflict between interest and duty; and, constituted as humanity is, in the majority of cases duty would be overborne in the struggle.

And yet this salutary rule has been made wholly ineffective to prevent unfair contracts between corporations through the agency of a common director by judicial decision that such contracts are valid when the vote of the interested director was not necessary to carry the resolution or his presence to constitute a quorum, and that even where his vote and presence were so necessary, the contract is voidable only in a proper proceeding taken for that purpose by the corporation, its shareholders, or its creditors, and is not absolutely null and void.

And yet everyone knows that it is the common practice in such cases for a director actively to interest himself in the discussions of such contracts and then have himself recorded as "not voting." Where the interested director is a representative of the fiscal agent of such corporation, it is unnecessary for him even to be present at meetings where such contracts are voted, for since he controls the supply of capital his will can not be disregarded.

This ruling of the courts has rendered actions to set aside such contracts so infrequent as to be almost negligible. Manifestly stockholders have but slight knowledge of the transactions of large corporations which are managed exclusively by a board of directors. Nor would knowledge alone suffice since they are under the necessity of producing evidence often carefully concealed and difficult of exposure. Even with the necessary evidence at hand, a suit against a large corporation or one of its directors is usually an expensive and protracted proceeding, and one which stockholders of moderate means will not often undertake. Even large stockholders may very well fear the power of the interlocked interests of such a director and his associates and conclude rather to bear the ills he has than fly to others that he knows not of.

Mr. Chairman, I would go still further than this bill, for whereas it has been provided that no person shall be a director in two or more commercial corporations either of which has capital of more than $1,000,000, I would extend the prohibition to prevent any person who is a stockholder to the extent of 10 per cent or more of the share capital of any corporation capitalized at $1,000,000 or more from being at the same time a director in any corporation capitalized at more than $1,000,000, except the corporations in which he is a stockholder. I can see no difference in principle in the one case than in the other. The evils to be avoided are identical, the conflict of interest is the same, the divided allegiance is equally evident.

The time has come, Mr. Chairman, to deal effectively with these abuses. The paternal control of a few self-constituted masters can not longer be suffered to obstruct the industrial activity which is the spirit of liberty and the very lure of life. In this bill we lay the ax to the root of the tree of monopolistic control. We seek to destroy the processes which make monopoly possible. And further fulfilling our pledges we make guilt personal. We declare then the offending individual shall himself answer for his offending. We seek to protect the commerce of the Nation and to allow it to flow in the natural channels of free and fair competition, to permit the individualistic spirit of America to find expression and our human resources to be utilized in the freedom of our industrial life. [Applause.] . . .

Mr. LEWIS of Maryland. Mr. Chairman, I should not undertake to discuss this provision further were it not for the deep respect I feel for the high-minded patriotism of the author of the amendment, Mr. NELSON, a compliment I wish to pay him in this public way. I think, however, he, with some others, is proceeding on an assumption with reference to these amendments which is not sustained by the actual conditions of the discussion. That assumption is that in some sort of a way Congress is giving to the farming organizations and to other mutual organizations the rights which they are to enjoy in the future. That is an error. Their right to exist and their conditions of existence will continue to spring from the legislation of the respective States; and the farming organizations in which my friend from Wisconsin [Mr. NELSON] is justly so much concerned can look with confidence to the legislature of his own State for their charters of privileges and their bills of rights.

Mr. NELSON. Mr. Chairman, I should like to ask the gentleman—

Mr. LEWIS of Maryland. Let me first complete this thought. It is only under conditions whereby any commercial organization may become a trust or monopoly that the jurisdiction of national legislation will attach to that organization at all. It is very misapprehensive of the situation to suggest any fear for the farming organizations which exist in this country, because in evidence of that we have the actual situation itself to dispel such fear. There is the well-known California Citrus Fruit Association, of the Pacific coast, which has reached very, very large proportions, and the operations of which are a matter of national notice. Yet, large and important as it is, there has been no effort to apply even the unamended Sherman antitrust law to its operations. There is, therefore, no ground to express the fear that the National Government is about to or may at ⊥ any time proceed against the farming organizations of the country. Their rights will continue to be the rights which are granted them by the respective States. Now I will yield to the gentleman from Wisconsin for his question.

Mr. NELSON. If the States can properly grant them the rights the gentleman mentions, why can not the Congress grant them also the right to be protected interstate?

Mr. LEWIS of Maryland. The Congress does grant that right under the present antitrust laws, especially as qualified and amended by this clause, section 7.

Mr. NELSON. One further question. The gentleman is a very able representative of labor, and as such he asked relief for labor organizations because they were always under the threat of being prosecuted under the Sherman law. Why does he not ask, in all fairness, that farmers be treated as he has insisted that labor should be treated?

Mr. LEWIS of Maryland. We do give them the same rights in the same clause and in the same language of section 7.

Mr. NELSON. Oh, but the gentleman—

Mr. LEWIS of Maryland. There was this difference: The labor organizations had been attacked, and successfully attacked, in the courts.

Mr. NELSON. But the farmers have also been attacked in Kentucky, as the gentleman knows.

Mr. LEWIS of Maryland. Both of them are relieved from that attack in the same provision. . . .

Mr. NELSON. The gentleman from Maryland is very fair, and I want to say to him that I am very sorry to see that labor has deserted its old-time ally, the farmer. Labor is specifically excluded, because of the two qualifications, "capital stock" and "conducted for profit." But what has the farmer, if he organizes a cooperative business association for profit?

Mr. LEWIS of Maryland. That introduces what I would wish to add to my remarks. What is it that the farmer of the United States wants? I do not believe he wants to raise prices, as a trust or monopoly is instinctively designed to do. What he wants is to get for his own products the prices that he knows the consumers of this country are paying for them. If we could give the farmer a method by which he could secure for his product what the consumers actually pay, I am sure he would be delighted; farming prosperity would be greatly augmented and the Nation itself blessed by such prosperity.

Now, there is nothing in this provision that is not designed to give him the fullest opportunities to organize with reference to the marketing of that product through mutual cooperation. But I am sure the gentleman recognizes that in dealing with the trusts the statutes must draw lines of distinction, and the statute in this particular case draws its line of distinction between the organization of men and the monopolizers of commodities. That distinction is sustained by the instincts of justice in the human race. The ordinary workman in the factory can combine his manhood, his intelligence, and his organizing instincts for mutual advantage. The farmer is explicitly mentioned as having the right to do the same thing. Now, to do otherwise would be to open the gates for, possibly, that citrus fruit association, if it ever should overgrow and overleap the bounds where national welfare becomes involved. I think that in all fairness to the gentleman from Wisconsin it can be claimed for this section 7, as it is now amended, that it is equally just to all forms of human labor, on the farm as well as in the factory. [Applause.] . . .

Mr. FALCONER. Mr. Chairman, I speak in favor of the amendment offered by the gentleman from Wisconsin [Mr. NELSON]. I believe there was something also in the statement of the gentleman from Pennsylvania [Mr. GRAHAM] a few minutes ago when he said that this bill seems to treat of several distinct lines of legislation. It is characteristic of this Congress to do an omnibus legislative business. I believe it would have been wiser for the Congress to have treated the question of labor and farm cooperative associations entirely separately from monopolies and trusts.

This bill—and I do not rely on my own judgment alone, but from general discussion of eminent gentlemen—is very much complicated; but there should be no misunderstanding regarding the rights of farm cooperative associations in an endeavor to obtain just consideration when organizing among themselves for the purpose of profitably marketing their own produce. . . .

Mr. MORGAN of Oklahoma. Mr. Chairman, I should not impose further remarks on the House if I did not really believe that there is great merit in the amendment proposed by the gentleman from Minnesota. The first paragraph of section 7 of the bill as reported by the committee and as amended by the amendment offered by the gentleman from North Carolina is as follows:

SEC. 7. That nothing contained in the antitrust laws shall be construed to forbid the existence and operation of fraternal, labor, consumers', agricultural, or horticultural organizations, orders, or associations instituted for the purposes of mutual help, and not having capital stock or conducted for profit, or to forbid or restrain individual members of such organizations, orders, or associations from carrying out the legitimate objects thereof, nor shall such organizations or orders or associations, nor the members thereof, be held or construed to be illegal combinations or conspiracies in restraint of trade under the antitrust laws.

Now, I have prepared what I think would be a proper substitute for the first paragraph of section 7, as quoted above. It is as follows:

SEC. 7. That nothing contained in the antitrust laws shall be construed to prevent the existence or operation of labor organizations; or to forbid such labor organizations or persons belonging thereto from entering into any contract, agreement, or arrangement with a view to lessening the hours of labor; or of increasing their wages; or of bettering their conditions; or to forbid the existence and operation of consumers' organizations; or to forbid such organizations or members thereof from entering into any contract, agreement, or arrangement with a view to lessening the cost to them of goods, wares, and merchandise, or of any agricultural or horticultural product; or to forbid the existence or operation of any farmers' organization or any agricultural or horticultural organization; or to forbid such organizations or the members thereof from entering into any contract, agreement, or arrangement with a view to reducing the cost to them of tools, implements, machinery, fertilizers, or of any other supplies needed by persons engaged in agriculture or horticulture; or with a view to collective bargaining in the sale of their products or to obtain better credit or lower interest; nor shall such organizations or orders or associations, nor the members thereof, be held or construed to be illegal combinations or conspiracies in restraint of trade under the antitrust laws.

My objection to section 7 as it has been amended is that under it only farmers' organizations without capital stock and not conducted for profit would be legal under this section. In other words, it exempts from antitrust laws only farmers' organizations organized for mutual help along social, literary, and educational lines. There has been no attempt to dissolve such farmers' organizations, so that the provisions of section 7 really give to farmers nothing. While we are considering this question we should in plain language give the farmers the right to organize, even with capital stock or for profit, so long as their organizations are along legitimate lines to aid them in marketing their products as cheaply as possible and in purchasing their supplies as cheaply as possible.

Now, the amendment offered by the gentleman of Minnesota [Mr. NELSON] is broad enough to give the farmers what they need and should have. I think it was Sir Horace Plunkett, who made a thorough study of American agriculture, and who has devoted his life largely in an effort to improve agricultural conditions in Ireland, who said that improvement in agriculture must come through better farming, better business, and better living, and that the first of these was better business in farming. Improvement in farming—the making of the farm what it should be in this country— must come through better transportation facilities, better educational advantages, and better organization among our farmers.

As a member of the Judiciary Committee I filed a minority report to this bill, in which I said:

The law not only should not prohibit but should encourage farmers to organize with a view to purchasing implements, machinery, and other farm supplies at less cost and with the view to collective bargaining in the sale of their products and in the purchase of supplies. In France, Germany, and other European countries farmers' organizations are authorized by law. The line along which these organizations can act is definitely defined. Governmental aid, direction, and assistance is given. Such organizations are encouraged to engage in a wide field of purely business transactions. These organizations have contributed immensely to the expansion of the agricultural interests of these countries. It would be exceedingly unfortunate at this time, when we are about to enter upon the important task of providing our farmers with better credit facilities, to enact a law which may be construed to make all farmers' organizations unlawful except such as are organized for the mutual benefit of members along literary, insurance, and social lines.

Practically every other business is highly organized but the business of farming. There are about 6,500,000 farmers. Something like 12,000,000 persons over 10 years of age toil on the farm. The farmers are at a great disadvantage. Labor is organized. Business is organized. Concentration, combination, cooperation everywhere except among the farmers. With the most intelligent farmers of the world, in business cooperation our farmers are far behind the less intelligent farmers of other countries. To aid our farmers in the line of greater cooperation has now become a national duty, and it would be hardly short of a public calamity to enact a statute which on its face restricts and limits to a narrow sphere the purposes for which agricultural associations may be formed.

⊥9578 ⊥ I know the gentlemen constituting the leadership on this committee have no desire to neglect the farmer. I know the gentleman from Maryland [Mr. LEWIS], who is the champion in the interest of labor, has no desire to do an injustice to the farmer, and yet, as I have studied this question, I believe that the National Government ought not only to permit farmers to organize, but that the National Government should make appropriation to encourage the farmers to organize.

The United States is doing more and has done more along the line of education for the farming interests than any nation on earth, but along the lines of teaching our farmers to organize for better business we are a quarter of a century behind the great European Governments. There is no question about that. . . .

Mr. WEBB. Wherein do the farmers get more in the Nelson amendment than we have given them in the amendment just adopted?

Mr. MORGAN of Oklahoma. I think there is some question of whether there can be a farmers' organization to aid the farmers in marketing the crops more cheaply, or in purchasing their supplies at a less price under the committee amendment which has been adopted. To carry on this kind of an organization it may be necessary to have capital stock, and it may be necessary that these organizations shall be for the purpose of profit. As long as we do not permit the farmer to organize trusts to elevate prices of cotton, wheat, or some other staple product, we are doing the country no injury.

We passed the tariff act, but we all know that under that act the farmer is largely placed in competition with the farmers of the world, however ignorant they may be, or however cheap the labor they may employ, or however cheaply they may be able to produce farm products. We passed the currency act, but you postponed the bill to give our farmers cheaper interest. What have you done for the farmer? Now, when you are passing a third great bill, you are about to place therein a section which, in my judgment, does not do the farmers of this country justice. I believe that it is in the interest not only of the farmer but in the interest of the great consuming masses of the country that we should encourage the farmers to organize to market their crops and in buying supplies.

Gentlemen who pose here as champions for labor are indirectly pleading against labor when they oppose the organization of farmers. We want the farmers to organize so that the products of the farm can come more directly to consumers with less cost and with a fewer number of middlemen. [Applause.] . . .

Mr. FLOYD of Arkansas. Mr. Chairman, I desire to oppose the amendment offered by the gentleman from Minnesota. In the exception made in section 7 as it is written we use the same language in reference to farmer's organizations that we do in reference to labor and other organizations mentioned. We believe to that extent they should be differentiated from industrial and other corporations organized for profit. Gentlemen, I represent a farming district, and I also represent one of the greatest horticultural districts in the United States, but I am opposed to incorporating a provision in this bill that will allow the farmers and the horticulturists of this country to enter into combinations to increase the price of their products, which are industrial commodities, when in the existing law we forbid manufacturers and other classes of citizens from entering into such combinations.

I come from the South, and the South produces three-fourths of the cotton in the world and perhaps more. I am opposed to any law that would allow the cotton farmers of the South to enter into combinations to control the price of cotton which at the same time would make it a crime for the manufacturers who purchase that cotton and manufacture it into cloth to enter into like combinations to raise the price of the manufactured product. For these reasons we think the amendment should be rejected. I represent the majority of the committee in opposing the amendment offered by the gentleman from Wisconsin, and I hope the House will vote it down. [Applause.]

Mr. WEBB. Mr. Chairman, just one word before we vote. The Illinois antitrust act, as my friend from Illinois knows, undertook to exempt agricultural products and live stock while in the hands of the producer and raiser. It was in these words:

> The provisions of this act shall not apply to agricultural products and live stock while in the hands of the producer and raiser.

That was in the antitrust act.

A man by the name of Connolly was the defendant when this particular act came to the notice of the Supreme Court.[5.550] When the Supreme Court came to pass upon it they said that that act was void because it undertook to exempt agricultural products and live stock. . . .

Mr. MANN. That was under a constitutional limitation on the power of the Legislature of Illinois, and that is not in the United States Constitution.

Mr. WEBB. I understand that perfectly. The fourteenth amendment forbids any State to deny every citizen the equal protection of the law. That is the ground on which the Supreme Court in this case puts its opinion in declaring the statute unconstitutional. But I want to call attention to this one sentence in the opinion of that great and good judge, Judge Harlan:

> We conclude this part of the discussion by saying that to declare that some of the class engaged in domestic trade or commerce shall be deemed criminals if they violate the regulations prescribed by the State for the purpose of protecting the public against illegal combinations formed to destroy competition and to control prices, and that others of the same class shall not be bound to regard those regulations, but may combine their capital, skill, or acts to destroy competition and to control prices for their special benefit, is so manifestly a denial of the equal protection of the laws that further or extended argument to establish that position would seem to be unnecessary.[5.551]

The proposition of my friend from Minnesota [Mr. NELSON] is to allow a certain class of people to form corporations with the avowed purpose of monopolizing certain products for the purpose of enhancing the prices of those products. If that be his amendment, I do not believe that any man ought to vote for it, because I do not see why one man should have the right to enhance the price of a certain class of products by monopoly whereas another man is denied that same right and is put in jail if he does it. . . .

Mr. NELSON. Therefore the gentleman feels that farm organizations should be properly under the Sherman antitrust law?

Mr. WEBB. No; I do not believe that they should, if they are organizations for mutual help, without profit, just like labor organizations, and this bill expressly legalizes their existence.

Mr. NELSON. Will the gentleman explain how any farm organization not organized for profit could possibly be in violation of the terms of the law?

Mr. WEBB. If a farmer or a doctor or a merchant or a manufacturer, or a combination of them, violates the law of the land, they ought to be punished for it. . . .

Mr. MANN. Under the Webb amendment which we have just agreed to, would it not be lawful for 10,000 or 100,000 farmers to join an organization not for profit?

Mr. WEBB. Absolutely.

Mr. MANN. To raise the price of wheat or the price of cotton or to refuse to sell it at a less price than a certain fixed price higher than the then market price?

[5.550] Connolly v. Union Sewer Pipe Co., 184 U.S. 540, 22 S. Ct. 431, 46 L. Ed. 679 (1902).
[5.551] 184 U.S. at 564.

Mr. WEBB. I do not know whether it would go that far or not. As long as the product is their own cotton or corn they can hold it as long as they please.

Mr. MANN. I asked the question, and the gentleman said a while ago that he did not believe in that; but is not that the effect of the amendment that we agreed to, as long as the organization is not for profit, that it shall not be considered as an organization in restraint of trade?

Mr. WEBB. That is what the amendment says; yes.

Mr. MANN. So that if a million farmers, if they could get them to agree, could agree not to sell cotton below a fixed price or corn or wheat or any other product below a fixed price, and that agreement would be lawful?

Mr. WEBB. So long as the farm products are in the hands of those who produce them.

Mr. MANN. It might not be in hand, but it might be in a warehouse.

Mr. WEBB. That is still in the producer's possession.

Mr. CARR. Would it not be for profit if it raised the price, and therefore illegal?

Mr. MANN. But it would not be an organization for profit.

Mr. CARR. That is what the gentleman says—organized for profit.

Mr. WEBB. I do not believe we ought to permit corporations organized for profit to monopolize any product and to depress or raise the price of any product, for such would be offensive to every principle of law against monopoly and restraint of trade.

The CHAIRMAN. The question is on agreeing to the amendment offered by the gentleman from Wisconsin.

The question was taken; and on a division (demanded by Mr. NELSON) there were—ayes 23, noes 59.

So the amendment was rejected.

Mr. BRYAN. Mr. Chairman, I offer the following amendment, which I send to the desk and ask to have read.

The Clerk read as follows:

Page 24, after the word "laws," at the end of the Webb amendment, add the following:
"There shall be no abridgment of the right of wage earners and producers to organize for the protection of wages and improvement of labor conditions."

Mr. BRYAN. Mr. Chairman, I claim no pride of authorship in this amendment. A very much greater Bryan than I is the man who wrote this amendment. I have copied it verbatim from the Democratic platform enunciated at Baltimore by the Democratic Party, and it is declared to be the last word of that party on this particular subject. . . .

Mr. Chairman, this is a part of the Democratic platform, and it gives me a great deal of pleasure to dish up to the Democrats here an amendment which ordinarily I know they would not adopt, but which, under the peculiar conditions existing, it being a part of their own platform, they will surely adopt.

It goes a good deal further than the amendment that has been adopted, for it provides that there shall be no abridgment of the right of labor to organize to promote higher wages and protect their own product, and it is true it might, under interpretation, grant labor a great deal more rights than labor has demanded. But it is a part of the Democratic platform. . . .

Mr. HENRY. Does the gentleman wish to adopt all of the Democratic platform?

Mr. BRYAN. I will say to the gentleman that I could hardly ask to put all of the Democratic platform in this bill, for if we were to do so we would save the Panama Canal.

Mr. HENRY. The gentleman knows that all of his amendment is in section 7 as amended?

Mr. BRYAN. If it is already in the bill, then it will not be out of place to call the matter to the attention of Congress and permit Congress to vote upon it. The Democratic platform has some good things in it, but I have noticed that it has not always been approved. I have noticed that on two or three occasions it has been denied recognition on the floor of this House, and I am anxious to see whether in this particular case the very words of the Democratic platform will prove to be obnoxious to the members of the Democratic Party on this floor. I ask that the amendment be adopted; it comes from such an eminent authority.

I now yield to the gentleman from Nebraska [Mr. SLOAN].

Mr. SLOAN. Speaking about the plank in the Baltimore platform, I want to ask the gentleman if he has read the latest bulletin to discover whether or not it is a slight interference and like a good many others it has been repudiated?

Mr. BRYAN. Well, I have not discussed the latest bulletin, but I recognize the fact that when we are on the Democratic platform, according to some precedents, we have to learn what the latest authority is about it, but I do not think in a case of this kind, in a matter involving the Democratic Party's interpretation of its duty to labor, that anybody would have to be consulted, and I think the fact that this amendment is a plank from the Democratic platform ought to be enough not to require any debate whatever, and I hope it will be adopted. . . .

The CHAIRMAN. The question is upon the amendment offered by the gentleman from Washington.

The question was taken, and the amendment was rejected.

Mr. HULINGS. Mr. Chairman, I offer an amendment, which I send to the Clerk's desk. I do not know it is in order [sic] at this time, because it is an amendment to the second paragraph.

The CHAIRMAN. It is not in order at present, the Chair will state to the gentleman. The Clerk will report the amendment offered by the gentleman from Illinois to the paragraph which is pending.

The Clerk read as follows:

Page 24, strike out lines 11 to 24, both included.

Mr. MANN. Mr. Chairman, this amendment— . . .

Mr. HULINGS. I understand the gentleman's amendment is to strike out the paragraph.

The CHAIRMAN. So the Chairman understands.

Mr. HULINGS. My amendment is to insert.

The CHAIRMAN. The gentleman from Illinois [Mr. MANN] has the floor at the present time.

Mr. HULINGS. The gentleman's amendment is to strike out, while the amendment I present is to perfect the section, and I assume it has precedence.

The CHAIRMAN. Such an amendment as the gentleman indicates would be a preferential amendment. . . .

Mr. CARLIN. Mr. Chairman, I want to make a suggestion to the gentleman while he is on his feet. I want to suggest to gentlemen who have amendments already prepared that they send them to the desk and there have them read, so that they can be included in the debate.

Mr. MANN. I hope this will not be taken out of my time. I suggest to the gentleman in charge of the time to yield to gentlemen to offer amendments. I am perfectly willing to delay, so far as I am concerned, until those amendments are disposed of. . . .

The CHAIRMAN. The gentleman from Oklahoma [Mr. FERRIS] is recognized.

Mr. FERRIS. Mr. Chairman, I offer an amendment, which I send to the Clerk's desk.

The CHAIRMAN. It is to be considered as pending?

Mr. FERRIS. Yes.

Mr. MANN. He offers the amendment, if it is in order, to perfect the text.

Mr. FERRIS. I thought the gentleman from Illinois wanted to go ahead.

Mr. TOWNER. Mr. Chairman, would it not be better if these amendments were offered in connection with the remarks of the gentleman from Oklahoma and other gentlemen?

Mr. WEBB. If the gentleman from Illinois will yield, I will recognize each one of these gentlemen to offer amendments.

Mr. MANN. I will yield.

Mr. FERRIS. Mr. Chairman, let my amendment be reported.

The CHAIRMAN. The Clerk will report the amendment offered by the gentleman from Oklahoma [Mr. FERRIS]. . . .

The Clerk read as follows:

Amendment by Mr. FERRIS:

"Page 24, line 24, after the word 'rates,' insert the following proviso: '*Provided*, That from and after the passage of this act it shall be unlawful for any corporation or any person or persons to transport the products of any mine or mines, including coal, oil, gas, or hydroelectric energy, either by rail, water, pipe line, transmission line, or otherwise from one State, Territory, or District of the United States to another State, Territory, or District of the United States, or to any foreign country, who shall not become a common carrier within the meaning and purposes of and subject to the act entitled "An act to regulate commerce," approved February 4, 1887.' "

Mr. WEBB. Mr. Chairman, I make the point of order that that is not germane. It does not sound germane from the reading of it.

Mr. FERRIS. I want to be heard on that, Mr. Chairman.

Mr. HULINGS. Mr. Chairman, I believe I have sent to the desk an amendment already.

Mr. FERRIS. The gentleman from North Carolina [Mr. WEBB] has made a point of order on my amendment. I want to be heard on the point of order.

The CHAIRMAN. The Chair will state that the gentleman from Pennsylvania [Mr. HULINGS] did not have the floor.

Mr. HULINGS. I had the floor to offer an amendment and was recognized by the Chair.

The CHAIRMAN. The Chair will state to the gentleman that an agreement was made by the committee to limit debate on this section.

Mr. HULINGS. I did not want to be run over; that is all.

Mr. FERRIS. Mr. Chairman, I hope argument on the point of order will not be taken out of my time. I want to be heard on the point of order.

This bill is to supplement existing laws against unlawful restraints and monopolies and combinations for unlawful purposes. This particular paragraph deals with common carriers and interlocking directorates and traffic arrangements.

Mr. MANN. Oh, there is nothing about interlocking directorates and traffic arrangements in this paragraph.

Mr. FERRIS. Listen a moment and let us determine who is right. This section provides:

Nothing contained in the antitrust laws shall be construed to forbid associations of traffic, operating, accounting, or other officers of common carriers for the purpose of conferring among themselves or of making any lawful agreement as to any matter which is subject to the regulating or supervisory jurisdication of the Interstate Commerce Commission, but all such matters shall continue to be subject to such jurisdiction of the commission, and all such agreements shall be entered and kept of record by the carriers, parties thereto, and shall at all times be open to inspection by the commission: *Provided*, That nothing in this act shall be construed as modifying existing laws prohibiting the pooling of earnings or traffic, or existing laws against joint agreements by common carriers to maintain rates.

The amendment I have offered, Mr. Chairman, is to amend and supplement the antitrust laws of the United States, and has to do with the particular paragraph under consideration, and has to do with the particular bill now pending before the House. Nothing can be more germane, nothing could be more in order, dealing precisely with the proposition of carrying in [sic] interstate business, and with the proposition laid down in this section and even in the title of the bill. . . .

Mr. WEBB. Is not that very question now pending in the Supreme Court of the United States on appeal from the State of Oklahoma, and is not the decision of that court expected on the 8th of this month?

Mr. FERRIS. It is. But this is to strengthen the law the Commerce Court sought to destroy. The Interstate Commerce Commission has for a long time been trying to bring pipe lines under their own jurisdiction, and they instituted a series of proceedings on their own motion to bring that about.[5.552] The Prairie Oil & Gas Co., with others, went in and enjoined the commission, and I hold in my hand the decision in the Prairie Oil & Gas case, which was decided by the Commerce Court,[5.553] and I think the dissenting opinion by Judge Mack is the correct law and ought to be the law; but I fear that the Supreme Court will not [sic] uphold the decision of the Commerce Court, and I want to write this amendment into the law so we will be sure to get relief.[5.554] This amendment was submitted to Secretary Lane, who probably knows more about this matter than most of us here, and he is heartily in favor of the adoption of such a principle. This is too important to pass by lightly.

Mr. WEBB. Mr. Chairman, our view is that while this amendment may be germane to some portion of the bill, it certainly is not germane to this particular paragraph of this section, which exempts certain traffic arrangements from the operation of the antitrust law.

In addition to that, the gentlemen from Oklahoma ought not to undertake to take two bites at the same cherry. They have submitted their controversy to the highest court in the land, and they ought to wait until the 8th day of this month, when the proceeding will probably be terminated, before they ask to put something new into this bill, and particularly in this paragraph of this section. . . .

Mr. CARTER. You expect to pass this bill before the 8th of this month, do you not?

Mr. WEBB. Yes; and you expect this decision by the 8th.

Mr. CARTER. Suppose you do not get the decision by the 8th of this month, and then this bill is passed?

Mr. WEBB. There is another branch of this lawmaking body where the gentleman may have his amendment offered.

Mr. CARTER. We should be very glad to offer it there, but we have not the privileges over there which we have in this House.

The CHAIRMAN. The paragraph under consideration provides that nothing contained in the antitrust laws shall be construed to forbid associations of traffic, operating, accounting, or other officers of common carriers for the purpose of conferring among themselves or of making lawful agreements, and so forth. The amendment offered by the gentleman from Oklahoma [Mr. FERRIS] provides that it shall be unlawful for any corporation or person or persons to transport the products of any mine or mines, including coal, and so forth, unless they become common carriers under the act of 1887. The Chair fails to see how the amendment offered by the gentleman from Oklahoma can be germane to this particular paragraph. It may be entirely germane to other sections of the bill which have not yet been reached, but upon that the Chair is not now called upon to rule.

Mr. FERRIS. If the Chair has any doubt about it, I confess that the section has two independent propositions in it. The first is purely a labor proposition, and the second is a carrier proposition. I will offer it as a separate section, section 7 1/2, and will strike out the word "provided."

The CHAIRMAN. The Chair will state that it is not in order to offer it as a separate section now, because we are considering section 7.

Mr. FERRIS. The chairman of the committee a moment ago, in answer to a question asked of him, said he was of the opinion that an amendment offered as a separate section would constitute an amendment to this paragraph and would come

---

[5.552] Pipe Lines, 24 I.C.C. 1 (1912) (pipelines are carriers under ICC jurisdiction).

[5.553] Prairie Oil & Gas Co. v. United States, 204 F. 798 (Commerce Ct. 1913) (Mack, J., dissent at 821). In reversing the ICC decision, the Commerce Court held that the 1906 amendment to the Interstate Commerce Act was unconstitutionally broad and that Congress exceeded its powers under the commerce clause in passing the amendment.

[5.554] The Pipe Line Cases, 234 U.S. 548, 34 S. Ct. 956, 58 L. Ed. 1459 (1914) (June 22). Representative Ferris' concern was unfounded. The Supreme Court reversed the Commerce Court, upholding the legality of the ICC's jurisdiction. The carriers involved in the case were: Ohio Oil Co., Standard Oil Co., Standard Oil of Louisiana, Prairie Oil & Gas Co., Uncle Sam Oil Co., and Tide Water Pipe Co. All were held to be subject to ICC jurisdiction except Uncle Sam Oil Co., which was held to be an intrastate carrier.

within the rule. If the Chair thinks otherwise, I will offer it as soon as the paragraph is disposed of.

The CHAIRMAN. The Chair will state that as long as there are any amendments to be offered to this particular paragraph it will be out of order to offer the amendment which the gentleman from Oklahoma proposes. The point of order is sustained.

Mr. FERRIS. I will withdraw the amendment at this time and will ask the Clerk to have it returned to me. . . .

Mr. VAUGHN. Mr. Chairman, I desire to offer an amendment.

The CHAIRMAN. The gentleman from Texas offers an amendment, which the Clerk will report.

The Clerk read as follows:

Add at the close of section 7 the following paragraph:
"Nothing in the antitrust laws shall be construed to forbid persons operating local telephone exchanges engaged in commerce from selling their local exchanges to competitors for local business or from acquiring local exchanges from competitors for local business when such sale or acquisition is not forbidden by any law of the State or locality where the exchange is situated and competition in the transmission of interstate toll messages is not interrupted nor interfered with."

Mr. FLOYD of Arkansas. Mr. Chairman, I desire to make a point of order against that amendment at this point. I do not think it is germane to this section or paragraph.

Mr. VAUGHAN. I think it is germane, and I should like to be heard on the point of order, but I would not like to have it taken out of my five minutes. . . .

The CHAIRMAN. Does the gentleman propose this as a separate paragraph or section?

Mr. VAUGHAN. I offer it as a separate paragraph to this section.

Mr. FLOYD of Arkansas. I make the point of order that it is not germane to this section.

The CHAIRMAN. The Chair does not think the amendment of the gentleman from Texas is in order at this time. It is not germane to the paragraph which is now under consideration.

Mr. VAUGHAN. Mr. Chairman, I should like to be heard on that for a moment, and to suggest that this paragraph proposes to exempt certain transactions from the operation of the antitrust laws. . . .

Mr. FLOYD of Arkansas. I will state to the gentleman that it seems to me if it is germane anywhere, it is germane to the section relating to holding companies, which is section 8. I will state to the gentleman that there are a number of exceptions in that section, and it seems to me that section 8 is the one that will make unlawful the transactions that the gentleman desires to exempt, if anything in this bill does make them unlawful, so that there would be the proper place to offer it, provided, of course, it should be held to be germane at that point.

Mr. VAUGHAN. That being the case I ask unanimous consent to withdraw the amendment now and offer it to section 8.

The CHAIRMAN. If there be no objection, permission will be granted to withdraw the amendment.

There was no objection. . . .

Mr. HULINGS. Mr. Chairman, I desire to offer an amendment.

The CHAIRMAN. The gentleman from Pennsylvania offers an amendment, which the Clerk will report.

The Clerk read as follows:

Page 24, line 21, strike out the colon after the word "commission" and insert a comma and the following:
"But no such agreement shall go into effect or become operative until the same shall have first been submitted to and approved of by the Interstate Commerce Commission." . . .

Mr. HULINGS. Mr. Chairman, it seems to me in reading this paragraph that as it stands it would give authority to these traffic associations to make pooling arrangements or lawful agreements as to any matter which is subject to the regulating or supervisory jurisdiction of the Interstate Commerce Commission, but it does not distinctly give the Interstate Commerce Commission authority over the rule or the agreement that is made.

Mr. WEBB. I should like to make a statement. It was the idea of the committee that these agreements could not go into operation until they were O.K'd by the Interstate Commerce Commission.

Mr. HULINGS. I presume so.

Mr. WEBB. We think that is a reasonable conclusion to draw from the section or paragraph.

Mr. HULINGS. I doubt whether the language is clear.

Mr. WEBB. That was our intention.

Mr. HULINGS. The amendment makes that thoroughly clear, and I ask that the amendment be again reported.

The CHAIRMAN. If there be no objection, the amendment will be again reported.

The amendment was again read.

Mr. WEBB. I call the attention of my friend to the fact that this agreement is subject to the regulation or supervision of the Interstate Commerce Commission.

Mr. HULINGS. No. There is just where I think the failure is. The agreement is not subject. The matter about which the agreement may be made is subject to the regulation of the Interstate Commerce Commission.

Mr. WEBB. Of course the association is under the control of the Interstate Commerce Commission.

Mr. HULINGS. In my judgment it requires the amendment to make it clear. . . .

Mr. MANN. Is not this the distinction between the provision in the bill and the gentleman's amendment: That under the gentleman's amendment the agreement to fix rates before it goes into effect must be approved by the commission, and under the bill the rates go into effect and after that the commission may revise the rates?

Mr. HULINGS. That is precisely the point.

Mr. WEBB. Mr. Chairman, the committee wants to be perfectly frank with the House on both sides. If there is any doubt about the intent and scope of the provisions in the bill we want to accept the amendment so as to make it perfectly clear.

Mr. FLOYD of Arkansas. Mr. Chairman, I would like to have the amendment again reported.

The CHAIRMAN. Without objection, the Clerk will again report the amendment.

The Clerk again read the amendment.

Mr. WEBB. Mr. Chairman, we will gladly accept that amendment.

The CHAIRMAN. The question is on the amendment offered by the gentleman from Pennsylvania [Mr. HULINGS].

The question was taken, and the amendment was agreed to. . . .

Mr. TOWNER. Mr. Chairman. I shall not occupy all the time yielded to me for the reason that I desired to submit an amendment to the same effect as that offered by the gentleman from Pennsylvania [Mr. HULINGS]. I congratulate the gentleman from Pennsylvania [Mr. HULINGS] for presenting an amendment that is acceptable to the committee and the committee for accepting the amendment. There is no question whatever but what it was absolutely necessary that such an amendment should be adopted in order to protect the people and to carry out the purpose and intent of the section. I yield back the balance of my time. . . .

Mr. LENROOT. Mr. Chairman, like the gentleman from Iowa, I was about to offer the same amendment, and like him I wish to congratulate the members of the committee on accepting the amendment offered by the gentleman from Pennsylvania [Mr. HULINGS]. But, Mr. Chairman, I would like to ask the members of the committee one or two questions with reference to the paragraph as it stands. It reads:

> Nothing contained in the antitrust laws shall be construed to forbid associations of traffic, operating, accounting, or other officers of common carriers for the purpose of conferring among themselves or of making any lawful agreement.

Now, I would like information wherein the antitrust laws now can possibly prohibit the conferring together and making of any lawful agreement.

Mr. WEBB. I want to say to the gentleman that we think the trust laws would not apply to that condition of affairs, but the Interstate Commerce Commission thought we ought to make the thing perfectly clear, and therefore the section.

Mr. CARLIN. The mere meeting is thought by many to come within the law and might be construed to be a combination, and they want to make it clear, and that is the object of the provision.

Mr. MANN. If the gentleman will yield, they may have in mind the fact that when the law regulating railroad rates was passed four years ago, as gentlemen will recall, a lot of railroad officials met, and it was proposed to raise the rates in advance of the passage of the law. The bill under consideration provided that the Interstate Commerce Commission might suspend the proposed rates. President Taft threatened to have proceedings begun under the Sherman antitrust law and indict these people, whereupon the rates went glimmering. I suppose this is designed to allow them to do the thing that they tried to do then.

Mr. LENROOT. I remember the circumstances very well, and it was the Sherman law alone that prevented the increase of rates at that time until the amended law went into effect so as to permit suspension. Now, then, Mr. Chairman, this is in the disjunctive. The antitrust laws do not prohibit the making of any lawful agreement. They do not do that now; of course not. But the gentleman says that the conferring among themselves may be a violation of the Sherman law, and they wish to permit such conferences.

Mr. Chairman, if the conferences lead to something that means a violation of law, they ought to be subject to the antitrust laws. . . .

Mr. FLOYD of Arkansas. I will state that in the opinion of the committee these meetings of the traffic managers and officers of railroads are absolutely essential in order that officers and managers of different railroads may carry on business without friction and without complication and without annoyance to the traveling public. They must understand each other, and since the laws regulating interstate commerce have been on the statute books they have been compelled by the necessities and the nature of their business to have these meetings, conferences, and enter into arrangements; and yet they have felt that possibly under the strict interpretation of the Sherman law, if they were ever charged in the courts with a violation of the law, they might be held guilty of a violation of the Sherman Act. This is intended to lift them from under the ban of the existing law and to allow them to meet, confer, and understand each other, and to make any lawful agreements; but the exceptions in the provision expressly provide that their agreements shall still be subject to the regulation and power of the Interstate Commerce Commission. The amendment which we have just adopted, offered by the gentleman from Pennsylvania, makes that clear. . . .

Mr. LENROOT. Mr. Chairman, now, to recall a little of the history in connection with this same question, this identical proposition was up four years ago, in 1910. I then took quite an active part in securing an amendment almost identical with the one which has now been adopted. Another amendment which was also adopted prohibited any agreement of any character between railroads which were directly competing with each other. These amendments, with the assistance of the solid Democratic side of the House, were incorporated as a part of the Mann bill.

After we had improved the bill in that respect, improved it more and to a greater extent than this section now stands, a motion was then made to strike the entire section out of the bill, and that motion prevailed, and every Democrat, I believe, voted "aye," so that the provision went out of the Mann bill; and I am, I confess, a little surprised to find that it again creeps into this bill, brought in by the Democratic Party, who were then unanimously opposed to it. I am frank to say that, with the amendment just adopted, I have such confidence in the Interstate Commerce Commission that I do not know that the public interests will be injured if this remains in the bill, but certainly it was a most dangerous proposition before the adoption or the acceptance of the amendment offered by the gentleman from Pennsylvania [Mr. HULINGS]. I voted to strike it all out in 1910, and I shall vote to strike it out to-day, because, I may add, I can see no possible good to come from it in the way in which it is framed. So far as lawful agreements are concerned, they are permitted now. You have accomplished nothing there. So far as conferences are concerned, they are not under the ban of the law now unless there is something injurious to the public interest going on in those conferences, and if there is, I know of no reason why they should not be under the ban of the law. . . .

Mr. [JOHN J.] ESCH [R., Wis.]. Mr. Chairman, many of the practices of interstate carriers, if the Sherman antitrust law were strictly construed, would be held subject to the penalties of the act. Those violations have been blinked at, however, to a certain extent. The necessity for some conference agreements has long been recognized, provided such conference agreements were subjected to the supervisory control of the Interstate Commerce Commission, and in this very provision in this bill the committee is practically seeking to carry out a recommendation contained in the Republican platform of 1908, which reads as follows:

We believe, however, that the interstate-commerce law should be further amended so as to give railroads the right to make public traffic agreements, subject to the approval of the commission, but maintaining always the principle of competition between naturally competing lines and avoiding the common control of such lines by any means whatsoever.

The amendment offered by the gentleman from Pennsylvania, just adopted, carries out that further suggestion—that such conference agreements should be subject to the regulatory power of the Interstate Commerce Commission. President Taft, in his special message to Congress on January 7, 1910, wherein he recommended to Congress amendments to the interstate-commerce act, stated, among other things, as follows:

The subject of agreements between carriers with respect to rates has been often discussed in Congress. Pooling arrangements and agreements were condemned by the general sentiment of the people, and, under the Sherman antitrust law, any agreement between carriers operating in restraint of interstate or international trade or commerce would be unlawful. The Republican platform of 1908 expressed the belief that the interstate-commerce law should be further amended so as to give the railroads the right to make and publish traffic agreements subject to the approval of the commission, but maintaining always the principle of competition between naturally competing lines and avoiding the common control of such lines by any means whatsoever. In view of the complete control ever [sic] rate making and other practices of interstate carriers established by the acts of Congress and as recommended in this communication, I see no reason why agreements between carriers subject to the act, specifying the classifications of freight and the rates, fares, and charges for transportation of passengers and freight which they may agree to establish, should not be permitted, provided copies of such agreements be promptly filed with the commission, but subject to all the provisions of the interstate-commerce act, and subject to the right of any parties to such agreement to cancel it as to all or any of the agreed rates, fares, charges, or classifications by 30 days' notice in writing to the other parties and to the commission. . . .

Mr. MANN. Mr. Chairman, this proposition now before us revives old times to me. I reported into the House four years ago a bill which became the amendment to the interstate-commerce act of 1910, containing a provision somewhat similar but better guarded than the one that is in this bill. The Committee on Interstate and Foreign Commerce had jurisdication of the subject matter, and knew something about it. The present proposition comes in a bill reported from the Committee on the Judiciary, which has never made any investigation of railroad matters, and I assume does not pretend to know very much about the subject. It was not in the bill as originally drafted. There were a great many committee prints of this bill, and this never appeared in one of the committee prints. Mr. Clayton introduced a bill in the House on April 14, 1914, of which the present bill is the issue, and this provision was not in that Clayton bill introduced on April 14. It had never been suggested to the Committee on the Judiciary, so far as I can learn, that any proposition of this kind should be put into the antitrust bill until just before the bill was reported. The committee, having decided to incorporate in the bill a provision exempting labor organizations and farmers' organizations from the operation of the antitrust law, concluded that it would even up the situation by a provision exempting railroads from the operation of the antitrust law.

What are the facts? The railroads everywhere do have some kind of an understanding as to rates between competitive points. I suppose it would be impossible between two points, where each of two railroads ran, for one to have one rate and the other to have a different rate. They have always in some way gotten together. Four years ago I proposed in the administration bill to insert a provision practically taken from the Republican platform authorizing railroads to make these agreements, the rates when made to be subject to the operation of law. This provision goes a little further than that in behalf of the railroads. This provision authorizes the officers of common carriers to confer among themselves without any restriction and without any limitation. There is a restriction now inserted in the bill that the rates they make must be approved by the Interstate Commerce Commission, but the right to confer is made absolute. You do not need anything more. They never need to make a rate by agreement when they can confer. The heads of a dozen railroads get together and stick their legs under the mahogany and say the rate from New York to Chicago shall be raised so much on a certain class of freight. There is no agreement necessary. All they need is the power to confer. There is no limitation in this section on the power to confer.

If they make an agreement and write it out, why, they have to submit that to the Interstate Commerce Commission, but after they confer each one goes out and has a rate sheet filed raising the rate. There is no agreement, only a conference, and the rate goes into effect.

Mr. BARTLETT. That is just as it was with the Steel Trust, which had its banquets and conferences.

Mr. MANN. Yes. Now, these conferences to-day are under the ban of the antitrust law. When the act of four years ago was to be passed and put upon the statute books, an act which gave the power to the commission to suspend a proposed rate, the railroads met, or their officials did, and after a conference each one said to himself or to somebody else, we will raise the rate. It was announced in the papers the rates were to be raised, but President Taft directed the Attorney General to file an injunction proceeding at St. Louis to restrain the railroads from putting into effect the proposed rates,[5.555] and there was in addition a prosecution under the criminal provisions of the law, and the railroads quit. But they would have that power under this. Now, do not misunderstand me. I reported the provision of four years ago, not so strongly in favor of railroads in that bill as in this bill, and thereupon the Committee of the Whole House on the state of the Union made various amendments to the section, one of them very similar to the amendment just agreed to, called the Hulings amendment. We inserted in that section this provision:

Provided, That the proposed agreement before being made, and the rates, fares, charges, and classifications specified therein, shall be presented to and approved by the Interstate Commerce Commission.

That amendment was agreed to. The distinguished Chairman of the present Committee on Interstate and Foreign Commerce, which committee has jurisdiction of these matters, then the ranking Democratic member of my committee, made these few remarks on the subject of this legislation, among others:

Now, what is the object of this thing? The object of it is plainly not to benefit the people; it is not intended to apply to rates at any points except competitive points. The way stations by thousands along single lines of road, with no competition, will never be benefited. They may appeal and pray for help, but they will never get it under this section or any other of that sort. The whole object of it is to enable carriers to agree upon a stable basis of rates that they will all work under and not begin to compete one with the other. That is all there is to it.

The present chairman of the committee, the gentleman from Georgia [Mr. ADAMSON], is one of the best-posted men in this country on the subject of railroad legislation. He has been on the committee studying it now for nearly 18 years. That was the Democratic view which he expressed at that time. And, again, he said:

I was proceeding to say that the desire of these carriers is to escape competition and underbidding at competitive points only. They can only do that by agreeing upon an ironclad system of rates that they will all stick to. Of course that would be in violation of the antitrust law, because it prevents carriers from bidding against each other; but would it benefit even the competitive points—

[5.555] United States v. Missouri Pac. Ry., 1 D. & J. 243 (C.C.E.D. Mo. 1910).

And so forth.

And there is another very distinguished Member of this House who has been for some time a member of the Committee on Interstate and Foreign Commerce, who was then and is now a Democratic Member from Tennessee [Mr. SIMS], and he had this to say about this proposition which the Democratic committee has now reported:

It was boldly admitted by the gentleman from Illinois—

That was myself—

that this section does repeal and render nugatory so much of the Sherman antitrust law as applies to these agreements. Does any gentleman in this House want to go out and ask for a renomination or a reelection to this House admitting that he would willfully and with full knowledge vote to repeal pro tanto the antitrust law in any respect?

And the committee after inserting what was then called the Martin amendment, along the same lines as the Hulings amendment here, had another amendment proposed. Mr. Kendall, of Iowa, offered this amendment:

Provided, That in considering agreements contemplated by this section due regard shall be had in the maintenance of the principle of competition between natural competitive carriers, and no such agreement shall be approved between the carriers directly and substantially competitive with each other.

That is not in the pending proposition, and that was inserted in the Committee of the Whole House on the state of the Union, and after that came the amendment of my colleague [Mr. MADDEN], who has a similar motion pending here, to strike out the section which was No. 7, as this is No. 7, and we had a vote upon that. The committee divided, and there were ayes 102, noes 102. The amendment was not agreed to at that point. Tellers were asked for, and on tellers there were ayes 110, noes 91, and every Democrat in this House voted "aye," and every insurgent Republican—that is what they were called then—voted "aye."

Mr. [CHARLES H.] BURKE [R., S.D.]. To strike out?

Mr. MANN. To strike out; and that was one of those times, which were not very numerous on propositions of that kind, when the gentleman from Illinois, in charge of the bill, got very badly licked. Just before this provision was stricken out in this bill in the House under these circumstances, a provision which then had been made much more beneficial to the people than this, the Senate considered a similar Senate bill and had stricken out the same section in the Senate. Of course, I can not comment upon how the individual Senators voted over there, but if I were not in a legislative body here I could say that every Democratic Senator voted to strike out. [Laughter and applause on the Republican side.]

Now, we have a provision brought in here by the committee which did not have jurisdiction of it, without consideration by the committee, to reverse the unanimous action of the Democratic side of this House four years ago, and the question with me is whether you have learned more and know more or whether you have forgotten what you did in the past. My distinguished friend from North Carolina might suggest that a committee with little knowledge on the subject found it easier to handle it than did a committee that had a great deal of knowledge on the subject.

The railroads have been trying to get this provision into the law ever since I have been a Member of this House. The Pennsylvania Railroad Co. and its counsel in every bill which has been suggested to be brought before this House on the subject of railroad legislation have asked that this provision be put into it. It has been suggested time and time again. The Interstate Commerce Commission has suggested it and urged it. President Taft urged it. President Roosevelt urged it. The railroads have all been for it. I do not say that it is a bad provision, because I supported a very similar one four years ago, although that one was better than this; but Congress, in close touch with the people and the shippers, has never been swerved from its opinion on this subject by the attitude of the men here who had been argued with by the big railroad officials.

The provision does destroy every semblance of competition between the railroads. It is true that the Interstate Commerce Commission has control over the railroad rates, but when this provision goes into the law there is no longer any competition. Now, competition is not merely over rates. Competition is largely over business, and while we never have proposed a pooling permit under the law, under this provision authorizing the railroad officials to confer lawfully they can make any sort of a conference or understanding they please in regard to rates or in regard to quantities of freight. But, of course, they will not be able to make a lawful agreement where they can find one railroad that does not live up to the agreement. Under the old system where railroads entered into these agreements there was a penalty imposed when a railroad broke the agreement. They can not make such an agreement as that unless it be approved by the Interstate Commerce Commission, but they can make their conferences and agreements in honor among themselves as they please.

⊥ And, after all, gentlemen, if you vote this in, do not ever chide me again. There never was a provision more bitterly opposed in this House than was this provision when I reported it four years ago. It takes you gentlemen on that side some time to catch up. I do not know that I am personally proud of being the leader of the Democratic side of the House four years in advance. Although I have pride in the Democratic membership, it takes four years for that membership to catch up. If you keep on you may catch up with the other good things I have proposed, but which you have voted down. [Laughter and applause.] . . .

Mr. STAFFORD. I would like to have the gentleman's opinion whether under this phraseology railroads could enter into agreements as to rates and other matters for 50 years, and if it had the approval of the Interstate Commerce Commission it would be binding upon the railroads for that time or a longer time?

Mr. MANN. Well, you will notice they have left out of this provision a provision which was in the bill which I reported to the House, which was in effect that they could not enforce these agreements; that is, that an agreement entered into might be withdrawn at any time without penalty on the part of any railroad. But there is no limitation in this, as I recall it. Here is an agreement which, if the Interstate Commerce Commission approves, is binding, although it may place a penalty of a million dollars upon the railroad company which fails to live up to the agreement. . . .

Mr. GREEN of Iowa. If this section is enacted in its present form, is there any object in enacting the next section, which is intended to prevent the acquirement by holding companies of competing railroads?

Mr. MANN. Well, I will not undertake to say about that.

Mr. GARNER. I want to ascertain whether the gentleman is in favor of this second paragraph in section 7.

Mr. MANN. Well, if the gentleman is here—as he seldom is [laughter]—when we vote, the gentleman will find out.

Mr. GARNER. The gentleman is making an argument now which consumes considerable time, instructing the House and its Members how they shall follow him, and I want to find out whether he is in favor of this, so that I can follow him. [Laughter.]

Mr. MANN. It contains considerable instruction, too.

Mr. GARNER. It has nothing to do with the merits of this law.

Mr. MANN. How is the distinguished gentleman from Texas going to vote?

Mr. GARNER. I am waiting for the gentleman from Illinois to indicate how he will vote. [Laughter.]

Mr. MANN. Oh, no. You usually vote four years after I do. . . .

Mr. HULINGS. Under the present arrangement there is nothing to prevent any of these railroads or their officers from conferring if they do not do anything, is there, under the present law?

Mr. MANN. If they confer for the purpose of raising rates, they are guilty under the law, or for the purpose of doing anything else that is in restraint of trade.

Mr. HULINGS. Can the railroads raise rates without the consent of the Interstate Commerce Commission?

Mr. MANN. They can not raise the rates if the commission suspends the rates, but ordinarily the rates are not suspended. The railway company files a rate sheet that goes into effect 30 days after it is filed unless the commission issues an order extending the time in which it shall go into effect. Then it may be extended for 10 months. . . .

Mr. GARDNER. I ask this question for my own information and enlightenment.

The evidence adduced at the time of the investigation of the United States Steel Corporation shows that the Interstate Commerce Commission is aware of the fact that railroad traffic agreements exist, and that it utilizes those agreements and that no one objects. Now, does this wording which is proposed here, this proposed change in the law, permit more than that which already exists as a matter of practice?

Mr. MANN. Oh, yes; it goes further than what now exists, although what now exists is contrary to law.

Mr. GARDNER. Does it go substantially further?

Mr. MANN. It goes substantially further.

The CHAIRMAN. The question is on the amendment. . . .

Mr. FLOYD of Arkansas. Mr. Chairman, I have listened with great interest to the gentleman from Illinois [Mr. MANN]. I hardly know how to answer his position, because I have been unable to discover what it is; but I want to say to the gentleman that assuming everything he has said about the record vote on the proposition four years ago to be correct—and I do not question his statement, although I have not looked it up—we who voted against it four years ago will be no more inconsistent in voting for it now than he who proposed it four years ago is inconsistent in offering a motion to strike it out.

Mr. MANN. I did not offer a motion to strike it out.

Mr. FLOYD of Arkansas. Then I beg the gentleman's pardon.

Mr. MANN. My colleague, Mr. MADDEN, offered the motion this time and four years ago.

Mr. FLOYD of Arkansas. I beg the gentleman's pardon. I misunderstood the parliamentary situation.

Now, I desire to make this explanation: We have not considered this bill in the light of what we may have done in the past upon these questions, but the committee in charge of this bill have endeavored to bring in legislation that would be of value, and if there are any defects in the present law we have endeavored to remove those defects by appropriate legislation.

Now, the gentleman says that the Committee on the Judiciary has not jurisdiction of this proposition. I desire to take issue with the gentleman on that proposition. If such conferences or agreements are unlawful, they are unlawful by virtue of the provisions of the Sherman antitrust law, and under the rules of this House the Committee on the Judiciary has jurisdiction over that question. This matter was brought to the attention of the Subcommittee on the Judiciary having the bill in charge, and it was thoroughly investigated.

The matter was brought to our attention by representatives of the railroads, who explained that in the very nature of things they were compelled to meet, compelled to have these conferences, compelled to make arrangements, in order to carry on and conduct the traffic business of the railroads in the interest of the general public and to prevent conflicts and frictions in their dealings with the public; that it was necessary to have these conferences and meetings, and that since the enactment of laws upon the subject of interstate commerce they had been having these meetings; and yet, with their knowledge of the Sherman law and of the interpretations placed upon that law by the courts, they had always felt that if the Government should proceed against them under the terms of the Sherman law they might be adjudged guilty of a crime and punished for doing what the very nature of their business and the interest of the public require them to do.

But we did not depend upon the representations of the railroad people. We then took the matter up with the Interstate Commerce Commission, which has jurisdiction over this matter. While we did not go to the Interstate Commerce Committee of the House for information on that subject, we went to the great body of men, the Interstate Commerce Commission, who for years have been administering the affairs of interstate railroads, to the great advantage and to the general satisfaction of the public, and obtained their views upon the subject; and I desire to say that the provision reported in this bill was drawn by the Interstate Commerce Commission, and will be found in a letter of James S. Harlan, chairman of the commission, which letter I will put into the RECORD at the conclusion of my remarks. I will read the provision which was so drawn by the Interstate Commerce Commission:

Nor shall anything contained herein or in said antitrust law be construed to forbid associations of traffic, operating, accounting, or other officers of common carriers for the purpose of conferring among themselves or of making any lawful agreement as to any matter which is subject to the regulating or supervisory jurisdiction of the Interstate Commerce Commission, but all such matters shall continue to be subject to such jurisdiction of the commission and all such agreements shall be entered and kept of record by the carriers parties thereto, and shall at all times be open to inspection by the commission: *Provided*, That nothing in this act shall be construed as modifying existing laws prohibiting the pooling of earnings or traffic, or existing laws against joint agreements by common carriers to maintain rates.

After this matter was brought to our attention, after we brought it to the attention of the Interstate Commerce Commission, and they had approved the proviso in the language which I have read to you, we incorporated that provision into the bill, instead of the provision that was incorporated in the bill originally, and the provision that we bring before you has the approval of the Interstate Commerce Commission.

I have no apology to offer for the position of the committee upon this question. We have been endeavoring to bring in this legislation in such form that it will be beneficial to the business interests of this country and beneficial to the American people. If the Sherman law has been so interpreted as to work harm, or to prevent legitimate or necessary things, your committee believes it ought to be amended. We believe that it has been so interpreted in regard to fraternal, labor, farmers', and other associations. We brought in a provision to relieve those associations; and we believed also, when this matter was brought to our attention, when we understood the facts, that the railroads were entitled to relief in this respect; and we compliment the gentleman from Illinois [Mr. MANN] on being in advance of us, if he thinks this provision is right. In the preparation of this bill we did not hesitate to seek and obtain information from any source, and I disclaim that in any provision of this bill we acted from any narrow point of view, or that we hesitated to do a thing in the interest of capital or business, when we were convinced that the demands of justice required it.

Now, I desire to submit at this point two letters from the chairman of the Interstate Commerce Commission, James S. Harlan, and ask that they be printed in the RECORD.

The letters are as follows:

Interstate Commerce Commission,
Washington, April 22, 1914.

Hon. H. D. Clayton,
Chairman Committee on the Judiciary,
House of Representatives, Washington, D. C.

DEAR SIR: I have the honor to acknowledge the receipt of your letter of this date inclosing confidential committee print of a bill offered by you to supplement existing trust laws. Immediately upon its receipt I called a conference of my colleagues, but in view of the absence of Commissioners Clements and Clark from the city we were not able to reach a conclusion this afternoon. I hope to convey to you the views of the commission early to-morrow afternoon.

Permit me to call your attention to the clause beginning in line 4 on page 6. It reads:
"But any agreement in the premises shall likewise continue," etc.
It occurs to me that the meaning would be made more clear by substituting:
"But any such matter that shall be made the subject of agreement by any such association shall likewise," etc. In other words, as I assume, it is the subject matter of the agreement and not the agreement itself that ought to continue under our regulating or supervisory jurisdiction.

Very truly, yours,

James S. Harlan, Chairman.

Interstate Commerce Commission,
Washington, April 24, 1914.

Hon. Henry D. Clayton,
Chairman Committee on the Judiciary,
House of Representatives, Washington, D. C.

DEAR SIR: Further acknowledging your letter of the 22d, inclosing a copy of the confidential committee print of a bill to supplement existing trust laws, and calling our attention to certain language in it commencing at the foot of page 5 and continuing through line 6 on page 6, I beg to say that the bill has had consideration by the commission.

We do not understand that the provision in any degree modifies existing laws forbidding the consolidation or merger of railroad corporations operating competing lines, but that it is intended to go no further than to legalize associations of officials of common carriers organized for the purpose of agreeing upon rates, classifications, operating rules, accounting, and other similar matters now subject to the jurisdiction of this commission.

Such associations have been in active existence for many years. They have stated and special meetings at which matters within our jurisdiction are the subject of discussion and conference and not infrequently of actual agreement; and often when no positive and affirmative agreement is reached such conferences are nevertheless followed by a concert of action among the participating carriers. These facts have been shown in contested cases before us, the testimony being offered by the complainants on the general theory that such agreements are unlawful. The commission, however, has never based any order on the hypothesis of unlawfulness in the action taken by the carriers as the result of any such conference or agreement, except in so far as any such agreement or concert of action might have some bearing upon the reasonableness or general lawfulness of the rate or practice in dispute before us.

The increasing stability in rates now observable in our transportation service results to no small extent from the conferences of the traffic associations of carriers. As a practical matter, therefore, we see no objection to what is sought by the provision in question. We do not understand that it is intended to modify the provisions of law forbidding carriers to enter into any contract or combination for the pooling of traffic or earnings, or to modify the prohibitions of law against agreements by which one carrier undertakes not to change a rate or rates except upon the consent of one or more other carriers. But to avoid any confusion on these points the following paragraph is suggested as a substitute for the paragraph of the bill commencing with line 24 on page 5:

"Nor shall anything contained herein or in said antitrust laws be construed to forbid associations of traffic, operating, accounting, or other officers of common carriers for the purpose of conferring among themselves or of making any lawful agreement as to any matter which is subject to the regulating or supervisory jurisdiction of the Interstate Commerce Commission, but all such matters shall continue to be subject to such jurisdiction of the commission, and all such agreements shall be entered and kept of record by the carriers parties thereto and shall at all times be open to inspection by the commission: *Provided,* That nothing in this act shall be construed as modifying existing laws prohibiting the pooling of earnings or traffic or existing laws against joint agreements by common carriers to maintain rates."

You will observe that the substitute above proposed embodies a clause requiring carriers to make a record of the agreements and understandings of their associations and to keep them open to inspection.

Very truly, yours,

James S. Harlan, Chairman.

• • • •

The CHAIRMAN. The question is on the amendment offered by the gentleman from Illinois [Mr. MADDEN].

The question was taken; and on a division there were—ayes 21, noes 36.

So the amendment was rejected.

Mr. GREEN of Iowa. Mr. Chairman, I offer the following amendment.

Mr. CARLIN. Mr. Chairman, I make the point of order that it is too late to offer an amendment under the agreement.

The CHAIRMAN. The Chair understands that the gentleman from Oklahoma is to offer a new section, but withholds that until the gentleman from Iowa can offer an amendment.

The Clerk read as follows:

At the end of the section strike out the period and insert a comma and add the following:
"Or authorize competing lines to make agreements with reference to the rates which shall be charged or the services rendered."

Mr. CARLIN. I understand, Mr. Chairman, that all time on this paragraph has expired.

Mr. MANN. Mr. Chairman, did I have any time left?

The CHAIRMAN. The gentleman had one minute.

Mr. MANN. I yield that one minute to the gentleman from Iowa.

Mr. GREEN of Iowa. That is all I want. I only desire to say a word with reference to this amendment. It is claimed here that the purpose of this bill is to further competition and not to restrain it. If this section is adopted as it stands, it will absolutely nullify the following section, which provides that holding companies may not hold or control competing lines. If gentlemen wish, in fact, to still preserve the competition feature of the present law, this amendment should be adopted.

The CHAIRMAN. The question is on the amendment offered by the gentleman from Iowa.

The question was taken, and the amendment was rejected.

Mr. FOWLER. Mr. Chairman, I desire to offer an amendment. On page 24, line 21, after the word "Commission," insert these words: "and any Member of Congress."

The CHAIRMAN. The Chair will state to the gentleman from Illinois that an amendment has been offered at that particular place and adopted by the committee.

⊥ Mr. FOWLER. I do not understand that the amendment as I have offered it has ever been offered to this part of the bill.

The CHAIRMAN. The Clerk will report the amendment.

The Clerk read as follows:

Page 24, line 21, after the word "Commission," add the following: "and any Member of Congress."

The CHAIRMAN. The question is on the amendment offered by the gentleman from Illinois.

The question was taken; and on a division (demanded by Mr. FOWLER) there were—ayes 8, noes 16.

So the amendment was rejected.

Mr. PLATT. Mr. Chairman, I offer the following amendment.

The Clerk read as follows:

Section 24, line 24, after the word "rates," add the following:

"*Provided further,* That nothing in this act shall be construed as applying to associations of manufacturers conducted purely for profit and not for their health or for pleasure.

[Laughter.]

The CHAIRMAN. The question is on the amendment.

The question was taken, and the amendment was rejected.

Mr. TOWNER. Mr. Chairman, I offer the following as a new section.

The CHAIRMAN. Are there any further amendments to this paragraph. If not, the Chair recognizes the gentleman from Oklahoma.

Mr. FERRIS. Mr. Chairman, I have hesitated to offer an amendment to this section, because the Committee on the Judiciary have done so well, and I commend them for their good work and I am in sympathy with many of the provisions of the bill. But I wish to offer the following amendment.

The Clerk read as follows:

Page 24, line 24, after the word "rates," insert the following as a new section:
"SEC. 7a. That from and after the passage of this act it shall be unlawful for any corporation or any person or persons to transport the products of any mine or mines, including coal, oil, gas, or hydroelectric energy, either by rail, water, pipe line, transmission line, or otherwise, from one State, Territory, or District of the United States to any other State, Territory, or District of the United States, or to any foreign country, who shall not become a common carrier within the meaning and purposes of and subject to the act entitled 'An act to regulate commerce,' approved February 4, 1887."

Mr. FLOYD of Arkansas. Mr. Chairman, I make the point of order on that. I do not think it is germane.

Mr. FERRIS. Mr. Chairman, the point of order comes too late. The amendment has been debated.

Mr. BARTLETT. Oh, it has just been reported.

Mr. FERRIS. Oh, but it has been reported heretofore, and the point of order comes too late.

Mr. BARTLETT. Mr. Chairman, it seems to me that the point of order was raised and sustained when the same thing was offered as an amendment to the second paragraph of section 7. It was then withdrawn with a view of offering it as a new section, and the gentleman now offers it as a new section.

HOUSE CONSIDERATION 1611

The CHAIRMAN. The Chair will state to the gentleman that the point of order was sustained when it was offered as an amendment to section 7. The gentleman now offers it as a new section.

Mr. FERRIS. And I proceeded to debate it, and did debate it, and after that some one asked that it be reported.

Mr. STAFFORD. But it was not reported.

Mr. FERRIS. It had been reported before, as I think the Chair will remember.

Mr. HARRISON. It had been offered as an amendment to the other paragraph.

Mr. BARTLETT. But it is offered now as a new section. It was withheld while these other amendments were offered.

Mr. HARRISON. It could not have been offered as a new section until now.

The CHAIRMAN. The RECORD shows that the amendment had not been reported. It was reported when it was offered as an amendment to the paragraph.

Mr. FERRIS. The Chair is not holding that it had not been read? It was read when I first offered it.

Mr. CARLIN. It was read out of place and out of time.

The CHAIRMAN. It was offered at that time as an amendment to the second section of paragraph 7, and it went out on a point of order. The gentleman now offers it again, and the Clerk has just reported it. What is the point of order made by the gentleman from Arkansas?

Mr. FLOYD of Arkansas. Mr. Chairman, I make the point of order that the amendment is not germane to the bill; that we have not undertaken in this bill, or in any paragraph of it, to regulate or define common carriers, but have been dealing with a criminal statute. What the gentleman seeks to amend is within the jurisdiction of another committee. This legislation is supplementary to the Sherman antitrust act regulating trusts and monopolies in restraint of trade. There is not a paragraph in it in which we undertake to assume jurisdiction over common carriers or to regulate in any way common carriers or define who shall be deemed common carriers or who shall not be deemed common carriers. The second paragraph of section 7, while it mentions common carriers, relates to certain agreements, conferences, or arrangements by common carriers, and is inserted for the specific purpose of relieving them from the operation of the Sherman antitrust law as a criminal statute in regard to such, and for no other purpose, and we submit that the amendment is not germane to any portion of this bill. That is a matter under the jurisdiction of the Interstate Commerce Committee. That is the committee that ought to deal with the matter embodied in this amendment. . . .

Mr. HARRISON. The amendment offered by the gentleman from Oklahoma proposes to amend the act of February 4, 1887, which is the Interstate Commerce Commission act, and this bill does not propose to amend that.

Mr. FLOYD of Arkansas. There is not a paragraph in the bill that undertakes to amend the provisions of law relating to common carriers or the Interstate Commerce Commission act. We are dealing simply with the Sherman Act.

Mr. FERRIS. Mr. Chairman, the very first section of the bill, on page 19, which begins with line 15, specifically amends three different statutes wholly foreign to this bill. Section 7, the very paragraph that we have just concluded, in the second paragraph of it, specifically deals with common carriers. The gentleman in charge of the bill on the Judiciary Committee says that they did not assume jurisdiction in one breath and in the next breath he asserts that that section relieves common carriers from the laws that we now impose upon them by the Sherman Antitrust Act. I submit to the Chair, if the committee has jurisdiction to relieve common carriers from certain obligations imposed upon them by law, I can not fathom why we have not the same jurisdiction and the same power to impose additional conditions upon them, and if the rule works one way I can not understand how the gentleman could contend that offering this as a new section the committee is without jurisdiction to consider it.

Mr. BARTLETT. Mr. Chairman, it seems to me this is clearly violative of the rule of germaneness. In order that an amendment be germane it must be not only germane to the paragraph and the section, but germane to the bill and the purposes which the bill has in view. The very face of the amendment itself discloses that it proposes to do something which it is contemplated will put these companies described in this amendment not under the act of 1890, known as the Sherman antitrust law, but under the act of 1887, known as the interstate-commerce law, to regulate common carriers.

Mr. FERRIS. Does not the exemption afforded them on page 24 from lines 11 to 24 to that extent mention the Sherman antitrust law, and on page 19 does not the language from lines 15 to 24 and on over to the next page specifically amend three statutes foreign to this bill; and if not, why not?

It is amazing that the whole bill can be made up of amendments of the various statutes in another section that comes from the existing law in this identical section, and that an amendment trying to do the same thing in another paragraph should be held out of order.

Mr. BARTLETT. It is amazing that a gentleman of the intelligence of the gentleman from Oklahoma should get on a hobby here and ride it eternally in the House as he has done this proposition.

Mr. FERRIS. It is a pretty good hobby when you are trying to ride the Standard Oil and the water-power trusts.

Mr. BARTLETT. Now, Mr. Chairman, on the point of order I say this bill has reference solely to the creation of an addition to the Sherman antitrust law. The Committee on the Judiciary has no jurisdiction to consider propositions relating to interstate commerce except as to the effect of the law relating to interstate commerce. Now they propose to say—what? That no corporation or person shall not do—what? Shall not transport the products which they produce between the States; who shall not become a common carrier under the act of 1887.

Mr. Chairman, this bill which we are considering does not propose to deal with common carriers at all. There is nothing in it, except this provision; and the second paragraph of section 7, relating to common carriers, has reference to agreements which violate the Sherman antitrust law as was known in what we call the Trans-Missouri Transportation cases and the Traffic Association cases, which happened to be the first consideration of the Sherman law adjudicated by the Supreme Court; so this is an amendment not to the antitrust law, but an amendment to the interstate-commerce law. Upon its very face it declares that they shall not transport their products unless they shall come within the meaning and purpose of the act of 1887, which has no reference to the control or regulating of trusts, but the sole purpose of the amendment is made to the act of 1887 and as amended in 1906 and 1910, and has reference solely to transportation and not to violations of the antitrust law. So that, upon its very face, it indicates that it is subject to a point of order, because it proposes to deal and does deal with an entirely different subject foreign to the one dealt with in this bill.

Mr. CAMPBELL. Mr. Chairman, if the gentleman from Oklahoma should introduce a bill embodying the subject matter of his amendment, then there is no question but the subject matter would direct that the bill be referred to the Committee on Interstate and Foreign Commerce rather than the Committee on the Judiciary. There is no question in my mind but this amendment covers the subject matter over which the committee reporting this bill now under consideration has no jurisdiction. The subject matter of the amendment is so important and so different from the subject matters that are referred to the Committee on the Judiciary that the Committee on Interstate and Foreign Commerce has sole jurisdiction, so that in my opinion the point of order is well taken.

Mr. FERRIS. Mr. Chairman, I do not desire to consume too much of the time of the committee, but I want to call the attention of the Chair and the committee just for a moment to this proposition. The Congress of the United States has begun on a trust program made up of three bills, the first of which is the trade-commission bill, which they said has nothing to do with pipe lines, common carriers, Standard Oil rates, and the water-power trust. That bill has been laid aside with a favorable recommendation. We are now considering a bill from the Committee on the Judiciary, dealing with all sorts of monopoly in every conceivable form and fashion and every conceivable way, and I want to ask the Chairman and the House if it is going to be the ruling of the Chair and if it is going to be the decision of the committee that a complete trust program shall be put through, ought we not to put through a measure dealing with the Standard Oil Trust or the water-power trust? We do not want to shoot wide of the mark; they are notorious monopolies in this country, and these are propositions with which we ought to deal. It is not enough to push them aside when we are dealing with trust legislation.

The section 3 that we amended Friday by including oil, gas, water power, and so forth, certainly is dealing with the subject, and, if for no other reason, that ought to render additional legislation on the same subject in order.

Again, this bill is wide in its scope. It deals with labor legislation in the first part of paragraph 7. It deals with stocks, bonds, and banking legislation in other sections. Why is it we can not deal with the most monumental of all trusts?

It is not sufficient for the House to say, it is not sufficient for the Chairman to say, every time a question is raised on a bill dealing with monopoly, that it is out of order, or it is germane, or not germane, when the identical section dealing with that particular proposition relates to carriers. It is remarkable in the extreme that the Committee on the Judiciary should in an amendment say they have the power to exempt carriers from certain obligatory duties, and in the next breath should say they have no right, and that it would be not germane to put upon a bill a provision putting duties upon them.

I do not know what the decision of the Chair may be, and I do not know what the disposition of the committee may be, but surely this House is in favor of declaring the pipe-lines and water-power trusts carriers to be common carriers and subject to the Interstate Commerce Commission. I can not fathom a proposition of running away from a question so important, so necessary, and so patent and so universally agreed to by everybody.

For years the Interstate Commerce Commission themselves upon their own motion have been trying to bring pipe lines under the jurisdiction of that commission. What happens? In comes the Standard Oil Co. and brings an injunction proceeding and enjoins them from coming under the protection of that law.

This is the first time, and it is the only time during this administration and this Congress, under the resolution adopted by the Democratic caucus, when we have any chance to get relief on this proposition. I believe a bill on trusts and monopolies might properly go to any extent and all its provisions would still be germane as parts of a bill that proposes to curb monopolies. What are the pipe lines? The worst monopoly in the country. What is the Standard Oil Co.? The worst monopoly in the country. What is the Water Power Trust? One of the worst monopolies in the country. Is there any reason why, in dealing with monopoly, we should not deal with the transportation question, which is the vital cord in the whole trust question.

It has been said, and well said, that he who controls the transportation controls the country, and it is very true. The men who control the pipe lines control the production of oil and the price of oil, both in the region of production and at the consumer's end; and even so with the power trust. I believe that a bill so comprehensive as to carry out the legislative antitrust program for an entire administration and for an entire Congress should include this transportation question. The Chair may be ready to hold that this section shall be considered at this time, or— . . .

Mr. CULLOP. Is not the purpose of this amendment to control the transportation of these products now, or regulate them where they are not controlled or regulated under the interstate-commerce law?

Mr. FERRIS. Precisely; and not alone that, Mr. Chairman, but the oil-transportation companies are all in the oil-production business themselves. The only market for crude oil that the independent producer has is the pipe-line company, which is a transporter, which transports it or refuses to transport it, as it elects to do. It then has it in its full control and sells it at what it will at its destination point.

Mr. CULLOP. Is not the further purpose of this amendment also to control a situation which now, because of the peculiar conditions of operating the pipe lines, can not be controlled by the Interstate Commerce Commission?

Mr. FERRIS. Absolutely; and the Commerce Court, under the Hepburn amendment, sought to do this very thing that I am trying to do; only I drew the amendment here a little more comprehensively, so as to be sure and include it. Then came along the Prairie Oil and Gas case, which I have before me, and knocked out this proposition of holding pipe lines as carriers. Judge Mack dissented in an able opinion, and the matter is now pending in the Supreme Court. This amendment does what the court indicated a former Congress could have done when we enacted that law. We can do it now. We ought to do it now. There is no use to postpone it. The American people deserve it. The trust question is being dealt with; we ought to do it now.

Mr. CULLOP. Mr. Chairman, as I read this amendment, it is not an attempt to amend the interstate-commerce law at all, but it is to put into this law a remedy for a condition which the Interstate Commerce Commission can not control for the want of legislation. There is no law upon that subject, and the language of the amendment very clearly shows that it does not attempt to amend the interstate-commerce law. It is an amendment to this bill on a matter that is not now regulated or under the supervision in any way of the Interstate Commerce Commission.

I want to call the attention of the Chair to the language:

> That from and after the passage of this act it shall be unlawful for any corporation or any person or persons to transport the products of any mine or mines, including coal, oil, gas, or hydroelectric energy, either by rail, water, pipe line, transmission line, or otherwise, from one State, Territory, or district of the United States to any other State, Territory, or district of the United States, or any foreign country—

Now, listen to the language—

> who shall not become a common carrier within the meaning and purpose of and subject to an act entitled "An act to regulate commerce," approved February 4, 1887.

Now, by the very language of the amendment it clearly shows that the subject matter embraced in this amendment is not a subject under any provision of the interstate-commerce law, but it is a matter entirely outside of it and a matter that it can not handle, and for that reason it has a proper place here, and it is proposed to place it under the supervision of the different sections of this bill.

Section 3 was amended so as to include oil and gas and water-power production, so as to make the language of that section clearly cover those articles of commerce. Now, as those articles of gas and oil are transported in some of the States, and especially in the State of the gentleman from Oklahoma [Mr. FERRIS], it does not come under the provisions or regulations of the interstate-commerce law; but the pipe lines are so regulated and conducted that the commission can not obtain jurisdiction of the subject matter at all because of the manner in which the oil is transported. The very language of this section shows that it is not an amendment to the interstate-commerce law, but clearly belongs to and is a part of the subject matter ⊥ to be regulated in the legislation now proposed to be adopted by this measure.

If the Chair will turn to section 3 he will observe that that section was amended by the adoption of an amendment offered by the gentleman from Oklahoma so as to cover these two articles of commerce. It was then contended that as this bill was drawn it did not cover the subject of oil and gas and hydroelectric energy, and the bill was so amended. And it is now contended that the transportation of both oil and gas in some sections of the United States is so manipulated and controlled that they avoid coming under the Interstate Commerce Commission, or the act to regulate commerce passed in 1887 or any amendment thereto.

If that be true—and I assume no one here will attempt to deny that condition in relation to this matter—then where does it belong if it does not belong in this bill, and when is the time to adopt the amendment or some provision to regulate that important matter, if not now in the handling of this trust legislation?

These two things—oil and hydroelectric energy—constitute two of the greatest articles of commerce, and are absolutely controlled to-day by the trusts of this country; and while we are adopting this antitrust legislation bearing directly on this subject and kindred subjects, is not this the time when something controlling these articles of commerce should be incorporated into this measure? I call the attention of the Chair to the language of the amendment, showing that it is not an amendment to the interstate-commerce law of 1887, because it distinctly provides that it is not any part of that law, but these are articles entirely outside of the purview of that legislation and all of the amendments that have been made of it. I submit that it is in order here, and I hope we will incorporate in this measure provisions which will control these twin giants of monopoly and which have been remorseless in their exploitation of the people of the entire country. We should see to it that these two great combinations are not permitted to escape all legislation which will make them amenable to strict regulation....

The CHAIRMAN. If the gentleman from Oklahoma [Mr. FERRIS] were to offer a bill containing in effect the provisions offered by him in this amendment, to what committee of this House would it go? In other words, what committee would have jurisdiction of it? Would it be the Committee on the Judiciary or the committee to which the gentleman belongs, the Committee on Interstate and Foreign Commerce?

Mr. CULLOP. I shall be glad to answer the Chair as I understand that matter. While I do not think that question is important here, or I do not think it could have any bearing in the consideration of this legislation, I do say that the jurisdiction of the subject matter of this bill was properly in the Interstate Commerce Committee and not the Judiciary Committee, and I agree with the distinguished gentleman from Illinois [Mr. MANN] upon that subject. Nearly every question dealt with in this legislation is a proper subject for the Committee on Interstate Commerce, and does not belong to the Judiciary Committee at all. But I submit the test in deciding this question is not to what committee a bill embracing this question should be referred, but does the amendment contain subject matter directly connected with the objects covered by this proposed legislation? Measured by that test it is clearly germane here and in order.

If that question had been raised at the inception of this legislation, the Speaker of this House doubtless would have referred the bill to the Committee on Interstate and Foreign Commerce instead of the Judiciary Committee, because the subjects embraced in it are proper subjects of legislation for the Committee on Interstate and Foreign Commerce and not the Judiciary Committee. But the question the Chair is now asking, I take it, is not the proper test and does not settle this question. The subject matter covered by this amendment is germane to the legislation here proposed and to the legislation that has been adopted all along in the sections of the bill we are now considering....

Mr. FERRIS. Mr. Chairman, my only thought was to supplement what the gentleman is saying by calling attention to the fact that on the second paragraph of section 7 that we have just disposed of and on which a long debate ensued the gentleman from Illinois debated what occurred two years ago. The bill from beginning to end is made up of matters that belong partly to this committee and to other committees, if caught at the inception, but they have gone to the committee, have received consideration, been reported here, and this House has jurisdiction of it, and we ought to go along with it.

Mr. CULLOP. Mr. Chairman, one thought further and I am through. Let me call the attention of the Chair to this proposition: That whenever any subject has been referred for regulation or supervision in any provision in this bill it has been referred to the Interstate Commerce Commission and not to the courts of this country. Running through every provision from the first word in it to the close of the provision the jurisdiction and settlement of questions in a primary sense are committed to the Interstate Commerce Commission and not to the courts in this country. The last amendment adopted here was a matter that did not put the regulation of it under any court in this country, but it put it under the regulation of the Interstate Commerce Commission. If that view of it be true, then this subject is germane here. If the standard of what committee it would be referred to is to be taken as a measure of the jurisdiction of this question, the last amendment was not germane, and a number of amendments that have been adopted during the course of the consideration of this bill are not germane, because the question was referred for arbitrament to the Interstate Commerce Commission and not to the courts of the land.

Mr. MORGAN of Oklahoma. Mr. Chairman, may I call attention of the Chair to a few points? In section 9, which provides—

> That from and after two years from the date of the approval of this act no person who is engaged as an individual, or who is a member of a partnership, or is a director or other officer of a corporation that is engaged in the business, in whole or in part, of producing or selling equipment, materials, or supplies to, or in the construction or maintenance of railroads or other common carriers engaged in commerce, shall act as a director or other officer or employee of any other corporation or common carrier engaged in commerce—

And so forth.

Now, Mr. Chairman, if the committee had jurisdiction to control who shall be the directors of common carriers, why would not an amendment such as the gentleman from Oklahoma offers be germane? If it is appropriate to say who shall be directors of a common carrier in this bill, then it is appropriate to legislate on any subject that applies to common carriers; and if this amendment goes out on a point of order, will not we be compelled to take out of this bill section 9?

Mr. LENROOT. Mr. Chairman, with reference to the Chair's question to the gentleman from Indiana as to whether, if this amendment was introduced as an original bill it would go to the Interstate Commerce Committee, I submit to the Chair that that can not decide the germaneness of the amendment, for the reason that the sole standard is whether or not there is anything in this bill as it now appears before the committee to which this amendment is germane. If there is, it must be admitted, although in the first instance it might have gone to the Interstate Commerce Committee. If the Chair will recall, a little later on in the bill the subject of directors of banks is dealt with. If that had been introduced as an original bill it would have gone not to the Judiciary Committee but to the Committee on Banking and Currency.

Now, with reference to the germaneness of this amendment, I wish to submit an observation that has not been mentioned to the Chair, and that is that this is clearly germane under section 3 of the bill. In other words, section 3 of the bill has dealt with this very subject, and having done so this proposed amendment becomes germane. Section 3 deals, as amended, with interstate commerce in the product of the mine. It is provided that the owner or person controlling the product, or the transporter engaged in selling, is prohibited from arbitrarily refusing to sell that product.

Let me read to the Chair the amendment as it now stands:

That is [sic] shall be unlawful for any corporation or any person or persons to transport the products of any mine or mines, including coal, oil, gas—

And so forth.

Now, then, we have dealt with the transporter of these very products in section 3, and this proposed amendment only does one thing. The section as it stands relates to arbitrarily refusing to sell, and all this does is to provide that they shall not engage in that transportation unless they shall become a common carrier. It has nothing whatever to do with any amendment of the interstate-commerce law in the slightest degree. It simply places a condition precedent on the transportation of this product of the mine which this committee has dealt with in section 3.

It seems to me clear that if this amendment had been proposed to section 3 after the adoption of the gentleman's amendment no one would have thought of raising the point of order upon it, and if that be true, it is certainly in order to offer it as a separate section. . . .

Mr. FERRIS. Supplementary to what the gentleman has said, on page 24, the first paragraph of section 7 deals with labor conditions, and if the Chair is going to say as a test that the committee had no jurisdiction, that portion should have been referred to the Committee on Labor.

Mr. LENROOT. Yes.

The CHAIRMAN. But the Chair did not mean to intimate that that would be the test. The gentleman from Indiana simply suggested it to the Chair, and that is the reason the Chair propounded the interrogatory.

Mr. WEBB. Mr. Chairman, just a word or two. We are dealing here not with the creation of interstate common carriers, but with the acts of interstate carriers already established and the acts of individuals. We are dealing with combinations, contracts in restraint of trade, and immoral business practices. We are not undertaking to create common carriers, and that is all there is to my friend's amendment. He wants the committee considering an antitrust bill to force certain corporations to become common carriers, because they transport their own product from one State to another. It is not necessary to discuss that phase of it, but I doubt very much whether Congress can say that because a man transports his corn from one State to another on his own shoulders or in his own wagon that he can be compelled to be a common carrier. This very identical question is now pending before the Supreme Court of the United States.[5.556] It comes from the Interstate Commerce Commission on an appeal, showing it is an interstate-commerce question, and I submit that this House in preparing an antitrust bill should not be put in the attitude of creating common carriers, and that therefore the amendment is not germane to this section or to the bill.

[Mr. DECKER addressed the committee. See Appendix.*]

The CHAIRMAN. The Chair is ready to rule. The gentleman from Oklahoma [Mr. FERRIS] has offered an amendment as a new section which relates to the transportation of the products of any mine and provides that it shall be unlawful for any corporation to transport such product unless it becomes a common carrier within the intent and purpose of the special act entitled "An act to regulate commerce," approved February 4, 1887. In ruling upon the point of order it is not the province of the Chair to pass upon the desirability of such legislation or the importance of the particular amendment. If the Chair were to express his personal opinion he might be in sympathy with a good deal of what the gentleman from Oklahoma has said. But the Chair must pass upon the point of order under the rules and procedure governing such matters. This amendment does not on its face refer to any monopoly or restraint of trade or seek to prevent a monopoly in restraint of trade. The bill under consideration is a bill to supplement existing laws against unlawful restraints and monopolies. Reference has been made to the second paragraph of section 7, but as the Chair construes that paragraph it is simply intended to relieve certain officers of common carriers from the operation of the Sherman antitrust law under certain conditions set forth in the paragraph. The Chair is unable to understand how the amendment proposed by the gentleman from Oklahoma can be germane to a bill framed for the purpose of supplementing existing laws against unlawful restraints and monopolies. The Chair does not say it will not be in order at some future time in the consideration of this bill, but it certainly seems to the Chair, so far as this particular portion of the bill is concerned, that it is not germane, and for that reason the Chair sustains the point of order. The Chair would like to state, in addition, reference having been made by the gentleman from Wisconsin to section 3 and the amendment adopted by the committee a day or so ago, as a reason why this amendment is germane, that if the gentleman will read that amendment he will see that it simply provides that those in control, either as owners or transporters of the products of any mine, etc., shall not have the right to withhold such products from any responsible purchaser or, in other words, to use them for the purpose of crushing out competition. Quite a different proposition from that which is presented in the amendment now proposed. The Chair thinks that the amendment is not in order to this particular paragraph or section of the bill and therefore sustains the point of order.

Mr. TOWNER. Mr. Chairman, I desire to offer a new section.

The CHAIRMAN. The gentleman from Iowa offers a new section, which the Clerk will report.

The Clerk read as follows:

Page 24, after line 24, insert as a new section:

"That in any city, town, or county of the United States wherein a cooperative association is established for the purpose of producing or marketing a food product or products any person who shall directly or indirectly for the purpose of destroying competition, discriminate in price in the purchase of such food products or the materials thereof within such city, town, or county, or use other means the effect of which is to destroy competition or secure a monopoly in commerce, shall be deemed guilty of a misdemeanor, and upon conviction thereof shall be punished by a fine not exceeding $5,000 or by imprisonment not exceeding one year, or by both such fine and imprisonment, in the discretion of the court."

Mr. TOWNER. Mr. Chairman, this attempts to reach, and I think reaches, a very great evil which exists to such an extent that many of the States of the Union have already legislated to overcome it. Wherever a cooperative association is formed among the producers of food products large dealers in the same line of business at once try to

---

* Not reprinted herein.

[5.556] See note 5.554 supra.

drive the cooperative association out of business, and for that purpose will send into that territory their agents to purchase the products from the producers and endeavor by paying higher prices to drive out the cooperative association. The payment of higher prices for a time is for the purpose of destroying the competition of the cooperative association, put it out of business, and thus control the prices themselves. There is no law now in existence that exactly meets that condition with regard to interstate trade. For instance, to give a concrete example of the way this matter works, a cooperative creamery is established in some small town. If control is sought of the market by some large company or great combination of that character in an adjoining State they will send their agents to the town where the cooperative association is located and establish a receiving station—centralizers, as they are called. . . .

Mr. WEBB. I thought that section 2 absolutely destroyed that practice.

Mr. TOWNER. I can not agree with the gentleman in regard to that. I can not even take the time to argue it. If that is the opinion of the committee, of course they will then be opposed to this amendment. But I think this amendment will make it so certain that there will be no question about it.

It is a very great evil. It injuriously affects more producers in this country than any other one thing to-day. In the State of Iowa there are many cooperative creameries established, and they are being put out of business by these "centralizers" from other States, who go into their markets and buy the products from the farmers at a higher price for a certain time, but whose sole object is to destroy the established creamery and control the market in their own interest. . . .

Mr. FLOYD of Arkansas. I did not catch the full purport of the gentleman's amendment. Can the gentleman briefly state it?

Mr. TOWNER. I can not state the purport more succinctly than to state its terms. My amendment reads:

> That in any city, town, or county in the United States wherein a cooperative association is established for the purpose of producing or marketing a food product or products, any person who shall directly or indirectly for the purpose of destroying competition discriminate in price in the purchase of such food products or the materials thereof within such city, town, or county, or use other means the effect of which is to destroy competition or secure a monopoly in commerce, shall be deemed guilty of a misdemeanor—

And so forth.

Mr. WEBB. Mr. Chairman, I want to make this suggestion to the gentleman: We have absolutely no authority to pass that sort of an amendment. The gentleman is asking Congress to go into a city or a little town or village and regulate the affairs of business there. That does not relate to interstate commerce at all.

Mr. TOWNER. Oh, the gentleman is mistaken. This amendment would be effective only with regard to those engaged in commerce, and your bill says "commerce" is interstate commerce. The gentleman should not think that I do not know this bill operates only in interstate commerce. That is the great difficulty now. Very many States have legislated and do control this matter in the States, but that is not the most serious trouble. The serious trouble comes from those large combinations outside of the States and which the States can not control. This bill is limited in its terms and applies only to operations in interstate commerce.

Mr. GARNER. But the gentleman's amendment does not say anything about interstate commerce.

Mr. TOWNER. Oh, I beg the gentleman's pardon. It does. It says "commerce," which you define by this bill to be interstate commerce. It is limited strictly to that. . . .

Now, Mr. Chairman, allow me to make a further statement in regard to this amendment. Certainly it meets a real evil, and if gentlemen desire to make this bill of benefit to the people of the United States they ought not to object to this amendment to it.

The products of the Iowa creameries last year sold in the Chicago market at the average price of 33 cents a pound, and yet the average price received by the farmers for their butter fat was only 25 cents a pound. The "centralizers," those controlling their market, made 36 per cent on the butter and had a margin of 20 per cent in addition on the overrun, for a pound of butter fat will produce 1.20 pounds of butter. Two of the cooperative concerns paid the farmers 34 1/4 cents a pound, or more than the Chicago prices.

Now, if you allow the destruction of these cooperative associations, not only of creamery and dairy products, but all other associations of that character—voluntary associations of the farmers who put directly their product on the market—if you destroy them and drive them out of business, you put into the hands of these "centralizers," who control the markets, the power to destroy competition and enable them to pay the farmers just what they choose for their product. . . .

Mr. METZ. In New York City we have no dairies and no cows, and we have got to get milk from outside. Now, suppose that across the line in New Jersey there is a town which has a cooperative concern like the one the gentleman speaks of. The milk dealer in New York City is shy in milk and must get a supply. He goes to New Jersey and buys milk from the farmers at a higher price than the cooperative concern is paying, for the purpose of getting milk to take it to New York. Would that be permissible under your amendment, or must the city of New York go without milk?

Mr. TOWNER. I will say to the gentleman that this bill could not apply in any case unless the object and purpose was to destroy competition or establish a monopoly or drive out a producer.

Mr. METZ. The purpose is to get the milk, and if they take it away that town has got no milk.

Mr. TOWNER. This amendment is limited strictly to cooperative associations. It meets directly a real need; it meets directly an evil that is growing throughout the United States and needs immediate relief.

Mr. METZ. You prohibit anybody buying from the dealer or producer at a higher price the thing which is purchased by the cooperative concern.

Mr. TOWNER. I will say to the gentleman that there can be nothing that will so bring down the price of food products to the ultimate consumer like the destruction of these combinations that control them. The middlemen are the people who raise the prices. Butter is sold in the Chicago market at an average price of 33.92 cents for a whole year, and yet the farmers receive less than 25 cents for their product. The farmers will receive a higher price and the consumers will pay a lower price if you will encourage cooperation in the production of food products. I sincerely hope this amendment may be adopted.

Mr. GREEN of Iowa. Mr. Chairman, if there is any necessity for section 2, there is also special necessity for the converse, which is found in the amendment of my colleague. Section 2 provides that any person who shall discriminate in price with intent to injure a competitor between different purchasers of commodities shall be subject to the penalties of the act. This amendment provides, in effect, that anyone who shall discriminate between sellers—that is, persons who are bringing various products to him to be sold—shall also be subject to the penalty where the object and purpose is to destroy competition or to obtain a monopoly. As my colleague has suggested, it strikes at an evil that has been maintained and been growing for a long time in the section of country which we represent. A very large creamery is maintained in the neighboring State of Nebraska, and that creamery makes a practice of overbidding and outbidding any concern that may start up in competition with it in the neighboring State. The only way this evil can be reached is by some such provision. I am very much inclined to think it ought to have been included in section 2.

I know it is said that these acts are already reached and covered by the Sherman Act. It is true they are, if there is any restraint of trade or if monopoly is intended to be acquired, as I think; but the gentlemen upon the other side have all along been contending that similar acts were not covered and not reached by the Sherman Act. If so, then this provision which has been introduced by my colleague [Mr. TOWNER] is absolutely necessary in order to reach actions of this character.

Mr. FITZHENRY. Mr. Chairman, I rise to oppose this amendment. It seems to me it should be defeated, if for no other reason than the manner in which it is drawn. It provides that in any city, town, or county in the United States where a cooperative association is established for the purpose of producing or marketing a product any person who shall, directly or indirectly, for the purpose of destroying competition, discriminate in price in the purchase of such food products or other material within such city, town, or county shall be subject to the penalties provided. It provides, first, for the location of the cooperative institution in a certain city, town, or county, and limits its operation to the city, town, or county, and clearly covers intrastate and not interstate commerce. It is true that in the following phrase these words are used:

> Or use other means the effect of which is to destroy competition or to secure a monopoly in commerce.

That is such a vague provision that it ought not to be written into the law at this place.

Any merit that there might be in this proposition is all covered by the Sherman antitrust law, and the adoption of this amendment at this time will simply limit the remedies of the people against the institution which it is aimed against. . . .

Mr. GREEN of Iowa. Is the gentleman aware that you have much the same provision in section 2 with reference to the discrimination in price of commodities, which uses similar language? It refers to "purchasers of commodities in the same section."

Mr. FITZHENRY. Section 2 is to promote competition and not to limit it as is the idea here, and then section 2 is aimed against monopoly, a concern being engaged in interstate commerce coming into a particular locality and lowering the price, destroying the competitor, and then raising the price again. It covers a train of events.

Mr. WEBB. If the evil practices detailed by the gentleman from Iowa are interstate in their operation and effect, he defines very clearly a case which would come within the provisions of section 2 of the Sherman antitrust law, which is plain and specific, and which would break up the practice which he inveighs against and which ought to be broken up. It reads:

> Every person who shall monopolize or attempt to monopolize or combine or conspire with any other person to monopolize any part of trade among the several States—

And so forth.

The acts which he complains of are covered by the Sherman antitrust law if they are interstate. If they are intrastate, he can not complain to Congress, because we have no power to remedy it. He must go to the State legislature and get them broken up by an act of that body, as we have done in North Carolina. Two or three months ago this same practice was tried on the people of the city of Wilmington, N. C., and the grand jury indicted them under the antitrust laws of our State and put them out of business and broke it up—the practice—by imposing fines on the parties to the practice.

Mr. GREEN of Iowa. Does the gentleman say that the acts attempted to be reached by section 2 are not done in restraint of trade?

Mr. WEBB. There it is the individual act, and the discriminating act itself is condemned.

Mr. GREEN of Iowa. That is what this is.

Mr. WEBB. Here you have a perfect monopoly described by the gentleman from Iowa [Mr. TOWNER] describing every detail, which makes it a monopoly or an attempt to monopolize, and comes within section 2 of the Sherman antitrust law.

Mr. GREEN of Iowa. It comes in the same way under the provision you have in section 2.

Mr. WEBB. This is not the place to offer the amendment. It would mutilate section 7 and has nothing to do with the preceding parts of the same section. The law is ample to cover the condition described, and I trust the House will not adopt the amendment.

The CHAIRMAN. The question is on the amendment offered by the gentleman from Iowa.

The question was taken, and the amendment was rejected.

The Clerk, proceeding with the reading of the bill, read as follows:

> SEC. 8. That no corporation engaged in commerce shall acquire, directly or indirectly, the whole or any part of the stock or other share capital of another corporation engaged also in commerce, where the effect of such acquisition is to eliminate or substantially lessen competition

between the corporation whose stock is so acquired and the corporation making the acquisition, or to create a monopoly of any line of trade in any section or community.

No corporation shall acquire, directly or indirectly, the whole or any part of the stock or other share capital of two or more corporations engaged in commerce where the effect of such acquisition, or the use of such stock by the voting or granting of proxies or otherwise, is to eliminate or substantially lessen competition between such corporations, or any of them, whose stock or other share capital is so acquired, or to create a monopoly of any line of trade in any section or community.

This section shall not apply to corporations purchasing such stock solely for investment and not using the same by voting or otherwise to bring about, or in attempting to bring about, the substantial lessening of competition. Nor shall anything contained in this section prevent a corporation engaged in commerce from causing the formation of subsidiary corporations for the actual carrying on of their immediate lawful business, or the natural and legitimate branches or extensions thereof, or from owning and holding all or a part of the stock of such subsidiary corporations, when the effect of such formation is not to eliminate or substantially lessen competition.

Nothing contained in this section shall be held to affect or impair any right heretofore legally acquired: *Provided*, That nothing in this paragraph shall make stockholding relations between corporations legal when such relations constitute violations of the antitrust laws.

Nor shall anything herein contained be construed to prohibit any railroad corporation from aiding in the construction of branch or short-line railroads, so located as to become feeders to the main line of the company so aiding in such construction, or from acquiring or owning all or any part of the stock of such branch line, nor to prevent any railroad corporation from acquiring and owning all or any part of the stock of a branch or short-line railroad constructed by an independent company where there is no substantial competition between the company owning the branch line so constructed and the company owning the main line acquiring the property, or an interest therein, nor to prevent any railroad company from extending any of its lines, through the medium of the acquisition of stock or otherwise of any other railroad company, where there is no substantial competition between the company extending its lines and the company whose stock, property, or an interest therein, is so acquired.

A violation of any of the provisions of this section shall be deemed a misdemeanor, and shall be punishable by a fine not exceeding $5,000, or by imprisonment not exceeding one year, or by both, in the discretion of the court.

Mr. VOLSTEAD. Mr. Chairman, I offer the following amendment.
The Clerk read as follows:

Strike out all of section 8 and substitute the following:
"SEC. 8. (a) That it shall be unlawful to own, hold, or otherwise use any share of any capital stock of any corporation so as to aid in carrying into effect, creating, or maintaining any contract combination in the form of trust or otherwise, or conspiracy in restraint of commerce or to own, hold, or otherwise use any such share so as to aid in effecting or attempting to effect a monopoly or any combination or conspiracy to monopolize any part of commerce. In addition to any punishments prescribed by existing law, it is provided that as a penalty for a violation of this provision all earnings that may accrue upon any share of capital stock while so unlawfully owned, held, or used shall be forfeited and belong to the stockholders of the corporations having issued the same whose shares are not then unlawfully owned, held, or used. And none of the shares of such stock while so unlawfully owned, held, or used shall entitle anyone to vote or otherwise participate in the election of any director, trustee, officer, or employee of the corporation having issued such share or to otherwise participate in the management or control thereof.

"(b) No corporation shall issue any share of capital stock or borrow any money to acquire any part of the capital stock of any corporation engaged in commerce, and the acquisition of any such stock by any such means is prohibited. Nor shall any share of capital stock of any corporation engaged in commerce be acquired by or on behalf of any other corporation by exchanging therefore directly or indirectly any share of the capital stock of another corporation. As a penalty it is provided that all earnings that may accrue upon any share of stock hereafter acquired in violation of this paragraph shall, while retained directly or indirectly by the corporation acquiring the same, be forfeited and belong to the other shareholders of the corporation having issued the same. And none of the shares of stock acquired in violation of this paragraph shall, while so retained, entitle anyone to vote for any director, trustee, officer, or employee of the corporation having so issued such stock, or to otherwise participate in the management or control thereof. This paragraph shall not prevent any bank, banking association, or trust company engaged as a business in receiving deposits from using such deposits to acquire, either by purchase or as security, any share of capital stock of a corporation engaged in commerce.

"(c) Unless otherwise authorized by the Commissioner of Corporations, no stock or any bond or obligation due more than two years from the date of issue shall be issued by any corporation engaged in commerce for less than par or until the fair market value thereof shall have been paid in cash into the treasury of the corporation. Said commissioner may, however, on application, permit any issue for less than par and for property in place of cash if it shall appear to him that it is reasonably necessary and that a fair consideration is actually received for such issue. Stocks, bonds, and obligations issued in violation of this paragraph shall be void.

"(d) That no corporation engaged in commerce shall declare any dividend except from the net profits arising from its business; nor shall it divide, withdraw, or in any way pay to the stockholders, or any of them, any part of the capital stock of such corporation, or any of the proceeds of the issue or sale of any such stock, unless it shall first be made to appear to the Commissioner of Corporations that it is reasonably necessary for the purpose of maintaining the credit of the corporation or to carry on its legitimate business. Any person who shall violate or participate in violating any provision of this paragraph or suffer or permit any violation thereof shall be individually liable for all the debts of the corporation and all shares of stock issued in violation of this paragraph shall be void.

"(e) That paragraphs (c) and (d) of this section shall not apply to any corporation whose capital stock, including bonds due more than one year from their date of issue, shall be less than $2,000,000 par value, unless the Commissioner of Corporations shall find and certify as to any corporation that it is a part of some combination that is so conducted as to make it substantially a business unit with more than $2,000,000 in capital including such bonds; or unless said commissioner shall find and certify as to any corporation that it controls more than one-half of all commerce in its line of commerce in any section that includes two or more States. Upon making such certificate, a copy thereof shall be delivered to the corporation affected, and from the date of such delivery this section shall apply to such corporation, and no part of this section shall apply to any corporation subject to regulation as a common carrier under the act entitled 'An act to regulate commerce,' approved February 4, 1887, and amendments thereto. Nor shall this section be construed to repeal any provision of the antitrust laws.''

Mr. VOLSTEAD. Mr. Chairman, I assume that it is useless at this time to try to make this law any stronger by offering any amendments. We have to-day exempted labor organizations from the Sherman Antitrust Act; we have also exempted railway companies so as to permit them to stifle competition, and now section 8 is submitted to authorize the formation of trusts. I called attention to this section some days ago. I have listened patiently for any explanation of this section that would show that my criticism is not justified, but so far I have heard no such explanation.

I again call attention to the third paragraph of this section 8, and again repeat that it clearly permits corporations to consolidate into trusts. Clearly permits the creation of a community of interests that will eliminate anything like competition. I am not going to explain this feature any further than I did a day or two ago. Anyone who will read it carefully will come to the same conclusion that I have come to. I want to explain briefly the nature of my amendment. The first paragraph of the amendment attempts to compel corporations to unscramble their own eggs. It attempts to make it unprofitable for corporations or individuals to hold stock in violation of the Sherman Antitrust Act, and as such to induce them voluntarily to separate and organize along legal lines. If we depend on the courts to set aside these combinations, we know from past experience that it is ineffectual. . . .

Mr. BARTLETT. I could not get the purport of the gentleman's amendment. Does his amendment, like the section, deal solely with holding companies?

Mr. VOLSTEAD. It deals with all combinations through stock ownership.

Mr. BARTLETT. I understand this section 8 deals with holding companies only.

Mr. VOLSTEAD. No; it deals with all combinations through stock ownership. Paragraph 3 of the section deals solely with holding companies, but paragraphs 1 and 2 deal generally with stock consolidation of corporations, whether holding companies or not. Paragraph 2 of the amendment which I have offered was suggested in the hearings on this bill. Almost the only method adopted by corporations in forming these consolidations is by the issue of their own stock in exchange for the stock of the corporation that they seek to acquire. Corporations do not invest surplus money which they may have in the corporate stock of another corporation. On the other hand, they create an additional amount of stock and take that stock and use it for the purpose of trading for the stock of the corporation they seek to acquire. I have drawn the second paragraph so as to prohibit that practice. If that practice was prohibited, I do not believe we should have very much trouble about the formation in the future of other consolidations of corporations by reason of stock ownership. The third and fourth paragraphs of my amendment present nothing particularly new; like provisions can be found in almost any statute that seeks to regulate corporations. . . .

Mr. Chairman, I have sought not to apply paragraphs 3 or 4 to the small corporations that only incidentally do an interstate business. I have limited those two provisions to corporations with a capital stock of $2,000,000, but in defining capital stock I include the bonds. You can find provisions like those two in the Massachusetts statute or in the New Jersey statute. It seems to me that when these corporations go into interstate commerce we have a right to say to them, "You must comply with provisions of this class, provisions that are recognized generally as reasonable." I simply submitted them as such. I realize it is useless for me to attempt to convince this committee, but I want to impress upon it that it is not safe to go before this country with a provision such as you have in section 8. Here is a provision that clearly wipes out for all practical purposes the Sherman Antitrust Act so far as it prohibits combinations in restraint of trade. The Democrats and the Republicans stand pledged to the maintenace of the Sherman Antitrust Act. Do you believe that you can deceive the people into the belief that you are passing an effective statute? In some way this statute may soon reach the courts. When it does the court will give it the construction that its plain language clearly warrants, and when they do you will have a reckoning. No doubt you expect this bill to be rewritten in the Senate. I do not believe you expect this bill to become a law or you would try to correct it in this House. It certainly does not add to the standing or dignity of the House by passing such a political makeshift as this.

Mr. [JOSEPH B.] THOMPSON [D., Okla.]. . . .

Mr. Chairman, I voted for the Thomas amendment this afternoon to the antitrust act, and I want to call attention to a report that is carried this afternoon in the Evening Star of an interview with the President which confirms me in the view that I took at that time when I voted for the Thomas amendment. I did not believe that the Webb amendment was broad enough to exempt labor and farmers' organizations from the terms of the antitrust act. The Star carries this report, in talking about the interview with the President:

> He was asked numerous questions as to pending legislation, and especially as to the amendments to the Clayton bill touching upon the exemption of labor unions from the operation of the Sherman antitrust law. He does not believe that the amendments agreed upon by the administration and Congress give the exemptions mentioned.

That is in exact accordance with the view that I had when I voted for the Thomas amendment. The article continues:

> On the contrary, he thinks there is no more immunity for labor and farm organizations, as far as violations of the law are concerned, than any corporation or other organization.

Mr. Chairman, I did not believe when I voted this afternoon that the amendment offered by the gentleman from North Carolina [Mr. WEBB] took care of labor and farmers' organizations, especially of farmers' organizations. I have not very many labor organizations in my own State, but we have a great many farmers' organizations, and I want to say this, that while that amendment might exempt the organization as such, it did not exempt the actions of the organization officials. Suppose the president of the farmers' union were to send down word to the organizations, or to the members of the union, to hold their cotton in the warehouse and not to sell it, to await a better price, is there any member of the Committee on the Judiciary who would say that that would not subject the member of the organization who sent down that word to prosecution under the Sherman antitrust law? If there is any Member, I would like for him to rise in his place and say so. The question was propounded here by Mr. GARNER this afternoon to the gentleman from Texas [Mr. HENRY], who is a genuine friend of the farmer, and Mr. HENRY did not answer the question. It was also submitted to the gentleman from Pennsylvania [Mr. GRAHAM], and he candidly admitted that it would subject these members of the farmers' union, the grange, and so forth, to criminal prosecutions under the Sherman antitrust law. Now, Mr. Chairman, I want to say this: These gentlemen come before us and say this amendment offered by Mr. WEBB is supposed to take care of the farmers' and labor organizations. If this amendment takes care of them, why are not you willing to go further and put in it that they shall not be subject to prosecution; that these organizations shall not be subject to the terms of the antitrust act?

If we want to do the thing, if you want to exempt these organizations why not put language in the bill that absolutely and plainly takes care of them, and not put language in there that would be subject to judicial construction. Now, I do not know what experience you gentlemen have had with Federal judges. I know, Mr. Chairman, that out in our State we have not very much regard for the opinion of a Federal judge on any question. Why, they have tied up our 2-cent fare rate, they have enjoined our taxation, they have attempted, Mr. Chairman, to enjoin statehood in Oklahoma in the face of an act of Congress. . . .

Mr. HENRY. The gentleman referred to my colleague asking me a question, and said that I did not reply to it. I did make a reply to it, and I want to add here that even if this exemption were not written into the law which we have written in the shape of the Webb amendment that the farmers of Oklahoma or of Texas could meet and agree to hold their cotton or their grain, and put it in a warehouse, and hold it there until they got ready to sell, and that would not be a violation of the terms of the Sherman antitrust law. . . .

I say, without this exemption the farmers of Texas could have met and agreed to put their cotton in the warehouse and keep it there until they got ready to sell, and it would not be a violation of the Sherman antitrust law. Now, this exemption makes assurance doubly sure, and they are exempted from the provisions of the antitrust law, both in State and interstate commerce, if they see proper to invoke the protection of it.

Mr. THOMPSON of Oklahoma. Does the gentleman mean to say to this House that if the farmers of Oklahoma were to put their cotton in a warehouse and hold it for a certain price they would not be guilty under this act?

Mr. HENRY. Even if this law were not passed now they could not be touched under the terms of the Sherman antitrust law.

Mr. THOMPSON of Oklahoma. Suppose the men who manufacture the cotton should put their manufactured goods in the warehouse to hold the manufactured goods for a certain price, would they be guilty under this act?

Mr. HENRY. If it entered into interstate commerce and becomes a part of interstate commerce, that is another proposition; but here is a purely local proposition, and it is not in violation of that statute. You can put every bale of cotton raised in Oklahoma or every bushel of corn or grain and hold it there until you get ready to sell, and that is not a violation of the Sherman antitrust law.

Mr. BARKLEY. I will say further this is exactly what was done in Kentucky with the tobacco raisers who pooled their tobacco—

Mr. THOMPSON of Oklahoma. And there was a fine imposed of $3,500—

Mr. BARKLEY. That is where they were charged with interfering with interstate tobacco by crossing the Ohio River. . . .

Mr. BARTLETT. Mr. Chairman, this provision, section No. 8 and the subsequent section of this bill, stretch the power of Congress over interstate commerce very far. In fact, Mr. Chairman, I have very serious doubts myself whether they do not go beyond the limit of the power of Congress to regulate interstate commerce by undertaking to regulate the internal management of corporations created by the States.

So far as I am concerned, Mr. Chairman, on another occasion I saw fit to give expression to my views on this subject in a minority report which I signed, emanating from the Committee on Interstate and Foreign Commerce of the House in 1910, and also to say what I thought about that subject on the floor during the discussion of that bill. I think there is more power in Congress and more reason for exercising it in regulating the matter of directors or the matter of transportation companies than it has to exercise it in this bill. I realize, Mr. Chairman, that the Democratic Party in its Baltimore convention adopted this in its platform:

We favor the declaration by law of the conditions upon which corporations shall be permitted to engage in interstate trade, including, among others, the prevention of holding companies, of interlocking directors, of stock watering, of discrimination in price, and the control by any one corporation of so large a proportion of any industry as to make it a menace to competitive conditions.

I am a pretty loyal Democrat, Mr. Chairman. I believe in following the declarations of party platforms, confiding in the wisdom of those who represent the party in the convention; and but for that declaration in the party platform I do not see how ⊥ I could bring myself to vote for the provisions of these sections 8 and 9, all of them. Nor, Mr. Chairman, have I yet brought myself to the conclusion that I can vote for them. I know, Mr. Chairman, it is not very fashionable to suggest that the Constitution stands in the way of legislation of any sort by Congress. But it would not be out of place, Mr. Chairman, to call attention of some—not many—of the adjudicated cases upon this subject, cases adjudicated by the Supreme Court of the United States.

I maintain, and the Supreme Court has decided, that the charters of the corporations granted by the States are their guide as to what they shall do in the internal management of those corporations. I do not believe it is a proper exercise of legislative authority by Congress under the commerce clause of the Constitution to say who shall or who shall not be directors of a corporation organized by a State. If we examine the law writers and the decisions of the courts that have passed upon those subjects we shall find that the regulation of the internal affairs of a corporation, what business it shall do, what the directors shall do, who they shall be, of whom the board of directors shall be composed, is an exercise of the police power of the States solely, and not a power authorized to be controlled by Congress.

Let us take the opposite view of it, Mr. Chairman, for a moment. Suppose Congress should undertake to say, in spite of State legislation, that there should be interlocking directorates; that there should be combinations of interstate railroads running from one State to another in spite of constitutional prohibitions. . . .

Suppose, Mr. Chairman, that Congress should declare that railroads that were engaged in interstate commerce might have interlocking directorates, and the States should forbid it. Is it to be presumed that Congress could authorize a thing of that sort? Yet, if Congress can forbid it, Congress can grant it.

Now, let us see what the Supreme Court of the United States says upon that subject. . . .

Mr. GREEN of Iowa. Is the gentleman speaking now of the provisions of section 9 instead of section 8?

Mr. BARTLETT. I said at the beginning that I was speaking of the provisions of sections 8 and 9. I am fully aware that the Supreme Court has decided in the Northern Securities case that holding companies, such as the Northern Securities Co., when they undertake to combine, and thereby interfere with commerce and have a monopoly, come within the purview of the act of 1890 by a divided court of 5 to 4. But I will read from the case of the Louisville & Nashville Railroad Co. v. Kentucky (161 U. S., 702). . . .[5.557]

This was a case where the Louisville & Nashville Railroad undertook to combine with another railroad and to purchase some of its stock and own it in contravention of the constitution of Kentucky, which said it should not be done. When attacked in the courts for doing it they set up that the statute of Kentucky was unconstitutional because it interfered with interstate commerce, both railroad companies being interstate railroads. In that case the court said:

It was said in Sherlock v. Alling (93 U. S., 99, 103, 104)[5.558] and quoted with approbation in Plumley v. Massachusetts (155 U. S., 461)[5.559] that "in conferring upon Congress the regulation of commerce it was never intended to cut the States off from legislating on all subjects relating to the health, life, and safety of their citizens, though the legislation might indirectly affect the commerce of the country. Legislation, in a great variety of ways, may affect

---

[5.557] 161 U.S. 677, 16 S. Ct. 714, 40 L. Ed. 849 (1896).
[5.558] 93 U.S. 99, 103-04, 23 L. Ed. 819, 820-21 (1876).
[5.559] 155 U.S. 461, 473, 15 S. Ct. 154, 158, 39 L. Ed. 223, 227 (1894).

commerce and persons engaged in it without constituting a regulation of it within the meaning of the Constitution, * * * and and it may be said, generally, that the legislation of a State not directed against commerce or any of its regulations, but relating to the rights, duties, and liabilities of citizens, and only indirectly and remotely affecting the operations of commerce, is of obligatory force upon citizens within its territorial jurisdiction, whether on land or water, or engaged in commerce, foreign or interstate, or in any other pursuit."

It has never been supposed that the dominant power of Congress over interstate commerce took from the States the power of legislation with respect to the instruments of such commerce so far as the legislation was within its ordinary police powers. Nearly all the railways in the country have been constructed under State authority, and it can not be supposed that they intended to abandon their power over them as soon as they were finished. The power to construct them involves necessarily the power to impose such regulation upon their operation as a sound regard for the interests of the public may seem to render desirable. In the division of authority with respect to interstate railways Congress reserves to itself the superior right to control their commerce and forbid interference therewith, while to the States remains the power to create and to regulate the instruments of such commerce so far as necessary to the conservation of the public interests.

If it be assumed that the States have no right to forbid the consolidation of competing lines, because the whole subject is within the control of Congress, it would necessarily follow that Congress would have the power to authorize such consolidation in defiance of State legislation—a proposition which only needs to be stated to demonstrate its unsoundness. As we have already said, the power of one railway corporation to purchase the stock and franchises of another must be conferred by express language to that effect in the charter, and hence, if the charter of the Louisville & Nashville Co. had been silent upon that point it will be conceded that it would have no power to make the proposed purchase in this case. As the power to purchase, then, is derivable from the State, the State may accompany it with such limitations as it may choose to impose. Its [sic] results, then, from the argument of the appellant that, if there be any interference with interstate commerce it is in imposing limitations upon the exercise of a right which did not previously exist, and hence if the State permits such purchase or consolidation it is bound to extend the authority to every possible case or expose itself to the charge of interfering with commerce. This proposition is obviously untenable.[5.560]

So that if the Congress has the right to exercise this power of prohibiting interlocking directorates in corporations simply because they engage in interstate commerce, then Congress has the power to permit interlocking directorates; and if the power is in Congress, the power is exclusive in Congress, and the whole power to regulate can be taken away from the States. In my opinion that can not be done.

I have another case here to which I desire to call the attention of the House, in volume 204, United States, page 152. That was a case where the State of New York levied a tax upon the transfer of shares of stock sold in New York. The tax was resisted upon the ground that the stock was sold to some one outside of the State, and that the tax was an interference with interstate commerce. The court held:

The protection of the commerce clause of the Federal Constitution is not available to defeat a State stamp-tax law on transactions wholly within a state, because they affect property without that State, or because one or both of the parties previously came from other States.[5.561]

Those are two decisions which I have cited, and to which I desire to call the attention of the committee. If they are the law, if it be true that the State and only the State has the right to regulate who shall be directors and who shall not, and what a railroad or a corporation shall do in reference to purchasing or owning the property of its competitor, then the Congress has no power such as this bill undertakes to exercise. I do not think it has the power. I may be mistaken. I know that the steps have been long and the strides have been far in the direction of controlling everything under the commerce clause of the Constitution.

I recall a letter written by Mr. Jefferson to Judge Sloan in 1816, as I recall the year, when, criticizing and condemning the effort to concentrate all power in the Federal Government here at Washington, Mr. Jefferson said that under the commerce clause of the Constitution they would undertake not only to regulate what was real

---

[5.560] 161 U.S. at 701–03.

[5.561] New York ex rel. Hatch v. Reardon, 204 U.S. 152–53, 27 S. Ct. 188, 51 L. Ed. 415 (1907). The Congressman read from the Court's syllabus, not from the opinion.

interstate commerce, but to bring under the control of Congress all manufacture and agriculture. If he could now revisit these scenes of his labors and see what has been done and what we are daily attempting to do he would see that the prophecy he made in 1816 had almost come to a dread realization.

So, Mr. Chairman, I find myself in this position of having very serious doubt as to the constitutionality of these sections and as to the power of Congress to enact them. I can not get away from that. It is no hobby. I have undertaken to study the question. I have given much thought to it on other occasions, as I have also upon this occasion, and I can not escape the conviction that Congress does not have the power, in regulating the instrumentalities of Congress, like railroads that pass from one State to another, to say how the internal affairs of such a corporation shall be managed.

To repeat what was said in the Kentucky case, would anyone presume for a moment that Congress would have the power to say that if the State law forbade it, that one competing railroad could absorb another, yet, in spite of said State law, should authorize such consolidation? Yet if Congress has the supreme and sole power and jurisdiction over the subject, it would have the right to permit it—as it does in this bill—permit traffic arrangements and permit railroad officers to confer together for the purpose of making agreements. If the State law forbids corporations within its domain from making these arrangements, Congress having the power to direct and saying that they can make these arrangements, and that one railroad could absorb another, you can not escape the conclusion and conviction that if Congress has the exclusive power to forbid these things it has the power to permit them.

So, Mr. Chairman, I come back to the proposition that these provisions of this bill give me serious concern and serious doubt as to what my duty in the matter is. I realize that I am liable to err as to how the law will be construed. When I read some recent decisions of the Supreme Court of the United States it looks, Mr. Chairman, as if they were ready to go even further than Congress wants them to go. The Supreme Court may decide this to be constitutional. As far as I am concerned I think they endanger the good provisions of the bill, and that in the platform, as it was written in Baltimore, the demands placed on the Democratic Members were made without considering whether they could be sustained in the courts or not. [Applause.]

Mr. GREEN of Iowa. Mr. Chairman, orders have been issued from the White House that the trust problem should be taken up at this session and some new law passed. These instructions have been issued in accordance with a theory, of which the President seems to be the chief exponent, that to cure any evil that exists it is only necessary to put a new law upon the statute books, and it matters little in what form the law is enacted. One part of this theory is that legislation upon any subject, no matter how complicated, can easily be drafted, and when once formulated should be accepted by Congress without any changes or amendments. At this particular time I doubt whether the country at large is as ready to accept this theory as it has been. It is getting some experience with half-baked legislation, and now in the bill before us we have some measures as to which the cookery has not even gone that far. We had already on our statute books undoubtedly the best law on the subject of trusts and combinations in restraint of trade possessed by any nation. It is a model of brevity, clearness, and of comprehensiveness. It has been tried again and again and never found wanting except when its failure was caused by incompetency, neglect, or something worse. It will not, of course, reach acts done in intrastate business. These can only be reached by the States themselves, although the framers of this bill seem to have overlooked this obvious rule.

Mr. Chairman, the bill is drawn on wrong lines. It undertakes to deal with specific acts, regardless of whether they are done in restraint of trade or for the purpose of creating a monopoly. In framing the bill it seems to have been forgotten that an act may be perfectly innocent and an aid to competition when done by a small dealer for the purpose of extending his trade, while the same act may be highly injurious when done by a large concern as a part of a far-reaching scheme for the purpose of creating a monopoly. It has been said by a member of the committee introducing the bill that the Sherman law merely reached acts done in restraint of trade, while this bill was intended to promote competition. Such a statement shows an utter misconception of the Sherman law. If restraint of trade be forbidden—and everyone concedes it is forbidden by the Sherman law—competition is free. We can not compel different concerns to compete, but we can compel them to give a free and fair field to competition with each other and forbid their combining with each other in restraint of trade and thus preventing competition. This is just what the Sherman law does. Restraint of trade, Mr. Chairman, is the exact converse of competition. Forbid restraint of trade and the door is thrown wide open for competition. The Sherman law provides for competition and at the same time it does not fetter business, because sales and contracts alike are left undisturbed where no restraint of trade is imposed.

Another great defect in the bill is that it undertakes to be specific, but finding that the attempt resulted in expressions either too broad or too narrow, it has been sought to remedy the difficulty by the use of indefinite terms. Who can even guess at the meaning of certain expressions used in the bill? For example, "wrongfully injure a competitor"; "arbitrarily refuse to sell"; "substantially lessen competition"; "legitimate purposes," and so forth. The committee itself seemed to be so uncertain of the effect of the bill that it not only inserted numerous provisos, but it was found necessary to follow these provisos with other provisos to the effect that no part of the bill should be construed to modify existing laws.

The result, if the bill becomes a law, will be to create doubt and uncertainty. The business man embarking upon a voyage of trade will not know which way to steer his vessel. The construction of the act will necessarily be involved in a fog of doubt, and until its uncertainties are settled the most honest may be in fear and the active will hesitate.

The bill will neither do the harm many expect nor the good which its authors anticipate. It is so crudely drawn that many of its provisions are meaningless, and it is so far from having any "teeth" that a corporation lawyer who could not drive a six-horse team and band wagon through nearly all of its provisions ought to be discharged at once. In some respects it actually weakens the Sherman law by providing a method of evading it.

Section 2 of the bill is a good example of the method which has been used in preparing the bill. This section forbids discrimination in prices in different localities, except such as is caused by making due allowance for transportation charges, and so forth. Yet the only way for a small concern to get a foothold in a new locality is to sell at first at a reduced price; otherwise it will be unable to get the business. In so doing competition is stimulated and a monopoly on the part of those who have been in control of that market can be prevented. But this section seems to place such transactions under the ban of the law. The large industries can easily establish branch houses in any desired locality, and thus evade the law entirely, although its purpose in lowering prices may be part of a plan to build up a monopoly and drive its competitors out of that locality. Thus the small concern may be punished, although its acts are not only innocent but in reality beneficial, while the big monopoly goes free. The effect of this section, if it has any effect, will not be to promote competition, but to destroy it, and its provisos legalize acts which are forbidden under the Sherman law when done as a part of a scheme to restrain trade.

Section 3 is so indefinite that no one can tell what it means. It is intended to compel those operating coal mines to sell to the public. It will have no such effect. No two persons have agreed as to what is the meaning of the word "arbitrarily," as used therein. If it means what the authors of the bill state, namely, "without any reason whatever," then the section has not the slightest effect. If it means what some others claim, it will embarrass the small dealer without in any way reaching the large dealer who has branch selling houses in each State. In any event, its meaning is so uncertain as to make its enforcement impracticable and its enactment useless, if not dangerous.

Section 4 strikes at the small dealer, who can not maintain an agency of his own in another State while the large dealer can maintain an agency therein, and by making his sales through such agency cause all such sales to be intrastate business and entirely escape the provisions of the section. Like the two preceeding sections it holds a club over the head of the small dealer and leaves open a wide door through which the big interests may escape.

Section 5 is included in the Sherman law as it now stands.

The first paragraph of section 7 does not include cooperative agricultural associations, and all amendments for that purpose were rejected. In its original form it contained nothing not already provided by law.

The second paragraph of section 7 is one of the most dangerous in the whole bill. It gives the railroads the privilege of making agreements with reference to rates and services which they shall perform regardless of whether they are competing lines or not. The railways have been trying for years to obtain this privilege, and heretofore Congress has always denied it. It is true that the bill excepts agreements to maintain rates, but this can easily be evaded as it does not forbid agreements to establish or fix rates. The provision that such agreements shall be approved by the Interstate Commerce Commission does not help the situation. Inevitably competition is destroyed when such agreements are made, rates will be raised, and service heretofore rendered will be denied. The railways can agree upon slow trains, upon onerous conditions for shippers, and to refuse privileges heretofore granted. Whether intended or not this paragraph conceals a "joker" of the most dangerous kind.

Section 8 is a sham, pure and simple. It pretends to be that which it is not and which it can not be. It pretends to forbid the consolidation of competing railroad companies by means of holding companies. As an actual fact it facilitates such consolidation. It pretends to strengthen the Sherman law while it actually weakens it. It pretends to forbid the use of holding companies for the purposes of consolidating companies engaged in commerce. It actually provides that such holding companies may be organized instead of commanding their dissolution.

Mr. Chairman, it was held in the Northern Securities Co. case—and since that time no lawyer has pretended to doubt ⊥ the principle—that competing lines of railways could not be joined by holding companies; that holding companies could not be organized that had even the potential power of preventing competition without violating the Sherman law. But under the provisions of this section, in order to establish a violation of the antitrust law we must go further and show that the competition has actually been lessened and prevented or a monopoly obtained. Nothing of that kind was required prior to the enactment of this section if it should become a law.

Mr. VOLSTEAD. Will the gentleman permit me to call his attention to the third paragraph of this section, that does not even condemn a monopoly?

Mr. GREEN of Iowa. I was about to allude to that. In the third paragraph of the section is found a series of exemptions which runs through the section until almost everything imaginable has been exempted. I read from one of the provisos:

> The section shall not apply to corporations purchasing stock for investment, or using the same by voting or otherwise to bring about a lessening of competition, nor shall it prevent a corporation engaged in commerce from causing the formation of subsidiary corporations, or from owning or holding all or part of the stock of such subsidiary corporations.

Under this provision, no matter how complete the monopoly, unless some action was taken by voting it would not fall under the ban of the law, while under the present law it is so well settled that a combination of competing lines is illegal that it is not necessary for the Department of Justice to bring a suit against railway companies which have been consolidated through a holding company or by the purchase of stock, whether one or the other. The simple statement of the Department of Justice that action will be brought to dissolve the combination has been sufficient to cause the railway companies attempting consolidation to yield immediately and consent to a dissolution.

Under this section (8) holding companies may be organized which can obtain the control of two competing lines, and then under the preceding section they may enter into any agreement that they choose to fix rates, to determine the service which they shall perform, and, in short, to absolutely eliminate competition.

This is what the committee has brought forward as something that will bring relief to the people. Why, Mr. Chairman, it is just what those in control of the railways have been seeking for. They now can say:

> This is the way I long have sought,
> And mourned because I found it not.

[Laughter.]

The majority of the Judiciary Committee have brought in what the railroads have been hounding the Interstate Commerce Commission for and demanding of Congress for lo these many years, and it has been refused them until this time. Now they have all the powers of consolidation they ever really wished and asked for in the two sections, and may consolidate under one section and agree on rates under the other. [Applause.]

Mr. Chairman, this section should be stricken out. It serves no purpose. There never was any demand or reason for it, nor have gentlemen undertaken to give any reason why it should be adopted. The relief afforded by the Sherman law was ample. As the gentleman fron Minnesota [Mr. VOLSTEAD] has stated, this section is likely to furnish the means of evading the most valuable portion of the Sherman law which we now have on our statute books.

Complaints against this and the preceding section are answered by gentlemen on the other side by calling attention to provisions to the effect that these sections shall not be construed to permit acts illegal under the present law. But if these provisos are relied upon, why keep these sections in the bill? Why should we enact a law which we so much fear partially repeals the Sherman Act, that we are obliged to follow it by a proviso that it shall not be so construed? Could anything be more useless or confusing?

Section 12 is the so-called "personal-guilt section." It is claimed by the authors that it will attribute the guilt of the corporation to its officers. As a matter of fact, it will do nothing of the kind. As originally drawn, while I do not think that its authors intended that it should conceal a "joker," it was in fact a joke. In order to convict any individual of a violation of the antitrust laws it required a conviction first of the corporation and then of the individual—in other words, two convictions to show one crime. As amended, it is questionable whether it is any better. It may not now require two trials, but it certainly will require more evidence than was necessary under the Sherman law, and unless further amended this section will weaken this important statute instead of strengthening it.

There are some of the provisions of the bill that meet with my approval. The section extending the statute of limitations while a suit is pending against a trust is an excellent one and ought to have been enacted long ago. The proviso authorizing an individual as well as the Government to commence an equity action to restrain a threatened injury by some monopoly is also a good one, although I doubt whether as much good will be received therefrom as was expected. Section 6, as amended in the Committee of the Whole House, is excellent in its purpose, although there may be some doubt about its constitutionality, and I have no fault to find with its provisions with reference to labor organizations, which, in my opinion, merely state the law according to the best authorities.

The bill, taken as a whole, is a political measure, framed for purposes which are political, rather than those which would be for the benefit of the country at large. It is evidently intended to hold it up before the country as an example of legislative activity on the part of the Democratic administration, which is determined to do something, "right or wrong." It demonstrates the inability of a Democratic Congress to frame constructive laws under which business can thrive; the laborer receive his just reward; competition be free; and predatory interests restrained. No great constructive measure has ever yet been made a law through that party which did not in a few months after enactment become so unpopular that the people could not repeal it soon enough. The form of this bill does not indicate any improvement in the capacity of that party for government.

The antitrust provisions of the bill are simply buncombe, designed to give the country the impression that the Democratic Party was redeeming its party pledges, and by the inclusion of some good provisions, to place the Republican Members of this House in a false light. If I should vote against the bill, I realize that it would be claimed that I was voting against measures which would tend to suppress the trusts and also against policies in regard to labor organizations which I have always favored. I do not propose to be put in such a position. For years I have worked to make the laws against trusts more efficient, and I have always been in favor of giving labor its just dues, although I have not been willing to select any particular class and grant it a special privilege. I am not in any way responsible for any of the defective provisions in this bill. I have repeatedly spoken in opposition to them on the floor of this House. I have offered amendments myself and have supported those offered by others which would have eliminated its evil features and made it more efficient in controlling trusts without in any way interfering with legitimate business. But amendment after amendment has been voted down regardless of their merit. It has become so plain, Mr. Chairman, that the Democratic majority is not intending to prevent acts which restrain trade or create monopolies that it is useless to offer amendments further. Their whole purpose is to make a showing regardless of whether anything is accomplished in the way of curbing monopoly. If there was any prospect that this bill would become a law in its present form, I would not give it my vote; but no one expects anything of the kind. The bill is introduced for appearance, well knowing that it never will become a law as it now stands, and in the expectation that it will not even be considered by the Senate before the congressional elections.

The hope is that its high-sounding phrases, which can be understood by no one, will deceive the people and ensnare their opponents. I will not walk into such a trap. As I have stated, I have long been working among the ranks of those who are opposed to trusts and monopolies. Years ago I was selected by the governor of Iowa as a delegate to and attended the convention held at Chicago to consider measures against trusts—the first ever held in this country for that purpose—and I have always been in favor of giving the laboring man the right to organize. On prior occasions when measures giving the workingmen their rights have been before the House I have supported them by my voice and by my vote. I decline now to be put in the attitude of opposing the principles which I have before advocated by reason of my vote upon a bill the antitrust provisions of which are a mere pretense and a sham.

The attempt which has been made in this bill is entirely in the wrong direction. The Sherman law, as I believe, is amply sufficient to reach all restraint of trade and monopoly exercised or attempted in interstate commerce. It is true that evils now exist, but they exist partly through lack of enforcement of the Sherman law and partly because the wrongful acts are committed in intrastate commerce—that is, wholly within the boundaries of a single State—and are not within the jurisdiction of Congress. Many, if not most, of the evils at which this bill ⊥ is aimed can only be reached through State laws. I regret to say that the laws of my own State are not what they should be on this subject, and we need therein a broad and comprehensive measure like the Sherman Act. We need, especially on the part of our national authorities, a fearless and thorough enforcement of the Federal law which, it is unnecessary to say, we are not receiving. We need also a Federal law requiring all concerns doing an interstate business to come under its jurisdiction, and a provision that as a penalty for a failure to observe such antitrust laws the privilege of transacting such business will be withdrawn. Then, and then only, in my judgment, will the great combinations which now are a menace to our national existence be properly curbed and restrained, and to this end I shall direct my best efforts.

Mr. MANN. Mr. Chairman, I would like to get the attention of the gentleman in charge of the bill if I might. On page 25 this language is inserted, this being the section in regard to holding of stock by one corporation in another corporation:

> This section shall not apply to corporations purchasing such stock solely for investment and not using the same by voting or otherwise to bring about, or in attempting to bring about, the substantial lessening of competition.

The first provision is:

> This section shall not apply to corporations purchasing such stock solely for investment.

Of course, that includes any stock that is purchased for investment, and all stock is purchased for investment when it is purchased at all. Then there is the exception—

> And not using the same by voting or otherwise to bring about, or in attempting to bring about, the substantial lessening of competition.

That would not apply to voting for the election of officers, would it? . . .

What does this exception mean? Here is a provision which says that this section shall not apply to corporations purchasing stock solely for investment, with an exception, and the exception is—

And not using the same by voting or otherwise to bring about, or in attempting to bring about, the substantial lessening of competition.

That would not prevent voting the stock they purchase.

Mr. CARLIN. I think not, unless they were voting it with that object in view.

Mr. MANN. How would it be possible to show that they were voting the stock for the purpose of bringing about the lessening of competition? They vote stock for officers, and they may vote stock as to the issuance of other stock or bonds, but they do not vote stock as to the policy of the corporation.

Mr. CARLIN. If they voted that stock for sale to a holding company, the object of which would be combination with a competing company, that would be one way in which they would bring themselves within the provisions of this statute.

Mr. MANN. But there is another provision in reference to holding companies.

Mr. CARLIN. Yes; but this is the holding company provision that we are discussing now. The gentleman is discussing the holding company provision of the bill.

Mr. MANN. Oh, no; I am discussing the question of where one company buys the stock of another. You say it shall not apply where they buy stock for investment, unless they vote it to lessen competition.

Mr. CARLIN. That is right.

Mr. MANN. They do not vote to lessen competition in any case.

Mr. CARLIN. They could vote stock in violation of section 9, which follows, in the election of interlocking directorates, and by reason of that fact competition might be lessened—any number of various specific acts which go to bring about the lessening of competition might be done through stock voting or otherwise.

Mr. MANN. Under this section one corporation can buy and own the stock of another, and it can vote that stock unless it be proven that it voted for the purpose of substantially lessening competition.

Mr. CARLIN. That is correct.

Mr. MANN. I do not think it means anything. . . .

[Mr. FARR addressed the committee. See Appendix.*] . . .

Mr. VOLSTEAD. Mr. Chairman, in connection with the colloquy that has just taken place between the gentleman from Illinois and the gentleman from Virginia, I desire to call to the attention of this House the Northern Securities Co. case. That case originated in my country, and I think I know a little about it. That company was formed for the purpose of holding stock purely as an investment. Upon the trial of that action the company showed that it had never given any direction whatever to the officers of the Northern Pacific or the Great Northern Railroad, the two railroad companies combined in the Northern Securities Co.

The company itself had no power whatever to run a railroad. Here was a case on all fours with the one you provide for in paragraph 3 of this section, but did the court take the view that this consolidation did not restrain trade? Not at all. As I said before, the court saw just as clearly as any man in his senses could see that such an organization necessarily destroyed competition, because when the Northern Securities Co. became the owner of the two railroads competition would necessarily cease. It would not be necessary to do anything to direct the officers of the two railroads not to compete. They knew that every dollar expended for the purpose of competition as between those two was money taken away from the Northern Securities Co., and as a consequence taken from the company for which they were working. Now, this bill clearly legalizes just that sort of an arrangement, and you know that practically every combination in restraint of trade that has been formed in this country in the last 15 or 20 years has been formed in this same fashion, and still you legalize that sort of a combination. It seems to me so clear that I must confess I can not understand how this committee expects to defend it. It can not be defended. I think you owe to the country a frank statement as to the purpose of this section. If it is for the purpose of wiping

---

* Not reprinted herein.

out the Sherman antitrust law, let us know it, and we will go before the country on that issue. If, on the other hand, you pretend that it does not, it seems to me we are entitled to an explanation before you write it into the statute.

Mr. CARLIN. Mr. Chairman, I ask for a vote.

The CHAIRMAN. The question is on the amendment offered by the gentleman from Minnesota.

The question was taken, and the amendment was rejected.

Mr. VAUGHAN. Mr. Chairman, I offer the following amendment.

The CHAIRMAN. The Clerk will report the amendment.

The Clerk read as follows:

Add, after the period in line 2, page 27, the following paragraph:
"Nor shall anything in the antitrust laws be construed to forbid persons operating local telephone exchanges engaged in commerce from selling their local exchanges to competitors for local business, or from acquiring local exchanges from competitors for local business, when such sale or acquisition is not forbidden by any law of the State or locality where the exchange is situated and competition in the transmission of interstate toll messages is not interrupted nor interfered with: *Provided,* That where such sale or purchase will affect commerce it shall not be permitted until the terms thereof have been submitted to and approved by the Interstate Commerce Commission." . . .

Mr. VAUGHAN. Mr. Chairman, the whole theory of all antitrust legislation is that competition for patronage is beneficial to the public, but there is at least one business in which it is not beneficial but is injurious to the public. The existence of two good, well-patronized telephone systems in any community makes it necessary for every business man in the community to ⊥ patronize both systems. I believe that every local telephone exchange should be owned by the municipality in which it is located or by the Government, and that all long-distance systems should be owned and operated by the Government. But whether or not we agree about that we certainly should not disagree upon the proposition that wherever there is real competition between any two local telephone exchanges it is a burden and not a benefit to the public in that locality.

The amendment I propose will simply authorize the owners of one exchange to purchase the exchange of another when not forbidden by the law of the State or locality, and when competition in the transmission of interstate-toll messages is not interfered with nor interrupted.

I happen to live in a town where we have two systems, one exchange is located in Texas and the other in Arkansas, and I wish to make it certain that my people will not always be compelled to patronize and maintain two telephone systems. I dare say there are other towns in the United States that are similarly located, and that feel the same burden that my town does. . . .

Mr. WEBB. Will the coalition of these two exchanges substantially lessen competition?

Mr. VAUGHAN. It will lessen competition for the patronage of the people. The people in the town will not be compelled to patronize two telephone systems.

Mr. WEBB. How about the interstate rates?

Mr. VAUGHAN. The amendment I propose provides that the purchase or acquisition shall be permitted only when competition for the transmission of interstate toll messages is not interfered with, and whenever commerce would be affected thereby, it is not permitted until it has been submitted to and approved by the Interstate Commerce Commission.

Mr. WEBB. Why do you say "where messages are not interfered with or interrupted"? Why not say "competition in the transmission of interstate toll messages is not substantially lessened"? That is the language that is used in other provisions.

Mr. VAUGHAN. If the committee will accept my amendment, I will agree to that change in the language.

Mr. WEBB. If it does not substantially lessen competition, it does not apply to the interstate telephone exchanges at all. That is already in the bill.

Mr. VAUGHAN. Why not make it plain that a transaction which could not injuriously affect but would benefit is not forbidden by this bill, which may be construed to forbid what the committee must admit can not be any violation of the spirit or the purpose of antitrust legislation? . . .

⊥9599   ⊥ [Mr. STEVENS of New Hampshire addressed the committee. See Appendix.*] . . .

Mr. [LATHROP] BROWN [D., N.Y.]. Mr. Chairman, I offer the following amendment:

The CHAIRMAN. There is an amendment pending. . . .

[Mr. HENRY addressed the committee. See Appendix.*] . . .

The CHAIRMAN. The question is on the amendment offered by the gentleman from Texas [Mr. VAUGHAN].

Mr. CARLIN. I thought I would allow the gentleman from New York [Mr. BROWN] to offer his amendment.

The CHAIRMAN. The amendment of the gentleman from New York [Mr. BROWN] will not be in order until this amendment is disposed of.

Mr. CARLIN. Then I will use a part of my time now and use a part of it later.

Mr. Chairman, this amendment is the most remarkable one that has been offered during the consideration of this bill. While it was stated that it is a simple little amendment seemingly, allowing States to regulate their own telephone exchanges, the fact is that this amendment exempts the American Bell Telephone Co. from a decree of the court rendered within the last few months in a dissolution proceeding on behalf of the United States Government.[5.562]

That company combined, as they admitted, in State after State, telephone company after telephone company until they had monopolized the telephone business of the United States, and when suit was threatened for dissolution they consented to the decree, and now we have an amendment which will eliminate that decree.

Mr. FLOYD of Arkansas. They bought out all the telephone exchanges in my part of the country, and as soon as they had done that the first thing they did was to raise the price.

Mr. BARTLETT. That is the usual course.

Mr. CARLIN. This amendment says:

> Nor shall anything in the antitrust laws be construed to forbid persons operating local telephone exchanges engaged in commerce from selling their local exchanges to competitors for local business, or from acquiring local exchanges from competitors for local business, when such sale or acquisition is not forbidden by any law of the State or locality where the exchange is situated.

And by the system of purchase and sale they have been able to form a great combination which the Government has just dissolved. It seems to me it needs but to mention it to show that the committee can not consent to accept this amendment, and that it has no place in this bill. . . .

Mr. [OTIS T.] WINGO [D., Ark.]. Let us use a concrete illustration. Suppose in the town of Horatio, Ark., the Southwestern Telephone Co. own [sic] not only the long-distance line but the local exchange. Suppose in the town of De Queen, Ark., 9 miles north, there is a company that owns both the local and the long-distance lines. The long-distance line runs into Oklahoma, the State line being only 8 miles away. The line also runs out over three or four counties having a rural system. Suppose that the Southwestern Telephone Co., at Horatio, should sell its local exchange to the man who owned the De Queen exchange and the country exchanges. Do you mean to say that that would be inimical to the public good? Do not you think that that ought to be permitted?

Mr. CARLIN. I am not sure that I understand the gentleman's question, but what I mean is that the combination of a number of competing telephone exchanges engaged in interstate business so that it is controlled by one corporation is a combination in restraint of trade.

Mr. WINGO. I agree with the gentleman.

Mr. CARLIN. And this is what this amendment permits.

Mr. WINGO. Oh, no. If I thought that, I would not advocate it. Does not the amendment say that one competitor may sell its local exchange to another competitor

---

* Not reprinted herein.

[5.562] United States v. American Tel. & Tel. Co., 1 D. & J. 483 (D. Ore. 1914) (consent decree).

so long as it does not violate the State law and does not restrain interstate commerce?

Mr. HENRY. Yes.

Mr. CARLIN. Oh, the gentleman from Texas is mistaken. The amendment reads:

> Nor shall anything in the antitrust laws be construed to forbid persons operating local telephone exchanges engaged in commerce from selling their local exchanges to competitors for local business or from acquiring local exchanges from competitors for local business when such sale or acquisition is not forbidden by any law of the State or locality where the exchange is situated and competition in the transmission of interstate toll messages is not interrupted or interfered with.

Mr. WINGO. Is not that what I said?

Mr. CARLIN. If the exchanges are within the State, we have no control over it.

Mr. WINGO. I call attention to this: Unfortunately for the situation, the gentleman from Texas—from Texarkana—has a concrete proposition. In my district there is a railroad that wiggles in and out across the State line. I have given you a concrete illustration of a sale which took place less than a week ago, and I know it is for the public good and does not create a monopoly, but tends to the betterment in the service.

The CHAIRMAN. The question is on the amendment offered by the gentleman from Texas.

The question was taken; and on a division (demanded by Mr. VAUGHAN) there were—ayes 11, noes 22.

So the amendment was lost.

Mr. BROWN of New York. Mr. Chairman, I offer the follow [sic] amendment.

The Clerk read as follows:

> Page 25, line 19, after the word "investment," add the words "or for investment and operation."

Mr. BROWN of New York. Mr. Chairman, I offer this amendment for the purpose of clarification only, because I do not know what the result of this paragraph is going to be. At the present time there is $5,500,000,000 invested in the securities of holding companies who operate public-utility companies subject to State regulation by the public-utility commissions in the various States. If these holding companies under State regulation do not bring about, or attempt to bring about, as the language of the bill reads, a substantial lessening of competition, I assume that this committee has no desire to interfere with the extension of their lawful business. But in the way the bill is drawn, Mr. Chairman, all future operations by holding companies may be unlawful for three reasons.

In the first place, in the district of Michigan two Federal judges recently held that for a corporation to sell its securities in more than one State constituted interstate commerce.[5.563] Again in the State of Texas it is held that ownership of a gas-producing company and an electric-light company in the same location, no matter how much they may be regulated as to price of output and quality of service, is ownership of technically competing companies. Again it might be well held that the distribution of supplies from the parent holding company to the various plants in the various States would be interstate commerce. Therefore, in order to clarify these matters, I trust that the committee will consent to the adoption of this amendment in order that public-utility holding companies may continue their lawful business under the operation not only of the present law, but also under the provisions of this very able bill.

Mr. FLOYD of Arkansas. Mr. Chairman, we oppose the amendment offered by the gentleman from New York. We think that we have made all exceptions in this provision of the bill that ought to be made. We have made so many exceptions that some of our friends on the opposite side claim that the provisions of this section amount to nothing. We think we have already placed and incorporated in the section proper limitations; and this amendment is as objectionable as the one voted down a few moments ago, and more so, for the reason that it is general, while that undertook to exempt a specific thing. This excepts broadly these investment companies, and we object to it.

[5.563] Alabama & N.O. Transp. Co. v. Doyle, 210 F. 173 (E.D. Mich. 1914).

Mr. WEBB. Mr. Chairman, I want to say that so far as the $5,000,000,000 [sic] are invested in public utility corporations, if they are legal now, they will continue to be legal notwithstanding this act, because we specifically exempt those which are not illegal at present. If they are not legal under the present law, we certainly would not want to be put in the attitude of legalizing them in this act, and therefore I think it would be a very dangerous provision to put in the bill at this time. I trust the committee will vote it down.

The CHAIRMAN. The question is on the amendment offered by the gentleman from New York.

The amendment was rejected.

The Clerk read as follows:

SEC. 9. That from and after two years from the date of the approval of this act no person who is engaged as an individual, or who is a member of a partnership, or is a director or other officer of a corporation that is engaged in the business, in whole or in part, of producing or selling equipment, materials, or supplies to, or in the construction or maintenance of, railroads or other common carriers engaged in commerce, shall act as a director or other officer or employee of any other corporation or common carrier engaged in commerce to which he, or such partnership or corporation, sells or leases, directly or indirectly, equipment, materials, or supplies, or for which he or such partnership or corporation, directly or indirectly, engages in the work of construction or maintenance; and after the expiration of said period no person who is engaged as an individual or who is a member of a partnership or is a director or other officer of a corporation which is engaged in the conduct of a bank or trust company shall act as a director or other officer or employee of any such common carrier for which he or such partnership or bank or trust company acts, either separately or in connection with others, as agent for or underwriter of the sale or disposal of such common carrier of issues or parts of issues of its securities, or from which he or such partnership or bank or trust company purchases, either separately or in connection with others, issues or parts of issues of securities of such common carrier.

That from and after two years from the date of the approval of this act no person shall at the same time be a director or other officer or employee of more than one bank, banking association, or trust company organized or operating under the laws of the United States either of which has deposits, capital, surplus, and undivided profits aggregating more than $2,500,000; and no private banker or person who is a director in any bank or trust company, organized and operating under the laws of a State, having deposits, capital, surplus, and undivided profits aggregating more than $2,500,000, shall be eligible to be a director in any bank or banking association organized or operating under the laws of the United States. The eligibility of a director under the foregoing provisions shall be determined by the average amount of deposits, capital, surplus, and undivided profits as shown in the official statements of such bank, banking association, or trust company filed as provided by law during the fiscal year next preceding the date set for the annual election of directors, and when a director has been elected in accordance with the provisions of this act it shall be lawful for him to continue as such for one year thereafter under said election.

No bank, banking association, or trust company organized or operating under the laws of the United States in any city or incorporated town or village of more than 100,000 inhabitants, as shown by the last preceding decennial census of the United States, shall have as a director or other officer or employee any private banker or any director or other officer or employee of any other bank, banking association, or trust company located in the same place: *Provided*, That nothing in this section shall apply to mutual savings banks not having a capital stock represented by shares: *Provided further*, That a director or other officer or employee of such bank, banking association, or trust company may be a director or other officer or employee of not more than one other bank or trust company organized under the laws of the United States or any State where the entire capital stock of one is owned by stockholders in the other: *And provided further*, That nothing contained in this section shall forbid a director of class A of a Federal reserve bank, as defined in the Federal reserve act, from being an officer or director or both an officer and director in one member bank.

That from and after two years from the date of the approval of this act no person at the same time shall be a director in any two or more corporations, either of which has capital, surplus, and undivided profits aggregating more than $1,000,000, engaged in whole or in part in commerce, other than common carriers subject to the act to regulate commerce, approved February 4, 1887, if such corporations are or shall have been theretofore, by virtue of their business and location of operation, competitors, so that an elimination of competition by agreement between them would constitute a violation of any of the provisions of any of the antitrust laws. The eligibility of a director under the foregoing provision shall be determined by the aggregate amount of the capital, surplus, and undivided profits, exclusive of dividends declared but not paid to stockholders, at the end of the fiscal year of said corporation next preceding the election of directors, and when a director has been elected in accordance with the provisions of this act it shall be lawful for him to continue as such for one year thereafter.

That any person who shall violate any of the provisions of this section shall be guilty of a misdemeanor and shall be punished by a fine of $100 a day for each day of the continuance of such violation, or by imprisonment for such period as the court may designate, not exceeding one year, or by both, in the discretion of the court.

Mr. CLINE. Mr. Chairman, I offer the following amendment on page 29, line 18, to strike out the word "entire" at the end of the line and insert the words "not less than three-fourths of the," so that the provision shall read:

Provided, That nothing in this section shall apply to mutual savings banks not having a capital stock represented by shares: *Provided further*, That a director or other officer or employee of such bank, banking association, or trust company may be a director or other officer or employee of not more than one other bank or trust company organized under the laws of the United States or any State where the entire capital stock of one is owned by stockholders in the other.

The CHAIRMAN. The Clerk will report the amendment.

The Clerk read as follows:

Page 29, line 18, strike out the word "entire" at the end of the line, and insert in lieu thereof the words "not less than three-fourths of the."

Mr. CLINE. Mr. Chairman, it is well known to every man in the House who has had any connection with the banking business, and especially with national banks, that in the last five or six years there has been organized, in conjunction with national banks, trust companies. The stock of the trust company has almost universally been owned by the bank of which the trust company was an auxiliary, but where a former stockholder happened to die and the stock has been distributed, it is sometimes impossible for the banking company to own the entire stock. I have one or two instances in mind where it would work a hardship to the bank that sought to control all the stock of the trust company which was organized for the purpose of carrying long-time loans or building loans for the benefit of the bank's customers.

It would be impossible after the distribution of the stock of a deceased stockholder in some instances to get all of the stock. Of course, I understand it is the purpose of the law to make the bank and the auxiliary institution one banking institution, but I do not understand why they can not be protected just as easily with a control of three-fourths of the stock or more as with a control of the entire stock. It still would constitute one banking institution. Take the instance I have in mind. It is impossible for the bank to secure $200 of outstanding stock, and that under the bill would compel the bank that has the trust company in connection with it to close out the trust company business, to close out the long-time or building loans that it is accommodating its customers with, and I am at a loss to see what advantage it would be to compel the bank to have the entire stock when three-fourths of the stock is as effectual to prevent evil effects arising from interlocking directorates as all of it would be. It seems to me that the full purpose is accomplished by compelling the bank to have three-fourths of the stock and not to require the banks that fall under these conditions to close out their trust-company business.

Mr. FLOYD of Arkansas. Mr. Chairman, we desire to oppose the amendment offered by the gentleman from Indiana. We do not think that there is anything in this interlocking-directorate provision in this bill that will cause anybody to close out their business. We have not undertaken in this bill to deal with the stocks or to prevent common ownership of stocks, but we are attempting to prevent a well-known evil in the business world, an evil not only to the general public, but an evil to every stockholder in this Nation. The corporate business, honestly and properly managed, is the most desirable system of business ever devised by man. While that is true, it furnishes the greatest opportunity for dishonesty of any form of business. Whenever you permit the directors of banks and of different concerns to control these different concerns, you may rest assured that those directors are going to control the business of the several concerns in such a way that they will get the greatest profit and advantage out of it to themselves or to the particular concern in which they are most deeply interested. To give you an illustration, before the Judiciary Committee, in an investigation of another matter, we had before the committee a director of two coal companies who was also a director of a railroad company. He negotiated a deal between the two coal companies. He was a director in both, and then approved it as the director of the railroad company, and he was asked by a member of the committee if he could see any possible way whereby his personal interests could suffer in such a transaction, and he frankly admitted that he could not. . . .

. . . The object of this whole provision is in the interest of honesty, not only in the interest of the general public, but in the interest of the stockholders of the corporations themselves. The objection to the amendment offered by the gentleman from Indiana is this: We have a provision in the bill that where the stockholders of one company own all the stock of the other, there may be interlocking directors.

Mr. CULLOP. But that bank would have to be located in a city or village of not less than 100,000 inhabitants.

Mr. FLOYD of Arkansas. Of more.

Mr. CULLOP. The provision in the bill is:

No bank, banking association, or trust company organized or operating under the laws of the United States in any city or incorporated town or village of more than 100,000 inhabitants.

It would not apply to banks in a city of 50,000.

Mr. FLOYD of Arkansas. That proviso would.

Mr. CULLOP. I do not think so.

Mr. FLOYD of Arkansas. The proviso would apply anywhere in any kind of a city where the stockholders of one own the entire stock of another.

Mr. CULLOP. Well—

Mr. FLOYD of Arkansas. Now, the object of this legislation is to prevent the concentration of capital under one control. In the Pujo investigation it developed that four or five concerns in New York, through a system of interlocking directorates, controlled practically the finances of this country, and then it finally centered in one great concern in New York. . . .

Mr. CLINE. But you provide in this bill that a national bank may have an auxiliary in the shape of a trust company.

Mr. CARLIN. May have one.

Mr. CLINE. Providing they own the entire stock. Now, what advantage does the law get in securing any of the stock above 75 per cent of the stock where they only seek to hold joint relationship with another company?

Mr. FLOYD of Arkansas. Well, the point is this: Where they own the entire stock the tendency would not be to concentrate, but would be rather to divide up, divide their capital; it is one ownership practically, and could at will draw the entire amount back into one concern, but if we except banks owning not less than 75 per cent of the stock of the other, it seems that we will leave a loophole that will permit the control and concentration of money that we are endeavoring to prohibit. . . .

Let me explain how this works. Your committee gave great consideration to this whole question, and especially to the question of the exemption of one trust company. Let me submit that since the adoption of the currency law the necessity that caused the creation of trust companies in connection with national banks does not exist to the same extent that it did previous to the adoption of that law, because under the old law a national bank could not lend money on real estate, and hence a trust company became an adjunct and handmaid of the national-banking system in order that they might do certain things which the banks were prohibited from doing under the law. . . .

. . . Now, we gave very careful consideration to this provision and to every phase of the question, and you will bear in mind we have no jurisdiction over the State banks. We excluded the private banker, the State bank director, and the trust company director from a directorship on national banks upon the theory and question of qualification. We are allowed to prescribe the qualifications of the directors of national banks, and in prescribing and fixing the qualifications of the directors of national banks we provide in this bill that the private banker, the State bank director, and the director in the trust company shall not be eligible to be directors in national banks. Now, if you permit common directors in two banks on a percentage system, then you provide a condition where through the trust company or the State bank these great national banking institutions can have an affiliated trust company, and if you permit that affiliated trust company the national bank can maintain these interlocking connections with State banks and trust companies, and you thus permit the evil of interlocking directorates which in a somewhat different way heretofore obtained, as we believe, to the detriment of the public and especially to the detriment of the stockholders of the banks. . . .

Mr. [M. F.] PHELAN [D., Mass.]. I do not wish to take issue with the committee, but can not you do it under this bill as it is framed where you allow the directors to be on a national bank and on a State bank at the same time, providing the stock is in the same ownership? It seems to me you allow the very thing you do not want to do.

Mr. FLOYD of Arkansas. That would be an extreme case.

Mr. PHELAN. But you are not limiting it to one of these cases.

Mr. FLOYD of Arkansas. It will be only one, and such a case would be rare indeed, and it would be of short duration where they own the entire stock, because the very moment a common ownership ceased and a part of the stock went into other hands there would be the inhibition of the law. . . .

Mr. MANN. The gentleman is talking about a provision that covers cases in my town which I am somewhat familiar with. Take, for example, the case of the First National Bank of Chicago. There is the First National Savings & Deposit Co.—

Mr. FITZHENRY. The First Trust & Savings Co.

Mr. MANN. Yes. It is fixed so that you can not sell the stock of the one without selling the stock of the other.

Mr. PHELAN. Yes. That is done in the case of a bank that I know of.

Mr. MANN. They do a trust business. In this case that I speak of there is no chance for the stock to become scattered. You can not buy the stock of the First Trust without buying at the same time the stock of the First National, and you can not buy the First National stock without buying the First Trust stock. There is some arrangement by which that is held in that condition. Now, of course, if that were not the case no one could tell whether they owned all the stock, or three-quarters of the stock, or half the stock. A man to-day might be a legal director and to-morrow he might be a criminal.

Mr. FLOYD of Arkansas. We provide against that.

Mr. MANN. I understand that.

Mr. CULLOP. I wanted to ask the gentleman from Illinois a question. . . .

In the case that the gentleman from Illinois speaks of as an illustration, that institution also deals with real estate, renting, mortgages, and so forth; guardianships; acts as administrator of estates, receiverships, and things that a national bank could not do.

Mr. MANN. It is a trust company.

Mr. CULLOP. It has outside earnings and outside profits and does business which national banks under the laws can not engage in, can they?

Mr. MANN. I do not say whether a national bank could or not. I think they do it sometimes.

Mr. CULLOP. A national bank could not collect rents from real estate and perform the duties incident to receiverships, guardianships, and things like that.

Now, I would like to ask the gentleman from Arkansas about a case that has been presented to me, where there is a national bank with deposits, profits, and capital stock of more than $2,500,000. Is there anything in this measure to prevent any director or stockholder or officer of that bank from being a director or other officer of a State or private bank that may be organized in the same county?

Mr. FLOYD of Arkansas. In the same place?

Mr. CULLOP. In the same county.

Mr. FLOYD of Arkansas. Certainly.

Mr. CULLOP. For instance, the stockholders of a national bank in a county seat will have, out in some little town, a State bank or a private bank, which becomes a feeder to the national bank at the county seat.

Mr. FLOYD of Arkansas. Did the gentleman say less than $2,500,000?

Mr. CULLOP. No; I said more than $2,500,000.

Mr. FLOYD of Arkansas. It is prohibited.

Mr. CULLOP. What is there in this measure to prohibit a director in a bank of that kind being a director in a State bank in the same county, in the same State, that will have perhaps $100,000 of capital stock and undivided profits, deposits, and so forth?

Mr. FLOYD of Arkansas. The wording of the bill prevents it.

Mr. CULLOP. I deny there is, and if there is I would like to have the gentleman point it out.

Mr. FLOYD of Arkansas. On page 29, on line 4, there is this provision:

> No bank, banking association, or trust company organized or operating under the laws of the United States in any city or incorporated town or village of more than 100,000 inhabitants, as shown by the last preceding decennial census of the United States, shall have as a director or other officer or employee any private banker or any director or other officer or employee of any other bank, banking association, or trust company located in the same place.

No; that is not the provision I had in mind.

Mr. CULLOP. Does not the gentleman mean to refer to page 28, beginning line 8.

Mr. FLOYD of Arkansas. Yes. The other was not the right provision. This provision reads:

> That from and after two years from the date of the approval of this act no person shall at the same time be a director or other officer or employee of more than one bank, banking association, or trust company organized or operating under the laws of the United States either of which has deposits, capital, surplus, and undivided profits aggregating more than $2,500,000—

Mr. CULLOP. That applies to national banks only, and does not refer to State or private banks.

Mr. FLOYD of Arkansas. Wait until I get through. I read further:

> And no private banker or person who is a director in any bank or trust company, organized and operating under the laws of a State, having deposits, capital, surplus, and undivided profits aggregating more than $2,500,000, shall be eligible to be a director in any bank or banking association organized or operating under the laws of the United States.

Mr. CULLOP. Now, if the gentleman will permit right there, in order to make that prohibition it would have to be a private bank with a capital and surplus and profits and deposits amounting to $2,500,000. It does not apply to State and private banks with a smaller sum.

If it was a bank of $100,000, then a director or officer in the national bank that had more than $2,500,000 could be a director in that State bank, and there is nothing here to prohibit it.

Mr. FLOYD of Arkansas. I think I can make the gentleman understand that it is absolutely prohibitive.

Mr. CULLOP. If there is anything, I shall be glad to have the gentleman do so. I am asking the question for information.

Mr. FLOYD of Arkansas. I will try to make it plain. I think it is prohibitive. It says:

> That from and after two years from the date of the approval of this act—

Mr. CULLOP. Where is the gentleman reading?

Mr. FLOYD of Arkansas. I am reading from line 8, page 28—

> No person shall at the same time be a director or other officer or employee of more than one bank, banking association, or trust company organized or operating under the laws of the United States either of which has deposits, capital, surplus, and undivided profits aggregating more than $2,500,000.

The words "either of which" would cover it. . . .

As I stated at the outset we deal with the eligibility of the bank directors, and if either of these banks specified has the capital, surplus, and so forth, then the person can not be at the same time a director in the two. That provision would exclude him. That is, if he was a director in the little bank, he would be ineligible to be a director in the large bank, for the reason that the provision relates to his eligibility, and he could not be in both of them. One might be a very small bank.

Mr. CULLOP. But if the gentleman will begin at the semicolon and read the next subdivision of the paragraph, and then construe that with the previous provision that he has read, I think he will find that if one of those banks is a private bank or a State bank there is nothing in this provision that will prohibit one of the directors in the national bank with a capital, deposits, and profits amounting to more than $2,500,000 from being a director in the private or State bank, provided it has not a capital, deposits, and surplus of more than $2,500,000. Now, I have asked that question because I have had bankers writing me about that subject from my district. A number of them are interested in small banks in different localities. I have examined the bill carefully, and I can find nothing to prohibit the same.

Mr. McCOY. Will the gentleman allow me—

Mr. FLOYD of Arkansas. I will answer the gentleman's question.

There is nothing in this bill to prevent that.

Mr. McCOY. I should like to call the gentleman's attention to line 14, page 28—

And no private banker—

Now go down to line 18—

shall be eligible to be a director in any bank or banking association organized or operating under the laws of the United States.

Does not that absolutely exclude private bankers?

Mr. CULLOP. Oh, no.

Mr. [ADOLPH J.] SABATH [D., Ill.]. Oh, no.

Mr. CULLOP. He can not be in two banks organized under the laws of the United States, but there is not a word excluding him from the State bank or private bank. If there is, I would be glad to have it pointed out.

Mr. FLOYD of Arkansas. I desire to say, further—

Mr. CARLIN. It was not intended to do that.

Mr. PHELAN. If the gentleman means two State banks, we can not prohibit his being a director of both. We have nothing to do with that, or at any rate we have not yet assumed jurisdiction if we have it.

Mr. FLOYD of Arkansas. When this bill was orginally drafted by the committee we made its provisions broad and covered in scope every kind of bank, but in the hearings—

Mr. CULLOP. But the gentleman from Virginia [Mr. CARLIN] said it was never intended to cover such a case as I am putting to the gentleman from Arkansas, and if there is, I want to know it.

Mr. FLOYD of Arkansas. As finally prepared, it was not intended to cover that. If the gentleman will read the first bills he will see that they contain a sweeping prohibition of interlocking directorates, but in the hearings we found that there were so many conditions that existed throughout the country that were perfectly harmless that we made many exceptions. We put in a limitation prohibiting common directors where either of the national banks has a capital, surplus, and undivided profits of $2,500,000. In that case they are prohibited from having common directors, although one may be the smallest kind of a national bank.

But when it comes to the question of a State bank, the limitation is $2,500,000. That disqualifies the private banker or State bank director from being a director of a national bank or national banking assocation outside of cities of 100,000 inhabitants.

Mr. CULLOP. Let me put this proposition: As I understand it, a director of a national bank, with its deposits and capital stock and undivided profits of $2,500,000, can be director in a State or private bank organized in the same locality, provided its capital stock, profits, and undivided deposits amount to less than $2,500,000?

Mr. FLOYD of Arkansas. If he is not within a city exceeding 100,000 inhabitants.

Mr. CULLOP. I want to call the gentleman's attention to provision on page 29:

No banking association or trust company—

No bank, banking association, or trust company organized or operating under the laws of the United States in any city or incorporated town or village of more than 100,000 inhabitants, as shown by the last preceding decennial census of the United States, shall have as a director or other officer or employee any private banker or any director or other officer or employee of any other bank, banking association, or trust company located in the same place.

Now, if the gentleman will observe, the rest of that section down to the word "bank," in line 23, is one continuous sentence, so that this provision as to $2,500,000 and the director in one bank being a director in another is applied only in cases where the bank with its $2,500,000 is located in a city of more than 100,000 inhabitants. . . .

Mr. CARLIN. I would suggest to the gentleman that we dispose of the pending amendment and then take this question up and discuss it.

Mr. CULLOP. That is what this amendment is.

Mr. SABATH. The amendment applies to this very provision.

Mr. FLOYD of Arkansas. If the gentleman from Indiana will permit me, I will explain the two provisions. If the two banks are in a city exceeding 100,000 inhabitants, then I understand that there can be no common directors, regardless of capital. The limitation of $2,500,000 does not apply in a city. It simply prohibits in cities exceeding 100,000 inhabitants there being common directors in national banks or banks operating under the laws of the United States, like those State banks which took advantage of the late act, without regard to capitalization or ⊥ without regard to the amount of capital, surplus, and undivided profits. In all other cases the rule is that $2,500,000 capital, surplus, and undivided profits applies throughout the country.

Mr. SABATH. You do make exception in this provision, and you mean that it shall apply to only cities having a population over 100,000.

Mr. FLOYD of Arkansas. No; that is not it. That inhibition is that there shall not be common directors at all, without regard to the limitation, in cities of 100,000 population.

Mr. FARR. What was the theory of the committee in discriminating against cities of that size?

Mr. FLOYD of Arkansas. On the theory that the banking interest is generally centered in cities. We had complaints before our committee, especially in the larger cities, that men who offered perfectly good security were, on account of the chain of banks having common directors, say, in a dozen different banks—a man perfectly responsible, with good security, would make application for a loan, and be refused by one bank, and then would be refused in turn by every other bank in the city, through the influence of that common director.

Mr. PHELAN. Mr. Chairman, I would like to ask the chairman of the committee a question. I am not quite clear as to lines 14 to 19, on page 29. Where it says the entire capital stock, that does not mean necessarily joint ownership of all the stocks in both banks? For instance, if you have two banks, one a State and one a national, with a million dollars capital, and one has 20 stockholders and one 10 stockholders, if five of the latter own all the stock of the former, that is enough to get the two banks within these provisions, is it not?

Mr. FLOYD of Arkansas. Yes.

Mr. PHELAN. Suppose, under these conditions, 10 men in a national bank own all the stock of a trust company, and there are common officers and directors in both banks. Suppose 1 of the 10 men sells his stock, does it follow that immediately the directors have to resign their positions and the officers have to get out? Is there any provision in the bill to prevent such a hasty change?

Mr. FLOYD of Arkansas. I am glad that the gentleman from Massachusetts has asked that question. We realize the importance of so wording the statute that a director might not be put in the attitude of being eligible one day and a criminal the next. So we provide that where the disqualification is based on capitalization, surplus, and undivided profit, you shall take the average for the preceding year, and that when he is eligible at the time of his election, his eligibility continues throughout the year.

Mr. PHELAN. Yes; but this is not in the capitalization, surplus, and undivided profit section. This is in a different paragraph. It is the stock and not the amount of the capitalization that applies on page 29.

Mr. FLOYD of Arkansas. I will say to the gentleman from Massachusetts that if that is not covered in the exceptions it ought to be.

Mr. PHELAN. I just mentioned it because I do not see it, and I thought possibly I might have missed it.

Mr. FLOYD of Arkansas. The gentleman will realize the difficulty in providing a definite rule making it a criminal offense for a man to act as a director under the conditions described here. We fix it so that if he is eligible at the time of his election his eligibility continues for a year, although the condition of his bank might change or the capitalization be increased so that he would be ineligible under the terms of the provision and also in regard to the other provision, as to population, we make similar exceptions and provide that if eligible when elected his eligibility continues for a year; but if the particular point raised by the gentleman from Massachusetts is not covered it certainly ought to be, and we ought to make it clear.

Mr. PHELAN. My impression is that it is not covered in this particular place.

Mr. FLOYD of Arkansas. I am glad the gentleman has called our attention to that, because the theory upon which we are proceeding is to provide that if the director is eligible under this law at the time of his election, no matter what happened in the meantime, he shall be eligible for a year, the usual period for which bank directors are elected. . . .

Yes. I am inclined to think that we overlooked that particular provision, and I desire to say frankly to the gentleman from Massachusetts that if we have it is important that an amendment should be offered to cure that defect.

Mr. PHELAN. I can offer that amendment later, can I not?

Mr. FLOYD of Arkansas. Yes. . . .

Mr. WINGO. Mr. Chairman, I want to ask for some information from either the gentleman from Virginia [Mr. CARLIN] or the gentleman from North Carolina [Mr. WEBB]. Is there anything in this section that reaches this proposition? Let us say there is a national banking association in Kansas City that owns and controls 45 banks in the States of Oklahoma and Arkansas, and there is one man who is a common director in them all. Is there anything in this that will prohibit that?

Mr. CARLIN. Oh, yes; if the capital of any one of them exceeds two and a half million dollars or if the bank be situated in a city of 100,000 inhabitants or more. If the capital is smaller or the population smaller it does not prohibit it.

Mr. WINGO. Suppose there is a private banker in Missouri who owns a controlling interest and is a common director in a great many small banks scattered through those different States. Does it reach that condition?

Mr. CARLIN. It does not reach any number of small banks unless the capital of some one of them, surplus and deposits, should amount to two and one-half millions of dollars, or unless the bank should be situated in a city of 100,000 inhabitants.

Mr. WINGO. Suppose it is a national banking association that has a capital of two and a half million dollars. In other words, take a banking association that comes within the prohibited class in Kansas City. Is there anything to prohibit it from owning and controlling through a joint director 45 State banks in Oklahoma and Arkansas?

Mr. CARLIN. The bank itself?

Mr. WINGO. Yes.

Mr. CARLIN. No. This bill does not deal with combinations relating to bank stocks.

Mr. WINGO. I say controlled through a common director.

Mr. CARLIN. They can not have a common director if at any time the capital, surplus, and deposits reach the sum of two and a half millions. He could not be a director in any other bank.

Mr. WINGO. That is a director in banks organized under the laws of the United States.

Mr. CARLIN. Yes; or those that are not. Of course, we can only reach State banks as they are related to national banks.

Mr. WINGO. It is provided on page 28 of the bill that no person shall be at the same time a director in more than one bank organized under the laws of the United States which shall have a capital of more than two and a half millions. There is nothing to prohibit that person from being a director in a national banking association having two and a half million dollars and at the same time being a director in 45 State banks in other States, is there? He can still be a director in a national bank of two and a half millions, and you do not prohibit—

Mr. CARLIN. If he is a director in a bank of two and a half millions surplus capital and undivided profits, he is prohibited from being a director in any other bank.

Mr. WINGO. Not in any other bank, but in any other United States bank.

Mr. CARLIN. In any national bank.

Mr. WINGO. But does it prohibit him from being a director in 45 State banks?

Mr. CARLIN. I think it does; yes.

Mr. WINGO. If they are State banks they are not organized under the laws of the United States.

Mr. CARLIN. We have authorized him to be a director in one State bank and under only one condition, and that is where a common stock ownership exists in the same party.

Mr. WINGO. I would like for the gentleman to point out in this section where you prohibit a man from being a director in a national bank of two and a half million capital and at the same time a director in a private or a State bank, however great their number may be.

Mr. CARLIN. We had that question up a moment ago.

Mr. CULLOP. And we settled it just against what the gentleman decided now.

Mr. CARLIN. No; we did not.

Mr. CULLOP. Exactly.

Mr. [JOHN B.] PETERSON [D., Ind.]. If the gentleman will see the beginning of section 9, it says:

> That from and after two years from the date of approval of this act no person at the same time shall be a director or other officer or employed in more than one bank.

Mr. WINGO. What kind of a bank? A bank organized and operated under the laws of the United States.

Mr. PETERSON. Any kind of a bank.

Mr. WINGO. But more than one bank or association or trust company can operate under the laws of the United States. In other words, that inhibition goes to the national bank directors.

The CHAIRMAN. The time of the gentleman has expired.

Mr. CARLIN. That is as far as we can carry it.

Mr. CULLOP. Mr. Chairman, I would like to have the attention of the gentleman from Arkansas. I think I understand this proposition just as the gentleman does, and that is if he means one director, a man may be a director in a bank of $2,500,000, capital, surplus, and deposits combined, organized under the laws of the United States, but he can not be a director in any other bank organized under the laws of the United States, but there is nothing to prohibit him from being a director in a State or private bank in this bill.

Mr. WINGO. There is nothing to prohibit, but I want to get the opinion of the gentleman from Indiana on this. As I understand, there is nothing to prohibit a Missouri preacher who happens to be a director in a Kansas City national bank also from being a director and having dominating control in 45 banks in Oklahoma and Arkansas.

Mr. CULLOP. Nothing, unless he has not the capital to own the stock.

Mr. FLOYD of Arkansas. That is only true where banks have less than $2,500,000 capital.

Mr. CULLOP. Yes.

Mr. CARLIN. That is the limit placed on it.

Mr. CULLOP. But a man can be a director in a national bank with a stock of $2,500,000 capital, deposits, and surplus and there is nothing to prohibit him from being a director in a State bank or private bank or in numerous banking concerns providing their capital does not run above $2,500,000.

Mr. FLOYD of Arkansas. That is what I explained to the gentleman from Indiana before.

Mr. CULLOP. But the gentleman from Virginia [Mr. CARLIN] was combating that proposition just a moment ago, and hence I raised the question again.

Mr. CARLIN. It was a misunderstanding, if that is the case. I tried to make it plain that the capital had to be $2,500,000.

Mr. CULLOP. But the gentleman did not state that, and that is why I called attention to the fact again. . . .

Mr. FLOYD of Arkansas. I think that the case referred to by the gentleman from Massachusetts is covered in lines 15, 16, and 17.

Mr. CULLOP. What page?

Mr. FLOYD of Arkansas. Page 30.

The eligibility of a director under the foregoing provision shall be determined by the aggregate amount of the capital, surplus, and undivided profits, exclusive of dividends declared but not paid to stockholders, at the end of the fiscal year of said corporation next preceeding the election of directors, and when a director has been elected in accordance with the provisions of this act it shall be lawful for him to continue as such for one year thereafter. . . .

Mr. PHELAN. I am not certain whether that covers it or not.

Mr. FLOYD of Arkansas. It refers to that act.

Mr. PHELAN. Whether or not it does with reference to the director, it does as to an officer or employee; but those are the words used on line 16 on page 29—"director or other officer or employee."

Mr. CULLOP. That refers to some other corporation than a bank. That does not apply to a bank. If the gentleman from Massachusetts [Mr. PHELAN] and the gentleman from Arkansas [Mr. FLOYD] will observe, commencing on line 24 of page 29, the language is—

That from and after two years from the date of the approval of this act no person at the same time shall be a director in any two or more corporations, either of which has capital, surplus, and undivided profits aggregating more than $1,000,000, engaged in whole or in part in commerce.

This has no reference to the banking business, but to other affairs.

Mr. CARLIN. That relates to industrial commerce.

Mr. CULLOP. Yes. That does not relate to banking. That relates to industrial and commercial corporations, or institutions of that kind, but has no reference whatever to the banking business.

Mr. FLOYD of Arkansas. I will state to the gentleman from Indiana that on page 29, in reference to the banking section, the same language is repeated again on line 1 of page 29:

And when a director has been elected in accordance with the provisions of this act it shall be lawful for him to continue as such for one year thereafter under said election.

Mr. CULLOP. Yes; but that refers back to the qualification on page 28 of the $2,500,000 capital, deposits, and surplus.

Mr. FLOYD of Arkansas. I think not. It says "in accordance with the provisions of this act." I think that is broad enough to cover it. He is eligible when he is elected. That is on lines 1, 2, and 3 of page 29. . . .

Mr. Chairman, I desire to repeat that if this provision is not clear in this respect we would be glad to have an amendment offered to clarify it.

The CHAIRMAN. The question is on agreeing to the amendment offered by the gentleman from Indiana [Mr. CLINE].

Mr. STAFFORD. Mr. Chairman, let us have this reported again. It has been some time since it was reported.

The CHAIRMAN. Without objection, the Clerk will report the amendment again.

The Clerk read as follows:

Amendment offered by Mr. CLINE:

Page 29, line 18, strike out the words "the entire," at the end of the line, and insert the words "not less than three-fourths of the," so that the lines as amended will read: "more than one other bank or trust company organized under the laws of the United States or any State where not less than three-fourths of the capital stock of one is owned by stockholders in the other," etc.

The CHAIRMAN. The question is on agreeing to the amendment.

The question was taken, and the amendment was rejected.

Mr. McCOY. Mr. Chairman, I offer the following amendment.

The CHAIRMAN. The gentleman from New Jersey [Mr. McCOY] offers an amendment which the Clerk will report.

The Clerk read as follows:

Strike out, on page 28, lines 8 to 25, inclusive, and on page 29, lines 1 to 23, inclusive, and insert in place thereof the following:

"Whenever an officer or director of a bank or trust company, member of a Federal reserve bank, shall be also a private banker, or an officer or director of any other bank or trust company, and it shall appear to the Federal Reserve Board upon proof, after due notice of hearing and an opportunity to be heard, that such officer or director is taking advantage of his position so as substantially to lessen competition between such banks or trust companies or any of them, or between himself and any such bank or trust company, or that he is exercising improper influence over any such bank or trust company in the granting or refusing of credit, the Federal Reserve Board shall remove such officer or director from one or all of said banks organized under the laws of the United States and may require the removal of such officer or director from such State bank or trust company, or in the alternative the retirement of such State bank or trust company from membership in said Federal reserve bank." . . .

Mr. McCOY. Mr. Chairman, the amendment which I have offered strikes out of the section in regard to interlocking bank directorates that part which controls and limits them by the amount of $2,500,000 in the one instance and by the population of the town in which the banks are situated in the other instance, and proposes to substitute for that a provision establishing two principles which it is believed should be followed in banking; and then it provides that if either of those principles be violated, on complaint of the violation being made to the Federal Reserve Board, the Federal Reserve Board, after a hearing, shall act.

Now, I introduced as drastic an interlocking directorate bill affecting banks as could possibly be imagined. That was before we had the hearings. But after the hearings I was satisfied that in order to remedy some admitted evils, of which I complained as much as anybody, and which exist principally in some of the large cities, we might easily go too far and hit a great many people who are directors in banks and who are entirely innocent of any attempt to do the sort of thing complained of. The complaints when boiled down were in substance that on the one hand banks suppress competition and on the other hand that they unfairly discriminate in making loans. Now, this amendment provides, in substance, that there must be competition, and that there must be no unfair discrimination in making loans. Then it provides, as I said before, that on complaint of the violation of either of those two general principles, the Federal Reserve Board shall remove the officer or director complained of from one or all of said banks organized under the laws of the United States; that is as far as we have power to go directly in the way of removal, and the proposed amendment provides that they may require the removal of such officer or director from such State bank or trust company, or the withdrawal of the bank or trust company from the Federal reserve bank. In other words they might say, "You must get out of the State bank or trust company," and failing that, in the alternative, might require the retirement of a State bank or trust company from membership in the Federal reserve bank.

Now, why does not that entirely take care of this whole situation? If the abuse exists, here is the power to remedy the abuse; but by making these artificial limitations—because they are purely artificial limitations—of $2,500,000 of capital, surplus, deposits, and undivided profits in the one instance, and of 100,000 population in the other, while we may remedy some of the evils, we are pretty certain to injure unnecessarily a great many people of the kind of whom no complaint has been made. . . .

Mr. BARTON. Under your amendment who makes the complaint?

Mr. McCOY. Anybody can make the complaint. It does not limit it to any particular person. Presumably it will be the person who has been injured.

As I say, from all over the country we have encountered, or have been informed in the testimony, of situations such as exist in and about Chicago, New York, St. Louis, San Francisco, and other places, and, moreover, in other parts of the country where they have no very large cities. . . .

Mr. KENT. Mr. Chairman, it seems to me that this is a sane and sensible proposition. This amendment seeks to cure an evil and not to stop the ordinary course of business. It seems to me it is a remedy for the trust evils of which we complain. The alternative is that those men who invest in bank stocks and who under this bill would be ineligible for directors would naturally put in dummies to act as directors for them. It is very much better that capable and able business men, who have a knowledge of credit, who have a knowledge of business, should act as directors of banks than that they, having invested in bank stocks, should put in dummies to represent them. No one could be more opposed than I am to the limitation of credit and the unfair practices that have debauched the commercial world; but I, of my own knowledge, know that men of capital who invest in bank stocks are naturally anxious to watch those investments and would not take the responsibility of banking shown in the double liability of national-bank stock unless they knew what was going on in the banks in which they were interested.

If at any time these directors, by collusion, by unfair practices, by blacklisting, refusal of credit, or combination, should do things that are contrary to the public welfare, under this amendment they can be disassociated from protection or control of their investments. But as things are to-day, to provide that men must be limited in their directorship in corporations in which they are interested, not on the ground of evil they may do by combinations contrary to law and to public policy, but merely on account of the fact of their caring for their investments, it seems to me that such a course must lead necessarily to the incompetence born of dummy directors and consequent chaos in business organization. [Applause.] . . .

Mr. FLOYD of Arkansas. Mr. Chairman, I desire to oppose the amendment offered by the gentleman from New Jersey [Mr. MCCOY] on the ground that he proposes to change the whole theory of this bill and to interject into the provisions of it a new and untried experiment, and to legislate the power to deal with bank directors to the Federal Reserve Board, which, perhaps, in the course of a very short time, will need regulating as badly as do the directors of banks now. That is his proposition.

Now, I believe in dealing with corporations as you would deal with individuals. This is a criminal statute and I believe in a criminal statute we should say to corporations and to persons acting as agents of corporations what they can do, and give them the widest latitude to do things not prohibited in the law; we should put them on notice of what is prohibited by statute, but when you adopt a system of creating boards and letting the board exercise favoritism on the one hand and their prejudices on the other, then indeed we will enter on an era of dissatisfaction, strife, and discontent in this country that will disturb the business interests of the entire country.

We believe in regulating and controlling, but not in disturbing, legitimate business. We believe that great evils have grown out of interlocking directorates, and everybody recognizes that condition who has given the subject any consideration.

The gentleman from California [Mr. KENT] says that it will only create dummy directors. What have we now? We have one great and powerful director, say, of a railroad company, director of the holding company, director of all the affiliated corporations owned by the railroad company and by the holding company, and who are the other directors? They select some employee of that company and of the affiliated companies, give him one share of stock, make him sign up a transfer to them in blank, and then appoint him a director. Is he not a dummy director, pure and simple? We desire to prevent this evil; we desire to do it in an intelligent and sensible way. We desire to put all men upon notice, so that they will know when they are violating the law and when they are not.

It has been argued that certain men are alone capable of carrying on the business of a great concern. What an absurdity. There is one phase of this legislation that has been overlooked largely. It was mentioned by the President, and that is the opportunities that will be offered by this legislation to thousands of young men now shut off from business opportunity and who are now mere hirelings. They are not getting a fair chance in the business world. It will open up a thousand avenues for them. Where we now have 1 man a director of 50 corporations we will have 50 capable men occuping [sic] places of importance in the business world, places of responsibility, and the result will be good to the business interests of this country. . . .

Mr. GARDNER. Mr. Chairman, the trouble with the majority is that they do not wish to injure any legitimate business, but nevertheless they do injure legitimate business. I have in mind an instance in my own district, and I have no doubt that similar instances could be found in every other district which is suburban to Boston. In the city of Salem in the Merchants Bank we have a director who is also a director in the Liberty Trust Co. in Boston, a large concern. He remains a director in the Merchants Bank of Salem out of local pride, greatly to the benefit of the community. There is no connection on earth between the Liberty Trust Co. in Boston and the Merchants Bank in Salem, and yet because the Liberty Trust Co. has over two and a half millions in assets and deposits, this bill says that we must deprive Salem of this director's services. I have no doubt the same situation exists in the district represented by the gentleman from Massachusetts [Mr. MITCHELL]. I have no doubt that the same situation exists in every district suburban to Boston. We are depriving the national banks in those suburban districts of the services of men who are actuated solely by public spirit. I prefer the amendment offered by the gentleman from New Jersey [Mr. MCCOY] to the amendment which I shall offer myself if his amendment is rejected. The McCoy amendment bears no relation to what the gentleman from Arkansas [Mr. FLOYD] has been saying. The gentleman has been talking about individuals who serve on 50 directorates.

Certain men may perhaps serve on a great number of miscellaneous directorates, but there is no man on earth who ⊥ serves on the boards of 50 national banks or trust companies. The amendment of the gentleman from New Jersey says this: Let us permit a man to serve on two or more national banks or trust companies, no matter what their size may be; but if he does wrong when so serving, then the Federal Reserve Board is to have him removed from his position and he will not be permitted to serve any longer. I consider that the gentleman from New Jersey has proposed a very liberal and proper amendment. My amendment, which I shall offer if his is defeated, is not so liberal. My amendment provides that the Federal Reserve Board may issue a revocable permit allowing a man to serve on the board of directors of two banking institutions, no matter what their size.

The amendment of the gentleman from New Jersey is just. If, however, you gentlemen are unwilling to agree that a man shall be permitted to serve in two large banking institutions until removed for misconduct, perhaps you will consent to my amendment. The gentleman from New Jersey proposes to allow service on two large boards, unless forbidden by the Federal Reserve Board. I propose to allow service on two large boards if specially permitted by the Federal Reserve Board. You gentlemen who come from country districts ought not to deprive us who live near large cities of the best banking talent we can find—so far, of course, as is consistent with the public welfare. . . .

Mr. AUSTIN. Mr. Chairman, I desire to have read from the Clerk's desk resolutions unanimously adopted by the Bankers' Association of Tennessee at their annual meeting held at Chattanooga on the 29th day of May. This association is composed of the National, State, and private bankers of that State, and its membership I should think politically is at least two-thirds Democratic.

The CHAIRMAN. Without objection, the Clerk will read:

There was no objection, and the Clerk read as follows:

Whereas Congress has now been in session almost continuously for more than a year; and

Whereas during that time a great amount of legislation has been passed, the entire tariff revised, the entire currency system of the United States has undergone a complete and fundamental change; and

Whereas it will take much time for the banking interests to adjust themselves to these new laws; and

Whereas there are now pending before Congress numerous bills which, if passed, will undertake the regulation of all business institutions with which banks are constantly doing business, and not only will banks be undergoing, as they are undergoing, a complete change of methods, but the business with which they are constantly in contact will themselves be undergoing a complete change: Be it

Resolved, That we believe that the country is sorely in need of a period of legislative rest while the business of the country is readjusting itself to the new currency and banking bill, and that we consider the passage of any great amount of new legislation by Congress at this time to be unhelpful to the general welfare of the country, and we believe the passage of such legislation will rather tend to further stagnate business than to stimulate it: Be it further

Resolved, That the secretary be hereby directed to forward to our Congressmen and our Senators a copy of this resolution. . . .

Mr. AUSTIN. Mr. Chairman, in connection with the discussion we have had to-night, participated in by the gentleman from Massachusetts [Mr. GARDNER], I wish to read an extract from a speech made by Daniel Webster 81 years ago in the Senate of the United States in reference to banks, corporations, and monopoly. This is taken from a speech by Mr. Webster in the Senate in 1833 and has a bearing on the pending measure:

There are persons who constantly clamor. They complain of oppression, speculation, and pernicious influence of accumulated wealth. They cry out loudly against all banks and corporations and all means by which small capitalists become united in order to produce important and beneficial results. They carry on mad hostility against all established institutions. They would choke the fountain of industry and dry all streams. In a country of unbounded liberty they clamor against oppression. In a country of perfect equality they would move heaven and earth against privilege and monopoly. In a country where property is more evenly divided than anywhere else they rend the air shouting against agrarian doctrines. In a country where wages of labor are high beyond parallel they would teach the laborer that he is but an oppressed slave. . . .

Mr. WEBB. Mr. Chairman, I hope the committee will not adopt the amendment of the gentleman from New Jersey. We feel that it would make this important provision in the bill practically useless. It is well known that the influences of interlocking directorates are such that you can not place your hand upon the sore spot, you can not place your hand upon the source where the damage to a business man is done. If you transfer the right to the Federal Reserve Board to discover where the wrong is done, you might as well throw it away, for in my opinion the reserve board would not find it. These influences are so subtle that a ferret could not find where a man was hurt. Complaint has been made about a string of banks in Boston before our committee. There are three or four different banks there in which directors were common in them all. A business man or two would apply to one of these banks for a loan. Nothing doing. He would then apply to another bank for a loan, and another bank, and finally he is shut out entirely. Now, the reserve board could not tell who did that, where the information came from, so the committee thought it better to make a hard and fast rule in order that no man could serve on these boards as an interlocking director, rather than transfer it to the board, which might never, or certainly would hardly ever, find the source of injury or wrong, and we think therefore it is better to adhere to the rule laid down in the bill, and I hope the committee will do so. . . .

Mr. [HENRY A.] BARNHART [D., Ind.]. The gentleman from Massachusetts [Mr. GARDNER] repeatedly said that under the pending amendment the reserve board would have the right to remove directors caught in wrongdoing, or words to that effect. Is there anything in the present law that would prevent the removal of directors under such conditions?

Mr. CARLIN. Nothing; any director caught in wrongdoing can be removed now. A clause in the banking and currency bill provides it. . . .

Mr. GARDNER. Can any director be removed to-day for any action which will lessen the competition between two banks in both of which he is a director?

Mr. CARLIN. Not for lessening competition; of course not.

Mr. GARDNER. That is the point of the amendment of the gentleman from New Jersey about which the gentleman from Indiana asked.

Mr. CARLIN. The difficulty with the gentleman from Boston is this—

Mr. GARDNER. I am not from Boston.

Mr. CARLIN. With the gentleman from Massachusetts is this: We are endeavoring to drive at a system, whereas this amendment undertakes to deal with individuals and specific cases.

Mr. GARDNER. The gentleman is driving at a system with which the gentleman has no experience in that part of the country from which the gentleman comes.

Mr. CARLIN. The gentleman is very much mistaken. I expect I have had as much experience if not more than the gentleman.

Mr. GARDNER. Well, perhaps.

Mr. WEBB. Mr. Chairman, I ask for a vote, if discussion is ended.

The CHAIRMAN. The question is on the amendment offered by the gentleman from New Jersey.

The question was taken, and the amendment was rejected.

Mr. BARTLETT. Mr. Chairman, I offer the following amendment.

The CHAIRMAN. The Clerk will report the amendment.

The Clerk read as follows:

Page 30, line 21, after the word "of" when it occurs the first time in the line, insert the words "not exceeding.". . .

Mr. BARTLETT. Mr. Chairman, the bill as it is now presented makes a flat fine of $100 a day, irrespective, and gives the court no discretion in the matter. The amendment I offer is simply to make it not exceeding $100 a day. There may be cases where the court would like not to impose the largest penalty, and this amendment simply gives the court some discretion in the matter so as to adjust the penalty to the case.

Mr. WEBB. Mr. Chairman, the committee sees no objection to the amendment. We think it is a fair one.

The question was taken, and the amendment was agreed to.

Mr. GARDNER. Mr. Chairman, I offer the following amendment.

The CHAIRMAN. The Clerk will report the amendment.

The Clerk read as follows:

"Page 29, line 3, after the word 'election,' insert '*Provided*, That the Federal Reserve Board may grant to any person a revocable permission to serve at the same time as a director or other officer or employee of an additional bank, banking association, or trust company, notwithstanding anything contained in this paragraph, whenever it is satisfied that such permission may be granted without detriment to the public welfare and without the creation of monopoly or restraint of trade; *Provided further*, That in his annual report the Secretary of the Treasury shall specify each permission granted in accordance with the preceding proviso, together with the reasons therefor.' "

Mr. WEBB. Mr. Chairman, of course the committee is opposed to that amendment because it changes the whole principle of the interlocking-directorates section of this bill.

The CHAIRMAN. The question is on the amendment offered by the gentleman from Massachusetts.

The question was taken, and the amendment was rejected.

Mr. REILLY of Connecticut. Mr. Chairman, I desire to offer an amendment, which I would like the Clerk to report.

The CHAIRMAN. The Clerk will report the amendment.

The Clerk read as follows:

On page 29, lines 6 and 7, strike out the words "one hundred thousand" and insert in lieu thereof the words "two hundred thousand."

Mr. REILLY of Connecticut. Mr. Chairman, I do not desire to discuss this amendment further than to say— . . .

All I desire to say or can say in the minute allowed me is that the frenzied financiering and unfair control by interlocking directorates that this bill seeks to rectify do not apply to cities of 100,000 or 200,000 inhabitants. In the banking business of New Haven, Bridgeport, Worcester, Fall River, and other New England cities there is no interlocking directors' evil and no need of this legislation. It looks as if the other cities of the country were being punished for the offenses of one or two great money centers and a few money kings. The limit should be raised to cities of at least 200,000, and might safely go beyond that figure.

The CHAIRMAN. The question is on agreeing to the amendment offered by the gentleman from Connecticut [Mr. REILLY].

The question was taken, and the amendment was rejected.

Mr. MANN. Mr. Chairman, I move to strike out the last word. . . .

Mr. Chairman, I am not in sympathy with the section, and, having said that much about the section, I would like to ask a question in reference to what it means. Section 9 provides—

> That from and after two years from the date of the approval of this act no person who is engaged as an individual—

Now what? Then it proceeds:

> Or who is a member of a partnership.

Now, if the gentleman can find anything that follows that that it relates to, I will be willing to give him a new suit of clothes. [Laughter.]

Mr. BARNHART. It would not relate to it if it would follow it.

Mr. MANN. I yield, Mr. Chairman, to know what that refers to, if anybody can tell me. All the language that follows it relates to a corporation. I suppose that the mere fact that an individual is "engaged" is not intended to prevent him from being an officer or director or employee of a corporation.

Mr. CARLIN. That section is intended to apply to the individual.

Mr. MANN. I know. I am not asking what the section applies to, but what this language applies to:

> No person who is engaged as an individual.

What?

Mr. CARLIN. An individual engaged in producing or selling equipment.

Mr. MANN. That is not what the bill says. The bill says:

> No person who is engaged as an individual, or who is a member of a partnership, or is a director or other officer of a corporation that is engaged in the business, in whole or in part, of producing or selling equipment—

And so forth.

All the language about equipment is related to and a part of the definition of "a corporation," and there is no language in the paragraph that relates to an individual or a partnership except that under the language a man that is "engaged," or a man who is a member of a partnership, can not become a director or other officer or employee of a corporation. Of course I do not expect the gentleman to correct it now, but, as a matter of credit to even the Democratic side of the House, I hope the gentleman will study grammar enough and rhetoric enough to make that language mean sense. [Laughter.]

Mr. CARLIN. I think the gentleman needs to become a student, and not the gentlemen on this side.

Mr. MANN. Oh, the gentleman can say that, but the gentleman can not answer the question.

Mr. CARLIN. I think the language is perfectly correct. That answers the question.

Mr. MANN. If you should leave that in the bill, and any school teacher looked at it, you would be forever discredited. [Laughter.]

Mr. CARLIN. I think the gentleman is mistaken about that.

The CHAIRMAN. The pro forma amendment will be considered withdrawn, and the Clerk will read.

The Clerk read as follows:

> SEC. 10. That any suit, action, or proceeding under the antitrust laws against a corporation may be brought not only in the judicial district whereof it is an inhabitant, but also in any district wherein it may be found.

Mr. CULLOP. Mr. Chairman, I move to strike out the last word for the purpose of asking the chairman a question. This is a section that should be amended to conform to the previous amendment about jurisdiction and service. I suppose the committee wants to offer an amendment, does it not?

Mr. WEBB. I believe the amendment we agreed to before, Mr. Chairman, was that after the word "found" we would insert the words "or has an agent."

Mr. CULLOP. I would like, Mr. Chairman, to suggest that there be incorporated in the amendment further the language "and wherever the cause of action accrues." That applies to bringing a suit; that any suit or action against a corporation may be brought not only in the judicial district whereof it is an inhabitant, but also in any district wherein it may be found or has an agent, and it ought to go further, and I think that was the agreement, and provide "or where the cause of action arises."

Mr. CARLIN. How will you get service there?

Mr. CULLOP. There is where it has an agency.

Mr. CARLIN. If you sue them where they have an agency, it does not make any difference where the cause of action arises. You would not help the bill any by adding what you suggest. I think if you include the words "or has an agent" you have got the whole thing.

Mr. CULLOP. If the committee are satisfied with that, I will not press the suggestion.

The CHAIRMAN. Does the gentleman from North Carolina offer an amendment?

Mr. WEBB. The amendment which I suggested, after the word "found," in line 4, on page 31, to add the words "or has an agent."

The CHAIRMAN. The gentleman from North Carolina offers an amendment, which the Clerk will report.

The Clerk read as follows:

Page 31, line 4, after the word "found," insert the words "or has an agent."

Mr. WEBB. And strike out the period, and insert a comma after the word "found."

The CHAIRMAN. The question is on the amendment offered by the gentleman from North Carolina.

The amendment was agreed to.

Mr. SUMNERS. Mr. Chairman, I move to strike out the last word, for the purpose of making a suggestion to the committee, and if necessary, of offering an amendment.

⊥ It seems to me very clear that when the bill comes to provide for the venue, it ought to add the words "where the cause of action or any part thereof arises."

That fixes the venue, and does not make the plaintiff depend upon the place where he may be able to find an agent.

Mr. Chairman, I withdraw the pro forma amendment if I may, and offer this amendment.

The CHAIRMAN. If there be no objection, the pro forma amendment will be withdrawn; and the gentleman from Texas offers an amendment which the Clerk will report.

The Clerk read as follows:

Page 31, line 4, strike out the period at the end of the paragraph, insert a comma, and add the following: "or where the cause of action or any part thereof arises."

Mr. MANN. I suggest that the gentleman offer it to come in after the amendment just agreed to.

Mr. SUMNERS. I meant to ask unanimous consent that it come in after the amendment just adopted.

The CHAIRMAN. If there be no objection, the amendment will be modified in the way indicated by the gentleman from Texas.

Mr. SUMNERS. Mr. Chairman and gentlemen of the committee, I am certain that this amendment ought to be adopted. There is no reason on earth why it should not be adopted. This amendment provides that suit may be instituted where the cause of action or any part thereof accrues. Now, why should it not be adopted? If a man suffers an injury in a given locality, why not bring the suit there?

Mr. WEBB. The bill provides that you can sue the corporation wherever it may be found, or wherever it has an agent, or wherever it resides. Now, how could you get service on a corporation unless it be found in a locality or unless it has an agent there?

Mr. SUMNERS. May I ask the gentleman a question before answering his? Has the gentleman any objection to permitting a man to bring suit at the place where he suffers the injury?

Mr. WEBB. You may not be able to find anyone to serve process upon.

Mr. SUMNERS. We can provide for the service of process later. The service of process is governed entirely by the laws which Congress may enact; and if it is necessary to have subsequent legislation in order to regulate the matter of service of process that is no reason why the suit should not be brought at the place where the cause of action arises.

Mr. WEBB. You might authorize suit against the property of the corporation, but you could not get personal service on the corporation unless it had an agent there, or was found there, or resided there.

Mr. SUMNERS. Unless Congress authorized service beyond the district, and we can do that.

Mr. WEBB. How can you get service of process?

Mr. SUMNERS. By sending your process to an officer of the Federal Government at the place where the corporation has its residence or an agency.

Mr. CARLIN. The gentleman's amendment does not provide for that.

Mr. SUMNERS. I know it does not; but there is no reason why that amendment could not be added. I will offer that amendment if it ought to be there. If you adopt this amendment, that does not interfere with the right of service of process, just the same as you have it under this bill. Suppose a corporation or individual goes into a certain locality and there inflicts an injury, and then withdraws its agent from that territory. Do you mean to tell me that this committee is in favor of driving the man who suffered the injury to a foreign jurisdiction to get his remedy? There is nothing fair or just about it, and I am sure that the committee do not intend to do that. I merely want to call your attention to it, and I hope the committee will agree to it. It does not weaken your bill by just adding that much more to it, and it gives the poor man who has suffered the injury that much additional opportunity to bring suit at or near his home. It can not hurt your bill.

Mr. WEBB. We have already broadened the provisions of the Sherman Act with reference to the bringing of suit and the service of process at any place where the corporation is an inhabitant, or wherever it is found, or wherever it has an agent. I can hardly conceive of a suit being brought otherwise than under these conditions, and it makes service by process easy, and therefore we oppose the amendment.

Mr. FOWLER. Mr. Chairman, I want to ask the gentleman in charge of the bill a question. The language of the bill is as amended "wherever it may be found," and the amendment is "or has an agent." What do you mean by the language "wherever it may be found"?

Mr. WEBB. Wherever it has an agent. The circuit court of appeals has so decided.

Mr. FOWLER. The antecedent of "it" is "corporation." Where may a corporation be found?

Mr. WEBB. Wherever it has an agent, and practically every State in the Union requires, before a corporation is allowed to do business within the borders of the State, that it must have an agent upon whom process can be served.

Mr. FOWLER. That is true, and that is the reason of my asking the question. This is a Federal proceeding and ought not you to enumerate the officers on whom service may be had? Ought you not to say the president, the vice president, any director, or any agent of the corporation, so that it would mean something? "It" stands for corporation in the language you have used.

Mr. WEBB. I am not sure, but I think there is a provision in the Federal law which allows you to serve the president, vice president, director, or agent of a corporation.

Mr. FOWLER. The gentleman means that the plaintiff is permitted to get service on the corporation by serving the president, vice president, director, or an agent?

Mr. WEBB. Yes.

Mr. FOWLER. I am not sure, and I want information on that. . . .

Mr. KONOP. I would like to ask a question. You say wherever it may be found or has an agent. Suppose a violator of the antitrust law is an individual? Would you refer to him as "it"?

Mr. WEBB. This refers to corporations who commit actions in restraint of trade.

Mr. CARLIN. This is in relation to suits against corporations.

Mr. FOWLER. The antecedent of "it" is "corporation." The only point I wanted to raise is as to the person on whom service would be had. My opinion is that the persons ought to be enumerated if they are not definitely enumerated in some Federal statute. . . .

Mr. FLOYD of Arkansas. I desire to call the gentleman's attention to the fact that the language he is discussing is found in section 7 of the Sherman antitrust law, where it says "in which the defendant resides or is found." There has never been any difficulty about service in regard to those words, and the gentleman from Illinois desires to put a limitation upon that language which would lessen it and narrow it. When you mention specific officers, agents, or individuals upon whom service may be had, like the president, vice president, and director, and so forth, you narrow the scope of the provision. The corporation is found wherever it is transacting business and has any kind of an agent.

Mr. FOWLER. Well, you must have some person definite on whom to get service before you can get a corporation into court. The gentleman from Arkansas is too good a lawyer not to know all that.

Mr. FLOYD of Arkansas. But when you say agent it includes every kind of an agent.

Mr. FOWLER. There is a difference between an officer of a corporation and the agent of a corporation. . . .

Mr. DAVENPORT. I have had occasion within the last few weeks to look up the Federal statutes in regard to the service of corporations. There is a statute that provides in substance that a suit against a corporation may be served on the president, vice president, or agent, or any officer of the corporation.

Mr. FOWLER. That is exactly the point I am raising. If there is a Federal statute providing that service shall be made upon representatives of a corporation in order to get it into court, I presume that this language is sufficient.

Mr. DAVENPORT. That is a fact, because I looked it up within two weeks.

The CHAIRMAN. The question is on the amendment offered by the gentleman from Texas.

The question was taken, and the amendment was rejected.

The Clerk read as follows:

SEC. 12. That whenever a corporation shall be guilty of the violation of any of the provisions of the antitrust laws the offense shall be deemed to be also that of the individual directors, officers, or agents of such corporation; and upon the conviction of the corporation any director, officer, or agent who shall have authorized, ordered, or done any of such prohibited acts shall be deemed guilty of a misdemeanor, and upon conviction therefor shall be punished by a fine not exceeding $5,000 or by imprisonment not exceeding one year, or by both, in the discretion of the court.

⊥ Mr. LENROOT. Mr. Chairman, I move to strike out the last word for the purpose of asking information of the chairman of the committee. Section 12 as it appears before us now is radically different from the section in the original bill. I would like to ask the chairman of the committee what the thought of the committee was in lines 12 and 13. The language is "the offense shall be deemed to be also that of the individual director, officers, or agents of such corporation." Was it the thought of the committee that each director of a corporation guilty of this offense should also be deemed personally guilty?

Mr. WEBB. As far as we are concerned, it would be read, in connection with line 13, after the semicolon, "and upon the conviction of the corporation any director, officer, or agent who shall have authorized, ordered, or done any such prohibited acts shall be deemed guilty of a misdemeanor," and so forth. I think it should be connected up with that provision.

I do not think that the officer of the corporation could be convicted unless you picked out the officer who had done the prohibited thing, and that is explained in lines 13 to 15, inclusive.

Mr. LENROOT. It ought to be so, but it certainly does not read so on its face. It would be open to construction and the construction seems to me to be uncertain.

Mr. FLOYD of Arkansas. What suggestion has the gentleman to make?

Mr. LENROOT. The original section read in this way:

> Shall be deemed to be also that of the individual directors, officers, and agents of such corporation authorizing, ordering, or doing any of such prohibition [sic] acts.

It limited the guilt to those actually responsible for the acts violative of the law. I am not offering an amendment, because I also want to raise another question.

Mr. FLOYD of Arkansas. While the gentleman is on that point, if he will notice the draft of the original provision he will find that it is connected with the preceding clause; but the committee, in order to make it clear that the conviction of the corporation did not of itself constitute the director's guilt, changed it so as to read:

> And upon the conviction of the corporation any director, officer, or agent who shall have authorized, ordered, or done any of such prohibited acts shall be deemed guilty of a misdemeanor—

And so forth.

Mr. LENROOT. I want to ask the gentleman if in seeking to avoid one difficulty he has not gotten into another?

Mr. FLOYD of Arkansas. If we did, we would be very glad to have any suggestion from the gentleman.

Mr. LENROOT. I am not entirely clear myself. I am asking for information.

Mr. FLOYD of Arkansas. The purpose we had was to make it clear that, when a corporation had been guilty, those officers, agents, and directors of the corporation that either authorized, ordered, or did the thing prohibited should be guilty. Under the existing law, and without that provision of the statute, the person who did the things would undoubtedly be guilty; but in the enforcement of the criminal provisions of the Sherman law, experience has demonstrated that both juries and courts are slow to convict men who have simply done acts authorized or ordered by some officers of the concern higher up, and the words "authorized" and "ordered" were introduced to reach the real offenders, the men who caused the things to be done; and if the language is susceptible of any ambiguity and is not clear, we desire to make it clear. I will state to the gentleman that we intended to give agents and officers a trial, and we do not mean that the guilt of the corporation shall attach to them without trial; but in order to obtain a conviction, it will be necessary for the Government to charge them specifically with authorizing, ordering, or doing of the thing prohibited, and, on proof, convict them. . . .

Mr. MANN. Under this language—

> and upon the conviction of the corporation, any director, officer, or agent who shall have authorized, ordered, or done any of such prohibited acts shall be deemed guilty of a misdemeanor—

would the corporation have to be convicted before any proceeding, information or otherwise, indictment, could be brought against the officers of the corporation for the offense?

Mr. FLOYD of Arkansas. I do not think so. It was not so intended.

Mr. MANN. Is not that what it says? The first part says:

> That whenever a corporation shall be guilty of the violation of any of the provisions of the antitrust laws the offense shall also be deemed to be that of the individual directors—

And so forth.

How can you tell when the corporation is guilty until you have tried the corporation?

Mr. FLOYD of Arkansas. I think the officers, directors, and agents might be guilty independently of the guilt of the corporation.

Mr. MANN. In the first part you have to find the corporation guilty before any of them can be convicted, and then you go on and say that upon conviction the others may be convicted.

Mr. LENROOT. Mr. Chairman, I appreciate the difficulty that the committee was in with reference to the original section to make it clear that merely upon conviction of the corporation the officers should not be convicted of the offense without trial, but in attempting to remedy that it seems to me the committee has gotten into another and even more serious difficulty. As suggested by the gentleman from Illinois [Mr. MANN], the first section now reads that the corporation itself must first be convicted before they can proceed against the officers; but that is not the most serious thing, for I am afraid, as the section reads, it will be construed in this way: That when the corporation is convicted the question of violation of law becomes a settled fact, and the only issue that the officers are entitled to be heard upon in the action against them is the simple one as to whether or not they ordered or authorized the act to be done, and denying them the opportunity to be heard as to whether the act itself was in fact prohibited by the law; but they certainly must have the right to have that question determined as well as the fact as to whether or not the particular act was ordered or authorized by them.

Mr. FLOYD of Arkansas. In other words, the gentleman from Wisconsin suggests that the language used might be interpreted to mean that the officers of the corporation would never be convicted unless the corporation was first convicted.

Mr. LENROOT. That is the way it reads.

Mr. FLOYD of Arkansas. I desire to say it was not the intention of the committee to give it any such construction and to repeat that if an amendment can be suggested that will cure the apparent defect the committee will be glad to accept it. We intended to provide that when the corporation was convicted that the offense should be deemed also the offense of the officers and agents authorizing, ordering, or doing the prohibited thing, and then to provide that these individuals should not be convicted except upon indictment and trial as to the facts charged. . . .

Mr. VOLSTEAD. Mr. Chairman, I offer an amendment.

The CHAIRMAN. The Clerk will report the amendment.

The Clerk read as follows:

Strike out section 12 and substitute:

"Any person who shall do, or cause to be done, or shall willingly suffer and permit to be done any act, matter, or thing prohibited or declared to be unlawful in the antitrust laws or shall aid or abet therein, shall be deemed guilty of such prohibited and unlawful acts, matters, and things and shall be subject to the punishments prescribed therefor in the trust laws."

Mr. FLOYD of Arkansas. Mr. Chairman, we desire to oppose the amendment offered by the gentleman from Minnesota.

The CHAIRMAN. The gentleman from Minnesota has the floor.

Mr. VOLSTEAD. Section 12, as it reads, I think clearly requires that there must be first a conviction of the corporation before there is any guilt on the part of the officers, because it provides that upon conviction the officers doing certain things shall be guilty of a misdemeanor; consequently it is necessary to establish first the guilt of the corporation. I assume that the committee did not intend any such result as that, because instead of making the guilt personal it would make it—

Mr. METZ. If the gentleman will permit me there, we are trying in all of these sections to deal with the corporation, with the corporate form of doing business. The individual is not touched in any shape or manner. The moment he incorporates under the State law he becomes a corporation. Now, a great majority of the corporations of this country are not corporations in the sense that their stock is for sale, but it is a one-man concern and is under the control of one man with dummy directors, and if he—

Mr. VOLSTEAD. I did not yield for a speech, but simply for a question.

Mr. METZ. My question is, How are you going to reach the one-man corporation?

Mr. VOLSTEAD. The amendment I have offered is practically a copy of a similar act that is applied to the railway corporations by the interstate-commerce act. It has this additional advantage over the one contained in the bill. It does not increase the punishment beyond the limit fixed in the various acts. Take, for instance, section 9. The punishment there is only $100, while the punishment provided in section 12 is $5,000.

Mr. WEBB. It is $100 a day in section 9.

Mr. VOLSTEAD. But you do not intend to change that item, you intend that the punishment shall be the same; that is, that the punishment of the individual shall be the same as the punishment of the corporation. Now, the amendment that I have offered— . . .

Mr. WEBB. I take it that we all agree that this section ought to be amended, and I ask unanimous consent to let this section go over until to-morrow and see if we can not draw up an amendment that will be acceptable to both sides.

Mr. TOWNER. I hope that will be granted.

The CHAIRMAN. Does the gentleman yield to that request?

Mr. VOLSTEAD. Yes.

Mr. TOWNER. Before leaving it, I would like to inquire of the chairman of the committee if this section might not be omitted altogether. I would like this question to be considered. The reason for that is this: Returning to page 20, you have defined there the word "person" to include also corporations. But that does not by any means mean that the word "person" always means a corporation. It means in the bill just as much as it ever did. It means a person, and if any person commits any of the acts that are prohibited by this act—that is, if his personal connection can be shown with any of those acts—will he not be deemed as a violator of the terms of this act?

Mr. VOLSTEAD. May I suggest to the gentleman that I think it is very essential that some prohibition of this kind should be made, because section 8, which deals with the question of stock consolidations, does not mention persons at all. It is simply a prohibition against corporations, and in order to prevent individuals from carrying out the consolidations prohibited in section 8 you will need that; otherwise you would have nothing at all.

The CHAIRMAN. The gentleman from North Carolina [Mr. WEBB] asks unanimous consent that section 12 be passed over. Is there objection?

There was no objection.

The CHAIRMAN. The Clerk will read.

The Clerk read as follows:

SEC. 15. That no preliminary injunction shall be issued without notice to the opposite party.

No temporary restraining order shall be granted without notice to the opposite party unless it shall clearly appear from specific facts shown by affidavit or by the verified bill that immediate and irreparable injury, loss, or damage will result to property or a property right of the applicant before notice could be served or hearing had thereon. Every such temporary restraining order shall be indorsed with the date and hour of issuance, shall be forthwith filed in the clerk's office and entered of record, shall define the injury and state why it is irreparable and why the order was granted without notice, and shall by its terms expire within such time after entry, not to exceed 10 days, as the court or judge may fix. In case a temporary restraining order shall be granted without notice in the contingency specified, the matter of the issuance of a preliminary injunction shall be set down for a hearing at the earliest possible time and shall take precedence of all matters except older matters of the same character; and when the same comes up for hearing the party obtaining the temporary restraining order shall proceed with his application for a preliminary injunction, and if he does not do so the court shall dissolve his temporary restraining order. Upon two days' notice to the party obtaining such temporary restraining order the opposite party may appear and move the dissolution or modification of the order, and in that event the court or judge shall proceed to hear and determine the motion as expeditiously as the ends of justice may require.

Section 263 of an act entitled "An act to codify, revise, and amend the laws relating to the judiciary," approved March 3, 1911, is hereby repealed.

Nothing in this section contained shall be deemed to alter, repeal, or amend section 266 of an act entitled "An act to codify, revise, and amend the laws relating to the judiciary," approved March 3, 1911.

Mr. MACDONALD. Mr. Chairman, I offer an amendment.

The CHAIRMAN. The gentleman from Michigan [Mr. MACDONALD] offers an amendment, which the Clerk will report.

Mr. MACDONALD. Mr. Chairman, beginning with the second paragraph on page

33, line 13, I move to strike out the remainder of the section and insert the language that I have sent to the desk.

The CHAIRMAN. The Clerk will report the amendment.

The Clerk read as follows:

Page 33, line 13, strike out the remainder of the section down to and including line 24, on page 34, and insert in lieu thereof the following:

"In construing this act the right to enter into the relation of employer and employee, to change that relation and to assume and create a new relation of employer and employee, and to perform and carry on business in such relation with any person in any place or do work and labor as an employee shall be held and construed to be a personal and not a property right. In all cases involving the violation of the contract of employment by either the employee or employer where no irreparable damage is about to be committed upon the property or property right of either no injunction shall be granted, but the parties shall be left to their remedy at law."

The CHAIRMAN. The question is on agreeing to the amendment offered by the gentleman from Michigan [Mr. MACDONALD].

Mr. MACDONALD. Mr. Chairman, the second paragraph of section 15, as I read it, does nothing to change existing law in regard to injunctions or the issuance of injunctions, except one thing, and that one thing is that the language of the section, by implication, creates a new and distinct class of cases in which injunctions can issue with notice. The paragraph provides—

That no temporary restraining order shall be granted without notice to the opposite party—

And so forth; and in continuation states no further jurisdiction in such cases than now exists under the present practice, thereby, by implication, creating another class of injunctions that can be granted with notice; and I am constrained to believe that a court could hold, and probably would hold, that that might authorize courts to issue injunctions in cases of invasion of personal rights where they are not so authorized to do now. That has been a long-mooted question in some aspects of this controversy—whether the right of issuing injunctions where property and property rights are threatened with irreparable injury and no adequate remedy exists at law, is not gradually being extended so as to take in, partially at least, personal rights. And I think that if this section of the law is passed as it now stands you leave room for argument, at least, that there is an express authorization of the statute which by implication permits the issuance of injunctions in that class of cases.

The language that I have offered as a substitute for this section is, as is well known, a part of the Bartlett bill, and is unobjectionable, and plainly states the object for which it is intended. I think that it is very important that this change should be made, so that there can be left upon the statute no question as to whether the right to extend the issuance of injunction to this field has been granted.

Mr. FLOYD of Arkansas. Mr. Chairman, I desire to oppose the amendment offered by the gentleman from Michigan [Mr. MACDONALD] and to explain this provision.

The language that the gentleman objects to is substantially the language of rule 73 of rules of practice for the courts of equity adopted by the Supreme Court of the United States.

The Clayton anti-injunction bill that was passed at the last session of Congress contained a similar provision, which was modified in this bill so as to make it conform to rule 73 adopted by the Supreme Court of the United States in equity cases. We did not desire to disturb that rule; but the fact that they have adopted it as a court rule is no reason why we should not incorporate it into the statute, especially when we are dealing with the general subject of injunctions.

Mr. MACDONALD. Is it true that there is nothing in this section but what is the practice now under the law and the rules?

Mr. FLOYD of Arkansas. I am not sure of that; but the point I make is that the first part of the language that the gentleman moves to strike out follows the language of rule 73 of the Supreme Court of the United States in equity cases, formulated and adopted by the Supreme Court since the passage of the Clayton bill in the Sixty-second Congress. I will incorporate that rule in my remarks:

Rule 73.
PRELIMINARY INJUNCTIONS AND TEMPORARY RESTRAINING ORDERS.

No preliminary injunction shall be granted without notice to the opposite party. Nor shall any temporary restraining order be granted without notice to the opposite party, unless it shall clearly appear from specific facts, shown by affidavit or by the verified bill, that immediate and irreparable loss or damage will result to the applicant before the matter can be heard on notice. In case a temporary restraining order shall be granted without notice, in the contingency specified, the matter shall be made returnable at the earliest possible time, and in no event later than 10 days from the date of the order, and shall take precedence of all matters, except older matters of the same character. When the matter comes up for hearing the party who obtained the temporary restraining order shall proceed with his application for a preliminary injunction, and if he does not do so the court shall dissolve his temporary restraining order. Upon two days' notice to the party obtaining such temporary restraining order, the opposite party may appear and move the dissolution or modification of the order, and in that event the court or judge shall proceed to hear and determine the motion as expeditiously as the ends of justice may require. Every temporary restraining order shall be forthwith filed in the clerk's office.

The other provisions of the section have been very carefully considered. No material change has been made in the other ⊥ provisions of the Clayton injunction bill, ⊥9611 which was thoroughly considered and passed at the last session of the Congress.

While in the past some courts have followed the general principles laid down in those provisions of this bill that relate to injunctions, I desire to call the attention of the gentleman from Michigan [Mr. MacDONALD] to the fact that we have many Federal courts in this country, and that a great many of the judges have adopted rules contrary to the principles laid down here and have enforced them in their respective courts; and the Committee on the Judiciary in preparing this injunction bill made an effort to follow the better line of decisions of the Federal courts and to put in the statute an inhibition that would prevent courts that had been abusing the writ of injunction by issuing it in cases in which we do not feel that the issuance of an injunction was justified from doing so in the future.

Mr. MacDONALD. Does the gentleman refer to cases of injunctions where it is doubtful whether the injunction is based upon threatened injury of personal rights rather than property or property rights?

Mr. FLOYD of Arkansas. We preserve that distinction in the bill.

Mr. MacDONALD. Not in terms.

Mr. FLOYD of Arkansas. I think so.

Mr. MURDOCK. Mr. Chairman, before the gentleman takes his seat— . . .

I should like to have the gentleman explain about this section. What is the time of the notice given in case of a restraining order where irreparable injury is claimed? How much of a notice is provided for in this bill?

Mr. FLOYD of Arkansas. It may be issued without notice, but unless the parties proceed within 10 days the suit abates and must be dismissed. The rule of the Supreme Court is more liberal than the provision of the bill passed at the last session, which provided for 7 days and a renewal of 7 days, which would make 14 days; but the rule of the Supreme Court which is incorporated here requires the parties to proceed within 10 days or the suit will abate and must be dismissed.

Mr. MURDOCK. The language of the bill is that no preliminary injunction shall be issued without notice to the opposite party. There must in every case be some notice.

Mr. BARTLETT. Unless—

Mr. MURDOCK. Unless irreparable injury to property is claimed.

Mr. FLOYD of Arkansas. Yes.

Mr. MURDOCK. The provisions of the second paragraph are precisely in keeping with the better practice now. Is that right?

Mr. FLOYD of Arkansas. Yes; that is what we understand.

Mr. MURDOCK. But you are writing into statutory law a rule of the Supreme Court. Is that right?

Mr. FLOYD of Arkansas. Yes; absolutely. In the consideration of this question we examined the decisions. One court would hold that a certain practice was lawful and would refuse to issue an injunction. Another court would proceed to issue an injunction, and it was this wrongful issuance of injunctions in cases where courts were not justified under the facts in issuing them that has given rise to this criticism of the Federal courts.

We propose to write the better practice of the Federal courts into the statute as a rule to govern all the courts, and not leave it to their discretion to issue injunctions on whatever state of fact may suit the fancy of the judge.

The CHAIRMAN. The question is on the amendment offered by the gentleman from Michigan.

The question was taken, and the amendment was rejected.

The Clerk read as follows:

SEC. 17. That every order of injunction or restraining order shall set forth the reasons for the issuance of the same, shall be specific in terms, and shall describe in reasonable detail, and not by reference to the bill of complaint or other document, the act or acts sought to be restrained, and shall be binding only upon the parties to the suit, their agents, servants, employees, and attorneys, or those in active concert with them and who shall by personal service or otherwise, have received actual notice of the same.

Mr. MURDOCK. Mr. Chairman, I move to strike out the last word. I wish the gentleman from North Carolina would explain section 17.

Mr. WEBB. The main purpose of the section is to bind nobody to the statute except the agent and those in active service; the parties enjoined are those who have actual interests.

Mr. MURDOCK. Is this as in the case of section 15 merely writing into the statutory law the practice of the court?

Mr. WEBB. Yes; I think the case of In re Lennon[5.564] is practically embodied in this section. It has not always been the practice in the Federal courts, but we are making or trying to make a uniform practice for all the courts.

Mr. FLOYD of Arkansas. We prohibit what is known as the blanket injunction. Courts have issued injunctions against parties without naming them and so a man might be in California and violate an order of the court in New York and not know it, and be brought into court for contempt in violating the order. The main purpose of this section is to prevent what is commonly known as the blanket injunction.

Mr. MURDOCK. This makes it specific?

Mr. WEBB. Yes; it does away with what as the gentleman from Arkansas says is a blanket injunction and protects every man who may come within the injunction law.

Mr. MANN. Mr. Chairman, I move to strike out the last word. I think there is to be some contest in regard to section 18, is there not?

Mr. WEBB. Yes, I thought the Clerk might read section 18 and then we would leave that open for amendment to-morrow.

The CHAIRMAN. Without objection, the pro forma amendments are withdrawn and the Clerk will read.

The Clerk read as follows:

SEC. 18. That no restraining order or injunction shall be granted by any court of the United States, or a judge or the judges thereof, in any case between an employer and employees, or between employers and employees, or between employees, or between persons employed and persons seeking employment, involving, or growing out of, a dispute concerning terms or conditions of employment, unless necessary to prevent irreparable injury to property, or to a property right, of the party making the application, for which injury there is no adequate remedy at law, and such property or property right must be described with particularity in the application, which must be in writing and sworn to by the applicant or by his agent or attorney.

And no such restraining order or injunction shall prohibit any person or persons from terminating any relation of employment, or from ceasing to perform any work or labor, or from recommending, advising, or persuading others by peaceful means so to do; or from attending at or near a house or place where any person resides or works, or carries on business or happens to be, for the purpose of peacefully obtaining or communicating information, or of peacefully persuading any person to work or to abstain from working; or from ceasing to patronize or to employ any party to such dispute, or from recommending, advising, or persuading others by peaceful means so to do; or from paying or giving to, or withholding from, any person engaged

---

[5.564] 166 U.S. 548, 17 S. Ct. 658, 41 L. Ed. 1110 (1897).

in such dispute, any strike benefits or other moneys or things of value; or from peaceably assembling at any place in a lawful manner, and for lawful purposes; or from doing any act or thing which might lawfully be done in the absence of such dispute by any party thereto.

Mr. WEBB. Mr. Chairman, the House has been in continuous session since 11 o'clock this morning, 10 hours and a half. It has been a very strenuous day, and on behalf of the committee I want to thank the Members who have stayed here and assisted us. Mr. Chairman, I move that the committee do now rise.

The motion was agreed to; . . .

HOUSE DEBATE
63d Cong., 2d Sess.
June 2, 1914

51 CONG. REC. 9652

The House met at 11 o'clock a. m.

The SPEAKER. The House automatically resolves itself into the Committee of the Whole House on the state of the Union for the further consideration of the bill H. R. 15657 and other bills embraced within the special order, and the gentleman from Tennessee [Mr. HULL] will take the chair. . . .

Mr. WEBB. Mr. Chairman, when we adjourned on yesterday evening we had finished reading section 18, and it is now open to amendment, as I understand, and I desire to send forward the following amendment, which is a committee amendment.

The CHAIRMAN. The Clerk will report the amendment.

The Clerk read as follows:

At the end of section 18, line 23, on page 36, strike out the period and insert a semicolon and add "nor shall any of the acts specified in this paragraph be considered or held unlawful."

Mr. MANN. Will the gentleman explain this?

Mr. WEBB. Yes, sir. If you will notice section 18, it says that in labor disputes no injunction shall be issued restraining a person from ceasing to work, commonly known as striking; no injunction shall be issued against a person for advising or persuading others to quit work—that is, to strike; no injunction shall be issued against a person or persons prohibiting them from assembling peacefully together at a place they may select; no injunction may issue against a person forbidding him to cease to patronize a party to the dispute; no injunction shall be issued against a person or persons or labor organizations forbidding them to pay strike benefits or withhold strike benefits.

Mr. VOLSTEAD. Would not this also legalize the secondary boycott? I want to call the gentleman's attention to lines 16 and 17, on page 36.

Mr. WEBB. Mr. Chairman, I do not think it legalizes a secondary boycott.

Mr. VOLSTEAD. Let me read the lines, if the gentleman will permit. And no such restraining order or injunction shall prohibit anyone—

From ceasing to patronize those who employ any party to such dispute, or from recommending, advising, or persuading others by peaceful means so to do.

Now, does not the word "others" in that instance refer to others than parties to the dispute?

Mr. WEBB. No; because it says in line 15:

From ceasing to patronize or employ any parties to such dispute.

Mr. VOLSTEAD. Can the gentleman suggest as to what the word "others" refers to if it does not refer to others and parties to the dispute? Can there be any doubt this is intended or does, in fact, legalize the secondary boycott?

Mr. WEBB. I will say frankly to my friend when this section was drawn it was drawn with the careful purpose not to legalize the secondary boycott, and we do not think it does. There may be a difference of opinion about it, but it is the opinion of the committee that it does not legalize the secondary boycott and is not intended to do so. It does legalize the primary boycott; it does legalize the strike; it does legalize persuading others to strike, to quit work, and the other acts mentioned in ⊥ section 18, but we did not intend, I will say frankly, to legalize the secondary boycott.

Mr. TOWNER. Is it not true, I will ask the gentleman, if these statements, every one of them contained in this paragraph of this section, have been time and time again declared by the supreme courts of the United States not to be illegal or unlawful acts?

Mr. WEBB. Not time and time again by the Supreme Court of the United States, but time and time again by various inferior Federal courts and the Supreme Court.

Mr. TOWNER. By the supreme courts, I said.

Mr. WEBB. Mr. Chairman, we are frank to say in our opinion everything set forth in section 18 is the law to-day.

Mr. VOLSTEAD. But would the gentleman be willing to accept an amendment which would expressly exclude the secondary boycott?

Mr. WEBB. Well, with our present view and understanding of the section we feel it is not necessary to accept such amendment.

Mr. VOLSTEAD. So there can be no doubt as to what it is, and it seems to me that we ought to know just what is intended to write into this law.

Mr. WEBB. The word "others" is confined to the parties to the dispute.

Mr. VOLSTEAD. Others than parties to the suit.

Mr. WEBB. It does not say "others than."

Mr. VOLSTEAD. Read lines 15, 16, and 17, on page 36. It seems to me the word "others" can refer to nobody else but others outside of the parties to the dispute.

Mr. WEBB. There may not be any others and probably will not be, and if there are others they must be parties to the dispute where the strike takes place.

Mr. VOLSTEAD. If the gentleman will accept an amendment, I will offer one.

Mr. WEBB. I will say this section was drawn two years or more ago and was drawn carefully, and those who drew this section drew it with the idea of excluding the secondary boycott. It passed the House, I think, by about 243 to 16, and the question of the secondary boycott was not raised then, because we understood so clearly it did not refer to or authorize the secondary boycott. . . .

Mr. HENRY. Mr. Chairman, this is a very important amendment that has been offered, and I think the House ought to thoroughly understand it. . . .

Mr. MURDOCK. Will the gentleman have the amendment read again, so that we can get it clearly in mind?

Mr. HENRY. Yes. I have no objection.

The CHAIRMAN. Without objection, the Clerk will again report the amendment.

The Clerk read as follows:

At the end of section 18, line 23, page 36, strike out the period and insert a comma, and add "nor shall any of the acts specified in this paragraph be considered or held unlawful. . . .

Mr. WEBB. Now, I will say to the gentlemen of the committee, having recognized and legalized the acts set forth in section 18, so far as the conscience side of the court is concerned, the committee feels that no harm can come from making those acts legal on the law side of the court, for anything that is permitted to be done in conscience ought not to be made a crime or forbidden in law.

That is the view we take of it, and that is the reason why we offer this amendment, which provides that the acts and things set forth in section 18 shall not be construed to be unlawful. That is as clear, Mr. Chairman, as I can make it, and I think it covers the section and is easily understood.

Mr. HENRY. Mr. Chairman, I regard this as a very important amendment. Section 18 may be truly regarded as a bill of rights for the labor organizations. This bill was passed through the House before. This section as a separate bill was held up in the Senate. I am glad that we are now about to make it a part of the antitrust program.

Some of us, after reading this section in connection with the other provisions of the general bill, did not believe that it was quite explicit, and that there ought to be some addition to section 18. So, on the evening of May 21 of this year, Mr. KITCHIN, of North Carolina; Mr. TOWNER; Mr. HINEBAUGH, of Illinois; Mr. GRAHAM, of Illinois; Mr. LEWIS, of Maryland; and myself met in the rooms of the Committee on Rules for the purpose of examining this section and certain other sections of the bill, and we came to the conclusion that this amendment which has been offered by Mr. WEBB and accepted by the Committee on the Judiciary should be made a part of the bill.

On that evening we formulated this amendment exactly as it has been tendered, and on Sunday morning submitted it to the American Federation of Labor, because we did not want any misunderstanding about this question. We believed that we ought to make history clear; that there ought not hereafter to be any cloudy or foggy history as there was after the Sherman antitrust law was passed. So in connection with the amendment, which was agreed to as a part of section 7, this amendment was agreed to, and we asked the officers of the American Federation of Labor to submit this amendment to their counsel in order that we might clearly understand it and cooperate with them.

They did so, and they have agreed that this amendment is appropriate and indeed necessary; and we concur with them, and the President and the Committee on the Judiciary has concurred with them, and for a very good reason. Section 18, as originally drawn in connection with the other parts of this bill, should be amended in this respect.

Section 18, in connection with other parts of the bill, only referred to the equity powers of the courts, and we thought that it ought to go further, and that there should be an amendment saying that the things mentioned in section 18, if they were done, should not be illegal, not only as far as the equity courts were concerned but that no court should be able to lay its hands upon the members of the organizations touching the rights guaranteed in section 18.

Now I will yield to the gentleman.

Mr. GRAHAM of Pennsylvania. I understand the gentleman to say that this has been submitted to the Committee on the Judiciary and approved by it. If so, I would like to know when and under what circumstances?

Mr. HENRY. I presume it was. It was submitted to the subcommittee. I have not been in attendance on the meetings of the committee, but suppose it was submitted to the members of the general committee. But this amendment is satisfactory to the American Federation of Labor; it is satisfactory to the President of the United States; and was and is satisfactory to the chairman of the Committee on the Judiciary and the members thereof with whom I have talked; and it ought to be added at the end of section 18 so as to preserve, protect, and perpetuate the rights that are given to labor organizations in section 18, and not only prohibit courts of equity from violating those rights, but also restrain the courts of law from undoing any of those things that we have guaranteed in this section. . . .

Mr. MANN. The gentleman has stated that conferences with certain Members of the House agreed upon this amendment and submitted it to the officers of the American Federation of Labor.

Mr. HENRY. Yes.

Mr. MANN. Is it not a fact that the officers of the American Federation of Labor submitted practically this amendment to the gentleman and other gentlemen of the House before this conference met at all?

Mr. HENRY. Yes; that is true, substantially.

Mr. MANN. So that this amendment did not originate, as the gentleman would have us believe—I will not say "as the gentleman would have us believe"—but as we might believe from the gentleman's statement as to this little conference, but this amendment originated with the officers of the American Federation of Labor?

Mr. HENRY. I think those gentlemen desired this kind of an amendment. And we did agree on certain language in two amendments.

Mr. MANN. This is the amendment which the American Federation of Labor submitted to the gentleman, is it not?

Mr. HENRY. Yes.

Mr. MANN. I read:

Nor shall any of the acts specified in this paragraph be considered or held unlawful—

By the courts of the United States?

Mr. HENRY. Yes; substantially. The amendment was submitted to us, and we agreed that it was correct, and that we must organize to make a fight for it, because the affable gentleman from Illinois had said, when the rule was debated, that he proposed to vote so as to make all the mischief possible for the Democratic Party, and we did not want to be taken unawares. So we were organizing to put this amendment through.

Mr. MANN. But the amendment did not originate with the gentleman.

Mr. HENRY. Oh, well, I have no pride of personal authorship. All I say is that I stand with these men for their amendment, and they ought to be exempted from the provisions of the antitrust laws, and this right ought to be written into all these statutes.

This amendment was submitted, considered, and agreed to in the conference held in the Committee on Rules, and the gentlemen there assembled obligated themselves to support and press it. . . .

Mr. WEBB. As far as the committee are concerned, the first time we ever heard of this amendment was when it was presented to the subcommittee by Mr. DAVID J. LEWIS, of Maryland, a Member of the House.

Mr. HENRY. That is the first time you ever heard of it?

Mr. WEBB. Yes.

Mr. HENRY. I am not taking any issue with the Judiciary Committee.

Mr. WEBB. Certainly not.

Mr. HENRY. I am not going into any controversy with them; but the fact remains that the Judiciary Committee had drawn their sections, 7 and 18, and they were not satisfactory, and we were trying to get together with the Judiciary Committee and shape up this matter so as to prove our friendship for the labor forces of this country and carry out our platform demands. Now, I have no pride of authorship about anything I may have suggested and do not claim anything, but do say we do not want any vague or doubtful history hereafter, and these things ought to be stated here and written down as they occur. Now I yield to the gentleman from Tennessee.

Mr. AUSTIN. In view of a statement in the editorial columns of a Philadelphia paper this morning that the President of the United States has changed his position on this legislation, I wish to know what the gentleman knows in reference to that statement?

Mr. HENRY. Changed his position when and on what?

Mr. AUSTIN. On this labor proposition.

Mr. HENRY. I do not think the President has ever changed his position. I think the President has always been in favor of complying with the Baltimore platform and giving labor everything to which it is entitled. I do not think he has changed his position. You surprise me.

Mr. WEBB. The President has not changed his position with reference to any of these amendments that have been adopted here.

Mr. AUSTIN. What contemplated provision was it that the President threatened to veto?

Mr. HENRY. I never knew of any threats to veto. I think the gentleman must be mistaken about that. The gentleman has got his information from some wild rumor printed in a newspaper.

Mr. AUSTIN. Printed in the local press here.

Mr. HENRY. Sometimes the local press do not always state things exactly as they occur, because they do not get the correct information. They print what they believe, but sometimes they make mistakes.

Mr. AUSTIN. But the statement was also carried in the Associated Press.

Mr. HENRY. Sometimes the Associated Press is misinformed and has to correct things, and it will have to correct this, because the President is not going to veto this bill.

Mr. MURDOCK. Mr. Chairman, I move to strike out the last word.

I think the amendment just offered by the gentleman from North Carolina [Mr.

WEBB] undoubtedly strengthens this section; but there are some things about the section that I should like to discover, and I am going to address myself to the gentleman from North Carolina [Mr. WEBB].

The section has two paragraphs, and the first paragraph, which I am going to read in order to get it into the RECORD, is the paragraph fixing jurisdiction in granting exemptions. It reads as follows:

SEC. 18. That no restraining order or injunction shall be granted by any court of the United States, or a judge or the judges thereof, in any case between an employer and employees, or between employers and employees, or between employees, or between persons employed and persons seeking employment, involving, or growing out of, a dispute concerning terms or conditions of employment, unless necessary to prevent irreparable injury to property, or to a property right, of the party making the application, for which injury there is no adequate remedy at law, and such property or property right must be described with particularity in the application, which must be in writing and sworn to by the applicant or by his agent or attorney.

Now, Mr. Chairman, I have compared this paragraph with former proposals, and in the Pearre bill and in the Wilson bill as amended—

Mr. MACDONALD. And also in the Bartlett bill.

Mr. MURDOCK. The gentleman from Michigan correctly says "also in the Bartlett bill"; but not in the Clayton bill. There was included, before the word "involving," as is now found, in line 23, on page 35, the word "or," which seemed to extend the area of this provision of exemption. The exemption proposed under the terms of this bill is to extend to any case—

Between an employer and employees, or between employers and employees, or between employees, or between persons employed and persons seeking employment, involving, or growing out of, a dispute concerning terms or conditions of employment.

Now, the inclusion of the word "or" before the word "involving" would, I think, undoubtedly increase the area of the exemption granted to labor. I will not ask the gentleman to answer me just now, but I will ask him to answer me a little later on, when I have also called his attention to the fact that the second paragraph of the section is tied to the first paragraph by the inclusion of the word "such" before the word "restraining" in line 6, page 36, for the second paragraph begins as follows:

And no such restraining order or injunction shall prohibit any person or persons from terminating any relation of employment, or from ceasing to perform any work or labor, or from recommending, advising, or persuading others by peaceful means so to do; or from attending at or near a house or place where any person resides or works, or carries on business or happens to be—

And so forth.

Now, that second paragraph, while granting certain rights, is so tied to the first paragraph that there is a probability, to my mind, that you have narrowed the exemption you intended to offer, because the abuse of the injunctive process occurred, as the gentleman knows, in a majority of cases in connection with strikes; and it seems to me the relation of employer and employee ceases when there is a strike, and strikers are not included here. The strikers are no longer employees, and the exclusion of the word "or," it seems to me, takes out of the purview of the first paragraph of exemptions the right of the striker.

Mr. WEBB. No; I think the gentleman is mistaken.

Mr. MURDOCK. I hope the gentleman has followed me. I think the point has merit.

Mr. WEBB. Mr. Chairman, I am sorry that this argument appears to me to be extremely technical. I can not understand the difference.

Mr. MURDOCK. I know; but that is a general statement. I suppose the gentleman believes that he has done that in this case. In the former bills, in the amended Wilson bill and in the Pearre bill and latterly in the Bartlett bill, the word "or" was inserted before the word "involving," and that seemed to extend the exemption granted to a case of strikers, who are no longer employees. I will ask the gentleman if he believes that strikers having struck are still in the relation of employees to a former employer? They may have been discharged.

Mr. WEBB. Exactly. Then what further does the gentleman want?

Mr. MURDOCK. It does not seem to me the definitions the gentleman has given there in the first paragraph—

In any case between an employer and employees, or between employers and employees, or between employees, or between persons employed and persons seeking employment—

and so forth, includes the case of a striker. I do not believe you can find it in those classifications.

Mr. WEBB. How would the gentleman include his suggestion?

Mr. MURDOCK. By including the word "or," and making it read:

In any case between an employer and employees, etc., or involving or growing out of a dispute—

And so forth.

⊥ Mr. WEBB. We have the word "involving" in the section now.

Mr. MURDOCK. Yes; but without the word "or" preceding it you do not include strikers. . . .

Mr. [WILLIAM P.] BORLAND [D., Mo.]. Is it not sufficient where it says "or growing out of a dispute"?

Mr. MURDOCK. If the word "or" were inserted, it certainly would be, but without the word "or" I do not believe it is. I am going to ask the gentleman if he will accept that amendment?

Mr. WEBB. Mr. Chairman, I could not agree to that. I think the phrase "involving or growing out of" is sufficient. I think that would include a strike, and that is what we intend it to include.

Mr. MURDOCK. Why not be certain about it by including the word "or"?

Mr. WEBB. I think the use of that word might make it uncertain.

Mr. MURDOCK. I would like to have the gentleman explain to me in what way it would make it uncertain.

Mr. WEBB. I will say to the gentleman that we have gone over this very carefully and drawn the section, having in view the decisions on the matter, and we passed it through this Congress two years ago just as it is written, although the gentleman was not here to vote for it, I believe, by a vote of 243 to 18, and I should feel loath to change the wording of it now.

Mr. MURDOCK. Will the gentleman take time to explain to me, and I will be obliged to him if he will, how strikers are included in this definition as given at the bottom of page 35 without the inclusion of the word "or," before the word "involving"? I would like to know if an employee who has severed his connection with an employer is still an employee; and if he is, how can you include him in this paragraph?

Mr. WEBB. After he has ceased work he cares nothing more about the relation, provided he can not be compelled to go back to work, and we do not permit that in the bill. He could not be punished for persuading others to do likewise, and how would the word "or" help the situation?

Mr. MURDOCK. But these prohibitions against the use of the injunctive process are confined to the classes of cases set forth in the first paragraph of section 18, and that does not include strikers.

Mr. WEBB. It covers the entire field of strikes, primary boycott, and everything incident to a strike. . . .

Mr. [FRANK] BUCHANAN [D, Ill.]. Mr. Chairman, my understanding is that strikers are employees who are seeking work under different condtions than they were working under when they struck. Strikers are really [sic] seeking work, but they are seeking their positions back under conditions which they desire.

Mr. MURDOCK. I do not think the gentleman can read that into the proposition.

Mr. BUCHANAN of Illinois. I do not think that as long as judges are going to construe laws in the narrowest possible way against labor that we will ever get anything right.

Mr. MURDOCK. That is what I am trying to guard against. I would like to ask the gentleman from Illinois if he can read into those various definitions of classes of cases where the position of a striker is included, and if the gentleman from Illinois realizes that the second paragraph of section 18 by the use of the word "such" in line 6 may narrow the very privileges that the gentleman is trying to expand?

Mr. BUCHANAN of Illinois. I would construe or define a striker as one seeking work under different conditions. As long as he is on strike he is certainly desirous of going back to work again on different terms. He is an employee until his place is filled, and as far as my understanding of it goes, while I do not believe we ought to leave any opening at all in regard to this, because our experience is that the judge has always put a narrow construction upon it— . . .

Mr. GARDNER. Mr. Chairman, where does the gentleman from Kansas suggest the insertion of the word "or"?

Mr. MURDOCK. Before the word "involving," in line 23, page 35, and I want to say to the gentleman from Massachusetts that my point was this: I may not have made it plain. The various definitions of classes of cases immediately preceding that line in the bill do not, to my mind, include strikers, and the abuse of the injunctive process which we are seeking here to cure has in the great majority of cases arisen from strikes. . . .

Mr. GRAHAM of Pennsylvania. Would not the insertion of the word "or" before the word "involving" destroy the symmetrical construction and the real meaning of the sentence, because you must go back in reading this section to the beginning and, skipping over what I shall omit, read it in this way:

> That no restraining order or injunction shall be granted by any court of the United States, or a judge or the judges thereof, in any case involving or growing out of a dispute concerning the terms or conditions of employment.

That is what it means.

Mr. MURDOCK. Now, if the gentleman will follow me, what I am attempting to do is to read that paragraph in this way:

> SEC. 18. That no restraining order or injunction shall be granted by any court of the United States, or a judge or the judges thereof, in any case between an employer and employees, or between employers and employees, or between employees, or between persons employed and persons seeking employment, or in any case involving or growing out of a dispute—

And so forth.

In other words, we want to add another class of cases to those already in the bill.

Mr. GRAHAM of Pennsylvania. I suggest to the gentleman that he has all of that in the language of the section as it now stands, because it reads, beginning at the beginning and proceeding on to line 20—

> In any case between an employer and an employee, or between employers and employees, or between employees, or between persons employed and persons seeking employment involving or growing out of—

And so forth. . . .

Mr. FLOYD of Arkansas. I desire to state that the insertion of the word "or" before "involving" would not improve the section, but, to my mind, would complicate it. "Involving" relates back to "case," and if you insert the word "or" I do not know what it would relate to.

Mr. MURDOCK. I grant that "involving" does refer back to "case," but by the inclusion of the word "or" you would make a new class of cases and include strikers. The gentleman from Arkansas knows that under this paragraph there are several kinds of classes to which are granted exemption; that is, cases between employer and employees, between employers and employees, and between two sets of employees, and between persons employed and persons seeking employment; but none of these classes of cases, to my mind, include strikers. And it was the strike which caused this proposition to be offered.

Mr. FLOYD of Arkansas. There is where I take issue with the gentleman.

Mr. MURDOCK. Will the gentleman explain how strikers are included?

Mr. FLOYD of Arkansas. I will give the gentleman my construction of it.

Mr. MURDOCK. I would like to hear it.

Mr. FLOYD of Arkansas. The provision reads:

SEC. 18. That no restraining order or injunction shall be granted by any court of the United States, or a judge or the judges thereof, in any case between an employer and employees, or between employers and employees, or between employees, or between persons employed and persons seeking employment, involving, or growing out of, a dispute concerning terms or conditions of employment—

And so forth.

I think in every case of a strike where the purpose of the strike relates to the terms and conditions of employment it is included in the language of the bill. I can not agree with the gentleman from Kansas that when strikers temporarily quit work, demanding better terms and conditions before they resume, that the relation of employer and employee has ceased. It may have ceased temporarily, but this broad language used in the provision would undoubtedly include them.

Mr. MURDOCK. I hope the gentleman is right. . . .

Mr. GARDNER. Now, will the gentleman from Kansas listen to me? He wishes to insert the word "or" before the word "involving," and that would make the clause read as follows:

SEC. 18. That no restraining order or injunction shall be granted * * * in any case * * * between employees * * * or involving or growing out of a dispute—

And so forth.

In other words, if an employee had a case against another employee, no matter what the cause, whether a labor dispute or anything else, under the gentleman's amendment no restraining order could issue. I believe the gentleman from Kansas is correct when he says that strikers are not employees; but I suggest an amendment which I think may fix it properly. In line 21, after the word "employees," insert the words "or persons seeking employment," so as to read:

That no restraining order shall issue in any case between employer and employees or persons seeking employment.

If the men were on strike, they would be seeking employment. Would not that amendment remove the difficulty?

Mr. MURDOCK. I suppose it would if you define persons seeking employment as referring to strikers. Yes; I think it would.

Mr. GARDNER. The same amendment must also be inserted in line 21, after the word "employees." I think if the gentlemen on the Judiciary Committee will turn their minds to the matter they will see that there is something in the contention of the gentleman from Kansas. . . .

Mr. [GEORGE E.] GORMAN [D., Ill.]. I have listened to the discussion with a great deal of interest, and have given some study and thought to the question. I have discussed it also with some Members. I had in mind, when the committee amendment was disposed of, to suggest an amendment which I hope the committee will adopt. I think the gentleman from Kansas has suggested a weakness that ought to be corrected. The amendment I had in mind to propose is, on page 35, line 21, after the word "employee," insert "or persons between whom the relation of employer and employee is temporarily suspended because of a strike or lockout."

As I view it, a man on a strike has not necessarily terminated his employment, but the employment is temporarily suspended. But it might be construed that it was a complete cessation.

Mr. WEBB. He is seeking employment.

Mr. GORMAN. It might be construed differently.

Mr. MURDOCK. I think the gentleman's amendment would include my suggestion.

Mr. DICKINSON. Mr. Chairman, if the gentleman will yield. I want to call attention to the language that strikes me may cover the situation. On page 35, line 23, suppose you were to add the words "or desiring" between the word "seeking" and the word "employment," in line 23. Would not that help the situation?

Mr. MURDOCK. I did not catch the language.

Mr. DICKINSON. In line 23, before the word "employment," insert "or desiring," so it shall read "seeking or desiring employment." I do not think that parties who are not either seeking employment or desiring employment, but who are simply creating trouble without wanting employment, ought to have any protection under this law, but those seeking or desiring employment should be protected.

Mr. MURDOCK. That would introduce a new element, and I am not prepared to say whether I would like it or not.

Mr. DICKINSON. If you put in the word "desiring" or "wanting employment," that would broaden it and cover that class of men who would strike and want employment, but leaves out that class of men who are trying to interfere between the employer and employee and do not want to work at all, and I suggest the addition of the words "or desiring employment."

Mr. DECKER. Mr. Chairman, I would like to ask the gentleman from Kansas if he would not make that plainer and entirely clear it up, and I would like to have the attention of the gentleman from Massachusetts [Mr. GARDNER] in connection with the point he raised. Would it not be better to insert, before "involving," the following words: "or in any case," so that the section would then read:

> That no restraining order or injunction shall issue in any case between the employer and employees or between employers and employees or between employees, or between persons employed and persons seeking employment, or in any case involving or growing out of a dispute—

And so forth. Now, the reason for that is this: As I understand this section, the word "involving" modifies the words "in any case." . . .

I will move to strike out the last word. Mr. Chairman, the trouble with the section, and the only trouble, is the word "involving" modifies the words "in any case," but being at the end of the paragraph and so far from the words "in any case," it might, at first reading, be thought to modify the word "employment," which it follows, and so I think the amendment should be "or in any case," inserted before the word "involving." . . .

Mr. GARDNER. Now, Mr. Chairman, I move to strike out the last two words. The amendment suggested by the gentleman from Missouri is the same amendment suggested by the gentleman from Kansas, only in a different form. It has the effect of which I complained in the case of the amendment offered by the gentleman from Kansas. The effect of inserting the language which the gentleman suggests would be that no restraining order could be granted by any court of the United States in any case between employees, whether the dispute referred to a labor difficulty or to some other kind of difficulty.

The result of the gentleman's wording is the same as the result of the wording suggested by the gentleman from Kansas. It would forbid the issuing of a restraining order in any case between employees, no matter what the cause was. The dispute might perhaps refer to the blocking of a water course. I suggest to the gentleman from Missouri that perhaps the words "or persons seeking employment" would not cover strikers inasmuch as strikers would not necessarily be seeking employment. Not being a lawyer, I feel a good deal of doubt as to my wisdom in making suggestions of this sort, but I suggest, in order to clear up this section and to leave the wording beyond peradventure of a doubt, that the members of the Judiciary Committee ought to insert some words in this section which would embrace strikers engaged in contest with their employers under the significance of the word "employees." . . .

Mr. HULINGS. What is the gentleman's idea of the effect if you simply strike out all in line 20 after the word "case" down to and including the word "employment," in line 23, so that it would read:

> That no restraining order or injunction shall be granted by any court of the United States, or a judge or the judges thereof, in any case involving or growing out of a dispute concerning terms or conditions of employment.

Mr. GARDNER. Now, I am not at all sure but what that is a solution of the whole question. . . .

Mr. PHELAN. Let me ask the gentleman if this will not take care of the whole thing? By changing the order of this clause what it really means is this:

That in any case involving or growing out of a dispute concerning terms or conditions of employment between employer and employee—

And so forth.

Now, that covers the case of strikers, because the case originally grows out of a dispute between the employer and employee. I think that is just what it means, but the order of the words should be changed for clearness. It says in any case between employer, and so forth, whereas it means a dispute arising between employer and employee concerning terms or conditions of employment.

Mr. GARDNER. I see the gentleman's point, and it strikes me as being very ingenious. The dispute, of course, must have originated when the strikers were still employees.

Mr. PHELAN. The case where a dispute arises is in the case of a strike. If the word "employee" does not include a striker, it does not mean anything in this case, but it would simply mean there shall not be a restraining order between an employee and the man at present employed.

Now, if you change the order of that wording I believe the whole thing will be taken care of and there will be no misunderstanding.

Mr. GARDNER. The gentleman is right in the idea that when the dispute arose it was between the employer and employees, but it has been suggested by one of the gentlemen near me that many times people are engaged in a strike who never were employees of the employer with whom the dispute arose. At the same time, so long as the whole matter arises out of a dispute between employers and employees, it seems to me that that is where the suggestion of the gentleman from Massachusetts is pertinent, and that is what we are trying to arrive at.

Mr. PHELAN. The section does not say you shall not have a restraining order against employees. It says you shall not have a restraining order where a dispute arose between employers and employees, and it does not classify those against whom the order is to be made.

Mr. GARDNER. I think the gentleman's idea is a good one. . . .

Mr. MANN. Mr. Chairman, we were told by the distinguished gentleman from Texas [Mr. HENRY] that this amendment had been submitted to the President, and met his approval. We have not yet been told by the distinguished gentleman from Kansas [Mr. MURDOCK] that this amendment has been submitted to Col. Roosevelt [laughter], although a few days ago the papers all carried the statements, repeated day after day, that the gentleman from Kansas and the members of the Progressive Party were going over to New York to find out what their attitude was on these labor amendments. [Laughter.]

We know that the Democratic side of the House does not know what its attitude is until the matter has been submitted to the President, and we were told that the Progressive Members of the House did not know what their attitude was until they had had a chance to consult Col. Roosevelt. Evidently, when the gentleman from Kansas went over and saw "the colonel" he did not derive very much comfort and did not get the information which he sought on this labor amendment, for yesterday, when the gentleman from Michigan [Mr. MACDONALD] offered an amendment to exempt all labor organizations and farmers' organizations from the operation of the antitrust laws, his colleague from Michigan [Mr. WOODRUFF], the other Progressive Member from that State, did not vote with him, and the chairman of the Congressional committee of the Progressive Party, a very distinguished gentleman of this House, for whom I have a high regard, my colleague [Mr. HINEBAUGH], did not vote with the gentleman from Michigan on his amendment. So I take it that when my friend from Kansas [Mr. MURDOCK] went to New York and asked "the colonel" what the gentleman from Kansas thought [laughter] on the subject of these labor amendments the colonel was not able to tell the gentleman from Kansas, and hence the Progressive Party yesterday was split up the back. [Laughter and applause.] . . .

Mr. MURDOCK. I know the gentleman from Illinois is a very busy man. I will ask him if he has ever read the Progressive platform on this proposition?

Mr. MANN. Oh, that would not make any difference, whether I had or not.

Mr. MURDOCK. The platform is very specific, and I want to say to the gentleman from Illinois, if he will let me answer all his question [sic], that "the colonel" stands on the Progressive platform, and the Progressive platform is all right.

Mr. MANN. How was it, then, that yesterday, when the gentleman from Michigan [Mr. MACDONALD] offered an amendment and voted one way, the other gentleman from Michigan [Mr. WOODRUFF], his compatriot Progressive, voted the other way, and that the gentleman from Kansas [Mr. MURDOCK], the leader of his party on the floor, voted one way and the gentleman from Illinois [Mr. HINEBAUGH], the chairman of the congressional committee of the Progressive Party, voted the other way? [Laughter.] Evidently they did not know how to read the Progressive platform [laughter], or else in that respect, as in many others, no one can tell, after reading it, what it means. [Renewed laughter.]

Mr. MURDOCK. Will the gentleman let me answer that question? He has asked the question why there was a division.

Mr. MANN. I have not asked any question. I have commented upon a fact, though if the gentleman denies the fact I will yield to him. . . .

Mr. MURDOCK. I will answer the gentleman's question by saying that the members of the Progressive Party, unlike those of the Republican Party and the Democratic Party, are not hog tied in this House. They vote their own sentiments. That is the genius of our party.

Mr. MANN. Exactly. [Laughter.]

Mr. MURDOCK. We leave the individual free.

Mr. MANN. Yes

Mr. MURDOCK. But I would make this exception, that the gentleman from Illinois—if the gentleman will permit me—

Mr. MANN. I would like to have a little of my own time. The gentleman from Kansas says that the Progressives vote their sentiments. That is true; but they do not know what their sentiments are until after the gentleman from Kansas goes over to New York and asks "the colonel" what the gentleman from Kansas thinks. [Laughter.] . . .

Mr. TOWNER. Mr. Chairman, referring again to the matter in controversy, I want to call the attention of the committee to this fact: I think the gentleman from Kansas [Mr. MURDOCK] was undoubtedly right in his contention; but I think he is wrong, and others are wrong, in saying that the phrase and others following it "involving or growing out of" refers back to "any case." If that were true, then there would be no necessity for the disjunctive "or."

But I call the gentleman's attention to this fact, that this is a prohibition against any restraining order being granted in cases, first, of a dispute between an employer and employee; second, between employers and employees; third, between employees; fourth, or between persons employed and persons seeking employment.

Now, if you desire another class, you will have to use another disjunctive "or," else the words following it are only qualifying or limiting words to the phrase:

Or between persons employed and persons seeking employment.

There is no question whatever about the grammatical effect of the words—

Involving or growing out of a dispute concerning terms or conditions of employment.

As it now is, it limits the statement immediately preceding "or between persons employed or persons seeking employment," because the words "or between persons employed and persons seeking employment" are one clause, and you should have following that the words "or in cases involving or growing out of a dispute concerning terms or conditions of employment" if you wish the section really to mean what you intend it to mean. I call the attention of the committee also to this fact, that however this may be interpreted, you certainly ought not to allow the comma to follow "of" in line 23, page 35. If you leave it there, it will further cloud the meaning of the section and ⊥ give rise to further controversy that may be disastrous. There is no reason for the insertion of the comma. As it is, it breaks the clause and makes its application uncertain. . . .

Mr. FLOYD of Arkansas. I desire to transpose the language so as to give the meaning as I understand it, without changing the wording, except transposing the words:

> SEC. 18. That no restraining order or injunction shall be granted by any court of the United States, or a judge or the judges thereof, in any case involving or growing out of a dispute concerning terms or conditions of employment between an employer and employees, or between employers and employees, or between employees, or between persons employed and persons seeking employment, unless necessary to prevent irreparable injury to property—

And so forth. That is exactly what it means as it is written; but by transposing the words you get the meaning more clearly.

Mr. TOWNER. I think if the gentleman will transpose those words it might have the effect that he desires, although—

Mr. FLOYD of Arkansas. That is what it means now. The word "involving" modifies the word "case" and nothing else.

Mr. TOWNER. No; the gentleman is mistaken about that. You can not take a lot of instances which are marked off from one another by the word "or" and then have these words "involving or growing out of a dispute" follow one of those disjunctive instances, without limiting its application to that disjunctive instance. That is very clear. It will serve the purpose the gentleman desires if he places it where he has just read it, because then it would not follow or modify or limit one of those clauses.

Mr. FLOYD of Arkansas. The purpose was to make the phrase "involving or growing out of a dispute" modify the word "case." We understand that is what it means now, and we are perfectly willing to transpose the words as indicated.

Mr. TOWNER. It might serve the purpose intended by transposition, but certainly it does not do so now.

Mr. FLOYD of Arkansas. The committee is convinced that that is what it means.

Mr. VOLSTEAD. Mr. Chairman, I offer an amendment.

The CHAIRMAN. The gentleman from Minnesota offers an amendment, which the Clerk will report. Without objection, the amendment will be considered as pending.

The Clerk read as follows:

> Page 36, at the end of the amendment offered by Mr. WEBB, add the words "but nothing in this act shall be construed to permit a secondary boycott."

Mr. VOLSTEAD. Mr. Chairman, I desire to call attention to this language, so that members of this committee may know just what they are voting for. I will read it, omitting matters not pertinent, so as to call to the attention of the committee the point I have in mind. The second paragraph of this section reads:

> No injunction shall prohibit any person from ceasing to patronize or to employ any party to such dispute, or from recommending, advising, or persuading others by peaceful means so to do.

That is the plain reading of the provision. In the light of decisions that we have had on the subject of a secondary boycott, can it be questioned that the amendment offered by the gentleman from North Carolina [Mr. WEBB] will legalize the secondary boycott? I want this House to know just what is proposed, so there can be no dispute in the future as to the attitude that we are assuming. While I have always strongly sympathized with labor, may not friends of labor hesitate? With this amendment we shall erase from the statute books practically every Federal law that can reach organized labor or any kind of labor. Is that what we desire? If it is, let us be frank enough to say so. There are two sides to this proposition.

If there is to be no law to protect property or the man who seeks to labor, if the courts are to be deprived of their power to protect property and personal rights, the only thing left is civil war. How long do you suppose the public is going to submit to such a program. A strike does not only injure the parties engaged in it. The community in which it occurs suffers severely. I recall very vividly the effect of the coal strike that occurred some ten or twelve years ago. The suffering which the country endured was very great. Should another strike of that kind occur, in what condition would we be in the absence of any law to protect persons or property and in the absence of the restraining influence of the courts? Would not public indignation write upon the statute books far more drastic laws than anything now complained of. It is true that State laws will apply to and condemn many acts, but such laws can not protect the free flow of interstate commerce, and without such commerce the country must suffer severely. Those who refuse to protect the people now may not then find it easy to explain their course.

Do we want to place ourselves in the attitude of exempting any class of our citizens from the operation of the law that applies to other citizens? It seems to me that this is the real question that is before this House, and one that you can not avoid or dodge. It seems to me that we ought to face it as it is, and not pretend that this section means something different from its plain reading. I have asked you to write an amendment into this act so as to make it plain that it means what you say it means. I do not believe the President will sign this bill with a provision in it which legalizes the secondary boycott. I do not believe any such law can be constitutional. A person not a party to the dispute may be absolutely ruined by such a boycott. Is he to have no remedy under the laws of this land?

Mr. [JAMES P.] MAHER [D., N.Y.]. Will the gentleman state what his opinion is of a secondary boycott?

Mr. VOLSTEAD. I can not go into that; it has been discussed in the courts, and it has always been condemned. I do not know that there ever was a decision in its favor.

Mr. MAHER. Some people do not know just what it means. I would like to have the gentleman's idea of a secondary boycott.

Mr. VOLSTEAD. A secondary boycott affects and injures a party not concerned in the dispute.

Mr. MAHER. In case of a dispute between railroad employees on a trolley road and their employers, where an employer locks them out, as it were, issues an order that on and after a certain day they will not be employed on account of their connection with a labor organization, and the merchant on the outside doing business down town takes the part of the employer and patronizes the employer, is he not taking the part of a secondary boycott?

Mr. VOLSTEAD. I am not going into a discussion of the different phases of a secondary boycott. The question of what is a secondary boycott is pretty well understood.

Mr. MAHER. It is from one side.

Mr. VOLSTEAD. I have not the time to go into it more fully. . . .

Mr. MOORE. The gentleman has been dealing with the secondary boycott in which property rights may be invaded, and where the injured party may not be concerned in the dispute between capital and labor. Will the gentleman explain what is meant by this language, on page 36, line 10:

And no such restraining order or injunction—

And so forth—

shall prohibit any person or persons from attending at or near a house or place where any person resides or works or carries on business or happens to be—

And so forth.

Does that mean any person or persons, organized or unorganized, may assemble in or at the house of a workingman?

Mr. VOLSTEAD. Yes; and in as large numbers as they choose.

Mr. MOORE. And interfere with his peace and right of employment. Is not that an invasion of personal liberty, to say nothing of the invasion of the rights of property? Does not this tend to restrict the liberty and labor of the person owning or occupying that house?

Mr. VOLSTEAD. I think it does. Mr. Chairman, I ask the other side to consume some of its time.

Mr. MOORE. I understood the gentleman to say that it does restrict personal liberty?

VOLSTEAD. Yes; it may. The fear inspired by large numbers may and often is as effective as the actual force, though no actual force is used.

Mr. WEBB. Mr. Chairman, I should vote for the amendment offered by the gentleman from Minnesota if I were not perfectly satisfied that it is taken care of in this section. The language the gentleman reads does not authorize the secondary boycott, and he could not torture it into any such meaning. While it does authorize persons to cease to patronize the party to the dispute and to recommend to others to cease to patronize that same party to the dispute, that is not a secondary boycott, and you can not possibly make it mean a secondary boycott. Therefore this section does not authorize the secondary boycott.

I say again—and I speak for, I believe, practically every member of the Judiciary Committee—that if this section did legalize the secondary boycott there would not be a man vote [sic] for it. It is not the purpose of the committee to authorize it, and I do not think any person in this House wants to do it. We confine the boycotting to the parties to the dispute, allowing parties to cease to patronize that party and to ask others to cease to patronize the party to the dispute.

⊥9659 ⊥ Mr. MOORE. I call the gentleman's attention to line 10, page 36, where one of the privileges against which restraining orders may not issue is "attending at or near a house or place where any person resides or works or carries on business or happens to be." Does not that mean an invasion of the constitutional right of the citizen, and that men, organized or unorganized, embittered against one of their number or prejudiced in the extreme, may sit on the doorstep in your house and discuss with your wife while she is preparing the evening meal your right to work?

Mr. WEBB. Oh, my friend does not mean to put that language in, because it is ridiculous.

Mr. MOORE. That is what it seems to say.

Mr. WEBB. I will not say ridiculous, but it is an absurd conclusion to draw from this language.

Mr. MOORE. You gentlemen, as lawyers, know that you have to take the text, and you propose to put this language into law. Now, I will not say the Federation of Labor, because I believe that to be a law-abiding body, but the Industrial Workers of the World. Under this paragraph they may go to your house or attend "at or near your house"—

Mr. WEBB. It does not say that they may go into a man's castle.

Mr. MOORE. You may have a little garden around your house, and they can go into that garden, and that is "at" your house.

Mr. WEBB. It does not say that you can go onto the premises that you are forbidden to enter. That is a man's castle and sacred all over the world where the Anglo-Saxon tongue is spoken. We do not authorize anything like taking charge of a man's home. A man can do these things to-day, if he does it in a peaceful way.

Mr. MOORE. We have recently heard of "gun men" going to a man's premises, revolvers in their pockets, "peacefully" to persuade a man not to go to work until some understanding has been had with him; and that in cities, where the people are packed together, not out in the country. I do not lay this to legitimate labor unions.

Mr. WEBB. What did the gentleman's city authorities do under those circumstances?

Mr. MOORE. Oh, the police authorities, if they can reach such men, do it.

Mr. WEBB. Do what?

Mr. MOORE. Seize the gun men.

Mr. WEBB. They can do the same thing under this act.

Mr. MOORE. I question whether they could in certain interstate relations.

Mr. WEBB. Mr. Chairman. I decline to yield further. My friend refuses to read the further portion of this same sentence.

Mr. MOORE. I know this pertains to a Federal injunction.

Mr. WEBB. It says for the purpose of peacefully obtaining or communicating information or of peacefully persuading any person to work or to abstain from work. The idea of peacefully assembling runs all the way through this entire section, and unless it is done peacefully it is in violation of the law.

Mr. MOORE. I understand the peaceful part of it thoroughly; but suppose we take the instance of Tarrytown, N. Y., and substitute a workman who is earning two or three dollars a day for John D. Rockefeller, jr. I presume he would be entitled to some protection. I presume the cause of the trouble did not originate in Tarrytown, N. Y., but out in Colorado.

Mr. WEBB. And does the gentleman want to deny to the laboring man—

Mr. MOORE. And I presume in that case your Federal injunction—

Mr. WEBB. Mr. Chairman, I decline to yield further, unless the gentleman will permit me to ask him a question or to answer one of his.

Mr. MOORE. This is a very important question, and the gentleman has limited the time for debate.

Mr. WEBB. Would the gentleman deny to a laborer or to any other person in the United States the right to peacefully assemble and discuss his grievance?

Mr. MOORE. I certainly would not.

Mr. WEBB. Then the gentleman should vote for this section.

Mr. MOORE. But I would vote to sustain the humblest individual in his right to have his home protected.

Mr. WEBB. This section does that, because it does not include the criminal law of the land.

Mr. MOORE. I think the gentleman can not have had very much experience with "peaceful persuasion."

Mr. WEBB. Whether it be a laboring man or a lawyer or a merchant or a banker who violates the law, the law will consider him.

Mr. MOORE. And when you permit the Industrial Workers of the World, who have a pretty broad field—and it is said that they also operate in Europe, where we can not reach them—to camp on the gentleman's doorstep in North Carolina, or on that of some laboring man who may not agree with them, it might be that he would like to have some court to go to when he found he was unable to protect himself. He ought to have some place to go.

Mr. WEBB. I want to tell the gentleman that we have courts to go to to protect ourselves under those circumstances, and if the gentleman has not in Pennsylvania, I invite him to come down to North Carolina.

Mr. MOORE. I am going to say something about the industrial conditions in the gentleman's State in a day or two, but I am referring now to the Industrial Workers of the World and others who may or may not respect the law.

Mr. WEBB. Does the gentleman mean the "I won't work" people?

Mr. MOORE. I believe the gentleman to be the friend of labor, as I believe all of us want to be, but I think most men in a great House like this, a deliberative assembly of the people's representatives, ought to be fair to all labor. We ought to deal with all of the workers of the land without specializing a few. It is a question whether under the badge of organization we are bound to pass laws here covering 30,000,000 wage earners in this country, most of whom are unorganized and not represented here at all. I question whether the hundred millions of people of this country do not look to this Congress to deal fairly with every man who has a right to protection under the Constitution of the United States.

Mr. WEBB. Mr. Chairman, while I like to hear my friend talk—

Mr. MOORE. Oh, I know, and thank the gentleman, but I have gotten in a little of something that ought to be said.

Mr. WEBB. After that beautiful piece of eloquence, I will ask the gentleman if he did not vote for the amendment which I offered yesterday?

Mr. MOORE. Which amendment?

Mr. WEBB. The amendment providing for the exemption of labor organizations and farmers' organizations.

Mr. MOORE. I was not here yesterday when that vote was taken. There are certain legal phases of that question which are open to dispute, but if I believed his amendment was in favor of a legal classification of labor against other classes of labor, I would have voted against it. . . .

Mr. MURDOCK. Mr. Chairman, I do not think the gentleman completed that colloquy. The gentleman from Pennsylvania [Mr. MOORE] indicates that he might have done differently from the other 207 of us.

Mr. MOORE. I think the 207 ran away like a flock of sheep yesterday. They were terrorized, too much terrorized to do the business of this country for a hundred million people, rather than for the few gentlemen who seem to hold this House in the hollow of their hands.

Mr. MURDOCK. The gentleman, then, would have voted against this proposition?

Mr. MOORE. I think I would have voted against almost anything the gentleman from Kansas brought in, because he does not know legislation or the rights of the people. . . .

Mr. MACDONALD. Mr. Chairman, just a word in regard to what the gentleman from Illinois had to say, facetiously, I presume, as to the position of the Progressive Party upon the amendment yesterday. In view of the fact of the condition of the Republican Party upon this trust legislation, as is shown by the varying minority reports that are filed by the Republican members of the Judiciary Committee, it seems to me that it ill becomes the gentleman from Illinois to comment upon any diversity of opinion upon any branch of this subject.

Mr. Chairman, the amendment that has been suggested here by a number of gentlemen, involving the use of the word "or" in line 23, unmistakably makes a new class of cases that will be included if the word "or" or language substantially accomplishing the same purpose is inserted. And I want to call attention again to the fact that has been mentioned by my colleague from Kansas, and that is that this becomes doubly important in view of the use of the word "such" in line 6 of the next paragraph, because by the use of the word "such" in line 6, the next paragraph—

Mr. CLINE. Will the gentleman yield?

Mr. MACDONALD. I just want to finish this. The equity power conferred in this part of the law is limited absolutely to four classes laid down in paragraph 1, and if you leave out the word "or," or its equivalent, you limit these cases to four classes only, and you leave out cases where strikes exist; but if you put the word "or," or its equivalent, in you make it five classes and include these cases. . . .

Mr. WEBB. What other case can the gentleman imagine could be included in this? Any case involved or growing out of a suit concerning terms or condition of employment. Does not that cover the whole range of strikes, employment, wages, hours of labor, and so forth?

Mr. MACDONALD. It says in any case growing out of a dispute between persons employed and persons seeking employment. Now, it has been argued, and I think it is true, that a person on strike or after he has struck or has been discharged is not a person seeking employment.

Mr. WEBB. He is seeking employment—that is why he strikes.

Mr. MACDONALD. But the language says, "or between persons employed and persons seeking employment," and the previous language is "in any case between an employer and employees or between employers and employees or between employees." Now, the use of the disjunctive makes a new class named herein, and clearly includes all involved in disputes of the character described in the language that follows.

Mr. WEBB. That is where the gentleman and I differ. It covers every case involving or covering every phase of employment.

Mr. MACDONALD. I desire to offer, and I shall offer, an amendment, page 35, line 23, after the word "employment," to insert the following: "In the case where a strike or lockout exists or is threatened, or in any other case"; and also, when we reach it, I wish to offer an amendment to strike out the word "such," in line 6, page 36. . . .

The CHAIRMAN. Without objection, the amendment offered by the gentleman from Michigan will be reported for information.

The Clerk read as follows:

Page 35, line 23, after the word "employment," insert the following: "In the case where a strike or lockout exists or is threatened, or in any other case."

The Clerk reported a second amendment of Mr. MACDONALD, as follows:

Page 36, line 6, strike out the word "such."

Mr. HULINGS. Mr. Chairman, the facetiae of the gentleman from Illinois indicates that the Democratic Party has all its inspirations from the gentleman at the White House. It seems to me he seems to indicate, in his opinion, that the gentleman from Kansas [Mr. MURDOCK] trails after Col. Roosevelt, and he gets his inspiration there and he spreads that among the members of the Progressive Party. Well, if this were true, it must be conceded that the Democrats have a good man to go to [applause on the Democratic side], and the Progressives have a good man to go to, but where in the world do the Republicans themselves have to go? [Laughter and applause.] It seems to me they have to go to the classic shades of Yale to get inspiration from a dead one. [Laughter and applause.] He charges the Progressives have no consistency, and for heaven sake if there ever was any inconsistency is not it demonstrated in the Republican ranks on this side, where a great many of them have been elected as Progressives, indorsing that platform and agreeing to stand by that platform, and coming down here and going in with the same old gang.

Mr. GREEN of Iowa. And a good many Progressives have been elected as Republicans who did not stand by that party.

Mr. MURDOCK. This is Exhibit A.

Mr. HULINGS. This is Exhibit A and that is Exhibit B. [Laughter.] Mr. Chairman, aside from jesting, and I want you to understand there is a whole lot of truth in that jest, but aside from that, referring to the thing right in point, it seems to me that all of this controversy can be set aside by striking out, in line 20, after the word "case" on page 35, down to and including the word "employment" in line 23, so that the language will read:

That no restraining order or injunction shall be granted by any court of the United States, etc., in any case involving, or growing out of, a dispute concerning terms or conditions of employment—

And so forth.

Now, without any question, there may be cases in which injunctions will be applied for as against or involving persons who are not employees, because when a labor organization orders a strike and men cease to work and march out they are in no sense employees. They may be joined by men who never were the employees of the party seeking the injunction, who are the very ones doing the things complained of. But the suggestion I make here would leave out all difficulty of that kind. You would include every person in any case involving or growing out of a dispute concerning terms or conditions of employment. I wish to bring that to the attention of the committee, and especially the gentleman from North Carolina, because I believe it will commend itself to him as a reasonable, rational, and very clear exposition of what is intended in this section. I yield back the balance of my time. . . .

Mr. Chairman, I desire to send this amendment to the desk and ask to have it read for information.

The CHAIRMAN. Without objection, the Clerk will report the amendment for information.

The Clerk read as follows:

Amendment by Mr. HULINGS:
Page 35, line 20, after the word "case," strike out all down to and including the word "employment," in line 23. . . .

Mr. MURDOCK. Mr. Chairman, I hope some one will send for the gentleman from Pennsylvania [Mr. MOORE]. Can not the gentleman yield to me later when he gets back?

Mr. HULINGS. I suggest the gentleman from Kansas go after him.

Mr. MURDOCK. No; I will let him come back. . . .

Mr. WEBB. Mr. Chairman, just one word. It is quite evident that Members of the House have a wide difference of opinion as to this particular section, and I want to say the committee has worked over it again and again and again, we have gone over it for two years, and that this particular language in this particular section has been indorsed probably by every labor union in the United States. It is an excerpt from what is known as the Bacon-Bartlett bill, and it covers in a proper way, we think, every possible angle of the strike situation. We think any sensible man will agree that a striker is a person who seeks employment, otherwise he would not strike, and those are the ones we ought to take care of, at least the labor organizations of America think so, and I trust that the committee will leave the section as it is. If you begin changing the section I do not know where it will land us.

Mr. HULINGS. Mr. Chairman, will the gentleman yield?

The CHAIRMAN. Does the gentleman from North Carolina yield to the gentleman from Pennsylvania?

Mr. WEBB. Yes.

Mr. HULINGS. What would you think, then, of the application of the section in a case of this kind. You are an employer of labor; your men cease work; I am in sympathy with them; I never was in your employment, and I do not seek any employment, but I go in and make common cause with them against you, and you take me into court. What would you do in that case?

Mr. WEBB. You would have no business hanging around there. You would have no business "butting in," if you are not a party in the dispute. That is labor's own cause, and if the employer and the employee grip on the proposition, we will take care of that.

Mr. HULINGS. In a section later you justify me in going in and making common cause against them. . . .

Mr. ALEXANDER. In the case mentioned by the gentleman from Pennsylvania this writ of injunction would not apply at all. This injunction would go against other people?

Mr. WEBB. Certainly. We want to confine the language to the parties to the dispute, and no others. . . .

Mr. GARDNER. The gentleman says that he thinks the language "persons seeking employment" covers persons on strike?

Mr. WEBB. Yes, sir. That is the opinion of the committee.

Mr. GARDNER. But section 18 does not mention disputes between "employers and persons seeking employment."

Mr. WEBB. Oh, yes. I think that is covered.

Mr. GARDNER. Oh, no. The wording relates to cases "between persons employed and persons seeking employment."

Mr. WEBB. I think that is covered.

Mr. GARDNER. Oh, no. A dispute between "persons employed and persons seeking employment" is a very different proposition from a dispute between employers and people seeking employment. There might be something in the gentleman's contention if the clause referred to cases "between employers and persons seeking employment." I call the gentleman's attention to line 22, which refers to cases "between persons employed and persons seeking employment." I think that that clause refers to disputes between persons known as "scabs" and the usual force of employees in any establishment.

Mr. WEBB. I do not know what you mean by "scabs," but it says "between persons employed and persons seeking employment."

Mr. GARDNER. It is all qualified by what goes before it. What is your objection to extending the definition of the word "employees" by a proviso at the end of the section. I suggest something like this: "The term 'employees' in this section shall be held to include persons whose status as employees has been suspended by a strike or lockout." What is your objection to that?

Mr. WEBB. You might weaken the section by doing it. . . .

Mr. MURDOCK. Mr. Chairman, the gentleman from Pennsylvania [Mr. MOORE] this morning took occasion to drive up to my front door and leave a bouquet. [Laughter.] I want to make acknowledgment of the fact.

Mr. MOORE. There were some thorns among the roses. [Laughter.]

Mr. MURDOCK. If the gentleman will permit me to go on, I will yield to him later. The gentleman from Pennsylvania makes a general charge of cowardice against the membership of Congress. When asked the simple question how he would have voted yesterday had he been here, he followed the characteristic Republican attitude, and dodged. How would the gentleman from Pennsylvania have voted in the House yesterday? Will the gentleman answer the question and stop dodging?

Mr. MOORE. If I had thought that a vote "aye" would have meant to specialize a certain class of the 30,000,000 of workers in this country, I would not have voted "aye," nor would I have played the game of buncombe which has been played since this agitation began.

Mr. MURDOCK. The gentleman from Pennsylvania typifies the political situation that prevails in the country. "Truth is mighty and will prevail." There is talk in New York and in Washington, with the aid of the press, in San Francisco and St. Louis, of amalgamation between the Progressive Party and the Republican Party. Do you think there is any chance of amalgamation between a set of men who want to go forward and a set of men, typified by the gentleman from Pennsylvania, who evade, dodge, and sidestep on everything? [Laughter and applause.]

Mr. MOORE. Mr. Chairman—

Mr. MURDOCK. The gentleman from Illinois [Mr. MANN] also demonstrates this morning, I think, the situation of the country, and proves that there is no prospect of harmony between the Progressive and Republican Parties. The gentleman from Illinois typifies by his charge against me—facetious enough in its way—precisely what has been the matter with him in the last six or seven years with respect to the political situation. He did not consult Col. Roosevelt enough. By having consulted Col. Roosevelt a little more he and his party would be—well, somewhere else than on the road to destruction and decay, as it is. [Laughter.] Col. Roosevelt can not be justly accused of dodging or evading any public question.

The three parties are shown precisely as they stand before the Nation in the attitude of the gentleman from Pennsylvania [Mr. MOORE], that of the gentleman from Illinois [Mr. MANN], and that of the gentleman from North Carolina [Mr. WEBB] and the Progressives on this floor. For a matter of four or five years, to my knowledge, under the leadership of Mr. Taft, backed up by the gentleman from Illinois [Mr. MANN], the reactionaries here and at the other end of this building absolutely locked away in committee every bit of remedial legislation that labor wanted. Every man within the sound of my voice knows that that is true.

In those days every time we succeeded in getting an amendment in favor of the exemption of organized labor we had to do it by revolution, over the protest and veto of the Republican leader in this country, Mr. Taft, and I think sometimes over a rather serious protest from the gentleman from Illinois [Mr. MANN], although I am not certain about that.

The Democrats came into power with a plain pledge in their platform to exempt labor, after a record of amendments in the House and Senate which gave in terms exemption. And what did the Democrats do? Why, they have followed their usual plan of action and have brought into the House for the indorsement of the Members an amendment that is ambiguous. If you put the Progressives in power, Mr. Chairman, we will not dodge as the Republicans have dodged, we will not be ambiguous as the Democrats have been ambiguous; we will bring in an exemption clause that will mean business. . . .

Mr. MOORE. Mr. Chairman, I have not dodged any issue, and I have not waited for a nod from the galleries to determine how I shall vote, as the gentleman from Kansas has persistently done throughout this debate. . . .

. . . I have not even changed the RECORD, as the gentleman from Kansas [Mr. MURDOCK] has done this morning. After pleasing our labor friends in the galleries by frequent glances up that way, and by smiles and nods, and after referring to the National Association of Manufacturers, possibly forgetting that the late Progressive candidate for governor in Massachusetts, Mr. Bird, was not only a Progressive but a leading member of the Manufacturers' Association which he denounced, and for which denunciation he received applause, the gentleman from Kansas changed the RECORD this morning so that instead of calling that association the "corrupt" National Association of Manufacturers he has, with Col. Bird, the Progressive, in mind, changed it to the "powerful" National Association of Manufacturers. I do not have to correct the RECORD in that way, because I am not constantly watching what Mr. Gompers and Mr. Morrison and that able band of labor leaders up there in the gallery are doing or thinking as to my vote. I should feel myself despicable indeed if I stood here as a representative of the people and voted to exempt Mr. Samuel Gompers or Mr. Frank

Morrison or others up there in the gallery from the operation of the criminal laws of this country and made a special class of them or any hundred of them. I would not exempt John D. Rockefeller from the operation of the criminal laws of this country, nor would I exempt Andrew Carnegie from the operation of those laws; but before and within the law I would hold each man responsible for his own acts, the man who employed and the man who was employed alike. I would not make fish of one and fowl of the other. And if it be a crime in the presence of the labor representatives who have been in the galleries dictating this legislation for the last 10 days to make this declaration in favor of the rights of the workingmen of this country regardless of union or nonunion, then I stand convicted before them; but before the people and before my conscience I am grateful for the opportunity to say that I would not vote for special legislation exempting crime nor for the amendment offered by the gentleman from Kansas, who is playing politics and has been playing to the galleries from one end of this debate to the other. . . .

Mr. MANN. Mr. Chairman, the gentleman from Kansas [Mr. MURDOCK], who was elected as a Republican—

Mr. CAMPBELL. And he could not have been elected if he had not been.

Mr. MANN (continuing). Like a number of other gentlemen in the House who were elected as Republicans—some of whom now have the courage to call themselves Progressives and abuse the Republican Party all the time, although they never were elected upon any ticket except the Republican ticket—will have the opportunity next November of running as Progressives. There has been talk of amalgamation, as the gentleman from Kansas [Mr. MURDOCK] says, but the so-called Progressives throughout the country, the men who voted for Col. Roosevelt the last time, are coming back to the Republican Party. It is not an amalgamation, and whatever the outcome may be, the gentleman from Kansas will be left out in the cold. He was elected as a Republican. He repudiated the party which he followed until he had been elected, and when the Progressives come back to the Republican Party, as the voters will, these little so-called leaders in the House, who can not think for themselves, who have no position upon any question until they have asked the colonel, and now can not find out from the colonel—they can still continue to be Progressives, but enough of the people will come back into the Republican fold until this House will be Republican the next time. [Applause on the Republican side.] . . .

The CHAIRMAN. The time of the gentleman has expired. The question is on agreeing to the amendment offered by the gentleman from Minnesota [Mr. VOLSTEAD] to the amendment offered by the gentleman from North Carolina [Mr. WEBB].

Mr. GRAHAM of Pennsylvania. May we not have the amendment reported again? After this desultory debate we have lost sight of the amendment.

The CHAIRMAN. The Clerk will report the amendment and the amendment to the amendment.

The Clerk read as follows:

Amendment offered by Mr. WEBB:
At the end of section 18, line 23, on page 36, strike out the period and insert a semicolon and add:
"Nor shall any of the acts specified in this paragraph be considered or held unlawful"
Amendment to the amendment offered by Mr. VOLSTEAD:
Page 36, at the end of the amendment offered by Mr. WEBB, add:
"But nothing in this act shall be construed to permit a secondary boycott."

The CHAIRMAN. The question is on the amendment to the amendment.

The question was taken, and the amendment to the amendment was rejected.

The CHAIRMAN. The question now is on the amendment offered by the gentleman from North Carolina.

The question was taken, and the amendment was agreed to.

Mr. WEBB. A division, Mr. Chairman.

Mr. FOWLER. Mr. Chairman, I ask for a division.

The CHAIRMAN. The Chair thinks the gentleman is too late.

Mr. GARNER. Mr. Chairman, the Chair did not state that the ayes seemed to have it, and therefore the gentleman from North Carolina was in time, because the

Chair announced that the ayes had it and hardly gave the gentleman from North Carolina an opportunity for division.

The CHAIRMAN. The Chair only heard one vote in the negative, and for that reason announced the result. The Chair is of the opinion that the request for division comes too late unless some gentleman was on his feet.

Mr. HENRY. The gentleman from North Carolina was on his feet as quickly as possible asking for a division.

The CHAIRMAN. The Chair thinks the request comes too late. The Clerk will report the amendments in the order in which they were offered.

The Clerk read as follows:

Amendment offered by Mr. MacDonald:
Page 35, line 23, after the word "employment," insert the following:
"In a case where a strike or lockout exists, or is threatened, or in any other case."

The CHAIRMAN. The question is on agreeing to the amendment.

The question was taken; and on a division (demanded by Mr. MacDonald) there were 15 ayes and 80 noes.

So the amendment was rejected.

The CHAIRMAN. The Clerk will read the next amendment.

The Clerk read as follows:

Second amendment by Mr. MacDonald:
Page 36, line 6, strike out the word "such."

The CHAIRMAN. The question is on agreeing to the amendment.

The question was taken, and the amendment was rejected.

The CHAIRMAN. The Clerk will report the next amendment.

The Clerk read as follows:

Amendment offered by Mr. Hulings:
Page 35, line 20, after the word "case," strike out all down to and including the word "employment," in line 23.

The CHAIRMAN. The question is on the amendment.

The question was taken, and the amendment was rejected.

Mr. CULLOP. Mr. Chairman, I offer the following amendment which I send to the desk as a new section.

Mr. FOWLER. Mr. Chairman, a parliamentary inquiry.

The CHAIRMAN. The gentleman will state it.

Mr. FOWLER. If an amendment is offered as a new section, will that deprive a Member of the right to offer an amendment to section 18?

The CHAIRMAN. The Chair will state to the gentleman that the committee has disposed of section 18. The gentleman from Indiana offers an amendment as a new section, but the Chair is unable to determine its application until the amendment is read.

Mr. BARTLETT. But we have not passed section 18. The gentleman from Illinois has an amendment to section 18, and he is entitled to offer it now.

Mr. CULLOP. Mr. Chairman, we had passed section 18 and the Chairman had instructed the Clerk to read, and I offered my amendment as an additional section.

The CHAIRMAN. The Chair has so stated to the committee.

Mr. FOWLER. Mr. Chairman, I do not desire to interfere with the gentleman from Indiana at all, except that I do not want to pass section 18 without the right of offering a very slight amendment.

The CHAIRMAN. The Chair will be obliged to hold that the gentleman must have unanimous consent to return to section 18.

Mr. FOWLER. Then, Mr. Chairman, I ask unanimous consent to return to section 18.

The CHAIRMAN. The gentleman from Illinois asks unanimous consent to return to section 18.

Mr. MANN. Reserving the right to object, Mr. Chairman, my colleague from Illinois arose and offered to submit a preferential amendment to section 18. We had not passed section 18, except to close debate, and the gentleman from Indiana proposed to offer an amendment as a new section. My colleague could not tell whether the gentleman from Indiana proposed to offer a new section or to amend section 18 until the gentleman from Indiana stated his purpose. When he did my colleague said that he desired to offer an amendment to section 18. Certainly that was in order as a preferential motion, not debatable, of course, because debate has been closed.

The CHAIRMAN. In any event the Chair hears no objection to the request of the gentleman from Illinois.

Mr. FOWLER. On page 35, line 20, I move to insert after the word "case" a comma.

The CHAIRMAN. The Clerk will report the amendment.

The Clerk read as follows:

Page 35, line 20, after the word "case" insert a comma.

Mr. FOWLER. Mr. Chairman, I have but one word to say.

Mr. MANN. Mr. Chairman, debate is closed.

The CHAIRMAN. Under the order of the committee the gentleman from Illinois can not be recognized to discuss his motion. The question is on the amendment offered by the gentleman from Illinois.

The question was taken; and on a division (demanded by Mr. FOWLER) there were—ayes 3, noes 27.

So the amendment was rejected.

The CHAIRMAN. The gentleman will now report the amendment offered by the gentleman from Indiana [Mr. CULLOP].

The Clerk read as follows:

Amend, page 36, by adding a new section to be known as section 18a:
"The jurisdiction of the courts of the United States under this act shall be concurrent with that of the courts of the several States, and no case arising under this act and brought in any State court of competent jurisdiction shall be removed to a court of the United States."

Mr. WEBB. Mr. Chairman, I reserve a point of order against that amendment, to its germaneness and to its insertion in this place in the bill.

Mr. MANN. Oh, let us have the point of order disposed of. I demand the regular order.

The CHAIRMAN. The regular order is called for.

Mr. CULLOP. Mr. Chairman, I would like to be heard on the point of order.

The CHAIRMAN. The Chair will hear the gentleman briefly.

Mr. GARDNER. Mr. Chairman, a parliamentary inquiry.

The CHAIRMAN. The gentleman will state it.

Mr. GARDNER. Has the point of order been made?

The CHAIRMAN. The Chair will hear the gentleman briefly on the point of order. The regular order has been called for. The Chair understood the gentleman from North Carolina to make the point of order.

Mr. WEBB. I make the point of order.

Mr. CULLOP. Mr. Chairman, this being an independent section, it can be introduced at any place in the bill. It is not dependent on any other section; it is not an attempt to amend any other section or to qualify other than extend the process of the courts or the jurisdiction of cases to be tried under the provisions of the act, so that it is not material whether it be introduced after section 18, after section 14 or 15, or any other section. It might come at the end of the bill, and would be ⊥ applicable there, so that not being an amendment to any particular section of the bill it is germane in any place in the bill at which it may be introduced, because it is a new section and a section that gives jurisdiction to State courts as well as the Federal courts in actions arising under the provisions of this act. . . .

Mr. BARTLETT. This amendment does not simply confine the right to sue in the State courts to the matter of granting injunctions, but it is general in its jurisdiction. Is that true?

Mr. CULLOP. That is true.

Mr. BARTLETT. In other words, that any proceeding under this bill to enforce the law provided for in the bill can be brought in a State court as well as in the Federal court?

Mr. CULLOP. Yes.

Mr. BARTLETT. In other words, it confers concurrent jurisdiction on the State courts with the Federal courts to enforce any part of this bill, either civil or criminal?

Mr. CULLOP. That is the object of it; but, of course, it would apply to civil cases. Mr. Chairman, if it was simply applying to any particular section of the bill in reference to the bringing of suits and the trying of cases, then its germaneness might be attacked, as it is now, because it should be made a part of the section to which it would be applicable under the circumstances; but being applicable to every provision of the bill, giving jurisdiction to State courts to try any violation defined under any provision of the bill, it is germane at any point in the bill, as an independent section.

The CHAIRMAN. The Chair thinks the amendment is in order.

The question is on agreeing to the amendment.

Mr. CULLOP. Mr. Chairman, I desire to be heard on the merits of the proposition. This amendment is offered for the purpose of bringing convenience to the people who may have litigation under any provision in this act which we are now considering. The language of this section is precisely the same as that enacted by Congress in 1910 in the employers' liability act, which reads:

> The jurisdiction of the courts of the United States under this act shall be concurrent with that of the courts of the several States, and no case arising under this act and brought in any State court of competent jurisdiction shall be removed to any court of the United States.

The language of this amendment is taken directly from the language of the amendment which was offered to the employers' liability act of 1910. Let me call the attention of the committee to this situation. Some of these Federal judicial districts are very large. Many people reside a long distance from the place where the courts are held. A gentleman from California the other day said that some of the people there were living 400 and 500 miles from the place where the courts were held. In such circumstances where there were violations of this act the suits could be brought in the State courts, tried and determined at home, and it would be a matter of convenience as well as economy to the litigants who might have to resort to the courts for redress of grievances under the act. . . .

Mr. GORDON. Where does the gentleman find authority in the Constitution of the United States giving this Congress the right to confer any jurisdiction, civil or criminal, on a State court?

Mr. CULLOP. Oh, that is too well settled to take up any time in the discussion of it here.

Mr. GORDON. Will the gentleman give me an authority for it?

Mr. CULLOP. Why, we have an act of Congress to which I have referred; that is the best of authority for it. Why not? This Congress has conferred jurisdiction of this character on the State courts. It is simply giving a cause of action under a statute, and Congress has a right to confer jurisdiction in the State courts. . . .

Mr. [NICHOLAS J.] SINNOTT [R., Ore.]. For the benefit of the gentleman from Ohio who asked the question, I will state that that matter has been decided in the Two hundred and twenty-third United States.[5.565]

Mr. GORDON. In a criminal case?

Mr. SINNOTT. No.

Mr. GORDON. Does the gentleman think we would have authority to confer jurisdiction in a criminal case?

Mr. SINNOTT. This is conferring jurisdiction in a civil case.

Mr. GORDON. And in a criminal case, also.

Mr. CULLOP. We are conferring the jurisdiction here in a civil case.

Mr. SINNOTT. I think it should be confined to a civil case.

Mr. CULLOP. The same is true under the national banking act. The benefit of this would be that people who have to resort to the courts for a redress of grievances under this statute would have the convenience of being able to do so in their own home

---

[5.565] Mondou v. New York, N.H. & H.R.R., 223 U.S. 1, 32 S. Ct. 169, 56 L. Ed. 327 (1912).

courts, which would be an economy, and the matter could be tried and determined just as well as in any Federal court; and I hope the amendment will be adopted for that reason.

Mr. FLOYD of Arkansas. Mr. Chairman, I desire to speak in opposition to the amendment. This legislation is supplementary to the Sherman Act. Jurisdiction under the Sherman Act is confined to the Federal courts, and I think properly so. There are a number of reasons why this proposed amendment of the gentleman from Indiana should not be incorporated into this bill. In the first place, it would be a burden to the State courts to have jurisdiction over these cases conferred upon them. This Federal Government has exclusive jurisdiction of this class and character of legislation and should retain full jurisdiction in the trial of such cases. Dissolution suits are under the control of the Attorney General of the United States. We have district courts throughout the country, with district attorneys employed by the United States to look after the Federal business, and I think that the proposition of the gentleman from Indiana to confer jurisdiction over these cases upon the State courts would be an injustice to the people of the States and to the courts of the States; and I oppose it for that reason. In the second place, this is a very broad and far-reaching statute in its provisions.

It deals with the business interests of people of all classes—railroads, manufacturers, industrial concerns, combinations, and conspiracies in restraint of trade—and we think it would likewise be an injustice to parties litigant to take them away from the jurisdiction of the Federal courts and confer jurisdiction upon State courts to try this character of cases. It broadens the scope of the law. It is one of those things which if attached to this legislation will make it all the more difficult to pass the legislation, and we do an injustice to the cause and principle which we seek to establish by this legislation if we broaden the measure with far-reaching and momentous questions such as the gentleman from Indiana offers as an amendment. Any friend of this legislation, as I am sure the gentleman from Indiana is, ought not to aid those who are fighting this legislation—the trusts and the combines of this country—by loading it down with questionable amendments that will tend to defeat it and destroy it in the end. For these reasons the committee opposes the amendment and hopes that it will be rejected. . . .

Mr. CULLOP. Mr. Chairman, I move to strike out the last word. Mr. Chairman, the doctrine just advocated by the distinguished gentleman from Arkansas [Mr. FLOYD] is a very dangerous doctrine, indeed. In its last analysis it means to many a denial of justice, and a failure to enforce the law in all its phases. Who are the parties that have been always running to the Federal courts? Has it been the individual or has it been the trusts and the big corporations? The answer is easy and is within the knowledge of all. It is the experience, I am confident, of every man on this floor that the men who seek cover under the ample folds of the Federal courts of this country are the owners of the trusts and big corporations of the country, and by so doing they are constantly forcing the poor man out of the benefits of such legislation as this by seeking that forum for the adjudication of their cases. Aye, gentlemen, if it is desired to protect the trusts, to protect the big corporations of this country, under this act, then confine its jurisdiction to the Federal courts and it will well nigh destroy the advantages of the legislation we are attempting to adopt here to-day for the relief of the people. Who is it that has been running to the Federal courts for the last quarter of a century? Who is it that has taken refuge in the Federal courts of this country? Has it been the poor individual or has it been the trusts and the big corporations which seek to be relieved from penalties and from punishment provided for in the law of the land? Go read the petitions for removals from the State to the Federal courts of this country, and it will be found that in every instance they are filed by the corporations or rich and powerful individuals for the purpose of escaping the penalties of the law. It has been their refuge for escape from deserved punishment. Cases are removed frequently for the purpose of getting away ⊥ from the scene where the injury has been inflicted and where the poor man will be unable to follow it up, take his witnesses to court, and conduct his litigation as it ought to be conducted. Why impose hardships on litigants? And yet the gentleman from Arkansas says that a measure that seeks to bring these cases at home and let the poor man try his case in the court where he resides, where the injury was inflicted, and where the witnesses reside, that such a measure is in the interest of the trusts and of the big corporations of this country. The gentleman will not stand by that declaration for a moment, because it is not only ridiculous, but it is contradicted by the facts, as the experience of every individual will verify. The reverse is true, and every man knows or ought to know it. . . .

Mr. FLOYD of Arkansas. I did not make the statement attributed to me by the gentleman from Indiana.

Mr. CULLOP. Then I misunderstood the gentleman from Arkansas, and I am glad to know he did not desire to be so understood.

Mr. FLOYD of Arkansas. The statement I made was this: That if we load this measure down with amendments of far-reaching import like this, it would tend to defeat the legislation, and that would result in the interests of the trusts.

Mr. CULLOP. I beg to disagree with the gentleman. How does this load it down? Are not the judges of the State courts as capable, as learned, as honest, and conscientious as the judges of the Federal courts to try and determine the questions involved in this legislation? Upon what meat does the Federal judge feed that makes him so much greater than a judge of a State court? [Applause.] Who are these judges of the Federal courts? They are the men who have been taken off the benches of the State courts from the bars over the country. What has made them more able to construe a statute than a State judge? Where and how is this measure loaded down with any such amendments? What complication does this amendment involve? I defy the gentleman or any other gentleman to point out how any harm may come from the adoption of this amendment. It simply gives the right of trial in the locality where the cause of action arises and at home where the witnesses are. It gives opportunity for a full and fair hearing of a cause. It assures economy in the administration of justice. It assures a speedy trial in a competent tribunal. Does anybody have objection to this? If so, let him state it. Can anyone who desires fair play in our courts take exceptions to it? If so, I would be pleased to have him do it. We are now legislating on a subject of much interest to the American people. Relief has been promised them from the extortions of remorseless organizations, in which greed and avarice have been the dominating features in their operations. They have stifled competition, bankrupted their weak and unfortunate competitors, and out of the ruins of the unfortunate created monopoly, through which the people have been unmercifully plundered. Let us furnish the best and easiest method for a redress of grievances, in order that the people may take advantage of its provisions and secure relief. With that end in view I offered this amendment, and no one will here deny but what it will afford great benefit in the administration of this law.

The people expect us to afford them a complete remedy and a convenient method for its administration. Their eyes are upon us; they are patiently scanning every move made, because they know how they have suffered for the want of appropriate and adequate legislation on this subject, how often it has been promised, and how often they have been deceived in this matter. They must not be deceived now, but we must afford them a full and complete means of relief and a convenient and economic method for the enforcement of the same. This amendment means much for the success of this legislation, and the poor man, the man who needs this legislation most, will hail its adoption with satisfaction and delight. The committee in charge of this bill and this House should be interested in its success. If it will assist in destroying monopoly, in dissolving combinations operating as a restraint in trade, in restoring competition, it will be hailed with delight by millions of people all over our country and will redound to the glory of all who helped enact it. The amendment under consideration will assist in carrying out the good purposes it proposes and will make it available to many who otherwise could never invoke its provisions or take advantage of the protection it affords. I hope it will be adopted, so that its provisions may become available to the poor as well as the rich, to the weak as well as the strong. [Applause.]

Every line and every word will be closely scrutinized by thousands of patriotic people who have suffered for the want of such legislation and who hope to secure relief through its provisions. They are watching every move made here, every vote cast, in order to know how each man stands, whether friendly to them or friendly to the special interests which have thrived at their expense. They have been promised means for relief; they demand every obligation contained in that promise be scrupulously kept and the fullest measure of relief afforded within the power of this lawmaking body. We will comply fully with the obligation if we adopt this amendment. [Applause.]

The CHAIRMAN (Mr. MURRAY of Oklahoma). The time of the gentleman has expired. The question recurs on the amendment offered by the gentleman from Indiana as a new paragraph to the section.

The question was taken, and the Chair announced he was in doubt.

The committee divided; and there were—ayes 35, noes 30.

Mr. WEBB. Mr. Chairman, I ask for tellers.

Tellers were ordered.

The committee again divided; and the tellers (Mr. CULLOP and Mr. WEBB) reported that there were—ayes 32, noes 34.

So the amendment was rejected.

The Clerk read as follows:

SEC. 20. That whenever it shall be made to appear to any district court or judge thereof, or to any judge therein sitting, by the return of a proper officer on lawful process, or upon the affidavit of some credible person, or by information filed by any district attorney, that there is reasonable ground to believe that any person has been guilty of such contempt, the court or judge thereof, or any judge therein sitting, may issue a rule requiring the said person so charged to show cause upon a day certain why he should not be punished therefor, which rule, together with a copy of the affidavit or information, shall be served upon the person charged with sufficient promptness to enable him to prepare for and make return to the order at the time fixed therein. If upon or by such return, in the judgment of the court, the alleged contempt be not sufficiently purged, a trial shall be directed at a time and place fixed by the court: *Provided,* however, That if the accused, being a natural person, fail or refuse to make return to the rule to show cause, an attachment may issue against his person to compel an answer, and in case of his continued failure or refusal, or if for any reason it be impracticable to dispose of the matter on the return day, he may be required to give reasonable bail for his attendance at the trial and his submission to the final judgement of the court. Where the accused person is a body corporate, an attachment for the sequestration of its property may be issued upon like refusal or failure to answer.

In all cases within the purview of this act such trial may be by the court, or, upon demand of the accused, by a jury; in which latter event the court may impanel a jury from the jurors then in attendance, or the court or the judge thereof in chambers may cause a sufficient number of jurors to be selected and summoned, as provided by law, to attend at the time and place of trial, at which time a jury shall be selected and impaneled as upon a trial for misdemeanor; and such trial shall conform, as near as may be, to the practice in criminal cases prosecuted by indictment or upon information.

If the accused be found guilty, judgment shall be entered accordingly, prescribing the punishment, either by fine or imprisonment, or both, in the discretion of the court. Such fine shall be paid to the United States or to the complainant or other party injured by the act constituting the contempt, or may, where more than one is so damaged, be divided or apportioned among them as the court may direct, but in no case shall the fine to be paid to the United States exceed, in case the accused is a natural person, the sum of $1,000, nor shall such imprisonment exceed the term of six months.

Mr. BARTLETT. Mr. Chairman, I move to strike out the last word, unless the gentleman from North Carolina has an amendment to offer.

Mr. WEBB. No; I have no amendment to offer.

Mr. BARTLETT. Mr. Chairman, this provision in this bill and subsequent provisions of it, especially that provision that requires that a party charged with indirect contempt of court must be accused, tried, or convicted of contempt by a jury as in criminal cases, is a step in the direction of proper trials in court in such cases. We boast, Mr. Chairman, those of us who live under the English system of laws, that the system of jury trials as handed down to us from English jurisprudence is the greatest palladium of the liberties of the English-speaking people, yet in a case which involves imprisonment and fine, forfeitures and punishment by both imprisonment and fine, we have been struggling in Congress for 20 years or more in order to have enacted into a statute of the United States the right of the American citizen to be tried by a jury of his peers in this class of cases when his liberty and property are at stake. We are about to realize a successful completion of the efforts of the men who have struggled long and patiently to obtain that end. The first bill I had the honor to introduce as a Member of

Congress, when I became a Member of it in 1895, was a bill to permit and require, when demanded by a man who might be charged with indirect contempt of the court, that the trial should be by jury.

I have at each succeeding Congress introduced a bill to that effect. It was never considered favorably by a Republican committee or House, but a bill of like character was favorably reported at the last Congress and passed by this House.

⊥ The Senate of the United States in 1896, at the instance of Senator Hill, of New York, did pass a bill, introduced by him, providing for jury trials in indirect contempt cases. It came to this House, and went to the Committee on the Judiciary of the House, where it slept the death that knew no waking. The Democratic platform in 1896 embodied a demand for the passage of that bill, and from 1896 down to 1912, again and again, it has been reiterated in every Democratic national platform that trials of indirect contempt cases in the courts shall be by jury when that demand is made by the accused.

Mr. Chairman, this bill gives to the American citizen, charged with the violation of an order or an injunction of the court in these cases that we know to be indirect contempts, the right that he ought to have had from the foundation of the Government—the right to have his case, when he is charged with a criminal offense or a quasi-criminal offense, tried by a jury of his peers. This bill further contains a provision giving a right which has not heretofore been enjoyed by those who undergo these trials, namely, the right of appeal. We know the history of these trials, and— . . .

. . . We who have investigated the matter and have kept pace with it know the history of these cases. It is shocking to my sense of justice; it has always been a matter that offended my sense of what the right of American citizens was, that when charged with crime the judge should be grand jury, prosecutor, and jury to find a verdict and then as judge to pronounce a sentence. Therefore, during all these years, at least since I have been a Member of this House—which on the 4th day of March next will be 20 years—the struggle has gone on, and during those years I have devoted whatever energy and ability I possess to the accomplishment of what this bill accomplishes; that is, to have the right of trial by jury enjoyed by the accused in these contempt cases.

I have been in a United States court, Mr. Chairman, and seen cases of constructive or indirect contempt tried by the judge when those cases were instigated, inaugurated, prosecuted, heard, and tried and judgment rendered and sentence pronounced by the judge who instigated and had the prosecutions started, and when the men thus accused, thus tried, thus convicted, and thus punished, undertook to find relief from what those who had investigated the case or heard it thought and believed to be an outrage upon the rights of a citizen, an illegal and unjust punishment, by appeal to a higher court, they would find that it was embodied as a principle in our jurisprudence that no appeal lay from any such judgment in any such case.

And so, when the American people had wakened up to the idea that there were cases where men could be criminally punished, could be criminally accused, could be tried and convicted as in a criminal case, could be imprisoned and placed in jail and within prison walls, and have their money and property taken from them and be incarcerated in prison; that there was not the right accorded to them which every American citizen and every man who lives under the Anglo-Saxon system of jurisprudence ought to have; when they realized this fact the campaign proceeded and has gone on and on, and the doctrine which was asserted, that the courts have in themselves the inherent power to punish for contempt, and that no one should decide that question except the judge, has been dissipated. These sections in this bill, and those that permit—or require, rather—criminal information and the facts to be set out in the trial of a man accused before a jury, give him a right that he never had before to appeal that case to a higher court and have it considered on its merits.

These are the things which the Democratic Party's platform has demanded, and these are the things which the Democratic Congress intends by this bill to place upon the statute books. It breaks the chains that bound the people to the unjust and tyrannous decisions of unjust judges. [Applause.] . . .

Mr. QUIN. Mr. Chairman, at least to my conception of law, justice, and right, this section, which gives a trial by jury in contempt cases, is writing into the statute laws of this land enlightened thought. It shows the spirit of the age—that we are moving away from the old archaic idea that all wisdom and all justice is within the cranium and heart of one man, that of a judge appointed for a term lasting until he is dead.

Gentlemen, that has been one of the prerogatives that the courts of this country have possessed since the Constitution was first adopted. It has been more abused than any other right that the courts have had, and I am proud to have the opportunity to vote for a bill that takes that right away from the courts. Not that the judge himself is not honest, but some judges get so far removed from the people that they can not feel for the man who is down in life. [Applause.]

I know from personal experience something of contempt cases, where a Federal court issued a sweeping injunction in a strike that covered every man in the community that was indirectly or remotely involved; and, regardless of what he did, he was amenable to that court under contempt proceedings, and no jury could he have.

I believe that this bill will give the people of the country more confidence in the courts. It will give them more respect for the courts, and it will give the courts to understand that the people have rights, and that those rights can be passed upon by their peers. . . .

Mr. GARDNER. Is it not the gentleman's opinion that one of the great causes of attacks upon the courts of this country is the fact that they have had imposed on them, or have assumed, the duty of trying persons without a jury for the violation of restraining orders issued in labor cases?

Mr. QUIN. I think the gentleman from Massachusetts is correct. However, I believe myself that some of the courts of the country have brought themselves into the contempt of the people because of that right being frequently abused by autocratic judges.

Mr. GARDNER. The gentleman ought not to understand—

Mr. QUIN. The American people ought to love the courts, but instead of doing that the usurped and assumed power by the courts has made them, in a measure, the object of contempt.

Mr. GARDNER. I hope the gentleman will not imbibe from my remarks the idea that I am blaming the courts. I am blaming the law or the practice which imposes on the courts the duty of trying without a jury those cases of contempt of court in the matter of labor injunctions. I do not blame the courts, however, for doing what they believed to be their duty. Fortunately it will no longer be their duty after this law shall have been passed.

Mr. QUIN. The gentleman is correct. But the long following of that rule leads the judge to entertain the idea that he is all-powerful, and sometimes he gets to be a tyrant. That is what the people of America complain of.

If the judge knew he would be on the bench only for a few years, and that his reappointment depended on his method of trying cases, it is very likely that he would always try to be in harmony with the people and the law. A judge can make mistakes as well as any other person.

And the judicial tyranny of this country is to-day written through the decisions. If you will read those decisions, you can see tyranny there that is equaled nowhere on earth except by the Czar of Russia or, perhaps, the ruling of some military court; and there is not a man in the United States who could ever have any respect for the ruling of a court-martial. I say that the courts of this country have had a power that they ought not to have had under the constitution of a republic. Some of them have used it properly, but others have used it improperly. It has been a method of oppression, a tool with which to oppress the people. [Applause.]

It has been too easy for the great and powerful corporations to be either directly or indirectly instrumental in naming the ⊥ Federal judges of this country. In many instances the judge has spent his life as the retained attorney of the special interests, and it matters not how honest he may be, he sees the law from a different viewpoint as distinguished from the ordinary citizen. The great corporate interests believe in the Federal courts, and the sweeping injunction is the weapon which they can always use in an unfair and unjust manner.

Every intelligent citizen knows that many judges have abused the right to adjudge a citizen to be in contempt of the court, and the same judge try and sentence him. In late years the freedom of the press has been abridged by some autocratic judges.

The United States is a Government of the people, and the original framers of our Constitution never intended that the courts should usurp any authority or infringe upon the liberties of the people. The privilege of a Federal judge to deny the right of trial by juries in contempt cases has grown to be one of the greatest abuses in our scheme of government. I do not believe any judge ought to hold his position for life, as there is too much danger of him growing to be an autocrat and intolerant of the views and the rights of others. This section in the antitrust bill which allows the persons charged with contempt to be tried by a jury is one good step in the right direction. Yet there is nothing in the bill to prevent the judge from charging the jury orally and from his seat of power tell the jury that he thinks the individual accused is guilty. He may not do it in so many words, but he will give the jury to understand that he thinks the fellow ought to be convicted. Gentlemen, that is the next evil Congress will be called on to correct. These Federal judges ought not to hold office over a certain term of years. The Constitution should be amended making the term of office of Federal judges for a period of four years, and if any judge holds longer it would be necessary for him to be reselected. I regard life tenure in any functionary position of the Government as indefensible. What good reason can there be assigned for making any man a judge on the bench for life? I am happy to vote to force the courts to grant the jury in contempt cases, and I will be still happier in voting to bar life appointments of judges. The people of this country can never rule in reality as long as the judges hold for life. The laws we are passing this week constitute a real bill of rights, a veritable Magna Charta in which the American citizenship can see hope for the future.

Mr. BRYAN. Mr. Chairman, I wish to offer an amendment.

The CHAIRMAN. The gentleman from Washington offers an amendment, which the Clerk will report.

The Clerk read as follows:

Page 39, line 4, after the word "months," add the following:
"In all trials for contempt in such cases the judge whose order has been disobeyed shall not be eligible to sit as presiding judge where any defendant files a motion for change of judge on the ground that he believes such judge to be prejudiced or that a fair and impartial trial can not be had before such judge."

Mr. BRYAN. Mr. Chairman and gentlemen, I think that amendment ought to receive the careful consideration of this House and be adopted. The gentleman from Massachusetts [Mr. GARDNER] just suggested that the burden imposed upon the courts in these matters is one of the reasons for the lack of confidence on the part of the people in the courts in a great many cases.

Mr. [WILLIAM F.] MURRAY [D., Mass.]. Will the gentleman suggest the origin of this duty of the court; how it came about that the courts have such authority?

Mr. BRYAN. The courts have held that in contempt cases they have inherent rights to try and punish. State judges have held that their rights are superior to the legislatures of the several States, and that their right to fine for contempt does not depend upon legislative enactment; and especially was that illustrated in the Idaho case, where an editor, whose name, I think, was Broxon, published a criticism by Theodore Roosevelt on the action of the court out there in shutting out Progressive electors, and the judges of that court said they were proceeding by inherent right and not under authority conferred by the legislature.[5.566] But that is aside from the question.

Mr. BARTLETT. How does the gentleman's amendment remedy that defect?

Mr. BRYAN. The gentleman from Massachusetts [Mr. MURRAY] led me off on that line. He probably did not intend to; but my amendment proposes that where a defendant is brought before a judge for violating an order of that judge, the judge who has issued the order is not to try the case if the defendant requests a change of judge. There is no reason why a judge who has been angered by the violation of one of his orders should sit and try the case. That has been spoken of here by the gentleman from

---

[5.566] McDougall v. Sheridan, 23 Idaho 191, 128 P. 954 (1913).

Georgia [Mr. BARTLETT]. That is sought to be remedied in this act by calling a jury of 12 men; but the judge who rules on the admission of testimony and who charges the jury and interprets the law can many times force a conviction from the jury, and it is not a fair and impartial tribunal where a man is haled before the court to be tried on a summons issued by direction of the court for violating an order that the judge of that court himself has issued. If you want to make this fair, if you want to make it so that a defendant before the court will have a chance of a fair trial, give him an opportunity to be freed from standing before the judge who has ordered him arrested.

The legislatures of a number of the States have provided that in any case where a man comes before the court and files his application for a change of judge and enters an affidavit stating that he believes the judge sitting on the bench is prejudiced against him and that he can not have a fair trial before that judge, then the judge sitting in that court must call in another judge to try that case. There are many Federal judges in this country, and these judges have their prejudices. I do not believe that a defendant ought to be compelled to go to trial before a judge under those conditions. It is true that you can not make this absolute. You can not get perfection. It may be that the second judge will feel the same way, and this amendment only provides for one change, one substitution; but there is at least a better chance at obtaining an impartial judge. It is very easy for the judge to call some one else to try the case. The same statute is on the books of the State of Washington. The same statute is on the books of the State of Ohio. There is nothing new or wrong or abborrent about it. There is no reason why it ought not to be adopted, especially in a contempt case.

THE CASE AGAINST GOMPERS, MORRISON, AND MITCHELL.

The decision of the Supreme Court [sic] of the District of Columbia in American Federation of Labor v. Buck Stove & Range Co. (33 App. Cases, D. C., 83)[5.567] is one that attracted tremendous attention. As an outcome of a violation of the "inherent right" of the court to punish for contempt, the head of the American Federation of Labor till a few days ago stood condemned to serve a term in a Federal prison. I shall not attempt to discuss this case except to cite it as one of unusual significance. Mr. J. W. Van Cleave was the principal owner of the Buck Stove & Range Co., of St. Louis. He was also the president of the National Manufacturers' Association, with its manipulations as a corruptionist and insidious lobbyist, with its Mulhall and its millions. The Buck Stove & Range Co. employed union and nonunion men. Thirty-five union men in one branch of the company's service got into a dispute with their employer over matters pertaining to hours of work. The difficulty was not satisfactorily adjusted and a strike ensued. The American Federation of Labor indorsed the action of the men, ordered a boycott of the products of the company, and placed its name upon the federation's "We don't patronize" list. The company applied to the Supreme Court of the District of Columbia for an injunction to restrain such boycott. On December 18, 1907, the court granted an injunction, pendente lite, restraining the defendants as prayed for in the bill.

The injunction granted pendente lite in this case was in violation of the Constitution, and the appellate court so decided. It was an absurd autocratic order that trampled upon individual freedom, the freedom of the press, and was entirely unjustified. This is established by the majority opinion of the appellate court, by which the absurd injunction was materially modified,[5.568] but, in my judgment, the dissenting opinion of Chief Justice Shepherd should have been the conclusion of the majority. The injunction both as originally granted and as modified by the majority opinion of the court prohibited the publication of the "We don't patronize" list in the American Federationist, the journal of the labor organizations.

The people of this country are not going to permanently stand for such power as permits a life-tenure judge to order an editor in advance of a trial on an ex parte hearing not to publish this or to publish that. Surely if the judge can say what the

---

[5.567] 33 App. D.C. 83 (D.C. Cir. 1909) (injunction upheld but modified), *dismissed per curiam,* 219 U.S. 581, 31 S. Ct. 472, 55 L. Ed. 345 (1911) (dismissed after settlement between parties). *See* note 5.522 *supra* and accompanying House debate.

[5.568] 33 App. D.C. 83.

editor can not publish, by the same token he can tell him what he must publish. The term "freedom of the press" becomes a silly and meaningless phrase under such conditions. The learned judge in his dissenting opinion cited Chancellor Kent, as follows:

> It has become a constitutional principle in this country that every citizen may freely speak, write, and publish his sentiments on all subjects, being responsible for the abuse of that right, and that no law can rightfully be passed to restrain or abridge the freedom of speech or the press.[5.569]

Chief Justice Shepherd continues:

> The true ground for the denial of jurisdiction to restrain the publication of a libel destructive of property is that the exercise of such jurisdiction would amount to an abridgement of the freedom of the press by establishing a censorship over the press so enjoined. The soundness of this view is demonstrated in an able opinion by Fenner, J., speaking for the Supreme Court of Louisiana, in such a case. (State, ex rel. Liversey, v. Civil District Judge, 34 La. Ann., 741, 745.)[5.570] He says: "There would be no safe course except to take the opinion of the judge beforehand or to abstain entirely from alluding to the plaintiff. What more complete censorship could be established? Under the operation of such a law, with a subservient or corrupt judiciary, the press might be completely muzzled and its just influence upon public opinion entirely paralyzed. Such powers do not exist in courts, and they have been constantly disclaimed by the highest tribunals of England and America. It has passed into a settled rule of jurisprudence that 'courts of equity will not lend their aid to enjoin the publication of libels or works of a libelous nature, even though the libelous publication is calculated to injure the credit, business, or character of the person against whom it is directed.' "
>
> In view, then, of the provision of the first amendment, I can come to no other conclusion than that the only remedy for libelous or otherwise malicious, wrongful, and injurious publications is by civil action for damages and criminal prosecution. There is no power to restrain the publication.
>
> For the reasons given I can not agree to the terms of the decree as modified. In my opinion it should be modified so as to restrain the acts, only, by which other persons have been or may be coerced into ceasing from business relations with the Buck's Stove & Range Co., but so as not to restrain the publication of the name of that company in the "we don't patronize" columns of the American Federationist, no matter what the object of such publication may be suspected or believed to be.[5.571]

Chief Justice Shepherd believes the attempt to enjoin Gompers, Morrison, and Mitchell from publishing this list in the American Federationist and from talking about the Van Cleave outfit as unfair was an infringement of the Constitution of the United States, and that Gompers, Morrison, and Mitchell had the right to print and talk about the matter and that no court could take that right from them. Is it surprising that Gompers, Morrison, and Mitchell believed the same thing?

THE COURT'S ORDER MUST BE OBEYED, THOUGH UNCONSTITUTIONAL.

The labor leaders at once appealed from the order to the higher court. They put up their bond on appeal, just like the Mulhall employers had put up their bond on obtaining the order. Notwithstanding the appeal, the order remained of full force till reversed. The fact that the appellate court would modify the order and deliver an opinion that it was an outrage on the Constitution could not abate in the slightest its "inherent"—from God descended—power. "What if it does violate the Constitution, this court's order must be obeyed." This is the uniform position taken by all courts as to their injunctions. It does not lie in the mouth of any puny man or labor leader to question a court's order—if it violates the Constitution, reverse it if you can by the regular, tedious, and expensive course of the law's delays, and by the order of a brother judge, but in the meantime, obey is the word.

It is worthy of note that obedience does not need be granted to a statute of Congress which violates the Constitution. Not for a moment. If Congress violates the Constitution in the enactment of a statute, no attention need be paid to it. Such a

---

[5.569] *Id.* at 130.

[5.570] State *ex rel.* Liversey v. Judge of Civil District Court, 34 La. Ann. 741, 745 (1882).

[5.571] 33 App. D.C. at 131-32.

statute is void ab initio. Anyone is at liberty to violate it with impunity; the quicker it is violated and wiped off the statute books the better for all concerned. If Congress were to enact into law the principles of the iniquitous injunction issued for Mulhall's overlords by the court, prohibiting certain publications and ordering people not to talk about the Mulhall crowd being unfair, no newspaper publisher would for a moment attempt to obey the statute. They would fall back on the Constitution and their rights, as they have done hundreds of times, and then the court would say, as it has said hundreds of times: "You did right; you did not need to obey Congress; the law was unconstitutional." And by its later doctrine the court has found that an "unreasonable" statute is absolutely void and need not be obeyed.

Not only are unconstitutional legislative orders void and entirely unworthy of notice or obedience, although solemnly passed by the House and the Senate and duly signed by the President, but Executive orders, presidential proclamations, treaties with foreign countries, and all forms of Executive demands are void and not worth the paper on which they are written if not in accord with the Constitution. All such may be held in contempt or may be totally ignored.

AN EX PARTE INJUNCTION IS PRIVILEGED ABOVE A STATUTE.

Not so when a judge at the behest of the Mulhall crowd orders men at the head of a great movement for the bettering of labor conditions to suspend exercising their constitutional rights. What if the order does violate the Constitution, it is the voice of the court. It is not the puny legislative or executive department that now speaks; it is the department of the judiciary, which rules like the Kings of England once ruled—by "inherent" right.

Gompers, Morrison, and Mitchell knew this, and they did their very best to obey the order. They took the Mulhall concern off the unfair list and tried to edit their paper to the liking of the court. While the order was on appeal, however, these three men were, on motion of an attorney who was a fellow employee of Mulhall, brought before court and ordered to pay heavy fines and to go to Federal prison, there to do hard labor for 12, 9, and 6 months, respectively, for "contempt" alleged to have been committed in the violation of the injunction. No trial by jury; of course not! Jury trials are designed for the other branches of the Government—the legislative and executive. This is the judiciary enforcing its decree. It makes no difference that the order was made ex parte, before trial, and is yet to be set aside by the United States Supreme Court. In this case the court is acting under powers superior to statute and the Constitution. It is acting under "inherent" rights derived from God Himself under procedure set in motion by Mulhall's associate, as an humble agent in the hands of God to work out His immutable decrees!

FACTS INVOLVING CONTEMPT VERY INDEFINITE.

Gompers had written and published editorials, had appealed for funds, and had advised the members of the federation as to their duty and their rights, and had made references to this suit and to labor's constitutional rights in campaign speeches. Morrison was in contempt because he had allowed old copies of the American Federationist to be circulated that had this "We don't patronize" list in them. They had obeyed the order and allowed the judge to edit their magazine to the extent of eliminating the "We don't patronize" list from all editions after the order was signed. Malefactor Morrison had also sent out printed copies of the printed official proceedings of a prior convention of the American Federation of Labor which contained a record of officers and committee reports of the convention relative to this very controversy. He had also sent out copies of the Federationist. Mitchell had violated the order of the judge against talking or printing by presiding at a convention of the United Mine Workers of America where a resolution was introduced calling upon the members of the union not to patronize this outfit of lobbyists and stove makers.

There is nothing in the record of this case to show that this National Manufacturers' Association was, through one of its representatives, just about this time attempting to bribe Gompers to throw down his work for organized labor and pass into a life of ease, in which case, of course, the case would have been dismissed and the contempt of court duly purged, so far as the court and the complaining lobbyists are concerned.

Of course, it is now well known that this contempt case has been settled by the order of the Supreme Court dismissing it.[5.572]

I have in mind other contempt cases not involving labor difficulties where the same rule should prevail. The Idaho case which I have already referred to, where C. O. Broxon, editor of the Boise Capital News, offended the feelings of some judges that ought to have been impeached by criticizing their decision by which Roosevelt electors were denied the right to have their names published on the official ballot.[5.573] These judges ordered Broxon and R. S. Sheridan and A. R. Curzen imprisoned; and they actually served their term of 10 days because of the publication of the Roosevelt criticism. It was an outrage against the spirit of our institutions that these judges could do this without a verdict of guilty from a jury to precede the sentence. Yet the judges said they were acting by inherent authority, and that the legislature had no right either to limit or regulate their authority in contempt matters.

Then, take the case of Col. Nelson, of the Kansas City Star. I do not remember all the details of that attempted judicial outrage, but it stands out to-day as an illustration of the absolute necessity of ordering the courts of this country to give up their self-assumed rights to imprison editors and others where they feel aggrieved. Except for the resourcefulness of Col. Nelson and the order of an appellate court he would have gone to jail.

In my own experience I was the editor and proprietor of a weekly paper published at Bremerton, Wash. I still own the paper, though it is now published in the adjoining town of Charleston, Wash. I was in a fight with a corporation-owned judge in that county, and I used to go to court to try my cases with an appeal bond in my pocket already signed in blank, so that I would be ready to perfect an appeal quick and save temporary incarceration for some unavoidable display of the contempt I felt for that judge.

I had urgent need of that bond, too, one day, and later I needed more than a contempt-of-court bond. But I will say that that particular judge is not in the State of Washington now; he is not away on a visit, either.

Mr. WEBB. Mr. Chairman, the committee will have to oppose this amendment, not because it is not meritorious, but because it is already provided for in the statutes of the United States.

Mr. BRYAN. Oh!

Mr. WEBB. Oh, yes; it is. The gentleman says "Oh," but I will read it to him. Section 23 of the Judicial Code says:

> Whenever a party to any action or proceeding, civil or criminal, shall make and file an affidavit that the judge before whom the action or proceeding is to be tried or heard has a personal bias or prejudice either against him or in favor of any opposite party to the suit, such judge shall proceed no further therein, but another judge shall be designated in the manner prescribed in the section last preceding, or chosen in the manner prescribed in section 23, to hear such matter. Every such affidavit shall state the facts and the reasons for the belief that such bias or prejudice exists.

That is all my friend asks.

Mr. BRYAN. Does it not leave it discretionary with the court?

Mr. WEBB. Oh, no; not at all.

Mr. BARTLETT. And the circuit court of appeals for the fifth circuit have decided that it is not discretionary; that the judge has to get off the case.

Mr. BRYAN. I thought it left it discretionary with the judge.

Mr. WEBB. I think it is already covered by the statute. I hope the gentleman will withdraw it.

[5.572] 219 U.S. 581 (1911).

[5.573] See note 5.566 supra.

Mr. BRYAN. Then I will withdraw it.

The CHAIRMAN. The gentleman from Washington asks unanimous consent to withdraw his amendment? Is there objection?

There was no objection.

Mr. GARDNER. Mr. Chairman, I move to strike out the last two words. When I interrupted the gentleman from Mississippi [Mr. QUIN] I was trying, very imperfectly, owing to my lack of legal training, to explain a thought which I have had for a long time, to wit, that the attack on the courts of the United States, so strikingly prominent in recent years, arose substantially from two causes: First, our Constitutions, State and National, impose on our courts the duty of passing on the constitutionality of legislative acts. That is an unpopular function for our courts to perform, but I believe it to be a function which our courts ought to perform. Second, upon our judges has been imposed, either by judicial decision in times past or by statute, the duty of trying without a jury persons charged with the violation of injunctions issued in connection with labor disputes. . . .

Mr. MURRAY of Massachusetts. May I ask my colleague whether there is any alternative to this position? Is it not a fact that there is not any statute imposing these duties except such statutes as may be declaratory of the common law? The difficulty in this regard is because of the crystallized abuse in which, in the first instance, the judges usurped this matter of issuing injunctions in labor cases.

Mr. GARDNER. The first instance, I have been told, occurred in Massachusetts.

Mr. MURRAY of Massachusetts. The first instance arose in England.

Mr. GARDNER. The fact is, I think, that some one or other made up his mind that a jury would not convict strikers. Yet a trial by jury under the terms of the Constitution is guaranteed to every man accused of crime. Some court somewhere—and I was under the impression that it was in my own State—devised the ingenious plan of converting a crime into a contempt of court by the simple process of ordering persons to refrain from acts which the statute had already declared to be crimes. Hence a practice arose under which a judge would step in and say, "Not only does the State declare in the law that this act which you are perhaps going to commit is a crime, but, what is more to the point, I, the judge, also say that it is a crime." Now, what was the object of that performance? Why sometimes, doubtless, it was this: If the person enjoined went ahead and committed the forbidden act, the question of the court's dignity became involved and the accused got punished, not for a crime but for contempt of court. I have very little patience with any device to deprive a striker or anyone else of his constitutional right to a jury trial by the issuance of an injunction designed to convert a crime into a contempt of court. For this and other reasons I give my approval to the anti-injunction and trial-by-jury features of this bill.

Great Britain has been going through pretty much the same sort of evolution which we are going through. Yet during this period of change and attack on old institutions the courts of Great Britain have not been assailed. The reason, in my opinion, is that the British courts have not been faced with the necessity of declaring laws to be unconstitutional, nor has the writ of injunction in Great Britain been used in such a way as to negative the right of jury trial which ought to be assured to every man accused of wrongdoing.

Mr. BRYAN. Mr. Chairman, I rise to oppose the pro forma amendment. Mr. Chairman, the section of the statute that the gentleman from North Carolina read is a new section put into the statutes since I had the matter under consideration in the State of Washington, when I introduced the same measure in the senate of that State. A number of lawyers and the attorney general declared that it was the most outrageous and ridiculous proposition they ever heard of. It was the hardest effort of my legislative life to keep the governor from vetoing the statute at the request and advice of the attorney general. I am glad to see that the same principle has been put into the Federal statutes. It is right, and the lawyers and litigants, as well as the judges, of the State of Washington know now that it is right, and it would be impossible to repeal it.

Mr. MANN. Mr. Chairman, I move to strike out the last two words. I do not propose to discuss the matter under consideration in the House, largely for physical reasons. I notice with great regret that it seems to be a very popular thing in this body to denounce the courts. During this debate I think I have heard no one on this floor say a word sustaining the integrity of the courts, but I have heard considerable denunciation.

Courts do not always decide cases the way I would like to have them decide them, or at least they did not when I was an active practitioner at the bar. I do not always agree with the decisions of the courts in their construction of legislative acts, nor do I agree with gentlemen on this floor when they say that the courts have lost the confidence of the people. I think the courts have the confidence of the people to a far greater degree than has this House. As far as I am concerned, I have faith in the integrity of the courts as courts, in the integrity of the judges who fill those positions in the courts, and I believe that when the time comes, if it ever does come, which God forbid, that the people really believe, as certain gentlemen have stated on the floor of this House to-day that they do believe that the courts have lost the confidence of the people of this country, that what we will receive is first anarchy and then absolutism. I do not think that time will ever come. I think the courts and the judges of the courts can probably afford to smile good-naturedly at the wild and foolish denunciations which are leveled at them, go ahead, following their duty as best they can, and that in the end they will find that the people sustain them and sustain the doctrine that the last resort in this country in a case of controversy is to judicial determination. [Applause.]

The Clerk read as follows:

SEC. 21. That the evidence taken upon the trial of any person so accused may be preserved by bill of exceptions, and any judgment of conviction may be reviewed upon writ of error in all respects as now provided by law in criminal cases, and may be affirmed, reversed, or modified, as justice may require. Upon the granting of such writ of error, execution of judgment shall be stayed, and the accused, if thereby sentenced to imprisonment, shall be admitted to bail in such reasonable sum as may be required by the court or by any justice or any judge of any district court of the United States or any court of the District of Columbia.

Mr. MURRAY of Oklahoma. Mr. Chairman, I offer the following amendment.

The Clerk read as follows:

After the word "Columbia," in section 21, line 15, strike out the period and insert a colon and add the following: "*Provided*, That the procedure for writ of error or appeal as in this act provided shall not be construed by any court to supersede the writ of habeas corpus, but the right of such writ shall never be denied to liberate any citizen from false imprisonment in charges of contempt."

Mr. MURRAY of Oklahoma. Mr. Chairman, it may be a bit difficult to explain the purpose of this amendment, but nevertheless I feel it ought to be suggested to the House. Section 20 provides a remedy for the trial of contempt cases. Section 21 provides the method of appeal. The contempt has been stated to be inherent in every court of record under common law. It is not a crime; it is inherent because of the necessity of some power for the self-preservation of the court. It will be a very sad day when the court will not exercise or have that power. However, we have found that there should be limitations upon that power, like there have been upon other powers.

In section 20, as I stated, we have provided for a jury trial. In section 21 we place the contempt along in the category of crimes, and we provide that it shall be under the law governing criminal cases.

Of course gentlemen may reply that the Constitution prohibits the suspension of the writ of habeas corpus, but it does not take away the power to supersede it with additional or other writs. Suppose in a certain jurisdiction it was not a violation to sell liquor and some one was imprisoned for selling it. In such a case there would be no remedy in criminal procedure, and the only relief would be the writ of habeas corpus. But suppose it was made a crime to sell liquor, then he could not be liberated under the writ, because the law making it a ⊥ crime would provide a procedure, so that the writ of habeas corpus in that case would be superseded. In this bill you have a writ of error, and it provides for a bond. The fellow who can not make the bond you have subjected to burdens, which could not be permitted under a writ of habeas corpus. If he can not make his bond, he will have to lie in jail, while the writ of habeas corpus, the highest writ of liberty, gives him a speedy relief, and I offer this amendment in view of those changes in the matter of procedure, and I think it essential to protect those men who happen to be fined for contempt, who would be unable to make bonds. I think it was an error to place contempt cases side by side with criminal trials.

Mr. WEBB. Mr. Chairman, this is a criminal matter. It has been generally known as criminal contempt we are dealing with. If that were not so, we would not be interposing a jury between the judge's sentence—

Mr. MURRAY of Oklahoma. Oh, no; that is a question only of limitation—the interposition of a jury, just as we have limited their powers in other branches, and it is not a question of crime.

Mr. WEBB. Wherever a judge can put a man in jail we regard that as a sort of criminal or quasi criminal action, and therefore we have no apologies to make for preserving the defendant's rights in this bill as rights should be preserved in all criminal cases. . . .

Mr. [EMMETT] WILSON [D., Fla.]. There is nothing to keep the defendant in a contempt case from suing out a writ of habeas corpus.

Mr. WEBB. Nothing.

Mr. MURRAY of Oklahoma. There are some classes that could not under this procedure.

Mr. WEBB. If he is indicted for murder or robbery, he always, of course, has the right of suing out a writ of habeas corpus.

Mr. MURRAY of Oklahoma. The gentleman does not undertake to say that in an indictment for murder a man could be liberated under the writ of habeas corpus except where he alleges that he was denied bail when he had the right to bail?

Mr. WEBB. He ought not to be allowed to do that in any case unless he alleges something entitling him to the writ.

Mr. MURRAY of Oklahoma. He can do it if he alleges that he is denied bail when he has the right to bail, but he can not relieve himself from the charge of murder by a writ of habeas corpus.

Mr. WEBB. Of course not.

Mr. MURRAY of Oklahoma. You place contempt as a crime. It is merely a disrespect of the court under a power given to the court for self-preservation only.

Mr. WEBB. Mr. Chairman, contempts are divided into criminal and civil contempts, and we are dealing with the criminal comtempt in this bill, and we preserve the right to appeal and the right to sue out a writ of habeas corpus if the defendant can show that the court has no jurisdiction or that he has been subjected to an unusual or cruel punishment or excessive bail, and so forth, has been required. In those circumstances he can then go to court and sue out a writ of habeas corpus as in all other criminal cases, and we have preserved the defendant's rights absolutely in this section, which seems to be satisfactory to our labor friends and all others, so far as I know, and I do not see the necessity of accepting this amendment, because the rights of every defendant under this bill are preserved. So far as the writ of habeas corpus is concerned, that is a constitutional right, and a defendant can always exercise it whenever he has a proper case.

The CHAIRMAN. The question is on agreeing to the amendment offered by the gentleman from Oklahoma.

The amendment was rejected.

The Clerk read as follows:

SEC. 22. That nothing herein contained shall be construed to relate to contempts committed in the presence of the court, or so near thereto as to obstruct the administration of justice, nor to contempts committed in disobedience of any lawful writ, process, order, rule, decree, or command entered in any suit or action brought or prosecuted in the name of, or on behalf of, the United States, but the same, and all other cases of contempt not specifically embraced within section 19 of this act, may be punished in conformity to the usages at law and in equity now prevailing.

Mr. MURRAY of Oklahoma. Mr. Chairman, I offer the following amendment, which I send to the desk and ask to have read.

The Clerk read as follows:

Amend, on page 39, line 25, after the word "prevailing," strike out the period and insert a colon and add the following: "*Provided,* That in no case shall a penalty or punishment be imposed for contempt until a trial is had and an opportunity to be heard is given the accused."

Mr. MURRAY of Oklahoma. Mr. Chairman, the unfortunate part of this paragraph is the closing words:

And all other cases of contempt not specifically embraced within section 19 of this act may be punished in conformity to the usages at law and in equity now prevailing.

What are these "usages"? In some jurisdictions the "usage" has been for the court to say, "Mr. Marshal, place the man in jail." I remember in the old Indian Territory, under the Federal jurisdiction, as a practitioner at the bar, I was fined $25 by the court without a word. That was the usage there. I remember on a subsequent occasion I said to the court that he had no power to charge the jury, because his court was less than a court of record under the common law. He ordered me to jail for three days, and on a writ of habeas corpus I was liberated. That is the usage in many jurisdictions.

Gentlemen seem to enjoy the fact that the court sent me to jail. He ordered me to jail, but I did not go. I have been fined for contempt many times, but I never have suffered the penalty.

Mr. MANN. The gentleman did not go to jail, and instead they sent him to Congress. [Laughter.]

Mr. MURRAY of Oklahoma. Yes; later.

Mr. CARTER. But not for the same offense. [Laughter.]

Mr. MURRAY of Oklahoma. No. . . .

Mr. MOORE. This is right in point. If they did not send the gentleman to jail, did they not send him to Congress?

Mr. MURRAY of Oklahoma. Those fellows did not send me to jail, but the people who limited their powers sent me to Congress. So in this provision in this law the only difference between it and the Oklahoma constitution is that wherever the United States is a party there is no jury trial. I think it is correct to provide in the law that the judges shall fine as for contempt where the contempt is in the presence of the court or is liable to obstruct the due process of justice. I think that is necessary and that the court should have the right without a trial by jury. But no man should be imprisoned without a hearing. The first element of contempt is the intent, just as is the "intent" coupled with an act which makes a crime. And so we placed in the Oklahoma constitution, and I think it is proper here, a provision that no man should be punished for contempt without a trial, without a hearing. You have provided over here a trial by the court or a trial by the jury, if the one committing the offense demands a trial by jury; but in this case, where the contempt is committed in the presence of the court, there is no trial, or in the case of the disobedience of a writ, where a suit is brought on behalf of the United States, which may be outside of the court, the defendant is not guaranteed a trial by court or by jury. I am not urging in this kind of cases that there ought to be a trial by jury, but I believe, as Judge Hurt, of Texas, said when Jerome Kirby cursed Judge Flint in the open court and the judge sent him to jail without writing the charge on the docket, that no man should be sent to prison without putting upon the docket why he was sent to prison. To do so would jeopardize the liberty of the citizen.

So, in this class of cases, let the trial be before the court; let him have a trial and let him have an opportunity to be heard and let him state whether it was intended or show such extenuating circumstances that might tend to liberate him so that the record might be made. . . .

Mr. MURRAY of Massachusetts. Would you have that trial take place before the same judge?

Mr. MURRAY of Oklahoma. Certainly I would; and then we have a record—

Mr. MURRAY of Massachusetts. And would the gentleman have it take place at the immediate time when the contempt was alleged to have been committed, or subsequent, or when?

Mr. MURRAY of Oklahoma. I would let the judge fine him for contempt, but no punishment to be had until the accused was heard and had a trial.

Mr. MURRAY of Massachusetts. Heard before whom?

Mr. MURRAY of Oklahoma. Before that same judge.

Mr. MURRAY of Massachusetts. When?

Mr. MURRAY of Oklahoma. At any time when it suited the judge, but he can not "punish" him, understand.

Mr. MURRAY of Massachusetts. Is not that a proceeding where the very fact there is any proceeding at all shows the judge who is going to do the trying says in advance there has been a contempt?

Mr. MURRAY of Oklahoma. Yes; but it does this: It gives opportunity to have a record made, and when the record is made he, when he is punished or attempted to be punished, may appeal to the higher court and in that case invoke the right of habeas corpus to liberate him upon the record that shows he ought to be liberated. . . .

Mr. MURRAY of Massachusetts. There might be a record of certain facts, but is there any record of impartial testimony or an impartial finding on impartial testimony?

Mr. MURRAY of Oklahoma. There is a record on both sides in the hearing in the one case, just as the judge makes a finding upon knowledge in his own mind. Under the proceeding I offer, you have the statement of the accused, you have both sides of the question, and you have a higher court to pass upon it.

Mr. MURRAY of Massachusetts. But in the first instance, before the higher court passes upon it at all, there is a decision of the judge that there has been contempt committed in his presence, and the judge in whose presence the contempt was committed would send this man to jail or—

Mr. MURRAY of Oklahoma. It does not follow in that case in his presence alone, if he violates any writ—

Mr. MURRAY of Massachusetts. Well, let us take first the direct contempt, committed in the presence of a judge. The gentleman's plan, as I understand it, is he would have the judge against whom the contempt was directed immediately suspend a trial that might be going on for the purpose of hearing the testimony in reference to the alleged contempt.

Mr. MURRAY of Oklahoma. No, sir; it is true the judge in the exercise of discretion left him under the law will wait until he is through with the case until an opportune moment, and then try, but he would not punish until he had that trial.

Mr. MURRAY of Massachusets. Well, I know, but my objection is not as to the time nor the manner in which the trial for contempt is had. I do not like the idea of the same judge who says the man has been in contempt, trying the man who he says had committed the contempt.

Mr. MURRAY of Oklahoma. I do not agree to the idea every time some man wants to swear a judge off the bench it ought to be permitted. I believe, in the first place, in giving the court enough power to preserve the dignity and strength of the court, and I believe in that doctrine thoroughly; but I do not believe in the case of contempt against the judge that some other judge ought to be summoned, but I do believe in giving the accused an opportunity to get in his evidence, and—

Mr. MURRAY of Massachusetts. Is not there as much opportunity of maintaining and preserving the dignity of the court by a proceeding before a jury or before a separate justice? Is it not a far better plan to preserve the dignity and security of the court to have the proceeding before a jury of impartial men than to have a finding by a man who says he was aggrieved when the man committed the contempt?

Mr. MURRAY of Oklahoma. Not in the case of a direct contempt. . . .

Mr. MANN. I could not hear what the gentleman said in reference to the provision in the Oklahoma constitution about not permitting people to be locked up until they had been tried; but I understood the gentleman to say that if a policeman arrested a drunk or disorderly or arrested a man committing a crime he could not lock him up until after he has been tried.

Mr. MURRAY of Oklahoma. Could not punish.

Mr. MANN. "Could not lock him up," the gentleman said a while ago.

Mr. MURRAY of Oklahoma. "Punish" is the word used in this amendment. He may hold him in custody.

Mr. MANN. Does not the gentleman make a distinction between locking up and punishing?

Mr. MURRAY of Oklahoma. Punishing and imprisoning.

Mr. MANN. Locking up is imprisonment; punishment may not be, but locking up is.

Mr. WEBB. Mr. Chairman, we can not agree to go so far as my friend from Oklahoma desires us to go in his amendment. This section provides that a judge may punish for contempt summarily those contempts committed in his presence.

Now, something has been said about the integrity of the courts, and I want to make this observation: If you take that power away from the courts, then you do destroy the very basis of the court's integrity and its power to protect itself. In other words, it ceases to be a court.

Another is where the contempt is committed not in the actual presence of the judge but so near thereto as to disturb the proceedings of the court; that is the business of the people.

The third is where a person violates an order in a suit brought by the United States. That provision was put in there, gentlemen, as most of you know, for the purpose of giving the court the power to enforce its orders in antitrust suits. . . .

Mr. MURRAY of Oklahoma. Does the gentleman understand that this amendment changes that a particle?

Mr. WEBB. Yes. You provide for a trial, and it would be a farce for a judge sitting on a bench to hear a man, say, break out in some cursing language or abusive language, or some violent outburst of temper, and then say, "I will try you to see if you did that," when he was sitting there himself and heard it. A farce like that ought not to be required in a courthouse.

Mr. MURRAY of Oklahoma. How does that trial lessen the dignity of the court when the judge of the court himself finally tries and passes upon the evidence and the law and fines the defendant? How does it check his ability to conduct the court?

Mr. WEBB. There are some things that ought not to be allowed in a court, and when a man infringes on the privileges of the court the judge ought to have the right to stop him right there, without going through the formality of a trial. . . .

Mr. MANN. Suppose a man on trial went into a court room with a dozen rotten apples in his pocket, and he fired one at the judge, and the gentleman from Oklahoma, acting as a judge, should postpone consideration of that until the man had fired another rotten apple, and still another, and so on until he had fired a dozen? [Laughter.]

Mr. WEBB. Do you say rotten apples?

Mr. MANN. Yes; or it might be rotten eggs, for that matter. . . .

Mr. MURRAY of Oklahoma. Do you object to the provision of this amendment that says he shall have a hearing? Would you be willing to strike out the word "trial" and say he shall not be punished until the accused has an opportunity to be heard?

Mr. WEBB. Mr. Chairman, in reply to that, there may be a few judges in this country who are so arbitrary as not to give a man a chance to purge himself of contempt; but I know very few of them, and rather than cast suspicion and reflection on every judge by passing this sort of an amendment I would prefer to take the chances of impeaching the judge who violates that rule in his practice. . . .

Mr. MURRAY of Oklahoma. Mr. Chairman, the gentleman from North Carolina [Mr. WEBB] urges that this is a reflection upon the courts. How much more a reflection is it to take away from the court entirely the trial of the case and put it before a jury? There is your first reflection upon the court.

Mr. WEBB. Let me answer the gentleman there.

Mr. MURRAY of Oklahoma. Let me finish, and then I will yield to the gentleman.

Mr. WEBB. When a crime is committed, say, 10 miles from the presence of the court, and it does not involve the organization and integrity of the court—

Mr. MURRAY of Oklahoma. Yes; and you except every writ and order and every decree and every command wherever a suit is brought on the part of the United States and in its behalf.

Mr. WEBB. That is to protect the big trusts of the country.

Mr. MURRAY of Oklahoma. And when that is brought, a man may be a thousand miles away, and under this provision he has not a jury trial. I am not urging that he has not even an opportunity to be heard in a case like that. Now why, if one is a reflection on the court, is not the other also a reflection on the court? I would be the last man in the world to reflect upon the courts as such. I believe in preserving to the courts power enough to protect the dignity of the courts.

Mr. WEBB. Did you ever hear of a case where a court did not give a man a right to purge himself of contempt?

Mr. MURRAY of Oklahoma. The usage in this bill is the old usage. It was the usage in the old Territory of Oklahoma. I have been fined myself more than once in that way. [Laughter.] . . .

Mr. CAMPBELL. Has it never occurred to the gentleman from Oklahoma that we are legislating here for other States than Oklahoma? [Laughter.]

Mr. MURRAY of Oklahoma. They do not do that now in Oklahoma, because this is in the constitution, and we have no difficulty in preserving the dignity of the court.

Mr. CAMPBELL. There is no such practice in other courts. Even if a man has been convicted, the court allows the defendant to say something before sentence is pronounced.

Mr. MURRAY of Oklahoma. That has been the practice in the inferior Federal courts. That is the usage, not the law.

Mr. CAMPBELL. That does not obtain in Kansas in any court, not even in a justice's court.

The CHAIRMAN. The time of the gentleman from Oklahoma has expired. The question is on agreeing to the amendment offered by the gentleman from Oklahoma.

The question was taken, and the Chairman announced that the noes seemed to have it.

Mr. MURRAY of Oklahoma. A division, Mr. Chairman!

The CHAIRMAN. A division is demanded.

The committee divided; and there were—ayes 31, noes 47.

So the amendment was rejected.

Mr. THOMSON of Illinois. Mr. Chairman, I move to strike out the last word.

The CHAIRMAN. The gentleman from Illinois [Mr. THOMSON] moves to strike out the last word.

Mr. THOMSON of Illinois. Mr. Chairman, the statements made this morning by one of the Washington papers as to my attitude on the Webb amendment to section 7 of the bill now pending so completely misrepresented my position in the matter that I wish to state on the floor here as clearly as I can just what my position was and is on the matters involved in that amendment. I did not vote for it. In my judgment, the contentions of Mr. MURDOCK and Mr. MACDONALD to the effect that the amendment is ambiguous and uncertain, and probably will prove ineffectual so far as the purposes sought to be accomplished by the labor organizations are concerned, are correct.

But assuming that it does go as far as its proponents say it does, it then exempts "fraternal, labor, consumers', agricultural, or horticultural organizations, orders, or associations"—to quote the language of the bill—from the operation of the antitrust laws.

The real friends of this amendment contend that in effect it excludes these organizations from the operation of the antitrust laws just as clearly as the amendment offered by Mr. MACDONALD, of Michigan, proposed to do in very plain terms. I am opposed to any such wholesale exemption of these or any other organizations from the operation of the antitrust laws.

I do not believe that the acts of combinations of labor should be regarded by the law precisely as the acts of combinations of capital are. Their legitimate objects are different, and the proper means employed to reach their ends are likewise different, and therefore their operations should be regulated differently by the law, but nevertheless the acts of both should be regulated. Laws should be enacted regulating the activities of each kind of organization—the one founded on capital and the one founded on labor.

I will admit that the so-called antitrust laws are designed primarily to regulate combinations involving capital. But they prohibit the doing of certain specified things and the making of certain kinds of contracts by anybody. These laws now are held by the courts to operate to prevent organizations of labor from doing certain things that I believe they ought to have the right to do under the law. A strict interpretation of the law might, as their leaders contend, threaten the very existence of the organizations. In these respects the laws should be changed. Organizations of the kind mentioned in this amendment have a right to exist. They have rendered a great service to civilization. They have a field of activity which is proper, is needed, and in the exercise of which the law should protect them.

But also the antitrust laws operate to prevent these organizations from doing certain other things that I believe they ought not to have the right to do under the law. The Webb amendment does not distinguish between these two classes of activities which such organizations indulge in, but with one stroke exempts such organizations from the law entirely, thus making it possible for them to engage not only in proper acts, but improper ones. For instance, under this amendment a labor organization could not only engage in a strike, entirely justified under conditions existing, which might operate to restrain interstate commerce, but it could establish a boycott or a secondary boycott.

It seems to me that a proper amendment would be one seeking to take out from the operation of the law not certain kinds of organizations, but the doing of certain acts. It is the act itself that should be the criterion. Certain acts should be prohibited and others permitted, and the law should apply to everybody and to all kinds of combinations. But to me it becomes unwarranted class legislation when we prohibit the doing of certain things and then provide that certain persons or combinations of persons shall not be bound by the law. That is what this amendment does, and therefore I could not support it.

The Sherman law declares that every "contract, combination in the form of trust or otherwise, or conspiracy in restraint of trade or commerce among the several States or with foreign nations is hereby declared to be illegal." That law also says that every person who shall make any such contract or engage in any such combination or conspiracy shall be deemed guilty of a misdemeanor and shall be punished as provided in the law. Further, the law says that every person who shall monopolize, or attempt to monopolize, or combine or conspire with any other person or persons to monopolize any part of the trade or commerce among the several States or with foreign nations shall be deemed guilty of a misdemeanor and on conviction thereof shall be punished as provided.

The Webb amendment will, if this bill passes, write into the law of this country a paragraph providing that fraternal, labor, consumers', agricultural or horticultural organizations, orders, or associations instituted for the purpose of mutual help, and not having capital stock or conducted for profit, and the members of such organizations "shall not be construed or held to be illegal combinations or conspiracies in restraint of trade under the antitrust laws."

I am as good a friend of labor as my Progressive colleague from Michigan [Mr. MACDONALD] or my Progressive colleague from California [Mr. NOLAN] or my colleague from Illinois [Mr. BUCHANAN] or any other Member of this House. I am against every form of oppression and unfair and unreasonable treatment that the laboring man has had to endure, and in some cases is still enduring. And I shall do all I can for the early enactment of every reasonable and proper law that seeks to put an end to such things. I will vote for all measures included in the program of social justice, but I could not support such an amendment as this. Labor organizations have long been seeking equality of treatment with organizations representing the other end of the economic structure. I think they should have that treatment, and am willing to do all I can to give it to them. But why they should have more than that I fail to see. I am just as much opposed to creating a privileged class out of the organizations specified in this amendment as I have always been to creating a privileged class out of organizations of capital. One practice is just as vicious as the other.

The Webb amendment goes to the length of saying that a monopoly or a restraint of trade shall not be indulged in by any kind of organization except those specified in the amendment. In determining what organizations or what kinds of organizations come or should come within the antitrust laws, the true test to apply is not what is the organization, one involving capital or one involving labor, but the true test is what does the organization do. Does it restrain commerce or not; is it a monopoly or is it not.

If a contract, combination in the form of trust or otherwise, or conspiracy, in restraint of trade or commerce among the several States or with foreign nations, is undesirable and is illegal, as it is declared to be by the Sherman law, it is so no matter who the person or what the organization may be that is involved. Can it be that a restraint of trade or a monopoly or conspiracy to that effect is bad where a corporation for profit is the actor involved but is perfectly harmless and quite proper where a labor union or a farmers' organization is the one involved? If monopolies or conspiracies in restraint of trade are a bad thing, they are a bad thing, no matter by whom, ⊥ no matter by what kind of an organization they are fostered. To prohibit them by legislation except where they are perpetrated by labor or fraternal organizations or farmers' associations or the members thereof is as clear an example of unwarranted class legislation as can be furnished.

It is mere folly to contend that simply because labor is a human attribute and capital is a mere inanimate thing that combinations of those who deal solely in the former ought not to be hampered in such acts as operate to restrain trade while those who deal in the latter commodity ought to be prohibited from doing any acts having such a tendency.

Again I say, if restraint of trade and monopoly and conspiracy to that end are wrong, what matters it whether that restraint is brought about by the manipulation of that which is a human attribute or that which is an inanimate thing? The antitrust laws relate to combinations of persons, not of capital nor of labor as such, and to certain acts by those persons. Capital in itself can do nothing, nor can labor. It is with the owners and the manipulators of these things and the way in which those owners use these things as distinguished from the things themselves that the laws should have to do.

But this amendment says that these laws shall not apply to these persons so long as the thing that they use and manipulate to restrain trade is a human attribute—labor—and that all such persons shall be exempt from the operation of the law.

If the Webb amendment had specified certain proper acts and kinds of acts usually engaged in by such organizations as are named in the amendment, and which are now prohibited by a strict construction of the antitrust laws, and had provided that they might be legally done notwithstanding the antitrust laws, I would have supported the amendment.

It is the acts proper in themselves that should have been excepted from the operation of the antitrust laws, and the laws, with the exceptions adopted, should apply to everybody and every kind of organization. But in excepting certain organizations and classes of individuals from the operation of the law not only acts proper in themselves, such as a peaceful strike, are legalized, but acts not proper in themselves, such as a secondary boycott, are legalized.

I am opposed to any exemption which has such an effect or which might be so construed, and therefore I did not support the Webb amendment, and I also voted against the MacDonald and Thomas amendments.

Mr. BRYAN. Mr. Chairman, section 22 includes among the exceptions any case in the name of or on behalf of the United States. Does not that exception include receivership cases, where railroads, for instance, would be in the hands of the court and the court would enter orders concerning them? Are not all those cases conducted in the name of the United States?

Mr. WEBB. No; this is where the United States is a party to the suit.

Mr. BRYAN. But it does not say that. It says—

In the name of, or on behalf of, the United States.

My present impression is that these orders in receivership cases are issued in the name of the United States in the Federal courts.

Mr. WEBB. I think this does not cover those cases.

Mr. BRYAN. I will not offer any amendment, but I think you will discover an indefiniteness here.

The Clerk read as follows:

SEC. 23. That no proceeding for contempt shall be instituted against any person unless begun within one year from the date of the act complained of; nor shall any such proceeding be a bar to any criminal prosecution for the same act or acts; but nothing herein contained shall affect any proceedings in contempt pending at the time of the passage of this act.

Mr. MORGAN of Oklahoma. Mr. Chairman, I desire to offer an amendment to come in as a new section.

The CHAIRMAN. Are there any amendments to perfect the text of section 23? . . .

Mr. BUCHANAN of Illinois. Mr. Chairman, I have not taken up any of the time of this committee during this debate. Those who desire the freedom of action of the labor people of the country expected that we were going to have the practically unanimous support of the House to those amendments that we believed would exempt the labor people of the country—organized labor—in their liberty of action that the Constitution of the United States is supposed to guarantee.

It was stated on the floor, in the discussion of section 7, that the amendments adopted were a compromise on the part of the representatives of labor. While I do not assume to speak for organized labor, and while I am not wholly familiar with their thoughts in regard to the matter, I believe it is safe to say that they consider the question of exemption from the operation of such laws as the Sherman antitrust law, and laws created for the purpose of preventing the monopoly of commodities, as being entirely separate and apart from the questions involved in the activities of organized labor. They consider it so important to have human beings in their normal activities freed from the operations of the Sherman antitrust law that there is absolutely no chance for them to agree to any sort of a compromise, so far as that is concerned. While it is true that those of us who considered this question of such great and vital importance to the wageworkers of the country at first desired an amendment providing that the antitrust laws shall not apply, we believed that the amendment finally agreed upon was fully as strong as the amendment that we had first proposed.

I wish to say we did not accept that amendment as any sort of a compromise. We believed that the Democratic Party, the Progressive Party, and even the Republicans, the great majority of the Members of this House, had seen the light in regard to this question. We believed that they had plainly seen the difference between commodities and living human beings; in other words, that they had come to the conclusion that humanity was in a different class from a ton of coal, a bolt of cloth, or a pile of bricks, and therefore did not consider this to be class legislation of any sort, or any special privilege. In other words, labor organizations do not desire to be permitted to buy up and monopolize any commodity for the purpose of profit, but they do want to be placed in the same status—in other words, to be restored to the same status—in which they were before the Sherman antitrust law was twisted to apply to their activities. On this question there could be no compromise. If it was simply a question of language that meant the same thing, then we were not so much concerned. While personally I believed in making the language short and clean-cut, so that there could be no doubt in regard to the matter, and while so far as I was concerned I was willing to make the issue a clean-cut one, I claim that it is high time that the people of this country know how their public servants stand on this question, whether or not they really mean to give to the labor people of this country, who bear the burdens of industry, that freedom of activity guaranteed them by the Constitution. They believe the time has now come when judges shall not be permitted to strangle justice and liberty by construing and applying laws contrary to the intention of the creators of the law. . . .

Mr. MORGAN of Oklahoma. Now, Mr. Chairman, may I offer my amendment?

The CHAIRMAN. The gentleman from Oklahoma offers an amendment, which the Clerk will report.

The Clerk read as follows:

Mr. MORGAN of Oklahoma moves to amend, on page 40, by adding a new section, to follow section 23, and to be numbered section 24, as follows:

"SEC. 24. That whenever any United States attorney shall have reliable information that any corporation engaged in commerce in the manufacture, sale, or distribution of any necessity of life, or of any article, product, or commodity in common use is a virtual monopoly, or by reason of the nature, character, or extent of its business the absence of effective competition or for any other cause possesses the power to arbitrarily control the price or prices of any necessity of life, or of any article, product, or commodity in common use, or controls the price or prices paid to the producers of any article, commodity, or product in common use, or controls the price or prices paid for the product of any mine, or of any oil or gas well, it shall be the duty of said United States attorney, under the direction of the Attorney General, to file a petition in the United States court against said corporation alleging the aforesaid facts, and praying that the said corporation shall be adjudged a quasi-public corporation and made subject to the control of the Commissioner of Corporations or subject to the control of any commission that, at the passage of this act or thereafter, may be the successor of the Commissioner of Corporations, in all its practices, prices, and charges in like manner and to the same extent that common carriers are now subject to the control of the Interstate Commerce Commission; and if the court shall find that the material facts alleged in the petition are true it shall render a decree adjudging the said corporation to be a quasi-public corporation, and adjudging the said corporation to be subject in all its practices, prices, and charges to the control of the Commissioner of Corporations or the commission, as the case may be, as prayed for in the petition: *Provided,* That thereafter the practices of said corporation in conducting its business and the prices at which it shall sell its products and the price or prices it shall pay the producer of any of the articles, commodities, or products mentioned in this section shall be just and reasonable."

Mr. MORGAN of Oklahoma. Mr. Chairman—

Mr. CARLIN. I desire to make the point of order that the amendment is not germane to this bill.

Mr. MORGAN of Oklahoma. I should like to be heard on that point of order. I did not quite get the ground of the point of order, and I wish the gentleman would state it again.

Mr. CARLIN. That it is not germane. As I understand, the amendment relates to the duties of the trade commission.

Mr. MORGAN of Oklahoma. No; it provides for a proceeding whereby we may control a virtual monopoly.

Mr. CARLIN. I withdraw the point of order. Let the gentleman discuss the merits.

The CHAIRMAN. The gentleman from Virginia withdraws the point of order.

Mr. MORGAN of Oklahoma. Mr. Chairman, I do not present this amendment as expressing my conception of what should be done as a broad, comprehensive, effective measure to control the industrial corporations of this country, commonly known as trusts.

In the bill No. 18711, which I introduced in the Sixty-second Congress and which I reintroduced in this Congress, I have presented my idea of the administrative machinery that is needed in the form of a Federal trade commission, the power that should be conferred upon this commission, and the laws that should be enacted to enable the Federal Government to exercise the proper and necessary control over our large industrial corporations in both their practices and prices. But we have completed the consideration of the bill to create an interstate trade commission without conferring any adequate power upon the commission to exercise the control over our large industrial corporations which is demanded for the proper protection of the people of this country.

We have had this bill—House bill 15657—under consideration for a number of days. The last section has been read, and I propose a new section to follow the last section, which I believe would add materially toward securing substantial and beneficial results under the bill.

While the amendment does not express my idea of what should be done, I am certain it is a step in the right direction, and if it were adopted splendid results would follow therefrom. Then, having ascertained that the majority in this House will not go as far as I think we should go, I present this proposition, hoping the majority will go a part of the way in the right direction, for a half of a loaf is better than none.

Mr. Chairman, I want the Members of the House to get clearly in mind that this provision only applies to corporations which arbitrarily control the price or prices of some necessity of life or of some article in common use among the people.

It does not apply to all industrial corporations, however much their capital or wealth may be, but it narrows it down to providing a procedure against a corporation that possesses the arbitrary power to control the prices of a product in common use or of some necessity of life. And before that power shall be exercised, under this section that I propose, the United States attorney is required to file a suit in court, citing and bringing the corporation into court, giving that corporation the right to defend, and if after a full hearing the court shall find on the single issue that the corporation does control the price of a product in common use or of some necessity of life, then the court is given authority to adjudge that corporation a quasi public corporation and subject to the control of the Commissioner of Corporations or the commissioner that may be made his successor in the same manner that common carriers are subject to the control of the Interstate Commerce Commission.

In proceeding under the Sherman antitrust law we have two remedies. We may dissolve the corporation or fine it. The amendment which I have offered provides a new remedy. And a new remedy is needed. Under the Sherman law the American Tobacco Co. and the Standard Oil Co. were dissolved. But it is generally believed that some of these companies still possess the power to control prices of their products, yet there is no remedy, no procedure, for relief. In my own State the Standard Oil Co., or one of the branches into which it was divided by the court, absolutely controls the price of petroleum and its products in that State. The same company controls the price of products throughout other States of the Union. Under the law as it now exists our people are powerless. There is no procedure by which they can free themselves from the monopolistic power of this gigantic corporation.

Now, when you undertake to dissolve a corporation under the Sherman antitrust law you must prove the conspiracy and you must prove many things before you get a decree against it. In this procedure there would be one single proposition to prove, one single issue—Does the corporation control the price of any necessity of life or of any product in common use among the people? If, after a hearing in court, this question shall be answered in the affirmative, say, that the corporation ought not to be brought under the control of the Federal Government, who will say such corporation should be permitted to continue with this power to levy tribute upon the people? Such corporation has ceased to be a mere private business concern, making reasonable profits under competitive conditions. It is not profits it makes, but it is levying tribute; for a great corporation, controlling the production and the prices of an article in common use, really possesses the taxing power.

Now, I appeal to you to let this section go into this law. Give the people an additional remedy. Give the people a procedure whereby they may go into court and determine what power a big corporation has to arbitrarily control prices of articles in daily use among the people.

We hardly realize, I think, to what extent the prices of products in common use in this country are within the arbitrary control of great corporations. The farmer goes to town, and perhaps he wants to buy coal. He visits the coal yards, and they have all the same price. He wants to buy lumber, and he visits the lumber yards, and they all make the same price. He goes into a dry goods store to buy clothing for his family, and he finds that they all sell at the same price. He wants to borrow some money, and he goes to the banks, one after another, and they all charge the same rate of interest. Now, the local merchants are not to blame; they must have a reasonable profit; but they buy of big corporations which practically fix the prices at which local dealers must sell. But the farmer comes to town to sell his corn, wheat, or cattle, or hogs. He finds the prices at which he must sell his products are largely fixed by big corporations doing business in the great cities, the centers of trade and commerce. This is what the people are complaining about. This is the thing from which they ask relief. Do you propose to pass this trust bill without giving the people a single additional remedy? Do you think the people will think you have done your duty when you have prohibited a few things? The things which you have prohibited in this bill will not materially change present conditions. All the provisions in this bill are not sufficient to destroy a single trust or to take away from a single corporation the power to control the prices of articles in common use. [Applause.]

In our antitrust legislation we should keep clearly in mind what we want to accomplish, the evil to be eradicated, the result to be attained. We should have a definite program in mind. As I see it, this is what we want to do: Destroy monopoly, maintain competition, prohibit unfair practices, prevent unjust discrimination, secure equality of opportunity, insure reasonable prices, give protection to the people, encourage enterprise, reward industry, and promote prosperity. The one thing that is dangerous in a large corporation is its power to arbitrarily control prices—the prices not only of what people buy, but the prices of what farmers and other producers have to sell. Now, this a power that no private corporation should have or can have with safety to the people. Now, then, I have suggested a procedure and the judicial and administrative machinery by which any corporation suspected of possessing this power may be brought into court and the question determined. If the corporation is found to possess this power, then I provide that its practices and the prices of its products shall be subject to the control of a Federal commission so long as that power exists. We control the rates and charges of our transportation companies and of our public utility companies solely on the ground that their charges are not controlled by competition. I submit that we have the same moral and legal right, and that there is the same public necessity to control the prices of the products of our great industrial corporations when they possess a like power to control the prices of articles in common use. More than this, it will have a great moral effect upon the great business concerns of this country when the Government may, by a judicial proceeding, determine what degree of monopolistic power they possess; and, in addition to this, when you have demonstrated to the people that either through effective competition or governmental control they shall be fully protected from monopolistic prices and charges, you will have taken a long step toward social and industrial peace. You will have contributed to the material progress of our country. You will have laid the foundation for the highest possible expansion of our trade and commerce. You will have strengthened the fabric of the Republic and added to the prosperity, contentment, and happiness of the American people.

Mr. BUCHANAN of Illinois. Mr. Chairman, labor's representatives do not consider that they have compromised in regard to the amendments to this bill. I do not consider that the President has made any compromise nor undergone any change. To bear out my position I want to read what the President said about this legislation in his speech accepting the nomination of the Democratic Party.

Mr. KINDEL. Mr. Chairman, I make the point of order that the gentleman is not talking to the matter before the House.

The CHAIRMAN. The gentleman from Colorado makes the point of order—

Mr. DAVENPORT. Mr. Chairman, I did not understand that the gentleman from Colorado made a point of order.

Mr. MURDOCK. The gentleman from Colorado has made the point of order, but the gentleman from Illinois is entitled to proceed.

The CHAIRMAN. The Chair understood the gentleman from Colorado to make a point of order that the gentleman from Illinois was not confining his remarks to the subject. The gentleman from Illinois will proceed.

Mr. BUCHANAN of Illinois. I want to say now that the gentleman from Colorado made an erroneous statement a short time ago when he said that I objected to his remarks. I did object to his inserting some matter in the RECORD in regard to the Colorado strike, but I never objected to the gentleman making a statement on the floor.

Mr. KINDEL rose.

The CHAIRMAN. For what purpose does the gentleman from Colorado rise?

Mr. KINDEL. I want to correct the gentleman from Illinois.

The CHAIRMAN. Does the gentleman from Illinois yield?

Mr. BUCHANAN of Illinois. No; I do not yield. As I was saying, the President stated in his speech accepting the Democratic nomination:

> The working people of America—if they must be distinguished from the minority that constitutes the rest of it—are, of course, the backbone of the Nation. No law that safeguards their life, that improves the physical and moral conditions under which they live, that makes their (the working people of America) hours of labor rational and tolerable, that gives them freedom to act in their own interests, and that protects them where they can not protect themselves, can properly be regarded as class legislation or as anything but a measure taken in the interest of the whole people, whose partnership in right action we are trying to establish and make real and practical. It is in this spirit that we shall act if we are genuine spokesmen of the whole country.

Therefore, I say, Mr. Chairman, that when the President lends his support to legislation such as the amendment labor desires to secure in this bill, he has not undergone a change. I want to say, in addition to what I have said, that those who can not distinguish the difference between human physical and mental activity and commodities, in my opinion, are mentally unfit to pass upon matters that concern humankind. Before they are capable of coming to the right conclusions in regard to the matter they must understand that labor is not in the same class with commodities, that a human being can not be placed in that class. In regard to the injunction, to me it is a reflection upon the republican form of government in this country where our forefathers spent their blood and lives for freedom and liberty that it becomes necessary to pass an act to give the citizens of our Republic that equality and liberty which the Constitution guarantees; and when we are passing measures to curb injunction judges, or, in other words, when judges enjoin citizens from exercising their legal and constitutional rights, they are usurping power and therefore committing a crime. I hear much said about the dignity of the judges, and I agree that the position of judge is a dignified position, but when those who are holding that position do not conduct themselves in accordance with the dignity of the position it is all the more reason why they should be criticized for the wrongs they commit.

The usurpation of power by the judges of our country has created public mistrust and contempt for our judiciary. When our judges are guided by the justice and patriotism of our forefathers, who freed us from the tyranny of monarchy, public respect and confidence will be restored; but when their decisions and constructions of the laws are influenced by the vicious combinations of the criminal rich they will continue to lose the confidence and respect of the great masses of the people.

Section 18 of this bill is a prohibition of restraining orders and injunctions by the courts of the United States. It does not legalize any act that is not already legal and constitutional, and therefore it is for the purpose of preventing judges from usurping power by issuing injunctions to prevent citizens from exercising their legal and constitutional rights.

I am unalterably opposed to government by injunction. I do not think that judges have any right to issue injunctions restraining citizens from violating the laws of the country, because in every State, county, city, District, and Territory of the United States the Government has its officials to enforce the laws, and in my judgment justice will be better served if the laws against violence and other necessary prohibitions are enforced in the regular way by giving a hearing and trial by jury, as provided in the Constitution and laws of the country. If wage workers violate the law they should be prosecuted the same as anyone else, no matter whether there is industrial strife or industrial peace; in fact, all they ask is to be on equal terms before the law with every other citizen.

The justice which affects men and women is not some impersonal, universal thing, but a force which accords them their rights in the relations with other men and women. Justice must be made effective in all the interests and phases of life. Since justice can only result through the conductivity of a human will, the human agent is the most important factor in securing it. Theoretically absolute justice is, of course, never realized in the actual, but we must at least approximate it. To be an agent of justice is a most serious function, requiring the highest qualities of heart and mind.

To do justice one must understand the past and the future. Whatever the judge knows of the past is part of his own mental background. Whatever he knows of the future is his prophetic instinct born of his knowledge of the human heart.

Knowledge is the mass of usable impressions and facts that have accumulated from environment, thought, and life. This knowledge is the means of interpreting the present. Whatever experience is not a part of one's knowledge can not influence the mind in deciding present problems. A judge whose mental capacity has never been keyed to the whir of modern industry and does not contain real experiences that enable him to step into the shoes of the man who works for an employer for wages can never get the viewpoint of those who view life from the machines of industry. If he can not get the viewpoint, he can never enter into that life to a sufficient degree to enable him to know justice for the affairs of that life, for he could never understand what it was all about. A man who does not take for granted the great things in human nature can not be an agent of justice, for he has no sense of the future into which the whole world is swinging. A judge who does not believe in the masses can apply only the letter of the law without understanding the spirit of justice.

Perhaps no more conspicuous example of the absence of the true judicial temperament can be found than Alston G. Dayton, Federal judge for the northern district of West Virginia. His official acts prove either that he is unable to understand the life of the masses of the people or that he has deliberately allied himself with a particular class interest against the welfare of the masses. Whichever is true, he is incapable of unprejudiced decisions and unable to perform duties in a manner requisite to justice.

In the article by Samuel Gompers, president of the American Federation of Labor, appearing in the current issue of the American Federationist some of Judge Dayton's official acts were discussed which have aroused condemnation of him as a judge and have brought criticism upon that which he represents. The miners in West Virginia endeavored to bring the judicial abuses of this judge before those authorized to remove him from office. Another effort to secure his removal is a resolution for impeachment proceedings against him introduced in this House by Congressman NEELY of West Virginia.

In the passage of the legislation embodied in this bill the Democratic Party is fulfilling its promises to the American wageworkers by enacting a law to protect them against judicial usurpation of authority and to secure to them full enjoyment of their rights, and it will secure for this administration and the Congress the confidence and support of the great masses of the American voters.

The CHAIRMAN. The question is on the amendment offered by the gentleman from Oklahoma.

The amendment was rejected.

Mr. WEBB. Mr. Chairman, I ask unanimous consent to return to section 9 to make a correction.

The CHAIRMAN. The gentleman from North Carolina asks unanimous consent to return to section 9. Is there objection?

There was no objection.

Mr. FLOYD of Arkansas. Mr. Chairman, I desire to offer the following amendment which I send to the desk and ask to have read.

The Clerk read as follows:

On page 28 amend as follows:
"In line 20, after the word 'director,' amend by inserting the word 'officer or employee.' On page 29, in line 1, amend by inserting after 'director' the words 'officer or employee.' And in the same line, after the word 'elected' insert the words 'or selected'; and in line 3, on the same page, amend by inserting after the word 'election' the word [sic] 'or employment.' "

The CHAIRMAN. The question is on agreeing to the amendments.

The amendments were agreed to.

Mr. FLOYD of Arkansas. Mr. Chairman, I offer the following further amendment, which I send to the desk and ask to have read.

The Clerk read as follows:

On page 30, after line 18, amend by inserting as a new paragraph the following:
"When any person elected or chosen as a director or officer or selected as an employee of any bank, or other corporation, subject to the provisions of this act, is eligible at the time of his election or selection to act for such bank or other corporation in such capacity, his eligibility to act in such capacity shall not be affected, and he shall not become or be deemed amenable to any of the provisions hereof by reason of any change in the affairs of such bank or other corporation, from whatsoever cause, whether specifically excepted by any of the provisions hereof or not, until the expiration of one year from the date of his election or employment."

The CHAIRMAN. The question is on agreeing to the amendment.

The amendment was agreed to.

Mr. MURRAY of Oklahoma. Mr. Chairman, I offer the following amendment, which I send to the desk and ask to have read.

The Clerk read as follows:

On page 28, line 14, strike out "$2,500,000," and insert "$1,000,000."

Mr. WEBB. Mr. Chairman, a parliamentary inquiry. Is that amendment in order unless the gentleman has unanimous consent to offer it?

Mr. MURRAY of Oklahoma. The gentleman returns to the section by unanimous consent, and he did not specify any particular amendment, and that opened section 9 for any other amendment.

The CHAIRMAN. The Chair is inclined to the opinion that under the terms on which this section was returned to the amendment would be in order.

Mr. WEBB. Mr. Chairman, this section 9 was not passed by unanimous consent. Section 12 was the only one that was passed by unanimous consent. I asked unanimous consent to return to section 9 to make some corrections.

Mr. MANN. It was for the purpose of offering amendments.

Mr. WEBB. That is true.

The CHAIRMAN. The gentleman from Oklahoma is entitled to offer his amendment, the Chair thinks, and the gentleman is recognized for five minutes.

Mr. MURRAY of Oklahoma. Mr. Chairman, I drafted this amendment while the gentleman was talking, and the amendment ought to apply not only to line 14 but also to line 18. The purpose of my amendment is this: The bill provides that only those corporations have a capital stock and surplus of $2,500,000 can come within this act, prohibiting interlocking directors. Without this lowering of the amount of $1,000,000 many large banks, trust companies, and other concerns will escape the prohibition against interlocking directors. I really believe that $1,000,000 stock banks is too high to reach the evil, but certainly $2,500,000 banks will let too many out to reach the evil. I therefore trust the committee will let this amendment go in.

The CHAIRMAN. The question is on agreeing to the amendment offered by the gentleman from Oklahoma.

The amendment was rejected.

Mr. MANN. Mr. Chairman, I ask unanimous consent to return to section 11, for the purpose of offering an amendment.

Mr. WEBB. But one amendment?

Mr. MANN. Yes

Mr. CARLIN. I suggest that the gentleman make it specific.

Mr. MANN. Mr. Chairman, I ask unanimous consent that we return to section 11, in order that the gentleman from Pennsylvania [Mr. GRAHAM], a member of the committee, may offer an amendment.

The CHAIRMAN. The gentleman from Illinois asks unanimous consent that the committee return to section 11 for the purpose stated. Is there objection?

Mr. FOWLER. Mr. Chairman, reserving the right to object, I would be glad if the gentleman would indicate what amendment he desires to offer.

Mr. WEBB. Mr. Chairman, I hope the gentleman from Illinois will not object. The committee is advised of what the amendment is.

The CHAIRMAN. Is there objection? [After a pause.] The Chair hears none, and it is so ordered. The Clerk will report the amendment.

The Clerk read as follows:

Page 31, line 9, after the word "district," insert:

"*Provided*, That no writ of subpoena shall be issued to run for more than 100 miles from the trial court without the permission of the court being first had, upon proper application, and cause shown."

Mr. GRAHAM of Pennsylvania. Mr. Chairman, section 11, as I understand it, has been introduced for the purpose of enlarging the scope of the service of a subpoena. By its terms as the section stands the subpoena will run now throughout the whole of the United States without any limit or hindrance; and when one remembers that a subpoena is a writ of right and that upon paying the fee a subpoena may issue one can readily see how this bill puts it in the power of a person to summon an individual from California to come to New Jersey and vice versa, or from one end of the country to the other. Now, that is an extraordinary power that would expose all of our citizens to a severe hardship. It might lead to the ruin and destruction of a man's business, besides the severe inconveniences to which it would subject him. . . .

Mr. CARLIN. I think if the gentleman would change the amendment so as to read the writ should run to the judicial district the committee might accept it.

Mr. GRAHAM of Pennsylvania. I want to say in answer I am perfectly willing, although the existing law permits service of a subpoena upon citizens living outside the district for not over 100 miles from the court.

Mr. FLOYD of Arkansas. I understand the existing law permits the running of a subpoena 100 miles outside of the State. If it was limited to 100 miles within the State, there are plenty of judicial districts in the United States—

Mr. GRAHAM of Pennsylvania. I beg leave to say that I am correct in my statement about the service.

Mr. FLOYD of Arkansas. Anywhere in the judicial district?

Mr. GRAHAM of Pennsylvania. And 100 miles from the courthouse for citizens living outside of the district. That is the law as it stands to-day. It may be necessary in some cases, there may be isolated exceptional cases, in which the power given in this bill ought to be exercised; but while we grant this power we should put a certain limitation upon it, that it must be made upon proper application and cause shown. It seems to me to be in the interest of all our citizens that this amendment should be allowed.

Mr. WILSON of Florida. Does the gentleman's amendment apply to criminal cases as well as civil?

Mr. GRAHAM of Pennsylvania. No.

The CHAIRMAN. The question is on agreeing to the amendment offered by the gentleman from Pennsylvania.

The question was taken, and the Chairman announced the noes seemed to have it.

Upon a division (demanded by Mr. GRAHAM of Pennsylvania) there were—ayes 59, noes 15.

So the amendment was agreed to.

Mr. TOWNER. Mr. Chairman, I have an amendment to offer to section 12.

The CHAIRMAN. That will not be in order without unanimous consent to return to section 12.

Mr. TOWNER. I am not asking for unanimous consent.

Mr. GARNER. Mr. Chairman, is this amendment to be offered by unanimous consent or by right of a Member?

Mr. MANN. We passed over section 12 yesterday.

The CHAIRMAN. The Chair stated that it will not be in order except by unanimous consent.

Mr. MANN. We passed over section 12, and I think the committee is entitled to recognition.

The CHAIRMAN. The Chair will recognize the gentleman from North Carolina [Mr. WEBB].

Mr. WEBB. Mr. Chairman, I ask to return to section 12, which was passed over yesterday, and I ask the Chair to recognize the gentleman from Arkansas [Mr. FLOYD], who has a substitute for section 12, and no other amendment.

The CHAIRMAN. The gentleman from Arkansas offers a substitute, which the Clerk will report.

Mr. FLOYD of Arkansas. Mr. Chairman, I send to the Clerk's desk a substitute for section 12, which I offer.

Mr. STAFFORD. Mr. Chairman, a parliamentary inquiry.

The CHAIRMAN. The gentleman will state it.

Mr. STAFFORD. Did the chairman of the committee ask unanimous consent to return to this section for the purpose of offering an amendment?

Mr. WEBB. It was passed over last night, and we have a right to return to it. That is the order of business now.

The CHAIRMAN. The Clerk will report the substitute.

The Clerk read as follows:

Page 31, amend by inserting in lieu of section 12 the following:

Mr. VOLSTEAD. Mr. Chairman, I make the point of order that there is already a substitute pending. I offered a substitute for this same section yesterday.

The CHAIRMAN. The present occupant of the chair was not present on that occasion.

Mr. STAFFORD. It is shown in the RECORD.

⊥ Mr. FLOYD of Arkansas. Mr. Chairman, I was not aware the gentleman from Minnesota had a substitute pending.

Mr. WEBB. Mr. Chairman, there is no doubt about the gentleman from Minnesota having offered a substitute, and I asked to pass over the section until to-day, hoping to get together on an amendment.

Mr. GARNER. I suggest the gentleman from Arkansas withdraw his substitute.

Mr. FLOYD of Arkansas. I withdraw my amendment for the present.

The CHAIRMAN. Without objection, the gentleman from Arkansas will be permitted to withdraw his substitute for the present. The Clerk will report the substitute offered by the gentleman from Minnesota on yesterday.

The Clerk read as follows:

Strike out section 12 and substitute:
"Any person who shall do, or cause to be done, or shall willingly suffer and permit to be done any act, matter, or thing prohibited or declared to be unlawful in the antitrust laws or shall aid or abet therein, shall be deemed guilty of such prohibited and unlawful acts, matters, and things and shall be subject to the punishments prescribed therefor in the trust laws."

Mr. VOLSTEAD. Mr. Chairman, I ask unanimous consent to change the word "and" in the second line to the word "or," and also by inserting in the last line the word "anti" before the word "trust," so as to make it read, "antitrust laws."

The CHAIRMAN. The Clerk will report the proposed modification.

The Clerk read as follows:

Modify the amendment by striking out the word "and" in line 2 of the amendment and substitute the word "or"; and in the last line place the word "anti" before the word "trust."

The CHAIRMAN. Is there objection? [After a pause.] The Chair hears none.

Mr. VOLSTEAD. Mr. Chairman, I would like to call attention to this and to some extent compare it with the amendment which was offered by the gentleman from Arkansas. I think this would meet the situation better than the one he has offered. In the first place, this does not undertake to change the extent of the punishments. This simply says that as to any act that is criminal under existing law, if any person does anything to aid or assist in doing that act, he shall be guilty just the same as the corporation. Now, that seems to me better, because you do not have to consider whether the punishment of $5,000 is the proper one, the sum mentioned by the amendment proposed by the gentleman from Arkansas. Different sections of this act provide for different punishments, some greater than others.

This amendment is drafted in line with a similar provision contained in the interstate-commerce law and seeks to accomplish the purpose of that provision in substantially the same language. It uses languages quite generally used in criminal statutes. I do not see why we should not go as far as this does. The amendment proposed by the gentleman from Arkansas [Mr. FLOYD] does not go nearly as far as this, because it only provides punishments in case the individual authorizes or orders an unlawful act.

Now, why should not a person who willingly suffers or permits a thing to be done or who aids or abets in doing a thing denounced as a crime be guilty under this statute, just as he is under almost any other criminal statute? It seems to me there is no reason why we should be so extremely lenient to these violators of the law. Why should we not apply to them a statute like the statutes we apply to other offenders?

I do not think that there is anything further that I care to add. It is a simple proposition. If you desire to draw this statute so as to make the crime personal and carry out the promises made in your stump speeches let us put it in language so that it means something.

Mr. FLOYD of Arkansas. Mr. Chairman, I desire to oppose the amendment offered by the gentleman from Minnesota [Mr. VOLSTEAD]. He has very correctly stated that his proposed amendment goes very much further than the amendment proposed in section 12 as it is now written, and further than the amendment I propose to offer as a substitute for section 12, in case this is voted down. I have several objections to the wording of this provision. I think it is indefinite. I think it is too drastic and goes too far. It not only proposes to make unlawful the act of any person that aids and encourages, but also makes unlawful the acts of those who assist in any way those who violate the antitrust laws.

Now, in the operations, these great corporations with which we are dealing, under the broad terms of this language, every man that aids in any way in carrying out any unlawful purpose of the corporation would come within the scope of this provision. . . .

Mr. MANN. Mr. Chairman, as I understand the purpose of this section, it is to make the act of the individual punishable, although he is an officer of the corporation, and to make the corporation itself punishable.

Mr. FLOYD of Arkansas. Yes; the corporation itself.

Mr. MANN. Why does not this language, inserted in a number of laws, cover the case identically—

When construing and enforcing the provisions of this act, the act, omission, or failure of any officer, agent, or other person acting for or employed by any corporation, company, society, or association, within the scope of his employment or office, shall in every case be also deemed to be the act, omission, or failure of such corporation, company, society, or association as well as that of the person.

Mr. FLOYD of Arkansas. Well, I think that is entirely different. That makes the act of the individual the act of the corporation and holds the corporation responsible for the act of the individual, and the purpose of that provision is entirely different from and the reverse of the purpose of this section.

Mr. MANN. It makes the act of the individual punishable as to the individual, and also punishable as to the corporation. I understood that was the purpose of this section.

Mr. FLOYD of Arkansas. Certainly; it makes the act of the individual punishable within itself, and also attributes to the corporation guilt on account of the act of the individual.

Mr. MANN. Yes. Here is an officer of a corporation who performs an act.

Mr. FLOYD of Arkansas. Our proposition is the reverse of that, in a sense.

Mr. MANN. The corporation must act through individuals. There is no other way for it to act. Now, you propose in a section, as I understand, that where an act is committed by a corporation, which, of course, must be committed through individuals, the individuals may be punished if they are officers or employees of the corporation. That is identically what is accomplished by this provision which I read, which I think, in the exact form it is in, was carried in the pure-food law, but it has also been carried in a number of acts passed since then. But it has met the construction that where an individual who is a member or an officer of a corporation fails to perform an act or commits an act the corporation can be punished for that and so can the individual.

Mr. FLOYD of Arkansas. That is correct; but I like the provision that we present much better than that provision. Under the existing law the corporation may be convicted. True, as the gentleman from Illinois states, the corporation can only violate the law through the acts of its agents, officers, or employees; but we are proposing and seeking by this provision to visit guilt upon the real offenders.

Now, under the existing law, the man who does the act which constitutes a violation of the law can be punished as an individual, just as the corporation can be punished on account of the unlawful act of its agents or officers. But we propose by this provision to hold as responsible under the criminal statutes the man who authorizes or orders wrongful things to be done. In other words, we are seeking to reach the directors and the high officers of these corporations who authorize or direct their employees to do acts which constitute violations of the antitrust laws, and we much prefer the language we have used to that proposed by the gentleman from Minnesota [Mr. VOLSTEAD] or that suggested by the gentleman from Illinois [Mr. MANN]. . . .

Mr. VOLSTEAD. I want to ask the gentleman from Arkansas this question: Are you quite sure that this does not make it necessary, first, to convict the corporation before you can indict the individual? I want to call your attention to the first part of this amendment. It says that "whenever a corporation shall be guilty, such offense shall be deemed also that of the individual directors." Now, are you quite sure that a court would not hold that you must first prove that the corporation is guilty?

Mr. FLOYD of Arkansas. In answer to the gentleman's question, I will state that if it said "whenever a corporation is convicted" it would mean what he suggests.

Mr. VOLSTEAD. It says "when they are guilty." They are not guilty in law until they are convicted.

Mr. FLOYD of Arkansas. I do not think the language here used would admit of that interpretation.

Mr. VOLSTEAD. It seems to me that this is open to the same objection as the original section. While it is true that the original section requires a conviction, this section requires first a showing that the corporation is guilty, because until there is proof of guilt the court could not say that the corporation is guilty. Nearly all our antitrust suits are brought as equity suits, because it is of very little use to bring a criminal suit against a corporation. Consequently this will practically shield the persons participating in the guilty act by making their conviction depend upon the conviction of the corporation, which is not likely to take place.

Mr. FLOYD of Arkansas. I will say to the gentleman from Minnesota that we do not make the conviction of an individual conditional upon the guilt of the corporation. We provide that where the corporation is guilty it shall be deemed the offense of the officers, directors, or agents authorizing, ordering, or doing the thing prohibited, but they may be guilty independently of that, and if guilty may be tried and convicted without reference to the guilt of the corporation.

Mr. VOLSTEAD. I know; but if you make the guilt of the officers dependent upon the guilt of the corporation, you can not convict the officers until you convict the corporation. There is only one way known to the law under which you can prove the guilt of the corporation, and that is by a conviction; you do not want that, because you are wasting your time and energy in proving the corporation guilty. What you want to do with the corporation is to bring your suit against it in equity. And you want to be at liberty to bring your criminal suit against the officers at the same time for any violation of the antitrust law.

Mr. FLOYD of Arkansas. I hope the House will vote down the amendment of the gentleman from Minnesota. . . .

Mr. BEALL of Texas. In the amendment which you have offered do you still include this phrase—

That whenever a corporation shall be guilty of the violation of any of the provisions of the antitrust laws—

Mr. FLOYD of Arkansas. Yes.

Mr. BEALL of Texas. Mr. Chairman, I think there is something in the suggestion made by the gentleman from Minnesota [Mr. VOLSTEAD]. I do not believe, if that phrase remains in the section, any officer of a corporation can be convicted of a violation of the antitrust laws until after the corporation of which he is an officer has been convicted of it.

Mr. BRYAN. Criminally guilty, too.

Mr. BEALL of Texas. Criminally guilty. Now let us look at it:

That whenever a corporation shall be guilty of the violation of any of the provisions of the antitrust laws, the offense shall be deemed to be also that of the individual directors, officers, or agents of such corporation, and upon the conviction of the corporation any director, officer, or agent who shall have authorized, ordered, or done any of such prohibited acts shall be deemed guilty of a misdemeanor, and upon conviction therefor shall be punished by a fine not exceeding $5,000, or by imprisonment not exceeding one year, or by both, in the discretion of the court.

Now, as a condition precedent to the convicting of any one of these officers or agents you have first to establish the fact that the corporation has been guilty of a violation of the antitrust law through a judicial conviction.

Mr. BRYAN. And you have got to put it in your indictment.

Mr. BEALL of Texas. It is true that the corporation acts only through officers and agents, but it seems to me it would be much more direct language, and a much plainer provision, if you should say that any person acting or purporting to act as the agent or as an officer of an offending corporation, who does any of the things forbidden by the antitrust laws shall be guilty of a misdemeanor, and shall be punished so and so, and eliminate this requirement which, if it remains, must be given some meaning. You are seeking to convict a man of some criminal offense, and one of the conditions which the prosecution will be required to meet will be to prove the fact that the corporation has been guilty of a violation of the provisions of the antitrust laws. I think the amendment of the gentleman from Minnesota [Mr. VOLSTEAD] is preferable. . . .

Mr. MCCOY. Is it not perfectly possible also that an officer of a corporation might commit an ultra vires act and the corporation not be liable, whereas all the while he might be doing something in violation of the law?

Mr. BEALL of Texas. That is true. A man who does something in violation of the provisions of the antitrust law may be doing something that is entirely beyond his authority as an officer or agent of the corporation, but yet the effect of his act is to bring about a violation and a transgression of the law as laid down in the antitrust statutes. It is my opinion that the amendment of the gentleman from Minnesota [Mr. VOLSTEAD] is in better form and reaches the evil which you are seeking to reach more directly and certainly and perhaps more efficiently than the amendment suggested by my colleague on the committee, the gentleman from Arkansas [Mr. FLOYD].

Mr. LENROOT. I should like to ask the gentleman whether it is not true that there are a great many acts which, standing alone by themselves, are not wrongful, are not within the condemnation of the antitrust law, but which become wrongful only when committed or performed in furtherance of an unlawful combination, and therefore you must have the unlawful combination in connection with the performance of the act in order to reach what we ought to reach by this amendment?

Mr. CARLIN. In other words, you must have the offense by the corporation.

Mr. BEALL of Texas. That may be true in some instances, but it is also true that there are certain things forbidden by this bill that we are now passing—certain specific acts that if a man commits he violates the antitrust law. He need not be in conspiracy with anybody. It is not required that he shall be cooperating with anybody. If he commits any one of these acts, he violates the antitrust law. Now, why not say that the man who does one of these forbidden things, acting as an officer or agent of a corporation, shall be guilty of a violation of the antitrust law, and in that way make his guilt personal? . . .

Mr. GREEN of Iowa. Mr. Chairman, I agree with the gentleman from Arkansas [Mr. FLOYD] that the language read by the gentleman from Illinois was intended to operate just the converse of what is intended by this section, namely, to make the corporation liable for the act of the individual; but I agree also with the gentleman from Texas [Mr. BEALL] who states substantially that the amendment of the gentleman from Arkansas [Mr. FLOYD] does not obviate the objections to the section as it now stands.

The section as it now stands undoubtedly requires two convictions before the guilt of the individual can be established and he be punished. As the gentleman from Texas has properly said, under the amendment proposed by the gentleman from Arkansas the conviction of the corporation will still be required as a condition precedent. The gentleman from Arkansas said he thought the amendment proposed by the gentleman from Minnesota was too drastic, but it only embodies a general principle of the criminal law that whoever aids, abets, assists, assents to, or consents in an affirmative way to any criminal act is liable to all the consequence of it and may be punished. . . .

Mr. MANN. The gentleman made a distinction between corporations being held responsible for the acts of the officer or agent and the agent and officer being held responsible for the acts of the corporation. Does the gentleman believe that if you convict the Standard Oil Co. of a criminal act, that that authorizes the conviction of every agent of the Standard Oil Co. throughout the United States in a criminal prosecution?

Mr. GREEN of Iowa. Oh, the gentleman either misunderstood me or I made a statement which I did not intend. As a matter of fact, I do not think this provision is needed at all.

Mr. MANN. As a matter of fact, can you convict a man of an offense of which he knew nothing and in which he did not participate?

Mr. GREEN of Iowa. No; and the amendment of the gentleman from Minnesota proposes nothing of the kind.

Mr. MANN. I am not talking about the amendment of the gentleman from Minnesota. The gentleman from Iowa undertook to distinguish between a corporation being held responsible for the acts of the officers and the agents, and the agent or officer being held responsible for the act of the corporation. That distinction I can not get through my cranium.

Mr. GREEN of Iowa. That distinction was made by the gentlemen who drew the bill, and not by me.

Mr. MANN. The gentleman from Iowa was supporting it.

Mr. GREEN of Iowa. No; the gentleman misinterpreted me.

Mr. MANN. If the gentleman does not change his remarks in the RECORD he will find that I am right.

Mr. GREEN of Iowa. Mr. Chairman, as I stated a moment ago, the amendment of the gentleman from Minnesota puts in force a principle of the criminal law that whoever assists a criminal to do a criminal act shall himself be liable. It is not a strange provision; it is one that has been applied in the Sherman law as it now stands. The amendment of the gentleman from Minnesota does not weaken the Sherman law, and I am inclined to think it strengthens it. Therefore I am in favor of the amendment of the gentleman from Minnesota. We ought to have in this bill at least one provision that does not detract from the present law, and here is an opportunity to get it. I hope the amendment of the gentleman from Minnesota will prevail.

Mr. HULINGS. Mr. Chairman, I move to strike out the last word. I believe that much of the failure of the antitrust law is because, in most cases, the courts simply fine the corporation. I believe all these restrictive punitive statutes on this subject fail greatly for that very reason. I can not quite understand, although I know the courts have so held, how a corporation, the creature of the law, having no existence save for authorized purposes, can do an illegal act. Every unlawful act of a corporation is ultra vires, and the corporation is, in strict logic, incapable of doing anything except that which is in the proper sphere of its creation. Anything wrong or unlawful that is done is the authorized act of an individual, a director, officer, or agent of that corporation. I believe if you make these punitive statutes apply strictly to the officers of corporations who willfully do these ultra vires acts that you will eradicate much of the evils of corporate management. We have seen that fines amount to nothing. The officers of the corporation, and in the name of the corporation, go on and repeat the acts in spite of the repeated fines, but if you punish the men who use the powers of the corporation outside of the proper sphere of their duty, you will stop these repeated violations of the law. If you take hold of these men and punish them by imprisonment, much of the present disregard of law will cease. That is the way to stop this sort of thing. The fining of corporations means nothing; they simply go on with the acts of monopoly and collect those fines again from the people. [Applause.]

For these reasons, Mr. Chairman, I believe it to be much more important that this section of the bill should clearly provide for the prosecution of the responsible officers and agents of corporations violating the antitrust laws, independently of any prosecution of the corporation, chiefly for the reason that such personal liability is the practical way to stop the abuse of corporate power and for the additional reason that, logically and ethically, a corporation, having no power except for lawful purposes, can not conceive the intent to commit a crime, although I know the courts have held that a corporation may be indicted for a crime.

The CHAIRMAN. The question is on the amendment offered by the gentleman from Minnesota.

The question was taken; and on a division (demanded by Mr. FLOYD of Arkansas) there were 39 ayes and 24 noes.

Mr. FLOYD of Arkansas. Mr. Chairman, I demand tellers.

Tellers were ordered, and the Chair appointed as tellers Mr. VOLSTEAD and Mr. WEBB.

The committee again divided, and the tellers reported that there were 40 ayes and 50 noes.

So the amendment was rejected.

The CHAIRMAN. The Clerk will report the amendment offered by the gentleman from Arkansas.

The Clerk read, as follows:

On page 31 amend by inserting in lieu of section 12 the following:

"SEC. 12. That whenever a corporation shall be guilty of the violation of any of the provisions of the antitrust laws the offense shall be deemed to be a misdemeanor, and such offense shall be deemed to be also that of the individual directors, officers, or agents of such corporation who shall have authorized, ordered, or done any of such prohibited acts, and any corporation violating any of the provisions of the antitrust laws or any director, officer, or agent thereof who shall have authorized, ordered, or done any such prohibited acts, upon conviction therefor shall be punished, if a corporation, by a fine of not exceeding $5,000; if a director, officer, or agent of a corporation, by a fine of not exceeding $5,000 or by imprisonment for not exceeding one year, or by both such fine and imprisonment in the discretion of the court." . . .

Mr. FLOYD of Arkansas. Mr. Chairman, I regard this as a very important proposition, and I hope that gentlemen will hear me in defense of it. . . .

Mr. GARNER. Does the gentleman's proposed amendment require the corporation to be convicted before a director or agent can be convicted?

Mr. FLOYD of Arkansas. I do not so understand it.

Mr. GARNER. I just read the amendment a moment ago, and I think it specifically states that when a corporation is convicted that then the acts of its agents and directors shall be considered—

Mr. FLOYD of Arkansas. Oh, I beg the gentleman's pardon, but it says guilty. . . .

Mr. THOMSON of Illinois. Who is to determine whether the corporation is guilty?

Mr. FLOYD of Arkansas. This is a question to be established by proof, as a matter of course.

Mr. THOMSON of Illinois. Then it would have to be established in court.

Mr. FLOYD of Arkansas. I desire to be perfectly frank. I desire to state that our idea was to so write the law that when one of those corporations had been found guilty that the parties who were responsible for that violation of law could be punished for the acts that constituted that violation of law as individuals.

If they commit acts held to be unlawful they can be punished now, as I suggest, but we can not reach the men who are really responsible, the men who authorize and direct the acts to be done. They shelter themselves under technical provisions of the law, and some subordinate or minor employee of the corporation, some man who is paid $5 a day for his services, as in the sugar case, is convicted and sent to the penitentiary, while the rich director or officer who sits back in his room and directs the employee to do the things prohibited and gives him $5 a week extra to violate the law is never touched and never convicted. Our purpose is certainly good, and if the House can help us in perfecting the amendment we will welcome their assistance. But we regard this section as important. If the individual now violates the Sherman law he can be convicted independently of the conviction of the corporation, but we seek to impute to the individual in this provision the guilt of the corporation, and subject him to punishment, but in all fairness we do not make him guilty without further trial. We provide he shall be indicted, tried, and proceeded against in the usual way. That is the purpose of this section. . . .

Mr. TOWNER. Would it not be absolutely necessary in any prosecution against any individual to allege in the indictment that the corporation had been convicted, and would not the indictment be subject to demurrer unless that allegation was made in the indictment?

Mr. FLOYD of Arkansas. Under this particular section I will state to the gentleman that that might be true, but still that very fact would enable us to reach a class of cases that we can not now reach under existing law. But if the individual independently had violated the Sherman law and was guilty of violation of it in any way as an individual, he could be convicted without ever convicting the corporation, while if the guilt of the corporation is imputed to his acts as an individual, and those acts as an individual would not constitute a violation of the Sherman law, then under this provision, if written into the law, such acts would become unlawful and the adoption of this provision would bring these forbidden acts within the purview of the law and make the director, officer, or agent guilty, the guilt of the corporation being imputed to him.

Mr. TOWNER. But the injurious effect would be that you never could convict any individual without previously convicting the corporation.

Mr. FLOYD of Arkansas. The purpose of this section is to enable the Government, when it has convicted the corporation, to reach those responsible officers who have been proven in the trial to be guilty of a violation of law by presentment of an indictment and trial. It authorizes their conviction not only for acts done but for acts authorized or ordered to be done, and gentlemen who think this would be any protection to the corporation or its directors, officers, or agents and would give them any leniency entirely misconceive the purpose of this provision. . . .

Mr. VOLSTEAD. Is not this true, that the Government very seldom indicts a corporation? It brings a suit in equity, while this compels a double action if you seek to hold the individual criminally. It compels first a criminal action against the corporation and then perhaps a suit in equity, while under the law as it now stands you can indict and convict the individual without paying any attention to the corporation, so far as any criminal procedure is concerned, and you can at the same time pursue your remedy in equity.

Mr. FLOYD of Arkansas. In answer to the gentleman's question I will say this: That this in no way affects the procedure under existing law, either criminal or civil. If an individual is guilty of violating the Sherman law, he can be indicted independently of this provision; but the series of acts which constitute a violation of the Sherman law are not crimes within themselves under existing law. If we adopt this provision, whenever a corporation is convicted of violation of the Sherman law and the guilt of the corporation is imputed to the individual officers or agents of the corporation, then acts done in furtherance of an unlawful combination become within this provision specifically indictable offenses that are not indictable now; and the result would be that you could indict and convict the officers and agents that were responsible for that violation on a state of facts on which they will go free now, no matter how often you indict them, because those isolated acts are not sufficient in themselves to constitute a violation of the Sherman law. . . .

Mr. RAKER. Under this provision you would have to indict and convict the corporation, and then in the indictment against the individual you would have to allege the fact that the corporation had been indicted and convicted before you could convict the individual personally.

Mr. FLOYD of Arkansas. I do not so interpret it, but I do admit that you would have to show by proof in that trial that the corporation had been guilty of violating the Sherman law, or else prove that it had been indicted and convicted. But I do not admit that you would necessarily have to convict the corporation before you could proceed against the individual; the first burden of proof would be upon the Government, to show that they had violated that law, before the guilt of the corporation could be imputed to the acts of its officers or agents. . . .

. . . I desire to make this point clear. Now, we think this provision very important. We all understand that under the Sherman law, as it is written, there have been no criminal prosecutions of any consequence. Take the extreme position which seems to be entertained by those who oppose this amendment. They would have you believe that before proceeding against individuals you would have to convict first the corporation. What has been lost by the Government in criminal prosecutions if their construction is correct? How many convictions have been had in criminal cases in the 24 years of the existence of that law? The criminal provisions of the Sherman antitrust law have proven a failure in the past, and we are seeking by this provision and by this legislation to strengthen it and reach the men who are really responsible for its violations, and if we can succeed in doing that we will have fewer violations of law, because the men connected with these great corporations do not desire to go to jail and do not desire to be convicted of crimes. . . .

Mr. VOLSTEAD. Does the gentleman contend that a person is not guilty under the present law if he authorizes or directs a violation of the law? Is there any question on that proposition?

Mr. FLOYD of Arkansas. I do not know how you can convict him if he has merely authorized and directed it. . . .

Mr. McCOY. Would the committee accept this as an amendment:

> Any person who, while acting or purporting to act as a director, officer, or agent of a corporation, shall authorize, order, or do any of the acts prohibited by the antitrust laws shall be deemed guilty of a misdemeanor—

And so forth?

Mr. FLOYD of Arkansas. Mr. Chairman, I reserve the balance of my time. . . .

Mr. TOWNER. Mr. Chairman, I would like to have the attention of the committee. The chairman of the committee is certainly right in saying that this is a very important matter. Nowhere else in the criminal law, either in State or Nation, is it necessary to convict two entities before one of them can be punished. By the provisions of this section it will be absolutely necessary to convict a corporation of which the individual is a member before you can ever convict any individual. In fact, it will be necessary that the indictment itself shall allege, in order to charge an indictable offense against the individual, that a conviction against the corporation of which the man is a member has been secured before the individual can be even placed on trial. I desire to call the attention of the committee further to this fact, that if you place any corporation on trial and it should be found that the act was not the act of the corporation, but was the act of an individual, ultra vires, without authority, then you would fail in the indictment against the individual, because you could not convict the corporation. The corporation would be acquitted, and you could secure no penalty against the corporation, and then you never could proceed against the individual, because, as a prerequisite to every indictment against an individual, if you adopt the form of amendment which the committee presents, it will be absolutely necessary to convict the corporation. I want to call the attention of the committee, if I can have it for a moment, to a substitute which I would like to have them consider, and this will be the only way, perhaps, to have it considered. It is to strike out all of the section and insert this:

> That in any case where a corporation has been convicted of a violation of any of the acts, matters, or things prohibited or declared to be unlawful in the antitrust laws the said conviction shall not be plead, offered, or received as defensive evidence or held as a prior conviction in a prosecution against any officer, director, agent, or member of such corporation.

I suggest to the committee that it will be necessary that you have some such provision if you intend to prosecute both the corporation and the individual, as I hope you do so intend. The section should contain a provision that the conviction of the corporation should not be held to be a prior conviction of an individual member of it. And then should follow this clause:

> And any officer, director, agent, or member of such corporation, who has authorized, ordered, or knowingly aided and abetted any act, matter, or thing prohibited or declared unlawful in the antitrust laws shall be deemed guilty of a misdemeanor, and upon conviction thereof shall be punished as provided in such antitrust laws.

It is in substance the same as the substitute offered by the gentleman from Minnesota and that suggested just now by the gentleman from New Jersey. I think it is in better form than either of them, and in addition to what they contain is the provision that the conviction of the corporation can not be plead as a prior conviction of any individual member of the corporation. I submit it for the consideration of the committee without much hope of its being adopted, but at least we will have discharged our duty if we try to make the bill what it ought to be. . . .

Mr. VOLSTEAD. Mr. Chairman, I want to oppose this proposition. It is evident there is a disposition on the part of the majority to weaken instead of strengthen the Sherman antitrust law. It would be infinitely better to leave the law as it stands and depend upon the general principles of criminal jurisprudence to apply its provisions to acts of individuals than to add a section such as that which is proposed.

There can be no question but that, under the proposed amendment, it would be necessary first to establish the guilt of a corporation before you could convict an officer; and, besides, there is nothing in this proposed amendment that broadens or in any way strengthens the criminal statute as it stands to-day.

Gentlemen complain that we have not succeeded in convicting men in the years past. That is not true. In a great many instances men have been convicted and punished under the Sherman Antitrust Act. In some instances they have been sent to prison, although as a rule they have not been sent there for any great length of time. Under the law as it stands they can be convicted, and are constantly being indicted and convicted.

Why should we take away the power we have to-day to protect commerce against unlawful restraints and monopolies? That is what you are trying to do. You are trying to place between the Government and these offenders an additional obstacle to conviction of the individual by first requiring the conviction of the corporation. You are asking the Government to prosecute a suit that is absolutely needless and useless in most cases. You can not put a corporation in jail—corporations must be reached under the equity powers of a court. But you are going to insist that before the individual can be punished the Government must waste its money on a criminal conviction of the corporation. This simply means that you are going to let go free the men who restrain commerce and create monopolies—the men who, in my judgment, are doing as much as anybody to increase the cost of living. [Applause.]

The CHAIRMAN. The gentleman from Minnesota [Mr. VOLSTEAD] consumed two minutes.

Mr. WEBB. Mr. Chairman, I yield one minute to the gentleman from New Jersey [Mr. MCCOY].

The CHAIRMAN. The gentleman from New Jersey [Mr. MCCOY] is recognized for one minute.

Mr. MCCOY. Mr. Chairman, I offer the following as a substitute for the committee amendment.

Mr. BRYAN. Mr. Chairman, a parliamentary inquiry.

The CHAIRMAN. The gentleman will state it.

Mr. BRYAN. Is an amendment in order now, at this time?

Mr. MCCOY. I offer my amendment as a substitute.

The CHAIRMAN. The gentleman from North Carolina [Mr. WEBB] yields to the gentleman from New Jersey [Mr. MCCOY] one minute. The Clerk will report the amendment.

The Clerk read as follows:

SEC. 12. Any person who while acting or purporting to act as director, officer, or agent of a corporation shall authorize, order, or do any of the acts prohibited by the antitrust laws shall be deemed guilty of a misdemeanor, and upon conviction therefor shall be punished by a fine not exceeding $5,000 or by imprisonment not exceeding one year, or by both in the discretion of the court.

Mr. STAFFORD. Mr. Chairman, a parliamentary inquiry. Do I understand this amendment is being read for information?

The CHAIRMAN. Yes. The gentleman has been yielded time.

Mr. MCCOY. Mr. Chairman, this amendment relieves the section from the criticism as it now stands or as the substitute proposes to do—that you must first convict the corporation before you can find any of these officers guilty. It simply provides that when any person acts or purports to act—and that would cover an ultra vires act—does the thing prohibited, he may be convicted. It makes guilt as personal as it can be. . . .

Mr. BRYAN. Mr. Chairman, I ask that my amendment be read. . . .

The CHAIRMAN. The Clerk will report the amendment.

The Clerk read as follows:

Page 31, strike out all of section 12 and substitute the following: "That any person or corporation that violates any of the provisions of the antitrust laws, or any director, officer, or agent of any corporation that authorizes, orders, or permits to be done any act done by any corporation in violation of the antitrust laws, shall be guilty of a misdemeanor, and upon conviction thereof shall be punished by a fine not exceeding $5,000 or be imprisoned not exceeding one year, or both, in the discretion of the court."

Mr. BRYAN. I think that is almost identical with the amendment offered by the gentleman from New Jersey [Mr. MCCOY], but it provides that in order to make the individual guilty he must have advised, permitted, or authorized something to be done that was actually accomplished by the corporation in violation of the law. . . .

Mr. LENROOT. Mr. Chairman, I believe the committee amendment has been improved upon, but is still open to criticism. I think the amendment of the gentleman from New Jersey [Mr. MCCOY] is subject to criticism in this, that the whole thought and purpose has been that where there was guilt upon the part of the corporation any officer, agent, or director responsible in any degree for contributing to that guilt should also be personally guilty. The amendment of the gentleman from New Jersey simply provides that where the officers, agents, or directors shall be guilty of any prohibited act they shall be punished, as I understand it. . . .

Mr. MCCOY. It provides that any officer, agent, or director who authorizes or commits—

Mr. LENROOT. Any prohibited act.

Mr. MCCOY. Any prohibited act.

Mr. LENROOT. That is just the trouble, because the act itself may not be prohibited by the antitrust law, and it takes the illegal combination and the act done in furtherance of it before it becomes a prohibitive act. Therefore we must have guilt on the part of the corporation, because in other cases your antitrust law without this section reaches the individual in every case.

Mr. WEBB. I thought the gentleman was one of those who did not want the necessity of proving guilt on the part of the corporation before we could reach the directors or officers.

Mr. LENROOT. I do not want to be compelled to convict the corporation before you can proceed against the officer, but I do ⊥ insist that you must show in your action against the officers that the corporation is guilty, and then that the man you are proceeding against has performed some act that has contributed to the violation by the corporation; and when he has, he ought to be punished.

Mr. WEBB. You can only prove guilt by a conviction.

Mr. LENROOT. Yes, certainly; but you can prove the guilt of the corporation in your proceeding against the individual, or for this purpose you might first prove the guilt of the corporation in an equity action, if your amendment was properly framed to cover that, though, of course, that would not bind the defendant in the criminal action. I shall offer an amendment which, I think, covers the case.

Mr. BARKLEY. Is not the real object of the section that there shall be unlimited power of prosecution, both of individuals and corporations, but the additional power that when the corporation itself is convicted the officers and directors shall also be guilty of the thing which is denounced by the law.

Mr. LENROOT. Not denounced by the law, but where they have contributed in any degree to the violation, although their act, standing alone, might not be a violation.

Mr. BARKLEY. The amendment covers this ground specifically.

Mr. LENROOT. My amendment is to strike out the balance of the section and insert, so that it will provide that whenever the corporation shall violate any of the provisions of the antitrust laws—not leaving it to be determined in a criminal action; it may be determined in an action in equity—such violation shall be deemed to be also that of the individual directors, officers, or agents of such corporation who shall have authorized or ordered or done any of the acts constituting in whole or in part any such violations. Those acts standing alone might be absolutely innocent, but if they have contributed in whole or in part to the violation by the corporation, then they make the party guilty. Then it goes on—

Mr. WEBB. I understand what the gentleman proposes. May I ask the gentleman from Minnesota [Mr. VOLSTEAD] if he agrees to the amendment of the gentleman from Wisconsin?

Mr. CARLIN. I think that is all right.

Mr. VOLSTEAD. Which amendment?

Mr. WEBB. The Lenroot amendment.

Mr. VOLSTEAD. I do not understand the provisions of it.

Mr. LENROOT. I ask that it be reported.

The CHAIRMAN. Without objection, the Clerk will report the amendment.

The Clerk read as follows:

Amend the committee's substitute by striking out all after the word "corporation" and inserting the following:

"That whenever a corporation shall violate any of the provisions of the antitrust laws, such violation shall be deemed to be also that of the individual directors, officers, or agents of such corporation who shall have authorized, ordered, or done any of the acts constituting in whole or in part such violation, and shall be deemed a misdemeanor; and upon conviction therefor of any such director, officer, or agent he shall be punished by a fine of not exceeding $5,000 or by imprisonment for not exceeding one year, or by both, in the discretion of the court."

Mr. WEBB. I will ask the gentleman from Minnesota [Mr. VOLSTEAD] if he is satisfied with this amendment?

Mr. VOLSTEAD. I am not able to discover where the difference comes in.

Mr. WEBB. I will ask that the amendment be again read, to see if we can not come to some agreement about it. . . .

Mr. LENROOT. I shall be glad to explain the difference if I can get the time.

Mr. WEBB. I understand the difference, and I think the House does. Mr. Chairman, I think the amendment offered by the gentleman from Wisconsin [Mr. LENROOT] expresses the judgment of the House on both sides; that is, that we wish to make guilt personal; that whenever a corporation violates any of the provisions of the antitrust laws the agents or directors, or those who are responsible for those violations, shall be deemed guilty of a misdemeanor, and fined or imprisoned. Now, I think that is exactly what my friend from Minnesota [Mr. VOLSTEAD] wants done, and we are perfectly willing to accept the amendment offered by the gentleman from Wisconsin [Mr. LENROOT].

The CHAIRMAN. Does the gentleman from North Carolina withdraw the committee amendment?

Mr. FLOYD of Arkansas. This is an amendment to the committee amendment. I offered the committee amendment, and I accept the amendment of the gentleman from Wisconsin.

Mr. McKENZIE. Mr. Chairman, I ask unanimous consent that the committee amendment may be read, and then the amendment offered by the gentleman from Wisconsin read in connection therewith, so that we may have an understanding of the whole matter.

Mr. FLOYD of Arkansas. If the gentleman from Illinois will permit, I will state that the amendment offered by the gentleman from Wisconsin [Mr. LENROOT] supersedes the entire amendment that I offered except the first word.

Mr. MANN. I ask for the regular order.

The CHAIRMAN. Without objection, the Clerk will again report the amendment of the gentleman from Wisconsin.

The Clerk again read the amendment. . . .

Mr. VOLSTEAD. I will yield two minutes to the gentleman from Wisconsin, in order that he may answer some questions. Does this include all of the gentleman's amendment?

Mr. LENROOT. It does. It is in the form of a substitute.

Mr. VOLSTEAD. What part of the original amendment does the gentleman retain?

Mr. LENROOT. The words "whenever a corporation shall"; that is all that is retained of the original amendment. Then it strikes out all of the balance of the amendment, so that it will read "whenever a corporation shall violate." and so forth.

Mr. WEBB. I hope the gentleman from Minnesota will accept the amendment.

Mr. VOLSTEAD. No, Mr. Chairman; I shall not accept the amendment. This amendment is still open to the same objection that I made to other amendments—that it does not take into consideration the fact that for some offenses under existing law the fine is one sum and for other offenses it is a different sum. This makes a uniform punishment of a fine of $5,000 for every offense. We have some provisions in this bill that provide for a fine of $100 a day. Now, will this mean $5,000 a day? And this amendment does not add a particle to the existing law.

I believe that under the existing law we can reach every offense that could possibly be reached under this provision and a number of others.

In years past we have been able to prosecute and convict people under the antitrust laws. The trouble has not been that we did not have law enough; the trouble has been that jurors did not want to convict and officers did not always want to prosecute. They have had some sympathy for the men who have had the genius to build up these great combinations and their industries. It was not the fault of the law. It was the fault of the men who sat in judgment on the men who committed the offenses.

I am not going to consent to weaken the law. I can not see how you add a single thing to the law; on the other hand, you limit it by expressly providing that an individual is only liable if he authorizes or directs an act to be done. It is a familiar principle of the criminal law that anyone who knowingly aids or assists in doing an illegal act is guilty. You do not have to authorize or direct. Anyone that participates in doing a criminal act is guilty. You require that the offense shall be done in a particular way, and thereby exclude other methods of committing the crime. This is not going to add a single thing to the law; on the other hand, I can see clearly that it is going to weaken it very much. The effect of this amendment is to shield the individual and make the law less drastic than it is to-day. [Applause.]

Mr. McCOY. Mr. Chairman, a parliamentary inquiry.

The CHAIRMAN (Mr. SIMS). The gentleman will state it.

Mr. McCOY. I understand the amendment of the gentleman from Wisconsin as a substitute for the committee amendment has been accepted.

The CHAIRMAN. The Chair understands it is offered as an amendment to the committee amendment.

Mr. McCOY. And the committee has accepted it.

Mr. LENROOT. It can not be accepted. It has to be voted upon.

Mr. McCOY. What is the status of the substitute which I offered for the committee amendment?

The CHAIRMAN. The present occupant of the chair understands the gentleman's amendment was simply read in his time for information.

Mr. McCOY. I got the time in order to offer it as a substitute, and the Clerk so read it.

The CHAIRMAN. The Chair understood that it was offered for information of the committee, to be offered in the regular order at the proper time.

Mr. McCOY. Assuming that is so, when is the time to offer it?

The CHAIRMAN. The agreement was made before the present occupant took the chair.

Mr. CARLIN. Under the unanimous-consent agreement all the amendments had to be offered. The amendment of the gentleman from New Jersey took its place as a substitute for the amendment which is pending. We have accepted the amendment of the gentleman from Wisconsin.

The CHAIRMAN. That arrangement was made before the present occupant took the chair.

Mr. MANN. There was no agreement about amendments. The agreement was as to debate.

Mr. CARLIN. The agreement was to close debate on the paragraph and all amendments.

Mr. MANN. Yes; but that does not close or shut off amendment. The committee offered an amendment, and the gentleman from Wisconsin offered an amendment to that amendment, and the gentleman from New Jersey offered a substitute to the amendment.

The CHAIRMAN. The Chair understands that the vote will come first on the amendment offered by the gentleman from Wisconsin to the amendment offered by the gentleman from Arkansas. Then the substitute will be voted upon.

Mr. MANN. The vote would come first on the amendment offered by the gentleman from Wisconsin to the committee amendment and then upon the substitute offered by the gentleman from New Jersey and finally upon the amendment as amended, if it should be amended.

The CHAIRMAN. The Chair so understands. The question is on the amendment offered by the gentleman from Wisconsin to the amendment offered by the gentleman from Arkansas.

The question was taken, and the amendment to the amendment was agreed to.

The CHAIRMAN. The question now is on the substitute offered by the gentleman from New Jersey [Mr. McCoy] for the amendment offered by the gentleman from Arkansas.

The question was taken, and the substitute was rejected.

The CHAIRMAN. The Chair understands the gentleman from Washington offered a substitute. The question is on the amendment offered by the gentleman from Washington [Mr. BRYAN] in the nature of a substitute.

The question was taken, and the amendment in the nature of a substitute was rejected.

The CHAIRMAN. The question now is on the amendment offered by the gentleman from Arkansas [Mr. FLOYD], a member of the committee, as amended by the gentleman from Wisconsin [Mr. LENROOT].

The question was taken, and the amendment as amended was agreed to.

Mr. RAKER. Mr. Chairman, I ask unanimous consent that the proposed amendment which I send to the desk, to section 10 of the bill, may be read; and after it is read, then it is my purpose to prefer a request for unanimous consent to return to section 10 in order that it may be offered.

The CHAIRMAN (Mr. HULL). The gentleman from California asks unanimous consent to return to section 10 in order to offer an amendment. Is there objection?

Mr. MANN. Mr. Chairman. I object. As the Chair states the request, it is to return to section 10.

Mr. RAKER. Mr. Chairman, my proposition is that this proposed amendment be first read, and then, after it is read, it is my purpose to ask unanimous consent to return to the section. I wish the gentleman from Illinois would let me have the amendment read.

Mr. MANN. What is it about? Is it about anything in the section?

Mr. RAKER. Yes; it covers the provisions of the section, and I will ask the gentleman to let me have it read.

The CHAIRMAN. The gentleman from California asks unanimous consent that the amendment be reported for information. Is there objection?

There was no objection.

The Clerk read as follows:

On line 3, page 31, after the word "inhabitant," amend by adding the following words: "or where the principal place of business of such corporation is situated"; and on line 4, page 31, after the word "district," insert the following words: "where the contract is made or is to be performed or where the obligation or liability arises or the breach occurs or," so that as amended it will read as follows:

"SEC. 10. That any suit, action, or proceeding under the antitrust laws against a corporation may be brought not only in the judicial district whereof it is an inhabitant or where the principal place of business of such corporation is situated, but also in any district where the contract is made or is to be performed or where the obligation or liability arises or the breach occurs, or wherein it may be found or has an agent."

Mr. RAKER. Mr. Chairman, I now ask unanimous consent that the committee return to section 10 for the purpose of considering the amendment.

The CHAIRMAN. The gentleman from California asks unanimous consent that the committee return to section 10 in order to consider the amendment just read for information. Is there objection?

Mr. WEBB. Mr. Chairman, I object. I now move that the bill as amended be laid aside under the rule with a favorable recommendation.

The CHAIRMAN. The question is on the motion of the gentleman from North Carolina that the bill as amended be laid aside with a favorable recommendation.

Mr. GRAHAM of Pennsylvania. Mr. Chairman, before that motion is put I desire to call the attention of the chairman of the committee to the fact that there should be a verbal correction made in one of the amendments which was presented and adopted.

Mr. WEBB. Mr. Chairman, that is right; and I ask unanimous consent that the gentleman may be permitted to offer his proposed amendment as amended.

The CHAIRMAN. To which section does the amendment apply?

Mr. WEBB. And I ask unanimous consent that we return to that section for that purpose alone. It is to section 11.

The CHAIRMAN. The gentleman from North Carolina asks unanimous consent to return to section 11 to permit the correction of an amendment. Is there objection?

Mr. RAKER. Mr. Chairman, reserving the right to object, let the amendment be reported first.

Mr. GRAHAM of Pennsylvania. Mr. Chairman, I will explain to the gentleman that the amendment offered has already been adopted by the committee, but that it was drawn hastily, and there are some verbal corrections necessary.

The CHAIRMAN. Without objection, the Clerk will report the proposed amendment for information.

The Clerk read as follows:

Amendment by Mr. GRAHAM of Pennsylvania:
Page 31, line 9, after the word "district," insert the following:
"*Provided,* That in civil cases no writ of subpoena shall issue for witnesses living out of the district in which the court is held at a greater distance than 100 miles from the place of holding the same, without the permission of the trial court being first had, upon proper application, and cause shown."

The CHAIRMAN. Is there objection?

Mr. RAKER. Does that limit the distance?

Mr. MANN. The gentleman offered his amendment a while ago, but as adopted it applies to criminal cases.

Mr. RAKER. That may be true; but if it is possible to keep out the question of distance, it ought to be kept out. In my State men have to travel four and five hundred miles in one district.

Mr. GRAHAM of Pennsylvania. Mr. Chairman, if the gentleman will permit, I will explain. It was the thought of districts like the gentleman's that suggested the importance of making this change. I know there are districts in which the extent from one end to the other would be four or five hundred miles, and therefore the limitation of 100 miles which applies with us in the eastern districts would not apply to them, because this amendment now leaves it so that the writ of subpoena runs all through the district, and the limitation is in the language of the old law, that where the witness resides outside of the district he can not be compelled to attend more than 100 miles.

Mr. RAKER. Outside the district?

Mr. GRAHAM of Pennsylvania. Yes; in conformity with the old statute. It is merely a verbal correction to make it conform to the law.

Mr. RAKER. With the amendment proposed by the gentleman, irrespective of what distance might be in the district—200, 300, or 500 miles—the subpoena will run to the outermost limits of that district?

Mr. GRAHAM of Pennsylvania. That is exactly the purpose of that amendment, and it does that.

The CHAIRMAN. Is there objection? [After a pause.] The Chair hears none. The question is on agreeing to the amendment offered by the gentleman from Pennsylvania.

Mr. MANN. That is to strike out the amendment that was inserted and insert this amendment in lieu thereof; practically it has to be done by unanimous consent.

Mr. WEBB. This is to be adopted in lieu of the amendment the gentleman offered an hour or so ago?

Mr. MANN. The gentleman asks unanimous consent to modify his amendment and adopt it as read.

The CHAIRMAN. The gentleman from Pennsylvania asks unanimous consent to modify his amendment previously adopted by the committee by inserting the amendment just read. Is there objection? [After a pause.] The Chair hears none, and it is so ordered.

Mr. WEBB. Mr. Chairman, I move that the bill as amended be laid aside with a favorable recommendation that it do pass.

The question was taken, and the motion was agreed to.

[Applause.] . . .

⊥ ORDER OF BUSINESS. ⊥9683

• • • •

Mr. MANN. Mr. Speaker, I ask unanimous consent, or suggest to the gentleman from North Carolina [Mr. WEBB] that he ask unanimous consent, to have the antitrust bill that was just laid aside and favorably reported reprinted as it has been amended by the committee.

Mr. WEBB. I make that request, Mr. Speaker. I think it is a good suggestion.

The SPEAKER. The gentleman from North Carolina [Mr. WEBB] asks unanimous consent to have a reprint made of the antitrust bill as agreed to in committee. Is there objection? Were any amendments adopted to it?

Mr. MANN. Yes; a number of them; but the reprint should not show that they are amendments. I think the whole thing, being a committee amendment, should be printed as agreed to in the committee.

The SPEAKER. Is there objection to the request? [After a pause.] The Chair hears none, and it is so ordered. . . .[5.574]

⊥ Mr. FESS. Mr. Chairman, I am in sympathy with the purpose of the program ⊥9697 that has been announced on the trust legislation by the authors of the bills. [Applause.] You are applauding too soon. The purpose of the legislation, as it is expressed in every speech made upon this floor in support of the various measures can not, I think, be objected to. Part of these bills I favor. I shall give my support to the interstate trade commission, and do it heartily, because I believe it supplements the Sherman law, that in a sense has been effective, but not entirely so. However, this ineffectiveness is due not to the law so much as to the administration of it.

I am not satisfied with this measure now before us and can not now give my approval of it. If it is amended along the lines suggested by Mr. STEVENS of Minnesota, I will support it. I hope it will be so modified. The measure that was laid aside to-day, the Clayton antitrust bill, is a measure seeking to do a thing that I have desired to see done for years. As a student for some time of the subject of concentration and control, as set forth by the investigations of Dr. Van Hise, Bruce Wyman, and a great number of experts, such as Dr. Ripley, Prof. Jenks, and Prof. Ely, I have well-defined convictions. This bill is designed by its proponents to regulate big business, without destroying the small man, but I can not see that this bill is reaching the thing that you men think it will reach. My belief is not the result of prejudice, not a desire to avoid responsibility. I have tried to be absolutely honest in my own mind. I have come to this proposition in this spirit of an open mind. If it were introduced in a Republican Congress and I could see my way to support it as a Republican measure, I would support it in this Democratic Congress, introduced by a Democrat. I have come with that open mind, rather to be fair to myself as a legislator. But if I am not mistaken, you are not striking the monopoly as you think you are, and you are striking the small business man as you think you are not. In other words, you are not hurting the enemy of business, but you are distressing the friend of it. When you deny the exclusive contract to the large business corporation, in order, as you profess, to insure competition for the small man, your limitation will not in this law interfere with monopoly, because you allow the big business concern to supersede the small dealer to

---

[5.574] The bill as agreed to in the Committee of the Whole House appears *infra* at 1728-38.

whom it sells its goods by putting in his place its legal representative, a man who becomes its agent, and upon a contract where the title does not pass from the corporation to the seller, but where the seller is simply a distributor of the goods of the corporation. In such a law you are not harming the corporation, you are not lessening the danger from the big man, but you are interfering with the little man, whom you are superseding by the agent of the big man.

By this act, if it becomes a law as it now stands, the great anthracite-coal corporations will cease to make exclusive contracts with the various retail dealers in the country, but it will not interfere with the corporation sending its agents as distributors to the various localities. No one will seriously contend that such displacement of the retailer will hinder the corporation in its monopolistic tendencies, but most people must see its effect upon the retailer. What is true of anthracite coal will be true of every big concern which approaches monopolistic dimensions. It will assist the tendency of concentration without providing the necessary control we all seek, and at the same time to the distress of the small dealer.

I tried to put these questions to the men who are the proponents of the bill. They say that my fears are unfounded; but I am confident that when the Standard Oil Co. does not sell to an individual under an exclusive contract, because of the limitation in this law, that will not interfere with the Standard Oil Co. putting a distributor of its goods into every little town. To-day the exclusive contract can be reached under the Sherman law if it can be shown that it either produces monopoly or is in restraint of trade. To-day this remedy can be reached without affecting the small business man. Under this law as proposed you invite the Standard Oil Co. to distribute its products through agents instead of through the middle man. You do not reach the company, but you do affect the thousands of middle men.

Mr. GORDON. Will the gentleman yield?

Mr. FESS. I yield for a question.

Mr. GORDON. Has not the Standard Oil Co. got a distributing agent in every town now?

Mr. FESS. Yes; it may have, but that does not change this provision any, and I am referring to that simply as an example. What it has done you invite every big concern to do under this bill, and I take it that is the thing you do not want to do. This injury to the small man is not confined to the exclusive contract in the bill. You do it in the price discriminating provision, if I can read the matter right, and I have tried to be honest in this matter with myself.

You forbid the sale of goods except upon quality and quantity at different prices. I know your purpose, which is good. But your purpose will not be realized. This feature will not hurt the monopoly, but it will hurt the small dealer.

I have no great dealers of monopoly proportions in my district, so far as I know. But I have a most highly intelligent group of small dealers. Note how this bill operates upon them. Take, for example, the shoe industry. My constituent can not enter the market in competition with the Douglas shoe concern. The latter has its organization represented by the hundreds of representatives. It does not need to discriminate in price to secure trade, to develop a new field. The campaign of advertising, the personal persuasion of its representatives are the means to do that. This law does not harm that firm. But take the small shoe manufactory in my district, limited in its output because of its inability of developing new trade. This concern, without its agents and its campaign for new business, is denied under this law to reduce the price upon the initiation of the contract, as an inducement to take consignment, unless the same reduction is made in places where trade is already established, upon penalty of a $5,000 fine, a year imprisonment, or both.

How will the small man compete in the market with the big man? How will he develop any new trade? Wherein do we see the harm to the big man? Wherein do we see the good to the small man? I can not see it in the bill.

This is not the only feature I fear. The denial of an operator of a mine to choose his own customer is serious. In a year I have an occasion, as the president of a college, to order about 300 tons of coal. Suppose I choose not to purchase from a coal dealer in my town. I order directly from the mine. This law, in section 3, compels the operator to sell to me if I am responsible. Who is to say whether I am responsible[?] If he refuses arbitrarily, whatever that means—and of course that will require the courts to say—he will be subject of a fine of $5,000 and a year's imprisonment or both.

That is not all; he must not sell to me higher than to another in my town. In other words, the only way the coal dealer can buy at less price is in the question of quantity. In that case the dealer must know how much I ordered to know what he can pay. What effect will such a provision have upon the hundreds of small operators of mines? What effect will it have upon the retail dealer in the country over? Again, you do not disturb so much the few great operators, but think of the confusion of the small operator and the retailer.

I voted for the amendment which declared that labor and farmer organizations as such shall not be considered as conspiracies under the Sherman law. I would not vote for any measure that would deny either labor or farmers the right to organize for mutual helpfulness. Upon the other hand, I would not vote for any law that would exempt either from punishment for the violation of law. This amendment which I supported allows organization of these various interests, but it subjects them to punishment under the law if they do unlawful acts. I have no doubt myself upon this provision; however, there seems to be some dispute among the Members. This feature should have been clearly stated so that the courts would not have been necessary to decide it. When the direct question was put to the chairman in charge whether the bill permitted a secondary boycott, he replied it did not, and he would not vote for a measure that did. Then an amendment was offered specifying that it did not authorize it. This the committee refused to accept. It should have accepted the amendment. The bill is at fault in the sense that it lacks clearness. It will take the courts to define its meaning. This is another reason for my withholding my support.

That being the case, for these reasons, as well as others, I will have to withhold my support of this measure. I believe it catches business going and it catches it coming. Business is already in the air, and it will be more so than ever before if this act becomes a law as it goes out of this House, especially if not modified materially.

Mr. Chairman, I do not believe that the country is as much interested in this particular line of legislation as you gentlemen think it is. It would like to have Congress adjourn. The people demand it. The press demands it. Business wants a rest. I do not think this Congress is interested in this line of legislation as much as you gentlemen think it is. I do not want to be cruel. It is my nature to approve. No man in this Chamber has heard me say anything ugly purely for partisan advantage, for it is not my nature to do so. But I want to prove to you that the Democrats in this House are not interested in this legislation. Some of us have been in constant attendance in this Chamber for the past 14 months. What does the small attendance upon the sessions signify? I have kept the roll of the Democratic side of the House for the last 10 days, making an actual record every 30 minutes, and I have it in my pocket, and I would like to read it to you to show that this Democratic Congress is not interested in this legislation. The only Democrats interested seem to be the President and the members of the Judiciary Committee. And even they, I am persuaded to think, would like to be relieved in response to the demands of the country. You are not here to take part in the discussion, and a quorum is not here now, and I can easily show you that even presidential persuasion is not sufficient to compel interest in these measures. . . .

Mr. [WILLIAM C.] ADAMSON [D., Ga.]. I thank the gentleman; he is always fair and courteous. I understand the gentleman's remarks just made apply to the bill which was laid aside to-day from the Judiciary Committee.

Mr. FESS. Yes; I refer to the last 10 days.

Mr. ADAMSON. And not to the stock and bonds bill?

Mr. FESS. No. I am not suggesting a lack of interest in your measure.

H.R. 15657 AS AGREED UPON IN THE COMMITTEE OF THE WHOLE HOUSE
63d Cong., 2d Sess.
June 2, 1914

Ordered printed as agreed upon in the Committee of the Whole House on the state of the Union.

A BILL

To supplement existing laws against unlawful restraints and monopolies, and for other purposes.

Be it enacted by the Senate and House of Representatives of the United States of America in Congress assembled, That "antitrust laws," as used herein, includes the Act entitled "An Act to protect trade and commerce against unlawful restraints and monopolies," approved July second, eighteeen hundred and ninety; sections seventy-three to seventy-seven, inclusive, of an Act entitled "An Act to reduce taxation, to provide revenue for the Government, and for other purposes," of August twenty-seventh, eighteen hundred and ninety-four; an Act entitled "An Act to amend sections seventy-three and seventy-six of the Act of August twenty-seventh, eighteen hundred and ninety-four, entitled 'An Act to reduce taxation, to provide revenue for the Government, and for other purposes,'" approved February twelfth, nineteen hundred and thirteen; and also this Act.

"Commerce," as used herein, means trade or commerce among the several States and with foreign nations, or between the District of Columbia or any Territory of the United States and any State, Territory, or foreign nation, or between any insular possessions or other places under the jurisdiction of the United States, or between any such possession or place and any State or Territory of the United States or the District of Columbia or any foreign nation, or within the District of Columbia or any Territory or any insular possession or other place under the jurisdiction of the United States.

The word "person" or "persons" wherever used in this Act shall be deemed to include corporations and associations existing under or authorized by the laws of either the United States, the laws of any of the Territories, the laws of any State, or the laws of any foreign country.

SEC. 2. That any person engaged in commerce who shall either directly or indirectly discriminate in price between different purchasers of commodities in the same or different sections or communities, which commodities are sold for use, consumption, or resale within the United States or any Territory thereof or the District of Columbia or any insular possession or other place under the jurisdiction of the

United States, with the purpose or intent thereby to destroy or wrongfully injure the business of a competitor, of either such purchaser or seller, shall be deemed guilty of a misdemeanor, and upon conviction thereof shall be punished by a fine not exceeding $5,000, or by imprisonment not exceeding one year, or by both, in the discretion of the court: *Provided*, That nothing herein contained shall prevent discrimination in price between purchasers of commodities on account of differences in the grade, quality, or quantity of the commodity sold, or that makes only due allowance for difference in the cost of transportation: *And provided further*, That nothing herein contained shall prevent persons engaged in selling goods, wares, or merchandise in commerce from selecting their own customers, except as provided in section three of this Act.

SEC. 3. That it shall be unlawful for the owner, operator, or transporter of the product or products of any mine, oil or gas well, reduction works, refinery, or hydroelectric plant producing coal, oil, gas, or hydroelectric energy, or for any person controlling the products thereof, engaged in selling such product in commerce to refuse arbitrarily to sell such product to a responsible person, firm, or corporation who applies to purchase such product for use, consumption, or resale within the United States or any Territory thereof or the District of Columbia or any insular possession or other place under the jurisdiction of the United States, and any person violating this section shall be deemed guilty of a misdemeanor and shall be punished as provided in the preceding section.

SEC. 4. That any person engaged in commerce who shall lease or make a sale of goods, wares, merchandise, machinery, supplies, or other commodities for use, consumption, or resale within the United States, or any Territory thereof or the District of Columbia or any insular possession or other place under the jurisdiction of the United States, or fix a price charged therefor, or discount from, or rebate upon such price, on the condition, agreement, or understanding that the lessee or purchaser thereof shall not use or deal in the goods, wares, merchandise, machinery, supplies, or other commodities of a competitor or competitors of the lessor or seller shall be deemed guilty of a misdemeanor, and upon conviction thereof shall be punished by a fine not exceeding $5,000, or by imprisonment not exceeding one year, or by both, in the discretion of the court.

SEC. 5. That any person who shall be injured in his business or property by reason of anything forbidden in the antitrust laws may sue therefor in any district court of the United States in the district in which the defendant resides or is found or has an agent, without respect to the amount in controversy, and shall recover threefold the damages by him sustained, and the cost of suit, including a reasonable attorney's fee.

SEC. 6. That whenever in any suit or proceeding in equity hereafter brought by or on behalf of the United States under any of the antitrust laws there shall have been rendered a final judgment or decree to the effect that a defendant has entered into a contract, combination in the form of trust or otherwise, or conspiracy, in restraint of trade or commerce, or has monopolized, or attempted to monopolize or combined with any person or persons to monopolize, any part of commerce, in violation of any of the antitrust laws, said judgment or decree shall, to the full extent to which such judgment or decree would constitute in any other proceeding an estoppel as between the United States and such defendant, constitute against such defendant conclusive evidence of the same facts, and be conclusive as to the same questions of law in favor of any other party in any action or proceeding brought under or involving the provisions of any of the antitrust laws.

Whenever any suit or proceeding in equity is hereafter brought by or on behalf of the United States, under any of the antitrust laws, the statute of limitations in respect of each and every private right of action, arising under such antitrust laws, and based, in whole or in part, on any matter complained of in said suit or proceeding in equity, shall be suspended during the pendency of such suit or proceeding in equity.

SEC. 7. That nothing contained in the antitrust laws shall be construed to forbid the existence and operation of fraternal, labor, consumers, agricultural, or horticultural organizations, orders, or associations instituted for the purposes of mutual help, and not having capital stock or conducted for profit, or to forbid or restrain individual members of such organizations, orders, or associations from carrying out the legitimate objects thereof; nor shall such organizations, orders, or associations, or the members thereof, be held or construed to be illegal combinations or conspiracies in restraint of trade, under the antitrust laws.

Nothing contained in the antitrust laws shall be construed to forbid associations of traffic, operating, accounting, or other officers of common carriers for the purpose of conferring among themselves or of making any lawful agreement as to any matter which is subject to the regulating or supervisory jurisdiction of the Interstate Commerce Commission, but all such matters shall continue to be subject to such jurisdiction of the commission, and all such agreements shall be entered and kept of record by the carriers, parties thereto, and shall at all times be open to inspection by the commission, but no such agreement shall go into effect or become operative until the same shall have first been submitted to, and approved by, the Interstate Commerce Commission: *Provided*, That nothing in this Act shall be construed as modifying existing laws prohibiting the pooling of earnings or traffic, or existing laws against joint agreements by common carriers to maintain rates.

SEC. 8. That no corporation engaged in commerce shall acquire, directly or indirectly, the whole or any part of the stock or other share capital of another corporation en-

gaged also in commerce, where the effect of such acquisition
is to eliminate or substantially lessen competition between
the corporation whose stock is so acquired and the corporation making the acquisition, or to create a monopoly of any
line of trade in any section or community.

No corporation shall acquire, directly or indirectly, the
whole or any part of the stock or other share capital of two
or more corporations engaged in commerce where the effect
of such acquisition, or the use of such stock by the voting
or granting of proxies or otherwise, is to eliminate or substantially lessen competition between such corporations, or
any of them, whose stock or other share capital is so acquired,
or to create a monopoly of any line of trade in any section
or community.

This section shall not apply to corporations purchasing
such stock solely for investment and not using the same by
voting or otherwise to bring about, or in attempting to bring
about, the substantial lessening of competition. Nor shall
anything contained in this section prevent a corporation
engaged in commerce from causing the formation of subsidiary corporations for the actual carrying on of their immediate lawful business or the natural and legitimate
branches or extensions thereof, or from owning and holding
all or a part of the stock of such subsidiary corporations,
when the effect of such formation is not to eliminate or
substantially lessen competition.

Nothing contained in this section shall be held to affect
or impair any right heretofore legally acquired: *Provided*,
That nothing in this paragraph shall make stockholding
relations between corporations legal when such relations
constitute violations of the antitrust laws.

Nor shall anything herein contained be construed to
prohibit any railroad corporation from aiding in the construction of branch or short line railroads so located as to
become feeders to the main line of the company so aiding in
such construction or from acquiring or owning all or any part
of the stock of such branch line, nor to prevent any railroad
corporation from acquiring and owning all or any part of the
stock of a branch or short line railroad constructed by an
independent company where there is no substantial competition between the company owning the branch line so
constructed and the company owning the main line acquiring
the property or an interest therein, nor to prevent any railroad company from extending any of its lines through the
medium of the acquisition of stock or otherwise of any other
railroad company where there is no substantial competition
between the company extending its lines and the company
whose stock, property, or an interest therein is so acquired.

A violation of any of the provisions of this section shall
be deemed a misdemeanor, and shall be punishable by a fine
not exceeding $5,000, or by imprisonment not exceeding
one year, or by both, in the discretion of the court.

SEC. 9. That from and after two years from the date of
the approval of this Act no person who is engaged as an

individual, or who is a member of a partnership, or is a
director or other officer of a corporation that is engaged in
the business, in whole or in part, of producing or selling
equipment, materials, or supplies to, or in the construction or
maintenance of, railroads or other common carriers engaged
in commerce, shall act as a director or other officer or
employee of any other corporation or common carrier engaged in commerce to which he, or such partnership or corporation, sells or leases, directly or indirectly, equipment,
materials, or supplies, or for which he or such partnership or
corporation, directly or indirectly, engages in the work of
construction or maintenance; and after the expiration of said
period no person who is engaged as an individual or who is
a member of a partnership or is a director or other officer of
a corporation which is engaged in the conduct of a bank or
trust company shall act as a director or other officer or employee of any such common carrier for which he or such
partnership or bank or trust company acts, either separately
or in connection with others, as agent for or underwriter of
the sale or disposal by such common carrier of issues or parts
of issues of its securities, or from which he or such partnership or bank or trust company purchases, either separately
or in connection with others, issues or parts of issues of securities of such common carrier.

That from and after two years from the date of the
approval of this Act no person shall at the same time be a
director or other officer or employee of more than one bank,
banking association, or trust company organized or operating under the laws of the United States either of which has
deposits, capital, surplus, and undivided profits aggregating
more than $2,500,000; and no private banker or person
who is a director in any bank or trust company, organized
and operating under the laws of a State, having deposits,
capital, surplus, and undivided profits aggregating more than
$2,500,000, shall be eligible to be a director in any bank or
banking association organized or operating under the laws
of the United States. The eligibility of a director, officer, or
employee under the foregoing provisions shall be determined
by the average amount of deposits, capital, surplus, and
undivided profits as shown in the official statements of such
bank, banking association, or trust company filed as provided by law during the fiscal year next preceding the date
set for the annual election of directors, and when a director,
officer, or employee has been elected or selected in accordance with the provisions of this Act it shall be lawful for him
to continue as such for one year thereafter under said election
or employment.

No bank, banking association, or trust company organized or operating under the laws of the United States in any
city or incorporated town or village of more than one hundred
thousand inhabitants, as shown by the last preceding decennial census of the United States, shall have as a director or
other officer or employee any private banker or any director
or other officer or employee of any other bank, banking

association, or trust company located in the same place: *Provided*, That nothing in this section shall apply to mutual savings banks not having a capital stock represented by shares: *Provided further*, That a director or other officer or employee of such bank, banking association, or trust company may be a director or other officer or employee of not more than one other bank or trust company organized under the laws of the United States or any State where the entire capital stock of one is owned by stockholders in the other: *And provided further*, That nothing contained in this section shall forbid a director of class A of a Federal reserve bank, as defined in the Federal Reserve Act, from being an officer or director or both an officer and director in one member bank.

That from and after two years from the date of the approval of this Act no person at the same time shall be a director in any two or more corporations, either of which has capital, surplus, and undivided profits aggregating more than $1,000,000, engaged in whole or in part in commerce, other than common carriers subject to the Act to regulate commerce, approved February fourth, eighteen hundred and eighty-seven, if such corporations are or shall have been theretofore, by virtue of their business and location of operation, competitors, so that an elimination of competition by agreement between them would constitute a violation of any of the provisions of any of the antitrust laws. The eligibility of a director under the foregoing provision shall be determined by the aggregate amount of the capital, surplus, and undivided profits, exclusive of dividends declared but not paid to stockholders, at the end of the fiscal year of said corporation next preceding the election of directors, and when a director has been elected in accordance with the provisions of this Act it shall be lawful for him to continue as such for one year thereafter.

When any person elected or chosen as a director or officer or selected as an employee of any bank or other corporation subject to the provisions of this Act, is eligible at the time of his election or selection to act for such bank or other corporation in such capacity his eligibility to act in such capacity shall not be affected and he shall not become or be deemed amenable to any of the provisions hereof by reason of any change in the affairs of such bank or other corporation from whatsoever cause, whether specifically excepted by any of the provisions hereof or not, until the expiration of one year from the date of his election or employment.

That any person who shall violate any of the provisions of this section shall be guilty of a misdemeanor and shall be punished by a fine of not exceeding $100 a day for each day of the continuance of such violation, or by imprisonment for such period as the court may designate, not exceeding one year, or by both, in the discretion of the court.

SEC. 10. That any suit, action, or proceeding under the antitrust laws against a corporation may be brought not only in the judicial district whereof it is an inhabitant, but also in any district wherein it may be found or has an agent.

SEC. 11. That in any suit, action, or proceeding brought by or on behalf of the United States subpoenas for witnesses who are required to attend a court of the United States in any judicial district in any case, civil or criminal, arising under the antitrust laws may run into any other district: *Provided*, That in civil cases no writ of subpoena shall issue for witnesses living out of the district in which the court is held at a greater distance than one hundred miles from the place of holding the same without the permission of the trial court being first had upon proper application and cause shown.

SEC. 12. That whenever a corporation shall violate any of the provisions of the antitrust laws, such violation shall be deemed to be also that of the individual directors, officers, or agents of such corporation who shall have authorized, ordered, or done any of the acts constituting in whole or in part such violation, and such violation shall be deemed a misdemeanor, and upon conviction therefor of any such director, officer, or agent he shall be punished by a fine of not exceeding $5,000 or by imprisonment for not exceeding one year, or by both, in the discretion of the court.

SEC. 13. That the several district courts of the United States are hereby invested with jurisdiction to prevent and restrain violations of this Act, and it shall be the duty of the several district attorneys of the United States, in their respective districts, under the direction of the Attorney General, to institute proceedings in equity to prevent and restrain such violations. Such proceedings may be by way of petition setting forth the case and praying that such violation shall be enjoined or otherwise prohibited. When the parties complained of shall have been duly notified of such petition, the court shall proceed, as soon as may be, to the hearing and determination of the case; and pending such petition, and before final decree, the court may at any time make such temporary restraining order or prohibition as shall be deemed just in the premises. Whenever it shall appear to the court before which any such proceeding may be pending that the ends of justice require that other parties should be brought before the court, the court may cause them to be summoned, whether they reside in the district in which the court is held or not, and subpoenas to that end may be served in any district by the marshal thereof.

SEC. 14. That any person, firm, corporation, or association shall be entitled to sue for and have injunctive relief, in any court of the United States having jurisdiction over the parties, against threatened loss or damage by a violation of the antitrust laws, when and under the same conditions and principles as injunctive relief against threatened conduct that will cause loss or damage is granted by courts of equity, under the rules governing such proceedings, and upon the execution of proper bond against damages for an injunction improvidently granted and a showing that the danger of irreparable loss or damage is immediate, a preliminary injunction may issue: *Provided*, That nothing herein contained shall be construed to entitle any person, firm, corporation, or association, except the United States, to bring suit in equity for injunctive relief against any common carrier subject to the provisions of the Act to regulate commerce, approved February fourth, eighteen hundred and eighty-seven, in respect of any matter subject to the regulation, supervision, or other jurisdiction of the Interstate Commerce Commission.

SEC. 15. That no preliminary injunction shall be issued without notice to the opposite party.

No temporary restraining order shall be granted without notice to the opposite party unless it shall clearly appear from specific facts shown by affidavit or by the verified bill that immediate and irreparable injury, loss, or damage will result to property or a property right of the applicant before notice could be served or hearing had thereon. Every such temporary restraining order shall be indorsed with the date and hour of issuance, shall be forthwith filed in the clerk's office and entered of record, shall define the injury and state why it is irreparable and why the order was granted without notice, and shall by its terms expire within such time after entry, not to exceed ten days, as the court or judge may fix. In case a temporary restraining order shall be granted without notice in the contingency specified, the matter of the issuance of a preliminary injunction shall be set down for a hearing at the earliest possible time and shall take precedence of all matters except older matters of the same character; and when the same comes up for hearing the party obtaining the temporary restraining order shall proceed with his application for a preliminary injunction, and if he does not do so the court shall dissolve his temporary restraining order. Upon two days' notice to the party obtaining such temporary restraining order the opposite party may appear and move the dissolution or modification to the order, and in that event the court or judge shall proceed to hear and determine the motion as expeditiously as the ends of justice may require.

Section two hundred and sixty-three of an Act entitled "An Act to codify, revise, and amend the laws relating to the judiciary," approved March third, nineteen hundred and eleven, is hereby repealed.

Nothing in this section contained shall be deemed to alter, repeal, or amend section two hundred and sixty-six of an Act entitled "An Act to codify, revise, and amend the laws relating to the judiciary," approved March third, nineteen hundred and eleven.

SEC. 16. That, except as otherwise provided in section fourteen of this Act, no restraining order or interlocutory order of injunction shall issue, except upon the giving of security by the applicant in such sum as the court or judge may deem proper, conditioned upon the payment of such costs and damages as may be incurred or suffered by any party who may be found to have been wrongfully enjoined or restrained thereby.

Sec. 17. That every order of injunction or restraining order shall set forth the reasons for the issuance of the same, shall be specific in terms, and shall describe in reasonable detail, and not by reference to the bill of complaint or other document, the act or acts sought to be restrained, and shall be binding only upon the parties to the suit, their agents, servants, employees, and attorneys, or those in active concert with them, and who shall, by personal service or otherwise, have received actual notice of the same.

Sec. 18. That no restraining order or injunction shall be granted by any court of the United States, or a judge or the judges thereof, in any case between an employer and employees, or between employers and employees, or between employees, or between persons employed and persons seeking employment, involving, or growing out of, a dispute concerning terms or conditions of employment, unless necessary to prevent irreparable injury to property, or to a property right, of the party making the application, for which injury there is no adequate remedy at law, and such property or property right must be described with particularity in the application, which must be in writing and sworn to by the applicant or by his agent or attorney.

And no such restraining order or injunction shall prohibit any person or persons from terminating any relation of employment, or from ceasing to perform any work or labor, or from recommending, advising, or persuading others by peaceful means so to do; or from attending at or near a house or place where any person resides or works, or carries on business or happens to be, for the purpose of peacefully obtaining or communicating information, or of peacefully persuading any person to work or to abstain from working; or from ceasing to patronize or to employ any party to such dispute, or from recommending, advising, or persuading others by peaceful means so to do; or from paying or giving to, or withholding from, any person engaged in such dispute, any strike benefits or other moneys or things of value; or from peaceably assembling at any place in a lawful manner, and for lawful purposes; or from doing any act or thing which might lawfully be done in the absence of such dispute by any party thereto; nor shall any of the acts specified in this paragraph be considered or held unlawful.

Sec. 19. That any person who shall willfully disobey any lawful writ, process, order, rule, decree, or command of any district court of the United States or any court of the District of Columbia by doing any act or thing therein, or thereby forbidden to be done by him, if the act or thing so done by him be of such character as to constitute also a criminal offense under any statute of the United States, or at common law, shall be proceeded against for his said contempt as hereinafter provided.

Sec. 20. That whenever it shall be made to appear to any district court or judge thereof, or to any judge therein sitting, by the return of a proper officer on lawful process, or upon the affidavit of some credible person, or by information filed by any district attorney, that there is reasonable ground to believe that any person has been guilty of such contempt, the court or judge thereof, or any judge therein sitting, may issue a rule requiring the said person so charged to show cause upon a day certain why he should not be punished therefor, which rule, together with a copy of the affidavit or information, shall be served upon the person charged, with sufficient promptness to enable him to prepare for and make return to the order at the time fixed therein. If upon or by such return, in the judgment of the court, the alleged contempt be not sufficiently purged, a trial shall be directed at a time and place fixed by the court: *Provided, however,* That if the accused, being a natural person, fail or refuse to make return to the rule to show cause, an attachment may issue against his person to compel an answer, and in case of his continued failure or refusal, or if for any reason it be impracticable to dispose of the matter on the return day, he may be required to give reasonable bail for his attendance at the trial and his submission to the final judgment of the court. Where the accused person is a body corporate, an attachment for the sequestration of its property may be issued upon like refusal or failure to answer.

In all cases within the purview of this Act such trial may be by the court, or, upon demand of the accused, by a jury; in which latter event the court may impanel a jury from the jurors then in attendance, or the court or the judge thereof in chambers may cause a sufficient number of jurors to be selected and summoned, as provided by law, to attend at the time and place of trial, at which time a jury shall be selected and impaneled as upon a trial for misdemeanor; and such trial shall conform, as near as may be, to the practice in criminal cases prosecuted by indictment or upon information.

If the accused be found guilty, judgment shall be entered accordingly, prescribing the punishment, either by fine or imprisonment, or both, in the discretion of the court. Such fine shall be paid to the United States or to the complainant or other party injured by the act constituting the contempt, or may, where more than one is so damaged, be divided or apportioned among them as the court may direct, but in no case shall the fine to be paid to the United States exceed, in case the accused is a natural person, the sum of $1,000, nor shall such imprisonment exceed the term of six months.

SEC. 21. That the evidence taken upon the trial of any person so accused may be preserved by bill of exceptions, and any judgment of conviction may be reviewed upon writ of error in all respects as now provided by law in criminal cases, and may be affirmed, reversed, or modified as justice may require. Upon the granting of such writ of error, execution of judgment shall be stayed, and the accused, if thereby sentenced to imprisonment, shall be admitted to bail in such reasonable sum as may be required by the court, or by any

	19	justice, or any judge of any district court of the United
	20	States or any court of the District of Columbia.
	21	SEC. 22. That nothing herein contained shall be con-
	22	strued to relate to contempts committed in the presence of
	23	the court, or so near thereto as to obstruct the administra-
	24	tion of justice, nor to contempts committed in disobedience
	25	of any lawful writ, process, order, rule, decree, or command
23	1	entered in any suit or action brought or prosecuted in the
	2	name of, or on behalf of, the United States, but the same,
	3	and all other cases of contempt not specifically embraced
	4	within section nineteen of this Act, may be punished in con-
	5	formity to the usages at law and in equity now prevailing.
	6	SEC. 23. That no proceeding for contempt shall be
	7	instituted against any person unless begun within one year
	8	from the date of the Act complained of; nor shall any such
	9	proceeding be a bar to any criminal prosecution for the same
	10	act or acts; but nothing herein contained shall affect any
	11	proceedings in contempt pending at the time of the passage
	12	of this Act.

HOUSE DEBATE
63d Cong., 2d Sess.
June 5, 1914

51 CONG. REC. 9909

The CHAIRMAN. The gentleman from Georgia [Mr. ADAMSON] moves that the committee do now rise and report the substitute—

Mr. MANN. And the other bills that have been laid aside with a favorable recommendation.

Mr. ADAMSON. That is right. I move, Mr. Chairman, that all bills under consideration embraced within the special order be reported to the House with favorable recommendation that they pass as amended.

Mr. MANN. There are just three that have been laid aside.

The CHAIRMAN. The gentleman from Georgia moves that the committee rise and report the bill H. R. 15613, the bill H. R. 15657, and the bill H. R. 16586, with sundry amendments, with the recommendation that the amendments be agreed to and that the bills as amended do pass.

The motion was agreed to.

Accordingly the committee rose; and the Speaker having resumed the chair, Mr. HULL, Chairman of the Committee of the Whole House on the state of the Union, reported that that committee, having had under consideration the bill (H. R. 15613) creating an interstate trade commission, to define its powers and duties, and for other purposes; the bill (H. R. 15657) to supplement existing laws against unlawful restraints and monopolies, and for other purposes; and the bill (H. R. 16586) to amend section 20 of an act to regulate commerce, and for other purposes, had directed him to report each bill with amendments, with the recommendation that the amendments be agreed to, and that the bills as amended do pass.

The SPEAKER. The Chairman of the Committee of the Whole House on the state of the Union reports that that committee, under the special rule, having had under consideration House bill 15613, House bill 15657, and House bill 16586, had directed him to report the same back with sundry amendments, with the recommendation that the amendments be agreed to and that the bills as amended do pass.

Mr. ADAMSON. I believe, Mr. Speaker, the rule provides that the previous question is ordered.

The SPEAKER. Yes; it is already ordered. . . .

⊥ . . . The next bill reported from the committee of the Whole is the bill (H. R. 15657) to supplement existing laws against unlawful restraints and monopolies, and for other purposes. Is a separate vote demanded on any amendment?

⊥ Mr. MANN. There is but one amendment.

Mr. GARDNER. There were other amendments.

Mr. MANN. They were amendments to the amendment.

Mr. GARDNER. Mr. Speaker, a parliamentary inquiry.

The SPEAKER. The gentleman will state it.

Mr. GARDNER. I rise to ask whether it is true that when a bill is reported back from the Committee of the Whole with a perfected amendment it is impossible to get a record vote on an amendment to that amendment adopted in committee?

The SPEAKER. It comes back to the House in the form of one amendment.

Mr. GARDNER. The reason I asked the question was that when the rule was introduced it was specifically stated that it would be possible to get a separate vote on certain amendments.

Mr. GARNER. That was in Committee of the Whole.

Mr. GARDNER. A record vote.

The SPEAKER. Who made that statement? The Chair did not.

Mr. GARDNER. The Chair did not state it.

The SPEAKER. There is only one amendment to this bill. The question is on the amendment.

The amendment was agreed to.

The bill as amended was ordered to be engrossed and read a third time, and was accordingly read the third time.

The SPEAKER. The question is on the passage of the bill.

Mr. WEBB. Mr. Speaker, I demand the yeas and nays.

Mr. MANN. Mr. Speaker, I ask for the yeas and nays.

Mr. MURDOCK. I ask for the yeas and nays, too, Mr. Speaker, if everybody is making the demand.

The SPEAKER. The gentleman from North Carolina [Mr. WEBB], the gentleman from Illinois [Mr. MANN], and the gentleman from Kansas [Mr. MURDOCK] demand the yeas and nays.

The yeas and nays were ordered.

The question was taken; and there were—yeas 277, nays 54, answered "present" 3, not voting 99, as follows:

YEAS—277.

Abercrombie	Bell, Cal.	Burnett	Connelly, Kans.
Adair	Bell, Ga.	Byrnes, S. C.	Conry
Adamson	Blackmon	Byrns, Tenn.	Copley
Aiken	Booher	Campbell	Covington
Alexander	Borchers	Candler, Miss.	Cox
Allen	Bowdle	Cantor	Cramton
Anderson	Broussard	Cantrill	Crosser
Ashbrook	Brown, N. Y.	Caraway	Cullop
Aswell	Bruckner	Carlin	Curry
Bailey	Brumbaugh	Carr	Davenport
Baker	Bryan	Cary	Davis
Baltz	Buchanan, Ill.	Casey	Decker
Barkley	Buchanan, Tex.	Church	Deltrick
Barnhart	Bulkley	Clancy	Deut
Barton	Burgess	Claypool	Dershem
Bathrick	Burke, S. Dak.	Cline	Dickinson
Beakes	Burke, Wis.	Coady	Dies

Dillon	Heflin	Maguire, Nebr.	Sherwood
Dixon	Helgesen	Mahan	Sims
Donovan	Henry	Maher	Sinnott
Doolittle	Hensley	Mapes	Sisson
Doremus	Hill	Mitchell	Sloan
Driscoll	Hinebaugh	Mondell	Small
Dupré	Hobson	Morgan, La.	Smith, Idaho
Eagle	Holland	Morgan, Okla.	Smith, J. M. C.
Edwards	Houston	Morrison	Smith, Md.
Elder	Hughes, Ga.	Moss, Ind.	Smith, N. Y.
Falconer	Hulings	Moss, W. Va.	Stafford
Farr	Hull	Murdock	Stedman
Fergusson	Igoe	Murray, Mass.	Stephens, Miss.
Ferris	Jacoway	Murray, Okla.	Stephens, Tex.
Fields	Johnson, Ky.	Neeley, Kans.	Stevens, N. H.
Finley	Johnson, S. C.	Neely, W. Va.	Stone
Fitzgerald	Johnson, Wash.	Nolan, J. I.	Stringer
FitzHenry	Keating	O'Brien	Sumners
Floyd, Ark.	Kelley, Mich.	O'Hair	Sutherland
Foster	Kelly, Pa.	Oldfield	Taggart
Fowler	Kennedy, Conn.	O'Leary	Talcott, N. Y.
Frear	Kennedy, Iowa	Page, N. C.	Tavenner
French	Kent	Palmer	Taylor, Ark.
Gallagher	Kettner	Park	Taylor, Colo.
Gallivan	Key, Ohio	Patten, N. Y.	Taylor, N. Y.
Gard	Kindel	Peters, Mass.	Temple
Gardner	Kinkaid, Nebr.	Peterson	Thacher
Garner	Kinkead, N. J.	Phelan	Thomas
Garrett, Tex.	Kitchin	Porter	Thompson, Okla.
Gilmore	Konop	Post	Thomson, Ill.
Glass	Korbly	Pou	Towner
Gocke	La Follette	Quin	Tribble
Good	Lazaro	Ragsdale	Tuttle
Goodwin, Ark.	Lee, Pa.	Rainey	Underhill
Gordon	Lenroot	Raker	Underwood
Gorman	Lesher	Rauch	Vare
Goulden	Lever	Rayburn	Vaughan
Gray	Lieb	Reed	Vollmer
Green, Iowa	Lindbergh	Reilly, Wis.	Walsh
Gregg	Linthieum	Riordan	Walters
Griffin	Lloyd	Roberts, Nev.	Watkins
Hamill	Lobeck	Rothermel	Weaver
Hamlin	Logue	Rouse	Webb
Hammond	Lonergan	Rucker	Whitacre
Hardwick	McAndrews	Rupley	Williams
Hardy	McClellan	Russell	Wilson, Fla.
Harris	McCoy	Sabath	Wingo
Harrison	McDermott	Saunders	Witherspoon
Hart	McGillicuddy	Scott	Woodruff
Hangen	McKellar	Scully	Woods
Hawley	McKenzie	Seldomridge	
Hay	McLaughlin	Shackleford	
Hayden	MacDonald	Sharp	

NAYS—54.

Anthony	Fess	Kless, Pa.	Sells
Austin	Gillett	Langley	Shreve
Bartholdt	Graham, Pa.	McGuire, Okla.	Slemp
Britten	Greene, Vt.	Madden	Steenerson
Browne, Wis.	Guernsey	Mann	Stevens, Minn.
Butler	Hamilton, N.Y.	Moore	Switzer
Calder	Hayes	Mott	Treadway
Chandler, N.Y.	Hinds	Nelson	Volstead
Danforth	Howell	Paige, Mass.	Wallin
Drukker	Humphrey, Wash.	Parker	White
Dunn	Johnson, Utah	Payne	Willis
Edmonds	Kahn	Platt	Winslow
Esch	Keister	Plumley	
Fairchild	Kennedy, R.I.	Powers	

ANSWERED "PRESENT"—3.

Bartlett	Fordney	Gerry

NOT VOTING—99.

Ainey	Eagan	Kreider	Reilly, Conn.
Ansberry	Estopinal	Lafferty	Roberts, Mass.
Avis	Evans	Langham	Rogers
Barchfeld	Faison	Lee, Ga.	Rubey
Beall, Tex.	Flood, Va.	L'Engle	Sherley
Borland	Francis	Levy	Slayden
Brockson	Garrett, Tenn.	Lewis, Md.	Smith, Minn.
Brodbeck	George	Lewis, Pa.	Smith, Saml. W.
Brown, W. Va.	Gittins	Lindquist	Smith, Tex.
Browning	Godwin, N.C.	Loft	Sparkman
Burke, Pa.	Goldfogle	Manahan	Stanley
Callaway	Graham, Ill.	Martin	Stephens, Cal.
Carew	Greene, Mass.	Merritt	Stephens, Nebr.
Carter	Griest	Metz	Stout
Clark, Fla.	Gudger	Miller	Talbott, Md.
Collier	Hamilton, Mich.	Montague	Taylor, Ala.
Connolly, Iowa	Helm	Moon	Ten Eyck
Cooper	Helvering	Morin	Townsend
Crisp	Howard	Norton	Walker
Dale	Hoxworth	Oglesby	Watson
Difenderfer	Hughes, W. Va.	O'Shaunessy	Whaley
Donohoe	Humphreys, Miss.	Padgett	Wilson, N.Y.
Dooling	Jones	Patton, Pa.	Young, N. Dak.
Doughton	Kirkpatrick	Peters, Me.	Young, Tex.
Dyer	Knowland, J.R.	Prouty	

So the bill was passed.
The following pairs were announced:
Until further notice:
Mr. GRAHAM of Illinois with Mr. SAMUEL W. SMITH.
Mr. REILLY of Connecticut (for the bill) with Mr. BARCHFELD (against).
Mr. PADGETT (for trust bill) with Mr. ROBERTS of Massachusetts (against).
Mr. YOUNG of Texas with Mr. HAMILTON of Michigan.
Mr. SLAYDEN with Mr. BURKE of Pennsylvania.
Mr. GARRETT of Tennessee with Mr. FORDNEY.
Mr. HILL with Mr. COPLEY.
Mr. TAYLOR of Alabama with Mr. HUGHES of West Virginia.
Mr. CALLAWAY with Mr. ROGERS.
Mr. AINEY with Mr. COLLIER.
Mr. OGLESBY with Mr. PROUTY.
Mr. CARTER with Mr. AVIS.
Mr. DOOLING with Mr. COOPER.
Mr. FLOOD of Virginia with Mr. KREIDER.
Mr. GOLDFOGLE with Mr. LAFFERTY.
Mr. SMITH of Texas with Mr. LANGHAM.
Mr. HOWARD with Mr. LINDQUIST.
Mr. HUMPHREYS of Mississippi with Mr. MANAHAN.
Mr. LEE of Georgia with Mr. MILLER.
Mr. SHERLEY with Mr. NORTON.
Mr. TALBOTT of Maryland with Mr. STEPHENS of California.
Mr. CAREW with Mr. YOUNG of North Dakota.
Mr. GITTINS with Mr. BROWNING.
Mr. SPARKMAN with Mr. DYER.
On this vote:
Mr. BARTLETT with Mr. MARTIN.
Mr. WATSON (for the bill) with Mr. PETERS of Maine (against).
Mr. WILSON of New York (for the bill) with Mr. MORIN (against).
Mr. DOUGHTON (for the bill) with Mr. METZ (against).
Mr. SMITH of Minnesota (for the bill) with Mr. PATTON of Pennsylvania (against).
Mr. RUBEY (for the bill) with Mr. GERRY (against).
Mr. BRODBECK (for the bill) with Mr. GRIEST (against).
Mr. DALE (for the bill) with Mr. LEVY (against).

Mr. DONOHOE (for the bill) with Mr. MERRITT (against).

Mr. MONTAGUE (for the bill) with Mr. GREENE of Massachusetts (against).

Mr. [PETER G.] GERRY [D., R.I.]. Mr. Speaker, I am paired with the gentleman from Missouri, Mr. RUBEY. I wish to withdraw my vote of "no" and answer "present."

The Clerk called the name of Mr. GERRY, and he answered "Present," as above recorded.

Mr. [JOSEPH W.] FORDNEY [R., Mich.]. Mr. Speaker, I voted "no." I find I am paired with the gentleman from Tennessee, Mr. GARRETT. I wish to withdraw my vote and answer "Present."

The Clerk called the name of Mr. FORDNEY, and he answered "Present," as above recorded.

Mr. [JOHN A.] MOON [D., Tenn.]. Mr. Speaker, I desire to vote "aye" on this bill. I do not know whether I am entitled to vote or not. I was in the committee room in the preparation of a matter that is to be presented to the House before adjournment. I did not hear the bell for roll call until a few moments ago.

The SPEAKER. The gentleman does not bring himself within the rule.

Mr. TOWNSEND. Mr. Speaker, can I be recorded on this vote?

The SPEAKER. What is the gentleman's request?

Mr. TOWNSEND. I wish to vote "aye" on this bill.

The SPEAKER. Was the gentleman in the Hall and listening when his name should have been called?

Mr. TOWNSEND. I was not, Mr. Speaker. I thought it was a call of the House.

The SPEAKER. The gentleman does not bring himself within the rule.

The result of the vote was then announced as above recorded.

On motion of Mr. WEBB, a motion to reconsider the vote whereby the bill was passed was laid on the table.

SENATE CONSIDERATION

SENATE DEBATE
63d Cong., 2d Sess.
June 6, 1914

51 CONG. REC. 9929

MESSAGE FROM THE HOUSE.

The message also announced that the House had passed the following bills, in which it requested the concurrence of the Senate: . . .

H. R. 15657. An act to supplement existing laws against unlawful restraints and monopolies, and for other purposes. . . .

HOUSE BILLS REFERRED.

The following bills were severally read twice by their titles and referred to the Committee on Interstate Commerce:

H. R. 15613. An act to create an interstate trade commission, to define its powers and duties, and for other purposes; and

H. R. 16586. An act to amend section 20 of an act to regulate commerce, to prevent overissues of securities by carriers, and for other purposes.

H. R. 15657. An act to supplement existing laws against unlawful restraints and monopolies, and for other purposes, was read twice by its title.

Mr. OVERMAN. I move that the bill be referred to the Committee on the Judiciary.

The motion was agreed to.

SENATE DEBATE
63d Cong., 2d Sess.
July 22, 1914

51 CONG. REC. 12468

Mr. [CHARLES A.] CULBERSON [D., Tex.]. From the Committee on the Judiciary I report back favorably with amendments the bill (H. R. 15657) to supplement existing laws against unlawful restraints and monopolies, and for other purposes, and I submit a report (No. 698) thereon.

The VICE PRESIDENT. The bill will be placed on the calendar.

REPORT OF THE SENATE COMMITTEE ON THE JUDICIARY
S. Rep. No. 698
63d Cong., 2d Sess.
July 22, 1914

Mr. CULBERSON, from the Committee on the Judiciary, submitted the following

REPORT.

[To accompany H. R. 15657.]

The Committee on the Judiciary, having had under consideration the bill (H. R. 15657) to supplement existing laws against unlawful restraints and monopolies, and for other purposes, report the same to the Senate with the recommendation that it be amended as shown on the face of the bill, and that, as amended, it do pass.

It is well, at the outset, to state the theory of the bill, both as it passed the House of Representatives and as it is proposed to be amended, for the general scope of the House measure is unchanged. It is not proposed by the bill or amendments to alter, amend, or change in any respect the original Sherman Antitrust Act of July 2, 1890. The purpose is only to supplement that act and the other antitrust acts referred to in section 1 of the bill. Broadly stated, the bill, in its treatment of unlawful restraints and monopolies, seeks to prohibit and make unlawful certain trade practices which, as a rule, singly and in themselves, are not covered by the act of July 2, 1890, or other existing antitrust acts, and thus, by making these practices illegal, to arrest the creation of trusts, conspiracies, and monopolies in their incipiency and before consummation. Among other of these trade practices which are denounced and made unlawful may be mentioned discrimination in prices for the purpose of wrongfully injuring or destroying the business of competitors; exclusive and tying contracts; holding companies; and interlocking directorates.

Existing antitrust acts are further supplemented by a provision that whenever a corporation shall violate the antitrust acts such violation shall be regarded as that also of the individual directors and officers of the corporation who shall have authorized, ordered, or committed any of the acts constituting such violation, thus fixing the personal guilt of the officials of the corporation who are responsible for the infraction of the law.

The other important and general purposes of the bill are to exempt labor, agricultural, horticultural, and other organizations from the operation of the antitrust acts; to regulate the issuance of temporary restraining orders and injunctions generally by the Federal courts, and particularly in labor controversies, and to make provision for the trial by jury of contempts committed without the presence of the court.

The following is the analysis of the bill as made by the Committee on the Judiciary of the House of Representatives in their report recommending its passage: . . .[5.575]

As heretofore stated, the general scope of the House bill is followed in the Senate amendments. The form of the substantive law and the remedies provided for its enforcement are, however, changed in several instances by the proposed amendments. These will appear in detail in this report, as the amendments to the sections of the bill will be considered separately and in order, but a reference to the more important of

---

[5.575] At this point, the Senate report reprinted most of the House Judiciary Committee's majority report analysis of the bill, H.R. REP. No. 627, 63d Cong., 2d Sess., pt. 1, 7-46 (1914), reproduced *supra* at 1089-121.

them at this point may not be amiss. In sections 2 and 4, which deal respectively with discrimination in prices and exclusive and tying contracts, instead of declaring that the acts named constitute offenses punishable by fine and imprisonment, as in the House bill, the proposed amendments declare the acts unlawful and provide for the enforcement of the sections through the agency of the Federal Trade Commission, to be created. So, also, in sections 8 and 9, which deal with holding companies and interlocking directorates, respectively, some changes have been made in the provisions of positive and substantive law; and the enforcement of the sections has been confided by the amendments to the Interstate Commerce Commission, in the case of common carriers, and to the Federal Trade Commission, in the case of individuals and corporations other than banks and common carriers. All the remedies provided in the bill and amendments are cumulative.

The proposed amendments will now be considered by sections of the bill:

SECTION 1.

This section, which is one confined exclusively to the definition of terms employed in the bill, is only amended in one respect; this is exempting the Philippine Islands from the operation of the act. The reasons for this exemption are stated in a letter of the Acting Secretary of War, as follows:

War Department,
Washington, June 9, 1914.

MY DEAR SENATOR: I find that in the bill H. R. 15657, which has now been referred to the Committee on the Judiciary, there are provisions which would, in part, extend the application of this act to the Philippine Islands.

It seems that it was the intention of the House committee having the bill in charge so to do. It is apparent, however, that the committee did not consider the present status of the Philippine Islands with reference to the laws which it is proposed to supplement by the contemplated legislation.

None of the acts enumerated in the enacting section of this bill are in effect in the Philippine Islands.

I hope that for the following reasons it may be possible to so modify the bill as not to include the Philippine Islands within its provisions:

1. The bill is in its terms supplemental to certain existing laws against unlawful restraints and monopolies and for other purposes, which laws do not apply to the Philippine Islands.

2. The instruments on which the execution of this law depends, such as the district courts of the United States, etc., do not exist in the Philippine Islands.

3. From the passage of the organic act of the Philippine Islands, July 1, 1902, in which act it was specifically provided that the statutory law of the United States should not extend to the Philippine Islands, it has been the policy to create in the Philippine Islands an autonomous government and to give to that government ample power to legislate on all matters of local concern. In this act extending to those islands amendatory legislation of legislation not applicable there, this principle is violated.

4. The Philippine Islands has an import tariff of its own quite distinct from that of the United States and in most of its schedules departing greatly from the rates in our own tariff. American exporters must enter that field in competition with foreign manufacturers of like goods and without the protection which is uniform in practically all other territory under our jurisdiction. Trade there is not a question of American firms competing with each other, but of American firms competing with foreign firms, and any restriction such as imposed in sections 2 and 4 of that act simply has the effect of placing American business at a great disadvantage in meeting foreign competition.

For the same reason that these sections are not made to apply to American trade with foreign countries they should not be made to apply to trade with the Philippine Islands.

Please understand that I make no suggestion as to the form of the bill, but desire to call attention to what was manifestly an oversight in making the bill apply to the Philippine Islands.

Sincerely, yours,

Henry Breckinridge,
Acting Secretary of War.

Hon. Charles A. Culberson,
Chairman Committee on the Judiciary, United States Senate.

Section 2.

This section relates to discrimination in price by persons engaged in commerce with the purpose and intent thereby to destroy or wrongfully injure the business of a competitor. The first Senate amendment to this section changes the form of the substantive law to a declaration of the illegality of the act, instead of the declaration of the House bill that the person committing the act shall be deemed guilty of a misdemeanor, and may be punished. This was done because it was thought best, especially in view of the experimental stage of this legislation, that the harshness of the criminal law should not be applied but that the enforcement of the section should be given to the Federal Trade Commission. Accordingly the penalty provision is stricken out, and the enforcement of the section is provided for in section 9b, under which the commission may arrest the practice by an order, failing in which it can apply to the courts where disobedience of such order may be redressed.

The words "in the same or different sections or communities," in the first part of this section, are stricken out because they are either surplusage, when applied to "commerce," as defined in the bill; or if they are used in a more restricted sense, in a sense which would apply them to local transactions merely, they would attempt to regulate intrastate commerce and be therefore void.

After full consideration it is deemed advisable to enlarge the exception in the first proviso to the section by adding that due allowance may be made for difference in the cost of "selling," as well as ⊥ transportation, and "discrimination in price made in good faith to meet competition and not intended to create monopoly," upon the ground that the enlargement will tend to foster wholesome competition. In the second proviso of this section, to the effect that nothing contained in the section shall prevent persons from choosing their own customers, the limitation is made by amendment that the selection must be made "in *bona fide* transactions and not in restraint of trade," which will enforce good faith and prevent restraint of trade by this method.

Section 3.

This section of the bill is a short one and is as follows:

SEC. 3. That it shall be unlawful for the owner, operator, or transporter of the product or products of any mine, oil or gas well, reduction works, refinery, or hydroelectric plant producing coal, oil, gas, or hydroelectric energy, or for any person controlling the products thereof, engaged in selling such product in commerce to refuse arbitrarily to sell such product to a responsible person, firm, or corporation who applies to purchase such product for use, consumption, or resale within the United States or any Territory thereof or the District of Columbia or any insular possession or other place under the jurisdiction of the United States, and any person violating this section shall be deemed guilty of a misdemeanor and shall be punished as provided in the preceding section.

The proposed Senate amendment is to strike out this section altogether, because, in the opinion of the committee, it would be unwise to enact such legislation as is contained in it. It would, primarily, deny freedom of contract to one of the parties, and consequently would be of doubtful constitutional validity. Passing from this consideration, the Committee believe that such an enactment, which would practically compel owners of the products named to sell to anyone or else decline to do so at the peril of incurring heavy penalties, would project us into a field of legislation at once untried, complicated and dangerous.

Section 4.

This section relates to exclusive and tying contracts. The first Senate amendment to the section changes the form of the declaration of substantive law by denouncing the acts as unlawful, instead of declaring, as in the House bill, that persons committing the acts shall be deemed guilty of misdemeanors, subject to the penalties prescribed. Following the course marked out in section 2, and for the same reason, the penalties provided in section 4 are stricken out and the enforcement of the section confided to the Federal Trade Commission by section 9b. It is believed section 4 is strengthened by the proposed Senate amendments to add "contracts for sale" to leases and sales denounced by the House provision, and to make the prohibition applicable whether the articles leased, sold, or contracted to be sold are "patented or unpatented."

Section 5.

This section, which gives any person injured by a violation of the antitrust acts the right to sue in the Federal courts for threefold the damages by him sustained, including the costs and reasonable attorney's fees, is not proposed to be amended in any particular.

Section 6.

In section 6 there are two paragraphs as it came from the House. The first paragraph provides in substance that whenever in any suit in equity hereafter instituted by the United States a final decree is rendered against a defendant for violating any of the antitrust laws said decree shall, to the full extent to which such decree would constitute in any other proceeding an estoppel as between the United States and such defendant, constitute against such defendant conclusive evidence of the same facts, and be conclusive as to the same questions of law, in favor of any other party in any action brought under the provisions of any of the antitrust laws. It is proposed to amend this by making the decree in favor of the United States *prima facie* evidence against the same defendant in any suit brought by any other party under the antitrust laws as to all matters respecting which said decree would be an estoppel as between the parties thereto. The material difference between the House provision and the Senate amendment is of course whether the decree in favor of the Government shall be *prima facie* evidence against the same defendant in a subsequent suit by another party or be conclusive against such defendant. The Committee think there are considerations of public policy which favor the House provision of conclusiveness, but in the state of the decisions of the Supreme Court of the United States in kindred cases they believe the law should go no further than to make the decree *prima facie* evidence. As a type of the opinions of the Supreme Court which have been examined by the committee in analogous cases attention is invited to the following:

Without going at length into the discussion of a subject so often considered, we think the conclusion reached by the courts generally may be stated as follows: It is competent for the legislature to declare that a tax deed shall be *prima facie* evidence not only of the regularity of the sale, but of all prior proceedings, and of title in the purchaser, but that the legislature can not deprive one of his property by making his adversary's claim to it, whatever that claim may be, conclusive of its own validity, and it can not, therefore, make the tax deed conclusive evidence of the holder's title to the land.

Mr. Cooley sums up his examination of the cases on this subject in the following statement: "That a tax deed can be made conclusive evidence of title in the grantee we think is more than doubtful. The attempt is a plain violation of the great principle of Magna Charta, which has been incorporated in our bill of rights, and, if successful, would in many cases deprive the citizen of his property by proceedings absolutely without warrant of law or of justice; it is not in the power of any American legislature to deprive one of his property by making his adversary's claim to it, whatever that claim may be, conclusive of its own validity. It can not, therefore, make the tax deed conclusive evidence of the holder's title to the land, or of the possible jurisdictional facts which would make out title. But the legislature might doubtless make the deed conclusive evidence of * * * everything except the essentials." Cooley on Taxation, 521, 5th ed., 1886. (Marx *v.* Hanthorn, 148 U. S., 183.)

By the second paragraph of section 6 of the House bill it is provided that whenever any suit in equity is brought by the United States under any of the antitrust laws, the statute of limitations in respect of every private right of action, arising under such antitrust laws, and based in whole or in part on any matter complained of in said suit by the Government, shall be suspended during the pendency of such suit. The proposed Senate amendment of this paragraph does not change its substance but the statute of limitations is extended from three to six years, except as to offenses heretofore committed.

SECTION 7.

This is the section which declares that nothing contained in the antitrust laws shall be construed to forbid the existence and operation of labor, agricultural, horticultural and other organizations, instituted for the purposes of mutual help, and not having capital stock or conducted for profit, or to forbid or restrain individual members of such organizations from lawfully carrying out the legitimate objects thereof; nor shall such organizations, or the members thereof, be held or construed to be illegal combinations or conspiracies in restraint of trade, under the antitrust laws.

The Senate amendments propose to strike out "fraternal" organizations, because, in the opinion of the Committee, not even a forced construction can bring them under the ban of the antitrust laws, and there is no reason for including them in this enactment. It is also proposed to strike out "consumers" in this paragraph. This is recommended by the Committee upon the ground that "consumers" in the economic sense in which the word is used in the bill, while probably intended to apply only to consumers of food products and clothing, is susceptible of much abuse if in the unrestricted sense it is applied, as possibly it may be in imaginable cases, to all character of consumers, including corporations generally, as they are unquestionably consumers. But the principal consideration which moved the Committee to strike out "consumers," which also applies in a less degree to "fraternal" organizations, is that they believe the only organizations which should be excluded from the operation of the antitrust laws are those where labor is the basis or one of the chief factors in the organizations, as in the case of labor organizations proper, and in agricultural and horticultural organizations The Committee rest this distinction upon the broad ground that labor is not, and ought not be regarded as, a commodity, within the purview of antitrust laws.

It is recommended that the last paragraph of this section be stricken out because it is not believed that such agreements, as those named, should be made whether approved or not by the Interstate Commerce Commission, nor that such traffic and operating associations as those mentioned should be formed.

SECTION 8.

This is the section of the bill directed against what are termed holding companies, and the object of the measure is stated in the report of the Committee on the Judiciary of the House of Representatives, heretofore reproduced herein, and to which reference is now again made.

Some of the Senate amendments to this section are minor ones. The word "commerce" is substituted for "trade" at two places, inasmuch as commerce is defined in the bill and trade is not. The words "in any section or community," as they appear in the first two paragraphs of the section, are stricken out, for reasons heretofore given under section 2.

The House provision that nothing contained in the section shall be held to affect or impair any right heretofore legally acquired, provided that nothing in the paragraph shall make stock-holding relations between corporations legal, when such relations constitute violations of the antitrust laws, is stricken out and a substitute proposed at the end of the section. This substitute is broader than the House provision, in that it is not limited to stock-holding relations of corporations, but reaches and extends to "anything prohibited and made illegal by the antitrust laws."

The House provision in this section that nothing contained therein shall be construed to prohibit any railroad corporation from aiding in the construction of branch or short-line railroads so located as to become feeders to the main line, etc., is amended so as to apply to any common carrier, thus including telephone and pipe lines, the committee believing that all common carriers should be given the same rights in this respect and that the extension of the rights to telephone and pipe lines would inure to the benefit of the public. Finally, in this section, the penalty provision is stricken out, for reasons heretofore given under section 2, and the enforcement of the section should be confided to the Interstate Commerce Commission, in the case of common carriers, and to the Federal Trade Commission, in the case of other corporations.

SECTION 9.

This is the section of the bill aimed at interlocking directorates in corporations. The purpose of the enactment is fully stated in the report of the Committee on the Judiciary of the House of Representatives, already reproduced in this report and to which reference is here made. The section, in its declaratory provisions, seeks to prevent the interlocking of directorates affecting three classes of corporations, namely, common-carrier corporations, industrial corporations, and banking and trust corporations. The first Senate amendment would substitute entirely new matter for the House provision in reference to directors of common carriers. The House provision in effect declares that from and after two years from the approval of the act no person who is engaged as an individual, or who is a member of a partnership, or is a director or other officer of a corporation that is engaged in the business of producing or selling equipment, material or supplies to, or in the construction or maintenance of railroads or other common carriers, shall act as a director or other officer or employee of any other corporation or common carrier engaged in commerce to which he, or such partnership or corporation, sells or leases equipment, material, or supplies, or for which he or such partnership or corporation engages in the work of construction or maintenance; and after the expiration of said period no person who is engaged as an individual or who is a member of a partnership or is a director or other officer of a corporation which is engaged in the conduct of a bank or trust company shall act as a director or other officer or employee of any such common carrier for which he or such partnership or bank or trust company acts, either separately or in connection with others, as agent for or underwriter of the sale or disposal by such common carrier of issues or parts of issues of its securities, or from which he or such partnership or bank or trust company purchases, either separately or in connection with others, issues or parts of issues of securities of such common carrier. The prime object of this provision is to prevent common or interlocking directors in corporations which occupy the relations to each other which are thus described; and is mainly intended to arrest the ⊥ practice of the same persons occupying conflicting and incompatible relations in the corporate dealings of common carriers, often being practically both seller and purchaser, lessor and lessee and trustee and beneficiary of the trust. While this evil is fully appreciated, the committee nevertheless recognize that, especially in the case of railroads, emergencies may arise when absolutely prohibitory law against such dealings would be most injurious to the public. In the case of railroads calamities of fire and flood might make it necessary in the shortest possible time and to a certain extent regardless of lesser consequences to replace engines, cars and bridges. The Committee have, therefore, recommended a substitute for the House paragraph on this subject, which, with the publicity, competitive bidding and the supervision of the Interstate Commerce Commission provided for, will, it is believed, minimize if not wholly cure the evil to be reached.

⊥48

The House provision in this section relating to interlocking directorates of industrial corporations is not proposed to be changed or amended in any respect.

A Senate amendment to this section strikes out the entire paragraph which relates to interlocking directorates of banks and trust companies. In proposing this amendment a majority of the Committee believed that such legislation as this more properly belongs to the domain of banking rather than of commerce and such additional regulation of bank directorates as may be wise and just should be made by amendments to the national bank acts, and the enforcement of it given to the Comptroller of the Currency and the Federal Reserve Board.

The penalty provision in this section is stricken out for reasons already given under sections 2, 4 and 8, but a penalty is expressly provided for violating the provisions of the amendment to the paragraph relating to interlocking directorates in the case of common carriers.

SECTION 9A.

This is an entirely new provision, fully explains itself, and is as follows:

SEC. 9a. Every president, director, officer or manager of any firm, association or corporation engaged in commerce as a common carrier, who embezzles, steals, abstracts or willfully misapplies any of the moneys, funds, credits, securities, property or assets of such firm, association or corporation, or willfully or knowingly converts the same to his own use or to the use of another, shall be deemed guilty of a felony and upon conviction shall be fined not less than $500 or confined in the penitentiary not less than 1 year nor more than 10 years, or both, in the discretion of the court.

Prosecutions hereunder may be in the district court of the United States for the district wherein the offense may have been committed.

SECTION 9B.

This is also an entirely new provision and is intended to provide the administrative agency through which sections 2, 4, 8, and 9 are to be enforced. It carries its own explanation and is as follows:

SEC. 9b. That authority to enforce compliance with the provisions of sections two, four, eight, and nine of this Act by the corporations, associations, partnerships, and individuals respectively subject thereto is hereby vested: In the Interstate Commerce Commission where applicable to common carriers and in the Federal Trade Commission where applicable to all other character of commerce, to be exercised as follows:

Whenever the commission vested with jurisdiction thereof has reason to believe, either upon information furnished by its agents or employees or upon complaint, duly verified by affidavit, of any interested person, that any corporation, association, partnership, or individual is violating any of the provisions of sections two, four, eight, and nine of this Act, it shall issue and cause to be served a notice, accompanied with a written statement of the violation charged, upon such corporation, association, partnership, or individual who shall thereupon be called upon, within a reasonable time fixed in such notice, not to exceed thirty days thereafter, to appear and show cause why an order should not issue to restrain and prohibit the violation charged. If upon a hearing held pursuant to such notice it shall appear to the commission that any of the provisions of said sections have been or are being violated, then it shall issue and cause to be served an order commanding such corporation, association, partnership, or individual forthwith to cease and desist from such violation, and to transfer or dispose of the stock or resign from the directorships held contrary to the provisions of sections eight or nine, as the case may be, within the time and in the manner prescribed in said order. Any such order may be modified or set aside at any time by the commission issuing it for good cause shown.

If any corporation, association, partnership, or individual charged with obedience thereto fails and neglects to obey any such order of a commission, the said commission, by its attorneys, if any it has, or by the appropriate district attorney acting under the direction of the Attorney General of the United States, may apply for an enforcement of such order to the district court of the United States for the district wherein such corporation, association, partnership, or individual is an inhabitant or may be found or transacts any business, and therewith transmit to the said court the original record in the proceeding, including all the testimony taken therein and the report and order of the commission. Upon the filing of the record, the court shall have jurisdiction of the proceeding and of the questions determined therein and shall have power to make and to enter upon the pleadings, testimony, and proceedings such orders and decrees as may be just and equitable.

On motion of the commission and on such notice as the court shall deem reasonable, the court shall set down the cause for summary final hearing. Upon such final hearing the finding of the commission shall be prima facie evidence of the facts therein stated, but if either party shall apply to the court for leave to adduce additional evidence and shall show to the satisfaction of the court that such additional evidence is material and that there were reasonable grounds for the failure to adduce such evidence in the proceeding before the commission, the court may allow such additional evidence to be taken before the commission or before a master appointed by the court and to be adduced upon the hearing in such manner and upon such terms and conditions as to the court may seem just.

Disobedience to any order or decree which may be made in any such proceeding or any injunction or other process issued therein shall be punished by a fine not exceeding $100 a day during the continuance of such disobedience or by imprisonment not exceeding one year, or by both such fine and imprisonment.

Any party to any proceeding brought under the provisions of this section before either the Interstate Commerce Commission or the Federal Trade Commission, including the person upon whose complaint such proceeding shall have been begun as well as the United States by and through the Attorney General thereof, may appeal from any final order made by either of such commissions to any court having jurisdiction to enforce any order which might have been made upon application of such commission as hereinbefore provided, at any time within ninety days from the date of the entry of the order appealed from, by serving notice upon the adverse party and filing the same with the said commission; and thereupon the same proceedings shall be had as prescribed herein in the case of an application by the same commission for the enforcement of its order as hereinbefore provided.

Any final order or decree made by any district court in any proceeding brought under this section may be reviewed by the Supreme Court upon appeal, as in cases in equity, taken within ninety days from the entry of such order or decree.

SECTIONS 10 AND 11.

These sections relate to the venue and issuance of process in suits arising under the antitrust laws. They are proposed to be amended in certain respects, as shown on their face, but the amendments require no special explanation here.

SECTION 12.

This is the personal guilt provision of the law. The substance of the section is not altered, but the Committee think the Senate amendment better expresses the purpose and is more direct. Instead of visiting the offense of the corporation over on its directors, officers and agents, as in the House provision, the amendment declares directly that they shall be guilty and somewhat enlarges the several acts which constitute the offenses denounced.

SECTION 13.

This section, which is existing law, is not proposed to be amended in any particular.

SECTION 14.

This section provides that any person, firm, corporation, or association shall be entitled to sue for and have injunctive relief in the Federal courts against threatened loss or damage by a violation of the antitrust laws, etc. It is proposed by a Senate amendment to make this Section apply expressly to Sections 2, 4, 8, and 9 of this bill, so that all doubt of the cumulative and not exclusive character of the remedy provided in section 9b may be removed. The House proviso in Section 14 is proposed to be stricken out because the Committee are of the opinion that actions under this section should lie against common carriers as well as other corporations.

SECTION 15.

The purpose of this section is to prohibit the issuance of preliminary injunctions in any case without notice to the opposite party, and to regulate the issuance generally of temporary restraining orders. The principal Senate amendment strikes out the words "property or property right of," so that a temporary restraining order may issue, if otherwise proper under the act, even though no property or property right is involved. Suits in equity by the United States may be instituted where no such property or property right may be involved, and there are classes of cases by private suitors where the same is true, and if the House provision were adopted no temporary restraining orders would be issuable in those cases. If the Senate amendment is adopted the provision will in this respect be practically Equity Rule 73 promulgated by the Supreme Court of the United States.

Cases may arise where it would be unjust that a temporary restraining order would necessarily and irrevocably expire at a time not to exceed 10 days after entry of the order, as is provided in the House bill. Accordingly it is proposed by a Senate amendment to insert the words "unless within the time so fixed the order is extended for a like period for good cause shown, and the reasons for such extensions shall be entered of record."

SECTIONS 16 AND 17.

Section 16 provides that no restraining order or interlocutory order of injunction shall issue except on the giving of bond by the applicant. Section 17 declares that every order of injunction or restraining order shall set forth the reasons for its issuance, shall be specific in terms, and shall describe in reasonable detail, and not by reference to the complaint or other document, the acts sought to be restrained, and shall be binding only upon the parties to the suit, their agents, servants, employees, and attorneys, or those in active concert with them, and who shall, by personal service or otherwise, have received actual notice of the same.

Neither section is proposed to be amended in any material respect.

SECTION 18.

This is the section which regulates the issuance of restraining orders and injunctions in labor controversies, to which several amendments are proposed.

The words "singly or in concert" are inserted in line 4, page 27, to guard the right of workingmen to act together in terminating, if they desire, any relation of employment, and to act together and in concert in doing or abstaining from doing any other of the acts named in that paragraph of the section. Some minor amendments also are made in this section, the reasons for which will appear obvious on examination.

The most important amendment to this section is that which strikes out the words, in lines 7 to 11, inclusive, page 27, namely, "or from attending at or near a house or place where any person resides or works or carries on business, or happens to be, for the purpose of peacefully obtaining or communicating information." This, as is well known, is what is termed picketing. The House provision declares that no restraining order or injunction in a labor case shall issue prohibiting any person from doing any of the acts quoted above, and if the Senate amendment, which was proposed by a majority of the Committee, is adopted the Federal courts will be left free to issue restraining orders and injunctions in such cases. The authorities as to the legality pro and con of picketing are collated in Martin's Modern Law of Labor Unions, pages 132 et seq.

SECTIONS 19, 20, 21, 22, AND 23.

These sections regulate the trial of contempts committed without the presence of the court. Only two amendments of consequence to these sections are proposed. In Section 19 the words "at common law" are stricken out, because the common law of England is not in force in the United States, and the words "under the laws of any State in which the act was committed" are inserted. It is proposed to amend Section 20 by adding at the end of the section the following:

Provided, That in any case the court or a judge thereof may, for good cause shown, by affidavit or proof taken in open court or before such judge and filed with the papers in the case, dispense with the rule to show cause, and may issue an attachment for the arrest of the person charged with contempt; in which event such person, when arrested, shall be brought before such court or a judge thereof without unnecessary delay and shall be admitted to bail in a reasonable penalty for his appearance to answer to the charge or for trial for the contempt; and thereafter the proceedings shall be the same as provided herein in case the rule had issued in the first instance.

The object of this amendment is to insure the presence of a party charged with contempt.[5.576]

[5.576] H.R. 15657 as amended by the Senate Committee on the Judiciary was reprinted on pages 53–83 of this report.

H.R. 15657 AS REPORTED BY THE SENATE COMMITTEE ON THE JUDICIARY
63d Cong., 2d Sess.
July 22, 1914

Reported by Mr. CULBERSON, with amendments.

[Omit the part struck through and insert the part printed in italic.]

AN ACT

To supplement existing laws against unlawful restraints and monopolies, and for other purposes.

Be it enacted by the Senate and House of Representatives of the United States of America in Congress assembled, That "antitrust laws," as used herein, includes the Act entitled "An Act to protect trade and commerce against unlawful restraints and monopolies," approved July second, eighteen hundred and ninety; sections seventy-three to seventy-seven, inclusive, of an Act entitled "An Act to reduce taxation, to provide revenue for the Government, and for other purposes," of August twenty-seventh, eighteen hundred and ninety-four; an Act entitled "An Act to amend sections seventy-three and seventy-six of the Act of August twenty-seventh, eighteen hundred and ninety-four, entitled 'An Act to reduce taxation, to provide revenue for the Government, and for other purposes,' " approved February twelfth, nineteen hundred and thirteen; and also this Act.

"Commerce," as used herein, means trade or commerce among the several States and with foreign nations, or between the District of Columbia or any Territory of the United States and any State, Territory, or foreign nation, or between any insular possessions or other places under the jurisdiction of the United States, or between any such possession or place and any State or Territory of the United States or the District of Columbia or any foreign nation, or within the District of Columbia or any Territory or any insular possession or other place under the jurisdiction of the United States: *Provided, That nothing in this Act contained shall apply to the Philippine Islands.*

The word "person" or "persons" wherever used in this Act shall be deemed to include corporations and associations existing under or authorized by the laws of either the United States, the laws of any of the Territories, the laws of any State, or the laws of any foreign country.

5.577 This version of H.R. 15657 incorporates language as finally passed by the House on June 5, 1914, and indicates the amendments which the Senate Judiciary Committee proposed to the House bill. Words scored through are House language the Senate committee proposed to delete, and words printed in italics are those the Senate committee proposed to add.

SEC. 2. That *it shall be unlawful for* any person engaged in commerce ~~who shall~~ either directly or indirectly *to* discriminate in price between different purchasers of commodities ~~in the same or different sections or communities~~, which commodities are sold for use, consumption, or resale within the United States or any Territory thereof or the District of Columbia or any insular possession or other place under the jurisdiction of the United States, with the purpose or intent thereby to destroy or wrongfully injure the business of a competitor, of either such purchaser or seller~~, shall be deemed guilty of a misdemeanor, and upon conviction thereof shall be punished by a fine not exceeding $5,000, or by imprisonment not exceeding one year, or by both, in the discretion of the court~~: *Provided*, That nothing herein contained shall prevent discrimination in price between purchasers of commodities on account of differences in the grade, quality, or quantity of the commodity sold, or that makes only due allowance for difference in the cost of *selling or* transportation *or discrimination in price in the same or different communities made in good faith to meet competition and not intended to create monopoly: And provided further*, That nothing herein contained shall prevent persons engaged in selling goods, wares, or merchandise in commerce from selecting their own customers *in bona fide transactions and not in restraint of trade*~~, except as provided in section three of this Act~~.

~~SEC. 3. That it shall be unlawful for the owner, operator, or transporter of the product or products of any mine, oil or gas well, reduction works, refinery, or hydroelectric plant producing coal, oil, gas, or hydroelectric energy, or for any person controlling the products thereof, engaged in selling such product in commerce to refuse arbitrarily to sell such product to a responsible person, firm, or corporation who applies to purchase such product for use, consumption, or resale within the United States or any Territory thereof or the District of Columbia or any insular possession or other place under the jurisdiction of the United States, and any person violating this section shall be deemed guilty of a misdemeanor and shall be punished as provided in the preceding section.~~

SEC. 4. That *it shall be unlawful for* any person engaged in commerce ~~who shall~~ *to* lease or make a sale *or contract for sale* of goods, wares, merchandise, machinery, supplies, or other commodities *whether patented or unpatented* for use, consumption, or resale within the United States, or any Territory thereof or the District of Columbia or any insular possession or other place under the jurisdiction of the United States, or fix a price charged therefor, or discount from, or rebate upon such price, on the condition, agreement, or understanding that the lessee or purchaser thereof shall not use or deal in the goods, wares, merchandise, machinery, supplies, or other commodities of a competitor or competitors of the lessor or seller ~~shall be deemed guilty of a misdemeanor, and upon conviction thereof shall be punished by a fine not exceeding $5,000, or by imprisonment not~~

3 ~~exceeding one year, or by both, in the discretion of the court.~~
4   SEC. 5. That any person who shall be injured in his
5 business or property by reason of anything forbidden in the
6 antitrust laws may sue therefor in any district court of the
7 United States in the district in which the defendant resides or
8 is found or has an agent, without respect to the amount in
9 controversy, and shall recover threefold the damages by him
10 sustained, and the cost of suit, including a reasonable
11 attorney's fee.
12   SEC. 6. ~~That whenever in any suit or proceeding in~~
13 ~~equity hereafter brought by or on behalf of the United States~~
14 ~~under any of the antitrust laws there shall have been ren-~~
15 ~~dered a final judgment or decree to the effect that a defend-~~
16 ~~ant has entered into a contract, combination in the form of~~
17 ~~trust or otherwise, or conspiracy, in restraint of trade or~~
18 ~~commerce, or has monopolized, or attempted to monopolize~~
19 ~~or combined with any person or persons to monopolize, any~~
20 ~~part of commerce, in violation of any of the antitrust laws,~~
21 ~~said judgment or decree shall, to the full extent to which such~~
22 ~~judgment or decree would constitute in any other proceed-~~
23 ~~ing an estoppel as between the United States and such~~
24 ~~defendant, constitute against such defendant conclusive evi-~~
25 ~~dence of the same facts, and be conclusive as to the same~~
1 ~~questions of law in favor of any other party in any action or~~
2 ~~proceeding brought under or involving the provisions of any~~
3 ~~of the antitrust laws.~~
4   ~~Whenever any suit or proceeding in equity is hereafter~~
5 ~~brought by or on behalf of the United States, under any of~~
6 ~~the antitrust laws, the statute of limitations in respect of each~~
7 ~~and every private right of action, arising under such antitrust~~
8 ~~laws, and based, in whole or in part, on any matter com-~~
9 ~~plained of in said suit or proceeding in equity, shall be sus-~~
10 ~~pended during the pendency of such suit or proceeding in~~
11 ~~equity.~~
12   *That a final judgment or decree rendered in any suit or*
13 *proceeding in equity brought by or on behalf of the United*
14 *States under the antitrust laws to the effect that a defendant*
15 *has violated said laws shall be prima facie evidence against*
16 *such defendant in any suit or proceeding brought by any*
17 *other party against such defendant under said laws as to all*
18 *matters respecting which said judgment or decree would be*
19 *an estoppel as between the parties thereto.*
20   *Any person may be prosecuted, tried, or punished for any*
21 *offense under the antitrust laws, and any suit arising under*
22 *those laws may be maintained if the indictment is found or*
23 *the suit is brought within six years next after the occurrence of*
24 *the act or cause of action complained of, any statute of limita-*
25 *tion or other provision of law heretofore enacted to the contrary*
1 *notwithstanding. Whenever any suit or proceeding in equity*
2 *is instituted by the United States to prevent or restrain viola-*
3 *tions of any of the antitrust laws the running of the statute*
4 *of limitations in respect of each and every private right of*
5 *action arising under said laws and based in whole or in part*
6 *on any matter complained of in said suit or proceeding shall*

be suspended during the pendency thereof: Provided, That this shall not be held to extend the statute of limitations in the case of offenses heretofore committed.

SEC. 7. That nothing contained in the antitrust laws shall be construed to forbid the existence and operation of ~~fraternal,~~ labor, ~~consumers,~~ agricultural, or horticultural organizations, ~~orders, or associations,~~ instituted for the purposes of mutual help, and not having capital stock or conducted for profit, or to forbid or restrain individual members of such organizations, ~~orders, or associations~~ from *lawfully* carrying out the legitimate objects thereof; nor shall such organizations, ~~orders, or associations,~~ or the members thereof, be held or construed to be illegal combinations or conspiracies in restraint of trade, under the antitrust laws.

~~Nothing contained in the antitrust laws shall be construed to forbid associations of traffic, operating, accounting, or other officers of common carriers for the purpose of conferring among themselves or of making any lawful agreement as to any matter which is subject to the regulating or supervisory jurisdiction of the Interstate Commerce Commission, but all such matters shall continue to be subject to such jurisdiction of the commission, and all such agreements shall be entered and kept of record by the carriers, parties thereto, and shall at all times be open to inspection by the commission, but no such agreement shall go into effect or become operative until the same shall have first been submitted to, and approved by, the Interstate Commerce Commission: *Provided,* That nothing in this Act shall be construed as modifying existing laws prohibiting the pooling of earnings or traffic, or existing laws against joint agreements by common carriers to maintain rates.~~

SEC. 8. That no corporation engaged in commerce shall acquire, directly or indirectly, the whole or any part of the stock or other share capital of another corporation engaged also in commerce where the effect of such acquisition is to eliminate or substantially lessen competition between the corporation whose stock is so acquired and the corporation making the acquisition, or to create a monopoly of any line of ~~trade~~ *commerce* ~~in any section or community~~.

No corporation shall acquire, directly or indirectly, the whole or any part of the stock or other share capital of two or more corporations engaged in commerce where the effect of such acquisition, or the use of such stock by the voting or granting of proxies or otherwise, is to eliminate or substantially lessen competition between such corporations, or any of them, whose stock or other share capital is so acquired, or to create a monopoly of any line of ~~trade~~ *commerce* ~~in any section or community~~.

This section shall not apply to corporations purchasing such stock solely for investment and not using the same by voting or otherwise to bring about, or in attempting to bring about, the substantial lessening of competition. Nor shall anything contained in this section prevent a corporation engaged in commerce from causing the formation of subsidiary corporations for the actual carrying on of their immediate lawful business, or the natural and legitimate branches or extensions thereof, or from owning and holding all or a part of the stock of such subsidiary corporations, when the effect of such formation is not to eliminate or substantially lessen competition.

~~Nothing contained in this section shall be held to affect or impair any right heretofore legally acquired: Provided, That nothing in this paragraph shall make stockholding relations between corporations legal when such relations constitute violations of the antitrust laws.~~

Nor shall anything herein contained be construed to prohibit any ~~railroad corporation~~ *common carrier subject to the laws to regulate commerce* from aiding in the construction of ~~branch~~ *branches* or short ~~line~~ *lines* ~~railroads~~ so located as to become feeders to the main line of the company so aiding in such construction or from acquiring or owning all or any part of the stock of such branch ~~line~~ *lines*, nor to prevent any ~~railroad corporation~~ *such common carrier* from acquiring and owning all or any part of the stock of a branch or short line ~~railroad~~ constructed by an independent company where there is no substantial competition between the company owning the branch line so constructed and the company owning the main line acquiring the property or an interest therein nor to prevent ~~any railroad company~~ *such common carrier* from extending any of its lines through the medium of the acquisition of stock or otherwise of any other ~~railroad company~~ *such common carrier* where there is no substantial competition between the company extending its lines and the company whose stock, property, or an interest therein is so acquired.

Nothing contained in this section shall be held to affect or impair any right heretofore legally acquired: Provided, That nothing herein shall be held or construed to authorize or make lawful anything prohibited and made illegal by the antitrust laws.

~~A violation of any of the provisions of this section shall be deemed a misdemeanor, and shall be punishable by a fine not exceeding $5,000, or by imprisonment not exceeding one year, or by both, in the discretion of the court.~~

SEC. 9. ~~That from and after two years from the date of the approval of this Act no person who is engaged as an individual, or who is a member of a partnership, or is a director or other officer of a corporation that is engaged in the business, in whole or in part, of producing or selling equipment, materials, or supplies to, or in the construction or maintenance of, railroads or other common carriers engaged in commerce, shall act as a director or other officer or employee of any other corporation or common carrier engaged in commerce to which he, or such partnership or corporation, sells or leases, directly or indirectly, equipment, materials, or supplies, or for which he or such partnership or corporation, directly or indirectly, engages in the work of construction or maintenance; and after the expiration of said~~

~~period no person who is engaged as an individual or who is a member of a partnership or is a director or other officer of a corporation which is engaged in the conduct of a bank or trust company shall act as a director or other officer or employee of any such common carrier for which he or such partnership or bank or trust company acts, either separately or in connection with others, as agent for or underwriter of the sale or disposal by such common carrier of issues or parts of issues of its securities, or from which he or such partnership or bank or trust company purchases, either separately or in connection with others, issues or parts of issues of securities of such common carrier.~~

After two years from the approval of this Act no common carrier engaged in commerce having upon its board of directors or as its president, manager, or purchasing officer or agent any person who is at the same time an officer, director, manager, or general agent of, or who has any direct or indirect interest in, another corporation, firm, partnership or association, with which latter corporation, firm, partnership or association or with such person such common carrier shall make purchases of supplies or articles of commerce or have any dealings in securities, railroad supplies or other articles of commerce or contracts for construction or maintenance of any kind with any such corporation, firm, partnership, or association to the amount of more than $50,000 in any one year, unless and except such purchases shall be made from or such dealings shall be with the bidder whose bid is the most favorable to such common carrier, to be ascertained by competitive bidding after public notice published in a newspaper or newspapers of general circulation, to be named and the time, character and scope of the publication to be prescribed by rule or otherwise by the Interstate Commerce Commission. No bid shall be received unless the names and addresses of the officers, directors, and general managers thereof, if it be a corporation, or of the members, if it be a partnership or firm, be given with the bid.

Any person who shall, directly or indirectly, do or attempt to do anything to prevent anyone from bidding or shall do any act to prevent free and fair competition among the bidders or those desiring to bid shall be punished as prescribed in this section.

Every such common carrier having any such transactions or making any such purchases shall within ten days after making the same file with the Interstate Commerce Commission a full and detailed statement of the transaction showing the manner and time of the advertisement given for competition, who were the bidders, and the names and addresses of the directors and officers of the corporations and the members of the firm or partnership bidding; and whenever the said commission shall have reason to believe that the law has been violated in and about the said purchases or transactions it shall transmit all papers and documents and its own views or findings regarding the transaction to the Attorney General.

If any common carrier shall violate this section, every

director or officer thereof who shall have knowingly voted for or directed the act constituting such violation or who shall have aided or abetted in such violation shall be deemed guilty of a misdemeanor and shall be fined not exceeding $25,000 and confined in jail not exceeding two years, in the discretion of the court.

~~That from and after two years from the date of the approval of this Act no person shall at the same time be a director or other officer or employee of more than one bank, banking association, or trust company organized or operating under the laws of the United States either of which has deposits, capital, surplus, and undivided profits aggregating more than $2,500,000; and no private banker or person who is a director in any bank or trust company, organized and operating under the laws of a State, having deposits, capital, surplus, and undivided profits aggregating more than $2,500,000, shall be eligible to be a director in any bank or banking association organized or operating under the laws of the United States. The eligibility of a director, officer, or employee under the foregoing provisions shall be determined by the average amount of deposits, capital, surplus, and undivided profits as shown in the official statements of such bank, banking association, or trust company filed as provided by law during the fiscal year next preceding the date set for the annual election of directors, and when a director, officer, or employee has been elected or selected in accordance with the provisions of this Act it shall be lawful for him to continue as such for one year thereafter under said election or employment.~~

~~No bank, banking association, or trust company organized or operating under the laws of the United States in any city or incorporated town or village of more than one hundred thousand inhabitants, as shown by the last preceding decennial census of the United States, shall have as a director or other officer or employee any private banker or any director or other officer or employee of any other bank, banking association, or trust company located in the same place: *Provided*, That nothing in this section shall apply to mutual savings banks not having a capital stock represented by shares: *Provided further*, That a director or other officer or employee of such bank, banking association, or trust company may be a director or other officer or employee of not more than one other bank or trust company organized under the laws of the United States or any State where the entire capital stock of one is owned by stockholders in the other: *And provided further*, That nothing contained in this section shall forbid a director of class A of a Federal reserve bank, as defined in the Federal Reserve Act, from being an officer or director or both an officer and director in one member bank.~~

That from and after two years from the date of the approval of this Act no person at the same time shall be a director in any two or more corporations, ~~either~~ *any one* of which has capital, surplus, and undivided profits aggregating more than $1,000,000, engaged in whole or in part in commerce, other than common carriers subject to the Act to regulate commerce, approved February fourth, eighteen hundred and eighty-seven, if such corporations are or shall have been theretofore, by virtue of their business and location of operation, competitors, so that ~~an~~ the elimination of competition by agreement between them would constitute a violation of any of the provisions of any of the antitrust laws. The eligibility of a director under the foregoing provision shall be determined by the aggregate amount of the capital, surplus, and undivided profits, exclusive of dividends declared but not paid to stockholders, at the end of the fiscal year of said corporation next preceding the election of directors, and when a director has been elected in accordance with the provisions of this Act it shall be lawful for him to continue as such for one year thereafter.

When any person elected or chosen as a director or officer or selected as an employee of any ~~bank or other~~ corporation subject to the provisions of this Act is eligible at the time of his election or selection to act for such ~~bank or other~~ corporation in such capacity, his eligibility to act in such capacity shall not be affected and he shall not become or be deemed amenable to any of the provisions hereof by reason of any change in the affairs of such ~~bank or other~~ corporation from whatsoever cause, whether specifically excepted by any of the provisions hereof or not, until the expiration of one year from the date of his election or employment.

~~That any person who shall violate any of the provisions of this section shall be guilty of a misdemeanor and shall be punished by a fine of not exceeding $100 a day for each day of the continuance of such violation, or by imprisonment for such period as the court may designate, not exceeding one year, or by both, in the discretion of the court.~~

SEC. 9a. *Every president, director, officer or manager of any firm, association or corporation engaged in commerce as a common carrier, who embezzles, steals, abstracts or willfully misapplies any of the moneys, funds, credits, securities, property or assets of such firm, association or corporation, or willfully or knowingly converts the same to his own use or to the use of another, shall be deemed guilty of a felony and upon conviction shall be fined not less than $500 or confined in the penitentiary not less than one year nor more than ten years, or both, in the discretion of the court.*

Prosecutions hereunder may be in the district court of the United States for the district wherein the offense may have been committed.

SEC. 9b. *That authority to enforce compliance with the provisions of sections two, four, eight, and nine of this Act by the corporations, associations, partnerships, and individuals respectively subject thereto is hereby vested: In the Interstate Commerce Commission where applicable to common carriers and in the Federal Trade Commission where applicable to all other character of commerce, to be exercised as follows:*

Whenever the commission vested with jurisdiction thereof

has reason to believe, either upon information furnished by its agents or employees or upon complaint, duly verified by affidavit, of any interested person, that any corporation, association, partnership, or individual is violating any of the provisions of sections two, four, eight, and nine of this Act, it shall issue and cause to be served a notice, accompanied with a written statement of the violation charged, upon such corporation, association, partnership, or individual who shall thereupon be called upon, within a reasonable time fixed in such notice, not to exceed thirty days thereafter, to appear and show cause why an order should not issue to restrain and prohibit the violation charged. If upon a hearing held pursuant to such notice it shall appear to the commission that any of the provisions of said sections have been or are being violated, then it shall issue and cause to be served an order commanding such corporation, association, partnership, or individual forthwith to cease and desist from such violation, and to transfer or dispose of the stock or resign from the directorships held contrary to the provisions of sections eight or nine, as the case may be, within the time and in the manner prescribed in said order. Any such order may be modified or set aside at any time by the commission issuing it for good cause shown.

If any corporation, association, partnership, or individual charged with obedience thereto fails and neglects to obey any such order of a commission, the said commission, by its attorneys, if any it has, or by the appropriate district attorney acting under the direction of the Attorney General of the United States, may apply for an enforcement of such order to the district court of the United States for the district wherein such corporation, association, partnership, or individual is an inhabitant or may be found or transacts any business, and therewith transmit to the said court the original record in the proceeding, including all the testimony taken therein and the report and order of the commission. Upon the filing of the record, the court shall have jurisdiction of the proceeding and of the questions determined therein and shall have power to make and to enter upon the pleadings, testimony, and proceedings such orders and decrees as may be just and equitable.

On motion of the commission and on such notice as the court shall deem reasonable, the court shall set down the cause for summary final hearing. Upon such final hearing the finding of the commission shall be prima facie evidence of the facts therein stated, but if either party shall apply to the court for leave to adduce additional evidence and shall show to the satisfaction of the court that such additional evidence is material and that there were reasonable grounds for the failure to adduce such evidence in the proceeding before the commission, the court may allow such additional evidence to be taken before the commission or before a master appointed by the court and to be adduced upon the hearing in such manner and upon such terms and conditions as to the court may seem just.

Disobedience to any order or decree which may be made in any such proceeding or any injunction or other process issued therein shall be punished by a fine not exceeding $100 a day during the continuance of such disobedience or by imprisonment not exceeding one year, or by both such fine and imprisonement [sic].

Any party to any proceeding brought under the provisions of this section before either the Interstate Commerce Commission or the Federal Trade Commission, including the person upon whose complaint such proceeding shall have been begun, as well as the United States by and through the Attorney General thereof, may appeal from any final order made by either of such commissions to any court having jurisdiction to enforce any order which might have been made upon application of such commission as hereinbefore provided, at any time within ninety days from the date of the entry of the order appealed from, by serving notice upon the adverse party and filing the same with the said commission; and thereupon the same proceedings shall be had as prescribed herein in the case of an application by the same commission for the enforcement of its order as hereinbefore provided.

Any final order or decree made by any district court in any proceeding brought under this section may be reviewed by the Supreme Court upon appeal, as in cases in equity, taken within ninety days from the entry of such order or decree.

SEC. 10. That any suit, action, or proceeding under the antitrust laws against a corporation may be brought not only in the judicial district whereof it is an inhabitant, but also any district wherein it may be found or ~~has an agent~~ *transacts any business; and all process in such cases may be served in the district of which it is an inhabitant, or wherever it may be found.*

SEC. 11. That in any suit, action, or proceeding brought by or on behalf of the United States subpoenas for witnesses who are required to attend a court of the United States in any judicial district in any case, civil or criminal, arising under the antitrust laws may run into any other district~~: Provided, That in civil cases no writ of subpoena shall issue for witnesses living out of the district in which the court is held at a greater distance than one hundred miles from the place of holding the same without the permission of the trial court being first had upon proper application and cause shown~~.

SEC. 12. That ~~whenever a corporation shall violate any of the provisions of the antitrust laws, such violation shall be deemed to be also that of the individual directors, officers, or agents of such corporation who shall have authorized, ordered, or done any of the acts constituting in whole or in part such violation, and such violation~~ *every director, officer, or agent of a corporation which shall violate any of the penal provisions of the antitrust laws, who shall have aided, abetted, counseled, commanded, induced, or procured such violation*, shall be deemed *guilty of* a misdemeanor, and upon conviction therefor of any such director, officer, or agent he shall be punished by a fine of not exceeding $5,000 or by imprisonment for not exceeding one year, or by both, in the discretion of the court.

SEC. 13. That the several district courts of the United States are hereby invested with jurisdiction to prevent and restrain violations of this Act, and it shall be the duty of the several district attorneys of the United States, in their respective districts, under the direction of the Attorney General, to institute proceedings in equity to prevent and restrain such violations. Such proceedings may be by way of petition setting forth the case and praying that such violation shall be enjoined or otherwise prohibited. When the parties complained of shall have been duly notified of such petition, the court shall proceed, as soon as may be, to the hearing and determination of the case; and pending such petition, and before final decree, the court may at any time make such temporary restraining order or prohibition as shall be deemed just in the premises. Whenever it shall appear to the court before which any such proceeding may be pending that the ends of justice require that other parties should be brought before the court, the court may cause them to be summoned, whether they reside in the district in which the court is held or not, and subpoenas to that end may be served in any district by the marshal thereof.

SEC. 14. That any person, firm, corporation, or association shall be entitled to sue for and have injunctive relief, in any court of the United States having jurisdiction over the parties, against threatened loss or damage by a violation of the antitrust laws, *including sections two, four, eight, and nine of this Act*, when and under the same conditions and principles as injunctive relief against threatened conduct that will cause loss or damage is granted by courts of equity, under the rules governing such proceedings, and upon the execution of proper bond against damages for an injunction improvidently granted and a showing that the danger of irreparable loss or damage is immediate, a preliminary injunction may issue: ~~Provided, That nothing herein contained shall be construed to entitle any person, firm, corporation, or association, except the United States, to bring suit in equity for injunctive relief against any common carrier subject to the provisions of the Act to regulate commerce, approved February fourth, eighteen hundred and eighty-seven, in respect of any matter subject to the regulation, supervision, or other jurisdiction of the Interstate Commerce Commission~~.

SEC. 15. That no preliminary injunction shall be issued without notice to the opposite party.

No temporary restraining order shall be granted without notice to the opposite party unless it shall clearly appear from specific facts shown by affidavit or by the verified bill that immediate and irreparable injury, loss, or damage will result to ~~property or a property right of~~ the applicant before notice ~~could~~ *can* be served ~~or~~ *and a* hearing had thereon. Every such temporary restraining order shall be indorsed with the date and hour of issuance, shall be forthwith filed in the clerk's office and entered of record, shall define the injury and state why it is irreparable and why the order was granted without notice, and shall by its terms expire within such time after entry, not to exceed ten days, as the court or judge may fix, *unless within the time so fixed the order is extended for a like period for good cause shown, and the reasons for such extension shall be entered of record.* In case a temporary restraining order shall be granted without notice in the contingency specified, the matter of the issuance of a preliminary injunction shall be set down for a hearing at the earliest possible time and shall take precedence of all matters except older matters of the same character; and when the same comes up for hearing the party obtaining the temporary restraining order shall proceed with ~~his~~ *the* application for a preliminary injunction, and if he does not do so the court shall dissolve ~~his~~ *the* temporary restraining order. Upon two days' notice to the party obtaining such temporary restraining order the opposite party may appear and move the dissolution or modification of the order, and in that event the court or judge shall proceed to hear and determine the motion as expeditiously as the ends of justice may require.

Section two hundred and sixty-three of an Act entitled "An Act to codify, revise, and amend the laws relating to the judiciary," approved March third, nineteen hundred and eleven, is hereby repealed.

Nothing in this section contained shall be deemed to alter, repeal, or amend section two hundred and sixty-six of an Act entitled "An Act to codify, revise, and amend the laws relating to the judiciary," approved March third, nineteen hundred and eleven.

SEC. 16. That~~, except as otherwise provided in section fourteen of this Act,~~ no restraining order or interlocutory order of injunction shall issue, except upon the giving of security by the applicant in such sum as the court or judge may deem proper, conditioned upon the payment of such costs and damages as may be incurred or suffered by any party who may be found to have been wrongfully enjoined or restrained thereby.

SEC. 17. That every order of injunction or restraining order shall set forth the reasons for the issuance of the same, shall be specific in terms, and shall describe in reasonable detail, and not by reference to the bill of complaint or other document, the act or acts sought to be restrained, and shall be binding only upon the parties to the suit, their *officers*, agents, servants, employees, and attorneys, or those in active concert *or participating* with them, and who shall, by personal service or otherwise, have received actual notice of the same.

SEC. 18. That no restraining order or injunction shall be granted by any court of the United States, or a judge or the judges thereof, in any case between an employer and employees, or between employers and employees, or between employees, or between persons employed and persons seek-

20 ing employment, involving, or growing out of, a dispute
21 concerning terms or conditions of employment, unless neces-
22 sary to prevent irreparable injury to property, or to a prop-
23 erty right, of the party making the application, for which
24 injury there is no adequate remedy at law, and such property
25 or property right must be described with particularity in
1 the application, which must be in writing and sworn to by
2 the applicant or by his agent or attorney.
3   And no such restraining order or injunction shall pro-
4 hibit any person or persons *whether singly or in concert* from
5 terminating any relation of employment, or from ceasing to
6 perform any work or labor, or from recommending, advising, or
7 persuading others by peaceful means so to do; ~~or from attending~~
8 ~~at or near a house or place where any person resides or works,~~
9 ~~or carries on business or happens to be, for the purpose of~~
10 ~~peacefully obtaining or communicating information,~~ or ~~of~~
11 *from* peacefully persuading any person to work or to abstain
12 from working; or from ~~ceasing to patronize or to employ~~
13 *withholding their patronage from* any party to such dispute,
14 or from recommending, advising, or persuading others by
15 peaceful *and lawful* means so to do; or from paying or giving
16 to, or withholding from, any person engaged in such dispute,
17 any strike benefits or other moneys or things of value; or
18 from peaceably assembling ~~at any place~~ in a lawful manner,
19 and for lawful purposes; or from doing any act or thing
20 which might lawfully be done in the absence of such dispute
21 by any party thereto; nor shall any of the acts specified in
22 this paragraph be considered or held ~~unlawful~~ *to be violations*
23 *of the antitrust laws*.
24   SEC. 19. That any person who shall willfully disobey
25 any lawful writ, process, order, rule, decree, or command of
1 any district court of the United States or any court of the
2 District of Columbia by doing any act or thing therein, or
3 thereby forbidden to be done by him, if the act or thing so
4 done by him be of such character as to constitute also a
5 criminal offense under any statute of the United States, or at
6 ~~common law~~ *under the laws of any State in which the act was*
7 *committed*, shall be proceeded against for his said contempt
8 as hereinafter provided.
9   SEC. 20. That whenever it shall be made to appear to
10 any district court or judge thereof, or to any judge therein
11 sitting, by the return of a proper officer on lawful process,
12 or upon the affidavit of some credible person, or by informa-
13 tion filed by any district attorney, that there is reasonable
14 ground to believe that any person has been guilty of such
15 contempt, the court or judge thereof, or any judge therein
16 sitting, may issue a rule requiring the said person so charged
17 to show cause upon a day certain why he should not be
18 punished therefor, which rule, together with a copy of the
19 affidavit or information, shall be served upon the person
20 charged, with sufficient promptness to enable him to prepare
21 for and make return to the order at the time fixed therein.
22 If upon or by such return, in the judgment of the court, the
23 alleged contempt be not sufficiently purged, a trial shall be

directed at a time and place fixed by the court: *Provided, however,* That if the accused, being a natural person, fail or refuse to make return to the rule to show cause, an attachment may issue against his person to compel an answer, and in case of his continued failure or refusal, or if for any reason it be impracticable to dispose of the matter on the return day, he may be required to give reasonable bail for his attendance at the trial and his submission to the final judgment of the court. Where the accused ~~person~~ is a body corporate, an attachment for the sequestration of its property may be issued upon like refusal or failure to answer.

In all cases within the purview of this Act such trial may be by the court, or, upon demand of the accused, by a jury; in which latter event the court may impanel a jury from the jurors then in attendance, or the court or the judge thereof in chambers may cause a sufficient number of jurors to be selected and summoned, as provided by law, to attend at the time and place of trial, at which time a jury shall be selected and impaneled as upon a trial for misdemeanor; and such trial shall conform as near as may be to the practice in criminal cases prosecuted by indictment or upon information.

If the accused be found guilty, judgment shall be entered accordingly, prescribing the punishment, either by fine or imprisonment, or both, in the discretion of the court. Such fine shall be paid to the United States or to the complainant or other party injured by the act constituting the contempt, or may, where more than one is so damaged, be divided or apportioned among them as the court may direct, but in no case shall the fine to be paid to the United States exceed, in case the accused is a natural person, the sum of $1,000, nor shall such imprisonment exceed the term of six months~~.~~: *Provided, That in any case the court or a judge thereof may, for good cause shown, by affidavit or proof taken in open court or before such judge and filed with the papers in the case, dispense with the rule to show cause, and may issue an attachment for the arrest of the person charged with contempt; in which event such person, when arrested, shall be brought before such court or a judge thereof without unnecessary delay and shall be admitted to bail in a reasonable penalty for his appearance to answer to the charge or for trial for the contempt; and thereafter the proceedings shall be the same as provided herein in case the rule had issued in the first instance.*

SEC. 21. That the evidence taken upon the trial of any persons so accused may be preserved by bill of exceptions, and any judgment of conviction may be reviewed upon writ of error in all respects as now provided by law in criminal cases, and may be affirmed, reversed, or modified as justice may require. Upon the granting of such writ of error, execution of judgment shall be stayed, and the accused, if thereby sentenced to imprisonment, shall be admitted to bail in such reasonable sum as may be required by the court, or by any justice, or any judge of any district court of the United

3 States or any court of the District of Columbia.
4 SEC. 22. That nothing herein contained shall be con-
5 strued to relate to contempts committed in the presence of
6 the court, or so near thereto as to obstruct the administra-
7 tion of justice, nor to contempts committed in disobedience
8 of any lawful writ, process, order, rule, decree, or command
9 entered in any suit or action brought or prosecuted in the
10 name of, or on behalf of, the United States, but the same,
11 and all other cases of contempt not specifically embraced
12 within section nineteen of this Act, may be punished in con-
13 formity to the usages at law and in equity now prevailing.
14 SEC. 23. That no proceeding for contempt shall be
15 instituted against any person unless begun within one year
16 from the date of the act complained of; nor shall any such
17 proceeding be a bar to any criminal prosecution for the same
18 act or acts; but nothing herein contained shall affect any
19 proceedings in contempt pending at the time of the passage
20 of this Act.

Passed the House of Representatives June 5, 1914.

SENATE DEBATE
63d Cong., 2d Sess.
August 5, 1914

51 CONG. REC. 13319

Mr. CULBERSON. I move that the Senate proceed to the consideration of House bill 15657.

Mr. [JACOB H.] GALLINGER [R., N.H.]. Let the title be read.

The VICE PRESIDENT. The bill will be read by title.

The SECRETARY. A bill (H. R. 15657) to supplement existing laws against unlawful restraints and monopolies, and for other purposes.

The VICE PRESIDENT. The question is on the motion of the Senator from Texas [Mr. CULBERSON].

The motion was agreed to; and the Senate, as in Committee of the Whole, proceeded to consider the bill (H. R. 15657) to supplement existing laws against unlawful restraints and monopolies, and for other purposes.

Mr. [HENRY F.] ASHURST [D., Ariz.]. I desire to give notice that to-morrow morning, immediately after the conclusion of the morning business, I shall submit some observations on the unfinished business, to the consideration of which the Senate has just proceeded.

SENATE DEBATE
63d Cong., 2d Sess.
August 12, 1914

51 CONG. REC. 13633

Mr. CULBERSON. I ask that the unfinished business, House bill 15657, be laid before the Senate and proceeded with.

The Senate, as in Committee of the Whole, proceeded to consider the bill (H. R. 15657) to supplement existing laws against unlawful restraints and monopolies, and for other purposes, which had been reported from the Committee on the Judiciary with amendments. . . .

Mr. CULBERSON. I ask unanimous consent that the formal reading of the bill may be dispensed with.

The VICE PRESIDENT. And that it be read for action on the committee amendments?

Mr. CULBERSON. And that it be read for action on the amendments of the committee first.

Mr. GALLINGER. It is not a very long bill, and I think it ought to be read. The Senate ought to know what is in it.

The VICE PRESIDENT. There is objection?

Mr. GALLINGER. I object.

The VICE PRESIDENT. The Secretary will read the bill.

SENATE DEBATE
63d Cong., 2d Sess.
August 13, 1914

51 CONG. REC. 13658

Mr. CULBERSON. I ask that the unfinished business be proceeded with.

The Senate, as in Committee of the Whole, resumed the consideration of the bill (H. R. 15657) to supplement existing laws against unlawful restraints and monopolies, and for other purposes.

Mr. CULBERSON. I ask unanimous consent that the formal reading of the bill may be dispensed with.

The VICE PRESIDENT. And that the bill be read for amendment?

Mr. CULBERSON. I will bring that question up later, Mr. President. I desire to present one proposition at a time.

Mr. [REED] SMOOT [R., Utah]. Mr. President, if we proceed with the bill at all, after the formal reading has been dispensed with, it will be for the consideration of committee amendments, and I think the Senator from Texas ought to include that in his request. Then, of course, any Senator can speak on any amendment.

The VICE PRESIDENT. As the Chair recalls, the Senator from Texas has once before preferred the same request, and there was objection.

Mr. CULBERSON. By the Senator from New Hampshire [Mr. GALLINGER].

Mr. [KNUTE] NELSON [R., Minn.]. The Senator from New Hampshire objected. The Chair is correct in that statement.

The VICE PRESIDENT. The Senator from New Hampshire objected.

SENATE CONSIDERATION

Mr. NELSON. And in view of his objection and on his account, I shall have to object now.

Mr. CULBERSON. I do not think the Senator from New Hampshire would object if he were present; but in view of the objection of the Senator from Minnesota, the bill must be read.

The VICE PRESIDENT. The Secretary will read the bill.

The Secretary read the bill, as follows: . . .[5.578]

⊥ Mr. ASHURST. Mr. President, I gave notice one week ago to-day that I would address the Senate upon House bill 15657, which had been favorably reported from the Committee on the Judiciary some time prior thereto. When, however, the shipping bill came before the Senate I felt it to be my duty, important as the pending bill is, not to project myself and my remarks into the time which was needed for the discussion of the shipping bill, because of the crisis which presented itself at that time. Subsequently the matter of the treaties for the advancement of the cause of general peace came before the Senate in executive session, and my notice was still further continued for a couple of days.

I am pleased, indeed, that intervening between the present moment and a week ago, when I gave my notice, two great subjects of legislation have been consummated—the shipping bill and the ratification of the peace treaties. Both were especially important, in view of certain eventualities in Europe; and I venture to make the observation at this time, in reply to some who have criticized the administration's policy of "watchful waiting," what a pity it is that in some of the chancelleries of Europe there could not have been exercised some of that "watchful waiting" which we all now commend, but which, while the waiting was going on, some persons apparently did not favor.

⊥ I rise, Mr. President, as I stated, to speak in behalf of House bill 15657; and as the hour is obviously late and Senators weary, I shall proceed as rapidly as I may, but after I shall have concluded, if it appears obvious that there are any historical inaccuracies in my remarks, I shall be glad to have them corrected.

⊥13661

⊥13662

There is a general impression that section 7 is the labor section of the bill. While that is true, sections 15 to 23, inclusive, are also denominated as the labor sections of the bill.

Some time since I clipped from Collier's Weekly the following interesting and pertinent article, entitled "Labor and the trusts":

The country was horrified recently by the discovery that the Steel Trust, which had paid fabulous sums to promoters and stockholders, worked many of its employees 12 hours a day 7 days in the week—worked them, too, at such low wages that, even if a man toiled his 12 hours each of the 365 days in the year, he could not earn enough to provide a decent living for a small family. The doctrine of legalized monopoly threatens to perpetuate the cause which made such conditions possible and which must breed similar evils in the future. That cause is the huge overweening power of the great trusts, the inexhaustible resources of organized capital, which enable it to prevent the organization of labor and to make the term "ironmaster" a reality. America must breed only freemen. It must develop citizens. It can not develop citizens unless the workingman possesses industrial liberty; and industrial liberty for the workingman is impossible if the right to organize be denied. Without the right to organize, short hours, high wages, and the best of working conditions, whether introduced by legislation or by the welfare departments of great corporations, can do no more than make slavery luxurious.

The great trusts have made the extermination of organized labor from their own works the foundation stone of their administration. Read this resolution, passed by the Steel Trust in 1901:

"That we are unalterably opposed to any extension of union labor and advise subsidiary companies to take firm positions when these questions come up and say they are not going to recognize it—that is, any extension of unions in mills where they do not now exist."

Here is a Steel Trust advertisement:

"Wanted—Sixty-two house men, tinners, catchers, and helpers to work in open shops; Syrians, Poles, and Roumanians preferred; steady employment and good wages to men willing to work; fare paid and no fees charged for this work. Central Employment Bureau, 628 Pennsylvania Avenue."

The result is that about 80 per cent of the unskilled laborers in the steel and iron business

---

[5.578] H.R. 15657 as passed by the House, reprinted *supra* at 1728-38, was read.

are foreigners of these classes. This ability of the great combinations of capital to overcome combinations of workingmen is confidently relied upon by the advocates of trusts as one of the savings of combination. Montague, in his Trusts of To-day, in explaining the trusts' "improved position in dealing with labor," says:

"By its preponderant influence in the business, the trust has an enormous advantage in its dealings with combined labor. In 1899, during the smelters' strike in Colorado, the American Smelting & Refining Co. closed the mills in which the strikers had been employed and transferred the work to its other mills; the effect was immediately to break the strike. The United States Steel Corporation had similar success in 1901 with the Amalgamated Association of Iron and Steel Workers. *Had the association been dealing with competing employers*, each eager to keep his mills running and to get orders which his recalcitrant rivals could not accept, *its demands would soon have been granted.*"

The success of the German Steel Trust appears to be due in part to this same ability to frustrate the aspirations of the workingman, as shown by the following passage quoted in President Van Hise's Concentration and Control:

"Another advantage obtained by the members from the existence of the cartel [trust] is in dealing with strikes and labor difficulties. Whenever a strike threatens the concern can transfer its quota to some other mill where there are no labor difficulties. Furthermore, the syndicate contract contains a provision releasing the mill from obligation to deliver goods whenever a strike is on. *Such an arrangement would have been impossible under the competitive system*, and losses growing out of strikes would undoubtedly have been much greater if the syndicate had not existed."

The italics in these quotations are ours. The labor policy of the Steel Trust is not exceptional. The Harvester Trust, the Beef Trust, the Smelter Trust, the Tobacco Trust, the Sugar Trust, and many others can all boast of their triumphs over organized labor. Denial to labor of the right to combine is a policy common to the great combinations of capital; and against that policy labor battles in vain. Its loosely banded, ill-provisioned forces, however valiant and self-sacrificing, are no match for the compact power of the huge trusts, with inexhaustible resources of money and of brains. Too great inequality in power is necessarily destructive of liberty—be it political or industrial. There is but one choice. We must keep democracy, or we must pass rapidly on to state socialism.

By the provisions of this bill United States courts are prohibited—

First. From issuing injunctions against persons on account of their ceasing to perform any work or labor.

Second. From issuing injunctions to prevent laborers from recommending, advising, or persuading others by peaceful means to cease work.

Third. From issuing injunctions enjoining laboring men from attending at or near a house or place where any person resides or works or carries on business or happens to be for the purpose of peacefully obtaining or communicating information or peacefully persuading any person to work or to abstain from work.

Fourth. From issuing injunctions enjoining laboring men from ceasing to patronize any party to a labor dispute.

Fifth. From issuing injunctions enjoining laboring men from recommending, advising, or persuading others by peaceful means so to do.

Sixth. From issuing injunctions enjoining laboring men from paying or giving to or withholding from any person engaged in any labor dispute any strike benefits or other moneys or other things of value.

Seventh. From issuing injunctions enjoining laboring men from peacefully assembling at any proper place in a lawful manner and for lawful purposes.

Eighth. From issuing injunctions enjoining laboring men from doing any act or thing which might lawfully be done in the absence of such labor dispute by any party thereto.

In other words, this proposed legislation purposes to place the laboring men upon the same equality under the law with every other citizen and requires an injunction in a case growing out of a labor dispute to be issued upon the same bill or cause of action and the same evidence as in any other case where a labor dispute is not involved. The injunction provisions of this bill give to labor a bill of rights on eight different propositions.

This legislation is rendered necessary by reason of the fact that some of the Federal courts have abused the writ of injunction, and in some instances have gone so far afield as to issue writs of injunction prohibiting laboring men from exercising the rights guaranteed by the Constitution of the United States to all persons in the United States.

SHERMAN ANTITRUST LAW.

The material advances in inventions, discoveries, transportation, and the mechanical sciences and arts during the nineteenth century were the cause of great increases in interstate commerce and in all its numerous ramifications and multiplications. These advances created, promoted, and enhanced opportunities for personal acquirement of disproportionate wealth, which opportunities, of course, strong and cunning men, as in every other age of the world, seized upon and employed to advance their own fortunes. Toward the close of the nineteenth century farseeing statesmen horoscoped the future and foretold that unless checked by law the then existing system would soon operate to put into the hands of a small minority of men in our Nation most, if not all, of the property which labor produced. Then arose a wide discussion as to the nature of the remedy to be applied. The discussion which took place was interesting and instructive, and it was pointed out that in the Governments of ancient as well as modern times grabbing and grasping monopolists sought by various ways and means and through various devices to acquire a disproportionate share of the wealth in the Nation.

In the examination of the various remedies proposed to curb monopoly there was pointed out and discussed the manner as to how in England the monopolies began to oppress the people during the reign of Queen Elizabeth, and we recall that in the colloquial debates in the English Parliament during the reign of Elizabeth on the bill introduced in Parliament for the purpose of checking and restraining her exercise of the royal prerogative with respect to granting monopolies to particular persons, Sir Francis Bacon delivered a speech, wherein he said:

With regard to monopolies, the case hath ever been to humble ourselves to Her Majesty and by petition desire to have our grievances remedied, especially when the remedy touched her so nigh in point of prerogative. I say, and I say it again, that we ought not to deal, to judge, or meddle with Her Majesty's prerogative. I wish, therefore, every man to be careful of this business.

This effusion by Sir Francis Bacon is precisely such a speech as we would expect to find the histories record of him. It was in keeping with his sycophantic and fawning spirit, which was always fearful, even to a fault, of offending the rich and powerful.

During the discussion of the bill Mr. Francis More said:

I know the Queen's prerogative is a thing curious to be dealt withal; yet all grievances are not comparable. I can not utter with my tongue or conceive with my heart the great grievances that the town and country for which I serve suffereth by some of these monopolies. It bringeth the general profit into a private hand, and the end of all this is beggary and bondage to the subjects. Out of the spirit of humiliation do I speak it, there is no act of hers that has been or is more derogatory to her own majesty, more odious to the subjects, more dangerous to the Commonwealth, than the granting of these monopolies.

Also, during the discussion of that bill, Mr. Martin said:

I do speak for a town that grieves and pines, for a country that groaneth and languisheth, under the burden of monstrous and unconscienceable monopolies of starch, tin, cloth, oil, vinegar, salt, and I know not what—nay, what not! The principalist commodities, both of my town and country, are engrossed into the hands of these bloodsuckers of the Commonwealth. Such is the state of my own town and country; the traffic is taken away; the inward and private commodities are taken away and dare not be used without the license of these monopolitans. If these bloodsuckers be let alone to suck up the best and principalist commodities which the earth there hath given us, ⊥ what will become of us, from whom the fruits of our own soil and the commodities of our own labor shall be taken by warrant of supreme authority, which the poor subject dare not gainsay?

Thus we observe that the people of our Nation are not the only people that have suffered from the greediness of some members of the human family.

The history of the Sherman antitrust law is instructive, and a short review of the parliamentary history of that law is pertinent to the present discussion.

On February 28, 1890, Fifty-first Congress, Senator Sherman, of Ohio, introduced his antitrust bill in the Senate. It was referred to the Committee on Finance. On March 22, 1890, the Committee on Finance introduced a substitute for the Sherman bill. On March 25, 1890, Senator Morgan, of Alabama, moved to commit the bill to the Judiciary Committee; it failed to carry on a vote of 16 yeas to 28 nays. On March 25, 1890, Senator Sherman offered a proviso to be added at the end of the first section of the bill, as follows:

Provided, That this act shall not be construed to apply to any arrangements, agreements, or combinations between the laborers, made with a view of lessening the number of hours of labor or the increasing of their wages; nor to any arrangements, agreements, or combinations among persons engaged in horticulture or agriculture, made with a view of enhancing the price of agricultural or horticultural products.

The amendment was agreed to in the Senate without any opposing votes.

On March 26, 1890, Senator Stewart, of Nevada, made the following comprehensive statement:

The original bill has been very much improved, and one of the great objections has been removed from it by the amendment offered by Senator Sherman (for Senator George), which relieves the class of persons who would have been first prosecuted under the original bill without the amendment.

Senator Stewart then added:

The bill ought now in some respects to be satisfactory to every person who is opposed to the oppression of labor and desires to see it properly rewarded.

During the debates in Congress on the Sherman antitrust law it was not suggested nor even hinted, so far as may be ascertained from the debates that have come down to us in the CONGRESSIONAL RECORD, that the exemption of labor organizations from the provisions of that law was improper class legislation. I do not assert that the contrary does not appear. I simply say, so far as I have been able to ascertain from the debate in the CONGRESSIONAL RECORD, that it does not appear. It was not the intention of the legislators to apply the Sherman antitrust law to labor organizations, although the courts, by strained and harsh constructions, have sought to apply it to labor organizations.

By judicial interpretations and legal precedents, and especially by the decision of the United States Supreme Court in the Danbury Hat case,[5.579] the terms of the law intended to apply to persons dealing in commodities were interpreted to apply to the energies and activities of associated laborers. Thus under the Sherman antitrust law labor organizations may be dissolved, their members fined or imprisoned, and the labor organizations mulcted by damages in civil suits.

In order, therefore, to secure to the workers the legal right to organized existence it is necessary by substantive law to remove and exempt the organizations of labor from the provisions of the antitrust laws, and section 7 and sections 15 to 23, inclusive, of the Clayton bill, H. R. 15657, provide for such exemption.

The proper energies and reasonable activities of labor organizations have been greatly injured and hindered by the improper use and the abuse of the injunction, because some courts have proceeded upon the hypothesis that labor power is property, such as mechanical and electrical contrivances, cattle, horses, and so forth. Some courts of equity have usurped jurisdiction and power to restrain laborers from doing the things they had a lawful right to do, and which in many instances it was necessary for them to do to promote their own interests and rise above the conditions of serfdom; for instance, injunctions have forbidden laborers to use the public highways and have forbidden them peacefully to consider their own condition. Laborers have been forbidden by injunction to pay strike benefits or to exercise the right of free speech. Therefore, in order to prevent any further abuse of this judicial power, these provisions

---

[5.579] Loewe v. Lawlor, 208 U.S. 274, 28 S. Ct. 301, 52 L. Ed. 488 (1908).

of sections 7 and 15 to 23, inclusive, of the Clayton bill have been written in this proposed legislation, and are known as the "laborers' bill of rights."

In this pending bill, disguise it as we may, dodge and evade as we may, there is one great question we must meet and settle, and that is the question as to whether this proposed law shall be directed against the combinations of capital that the Sherman antitrust law was designed to be directed against or whether the antitrust laws shall be shifted, partially at least, and turned as an engine of oppression and destruction against some of the very people they are designed to protect.

A vast deal of discussion has occurred regarding what class of people the antitrust legislation was directed against, but those who search the records with even a moderate degree of diligence will be rewarded by complete freedom from any doubt upon the subject. The statesmen who framed this legislation—the Sherman law—had no doubt as to whom the legislation was directed against.

Senator Sherman, the nominal author of the Sherman law, had no doubt as to this question, and in the debate in the Senate, on March 24, 1890, he said:

> Now, let us look at it. The bill as reported contains three or four simple propositions which relate only to contracts, combinations, agreements made with a view and designed to carry out a certain purpose which the laws of all the States and of every civilized community declare to be unlawful. It does not interfere in the slightest degree with voluntary associations made to affect public opinion to advance the interests of a particular trade or occupation. It does not interfere with the Farmers' Alliance at all, because that is an association of farmers to advance their interests and to improve the growth and manner of production of their crops and to secure intelligent growth and to introduce new methods. No organizations in this country can be more beneficial in their character than farmers' alliances and farmers' associations. They are not business combinations. They do not deal with contracts, agreements, and so forth. They have no connection with them. And so the combinations of workingmen to promote their interests, promote their welfare and increase their pay, if you please, to get their fair share in the division of production, are not affected in the slightest degree, nor can they be included in the words or intent of the bill as now reported.

Nothwithstanding the disclaimer on the part of Senator Sherman and many others in the Senate at that time as to the class of people designed to be reached by that legislation, Senator George introduced an amendment at that time as follows:

> *Provided*, That this act shall not be construed to apply to any arrangements, agreements, or combinations between the laborers, made with a view of lessening the number of hours of labor or the increasing of their wages; nor to any arrangements, agreements, or combinations among persons engaged in horticulture or agriculture, made with a view of enhancing the price of agricultural or horticultural products.

Although Senator Sherman and many others at that time emphatically stated that the language of the bill was plain without such an amendment, the amendment was finally incorporated in the bill as it passed the Committee of the Whole in the Senate. The bill was thereupon sent to the Judiciary Committee, and when it returned from the Judiciary Committee it was passed without this amendment, which had been stricken out in the committee as unnecessary. I assert that it was the contemporaneous opinion of Senators at that time that the amendment was unnecessary.

When the bill was being debated in the Senate Senator Hoar expressed the general attitude of the students of the question at that time in the following words which remove all doubt. Speaking in the Senate on March 27, 1890, Senator Hoar said:

> When you are speaking of providing to regulate the transactions of men who are making corners in wheat, or in iron, or in woolen or in cotton goods, speculating in them or lawfully dealing in them without speculation, you are aiming at a mere commercial transaction, the beginning and end of which is the making of money for the parties, and nothing else. That is the only relation that transaction has to the State. It is the creation or diffusion or change of ownership of the wealth of the community. But when a laborer is trying to raise his wages or is endeavoring to shorten the hours of his labor, he is dealing with something that touches closely, more closely than anything else, the Government and the character of the State itself.
>
> The maintenance of a certain standard of profit in dealing in large transactions in wheat or cotton or wool is a question whether a particular merchant or a particular class of merchants shall make money or not; but the question whether the standard of the laborer's wages shall be

maintained or advanced, or whether the leisure for instruction, for improvement shall be shortened or lengthened is a question which touches the very existence and character of government of the State itself. The laborer who is engaged lawfully and usefully and accomplishing his purpose in whole or in part in endeavoring to raise the standard of wages is engaged in an occupation the success of which makes republican government itself possible, and without which the Republic can not, in substance, however it may nominally do in form, continue to exist.

I hold, therefore, that as legislators we may constitutionally, properly, and wisely allow laborers to make associations, combinations, contracts, agreements for the sake of maintaining and advancing their wages, in regard to which, as a rule, their contracts are to be made with large corporations who are themselves but an association or combination or aggregation of capital on the other side. When we are permitting and even encouraging that, we are permitting and encouraging what is not only lawful, wise, and profitable, but absolutely essential to the existence of the Commonwealth itself.

When, on the other hand, we are dealing with one of the other classes, the combinations aimed at chiefly by this bill, we are dealing with a transaction the only purpose of which is to extort from the community, monopolize, segregate, and apply to individual use, for the purposes of individual greed, wealth which ought properly and lawfully and for the public interest to be generally diffused over the whole community.

These are the words of the late Senator Hoar, a distinguished Senator from Massachusetts, a statesman of untarnished public and private character and of highly cultivated mind, yet conservative withal.

Mr. [JOHN W.] KERN [D., Ind.]. And who wrote every word of the Sherman antitrust law as it was finally passed.

Mr. ASHURST. And, as is suggested to me, the man who wrote every word of the Sherman antitrust law as it is now on the statute books.

Senator Edmunds, Senator Stewart, Senator Teller, Senator Reagan, Senator George, and others—all without any question agreed that the bill as it was presented to the Senate for final passage left no doubt as to the fact that it was not intended to include fraternal orders, labor organizations, or farmers' alliances. I will insert these views of Senators in the RECORD.

[Senate, page 2729, March 27, 1890. Mr. Hoar.]

I said the object of this bill was to prevent the speculation in and engrossing of wheat and similar commodities. I did not speak in that connection of corporations. I said, in speaking generally of the lawfulness and propriety of laborers combining in the matter of wages, that the persons with whom they were to contract were very largely the corporations which were themselves nothing but a combination or aggregation of capital for that purpose. I made no such suggestion as that corporations were the persons aimed at by this bill. That was in a different connection.

[Senate, page 2606, March 25. Mr. Stewart.]

Again, suppose that the employers, railroad companies, and manufacturing establishments should say that labor should be put down to two bits a day. Suppose that capital should combine against labor, as it is very much inclined to do, and there should be a combination among the laborers which would increase the cost of production and increase the cost of all articles consumed. Suppose there should be a combination among the laborers to protect themselves from grasping monopolies; they would all be criminals for doing it.

[Senate, page 2562, March 24, 1890. Mr. Teller]

I know that nobody here proposes to interfere with the class of men I have mentioned. Nobody here intends that by any of these provisions, either in the original bill or in any amendment, and I have only called attention to it to see if the efforts of those who have undertaken to manage this subject can not in some way confine the bill to dealing with trusts, which we all admit are offensive to good morals.

[Senate, page 2562, March 24, 1890. Mr. Teller.]

I want to repeat that I am exceedingly anxious myself to join in anything that shall break up and destroy these unholy combinations, but I want to be careful that in doing that we do not do more damage than we do good. I know how these great trusts, these great corporations, these large moneyed institutions can escape the provisions of a penal statute, and I know how much more likely they are to escape than the men who have less influence and less money. Therefore I suggest that the Senators who have this subject in charge give it special attention, and by a little modification it may be possible to relieve the bill of any doubt on that point.

Mr. President, I stated a moment ago that harsh and unreasonable constructions had been placed upon the Sherman antitrust law so as to bring labor organizations within its purview, and in making that statement I am not alone in sounding a danger signal as to the drastic and harsh injunctions that have proceeded from some of our Federal courts against the laboring men of the country.

In October of 1907 Justice Moody, late of the Supreme Court of the United States, said:

I believe in recent years the courts of the United States, as well as the courts of our own Commonwealth (Massachusetts), have gone to the very verge of danger in applying the process of the writ of injunction in disputes between labor and capital.

Hon. Thomas M. Cooley, sometime president of the American Bar Association, said:

Courts with their injunctions, if they heed the fundamental law of the land, can no more hold men to involuntary servitude for even a single hour than can overseers with a whip.

Judge M. F. Tuley, of the appellate court of Illinois, used these words:

Such use of injunction by the courts is judicial tyranny, which endangers not only the right of trial by jury, but all the rights and liberties of the citizens.

Gov. Sadler, of Nevada, said:

The tendency at present is to have the courts enforce law by injunction methods, which are subversive of good government and the liberties of the people.

Prof. F. J. Stimson, of Harvard University, in his new work on Federal and State Constitutions, after citing many authorities, says:

These are sufficient to establish the general principle that the injunction process and contempt in chancery procedure, as well as chancery jurisdiction itself, is looked on with a logical jealousy in Anglo-Saxon countries as being in derogation of the common law, taking away the jurisdiction of the common-law courts and depriving the accused of his trial by jury.

Judge John Gibbons, of the circuit court of Illinois, declared that—

In their efforts to regulate or restrain strikes by injunction they (the courts) are sowing dragons' teeth and blazing the path of revolution.

In order that I may not be deemed to have overshot myself and allowed an intemperate or imprudent statement to escape my lips on this subject, I will insert in the RECORD at this point a few samples calling attention to some of the harsh and unreasonable decisions of the courts on this subject.

LABOR DECISIONS AND INJUNCTIONS.

Refusing to haul cars a conspiracy (T., A. & N. M. Ry. v. Pennsylvania Co., 54 Fed. Rep., 730, Apr. 3, 1893).

Quitting work is criminal (same, Apr. 3, 1893).

A workman considered "under control" (T., A. & N. M. Ry. v. Pennsylvania Co. et al., 54 Fed. Rep., 746, Mar. 25, 1893. Ricks, circuit judge).

Serving of injunction notice unnecessary (In re Lennon, 166 U. S., 548. Brown, judge).

The black list lawful (N. Y., C. & St. L. Ry. Co. v. Schaffer, 65 Ohio, 414. Jan. 21, 1902).

Effort to unionize shop unlawful (Loewe et al. v. Lawlor et al., 208 U. S., 274, Feb. 3, 1908).

Contract work to union house is void (State v. Toole, 26 Mont., 22).

Constitutional to require men to leave union (People v. Harry Marcus, 185 N. Y., 257, May 25, 1906).

Union labor has no right to conduct a strike (Alfred W. Booth & Co. v. Burgess et al., 65 Atl. Rep., 226, Nov. 26, 1906).

Unlawful to induce nonunion men to quit work (Enterprise Foundry Co. v. Iron Molders' Union, 112 N. W., 685, July 1, 1907).

The unfair list forbidden (Wilson et al., 232 Ill., 389, Feb. 20, 1908).

Employer has right to bar out unions (Flaccus v. Smith, 199 Pa. St., 128).

Antitrust act applies to labor unions as well as to combinations of capitalists (U. S. v. Workingmen's Amalgamated Council, 54 Fed. Rep., 994; Loewe v. Lawlor, 208 U. S., 274).

The boycott is unlawful (Loewe v. Lawlor, 208 U. S., 274).

Members of labor unions liable to threefold damages for injuries in business or property sustained by individuals or firms by reason of a boycott (Loewe v. Lawlor, 208 U. S., 274).

A combination of men to secure or compel the employment of none but union men is unlawful (U. S. v. Workingmen's Amalgamated Council, 54 Fed. Rep., 994).

Unlawful to threaten a strike (John O'Brien v. People ex rel. Kellogg Switchboard & Supply Co., 216 Ill., 354, June 23, 1905).

Effort to unionize a house is unlawful (J. L. Purvis et al., Local No. 500, U. B. of Carpenters and Joiners, 214 Pa. St., 348, Mar. 19, 1906).

The boycott is unlawful (Shine et al. v. Fox Bros. Mfg. Co., 156 Fed. Rep., 357, Oct. 19, 1907).

Unions liable to suit for damages (Leucke v. Clothing Cutters and Trimmers' Assembly, 77 Md., 396, Mar. 16, 1893).

The closed shop is illegal (A. R. Barnes & Co. et al. v. Berry et al., 156 Fed. Rep., 72, Oct. 21, 1907).

Unlawful to ask reasons for discharge (Wallace v. Georgia, Carolina & Northern Ry. Co., 94 Ga., 732, June 18, 1894).

Blacklisting can not be prohibited (Wisconsin ex rel. Theodore Zillner v. Louis Kreutzberg, 58 L. R. A., 748, May 18, 1902).

Maintaining a picket is unlawful (A., T. & S. F. Ry. Co. v. Gee et al., 139 Fed. Rep., 152, July 10, 1905).

Can not limit hours of labor by law (Holden v. Hardy, 169 U. S., 366, Feb. 28, 1898).

Payment in checks legal (Kentucky Court of Appeals, Avent-Beattyville Coal Co., appellant, v. Commonwealth of Kentucky, Dec. 1, 1894).

Employer has right to discharge a union man (Wisconsin Supreme Court, State of Wisconsin ex rel. Theodore Zillner, plaintiff in error, v. Louis J. Kreutzberg, 58 L. R. A., 748, May 19, 1902).

Eight-hour day unconstitutional (Nebraska Supreme Court, Charles G. Low, plaintiff in error, v. Rees Printing Co., 24 L. R. A., 702-708).

Eight-hour law illegal (Ohio Supreme Court, City of Cleveland, plaintiff in error, v. Clements Bros. Construction Co., 59 L. R. A., 775).

Protection of laborers illegal (Colorado Supreme Court, re Thomas A. Morgan, 47 L. R. A., 52, July 17, 1899).

Limiting check payment unconstitutional (Indiana Supreme Court, Nathan G. Dixon, appellant, v. James H. Poe, 60 L. R. A., 308, Nov. 25, 1902).

Unlawful to fix wages by law (New York Supreme Court, People ex rel. William J. Rodgers, respondent, v. Bird S. Coler, appellant, 166 N. Y.; 52 L. R. A., 814).

Protection of labor not required (New York Court of Appeals, Sarah Knisley, respondent, v. Pascal P. Pratt et al., appellants, 148 N. Y., 362; 32 L. R. A. 367).

No extra pay for extra hours (New York Court of Appeals, People, respondent, v. James H. Phyfe, appellant, Jan. 17, 1893).

Employer not responsible for death of employee (**Circuit Court of Appeals,** Eighth Circuit, Mar. 19, 1900; Westland v. Gold Coin Mines Co., 101 Fed. Rep., 59, 64, 65, and 66).

Labor check payments are legal (Massachusetts Supreme Judicial Court, Commonwealth of Massachusetts v. Josiah Perry, 14 L. R. A., 326).

No remedy for labor except personal suit (Massachusetts Supreme Judicial Court, Dianah Worthington et al., appellants, v. James Warring et al., 157 Mass., 421).

Employers need not furnish doctor to injured (Massachusetts Supreme Judicial Court, Alexander Davis, by next friend v. William H. Forbes, 171 Mass. 548).

Employers not liable for injuries (Massachusetts Supreme Court, William O'Mailly v. South Boston Gaslight Co., 158 Mass., 135).

Altering contract is legal for employers (Illinois Supreme Court, Richard Pemsey appellant, v. People of Illinois, 17 L. R. A., 853).

Employers need not recommend satisfactory employees (Illinois Supreme Court, C., C., C. & St. L. Ry. Co., appellant, v. Charles Jenkins, 174 Ill., 398).

Legal to jail a man a month without trial (Oregon Supreme Court, Longshore Printing & Publishing Co., appellant, v. George H. Howell et al., 26 Oreg., 527).

The right to blacklist upheld (Kentucky Court of Appeals, John Hundley, appellant, v. L. & N. Ry. Co., 105 Ky., 162).

Any willful attempt of employees of a railroad in the hands of a receiver to impede or hinder the operation of the road is contempt of court (Thomas v. C., N. O. & T. P. Ry. Co., 62 Fed. Rep., 803).

To instigate a strike on a road in the hands of a receiver is unlawful and a contempt of court (Thomas v. C., N. O. & T. P. Ry. Co., 62 Fed. Rep., 803).

A boycott is an unlawful conspiracy (Thomas v. C., N. O. & T. P. Ry. Co., 62 Fed. Rep., 803).

A sympathetic strike is an unlawful conspiracy by reason of its purpose whether such purpose is effected by means usually lawful or otherwise (Thomas *v.* C., N. O. & T. P. Ry. Co., 62 Fed. Rep., 803).

Any obstructing or retarding the mails by strikers is an unlawful conspiracy in violation of section 3975, Revised Statutes, although the obstruction is effected by merely quitting employment (Thomas *v.* C., N. O. & T. P. Ry. Co., 62 Fed. Rep., 803).

⊥ A law forbidding discrimination against an employee because of his membership in a labor union and making it a misdemeanor for an employer to discharge an employee because of membership in a labor union is unconstitutional (Adair case, 208 U. S., 161). ⊥13665

I also insert in the RECORD a copy of a final decree issued in June of this year by Judge Humphrey, of the United States District Court for the Southern District of Illinois, which is as follows:[5.580]

UNITED STATES OF AMERICA, SOUTHERN DISTRICT OF ILLINOIS, SOUTHERN DIVISION—IN THE UNITED STATES DISTRICT COURT, JUNE TERM, A. D. 1914.

American Steel Foundries, a corporation, complainant, *v.* The Tri-City Central Trades Council, Harry McKenny, Ted Ishmann, Earl Galloway, William Thornburg, C. Holmes, C. L. Burton, Eddie Roach, John Aldridge, Isaac Cook, Benjamin F. Lamb, J. P. McDonough, and C. E. Gerlich, defendants. In equity for injunction.

FINAL DECREE.

This cause came on to be heard at this term on the 9th day of June, A. D. 1914, and was argued by counsel; and thereupon upon consideration thereof it was ordered, adjudged, and decreed as follows, viz:

That the restraining order heretofore issued on May 18, 1914, and which on May 28, 1914, was continued in force as a temporary injunction, be and is hereby made permanent as to all of said defendants, with the exception of the defendant C. L. Burton, and as to the said C. L. Burton the said restraining order and temporary injunction be and is hereby vacated.

It is further ordered, adjudged, and decreed by the court that the said defendants the Tri-City Central Trades Council its officers and agents, and Harry McKenny, Ted Ishmann, Earl Galloway, William Thornburg, C. Thornburg, Tom Churchill, Clay Holmes, Eddie Roach, John Aldridge, Isaac Cook, Benjamin F. Lamb, J. P. McDonough, and C. E. Gerlich and each of them and all persons combining with, acting in concert with or under their direction, control, or advice, or under the direction, control, or advice of any of them and all persons whomsoever be and are hereby perpetually restrained and enjoined from in any way or manner whatsoever by use of persuasion, threats, or personal injury, intimidation, suggestion of danger or threats of violence of any kind, from interfering with, hindering, obstructing, or stopping any person desiring to be employed by said American Steel Foundries in its said tion [*sic*] with its business or its foundry in the city of Granite City, county of Madison, State of Illinois, or elsewhere, and from interfering by persuasion, violence, or threats of violence in any manner with any person desiring to be employed by said American Steel Foundries in its said foundry or plant; and from inducing or attempting to compel or induce by persuasion, threats, intimidation, force, or violence or putting in fear or suggestions of danger any of the employees of the American Steel Foundries or persons seeking employment with it so as to cause them to refuse to perform any of their duties as employees of the American Steel Foundries; and from preventing any person by persuasion, threats, intimidation, force, or violence, or suggestion of danger, or violence, from entering into the employ of said American Steel Foundries; and from protecting, aiding, or assisting any person or persons in committing any of said acts, and from assembling, loitering, or congregating about or in proximity of the said plant or factory of the American Steel Foundries for the purpose of doing or aiding or encouraging others in doing any of the said unlawful or forbidden acts or things, and from picketing or maintaining at or near the premises of the complainant or on the streets leading to the premises of said complainant any picket or pickets and from doing any acts or things whatever in furtherance of any conspiracy or combination among them, or any of them, to obstruct, or interfere with said American Steel Foundries, its officers, agents, or employees, in the free and unrestrained control and operation of its plant, foundry, and property, and the operation of its business, and also from ordering, directing, aiding, assisting, or in any manner abetting any person committing any or either of the acts aforesaid and also from entering upon the grounds, foundry, or premises of the American Steel Foundries without first obtaining its consent, and from injuring or destroying any of the property of the said American Steel foundries.

It is further ordered, adjudged, and decreed that the complainant shall cause not less than 100 printed copies of this final decree to be posted in conspicuous places about and in the

---

[5.580] This decree was not printed in the *Federal Reporter*.

vicinity of its said plant at Granite City, Ill.; that the affidavit of the agent of the complainant so posting said notices shall be filed in the clerk's office, stating when and where such notices were posted, and such affidavit shall be prima facie proof of the posting of such notices at such time and places as shall be therein stated.

It is further ordered, adjudged, and decreed that this injunction shall be binding upon each and all of the above-mentioned defendants and upon all other persons from and after the date of this decree.

It is further ordered, adjudged, and decreed that the defendants pay the costs of the above-entitled cause to be taxed by the clerk.

Otis Humphrey,
Judge United States District Court
for the Southern District of Illinois.

It will be seen from reading this final decree that this judge believes that the American Steel Foundries should be protected from certain individuals, who are named therein, against the use of "persuasion," which that "downtrodden" corporation fears some person may exercise, and thus do it an injustice. The very reading of this decree, if nothing further were called to our attention, makes necessary this substantive labor legislation in this Clayton bill, which has passed the House of Representatives, and, indeed, Mr. President, in my judgment, it is our duty to enact the labor provisions of the Clayton bill as they came to the Senate from the House of Representatives.

I now submit and include in the RECORD a list of over 100 decisions of Federal courts on labor cases where injunctions were issued, conspiracies charged, and allegations set up that the antitrust law was violated.

The VICE PRESIDENT. Without objection, it will be so ordered.

The matter referred to is as follows:

Allis-Chalmers Co. *v.* Reliable Lodge (111 Fed. Rep., 264; U. S. Labor Bul. 38, p. 183).
Allis-Chalmers Co. *v.* Iron Molders' Union No. 125 et al. (150 Fed. Rep., 155; U. S. Labor Bul. 70, p. 734; 166 Fed. Rep., 45; U. S. Labor Bul. 83, p. 157).
Aluminum Casting Co. *v.* Local 84 of International Molders' Union of North America et al. (197 Fed. Rep., 221).
American Steel & Wire Co. *v.* Wire, etc. (90 Fed. Rep., 608).
Armstrong Cork Co. *v.* Anheuser-Busch Brewing Co. (1914).
Arthur *v.* Oakes (63 Fed. Rep., 301).
Atchison, Topeka & Santa Fe R. R. Co. *v.* Gee—Cir. Ct. Southern District of Iowa (139 Fed. Rep., 582; 140 Fed. Rep., 153).
Bender *v.* Local Union 118, Bakers' Organization (34 Wash. Law Repr., 574; U. S. Labor Bul. 67, p. 894).
Barnes, A. R., & Co. *v.* Berry (156 Fed. Rep., 72; U. S. Labor Bul. 74, p. 259; 157 Fed. Rep., 833).
Beck et al. *v.* Railway Trainmen's Protective.
Besette *v.* Conkey & Co. (194 U. S., 324; 24 Sup. Ct. Repr., 665).
Blindell et al. *v.* Hogan et al. (54 Fed. Rep., 40).
Boutwell et al. *v.* Marr et al. (42 Atl. Repr., 607).
Bowels *v.* Indiana Railway Co. (62 N. E. Repr., 94).
Boyer et al. *v.* Western Union Telegraph Co.—C. C. E. D. Missouri (124 Fed. Rep., 246).
Bucks Stove & Range Co. *v.* American Federation of Labor (35 Wash. Law Repr., 797; U. S. Labor Bul. 74, p. 246).
Bucks Stove & Range Co. *v.* American Federation of Labor (36 Wash. Law Repr., 822; U. S. Labor Bul. 90, p. 124 and No. 86, p. 355).
Bucks Stove & Range Co. *v.* American Federation of Labor—Court of Appeals of District of Columbia (37 Wash. Law Repr., 154; U. S. Labor Bul. 33, p. 169; 31 Sup. Ct. Rep., 492; U. S. Labor Bul. 95, p. 323; 40 Wash. Law Repr., 412; U. S. Labor Bul. 112, p. 155).
Brewing & Malting Co. *v.* Hansen (Seattle) (144 Fed. Rep., 1011; U. S. Labor Bul. 68).
Barnes, A. R., & Co. *v.* Chicago Typographical Union (83 N. E. Repr., 932; U. S. Labor Bul. 76, p. 1016).
Barnes, A. R., & Co. *v.* Berry (157 Fed. Rep., p. 883; U. S. Labor Bul. 76, p. 1019).
Boyer et al. *v.* Western Union Telegraph Co. (124 Fed. Rep., 246; U. S. Labor Bul. 50, p. 202).
Callan *v.* Wilson (127 U. S. 540–555).
Carter et al. *v.* Fortney et al. (170 Fed. Rep., 463; also 172 Fed. Rep., 72).
Central District & Printing Tel. Co. *v.* Kent (156 Fed. Rep., 173; U. S. Labor Bul. 74, p. 256).

Coeur d'Alene Con. Min. Co. v. Miners' Union of Wardner, Idaho (51 Fed. Rep., 260-267).
Commonwealth v. Hunt (4 Metcalf's Rep., 111).
Conkey (W. B.) Co. v. Russell et al. (111 Fed. Rep., 417).
Construction Co. v. Cameron et al. (80 N. S. Rep., 478).
Contempt—nature of proceedings, appeals, Gompers et al. v. Bucks Stove & Range Co., Court of Appeals of the District of Columbia (37 Wash. Law Repr., p. 708; U. S. Labor Bul. 86, p. 355).
Campbell et al. v. Johnson (167 Fed. Rep., p. 102; U. S. Labor Bul. 82, p. 682).
Carter et al. v. Fortney et al. (170 Fed. Rep., p. 463; U. S. Labor Bul. 86, p. 370).
Casey v. Typographical Union (45 Fed. Rep., 135).
Delaware, Lackawanna & Western Railroad Co. v. Switchmen's Union of North America (158 Fed. Rep., 541-690; U. S. Labor Bul. 77, p. 389).
Donovan et al. v. Penn Co. (26 Sup. Ct. Rept., 91; U. S. Labor Bul. 63).
Debs, In re Petitioner (158 U. S. 564).
Doolittle and United States (23 Fed. Rep., 544-547).
Doolittle and United States v. Kane, supra, re Higgins (27 Fed. Rep., 443).
Farmers' Loan & Trust Co. v. The Northern Pacific Railroad Co., C. C. E. D. Wisconsin (60 Fed. Rep., 803).
Frank et al. v. Herold et al. (52 Atl. Rep., 152).
Fordahl v. Hayde (82 Pac. Repr., 1079).
Garrigan v. United States (163 Fed. Rep., 16; U. S. Labor Bul. 79, p. 961).
George Jonas Glass Co. v. Glass Blowers' Association (54 Atl. Rep., 567; 79 Atl. Repr., p. 262; U. S. Labor Bul. 95).
Glass Co. v. Glass Bottle Blowers (66 Atl. Repr., 593; U. S. Labor Bul. 72, p. 629; 79 Atl. Rep., 262; U. S. Labor Bul. 95, p. 312).
Goldfield Consolidated Mines Co. v. Goldfield Miners' Union 220 et al. (159 Fed. Rep., 500; U. S. Labor Bul. 73, p. 586).
Gray v. Trades Council (97 N. W. Repr., 663).
Guaranty Trust Co. v. Haggarty (116 Fed. Rep., 510; U. S. Labor Bul. 43, p. 1291).
Hammond Lumber Co. v. Sailors' Union of the Pacific (149 Fed. Rep., 577).
Hitchman Coal & Co. v. Mitchell (172 Fed. Rep. 963; U. S. Labor Bul. 87, p. 686).
Hopkins v. Oxley Stave Co. (83 Fed. Rep., 152, 912).
Huttig, etc., Co. v. Fuette et al. (163 Fed. Rep., 363).
Illinois Central Railroad v. International Association of Machinists (190 Fed. Rep., 910; U. S. Labor Bul. 98, p. 495).
In re Debs, petitioner (158 U. S., 564).
In re Doolittle and United States (23 Fed. Rep., 544-547).
In re Doolittle and United States v. Kane, supra, re Higgins (27 Fed. Rep., 443).
In re Lennon (166 U. S., 548).
Irving v. Joint District Council, United Brotherhood of Carpenters, etc., United States Circuit Court of Southern District of New York (180 Fed. Rep., p. 896; U. S. Labor Bul. 92, p. 289).
Iron Molders' Union No. 125, of Milwaukee, v. Allis-Chalmers Co. (166 Fed. Rep., 45; U. S. Labor Bul. 83, p. 157).
In re Reese (107 Fed. Rep., 942).
Jensen v. Cooke (81 Pac. Repr., 1069).
Jersey City Printing Co. v. Cassidy et al. (53 Atl. Repr., 230).
Jonas, George, Glass Co. v. Glass Blowers' Association of United States and Canada et al., Court of Chancery of New Jersey (54 Atl. Repr., p. 567; U. S. Labor Bul. 48, p. 1124).
Knudsen et al. v. Benn et al. (123 Fed. Rep., 636; U. S. Labor Bul. 50, p. 205).
Kargis Furniture Co. v. Local Union No. 131 (75 N. E. Repr., 877).
Keegan-Pope Motor Car Co. v. Keegan (150 Fed. Rep., 148; U. S. Labor Bul. 70, p. 757).
⊥ Kemmerer v. Haggerty (139 Fed. Rep., 693).
Kolley et al. v. Robinson et al. (187 Fed. Rep., 415).
Lawlor v. Loewe et al. (187 Fed. Rep., p. 522; U. S. Labor Bul. 96, p. 780; 148 Fed. Rep., 924; U. S. Labor Bul. 70).
Loewe v. Lawlor (28 Sup. Ct. Repr., 301; 130 Fed. Rep., 833; 142 Fed. Rep., 216; 148 Fed. Rep., 924; U. S. Labor Bul. 70, p. 710, and 75, p. 622).
Loewe et al. v. California Federation of Labor (139 Fed. Rep., 71; 189 Fed. Rep., 714).
Loewe v. Lawlor (208 U. S., 274).
Lennon, In re (166 U. S., 548).
Lindsay & Co. v. Montana Federation of Labor et al. (96 Pac. Repr., p. 127; U. S. Labor Bul. 78).
Mackall v. Ratchford et al., C. C. D. W. Va. (82 Fed. Rep., 41).
March v. Bricklayers, etc. (63 Atl. Repr., 291).
Mobile & Ohio Railroad v. E. E. Clark et al. (May, 1903).

Montana Federation of Labor et al. *v.* Lindsay & Co. (96 Pac. Repr., p. 127; U. S. Labor Bul. 78).
National Telephone Co. of West Virginia *v.* Kent (156 Fed. Rep., 173; U. S. Labor Bul. 74, p. 256).
National Fireproofing Co. *v.* Mason Builders' Association (169 Fed. Rep., 259; U. S. Labor Bul. 84., p. 427)
Newport Iron & Brass Foundry *v.* Molders' Union (1904).
O'Neil *v.* Behanna (37 Atl. Repr., 843).
Otis Steel Co. (Ltd.) *v.* Local Union No. 318, Cleveland, Ohio (110 Fed. Rep., 698; U. S. Labor Bul. 40, p. 638).
Oxley Stave Co. *v.* Coopers' International Union of North America (73 Fed. Rep., 695).
Pickett *v.* Walsh (78 N. E. Repr., 753).
Pope Motor Car Co. *v.* Keegan (150 Fed. Rep., 148; U. S. Labor Bul. 70, p. 757).
Pope Motor Car Co. *v.* J. H. Stitart or Steiert (June 9, 1906).
Rocky Mountain Bell Telephone Co. *v.* Montana Federation of Labor (156 Fed. Rep., 809; U. S. Labor Bul. 78, p. 804).
Reese, In re (107 Fed. Rep., 942).
Reinecke Coal Mining Co. *v.* Wood et al. (112 Fed. Rep., 477; U. S. Labor Bul. 41, p. 856).
Southern Railway Co. *v.* Machinists' Local No. 14 et al. (111 Fed. Rep., 49; U. S. Labor Bul. 39, p. 496).
Shine *v.* Fox Bros. Manufacturing Co. (156 Fed. Rep., 357; U. S. Labor Bul. 74, p. 244).
Southern California Railway *v.* Rutherford et al., C. C. S. D. California (62 Fed. Rep., 796).
State *v.* Stockford (38 Atl. Rep., 769).
State *v.* Coyle, Oklahoma (130 Pac. Repr. 316).
Southern Railway Co. *v.* Machinists' Local (111 Fed. Rep., 49).
Thomas *v.* Cincinnati, New Orleans & Texas Pacific Railway Co., C. C. S. D. Ohio, N. D. (62 Fed. Rep., 669).
Thomas *v.* Cincinnati, New Orleans & Texas Pacific Railway Co., in re Phelan, C. C. S. D. Ohio, W. D. (62 Fed. Rep., 803).
Toledo, Ann Arbor Railroad *v.* Arthur and Railroad Companies (54 Fed. Rep., 730).
Toledo, Ann Arbor Railroad Co., and Northern Michigan Railway Co. *v.* Pennsylvania Railroad Co. (54 Fed. Rep., 738-746).
Union Pacific Railway Co. *v.* Ruef, United States Circuit Court for District of Nebraska (120 Fed. Rep., 102; U. S. Labor Bul. 47, p. 267).
Underhill *v.* Murphy, Typographical Journal of August 15, 1901 (174—).
Union Pacific Railway Co. *v.* Ruef (120 Fed. Rep., 102).
United States *v.* Agler (62 Fed. Rep., 82).
United States *v.* Cassidy (67 Fed. Rep., 698).
United States *v.* Debs et al. (64 Fed. Rep., 724).
United States *v.* Elliott (62 Fed. Rep., 801; 64 Fed. Rep., 27).
United States ex rel. Guaranty Trust Co. of New York *v.* Haggarty et al., C. C. N. D. W. Va. (116 Fed. Rep., 510).
United States *v.* Shipp, the Farmers' case (27 Sup. Ct. Rep., 165; 203 U. S. 563).
United States *v.* Kane (23 Fed. Rep., 748).
United States *v.* Patterson (53 Fed. Rep., 605-641).
United States *v.* Sweeney (95 Fed. Rep., 434).
United States *v.* Weber et al. (114 Fed. Rep., 950).
United States *v.* Workingmen's Amalgamated Council of New Orleans et al. (54 Fed. Rep., 994).
Vegalahn *v.* Guntner (167 Mass., 92).
Western Union Telegraph Co. *v.* Boyer et al. (124 Fed. Rep., 246; U. S. Labor Bul. 50, p. 202).
Wabash Railroad Co. *v.* Hannahan et al. (121 Fed. Rep., 563; U. S. Labor Bul. 49, p. 1374).
Weber et al. (114 Fed. Rep., 590; U. S. Labor Bul. 43, p. 1295).
Waterhouse et al. *v.* Comer (55 Fed. Rep., 149).

Mr. ASHURST. Thus, Mr. President, we see that the very law that was intended to be used to curb monopolies and to preserve equality of opportunity among the American people has been used as a means of annoying, harassing, vexing, and in many instances oppressing a large number of the very people the makers of the law declared it should not be used against—the laborers.

I feel confident that in this presence I may call attention to the Democratic national platform adopted at Baltimore in 1912, which contains the following provision:

Questions of judicial practice have arisen, especially in connection with industrial disputes. We believe that the parties to all judicial proceedings should be treated with rigid impartiality, and that injunctions should not be issued in any case in which an injunction would not issue if no industrial disputes were involved.

The expanding organization of industry makes it essential that there should be no abridgement of the right of the wage earners and producers to organize for the protection of wages and the improvement of labor conditions, to the end that such labor organizations, and their members, should not be regarded as illegal combinations in restraint of trade.

I believe the same plank was in the platform of 1908.

Mr. KERN. It was copied from the 1908 provision.

Mr. ASHURST. Yes; the 1912 provision on the subject was copied from the 1908 provision.

The observation has been made that it is beyond the constitutional power of the National Legislature to exempt any persons from the operation of this law. A mere reference to the case of the International Harvester Co. of America against State of Missouri[5.581] decided by the Supreme Court of the United States June 8, 1914, upholding the constitutionality of the Missouri antitrust law, which, by omission, removed labor organizations from its provisions, is a definite answer to those who assert the unconstitutionality of the labor provisions of this proposed law. In that case Mr. Justice McKenna, delivering the opinion of the court, inter alia, said:

* * * * * * *

The assignments of error necessarily involve a consideration of the statutes. The relevant provisions are contained in section 10301 of the Revised Statutes of the State of 1909 and section 8966 of the Revised Statutes of 1899.

Section 10301 provides "that all arrangements, contracts, agreements, combinations, or understandings made or entered into between two or more persons, designed or made with a view to lessen, or which tend to lessen, lawful trade or full and free competition in the importation, transportation, manufacture, or sale" in the State "of any product, commodity, or article, or thing bought or sold," and all such arrangements, etc., "which are designed or made with a view to increase, or which tend to increase, the market price of any product, commodity, or article or thing, of any class or kind whatsoever, bought and sold," are declared to be against public policy, unlawful, and void, and those offending "shall be deemed and adjudged guilty of a conspiracy in restraint of trade, and punished" as provided.[5.582]

* * * * * * *

In State *v.* Standard Oil Co. (218 Mo., 1, 370, 372) the supreme court held that the antitrust statutes of the State "are limited in their scope and operations to persons and corporations dealing in commodities, and do not include combinations of persons engaged in labor pursuits." And, justifying the statutes against a charge of illegal discrimination, the court further said that "it must be borne in mind that the differentiation between labor and property is so great that they do not belong to the same general classification of rights or things, and have never been so recognized by the common law or legislative enactments."[5.583]

* * * * * * *

We said in Atchison, Topeka & Santa Fe Railway Co. *v.* Matthews (174 U. S., 96, 106), by Mr. Justice Brewer: "The very idea of classification is that of inequality, so that it goes without saying that the fact of inequality in no manner determines the matter of constitutionality." Therefore it may be there is restraint of competition in a combination of laborers and in a combination of purchasers, but that does not demonstrate that legislation which does not include either combination is illegal. Whether it would have been better policy to have made such comprehensive classification it is not our province to decide. In other words, whether a combination of wage earners or purchasers of commodities called for repression by law under the conditions in the State was for the legislature of the State to determine.[5.584]

* * * * * * *

And so in the case at bar. Whether the Missouri statute should have set its condemnation on restraints generally, prohibiting combined action for any purpose and to everybody, or confined it, as the statute does, to manufacturers and vendors of articles and permitting it to purchasers of such articles; prohibiting it to sellers of commodities and permitting it to sellers of

---

[5.581] 234 U.S. 199, 34 S. Ct. 859, 58 L. Ed. 1276 (1914).

[5.582] 234 U.S. at 207-08.

[5.583] *Id.* at 208-09.

[5.584] *Id.* at 210.

services, was a matter of legislative judgment, and we can not say that the distinctions made are palpably arbitrary, which we have seen is the condition of judicial review. It is to be remembered that the question presented is of the power of the legislature, not the policy of the exercise of the power. To be able to find fault, therefore, with such policy is not to establish the invalidity of the law based upon it.

It is said that the statute as construed by the Supreme Court of the State comes within our ruling in Connelly [sic] v. Union Sewer Pipe Co. (184 U. S. 540), but we do not think so. If it did, we should, of course, apply that ruling here. * * *[5.585]

I have received a number of letters and telegrams from various persons stating that the labor provisions of this bill were unjust and without precedent—and many of these communications stated that this proposed law, to use Thomas H. Benton's pleonastic phrase, "stood out solitary and alone"—and was without parallel in the history of parliamentary enactments. Some of these letters have especially inveighed against that provision of the bill which is as follows:

"And no such restraining order or injunction shall prohibit any person or persons from terminating any relation of employment, or from ceasing to perform any work or labor, or from recommending, advising, or persuading others by peaceful means so to do; or from attending at or near a house or place where any person resides or works, or carries on business, or happens to be, for the purpose of peacefully obtaining or communicating information, or of peacefully persuading any person to work or to abstain from working."

In truth and in fact, however, the language just above quoted is really a rescript of paragraph 2 of chapter 47 of an act to provide for the regulation of trade-unions and trade disputes, enacted by the Parliament of Great Britain December 21, 1906, and is to be found on pages 246 to 247 of volume 44 of the law reports of the statutes passed during the reign of King Edward VII. I here quote that act in extenso:

Be it enacted by the King's Most Excellent Majesty, by and with the advice and consent of the Lords Spiritual and Temporal, and Commons, in this present Parliament assembled, and by the authority of the same, as follows:

1. The following paragraph shall be added as a new paragraph after the first paragraph of section 3 of the conspiracy and protection of property act, 1875:

"An act done in pursuance of an agreement or combination by two or more persons shall, if done in contemplation or futherance of a trade dispute, not be actionable unless the act, if done without any such agreement or combination, would be actionable."

2. (1) It shall be lawful for one or more persons, acting on their own behalf or on behalf of a trade-union or of an individual employer ⊥ or firm in contemplation or furtherance of a trade dispute, to attend, at or near a house or place where a person resides or works or carries on business or happens to be, if they so attend merely for the purpose of peacefully obtaining or communicating information, or of peacefully persuading any person to work or abstain from working.

(2) Section 7 of the conspiracy and protection of property act, 1875, is hereby repealed from "attending at or near" to the end of the section.

3. An act done by a person in contemplation or furtherance of a trade dispute shall not be actionable on the ground only that it induces some other person to break a contract of employment, or that it is an interference with the trade, business, or employment of some other person or with the right of some other person to dispose of his capital or his labor as he wills.

4. (1) An action against a trade-union, whether of workmen or masters, or against any members or officials thereof on behalf of themselves and all other members of the trade-union in respect of any tortious act alleged to have been committed by or on behalf of the trade-union, shall not be entertained by any court.

(2) Nothing in this section shall affect the liability of the trustees of a trade-union to be sued in the events provided for by the trades-union act, 1871, section 9, except in respect of any tortious act committed by or on behalf of the union in contemplation or in furtherance of a trade dispute.

5. (1) This act may be cited as the trade disputes act, 1906, and the trade-union acts, 1871 and 1876, and this act may be cited together as the trade-union acts, 1871 to 1906.

(2) In this act the expression "trade-union" has the same meaning as in the trade-union acts, 1871 and 1876, and shall include any combination as therein defined, notwithstanding that such combinations may be the branch of a trade union.

(3) In this act and in the conspiracy and protection of property act, 1875, the expression

---

[5.585] *Id.* at 215.

"trade dispute" means any dispute between employers and workmen or between workmen and workmen, which is connected with the employment or nonemployment or the terms of the employment or with the conditions of labor of any person, and the expression "workmen" means all persons employed in trade or industry, whether or not in the employment of the employer with whom a trade dispute arises; and, in section 3 of the last-mentioned act, the words "between employers and workmen" shall be repealed.

This parliamentary enactment gave legislative relief against the judicial theory of criminal conspiracy under the common law, under which the oppressors of labor took refuge behind the doctrine of civil conspiracy.

Neither in England, France, Germany, nor in any other enlightened government, except in the United States, may laborers be arrested and punished for unitedly asking an increase of wages or for combining to do any lawful thing which means the bringing about a betterment of their condition; and it is a painful commentary upon the vicissitudes of our country to realize that the laborers must look, in some instances, to monarchical forms of government for light and hope in leadership on this particular subject rather than to the Members of Congress here in our elective Republic. From a study of labor leaders, I am convinced that the labor leaders in America are the ablest, the most conservative, and the most experienced which the world affords. They are much less radical than the labor group in the English Parliament, the Chamber of Deputies in France, or the German Reichstag.

Labor demands, and is on tenable ground in demanding, that we recognize a fundamental difference between labor power and real, personal, and mixed property. Labor power is not, strictly speaking, property, but labor power creates property. Labor power is not property, because it can not be separated from the laborer. Labor power can only be exerted and applied during the worker's life, and it ends with his death; hence it will be seen at a glance that labor power is not to be treated as property.

The statute against monopolies in England was enacted as a rampart against the greed of rapacious men who desired to acquire a disproportionate share of property, and for a like reason the Sherman antitrust law of 1890 was enacted for the purpose of curbing the rapacity of the selfish ones in our Nation, as I have pointed out in the beginning of this address; for it is a truth demonstrated to us and illustrated by the history of the world that some men are disposed to avail themselves improperly of the property of their fellow men, and in availing themselves improperly of the property of other men they also resort to availing themselves of the services, efforts, energies, and labors of their fellow men without rendering an equivalent.

Martin, at page 2 of his book, Modern Law of Labor Unions, defines labor unions as follows:

Perhaps as good a definition or description of a labor union as any is an association of workingmen of the same or of allied trades or occupations, the usual purposes of which are the regulation of their relations with their employers, the securing of better terms of employment, the elevation of their moral, social, and intellectual condition, and the assistance, financially or otherwise, of members in time of sickness, poverty, and distress.

Until recent years—that is to say, about the time of the trade-union act in 1871— laboring men in England were treated with much severity for combining to enforce their demands for higher wages. In Rex against Mawbey, decided in 1796, it was said that combinations of workingmen to raise wages constituted an indictable conspiracy at common law.

As late as 1834, in England, six agricultural laborers were convicted and sentenced to seven years' penal servitude for unitedly asking for an increase in wages of 1 shilling per week. Under the laws in force in England at that time this was treated as a conspiracy and these men were promptly convicted and transported to Australia. They became famous in history as the "six men of Dorset." One of these, George Lovelace, wrote in his diary a vivid description of the horrors they underwent while being transported. Then arose in England a tremendous agitation for their release, and 50,000 workingmen, in a procession, marched by the official residence of the then premier, Lord Melbourne, to present a petition in behalf of the "six men of Dorset." Their release finally came in 1837, and in May of last year a monument was erected in their native village in Dorsetshire to these martyrs in the cause of industrial liberty. I digress long enough to say that the very ship which took those men from England to Australia was recently in the harbor of Washington City. I refer to the ship *Success.*

I again quote from Martin on the Modern Law of Labor Unions, pages 9, 10, 11, 12, and 13, as follows:

> Whatever may have been the law in England in respect of combinations of workmen, it never obtained much foothold in America and was expressly repudiated in a Massachusetts decision of a comparatively early date, in which a very exhaustive opinion was written by Chief Justice Shaw. * * *
>
> In some jurisdictions where there are statutes authorizing it, and in others, in the absence of statutory authorization, it is now well settled that workmen may combine and associate themselves together for the purpose of bettering their condition either financially or socially by legitimate and fair means. Such a combination or association, it has been held, is not a monopoly or in restraint of trade; personal service—an occupation—can not be the subject of a monopoly. The right of workmen to form unions is expressly conferred by statute in many jurisdictions, and in a majority of the States the right is impliedly recognized by legislation enacted for the protection of unions from infringement of their labels, for it is obvious that where statutes expressly create or recognize the right of labor unions to be protected in the use of labels for labor union purposes, any suggestion that the union is an unlawful association falls of itself. It has also been held that the right to combine into unions has been raised to the dignity of a constitutional right by State constitutional provisions; that all men are born free and equal and have certain natural, essential, and inalienable rights, among which is the right of acquiring, possessing, and protecting property. But aside from any constitutional or statutory provision, the better view is that the right of laborers to organize into unions is an exercise of the common-law right of every citizen to pursue his calling, whether of labor or business, as he in his judgment thinks fit, and the law not only permits but encourages combinations of this character. An underlying law of human society, it is said, moves men to unite for the better achievement of a common aim, and this social principle justifies organized action. Organization or combination is a law of human society. It is open to all orders of men who desire to accomplish some lawful purpose through the greater strength and effectiveness which organization offers over individual effort. A very strong reason for permitting labor combinations is this: In an age when vast combinations of capital and the number of individual employers of labor are common, and in consequence competition for labor by employers enormously reduced, combination on the part of labor is an absolute necessity if the wage earner is to obtain his fair share in the distribution of the earnings which are the joint product of capital and labor. Combination on the part of capital is powerful. Combination on the part of labor is the necessary and desirable counterpart if the battle is to be carried on in a fair and equal way. The natural tendency of combined capital is to seek to obtain the cheapest labor, and unless resisted by combination on the part of the wage earner it would inevitably result in oppression and injustice. As was said by Attorney General Olney: "To-day, the mass of wage earners can no longer be dealt with by capital as so many isolated units. The time is passed when the individual workman is called upon to pit his feeble strength against the might of organized capital."

Mr. President, we might as well now as hereafter bid adieu to our antiquated ideas of the "law of supply and demand" doctrine regulating the price of labor, the hours of labor, and the conditions under which labor must be performed, for this "supply and demand" idea is a twin brother of the "might makes right" doctrine. Many, if not most, thoughtful persons are now beginning to realize and frankly admit that as a general rule the economic position of the individual employee is too weak for him to hold his own in the unequal contest he is obliged to wage with capitalism. The individual employee is frequently unable to insist upon the "square deal"; that is to say, he may be able to insist upon the "square deal," but he is without power to galvanize and translate his insistence into full life and realization unless he act in concert with his brother employees. In many instances the power of the employer to withhold a subsistence is a more effective weapon than the power of the employee to refuse to labor. Under such circumstances the law of "supply and demand" doctrine as applied to labor should really be called "despotism in contract." In other words, the relative position of the employee and the capitalist is not the same. The worker is sometimes in the position occupied by Esau when he surrendered his birthright for a mess of pottage, except the workingman is sometimes called upon to surrender his birthright and not get the pottage either.

The humanitarian spirit that is pervading our Nation and the demand for social justice which has taken hold of the hearts of men and women declare that the doctrine of the brutal Manchester school which held that human labor is a commodity to be bought and sold at the lowest possible market price, as machinery, oil, coal, wheat, flour, wool, and oats, and used until its supply is consumed or its efficiency exhausted, is vicious in morals and unsound in economics. The modern thinkers take exactly the opposite view, to wit, that labor can not and ought not be treated as a commodity, such as coal, wheat, flour, oil, machinery, broadcloth, raisins, lemons, and so forth, and insist that laborers are as much a human element in our civilization as bankers, lawyers, clergymen, merchants, or any other persons. Therefore, Mr. President, I take my stand for the humanitarian policy of dealing equitably and with strict justice toward those whose grime and sweat, blood and toil have built up our splendid civilization.

"Labor has, and ought to have, the right to organize." That is an expression we hear very often, and I doubt if there may be found any dissentient thereto.

Many years ago I visited this Capitol; I sat in the gallery of the Senate and looked down into this historic Chamber with a fevered ambition, hoping the evolution of politics would some day bring me to a seat in the Senate. While sitting in the gallery, I heard fall from the lips of a distinguished Senator a sentence I never have and probably never will forget, which was: "It is idle and vain to give a man a right unless you also give him the power to enforce that right." This sentence lived because it was true, and it might be applied to-day to the labor situation in our country. It is idle merely to say labor has the right to a living and decent wage unless we supplement that assertion by granting labor the power to enforce its demand for a living wage. When I use the term "living wage," I do not mean a wage which affords "bread alone," but I mean a wage which will afford proper food, clothing, shelter, some leisure time to devote to the family, to books, music, philosophy, and, in general, an opportunity to have sufficient respite from exacting toil to enjoy some of the idealistic, aesthetic, and spiritual side of life which adds zest, grace, and beauty to human existence.

It has been asserted that it is dangerous for laborers to possess the power to compel a compliance with their demands for a living wage. I reply that such power is indeed dangerous—to monopoly, oppression, tyranny, avarice, and greed—but is wholesome to the general welfare and to public tranquility. Internal dangers to a State need never be apprehended from a general desire and effort on the part of the creators of wealth to promote their own efficiency, improve and exalt their own station, for if laborers were to refuse to try to improve their own condition it would be tantamount to their seeking wantonly their own self-destruction.

Let us inquire, for what persons do the labor provisions of this bill seek "social justice" and industrial liberty? The reply to this question is that the proposed law is not especially solicitous as to those persons who might aptly be compared to the drones described in Maeterlinck's "Life of the Bee." We all remember how interestingly and with what vivid genius Maeterlinck wrote of the drones in the hive. He said:

These (the drones) comport themselves in the hive as did Penelope's suitors in the House of Ulysses, wasteful, sleek, and corpulent, fully content with their idle existence * * * they feast and carouse, throng the alleys, obstruct the passages, and hinder the work, jostling and jostled, fatuously pompous, swelled with foolish, good-natured contempt for the workers * * *. For their pleasant slumbers they select the snuggest corners of the hive; then, rising carelessly, they flock to the open cells where the honey smells the sweetest, and soil with their excrement the combs they frequent. The patient workers, their eyes steadily fixed on the future, will silently set things right. From noon till 3, when the purple country trembles in blissful lassitude beneath the invincible gaze of a July or August sun, the drones will appear on the threshold. They have a helmet made of enormous black pearls, two lofty, quivering plumes, a doublet of iridescent, yellowish velvet, an heroic tuft, a fourfold mantle, translucent and rigid. They create a prodigious stir, brush the sentry aside, overturn the cleaners, and collide with the foragers as these return laden with their humble spoil. These drones have a busy air, the extravagant, contemptuous, supercilious gait of indispensable gods who should be simultaneously venturing toward some destiny unknown to the vulgar. One by one these drones sail off into space, irresistible, glorious, and tranquilly make for the nearest flowers, where they sleep till the afternoon freshness awakes them. Then, with the same majestic pomp, and still overflowing with magnificent schemes, they return to the hive, go straight to the combs, plunge their heads up to the neck in the vats of honey and fill themselves as tight as a drum to repair their exhausted strength; whereupon, with heavy steps, they go forth to meet the good, dreamless, and careless slumber that shall fold them in its embrace till the time for the next repast.

No, Mr. President, the labor provisions of this bill do not especially demand "social justice" and industrial liberty for such persons unless they be willing to leave off their slothful, wasteful habits, but do demand "social justice" and industrial liberty for those persons without whose industry, resoluteness, patience, sacrifices, physical strength, cool heads, skillful hands, and unremitting toil we never could have mastered the mechanical arts and the physical sciences. This bill secures a measure of "social justice" and industrial freedom for those who amid the thud of the drill and the rising and falling of picks and shovels in the mines dig our copper ore and convert it into watch movements, magnetoes, wire, and electric lamps; for those who dig the coal which transports the commerce of the Nation; for those who dig our iron ore and convert it into railroad steel, machinery, cutlery, and all the ingenious mechanical and electrical contrivances that make life broader, more useful, and beautiful; for those who convert our crude oil into lubricants and gasoline; for those who convert our forests into houses, chairs, desks, tables, and bookcases; for those who cultivate and fructify our land; for those who produce; for those who transform the wool into clothing, the hides into boots and shoes, harness and saddles; for those who make engines, reapers, locomotives, and the thousands of other forms of manufactured commodities; for those who with good cheer face the rising morn, are loyal to their day's work, and are constantly pouring forth costly sacrifices—their time and strength—for the common good of all; for those who uncomplainingly meet danger on the trains, in the mines, in the smelters, and in the foundries; for those who with high but baffled ambition invincibly face the isolation and monotony which comes when poverty has deprived life of its sublimity and ideality and reduces it to a remorseless and deadly grind for a subsistence.

This bill recognizes that labor power is the noble force for the great social and industrial achievements of our Nation's future.

We need not suffer ourselves to be misled with any delusions. No nation will truly be great—indeed, no nation will survive—if it oppresses its own producers. The workers of our Nation have built up a surpassingly great fabric of mechanical industry, and history teaches us that powerful nations of ancient times fell prone and helpless not because of invasions or external barbaric strength but because of social injustices. If danger ever comes to us it will not come from abroad; it will rise up from among ourselves.

The American people have accomplished more salutary reform and progress than any other nation in the files of time. Let us add one more great achievement to the long list of American achievements by adopting this bill.

I thank the Senate for its attention, and ask that as an appendix to my remarks I may include a letter written by Gov. George W. P. Hunt, of Arizona, to the Popular Government League.

The VICE PRESIDENT. Without objection, that may be done.

The matter referred to is as follows:

ARIZONA'S GOVERNOR TELLS OF STATE'S GREAT PROGRESS UNDER POPULAR GOVERNMENT BANNER.

At a meeting of the popular government conference held at Washington the purposes of the meeting were stated as follows:

"To present the necessity for the proposed 'gateway amendment,' which will afford an easier method of amending the Federal Constitution; to discuss the dangers which now threaten the movement for the initiative, referendum, and recall; to consider the preferential ballot; to emphasize the need of the public school as a civic center; to organize the national popular government league."

Gov. Hunt had been invited as the representative of the "most advanced State in the Union," but was unable to attend. Under these circumstances Gov. Hunt wrote the following address, which was read by the secretary:

"Fellow friends of popular government: History continues an insistent repeater—an institution of parallels and similitude.

"Since the dawn of time humanity has been struggling toward the light—in philosophy, science, religion, and government. And in every age and every field this irresistible movement, always gaining toward the shining goal, has been combated, retarded, temporarily defeated by a self constituted, self-loving, self-interested aristocracy.

"Sometimes an aristocracy of blood, insolently assuming the dynastic right of perpetual dominion; sometimes an aristocracy of learning, solemnly averring itself the sum and substance, the beginning and the end, of knowledge and wisdom; sometimes of force, brutally proving its claim with bow, battle-ax, and sword; sometimes of charlatanic virtue, proclaiming from gilten temples the possession of all excellence.

"Sometimes it is an aristocracy of wealth—but of that, a word later.

"At all times and in all places an aristocracy of selfishness, of greed, egotism, and intolerance; of indifference to the rights of the many, deafness to the voice of humanity.

"Ever and everywhere it has first ignored, then derided, then crushed—if it could—those who dared question its absolutism, its ends, or its means.

"Its weapons? The weapons of evil, always. Ancient, medieval, modern, they have varied little. The first to hand, good enough—none too base, none too cowardly, none too cruel, and it would serve their purpose.

"Scheming, conniving, when need be; slaughtering to retain their grip of power, the resources and weapons of these self appointed rulers have ever been turned against those who dared stand forth for the right, for equality for justice, for progress. In the struggle valiant leaders have often succumbed, the battle been turned aside, victory ⊥ delayed. But ever the cause has lived and revived and grown, and to-day, as never before, humanity is marching forward. Where for long it groped it is now making its way swiftly, surely, steadily toward the light.

"Arizona has played and is playing her part in the latest act of this ages-old drama. Here we had, for many years and in almost unlimited power, the aristocracy of wealth, with all that it implies—government for the people but not of them; boss-ridden political parties, corrupted legislatures, burdensome laws, unequal taxation, special privileges for the few.

"The system has been changed; not, I must admit, absolutely revolutionized, but decisively, effectively.

"The new order came with statehood, not of slow growth, varying fortune, and gradual success, as great reforms usually come, but with suddenness—surprising, startling, almost wholly unexpected suddenness. The people, aroused into an activity to which, under the prevailing system, they had long been strangers became quickly prepared for a change in their interest. But the political parties, run as all aristocracies of wealth run political parties—by machines— were not ready. The popular government was a thing too remote, too different from the old Arizona plan, too entirely out of joint with the existing order, to be of a sudden feared. A cloud out of a clear sky for the aristocracy of wealth, it looked ominous but it simply would not, could not, open and let fall its flood. That's how the bosses—the old-time, always successful, self-satisfied bosses—sans reason, reasoned it out, and their masters, the aristocracy, took their word for it. There wasn't time for much of anything else.

"But the movement swept the Territory, soon to become a State. The people, charged with the making of a constitution, first became alive to their responsibility, and then awakened to the possibility. There was opportunity to become their own masters, and they felt qualified to assume the sovereignty. One old-time machine—the Democratic—was captured by assault; another run over and crushed—crushed out of all recognition, and to this day it lies a broken, shapeless mass, a testimonial to the persistence, the stubbornness, the insatiable greed of the aristocracy of wealth.

"The constitutional convention was held, and popular government reserved and defined in the organic law became an assured fact in Arizona.

"Do not think this brilliant achievement was unaccompanied by a struggle, or that the struggle ended with the constitutional reservation to the people of the right to control their own affairs. When has any one heard of an aristocracy of anything, and particularly of wealth, surrendering its prerogatives calmly, amiably, or at all if possible to prevent, or of suffering their continued loss while a chance of regaining any portion of the lost ground remained?

"On the contrary, the fight for a people's constitution in Arizona, unexpectedly as it came up, suddenly as it flared into life, was probably as fierce, as bitter, as uncompromising, as sensational, and, metaphorically speaking, as sanguinary a contest as has occurred in the United States for many a long year. Nor is the reference to its bloodiness so very far-fetched, for when the smoke of battle had cleared away many a political corpse lay stretched upon the field.

"One beauty—the beauty—of the contest was its clear-cutness. There was no doubting the issue which divided the forces. 'Shall the people rule?' was the paramount question. Of course, both sides answered, 'Yes'; but while one side said, 'through us,' the other said 'through themselves.' And the people proceeded to equip themselves to rule, not through the machines of the aristocracy of wealth, but through and by and for themselves.

"In the campaign out of which came a 'people's rule' constitution the machine, by its agents and instruments, villified, abused, and denounced the advocates of popular government as advocates of all movements for progress, of all movements to reduce the aristocracy to a position of political equality, have been villified, abused, and denounced—and frequently executed—in times and ages past.

"The proposed initiative, referendum, and recall were violently assailed as something totally impractical, subversive of republicanism, anarchistic—that was a favorite term—and most frequently by men who to be confounded needed only to be asked to explain what these terrible triplets were. They actually could not explain, literally they did not know. The three-headed monster had come upon them so suddenly that they had no time to identify the species. But that it was an insatiable, devouring beast they were certain, for their masters had so advised them, and in the battle for extinction, 'Theirs not to reason why; theirs but to do and die.'

"Other essential features of popular government were not forgotten by the people's advocates, but the battle waged about the initiative, referendum, and recall.

"And the initiative, referendum, and recall, if the opponents of reform were to be believed, would strike at the very foundation of our republican form of government; they were unconstitutional, unwieldy, impossible; they were weapons of the mob, the resort of anarchists. The champions of them were held up to ridicule and scorn, loaded with all the epithets that hatred and malignity might suggest or invent—Socialists, demagogues bogus reformers, ranting hypocrites, blatherskite orators, blithering idiots. No appellation too vile, no charge too nasty, no means too low if aimed toward undoing the efforts of those who upheld the people's fight and toward defeat of the people's fight. And in this history, for the thousandth time, was repeating.

"Then, too, the most direful results, if this monstrous calamity should befall, were predicted—aye, prophesied as of a certainty and finally threatened as an awesome bugaboo is held before a naughty child. That the Government would fall to pieces was the least of the terrible results that might be looked forward to. Business would be paralyzed, development would cease, capital would withdraw and never come again, the name of the State would be a byword and a scorn. On the contrary, if the safe and sane rule of the aristocracy of wealth were continued, prosperity would abound, capital would pour in, the industries would forge ahead, there would be universal plenty. The prophecies and representations, arguments, threats, and promises all were borrowed from the oft-copied pages of history—from the pages of history reciting other attacks upon the castles of tyrant rulers.

"But neither abuse, ridicule, threats, nor cajolery served the purpose of the machine. The people won—that is, so far as the returns went.

"Then the machines went to work upon the members-elect of the constitutional convention. They were bound by solemn pledges: they were instructed to insure the people's rule, but, argued the insidious agents of the aristocracy of wealth, what of that? Often before platform pledges had been ignored; in fact, it was generally understood that platforms were merely to get in on; now they were in, a good political trick has been turned let's get down to brass tacks—down to good, hard practical common sense. So the machine, as always, worked upon the weak-kneed and faint-hearted, the timid, the susceptible, and the corrupt. Abuse and villification somewhat continued, but largely gave way to subtler methods—to plausible representations, to the well-known ways of the lobbyist, to entreaties and to threats.

"As indicative of the methods employed, an incident may be related. A member-elect of the convention—a young man, with the promise of a political career before him—was approached by an agent of the machine. If the young man, with a future so full of hope, persisted in his unreasonable course, he would be crushed. He and his intemperate cause might triumph for a day, but it would not be long before he would be ground under the wheels of the aristocracy. It is indicative of the spirit which brought the convention to complete fulfillment of its duty that the young man replied: 'It may so so. Socrates was forced to drink the hemlock, but his philosophy survives the centuries; Columbus, ridiculed, reviled, and scorned, died a pauper's death, but he opened the door of a new world, and the glory of his name can never be dimmed. I am neither a Socrates nor a Columbus, but I can do my best.'

"The threat was freely used that unless the radical demands of the reformers were abandoned, there would be no statehood. No constitution containing the initiative, referendum and recall—and particularly the recall—could run the gantlet of Congress and the President. It was boldly asserted, on authority of the President, and confirmed by his spokesmen in the territory.

"But the people of Arizona are a courageous, determined race; and their representatives in that convention were largely of them—really and truly of them. In spite of every effort of the opposition, in spite of all obstacles, there was little hesitation in the carrying of the people's instructions.

"Then came the most dangerous period. When it became certain that the initiative, referendum, and recall would be features of the proposed constitution—when it was definitely known that the platform pledges were to be in some manner and measure redeemed—many were the schemes concocted to nullify their effects. The jokers proposed would fill a respectable volume—that is, they would fill a volume respectable in size.

"Among those it was proposed that, inasmuch as the details would be purely legislative, only a mandate to the legislature should be placed in the constitution. Or the question should be submitted to the people at the first State election. To the first proposal it was pointed out that the failures, refusals, and weaknesses of legislatures were responsible for the demand for direct legislative powers; to the latter reply was given that the people had already most emphatically spoken. Next appeared suggestions of the high and unworkable percentages, of requirements that petitions should come from a majority of counties, of a dozen things designed simply to reduce popular government, as it should be provided for in Arizona's constitution, to an empty phrase.

"Every scheme was bared, every proposal to restrict the power of the people was brushed aside. That convention did its duty. The initiative, referendum, and recall, in self-executing, workable detail, were placed in the constitution, and along with them the instrument was made most easily amendable, and practically all features known to the modern system of popular government were provided. Oregon's advisory vote for United States Senators was borrowed, provisions for the prevention and prohibition of trusts and monopolies and the regulation of public-service corporations were embodied, the proper safeguarding of the rights of labor was attended to. As a people's victory, it was quite complete.

"The scene changed to Washington, but the fight against popular government in Arizona did not cease. The proposed constitution, ratified by 85 per cent of Arizona's electorate, was attacked from within and without. It was a national struggle, with which all friends of popular government are familiar. An incident of the fight, local both in its purpose and effect, was a declaration, addressed to the President and Congress, and signed by something like 50 of the old machine Democrats of the State, acting on behalf of the aristocracy of wealth, to the effect that the proposed constitution was not the work of the Democratic Party, and petitioning for its disapproval. That document is still occasionally exhumed and the signers asked to explain.

"After a protracted struggle Arizona was admitted, its constitution unimpaired except for a concession insisted upon by President Taft to save his face—the excepting of the judiciary from the recall's provisions—and the rectification of that alteration constituted the electorate's first application of its constitutional powers.

"And what of the disaster—civil, political, industrial disaster—that was to follow the inauguration of these "innovations," these radical, impractical, anarchistic notions of the mob?

"It has not happened. Mines are running, farms are spreading, herds are increasing, homes are multiplying, towns are building; there is more prosperity to the square inch in Arizona than ever before, and the future's promise is roseate.

"Not a dollar of capital, as far as I know, has retired; rather, it has accepted many of the conditions imposed, and while still fighting for the domination to which it has been accustomed, is prepared to accept the legitimate return which the laws do not, by any means, deny. Business activities have shown no sign of abating, and, altogether, industrial conditions are pursuing to an even and far more normal tenor.

"The initiative, referendum, and recall have demonstrated their practicability, their utility, their success. The intelligence of the voters has been demonstrated and their interest in legislation illustrated in a most practical manner. Perhaps I can no more clearly set this forth than to quote from my message of last February to the legislature:

" 'Of particular and extraordinary interest at this time is the splendid and convincing vindication of the principle and as well the practice of direct legislation as embodied in the results of the election held November 5, but also by other occurrences of recent months. Notable among these may be mentioned the somewhat curious fact that whereas during the period in which the framing of Arizona's constitution was an issue, the Democratic Party was forced to make a single-handed fight for the direct-legislation cause, so well established has this principle now become that during the last campaign every political party, young or old, represented in the State, made platform indorsement of the initiative and referendum.

" 'The legislature submitted to the people four proposed amendments to the constitution, while the people, taking advantage of the power reserved to them under the constitution, initiated an amendment to the suffrage and elections article providing for woman suffrage. All of these proposed amendments were of the greatest importance and elicited the interest they deserved. The vote on them was as follows:

" 'Recall of judicial officers: For, 16,272; against, 3,705.

" 'Right of State to engage in industrial pursuits: For, 14,928; against, 3,602.

" 'Permitting greater latitude in the enactment of taxation laws: For, 15,967; against, 2,283.

" 'Permitting the additional bonding of incorporated towns and cities for municipal water and light plants and sewers: For, 15,358; against, 2,676.

" 'Equal suffrage: For, 13,442; against, 6,202.

" 'In addition to these constitutional amendments, the referendum was invoked on eight measures enacted by the legislature. It is worthy of consideration in estimating the absolute fairness and practicability of this method of legislation that in all of these cases save two resort to the people, which should always be the court of final appeal, was had by and at the instance of corporations which were, while Arizona's constitution was being framed and during the period when its fate, with that of statehood, hung in the balance at Washington, in bitter opposition to the initiative and referendum features of the charter. Not only were these corporations first to invoke the referendum, but they took occasion, in the literature forming a part of an elaborate campaign made to defeat the measures to which objection was had, to commend the "wise provision" of the constitution permitting the people to pass judgment on all laws enacted by the legislature.

" 'Never could the interest of the people in legislation affecting their welfare or the welfare of any class of citizens, or their ability to judge of the merits or demerits of proposed measures, be more strikingly illustrated or more definitely settled than was done in this instance. On one hand certain powerful interests, violently objecting to the measures enacted by the legislature, after invoking the referendum, entered upon an elaborate, exhaustive, systematic, and, doubtless, very expensive campaign to defeat the measures at the polls. Speakers were employed to tour the State; printed literature in large quantities and personal letters signed by prominent and influential officers of the corporations chiefly concerned flooded the mails; personal workers were interested, and such employees as could be influenced were advised as to what were for the 'best interests of the company,' while great spaces were used in many newspapers in the State, not only in the advertising columns, but in the news columns, and very frequently in the editorial departments. Nor did any political party champion the cause or lend its moral support. As required by law, publicity pamphlets were sent out by the secretary of state; a few speeches were made in the larger towns by advocates representing the labor organizations; and the people, alive to every phase of the situation, discussed it among themselves. That was the extent of the affirmative campaign. And in spite of the efforts put forth to convince them to the contrary, the people decided that the measures were good ones.

" 'The favorite claim made by the opponents of direct legislation, that the people will not take an interest in measures referred to or instituted by them, is here totally disproved, since an average of 18,887 votes were cast on the constitutional amendments and 17,884 on the referred laws, as against an average vote of 23,483 for presidential electors and 23,545 for all candidates for Congress.

" 'It were [sic] difficult to conceive of a more emphatic demonstration of the thorough utility of Arizona's direct-legislation provision than has thus been afforded at its first trial.'

"Altogether Arizona is wonderfully satisfied with her trial of popular government. It has not proved that perfection has been reached, and perfection is by no means claimed, but it has generously shown that the people may be safely intrusted with the management of their own affairs. They may make mistakes—who does not?—but they are quick to see, and with the power to do so, quick to remedy them. They are not rash, impulsive, or unfair, as the opponents of popular government would endeavor to make the people themselves believe, but, on the contrary, may be depended upon to treat fairly with all interests and classes.

"Not yet are they, with this weapon of self-government in their hands, out of danger from the exactions of the aristocracy of wealth, for at all times, day and night, early and late, under all conditions and circumstances, the machinery of that vast organization is working, if not to hold its unwarranted dominion, to regain that which it has lost. It is not quite sufficient that the people shall have the means to control and direct their government; they must be alert to do so. Thus far the people of Arizona have been watchful and alert and have proved their capability and intelligence. With the power at their command, reserved to them by the constitution they framed, they have only to continue so.

"Arizona will welcome the day when all the States of the Union shall respond to the demand for this genuinely democratic system of government, when the United States Government itself shall, through the medium of salutary reforms, become more sensitive to the majority's will. To this latter end the proposed "gateway" amendment constituted a highly commendable movement. No question could be of greater importance at the present time than the breaking down of the ancient barriers interposed between the people and their organic law. That done, and many needed reforms will follow. That done, and it will be a question of but a few years when the Government of the United States will become in fact as well as in theory an example of genuine popular government.

"Consecrated to such a cause, the National Popular Government League may well be proud of its mission. My heartiest support is hereby pledged."

RECESS.

Mr. CULBERSON. I move that the Senate take a recess until 11 o'clock tomorrow morning.

The motion was agreed to; and (at 5 o'clock and 44 minutes p. m., Thursday, August 13, 1914) the Senate took a recess until to-morrow, Friday, August 14, 1914, at 11 o'clock a. m.

SENATE DEBATE
63d Cong., 2d Sess.
August 17, 1914

51 CONG. REC. 13844

Mr. CULBERSON. I ask that the unfinished business be laid before the Senate.

The Senate, as in Committee of the Whole, resumed the consideration of the bill (H. R. 15657) to supplement existing laws against unlawful restraints and monopolies, and for other purposes.

Mr. [WILLIAM H.] THOMPSON [D., Kan.]. Mr. President, one of the most important features of the pending bill, commonly known as the Clayton bill or antitrust bill—H. R. 15657—is the exemption of labor and farmers' organizations from the operation of the antitrust laws. It was never intended that these organizations should be included within the terms of the Sherman Antitrust Act, and it was a source of great surprise to the country when some of the courts took a different view. The law was originally designed to cover industrial combinations, as is clearly demonstrated by a review of the various speeches made in 1890, at the time of the passage of the act.

The senior Senator from Arizona [Mr. ASHURST] a few days ago, in a very able and convincing argument on this subject, read into the RECORD the expressions of the author of the law, Senator Hoar, and also remarks from Senator Teller, which I again call attention to.

I desire to have these inserted as part of my remarks. They have already been read, and I will not again read the arguments used at that time.

The PRESIDING OFFICER (Mr. WALSH in the chair). Is there any objection? The Chair hears none, and it is so ordered.

The matter referred to is as follows:

[Senate, page 2729, March 27, 1890, Mr. Hoar.]

When you are speaking of providing to regulate the transactions of men who are making corners in wheat, or in iron, or in woolen or in cotton goods, speculating in them or lawfully dealing in them without speculation, you are aiming at a mere commercial transaction, the beginning and end of which is the making of money for the parties, and nothing else. That is the only relation that transaction has to the State. It is the creation or diffusion or change of ownership of the wealth of the community. But when a laborer is trying to raise his wages or is endeavoring to shorten the hours of his labor, he is dealing with something that touches closely, more closely than anything else, the Government and the character of the State itself.

The maintenance of a certain standard of profit in dealing in large transactions in wheat or cotton or wool is a question whether a particular merchant or a particular class of merchants shall make money or not; but the question whether the standard of the laborer's wages shall be maintained or advanced, or whether the leisure for instruction, for improvement shall be shortened or lengthened is a question which touches the very existence and character of government of the State itself. The laborer who is engaged lawfully and usefully and accomplishing his purpose in whole or in part in endeavoring to raise the standard of wages is engaged in an occupation the success of which makes republican government itself possible, and without which the Republic can not, in substance, however it may nominally do in form, continue to exist.

I hold, therefore, that as legislators we may constitutionally, properly, and wisely allow laborers to make associations, combinations, contracts, agreements for the sake of maintaining and advancing their wages, in regard to which, as a rule, their contracts are to be made with large corporations, who are themselves but an association or combination or aggregation of capital on the other side. When we are permitting and even encouraging that, we are permitting and encouraging what is not only lawful, wise, and profitable, but absolutely essential to the existence of the Commonwealth itself.

When, on the other hand, we are dealing with one of the other classes, the combinations aimed at chiefly by this bill, we are dealing with a transaction the only purpose of which is to extort from the community, monopolize, segregate, and apply to individual use, for the purposes of individual greed, wealth which ought properly and lawfully and for the public interest to be generally diffused over the whole community.

[Senate, page 2562, March 24, 1890. Mr. Teller.]

I know that nobody here proposes to interfere with the class of men I have mentioned. Nobody here intends that by any of these provisions, either in the original bill or in any amendment, and I have only called attention to it to see if the efforts of those who have undertaken to manage this subject can not in some way confine the bill to dealing with trusts, which we all admit are offensive to good morals.

* * * * * * *

I want to repeat that I am exceedingly anxious myself to join in anything that shall break up and destroy these unholy combinations, but I want to be careful that in doing that we do not do more damage than we do good. I know how these great trusts, these great corporations, these large moneyed institutions can escape the provisions of a penal statute, and I know how much more likely they are to escape than the men who have less influence and less money. Therefore I suggest that the Senators who have this subject in charge give it special attention, and by a little modification it may be possible to relieve the bill of any doubt on that point.

Mr. THOMPSON. The Court of Appeals of the District of Columbia in the initial decision on this question in the case of American Federation of Labor v. Buck's Stove & Range Co. (33 App. Cases D. C., 83), recognizes the absolute right of labor to organize, to conduct peaceable strikes, and to resort to all lawful means to accomplish any lawful purpose, as shown in the opinion on pages 114 and 115:

The right of laboring men to organize into unions and the right of these unions to conduct peaceable strikes is justified because of their inability to compete single-handed in contests with their employers. In this competition any peaceable and lawful means may be resorted to, and it is only when the means employed becomes unlawful that the courts will interfere. The law recognizes the right of both labor and capital to organize. The contest between employer and employee is one which courts of equity should recognize as entitled to be fought out upon the basis of equality; and the rule applied by the courts to the strike is based, I think, upon that principle. The fundamental principle underlying this contest is that the employer who employs 1,000 workmen is in possession of the same competitive power to force those workmen to his terms as the 1,000 men, by the most powerful lawful organization, have to force him into a compliance with their terms. The contest, therefore, opens with the one on one side and a thousand on the other upon a substantial basis of equality. The employer has a property right in his business which he asks the courts to protect, and which is entitled to protection. It consists, among other things, in his right to employ whom he pleases. He may use in his business such types of machinery and appliances as he may think adapted to carry on his work most successfully, so long as they are reasonably safe and sanitary. The law protects him in these rights, and the courts will require others to respect them. On the other hand, the thousand employees have a property right in their labor, which is equally sacred with that of the employer. They have a right to engage their services wherever and to whomsoever they can secure the largest rewards and the fairest treatment. They have a right to cease working for their employer, with due regard for their contractual relations, when, in their judgment, they can better their condition by so doing. They have a right to organize for this purpose, and they have a right to advise others to join their organization, and the law will protect them in the exercise of these rights equally with the rights of the employer. The refusal of the employees to work for the employer may result in his financial ruin, but the loss will be no greater than the damage his refusal to employ the 1,000 laborers may work in the aggregate upon them and those dependent upon their labor. In this contest between employer and employed, it should be remembered that the one who most strictly recognizes and observes the legal and equitable rights of the other enters the struggle with tremendous odds in his favor.[5.586]

[5.586] 33 App. D.C. at 114–16 (concurring opinion).

It was also the doctrine of the common law that a thing which is lawful when done by one person does not become unlawful when done by two or more persons in combination, provided no unlawful means is agreed upon or used.

The courts have held, and I refer now to this same labor decision which was against labor at that time:

Employees have a perfect legal right to fix a price upon their labor and to refuse to work unless that price is obtained. They have that right both as individuals and in combinations. They may organize to improve their condition and to secure better wages. They may even use persuasion to have others join their organization. They have an unquestionable right to present their cause to the public in newspapers or circulars in a peaceable way, but with no attempt at coercion. If ruin to the employer results from their peaceable assertion of these rights, it is a damage without remedy. But the law does not permit either employer or employee to use force, violence, threats of force, or threats of violence, intimidation, or coercion. (My Maryland Lodge, No. 186, of Machinists, *v.* Adt (1905), 100 Md. 238, 249; 68 L. R. A., 752. See also National Protective Asso. *v.* Cumming, 170 N. Y., 315, 321; 58 L. R. A., 135.)[5.587]

The opposition claim that the exemption of labor and farmer organizations would be unconstitutional by reason of discriminating between classes of citizens, and therefore denying the equal protection of the laws guaranteed by the Constitution of the United States, and that such legislation is new and unheard of in the operation of general laws.

In answer to this argument I call attention to the exemption provision of the section imposing a tax on corporations under the tariff law of 1909, approved and signed by President Taft, as follows:

Provided, however, That nothing in this section contained shall apply to labor, agricultural, or horticultural organizations, or to fraternal beneficiary societies—

And so forth. I also refer to a decision of the Supreme Court of the United States in the case of Flint *v.* Stone, Tracy & Co. [sic] (220 U. S., 107)[5.588] on the validity of this provision, wherein the court held:

As to the objection that certain organizations, labor, agricultural and horticultural, fraternal and benevolent societies, loan and building associations, and those for religious, charitable, or educational purposes, are excepted from the operation of the law, we find nothing in them to invalidate the tax. As we have had frequent occasions to say, the decisions of this court from an early date to the present time have emphasized the right of Congress to select the objects to excise taxation, and within this power to tax some and leave others untaxed, must be included the right to make exemptions such as are found in this act.[5.589]

That there is nothing uncommon or pernicious in provisions of this kind is further shown by a similar provision in the Simmons-Underwood tariff law recently enacted by Congress. In the section dealing with the income tax is found the following provision:

Provided, however, That nothing in this section shall apply to labor, agricultural, or horticultural organizations, or to mutual savings banks not having a capital stock represented by shares, or to fraternal beneficiary societies—

And so forth. Farmers are specifically exempted from the benefits of the Federal bankruptcy law. If it was legal to single out and deprive farmers as a class of the benefits given others under the bankruptcy law, it should also be legal to give them whatever advantage they may derive of exemption from the antitrust laws.

It will also be remembered that all annual incomes under $3,000 are exempt under the income-tax law, and that the compensation of all officials and employees of a State, or any political subdivision thereof, is exempt except when paid by the United States Government. The question is not whether a distinction is actually made, but whether such distinction is just and equitable and whether the results in making the distinction promote the welfare of the greatest number of the people and thereby contribute to the general good of the Government.

[5.587] *Id.* at 127 (dissenting opinion).

[5.588] The correct citation is Flint v. Stone Tracy Co., 220 U.S. 107, 31 S. Ct. 342, 55 L. Ed. 389 (1911).

[5.589] 220 U.S. at 173.

In the construction of a State statute involving almost the identical language in question, in the case of State *v.* Coyle, criminal court of appeals of Oklahoma (130 Pacific Reporter, 316),[5.590] where the contention was made that this exemption of labor combinations is unconstitutional as discriminatory between classes of citizens and not affording the equal protection of the laws which the Constitution of the United States guarantees, Judge Furman in his opinion answered the question in the following forceful manner:

I desire, without reading, to have it incorporated as a part of my remarks.

The PRESIDING OFFICER. It will be so ordered.

The matter referred to is as follows:

A careful consideration of this matter will show that the contention of counsel for appellees is not tenable. It must be conceded that the legislature has the right and power to make reasonable classifications with reference to any proper subject of legislation. The assumption of counsel for appellees is that the rights of capital are equal to the rights of labor. Good morals do not sustain this assumption. While labor and capital are both entitled to the protection of the law, it is not true that the abstract rights of capital are equal to those of labor, and that they both stand on an equal footing before the law. Labor is natural; capital is artificial. Labor was made by God; capital is made by man. Labor is not only blood and bone, but it also has a mind and a soul, and is animated by sympathy, hope, and love; capital is inanimate, soulless matter. Labor is the creator; capital is the creature. But if we concede that the assumption of counsel for appellees is well founded and if we arbitrarily and in disregard of good morals place capital and labor upon an absolute equality before the law, another difficulty confronts them. Capital organizes to accomplish its purposes. Then, according to their own logic, it would be a denial of equal rights to labor to deny to it the right to organize and act without a breach of the peace to meet the aggressions of capital.

We therefore hold, from either view, that the provisions of the statute constitute a reasonable classification, such as the legislature had the right to make, and that the antitrust law does not, on this account, violate the clause of the Constitution of the United States which guarantees equal protection to all of the citizens of the United States. We deny that trusts and monopolies are entitled to protection as citizens of the United States.[5.591]

Mr. THOMPSON. Whether the original decision against labor in the Buck's Stove case was correct or not, it is perfectly clear that we have a legal right to exempt labor from the operation of this law. That it is desirable to do so, few will deny. Labor is not property any more than the air we breathe. That it is necessary to organize to preserve the rights of labor can not be successfully denied. Without organization labor would be completely crushed by capital.

Mr. Gompers, president of the American Federation of Labor, when before the House committee, summed up his argument most convincingly in the following language:

Our existence is justified not only by our history, but our existence is legally the best concept of what constitutes law. It is an outrage—it is an outrage of not only the conscience, it is not only an outrage upon justice, it is an outrage upon our language to attempt to place in the same category a combination of men engaged in the speculation and the control of the products of labor and the products of the soil, on the one hand, and the associations of men and women who own nothing but themselves and undertake to control nothing but themselves and their power to work.

In another address to Congress on this same subject Mr. Gompers said:

That which we seek is not class legislation. It is a common custom in speaking to couple together the words "labor" and "capital" as though they stood for things of similar natures. Capital stands for material, tangible things, things separate and distinct from personality; labor is a human attribute indissolubly bound up with the human body. It is that by which man expresses the thought, the purpose, the self that is his own individuality; if he is a free man, he has the right to control this means of self-expression. This he values above all, for if he lose [*sic*] this right to decide the granting or withholding of his own labor, then freedom ceases and slavery begins. * * * Labor power is not a product; it is human ability to produce. Because of its very nature it can not be regarded as a trust or a corporation formed in restraint of trade.

[5.590] 8 Okla. Crim. 686, 130 P. 316 (1913).

[5.591] 8 Okla. Crim. at 695–96.

Any legislation or court construction dealing with the subject of organizations, corporations, or trusts which curtail or corner the products of labor can have no true application to the association of free men in the disposition or withholding of their labor power.

If it was a surprise when labor organizations were included in the terms of the antitrust law by the courts, it was certainly a greater astonishment when farmer organizations were also included. There seems, however, to have been but one prosecution of organizations of this kind that ever reached the higher courts, and it seems also to have been one of the very ⊥ few proceedings directly under the criminal section of the Sherman Act in any case. It is certainly a little strange that with all of the every-day violations of the antitrust laws by trust magnates in every section of the country that the poor farmers and laborers should have been selected as the only men to make an example of in cases of this character by criminal prosecution. I have always believed that if the men who sat at their desks in their offices in Wall Street in 1899 and deliberately planned and formed the Standard Oil Co., with its $100,000,000 capital stock, taking over and practically wiping out of existence 400 independent oil companies throughout the United States, giving themselves the practical control of 90 per cent of the domestic and export trade in oil, and who also at the same time planned and formed the Amalgamated Copper Co., with its $175,000,000 capital stock, for the purpose of purchasing and operating all of the copper-producing properties of the country without engaging in the mining business at all, neither owning nor operating a single mine, but acting simply as a security holding corporation, with its assets consisting only of stocks of other operating corporations, and the officers and directors associated with them in the formation of these companies had all been proceeded against criminally, convicted, and sentenced to the penitentiary, it would have done more toward putting a stop to monopolistic organizations than all of the laws we could pass in 100 years. It would have simply "nipped in the bud" all the unlawful high-finance schemes invented by the financial pirates of this country which have caused so much trouble to the business world in the last few years.

During the first 17 years of operation of the Sherman antitrust law the only persons convicted and sentenced under the criminal section of that act were eight farmers of Grant County, Ky. Twelve prominent farmers of that county were charged with the crime of conspiracy in restraint of interstate trade and commerce, the action was dismissed against 1 and acquittal was had in 3 cases and the remaining 8 were convicted and severally sentenced to pay heavy fines. The case is entitled Steers against United States,[5.592] and is reported in One hundred and ninety-second Federal Reporter, at page 1. A fair statement of the case is given by the defendant, J. G. Steers himself, as follows:[5.593]

The facts in brief are these: In the fall of 1907 Mr. W. T. Osborn was solicited to pool his tobacco. He refused kindly but positively. Then he proposed and promised to R. L. Conrad and several others of our good men that he would hold his tobacco until the 1907 pool was sold. We believed him sincere and trusted him to hold his tobacco.

Some time in November, 1907, he prized the tobacco, and in the week of the 29th of November, 1907, he hauled it to the Dry Ridge depot and received a bill of lading for shipment to Cincinnati.

This tobacco was in depot several days, and on Thanksgiving Day, November 28, 1907, a meeting of our local was called; a general rumor seemed to be going the rounds that something might happen to this tobacco that night. I and many others made talks urging peace, law, and order, and some one suggested that a committee be sent to see Mr. Osborn, to see if he would yet hold his tobacco. Then his best friends were looked for, and J. S. Carter, a brother-in-law of Osborn, and A. C. Webb, a lifelong neighbor and friend, were made a committee to go at once and see what he would do.

A young man, Hugh Lee Conrad, furnished a rig and drove it, so the three—Conrad, Webb, and Carter—drove out to see him, and the rest of us waited at the lodge for their return. They reported a very pleasant, social meeting with Mr. Osborn; they told him what the general rumor was and he said, "He was already uneasy about it and thought he had made a mistake." He was asked to take it back home, but would not do it. Then they proposed he let them put it in some place and hold it here; to this he said, "No; I won't do that; but if you

---

[5.592] 192 F. 1 (6th Cir. 1911).

[5.593] This statement does not appear in the reported decision.

will haul it back to my barns I will let it lay there until you say for me to sell it." To this the committee agreed, and all separated as the best of friends. Osborn followed them to the road and thanked them and invited all back to see him.

The local received the news with rejoicing and all going home feeling very kindly toward Mr. Osborn. On the next morning 200 or 300 men, some on foot, some on horseback, and some in buggies, and four wagons met at the depot, loaded the four hogsheads of tobacco on four wagons and had a little parade and marched two by two toward Mr. Osborn's. The tobacco was delivered in good shape and a general good feeling, love feast, engaged in by all present. If there was a threat made by anyone I never heard it nor heard of it. We were unable to even locate the rumor. I called on the local to know if there was a man in the house who knew of anyone who would likely do violence or make any threats against Mr. Osborn or his tobacco, and I failed to find any, only several seemed to have heard the rumor, but could not tell where or from whom.

(Signed) J. G. Steers.

This statement does not differ substantially from the statement of the case in the opinion of the court, except on the question of the threats against Osborn who had arranged to ship his tobacco, and defendants all claimed that there were no threats of any character made, and no force, coercion, or other unlawful means used or attempted by those who finally persuaded Osborn to hold on to his tobacco for a higher price. How these facts or circumstances could possibly amount to a violation of section 2 of the Sherman Antitrust Act is difficult to understand. In any event the conviction obtained under the facts in the case appealed so strongly to President Taft that he gave a full pardon to each of the defendants.

The Farmers' Union News of April 27, 1910, had this to say concerning the Kentucky convictions. I will ask leave to have it inserted as a part of my remarks without reading.

Mr. [JOHN F.] SHAFROTH [D., Colo.]. I wish the Senator would read that extract. It is very interesting and I should like to hear it read.

Mr. THOMPSON. I will be glad to read it.

THE KENTUCKY CONVICTIONS.

Eight of the eleven Kentuckians recently indicted by a United States grand jury have just been convicted in the United States district court and sentenced to pay fines ranging from $100 to $1,000. These eight were convicted under what is called the penal section of the Sherman Antitrust Act of 1890. They were convicted of "restraining interstate commerce." That is the heinous offense. The facts are simply these: Two or three years ago these men, who are excellent citizens of Grant County, Ky., and who stand high in the good opinions of their neighbors, persuaded one of their neighbors to haul his white-leaf tobacco back from the railroad station where he had taken it and had consigned it to a commission broker in Cincinnati, Ohio, just across the State line. For merely persuading a fellow friend and neighbor into withdrawing his products from the railroad's custody, which the shipper, the neighbor, had a perfect legal right to do, and where he had taken it and consigned it to a point in another State under the mistaken notion that the planters were no longer holding their tobacco, these eight men have been indicted and convicted of a crime. If the tobacco had been consigned to any town or city in Kentucky, the indictment and convictions could not have been, under the Sherman Act, which deals only with interstate and foreign commerce. What do you think of that? Much has been said on the Fourth of July and other patriotic occasions about this being a free country and about the inalienable rights of freedom of speech and the precious liberties we all enjoy in free America. But, Mr. Farmer, although the big trusts and monopolies have been allowed to run at large plotting, planning, and skinning you, both coming and going, the minute you get together or even talk of getting together in order to have some say about what you will take for your products or tell some friend he ought to hold his farm products, if they happen to have been consigned to a railroad company for shipment out of the State, you can be indicted and convicted of a crime under the Sherman Antitrust Act, which everybody knows was never intended to be used against anything or anyone except the big, thieving, robbing, oppressive monopolies and trusts. What is the matter with having Congress repeal that atrocious act, so ineffective against the trusts, and so outrageously unjust, and to our mind such an infringement of our liberties, both constitutionally and unconstitutionally?

Although the antitrust act was passed for the purpose of destroying trusts and the punishment of their promoters and others engaged in monopoly, it being clearly understood by the Members of Congress at the time of the passage of the act that it was not meant to apply and could not possibly be construed by anyone as applying to organizations of farmers or laboring men, yet farmers' societies and members of labor unions were the only persons indicted and convicted, all the big trust magnates being permitted to go their way and not a single one indicted until 1912 when the Cash Register people were convicted and sentenced.[5.594] The conviction of the eight Kentucky farmers, the leading citizens of their community, is an illustration of the way the administration of the laws through the courts is sometimes used in a manner not anticipated, where the laws are turned against the supposed beneficiaries by those at whom the legislation was originally aimed.

Mr. SHAFROTH. I understood the Senator to say—and I have listened to his address—that up to this time the first convictions or the only convictions had under the Sherman antitrust law were against combinations of either laborers or farmers?

Mr. THOMPSON. That is my understanding.

Mr. SHAFROTH. To what time?

Mr. THOMPSON. Up to 1907.

Mr. SHAFROTH. Thank you.

Mr. [CHARLES S.] THOMAS [D., Colo.]. The Senator from Kansas is making a most interesting and learned discussion on a very important feature of the pending measure. I want to call attention to the fact that, with the single exception of the Senator from Washington [Mr. JONES], sitting on this side of the Chamber, every seat upon the other side is vacant, and that three Senators upon the other side are engaged in a very earnest social or business discussion in one of the corners of the room.

Mr. THOMPSON. I hope it is not my speech that caused them to leave the Chamber. I notice it is a common practice indulged in by the other side whenever any Democrat speaks. So I do not feel at all slighted.

Mr. President, with the organization of the Consolidated Tobacco Co., in 1901, with its capital stock of over $500,000,000, acquiring or wiping out of existence about 150 concerns, the price of the finished manufactured product sold by the trust went soaring upward, and the price of the new unmanufactured tobacco raised and sold by the farmers to the trust went rapidly downward. The raw product of the farmers continued to go down to such a low point that there was not a decent living in its production for the Kentucky and other southern tobacco growers who, through dire necessity, were compelled to get together in a lawful organization to protect themselves against the unlawful acts of the Tobacco Trust. The trust had to have this white burley tobacco to use in the manufacture of certain proprietary brands. The white burley leaf was grown only in limited area in central Kentucky. The trust was obliged to send its officials to bargain with a committee representing practically all of the tobacco growers instead of sending its agents to the individual growers, as it had theretofore done, to beat down the price by making all kinds of misrepresentations to compel the growers to accept whatever the trust offered. Consequently the price of raw tobacco gradually went up.

The tobacco growers became contented and prosperous. They thought the problem had been solved and that they were getting their just share for the product of their own toil. In the meantime the managers of the Tobacco Trust were watching for an opportunity to prosecute the growers under the Sherman Antitrust Act. This chance finally came when a single grower, Mr. W. T. Osborn, and his two tenants, of Grant County, Ky., although not members of the farmers' organization known as the Society of Equity, or the Burley Society, which had pooled and was holding at its warehouse all the tobacco of its members until they could get a higher price, thinking the growers were selling, took their tobacco to the railroad station at Dry Ridge and consigned it to a commission firm just across the river in Ohio. But upon being told by several members of the farmers' society that they were not selling yet finally joined them by canceling the sale and hauling the tobacco back home. These eight men, who resorted simply to the right of "free speech," were indicted and convicted of the crime of conspiring to restrain interstate trade and commerce.[5.595] At the same time the big trusts, such as the Standard Oil, Tobacco Trust, and other trusts, which were being

---

[5.594] The conviction was later overruled, Patterson v. United States, 222 F. 599 (6th Cir.), *cert. denied*, 238 U.S. 635 (1915).

[5.595] *See* United States v. Steers, 192 F. 1 (6th Cir. 1911) (affirming the unreported conviction).

proceeded against in the courts, and although found guilty were merely called into court and told to dissolve, and no attempt whatever was made under section 6 of the act to forfeit their property engaged in interstate commerce. No wonder President Taft pardoned all of the farmers convicted in the prosecution against them.

They had simply peaceably agreed to hold their crop until they could get a higher price—a price sufficient to reasonably compensate them for their labor. There could certainly be nothing wrong in this, any more than if we Senators were all wheat growers and would agree among ourselves to hold our crop until we could get $1 per bushel. I formerly knew an old successful farmer who always held his crops, and encouraged his neighbors to do likewise, until he received at least 30 cents per bushel for his corn and at least 50 cents per bushel for his wheat. He figured that he had to receive this price in order to get back the cost of growing, with a fair profit for his time and labor. This farmer lived to be nearly a hundred years old, and was worth a round $100,000 when he died, showing an average of $1,000 savings for every year of his life. This was only common-sense business prudence, and no one ever imagined that he was in any way violating the antitrust law.

Farming in this country is one of the most honorable and useful occupations in which our citizens can engage. Daniel Webster said concerning farmers:

> The farmers are the founders of human civilization. Not only that, they are the lasting foundation. Let us never forget that the cultivation of the earth is the most important labor of man. Unstable is the future of a country which has lost its taste for agriculture. If there is one lesson of history that is unmistakable, it is that national strength lies very near the soil.

Although farmers are perhaps imposed upon more than any other class of citizens, they are the most law-abiding and patriotic people of the country. They perform the most important duties required for the highest type of citizenship. We could go longer without the followers of any other occupation much easier than without the farmer. Farmers are the real producers of the country, and without them the entire populace would eventually starve. They receive less for the value of their toil than any other laborers. They pay more taxes in proportion to the benefits received than any other citizen. They are therefore entitled to the highest protection of the law and of every reasonable favor in exemption that can legally and properly be extended to them in legislation or otherwise. This exemption from prosecution for associating together to protect themselves in order to secure just compensation for their products is certainly right and clearly legal for the reasons already stated. Organized labor and the farmer are seeking only legislative relief that they may not be prohibited from doing the things "not in themselves unlawful." That there is demand for this legislation is clearly shown by the action of the national meeting of the Farmers' Educational and Cooperative Union, which was held in my State at Salina last September, and adopted the following resolution.

I ask that the resolution be made a part of my remarks without reading.

Mr. SHAFROTH. I hope the Senator will read it. I am very much interested in his address, and I would like to hear the resolution read.

Mr. THOMPSON. Very well. I will gladly read it.

> Whereas according to the debates and statements made by Senators and Congressmen in charge of the bill on the floor of Congress in 1888 to 1890 it was never intended that the Sherman Antitrust Act should apply to aggregations of individuals, but only to aggregations of capital engineered by a few big speculators seeking unreasonable prices and profits; and
> Whereas during the first 17 years of the act the only convictions under the criminal section were farmers, promptly pardoned as a plain miscarriage of justice, the courts misinterpreting and misconstruing the act even to the extent of judicially legislating the word "unreasonable" into the law, wrongfully holding that trade meant traders, and that any interference with trade when done by farmers or by any persons, except, apparently, the big trust magnates, was criminal restraint of trade: Therefore be it
> *Resolved,* That the Farmers' Educational and Cooperative Union of America commend the action of Congress in limiting the $300,000 appropriation to the aggressive enforcement of the act and the real objects of the legislation, namely, the big trusts, and urge the importance of legislation that will correct the judicial legislation of the courts which have wrongfully decided

that it means things Congress never intended and the people never expected and the construction placed upon the said law by the former and present President of the United States.

This farmers' organization is composed of over 3,000,000 farmers, completely organized in 21 States of the Union and with auxilliary local organizations in 11 other States.

The Democratic platform in 1908, repeated in 1912, on this important question, declared as follows:

> The expanding organization of industry makes it essential that there should be no abridgment of the right of wage earners and producers to organize for the protection of wages and the improvement of labor conditions to the end that such labor organizations and their members should not be regarded as illegal combinations in restraint of trade.

President Wilson in his speech of acceptance of the presidential nomination spoke concerning working men as follows:

> The working people of America—if they must be distinguished from the minority that constitutes the rest of it—are, of course, the backbone of the Nation. No law that safeguards their life, that improves the physical and moral conditions under which they live, that makes their (the working people of America) hours of labor rational and tolerable, that gives them freedom to act in their own interests, and that protects them where they can not protect themselves can properly be regarded as class legislation or as anything but a measure taken in the interest of the whole people, whose partnership in right action we are trying to establish and make real and practical. It is in this spirit that we shall act if we are genuine spokesmen of the whole country.

Therefore, the exemption of the farmer and labor organizations as contemplated in this act, being right, legal, and clearly in accordance with the Democratic policy on this subject, I hope that the proposed legislation will be enacted.

Mr. SHAFROTH. I should like to ask the Senator whether he has examined into the statistics as to the number of antitrust indictments that have been made against labor organizations and farmers' organizations, and also whether he has examined as to how many indictments have been found among the large business people against those who combined for interference with interstate commerce? . . .

Mr. ASHURST. If the Senator will permit me I will state that upon an examination recently made by myself I find that the Sherman antitrust law has been brought into requisition in 101 cases against farmers' and labor organizations.

Mr. SHAFROTH. How many against the big trusts?

Mr. ASHURST. I am sure that the same zeal that was used against the farmers' and laborers' organizations has never been exercised and used against the trusts.

Mr. THOMPSON. I will say for the information of the Senator from Colorado that I think there is a list published and it is furnished by the document room. My attention was called to it. I did not take the pains to count them to ascertain just how many; but I did look through it hurriedly to find that the first criminal prosecution of any sort was against farmers under the criminal section of the statute. . . .

Mr. [WESLEY L.] JONES [R., Wash.]. I desire to get the views of the Senator from Kansas as to how far he thinks this provision of the proposed law goes. Does it go any further than recognizing the legality of these organizations as organizations, or does it permit these organizations, after they are organized, to then go on and do things in restraint of trade and exempt them from prosecution for such acts?

Mr. THOMPSON. I think it exempts them simply as lawful organizations; but, of course, if they do anything unlawful or use any unlawful means, they are subject to prosecution under the antitrust law and under the general laws on the subject without regard to the antitrust law.

Mr. JONES. That is what I wanted to get at; that is about my idea with reference to how far this provision goes.

⊥ Mr. THOMPSON. The provision only protects such organizations in the performance of lawful acts, as I understand.

Mr. JONES. It prevents the court from holding as a conspiracy in violation of the Sherman law simply because of their organization?

Mr. THOMPSON. That is the intention, as I understand.

Mr. JONES. As I understand, that is the Senator's idea as to the extent to which this provision goes?

Mr. THOMPSON. Yes, sir.

Mr. JONES. I saw a statement purporting to come from the President that this provision, in effect, simply recognizes as lawful what many of the courts already hold is legal, and does not go any further; and, as I understand, the chairman of the Judiciary Committee of the other House gave out a statement to the press in which he held the same view; in other words, as the Senator understands, this provision does not really exempt any of these organizations from prosecution for the commission of acts which would, in fact, be in restraint of trade, and therefore prohibited by the Sherman antitrust law, but it does recognize their right to exist as organizations; the mere fact that they are organizations does not warrant any prosecution against them?

Mr. THOMPSON. No; nor for performing lawful acts in connection with the purposes of the organization.

Mr. JONES. Of course, they could not be prosecuted for performing lawful acts.

Mr. THOMPSON. Withholding crops for higher prices, refusing to work for certain wages, and acts of that character would not be unlawful; nor could you prosecute them for the mere fact that they are organized to protect themselves any more than you could prosecute the Masons or Odd Fellows or any other secret society by reason of their organization for the common good of all their members.

Mr. JONES. I merely wanted to get the Senator's idea. That was and is my idea as to what this section means.

Mr. CULBERSON. Mr. President, out of consideration for the Senate, as well as for myself, it is not my purpose to deliver any extended remarks on this measure; but I desire to invite the attention of the Senate briefly to the general outlines of the bill.

As is well known to the Senate, four general legislative purposes are sought to be accomplished by the bill under consideration:

First. It is proposed, without amending the Sherman Antitrust Act, approved July 2, 1890, to supplement that act by denouncing and making unlawful certain trade practices which, while not covered by that act because not amounting to restraint of commerce or monopoly in themselves, yet constitute elements tending ultimately to violations of that act. The trade practices made illegal by the bill are discrimination in prices for the purpose of unlawfully injuring or destroying the business of competitors, exclusive and tying contracts, holding companies, and interlocking directorates.

Second. It is proposed by the bill to further supplement existing antitrust acts by a provision that whenever a corporation shall violate the antitrust laws such violation shall be deemed as that also of the individual directors and officers who shall have authorized or participated in the acts constituting such violation, thereby establishing the personal guilt of the officials of the corporation who are really responsible for its illegal conduct.

Third. Following the original purpose of the framers of the Sherman antitrust law, the bill proposes expressly to exempt labor, agricultural, horticultural, and other organizations from the operation of the antitrust laws.

Fourth. The bill seeks to regulate the issuance of temporary restraining orders and injunctions generally by the courts of the United States, and particularly in labor controversies, and to make provision for the trial by jury in contempts which are committed beyond the presence of the court.

Many amendments to the bill are proposed by the committee, but the general scope of the bill is not altered by these amendments. While the amendments do not propose to depart from the general object of the bill, yet in some instances the form of the substantive law, as well as the remedies provided for its enforcement, are proposed to be changed. In sections 2 and 4, which deal with price discriminations and exclusive and tying contracts, respectively, instead of providing that the acts named shall constitute offenses punishable by fine and imprisonment, as in the House bill, the proposed amendments declare the acts unlawful and provide for the general enforcement of the sections through the agency of the Federal trade commission, the creation of which is provided for in a bill which recently passed the Senate and is now in conference. In sections 8 and 9, which deal with holding companies and interlocking directorates, respectively, some changes have been made in the provisions of positive law, and the general enforcement of the sections has been confided by the amendments to the Interstate Commerce Commission in the case of common carriers and to the Federal trade commission in the case of individuals, partnerships, and industrial corporations.

The pertinency and effect of the other amendments proposed by the committee will appear as we proceed with their consideration. I now ask unanimous consent that the bill may be read for the consideration of the committee amendments.

Mr. GALLINGER. Does the Senator ask that the formal reading of the bill be dispensed with?

Mr. CULBERSON. The formal reading has been had. The bill has been read at length.

The PRESIDING OFFICER. Is there objection to the request of the Senator from Texas? The Chair hears none. The Secretary will state the first amendment reported by the committee. . . .

Mr. GALLINGER. Mr. President, when the Senator from Texas was proceeding to ask that the bill should be read for amendment, and that the amendments of the committee should be first considered, there were only a few Senators in the Chamber, and I thought it but fair that Senators should have an opportunity to be present. I want the Senator to know that I did not call for a quorum for the purpose of delay at all. I do not expect to say a word on this bill, and I hope it will be speedily considered; and it is likely I shall not again call for a quorum; but I thought that the Senators perhaps were not aware of the fact that the bill was being considered, and as 60 Senators had answered to their names a little while ago, I thought we would secure a quorum speedily, and that the call would not create much delay.

The PRESIDING OFFICER. The Secretary will state the first amendment reported by the committee.

The first amendment of the Committee on the Judiciary was, in section 1, page 2, line 17, after the name "United States," to insert, "*Provided*, That nothing in this act contained shall apply to the Philippine Islands," so as to make the clause read:

"Commerce," as used herein, means trade or commerce among the several States and with foreign nations, or between the District of Columbia or any Territory of the United States and any State, Territory, or foreign nation, or between any insular possessions or other places under the jurisdiction of the United States, or between any such possession or place and any State or Territory of the United States or the District of Columbia or any foreign nation, or within the District of Columbia or any Territory or any insular possession or other place under the jurisdiction of the United States: *Provided*, That nothing in this act contained shall apply to the Philippine Islands.

The amendment was agreed to.

Mr. CULBERSON. Mr. President, when the Committee on the Judiciary made their report on this bill, they proposed a number of amendments to section 2. Since then the Federal trade commission bill has passed the Senate and is now in conference. Under that bill all questions affecting unfair competition are to be submitted to that tribunal. I am now authorized by the committee to abandon the amendments to section 2, and to move in lieu thereof that the entire section 2 be stricken out, for the reason that the general subject embraced in that section can be dealt with by the Federal trade commission, as provided for in the trade commission bill.

The PRESIDING OFFICER. The question is on the motion of the Senator from Texas to strike out section 2.

The motion was agreed to.

The next amendment of the Committee on the Judiciary was, on page 3, after line 24, to strike out section 3, as follows:

SEC. 3. That it shall be unlawful for the owner, operator, or transporter of the product or products of any mine, oil or gas well, reduction works, refinery, or hydroelectric plant producing coal, oil, gas, or hydroelectric energy, or for any person controlling the products thereof, engaged in selling such product in commerce to refuse arbitrarily to sell such product to a responsible person, firm, or corporation who applies to purchase such product for use, consumption, or resale within the United States or any Territory thereof or the District of

Columbia or any insular possession or other place under the jurisdiction of the United States, and any person violating this section shall be deemed guilty of a misdemeanor and shall be punished as provided in the preceding section.

Mr. JONES. Mr. President, I should like to know why that section is proposed to be stricken out. It is a provision of the House bill and affects certain enumerated products. I should like to know whether there is any special reason why those products should not be brought under the terms of this bill.

If we strike out that section, it would seem to permit a dealer in the products enumerated to refuse arbitrarily to sell to anyone.

Mr. CULBERSON. If we strike out the section, the question is left open like all other sales questions are left open for the parties. I will read the reasons given in the committee report recommending that section 3 be stricken out. They are as follows:

> The proposed Senate amendment is to strike out this section altogether, because, in the opinion of the committee, it would be unwise to enact such legislation as is contained in it. It would, primarily, deny freedom of contract to one of the parties, and consequently would be of doubtful constitutional validity. Passing from this consideration, the committee believe that such an enactment, which would practically compel owners of the products named to sell to anyone or else decline to do so at the peril of incurring heavy penalties, would project us into a field of legislation at once untried, complicated, and dangerous.

Those are the reasons which impelled the committee to recommend that section 3 be stricken out.

Mr. JONES. Was the committee unanimous in that conclusion?

Mr. [LEE S.] OVERMAN [D., N.C.]. Yes.

Mr. CULBERSON. I think so.

The PRESIDING OFFICER. The question is on the amendment reported by the committee to strike out section 3.

The amendment was agreed to.

Mr. CULBERSON. What I said a moment ago, Mr. President, with reference to section 2, applies with equal force to section 4. That is one of the matters pertaining to unfair competition, and as that general subject has been treated in the bill which has passed the Senate and is now in conference, the committee, instead of recommending the amendments to the section, withdraw those proposed amendments and suggest that the entire section 4 be stricken out.

The PRESIDING OFFICER. The question is on the motion of the Senator from Texas to strike out section 4.

The motion was agreed to.

Mr. JONES. Mr. President, before we proceed to the next committee amendment I should like to ask the chairman of the committee if it is his judgment that section 5 would apply to violations of the trade commission bill when it shall become a law?

Mr. CULBERSON. I do not think it will.

Mr. JONES. The Senator does not think that that act will constitute one of the antitrust laws within the meaning of section 5?

Mr. [ALBERT B.] CUMMINS [R., Iowa]. Mr. President, that would depend entirely on whether the definition of the antitrust laws remains as it is in the trade commission bill. If that definition is broadened so as to include the trade commission bill as one of the antitrust laws, then this section would cover any violation of that law.

Mr. CULBERSON. This bill itself does not provide that the trade commission bill, when it finally becomes a law, shall be included within the antitrust laws as named in this bill, nor does the Federal trade commission bill so provide, as I remember.

The next amendment was, on page 5, line 12, after the words "Sec. 6," to strike out:

> That whenever in any suit or proceeding in equity hereafter brought by or on behalf of the United States under any of the antitrust laws there shall have been rendered a final judgment or decree to the effect that a defendant has entered into a contract, combination in the form of trust or otherwise, or conspiracy, in restraint of trade or commerce, or has monopolized, or attempted to monopolize or combined with any person or persons to monopolize, any part of commerce, in violation of any of the antitrust laws said judgment or decree shall, to the full extent to which such judgment or decree would constitute in any other proceeding an estoppel

as between the United States and such defendant, constitute against such defendant conclusive evidence of the same facts, and be conclusive as to the same questions of law in favor of any other party in any action or proceeding brought under or involving the provisions of any of the antitrust laws.

Whenever any suit or proceeding in equity is hereafter brought by or on behalf of the United States, under any of the antitrust laws, the statute of limitations in respect of each and every private right of action arising under such antitrust laws and based, in whole or in part, on any matter complained of in said suit or proceeding in equity shall be suspended during the pendency of such suit or proceeding in equity.

And to insert:

That a final judgment or decree rendered in any suit or proceeding in equity brought by or on behalf of the United States under the antitrust laws to the effect that a defendant has violated said laws shall be prima facie evidence against such defendant in any suit or proceeding brought by any other party against such defendant under said laws as to all matters respecting which said judgment or decree would be an estoppel as between the parties thereto.

Any person may be prosecuted, tried, or punished for any offense under the antitrust laws, and any suit arising under those laws may be maintained if the indictment is found or the suit is brought within six years next after the occurrence of the act or cause of action complained of, any statute of limitation or other provision of law heretofore enacted to the contrary notwithstanding. Whenever any suit or proceeding in equity is instituted by the United States to prevent or restrain violations of any of the antitrust laws the running of the statute of limitations in respect of each and every private right of action arising under said laws and based in whole or in part on any matter complained of in said suit or proceeding shall be suspended during the pendency thereof: *Provided*, That this shall not be held to extend the statute of limitations in the case of offenses heretofore committed.

Mr. THOMAS. Mr. President, I suggest that, after the word "equity," on line 13, page 6, there should be inserted the words "now pending or hereafter," so that it would read:

That a final judgment or decree rendered in any suit or proceeding in equity now pending or hereafter brought by or on behalf of the United States—

And so forth.

It seems to me the public should have the benefit of the provisions of the proposed amendment both as to suits that are now pending, and which have not proceeded as far as judgment or decree, and as to those which may be brought after the bill becomes a law.

Mr. CUMMINS. Mr. President, I have not considered the constitutional phase of the matter very carefully, but as I look at it the amendment proposed by the Senator from Colorado would be a limitation upon the amendment rather than an enlargement of it. As I understand this section, it applies to all decrees heretofore rendered as well as to decrees hereafter rendered, and makes those decrees prima facie evidence in suits brought by individuals for the recovery of damages.

Mr. THOMAS. If the Senator is correct, then, of course, my amendment would be a limitation, but I do not so understand the phraseology of the amendment. Generally speaking, I think it may be said that the presumption is against the retroactive character of legislation. There must be something in express terms to make it retroactive.

Mr. CUMMINS. May I suggest—

Mr. THOMAS. I would suggest, if the Senator will pardon me, that perhaps in the amendment, instead of using the words "now pending or hereafter," we might use the words "heretofore or hereafter," so that it would read:

That a final judgment or decree rendered in any suit or proceeding in equity heretofore or hereafter brought—

And so forth.

Mr. CUMMINS. As I understand, this section is prospective so far as it relates to suits brought by individuals; that is, suits that may be hereafter brought. That would be, I think, the construction given by the courts.

⊥ Mr. THOMAS. Yes; it is for the benefit of individual litigants hereafter.

Mr. CUMMINS. But when the suit is brought, then the judgment or decree of the court in the suit that has been brought by the Government would be prima facie evidence of violation of the antitrust law, no matter whether that decree is rendered hereafter or whether it has already been rendered; and I see no constitutional objection to making it so. In other words, it is simply a rule of evidence.

Mr. THOMAS. There might be, Mr. President, constitutional objection to making a judgment prima facie evidence in some suit thereafter brought when the judgment was rendered prior to the enactment of the law. There could be none with reference to pending cases in which judgment would be subsequently rendered. Of course, I do not mean to say that there is a constitutional objection in either case, but I think there is an ambiguity here— . . .

. . . I think there is an ambiguity here to which the principle that legislation will not be presumed to be retroactive would apply if we do not make it clear.

I now yield to the Senator from Minnesota.

Mr. NELSON. I desire to say to the Senator that I think he is decidedly right. The general rule of construction about statutes of this kind is that unless it expressly otherwise appears from the phraseology of the statute it has no retroactive effect; it applies only to future cases. I do not think this provision in lines 12, 13, 14, and so on, applies to anything except future cases as the language stands now.

Mr. THOMAS. Inasmuch as there is room for difference of opinion, which is quite evident, I think it should be amended so that it will read:

That a final judgment or decree rendered in any suit or proceeding in equity heretofore or hereafter brought.

So that there could be no question about it.

Mr. CUMMINS. "Heretofore brought or now pending or hereafter brought."

Mr. THOMAS. My first amendment was "now pending or hereafter brought," and the Senator objected to that.

Mr. CUMMINS. Unless there is a constitutional objection I should be very sorry to see it limited to decrees or judgments rendered in cases pending or hereafter brought.

Mr. THOMAS. Then the word "heretofore" would answer the purpose the Senator has in mind.

Mr. CUMMINS. For instance, take the decree in the American Tobacco case[5.596] or the Standard Oil case.[5.597] Suppose a person injured by either of those companies should bring suit to recover damages. I see no reason why the decree already rendered against those companies should not be made prima facie evidence in favor of the individual who brings the suit for damages.

Mr. THOMAS. I have no objection to that, Mr. President, but I think the amendment is necessary in order that the purpose which the Senator has in mind may be certainly and effectively carried out.

Mr. CUMMINS. I am rather inclined to agree with that. . . .

Mr. CULBERSON. I will read from the syllabus in the case of Union Pacific Railroad Co. versus Laramie Stockyards Co., in Two hundred and thirty-first United States:

The first rule of construction of statutes is that legislation is addressed to the future and not to the past. This rule is one of obvious justice.[5.598]

So I suggest that if we amend this language in any respect we ought to insert the word "hereafter" instead of the word "heretofore," because the rule of the Supreme Court of the United States is, as suggested by the syllabus I have just read, that it is a rule of obvious justice that statutes shall only act prospectively and not retroactively.

Mr. CUMMINS. Mr. President, I do not agree that it is universal law that there

---

[5.596] United States v. American Tobacco Co., 221 U.S. 106, 31 S. Ct. 632, 55 L. Ed. 663 (1911), portions of which are reprinted *supra* at chapter 1.

[5.597] Standard Oil Co. v. United States, 221 U.S. 1, 31 S. Ct. 502, 55 L. Ed. 619 (1911), portions of which are reprinted *supra* at chapter 1.

[5.598] 231 U.S. 190, 199, 34 S. Ct. 101, 102, 58 L. Ed. 179, 182 (1913).

can be no retroactive effect of a statute without coming into collision with the Constitution. A great many of our statutes are retroactive; but it would not be a retroactive statute in this case to make a judgment heretofore rendered, assuming that we have the right to deal with it in that manner, prima facie evidence in a suit hereafter brought. It is prospective in regard to the suits in which the judgment shall be evidence, and is not retroactive in the sense of the suggestion made by the Supreme Court in the case just cited.

There is no difference in principle between making a judgment already rendered between third parties prima facie evidence in another suit and doing the same thing as to judgments hereafter rendered. The person who is to be affected can not be admitted as a party in any suit hereafter brought nor to any decree hereafter rendered, so that the principle of the rule is just the same in either case.

Mr. THOMAS. Mr. President, the rule as announced by the Supreme Court in the case cited by the Senator from Texas is the universal rule, and it is, as there stated, an obviously just one, but it does not apply to statutes which in terms take effect prior to the time of their enactment. There are many State constitutions which forbid retroactive legislation of any sort. The Federal Constitution forbids Congress from enacting any ex post facto law, which, of course, has a technical meaning, and is applied to criminal statutes.

I quite agree with the Senator from Iowa that a decision favorable to the Government, rendered in a case brought by the United States against violators of the antitrust acts, should be prima facie evidence in actions brought by individuals against the same concern to recover damages which they have suffered from that violation or any other of similar character; but there are a great many cases pending in which, if this obvious construction be given to the statute as the amendment is phrased as reported here to the Senate, the litigants interested would be excluded from the prima facie effect which this statute gives to judgments rendered in cases brought after the bill shall become law.

Personally, I see no room for distinction, in justice and fairness, between the application of this principle in the Tobacco case or the Standard Oil case or any other case which has heretofore gone to judgment, as regards litigants bringing suit under this bill after its enactment, and its application to judgments rendered under suits brought by the Government after its enactment. The decision to which the Senator has referred makes the amendment which I suggest absolutely necessary, unless the Senate intends that it shall be only prospective in its operation.

Mr. [WILLIAM E.] CHILTON [D., W. Va.]. Mr. President, I should like to ask the Senator whether the application of the decision read by the Senator from Texas does not depend upon the meaning of the word "rendered"?

Mr. THOMAS. No; I think not.

Mr. CHILTON. The provision reads:

> That a final judgment or decree rendered in any suit or proceeding.

Mr. THOMAS. No; I think the word "brought" controls.

Mr. CHILTON. Does not that mean a decree or judgment hereafter rendered?

Mr. THOMAS. No; I think the word "brought" in this sentence, when the principle of the decision in Two hundred and thirty-first United States is applied to the amendment, would have that effect and would have reference to suits brought by the Government subsequently to the enactment of the law.

Mr. CHILTON. Mr. President, I can hardly agree with the Senator. This language refers to judgments or decrees rendered in any suit. Under the well-settled principle read by the Senator from Texas, of course, the word "rendered" there would be construed prospectively—that is, it would be held to apply to decrees hereafter rendered. I understand that is the meaning of the decision read by the Senator from Texas, and I take it that if we want it to mean something else it will have to be amended.

Mr. CULBERSON. I notice that on page 5, in the provision which we strike out and propose to amend in this respect, the House uses the word "hereafter" before the word "brought"; and I think it means the same as the Senate amendment in that respect.

Mr. CHILTON. I think, though, our attention should be centered upon when the decree was rendered. When the suit was brought makes no difference. The fact that the suit was brought 10 years ago, and has not yet reached judgment or decree, would make no difference. This is purely a matter of evidence.

Mr. CULBERSON. If the suit should be brought hereafter, the judgment could not be rendered prior to that, of course.

Mr. CHILTON. Certainly not; and that only emphasizes what I am saying. We are legislating as to certain decrees rendered. Now, under the law that means decrees hereafter rendered, and it makes no difference when the suit is brought. It is purely making it a matter of evidence, which is within our power, and I take it that under this language it means decrees hereafter rendered. I should think there would be no doubt about that.

Mr. [ATLEE] POMERENE [D., Ohio]. Mr. President, I am disposed to agree with the construction which the Senator from West Virginia places upon that language, but would it not avoid all uncertainty to insert the word "hereafter"?

Mr. CHILTON. It depends upon what is the judgment of the Senate. As the language is now, it is perfectly clear that it has a prospective meaning, and it refers to judgments and decrees hereafter rendered. It depends upon what is the judgment of the Senate finally as to what it wants. I am speaking of the language used.

Mr. [THOMAS J.] WALSH [D., Mont.]. Mr. President, referring to the remark made by the chairman of the committee [Mr. CULBERSON], I call the attention of the Senate to the fact that the word "hereafter" is quite appropriate in the House provision, which proceeds upon an entirely different basis. The House provision makes the judgment rendered conclusive of the facts and the law therein determined. Of course you could not make a judgment rendered in the past conclusive when it was not at the time it was rendered; and therefore, to give any force or effect at all to the House provision, you must have the word "hereafter" there. Indeed if the word "hereafter" were not in the House provision, the courts would so construe it anyway. It is, however, entirely unnecessary in order to give validity to the provision made by the Senate committee, because the Senate committee's amendment makes the judgment simply prima facie evidence; and the principle is thoroughly well established that you can declare a judgment rendered in the past to be prima facie evidence in the future, but you can not, as a matter of course, make it conclusive.

Mr. President, now that this matter has been precipitated, I desire to say that when this Senate amendment shall have been perfected it is my purpose to ask the Senate to reject the amendment and to stand upon the House provision; and if the Senate will bear with me a little while I desire to speak about that matter now.

The essential difference between the House provision and the Senate amendment is that under the House provision all judgments rendered in antitrust cases are made conclusive, both as to the facts and as to the law, in any action thereafter brought by a private individual against the corporation adjudged to have offended against the antitrust law, while the Senate provision makes the judgment simply prima facie evidence of the facts therein determined.

The operation of the thing is this: If the United States shall proceed against any organization said to be a combination in violation of the Sherman Act, and eventually, after a judicial proceeding going through all the courts, it shall be determined and decided that the organization is a combination in violation of the Sherman Act, that judgment stands and can be availed of by anybody who claims to have been damaged by reason of the existence of the combination. The party seeking to take advantage of it will not be obliged to travel again, step by step, over the entire field which the Government has been obliged to traverse in order to reach the judgment at which it arrived; but he will start in where the Government left off, the judgment being conclusive, establishing the facts and the law so far as it goes, and allowing him simply to establish and putting upon him the burden of establishing the actual damages which he has suffered. In other words, we give to the private individual the benefit which accrues by reason of the long litigation pursued by the Government in endeavoring to secure the judgment.

The amendment proposed by the Senate committee, however, simply makes that judgment prima facie evidence, so that when the individual citizen, claiming to be damnified by reason of the organization thus adjudged to be in violation of law brings his action to recover damages, he may submit in evidence the judgment and then prove his damages; but, although that will make a case for him, the organization still has a right to submit other evidence, to have a further trial upon the matter, and eventually to get a judgment overturning, if it can, the judgment that was rendered in the action brought by the United States Government.

What does that mean? That means that every private individual seeking to recover damages must go into court recognizing that he will be obliged to meet any additional evidence that the outlawed corporation may be able to command in order to arrive at a different result in the proceedings, and, as a matter of course, he must make his own provision in order to meet that testimony. We all know that the private individual is always at a disadvantage. He is never armed with the means at his command to cope with these great organizations; and that was the very reason why this act was passed—in order that the Government, with its great powers, might meet on something like equal terms the great aggregations of capital against which the statute was leveled.

I may say here—and I think I violate no confidence in saying it—that the force of these suggestions appealed powerfully to every member of the Judiciary Committee; and I believe that were it not for the fact that most of those members believed that the House provision violated constitutional principles the amendment suggested never would have been proposed at all. . . .

Mr. CULBERSON. On the point to which the Senator has just alluded, if he will permit me, I will read him a sentence or two from the report of the committee:

> The material difference between the House provision and the Senate amendment is, of course, whether the decree in favor of the Government shall be prima facie evidence against the same defendant in a subsequent suit by another party or be conclusive against such defendant. The committee think there are considerations of public policy which favor the House provision of conclusiveness; but in the state of the decisions of the Supreme Court of the United States in kindred cases they believe the law should go no further than to make the decree prima facie evidence.

Mr. WALSH. I am very glad the Senator has called the attention of the Senate to the report of the committee confirmatory of the suggestions I have been making, and I believe the wisdom of the policy of the House provision will address itself, upon the very slightest consideration, to every Member of this body. So it becomes simply a question whether we may, consistently with the provisions of the Constitution, make a judgment rendered in an action brought by the Government of the United States conclusive in subsequent proceedings brought by a private individual to recover damages sustained by him in consequence of the conduct of the defendant in the Government's suit. With all deference to the opinions of my colleagues upon the Judiciary Committee—and I speak with entire respect—I say that I am unable to understand the argument which would condemn an act of that character as in violation of the Constitution.

Why, Mr. President, the defendant, the violating corporation, has had its day in court. It has had an opportunity to try out before a court, with all the forms of the law, every question involved in the lawsuit. It has tried them, and all of the issues have been determined against it. I ask, Mr. President, upon what principles of constitutional law can it rely for justification of a second trial of these very same issues? . . .

Mr. THOMAS. Suppose the Senator from Montana were a defendant in a suit brought by the Senator from Nebraska, who prevailed in the action, obtaining a judgment against the Senator from Montana. Subsequently I bring an action growing out of the same transaction. Does the Senator believe that a statute making the judgment of the Senator from Nebraska against the Senator from Montana conclusive in the action which I brought would be constitutional?

Mr. WALSH. I should say not.

Mr. THOMAS. I do not myself perceive any distinction between the case supposed and that of a suit brought by the Government against an offending corporation.

Mr. WALSH. I think I can demonstrate it very readily. I was going to try to do so.

Mr. THOMAS. I shall be very glad to have the Senator do so.

Mr. WALSH. The Senator has asked me whether a judgment taken by him against the Senator from Nebraska could be made conclusive in a subsequent action which he brought against me involving exactly the same facts.

Mr. THOMAS. Oh, no; the Senator is slightly in error in his statement. I supposed a case brought by the Senator from Nebraska against the Senator from Montana resulting in final judgment. I then supposed a case brought by myself against the Senator from Montana growing out of the same transaction, and asked whether a statute making the former judgment conclusive against the Senator from Montana in the case brought by me would be constitutional. I understood the Senator to say "No." My further query was as to the difference between the case supposed and one brought by the Government against an offending corporation under the antitrust act.

Mr. WALSH. I am unable to perceive any differnce between the condition of facts now stated by the Senator from Colorado and the condition of facts that I have stated. I will say that, depending upon the relations that subsist between the Senator from Nebraska and myself, a judgment against him might be very easily made conclusive against me.

In fact, Mr. President, there are many relations in life and in business under which a judgment taken against one man is made conclusive against another man, to which I desire to advert. A judgment taken against an agent is under many circumstances made conclusive against the principal. A judgment taken against one individual of a class is very often made ⊥ conclusive against everyone belonging to the same class. A judgment taken against a city in a suit brought by a single taxpayer or a citizen of the city is often made conclusive in any proceeding subsequently brought by another citizen. Oftentimes an action is brought, for instance, by a citizen, a taxpayer, against the city and against parties said to be in collusion with the officers of the city in the transaction of certain business.

The judgment goes against that party adjudging that the proceeding was under the law and was warranted. That judgment becomes conclusive against any other citizen of the city desiring to prosecute the same character of action.

So, Mr. President, in all these antitrust prosecutions the Government of the United States prosecutes the action for the benefit of every one of its citizens. Otherwise there is no justification for the law at all. The Government of the United States sues in the action as parens patriae, the father of all its children, and for their benefit. That is the relation which exists between the United States suing under one of these antitrust acts and all others of its citizens, and there is no reason at all why the judgment, so far as it goes, should not be made conclusive against a corporation when it is sued for damages to it resulting from the very acts complained of.

Mr. President, this is what might result under the existing state of the law or under the amendment proposed by the Senate committee. A judgment will have gone against the corporation adjudging it to be in existence in violation of the Sherman Antitrust Act. That lawsuit will have been fought out bitterly, desperately, through a long series of years at an enormous expense to both the litigants thereto, the contest being upon both the facts and the law, and judgment finally goes against the corporation. Then, Mr. President, you not only open up the matter and allow the corporation to put in additional evidence as against a private individual suing to recover his damages on account of the unlawful corporation, but legal principles are again opened up for determination, and in the action brought by the private individual, after harrying him clear through the courts to the court of last resort, you may find different legal principles even announced and principles that would have defeated the action in the first instance. In other words, unless you make this complete, it practically amounts to no assistance whatever to the man who desires to recover damages by reason of the combination adjudged to be unlawful.

Mr. President, in view of the relationship which exists between the Government upon the one hand and its citizens upon the other, I entertain no doubt whatever that when the law and the facts are tried out in the action brought by the Government on behalf of every one of its citizens, any one of them is entitled to have the benefit of that judgment, and to say these matters are all foreclosed and determined, and to insist that the only question which remains for consideration is the damages suffered by it.

Accordingly, I believe, Mr. President, that the House provision ought to remain in the bill, but, of course, if it does, you must leave the word "hereafter" there, because obviously the conclusive effect can not be given to judgments heretofore rendered.

Mr. [WILLIAM] HUGHES [D., N.J.]. Let me ask the Senator a question. I have heard only the latter part of the Senator's argument. It seemed to me that the provision of the Senate conmittee is quite an original departure from the House bill, and I wondered what the effect would be of striking out the word "hereafter." It seems to me that it would give a retroactive effect to past judgments and decrees.

Mr. WALSH. I stated to the Senate, in opening, that to my mind when the judgment is made only prima facie evidence that character can be given not only to judgments rendered in the future, but it may be equally attributed to judgments rendered in the past; but if you seek to give a conclusive character to it, it can of course only apply to judgments in the future.

Mr. CUMMINS. I desire to ask the Senator from Montana a question. He has raised a very interesting inquiry. I turn it around a little and put it in this way: Suppose the State of Montana were to institute a criminal proceeding against one of its citizens for larceny and a conviction followed, could the State make that conclusive evidence in a suit brought by the owner of the property against the defendant for recovery?

Mr. WALSH. I should say unhesitatingly that it could, and I was referring to a lot of those things by way of illustration.

Mr. CUMMINS. I am not asserting now any opinion of my own about it, but I see that that might be a parallel instance. The Senator from Montana says that the judgment or conviction of the defendant could be made conclusive evidence against the defendant in a suit brought by the owner of the property for the recovery of its value.

Mr. WALSH. I do not see why it could not. Let me go on. Here is a man charged with the larceny of my horse. In order to establish the action it is necessary to prove that it was my horse and that the defendant took it and converted it to his own use. I make the complaint against him. I charge that it was my horse and that he feloniously took it and converted it to his own use. We go on and try that matter, and the jury is charged that they shall acquit him unless they believe that he wrongfully took my horse and converted it to his own use. I should like to understand upon what constitutional ground it can be said that when I go into a civil action to recover damages for the taking of that horse the defendant is entitled to have another jury trial of that issue.

Mr. THOMAS. Mr. President, right there I should like to ask this question. Suppose that the act of larceny consisted of the felonious taking of a horse belonging to the Senator and another horse belonging to me, all in the same transaction. The Government proceeds by indictment against the defendant, including the horse of the Senator from Montana with my property in the indictment. Subsequently I bring suit for the recovery of the value of the horse taken from me. Could the conviction resulting from the indictment for the larceny of the horse of the Senator from Montana be made conclusive in the suit which I have instituted?

Mr. WALSH. Certainly not. The question of the taking of the horse of the Senator from Colorado was not in issue at all.

Mr. THOMAS. Is it not the fact that a great many, if not all, the suits brought for damages would be analogous to that situation, involving the precise, substantial property in the first suit?

Mr. WALSH. The judgment in the antitrust case would be determinative of merely the issues raised in that case. They would be conclusive just so far as they were issues of law and issues of fact in that case and no further.

Mr. THOMAS. I wish to say that I am in hearty sympathy with the argument of the Senator from Montana, because I can perceive very easily—all of us can—the consequences of making this judgment prima facie instead of conclusive. The result would be precisely as the Senator has predicted. I am unable as yet to bring my mind in harmony with the Senator from Montana on the constitutional question.

Mr. WALSH. Let me go a little further, Mr. President, and offer some further illustrations. A man is charged with the malicious destruction of personal property belonging to A. A makes complaint and the man is proceeded against criminally. He is tried and is found guilty upon evidence convincing a jury beyond a reasonable doubt that he maliciously destroyed the property of A. Then A begins action to recover damages against him. What constitutional right of his is transgressed by a statute which would make the judgment in that criminal proceeding conclusive in the action brought to recover the damages?

Mr. CUMMINS. I ask the Senator from Montana whether he knows of such legislation in the various States? It is a new subject with me.

Mr. WALSH. I will state that I searched very diligently and was unable to find any adjudication whatever upon the legal proposition which is here at issue between the House provision and the Senate committee amendment.

Mr. CUMMINS. One more question. If the House provision limited its operation to suits in equity brought by the Government, does the Senator know why it was not extended to criminal prosecutions as well?

Mr. WALSH. No; I do not. I was going to instance the case of a criminal libel. A newspaper publisher is indicted, charged with having published a criminal libel against A. A makes complaint and has him prosecuted criminally for publishing that libel. The question is whether he did publish it and whether it is libelous. He is adjudged to be guilty and is punished accordingly. Then A sues to recover damages by reason of the publication of that libel. Why in that civil action should he be called upon to do anything more than prove the actual damages, and upon what principle, under what provision of the Constitution can a man have a second trial of the very issues that were tried in the criminal case?

Instances of this kind might be multiplied. I must confess, Mr. President, that I am myself unable to find any satisfactory answer to them.

Mr. OVERMAN. I will ask the Senator whether the State could make a tax deed conclusive evidence as to the title of land?

Mr. WALSH. Many States have statutes making the deed conclusive evidence of every question, not going to the groundwork of the tax; that is to say, to the assessment and levy of the tax. It is held, I believe, that the tax deed can not be made conclusive evidence upon those questions.

Mr. CHILTON. Mr. President, as the Senator from Montana has very properly said, there was no division in the Committee on the Judiciary upon the desirability of making these judgments and decrees obtained by the Government against trusts conclusive. So far as it was expressed there, everyone would like to have it so that these judgments and decrees should be available by anyone who might be injured by reason of the machinery and the machinations of the trusts, so that the burden of a new trial would not be put upon private individuals.

But, Mr. President, in our zeal to do something for the people and to get legislation which has "teeth in it" we must remember that every person under the Constitution of the United States has rights. One of the fundamental rights of every person and every corporation in the United States is that he must have a day in court, and he must have his day in court on his case and on his facts. For instance, if we would make a judgment conclusive as against a defendant it shocks any man's sense of justice and right to fail to make it conclusive as against a plaintiff. Certainly no Senator can stand here and argue the proposition that if A and B would have a lawsuit he would make the facts found and the judgment rendered conclusive as against B and not make it conclusive as against A. I do not care what might be the necessity nor what might be the condition; I do not care what might be the evil and what might be suggested to me as a remedy, I am unwilling to stand upon this floor and vote for something that means that a law is applicable to one party in a litigation and not applicable to another.

If we can make a decree conclusive as to those not parties, and would make this a just law, we should make it so that this decree shall be conclusive for all purposes as against the plaintiff and as against the defendant. If made conclusive, we should make it conclusive for all purposes and for both sides. If we want to enact just legislation, legislation that shows to the country that we are trying to be fair and right about this thing and not trying to yield to prejudice, we would enact that kind of legislation. If we would do otherwise, then we would be in an indefensible position. Here the great Beef Trust has recently been prosecuted. A verdict of acquittal was rendered for them. Shall we stand here and give life to a system of laws that would make that Beef Trust forever innocent under the laws of the United States? Certainly not. And yet we will enact just such a one-sided law unless we adopt the Senate amendment.

Mr. President, this is not a new question in the courts. It has been settled by the authorities, and the fundamental principle is that if you make anything evidence in a case, anything that has been properly adjudicated, you must preserve one principle, and that is a man must have his day in court, to submit to the court in his case any evidence that bears upon a matter that is essential to the judgment or decree which may be rendered. For instance, take the case supposed by the Senator from Montana. Here is a suit brought by A against B. It is concerning the same transaction as to which C has a suit against B. But, Mr. President, A and B may enter a collusive judgment, which should not bind C. The judgment against B may have been brought about by testimony that is conceded at the time of the trial between A and B to have been perjured, to have been false, and when C and B try their suit everybody in the courthouse, the judge and the jury and both parties to the litigation, might be willing to concede that every witness who testified against B testified falsely, and yet the House bill provides that C can not show it in his case. It is for that reason that the courts have said that they will never allow anything to be made conclusive in a suit between parties if it goes to the extent of precluding either of the parties from showing any facts that bear upon the issue.

On that proposition I want to read to the Senate some of the authorities. One of them is in Two hundred and nineteenth United States, the case of the Mobile Railroad against Turnipseed. I do not want to read all of it. I read from page 43, Two hundred and nineteenth United States:

If a legislative provision not unreasonable in itself prescribing a rule of evidence, in either criminal or civil cases, does not shut out from the party affected a reasonable opportunity to submit to the jury in his defense all of the facts bearing upon the issue, there is no ground for holding that due process of law has been denied him.[5.599]

The court goes further and discusses that proposition. I do not want to read all of the decision, but I shall insert so much of it as may bear upon this matter. I merely wished to read that to make plain that one fundamental principle that runs through all of the decisions. It is that you can make a judgment or decree prima facie evidence, you can make it anything you want, provided you do not shut out the party who is interested in the litigation and who will be affected by it from his right to show any evidence that he may want to show and from introducing any fact that bears upon the issue, and that there is preserved to the litigant the right to have the court or jury pass upon that evidence and give due consideration to those facts. . . .

Mr. [MOSES E.] CLAPP [R., Minn.]. As I read the amendment proposed by the Senate committee, it is subject to the criticism to which the Senator has referred, that a judgment or decree is only made prima facie evidence against the defendant. If the criticism is a good one as applied to the House provision, it seems to me it is equally good as to the amendment reported by the committee.

Mr. CHILTON. Not at all, Mr. President, and for this reason: What we are trying to do is to frame legislation under which, whenever the Government institutes a prosecution against trusts, where it is necessary to employ detectives and lawyers and investigators, costing thousands and thousands of dollars, any citizen might have the benefit of the results obtained by the Government in any suit which he might bring. We were not worrying about the cost to the trusts, which can get lawyers and investigators and experts whenever they want them; that part of it did not bother me any. I would not mind making it prima facie as to both parties. I think that it is probably right and that we should do so; but where you make it conclusive you have a different proposition; there you end the suit; you prevent anybody afterwards from putting in evidence what everybody might agree to be the exact facts. You are bound by the decree, and it can be used as an estoppel in favor of some one else who was not a party to the litigation. . . .

Mr. CLAPP. I think it should be made conclusive; and I think it should be made

---

[5.599] Mobile, J. & K.C.R.R. v. Turnipseed, 219 U.S. 35, 43, 31 S. Ct. 136, 138, 55 L. Ed. 78, 81 (1910).

conclusive only against the defendant for the identical reason which the Senator from West Virginia is giving why it should be made prima facie only against the defendant. I am not solicitous for the trusts; but if it is a just criticism that being final it should be final as to both, I insist that the same criticism would make it prima facie as to both.

Mr. CHILTON. Mr. President, the Senator says he is in favor of making it conclusive, and I know that he believes we have the constitutional right to do so; I take it that the Senator would not want to put on the statute books a law which would be inoperative and which the courts would be compelled to hold unconstitutional. It was to that point I was alluding. I am as much in favor as is the Senator of making it conclusive as to both parties, if we could do so. It is a peculiar kind of litigation that in its very nature ought to be made conclusive, if possible. It affects the public, and every decree should, if possible, settle the facts found for everybody. Business does not thrive upon litigation or uncertainty. . . .

Mr. WALSH. I want to inquire of the Senator from West Virginia if the trusts should escape and be acquitted in one action brought by the Government of the United States, whether he thinks they would be in very much peril from an action brought by a private individual on the same ground?

Mr. CHILTON. No; I do not; and I am no more worried about their peril than is the Senator from Montana. The Senator need not question me about that, because during a long service on the committee with him I think he has found that I have not been shuddering about the peril of the trusts and the dangers to which they may be subjected. I have, however, in good faith been trying to report to the Senate a proposed statute that I could maintain as a Senator here and retain my own self-respect, and could truthfully say to the Senate that I thought it conformed to the Constitution of the United States; and I would not agree to report any other kind of measure. It is because of my fears of the constitutionality of the House bill that I took the position which I did, and favored the Senate amendment.

Mr. WALSH. Mr. President, I want to bear testimony to the unfailing diligence of the Senator from West Virginia in the effort to frame legislation appropriate to the case and to my belief in his entire good faith in the position he has taken in the matter. I asked the question simply to indicate as forcefully as I could that the peril he sees in not making the estoppel reciprocal is one that is very vague and dim.

Mr. CHILTON. So far as the offending trust is concerned and so far as the question of injuring the trust is concerned I do not care to press the point, but so far as it may affect the courts and their reason for holding this legislation valid or invalid, my reason is not dim. I take it that we do not want to put upon the statute books one-sided legislation. We want to put on the statute books something that in our conscience we believe is right and fair. So far as I am concerned, if we are to enact a statute on this subject I want it to treat both sides alike, both the prosecutors, the Government, and the defendant. I do not assume that everyone who will be prosecuted under these laws will be guilty. It is entirely possible that some innocent people will be prosecuted under them, and if they are innocent I want them to have the benefit which every other citizen has under the law; and I am not afraid to say so in the Senate of the United States nor in any other place; and I have been just as zealous in putting teeth into the antitrust laws as any other member of the Judiciary Committee.

The next citation which I want to call to the attention of the Senate is the case of Chicago Railway Co. *v.* Minnesota (134 U. S., p. 456).[5.600] In that case the Supreme Court of Minnesota had put a construction upon a statute of the State, and the Supreme Court of the United States in determining the validity of that statute, construed the statute as had the supreme court of the State, and, so construing it, held it to be invalid. This is what the court says about it:

> The supreme court (of that State) authoritatively declares that it is the expressed intention of the Legislature of Minnesota, by the statute, that the rates recommended and published by the commission, if it proceeds in the manner pointed out by the act, are not simply advisory, nor merely prima facie equal and reasonable, but final and conclusive as to what are equal and reasonable charges; that the law neither contemplates nor allows any issue to be made or

---

[5.600] Chicago, M. & St. P. Ry. v. Minnesota, 134 U.S. 418, 10 S. Ct. 462, 33 L. Ed. 970 (1890).

inquiry to be had as to their equality or reasonableness in fact; that under the statute the rates published by the commission are the only ones that are lawful, and, therefore, in contemplation of law, the only ones that are equal and reasonable; and that, in a proceeding for mandamus under the statute, there is no fact to traverse except the violation of law in not complying with the recommendations of the commission. In other words, although the railroad company is forbidden to establish rates that are not equal and reasonable, there is no power in the courts to stay the hands of the commission if it chooses to establish rates that are unequal and unreasonable.[5.601]

For that reason the court decides the law to be unconstitutional and invalid.

The next authority I want to call to the attention of the Senate is Cooley's Constitutional Limitations, seventh edition, page 526. Speaking of matters made evidence by statute it is said:

But there are fixed bounds to the power of the legislature over this subject which can not be exceeded. As to what shall be evidence and which party shall assume the burden of proof in civil cases its authority is practically unrestricted so long as its regulations are impartial and uniform, but it has no power to establish rules which, under pretense of regulating the presentation of evidence, goes so far as altogether to preclude a party from exhibiting his rights. Except in those cases which fall within the familiar doctrine of estoppel at the common law, or other cases resting upon the like reasons, it would not, we apprehend, be in the power of the legislature to declare that a particular item of evidence should preclude a party from establishing his rights in opposition to it.

If the courts go to that extent as to a matter of evidence as between the same parties, what shall we say of the effort here to make a record in a suit between A and B binding in favor of the whole world besides, who have had no opportunity to participate in that trial and probably did not know at the time that their rights would ever be involved in the same set of circumstances or in the same class of litigation?

Proceeding, the same authority says:

In judicial investigation the law of the land requires an opportunity for a trial—

That means an opportunity for a trial to each litigant as to every matter which has not been adjudicated as between him and the party with whom he may be litigating at the time.

Reading further:

And there can be no trial if only one party is suffered to produce his proofs. The most formal conveyance may be a fraud or a forgery; public officers may connive with rogues to rob the citizen of his property; witnesses may testify or officers certify falsely, and records may be collusively manufactured for dishonest purposes; and that legislation which would preclude the fraud or wrong being shown, and deprive the party wronged of all remedy, has no justification in the principles of natural justice or of constitutional law.

And the authorities cited amply support that doctrine.

Mr. President, let me further illustrate: A brings a suit against a trust. Certain evidence is brought out. It may be in the power of one of the parties to that litigation afterwards to show that every witness who testified was mistaken; that the witnesses either perjured themselves or were mistaken as to the facts. It may be that the court and the jury and the public would be in such a state of mind as to want to render a different verdict. It is abhorrent to my mind that a statute can be constitutional which will put me in such a position that I who have not been a party to a litigation at all may be bound by a judgment rendered between other parties, although I have had no notice of the litigation, no opportunity to be heard, and may be in such a position that I can show the very contrary to be the fact.

I need not reiterate that the Committee on the Judiciary, without a single exception, was desirous of enacting a statute with teeth in it, as the expression is commonly used, one that would accomplish some good and would not merely play with this great subject; but when we came to investigate the question of the extent to which we could go a majority of that committee reached the conclusion that we could not go further than to make judgments or decrees rendered in a prior suit between other

---

[5.601] 134 U.S. at 456.

parties prima facie evidence. What does prima facie evidence mean? It means evidence sufficient to make out a case and to entitle one to recover unless overcome by proof. In other words, if A recovers judgment against B, then, in a suit brought by C against B, the former judgment that B has violated the law will entitle C to recover until and unless B shall overcome the prima facie case by competent evidence; and even then C is not precluded from introducing other evidence to support the prima facie case. It is an immense advantage for one to begin a lawsuit with sufficient evidence to entitle him to win; and that far we can go in safety. . . .

Mr. CUMMINS. A judgment when it is introduced in evidence in any suit operates by way of estoppel, and ordinarily an estoppel must be mutual in order to be operative. But, apart from that, the antitrust law gives to anyone who is injured the right to recover treble damages for the injury and attorneys' fees. The person injured is not compelled to wait for the action of the Government either in the way of bringing a criminal proceeding or a suit in equity. Now, suppose that we were to attempt to say that in a suit in equity or in a criminal proceeding brought by the Government to enforce the law a judgment in favor of the defendant or defendants should be conclusive evidence against the right of an individual to recover the damages which he had suffered by reason of the violation of the law or by reason of a wrongful act in restraining trade. That would involve the same principle of law precisely, would it not?

Mr. CHILTON. And would be abhorrent to a sense of justice.

Mr. CUMMINS. It would involve the same principle of law?

Mr. CHILTON. Exactly the same.

Mr. CUMMINS. That is to say, if there is such a privity between the United States as a governmental organization and its citizens as to enable us to make a judgment in favor of the Government binding upon all its citizens, we could in the same way make a judgment against the Government representing all its citizens conclusive against the right of any one of them to recover against the offender.

Mr. CHILTON. Does not the Senator think that if we make it conclusive against one we ought to make it conclusive against the other, in view of these authorities?

Mr. CUMMINS. I am not so sure about that, because there are reasons which might be sufficient to remove this from the ordinary rule.

Mr. CHILTON. Yes; there might, but they do not occur to me now.

Mr. CUMMINS. The strength of the one and the weakness of the other; but I think it shows beyond any question that we can not make it conclusive in favor of one or of the other. We can not make it conclusive against a person who is injured by such a wrongful act, nor can we make the judgment conclusive in favor of the person who has suffered from such wrongful act. In either case the person must be left, under the Constitution, to pursue his remedy, which is to recover these damages. I have always thought the utmost we could do would be to give the former legal proceedings prima facie effect in any suit brought by the individual. . . .

Mr. CLAPP. It does seem to me that the distinction there is too plain to admit of very much discussion. A suit is brought against a trust by the United States Government. That trust has its day in court. It is there with its lawyers and its witnesses. There is a vast difference between that trust, after having its day in court, being bound by that judgment, and a man who has been injured by the trust and who has not had his day in court, who has had no opportunity to present his case, being bound by the verdict against the Government.

Mr. CHILTON. If the Senator will let me answer him, let us suppose that we have a case against a labor organization, which both the Senator and I believe should not be prosecuted merely as such under the statute. No doubt the Senator will vote with me upon that clause. Suppose it should be convicted. Must it remain forever under the ban of that decision, no matter what the fact may be?

The Senator is proceeding upon the idea that nobody will be prosecuted here but guilty people. Is it possible that you want one judgment rendered against a labor organization, if it should be rendered, to stand forever to bind it in other cases?

Take this case: A decree has been rendered in West Virginia holding a labor organization to be a criminal and violating the laws of the State. That judgment was rendered in the courts of West Virginia. Now, suppose other suits were brought against it and it could come in and show that the witnesses in the first case were mistaken, or swore falsely. Does the Senator want it to rest forever under that ban?

Mr. CLAPP. Mr. President, I will answer the Senator's question.

Mr. CHILTON. All right.

Mr. CLAPP. There is no way on earth, in human affairs, of avoiding, sometimes, perhaps, a wrong; but when a judgment is rendered against me upon false testimony I have a time under the law in which I may present proof of the falsity of the testimony; and if the time goes by in which the court can interpose and grant a new trial, wrong and unjust as it is, it is one of the infirmities attendant upon human administration of affairs, and I have no escape from it.

Carrying out the same analogy of the ultimate finality of judicial proceedings, when a combination, a trust, or a company or an individual has had its day in court at the complaint of the public, and the time has expired within which, under the rules of law and equity, it may ask for a new trial upon the ground of newly discovered evidence, that witnesses have been bribed, or any other occasion for which courts may relieve it from the judgment, there is no reason to my mind why the person who has suffered at the hands of the alleged wrongdoer should not have, equally with all the public, the benefit of that verdict and that trial, and not be compelled to travel the same weary, dreary course that the Government traveled in getting its verdict.

There is that difference between making the judgment prima facie evidence or conclusive evidence—for in this respect there can be no difference of opinion—as against the man or the combination that has had his or its day in court and making it conclusive or prima facie evidence against the man who has not been in court at all. . . .

Mr. CUMMINS. We are now looking at the question from the legal standpoint alone, not from the sympathetic point of view nor from what might be called the standpoint of public policy. We have a Constitution; this is a country of law, and it is idle for us to enact a statute which will be stricken down by the courts.

I put to the Senator from West Virginia a case, and the Senator from Minnesota answered it by asserting a difference between the case I put and the case involved in the provision of the House bill. Let us see.

The Senator from Minnesota begins his argument by saying that in the case provided for in the House bill the corporation defendant has had its day in court. That statement assumes the whole controversy. The constitutional question is whether, under such circumstances, the defendant has had his day, or its day, in court. The argument of the Senator from Montana, which is persuasive, although, to my mind, not convincing, is that inasmuch as the Government of the United States represents all of the people of the United States, and all the people of the United States are privy with the Government in any suit that it brings and carries forward, therefore a judgment rendered in any such suit, if it be in favor of the Government, is a judgment rendered in favor of every citizen of that Government against the particular defendant who was being prosecuted. Upon that theory the well-known principle of the law, without any legislation whatever, would make the decree or judgment rendered in the suit conclusive as between all the citizens of the Republic; and it is only that reason that can bring the proposal within the scope of the Constitution. . . .

I want to show that the Senator from Minnesota assumed the real question in controversy when he made his first statement.

When the Government brings its suit and recovers, it is upon that theory adjudged, as between all the people and against the person or corporation against whom the recovery goes, that the facts are so-and-so and the law is so-and-so, just as I think it follows, if that reasoning be good, that if the judgment goes against the Government the person who asserts damages has had his day in court in the same way. He has had it through his own Government, which has prosecuted his case for him but has failed; and he therefore has had the same opportunities through his agent that many of these privies have had in the adjudicated cases with regard to a judgment covering a collection of persons. It seems to me pretty clear that if we can make the judgment conclusive in favor of the person who has been injured we can also make an adverse judgment conclusive against the citizen who asserts that he has been injured. I believe no one would contend that constitutionally we can do the latter. . . .

Mr. WALSH. I will say to the Senator from Iowa that I so contend, and I think I shall be able to demonstrate that there is not any question about it.

Mr. CUMMINS. That it could be made conclusive against the person?

Mr. WALSH. Against the citizen, of course.

Mr. CUMMINS. The Senator from Montana is sometimes startling, but he is always logical. I simply wanted to have the proposal so clear that we could see it from every point of view. . . .

Mr. CHILTON. I want to read just one other authority.

In the Encyclopedia of Evidence, volume 3, page 292, the principle is stated in this way:

> But a law which would cut off the right of a party to offer evidence bearing on the question to be determined, by providing that certain matters or facts shall be conclusive evidence of the truth of the charge, or of that which is to be proved, would be unconstitutional and void, and could not therefore be upheld as a valid act of legislation. Hence a legislature can not lawfully declare what specific facts shall constitute conclusive proof of any matter sought to be judicially determined and established.

That statement is supported by a long line of authorities from practically all the States of the Union. There are very few of them that have not decided this to be the law.

Mr. President, after all, in my judgment, the worst enemy of reform in these matters, no matter how good his intentions may be, is the legislator who would take any chance as to the legislation which we may adopt being constitutional. We have a broad enough field within the Constitution. We are not restricted in a great many lines. There is just a little narrow line that we have struck here where there is at least great doubt as to this legislation. So far as I am concerned, I would prefer to take the open track, where we know we are right, and where we will not subject the citizen and the Government to long litigation and possibly, very probably, have some legislation we enact here declared unconstitutional and thereby make a gap in our legislation, or make it one sided, when there is no good reason for it. There is no good reason from the standpoint of policy, there is no good reason in the situation which confronts us, to suggest the taking of a desperate chance.

When you come to consider the difference between the making of a judgment conclusive and its being prima facie evidence, the advantage of the one over the other is not sufficient to warrant us in taking the chance. Why does anyone want to make a judgment against anybody, whether it be a trust or a citizen, a corporation or an individual, conclusive, and preclude him forever from showing the fact, if the fact be against the decree or judgment?

We are here to uphold justice between parties. We are not here to persecute anyone. There is no need of it. There is plenty of public sentiment against a trust which violates any of these statutes or the Sherman antitrust law to convict it if there be a proper case. In the one we say they shall not defend; in the other we say that there shall be a prima facie case against them.

Take all of these statutes in the States where they are enforcing prohibition laws, laws against the carrying of pistols, and so on. They never go beyond making a fact prima facie evidence. For instance, the carrying of liquor about your person, or being seen with liquor, is only prima facie evidence. They only make having the Government stamp or the payment of the Government tax prima facie evidence. We have a number of statutes of that kind in the various States; and this is the first attempt I have ever seen made anywhere to make a judgment between A and B conclusive evidence as between A and C or as between B and C. We are discussing something that never will be really material. Any citizen can have all the advantage from a prima facie case that he could have from a conclusive case.

Are we not now going beyond the real condition, the real trouble, that we started in to remedy? What we tried to do was to have some way by which the citizen could have the advantage of the evidence collected and produced by the Government. That is all that has been asked by the people. That is all that has been asked by those who have found difficulty in prosecuting these trust cases.

The Government goes out, under its great advantages and with its powers and its great resources, and makes a case against one of these trusts. Now, the citizen does not ask us to go into the field of conjecture and get him into trouble. He has not asked us to do that. He has not asked us to pass a doubtful statute which may get him into further difficulty and subject him to heavy costs. The citizen has simply asked us to give to him the benefit of the Government's case and make it prima facie evidence; to let him have that evidence certified in the other case against the trust concerning the same transaction or the same wrong. Therefore we are really, in my judgment, about to do as needless as a vain thing. What the people have asked for is the practical thing. It is a real reform. It will do some good. Why should we take chances?

So far as I am concerned, I have not much doubt that the courts will declare the House bill unconstitutional the first time it is put to the test. Believing that, I have voted for the amendment of the committee to make the judgment of decree prima facie evidence. In doing so I feel that we are giving the citizen and the country every advantage which justice demands. Until the authorities which I have cited shall be overthrown, or some one points out a precedent that justifies it, I can not vote for a law that makes a decree binding in favor of one not a party to the litigation in which it was rendered. Because of the large interest of the public in controlling these trusts, I will go to the limit of our power, and I believe that the Senate bill marks that limit.

Mr. WALSH. The Senator from Iowa [Mr. CUMMINS] stepped out, but I hope he may come in. The Senator from Iowa seems to labor under the impression that it is a sufficient answer to the contention made by me in this connection to say that it is beyond the power of Congress to make the judgment conclusive against the citizen as well as in his favor, and therefore it follows that the judgment can not be made conclusive in his favor.

Mr. President, I am not at all ready to accept the idea of the Senator from Iowa that it is beyond the power of Congress to make the judgment in an antitrust case conclusive against the citizen. In fact, I entertain no doubt whatever about the power of Congress to do that much. About that I believe there can be no two opinions upon serious reflection, because the citizen has a right of action at all merely because the statute gives it to him. If there were no statute, he would have no right of action.

It is true, Mr. President, that it is not necessary to convey the right of action in express terms, but as was declared here upon the floor a few days ago the bare fact that the law denounces these acts as unlawful gives a right of action to anyone who may be damaged by the acts thus put under the ban of the law. But the law simply carries by implication the right of action to the man who has been injured. In other words, his right of action rests upon the law; it has its origin in the statute. Congress gives to him the right of action, and when Congress gives to him the right of action Congress may attach to it any conditions it may see fit. . . .

. . . It may develop that although the acts denounced in the statute are unlawful, no citizen shall have right of action by reason of any damages sustained in consequence thereof until after judgment shall have been rendered in an action brought by the Government. I yield to the Senator from Iowa.

Mr. CUMMINS. I have no doubt whatever about the last statement of the Senator from Montana. We have just such a provision as he has mentioned in the interstate-commerce law. A shipper who claims to have been overcharged can not bring a suit in the Federal courts until the rate has been found to be unreasonably high by the Interstate Commerce Commission. That is a condition precedent to the institution of a suit of that character. We could do so here. We could say that no suit shall be tried under the laws of the United States until a proceeding had terminated favorable to the United States in a suit brought for that purpose. That was not my proposition. We have given this cause of action. Those who suffer have the cause of action; and we are preparing a rule of evidence here. It was my proposition that, leaving the cause of action as it is, we could not say that the citizen could not prosecute that cause of action if a judgment against the Government had been rendered in a suit brought for the enforcement of the law.

Mr. WALSH. The Senator is talking about a cause of action which has already accrued.

Mr. CUMMINS. I am talking about leaving the statute as it is, with the cause of action in the hands of the citizen who is injured. We can, of course, destroy that cause of action entirely. We can repeal the provision of the antitrust law—there is no doubt of that—so that neither the Government nor citizen shall have any cause of action; but so long as we leave the cause of action I do not believe we can say that a judgment rendered between different parties shall be conclusive as between the injured citizen and the offending corporation.

Mr. WALSH. The Senator did not let me quite finish the line of the argument. However, he agrees with me now that we could amend the Sherman Antitrust Act so that it should provide that in the future no citizen shall be entitled to prosecute an action for damages resulting from the violation of the law until after a suit shall have been prosecuted by the United States and a judgment rendered in the action in favor of the Government. Therefore, if a suit was brought by the Government of the United States and failed, but a judgment were rendered against the Government, then the effect of a statute making that judgment conclusive against the citizen in an action brought by him would have exactly the same effect as a statute such as I first indicated, which denied to anyone the right to recover in an action unless first a judgment were rendered by the Government of the United States. In other words, a statute providing that no one could recover in an action of that character until after a judgment had been rendered in favor of the United States would be exactly the same as if it said that a judgment rendered in favor of the corporation shall be conclusive evidence against anyone prosecuting a private action for damages resulting from the unlawful combination. The two statutes would have exactly the same force and effect, and if you admit the power of Congress to pass the one you must admit the power of Congress to pass the other. So to my mind there is not any question about the right of Congress to make the judgment in the action prosecuted by the Government of the United States conclusive evidence against a citizen who prosecutes a private action for damages resulting from the act.

Mr. President, if we can pass that kind of a statute, why can we not pass the reciprocal of it; in other words, a statute providing that it shall be conclusive evidence when the judgment goes in favor of the judgment [sic] of the United States.

Now, just one other thought. The Senator recognizes the principle of the binding force of judgments by representation, a judgment in favor of a single individual binding upon all the members of the class which he represents, and he indicates that there is a close analogy, as undoubtedly there is, between a judgment of that character and a judgment in a suit brought by the Government of the United States, which represents all the citizens of the United States. I do not think that the principle of representation has ever been extended so far as to embrace all the citizens of a State in an action brought by the State; but why should it not? Is it not a perfectly arbitrary rule that excludes it? Where are you going to draw the line? Does not the Government of the United States in these prosecutions truly and rightly and justly represent its citizens in the prosecution of the action? It would be only a very little extension of the principle to include judgments brought in actions prosecuted by the Government or by the State.

I want to say just a word with reference to the authorities to which the attention of the Senate has been invited by the learned Senator from West Virginia [Mr. CHILTON]. Nobody questions them. They all lay down the rule that in an action brought against an individual who has never theretofore had his day in court you can not make a certificate or a recital or an order of an administrative board or anything of that kind conclusive evidence against him. You may make it prima facie evidence. A tax deed is made prima facie evidence of the truth of all its recitals. The notice of a mining claim filed in the office of the county recorder is prima facie evidence of all the facts recited in it and required to be recited in it by the statute; indeed the principle is general that whenever the law requires a certain document to be filed containing certain recitals that document becomes prima facie evidence of the truth of the recitals therein, and you can not make it conclusive. That is quite a different thing. Here the party has had his day in court. He has tried every issue, and it is simply a question, now that he has had it tried, whether he may insist upon a second trial.

Let me say, Mr. President, that we are proceeding against organizations denounced as unlawful by this law as guilty of crime, as a peril to the State, as a menace to ordinary business transactions, as fraught with danger to the public. That is the kind of an organization we are dealing with, and there is a judgment rendered by the court to the effect that it is so guilty.

Mr. President, I submit that that is a different kind of a judgment from one which would ordinarily be rendered in an ordinary private controversy between two citizens, and I submit that you violate no principle of justice by making that judgment conclusive against the party who thus is adjudged to be a violator of the law and leave it still subject to prosecution by a private party. They can not be put upon the same ground. They stand upon an entirely different footing.

I assert, sir, that there is no element of injustice in the policy expressed by the House bill that these judgments are to be conclusive against the corporation, leaving the private citizen, if he desires to take upon himself the burden of a subsequent prosecution at his own expense, the right to do so.

When a trust or a combination of any kind has been prosecuted by the great Government of the United States, and has been victorious in that fight, coming out of it with a judgment of acquittal, I wonder how many there are of us who are fearful that some private individual will thereafter harass and annoy the corporation by the institution and prosecution of another suit at his own expense? There is no need for a provision of that character; and, Mr. President, the law is not open to the charge of injustice when it does not give the right to the corporation or the combination, whatever it may be, to assert the conclusive character of the judgment which was rendered in its favor when it is brought again to the bar by a private individual.

So, Mr. President, it occurs to me that there is no constitutional objection to the House provision, and that it embodies a wise policy the argument upon all sides admits.

Mr. President, I desire to submit in connection with my remarks a brief portion of a late editorial in Harper's Weekly upon this subject, which I ask may be read from the desk.

The VICE PRESIDENT. Is there objection? The Chair hears none. The Secretary will read.

The Secretary read as follows from Harper's Weekly for August 15, 1914:

> The Clayton bill, as it passed the House, carried out the President's suggestion effectively by providing that a judgment for the Government shall be conclusive evidence in damage suits by private individuals. The Judiciary Committee of the Senate, however, has changed the provision so as to keep the word of promise to our ear and break it to our hope. As reported to the Senate, the provision is that the judgment for the Government shall be merely prima facie evidence in private suits. This destroys the expected benefit. In order to overcome the prima facie effect of the Government's judgment, the trusts will only have to introduce some new evidence, and then the whole matter will be open for determination by a jury. No private individual will be able to sue without being ready to prove over again all that the Government proved. This is something that small victims of the trusts can not afford to do. It is essential that the Government's judgment should be conclusive evidence of the violation of the antitrust law, and the Senate should see that it is made so, as the House did.

Mr. CHILTON. If the writer of that article does not know anything more about this subject than he knows about what prima facie evidence means, we can well submit the question to the Senate without any reference to the knowledge that writer has of the law of the land.

Mr. THOMAS. Mr. President, the Senator from Nebraska has suggested what I think is an improvement upon my proposed amendment. He has suggested that the words "heretofore or hereafter" be inserted after the word "decree," in line 12. I ask leave to change the amendment which I offered, so as to correspond with that suggestion. The clause would then read:

> That a final judgment or decree heretofore or hereafter rendered in any suit or proceeding—

And so forth.

The VICE PRESIDENT. The question is on the amendment of the Senator from Colorado to the amendment.

Mr. CHILTON. I should like to have it reported, Mr. President.

The VICE PRESIDENT. It will be reported.

The SECRETARY. On page 6, line 12, in the proposed committee amendment, after the word "decree" insert the words "heretofore or hereafter," so as to read:

That a final judgment or decree heretofore or hereafter rendered in any suit or proceeding in equity—

And so forth.

The VICE PRESIDENT. The question is on the amendment of the Senator from Colorado to the amendment of the committee. [Putting the question.] The ayes seem to have it.

Mr. HUGHES. I ask for a division. I am not sure that I understand it, but I was drawing an amendment intended to clear what I considered as an ambiguity in the section. Will not the Senator from Colorado allow his amendment to go over until I have a chance to read it in connection with the amendment I desire to offer?

Mr. THOMAS. I think I can explain it in a moment. The purpose of the amendment is to make the decrees heretofore rendered as well as those hereafter rendered prima facie evidence.

Mr. HUGHES. I will ask the Senator to let it go over until I have had a chance to compare it with an amendment that I intended to offer.

Mr. THOMAS. I have no objection.

The VICE PRESIDENT. Does the Senator from Colorado withdraw his amendment to the amendment?

Mr. THOMAS. No. It goes over without objection, I understand.

Mr. HUGHES. To be pending.

The VICE PRESIDENT. The committee amendment will have to go over, then.

Mr. CULBERSON. I think we can determine this matter without its going over. I suggest to the Senator from New Jersey that the amendment to the amendment is plain enough. The only question is whether the Senate wants to adopt it.

Mr. HUGHES. Then I want to debate it.

Mr. CULBERSON. Very well.

Mr. OVERMAN. Can we not take the vote on the motion of the Senator from Montana [Mr. WALSH] to strike out or disagree, and if the Senate disagrees to the amendment there will be no need of the amendment proposed by the Senator from Colorado?

Mr. CULBERSON. The question is on the adoption of the amendment proposed by the Committee on the Judiciary.

Mr. OVERMAN. If that is adopted, it can be amended subsequently.

The VICE PRESIDENT. The Chair understands the situation exactly. There has been an amendment offered to the committee amendment, and the Chair can not put the question on the amendment of the committee until the amendment to the amendment has been disposed of.

Mr. CHILTON. In other words, the Senate has a right to perfect the amendment before it is voted upon.

Mr. WALSH. Assuming the condition to be as the Chair has indicated, I have not yet offered my amendment. When the committee amendment is perfected, I imagine that the motion will be in order.

Mr. CULBERSON. I understood the proposition of the Senator from Montana to be to retain the House provision instead of the committee amendment. That question ought to be determined upon the proposition as to whether the committee amendment shall prevail.

The VICE PRESIDENT. There is no question about that. The committee amendment before the Senate has been proposed to be amended by the Senator from Colorado. The Chair asked the Senator from Colorado whether he would withdraw his amendment. He said "no."

Mr. OVERMAN. I suggest to the Senator from Colorado to withdraw it. He can offer it in the Senate and we can proceed with this legislation in Committee of the

Whole. He can withhold it and let us take the question on agreeing to the amendment of the committee.

Mr. HUGHES. It seems to me that the Senator from Colorado has a right to attempt to perfect the text.

⊥ Mr. OVERMAN. He can do that hereafter. ⊥13858

Mr. HUGHES. It seems to me this is the most convenient way to get at it. I will simply state what I have to say on the amendment of the Senator from Colorado and call his attention to what I regard as its vice, as I have already called it to the attention of the various members of the committee. The House provision contains the word "hereafter"; it reads:

> That whenever in any suit or proceeding in equity hereafter brought—

And so forth.

Mr. THOMAS. The provision makes it conclusive.

Mr. HUGHES. That a final judgment hereafter rendered shall operate in a certain way. The Senator from Colorado seeks to provide that a final judgment or decree heretofore or hereafter rendered shall operate in a certain way. The difficulty about that is we are opening up a vast field of litigation with reference to transactions that have passed and gone. This may well be productive of more litigation than anybody here dreams of; in fact, I know that it will be.

There is this also to be said, that in a great many of these cases consent decrees were entered by agreement and arrangement between the Government and the parties who were charged with offenses, and it does not seem to me fair that the Government, which induced these men, in order to save it the expense and trouble and time of litigation, to consent to a decree, which the Government might not have been able to obtain by regular procedure, before the case was tried, before a judgment was had, should afterwards, when that decree has been obtained by their consent, change the law and put them in a position which leaves them absolutely no redress or no recourse of any kind.

If Senators would stop for a moment to consider this they would realize that a great many of these consent decrees have been entered, and in every case thousands of individuals may claim that they have been injured and come in under the shelter of a consent decree and proceed against the defendant who consented to it probably because it desired to conduct its business in the way the Government said that it should. Without admitting that it had violated the law, but in order to make its peace and continue along the line mapped out for it by the Government, friendly cooperation existing between the defendant charged with an offense and the Government, the corporation may have given its consent to the entering of a decree, saying, "Very well, we will consent that in the future we shall not be permitted to do this."

This amendment opens that whole subject up to the time of the entering of the decree. I want Senators to understand that before they vote on it. I certainly would not vote for the amendment of the Senator from Colorado. The language of the bill as it came from the House provided explicitly that all the decrees entered hereafter should be of the binding force and effect sought to be given by this proposed statute. My understanding from the talk I have had with the various members of the committee is that it has been their idea and their intention that this proposed act should operate prospectively and not retrospectively.

Mr. THOMAS. Mr. President, there is no question but that the House provision is intended to operate prospectively, the only way it could operate if Congress has power to make such judgments conclusive.

Mr. CHILTON. The Senate amendment, also, is prospective.

Mr. THOMAS. The Senate amendment, however, is one which makes the judgements [sic] prima facie evidence. That being so, when the judgment is introduced as being prima facie evidence, it does not preclude the defendant against whom the judgment was rendered from explaining away its force and effect, that constituting the chief defect of the section, as the Senator from Montana [Mr. WALSH] has so well shown.

It is true that there are judgments which have been entered and decrees which have been entered by consent in some of these cases, but there are no cases in which any corporation was a defendant which I can now call to mind in which a consent decree was entered but that such decree would have been entered after final trial, the consent decree being influenced by what the inevitable result of the case would be. The mere fact that it is a consent judgment does not, it seems to me, detract from the privilege, if it be one, which this proposed statute gives of making the decrees prima facie evidence; and I am unable to distinguish between the justice of making a decree rendered upon a suit brought after this bill becomes a law prima facie evidence and making a decree rendered upon similar suits brought before this bill becomes a law prima facie evidence. Hence the amendment which I have suggested, that final judgment heretofore or hereafter rendered shall be prima facie evidence.

The VICE PRESIDENT. The question is on the amendment proposed by the Senator from Colorado [Mr. THOMAS]. [Putting the question.] The ayes seem to have it.

Mr. HUGHES. I call for a division.

The VICE PRESIDENT. Those in favor of the amendment will rise. Those opposed will rise. The amendment is carried.

Mr. HUGHES. I ask for the yeas and nays.

The yeas and nays were ordered, and the Secretary proceeded to call the roll.

Mr. CHAMBERLAIN (when his name was called). I announce my pair and withhold my vote.

Mr. CULBERSON (when his name was called). Again announcing my pair with the Senator from Delaware [Mr. DU PONT], I transfer that pair to the Senator from Arizona [Mr. SMITH], and vote "nay."

Mr. THOMAS (when his name was called). In the absence of my pair, I withhold my vote.

The roll call was concluded.

Mr. GALLINGER. I have a general pair with the junior Senator from New York [Mr. O'GORMAN]. I transfer that pair to the Senator from Illinois [Mr. SHERMAN] and vote "nay."

Mr. GRONNA (after having voted in the negative). I inquire whether the senior Senator from Maine [Mr. JOHNSON] has voted?

The VICE PRESIDENT. The Chair is informed that he has not.

Mr. GRONNA. I have a general pair with that Senator, and therefore withdraw my vote.

Mr. LEA of Tennessee. I transfer my pair with the senior Senator from South Dakota [Mr. CRAWFORD] to the Senator from Illinois [Mr. LEWIS] and vote "yea."

Mr. REED. The conditions of my pair are that I may vote in order to make a quorum; and if we are lacking a quorum, and I am advised of that fact, I will vote.

Mr. THOMAS. I transfer my pair with the Senator from New York [Mr. ROOT] to the Senator from South Carolina [Mr. SMITH] and vote "yea."

Mr. SMITH of Georgia (after having voted in the negative). I have a general pair with the senior Senator from Massachusetts [Mr. LODGE], which I transfer to the junior Senator from Georgia [Mr. WEST], and allow my vote to stand.

Mr. STONE. I inquire whether the Senator from Wyoming [Mr. CLARK] has voted?

The VICE PRESIDENT. The Chair is informed that he has not.

Mr. STONE. I have a pair with that Senator, and therefore withhold my vote.

Mr. REED. Under the circumstances I desire to vote. I vote "yea."

Mr. OWEN. If my vote is necessary to make a quorum, I have the right to vote, and I vote "yea."

Mr. JAMES. I transfer the general pair I have with the junior Senator from Massachusetts [Mr. WEEKS] to the senior Senator from Virginia [Mr. MARTIN] and vote "yea."

Mr. GORE. I have a pair with the junior Senator from Wisconsin [Mr. STEPHENSON], and therefore withhold my vote.

Mr. REED. Before the vote is announced I desire to know whether a quorum has voted.

Mr. GORE. I understand that my vote will be necessary to make a quorum. Under such circumstances I have the right to vote, and I vote "yea."

The result was—yeas 23, nays 23, as follows:

YEAS—23.

Ashurst	Jones	Pittman	Thomas
Bristow	Kern	Pomerene	Thompson
Cummins	Lane	Reed	Vardaman
Gore	Lea, Tenn.	Shafroth	Walsh
Hitchcock	Lee, Md.	Sheppard	White
James	Owen	Shively	

NAYS—23.

Bankhead	Gallinger	Newlands	Smoot
Bryan	Hughes	Overman	Sterling
Burton	Lippitt	Poindexter	Swanson
Chilton	McCumber	Ransdell	Thornton
Clapp	Martine, N. J.	Simmons	Williams
Culberson	Nelson	Smith, Ga.	

NOT VOTING—50.

Borah	Fall	Norris	Smith, Mich.
Brady	Fletcher	O'Gorman	Smith, S. C.
Brandegee	Goff	Oliver	Stephenson
Burleigh	Gronna	Page	Stone
Camden	Hollis	Penrose	Sutherland
Catron	Johnson	Perkins	Tillman
Chamberlain	Kenyon	Robinson	Townsend
Clark, Wyo.	La Follette	Root	Warren
Clarke, Ark.	Lewis	Saulsbury	Weeks
Colt	Lodge	Sherman	West
Crawford	McLean	Shields	Works
Dillingham	Martin, Va.	Smith, Ariz.	
du Pont	Myers	Smith, Md.	

⊥ The VICE PRESIDENT. On the amendment proposed by the Senator from ⊥13859 Colorado the yeas are 23, the nays are 23. Senators CHAMBERLAIN, GRONNA and STONE are present and have announced their pairs. That makes a quorum as the Chair figures it. The Chair votes "yea," and the amendment is adopted.

Mr. CHAMBERLAIN. I desire to say in that connection that I have no understanding with my pair allowing me to vote in order to constitute a quorum, but I have no objection to being counted as present.

SENATE DEBATE
63d Cong., 2d Sess.
August 18, 1914

51 CONG. REC. 13897

The Senate, as in Committee of the Whole, resumed the consideration of the bill (H. R. 15657) to supplement existing laws against unlawful restraints and monopolies, and for other purposes.

The VICE PRESIDENT. The pending question is on the amendment of the committee, on page 6, line 12, as amended.

Mr. POMERENE. Mr. President, with the permission of the Senate, I desire to address myself this morning to the so-called labor provisions of the bill.

Mr. CULBERSON. I suggest to the Senator from Ohio that we have not yet reached the labor provisions of the bill, and if it would suit him just as well I would be glad if he would postpone his remarks until we reach that section. We are on section 6.

Mr. POMERENE. If that is the desire of the chairman, I will defer my remarks until later.

Mr. CULBERSON. I would be glad if that would be done.

Mr. POMERENE. I should like during the day to speak upon that matter as soon as the section is reached.

Mr. CULBERSON. The Senator certainly will have an opportunity to do so.

Mr. POMERENE. Under those circumstances I will yield the floor.

The VICE PRESIDENT. The question is on the amendment reported by the committee, on page 6, line 12, as amended.

Mr. [NATHAN P.] BRYAN [D., Fla.]. Mr. President, on page 6, I move to strike out the words "in equity," in line 13, so that a final judgment or decree may be used as evidence regardless of whether or not the suit was in equity. I see no reason why a distinction should be made between a common-law suit, a criminal prosecution, and a suit in equity in the use of the record.

The VICE PRESIDENT. The question is on the amendment to the amendment proposed by the Senator from Florida.

Mr. CULBERSON. Mr. President, I suggest to the Senator from Florida that it would be better, and make it clearer, if, after the language in line 12, instead of striking out the words "in equity" there were inserted the words "in any criminal prosecution or."

Mr. BRYAN. That is perfectly satisfactory, Mr. President; it accomplishes the same purpose, I think. If my amendment to the amendment should prevail, it would read:

> That a final judgment or decree heretofore or hereafter rendered in any suit or proceeding.

Certainly a criminal prosecution is a suit; and the language then would cover all classes of suits, whether they be criminal prosecutions or common-law suits or suits in equity, by simply striking out the words "in equity." I have no objection, however, if the Senator prefers his amendment.

Mr. CULBERSON. We do not ordinarily refer to a criminal prosecution as a suit, I think.

Mr. [WILLIAM E.] BORAH [R., Idaho]. We would not refer to a criminal prosecution as a suit.

Mr. BRYAN. I have always heard it so referred to. I never heard it questioned that it was a suit.

Mr. BORAH. Oh, well, it is not a suit in the sense in which we use that term in referring to a suit in equity.

Mr. BRYAN. However, I am not particular about the phraseology. I think it ought to be so that a record in a criminal suit or prosecution could be used in a subsequent proceeding with the same force and effect as if it had been a suit in equity.

Mr. [JAMES A.] REED [D., Mo.]. Mr. President, it occurs to me that the matter suggested by the Senator from Florida—though I am not sure that I am in accord with him—would be covered by inserting, in line 13, between the words "in" and "equity," the words "law or," so that it would read "proceeding in law or equity," and after the word "equity" by inserting "or in any prosecution."

Mr. BRYAN. Mr. President, that is practically the same language as suggested by the chairman of the committee. I understand his suggestion is, in line 12, after the word "rendered," to insert "in any criminal prosecution or," so that it would read:

> That a final judgment or decree heretofore or hereafter rendered in any criminal prosecution or in any suit or proceeding in equity.

I am not at all particular about the phraseology.

Mr. REED. Leave out the words "in equity," and let it read "any suit or proceeding." That would cover any kind of proceeding.

Mr. BRYAN. That was my motion.

Mr. CULBERSON. There is no suit authorized by any of these statutes by the United States except a criminal prosecution or a suit in equity. The United States does not bring a suit at law for damages.

Mr. BRYAN. It occurs to me, Mr. President, that if the words "in equity" were stricken out, so that it would read "rendered in any suit or proceeding brought by or on behalf of the United States under the antitrust laws," it would be as broad as the antitrust law itself; but I am not interested in the phraseology. So I accept the suggestion of the Senator from Texas, and adopt his language, and offer it, withdrawing my first amendment.

The VICE PRESIDENT. The Secretary will state the amendment to the amendment.

The SECRETARY. On page 6, in the committee amendment, in line 12, after the word "rendered," it is proposed to insert the words "in any criminal prosecution or," so that, if amended as proposed, it will read:

> That a final judgment or decree heretofore or hereafter rendered in any criminal prosecution or in any suit or proceeding in equity brought by or on behalf of the United States.

The VICE PRESIDENT. The question is on agreeing to the amendment to the amendment.

The amendment to the amendment was agreed to.

The VICE PRESIDENT. The question recurs on the amendment as amended.

Mr. WALSH. Mr. President, that now brings up the question of whether we shall adhere to the House provision or adopt the provision recommended by the Senate committee; in other words, whether we shall make the judgment in the proceedings in which it is decreed that the defendant is a trust in violation of the statute conclusive, or whether it shall be held as prima facie evidence of the facts. I feel like taking the time of the Senate for just a few moments more this morning upon that question.

It will be borne in mind, first, that if you make it prima facie evidence only you leave entirely open every question of law that was litigated and determined in the original proceeding; you leave the question of fact open as well. You simply throw the burden of proof upon the defendant, when otherwise it would be upon the plaintiff. That is the whole force and effect of the statute that you are proposing to pass—simply to transfer the burden of proof.

As was well said in the editorial read from the desk yesterday, the whole purpose of the proposed statute is emasculated; its whole effect is destroyed. You are really giving nothing, for all practical purposes, by the provision here inserted.

I indicated yesterday that, in my judgment, in the prosecution of one of these cases the United States prosecutes as the representative of all of its citizens, and that there is no violation at all of legal principles when any one of its citizens subsequently takes advantage of the adjudication that is made in the primary suit. . . .

Mr. [FRANCIS S.] WHITE [D., Ala.]. There is just one question right at that point which I should like to ask the Senator, and that is where that would leave an alien who might become interested, the same as a citizen?

Mr. WALSH. Perhaps the word "citizen" is not technically correct. The United States brings the action in behalf of anybody who might be interested, which would include everybody who may claim the protection of this Government.

Mr. WHITE. The Senator gave more significance to the word "citizen" than he really intended.

Mr. WALSH. I did not use it in any technical sense.

I was going to say that this principle has received so broad an application that it has even been held when a judgment is taken against a town that judgment may be enforced by satisfaction out of the private property of the citizen [sic] of the town by virtue of a statute so providing. Indeed, Mr. President, that is the ordinary way of satisfying a judgment taken against the town in most of the New England States. It is a practice that prevails in Massachusetts and in the State of Maine. When a suit is instituted against a town every taxpayer of the town is so far included in the proceedings that execution may issue in the action, and his property may be levied upon. Not only that, Mr. President, we are not seeking to make a judgment operative against a citizen, but it is simply an estoppel against the defendant who has had his trial, who has had his day in court.

I want to add, Mr. President, that, in my estimation, constitutional rights are rights that are simply of substance; they do not include mere procedure or forms of law. Those may be changed at the will of the legislative body so long as the substance of the right is not destroyed.

Now, what is the constitutional provision which it is said is transgressed by legislation of this character? It is no other than the rule that no man shall be deprived of his property without due process of law. What is due process of law? Webster defines it as that law which hears before it condemns. In these cases the party has been heard; he has had every opportunity to defend against the claim, and the bill simply provides that when he has had that opportunity and the judgment has gone against him it shall be available not only to the United States, who is a party to the proceedings, but to any citizen of the United States or denizen of the country who desires to take advantage of it. I do not conceive, Mr. President, that this can be of the substance of the right at all. I ask for the yeas and nays on the amendment.

Mr. CULBERSON. Mr. President, I do not propose to argue this question, but I wish to suggest that the statement of the rule of prima facie evidence announced by the Senator from Montana is not so strong as that which the law books lay down. In other words, as I understand, the Senator says that the effect of the committee amendment will only be to shift the burden of proof, whereas the rule as announced by the Supreme Court of the United States is to the general effect that prima facie evidence is such evidence as will support a judgment at law, either criminal or civil, against those whom the rule of prima facie evidence is sought to be invoked, unless rebutted by contrary evidence.

I call attention to an opinion of the Supreme Court of the United States on that question, reported in the Two hundred and nineteenth United States, in the case of Bailey against the State of Alabama,[5.602] page 234, and I will read the paragraph to which I refer:

> Prima facie evidence is sufficient evidence to outweigh the presumption of innocence, and if not met by opposing evidence to support a verdict of guilty. "It is such as in judgment of law is sufficient to establish the fact, and if not rebutted remains sufficient for the purpose." Kelly v. Jackson (6 Pet., 632).[5.603]

Mr. President, in view of that rule announced by the Supreme Court of the United States, and in view of the trend of the decisions of that court to the effect that we can not make a judgment conclusive in which the party claiming it was not a party to the original judgment, I suggest that it is at least dangerous to insert such a doctrine in important legislation of this kind.

Mr. BORAH. Mr. President, I should like to have this section read just as the Senator from Montana desires it to read, and I have a very high regard for his judgment of the law. I must say, however, that I am unable to bring myself to the conclusion that we are not treading upon dangerous ground. I do not say that it might not be possible to sustain that position, but we must find, it seems to me, or ought to find, some distinct precedent for it before we insert it in this bill. There are a number of precedents although not clearly upon the matter as it is here presented, of course, which would lead us to the conclusion that it would not be constitutional, and I am rather inclined to share the view of the Senator from Texas that for that reason we ought not to tread upon that dangerous ground. I think it is safer to proceed upon the other theory.

The VICE PRESIDENT. The Senator from Montana requests the yeas and nays on the committee amendment.

Mr. REED. Mr. President, I should like to ask the Senator from Montana his construction of this section. The section reads as now amended:

> That a final judgment or decree heretofore or hereafter rendered in any criminal prosecution or in any suit or proceeding in equity brought by or on behalf of the United States under the antitrust laws to the effect that a defendant has violated said laws shall be prima facie evidence against such defendant in any suit or proceeding brought by any other party against such defendant under said laws as to all matters respecting which said judgment or decree would be an estoppel as between the parties thereto.

Does the Senator from Montana believe that under that language as it now stands the judgment of the court as to the law involved would be binding as prima facie evidence in the same way that a judgment as to the facts would be binding?

Mr. WALSH. Why, Mr. President, of course the language says that it shall be

---

[5.602] 219 U.S. 219, 31 S. Ct. 145, 55 L. Ed. 191 (1911).
[5.603] 219 U.S. at 234.

prima facie as to all of the matters determined, but the term "prima facie" is not properly applied at all as to the legal principles.

Mr. REED. Does the Senator desire to have the judgment made conclusive both as to the law and the facts?

Mr. WALSH. I do, of course.

Mr. REED. Now, let me put this question to the Senator—

Mr. WALSH. I criticize this provision because you give no effect whatever to the principles of law that have been settled in the primary suit. Every proposition of law is open on the second action.

Mr. REED. Then, Mr. President, the position of the Senator from Montana is that a judgment having been once rendered between the Government and any defendant should thereafter be conclusive in any other suit brought by any other party both as to every question of law and every question of fact involved in the original suit; that is what he desires to accomplish.

What I am saying is not by way of controversy, but to try to clear up this matter. Let me suppose this kind of a case: Let us suppose that an action is brought in a United States circuit court against an individual or corporation for violating the antitrust act; that in that action the court declares the law to be a certain way; that the case is decided against the defendant, and that, thereupon, an appeal is taken to the Supreme Court of the United States, and the Supreme Court of the United States affirms the decree, so that it is a final judgment between the parties. Thereafter an individual brings a suit against the same defendant; but in the meantime the Supreme Court of the United States in another case has absolutely reversed its position upon the law and has held the law as it declared it to be in the case just cited in my illustration to be bad law.

Now, under those circumstances would the Senator say that for all time the bad law declared in that case should be forever enforced against that defendant?

Mr. WALSH. I will answer the Senator by saying that that is just exactly what would happen. Notwithstanding the Supreme Court might subsequently reverse its decision, that bad law would at all times be enforced against the original defendant, and he would be enjoined by the final decree in that action from doing the very things which subsequently the Supreme Court in another case would allow the defendant in that case to continue to do.

Mr. REED. No, Mr. President; the Senator, I think, is inaccurate. It is true that if I have a suit with A, and he defeats me, and final judgment is rendered, the fact that that final judgment is an erroneous and bad judgment and that the law is afterwards otherwise declared does not relieve me of the hardship of bowing to and conforming to that decision. That rule exists, because it is said in the law that there must be an end to litigation. That binds me in that one case; but the fact that I must suffer the hardship of obeying a judgment which is founded upon erroneous considerations in the case I have with A is no reason why, when the law is correctly declared, B, C, D, and E should be enabled to bottom their cases upon a principle which the courts have afterwards declared is a wrong principle. You are extending it. Now, if you make the judgment prima facie, then, of course, as to questions of law, if there is afterwards a reversal of the point—not of the case, but of the law declared in the case—the remedy is there.

The Senator understands perfectly my feeling. I want to make this law as strong as he wants to make it, and he wants to make it as strong as I do. If, however, we were to put into this law a provision making the judgment absolutely conclusive, and if a case such as I have used in my illustration were brought before a court, would not a court be very likely to say: "You are deprived of your day in court; you are deprived of due process of law, because in litigation which did not exist at all at the time the first action was decided you are compelled to submit to a rule of law which is no longer the law of this land"? Indeed, Mr. President, are we not in danger, even if the decision were based upon a statute, and the statute were afterwards repealed, of seeking to bind a defendant conclusively and for all time by a decision bottomed upon such a statute?

Mr. WALSH. If the Senator from Missouri will permit me, I desire to say that you can not possibly minimize the wrong and the hardship that is suffered as the result of a final decision of a court against a man in a case in which the court eventually reaches the conclusion that it was wrong. The man against whom the judgment goes has no redress. He may lose his entire estate, and the law affords no remedy whatever to him. You can not urge that this provision is not sound by supposing a case in which an additional hardship will be wrought where the court originally decides erroneously.

That is all I care to say about the matter; but while I am on my feet I should like to say to the Senator from Idaho— . . .

Mr. [WILLIAM S.] WEST [D., Ga.]. Before the Senator passes from that subject, I should like to ask him a question.

Mr. WALSH. I shall be glad to recur to it, if the Senator will pardon me.

I should like to say to the Senator from Idaho and the Senator from Texas that they need give themselves no deep concern about the possibility of our being wrong about this matter. I was interrogated the other day by the Senator from North Carolina as to whether it was within the power of the legislature to make a tax deed conclusive evidence. I indicated my view about the matter, that it is within the power of the legislature to make the tax deed conclusive of every fact, except such facts as go to the groundwork of the tax; but statutes have been passed which have undertaken thus to make the tax deed conclusive as to every fact recited in the deed; and what has been the holding? It has been that it will not be conclusive evidence, but it will be merely prima facie evidence of the existence of those facts. So, Mr. President, if we should adopt the House provision, declaring that the judgment shall be conclusive, and there are constitutional objections to that, the court will give all the force it can to the statute; namely, it will make it just exactly as the Senators want it—prima facie evidence.

Mr. BORAH. Mr. President, that would be clearly imposing upon the court the duty of legislating—something for which the courts are being very much criticized these days, although often without justification. The Legislature here has up the question whether it shall make a judgment or decree of this kind prima facie or conclusive evidence. We reject the proposition of making it prima facie, and we say that it shall be conclusive. Shall the court have the right to assume that if we could not make it conclusive we would have made it prima facie? In any event I feel that it is our duty to exercise our judgment and not shift responsibility.

Mr. WALSH. Why, Mr. President, it is perfectly obvious that we are trying to make it as valuable as evidence as we can, and the court does not legislate at all. It says that we went further than we had any right to go, but it will give it effect so far as constitutional principles will permit.

Mr. BORAH. May I ask the Senator another question?—because I am going to support the Senator if I become convinced of the legal proposition, and the Senator has great capacity to convince people. Has the Senator any authority or decision, other than those he has cited, with reference to making a judgment against a town conclusive against a citizen of the town? I can see a relationship existing between the citizen and the town which does not exist here. Has the Senator any authority, or has there been any decision, sustaining the proposition, except in the cases where there is relationship between the citizen and the town, or where there is a distinct rule which applies with reference to tax deeds?

We all know that the courts have said that with reference to tax deeds a rule will be applied which does not apply elsewhere, because of the absolute necessity of the Government having a hasty method of collecting its taxes, and to protect those who take the chance of buying tax deeds; but unless there is some other authority than those I should still feel the matter to be in doubt.

Mr. SHAFROTH. Mr. President—

Mr. WALSH. I said on yesterday to the Senator that a very diligent search had failed to reveal any decision which seemed to me bore directly upon the proposition, either one way or the other.

Mr. BORAH. The difficulty of the situation here, it seems to me, is that there is no privity between these parties as there is between the town and its citizen. He is represented in a certain sense there. He is a member of a municipal corporation, a legal entity. He helps to elect the officers. They represent him. He helps to elect the city attorney. He represents him; and there is a certain privity which the courts have found sufficient to sustain that kind of a judgment.

Mr. WALSH. We are supposed to elect a President of the United States, and thereby the Attorney General as well. Can the Senator see any distinction in principle?

Mr. BORAH. I see quite a distinction between electing a President of the United States and having him appoint an Attorney General, and myself as a citizen, where I am a taxpayer, electing the members of an organization of which I am a member. In one instance I am a member of the body politic; in the other I am a member of a legally constituted municipal corporation.

Mr. WALSH. The Senator contributes to the support of the General Government just the same as he does to the support of the local government.

Mr. BORAH. Yes; but the law contemplates that when residing in a city I am a member of a legal entity, a member of a corporation, and that the legal entity represents me the same way as it does the stockholders in other instances: and that is a reason, in my judgment, why the law has thus gone to such an extent in those instances. I confess that I am arguing this matter, however, without having made any examination of the authorities, and simply upon original principles.

Mr. WALSH. I shall be glad now to answer the question of the Senator from Georgia.

Mr. WEST. Mr. President, injected here it would hardly be pertinent to the subject which was discussed, so I shall not propound the question now.

Mr. WHITE. Mr President, in many instances I think the provisions of the House bill contended for by the Senator from Montana [Mr. WALSH] would be useful; but there may be circumstances where it would work great hardship and it may be true— and I am afraid it is true—that it would be unconstitutional. I am afraid we are undertaking to exercise judicial power. When we say that certain facts or certain conclusions are binding on those who are not parties to the litigation, it occurs to me that we are exercising judicial power or invading the domain of the judiciary. If we can do that, can we not deny persons their right to be heard their day in court, as it is termed? And if we do that of course we invade the judicial province.

If we adopt the provisions of the House bill contended for by the Senator from Montana, we are putting ourselves in conflict with a long and well-established principle, a principle that was founded in the common law, namely, that judgments and decrees should bind only parties and privies. Evidently that is founded upon reason; and while we may not have had transmitted to us the reasons on which the principle is grounded we have had the principle itself handed down. It is a principle, as I have said, that had its foundation in the common law, and has existed up to this time. Now, we are changing that. We are declaring by this bill that these judgments and decrees shall be binding upon persons who are not parties or privies to the litigation.

There are good reasons why persons not parties or privies to the action should not be bound. There may be cases where the consequences are insignificant as between the immediate parties involved; for that reason little attention may be given them. It may not be of such vital importance as it afterwards becomes in a controversy between others not then parties to the suit. New burdens may be thrust upon the losing party to the litigation not contemplated or the consequences of which could not have been foreseen at the first trial. I think we ought to be careful and considerate before taking this step.

Again, Mr. President, the fact that we can find no precedent for this legislation either in England or in this country, either by Congress or by the legislatures of the several States, is to me a strong argument why the provisions of the House should not be adopted. If this kind of legislation is beneficial, if it is proper, if it is constitutional, why is it that this legislative weapon has never before been used? I think its disuse through the ages is a strong argument against its use to-day. It is a new field upon which we are entering, a field upon which I hesitate to enter.

Mr. President, another thing: I do not know just what courts have held. If, as the Senator contends, in case the conclusive effect intended can not be given to the act it will be given prima facie effect, I would think better of it. Of course, if I was convinced that the Supreme Court of the United States had or would so decide, that would remove the fear I have on this subject, and that fear is this, that the act will be declared unconstitutional and litigants will lose, because we can not make it conclusive, the prima facie effect of these judgments and decrees which they will have if the committee amendment is adopted. To make the decrees or the judgments of the court prima facie evidence is of vast importance to the litigants of the country. After long years of experience in active practice, I believe, Mr. President, that as many cases are lost or won upon the question as to who shall carry the burden of proof as are lost or won upon a consideration of all the evidence in the case.

Then, Mr. President, as has been said, it is burdensome enough to require parties to the litigation themselves to be bound by the findings of a court or jury in a particular case. So many things that we can not at the time possibly foresee influence such decisions. The way in which the evidence is produced may have its effect upon a jury or a court.

The manner in which the case is handled by the lawyers employed may determine in the mind of a jury or a court what the verdict or the judgment shall be, and yet, Mr. President, those things should probably not have been controlling influences in the conclusions reached. It is hard enough, sir, to make them binding forever upon the parties and the privies to the suit. It is possible that because of the inability of one of the parties to obtain evidence the verdict or judgment was rendered in the way it was, and that it would not have been rendered in that way if the missing evidence had been obtained. One of the parties may have been required to submit his case to a jury upon a showing, as we lawyers term it, which produced the proper effect upon the mind of the judge, but which was not worth the paper upon which it was written when it came to producing an impression upon the mind of a jury.

All these things, I say, argue strongly against making these judgments and decrees binding upon anyone except the parties to the suit. It would not be made binding upon them for a moment if it were not for a public necessity. Courts would not hesitate, they never would have hesitated, to have relieved against wrong and injustice but for the fact that in doing it they would have wronged society by removing from the judgments and decrees the stability that they must have in the interest of society.

Mr. President, in my own State—and I use this as an illustration—our supreme court properly held that when it had once decided a case, ever afterwards, when that case was being considered by the court on a subsequent appeal, the decision first rendered in the case was the law of that case, even though the decision was overruled in some other case; thus the court found itself in the position of having to say that that case which had been overruled was binding in the one case when not binding in any other case. To avoid the hardships imposed by this situation, our legislature enacted a law declaring that the supreme court should no longer adhere to any such rule as that, and that in the future consideration of that case it should be treated as any other case here.

Mr. President, it is with regret that I can not go with the Senator from Montana in supporting the provisions of the House bill. I see in some instances that great good might result from such a course; but I fear that greater harm may come. I fear, too, that it may be unconstitutional, and I fear that we may lose that which we will get by adopting the committee amendment—that is, the prima facie effect of these judgments and decrees. I will therefore vote for the committee amendment.

Mr. WEST. Before the Senator from Alabama takes his seat, I should like to ask him a question. As prima facie evidence, would decrees or judgments rendered change the burden of proof in a subsequent case? I notice the Senator alluded to it a few moments ago in his remarks.

Mr. WHITE. Of course, the judgment and decree rendered in a case would be prima facie evidence under the committee amendment in the cases mentioned in the amendment.

Mr. WEST. But would it shift the burden of proof in any subsequent case?

Mr. WHITE. It would shift the burden of proof in all cases covered by the amendment.

Mr. CUMMINS. Mr. President, I shall vote to sustain the amendment proposed by the committee, although I have grave doubt with respect to its efficiency in accomplishing any great, or even material, good. It would be impossible for me to vote for the proposal in the House bill, first, because I doubt very much its constitutionality, and, second, because I have never been able to understand one feature of the House provision. It is this, that on a decree in any suit in equity brought under the antitrust laws in which a final judgment has been rendered and in which it has been found "that a contract, combination in the form of trust or otherwise, or conspiracy in restraint of trade or commerce, or has monopolized or attempted to monopolize or combined with any person or persons to monopolize any part of commerce, in violation of any of the antitrust laws, said judgment or decree shall, to the full extent to which such judgment or decree would constitute in any other proceeding an estoppel as between the United States and such defendant, constitute against such defendant conclusive evidence of the same facts."

I have racked my mind in vain to imagine any other proceeding that could be brought by the United States in which the former judgment would operate as an estoppel, and I have been unable to conceive how, therefore, the House provision would make the former judgment or decree evidence of anything, inasmuch as I can not imagine how it could be evidence either for or against the United States in any subsequent proceeding. I know no other proceeding which the United States could institute against that defendant upon that cause of action or any other like it.

But there is another objection to it, and the objection I now state is in a measure an objection against the committee amendment. Whenever we pass this provision we will have effectually put an end to all consent decrees. More than one-half, I fancy, of all the decrees which have been entered adjudging that a defendant or defendants have been guilty of a violation of the antitrust laws—I mean those suits against commercial and industrial organizations—have been entered by consent. The defendant or defendants have been willing to cease to do the thing which they were charged with doing and they agreed to a decree, they submitted to the general policy enforced by the Department of Justice, and they are enjoined against a continuation of these practices. . . .

Mr. WHITE. Does not the Senator suppose that they gave consent to these decrees because they knew that the same end would be reached in a trial?

Mr. CUMMINS. Not always. I think in many cases they have been willing to abandon the courses or practices which they have pursued in order to avoid litigation and because the profit in so doing was not sufficient to warrant the trial. But if that consent decree is to be made conclusive evidence in favor of any plaintiff that might thereafter sue the defendant for damages, it goes without saying that the defendant in the Government suit would insist upon a complete trial and a vindication if possible.

I think that a code of business morals has grown up partially through these consent decrees, and that it would be very unfortunate from a high standpoint of public policy to say that these decrees should be conclusive evidence against the defendant of all the things that were charged in the bill of complaint and which may have been covered by the decree. I think it would be far better to make the judgment or decree prima facie evidence. I am a little at sea with regard to just what that means. All these great combinations which have been adjudged guilty of violations of the antitrust law have been guilty of a series of acts, thousands of acts, which joined together constitute a restraint of trade. Very few, I think, have been adjudged guilty of a violation of the law because of any single act.

When a decree is rendered, therefore, holding that there has been a combination in restraint of trade, of what particular act does that decree become either conclusive or prima facie evidence? Take the Standard Oil Co., for instance. It is a prolific illustration. One of the things that it did was to reduce prices in a given locality in order to eliminate a competitor who may have arisen in that locality. That was one thing that this great corporation did and did repeatedly, and it is one of the things, taken with a hundred others, for which it was condemned in the decree of the court. Now, let me turn to the antitrust law. I should like to know precisely what the application of this provision would be. Section 7 declares:

> That any person who shall be injured in his business or property by any other person or corporation, by reason of anything forbidden or declared to be unlawful by this act, may sue therefor in any circuit court of the United States and recover threefold damages.

Suppose that this competitor who had been driven out of business on account of a reduction in price in a particular locality were to sue the Standard Oil Co. to recover damages, of what would the decree that was rendered in the suit against the Standard Oil Co. be—conclusive evidence or prima facie evidence? It would be prima facie evidence, we may assume, of the fact or the compound of law and fact that the Standard Oil Co. had throughout the United States and in all its practices been guilty of a violation of the antitrust law. But in order to recover the person injured must show that he was injured by reason of something forbidden or declared unlawful by the act.

Now, if the thing was a single transaction, if it was a single act, there would be no difficulty about it; but when the thing forbidden, or the thing of which the Standard Oil Co. was found guilty, is a long series of acts and combinations and incorporations, it is my opinion that what we propose to do now, whether we make it prima facie evidence or whether we make it conclusive evidence, will be of little avail to the person who sues to recover. I think he will still have to show that the thing by which he was hurt was a violation of the antitrust law, and in nine cases out of ten the decree does not adjudge that that particular thing was a violation of the antitrust law. I should like in some way, although I do not know how we could do it, to make it much clearer than it is. . . .

Mr. WALSH. I was going to suggest to the Senator from Iowa that I assume that in all of these cases findings of fact are made.

Mr. CUMMINS. Oh, no.

Mr. WALSH. It may be charged, for instance, that local price cutting was practiced with intent to drive Jones or Smith or some one else out of business, and—

Mr. CUMMINS. I think there are very few cases in which there are findings of fact of the sort the Senator from Montana has in mind.

Mr. WALSH. If that is the case, the rule of implied findings would apply.

Mr. CUMMINS. The court reviews the evidence generally, the history of the defendant corporation, and says that all its history shows a violation of the antitrust law or a restraint of trade or an attempt to monopolize. I have never been able to see just how that opinion or that finding or that decree in the case in which the whole field was surveyed could be made available to a particular person who may have been injured by a particular act, which act, taken in connection with all the other acts, constitutes a restraint of trade, but which, taken alone, may not so constitute a restraint of trade.

However, I am expressing that view simply because I did not want it hereafter to be said that I, at least, thought that this section either as passed by the other House or as reported by the Senate committee would solve the problem or would render to the persons who have been injured by specific acts of an offending corporation the relief to which they are entitled, if we could conceive any way to award it to them.

In concluding, Mr. President, I will say that I think it is much better to go slowly with the movement, at any rate, and not to tempt total failure by making a judgment conclusive evidence in the face of the doubt that so many lawyers feel with respect to our power in that respect.

Mr. REED. Mr. President, I think this is a question presenting many grave difficulties, and that it is one that we ought to approach in as calm and judicial a spirit as possible. There can be no difference of opinion among the friends of this bill as to the object which we desire to attain, but in seeking to attain that object it is entirely possible we may defeat our purposes by endeavoring to do something which we are without power to do; or, again, we may defeat our object in its spirit by doing something which is ill-advised.

I grant that in the ordinary case a judgment, having been rendered, might well be made conclusive if we do not run counter to the principle that we are denying the individual his day in court. I do not think that question is without its doubts.

What is meant by your day in court? I think that when a court comes to consider the question of whether a litigant has had his day in court the court is likely to take the position that that expression has a pretty well defined meaning in the law, and that it means in the case where the judgment is about to be rendered that the litigant must be entitled to his full right to put in his evidence and take the judgment of a court or jury upon the facts thus presented in that particular case.

When you simply provide by law that a certain condition of facts shall constitute a prima facie case you do not violate the rule, because the individual still has his right to overcome that evidence, to fight that question out, and to take the judgment of a court or jury upon the whole case. When you make it conclusive a different question is presented.

I am not going to arrogate to myself such wisdom as to say that if you do make it conclusive you are necessarily impinging upon the constitutional right of a citizen, but it occurs to me that it is an exceedingly dangerous thing to do, and that we may by attempting to do too much succeed in doing nothing. When, however, on the other hand, we use the term "prima facie" I think we use a term that is too weak.

When we come to the definitions of "prima facie" we find they vary. I can illustrate that. In "Words and Phrases" I find this definition:

A prima facie case is that state of facts which entitles the party to have the case go to the jury.

If that were the universal rule, I think I could be content with this language as it now is in the bill. Again it is said:

Making it a prima facie case does not necessarily or usually change the burden of proof. A prima facie case is that amount of evidence which would be sufficient to counterbalance the general presumption of innocence, and warrant a conviction if not then encountered and controlled by evidence tending to contradict it and render it improbable, or to prove other facts inconsistent with it.

There we come to a very dangerous doctrine. If a prima facie case is made by laying down the decree in a trust suit, and it is ⊥ sufficient to enable the party who has produced that decree to go to the court or jury, no matter what other evidence is produced, and to have that evidence considered by the jury and to have it regarded by the court as sufficient to sustain the verdict of the jury or the judgment of the court, well and good; but if the court takes the view suggested in the latter definition which I have read, that prima facie is only sufficient to throw the burden upon the other man and to require him to produce evidence, and that when he has produced that evidence the force and effect of the prima facie case is overthrown, you have a doctrine which, if it were held with reference to the legislation we are about to enact, would result in emasculating it. So I have great sympathy for the desire—indeed, I am in perfect accord with the desire—of the Senator from Montana to make these judgments really effective.

How slight a thing a prima facie case may be is well illustrated in a case which I find on momentary examination from my own State—the case of Gilbert [sic] against The Missouri, Kansas & Texas Railway,[5.604] reported in One hundred and ninety-seventh Missouri. The syllabus of that case reads in part:

Under the statute giving to the owner damages for stock which go onto a railroad not "inclosed by a good fence" and are injured no liability attaches to the railroad company for failure to put a cattle guard at the place where the stock enters if to do so would endanger the lives or limbs of the company's employees. No such express exception is written in the statute, but to construe it otherwise would make its meaning unnatural.[5.605]

The third syllabus is the following:

The owner of a horse which went onto a railroad track and was killed makes out a prima facie case of negligence on the part of the railroad by showing that there was no cattle guard at the crossing where the horse entered upon the track, and because of that fact the horse got on the track and was killed. And if his evidence stops there, he has made out a prima facie case, which casts the burden on the railroad company to show that a cattle guard could not have been maintained there without imperiling the lives of railroad employees whose business required them to walk over it. But if, in order to show the condition of the crossing at the particular place, it becomes necessary for plaintiff to show the whole condition, and in doing so he shows a condition which speaks for itself and suggests the question of whether or not a cattle guard could be maintained at the place without endangering the lives of the company's employees whose business in operating trains compelled them to pass over it, the burden was

---

[5.604] The correct citation is Gilpin v. Missouri, K. & T. Ry., 197 Mo. 319, 94 S.W. 869 (1906).

[5.605] 197 Mo. at 319 (quote from the court's syllabus).

not cast upon defendant; but plaintiff, under such circumstances, is not entitled to ask the jury for a verdict until he has shown by some explanatory evidence that a cattle guard could have been maintained there without imperiling the lives and limbs of the railroad employees.[5.606]

It will be observed by the few Senators who are giving this bill consideration that in that case the statute which declared that a certain showing was prima facie was reduced so that it simply made the shadow of a showing, which could be blown aside by very slight evidence to the contrary.

I think it would be very wise if we passed by this section this morning, and let us see if we can not determine on some language which will strengthen it in this regard. I am afraid to vote for the amendment offered by the Senator from Montana, because I fear it might destroy the whole law. I am afraid to vote for it for another reason....

... It is that I can see cases where it might do a great injustice. As I observed a little while ago, this judgment would be conclusive, both as to law and as to fact; and it might be that after a judgment was rendered and the law declared in a certain manner, the highest authority in the country might declare that law to be bad law; and yet, for all time that judgment would stand, and any person could invoke it and it would be conclusive upon the party against whom it was rendered, although the Supreme Court of the United States might have otherwise declared the law....

⊥13906   ⊥ The PRESIDING OFFICER. The question is on the amendment reported by the committee, as amended.

Mr. WALSH. I ask for the yeas and nays, Mr. President.

The PRESIDING OFFICER. The Senator from Montana asks for the yeas and nays.

Mr. OWEN. Let the amendment be stated before the question is put.

The PRESIDING OFFICER. Is the demand for the yeas and nays seconded?

The yeas and nays were ordered.

The PRESIDING OFFICER. The Secretary will call the roll.

The Secretary proceeded to call the roll, and Mr. ASHURST voted in the negative.

Mr. [ROBERT L.] OWEN [D., Okla.]. Before the Chair ordered the roll called, I had requested that the amendment might be stated.

The PRESIDING OFFICER. The amendment is to strike out section 6 of the House bill and to insert the provision reported by the Senate committee as amended. The Secretary will call the roll.

Mr. WALSH. Mr. President, if I may be permitted—

Mr. OWEN. I do not know what that amendment is, and I want it stated.

The PRESIDING OFFICER. The Senator is now too late. The yeas and nays have been ordered, and the roll call has been begun.

Mr. OWEN. But the request was made—

The PRESIDING OFFICER. The amendment may be stated by unanimous consent. That is the only way it can be done.

Mr. OWEN. The request was made of the Chair before the roll call was begun.

The PRESIDING OFFICER. If there be no objection, the Secretary will restate the amendment. The Chair hears none.

The SECRETARY. On page 5, line 12, after the words "Sec. 6," it is proposed to strike out:

That whenever in any suit or proceeding in equity hereafter brought by or on behalf of the United States under any of the antitrust laws there shall have been rendered a final judgment or decree to the effect that a defendant has entered into a contract, combination in the form of trust or otherwise, or conspiracy, in restraint of trade or commerce, or has monopolized or attempted to monopolize or combined with any person or persons to monopolize, any part of commerce, in violation of any of the antitrust laws, said judgment or decree shall, to the full extent to which such judgment or decree would constitute in any other proceeding an estoppel as between the United States and such defendant, constitute against such defendant conclusive evidence of the same facts, and be conclusive as to the same questions of law in favor of any other party in any action or proceeding brought under or involving the provisions of any of the antitrust laws.

[5.606] *Id.*

Whenever any suit or proceeding in equity is hereafter brought by or on behalf of the United States, under any of the antitrust laws, the statute of limitations in respect of each and every private right of action arising under such antitrust laws and based, in whole or in part, on any matter complained of in said suit or proceeding in equity shall be suspended during the pendency of such suit or proceeding in equity.

And to insert:

That a final judgment or decree heretofore or hereafter rendered in any criminal prosecution or in any suit or proceeding in equity brought by or on behalf of the United States under the antitrust laws to the effect that a defendant has violated said laws shall be prima facie evidence against such defendant in any suit or proceeding brought by any other party against such defendant under said laws as to all matters respecting which said judgment or decree would be an estoppel as between the parties thereto.

Any person may be prosecuted, tried, or punished for any offense under the antitrust laws, and any suit arising under those laws may be maintained if the indictment is found or the suit is brought within six years next after the occurrence of the act or cause of action complained of, any statute of limitation or other provision of law heretofore enacted to the contrary notwithstanding. Whenever any suit or proceeding in equity is instituted by the United States to prevent or restrain violations of any of the antitrust laws the running of the statute of limitations in respect of each and every private right of action arising under said laws and based in whole or in part on any matter complained of in said suit or proceeding shall be suspended during the pendency thereof: *Provided,* That this shall not be held to extend the statute of limitations in the case of offenses heretofore committed.

The Secretary resumed the calling of the roll.

Mr. CHAMBERLAIN (when his name was called). I have a general pair with the junior Senator from Pennsylvania [Mr. OLIVER]. He being absent, I withold my vote.

Mr. CULBERSON (when his name was called). I transfer my general pair with the Senator from Delaware [Mr. DU PONT] to the Senator from Arizona [Mr. SMITH] and vote "yea."

Mr. GALLINGER (when his name was called). I have a pair with the junior Senator from New York [Mr. O'GORMAN]. He is absent from the Chamber, and I transfer that pair to the Senator from Illinois [Mr. SHERMAN] and vote "yea."

Mr. GORE (when his name was called). I have a pair with the junior Senator from Wisconsin [Mr. STEPHENSON]. I therefore withhold my vote.

Mr. OWEN (when his name was called). I have a pair with the Senator from New Mexico [Mr. CATRON]. If I were at liberty to vote, I should vote "nay."

Mr. REED (when his name was called). I have a general pair with the Senator from Michigan [Mr. SMITH]. In his absence I withhold my vote.

Mr. SMITH of Georgia (when his name was called). I have a general pair with the senior Senator from Massachusetts [Mr. LODGE]. In his absence I withhold my vote.

Mr. STONE (when his name was called). I have a standing pair with the Senator from Wyoming [Mr. CLARK]. In his absence I withhold my vote.

Mr. TILLMAN (when his name was called). I have a pair with the Senator from West Virginia [Mr. GOFF]. In his absence I withhold my vote.

The roll call was concluded.

Mr. THOMAS. I have a general pair with the senior Senator from New York [Mr. ROOT]. In his absence I withhold my vote.

Mr. GRONNA. I wish to inquire if the senior Senator from Maine [Mr. JOHNSON] has voted?

The PRESIDING OFFICER. The Chair is informed that he has not.

Mr. GRONNA. I have a pair with that Senator, but I will transfer that pair to the Senator from California [Mr. WORKS] and vote "nay."

Mr. POINDEXTER. Mr. President, a parliamentary inquiry. I understand that the vote is directly upon the amendment of the committee to section 6 of the bill?

The PRESIDING OFFICER. It is.

Mr. POINDEXTER. I vote "nay."

Mr. WILLIAMS (after having voted in the affirmative). I inquire if the senior Senator from Pennsylvania [Mr. PENROSE] has voted?

The PRESIDING OFFICER. The Chair is informed that he has not.

Mr. WILLIAMS. I was so informed a moment ago; but I thought the Senator was in the Chamber, and I voted. I transfer my pair with him to the junior Senator from South Carolina [Mr. SMITH] and will let my vote stand.

Mr. LEA of Tennessee. I have a general pair with the senior Senator from South Dakota [Mr. CRAWFORD]. In his absence I withhold my vote. If at liberty to vote, I would vote "nay."

Mr. SMOOT. I desire to announce the unavoidable absence of my colleague [Mr. SUTHERLAND], and will let the announcement stand for the day. He has a general pair with the senior Senator from Arkansas [Mr. CLARKE].

Mr. GALLINGER. I am requested to announce the pair of the Senator from Maine [Mr. BURLEIGH] with the Senator from New Hampshire [Mr. HOLLIS]; of the Senator from Rhode Island [Mr. MCLEAN] with the Senator from Montana [Mr. MYERS]; of the Senator from Michigan [Mr. TOWNSEND] with the Senator from Arkansas [Mr. ROBINSON]; and of the Senator from Wyoming [Mr. WARREN] with the Senator from Florida [Mr. FLETCHER].

The result was announced—yeas 35, nays 16, as follows:

YEAS—35.

Bankhead	Gallinger	Nelson	Smoot
Borah	Hitchcock	Newlands	Sterling
Bryan	Hughes	Overman	Swanson
Burton	Kenyon	Perkins	Thornton
Camden	Lane	Pomerene	Weeks
Chilton	Lee, Md.	Ransdell	West
Culberson	Lippitt	Shafroth	White
Cummins	McCumber	Simmons	Williams
Fall	Martin, Va.	Smith, Md.	

NAYS—16.

Ashurst	James	Martine, N. J.	Sheppard
Bristow	Jones	Norris	Shively
Clapp	Kern	Pittman	Thompson
Gronna	Lewis	Poindexter	Walsh

NOT VOTING—45.

Brady	Goff	Page	Stephenson
Brandegee	Gore	Penrose	Stone
Burleigh	Hollis	Reed	Sutherland
Catron	Johnson	Robinson	Thomas
Chamberlain	La Follette	Root	Tillman
Clark, Wyo.	Lea, Tenn.	Saulsbury	Townsend
Clarke, Ark.	Lodge	Sherman	Vardaman
Colt	McLean	Shields	Warren
Crawford	Myers	Smith, Ariz.	Works
Dillingham	O'Gorman	Smith, Ga.	
du Pont	Oliver	Smith, Mich.	
Fletcher	Owen	Smith, S. C.	

So the amendment as amended was agreed to.

Mr. POMERENE. Mr. President, I desire to speak this afternoon on the subject of the labor provisions contained in this bill. Since I have been in the Senate it has been my pleasure to aid in the establishment of a Department of Labor, the establishment of a Children's Bureau, to vote for the eight-hour law in the District of Columbia, to support the workmen's compensation bill, and to support a great may [sic] other measures which I conceived would aid in relieving the burdens of labor and redound to the general welfare. There are many provisions in this bill on this subject which have my hearty concurrence. I am unqualifiedly in favor of requiring notice to be given before an injunction or restraining order is issued whenever it is possible to give notice and subserve the ends of justice.

I am heartily in favor of jury trials in cases of indirect contempt. In this country we believe in jury trials. There is very little sentiment opposing jury trials in any issue of fact in a law case or in criminal cases, and if we believe in jury trials where the rights of litigants are at stake, it seems to me that there can be no good reason assigned why we should not have a jury trial in the case of indirect contempt.

When a court issues its order it is, so to speak, the statute in that particular case until it is modified or set aside. If the delinquent is found guilty, he is punishable in the discretion of the court either by fine or by imprisonment or by both. The contempt charged may have been committed miles away from the presence of the court; the court can have no knowledge upon the subject save such as the information contains and such as the testimony produced before it affords; and in these cases we know, as a matter of fact, that often there is the most intense feeling prevailing on both sides of the case, and, I regret to say, that it sometimes extends even to the court whose order it is alleged has been trampled under foot. That being the situation, it seems to me that we are only furthering a general principle which we have recognized time out of mind when we say that in those cases a trial by jury shall be granted to the delinquent.

There are other features, however, in the pending bill which give to me serious trouble. I refer particularly to sections 7 and 18.

I am a friend of the Sherman law. For a long time it was a dead letter upon the statute books; new life has been breathed into it; and I would regret to see any exemption made as to any of its provisions for any class of citizens, high or low, rich or poor. I take this position because I believe, first, that it would be inimical to the public welfare, and, secondly, I think I shall be able to demonstrate before I shall take my seat that it would be hostile to the interests of the laboring classes themselves.

Mr. President, I recognize the fact that the Sherman law has been severely criticized. It has been criticized by all classes, whether they be of the employer class or the employee class, when they come in contact with its provisions. I know that the friends of the pending measure are prone to say that there is no such thing as a trust in labor; that in that respect it is differentiated from capital; and I concede that to be so; but I do not think that an examination of the Sherman law justifies the contention that is made by the friends of the pending bill to the effect that it has ever been claimed that labor is a trust.

The present Sherman law is not in the same form as when it was first introduced in the Senate by Senator Sherman. I want to place emphasis upon that fact.

My very good friend from Arizona [Mr. ASHURST] the other day quoted at length from speeches made on the floor of the Senate by Senator Sherman, Senator Teller, Senator Stewart, and perhaps one or two others, to the effect that it was not intended to cover labor or its derelictions, if any, by the provisions of the bill. There was such a contention as that in the earlier discussion of the bill and before it was finally passed.

The bill was introduced on December 4, 1889. It was referred to the committee, reported to the Senate with amendments, and the discussion, in which it was said that it was not intended to cover labor organizations or their operations, took place before the bill assumed final form. Such was the view expressed on March 24 by Senator Teller, on March 25 by Senator Stewart, and on March 27 by Senator Hoar. On the other hand, Senator Edmunds, on March 27, 1890, as will be seen by referring to the CONGRESSIONAL RECORD of that session, page 2729, spoke in part as follows:

> On the one side you say that it is a crime and on the other side you say it is a valuable and proper undertaking. That will not do, Mr. President. You can not get on in that way. It is impossible to separate them and the principle of it therefore is that if one side, no matter which it is, is authorized to combine the other side must be authorized to combine or the thing will break and there will be universal bankruptcy. That is what it will come to, and then the laborer, whose interest and welfare we are all so really desirous to promote, will turn around and justly say to the Senate of the United States, "Why did you go to such legislation as that? Why did you attempt to stimulate and almost require us to combine against our employers, and thus break down the whole industry of the country and leave us all beggars? When you allowed us to combine and to regulate our wages why did you not allow the products that our hands produced to be raised in price by an arrangement, so that everybody that bought them might pay the increased price and everybody that was making them all around for whom we were working could live also?" I do not think, as a practical thing, Mr. President, that anybody will thank us for making a distinction of that kind.

If those on one side of a proposition are to be compelled to respond to a criminal statute, it is difficult to conceive why those who are on the other side of that question should not ⊥ also be required to respond to its criminal or civil provisions, as the case may be.

I refer to the earlier discussion of the Sherman law for the purpose of calling the attention of the Senate to the fact that the bill which was under consideration at the time these expressions were made by Senators Hoar, Teller, and Stewart was not the bill as it passed the Senate. During the discussion and after the question was raised as to whether or not the provisions of the bill as it was originally introduced or as it was thereafter modified by the committee were broad enough to embrace labor and agricultural organizations, Senator Sherman submitted an amendment in the following words:

Provided, That this act shall not be construed to apply to any arrangements, agreements, or combinations between laborers made with the view of lessening the number of hours of their labor or of increasing their wages, nor to any arrangements, agreements, associations, or combinations among persons engaged in horticulture or agriculture made with a view of enhancing the price of their own agricultural or horticultural products.

The same amendment was later offered by the then Senator from Rhode Island, Mr. Aldrich.

On March 27, 1890, the bill was recommitted to the Judiciary Committee, and on April 2 it was reported out, completely changed in its form and its provisions. The exemption clause which had been engrafted upon it by a committee amendment before its recommittal was entirely eliminated from the bill. After that—and I think I speak advisedly from a considerable examination which I have given the record myself, as well as by valuable assistants in my office—no reference was made to the question of the application or nonapplication of the provisions of the Sherman law to labor or agricultural organizations. So much it seems to me should be said in the interest of the history of that legislation. The fact that such exemptions were placed in the bill and later taken out by the committee, and its action afterwards confirmed by the Senate, clearly indicates an intention on the part of the Congress to make no exemptions.

Now, I desire to call attention particularly to the provisions of the Sherman law as it passed on July 2, 1890. The title of the bill had been changed. The title of the bill as introduced by Senator Sherman was:

A bill to declare unlawful trusts and combinations in restraint of trade and production.

I offer, without reading it, the first section of that bill, and ask that it be incorporated in my remarks.

The PRESIDING OFFICER (Mr. GRONNA in the chair). In the absence of objection, it is so ordered.

The section referred to is as follows:

Be it enacted, etc., That all arrangements, contracts, agreements, trusts, or combinations between persons or corporations made with the intention to prevent full and free competition in the importation, transportation, or sale of articles imported into the United States, or in the production, manufacture, or sale of articles of domestic growth or production, or domestic raw material, that competes with any similar article upon which a duty is levied by the United States, intended for and which shall be transported from one State or Territory to another for sale, and all such arrangements, contracts, agreements, trusts, or combinations between persons or corporations, intended to advance the cost to the consumer of any such articles, are hereby declared to be against public policy, unlawful, and void.

Mr. POMERENE. Mr. President, the title was amended so that it now reads:

An act to protect trade and commerce against unlawful restraints and monopolies.

It is not a law against organizations per se, whether they be of labor, or of capital, or what not. It was recognized in the early history of that law that most of the restraints of trade were occasioned by unlawful combinations of capital and monopolies, but it was also likewise recognized that a restraint of trade was in itself inimical to the public good no matter what its origin. The first section of the law, in part, reads as follows:

Every contract, combination in the form of trust or otherwise, or conspiracy, in restraint of trade or commerce among the several States, or with foreign nations, is hereby declared to be illegal.

So we see that the ultimate object of this law was not to prevent combinations of any kind, but its primary purpose was to prevent restraints of trade. Conceding for the moment that a restraint of trade ought to be prohibited, it seems to me that it makes but very little difference whether that restraint of trade is made by one class of citizens or by another class. The effect, so far as the public is concerned, is one and the same.

Mr. President, if there ever was any question as to the construction which is to be placed upon this act, it was ended for all time when the Supreme Court, in the Standard Oil Co. case and in the American Tobacco Co. case, said that the words "restraint of trade" meant only an undue restraint of trade. Conceding that to be the proper construction to be placed upon this act, can anyone say for one minute that a combination or organization of laborers for the purpose of obtaining a reasonable wage, or for the purpose of shortening hours, or for the purpose of obtaining reasonably good labor conditions is an undue restraint of trade? The proposition only needs to be stated to fall.

I submit this statement again: If a restraint of trade is a thing that ought to be guarded against by the laws of the United States, it can make no difference, so far as the public welfare is concerned, whether that restraint of trade is due to one class or to another class; the result is the same.

I recognize the fact that there is considerable sentiment in this country among our laboring friends asking for this exemption. I do not believe they would ask it if they understood what the law in fact is.

It is charged that it has been resorted to too frequently; that labor has been made to suffer unduly. The law was passed July 2, 1890, twenty-four years ago. Since that time the Department of Justice has begun 166 cases, and I have on my desk here two letters from the Assistant Attorney General showing that in the 24 years only 13 of these cases have been brought by the department against labor organizations. . . .

Mr. CUMMINS. I desire to recall to the Senator from Ohio a statement made by him a moment ago concerning which I wish to ask a question and upon which my own mind is not at all clear.

The Senator from Ohio said that it has never been claimed that a labor organization the purpose of which is to secure reasonable wages for its members is a combination in restraint of trade. I should like to know whether the Senator from Ohio attaches any significance to the use of the word "reasonable"? Suppose a combination of workingmen were to come together to secure what some people would call unreasonable wages; would such a combination be in violation of the antitrust law? If so, who is to determine whether the demand of the organization is reasonable or unreasonable?

Mr. POMERENE. Mr. President, I used the word "reasonable" at the time, I think, without attaching any considerable importance to it. My belief is, under the law, that when it comes to contests for an increase of wages, for betterment of hours, for betterment of conditions, so long as it is by peaceful means, this law would not apply, no matter whether the demands are reasonable or not; and I wish in a little while to take up this proposition and discuss it from a legal standpoint. In order that I may do this in the logical order, I desire to call attention to a statement of the law as it is believed to be by the American Federation of Labor.

I read from the report of the Judiciary Committee, on page 10—there is a little more to it in the report of the testimony, but I shall content myself with reading from the report of the Judiciary Committee.

Mr. WEST. Mr. President, before the Senator starts, may I ask whether that is the report of 1890?

Mr. POMERENE. No; it is contained in the report of 1914 submitted on this bill by the chairman of the committee.

Mr. Gompers, in discussing the subject, said:

> Gentlemen, under the interpretation placed upon the Sherman antitrust law by the courts, it is within the province and within the power of any administration at any time to begin proceedings to dissolve any organization of labor in the United States and to take charge of and receive whatever funds any worker or organization may have wanted to contribute or felt that it is his duty to contribute to the organization.

Mr. WEBB. Are there any suits pending in the courts now looking to this end, Mr. Gompers?

Mr. GOMPERS. There are no suits now pending, but an organization of workingmen, the window-glass workers, was dissolved by order of the court under the provisions of the Sherman antitrust law, charged with conspiracy as an illegal combination in restraint of trade. And while that organization was dissolved by action of the court, yet it created no furor, for this reason: I have no desire to reflect upon the men who are in charge of that organization as its officers and representatives, but it was, in my judgment, supine cowardice for them not to resist an attempt of the dissolution of their associated effort as a voluntary organization of men to protect the only thing they possessed—the power to labor.

It will be noted that there are not enough of the accompanying facts to advise us as to what the conspiracy was or the nature of it. . . .

Mr. WEBB. Have you any case where a labor organization has been dissolved simply because they themselves united in asking or fixing a certain wage and went no further in uniting with the manufacturers?

Mr. GOMPERS. I can not tell you, sir, about that. But that is the very essence of the life of the organization. What I want to convey is ⊥ this, that there are probably, of these 30,000 or more local associations of workingmen, what we call local unions of workingmen and workingwomen, probably more than two-thirds of whom have agreements with employers. As a matter of fact, I think that every observer and every humanitarian who knows greeted with the greatest satisfaction the creation of the protocol in the sweated industries of New York City and vicinity which abolished sweat shops and long hours of labor, and the burdensome, miserable toil prevailing, and established the combination of employers and of workmen and workwomen by which certain standards are to be enforced, and no employer can become a member of the manufacturers' association in that trade unless he is willing to undersign an agreement by which the conditions prevailing in the protocol will be inaugurated by him. Yet, under the provisions of the Sherman antitrust law, that association of manufacturers has been sued, I think, for something like $250,000, because it is a conspiracy in restraint of trade.

What I mean to say is this: I am perfectly satisfied in my own mind that the Attorney General of this administration, the Attorney General of the United States under the present administration, is not going to dissolve or make any attempt to dissolve the organizations of the working people of this country. I firmly believe that if there should be any of them, any individual or an aggregation of individuals, guilty of any crime, that the present administration would proceed against them just as readily, and perhaps more so, as any other; I am speaking of the procedure against the organizations themselves and the dissolution of them.

But who can tell whether this administration is going to continue very long, or whether the same policy is going to be pursued; that is, the policy of permitting these associations to exist without interference or attempts to isolate them? Who can tell what may come, what may not the future hold in store for us working people who are engaged in an effort for the protection of men and women who toil to make life better worth living? We do not want to exist as a matter of sufferance, subject to the whims or to the chances or to the vindictiveness of any administration or of any administration officer. Our existence is justified not only by our history, but our existence is legally the best concept of what constitutes law. It is an outrage; it is an outrage of not only the conscience, it is an outrage upon justice, it is an outrage upon our language, to attempt to place in the same category a combination of men engaged in the speculation and the control of the products of labor and the products of the soil on the one hand and the associations of men and women who own nothing but themselves and undertake to control nothing but themselves and their power to work.

Mr. FLOYD. I want to see if I understand your position. If I understand your position under the existing status of the law as determined by the Federal courts, if the Attorney General should proceed to dissolve any of your labor organizations they could be dissolved. Is that your proposition.

Mr. GOMPERS. Yes, sir.

Mr. FLOYD. And that your existence, therefore, depends upon the sufferance of the administration which happens to be in power for the time being?

Mr. GOMPERS. Yes, sir.

Mr. FLOYD. What you desire is for us to give you a legal status under the law?

Mr. GOMPERS. Yes, sir.

Mr. FLOYD. So you can carry on this cooperative work on behalf of the laborers of the country and of the different organizations without being under the ban of the existing law?

Mr. GOMPERS. Yes, sir.

Mr. President, if that were the law as stated, I would vote for its repeal; but I submit that no respectable court has ever so held. All organizations are legal unless there is something in the law which makes them illegal. Labor organizations have been recognized time out of mind, and I hope they always will be. If I were a laboring man, I would be an organization man; and if I were an employer of labor, I would encourage my men to be organization men, because I believe labor organizations have been an instrumentality of very great good in this country.

I now yield to the Senator from Idaho.

Mr. BORAH. Mr. President, as I understand the case to which Mr. Gompers referred in his testimony there, the Glassworkers' case, in which it is said that the organization was proceeded against under the Sherman law, it was a case arising in the Senator's State. I was going to ask the Senator if it is his purpose to discuss that case, or if he is familiar with the facts?

Mr. POMERENE. I am not familiar with the facts in the case.

Mr. BORAH. I have made some investigation in regard to it, and my investigation leads me to the conclusion—it was a case of a nisi prius court—that it was not a proceeding under the Sherman law at all, but under the common law and the statutes of the State of Ohio.

Mr. POMERENE. I am very much obliged to the Senator for his statement.

Mr. BORAH. I shall not take up the time of the Senator now in discussing it. . . .

Mr. CULBERSON. I should like to ask the Senator from Ohio if he has examined the case in West Virginia, the opinion in which was delivered by Judge Dayton a year or two ago, in which it was held under the Sherman law that labor organizations were illegal?[5.607]

Mr. POMERENE. I have not. But does the Senator say that that was so held without any other accompanying facts?

Mr. CULBERSON. I have sent for the book. I make the general statement that labor organizations were held to be illegal by Judge Dayton. . . .

Mr. POMERENE. . . . If that be true, it has not been recognized as a precedent; and if it be true, the judge made a mistake—just such a mistake as he could make or any other judge that was not well informed as to the law. . . .

Mr. HUGHES. I desire to ask the Senator if he is familiar with the various decisions that were handed down in the Danbury Hat case?

Mr. POMERENE. I am.

Mr. HUGHES. The Senator, then, doubtless will remember that in one of the courts—I forget whether it was the Supreme Court or the other court—the opinion held that the Sherman antitrust law acted in the Federal jurisdiction as the common law acted in the various States, and that it was even broader than the common law so far as restraints and monopolies were concerned. If that be so, of course the Senator is familiar with the fact that in the absence of a statute and under the common law of England any three or more men who simultaneously withdraw from an employer's employment are guilty of a conspiracy.

Mr. POMERENE. Oh, Mr. President, I am not going to take time to discuss the common law of England, except to say that the hostile and vicious decisions which are rendered by the English courts—and I speak generally now; there may be exceptions—were under statutes passed by Parliament and not under the common law; and whatever may have been the common law or statute law in England upon that subject, the rule has never obtained in the United States that an organization of laboring men did not have the right to organize and strike for higher wages or for shorter hours or for better conditions.

Mr. HUGHES. Mr. President, I know the Senator does not wish to make a misstatement.

Mr. POMERENE. Certainly not.

Mr. HUGHES. I wish to call his attention to a case which arose in my own State. It was brought home to me with peculiar force by reason of the fact that the craft which was affected was a craft of which my own father was a member. He was at that time an iron molder in the city of Paterson. The strike occurred in a molding shop, and 14 or 15 iron molders simultaneously withdrew from that employment. They were

---

[5.607] Hitchman Coal & Coke Co. v. Mitchell, 202 F. 512 (N.D. W. Va. 1912), *rev'd*, 214 F. 685 (4th Cir. 1914), *rev'd*, 245 U.S. 229 (1917) (decree of district court modified, and, as modified, affirmed).

indicted as common-law conspirators and were sent to the penitentiary. The Legislature of the State of New Jersey at its next meeting passed an act which is in substance the act which is before us now, providing that these men could do these very things, and that they would not be conspirators under the common law.

Mr. POMERENE. Mr. President, I think I limited my statement to the general proposition. If there has been a case here and there in which the law has been too severe in its provisions or administration, we can not correct that by this kind of legislation. The matter to which the Senator has referred was a local matter, under a local statute, or under the local common law. . . .

Mr. NELSON. I dislike to interrupt the Senator; but I simply rose for the purpose of calling his attention to the fact that, under the practice and procedure of the United States Government, we have no common-law offenses.

Mr. POMERENE. Very true.

Mr. NELSON. All criminal offenses against the United States are statutory offenses; and the cases to which the Senator from New Jersey has referred were cases arising under the local law in that State. I may further add that, I think, in most of the States they have few if any common-law offenses; they are nearly all statutory offenses of the State.

Mr. POMERENE. I think the Senator has correctly stated the proposition.

Now, Mr. President, if I may be permitted to proceed with my argument without any further interruption, I shall appreciate it. It is very warm, and I feel that my strength will not permit me to continue for the entire afternoon.

⊥ I desire now to call the attention of the Senate to the law as I conceive it to be in the United States; and I wish to read a paragraph from United States v. Cassidy (67 Fed. Rep., 700):

> The employees of railway companies have a right to organize for mutual benefit and protection and for the purpose of securing the highest wages and the best conditions they can command. They may appoint officers, who shall advise them as to the course to be taken in their relations with their employer, and they may, if they choose, repose in their officers authority to order them, or any of them, on pain of expulsion from their union, peaceably to leave the employment because the terms thereof are unsatisfactory. But it is unlawful for them to combine and quit work for the purpose of compelling their employer to withdraw from his relations with a third party for the purpose of injuring that third party.[5.608]

This follows the opinion of Judge Taft in Thomas v. Railway (62 Fed., 817).[5.609]

Again I wish to call the attention of the Senate to the case of United States v. Workingmen's Amalgamated Council (54 Fed., 994).[5.610] Paragraph 5 of the syllabus reads:

> The fact that a combination of men is in its origin and general purposes innocent and lawful is no ground of defense when the combination is turned to the unlawful purpose of restraining interstate and foreign commerce.
>
> A combination of men to secure or compel the employment of none but union men becomes a combination in restraint of interstate commerce within the meaning of the statute when, in order to gain its ends, it seeks to enforce, and does enforce, by violence and intimidation, a discontinuance of labor in all departments of business, including the transportation of goods from State to State and to and from foreign nations.[5.611]

This is one of the cases which has been referred to repeatedly before our committees as being in support of the proposition that an organization of this character was per se a violation of the law, but an examination of the opinion delivered by Billings, district judge, shows that there were acts of violence of the rankest kind, and a part of the evidence in the case shows this:

> To the representative of a morning paper Assistant State Organizer Porter said the outlook for successful strike was most excellent and promised that every union in the city would stand

---

[5.608] 67 F. 698, 700 (N.D. Cal. 1895). The quoted material is a headnote.

[5.609] Thomas v. Cincinnati, N.O. & T.P. Ry., 62 F. 803 (C.C.S.D. Ohio 1894).

[5.610] 54 F. 994 (C.C.E.D. La.), aff'd, 57 F. 85 (5th Cir. 1893).

[5.611] 54 F. at 994-95. The quoted material is from the headnotes.

by the locked-out workmen. He said it was possible a general strike would be ordered and that labor is determined to win this struggle. A union man who was with Mr. Porter is represented to have said that the strike will be made a victory of the laboring classes of the city, and unless the unions are recognized there will be more bloodshed than imagined. Mr. Porter is reported to have added, "We propose to win by peace if we can, but if we are pushed to the wall force will be employed."[5.612]

In this particular case the entire commerce of the city, interstate in character, had been interfered with.

Mr. President, I have here a large number of authorities, and, without taking the time of the Senate to read them all, I ask permission to incorporate them in my remarks.

The PRESIDING OFFICER. Without objection, it is so ordered.

The matter referred to is as follows:

Trades-unions are not unlawful combinations so long as they do not resort to acts tending to destroy freedom of action, such as intimidation, threats, or violence. Hence it is not contrary to public policy or illegal for a member of a union to combine with others for the purpose of maintaining wages or limiting the number of apprentices. (Longshore Printing Co. v. Howell, 46 Am. St. Repts., p. 640.)

Trades-unions and labor organizations must depend for their membership upon the free choice of each member and his perfect freedom of action. No resort can be had to violence, threats, intimidation, or other compulsory methods in matters concerning membership, or to enforce the observance of their laws, rules, and regulations.

Strikes among workingmen are not necessarily unlawful, though they may become both illegal and criminal by the means employed to enforce their objects. Employees may lawfully quit their service either singly or in a body, but if unlawful means are used to uphold or maintain a strike, or if the end to be attained is unlawful, then the strike itself is unlawful. (Longshore Printing Co. v. Howell, 46 Am. St. Repts., 640.)[5.613]

In the above-cited case, Judge Wolverton, at page 646, in discussing the statement "that there is no such thing as a legal or peaceful 'strike,'" cites the following case:

Justice Harlan, in the now celebrated case of Arthur v. Oakes (63 Fed. Rep., 327), says: "We are not prepared, in the absence of evidence to hold, as a matter of law, that a combination among employees having for its object their orderly withdrawal in large number or in a body from the service of their employers, on account simply of a reduction in their wages, is not a 'strike' within the meaning of the word as commonly used. Such a withdrawal, although amounting to a strike, is not, as we have already said, either illegal or criminal."[5.614]

An employee has an unquestionable right to place a price and impose conditions upon his labor at the outset of his employment, or, unless restrained by contract obligations, upon the continuance of his labor at any time thereafter, and, if the terms and conditions are not complied with by the employer, he has a clear right to engage, or having engaged in the service to cease from work, and what one may do all may lawfully combine to do for the purpose of rendering their action more effective. But this right of combination and to strike or quit the employment must be exercised in a peaceable and lawful manner, without violence or destruction of property or other coercive measures intended to prevent the employer from securing other employees, or otherwise carrying on his business according to his own judgment.

It is the right of labor to organize for lawful purposes, and by organic agreement to subject the individual members to rules, regulations, and conduct prescribed by the majority; and the courts can not enjoin the officers or committees of such an organization from counseling or ordering a strike in the exercise of authority given them by the laws and sanctioned by a majority of its members, nor can such action be made the basis of a charge of malicious conspiracy. (Wabash R. R. Co. v. Hannahan et al., 121 Fed., 563.)[5.615]

The members of a labor union may, singly or in a body, quit the service of their employer; and for the purpose of strengthening their association they may persuade and induce other workmen to join their union, and as a means to that end refuse to allow their members to work where nonunion labor is employed.

[5.612] *Id.* at 998.

[5.613] 26 Ore. 527, 38 P. 547, 46 Am. St. R. 640 (1894). The quoted material is from the headnotes in *American State Reports*, 46 Am. St. R. at 640. It does not appear in the official report.

[5.614] 26 Ore. at 542–43.

[5.615] 121 F. 563 (C.C.E.D. Mo. 1903). The quoted material is from the headnotes.

It is not unlawful for members of a labor union to go upon premises, with the owner's permission, for the purpose of enticing or ordering their associates to desist from work thereon unless their conduct is so persistent and annoying to the owner or contractor as to constitute a nuisance. (Gray v. Building Trades Council, 103 Am. St. Rep., 477.)[5.616]

In the above cited case Judge Brown, at page 485, says

Labor may organize, as capital does, for its own protection and to further the interests of the laboring class. They may strike and persuade and entice others to join them; but when they resort to unlawful means to cause injury to others with whom they have no relation, contractual or otherwise, the limit permitted by law is passed and they may be restrained.[5.617]

In National Protective Association v. Cummings (170 N. Y., 321),[5.618] Chief Justice Parker says:

What one man may do alone he may do in combination with others, provided they have no unlawful object in view. Mere numbers do not ordinarily affect the quality of the act. Workingmen have the right to organize for the purpose of securing higher wages, shorter hours of labor, or improving their relations with their employers. They have the right to strike; that is, to cease working in a body by prearrangement until a grievance is redressed, provided the object is not to gratify malice or inflict injury upon others, but to secure better terms of employment for themselves. A peaceable and orderly strike, not to harm others but to improve their own condition, is not in violation of law.[5.619]

This principle was laid down by the lower court and affirmed by the Court of Appeals of New York:

Laborers have a right to organize, and they will not be restrained by injunction from leaving the service of their employers, even though their action in so doing involves a breach of contract; but when the union and its officers and members agree together to prevent the employers from hiring other persons, by calling a strike and using force, threats, intimidation, and picketing, they have entered into an unlawful undertaking, which may be enjoined by a court of chancery. (Franklin Union v. The People, 220 Ill., 357 [sic].)[5.620]

In the foregoing case of Franklin Union v. The People (220 Ill., 357), at page 377, Judge Hand says:

It will be readily conceded by all that labor has the right to organize as well as capital, and that the members of Franklin Union, No. 4, had the same legal right to organize said union as the members of the Chicago Typothetae had to form that association, and that the members of Franklin Union, No. 4, had the legal right to quit the employment, either singly or in a body, of the members of said association, with or without cause, if they saw fit, without rendering themselves amenable to the charge of conspiracy, and that the courts would not have been authorized to enjoin them from so doing even though their leaving the employment of the members of the association involved a breach of contract.[5.621]

(Ohio, 1889) Workmen have the right to organize into unions for the common benefit of their members, for the purpose of advancing their scale, and for mutual charities. (Parker v. Bricklayers' Union, 10 Ohio, Dec. 458.)

Since the act of 1883 (Rev. Sup., p. 774, N. J.), it is not unlawful in this State for the members of an association to combine together for the purpose of securing control of the work connected with their trade, and to endeavor to effect such purpose by peaceable means. (Mayer et al. v. The Journeymen Stonecutters' Association, N. J. Eq., 47, 519.)[5.622]

1. Under the Declaration of Rights, article 1, guaranteeing to all men the right of acquiring, possessing, and protecting property, laborers can legally combine into a labor union, with

---

[5.616] 91 Minn. 171, 97 N.W. 663, 103 Am. St. R. 477 (1903). The quoted material is from the headnotes in *American State Reports*. It does not appear in the official report.

[5.617] 91 Minn. at 182–83.

[5.618] The correct citation is National Protective Ass'n of Steam Fitters & Helpers v. Cumming, 170 N.Y. 315, 63 N.E. 369 (1902).

[5.619] 170 N.Y. at 321.

[5.620] The correct citation is Franklin Union No. 4 v. People, 220 Ill. 355, 77 N.E. 176 (1906) (Hand, J.). The quoted language is from a headnote, 220 Ill. at 356, and not from a New York case as suggested by the speaker.

[5.621] 220 Ill. at 377.

[5.622] 47 N.J. Eq. 519, 20 A. 492 (Ch. 1890).

limitation on what it can do by the existence of the same right in every other citizen to pursue his calling as he may deem best, and the further limitation, coming from the increased power of organization, that what is lawful for an individual is not necessarily lawful for a combination. (Pickett *v.* Walsh, 78 N. E. Rep., 753.)[5.623]

At one time it was held by the courts that combinations of workmen to effect a desired end were illegal and indictable, but the later authorities both English and American, agree that trade-unions, in the ordinary acceptance of that term, are not unlawful combinations so long as they do not resort to acts of violence or endeavor to accomplish some end that is contrary to public policy. It is then not illegal per se for a union to adopt and endeavor to maintain a scale of wages, or to endeavor to limit and regulate the employment of apprentices.

A "strike" among workmen is not per se illegal or criminal, though it may become both by the means employed to enforce its objects. Workmen may quit the services of an employer, either singly or in a body, as they may see fit, and they may not be either enjoined or prosecuted for so doing unless the end to be attained or the means used to attain it be unlawful. (Longshore Printing Co. *v.* Howell, 26 Oreg. Repts., 527.)[5.624]

In Lake Erie & Western Railway *v.* Bailey District Judge Baker, in his opinion at page 495 (Fed. Rep., 61), says:

The court recognizes the right of any man or number of men to quit the service of their employers, and it recognizes the right of men to organize if they deem it expedient to better their condition. It also recognizes the hardships of the life of the average laboring man. Their conditions are often such as to touch the sensibilities of a feeling heart. The court is also aware of the scanty wages which they often receive, and of their long and arduous hours of service, frequently exposed to the rigors of an inclement season. * * * I confess I can not look with any degree of tolerance on the false and dangerous teachings of those who actively, or by their silent acquiescence, are teaching labor organizations to think that because they are organized in associations they have the right to seize property or by intimidation to prevent well-disposed people from laboring. * * * I think that such organizations for lawful purposes are to be commended; but when they combine and confederate for the purpose of seizing other men's property, or when they undertake by force and intimidation to drive other men away from employment, and thus deny them the right of earning a livelihood, they commit a crime. There ought to be blazed on the mind of every man that belongs to a labor organization, as with a hot iron so that he shall know and understand it, that while it is lawful and commendable to organize for legitimate and peaceful purposes, it is criminal to organize for the invasion of the rights of others to enjoy life, liberty, and prosperity.[5.625]

Mr. POMERENE. I wish to read a paragraph from the work of Frederick H. Cooke on "Combination, Monopolies, and Labor Unions." In discussing the legality of strikes, at paragraph 53, he says:

As has been seen, there has existed a tendency at least to apply the element of combination as a test of liability for acts of employees. Such tendency has been manifested in the alleged doctrine that a mere combination to obtain an increase of wages is illegal as a criminal conspiracy. The origin of this supposed doctrine appears on a consideration of the social conditions that had prevailed in England for centuries, producing a series of statutes dating as far back as the fourteenth century, operating most oppressively on the laboring classes. But this doctrine never gained foothold in this country, where it has been generally repudiated, and it may be regarded as established here, as a common-law principle, that a combination among wageworkers for the purpose of obtaining an increase of wages as well as for any other lawful purpose is entirely lawful, the only question of legality being as to the means employed. And as a result of recent elaborate investigation it must be considered as settled that the alleged doctrine never existed in England, independently of statute.

Again I desire to read from Judge Anderson in his instructions to the jury in the dynamite cases. He said:

It was not unlawful for the structural ironworkers to organize the union to which they belong. It is not unlawful for the defendants to be members of that or any other labor organization. Men have the right to use their combined power through such organizations to

---

[5.623] 192 Mass. 572, 78 N.E. 753 (1906). The quoted language is a headnote appearing in the *North Eastern Reporter*, 78 N.E. at 753–54, but not in the official report.

[5.624] 26 Ore. at 527. The quoted material is from the court's syllabus.

[5.625] 61 F. 494, 495–97 (C.C.D. Ill. 1893).

advance their interests in any lawful way; but they have no right to use this power in the violation of the law. Organized labor is not on trial here nor is the right of labor to organize an issue; but members of labor organizations owe the same obedience to the law and are liable to the same punishment for its violation as persons who are not members of such organizations.

(Page 1078 of the hearings before the subcommittees of the Committee on the Judiciary, United States Senate, which had under consideration H. R. 15657, Jan. 6, 1913.)

A very interesting work upon this subject of labor conditions is the late work of Martin on The Modern Law of Labor Unions. Sections 9, 10, 11, 12, 13, and 15 of this work read as follows:

Section 9: The purposes for which combination is permissible—in general.

Broadly speaking, workmen may combine to obtain any legitimate advantage. They may combine for the purpose of raising their intellectual, moral, and social condition, for social enjoyment, to afford members assistance in times of poverty, sickness, and distress; for the advancement and development of the intelligence of the members, and in consequence their skill in their trade or calling; to redress grievances of members; to improve or regulate their relations with their employers; to secure employment for their members; and, according to some decisions, to secure the employment of members in preference to and to the exclusion of other workmen, or to secure control of the work connected with their trade, although, as will be subsequently shown, there is authority which denies the correctness of these last two propositions (pp. 14 and 15).

Citing State *v.* Stockford (77 Conn., 227),[5.626] Karges Furniture Co. *v.* Amalgamated Woodworkers' Local Union (165 Ind., 421),[5.627] Com. *v.* Hunt (4 Met. (Mass.), 111, 129),[5.628] Coeur d'Alene Consol. Min. Co. *v.* Miners' Union (51 Fed., 260),[5.629] Parker *v.* Bricklayers' Union (10 Ohio Dec., 458), Cigar Makers' Union *v.* Lindner (3 Ohio Dec., 244),[5.630] Jacobs *v.* Cohen (183 N. Y., 212 [sic]),[5.631] Natl. Protective Asso. *v.* Cumming (170 N. Y., 315),[5.632] Hey *v.* Wilson [sic] (232 Ill., 389),[5.633] Pickett *v.* Walsh (192 Mass., 572),[5.634] Curran *v.* Galen (152 N. Y., 33),[5.635] Mills *v.* U. S. Printing Co. (99 N. Y. App. Div., 605).[5.636]

Section 10: To maintain or advance the rate of wages.

So one of the foremost purposes of organization among workmen is to secure the best wages obtainable, and whatever views may have been formerly entertained on the subject it is no longer open to question that a combination of workmen formed for the purpose of maintaining or advancing the rate of wages is a perfectly legitimate one. They are entitled to the highest wages and the best conditions that they can command. They may fix the price of labor and refuse to work unless it is obtained, and they may have that right both as individuals and in combination. It is of benefit to them and to the public that laborers should unite in common interest and for lawful purposes. They have labor to sell. If they stand together, they are often able, all of them, to command better prices for their labor than when dealing singly with rich employers, because the necessities of the single employee may compel him to accept any terms offered him. It has been well said that if it is lawful for the stockholders and officers of a corporation to associate together for the purpose of reducing the wages of its employees or of devising other means for making their investment profitable, it is equally lawful for organized labor to associate, consult, and confer with a view to maintain or increase wages (pp. 16 and 17).

[5.626] 77 Conn. 227, 58 A. 769 (1904).

[5.627] 165 Ind. 421, 75 N.E. 877 (1905).

[5.628] 45 Mass. (4 Met.) 111 (1842).

[5.629] 51 F. 260 (C.C.D. Idaho 1892).

[5.630] Cigar Makers' Protective Union No. 4 v. Lindner, 2 Ohio N.P. 114 (Hamilton County C.P. 1895).

[5.631] The correct citation is 183 N.Y. 207, 76 N.E. 5 (1905), *motion for reargument denied*, 184 N.Y. 524, 76 N.E. 1097 (1906).

[5.632] National Protective Ass'n of Steam Fitters & Helpers v. Cumming, 170 N.Y. 315, 63 N.E. 369 (1902).

[5.633] The correct citation is Wilson v. Hey, 232 Ill. 389, 83 N.E. 928 (1908).

[5.634] 192 Mass. 572, 78 N.E. 753 (1906).

[5.635] 152 N.Y. 33, 46 N.E. 297 (1897).

[5.636] 99 App. Div. 605, 91 N.Y.S. 185 (1904).

Citing numerous cases in all States of the Union.

Section 11: To obtain reduction of hours of employment.

So workmen may lawfully combine to obtain a reduction of the hours of employment, for the same reason that authorizes a combination to advance or maintain the rate of wages. A demand that wages should be paid during working hours amounts merely to a demand for a shorter day and the attainment thereof is a legitimate object of a combination (p. 16).

Section 12: To secure careful and competent fellow workmen.

The securing of careful and competent fellow servants in order to diminish the risk incident to employment is a legitimate object of a combination among laboring men. The reason for this is obvious. In the event of injury by the negligence of a fellow servant, except where the rule is changed by statute, the burden would have to be borne by the injured servant without compensation by the master, and with no financial responsibility as a general rule on the part of those causing the injury (p. 16).

Section 13: To accumulate strike fund or fund for unemployed members.

The accumulation of a strike fund for the support of those who feel that the wages offered are below market prices is one of the legitimate objects of a labor organization, as is also the accumulation of a fund for the unemployed members of the association (p. 17).

Citing Thomas v. Cincinnati R. Co. (62 Fed., 803);[5.637] see Hitchman Coal Co. v. Mitchell (172 Fed., 963).[5.638]

Section 15: Limitations on the right of combination.

The limitation on the right of workmen to combine for their own benefit and protection is that in the exercise of this right the property and rights of others must be respected. A labor union being an organization brought about by the exercise on the part of its members of the right of every citizen to pursue his calling as he thinks best is limited in what it can do by the existence of the same right in each and every other citizen to pursue his or their calling as he or they may think best. Workmen who have combined into a union can not have, under the law of equal rights, a liberty of contracting as they please, working when they please, and quitting when they please, which does not belong alike to nonunion men and employers of labor. It was said by an early commentator on the law of trade unions that "every person has a right under the law, as between him and his fellow subject, to full freedom in disposing of his own labor or his own capital according to his own will. It follows that every other person is subject to the correlative duty arising therefrom, and is prohibited from any obstruction to the fullest exercise of this right which can be made compatible with the exercise of similar rights by others." The law sanctions no combinations either of employers or employees which have for their immediate purpose the injury of another or the unjustifiable interference with his rights and privileges. It is the absolute, unqualified right of every employee, as well as of every other person, to go about his business unmolested and unobstructed, and free from intimidation, force, or duress (pp. 18 and 19).

Mr. President, I dare say that there will be few if any authorities found in conflict with the general principles which have been laid down in the opinions which I have cited or in the text writers to which I have referred.

Now, what becomes of the proposition which is made the basis of this legislation that labor has no right to organize, no right to strike for higher wages or shorter hours or better conditions? No authority has been cited, and, I dare say, none can be cited in this country, where the right to organize, to strike, and to do peaceful picketing is denied, unless it be prohibited by some special statute of some State.

It seems to me that it is unfair to the laboring men themselves, it is unfair to the country, it is unfair to Congress, it is unfair to the courts, to say that there is any principle of law recognized in this country which would permit the dissolution of an organization of employees unless they have been guilty of some unlawful acts. I take it that the friends of this bill would not contend for one moment that if an organization had been once properly organized and set out in a criminal course to do criminal acts that the law ought not to intervene even to the extent of using drastic measures, not to say decreeing dissolution.

Mr. President, under the law, as I conceive it, in this country men may strike for better wages, shorter hours, or, in general, for the betterment of their condition, and

---

[5.637] Thomas v. Cincinnati, N.O. & T.P. Ry., 62 F. 803 (C.C.S.D. Ohio 1894).

[5.638] Hitchman Coal & Coke Co. v. Mitchell, 172 F. 963 (C.C.N.D. W. Va. 1909).

they may do peaceful picketing. Why, then, should we attempt to change this law, and to change it in the form that it is here in section 7? This section, note, attempts to say "that nothing in the antitrust laws shall be construed to forbid the existence and operation of labor, agricultural, or horticultural organizations, instituted for the purposes of mutual help," and so forth, or to forbid or restrain individual members of such organization [sic] from lawfully carrying out the legitimate objects thereof; and then the last paragraph says:

> Nor shall such organizations or the members thereof be held or construed to be illegal combinations or conspiracies in restraint of trade under the antitrust laws.

The first part of this section permits their operation without any qualification of any kind. When it comes to the individual members it says, "or to forbid or restrain individual members of such organization from lawfully carrying out the legitimate objects thereof." There is no qualification at all on the operation of the organization. The individual must act lawfully. Applying the usual rules of construction, it follows that the operation of the organization may be either lawful or unlawful, legitimate or illegitimate. Why limit the individual to lawfully carrying out the legitimate objects of the organization and place no limitation on the organization?

Again, what are the legitimate objects? Why not attempt to define them? No one has attempted it. Does the word "legitimate" not cover every attempt that may be made to accomplish their purpose? Does it mean that the commerce of the country may be entirely tied up by the efforts of some men who do not appreciate the obligation of citizenship? Does it mean that it shall be confined to efforts to obtain a reasonable wage or a wage that would be concededly unreasonable under any and all circumstances? Does it mean to apply only to the obtaining of reasonable hours, or does it permit them to demand unreasonably short hours? Does it mean they may strive for reasonably good conditions, or for conditions which it would be impossible for the average employer to bestow? It seems to me that if this is to become the law there ought to be some attempt to explain what was in the mind of Congress when it attempted to place it upon the statute books. Again, the last paragraph:

> Nor shall such organizations or the members thereof be held or construed to be illegal combinations or conspiracies in restraint of trade under the antitrust laws.

Does it mean under no circumstances? Does it mean no matter what their acts are, they shall not be amenable to the law?

Mr. President, most of the laboring men are high-class men, of high purpose and high character. They want their rights and they want to be law-abiding citizens. It is not for that class of men that laws are made. We all recognize the fact that in every avenue of life there are men who will transgress the law and who do transgress the law. I recognize the fact that there are many employers in this country who have ground their labor down, and for them I have no word of sympathy of any kind. On the other hand, we must be entirely fair in this matter and at the same time we have in mind the employers who are unfair we must remember that there are some men who are speaking in the name of labor who likewise are unfair. Laboring men should not be placed at the mercy of the merciless employer. On the other hand, the good employers—and that embraces the greater part of them—ought not to be placed at the mercy of a few labor leaders who do not have a proper appreciation of their duty to the public. There are two sides to this question, as there are to most questions.

Mr. President, I know it is contended that the arm of injunction should never be used in connection with these disturbances. I concede that it has been too frequently used—used when it ought not to have been used—and injunctions granted without notice. Of course, that should be corrected; but, on the other hand, permit me to say that I believe the injunction has often prevented violence which all would regret had it occurred. I recognize the fact that most of the labor leaders of this country abhor violence; that they teach and speak against it; that they give their commands against it. But we all know that it sometimes happens that the wisest and most influential of leaders can not control some of their men. What is to be done under those circumstances?

Mr. President, when there is a labor disturbance generally the first desire is to have some sort of mediation or adjustment. I wish that were always true. The second is, if there is likely to be any disturbance the officers of the peace are called in. If that fails then the practice has been to invoke the equity arm of the court to stay any effort at violence. If that fails, what next? There is only one other recourse, and that is to call in the military where there is such a disturbance as can not be controlled by other means.

Am I wrong when I say that by so much as you cripple the arm of injunction in a proper case, by so much you are increasing the possibility of calling out the military? I hope the day will never come in this country when the military will be called out to stay any labor difficulty of any kind. The public will not tolerate violence. The peace must be preserved. If it can not be done by the police or the courts, the military will be summoned. Ought we not to use the courts where we can, and only resort to the military when all other possible means have failed?

Mr. President, my belief has always been that labor and capital are not to be treated as if in two separate camps. They are partners in a common purpose. They ought to be together. I believe in industrial peace. I do not believe in industrial war, and that is the basic thought in this section in my judgment. Section 7 and section 18 treat this subject as if employer and employee were in two opposing camps. You are never going to get these two elements of our society together by that kind of means. I will do anything in my power to bring them together, either by vote or voice. I will not do anything consciously to get them apart, and if there is a proper disposition exercised by employer and employee there will be less of trouble in this country.

Permit me to call the attention of the Senate to a beautiful picture of the relations which exist between one of the great employers in Ohio and his employees. I read a paragraph from a speech delivered by Col. James Kilbourne, president of the Kilbourne & Jacobs Manufacturing Co., in the city of Columbus, one of the largest employers of labor in central Ohio. Speaking of the hard times during the panic of 1893, 1894, and 1895, he says:

I could relate innumerable instances showing their loyalty—

Referring to his employees—

and devotion to our interests, but one will, I think, suffice, the like of which I have never heard of before or since. Some weeks after the beginning of the great panic of 1893, when trouble and desolation were spreading over the land, there filed into my office at our shops one morning some 15 or 20 men, representing the different shops of our works. They bore serious countenances and a serious manner, and my heart sank within me. One of my most earnest hopes had been that there should never be any trouble between our employees and myself, and I thought, "Here it has come at last."

Finally one of the men arose and said: "Mr. Kilbourne, we have hesitated about coming here; we have thought about it a great deal, and believe we are right, and we hope you will receive the suggestion we have to make in the spirit in which it is offered. We have seen in the daily papers accounts of the failure of this firm and that firm and the other firm, which had existed for many years, and were thought to be strong enough to resist any panic. We know that your warehouses are filling up with goods. We know that, as is the case with other manufacturers, you can not sell the goods you are making to-day and can not get your pay for the goods you have sold. We do not know what your circumstances are, but we fear they may be like those of other men who have failed. Some of us have been here a few years, some of us many years, some of us almost a generation. We have had good pay, we have been able to save up some money, and while the individual savings are not very large, the aggregate is a very considerable sum. We have come to tell you that it is all yours, to do with it what you please, if you need it in the interests of your company."

That is a picture of conditions as they ought to prevail in every factory, and that is a condition which would prevail in many instances if the extremists on both sides of this proposition were more disposed to get together, and I trust that the Congress will help them to get together.

Mr. President, I want to call the attention of the Senate to another peculiar provision of this section 7. For some unaccountable reason it has been sought to place in this section a provision exempting agricultural associations from the provisions of the Sherman law. I should like to know where the sentiment comes from that demands it. We have agricultural organizations galore in my State, doing splendid work. I have not heard from a single one who asked that agricultural organizations should be included in an exemption under this law.

On the contrary, Hon. A. P. Sandles, president of the Agricultural Commission of Ohio, writes me under date of July 10, 1914:

> You are right in opposing exemption of farmers from provisions of antitrust laws.
> Farmers ask no favors. Justice and equal consideration in governmental affairs is their creed and demand.

During the past week or 10 days the papers of the country have been calling attention to the increasingly high cost of living. Products of all kinds that are offered in the markets are going higher and higher. It has attracted the attention of the President himself. Congressmen have desired it to be investigated. All over the United States social organizations are inquiring into it. Everybody regrets it. We thought we were about to reduce the price of living, and I think, all things considered, we have done so by some of our legislation. And now comes a proposition whereby the Congress is putting itself on record to legitimatize agricultural organizations for the purpose of increasing the cost of living. Consistency ought to be a jewel now as it has been in other days.

One of the peculiar ironies of this section is this: There are consumers' leagues all over the country, and one of their objects is to reduce the cost of living, and they are eliminated from this bill. So if consumers were to get together and combine in interstate matters in an effort to reduce the cost of articles and thereby restrain trade, they would be amenable to the law; but the bill allows the producers of the country to get together for the purpose of increasing the price. It denies to the consumer the right to combine to reduce the cost of living while it gives the producer the right to combine to increase the price of his produce.

Mr. President, the labor and agricultural provisions of this bill received consideration at the hands of Congress during the closing days of the administration of President Taft. He vetoed the sundry civil appropriation bill at the time for two reasons—first, because he doubted its constitutionality, and, secondly, because he doubted the policy of it. I do not care this afternoon to discuss the question of the constitutionality of this provision. I am frank to say that I am disposed to think that Congress in its wisdom might eliminate both classes from the operation of the Sherman law, though I am not certain about it. I address myself only to the question of the policy.

Later on, when this same bill was passed by the present Congress, President Wilson said in signing the bill:

> I have signed this bill because I can do so without, in fact, limiting the opportunity or the power of the Department of Justice to prosecute violations of the law by whomsoever committed.
>
> If I could have separated from the rest of the bill the item which authorized the expenditure by the Department of Justice of a special sum of $300,000 for the prosecution of violations of the antitrust law, I would have vetoed that item, because it places upon the expenditure a limitation which is, in my opinion, unjustifiable in character and principle. But I could not separate it. I do not understand that the limitation was intended as either an amendment or an interpretation of the antitrust law, but merely as an expression of the opinion of the Congress— a very emphatic opinion, backed by an overwhelming majority of the House of Representatives and a large majority of the ⊥ Senate, but not intended to touch anything but the expenditure of a single small additional fund.

If it was wrong in principle at that time to exempt any element of society from the provisions of the law it seems to me that the same rule should obtain now.

Mr. President, section 18 of this bill is to my mind of somewhat uncertain phraseology. I have been trying to find out what it means. I trust I am guilty of no impropriety when I say that I have had three different opinions from members of the Judiciary Committee: One to the effect that it legalizes the secondary boycott; another to the effect that it does not; and the third to the effect that he did not know. I should like to know whether it does or not. It is pretty difficult to understand the language which is used in the middle of this section:

And no such restraining order or injunction shall prohibit any person or persons whether singly or in concert from terminating any relation of employment or from ceasing to perform any work or labor, or from recommending, advising, or persuading others by peaceful means so to do; or from peacefully persuading any person to work or to abstain from working; or from withholding their patronage from any party to such dispute, or from recommending, advising, or persuading others by peaceful and lawful means so to do.

Does that apply simply to the employer and the employee or does it apply to the use of means in connection with a third party? I do not know. If it is simply a legalizing of the primary boycott it is legal now; if it is an attempt to legalize the secondary boycott I am opposed to it, and I understand that most of the States have legislation upon that subject. I think that in principle it is altogether vicious.

Let me call attention to some of the examples of secondary boycott.

I take a different view of this subject from that of some of my friends. I do not believe that this struggle is going to be fashioned after the manner of war. If there is a difference between the employer and the employee and they can not agree, the employees can strike or there can be a lockout, and all the peaceful means incident to such methods may be employed; but because I, as an employee, have a difference with a company employing me and we can not agree, is that any reason why I should attempt to embroil somebody who may be in California in his relations with my employer? There must be an end somewhere.

Let me suggest, before I go into this matter further, that this bill, if it should be enacted, can have no effect upon intrastate commerce; it only applies to interstate commerce. When we are trying to weigh the merits and the demerits of a bill we ought to give grave consideration to the question as to whether or not the good that is to be accomplished is outweighed by the evil that may be consequent upon such legislation.

If this section means to legalize the secondary boycott, there is no limitation here of any kind; it legalizes all kinds of boycotts. Now, let us see how good a weapon that is. It was employed in the anthracite coal strike, and there is a splendid report on that subject by the commission which was appointed by President Roosevelt, consisting of Brig. Gen. John M. Wilson, Mr. E. W. Parker, Judge George Gray, Mr. Edgar E. Clark [,] Mr. Thomas H. Watkins, and Bishop John L. Spalding. Under date of March 18, 1903, they submitted their report. I want to read a paragraph from it:

Examples of such "secondary boycotts" are not wanting in the record of the case before the commission. A young schoolmistress, of intelligence, character, and attainments, was so boycotted and her dismissal from employment compelled for no other reason than that a brother, not living in her immediate family, chose to work contrary to the wishes and will of the striking miners. A lad, about 15 years old, employed in a drug store, was discharged, owing to threats made to his employer by a delegation of the strikers, on behalf of their organization, for the reason that his father had chosen to return to work before the strike was ended. In several instances tradesmen were threatened with a boycott—that is, that all connected with the strikers would withhold from them their custom and persuade others to do so—if they continued to furnish the necessaries of life to the families of certain workmen, who had come under the ban of the displeasure of the striking organizations. This was carrying the boycott to an extent which was condemned by Mr. Mitchell, president of the United Mine Workers of America, in his testimony before the commission, and which certainly deserves the reprobation of all thoughtful and law-abiding citizens. Many other instances of boycott are disclosed in the record of this case.

Again, at page 78 of the report, the commission says:

The practices which we are condemning would be outside the pale of civilized war. In civilized warfare, women and children and the defenseless are safe from attack, and a code of honor controls the parties to such warfare which cries out against the boycott we have in view. Cruel and cowardly are terms not too severe by which to characterize it.

If you will turn to the record of the testimony of this case you will find that the words "cruel and cowardly" were the words used by Mr. Mitchell himself; and yet if this section legalizes the secondary boycott, the Congress of the United States is called upon to give an indorsement to conduct of this kind which is cruel and cowardly. The report continues:

The commission is of opinion, however, that there should be a positive utterance on its part relative to discrimination, interference, boycotting, and blacklisting, and this opinion it has put in the form of an award, as follows:

"It is adjudged and awarded: That no person shall be refused employment, or in any way discriminated against, on account of membership or nonmembership in any labor organization; and that there shall be no discrimination against, or interference with, any employee who is not a member of any labor organization by members of such organization."

Mr. President, I want to call to the attention of the Senate the views of some of the labor leaders themselves upon the question of boycott. I have here at my desk the work of Harry W. Laidler on Boycotts and the Labor Struggle. On page 97 the author quotes from the reports of the bureau of statistics and labor of New York State, and I ask to introduce that without reading, because I do not care to take the time to do so.

The PRESIDING OFFICER (Mr. WALSH in the chair). In the absence of objection, permission to do so is granted.

The matter referred to is as follows:

The boycott is not in this country attended with violence, except in the case of foreigners.

Organized labor has attained that period in its development when it can see the necessity of wielding this potent weapon with extreme caution. Time was when the boycott was declared at the slightest provocation. Not so now, for the record proves that the organizations are loath to use it except in a prudent way, and then as a last resort.

The injury to labor of any abuse is thus stated:

It (the boycott) has nearly always proved successful when the parties who applied it represented a public or moral sentiment. If it is allowed to degenerate into a simple fight between competing firms, and if the pretended leaders of the labor movement assume to apply it indiscriminately, foolishly, and maliciously, it will result in complete disaster to the movement itself.

The attitude of labor leaders concerning the boycott's use is thus set forth:

It may be remarked that the more advanced thinkers in the ranks of labor disapprove of the boycott except in extreme cases in which no ordinary remedy is attainable.

Mr. POMERENE. Again, on page 107, the author says:

If wielded thoughtlessly the boycott on the transportation system could undoubtedly play havoc with the business of the country. On the other hand, there is no business in which the abuse in the conduct of this weapon brings a more immediate and pronounced condemnation from the public.

At page 110, the author says, with respect to the convention of the American Federation of Labor held in 1885:

In this convention the unscrupulous use of the boycott by other organizations, presumably the Knights of Labor, was vigorously condemned. These organizations were accused of employing this weapon on "frivolous, trivial, and imaginary grievances" without giving the question the attention and thorough investigation which it required. The convention voted that no boycott be approved by the federation, until it had been carefully considered by the legal committee.

*   *   *   *   *   *   *

In its convention in 1886 the author says:

It advocated only the boycott's careful and energetic use as a last resort.

*   *   *   *   *   *   *

On page 111 the author says:

The federation, in 1898, took a decided stand against the circularizing of its unions with boycott literature without its official indorsement, declaring that "the continuous and overwhelming flood of boycott circulars leads to confusion and ineffectiveness." The same year it took steps toward limiting particularly boycotts of those firms employing union men. The resolution read:

"Whereas the placing of a boycott upon any product the manufacture of which is participated
 in by two or more crafts may and often does work an injury to union workers: Therefore
 be it

"*Resolved*, That the American Federation of Labor shall indorse no boycott where the products of several organized unions will be affected thereby until every possible effort has been made to secure a settlement, and all organizations to be affected shall be given a hearing and an opportunity to assist in securing a settlement in which the existing grievance may be settled."

On page 112 the author says:

The boycott committee in 1904 clearly voiced the sentiment of the delegates in its declaration that "if anyone is unjustly placed on the unfair list it tends to injure not only the organization directly in interest, but the entire labor movement."

In 1905 (see Laidler on Boycotts, p. 113) Owen Miller, chairman of the boycott committee of the American Federation of Labor, reported to the convention:

We must recognize the fact that the boycott means war, and to carry on a war successfully we must adopt the tactics that history has shown are most successful in war. The greatest master of war said that war was the trade of a barbarian and the secret of success was to concentrate all forces upon one point of the enemy—the weakest if possible.

In view of these facts the committee recommends that the State federations and central bodies lay aside minor grievances and concentrate their efforts and energies upon the least number of unfair parties or places in their jurisdiction. One would be preferable. If every available means at the command of the State federations and central bodies were concentrated upon one such and kept up until successful, the next on the list would be more easily brought to terms, and within a reasonable time none opposed to fair wages, conditions, or hours, but would be brought to see the error of its ways and submit to the inevitable.

President Gompers, in speaking of the boycott, said (see Laidler on Boycotts, p. 114):

The workers fully realize that the boycott and strike are means to be used to maintain their rights and to promote their welfare when ⊥ seriously threatened by hostile, greedy, and unfair employers when no other remedy seems available. With the boycott cleared of wrongful charges and misapprehension and recognized as a lawful right we will find its use diminishing. It will be a power held in reserve and used only when no other remedy is adequate.

We have this anomalous situation: We are asked to legalize an instrument like the secondary boycott, which has been fraught with so much harm not only to the country at large but, according to these authorities and the declaration of the Federation of Labor itself, often to the labor organizations. We are asked to say that there shall be no restraint in the handling of this instrument, save the free will of those who use it.

According to Mr. Gompers:

With the boycott cleared of wrongful charges and misapprehension and recognized as a lawful right, we will find its use diminishing.

In other words, when it is not recognized, when there is no statute regulating it, there will be more perfect peace. "We do not want Government regulation of this instrument, and then we will cease to use it." A defiance of the law by a few—and there are only a few who do it—never breeds respect for any law or any man's rights. By the force of this same logic we should repeal all statutory laws making certain acts penal, because if we did there would be more respect shown for the rights of men.

Mr. President, when we do know that the boycott has been used in such ways as to bring down the condemnation of the labor leaders themselves, such as John Mitchell, it is not quite the right time to come in and legalize that which, in John Mitchell's own words, sometimes, as in the case of the anthracite coal strike in the instances to which I have referred, is "cruel and cowardly."

Mr. President, I fear that in the consideration of this subject we sometimes lose sight of the great third party—the public. I have never heard of a struggle between employer and employee that I did not feel that there were three parties to be considered—the employee, the employer, and the great third party, which embraces both of them, the public.

While we recognize the right to strike—and I would not have it otherwise—it is not always a means of securing what is desired. Workingmen now have a right to strike, but everyone must concede that the fewer times that right is exercised the better. It is of inestimable value, but, paradoxical as it may seem, the less it is used the greater its value.

Let me call the attention of the Senate to some of the statistics upon this subject. I take the following figures from the twenty-first annual report of the Labor Bureau, made in 1906, on the subject of strikes and lockouts, as contained in House Document No. 110:

In the period of 25 years (1881 to 1905) there were in the United States:

Strikes	36,757
Lockouts	1,546
Total disturbances	38,303
Strikes occurred in ....establishments	181,407
Lockouts occurred in ....do	18,547
Total	199,954
Total persons involved during said period in strikes	6,728,048
Number of persons locked out	716,231
Total	7,444,279

Total number during said period thrown out of employment:

By strikes	8,703,824
By lockouts	825,610
Total	9,529,434

Of the 36,757 strikes from 1881 to 1905, there were:

	Per cent
Ordered by labor organizations	68.99
Begun by employees who were not members of organizations, or who, if members, went on strike without sanction of the organizations	31.01

Of the 181,407 establishments involved in strikes, 90.34 per cent were included in strikes ordered by organizations.

Strikes ordered by labor organizations included 79.69 per cent of all strikers and 77.45 per cent of the total persons thrown out of work in establishments involved in strikes.

Average duration per establishment:

	Days
Of strikes	25.4
Of lockouts	84.6

Employees won all demands undertaken by strikes in 47.95 per cent of the establishments, succeeded partly in 15.28 per cent of the establishments, failed to win any of their demands in 36.78 per cent.

Lockouts resulted favorable to employers in 57.20 per cent of the establishments, succeeded partly in 10.71 per cent of the establishments, failed in 32.09 per cent.

Strikes ordered by labor organizations were wholly successful in 49.48 per cent of the establishments involved, partly successful in 15.87 per cent, failed in 34.65 per cent.

Strikes not ordered by labor organizations were successful in 33.86 per cent of the establishments involved, partly successful in 9.83 per cent, failed in 56.31 per cent of the establishments.

Eleven thousand eight hundred and fifty-one strikes, or 32.24 per cent of all strikes, were for increase of wages alone; 3,117 strikes, or 40.72 per cent of all strikes, due in whole or in part to demands for increase of wages.

The next most fruitful cause of strikes was disagreement concerning recognition of union and union rules. This cause alone produced 18.84 per cent of all strikes, and both alone and combined with other causes, 23.35 per cent of all strikes.

Objection to reduction of wages alone and combined with other causes produced 11.90 per cent of all strikes.

Demands for reduction of hours alone and combined with other causes produced 9.78 per cent of all strikes.

The most important cause of lockouts was disputes concerning recognition of union and union rules and employers' organization, which cause, alone and combined with various causes, produced nearly one-half of all lockouts and included more than one-half of all establishments involved in lockouts.

Now, Mr. President, let us see how expensive these strikes were. I refer to these matters because I have always felt that if those who are interested on both sides of this problem would in a proper spirit try to get together two-thirds at least of the labor troubles could be avoided and both would profit thereby. Mr. Carroll D. Wright, in an article on arbitration in a book entitled "Labor and Capital," at pages 153 and 154, says:

> The record of strikes in the United States for the 20 years ending December 31, 1900, as shown by the United States Department of Labor, would seem to indicate that at times, at least, some drastic measure for the prevention of conflicts might be desirable. This record is that during the period named there were 22,793 strikes, with a wage loss of $257,863,478, a loss through assistance rendered by labor organizations of $16,174,793, and a loss to employers of $122,731,121. The lockouts during the same period numbered 1,005, with a wage loss to employees of $48,819,745, a loss through assistance rendered by labor organizations of $3,451,461, and a loss to employers of $19,927,983. The total losses by strikes and lockouts reached the vast sum of $468,968,581.

Four hundred and sixty-eight million dollars! Is it not worth while to get both employer and employee together rather than to attempt to pass some legislation which treats the subject as if they were warring factions?

Mr. President, I want to call the attention of the Senate to this fact especially: This legislation will not affect those who are engaged purely in manufacturing or mercantile or mining occupations unless the transaction assumes an interstate character. It does affect all those who are engaged in transportation of every character—a matter which is peculiarly a subject for congressional control; a matter to which we ought always to give our most considerate attention. As a matter of fact, the legislation that is here asked is not in the interest of the whole people; it is not in the interest of the laboring classes as a whole; but rather, in view of its interstate character, it should be called legislation in favor of a part of labor as against all labor and as against all the rest of the 100,000,000 inhabitants of the United States.

Let us see how this will operate. A little more than a year ago Congress was called upon suddenly one morning to pass a law providing for mediation of the differences existing between the railways east of Chicago and their employees. We were told that if the bill did not pass within 48 hours all traffic east of Chicago would be tied up. Do we appreciate what that would mean? The bill was passed. The matters were submitted to arbitration. They were settled. A part of the demands of the employees were granted, but not in full. If that award means anything it means that they were reasonable in a part of their demands and they were unreasonable in a part of their demands.

Now, let us suppose that instead of a threatened strike the railways had gotten together and had said, "It is going to be to our interest to combine together and reduce the wages of these employees below a living wage," what would have been the result? The men would have left their employment, and properly so; but the consequence would have been that transportation east of Chicago would have been stopped, and in 10 days centers of population like New York, and Boston, and Philadelphia, and Pittsburgh, and Cleveland would have been starved. . . .

On the other hand, suppose, for the sake of the argument, that the demands of the brotherhoods of railway men had been excessive; that they had asked for something which the transportation lines could not pay; that they had asked for something which in the minds of all reasonable men would have been excessive, and, their demands having been denied, they strike. Traffic would have stopped. Transportation would have stopped. The result on the great centers of population, like New York, and Philadelphia, and Boston, and Pittsburgh, and Cleveland, would have been the same. It is the restraint of trade that we are looking to, and that should be the object of our most respectful attention. What would have been the consequences if they had arbitrarily assumed a stand of this character and their demands had been unreasonable? Who would have suffered in either instance? Would it have been the rich men of New York City or any other of these centers of population? Would it have been the employer class? Yes; but the suffering of the employer would not have been a tithe compared with the suffering of the laboring men in these great cities and of their wives and families, though their relations with their employers might have been most harmonious in character.

Let us take another illustration: Suppose this had been in the dead of winter, and in the anthracite regions of Pennsylvania or the bituminous regions of West Virginia the coal was being taken out. We will assume that the relations between the employers and the miners were most harmonious. They were getting out their coal, ready to ship it to the centers of population to keep the men and the women and the children there from freezing, and the only thing that stood in the way was the lack of means of transportation. The employers in the mining regions, if they could not market their coal, could not pay their men, and the result would be suffering and distress there.

I do not think this situation is likely to arise; but we know we have been on the very brink of such a situation; and only a few days ago one arose with reference to the transportation lines west of Chicago, and we were told that in a short day there was a probability that all the traffic west of Chicago would be tied up if there were not an adjustment. I more than appreciate the splendid efforts of the men on both sides of that controversy to get together and agree to arbitrate and to adjust their differences; but we know, as a matter of experience, that there have been cases in this country which they did not arbitrate. They could not, it seemed. Because of the passion that may have prevailed on both sides, they were not able to arbitrate. Beyond that, let us go a little further. If everyone during a situation such as I have described would keep an even temper, all might go well; but we know that in cases of excitement such as I have referred to there are men who do not control their tempers. They may be sometimes leaders of men on both sides of the proposition, and a little encouragement is given here, a little encouragement there, and the first thing we know the match is applied to the magazine, and there is an explosion that distresses the entire country; and with these strikes there come threats, intimidation, and violence to both person and property.

I am not saying that one side is any more to blame than the other, but I do say that when it comes to a proposition such as this the Government should not tie its hands and prevent itself from making, not an undue use of the power of injunction, but a proper use of the power of injuction. As injunction tends to peace, not to violence. When violence begins the cause is losing ground.

I want to say that while I have the most profound respect for the men who are at the head of the American Federation of Labor and at the heads of the various brotherhoods, we know that sometimes wrongs occur. The best of us may to-day be in a perfectly equable frame of mind, but to-morrow lose our tempers in the intensity of excitement; and we are not always responsible for things which may be done, and if we do control ourselves we are not always able to control those who may be under us.

Let me make a further suggestion in this connection. Let us suppose there should be a strike; that transportation should be tied up; that the courts of equity are not open. We have bound their hands. The public becomes excited. If we were to prohibit the issuance of injunctions what might not happen? If we were to pass a bill which in a proper case would prevent the use of the equity arm, what would our Senators from the South say to the cotton farmer when he could not market his product because transportation was stopped and strikers would not permit the management to resume? What are Senators from the great wheat-growing regions going to say to their constituents when transportation in that region is tied up? What are Senators from the great centers of population going to say if we cripple the hands of the courts so that fuel in the wintertime and food products at all times may not be brought to warm those who are cold and freezing and to feed the hungry?

I recognize the fact that courts have made mistakes, but I want to say at the same time that while some judges have issued wrong decrees they are the exception and not the rule. I am not willing to say, when it comes to a proposition such as this, that the courts are always wrong and that the organizations are always right. I hope there may never be another excuse for applying to a court in any labor struggle of any kind, but I do think a study of poor, weak human nature shows that it is sometimes necessary.

Mr. President, I want to call the attention of the Senate to another very interesting feature of section 18. I read only that part of the section which is pertinent to the point I have in mind:

That no restraining order or injunction shall be granted by any court of the United States, or a judge or the judges thereof—

In controversies between employers and employees—

unless necessary to prevent irreparable injury to property or to a property right.

You must show that there is an irreparable injury to property or to a property right before an injunction shall be granted. In other words, if the employer's property is threatened with violence, if some one goes down in the midst of the trouble and threatens the business, the property, the machinery, the plant itself, and there is no adequate remedy at law, in order to protect that property and that property right an injunction may be issued; but if the men who are employed there are threatened, if they are to be fired at, you can not protect them by the power of injunction. Under section 18, as it is drawn, we have the anomalous situation that property has become more sacred than life or limb or safety!

Mr. President, I have occupied more of the time of the Senate than I had expected to occupy. I say, as I began, that with most of the provisions of this bill I am in entire accord; but I can not give my consent to the exemption of any organization from the operation of the Sherman law. My belief is, as I have instanced in the case of the transportation companies, that the possibilities of harm to the laboring classes and to all classes of our population by the enactment of those parts of this bill to which I have registered my objections would far outweigh any possible good to the laboring classes. . . .

Mr. HUGHES. I want to get the Senator's idea of the effect of the present law upon these transportation strikes. The Senator described a set of circumstances which existed a few days ago and which threatened to involve all the railroads west of Chicago, I think the Senator said, in a general strike. He followed that up by saying that the natural result of that would be a terrific restraint of trade. Now, if that had happened; if that restraint of trade had occurred; if there had been a combination or agreement or conspiracy—call it what you will—of all the employees of all those railroads west of Chicago, and that had resulted, as it necessarily must have resulted, in an absolute restraint or cessation of trade, does the Senator think those conspirators or those in that combination or agreement would have come within the terms of the Sherman antitrust law?

Mr. POMERENE. On the Senator's statement of facts alone, I do not think so; but there are always, let me say—

Mr. HUGHES. I will ask the Senator—

Mr. POMERENE. Pardon me a moment, please. Let me suggest that it is easy enough to pick out a few innocent facts in these matters, on the one hand—

Mr. HUGHES. I am taking the facts the Senator set out.

Mr. POMERENE. Just a moment. Or, on the other hand, to select out all adverse facts; and when we do that, on either side, we are not presenting the situation properly. We know, however, that when there is a condition such as I have described there are always other circumstances which become involved, which, together with what I have described, would make out a perfect case under the law.

Mr. HUGHES. It seems to me that if anything is plain it must be plain that the simultaneous withdrawal from employment on the part of men who are engaged in carrying goods from State to State must result in a restraint of trade. If the Senator thinks it does not, and says so, why, that is all I have to say. I can not imagine a more complete restraint of trade.

Mr. POMERENE. Not those facts alone, but—

Mr. HUGHES. The Senator said in his speech that it would be a restraint of trade.

Mr. POMERENE. I understand all that. It would be a restraint of trade, but the facts which I have referred to alone, perhaps, in the hurried argument I was making, might not make out a case; but there are often other facts and circumstances accompanying these strikes. For instance, if the railroads ⊥ should attempt to move their trains by the employment of other men, and were to be interfered with, then certainly a court would interfere.

Mr. HUGHES. I just want to get at the Senator's view, because it is very important. The Senator, then, thinks that the simultaneous withdrawal of a lot of engineers and firemen which resulted in tying up all the railroads west of Chicago, so that no commerce at all could be moved by rail, would not be a restraint of trade unless it was accompanied by violence?

Mr. POMERENE. It is a restraint of trade. Those facts alone, however, without any other complications, might not be a violation of this law.

Mr. HUGHES. It would be a restraint of trade; would it not?

⊥13916

Mr. POMERENE. Certainly it would; but the restraint of trade—

Mr. HUGHES. The statute is directed against restraints of trade.

Mr. POMERENE. Undue restraints.

Mr. HUGHES. It is directed against restraints of trade. The Senator knows that.

Mr. POMERENE. As construed by the Supreme Court, it is an undue restraint of trade.

Mr. HUGHES. An unreasonable restraint of trade.

Mr. POMERENE. Yes.

Mr. HUGHES. Well, surely, if any restraint of trade would be unreasonable, a restraint of trade would be unreasonable which involved every railroad west of Chicago and cut the country in half, and left one half of it with its goods piling up and the other half of the country starving for them. No court could hold that that was reasonable.

Mr. POMERENE. Under those circumstances, would you cripple the law as it now is?

Mr. HUGHES. Would I cripple it? Would I interfere with the right of those men to withdraw?

Mr. POMERENE. Would you interfere with the enforcement of this law if it could be enforced, or if the circumstances were such as to justify it?

Mr. HUGHES. I would interfere with any law that attempted to prevent any American workingman from quitting his job when he got ready, either singly or in combination with anybody else.

Mr. POMERENE. So would I.

Mr. HUGHES. But the Senator does not say that.

Mr. POMERENE. I do say that, and I say it now.

Mr. HUGHES. The Senator turned to me and challenged my statement, and asked me if I would interfere with the law if it prevented that thing.

Mr. POMERENE. My question was whether you would cripple the law under the circumstances.

Mr. HUGHES. I would cripple the law. What would the Senator do?

Mr. POMERENE. I would protect the public, always.

Mr. HUGHES. Very well. Then the Senator would prevent those men from withdrawing simultaneously from that employment.

Mr. POMERENE. If the facts and complications were such as to justify it, under the law, I certainly would do it.

Mr. HUGHES. That is all I want to know.

Mr. [HENRY F.] HOLLIS [D., N.H.]. Mr. President, I desire to place in the RECORD a reference to the opinion by Judge Dayton which was referred to a short time ago by the Senator from Texas [Mr. CULBERSON]. It is in the case of Hitchman Coal & Coke Co. against Mitchell et al., in the United States District Court for the Northern District of West Virginia, decided December 23, 1912, and reported in Two hundred and second Federal Reporter, at page 512. At the conclusion of his opinion Judge Dayton says:

> In Loewe *v.* Lawlor (208 U. S., 274; 28 Sup. Ct., 301) it was held that the Sherman Antitrust Act "prohibits any combination whatever to secure action which essentially obstructs the free flow of commerce between the States, or restricts, in that regard, the liberty of a trader to engage in business; and this includes restraints of trade aimed at compelling third parties and strangers involuntarily not to engage in the course of interstate trade except on conditions that the combination imposes," and that it "makes no distinction between classes. Organizations of farmers and laborers were not exempted from its operation, notwithstanding the efforts which the records of Congress show were made in that direction," and that "a combination of labor organizations and the members thereof, to compel a manufacturer whose goods are almost entirely sold in other States, to unionize his shops, and on his refusal so to do to boycott his goods and prevent their sale in States other than his own until such time as the resulting damage forces him to comply with their demands," is a "combination in restraint of trade."

That is found in Two hundred and second Federal Reporter, at page 556. . . .

The VICE PRESIDENT. The Chair orders inserted in the RECORD a telegram from the Ohio Manufacturers' Association, protesting against the further consideration of this bill.

The matter referred to is as follows:

Columbus, Ohio, August 18, 1914.

Hon. Thomas R. Marshall,
President of the Senate, Washington, D. C.:

The Ohio Manufacturers' Association earnestly urges that action upon the pending Clayton bill be postponed until a later session of Congress, and we do this irrespective of the possible merits of the legislation contemplated by the bill. We call your attention to the facts, doubtless well known to you, that the industry and commerce of this country have been called upon within a very brief period to meet many changes in the fundamental laws and conditions governing every phase of our transactions. The currency and tariff in themselves require drastic readjustment, while the trade-commission bill recently enacted will impose upon business new and uncertain conditions difficult to meet at a time like this. To further complicate the situation, we are now faced by a world war involving commercial problems of absolutely unique character. We do not feel that we are unreasonable in beseeching your honorable body to postpone action upon a further measure, more unsettling in character, more threatening in aspect than any which have preceded it. We submit that the passage of this measure at this time would not "relieve business of uncertainty," but would greatly add to the perplexities which now beset business men. If the Clayton bill is a wise and just measure, it will unquestionably be passed by a later Congress and loyally accepted by the business men of the country. Nothing sub⊥stantial will be lost by a reasonable delay, through which, in the face of the present crisis, disaster may be avoided. Representing the second largest industry in the State of Ohio, we earnestly beseech your consideration of this appeal.

By order of the executive committee of the Ohio Manufacturers' Association.

Attest:

Malcolm Jennings, Secretary.

Mr. BORAH obtained the floor.

Mr. HUGHES. If the Senator from Idaho will allow me, I desire to read a few lines from the syllabus in the case of Loewe *v.* Lawlor (208 U. S., 275). I wish to call the attention of the Senate to it in connection with the argument which was just made by the Senator from Ohio [Mr. POMERENE]. He made the statement during the course of his argument that the courts held that the Sherman antitrust law in its application to interstate transactions of this character was broader than the common law. This is the syllabus, showing that view was fully sustained by the court:

The antitrust act of July 2, 1890, makes no distinction between classes. Organizations of farmers and laborers were not exempted from its operation, notwithstanding the efforts which the records of Congress show were made in that direction.

Mr. BORAH. I understand that section 7 is now before the Senate for consideration.

The VICE PRESIDENT. The Chair so understands.

Mr. CULBERSON. I think the last paragraph of section 6 is now before the Senate.

The VICE PRESIDENT. That was agreed to by a yea-and-nay vote.

Mr. CULBERSON. I am very glad to hear it, but I do not think it was done. It was not even read. The first paragraph of section 6, on page 6, was read and adopted. The second paragraph has not even been read, I understand.

The VICE PRESIDENT. The Secretary says it has been read. It was treated as one amendment, and both paragraphs have been adopted.

Mr. CULBERSON. If the record shows it, all right.

The VICE PRESIDENT. The next amendment of the Committee on the Judiciary will be stated.

The SECRETARY. On page 7, line 12, before the word "labor," strike out the word "fraternal"; after the word "labor," strike out the word "consumers"; in line 13, after the word "organizations," strike out the words "orders, or associations"; in line 16, after the word "organizations," strike out the words "orders, or associations"; in the same line insert the word "lawfully"; and in line 18, after the word "organizations," strike out the words "orders, or associations," so as to make the first paragraph of section 7 read:

That nothing contained in the antitrust laws shall be construed to forbid the existence and operation of labor, agricultural, or horticultural organizations, instituted for the purposes of mutual help, and not having capital stock or conducted for profit, or to forbid or restrain individual members of such organizations from lawfully carrying out the legitimate objects thereof; nor shall such organizations or the members thereof be held or construed to be illegal combinations or conspiracies in restrain [sic] of trade under the antitrust laws.

Mr. BORAH. Mr. President, section 7 in its entirety as reported by the committee reads as follows:

SEC. 7. That nothing contained in the antitrust laws shall be construed to forbid the existence and operation of labor, agricultural, or horticultural organizations, instituted for the purposes of mutual help, and not having capital stock or conducted for profit, or to forbid or restrain individual members of such organizations from lawfully carrying out the legitimate objects thereof; nor shall such organizations or the members thereof be held or construed to be illegal combinations or conspiracies in restraint of trade, under the antitrust laws.

Mr. President, it is not only the right but, in my opinion, the duty of labor to organize. I have no doubt that union labor has not only been of great value and benefit to the members of the organizations, but, indirectly, of benefit to those who are not members of the organization. The unionization of labor has assisted in maintaining a higher and better wage, better conditions with reference to the place where the work was to be performed, and has generally improved the conditions of labor, not only, as I said, with reference to those who are immediately members of the organization, but, indirectly, all labor has been benefited thereby.

I do not think that anyone at this time controverts the proposition or would argue against not only the right but the duty of labor to organize, in view of the thorough organization of the business world, with which labor has to deal. The only wonder to me has been that so many remain outside of the unions. Laborers have a right to organize, as I understand it, under the law as it now exists. They have a right to organize for the purpose of protecting their wages and for the purpose of raising their wages. They have the right, either singly or collectively as an organization, to refuse to work and to go upon a strike unless the wage is satisfactory. They may, in my opinion, notwithstanding the Sherman law, combine to raise wages and to strike if those wages are not conceded, and to carry out their strike in all peaceful and lawful ways.

Incidentally to this, of course, is the right to take care of strikers, to furnish funds during a strike, to take care of the families of strikers, and to generally carry on, through any peaceful or lawful methods, the cause of securing better wages and better conditions. They may strike for any reason they see fit to assign or for no reason. They may strike through sympathy, or they may strike because of a substantial and direct injury to themselves.

Mr. President, I read this section 7 as in no wise changing the law as it now exists from what I contemplate and conceive the law to be. I understand, of course, that there are those who believe that without such a provision as this, labor organization [sic] per se pursuing their ordinary and legitimate purposes would be in danger. I do not think so. I think they may, in fact, do now all that they may do after this section becomes the law. I know that a different view is entertained not only by members of labor organizations, but by very noted and distinguished lawyers. An article was published in the eastern papers some time ago by a distinguished member of the bar, in which he said:

The mere combination of employees in a given industry in the form of an organization to secure better wages, followed by any overt act, such as the demand for a higher wage or the refusal to work unless the same is conceded, is in restraint of trade and in violation of existing law. * * * The controlling circumstance that the free flow of competition in the trade in human labor has been restrained by this agreement among the workmen not to sell their labor except upon terms agreed upon between them stamps the combination as a conspiracy in restraint of trade.

In my opinion no decision of the courts can be found to sustain that view. On the other hand, speaking with all due respect, I think the authorities lay down the very opposite view.

So far as those who view the law as there expressed by this attorney and by some who are members of labor organizations are concerned, I can see a perfectly good reason for the enactment of this statute. But I was not willing, Mr. President, for this section to be adopted by my vote or with my apparent approval without stating what I conceive to be the law now and what the law will be when this section is adopted. I think no one should be misled and I feel that it is entirely proper to make known what we do not do as well as what we propose to do. The only effect of it, in my judgment, will be to remove the possibility of an attack upon the organization as such, which in my judgment at this time could not be successfully made. In other words, it removes a fear, possibly well grounded, but in my judgment unfounded in the law as it now exists. This section gives these organizations a status and permits them to lawfully carry out their legitimate purposes.

Doubtless the impression prevails among workingmen of this country that, according to the decisions of the court, labor organizations of themselves, organized for the purpose of protecting their wage, when guilty of any overt act in raising the wage are within the prohibition of the Sherman law. If such were the law, no one would want it so; but that such is not the law I entertain no doubt. The only effect of this section, therefore, standing alone and as reported from the committee, is to set at rest the fear that these organizations per se may be attacked and dissolved under the Sherman law.

If I entertained the opinion held by some, I would not only be in favor of this law, for the reasons which I have stated, but I would be in favor of it for the reason that I do not believe there is any desire upon the part of the public nor anything to be gained upon the part of the public in destroying labor organizations in their legitimate function, in performing the purposes for which ordinarily we regard them as organized to perform.

But it is not true, Mr. President, that labor organizations guilty of an overt act in raising their wages or in demanding higher wages are now inhibited by the Sherman law, notwithstanding the view expressed by learned attorneys. I believe that labor has a perfect right under the law now to strike because wages are lower than labor desires wages to be, and demand a higher wage, even if it stops every wheel rolling between the Atlantic and Pacific. . . .

Mr. HUGHES. The Senator qualifies his statement by interjecting into it the fact that wages must be lower. I should like to know how the Senator looks at the proposition that they would have a right to stop for that reason or for any other reason, or for no reason.

Mr. BORAH. For no reason. There is no law in this country and there never has been any law established by any court that I am familiar with to the effect that a man may not quit his employer's employment for the purpose of securing a better wage, or for any other reason satisfactory to the laborer himself, whether sanitary conditions, the betterment of labor generally, or for no reason assigned whatever. You can not compel a man to work under any system that we have so long as the Constitution of the United States has the salutary provision in it that it has now.

Mr. HUGHES. Does the Senator agree with me that under his conception of what the law is laborers would have a right to simultaneously withdraw from employment in order to coerce another employer who is having difficulty with his employees?

Mr. BORAH. No; I do not go to that extent, unless it is understood that it is voluntary all along the line. If all who quit do so voluntarily, they may do so; but men who have quit can not coerce or interfere with others to make them quit.

Mr. HUGHES. Then the Senator does not think that they can simultaneously withdraw or strike for no reason; that they must have good reason.

Mr. BORAH. No; I do not say that. What I say is that labor organizations may, so far as the relationship between the employer and employee is concerned, cease to work; and if that has the effect of producing nonemployment or cessation of work upon the part of the laborers elsewhere, it is an incident to it; but a labor organization can not demand that some one who is not dissatisfied with the employment at all shall not be permitted to labor.

Mr. HUGHES. But suppose this situation—I merely want to get the Senator's view—suppose there is a strike in a certain industrial establishment and another industrial establishment is furnishing raw material to the first establishment. In the Senator's view would the laborers in the second establishment, which is engaged in furnishing raw material to the industrial establishment having difficulty, be justified in going on a strike?

Mr. BORAH. I have no doubt that if the employees of one industry and the employees of another industry agree to quit both may quit, although one of the industries is not dissatisfied; but if the employees of one industry are satisfied and the others insist and interfere with their going ahead with their employment, then a different question arises.

Mr. HUGHES. There is no question of interference at all.

Mr. BORAH. I misunderstood the Senator. It is the proposition whether or not men have a right to quit work for any reason or for no reason—yes, absolutely.

Mr. HUGHES. I want to ask the Senator's opinion of the situation set out by the Senator from Ohio [Mr. POMERENE]. That Senator says that the present law does not in any way prevent the sudden, simultaneous cessation of employment on the part of labor. The Senator suggested the case of a strike taking place on all railroads west of Chicago. That would undoubtedly greatly inconvenience the people depending upon that line of transportation for goods, and it would amount not only to a restraint of trade to all practical purposes, but to an absolute cessation of trade between certain cities. Does not the Senator think that a situation like that, with the city of Chicago absolutely shut off from San Francisco and New York by the cause of simultaneous withdrawals from employment of the railroads of their men, it would constitute under the law as it stands a restraint of trade and commerce?

Mr. BORAH. No; I do not, if the men who struck or quit work in no wise interfere with the employers in securing other labor or in no wise interfered with the operating of the trains in any other method than through themselves, I entertain no possible doubt that the employees of the railroad, the entire employment may cease to work for the railroad company at any hour they see fit.

We are not talking about instances where they are under contract to work for a certain length of time, but where the contractual relations do not appear they may cease to work for the railroad at any time they see fit. The fact that the cessation of trade occurs is an incident to the superior right of the laborer to quit work.

Mr. HUGHES. Yes; but where is that superior right set out? That is what I would like to ascertain from the Senator.

Mr. BORAH. I will reach that in a few moments, but it is set out in the Constitution of the United States, as will be disclosed by Judge Harlan's opinion.

Mr. HUGHES. Take this case: Suppose they had no organization, but they proceeded to form one, the avowed purpose of the organization being to cause a cessation of commerce between two States over a particular line, that being the only railroad line running between those States—and there are points in the United States to which there are no wagon roads, which are absolutely dependent upon railroad transportation as a means of commerce between the States. Now imagine the case of men combining and agreeing together that they would do certain acts, the necessary result of which would be a cessation of commerce, I can not for the life of me conceive why that would not be a restraint of commerce.

Mr. BORAH. The Senator has raised there a different question entirely. In that case the men come together with the intent to restrain trade, for the purpose of preventing commerce between the States. It is a combination to restrain trade which they or no one else can do or should be permitted to do; but if restraint of trade follows from the mere fact of quitting work it is an injury for which there is no damage, and for which the men quitting work are not liable.

Mr. HUGHES. But the Senator a while ago agreed with me that they would have a right to quit for any reason or for no reason.

Mr. BORAH. Exactly. But you are not presenting the case of quitting work; you are talking about a combination which is made to restrain trade.

Mr. HUGHES. They do not have to set out their reason, and they do not set out their reason; but they are responsible for the reasonable consequences that follow from their acts and it is admitted that the reasonable consequence of this act of theirs in simultaneously withdrawing from the common employment is going to be an absolute cessation of commerce between two points in two different States. For the life of me, as I said a while ago, I can not see why an agreement, a combination, or conspiracy to bring about that result would not be a restraint of commerce under the Sherman antitrust law, which speaks of restraints of trade and agreements and combinations to interfere with and restrain interstate commerce.

Mr. BORAH. Well, Mr. President, as we proceed with the matter I shall be very glad to discuss it further with the Senator. I think I had better take up some of the decisions, perhaps, and get my views more thoroughly before the Senate.

Mr. President, one of the best statements of the law that has ever been made was made by Mr. Justice Harlan in a noted case, with which Senators are all, no doubt, familiar, but it is perhaps worth while to refresh our recollection in regard to it, because, with no exception, it is coming to be the recognized law with reference to this subject in this country, and I think has been pretty generally and clearly approved by the Supreme Court of the United States. It is true that the Sherman antitrust law itself was not the specific subject under investigation or discussion by the court at the time the opinion was rendered, but the opinion was rendered after the Sherman law was passed and relates to the employees of railroad companies, which railroad companies were operating between different States, and were, therefore, engaged in interstate commerce. I quote from the case of Arthur against Oakes in Sixty-third Federal Reporter, page 317, in which Justice Harlan said:

But the vital question remains whether a court of equity will, under any circumstances, by injunction prevent one individual from quitting the personal service of another? An affirmative answer to this question is not, we think, justified by any authority to which our attention has been called or of which we are aware. It would be an invasion of one's natural liberty to compel him to work for or to remain in the personal service of another. One who is placed under such constraint is in a condition of involuntary servitude, a condition which the supreme law of the land declares shall not exist within the United States or in any place subject to their jurisdiction. Courts of equity have sometimes sought to sustain a contract for services requiring special knowledge or peculiar skill by enjoining acts or conduct that would constitute a breach of such contract. To this class belong the cases of singers, actors, or musicians, who, after agreeing, for a valuable consideration, to give their professional service at a named place and during a specified time for the benefit of certain parties, refuse to meet their engagement and undertake to appear during the same period for the benefit of other parties at another place. (Lumley v. Wagner, 1 De Gex, M. & G., 604, 617; id., 5 De Gex & S. 485, 16 Jur., 871; Montagne v. Flockton, L.R. 16 Eq., 189.) While in such cases the singer, actor, or musician has been enjoined from appearing during the period named at a place and for parties different from those specified in his first engagement, it was never supposed that the court could by injunction compel the affirmative performance of the agreement to sing or to act or to play. In Powell Duffryn Steam-Coal Co. v. Taff Vale Ry. Co. (9 Ch. App., 331, 335) Lord Justice James observed that when what is required is not merely to restrain a party from doing an act of wrong, but to oblige him to do some continuous act involving labor and care, the court has never found its way to do this by injunction. In the same case Lord Justice Mellish stated the principle still more broadly—perhaps too broadly—when he said that a court can only order the doing of something which has to be done once for all, so that the court can see to its being done.

The rule, we think, is without exception that equity will not compel the actual affirmative performance by an employee of merely personal services any more than it will compel an employer to retain in his personal service one who, no matter for what cause, is not acceptable to him for service of that character. The right of an employee engaged to perform personal service to quit that service rests upon the same basis as the right of his employer to discharge him from further personal service. If the quitting in the one case or the discharging in the other is in violation of the contract between the parties, the one injured by the breach has his action for damages; and a court of ⊥ equity will not, indirectly or negatively, by means of an injunction restraining the violation of the contract, compel the affirmative performance from day to day or the affirmative acceptance of merely personal services. Relief of that character has always been regarded as impracticable. (Toledo, A. A. & N. M. Ry. Co. v. Pennsylvania Co., 54 Fed., 730, 740, Taft, J., and authorities cited; Fry, Spec. Perf., 3d Am. ed., 11, 87–91, and authorities cited.)

It is supposed that these principles are inapplicable or should not be applied in the case of employees of a railroad company, which, under legislative sanction, constructs and maintains a public highway primarily for the convenience of the people and in the regular operation of which the public are vitally interested. Undoubtedly the simultaneous cessation of work by any considerable number of the employees of a railroad corporation without previous notice will have an injurious effect and for a time inconvenience the public. But these evils, great as they are, and although arising in many cases from the inconsiderate conduct of employees and employers, both equally indifferent to the general welfare, are to be met and remedied by legislation restraining alike employees and employers so far as necessary adequately to guard the rights of the public as involved in the existence, maintenance, and safe management of public highways.

In the absence of legislation to the contrary, the right of one in the service of a quasi public corporation to withdraw therefrom at such time as he sees fit, and the right of the managers of such a corporation to discharge an employee from service whenever they see fit, must be deemed so far absolute that no court of equity will compel him, against his will, to remain in such service, or actually to perform the personal acts required in such employments, or compel such managers, against their will, to keep a particular employee in their service. It was competent for the receivers in this case, subject to the approval of the court, to adopt a schedule of wages or salaries, and say to employees, "We will pay according to this schedule, and if you are not willing to accept such wages you will be discharged." It was competent for an employee to say, "I will not remain in your service under that schedule, and if it is to be enforced I will withdraw, leaving you to manage the property as best you may without my assistance." In the one case, the exercise by the receivers of their right to adopt a new schedule of wages could not, at least in the case of a general employment without limit as to time, be made to depend upon considerations of hardship and inconvenience to employees. In the other, the exercise by employees of their right to quit in consequence of a proposed reduction of wages could not be made to depend upon considerations of hardship or inconvenience to those interested in the trust property or to the public. The fact that employees of railroads may quit under circumstances that would show bad faith upon their part, or a reckless disregard of their contract or of the convenience and interests of both employer and the public, does not justify a departure from the general rule that equity will not compel the actual, affirmative performance of merely personal services, or (which is the same thing) require employees, against their will, to remain in the personal service of their employer.[5.639]

Mr. HUGHES. The Senator, of course, knows as well as I do that that is altogether beside the question we were discussing. I never dreamed that anybody would even make application to a court of equity to compel a man specifically to perform a personal service. One of the first things which I was taught in law school was that a court of equity would not compel partners to remain together and would not compel a man to remain in employment. He might quit the employment, but he was responsible for the necessary consequences that followed from the fact that he violated his contract.

Now, admitting what Justice Harlan says to be the law, as it undoubtedly is, yet the fact remains that when these men did simultaneously cease work in the employment in which they were engaged they were still responsible for the reasonable consequences that flowed from that act.

Mr. BORAH. Oh, no, Mr. President. The court says that they had the constitutional right to quit, the constitutional right to be relieved from the employment for any reason that they might have. It was not alone a question of the power of injunction, but as a fundamental, elemental, constitutional right they might quit and could be neither punished under the common law or held in damages.

Mr. HUGHES. The court, as I understand, intimates that legislation might regulate in some way the rights of those men, so far as the public were concerned. It says so in that opinion, but it does not go any further than to say that the court will not issue an injunction commanding a man to stay in a certain employment.

Mr. BORAH. Does the Senator say the court does not say that?

Mr. HUGHES. The court does not go further than to say that it will not issue an injunction commanding a man to stay in a certain employment and to render a certain service. It will not do that. But the court does not say that in a criminal court or in a court of law, where damages merely were sought, they would be free from responsibility.

Mr. BORAH. Mr. President, I can not conceive of a man recovering damages from

---

[5.639] 63 F. 310, 317-19 (7th Cir. 1894).

another man for doing a thing which the Constitution of the United States guarantees him the right to do. That is what the court says here, that they have under the Constitution the absolute right to quit the employment of an interstate carrier. Now, suppose after quitting it had been the purpose of someone who was injured by their quitting to recover damages. The complete defense would have been their constitutional right to quit work. Or suppose an action had been brought under the Sherman law to dissolve their unions. The complete answer would have been that under the Constitution we had the right to quit, and the fact that it interfered with commerce was subordinate and incident to the absolute and perfect right under the Constitution to cease the employment. They would have said further, in answer to the charge, We have done nothing other than that which is right and legal for us to do under the Constitution. Oh, no; this case is not to be limited to the mere power to issue an injunction to prevent their quitting.

Mr. HUGHES. But the Senator knows that a man has a constitutional right to libel another, that the court will not enjoin him from publishing the libel, and that a jury under the Constitution must pass upon whether or not the libelous matter is true or false; but still he is liable in damages.

Mr. BORAH. Well, does the Senator think that the constitutional provision with reference to the freedom of the press and a man being responsible in damages for what he says is the same proposition as that a man can not be compelled to work in penal servitude?

Mr. HUGHES. I think it is fairly parallel.

Mr. BORAH. I do not think the similarity is great.

Mr. HUGHES. In any event, the position the Senator takes—and I want to agree with him, although in supporting this legislation I can not altogether agree with him, for I believe the legislation is absolutely necessary—the position the Senator takes is that it was never intended by the antitrust legislation to interfere with laboring men at all, so far as their simultaneous cessation of work is concerned.

Mr. BORAH. I have no doubt about that.

Mr. HUGHES. I agree with the Senator that such a conception never was in the mind of the author of the act. The debates clearly show that fact.

Mr. BORAH. I have no doubt the framers of the law never intended that the cessation of work upon the part of labor unions should constitute such a restraint of trade as would render laborers liable under the Sherman law; but there are conditions under which they would be liable under the Sherman law, which we will discuss later. The cessation of work, however, is not one of those conditions.

The judge says further here:

> It was equally their right, without reference to the effect upon the property or upon the operation of the road—

This comes pretty close to the question of damages, as the distinguished Senator will observe—

> It was equally their right, without reference to the effect upon the property or upon the operation of the road, to confer with each other upon the subject of the proposed reduction in wages and to withdraw in a body from the service of the receivers because of the proposed change. Indeed, their right, as a body of employees affected by the proposed reduction of wages, to demand given rates of compensation as a condition of their remaining in the service, was as absolute and perfect as was the right of the receivers, representing the aggregation of persons, creditors, and stockholders interested in the trust property, and the general public, to fix the rates they were willing to pay their respective employees.[5.640]

There can be no question as to the purport and the far-reaching effect of that statement. They had a perfect and complete right to quit singly or as a body, regardless of the effect upon the public or the injury which it might be to property.

Mr. HUGHES. Of course I maintain that all that decision sets out is that the court would not enjoin them to the contrary.

[5.640] *Id.* at 320.

Mr. BORAH. I understand the Senator's position.

Mr. President, I call attention next to the case of Hopkins v. The United States (171 U. S., 593).[5.641] This was an action under the Sherman antitrust law. The decision, of course, is not dealing with a labor organization or labor union, but it lays down the proposition that the restraint of interstate commerce must not be merely incidental to some other acts which the party has a right to perform, but must be substantial and direct before it comes within the provisions of the Sherman antitrust law, and it cites the particular kind of cases with which we are dealing as an illustration of the view of the courts. The court says:

> It is not difficult to imagine agreements of the character above indicated. For example, cattle, when transported long distances by rail, require rest, food, and water. To give them these accommodations it is necessary to take them from the car and put them in pens or other places for their safe reception. Would an agreement among the landowners along the line not to lease their lands for less than a certain sum be a contract within the statute as being in restraint of interstate trade or commerce? Would it be such a contract even if the lands, or some of them, were necessary for use in furnishing the cattle with suitable accommodations? Would an agreement between the dealers in corn at some station along the line of the road not to sell it below a certain price be covered by the act because the cattle must have corn for food? Or would an agreement among the men not to perform the service of watering the cattle for less than a certain compensation come within the restriction of the statute? Suppose the railroad company which transports the cattle itself furnishes the facilities, and that its charges for transportation are enhanced because of an agreement among the landowners along the line not to lease their lands to the company for such purposes for less than a named sum, could it be successfully contended that the agreement of the landowners among themselves would be a violation of the act as being in restraint of interstate trade or commerce? Would an agreement between builders of cattle cars not to build them under a certain price be void because the effect might be to increase the price of transportation of cattle between the States? Would an agreement among dealers in horse blankets not to sell them for less than a certain price be open to the charge of a violation of the act, because horse blankets are necessary to put on horses to be sent long journeys by rail, and by reason of the agreement the expense of sending the horses from one State to another for a market might be thereby enhanced?
>
> Would an agreement among cattle drivers not to drive the cattle after their arrival at the railroad depot at their place of destination to the cattle yards where sold, for less than a minimum sum, come within the statute? Would an agreement among themselves by locomotive engineers, firemen, or trainmen engaged in the service of an interstate railroad not to work for less than a certain named compensation be illegal because the cost of transporting interstate freight would be thereby enhanced? Agreements similar to these might be indefinitely suggested.
>
> In our opinion all these queries should be answered in the negative.[5.642]

I entertain no doubt, Mr. President, but that the employees, the engineers, the firemen, and the brakemen could all agree to quit work, and to quit work at any time they saw fit, leaving out for the present the discussion of a contractual relation running for a certain time, notwithstanding the fact that it might prevent the operation of the train and thereby actually stop commerce, because it is an incident to their superior right, to their perfect and complete right under the Constitution, to quit work whenever they see fit to do so. The correlative proposition would be that it would be within the power of the courts or in the power of the law to compel these men to remain in the employ of the company until such time as in the judgment of the court it might be deemed wise for them to quit. If they can not quit work, if we have the power to prevent them from ceasing labor because incidentally it stops commerce, the other proposition must be true, that there is some power under the Constitution in the laws and in the courts to compel them to continue in the employment, which would be, in my judgment, absolutely in the teeth of the Constitution of the United States, as cited by Justice Harlan.

An agreement may in a variety of ways affect interstate commerce just as State legislation may, and yet, like it, be entirely valid, because the interference produced by the agreement or by the legislation is not direct.

[5.641] 171 U.S. 578, 19 S. Ct. 40, 43 L. Ed. 290 (1898).

[5.642] 171 U.S. at 593–94.

Mr. HUGHES. Mr. President, I do not like to be constantly interrupting the Senator if it annoys him.

Mr. BORAH. No; not at all.

Mr. HUGHES. I simply wish to call his attention to the fact that the court there is dealing with an agreement which has not been acted upon, an agreement which apparently all hands have agreed to—the railroads and their employees. The court does not go so far as to say that if, in order to get that agreement, these men had committed certain overt acts, such as ceasing at once their employment, it would be as innocent as it is without those overt acts.

Mr. BORAH. Oh, the court is not dealing with any agreement.

Mr. HUGHES. The court cited, as an example of an innocent agreement which would not be violative of the law, an agreement between locomotive firemen or engineers.

Mr. BORAH. The court is using the word "agreement" there as we use it in popular parlance. The effect of the court's decision is simply that they might have an understanding or agreement or coming together, and all quit at once as the result of that agreement.

Mr. HUGHES. No; I am addressing myself to the other part of the statement.

Mr. BORAH. The particular part to which I have reference is:

Would an agreement among themselves by locomotive engineers, firemen, or trainmen engaged in the service of an interestate [sic] railroad not to work for less than a certain named compensation be illegal?

Mr. HUGHES. That means, "Would a union for that purpose be illegal?" The court says: "No; a union for that purpose would not be illegal;" but the court does not say that a union would be innocent which might have not only that for its purpose but an intention to strike.

Mr. BORAH. I have no doubt of the proposition, which to me is an entirely different proposition, that for a union or a labor organization or laboring men to go out with the intent and for the purpose of stopping an interstate train and preventing anybody from operating such a train, thereby making it their prime object and the purpose for which they are operating and acting, would be within the Sherman law; but that is an entirely different proposition from the one I am arguing, which is that the members of a labor organization have a perfect right to stop work for any reason they want to, although the result of it is to prevent the operation of a train and to stop commerce.

Mr. HUGHES. I can not see how the Senator can reconcile those two statements. That is the way it appears to me. I do not want to be captious, but that is the way I honestly think on the subject.

We will take the case—and it is not a fanciful case, either—of a group of men who are in practically entire control of a certain branch of industry. Take the locomotive engineers: There is not any doubt in my mind that on any great railroad, if the locomotive engineers went on a strike, there would not be a sufficient number of unattached locomotive engineers outside of their organization competent and capable of filling their places, or any respectable percentage of their places; so you can easily assume a case where locomotive engineers, by going on strike, would cause an absolute cessation of commerce. Now, a while ago I asked the Senator whether those men would have a right to strike for a reason satisfactory to themselves or for no reason—for any reason or not [sic] reason at all. The Senator agreed with me then, I think.

Mr. BORAH. I agree with you now.

Mr. HUGHES. But if their purpose or reason is to cause that cessation of commerce, as the Senator said a minute ago, as I understood, they would be operating in violation of the law.

Mr. BORAH. I have no doubt at all of the proposition that the organized engineers, although they might be the only engineers who could run the trains properly, could quit work. They could assign a reason or not assign a reason, just as they pleased. If they went a step further, however, and if the road was prepared to operate and they interfered with its operation through the instrumentalities which the road might choose to employ, incompetent engineers or otherwise, they would be within the provisions of the Sherman law. In one instance—to wit, in quitting work—they are exercising a right; in the other instance, where they interfere with others from operating a train, they are not exercising a right, but doing a wrong, and the consequences which flow from doing a thing we have a right to do and the thing we have not a right to do may be physically the same, but the legal liability is different.

Mr. HUGHES. I agree with the Senator absolutely as to that. Of course I think they are within it now.

Mr. BORAH. Mr. President, of course there never has been any decision upon all fours, as we use the term sometimes at the bar, with this proposition, but I do challenge my friends who think that there has been a different rule to cite a single case which has been sustained on appeal and has become the final voice of the court, in which the Federal courts have ever interfered with the right of the members of a labor organization to quit work whether they did it singly or collectively and whether it had the effect of stopping commerce or whether it did not. I do not believe any authority can be cited to the effect that they must continue in the employment, not according to their wishes, but according to the demands or the interests or the welfare of commerce. If any such case should be cited, I would agree perfectly with those who think there is a justification for this statute.

I understand that there are well-grounded fears on the part of honest men in regard to it, and in so far as it accomplishes the things which I believe now to exist, and which ought to be accomplished, I stand with them, and do not oppose the statute for that reason.

But, Mr. President, let me call attention to another case, and that is the case of Adair against United States, in Two hundred and eighth United States, page 178:

> Manifestly, any rule prescribed for the conduct of interstate commerce, in order to be within the competency of Congress under its power to regulate commerce among the States, must have some real or substantial relation to or connection with the commerce regulated. But what possible legal or logical connection is there between an employee's membership in a labor organization and the carrying on of interstate commerce? Such relation to a labor organization can not have, in itself and in the eye of the law, any bearing upon the commerce with which the employee is connected by his labor and services. Labor associations, we assume, are organized for the general purpose of improving or bettering the conditions and conserving the interests of its members as wage earners—an object entirely legitimate and to be commended rather than condemned. But surely those associations as labor organizations have nothing to do with interstate commerce as such. One who engages in the service of an interstate carrier will, it must be assumed, faithfully perform his duty, whether he be a member or not a member of a labor organization. His fitness for the position in which he labors and his diligence in the discharge of his duties can not in law or sound reason depend in any degree upon his being or not being a member of a labor organization. It can not be assumed that his fitness is assured, or his diligence increased, by such membership, or that he is less fit or less diligent because of his not being a member of such an organization.[5.643]

A single paragraph, Mr. President, from the case of Gompers against The Buck's Stove & Range Co., in Two hundred and twenty-first United States, at page 439:

> The law, therefore, recognizes the right of workingmen to unite and to invite others to join their ranks, thereby making available the strength, influence, and power that come from such association. By virtue of this right, powerful labor unions have been organized.

The case of National Protective Association against Cumming, in One hundred and seventieth New York, page 321, is a case familiar to us all, and has often been cited. Along with the opinion of Justice Harlan, it states the rights of labor unions as I conceive them to be, and as I believe the authorities will finally permanently and unmistakably establish them in this country:

> It is not the duty of one man to work for another unless he has agreed to, and if he has so agreed, but for no fixed period, either may end the contract whenever he chooses. The one may

---

[5.643] 208 U.S. 161, 178–79, 28 S. Ct. 277, 282, 52 L. Ed. 436, 444 (1908).

work, or refuse to work, at will, and the other may hire or discharge at will. The terms of employment are subject to mutual agreement, without let or hindrance from anyone. If the terms do not suit, or the employer does not please, the right to quit is absolute, and no one may demand a reason therefor. Whatever one man may do alone he may do in combination with others, provided they have no unlawful object in view. Mere numbers do not ordinarily affect the quality of the act. Workingmen have the right to organize for the purpose of securing higher wages, shorter hours of labor, or improving their relations with their employers. They have the right to strike; that is, to cease working in a body by prearrangement until a grievance is redressed, provided the object is not to gratify malice or inflict injury upon others, but to secure better terms of employment for themselves.[5.644]

Mr. HUGHES. Mr. President, if the Senator will permit me, he will notice there that the court qualifies their right to strike. That was the point I was trying to make. The court itself there qualifies their right to strike, and insists upon their having a good reason or a reason satisfactory to the court.

Mr. BORAH. Oh, no—

They have the right to strike—that is, to cease working in a body by prearrangement until a grievance is redressed—provided the object is not to gratify malice or inflict injury upon others—

Mr. HUGHES. Yes; but that qualifies it, nevertheless.

Mr. BORAH (reading):

But to secure better terms of employment for themselves.

Mr. HUGHES. You see how narrow that is.

Mr. BORAH. Of course if they are interfering with other people, that is another thing.

Mr. HUGHES. They necessarily interfere. If the Senator has had any experience with injunction cases—

Mr. BORAH. I have had some.

Mr. HUGHES (continuing). He will know that away down at the tail end of an injunction in a labor dispute there is a clause to this effect:

Nor shall these defendants in any other manner interfere with complainant's business.

The terrifying language with reference to coercion, intimidation, threats, battle, murder, and sudden death which is used to excuse the injunction, but which in very many cases is absolutely unjustified, is followed by this simple little clause:

Nor shall these defendants in any other manner interfere with the business of the complainant.

Now, to remain away from his employment in a great many trades is the most effective manner of interfering with his business.

Mr. BORAH. Does the Senator know of any instance in which a court has ever enjoined the members of a labor union from quitting work or from striking for higher wages?

Mr. HUGHES. Yes; I do. I do not remember the titles of the cases, but it seems to me that Judge Dayton—

Mr. BORAH. That case—

Mr. HUGHES. I am speaking now of some of the more remote activities of Judge Dayton, and not of this last case. There are one or two other West Virginia Federal judges who have done things of that kind. I do not say that the Supreme Court or any appellate court has ever upheld them, but back something like 15 or 20 years ago, according to my recollection, it was a common thing for receivers to make application to Federal judges to enjoin men from leaving their employment.

Mr. BORAH. Yes; but they have never done that since Justice Harlan rendered his opinion in the Oakes case.[5.645] The Dayton case does not go to the extent claimed and has been overruled besides.

Mr. HUGHES. I am quite prepared to believe that to be true.

[5.644] 170 N.Y. at 320-21.

[5.645] 63 F. 310 (7th Cir. 1894).

Mr. BORAH. I have never known of an instance. I have never been able to find it.

Mr. HUGHES. But the injunctions have been issued, and the very thing has been done which the Senator says constitutional rights and human rights forbid being done. That is, the attempt was made to compel men to remain in a certain employment, to give their service, to force them into involuntary servitude, and the writ of injunction was invoked for that purpose; and that was the beginning of the movement against the writ of injunction which has culminated in the proposed legislation which now appears before us. . . .

Mr. WHITE. My recollection is, though I may be mistaken, that Judge Taft punished an employee of a railroad that was being operated by a receiver because that employee quit work.

Mr. BORAH. If the Senator will investigate, he will find that that is a mistake. Judge Taft was too able a judge to have so held.

Mr. WHITE. That is my recollection.

Mr. BORAH. I think the Senator will find that he is in error as to that proposition. That was attempted to be done in the case of Arthur against Oakes. That was not Judge Taft's opinion; it was the opinion of Judge Woods, if I remember correctly; but, anyhow, it was not Judge Taft. But that was the portion of the injunction order which Justice Harlan struck from the decree. That is the only instance I know of; but you will find that Judge Taft did not lay down that rule. . . .

Mr. [THOMAS] STERLING [R., S.D.]. I think the Senator from Alabama must have the Phelan case[5.646] in mind.

Mr. WHITE. I think that is the style of the case.

Mr. STERLING. Yes; that is the style of the case or proceeding. The facts were not quite as the Senator supposes. If I remember the case correctly, Phelan was punished for disobeying the decree of the court in inciting others to violence and intimidation.

Mr. WHITE. I am glad to be corrected, but that was my recollection.

Mr. BORAH. Here is the Phelan case, and this is the language of Judge Taft. I cite from Sixty-second Federal Reporter, at page 817:

> Now, it may be conceded in the outset that the employees of the receiver had the right to organize into or join a labor union which should take joint action as to their terms of employment. It is of benefit to them and to the public that laborers should unite in their common interest and for lawful purposes. They have labor to sell. If they stand together they are often able, all of them, to command better prices for their labor than when dealing singly with rich employers, because the necessities of the single employee may compel him to accept any terms offered him. The accumulation of a fund for the support of those who feel that the wages offered are below market prices is one of the legitimate objects of such an organization. They have the right to appoint officers who shall advise them as to the course to be taken by them in their relations with their employer. They may unite with other unions. The officers they appoint, or any other person to whom they choose to listen, may advise them as to the proper course to be taken by them in regard to their employment, or, if they choose to repose such authority in anyone, may order them, on pain of expulsion from their union, peaceably to leave the employ of their employer because any of the terms of their employment are unsatisfactory. It follows, therefore (to give an illustration which will be understood), that if Phelan had come to this city when the receiver reduced the wages of his employees by 10 per cent and had urged a peaceable strike, and had succeeded in maintaining one, the loss to the business of the receiver would not be ground for recovering damages, and Phelan would not have been liable for contempt even if the strike much impeded the operation of the road under the order of the court. His action in giving the advice or issuing an order based on unsatisfactory terms of employment would have been entirely lawful. But his coming here and his advice to the Southern Railroad employees, or to the employees of other roads, to quit had nothing to do with their terms of employment. They were not dissatisfied with their service or their pay. Phelan came to Cincinnati to carry out the purpose of a combination of men, and his act in inciting the employees of all Cincinnati roads to quit service was part of that combination. If the combination was unlawful then every act in pursuance of it was unlawful, and his instigation of the strike would be an unlawful wrong done by him to every railway company in the city, for which they can recover damages and for which, so far as his acts affected the Southern Railway, he is in contempt of this court.

[5.646] Thomas v. Cincinnati, N.O. & T.P. Ry., 62 F. 803 (C.C.S.D. Ohio 1894).

Mr. WHITE. The cause was quitting, not inciting other men to quit.

Mr. BORAH. If the Senator will refer to the opinion, he will find what was decided.

Mr. WHITE. I am speaking of the opinion of the court. The court would seem to base it upon that rather than inciting them to quit.

Mr. CUMMINS. It has been some time since I read the opinion, but the case, as I remember it, involved the question of a secondary boycott against the Pullman Palace Car Co. Mr. Phelan was endeavoring to induce some employees of the railroad company to refuse to haul a train that contained a Pullman palace car.

Mr. BORAH. That is correct.

Mr. CUMMINS. It was upon that ground that he was held guilty of a contempt of court. Of course the final outcome as to the railroad would be that if the railroad company insisted on carrying the Pullman car, then the employees of that railroad refused to longer remain in the service, so far as hauling that train was concerned. They did not quit service; they simply refused to assist in moving a train that had a Pullman car in it.

Mr. BORAH. The point was that the men wanted to stay in the service, but they refused to haul a particular car.

Mr. WHITE. They had the lawful right to do that, I understand, and Phelan was punished because he had incited men to do that which they had a lawful right to do.

Mr. BORAH. Phelan did not have a lawful right to do it.

Mr. WHITE. I say he was punished for inciting men to do that which they had a lawful right to do.

Mr. HUGHES. Whether Senators believe it is the law that men have or have not the right to strike for any reason or for no reason, what the Senator from Iowa calls the secondary boycott is not a boycott; it is what the labor men call a sympathetic strike.

Mr. BORAH. I did not understand the Senator from Iowa that way at all.

Mr. HUGHES. It was precisely that.

Mr. BORAH. If a body of workingmen are working, we will say, for the Union Pacific Railroad Co., and another body of workingmen are working for the Northern Pacific Railroad Co., and if the Union Pacific Railroad Co. has trouble with its employees, there is no doubt that if out of mere sympathy the Northern Pacific employees want to quit they have a perfect right to quit. But if the Northern Pacific men are willing to continue and are satisfied with their situation, and the Union Pacific men undertake to menace by threats or violence, or otherwise to interfere with them, a different case is presented.

Mr. HUGHES. Let us leave out all that fustian about threats, intimidation, and violence; no one wants to legalize acts of that kind.

Mr. BORAH. I will try to keep fustian out of my speech.

Mr. HUGHES. I hope we will at least be able to keep it out of our colloquy so that we can get this matter cleared up. I am in sympathy with the Senator, but his position does not seem to me to be entirely clear.

I want to put this case to the Senator: The Pullman Co. has trouble with their men. They go on a strike. The strike is being carried on. There is no suggestion of violence or menace or coercion or anything of that sort so far as the Pullman employees are concerned, but they go to the employees of the railroad company which hauls certain Pullman cars and they pursuade the employees of the railroad company to a certain course of action; and as a result of what they say to them, as a result of the persuasion of the employees of the Pullman Co., the employees of the railroad company say to their employers and threaten them that they will quit, and commerce will be paralyzed unless the company refrains from hauling Pullman cars. Then, if the railroad company continues to haul the Pullman cars and its men quit, that would be a sympathetic strike; but the Senator from Iowa [Mr. CUMMINS] calls it a "secondary boycott." I should like to know whether the Senator from Idaho thinks the employees of that railroad company had a right to do that—to go to these men under those circumstances and induce them to quit unless their employers agreed that they would not haul a Pullman car; and would the latter have the right to quit?

Mr. BORAH. I have no doubt about it. I have no doubt that the one class of laborers or one organization may meet with another organization and discuss with them and say to them, "We do not think it is to the interest of labor that you should continue in their work." I have no doubt in the world that they may do that and they could not be restrained. I do not know of any instances where that kind of persuasion separated entirely from menace or threat or violence has ever been restrained.

Mr. HUGHES. I am not speaking about persuasion. I am speaking of the effect on the railroad employees because the railroad employees go to the president of the railroad and say certain things, which result in a threat on their part to quit, to tie up interstate commerce, although they say, "Our conditions are satisfactory; our wages are satisfactory; we are perfectly satisfied with everything surrounding us, but our brother employees are engaged in a death grapple with the Pullman Co., and you are helping the Pullman Co. to succeed by hauling their cars. If you continue to haul their cars, we will not permit you to haul your trains so far as we can prevent it."

Mr. BORAH. I have no doubt they have a right to do that. I am assuming now that the men who are quitting are doing so purely through sympathy, not by reason of threats or menaces or against their own desires.

Mr. HUGHES. That is what the Senator from Iowa called a secondary boycott.

Mr. CUMMINS. I did call it a secondary boycott. It is in every sense such a boycott, although it may have been also a sympathetic strike.

But the real difficulty in the Phelan case was not that the employees of these railroads asserted the right to strike because they were hauling Pullman cars. They asserted the right to remain in the employ of the railroad company, but declined to handle any train that had in it any Pullman car.

Mr. HUGHES. And if they were compelled to handle them they would quit.

Mr. CUMMINS. I am not asserting any sympathy with or my concurrence in the reasoning in the Phelan case. I may be wrong about some of the facts, because I have not read it for many years, but the strikers were trying to secure redress against the Pullman Palace Car Co., and the railroad companies which were made the victims of the boycott were innocent of any offense against the strikers. It is a little difficult always to draw the line, but what I term a secondary boycott is where strikers attempt to injure an innocent man in order to work out their plan. It is exactly like the ordinary case where wageworkers go to a merchant who is dealing with the employer with whom the strikers have their dispute. They say to him: "If you do not cease to deal or have relations with the unfair employer, then we will cease to deal with you, not only with regard to the goods that may be purchased by you of the unfair employer, but as to all goods in which you deal, without regard to the source from which you get them. I think there is a striking similarity between the case of refusing to haul a train in which there was a car of an offending employer and the case of concerting and combining to withdraw patronage from a merchant who was entirely innocent of the transaction, but who may have some dealings with the unfair employer. That is the reason I call it a secondary boycott. As I remember, it is so termed in one of the opinions that involved the transaction.

Mr. HUGHES. If the Senator from Idaho will permit me further to trespass upon his patience, I want to say that I thoroughly agree with the Senator from Iowa as to what constitutes a sympathetic strike. When you come to legislate against a secondary boycott you must legislate against a sympathetic strike, and that is the reason why I want to clear it up if I can. Men, in my opinion, have a right to strike; they have a right to institute a sympathetic strike; an unreasonable strike; or a strike for any reason or for no reason.

Mr. BORAH. I agree with the Senator that they have the right. I disagree with him in the view of the fact that he seems to think the authority they have—

Mr. HUGHES. The Senator from Iowa seems to think they have not the right.

Mr. CUMMINS. I have no doubt of their right to strike.

Mr. HUGHES. But the Senator referred to a secondary boycott.

Mr. CUMMINS. The Senator will remember I said I did not express any sympathy or concurrence with the reasoning of the opinion.

Mr. HUGHES. I understand that. I am asking the Senator about the law. I am not trying to find out what he thinks the law ought to be.

Mr. CUMMINS. I have no doubt the law is as stated by the Senator from Idaho, that the employees have a right to strike for a good cause, or a bad cause, or for no cause at all. It is a right superior to any inconvenience that it may occasion either the employer or the public. It is a right which I think is inherent in man.

Mr. HUGHES. The Senator, then, thinks that the railroad employees in the Pullman case had a right to refuse to haul the cars if the trains carried Pullman cars.

Mr. CUMMINS. I think the employees of those railroads had a right to strike for any reason, but it does not follow that the acts of Phelan were justifiable under the law.

Mr. STERLING. Mr. President, if the Senator from Idaho will yield to me for just a moment, whether that be the basis of Judge Taft's decision or not, I thought I could not be mistaken in regard to some of the facts in the Phelan case, namely, those relating to violence and intimidation and his activities in inciting men thereto. I have the case before me. The court says:

We come now to consider the question of fact, whether Phelan in any of his speeches advised intimidation, threats, or violence in carrying out the boycott.[5.647]

The court calls it a boycott, not a secondary boycott.

Mr. CUMMINS. I remember there was a boycott, and in the very nature of things I thought it was a secondary boycott.

Mr. STERLING (reading):

He is charged with having said, on Thursday night, June 28, at the meeting at West End Turner Hall, that the strike was then declared on; that it was the duty of every A. R. U. man to quit work, to induce and coax other men to go out, and if this was not successful to take a club and knock them out.[5.648]

And much more to the same effect. If the Senator from Idaho will excuse me a moment further, I will read briefly from the court's opinion, and then Senators may judge upon what ground the court bases the decision made.

But the combination was unlawful without respect to the contract feature. It was a boycott. The employees of the railway companies had no grievance against their employers. Handling and hauling Pullman cars did not render their services any more burdensome. They had no complaints against the use of Pullman cars as cars. They came into no natural relation with Pullman in handling the cars. He paid them no wages. He did not regulate their hours, or in any way determine their services. Simply to injure him in his business, they were incited and encouraged to compel the railway companies to withdraw custom from him by threats of quitting their service, and actually quitting their service. This inflicted an injury on the companies that was very great, and it was unlawful, because it was without lawful excuse. All the employees had the right to quit their employment, but they had no right to combine to quit in order thereby to compel their employer to withdraw from a mutually profitable relation with a third person for the purpose of injuring that third person, when the relation thus sought to be broken had no effect whatever on the character or reward of their service.[5.649]

Mr. BORAH. Mr. President, coming back to the point from which I was diverted, I was reading from the case of the National Protective Association against Cumming, which opinion was written by Chief Justice Parker:

A peaceable and orderly strike, not to harm others, but to improve their own condition, is not in violation of law.[5.650]

* * * * * * *

The same rule applies to a body of men who, having organized for purposes deemed beneficial to themselves, refuse to work. Their reasons may seem inadequate to others, but if it seems to be in their interest as members of an organization to refuse longer to work, it is their legal right to stop. The reason may no more be demanded as a right of the organization than of an individual, but if they elect to state the reason their right to stop work is not cut off because the reason seems inadequate or selfish to the employer or to organized society. And if the conduct of the members of an organization is legal in itself, it does not become illegal because the organization directs one of its members to state the reason for its conduct.

[5.647] *Id.* at 813.
[5.648] *Id.*
[5.649] *Id.* at 818.
[5.650] 170 N.Y. at 321.

The principles quoted above recognize the legal right of members of an organization to strike—that is, to cease working in a body by prearrangement until a grievance is redressed—and they enumerate some things that may be treated as the subject of a grievance, namely, the desire to obtain higher wages, shorter hours of labor, or improved relations with their employers, but this enumeration does not, I take it, purport to cover all the grounds which will lawfully justify members of an organization refusing, in a body and by prearrangement, to work. The enumeration is illustrative rather than comprehensive, for the object of such an organization is to benefit all its members and it is their right to strike, if need be, in order to secure any lawful benefit to the several members of the organization as, for instance, to secure the reemployment of a member they regard as having been improperly discharged, and to secure from an employer of a number of them employment for other members of their organization who may be out of employment, although the effect will be to cause the discharge of other employees who are not members.

And whenever the courts can see that a refusal of members of an organization to work with nonmembers may be in the interest of the several members, it will not assume, in the absence of a finding to the contrary, that the object of such refusal was solely to gratify malice and to inflict injury upon such nonmembers.[5.651]

I now read a paragraph from the New Jersey Equity Reports, volume 63, page 759.[5.652] It states the principle in a very clear and concise but comprehensive way:

From an examination of the cases and a very careful consideration of the subject I am unable to discover any right in the courts, as the law now stands, to interfere with this absolute freedom on the part of the employer to employ whom he will, and to cease to employ whom he will; and the corresponding freedom on the part of the workman, for any reason or no reason, to say that he will no longer be employed; and the further right of the workmen, of their own free will, to combine and meet as one party, as a unit, the employer, who, on the other side of the transaction, appears as a unit before them. * * *[5.653] Union workmen who inform their employer that they will strike if he refuses to discharge all nonunion workmen in his employ are acting within their absolute right, and, in fact, are merely dictating the terms upon which they will be employed.[5.654]

Now, Mr. President, I might cite many other decisions to the same effect, but these suffice. Whatever divergence may be found, if any, from principles here announced, these cases disclose the unmistakable trend of opinion and the law as it is and as it is to be. These decisions show the true attitude of the courts toward labor. In brief, what do these authorities hold? They hold the right of laborers singly or collectively, for good reason or no reason, to quit work, and that this right is absolute and guaranteed and protected by the Constitution. That the fact that the employees quitting work are in the employ of an interstate carrier and that interstate commerce is thereby interfered with does not change the rule or modify the right. That the fact that interstate commerce must suffer, and the public be inconvenienced, must all yield to the superior and protected right of the laborer to be free to do as he will with his labor. In other words, they clearly recognize the distinction between a commodity and labor. No combination would have a right to combine and to withhold the products of commerce through an intention of enforcing higher prices. It is further clearly held that the reasons for quitting work are reasons to be assigned by labor itself. The reasons may seem to be to the public wholly insufficient, but neither the public nor the courts can judge of the sufficiency of the reasons so long as the laborer in quitting acts upon his own volition, according to his own wishes, and not by reason of menace or fear of violence. It further appears clearly from these authorities that the courts have recognized that the combinations of laboring men to secure wages and refusal to work, though interfering with interstate commerce in a most pronounced way, are not within the provisions of the Sherman antitrust law; that the interference of interstate commerce is incidental, indirect, and subordinate to the positive and constitutional right of the laborer to work or not to work as he chooses. Moreover, it clearly appears from these authorities that the courts have universally commended and encouraged laborers to organize. It seems to me that these cases clearly establish these principles. In other

---

[5.651] *Id.* at 321–22.

[5.652] Jersey City Printing Co. v. Cassidy, 63 N.J. Eq. 759, 53 A. 230 (Ch. 1902).

[5.653] 63 N.J. Eq. at 761.

[5.654] *Id.* at 762.

words labor organizations may exist now and may demand higher wages and may refuse to work unless they get the wages, and that by so doing are not subject to the Sherman antitrust law. They may carry out all the legitimate objects of labor unions in a lawful way. If any decisions can be found to the contrary they were most erroneously decided. I have seen no such decisions and none are here presented. . . .

Mr. BRYAN. I ask the Senator from Idaho if it would be agreeable to him to continue his remarks to-morrow. If so, I would prefer a request for a meeting to-night, at the suggestion of several Senators. If agreeable to the Senator, I will prefer it now.

Mr. BORAH. Does the Senator desire to move an adjournment?

Mr. BRYAN. I was going to ask unanimous consent to hold a session to-night.

Mr. BORAH. Mr. President, I shall close my remarks in 20 minutes.

Mr. BRYAN. I hope the Senator will understand that I did not mean to take him off the floor or to suggest that he curtail his remarks.

Mr. BORAH. I shall close my remarks in a very few minutes.

Mr. President, I have taken this much time of the Senate apparently without any justification, for I am not going to oppose this section; but I was not willing to support the section with the construction which has been placed upon it by some others who have discussed it, both in this Chamber and elsewhere.

Mr. President, I secured my intimate acquaintance with labor organizations in a manner which was not calculated to unduly prejudice me in their behalf. There were conditions which brought me in touch with labor organizations which I do not propose to discuss here, but which were certainly not calculated to lead me into a fulsome eulogy or bias me unduly in favor of such organizations. But even in these same controversies I learned to sympathize thoroughly with the rights of labor organizations and became thoroughly convinced that it was impossible for labor to deal with the great organized business interests of the world without thorough organizations of their own. My sympathies were thoroughly aroused in favor of a just, proper, and lawfully conducted organization, and I have never changed my view upon that question. I saw very clearly how it was absolutely impossible for laborers to protect their wage, to protect their conditions of employment, and to secure for themselves their fair proportion of the world's pleasures and comforts without thorough organization.

I am in favor of any measure which is deemed essential to protect and shield fully labor unions as such from the condemnation of the Sherman antitrust law or any other law. I do not believe that unions are now condemned by that law or in anywise prohibited. I do not believe that any well-considered decision of the court can be found to that effect. But if there is fear that such decision may be had, or if there is belief that any court has assumed to go thus far and to say that the organization of labor unions is of itself a restraint of trade, then this legislation is justified to that extent and I cordially support it to that extent. The time has long since passed when any right-thinking man would do other than encourage labor unions in all legitimate and lawful acts. They are essential ⊥ to enable labor to protect the laborer in his wage and to help the well-being of his family. It seems to me incredible that any court would say such unions were in violation of the antitrust law. It would be a distinct and notorious perversion of the law.

These unions are no more in violation of the law than a corporation or association of business men are in themselves a violation of the law. Whether they come under the condemnation of the law depends not upon the fact as to the union, but entirely upon what as unions they do. They may combine, they may do all those things which look to the betterment and the welfare of the members, they may determine upon a wage, they may demand an increase of wage, and they may quit work singly or collectively in order to enforce their demands. All these and similar acts are not in violation of law and should not be, for they are essentially right and proper. They are within the legitimate scope and design and purpose of labor unions. But, Mr. President, we are asked by some to declare that the labor unions may go further and affirmatively and effectively and with design interfere with or restrain interstate commerce; that while we condemn all other interests and punish if they restrain trade or monopolize interstate commerce, we will except labor unions. This, Mr. President, I can not do. I could not support such a measure as a citizen or a Senator, and if I were a laboring man I am convinced I would not ask it. I do not believe that as a body labor does ask it.

Why did we pass the law of 1890; why do we keep it on the statute books? Because we thought then and think now that to restrain or embarrass interstate commerce wrongs and injures the whole people; that it works evil to the entire body politic. We thought then and we think now that to restrain or monopolize interstate trade would injure labor, and that in the end labor would suffer with all the rest of us. Now, the injury which would flow to the public from stopping commerce would be just the same regardless of who stopped it. If divine interposition through a war of the elements should stop interstate commerce, the great loss to the whole country would be just the same as if it were interfered with by some great monopoly. Labor can not thrive and the laboring man can not find work unless commerce moves, and I have no fear that labor will not see that this is true upon reflection. There are people in this country—and I am one of them—who believe very earnestly in the principle of the Sherman antitrust law. They believe that it is vital to our national welfare. So believing I could not for a moment weaken it and in the end destroy it by relieving a portion of our people from its operation while insisting upon its drastic enforcement as to others. That is not the kind of a government we built.

Neither do I believe the farmers of this country are asking to be relieved from the operation of any law deemed to be of general benefit to the people of the country. It is not like the farmer to ask any such exceptions in his favor. He knows this law of 1890 declared for a great, essential, and indispensable principle of trade and commerce, to wit, the free flow of commerce through the channels of interstate trade. He knows it declared that such commerce should be forever and at all times unembarrassed, unvexed by the restraint of monopoly. He knows there is no rule of more concern to the people as a whole, from a business and economic standpoint, than the rule declared by the statute of 1890, known as the Sherman antitrust law. He knows when our commerce is embarrassed, hindered, or restrained through combinations by reason of unnatural causes or through monopolies, when it is disturbed in any improper and illegal way, industrial stagnation, business distress, lower prices, lower wages, lockouts, and general unrest must inevitably follow.

The farmers, in my judgment, are willing and anxious to abide by this law. They are desirous of seeing it enforced fully and completely. Nothing could serve them more advantageously than the thorough enforcement of this law. What they are asking is that it be enforced alike as to all and that there be no exceptions, either by law or other political favoritism. If there is anyone in the country that is opposed to all forms of monopoly, it is the farmer. If there is anyone in favor of equality before the law, it is the farmer, and he will be the last man, in my judgment, to ask any exception or special privilege.

No, Mr. President; give the agricultural interests equality, an equal chance with other industries, and they will thrive and be content. Give the farmer an equal chance under the tariff laws with the manufacturer. Give him a system of rural credits by which he can utilize his credits and secure his loans for a reasonable rate of interest. Help him to build and construct good roads and be assured he will ask no favor of that kind; he will neither need it nor want it. Do not insult his intelligence or impeach his good citizenship and his patriotism by offering him some little special privilege or favor which will not greatly benefit him if at all and will greatly injure the country. Do not hope to secure his approval by withholding great and essential things which he should have and giving him the unfair and unessential things which he ought not to have and does not want.

Mr. President, I represent in part upon this floor a constituency made up very largely of farmers and laboring men. They constitute not only the great voting strength of the State, but in a large measure its wealth and moral force. We have but few manufacturing establishments and but few of those combinations such as it is said ought to come particularly and alone within the inhibition of this trust law. If a measure were proposed here which would have the effect of relieving the farmer and the laborer wholly from the operation of the Sherman antitrust law and I should vote for the same because they constitute largely my constituency, I would feel myself forever estopped from inveighing against the constituency of my colleagues engaged, as they are, in a different kind of business. Yes; I would feel myself a shuffling coward and wholly unworthy of my constituency.

If there is anybody in this world that ought to stand firm and unbroken for the enforcement of all laws which restrain trade and foster monopoly, it is the farmer and the laborer. If there is any power which seems to rise above the law and above apparently any ingenuity which the law can invoke to control the price of farm products and to oppress labor, to enforce child employment, and curtail and curb prices, it is these vast monopolies, which the Sherman law is designed to destroy and which it will destroy if we ever find men with courage enough to enforce it. So far as I am concerned, I do not propose at any time to do anything which in my judgment will weaken either legally or morally our capacity to destroy monopolies in this country. We may all have to make some sacrifices, but whatever sacrifices are necessary to be made should be made without hesitation to accomplish this great end. If we begin to tear down the Sherman law in one instance to relieve its operations in certain directions, it will not be long until it will be torn down in another instance and until the principle will be wholly emasculated, the Sherman law finally repealed or made a dead letter, and the great monopolies of this country will reign supreme over the farmer and the laborer, the consumer, and all who are not within the circle of their favors. When we come to the conclusion that monopoly in this country is a good thing, let us repeal the law as a whole and venture, if we dare, upon that era of industrial autocracy. If we do not believe in such an era, let us stand firm and make whatever sacrifices necessary to its absolute destruction.

The VICE PRESIDENT. The question is on the amendment.

Mr. CUMMINS. What is the amendment, Mr. President?

The VICE PRESIDENT. To strike out the work "fraternal" in line 12. The question is on agreeing to the amendment. [Putting the question.] The ayes have it.

Mr. REED. Mr. President, I was trying to get the attention of the Chair; and I suppose the matter is still open to debate, is it not?

The VICE PRESIDENT. Yes; if there is any objection to the word "fraternal" going out.

Mr. REED. If that is the only change proposed, I do not desire to discuss it.

The VICE PRESIDENT. That is the only word proposed to be stricken out. The amendment is agreed to. The next amendment reported by the committee will be stated.

The SECRETARY. In section 7, page 7, line 12, after the word "labor," it is proposed to strike out the word "consumers," so as to read:

SEC. 7. That nothing contained in the antitrust laws shall be construed to forbid the existence and operation of labor, agricultural, or horticultural organizations.

SENATE DEBATE
63d Cong., 2d Sess.
August 19, 1914

51 CONG. REC. 13963

Mr. CULBERSON. I make the suggestion that the unfinished business be laid before the Senate.

There being no objection, the Senate, as in Committee of the Whole, resumed the consideration of the bill (H. R. 15657) to supplement existing laws against unlawful restraints and monopolies, and for other purposes.

The VICE PRESIDENT. The pending amendment is an amendment of the committee, in section 7, page 7, line 12, to strike out the word "consumers."

Mr. OVERMAN. Mr. President, I voted to strike from the bill section 2 and section 4. Certain Senators were absent from the Senate when the motions were carried eliminating those sections. While I still favor striking those sections from the bill, at their request I make the motion to reconsider the votes by which that was done, and ask that the motion go over until the conclusion of the consideration of the committee amendments, then to be taken up. In order to be within my parliamentary rights I make the motion to-day to reconsider the votes by which those two sections were stricken from the bill.

The VICE PRESIDENT. Does the Senator from North Carolina move to reconsider the vote to which he refers, or does he enter a motion to reconsider?

Mr. OVERMAN. I enter the motion to reconsider.

Mr. REED. To reconsider the vote by which section 2 and section 4 were agreed to?

Mr. OVERMAN. Yes.

Mr. REED. The form which the Senator's motion takes is to enter a motion to reconsider?

Mr. OVERMAN. I enter a motion to reconsider the vote. The understanding is that the motion is not to be taken up at this time, because I wish the Senate to go on with the bill. I repeat, I am still in favor of striking those sections from the bill, but some Senator who voted in favor of striking them out will have to enter the motion to reconsider. I therefore enter the motion to-day, in order that I may not lose my right to do so.

Mr. REED. Very well. I desire to call up the matter to-morrow.

The VICE PRESIDENT. The question is on striking out the word "consumers" in line 12, page 7, section 7, of the bill as reported by the committee. [Putting the question.] The noes seem to have it.

Mr. CULBERSON. I call for a division.

The VICE PRESIDENT. All in favor of striking out the word "consumers" will rise. [A pause.] All those opposed will rise. [A pause.] The amendment is agreed to.

Mr. [MILES] POINDEXTER [Prog., Wash.]. I ask for the yeas and nays.

The yeas and nays were ordered, and the Secretary proceeded to call the roll.

Mr. BRANDEGEE (when his name was called). I am paired with the junior Senator from Tennessee [Mr. SHIELDS], and therefore withhold my vote.

⊥ Mr. CHAMBERLAIN (when his name was called). I have a general pair with the junior Senator from Pennsylvania [Mr. OLIVER]. In his absence I withhold my vote.

Mr. CULBERSON (when his name was called). I have a general pair with the Senator from Delaware [Mr. DU PONT]. I transfer that general pair to the Senator from Arizona [Mr. SMITH] and vote "yea."

Mr. FLETCHER (when his name was called). I am paired with the Senator from Wyoming [Mr. WARREN], and therefore withhold my vote.

Mr. GALLINGER (when his name was called). I transfer my general pair with the junior Senator from New York [Mr. O'GORMAN] to the Senator from Illinois [Mr. SHERMAN] and vote "nay."

Mr. GORE (when his name was called). I have a pair with the junior Senator from Wisconsin [Mr. STEPHENSON], and therefore withhold my vote.

Mr. GRONNA (when his name was called). I have a general pair with the senior Senator from Maine [Mr. JOHNSON]. Not seeing him in the Chamber, I withhold my vote.

Mr. MYERS (when his name was called). I have a pair with the Senator from Connecticut [Mr. MCLEAN]. In his absence I withhold my vote.

Mr. THORNTON (when Mr. O'GORMAN's name was called). I am requested to announce the necessary absence of the junior Senator from New York [Mr. O'GORMAN]. I ask that this announcement may stand for the day.

Mr. SAULSBURY (when his name was called). I have a general pair with the junior Senator from Rhode Island [Mr. COLT]. In his absence I withhold my vote. If at liberty to vote, I should vote "yea."

Mr. SMITH of Georgia (when his name was called). I have a general pair with the senior Senator from Massachusetts [Mr. LODGE]. If permitted to vote, I should vote "yea." If it should develop that my vote is necessary to make a quorum, I will take the liberty of voting.

Mr. THOMAS (when his name was called). I have a general pair with the senior Senator from New York [Mr. ROOT]. In his absence I withhold my vote.

Mr. TILLMAN (when his name was called). I have a general pair with the

Senator from West Virginia [Mr. GOFF]. In his absence I withhold my vote.

Mr. CLARK of Wyoming (when Mr. WARREN's name was called). My colleague [Mr. WARREN] is unavoidably detained from the Chamber. He has a general pair with the senior Senator from Florida [Mr. FLETCHER]. I make this announcement for this legislative day.

Mr. SMOOT (when Mr. SUTHERLAND's name was called). I desire to announce the unavoidable absence of my colleague [Mr. SUTHERLAND]. He has a general pair with the senior Senator from Arkansas [Mr. CLARKE]. I ask that this announcement may stand for the day.

Mr. WILLIAMS (when his name was called). I transfer my general pair with the senior Senator from Pennsylvania [Mr. PENROSE] to the junior Senator from South Carolina [Mr. SMITH] and vote "nay."

The roll call was concluded.

Mr. LEA of Tennessee (after having voted in the affirmative). I neglected to announce my pair when I voted. I transfer my pair with the senior Senator from South Dakota [Mr. CRAWFORD] to the senior Senator from Illinois [Mr. LEWIS], and will let my vote stand.

Mr. SMITH of Georgia. I transfer my pair with the senior Senator from Massachusetts [Mr. LODGE] to the junior Senator from Maryland [Mr. LEE] and vote "yea."

Mr. CHILTON. I desire to inquire whether the Senator from New Mexico [Mr. FALL] has voted?

The VICE PRESIDENT. The Chair is informed he has not.

Mr. CHILTON. I have a pair with that Senator, and in his absence I withhold my vote.

Mr. GRONNA. I desire to inquire if the senior Senator from Maine [Mr. JOHNSON] has voted?

The VICE PRESIDENT. The Chair is informed he has not.

Mr. GRONNA. I transfer my pair with that Senator to the Senator from California [Mr. WORKS] and vote "nay."

Mr. DILLINGHAM (after having voted in the affirmative). I inquire if the senior Senator from Maryland [Mr. SMITH] has voted?

The VICE PRESIDENT. The Chair is informed he has not.

Mr. DILLINGHAM. I withdraw my vote, having a general pair with him.

Mr. GALLINGER. I am requested to announce the pairs between the Senator from New Mexico [Mr. CATRON] and the Senator from Oklahoma [Mr. OWEN] and between the Senator from Michigan [Mr. TOWNSEND] and the Senator from Arkansas [Mr. ROBINSON].

I will also state that the junior Senator from Maine [Mr. BURLEIGH] is necessarily detained from the Senate, and that the junior Senator from Vermont [Mr. PAGE] is detained at his home because of serious illness in his family. I will let this statement stand for the day.

The result was announced—yeas 38, nays 14, as follows:

YEAS—38.

Ashurst	Hughes	Pomerene	Swanson
Bankhead	James	Ransdell	Thompson
Borah	Kern	Reed	Thornton
Bryan	Lea, Tenn.	Shafroth	Vardaman
Burton	Martin, Va.	Sheppard	Walsh
Camden	Nelson	Shively	Weeks
Culberson	Newlands	Simmons	West
Cummins	Overman	Smith, Ga.	White
Hitchcock	Perkins	Sterling	
Hollis	Pittman	Stone	

NAYS—14.

Bristow	Jones	McCumber	Smoot
Clark, Wyo.	Kenyon	Martine, N. J.	Williams
Gallinger	Lane	Norris	
Gronna	Lippitt	Poindexter	

NOT VOTING—44.

Brady	du Pont	Myers	Smith, Ariz.
Brandegee	Fall	O'Gorman	Smith, Md.
Burleigh	Fletcher	Oliver	Smith, Mich.
Catron	Goff	Owen	Smith, S. C.
Chamberlain	Gore	Page	Stephenson
Chilton	Johnson	Penrose	Sutherland
Clapp	La Follette	Robinson	Thomas
Clarke, Ark.	Lee, Md.	Root	Tillman
Colt	Lewis	Saulsbury	Townsend
Crawford	Lodge	Sherman	Warren
Dillingham	McLean	Shields	Works

So the amendment of the committee was agreed to. . . .

Mr. [PORTER J.] McCUMBER [R., N.D.]. Mr. President, a parliamentary inquiry. I desire to ask whether or not the status of the bill is such that I can move at this time to strike out section 7?

The VICE PRESIDENT. Not until the committee amendments have been disposed of, in the opinion of the Chair.

Mr. McCUMBER. Is the bill before the Senate now?

The VICE PRESIDENT. The opinion of the Chair is that, as the unfinished business was laid aside and consent was given to take up the bill in which the Senator from Missouri was interested, technically speaking the trust bill is not before the Senate until permission has been obtained to put it before the Senate again.

Mr. CULBERSON. Mr. President, I ask that the bill may be presented to the Senate for consideration. I desire to say in this connection that, it being clearly against the spirit of the rule, in my judgment, I must refrain from consenting to lay it aside for the consideration of emergency measures while the bill is pending.

The VICE PRESIDENT. Is there any objection? The Chair hears none.

⊥ The Senate, as in Committee of the Whole, resumed the consideration of the bill (H. R. 15657) to supplement existing laws against unlawful restraints and monopolies, and for other purposes.

The VICE PRESIDENT. The Secretary will state the pending amendment.

The SECRETARY. On page 7, line 13, it is proposed to strike out the words "orders, or associations."

Mr. McCUMBER. Mr. President, what I have to say upon this bill may as well be said upon this amendment as upon any other particular feature, and I shall ask the attention of the Senate for a very few moments only.

David, the Psalmist, says:

Nevertheless, they did flatter me with their mouths and lied unto me with their lips.

For the benefit of Senators generally I will say that that language will be found in the Seventy-eighth Psalm, at the thirty-sixth verse. I quote it because I consider that it is exceedingly applicable to the bill now under consideration.

Mr. President, on the 4th day of July, 1776, a band of patriots had gathered in this land. They were the wise men of their day. They were the great scholars and philosophers of their time. They lived in the morn of a great political awakening, when the divine rights of kings were being questioned and the God-given rights of man were being proclaimed.

If, on the one hand, they were lacking in many acquirements which modern science and progress have opened to the human mind, they had escaped, on the other hand, the thousands of questions which arise to vex us in our present advanced civilization, and therefore had the leisure to direct their research into the realms of governmental philosophy. They were versed in the history of the world. They knew the abuses of monarchial governments and the weaknesses of democracies. They were neither sycophants nor demagogues. They flattered neither the king nor the citizen.

They were met a great body of wise men on a solemn occasion. They were to lay the foundation of a new government. They were to place as its corner stone a mighty principle for which men could lay down their lives; and these were the words they wrote:

We hold these truths to be self-evident: That all men are created equal; that they are endowed by their Creator with certain inalienable rights; that among these are life and liberty and the pursuit of happiness; that to secure these [equal] rights governments are instituted among men deriving their just powers from the consent of the governed.

That all men are created equal and endowed by their Creator with inalienable rights rang to the world the birth of a new principle that should thenceforth be the basis of all civil and political governments. The lowly toiler heard it and raised his head in the pride of his right. The Slavic serf heard it and raised his shackled arms for the blow that should sever his chains. The impulsive sons of France heard it and planted the tree of liberty which, though hacked and bruised, still spreads its sturdy branches to every political tempest. The world heard it and felt the heart throbs of a new inspiration. Around that mighty principle we rallied the patriotism of our colonial fathers. For that principle they suffered and died. Orators have proclaimed and scholars have expounded the meaning of those words, but none clearer than our own Lincoln, when he declared that they do not mean that we are equal in intelligence or character or color but in our rights—our equal rights—under the law.

For 138 years we have maintained a Government based upon the equality of each and every citizen. For 138 years we have maintained a Government based upon the principle that every law shall operate with equal force upon every person; that none shall be too powerful to be above the restrictions of the law and none too lowly to be deprived of its protection.

With that principle written upon our national banner and given expression in every legislative act since the beginning of our Government, our progress has astounded the world, and the success of our free Government has belied all the prophecies of the downfall of our republican form of government.

To-day, while monarchies and republics are in a death struggle in the Old World, while the issue of imperialism and democracy, militarism and nonmilitarism are reddening the plains of Europe with the blood of millions of men, we, the great exponent of individual equality of citizenship under the law, we who founded our Government on that principle, have taken the first backward step. We for the first time have declared to our own people and to the world that our laws shall not operate with equal force on all our people; that an act committed by one class or individual shall be an offense, but when committed by another class or individual shall not be an offense. We, the originators of the great principle, are the first to strike a blow to that principle of equality.

You excuse this on the ground that such legislation is in the interest of labor. I deny it. You say you are the friend of the laboring man. I say you are his worst enemy. He who proposes to give me rights that are not allowed to my fellow citizen is not my friend. He who flatters me with a declaration that I am entitled to rights not granted to every other citizen flatters me with his mouth and lies unto me with his lips. You know and I know that when I begin to exercise a right that is not accorded to my fellow citizen you outlaw me from the sympathy and good will of that citizen. You know that the sentiment of the people will not long stand for this principle of inequality. It is repugnant to human nature and doubly repugnant to the American idea.

Nor is this all. Human nature is the same in every walk of life. Privileges exercised by the titled aristocracy of France brought on the first French revolution, when the incessant stroke of the guillotine wiped out the recipients of special privileges. Class inequality can not long continue in this land; the American people will not stand for it, though you clothe it with legislative sanction. Mr. President, justice and equality are not the strongest impulses of the human heart. Selfishness preponderates over both. Justice and equality are maintained in the world only by laws which recognize and enforce them. Withdraw the law of equality and injustice will always prevail.

What is the duty of the Government toward the American laborer? The first duty is to so legislate and conduct the internal affairs of the Government and so regulate our commercial relations with foreign Governments as to give the greatest possible employment to American labor. Give the American laborer the American market and you will show him an act of true friendship a thousandfold more valuable to him than any special privilege could possibly ever be. Giving him rights or exempting him from obligations that are not accorded or exempted to others does not create a demand for the only thing he has to sell in the market—his skill and his strength.

There is no living man possessing ordinary human sentiments who does not want to speed the day when labor will reap its legitimate reward, its legitimate wage in every article produced by that labor; who will not wish to speed the day when inequalities between the several kinds of labor and between labor and business vocations generally shall be wiped away and when the only difference in the wage or earnings of all classes shall be measured by the time used in the preparation for the labor, the hours employed, and the skill required.

But you secure none of these by destroying the very life principle of our Government—equality under the law. I know there are a great many labor leaders who believe that they are solving all inequalities by securing exemptions from liabilities. It may be that some temporary advantage may be secured, but it will be temporary only. The legislator who says to a laboring man, "We have authorized you to do acts which we have made criminal when committed by others," flatters him to his injury.

There is no question here presented against organization of labor. Without this new law laborers have organized and still maintain their organization. Their rights are not dependent upon this law. They may do any lawful thing under the present law to effectuate their purpose and better the conditions of labor, both as to wages and as to conditions and environments. They can strike whenever they believe their wages are not sufficient. They can strike to shorten hours of labor. They can enforce every one of their just demands through organized effort.

I know there are those on this floor who insist that nothing else is secured by this act; but, Mr. President, no matter how cunningly devised, this bill does go further. It gives authority to destroy the property rights of others in order to enforce demands. If it does not do this, if it gives no rights in advance of what the law now gives, then why is it placed in this bill? If it does not do so, then it is a piece of deception, a fraud upon those whose interest you declare you are furthering. There is no question but that you attempt to legalize the secondary boycott.

I do not believe that the great mass of American laborers are asking for this un-American legislation. I believe the sentiment of equality under the law is just as strong with them as with any other class of people. I believe they are endowed with too much good sense and judgment ever to believe that an unjust, unequal law can work ultimate good to them.

Mr. President, another feature of this proposed law is the destruction of judicial authority. A subservient judiciary is destructive of human freedom. The judiciary of our country must ever stand as a balance to check the tendencies of the executive to usurp the functions of the legislative branch. It must ever stand guard over the ancient and traditional rights ⊥ of the individual and shield him from unlawful injury and his property from destruction or confiscation.

The executive power can shield itself through the use of the agencies of the Government. The whole Army and Navy are at its disposal and subject to its command. The legislative arm can, in a degree, shield itself through its control over the revenues of the Government. The courts can only protect themselves through the power to enforce their judgments, and the only process by which it can enforce its writs and its orders is through proceedings for contempt. To deprive it of that power destroys its use and deprives the individual citizen of the only power of maintaining his civil and political rights. There are no people in this country who are more deeply concerned in maintaining the constitutional power of the courts than are our laboring people. Paralyze the arm of the court, and a tyrannical power will take its place in the future, as it has always taken its place in the past, and the laboring man ought to know that tyranny always ranges itself on the side of wealth and power. Let every laboring man pause before he strikes the protector of his own liberties.

I am making no objection to any procedure that shall require those things which are merely condemnatory of the court's action to be submitted to a jury. On the contrary, I am liberal enough to believe that if the court has the power to enforce all its judgments it need not pay very much attention to criticism against the authority that it is exercising. In other words, I do not believe honest criticism of judicial action, no matter how severe, should ever be regarded as a contempt.

Mr. President, this is a country governed by law and not by men. You can not deprive the court of its constitutional right to make its judgments effective. You may limit it and change its procedure, but you can not, by legislative act, deprive it of the means of enforcing its constitutional power. If A obtains a judgment against B through proceedings at law or in equity, you can not submit the question of the right of A to enforce his judgment to any jury. If A demands a writ of execution and B obstructs the execution of that writ, you can not compel A to submit to a jury whether he should allow B to continue the obstruction; and it is immaterial what the form of the obstruction and whether directed against an execution or injunction.

Mr. President, this deception practiced upon the laborer is bad enough, but you seek to cover up the vice of class legislation by increasing the size of the class, and so you say that the farmers shall also be exempt from the provisions of the trust law.

Why should you include farmers? You just now voted out a provision that the consumers might also be exempted. You say the consumers shall not be exempted from the trust laws; that they can not organize to protect themselves against exorbitant prices and charges. Why do you insist that they should be prohibited from so organizing? Their organization would not affect laborer, farmer, or manufacturer, but would only be directed against exorbitant retail prices.

Mr. President, what farmer has ever asked you to exempt him from a general law which declares that a certain act shall be an offense against public policy? I want to say to this Senate, in defense of that great class of toilers in our fields, the American farmers, that the farmer is American through and through, imbued with the American idea of equality; and even if he could obtain a special benefit from such legislation, from a law that would give him a right that the blacksmith and the grocer would not have, he would spurn the advantage; and if he would spurn that offer of advantage, you may be sure of his contempt for the sop you offer him. In the one instance you insult his sense of justice; in the other, his intelligence; and this seems to have been your attitude for a number of years. You have played the laboring man against the farmer and the farmer against the laboring man. You have declared in your political campaigns that you would reduce the price of the farmer's product to the laboring man; that you would give him cheaper food; you would give him cheaper eggs and butter, meat and flour. To the farmer you have declared that you would maintain his prices against the laborer and yet give him cheaper machinery and clothing and other articles of consumption. You have flattered them both with your mouths and lied unto them both with your lips.

There are 33,000,000 people in the United States engaged in farming. At least 30,000,000 of them are raising eggs. They are raising them on nearly every section of land from Canada to Mexico and from the Atlantic to the Pacific. They are selling those eggs every day over all of this vast territory to 70,000,000 customers. Tell me, then, how these egg producers can proceed to fix the price of eggs. You know they can not do it; and you know further that, being fearful that eggs might reach a price satisfactory to the farmer, you opened wide the bars for the free admission of all of the eggs of all of the hens on the face of the earth; and having by your laws placed the farmer where you know and where he knows it is impossible for him to combine to fix the price of his eggs, you laconically turn to him and say: "You can fix your own prices; we have exempted you from the law against combinations in restraint of trade." What is true of eggs is true of poultry and grain and meat and wool and practically everything the farmer produces. After you have placed him at the mercy of the whole world, then you serenely tell him he can fix his own prices for his crops.

You have not reduced the price of a single thing that the farmer purchases. Why? Because you know that the protection accorded any ordinary article in the shape of a duty is so infinitesimal when compared with the retail price of the articles that it is seldom taken into consideration at all. The ultimate consumer never recognizes the change. While eggs and butter in my State have gone down by reason of the lack of protection the great bulk of laborers throughout the United States have had no advantage of that reduction, and that is true of their meats and their flour and all other food products. Though our barley went down about 50 per cent the products of barley have remained substantially unchanged. Though our oats dropped 50 per cent in value, your laborer pays the same old price for a package of Quaker Oats.

Of course the great war raging in Europe has made many changes in the value of farm and other products for which you are in no way responsible. If our people have had some loss by reason of this war, it is not your fault. If it has given us some benefits, it is not due to the virtue of your policies. I can only say that you are exceedingly lucky that the war diverts the attention of the great American public from the political and industrial conditions brought about by your tariff revision, and which were becoming more and more stringent until the foreign demand was increased by that war.

The American farmer is not asking you for any favors. He is asking you for justice, and when you give him that he will excuse you from legislating any special rule exempting him from the laws of the land.

You have attempted, and I think successfully, in this bill to legalize a system that can not be but regarded as pernicious by all right-thinking men. The farmer, you know well enough, as I have stated, can not fix the price of his product to the laboring man. The laboring man, through his organization, can, with the assistance of this law, enforce the thing he has to sell as against the farmer. And right here, the farmer who must hire labor can not forget that while by law you have prohibited the importation of laborers, to the end that labor may not become too plentiful, and therefore remain more valuable, you have, on the other hand, invited the products of all the world to make the farmer's product more than plentiful, and therefore less valuable. The farmer can not send his agent and say to every other farmer and to every grocer, "Do not sell to this laboring man, he is not our friend." His effort would be laughed at as the folly of all follies. But how about the farmer who has a field of wheat which is ripe or an orchard of fruit which needs immediate gathering? Before his gate the agent of the laborer may walk back and forth, under the provisions of this bill, with impunity, bearing a placard: "Boycott this farmer. He works 16 hours a day and demands that his employees shall work 10 hours. See that his crops shall rot. He has committed no act against us, but insists that he ought to employ his labor at such a price as will enable him to support his family. Let us see to it that such audacity has its due and proper punishment." Of course, I have no fear of any such acts against the farmers of my State. They are every one of them courageous, and the placard artist would not long remain at that farmer's gate.

I do not question for one moment the right of the laborer, organized or unorganized, to declare that he will not accept employment under this farmer unless such employment is restricted to eight hours per day and to such a price as he himself may fix, but I do deny his right to institute a boycott against this farmer or against his neighbor whose only crime is that he loaned to the farmer his son to help him save a little of his year's labor. If I am right as to the farmer, I am right in every other line of business. There can be no principle that is unjust when applied to the farmer that the farmer at least will not consider unjust when applied to others.

You can just leave the American farmer out of this bill. If you want to be sincere with the American farmer, if you want to be just with the American farmer, give him the American market for 10 years as you have given the same to the merchant or manufacturer for 50 years. He has earned these markets. You deprive him of those markets. You depress the value of his products. You subject him to the competition of the whole world in his own country, and then you add insult to that injury by telling him he need not obey the law prohibiting combinations to fix his prices. If you fool him with that sop, then I shall admit that I have overestimated the intelligence of the farming public.

I shall hope, Mr. President, that we will at least strike out the words "agricultural and horticultural associations" from this bill and leave the farmer where he can hold up his head and look straight into the eye of every other American citizen, capitalist and laborer, and say, "I am your equal and you are not more than my equal under the laws of the land."

Mr. POMERENE. I wish to ask the Senator a question. The Senator's State is almost exclusively an agricultural State. I wish to ask him whether there is any demand among the farmers of his State for any exemption of this character?

Mr. McCUMBER. There is no demand among the farmers of my State or any other State, so far as I know, for this unequal legislation.

Mr. HOLLIS. Mr. President, I desire to speak briefly on the labor-union exemption clause in the Clayton bill.

The Sherman Antitrust Act was passed in 1890, for the purpose of preventing industrial monopoly. It was frankly aimed at the "trusts," those great industrial combinations which were controlling various branches of interstate commerce through restraint of trade, greatly to the profit of their stockholders and much to the disadvantage of citizens at large. Familiar examples were the Standard Oil Co. and the American Sugar Refining Co.

At that time no one imagined that labor unions or farmers' associations would come within the act. No abuses from such organizations challenged attention.

But subsequently the language of the act was tortured into a meaning that has worked much hardship on workingmen and farmers. From an instrument which was intended for the relief of the plain people, it is transformed into an instrument for their oppression.

Section 7 of the pending bill is intended to place "labor, agricultural, or horticultural organizations" outside the provisions of the Sherman Act. In other words, such organizations are left to be dealt with at the common law. No matter what they do they can not be punished as "illegal combinations or conspiracies in restraint of trade, under the antitrust laws." Their members do not come in conflict with the antitrust laws as long as they carry out the legitimate objects of their organizations by "lawful" means.

Some of the legitimate objects of an agricultural organization are fair terms of shipment and sale of the products of its members, fair prices, and prompt collections. Some of the legitimate objects of a labor organization are fair wages, reasonable working hours, and wholesome conditions of labor.

In the attainment of these objects labor and farming organizations are not to be restrained by the antitrust laws so long as they act "lawfully." An act will be lawful in this connection unless it is prohibited by some special statute or by the common law.

For example, a labor union may vote to call its members out on strike to force higher wages, shorter hours, or better sanitary conditions. Its members may use peaceful persuasion to induce other workmen to join them, but any attempt at violence, coercion, threats, or intimidation would be "unlawful," and bring them into conflict with the antitrust laws.

The usual case of a strike or a boycott would present no difficulty, but when the regions of sympathetic strikes and secondary boycotts are reached opinions may differ. My own opinion is that so long as only peaceful means are resorted to, so long as there are no threats, no intimidations, no violence, no coercion, so long as the objects sought are the eventual good of the members of the unions, the acts are lawful. But the courts must decide when the facts are in dispute, or when the acts are close to the line.

But whether the acts constitute a restraint of trade will be immaterial if the bill passes in its present form.

Some distinguished Senators believe that labor unions do not now come within the provisions of the Sherman Act. How they can hold to this view in the face of Loewe v. Lawlor (208 U. S., 274) I do not understand, but it makes little difference here. If they believe it does not cover labor organizations, they can not object if the point is definitely settled. At all events, labor unions and their friends will be much relieved to know certainly that they are not to be classed with the Standard Oil Co. and the Sugar Trust.

But there is another class of persons who believe that labor organizations are prohibited by the Sherman Act and who vigorously oppose the exemption contained in the pending bill. I have had many letters and telegrams from men of this class. They may be referred to broadly as "capitalists."

Capitalists oppose this exemption of labor unions for a real reason. They wish to deprive organized labor of its only efficient weapon. But they proffer as an argument the proposition that the exemption of labor unions is "class legislation." I freely concede that it is class legislation, but I can not see why class legislation is not in this case highly proper and desirable. Let us see.

With the advent of steam, manufacturing was diverted from the workman's cottage to the factory. At the outset every employer of labor was permitted to run his business as he pleased. He fixed the hours of labor, he fixed the wages, he hired women and children, he guarded his machinery or he left it unprotected, he paid much or little attention to sanitary conditions, he made conditions hard or easy. No one undertook to prescribe any limits to his power and authority. Manufacturers look back to those early days as the days of the "old freedom."

At the beginning the capitalist lived near his mill; he knew his help and their families; he took pride in having his town or village prosperous, in having his employees well fed and well dressed. His own sons and daughters worked at the loom and in the countingroom. They intermarried with the families of the workingmen. There was one speech, one purpose, one prosperity, one God.

But some employers grew greedy. Some were cruel and inhuman. They worked longer hours than their rivals; they paid smaller wages; they employed more women and younger children; they provided less safeguards; they spent less on sanitary improvements. Such men secured an industrial advantage over their competitors.

And then the community exercised its power of protecting itself. It prescribed the conditions under which manufacturers might conduct business. It provided penalties by fine and imprisonment for those who disobeyed the labor laws.

In most States the first interference with the liberty of the capitalist took the form of limiting the number of hours of labor in mills for women and children. At first the limit was placed at 60 or even 72 hours per week. In the District of Columbia the present Congress has limited the hours of labor for women and children to 48 hours per week. The measure passed this Senate and the House without a dissenting vote. No one has questioned the right of Congress to pass the law; few have questioned the wisdom and policy of the law.

But in this law for the protection of women and children in the District of Columbia, enacted so easily, are contained all the elements of class legislation which are inveighed against so roundly in the discussion of the labor-union exemptions in the Clayton bill.

In the first place, the 48-hour law is frankly "class legislation," for it applies only to women and children. Women and children are made a class apart from adult males, and the law applies only to this particular class.

More than that, the law does not apply to all women and children. It is confined to those women and children who work in factories and stores. It does not apply to women and children who work on farms or at housework. Here again the law is limited to a certain class of a certain class—to those women and children who work in factories and stores.

It is readily seen that class legislation is very common, and very desirable in many cases. Many laws have been passed in the various States of a similar nature, such as child-labor laws applying only to children, to children employed in certain pursuits, and to children of a certain age. Here are three class distinctions; but who says that child-labor laws are void or wrong because they are "class legislation"?

There is the "phossy jaw" law, applying only to the class which makes lucifer matches; the sanitary-inspection law, applying only to factories; the boiler-inspection law, applying to a certain class of power plant; the milk-inspection law, applying to a certain class of food; the betterment-tax law, applying only to real estate of a certain class, and so on, indefinitely.

A good illustration of "class legislation" is found in the income-tax law passed during the present Congress. All persons having an income below a certain sum are placed in one "class"; married men are placed in a different "class" from unmarried ones; and there are numerous "classes" with different rates of tax, graded according to the amount of income.

The only constitutional provision is, not that all classes shall be treated alike, but that all persons of a designated class shall be treated alike. Few will dispute these propositions.

The dispute comes not in the power of Congress to pass class legislation, but in the wisdom and policy of the particular legislation under consideration. I have no hesitation in saying that I believe it is wise to make the provisions of the Sherman Act much more drastic as applied to combinations of capital in restraint of trade, for the evils springing from such combinations are great and increasing. But I am equally certain that labor organizations are a good thing, and they should be encouraged rather than embarrassed by Federal laws.

A very good case may be made out, in the way of a distinction between labor and capital, as was done by Judge Furman, of the Oklahoma court, in State *v.* Coyle (130 Pac. Rept., 316), but I am content to rest my vote on the broad proposition that public policy is best served by exempting labor unions from the operation of an "antitrust" act.

The time may come when labor unions may oppress their employers or may act in such a way as to procure for their members more than their fair share of what is produced in the Nation. I believe that that time is not here yet, and if it is ever to come, it is a long way in the future.

But if that time shall ever come, let organized labor have a hearing, and fair consideration, and a law of its own. Let it be regulated by a statute that shall apply to its peculiar conditions and aims, its special advantages, and it special weaknesses. Let it not be insulted by being classed with malefactors of great wealth.

It would be funny, if it were not so unjust and pathetic, to picture the humble wage earner, paying his few cents a week for the protection of his trades-union, congratulating himself that the antitrust law will save him from the high prices imposed by monopoly, and suddenly realizing that he is himself classed with the monopolists and trust managers, and liable, like them, to fine and imprisonment under an antitrust act. This joke is hugely relished, no doubt, by monopolists and their attorneys, but it is the duty and the privilege of the Congress of the United States to put an end to all jokes and jokers of this character.

Mr. HUGHES. Mr. President, I desire to submit a few remarks with reference to this section of the bill, although I am not at this moment prepared to make any comprehensive or detailed argument. Still, I do not want the occasion to pass without submitting some of the reasons why I think this legislation is both necessary and wise.

First, I desire to direct my remarks to arguments which have been made on the other side of the Chamber with reference to the viciousness of class legislation. It is a strange thing to me that a Republican Senator should have the temerity to denounce class legislation, inasmuch as the existence of the Republican Party since it came into being has depended upon its ability to deliver class legislation.

I hold in my hand a book containing the Republican platform of 1908, and I find in it this language under the caption "Help to workers":

> The wise policy which has induced the Republican Party to maintain protection to American labor, to establish the eight-hour day in the construction of all public work, to increase the list of employees who shall have preferred claims for wages under the bankruptcy law, to adopt a child-labor statute for the District of Columbia, to direct the investigation into the condition of the working women and children and later of the employees of telephone and telegraph companies engaged in interstate business, to appropriate $150,000 at the recent session of Congress in order to secure a thorough inquiry into the causes of loss of life in the mines, and to amend and strengthen the law prohibiting the importation of contract labor will be pursued in every legitimate direction in Federal authority to lighten the burdens and increase the opportunity for happiness and the advancement of all who toil.

So, you can go through every declaration of the Republican Party set forth in its various platforms almost from the birth of that party down to the date of its last convention and you will find that it justifies enormous tariff exactions on the theory that the high prices made necessary by those exactions, going into the pockets of the manufacturer, are to be by him doled out to the American laboring man. If forbidding the American people to purchase their goods where they can purchase them cheapest and compelling them to purchase from a selected class of individuals is not class legislation, I am at a loss to know what class legislation is.

While we are speaking of class legislation, where could we find a more beautiful illustration of the ease with which class legislation is accepted when certain powerful interests are involved than the spectacle exhibited in this body the other day, when a statutory monopoly was permitted to continue its exactions, permitted to continue to mulct the American people for carrying their goods, even in the face of a great exigency, a great war emergency? Here was a little selected class of American citizens who have the privilege of operating vessels plying from port to port in the United States, while an American ship, flying the American flag, sailing from the port of Liverpool, for example, to the port of New York and discharging her cargo there can not pick up another cargo at the port of New York and carry it to a Gulf port in order to pay its expenses for that part of the trip, but must confine its operations to American commerce transported abroad. Why? Because if it were permitted to engage in the coastwise trade it would interfere with the privilege of a class of American citizens who own and operate coastwise ships and a class of American citizens who build those ships for those men to own and operate.

Now, let us drop all this nonsense; let us put that behind us. We are constantly engaged in class legislation. I am not discussing the merits of the shipping bill or of the conference report which was recently defeated in this body. I am simply calling attention to the fact that class legislation is not denounced and never has been denounced in this body since I have been here, unless the class attempted to be helped were the laboring people of the United States. As I have said, the Republican Party, the representatives of which are denouncing this legislation as class legislation, has held itself out as the exponent and proponent of class legislation in every campaign of which I have any recollection. I can not remember the time when the Republican orators did not claim that the principle of protection, the principle of forbidding the American people to purchase their goods where they might and compelling them to restrict their purchases and their operations to a limited number of known and designated men, was not the cause of the wonderful prosperity of the United States. They went further than that and stated that the reason why they did these things, the reason why they restricted the operation of the American people and compelled them to buy in a restricted market, ofttimes without competition, was not to benefit that class; no; it was another class they had in mind; the class they had in mind is the class that we are now really trying to help. They put the burden of that policy on the shoulders of the American laboring man.

They talk about demagogues and talk about claptrap and efforts to catch votes. What has their whole history been? What has it been with reference to this question but a succession and continuation of claptrap and buncombe, intended not only to get votes but to cheat the men from whom they got the votes? They have cheated them, but as soon as the men whom they cheated discovered the partnership and the connection between the Republican Party and those who were fighting the laboring people of this country that party was swept from power.

I listened to the argument of the Senator from Ohio [Mr. POMERENE] yesterday. He advanced, so far as I was able to discover, nothing that had not been advanced by the attorneys of the Manufacturers' Association years and years ago. Those gentlemen have been active in this fight ever since I can remember. On several occasions I came in contact with their agents in my district, and I was frankly informed that any man who stood for the legislation for which I stood could not be elected until every resource at the command of the Manufacturers' Association had been exhausted against him.

To-day I was handed a copy of a night letter which is being sent to Senators at this time, and I will read the body of it without putting in the name of the individual to whom it is addressed. It carries me back a good many years to the time when I was a younger man than I am now, but it is the same in form and the same in substance. This discredited organization, which was utterly disgraced and should have been shamed into silence, is as active to-day as ever it was, but it no longer has the influence it formerly had; it no longer can hold the club, and its threats have no force. Members of the House and Members of the Senate no longer fear the Manufacturers' Association.

I will read this communication now:

The Clayton bill, exempting labor combinations from the Sherman Act, providing trial by jury for contempts, and radical regulations for business, is now pending in the United States Senate. To overcome belief existing in many quarters that business men are indifferent to this vicious measure and to assist in securing illuminating debate, will you not immediately request and urge your members to make determined and persistent protest against it to your Senator and to ask their associates to do likewise? Immediate action is imperative.

National Association of Manufacturers,
George S. Boudinot, Secretary.

The National Association of Manufacturers have a perfect right to send out that communication, and I am not objecting to it. It is entitled to all the weight that a communication from such an association is entitled to. I have no quarrel with them. I never had any quarrel with them. Their opposition to me was the source of my greatest strength. The opposition of the National Manufacturers' Association to-day would be the greatest asset I could have in the State of New Jersey. My only fear is that perhaps they will not oppose me; so I look upon their activity now more in sorrow than in anger, and sympathize with them, knowing that they have lost the invaluable services of the delectable Col. Mulhall, although they seem to have enlisted a number of new recruits under their banner. Still, I can not help feeling that the close, intimate, and personal activities of the colonel will be but illy compensated for by the activities of the new recruits to the Manufacturers' Association, so far as I have been able to observe their activities.

I became interested in the Sherman antitrust law and its application to organizations of labor as soon as it was intimated that the law was intended to apply to organizations of labor; and in another body I introduced and had printed—I think I got that far—an amendment providing that it should not so apply. I made a study of the debates, and became familiar with the history of the legislation, and particularly the history of the legislation so far as it referred to its effect upon organizations of labor, and I discovered that nothing in the world was further from the mind of the author of what was known as the Sherman antitrust law than that it should in the slightest degree affect organizations of labor.

The question was raised on the floor of the Senate. I do not like to bore my colleagues with a repetition of these facts. They have been set out over and over again, more than once by me, and a great many times by other Senators. Nevertheless, I will pause to take the time to set out the main features of the history of this legislation so far as it relates to these organizations.

Although the bill apparently, by its terms, and having in mind the object and intent of the legislator who offered it and the legislators who discussed it, had absolutely no application to these men and these organizations. The question was raised on the floor of the Senate, as I recollect, by Senator George, of Mississippi, first. At that time there was a great and powerful organization of labor known as the Knights of Labor. For that matter, they are still in existence and still interested in this sort of legislation. The question was asked whether or not the bill, if enacted into law, would interfere with them in their operations. The answer was that it would not. The answer by the author of the bill was that it could not possibly, by any stretch of the imagination, in any way interfere with the operations of these men. These men were then engaged in doing what the ordinary labor organization is doing to-day. Their organization was practically the same as it is now. Their operations then were about what they are now.

Senator Hoar, of Massachusetts, not satisfied with the explanation of the author of the bill, asked further assurances that it was not the intent of the author of the measure or of those who supported it to interfere with these organizations. He called attention to how necessary they were. He called attention to the beneficent results which flowed from their activities. He called attention to the fact that they had inherent and natural rights which must be respected, and that in the effort of the legislature to control and curb the operations and practices of the great combinations of capital which then were afflicting the body politic, great care must be exercised to see that no harm was done to these beneficent organizations, which were interested only in the rights of men and women and children, the blood and bone and sinew of this country, without which the country was nothing; and he, too, was assured by the author of the bill that nothing was further from the minds of the legislators who offered it or of those who supported it.

Not satisfied with that, Senator George then offered an amendment providing in terms that the bill should not affect organizations of labor. That amendment was adopted by the unanimous vote of the Senate.

A peculiar situation existed in this body at that time. There were [sic] all sorts of opposition to the Sherman antitrust law. There was open opposition and there was hidden opposition. The hidden opposition took the shape of offering amendments to the bill which were not offered in good faith, and which were not offered with the purpose or object of improving the bill, but in the hope that it would be loaded down and made so objectionable and so obnoxious that on the final vote it could not pass.

The author of the bill called attention to what was going on. He said he was familiar with the methods and the practices that were then being employed. He called the attention of the Senate to the fact that these Senators were not trying to improve or benefit his bill, but that they were trying to load it down with amendments which would make it impossible for even him to vote for it. So far, however, as this amendment was concerned, he said that he was in favor of it; that if it was necessary to keep the courts from attempting to apply this law to organizations of labor, then he wanted it; he would have written it himself. He accepted it fully and completely.

Various other amendments, however, he resisted most vigorously, but in spite of all he could say or do they went in the bill; and at last, when the Senate and the opponents of the legislation had worked their will upon the Sherman antitrust bill as it was first presented, it was in such shape that he himself could not vote for it. His opponents had succeeded in their purpose, and they had so loaded it down with objectionable amendments that the author of the bill himself would not vote for it, and he asked that it be recommitted. As I recollect, he himself asked that it be recommitted to the Judiciary Committee. It went to that committee, and five or six days later it emerged therefrom, and contemporaneous historians say that in the committee it was redrafted, recast, and rewritten by the Senator from Massachusetts, Mr. Hoar. That seems to be the general understanding and the general agreement now. I am indebted for that piece of information to the junior Senator from Indiana [Mr. KERN], who says Senator Hoar sets it out in his autobiography. Senator Edmunds, who for years was regarded as the author of the bill, admits that Senator Hoar really wrote it when it was recommitted to the Judiciary Committee. That Senator, with the sentiments in his breast which caused him to question the legislation, to insist upon its amendment, to ask for a declaration by the author as to what its object was, to point out the beneficent character of these organizations of labor, wrote the bill that we are asked to believe was intended to apply to labor organizations as well as to the Standard Oil Co. and the Sugar Trust, which were then almost the sole objects of the legislative action, because we did not have the brood of trusts and gigantic corporations then that we have to deal with now.

There were, as I recollect, but two industrial combinations which then were raiding the American people, and the legislators had them in mind, and had nothing else and no one else in mind. Senator Hoar of Massachusetts, when he wrote that legislation, had them in mind, and expressly stated that he not only did not have organizations of labor in mind, but that he wanted to protect them, so that by no mischance should they come within the provisions of this drastic law. Yet the highest courts have solemnly said that there is nothing in the bill or in the debates to show that it was not the intention of the Congress to make this law apply to everybody—individuals, corporations, and organizations of every character. . . .

Mr. CUMMINS. I have heard the phase of the history of this law just suggested by the Senator from New Jersey developed here several times; but there is one view of it which I think ought to be borne in mind, and which very greatly strengthens the position now taken by the Senator from New Jersey.

The Sherman bill was not at all like the antitrust law. The thing that was prohibited or made unlawful in the Sherman bill, over which the debate raged for a year or two, and to which the amendment of the Senator from Mississippi, Mr. George, was offered, was interference with free, full competition. The words "restraint of trade" were not used in that bill. It was thought by some that a prohibition against free, full competition might include labor unions. When, however, the bill went to the Judiciary Committee for the first time—it had theretofore been dealt with in the Finance

Committee—and when either Senator Hoar or Senator Edmunds, it makes no difference which one of them it was, wrote a substitute for the bill, the words used were "restraint of trade or commerce," and the thing made unlawful was the restraint of trade or commerce, or monopoly. In my opinion, it never entered the mind of any man of that time that a labor union organized for the benefit of its members and to advance their interests in wages, in hours, in conditions, could be regarded as a restraint of trade. That suggestion was left for a much later period; and I have always thought that this difference between the Sherman bill as it was debated on the floor of the Senate and what we know as the antitrust law emphasized the point that has just been made by the Senator from New Jersey.

I am not saying, of course, that the members of a labor union can not do something that will restrain trade. That is a mere matter of what they do; but a labor union in and of itself, brought together for the purpose of advancing the wages of the members or bettering their condition, was never dreamed of at that time as being in any possible event a restraint of trade.

Mr. HUGHES. I am very much obliged to the Senator from Iowa for his contribution to this discussion. I can see the extreme importance and the relevancy of what he has said, although I confess that if I ever did know it I have forgotten it. I am speaking now entirely from memory, without notes, and ⊥ relying upon my general recollection of past investigations; but if it is necessary, if there is any honest doubt remaining in the mind of any man—and I confess that for the life of me I can not see how there can be—that it was not the intent of the legislators to make this drastic law apply to organizations of labor, it seems to me it must be dissipated by this fact:

Since the passage of this law, unless these men were either impliedly or expressly exempted from it, they have been existing and operating, a great many of them at least, in absolute and utter violation of it. Can anyone doubt that a strike threatened or carried into effect by a body of men like the Brotherhood of Railroad Engineers of the United States would be a violation of the Sherman law, if it is once admitted that the law is intended to include them within its terms?

We talk about the operations of the Danbury Hat Co. as in some indirect and far-fetched way affecting interstate commerce because it prevented the sale of an article in one State when made in another. But what about the explicit express and intended act of an organization the object of which is to prevent commerce between two States?

The Senator from Ohio [Mr. POMERENE] yesterday called attention to a threatened strike of the railroad employees west of Chicago a week or two ago, and he seemed to deplore the fact that this law would make it impossible to enjoin those men in that strike. But suppose the controversy had not been settled and that strike had been called, it was admitted by everybody and it must be admitted by everyone that that would not only restrain commerce, but it would absolutely for the time being destroy it.

Here is an organization of men banded together in combination under an agreement to do something that is not only going to restrain commerce, but is going to end commerce for the time being. Not only that, but they threaten in advance that they are going to conspire together, and then they are going to commit acts in conspiracy. If the Sherman antitrust law applies to organizations of labor, dealing directly or indirectly with goods which enter into interstate commerce, certainly every trainmen's organization operating over a road which traverses two or more States must be in utter violation of this law by the very purpose of its existence.

The primary purpose of its existence is to bargain collectively with their employers for its members. It is to relieve them, to take away the terrific handicap which the individual labors under when he goes to his incorporated employer and tries to make a bargain. They found out a good many hundred years ago that they could make a better bargain with one man speaking for all than when going individually. The union was forced into existence because of hard conditions placed upon employees by employers.

You could destroy every union in the United States in six months, you could destroy a union anywhere as soon as the members of the union became convinced that their employers were men of such character that they would always receive what their services were worth and that they would be treated as they should be treated. The union is only a shield, a protection, a growth made necessary by the hard conditions imposed upon the weak by the strong.

What is the object of the union? The object is to bargain collectively. What power have they? They walk into the office of the president of a railroad company and say, "We are not receiving enough wages," or "We are working too many hours," or "We have to lie over too many hours at this place or that place and waste time away from home for which we do not get paid." The president of the railroad company listens to the demand, talks with them, pleads with them, and argues with them, reasons with them. Why does he do that instead of dismissing them and sending them out? He knows that the members of these railroad unions can work or not, as they like. He knows that these men have the power to stop the wheels of his trains and his locomotives. He knows that these men have the power to stop commerce, to restrain commerce, perhaps to destroy for the time being commerce throughout the territory served by the railroad company.

Is there any question about that? We read frequently in the newspapers of the ultimatums presented by men and the reply by the owners of railroads. Do they not even vote upon it? Have not the polls been published in the newspapers of the United States? No one can doubt, no one ever could doubt but that here was an organization of men the very purpose of which was to restrain, to destroy, if necessary, for the time being commerce between the States, and the more effectively they could make their interruption or restraint of commerce the more likely they were to succeed.

Why is it that for all those years from 1890 down no one has attempted to invoke that law against these railroad organizations? I will tell you why. The railroad organizations are too powerful. The railroad organizations are in a position to interfere with trade and commerce. If the provisions of the law did include them the railroad presidents would be loath to invoke it against them.

But here and there is an organization of men who are not powerful, who are not rich, who have not many connections, and these men have been selected by district attoneys [sic] here and an attorney general there for the purpose of testing out this law, of carrying it on, encroaching further and further upon the rights of the laboring people of the country, until within a year or two they became convinced that unless this law was repealed or modified a great war was coming; that, as soon as the heads of the great corporations of the country were satisfied of their position and satisfied of their power, the attempt would finally be made to make that law mean what some boldly say now it means, that every combination, organization, or association that has for its purpose directly or indirectly the impeding or restraining of commerce between the States falls within the provisions of the Sherman law, and that these organizations are criminal per se.

There was a situation existing in another body when this matter first came up which made it impossible for that body to act along certain lines. Bills could be introduced, amendments could be introduced, but careful arrangements had been made that those bills and those amendments should never get beyond the committees to which they were referred. It was comparatively easy to make such arrangements, and they were made. Nevertheless, it was sought to test the sentiment of the other body on this particular question, and an amendment was offered to an appropriation bill four years ago, as I recollect it, and that House, then Republican overwhelmingly, passed that limitation on an appropriation bill which said in effect, which said as nearly as could be said in the limited way in which the House can legislate in that manner, that this law did not and should not be applied to organizations of labor.

That started this fight. The manufacturing associations and the Federation of Labor joined issue in the next campaign. Lists were published of the Members who voted for and of the Members who voted against. The Manufacturers' Association furnished a list of every man who voted in favor of this limitation on the Attorney General's fund which prevented him from the prosecution of organizations of labor under the law; the American Federation and allied organizations furnished a list of the men who voted in favor of the limitation; and those two great organizations, one of them was a great organization and the other was supposed to be a great organization, joined issue and fought that contest on that limitation.

It was some time ago, and I have not paid any attention to it for a long time, but it is my recollection that something like 30 Members of the other body, who took the national manufacturers' side of that question, after a thorough discussion in the campaign, were defeated at the polls, and if my recollection serves me correctly not a single Member who was attacked by the Manufacturers' Association for his vote upon that limitation failed to come back to the House.

It was in that situation that the Democratic Party took control of the House of Representatives, and I had the personal assurance of not less than 10 Republican Members of Congress that the reason why they were defeated was that they had voted against this attempt to take the organizations of labor, as the House could do it at that time, out from within the provisions of the Sherman antitrust law.

The American people do not want organizations of labor classed with the Standard Oil Co. and the Sugar Trust. They can see the difference, whether legislators or judges can or not. They know that there is a world of difference between these organizations as organizations and between their acts and practices, and they know there is a world-wide difference between the effect that the acts and practices of the Standard Oil Co. have upon the people of the United States and the effect that the operations of the American Federation of Labor has upon the people of the United States.

I can assure my colleagues in this Chamber that the American people have no difficulty at all in making this distinction. They have made it already, and I can say to my brethren in this body that they, too, should be able to make the distinction.

These men have been conducting this fight against terrific odds for years and years, and the inherent justice of their cause, in my judgment, regardless of what this body or any other legislative body will do for them, has triumphed. Public opinion aroused by them, aroused by the mere exhibition of their wrongs and their grievances, has won this fight for them. We are halting lamely behind that public opinion. When we ⊥ pass this law we are scarcely abreast of the foremost judges of the land.

The Senator from Idaho [Mr. BORAH] and I had a controversy yesterday with reference to whether this legislation was needed or not, and as somebody said about the Equator, a great deal is to be said on both sides. There are judges who are as far apart on this very question as the poles. There are judges who believe that every organization of labor which is in a position to affect directly or indirectly interstate commerce is within the provisions of this law. There are opinions, only recently rendered by the courts, which take the opposite view. We can not afford to leave to occupants of the Federal bench who qualified for their places by serving the National Manufacturers' Association the decision of this question—men who as legislators served other masters than the people; who earned the condemnation of the people and were turned from their service, repudiated; men upon the bench who for those reasons were embittered by their defeat, with their inherent hatred of the laboring people of the country intensified by their humiliation, vented their spleen by racking their brain for a more and more drastic provision to put in their restraining orders. There are some of these gentlemen on the bench yet. I do not want it to be within the power of a single one of them to point to any legislative warrant for what he does.

I regret, of course, that the Judiciary Committee on this side, and on the other side, too, for that matter, did not have the courage of the British Parliament, that they were not as downright thoroughgoing and honest as the British Parliament, which said in terms by means of the trade disputes act that laws of any kind which would interfere with the operation of these bodies should not apply to them. And understand, when we pass this law we leave every organization of labor subject to the laws of the State in which it is located.

I say for the comfort of the gentlemen who in their hearts hate these men, that there is still law enough to fill the penitentiary with representatives of organized and unorganized labor in this country; that every State in the Union, every county prosecutor can harass them, any sheriff can arrest them, every county judge can try them, grand juries can indict, and local juries can convict them and send them to the penitentiary. It is not so in England. The Parliament acted by means of the trade disputes act and said these men should be permitted to conduct their organizations and do a great many of the things we propose to permit them to do here, and a great many other things at which we throw up our hands in holy horror. . . .

Mr. CULBERSON. Probably I did not understand the Senator correctly, but do I understand him to make the assertion that the Congress of the United States has power to legalize the existence of labor organizations against the laws of the separate States?

Mr. HUGHES. No; the Senator misunderstood me. I may have given that impression but that is not the point I am trying to make. I think I will clear it up in a minute or two. I was simply calling attention to the action of the British Parliament. The criticism I made in which the Senator would be interested was an expression of regret. I am not criticizing the Senator or criticizing his committee. I am as familiar with the history of this legislation as anybody can possibly be and with the history of the present attempt to cure the evils complained of. I have no criticism to make of the Senator. On the contrary, I have found him and the members of his committee to be eager and anxious to cooperate in this movement to the extent that they thought it would be possible to go. I regret that it was not possible to go as far as the British Parliament went. Then I said that when the British Parliament acted it was not acting only upon members of organizations who were engaged in interstate commerce directly or indirectly but that the law ran into every hamlet in England and controlled every county prosecutor and every grand jury and every petit jury and every judge.

Mr. CULBERSON. The Senator of course understands that that would be impossible under our form of government.

Mr. HUGHES. Of course, I understand that it would be impossible. I am just calling attention to the fact that this legislation falls far short, in a Federal way, of what the British Parliament granted to its workingmen. Yet we are compelled because of our dual system of government to leave it subject to the laws of the various States. What would the laboring people have been getting if you had taken them out from within the provisions of this act? What would they have been getting from the Federal Government, when it is admitted that we leave them subject to the laws of every State? Was it too much to ask that they be exempted entirely from the operation of that law? . . .

Mr. BORAH. The Senator says that they are left to the laws of each and every State. I do not suppose the Senator means it that way; but it is so often said here that this and that must be left to the States, as if there were a superior virtue in the Congress of the United States to that which exists in the legislatures of the respective States.

I do not think there are any more competent bodies to pass upon questions in the respective States than the legislatures of those States. They make mistakes because they are human, but I do not think that because these matters are left to the States there is any reason to suppose that the States are going to be unfair in the laws which they pass. We have every reason to believe that the laboring men will share in as wise and just legislation at the hands of the States, with reference to those matters which are peculiar in the States, as they would in Congress. Does not the Senator think so?

Mr. HUGHES. I do not think anything to the contrary. I was not referring to the fact that this legislation ought to be left to the States. I was simply calling attention to the fact that there is now legislation in practically every State of the Union on this subject of one kind or another, but none going so far as the British Parliament went in the trades-disputes act. No matter if they are not prosecuted under the Sherman Antitrust Act, or if not prosecuted under the modified law which it is hoped we may here pass, they are still subject to prosecutions in the various counties of the States in which they live. We can not do much for them in the nature of things. Every one of these organizations has its local habitation and its name. It operates through its organization and its officers.

Mr. BORAH. I know, so far as my State is concerned, the legislature enacted labor legislation which was satisfactory to labor in reference to eight hours a day, and protecting them in the mines, and so forth, years before Congress acted upon it.

Mr. HUGHES. Exactly. I do not know whether I am making myself clear or not, but I am simply calling attention to the fact that these men are now resting under a double load of adverse legislation, because their activities are circumscribed, to a greater or less extent, in every State in the Union. There is not a single State in the Union of which I have any knowledge which has given them legislation as favorable as the British Parliament has given to the workingmen of England. There was no legislature that had the courage to stand up against the assaults of this discredited organization, powerful, indeed, at one time; I have seen its agents go to high places in public life in this country. There has not been a legislature of a State in the Union, so far as I know, which was courageous enough to stand up and look this outfit in the eye and do what the British Parliament did for the degraded pauper labor of England and Europe, as the phrase goes. The Senator is undoubtedly familiar with it. . . .

Mr. CHILTON. Does not the Senator think that his expression and the expression of the Senator from Idaho that we are leaving anything to the States is the rankest kind of reasoning, but in which the Senator has unfortunately drifted? We can not leave anything to the States. The States are all powerful, except as they grant some power to us. We are now attempting to give within the powers that are granted to us to guarantee such rights and to extend such freedom to labor as we are enabled to do. Can the Senator suggest any other field in which we can legislate except under the grant to regulate interstate commerce? Can the Senator suggest that we can go further in those lines than the House and the Senate seem willing to go at this time?

Mr. HUGHES. I seem to be very unfortunate in my attempts to make myself clear. I did not want anyone to understand that I thought Congress or the Senator's committee should not attempt to legislate on this subject or take away the rights of the States to legislate.

Mr. CHILTON. That is all right. I did not want to interrupt the Senator, but I knew he wanted to be clear about it.

Mr. HUGHES. I am simply trying to call attention to the fact that even if we give everything that is in our power, even if in the express terms we should take these men from ⊥ within the provisions of the law, we would still leave them subject to the jurisdiction of the various States of the Union, which have all sorts of laws on this subject and none of which are as liberal as the British act of which I spoke, which operates in every part of England. That is all I desire to say.

Mr. CHILTON. Just in this connection, if the Senator will permit me—

Mr. HUGHES. Certainly.

Mr. CHILTON. Of course that law operates in England, because there is no constitutional limitation there on Parliament.

Mr. HUGHES. I said that in the beginning. I said on account of our dual form of government it was not possible for Congress to do the same thing. I do not want any member of the committee to think in anything I am saying that I am implying criticism. I realize that the members of this committee have gone as far as they thought they could go, and I agree with them. I am in absolute and utter harmony with them, but I would like to go farther. We know the hue and cry that can be and has been raised and is being raised now against all this sort of legislation. We take what we can get. The laboring men of the United States of America have been taking what they could get ever since I can remember. They have, with hat in hand, been haunting the corridors of this Capitol, begging for a chance to be heard. They have been humble and suppliant; they have been asking for a chance to keep their organizations and to perfect them; they have asked for legislation which would put into effect other legislation which was granted to them before a presidential campaign, but which was suspended by the decision of the Attorney General after the campaign. They spent years and years in getting an eight-hour law upon the statute books, a law providing that eight hours should constitute a day's employment on work done by or for the Government. That law had been enacted, I think, back in 1892, with a great flourish of trumpets, and the gentleman who introduced it in the other body went into the campaign in the State of Ohio as the author of that great measure. Although he had previously been defeated for Congress, he introduced that measure in the short session, during which he had yet to serve before his term expired, and the bill was passed. He then went into the campaign as the author of that bill and was returned as governor of the State by an overwhelming majority, and afterwards became the President of the United States as the father of the eight-hour law, a law which was suspended by a decision of the Attorney General before the returns were counted. From that time on—

Mr. BORAH. The eight-hour law was suspended by the Attorney General?

Mr. HUGHES. I do not mean actually suspended by order of the Attorney General, but they put a comma in or took a comma out of the law, and then building, construction, and other work done by or on behalf of the Government could be carried on under an 8-hour day or a 16-hour day or any other kind of a day.

I called the attention of the man who is now supposed to be the great exponent of the laboring people of this country, then President of the United States, Theodore Roosevelt, to the fact that there was being built a great reservoir in the city of Washington, that there was an eight-hour law upon the statute books, that the Republican Party had taken great pride in the fact that it had passed that law, that a revered and honored member of their party, then dead, had been pointed to as the author of that law; and I told him that I had been on the ground and had seen the work being carried on; that the work was being done by and for the Government directly, without the intervention of any contractor, the Government engineers being in charge and in control of it, and that they were operating under a 10-hour day, working two shifts 10 hours each, one shift working by electric light. I called his attention to that myself in person so that there would not be any question about it. I wanted to ascertain the facts. That was in the old days when public men did not have to be sincere, when men were only expected to make pretense about election time. They did not rely upon the people for nomination; they did not rely upon the people for election. Politics was a game of buncombe; and the man who most successfully practiced buncombe was the most successful politician. That day has passed.

Mr. BORAH. It must be since the Panama Canal tolls bill was passed.

Mr. HUGHES. I will not permit the Senator from Idaho to divert me. I called the attention of the then President of the United States to the fact that this vaunted eight-hour law had virtually been suspended by the decision of the Attorney General in various instances, and that, whatever the merit of the Attorney General's decision was, there could not be any question in this particular case that that $3,000,000 worth of work was being done in the District of Columbia for the Government and by the Government, and that the law was being violated. To make a long story short, there was considerable correspondence which I returned by request. I was informed that this was an emergency proposition. I did not even take the trouble to call the attention of the President to the fact that on an emergency proposition they could work 24 hours a day instead of 20 hours, three 8-hour shifts instead of two shifts of 10 hours. That was in 1904, as I recollect. It was not until last year or the year before last that the laboring people of this country where able to get on the statute books legislation overcoming that decision of the Attorney General.

They have not asked for much and they have gotten a great deal less. I started out by saying that I would like to have seen the Congress of the United States pass an act reading something like this:

Be it enacted, etc., That an act done in pursuance of an agreement or combination by two or more persons shall, if done in contemplation or furtherance of a trade dispute, not be actionable unless the act, if done without any such agreement or combination, would be actionable.

I wish we could even have gotten that far. There is nothing in this bill which goes so far as that. The first paragraph of the British trades-dispute act—and, as I said a while ago, that act runs into every nook and corner of the Kingdom and is controlling upon every prosecuting officer and every grand and petit juror—reads:

It shall be lawful for one or more persons, acting on their own behalf or on behalf of a trade-union or of an individual employer or firm in contemplation or furtherance of a trade dispute, to attend, at or near a house or place where a person resides or works or carries on business or happens to be, if they so attend merely for the purpose of peacefully obtaining or communicating information, or of peacefully persuading any person to work or abstain from working.

That meat was too strong for the gentle stomachs of the American people, as their views are expressed by the Manufacturers' Association and kindred associations. That language could not have been adopted; that language is not in this bill. The act continues:

An action against a trade-union, whether of workmen or masters, or against any members or officials thereof on behalf of themselves and all other members of the trade union in respect of any tortious act alleged to have been committed by or on behalf of the trade-union, shall not be entertained by any court.

They seem to have gone mad over there. Parliament seems to be absolutely and utterly bereft of reason. Evidently they can not see any relation at all between an ordinary conspirator who is conspiring to murder somebody or to burglarize his house and labor unions. The British Parliament sees the widest distinction between those two kinds of conspirators. They seem to think that the interests of the British workmen are paramount and supreme over the necessities of everybody else in the land, and that they can permit them to organize and encourage them to organize and make it possible for them to procure reasonable wages and to enforce sanitary conditions, and that they in turn perhaps will be able to educate and feed their children and bring them up as they should be brought up. They seem to have some sort of an illusion that that will be a good thing for the British Empire.

We are under no illusion over here. There is not a State in the Union, so far as I know, that has an act of this kind or one so liberal as this. We know that it is not even attempted here to come within miles of it; and it is known that even if we did we still would leave these men subject to the various jurisdictions in which they live and operate. No; we prate about the American workman in our political platforms and we excuse the system of tariff robbery on the ground that the robbers are going to hand their plunder down to the workers. There is only one way in which they can be compelled to hand it down; there is only one weapon that will permit an American workman to plunge his hand into the employer's pocket and get his share of the loot that has been wrung from the American people, and that is the strike. One of these conspiracies, one of these combinations and agreements that may be in restraint of trade is the only weapon he has had, but you have given his employers themselves many; you have permitted them to capture this loot, and you have said you have done so on behalf of these American workmen. That is what you said; your platforms reek with it; there is not a platform that you have adopted for the past 25 or 30 years that does not say that. You pride yourselves upon being class legislators. You have two classes—employers and employees. You give the employers the right to loot and plunder, and you say we do so because we know they will pass it down. As the present Secretary of State one time said, you have appointed the employers trustees, you have made them executors or administrators, but you have not asked them to give bond....

Mr. [JOHN W.] WEEKS [R., Mass.]. It is hardly necessary, I think, to comment on the language of the Senator referring to the benefits of a protective tariff.

Mr. HUGHES. I do not insist that the Senator comment on it.

Mr. WEEKS. But it seems to me that if there is any connection between high wages and the legislation to which the Senator has been referring as prevailing in Great Britain we would naturally expect to see better wages in Great Britain than here; and he knows, just as everybody knows, that the wages here are from 25 to 100 per cent higher in the same industries than they are in that country.

Mr. [JAMES E.] MARTINE [D., N.J.]. The American workman possibly performs from 25 to 100 per cent more work than does the average Englishman. Our workmen do not get any more than they are entitled to at that.

Mr. HUGHES. What difference does the suggestion of the Senator from Massachusetts make? I do not care to discuss that with the Senator. I can reply to the Senator by saying that even if his statement is true, which it may or may not be, yet—

Mr. WEEKS. The Senator knows it is true, does he not?

Mr. HUGHES. No; I do not know that it is true, as the Senator states it; but even assuming that it is true, the British workman is getting twice as much—and perhaps that is as nearly true as the Senator's statement—as is his French brother, who is living under a high protective policy; but I do not care to go into that.

Mr. WEEKS. But that statement, Mr. President, is not correct.

Mr. HUGHES. I think it is more correct than the Senator's statement; but we can not decide that now.

The fact remains that the Senator will probably vote against this bill. I do not know as to that. I hope he will not do so; but he probably will vote against it, or against this provision at any rate. He never had any idea in his mind when he voted for the protective tariff to do anything except to benefit the laboring people of this country, but I want to tell him now that if he wants to benefit the laboring people of this country he should give them a chance to combine and organize, to enter into combinations and agreements which may or may not restrain trade, so that they can deal collectively and effectively with their employers. Then they will get even higher wages than the wages which the Senator thinks now are so generous, but which the laboring people of Fall River did not think were so generous a year or two ago, which my people in the city of Paterson did not think were so generous, and which I myself do not think were generous.

Mr. WEEKS. But the Senator puts words in my mouth which I did not use.

Mr. HUGHES. Then I withdraw them.

Mr. WEEKS. I did not say that wages were generous or overgenerous; I said that wages were materially higher, and if the laws of Great Britain were so favorable to the laboring men, we would naturally suppose that they would benefit because of them.

Mr. HUGHES. The Senator does not have to take my opinion with reference to the laws of England being favorable to the laboring men. The Senator can read the proposed legislation now pending, and he can read the law which is on the statute books of England, and I will take his judgment as to whether or not the English law is more favorable on this particular question.

Now, I can not be diverted into a tariff discussion. The Senator is familiar with my views on that subject and I am familiar with his. The tariff has not anything to do with this matter, except that your tariff has been perpetrating a fraud and humbug upon the laboring people of this country for years by pretending that a high tariff rate is for the benefit of the laboring people. If you were interested in the laboring people you would be in favor of legislation which would permit them to organize and to operate as organizations in order to protect themselves against combinations of capital which are so much more powerful than they are. . . .

Mr. [GEORGE W.] NORRIS [R., Neb.]. Mr. President, since the Senator has so often in his remarks undertaken to make a partisan question of this matter and has charged up to a political party all the sins that have come from bad legislation on this particular subject, I want to ask him if he charges the deficiencies of this legislation now pending to the Republican Party? If he claims that the bill now before the Senate does not go to the extent to which he thinks it ought to go, why not, then, put the responsibility on the Democratic Party, for they are certainly in power now?

Mr. HUGHES. They are perfectly willing to take that responsibility.

Mr. NORRIS. The Senator ought to place the responsibility where it belongs, then.

Mr. HUGHES. The Senator is as familiar with the situation that exists here as I can possibly be.

Mr. NORRIS. I think I understand the situation.

Mr. HUGHES. The Senator has had legislative experience enough to know that frequently a party may be in control, and yet the defection of a few men, united with a determined minority, can defeat legislation.

Again, I wish to say that I do not expect the Democratic Party to follow me blindly in these matters, or to go as far as I would have them go. I am simply trying to show you where I should like to have them go. I do not want the Senator to say that I am attempting to give a partisan tinge to this question.

Mr. NORRIS. I do not want to do so; but I have been surprised somewhat at some of the things the Senator has said, because I have been familiar with the Senator's activities in Congress. I entered the House at the same time he did, and I voted for certain propositions there affecting labor, just as he did; but he undertakes here every little while to put the responsibility for the lack of legislation on the Republican Party, and then gives a bouquet to the Democratic Party for what they are doing, and in the next breath says that what is being done now is not at all satisfactory; that it is not at all equal to what has been done over in England. Just as a matter of fairness, it seems to me that the Senator—

Mr. HUGHES. I think I have been absolutely fair—

Mr. NORRIS (continuing). Ought to place the responsibility where it properly rests.

Mr. HUGHES. I have not thrown any bouquets at anybody. I very frankly stated that, even if we did everything that the British Parliament did with reference to this question, we would still be leaving the laboring men subject to the laws of the various jurisdictions.

Mr. NORRIS. But we are not doing that; we do not propose to do that by the bill now pending. Does the Senator think that the President would like to have that done?

Mr. HUGHES. I think so.

Mr. NORRIS. It is true that when he signed the bill that was once vetoed by President Taft containing the restriction as to the use of funds allotted for prosecutions under the Sherman law, he also signed a notation in connection with it in which he expressed the same views that President Taft had expressed when he vetoed the same proposal.

Mr. HUGHES. I will say that I do not know whether or not the President would be as willing to go as far as the trades-dispute act goes, because I have never discussed that question with him. I was not a member of either committee having jurisdiction of the matter, and I had no desire to be officious or to attempt to shape legislation with which I had no particular or exclusive connection. I will say, however, that I am perfectly familiar with the reasons why the President made the memorandum with reference to the limitation on the sundry civil bill, and I agree with him in the main. The amendment to the sundry civil bill, as the Senator will recollect, was offered because of a situation which existed in a certain body with which the Senator is more familiar than any man in the United States. The Senator is not going to deny, I know, that committees were choked in a certain legislative body, and that action could not be had along certain lines. The Senator was as vigorous an opponent of the policy that resulted in those things as there was anywhere in the United States—I might say the most vigorous opponent. . . .

That amendment was offered as a limitation upon an appropriation bill for the purpose of testing the sense of the other House. It tested the sense of the House, and served its purpose. I do not think it is wise legislation to tie up a fund with a limitation; I do not think it is good legislation to abolish a judge by refusing to appropriate for his salary; I think the best way is to honestly abolish his office, and if I had been the President of the United States I would have been tempted to ⊥ say something such as he said. I was the author of the amendment. . . .

Mr. NORRIS. Mr. President, I recognize that the Senator was the author of that amendment, and he offered it in the House of Representatives before the present administration came into power. I was one of the Senator's supporters on that occasion and helped in my weak way to put that proposition on an appropriation bill. Then later a similiar provision was put on an appropriation bill that was sent to President Wilson.

Mr. HUGHES. I can not accept the Senator's statement as to his help being weak.

Mr. NORRIS. The Senator was not asserting when he was putting the question up to a Republican President that it was improper to enact such legislation, but when a Democratic President takes the same ground he assists him in making his apology. Now, I can see only this difference—and I am surprised to-day that the Senator has so often intimated it in his remarks, because I have always thought a great deal of his independence in the stand that he has taken since he has been a Member of Congress— that he condemns an action if it originates in one political party and apologizes for it when it is consummated by another political party.

Mr. HUGHES. The Senator insists on quarreling with me, but I do not want him to quarrel with me, because he is too good a friend of mine and we have fought shoulder to shoulder on too many occasions for us to part over a fancied difference now, for there is no real difference between us.

Mr. NORRIS. I am not quarreling with the Senator on this provision of the bill; I am in favor of this provision.

Mr. HUGHES. I understand that; I know that without asking.

Mr. NORRIS. And I want to see it enacted into law; but the Senator is not satisfied with it. I am not saying that his proposition would not be better than the one proposed, but because he wants to go further, it seems to me—perhaps I am wrong in my conclusions—because this provision in the bill does not suit him, he is condemning another political party, that is now out of power, because they have not enacted any law along the lines of the British law, and then he turns to his party, which is in power, and says, "You have gone as far as you could be expected to go; you have done well; it is all right; everything is lovely; you have done just what you ought to have done." It occurs to me the rule ought to work both ways.

Mr. HUGHES. Mr. President, the Senator does me a great injustice there. When I referred to our attempt to get another party to act, I was referring to the eight-hour bill, which was enacted into law precisely as we had been attempting and as I had been attempting to get another party to enact it into law.

The laboring people of the United States are satisfied with this legislation. They are afraid to jeopardize their chances of getting any legislation, because they have not much confidence in the real regard of the Congress—I will put it in that way—for them, and they are afraid to jeopardize their chances of getting any legislation by insisting upon getting more than there is in this bill as it came from the House. They are satisfied, and nobody is authorized to go any further in their name. So much for that.

I have been constantly referring to the attitude of the Republican Party toward the laboring people of this country, because the speeches which have been made against this proposition have been made against it in the main on the ground that it was class legislation. It is unfortunate that I have not made myself clear. I have a vivid recollection of the service that was rendered by the Senator from Nebraska and a great many other members, not only of the Progressive Party but a great many members of the Republican Party, for the limitation upon the Attorney General's fund went on a bill in a Republican House. The first time that it ever was offered and the first time, in my recollection, that either House of Congress had expressed its opinion as to whether or not the Sherman law did include or ought to include organizations of labor was at that time when the House was under Republican control.

I regret if I have appeared to show any spirit of partisanship in this matter, because it is not a partisan matter, and ought not to be a partisan matter. It is within the power of the Senate now to give the organizations of labor everything for which they are asking in this bill. Practically, it is possible to take organized labor out of politics in this country and let them divide along natural lines, as they ought to divide. Nobody would deplore more than I the building up of a class-conscious party of any kind in this country. . . .

Mr. [HENRY F.] LIPPITT [R., R.I.]. I have been rather interested in the Senator's views as to how labor can get higher wages. As I understand the Republican policy which he criticizes so severely, its purpose is to put a larger sum into the countingroom. The desire of the Senator from New Jersey is that out of the sum that goes into the countingroom a larger precentage shall go to labor, but he criticizes the policy which gives a larger sum to divide.

It seems perfectly evident to me that a policy which tries to put a dollar where it can be divided between capital and labor is infinitely superior to a policy which only puts 50 cents where it can be so divided, and that the division which goes to labor, even if it is only 75 per cent, is immensely greater when it is 75 per cent of a dollar than though it were 85 per cent of a half dollar. Neither labor nor capital can obtain more than the whole of what exists. The Republican policy, from the origination of that party, has been to make a larger fund that can be divided between the parties between whom it must be divided—those who contribute the labor and those who contribute the capital.

Mr. HUGHES. That is true; that is what I was trying to say; but the Senator has said it better than I could possibly have said it. I do not want to get into a discussion of the protective policy; I was only calling attention to it incidentally, as I tried to explain, to show that the Republican Party is not opposed to class legislation, because the Republican tariff laws have been class legislation. You are then legislating for a class, a class of employers and employees. I only touched on that incidentally. . . .

Mr. LIPPITT. The Senator has said several times in the last 10 minutes that he did not want the tariff question to enter into the discussion of the matter which he is considering, but almost before the words are out of his mouth he begins again to attack the tariff policy of the Republican Party. It is very comfortable for him to say "I will attack a Republican policy, but Senators on the other side must not say a word, because I do not want that policy discussed." If the Senator does not want it discussed, would it not be well to refrain from attacking it?

Mr. HUGHES. I have to carry on this discussion in my own way. I am not compelled to yield to the Senator; I can do as he did a day or two ago and decline to yield.

Mr. LIPPITT. On what occasion?

Mr. HUGHES. When the Senator made his last speech, as I recollect, he signified a desire not to be interrupted.

Mr. LIPPITT. I have no recollection of having done so. I think one year ago or so I made a carefully prepared speech, and may then have expressed a desire of that kind.

Mr. HUGHES. I have a right to carry on this discussion in my own way.

Mr. LIPPITT. I have no desire to interrupt the Senator, if he does not want to be interrupted.

Mr. HUGHES. I have not said that I did not want to be interrupted, but I do not like the Senator to direct my remarks into channels which are foreign to the purpose of my argument. I am going to say now that I have not made any attempt to discuss the protective theory as a policy. I have simply called attention to the fact—and I know the Senator will admit it—that the Republican Party is devoted to that theory. It believes in the protective principle. The Senator will admit that, undoubtedly.

Mr. LIPPITT. I even glory in it.

Mr. HUGHES. Yes; undoubtedly. The Senator will also admit that the protective theory contemplates that a man will have the privilege, which is denied to others, of doing business in a certain territory, the aim being for him to get—

Mr. LIPPITT. I will admit that it involves the theory of having an American citizen do things in America that are denied to a German or to an Englishman or to a Frenchman. I do not admit that it denies to any one American citizen the right to do what any other American citizen can do.

Mr. HUGHES. Exactly; I understand the Senator's position; but the protective theory is that a manufacturer will get a little more money for his goods than he would if the country were opened up to foreign competition, and that in turn he will be enabled to pay more wages than he would be able to pay if the country were opened up to foreign competition. The Senator will surely admit that?

Mr. LIPPITT. I would not put it just that way. I would put it a little differently; but the Senator says he does not want to discuss the tariff, and if we go on we will have a very lengthy discussion.

Mr. HUGHES. I know. I do not want to discuss it; but I thought those were protective axioms. I did not know that I was stating anything debatable; and I was then calling attention to the fact that the Senator's party was on record as desiring to favor the American laboring people as a class.

Mr. LIPPITT. Surely.

Mr. HUGHES. That it was class legislation, and they would stand for it so far as it was involved in the protective theory; that is all. I never made a single word of attack upon the protective theory.

Mr. LIPPITT. If the Senator would not confine his remarks to the statement that the protective policy is designed to favor the laborer entirely, to the exclusion of other people in the United States, I might agree with him. I do not understand that the Republican protective policy means that. I understand that the benefit Republicans think accrues from that policy is distributed over the entire American people.

Mr. HUGHES. Yes; I know. The benefits that will flow from this policy will be distributed over the entire United States, but the direct beneficiaries of the protective tariff—

Mr. LIPPITT. Are the people of the United States.

Mr. HUGHES. Well, the direct beneficiary, first, is the man who gets a little more for his goods than he would get if the country were opened up to foreign competition. Surely the Senator and I can agree on that. The Senator ought to be fair and candid with me. I am trying to be fair and candid with him.

Mr. LIPPITT. The Senator is leading me into strange paths, however, or trying to do so.

Mr. HUGHES. I think the Senator finds those paths fairly familiar, but I shall not pursue the discussion any further now. I must insist on saying, however, whether it harrows the Senator's feelings or not, that the Republican Party has claimed to be guilty of class legislation in favor of the laboring people of the United States. I do not think they have. I acquit them, so far as I am concerned; but they have claimed, and they have written it into their platforms, that they have legislated and that they are going to legislate in the interest of the laboring people. They are going to tax, they are going to keep the protective policy in force, not because of its inherent virtues and beauties altogether, but because, directly or indirectly, it helps the laboring men of the United States of America.

Mr. LIPPITT. I agree with that.

Mr. HUGHES. Of course the Senator agrees with that, and that is what I have been saying all along.

Mr. LIPPITT. But I do not agree that it helps only the laboring people.

Mr. HUGHES. Of course the Senator's theory is that after that those benefits are handed down. That is the difference between the Senator's theory and mine.

Mr. LIPPITT. And that is all the difference between the position in which the Senator is trying to place this tariff policy and the position in which I place it. He is trying to argue that it favors only one class. He then goes on to say that it favors all classes, which I agree with.

Mr. HUGHES. I say that the Senator believes it favors all classes. There is no use in my saying to the Senator that I do not believe in his theory. I do not believe in it any more than he believes in mine, but I do not want to discuss it. We have not the time to discuss it. I am simply calling attention to the fact that it does not lie in the mouth of the Senator to criticize this side of the Chamber, or any other body, for passing so-called class legislation, because his whole theory—

Mr. LIPPITT. Does the Senator believe class legislation is right?

Mr. HUGHES. Yes; I believe in class legislation.

Mr. LIPPITT. The Senator believes in passing laws that favor one particular class in opposition to other particular classes?

Mr. HUGHES. Yes. For instance, take this provision in this bill—

Mr. LIPPITT. I just wanted a statement of the broad, general principle. The Senator says he thinks class legislation is right.

Mr. HUGHES. The Senator has just admitted that the protective theory involves a favor to the working class.

Mr. LIPPITT. I have not admitted it at all in the way the Senator means it. I have said, over and over again, that it involves a benefit to all people. Now, the Senator says that he believes legislation ought to be passed which favors one class to the disadvantage of the others.

Mr. HUGHES. Why, certainly. The Constitution of the United States provides for a class. The Constitution of the United States provides that the press shall be free. If I threaten you with an injury, you may bind me over to keep the peace; you may take other steps; but if a newspaper of the United States threatens to make an attack on you, which may destroy you politically and socially, it is permitted to do it. It takes the consequences and pays for the consequences afterwards; but it can do it. You will find other classes provided for in the Constitution of the United States. Let me call your attention to a class in the bill now before us as it came over from the House. It has been stricken out by the Senate committee, for what reason I do not know; I hope not for the reason that it was class legislation.

Mr. McCUMBER. Mr. President, let me ask the Senator right there, if he will, whether I understand him correctly. If I understood him aright, he said that the press had rights that individuals do not have?

Mr. HUGHES. A man in the newspaper business has rights that other men have not.

Mr. McCUMBER. What right has he to defame another man's character, or to make any false statement, or to do anything else, that an individual has not?

Mr. HUGHES. Why, he has an absolute right to do it. He can not be prevented by injunction from doing it, under the Constitution.

Mr. McCUMBER. Neither can the individual.

Mr. HUGHES. The individual can be prevented from doing lots of things.

Mr. McCUMBER. I should like to know just one thing, if the Senator can point it out to me, that the owner of a paper can do through the instrumentality of his paper that an individual can not do.

Mr. HUGHES. He can injure a man; he can publish a defamatory statement about a man; he can give notice that he is about to do it, and he can continue to do it.

Mr. McCUMBER. Would that protect him any more than it would an individual?

Mr. HUGHES. Why, yes; the individual—

Mr. McCUMBER. Is there any difference between the law of libel and the law of slander, so far as the rights of the citizen are concerned, whether he be libeled by the press or slandered by the individual?

Mr. HUGHES. Why, yes. An individual can be bound over to keep the peace. If he were making verbal statements or written statements calculated to provoke a breach of the peace, he could be bound over. You can not bind a newspaper over.

Mr. McCUMBER. I admit that the press can not threaten that it will do anything of itself against a man.

Mr. HUGHES. A newspaper can go on publishing from day to day defamatory and libelous articles about the Senator, and he can not enjoin it. He can not stop it.

Mr. McCUMBER. But the Senator can have his action for damages against the newspaper, the same as he would against the individual.

Mr. HUGHES. Oh, yes; I started out by saying that.

Now, I want to read another specimen of class legislation which I approve of absolutely—that is, so far as any objection to it is concerned on account of its being class legislation. With the merits of the matter I am not familiar. I do not pretend to be familiar with it, but as this bill came over from the House it contained the language I am about to read. Now, this is a bill which prevents the existence of certain combinations and groups of men, and all that, and prevents combined action along certain lines. It contains this language:

> Nothing contained in the antitrust laws shall be construed to forbid associations of traffic, operating, accounting, or other officers of common carriers for the purpose of conferring among themselves or of making any lawful agreement as to any matter which is subject to the regulating or supervisory jurisdiction of the Interstate Commerce Commission, but all such matters shall continue to be subject to such jurisdiction of the commission, and all such agreements shall be entered and kept of record by the carriers, parties thereto, and shall at all times be open to inspection by the commission, but no such agreement shall go into effect or become operative until the same shall have first been submitted to, and approved by, the Interstate Commerce Commission: *Provided*, That nothing in this act shall be construed as modifying existing laws prohibiting the pooling of earnings or traffic, or existing laws against joint agreements by common carriers to maintain rates.

I quote that simply for the purpose of showing that when you are drawing a broad, comprehensive, and sweeping statute which is going to apply all over the United States of America it is likely to come in contact not only with other laws, but with customs and practices, and by virtue of being a later enactment wipe them out. Of course, it is class legislation. The interstate-commerce act is class legislation. I can charge a poor, unfortunate client of mine as much money as I can get from him for my services as a lawyer; but the Erie Railroad, which runs through my town, can not charge me what it likes to carry me to the city of New York, because we have made a class out of railroads. A corporation is permitted to do certain things which individuals can not do. Individuals are permitted to do certain things which corporations can not do. The man who holds the stock of a corporation can limit his liability in business to the assets of the corporation, because we have made a class out of corporations. The individual, on the other hand, may have all his earthly goods swept away by an industrial calamity.

We have provided that workingmen who are in the employ of a concern which goes bankrupt shall be preferred; and the first act that a receiver performs when he comes into possession of the assets of the derelict industrial concern is to make the necessary arrangements at the bank and pay wages. That is absolutely class legislation. I am in favor of certain kinds of class legislation and I am in favor of this legislation. . . .

Mr. CUMMINS. If the Senator from New Jersey has finished with this particular subject I should like to ask him to return to another with which he has already dealt. I do not quite like the way in which he has left the comparison of the English statute with the laws of the United States. The English statute in substance abolishes the distinction between individual action and combined action. That is all it does.

Mr. HUGHES. Oh, it does more than that.

Mr. CUMMINS. Yes; it does. It says, in substance, that people can not be held liable for concerted action if the same thing done by an individual would have been lawful.

Mr. HUGHES. Of course that is a tremendous addition; but that is not all.

Mr. CUMMINS. I will call attention to that. Now, that is all right. Of course the Congress of the United States could not do that, but I think the Senator from New Jersey entirely misunderstands what the application of the English doctrine would be under the antitrust law.

The antitrust law forbids restraint of trade. It makes no difference whether the restraint of trade is accomplished by an individual, by one man, or by 100 men, whether it is accomplished singly or in concert. If we had the English statute, whoever restrained trade would be liable under the law, whether a single person restrained it or whether a thousand persons acting together restrained it. In other words, the offense under our statute is not the combination to restrain trade, but it is the restraint of trade; and therefore, if the English statute were in full force in the United States and in all the States, the result would be just the same. If to do certain things would be to restrain trade, and the English had such a statute as ours, that act would be unlawful.

Mr. HUGHES. I agree with the Senator. I did not mean to be understood as saying that the literal language of the British act would be satisfactory here, or would meet the needs and requirements of the situation here as I see them. I am simply calling attention to the difference between the attitude of the British Government and the attitude of the American Government.

I will say, in deference to my friends here who have been disposed to criticize me for being partisan on this subject, that in the Taff Vale case,[5.655] when it was demonstrated that organizations of labor in England could be held responsible for going on strike when that strike took the shape of a conspiracy and resulted in damages to an employer of labor, and those damages could be traced back to the men who went on the strike, to their friends who paid them while they stayed out, to their organization which kept them in funds and which encouraged them and persuaded them to persist in the strike—when it became demonstrated that the unions could be held liable for that, and when they were held liable for a large sum of money, £ 150,000, which they paid, then the British Parliament acted.

Mr. CUMMINS. I am not at all disparaging the English statute, nor am I suggesting that it has not a very great effect. I am only saying that so far as restraint of trade is concerned it would do no good whatsoever to enact the English statute.

Mr. HUGHES. No; I agree with that.

Mr. CUMMINS. There is a difference, in the broad field of human activity, between the lawfulness of the action of a single man and the action of a hundred men in conspiracy or in combination. One man may often do something that would be entirely innocent for the man to do, but which would be criminal for a hundred or a thousand men to do in combination. Therefore, the English statute had a great field for operation; but so far as the restraint of trade is concerned, that is the unlawful thing, and it is just the same whether it is restrained by one man or by a thousand men.

Mr. HUGHES. Yes; but the restraint of trade was the thing in the Taff Vale case. . . .

Mr. NELSON. I think the Senator from New Jersey is laboring under a great misapprehension as to the scope of the English trade legislation. While in some respects it is very liberal, yet it contains restrictions that we have not known of or thought of in this country. I want to read to the Senator, with his permission, section 5 of the act of August 13, 1875:

> Where any person willfully and maliciously breaks a contract of service or of hiring, knowing or having reasonable cause to believe that the probable consequences of his so doing, either alone or in combination with others, will be to endanger human life or cause serious bodily injury or to expose valuable property, whether real or personal, to destruction or serious injury, he shall, on conviction thereof by a court of summary jurisdiction or on indictment as

---

[5.655] Taff Vale Ry. v. Amalgamated Soc'y of Ry. Servants, [1901] A.C. 426.

hereinafter mentioned, be liable either to pay a penalty not exceeding £20 or to be imprisoned for a term of not exceeding three months with or without hard labor.

Then I read section 7 of the same act, which is still in force:

Every person who, with a view to compel any other person to abstain from doing or to do any act which such other person has a legal right to do or abstain from doing, wrongfully and without legal authority—

1. Uses violence to or intimidates such other person or his wife or children or injures his property; or
2. Persistently follows such other person about from place to place; or
3. Hides any tools, clothes, or other property owned or used by such other person or deprives him of or hinders him in the use thereof; or
4. Watches or besets the house or other place where such other person resides or works or carries on business or happens to be or the approach to such house or place; or
5. Follows such other person with two or more other persons in a disorderly manner in or through any street or road—

shall, on conviction thereof by a court of summary jurisdiction or on indictment as hereinafter mentioned, be liable either to pay a penalty not exceeding £20 or to be imprisoned for a term not exceeding three months with or without hard labor.

Now, the change in the legislation of Great Britain which the Senator from New Jersey lauds so much is subject to all those restrictions which I have quoted from the act of Parliament of 1875. There was an amendatory act passed in December, 1906, but it does not modify any of the provisions I have indicated. The only modification in it is that it authorizes peaceful picketing. So while on the one hand, if the Senator will allow me—and I speak by his permission—the British trade-union act seems to be a great deal more liberal than our legislation here is, yet on the other hand it is subject to a class of restrictions that are not found in our statute books, and that would be found very burdensome and onerous to labor in this country.

Mr. HUGHES. I will simply say that British workmen have found the trade-dispute act recently enacted eminently satisfactory. It has enabled them to do what the laboring men of America want to be enabled to do, to preserve and keep their organizations, to withdraw simultaneously from employment, and to do the usual things, subject always to the law of the community in which they are done, during the periods when strikes are on or declared.

Mr. NELSON. But did the Senator observe section 5 of the British act, to which I called attention and which I read?

Mr. HUGHES. Yes; I observed it, and I simply want to call the Senator's attention to this—

Mr. NELSON. What has the Senator to say to that? Does he approve that provision or is he against it?

Mr. HUGHES. I do not recollect the provision.

Mr. NELSON. I will read it again.

Mr. HUGHES. I do not care to have it read to me now.

Mr. NELSON. I should like to know how the Senator stands on that question. Would he like to have such a provision incorporated into our law, or is he opposed to it?

Mr. HUGHES. I should like to have a law as good as the British trade-dispute act; yes; and I know the Senator would not vote for such an act.

Mr. NELSON. I will quote it again, with the Senator's permission.

Mr. HUGHES. I do not want the Senator to read it again.

Mr. NELSON. No; I do not suppose the Senator does.

Mr. HUGHES. The Senator can put it in the RECORD if he likes. I am so indifferent to it that I will let the Senator put me down as being either for it or against it; he can use his own judgment.

I know this: I know that the British Parliament rose at once to the emergency when it saw the difficult situation into which the labor organizations of England had drifted. They had friends in the Parliament, and the friends enacted the legislation they asked, and under that legislation there has not been a single case such as littered the calendars of the courts before. I know that. I know that the question was settled. I should like to have the Senator help me settle it in this country.

American workmen are entitled to as good treatment as British workmen or the workmen of any other country. They do not get it. The legislation in this country is less favorable to workmen than that of any other civilized country in the world, and the Senator knows it, and has helped to keep it as it is.

I have said a good deal more than I intended to say, Mr. President. I think this is a tardy compliance with the just and reasonable demands of the laboring people of this country. In my judgment, there is nothing in this section which justifies the secondary boycott or a boycott of any kind. It simply makes legal that which we all have been taught to believe was legal. It simply interposes the barrier of the arm of this law before an unfriendly Attorney General, who might with great reason and force, it seems to me, go into a court of equity and dissolve by injunction every organization of railroad trainmen, firemen, or engineers who were organized for the purpose of simultaneously ceasing their employment whenever necessary to enforce their demands. That is all it does, in my opinion.

It is possible that at a later time I may have something to say with reference to the other provisions of the bill.

Mr. BORAH. Mr. President, I have been somewhat surprised at some of the views which the Senator from New Jersey expressed, although I agree perfectly with his closing sentence. I think the labor organizations of this country ought to have the right which the Senator says he thinks they ought to have, if we are to measure that right according to his closing paragraph; but there were some views expressed during his able and earnest presentation of this matter that I do not entirely accept.

He eulogizes the British trades act. There are some things in the British trades act which may be commendatory, and which, in so far as our framework of government would admit, might be very properly transmitted to this country. But when the Senator goes further and says that the legislative condition and the general condition of labor in Great Britain are better than in America, I am sure the Senator in his zeal has overstepped the actual facts.

Mr. HUGHES. Mr. President, I do not think I said that, and I did not intend to say it. I said that simply from a legislative standpoint there had been more legislation enacted for the benefit of English workmen than had been enacted for the benefit of American workmen. I want to make that absolutely clear. If there is any doubt about it, I will call the Senator's attention to the pension laws that have been enacted and various other social measures.

Mr. BORAH. I am aware that there are some things that, as I say, are commendatory; but if the weather should turn cool before this debate closes I propose to present the condition of legislation in England with reference to labor and the condition of labor in England with reference to the condition of labor in America, because it will be a startling contrast, not a comparison but a contrast, altogether to the advantage of the workmen of America, of which we ought to be very glad. Labor is not so well paid, not so well housed, not so well clothed, not so well governed as in America.

But that is no reason, Mr. President, why we should not go forward and do whatever is right and proper to be done for the laboring men of this country. I repeat, as I said yesterday, that in so far as it is necessary to protect union labor to go forward and do the things which ordinarily and legitimately any reasonable man would say belongs to union labor to do, I am in favor of going that distance. In fact, Mr. President, I believe I may say, speaking in a general way, that I could go all the way with labor on the hither side of threats and intimidation and violence. I do not believe that there is anything on the hither side of these that I would not be willing to do for laboring men and to enable them to do so far as the Federal Government has power to legislate on the subject. I would protect fully and completely their right to organize, their right to strike, and their right to enforce the strike in all peaceful and lawful ways.

Now, just a word with reference to the protective tariff, which was brought into this matter. He assails the Republican Party most severely and denounces it for legislating for the rich as against the poor, of building up monopoly against the rights and at the cost of labor. It may be that the protective tariff has not been the benefit to the laboring men of this country which men during the campaign assured them that it would be. It may be that their share of the profits have not drifted down to them, and that they have not had their proportion of the world's blessings and comforts. I believe that that is true. I do not believe that labor has had its fair proportion of our prosperity in past years. But, Mr. President, to-day there is estimated to be by laboring men themselves at least 500,000, if not a million, men out of employment. What has brought that condition about I am not going into details at this time to say, but it is the honest, the solemn judgment and conviction of the advocates of a protective tariff that it would assist in ameliorating that condition if it were restored in a uniform way in this country. I may be in error in regard to that, but those who believe in the other policy have not been able to find employment for the 500,000 or million of men who are out of employment in this country to-day. Neither have they by their system of spotted free trade reduced the cost of living to those who have employment, to say nothing of the condition of those out of employment.

But, Mr. President, what is the protective tariff? When does it take and when does it not take? When does it apply and when does it not apply? If there is any particular form of a protective policy found in this country that is peculiarly offensive to Democracy it is in regard to the coastwise shipping in the United States. You have denounced it on every stump and filled the debates here with anathemas. If there is any form of protective policy which has been designated, individualized, and legalized and made a monopoly, it is the coastwise shipping proposition which we had before us a few days ago in this Senate Chamber.

Last Friday when we adjourned and that matter was before the Senate there was scarcely a quorum to be found in Washington, and the lack of interest and apathy upon the part of legislators was phenominal [sic]. But the legislation having been postponed from Friday until Monday, practically every Senator of the United States was then in his seat, and the forces and the influence which have sustained this form of protection in this country in its most aggravated and indefensible form were in Washington before Monday morning's sun had risen. And the party always denouncing this monopoly, this form of protection, retreated from their report and from the report of their party and perpetuated further the most offensive form of monopoly that protection could possibly foster in this country, as our Democratic friends view it. . . .

Mr. KERN. I was about to say—

> Thou canst not say I did it; never shake
> Thy gory locks at me.

Mr. BORAH. That is true; and I could say more than that in compliment to the Senator. I am far from criticizing his course on this or other things. . . .

Mr. ASHURST. Supplementing what our distinguished leader the Senator from Indiana [Mr. KERN] has said, I wish to say also that I claim to be one who has stood by the true Democratic doctrine and stood by the report of that conference committee and voted last Friday as I voted on the 11th of June upon the amendment offered by the Senator from Missouri [Mr. REED] to permit all ships to enter our coastwise trade.

Mr. BORAH. Mr. President, I was not looking at the Senator from Indiana or the Senator from Arizona. I will confine my "looks" now entirely to this side of the Chamber in order that I may not be supposed to criticize anyone, in person or in particular.

Now, Mr. President, I believe in a protective policy and in the principle of protection. I do not believe in its application in spots or in sections. I do not believe in protecting shipbuilding and protecting peanuts in the State of Virginia and in putting wheat and barley upon the free list. It is but a question of applying the principle. If it is applied with universal effect, so that it may reach Nation wide, building up industries, energizing labor, affording opportunity and inducing initiative, it is a great system. If it is not thus applied, it becomes a special privilege, and is intolerable and indefensible.

Mr. President, a word with reference to the limitation on the sundry civil bill to which the Senator from New Jersey [Mr. ⊥ HUGHES] referred. He said it was put into the bill for the purpose of testing the sense of the House—a Republican House—and that when it was brought over here it had served its purpose. But the Senator from New Jersey, in a very earnest speech upon this floor, advocated its passage through the

Senate for the same reason, I presume, that he urged its passage through the House—not to test the sense of the Senate and not to test the sense of the House, but because he said that the great organization of which he was a humble member was now prepared to do justice to the laboring men, who had been so long delayed in securing the justice to which they were entitled.

I took occasion to say upon the floor of the Senate at that time that attaching that limitation to that bill was a piece of hypocrisy and a fraud. I read in Mr. Gompers's great association paper within six months thereafter that it was a fraud, that the prosecutions wherever they arose proceeded just the same, that the law was enforced just the same, and that while they had asked for bread they had been given a stone.

Furthermore, Mr. President, the Senator tells us that certain Members of the House, as I understood, after serving the Manufacturers' Association and doing their work on the floor of the House, were selected out and put upon the Federal bench for the purpose apparently of protecting the manufacturers and the monopolies of this country. It was a serious charge to make. It was a direct impeachment of the honor of a Republican President and a most serious assault upon the bench. If any man has been placed upon the Federal bench for that purpose and there is any proof of that fact, it is not too late yet to know whether or not he is serving his masters who placed him there, and it should be investigated. I hope the Senator, in the cause of good and decent government, will withhold no fact.

But again, Mr. President, if the Senator wants to raise the question of serving monopolies, and of the close relationship between political parties and the interests, and selecting men who represent the monopolies to go into high place, what is the difference between selecting some single individual from the House of Representatives to go upon the Federal bench, where he is checked up by other judges and his opinions supervised and reviewed by the great Supreme Court of the United States, and selecting as the representative of one of the condemned monopolies of this country a man who had helped to build it up and defend it to take charge of the currency of the country, which indeed is no less than the lifeblood of the Nation? Does the Senator think that his party in these days is in a position to boast or to flaunt the record of anyone?

Give me the power to control the currency of this country, to contract and to inflate the currency, and I do not care who renders your decisions; I will build my fortune so high and spread my influence so far that no petty Federal judge can reach my power.

I would rather if I were seeking power and wanted to have close and effective alliance between government and monopoly to have control of the Federal Reserve Board than any single place in the whole structure of government. I am not impeaching the action of anyone, but it requires some effrontery, in view of lately written history, for Democracy to be talking of close alliance with the "interests."

Mr. President, it is a common, and, I think a deplorably common thing in these days to be always assailing the courts. I do not sympathize with this wholesale assault.

I do not claim that the courts do not err; they sometimes err signally and pronouncedly. I do not claim that they always administer justice with an even and exact hand, for judges are human and the passions and prejudices, the limited vision and the clouded mind which sometimes attach to their kind are also theirs. I do not claim that they are always free from political bias or at all times wholly exempt from that strange attachment which in a republic sometimes places party above the common welfare, for Presidents and governors and electorates in selecting judges do not always seek men most likely to resist such influences. But I do claim that of all the methods and contrivances and schemes which have been devised by the wit of man for the adjustment of controverted judicial questions and the administration of justice the courts and the machinery of the courts, built up from decade to decade and from century to century, built of the experience and the wisdom of a proud and freedom-loving race, the courts as they are built into our system, though not perfect, are the most perfect. They will not always be abreast of the most advanced opinions in the march of progress, but that they will in due time mortise and build into our jurisprudence all that is permanent and wise and just, all that a settled and digested public opinion finally indorses, no one familiar with the history of our jurisprudence can for a moment doubt. Not only that, but more than once the courts, both in England and America, have stood as the sole protector in the hour of turmoil and strife for the rights of the weak and the poor, the oppressed and the hunted, when the executive and the legislature have yielded to the whip of the strong and the powerful. I need recall only one instance in the hurry of this debate, though I might recall a hundred, beginning with the days of Coke's courage, and that is the instance wherein our own great Supreme Court preserved against the encroachments of war and the hunger of hatred the right of trial by jury, a most sacred right of the American citizen and without which the whole scheme of a republic would be but a delusion and a torment.

After the courts then what? When the courts can no longer stay the steps which may lead to violence and bloodshed, then what? When the arm of equity can no longer be extended to hold things in abeyance until rights can be adjudicated and reason and counsel can have a hearing, then what? Be not deceived. The alternative is the soldier and the bayonet. One can not be oblivious to the alacrity with which wealth in these days is prone to appeal to the soldier. When a delegation of workingmen informed me a few months ago that their fellow workmen had been arrested without warrant, tried without a jury, sentenced by no court—that at a time when the courts were open and in the midst of an intelligent, prosperous, modern American community men had been herded before a military tribunal, given the semblance of a trial, and sent to prison, it seemed incredible. For nearly 600 years no such repulsive scene had marred the story of the orderly development and growth of Anglo-Saxon jurisprudence. Our English ancestors had executed the petty tyrants who had last attempted it. I did not suppose that here, where jury trials and common-law courts were a guaranty—a part of our system of law and justice—that anyone would be so blind, so cruel, so witless as to covet the infamy of rehabilitating that discarded and detested dogma—the power of suspension. Nevertheless it was true. Since that time, in three other States, the workingman has settled his troubles out of court where counsel may be heard and witnesses testify, settled them at the point of the bayonet. What a glutton arbitrary power is for the rights and the interests of the weak. It generally comes forward at the bidding of the rich and the powerful and preys upon the interests and rights of the poor and the helpless.

These men who came to me were asking for what? They were asking for a hearing in the courts, before this tribunal, whose judgments they informed me they were willing to take. They were praying for the common-law court and its machinery just as it had been worked out and fought for in the humble days of our English ancestors to the humble days of their descendants on Paint and Cabin Creek in one of the great Commonwealths of this Union. And what was the answer to the charge when we arrived upon the ground? When we asked why have these men charged with offenses under the statute and guaranteed a trial in a common-law court been denied the right of the humblest citizen when charged with crime, what was the answer? The answer was not that riot and war had closed the courts, but that excitement and feeling in the community would render them ineffective in all probability. When we inquired further, the fear was that these laboring men would likely be acquitted. What, before the courts, acquitted under the processes and according to the manner that guilty men have been punished and innocent men acquitted for ten centuries? Then they must be innocent. But the logic seemed to be that, guilty or innocent, they must be punished. Force must be established and certainty as to results must be had. So, the strong fled from the courts of justice, suspended—what an infamous lie—yes, suspended by force the constitution of the State and the Nation, selected a military tribunal, called the judges from the guards who were in charge of the prisoners, tried them in groups, and sent them in droves to the penitentiary. Do not the workingmen understand that in the end their fight will be to maintain these courts in all their purity, independence, and strength? Do they not understand that if we can not have somewhere an independent tribunal, free from the passions and conflicts of contestants, to distribute justice, civilization must do again what it has done in the past—crumble and fall? Does not the average citizen of this country, whoever and wherever he is, understand that in the end he must find justice here in these tribunals or not find it at all? Does he not understand that after they are gone and law and order have departed he will shortly come to be the victim of violence and cruelty and injustice, the plaything of arbitrary power?

There comes a time, Mr. President, when every man and when the people in every walk of life seek shelter under the calm, ⊥ determined, beneficent power of a great government, rely upon its impartial strength, and accept with gratitude its means and methods of measuring and distributing justice. Men should seek to build a government which has no classes, grants no special privileges, recognizes no creed, and fosters no religion. It is a blind and shortsighted policy to suppose that you can curtail the functions of government in order to bestow favors, for when you have done so you have already weakened government for the prevention of wrongs. The fruits of industry, the wages of the toiler, the income of capital are all affected, fostered, encouraged, and sustained to the extent that order and law obtain throughout the land. While a strong and fearless government may sometimes seem quick to prevent those steps and block those paths which seem to lead to violence and bloodshed, yet ultimately the benefits to flow from such procedure must redound to the peace and happiness, the contentment and prosperity of the whole people. It was Liebknecht, the great socialist, who truly said, "Violence has been for thousands of years a reactionary factor." Show me a country without courts fully equipped in every way to deal with all the intricacies of each particular case as the facts appear; show me a country with its business and industry under the clamp of bureaucracy, its courts weakened, cowardly, and powerless, and I will show you a country where the laborer is no better than a slave—the miserable, ignorant, unclad dupe and plaything of arbitrary power.

The VICE PRESIDENT. The question is on the amendment of the committee, which the Secretary will state.

The SECRETARY. On page 7, line 13, after the word "organizations," strike out the words "orders, or associations."

The amendment was agreed to.

The VICE PRESIDENT. The Secretary will state the next amendment.

The SECRETARY. On page 7, line 16, after the word "organizations," strike out the comma and the words "orders, or associations."

The amendment was agreed to.

The VICE PRESIDENT. The next amendment of the committee will be stated.

The SECRETARY. On page 7, line 16, after the word "from," strike out the word "lawfully."

Mr. CUMMINS. Mr. President, this may be as appropriate a time as any other to express some views I hold with regard to the subject embodied in this seventh section.

I am not satisfied with the legislative expression found in the section now under consideration, but before I point out wherein I believe it might be strengthened and bettered I desire to pay some attention to the remarks of the Senator from North Dakota [Mr. MCCUMBER] and other Senators who have viewed the matter from his standpoint. He assailed this legislation, and many eminent citizens have assailed it, because it is alleged that it is class legislation, because it is said that we are here permitting certain people to do an act which if done by others would constitute a violation of the law.

I am not myself opposed to class legislation. Three-fourths of all the legislation adopted by Congress is class legislation. It is necessarily so because a general law will not accomplish the purpose that Congress has in view. But this particular legislation does not fall within the objection.

We have a statute which prohibits and makes unlawful restraints of trade. I agree with the Senator from North Dakota that a restraint of trade is as objectionable if brought about by a labor union as though brought about by a monopoly. But it is not always true that an interference with commerce on the part of a labor union is a restraint of trade.

I intend presently to ask the attention of the Senate to some observations with regard to the law of the matter, but just now I bespeak your consideration for one phase of this subject that hitherto has not been touched upon.

Labor organizations brought together for the purpose of enhancing or advancing wages, bettering the conditions of labor or lessening the hours of labor, can not in the very nature of things be a restraint of trade or commerce. Mark you, I am not now considering what the individual members of a labor organization may do. I am not considering how they may impede commerce in the execution of the objects of their organization. I am simply suggesting that an organization of workingmen who associate themselves together for the purpose of lifting up the plane upon which they live and labor can not be a restraint of trade.

I wonder if it is constantly in our mind that labor, even in a country as fortunate as our own, does not receive a compensation that will enable those who work for wages to adequately discharge their duties as citizens. We have in this country 20,000,000 people who may be called wageworkers. I have no information and can get none with regard to the average compensation of these 20,000,000 wageworkers, but I have information concerning a portion of them which I desire that Senators shall hear and remember during the remaining part of this debate. In the census of 1910 those who were collecting the information investigated the manufacturing establishments of the United States as defined in the law providing for the Thirteenth Census. I want, first, to read what the word "establishment" means, in order to show the scope of the investigation:

> The word "establishment," as used in the Thirteenth Census, is defined as meaning one or more factories, mills, or plants owned, controlled, or operated by a person, partnership, corporation, or other owner located in the same town or city, and for which one set of books of account is kept.

In these establishments turning out a product of $500 or more there was an investigation made, and they numbered, in all, 268,491. In these 268,491 establishments there were employed an annual average of 6,615,046 men and women.

I have just stated the average number employed in these establishments during the year 1909. These employees or wageworkers were paid, and I am confining my remarks now to wageworkers exclusive of clerks and salaried officers. The amount paid to these 6,000,000 and more wageworkers during the year 1909 was $3,427,038,000. So the average amount received by each of these 6,000,000 of wageworkers in the establishments to which I have referred was $518 per year. If I could have gathered the information respecting the 20,000,000 comprising all the wageworkers of the United States, I venture to say the average received by all of them would be under rather than over the sum I have mentioned. So we are expecting these 20,000,000 of men and women who constitute the bone, the sinew, the strength of the Republic to live; we are expecting them to support families and educate their boys and girls and train them into good citizens, to feed and clothe them, so that they may be respected members of society, upon $518 per year.

If this be true of the most fortunate Nation on the face of the earth, where opportunity is wider, where the rewards of enterprise and energy are richer than in any other country in all the world, I ask the question of those who seem to doubt the wisdom or the propriety of aiding these working people in enlarging their compensation and in bettering the conditions of their labor if they do not know that the life and the safety of the country depend upon the enlargement of the opportunities and the increase of the wages of our working men and women? Do you not know that unless we are able in some way to put into their hands as compensation for their labor a sum sufficient to inspire hope in their hearts and ambition in their souls, to enable them to hold their confidence in their country's institutions and their hope in the future, the experiment which we have been so brilliantly trying in the last century is doomed to dismal failure? These 20,000,000 of working men and women must be hopeful; they must be intelligent; they must be virtuous; they must be honest; they must be ambitious for themselves and their families, if free institutions in the world are to survive.

Then, why should not these workingmen and working women combine, associate themselves together, in order that their wages may be increased and the conditions under which their labor is performed may be bettered? There is no danger, Mr. President, that the workingman or the working woman will ever receive more than an adequate compensation for the labor performed. There is a potential competition always confronting wageworkers that will inevitably reduce the compensation far below the point at which it should in equity and in good conscience rest. These men and women grow hungry, and they must eat; they must clothe themselves; they must support their families; and these necessities compel them to work at whatsoever wages they may be able to secure. Idleness for any great length of time and among any great proportion of them is absolutely unthinkable and impossible.

For these reasons, Mr. President, I have never been one of those who have had any fear of combination among wageworkers. I believe that it ought to be the policy of this Government to encourage such combination and association. I believe we ought to lend a helping hand to their efforts to advance their condition in life, knowing that with all their energy and with all the assistance we can give them they will never be advanced in fortune or in property beyond the point necessary for comfort and happiness.

This is the beginning, I think, of all consideration of this subject. I do not see how anyone can investigate it without first learning and pondering upon the facts that I have so meagerly stated.

Let us take the next step. We have been debating this bill, and I have heard the subject debated a thousand times upon ⊥ the hypothesis that the labor of a human being is of the same quality and order as a bale of cotton, a barrel of flour or a bushel of corn. I repudiate the parallel and the comparison. It is because we have been in the habit of thinking of labor as a commodity that we have fallen into many mistakes which now impair and mar, I think, both legislation and judicial opinion. The labor of a human being, whether it be of the mind or of the hand, is not a commodity. While we are in the habit I know, of saying that a workingman has nothing to sell but his labor it is a confusion in thought and in terms. Labor is not a commodity; it is not an article of commerce; and when the Constitution of the United States gave to Congress the authority to regulate commerce among the States, it did not give it the right to regulate labor, the disposition of the energy of the human being.

If we would begin as we ought to begin, with the understanding that the power of a human being to work, to produce something, is not a commodity or a subject of commerce, we would reach a saner and better conclusion than we have heretofore announced.

It may be said that the distinction that I have drawn is technical rather than substantial. Not so, because out of it grows this proposition which is now admitted everywhere, which was declared in the Senate yesterday without dispute, namely, that it is the right of a human being to work or to refrain from working, as he deems best. Under our form of government it is not a thing that can be or ought to be controlled by the law. We have a right to say that one who refuses to work, and in that way becomes a burden upon society, shall no longer be a member of that society; we have a right to expel him from society; but we have no right under our form of government to say that he shall work; we have no right to say for whom he shall work or the vocation in which he may choose to employ his power of body or of mind. There is no inconvenience to organized society brought about by the refusal of a man or of a woman to work which can override the inherent and fundamental right to refuse to work or to refuse to work at a particular employment for a particular compensation or for a particular employer.

Therefore, when we speak of a restraint of trade or of commerce, when we prohibit, as we did in 1890, any person or any combination of persons from restraining trade or commerce, we did not prohibit one man alone, a thousand, or a million men from refraining from work, and we did not and we could not make it a crime for that one man or a thousand men in concert to advise or persuade other men to refrain from work.

Why, Senators, there is a propaganda going on all the time, and has been for years in this country and every other, for a complete change in the form of government. It might just as well be alleged that the movement for socialism is a restraint of trade and commerce as it is to allege that a strike or that the persuasion on the part of strikers brought to bear on those who are still at work to cease to work is a restraint of trade or commerce. After all, it is the privilege of free speech, it is the privilege of carrying forward a movement respecting the rules of society—respecting the belief of individual members of society; and I have never been able to understand how any man could believe that a labor union, the purposes of which are to advance the standard of wages, lessen the hours of employment, or better the conditions under which labor is performed, is a violation of the antitrust law.

But there are a great many people in the country who do believe it is a violation of the antitrust laws, precisely as it would be a violation of the law if a hundred manufacturers were to come together and agree that their products should be sold at a common price without any rivalry or competition between them. A combination or contract of that sort would be a violation of the antitrust law before a single act was performed, save the mere execution of the contract itself. That contract has to do with commodities, with the subjects of commerce, with articles that are transported from place to place and bought and sold in the markets of the world. A contract or an arrangement between men who have nothing to give but themselves, nothing to employ except the power of their own bodies or of their minds which they have, and which they can give or refuse as they choose, such a contract or arrangement as that, as it has always seemed to me and as I believe the better opinion of the courts is, can not be adjudged to be a restraint of trade.

For that reason I repudiate entirely the argument that we are here segregating a class, and exempting that class from the operation of the law and permitting its members to do the very things which other members of society are not permitted to do. That is not true; and if it had not been for the ill-considered judgment of some courts, if it had not been for the hasty and ill-advised expression of some judges, the matter contained in section 7 could never have been brought to the attention of Congress.

There never has been a decision—I emphasize the word "decision"—by any court that a labor union for the purpose I have so often described is in and of itself a violation of the law, or, in other words, a restraint of trade or commerce. There has been much argument that such a union ought to be considered as a violation of the antitrust law, but I think I speak advisedly when I say that no court has ever decided that such a union is within the prohibition of the antitrust law—I mean, now dissociated from any act performed either in the collective capacity of the union or by individual members of the union.

It is, however, as it seems to me, fair and just, in view of the disputes that have arisen from time to time and the differences of opinion which are everywhere manifest, to make it perfectly clear not by exempting a class and saying that we will not hold that class responsible for a violation of law, but by giving a legislative interpretation or construction of the law, by declaring, as we ought to declare, that labor is not a commodity, and that associations of laboring men for the purpose of lifting the level of their lives and increasing their compensation and other things that make existence a little more tolerable do not constitute a restraint of trade. We are not excepting them; we are simply declaring, so that all men may understand, so that hereafter there may be no difference with respect to it, that these unions thus organized are not restraints of trade. We ought to have done it long ago and preserved this country from many a disastrous and irritating controversy.

I have spoken about the right of the employee, the wage earner, to work for whomsoever he pleases or not to work at all. On the other hand, the right of the employer is corelative. The employer has a perfect right to hire whomsoever he pleases or to hire no one. His right in that respect, so far as labor is concerned, is just as well intrenched in the law and in the civilization of the time as is the right of the employee. We can not compel an employer—I am now passing over the question of public corporations which have assumed a duty under the law of the public—but in ordinary industry we can not compel an employer to employ men; we can not compel him to continue his business, to continue the risk of the capital he has invested or the operations which have been theretofore a part of his business; and his refusal to employ men or women can not constitute a restraint of trade.

If we are to recognize this higher right of labor to be dealt with in the manner I have already described, the question then always is—and we might as well look at it plainly and courageously—not whether labor organizations may be brought together for the purpose of general improvement, but what may the members of the associations lawfully do in order to accomplish their purposes?

There has never been any serious dispute hitherto with regard to the mere existence of a labor union, but there has been a very wide range of dispute with regard to what the members of the union can properly do in order to make effectual the purposes of the union, and the whole war has gathered around that issue. Let us see. If it be taken for granted that my view of labor is the correct view and that men may strike or quit their employment when they please, singly or in concert, and that they may persuade other laboring men to quit employment, singly or in concert, the next question—and it is the most difficult and perplexing question of all—is, What may these employees who choose thus to exercise their unquestioned right fairly do in persuading those whom their former employer desires to substitute in their places to refrain from working?

I believe that nine-tenths of all the cases and the overwhelming proportion of all the trouble that has arisen has arisen in the attempt to draw that line; that is, to determine the extent to which the strikers may go in interfering with the admitted right of the employer to substitute other wageworkers in the stead of those who have quit his employment.

The second question, which is of equal difficulty, is, How far may the employees who have thus quit employment go in interfering with the business of their employer; that is, with the sale and distribution of the commodities or articles produced by their employer?

These are the two things that are material in this bill. All that part of the bill which relates to the strike, which relates to the organization itself, is simply the expression of a universal understanding of the subject; but when we come to determine just how far the strikers may go in order to render their cause successful or their strike effectual we meet a difficulty that is not easy of solution.

This particular section does not deal with that question at all. There is a section in the bill, however, which does deal with it; and when the proper time comes I intend to offer a substitute for section 7 which shall declare the law as to labor unions, which shall recite what they may do, and leave the power of the courts in administering their rights as it now is.

I have never thought it wise, as is done in section 18, to attempt to declare that an injunction shall not be issued to restrain a person from doing so and so. I have believed that we ought to say that it is not unlawful for persons to do so and so; and if the act itself be not unlawful, no court can prohibit it by way of injunction, nor can any court penalize it by way of damages. Our code with regard to labor unions ought to be contained in section 7 instead of section 18. I shall present at the proper time—I do not think this is the proper time—a substitute for that section, dealing with it in that way.

Now, a word or two with regard to the section itself as it now is. I said I was not satisfied with it. I am not. I am not satisfied with it, first, because in the description of labor organizations the purposes for which the members of such an organization can combine are not stated. What are labor organizations? We understand fairly well what a labor union is, but a labor organization, as stated in the bill, may be anything that pertains to labor; and if it be confined to laboring men, as it is not always, there is not a suggestion as to the purposes for which they can lawfully organize. No one would contend that the members of a labor organization could come together for the purpose of destroying the property of an employer. No one would contend that a labor organization could embody in its articles of association any immoral or any unlawful purpose; and yet the bill as it was proposed in the House, and as it came to the Senate, and as it still is, does not attempt to define the purposes for which a labor organization can be created. . . .

Mr. CULBERSON. The Senator says the bill does not attempt to state the purposes for which the organization may be created. I call the Senator's attention to the fact that the bill provides that labor organizations instituted for purposes of mutual help, and not having capital stock or conducted for profit, are legalized.

Mr. CUMMINS. Of course every association is for mutual help.

Mr. CULBERSON. I was not arguing the sufficiency of the designation, but I wanted to attract the attention of the Senator to the fact that the attempt was made in the bill.

Mr. CUMMINS. Yes; I understand. The point I make is this: We recognize the wisdom, indeed the necessity, for the organization of laboring men, the purposes being to increase their compensation, to lessen the hours of their labor, and to render more tolerable the conditions of labor. Those are the objects of such a labor organization as should be authorized and encouraged in the law; but we, very inadvisedly, and I think with hardly a fair comprehension of the subject, have simply denominated these organizations which are declared to be not within the antitrust law labor organizations organized for mutual help. I am sure that when we reflect upon it we will go back to the old definition, the definition contained in the English trade act, the definition contained in every act that I have ever known to be presented here until this one, namely, labor unions or labor organizations for the purpose of increasing wages, lessening hours of labor, and bettering the conditions of labor. We can not afford to say that every labor organization, no matter what its purposes may be, is unobjectionable under the antitrust law.

I pass on now to the next part of the section. I have already given my view with regard to the character of labor and why laboring men have a high right to combine with each other to advance their own interests. We find in this section a proposal to extend the same immunity to agricultural organizations and horticultural organizations.

I should like some person who understands the subject better than I do to tell the Senate what an agricultural organization is. I venture to say that an organization of Chicago packers, for the purpose of buying all the live stock of the country, is an agricultural organization. I venture to say that an association which was to take into one ownership as trustee all the cereals of the United States or all the cotton of the Southern States would be an agricultural organization.

It does not confine the immunity to farmers' organizations. I would not be for it even if it were so confined, for I do not believe the farmers of this country desire that their commodities should be so treated. They deal in commodities precisely as a manufacturer deals in commodities. The farmer produces a commodity, and he produces it either for consumption or for sale. I venture to say that the farmers of this country do not desire the privilege of uniting their commodities in a single association or under the control of a single association so as to enhance by that combination the prices at which these commodities shall be sold. . . .

Mr. POMERENE. The Senator comes from a State which, perhaps, has the largest agricultural product of the country, and that is a good deal for one from Ohio to admit. I wish to ask the Senator whether, in his State, there is any sentiment among the farmers in behalf of this exemption? I have not learned of any from my State.

Mr. CUMMINS. If the Senator means to ask me whether there is any demand among the farmers of my State for an amelioration or change in the law that would permit agricultural products to be monopolized, and thus affect their prices, there is no such demand. If, on the other hand, he means to ask me whether they desire to continue to have county fairs and harvest homes and old-settlers' picnics and other organizations of that kind, largely composed of farmers in my State, I say unhesitatingly "yes." I have never heard it suggested, however, that these associations where farmers gather together in a neighborhood, a county, a State, for the purpose of exchanging information, of increasing acquaintance, of cultivating good fellowship, were contrary to the antitrust law. I have never heard anybody suggest anything of that kind, and I think it has never been asserted. If this clause with regard to agricultural associations has any effect whatsoever, it must be that it is intended to allow associations that can control the commodities which farmers produce as to their prices. I assume that a provision which would permit an association to control their prices in an upward way and would also permit some other association to control their prices in a downward way.

I ask again, What is an agricultural organization? I have referred to the dictionary and other sources of information with regard to the meaning of the word "agricultural," and I find that the very first definition of the word is "of or pertaining to agriculture; connected with agriculture." It would be entirely within the meaning of the words "agricultural organization" if we were to find an association not one member of which was a farmer or who produced the commodity, but the members of which were associated together for the purpose of affecting agricultural products.

I almost fear that such an association as the International Harvester Co. is an agricultural organization. If it were not a corporation organized for pecuniary profit, it certainly would be an agricultural organization; and it would be the easiest thing in the world to organize a like concern the purpose of which was to benefit pecuniarily its members, and in which the organization itself would have no pecuniary profit and no capital stock.

I am not in favor of this invasion of the antitrust law. It is wholly different from the subject of labor, for it deals in commodities and in articles of commerce and not in the human power which produces commodities or articles of commerce. We shall regret it if we make this inroad upon a statute upon which we have come to rely with so great confidence.

If the section is limited merely to those associations of farmers and of fruit growers who come together, as we see every year, for mutual help—that is, mutual information—that is another thing. We have these associations in every vocation and every industry in the United States. We have the farmers' organizations; we have the retail dealers' associations; we have the wholesale dealers' associations; we have the manufacturers' associations. We have associations, I think, in every vocation in which people are engaged. No one has ever pretended that these organizations are in restraint of trade. It is absurd. We are in danger of becoming hysterical with regard to the construction of the antitrust law.

It was not designed to prevent cooperation of the sort I have indicated, and there is no demand for introducing the clause I have recited in this section unless it is intended that through these organizations there may be a monopolistic price attached to some commodity produced through agriculture or through horticulture. I know that the country not only does not demand a change of that sort, but it will resent a change of that kind.

When the time comes, Mr. President, I intend to offer a substitute for the section. I have it before me now. It may not be literally perfect, but it expresses my view of the matter vastly better than the provisions of this bill. While I do not offer it ⊥ now, I intend to take the liberty of reading it just at this moment, so that Senators may be advised of its general scope:

> SEC. 7. The labor of a human being is not a commodity or article of commerce, and nothing contained in the antitrust laws shall be construed to forbid the existence and operation of labor organizations having for their objects bettering the conditions, lessening the hours, or advancing the compensation of labor, nor to forbid or restrain individual members of such organizations from carrying out said objects in a lawful way; nor shall said laws be construed to prevent or prohibit any person or persons, whether singly or in concert, from terminating any relation of employment or from ceasing to work or from advising or persuading others, in a peaceful, orderly way, and at a place where they may lawfully be, either to work or abstain from working, or from withholding their patronage from a party to any dispute growing out of the terms or conditions of employment, or from advising or persuading other wageworkers, in a peaceful and orderly way, so to do, or from paying or giving to or withholding from any person engaged in such dispute any strike benefits or other moneys or things of value, or from assembling in a peaceful way, for a lawful purpose, in any place where they may lawfully be, or from doing any act or thing which might lawfully be done in the absence of such dispute.

So much of it refers to labor. I cover the remainder of the section in this way:

> Nothing contained in said antitrust laws shall be construed to forbid the existence and operation of agricultural, horticultural, or commercial organizations instituted for mutual benefit, without capital stock, and not conducted for the pecuniary profit of either such organizations or the members thereof, or to forbid or restrain such members from carrying out said objects in a lawful way. . . .

Mr. [JOHN SHARP] WILLIAMS [D., Miss.]. I should like to ask the Senator from Iowa a question. If his substitute were adopted, and laboring men anywhere in a laboring man's newspaper should publish, under the head "We do not patronize," the names of JOHN SHARP WILLIAMS and various other people, could not they be prosecuted under the law as it then would be?

Mr. CUMMINS. Mr. President, I do not think so, if I understand the question of the Senator from Mississippi. I may state my purpose in this amendment, so that the Senator may at least read it in the light of my object.

Mr. WILLIAMS. Yes; I listened to the Senator.

Mr. CUMMINS. I believe in the strike. I believe the direct boycott of the offending or unfair employer is a fair weapon. I do not believe in the secondary boycott. I do not believe labor unions or any other organizations ought to be permitted to combine together to injure or destroy an innocent man because he may have dealings with a person who may be unfair to labor.

Mr. WILLIAMS. That is not quite the point I had in mind. I understand that; and I, like the Senator, believe in "boycotts," in the sense in which he is now using—that is, the right to refuse to patronize—not, of course, in the original sense of the word as derived from the fate of the unfortunate Capt. Boycott. When our forefathers made ready to resist Great Britain, the first thing they did was to boycott British goods; and I remember a time in the hard struggles of carpetbag days down South, when a man who was a large manufacturer in Indiana gave utterance to some very bitter expressions about the southern people, when mass meetings were held everywhere, and resolutions were passed that they would not buy any of his manufactured products, and they did not until he apologized by the explanation route, all of which I believe to be perfectly right. I go further. A man might come out to-morrow—take my own church as an instance, not that I am much of a churchman—and say that Episcopalians were all sorts of wicked and bad things, and tell all sorts of lies about them. I think the Episcopalians would have the right to agree, not only one Episcopalian but all of them, in one combined voice that they would not patronize that man, and ask fair-minded men everywhere not to patronize him.

Mr. CUMMINS. Undoubtedly. That is the primary boycott.

Mr. WILLIAMS. I believe civilization depends very largely upon the operation of the moral sense of a community, through ostracism, at times, if necessary, and frequently through what may be called a qualified boycott, but the point I had in view was the direct one, not the secondary one at all.

The Senator will remember that the labor unions were enjoined from putting upon a black list a certain manufacturer of hats, and that after that, obeying that injunction, they merely published the name of that manufacturer of hats under the heading: "We do not patronize."[5.656]

Now, that was all there was to it; and yet, under that, and because of that, those men were held up for violating the injunction and were about to be punished for contempt. I do not know whether they ever have been punished or not. I believe the statute of limitations intervened somewhere and they were not punished. I regarded that as one of the most high-handed pieces of judicial tyranny that ever has been perpetrated in any country in the world.

Mr. CUMMINS. So it was.

Mr. WILLIAMS. The Senator will also remember another case where certain men were enjoined from quitting work. Now, that was a sympathetic strike; but I never could see a reason why a man should not quit work for any reason that was good to him, or without giving or having any reason.

Mr. CUMMINS. Nor I, either.

Mr. WILLIAMS. Nor why any number of men should not combine to quit work for any reason that was good, or without any reason.

Mr. CUMMINS. I have insisted on that so often this afternoon that I am simply guilty of gross reiteration when I say that I believe so, too. I think a man has a right to quit work alone or with his companions, with agreement or without agreement.

Mr. WILLIAMS. Primarily or sympathetically.

Mr. CUMMINS. It does not make a bit of difference; but the point I make is this: Here were certain hat makers in Danbury, Conn. They had a dispute with their employer, and it grew into a bitter warfare.

I am looking at it now from my own point of view. The employees had a perfect right to say "We will buy no hats made by this concern, and we will ask everybody else to wear no hats made by this concern," but they come to a dealer in my town, a clothing man. Hats are simply one of a great many articles that he carries. There are cuffs, collars, neckties, shirts, and a thousand other things in his stock. I do not believe

---

[5.656] Reference is to Loewe v. Lawlor, 208 U.S. 274, 28 S. Ct. 301, 52 L. Ed. 488 (1908) (the *Danbury Hatters* case).

that they have any right to come to him and combine and say "Unless you quit buying hats of the Danbury man we will not buy anything from you; we will cease to buy your neckties and your shirts and your clothing and your boots and shoes and everything else that you may have to sell." I do not believe that that is a fair weapon in the war.

Mr. WILLIAMS. Mr. President, I agree with the Senator that that is going to a very unwise and extreme extent; but that does not touch the question of right. Have I not a right to refuse to deal with a man for any reason, say, because he is red-headed, and have I not a right to agree with other people not to deal with him because he is a red-headed man?

Mr. CUMMINS. You have a perfect right to refuse to deal with him, but you have no right to combine or to enter into a conspiracy with a thousand other people that they will not deal with a certain man because he is red-headed.

Mr. WILLIAMS. Leaving that out, we both agree, at any rate, that that would be carrying things to what I consider an unfair extreme.

Mr. CUMMINS. Yes; that is what I claim for it.

Mr. WILLIAMS. But a man has a right, to carry it to that extent, as far as I can see, in combination or otherwise, though it may be a right which it is foolish or even not fair to exercise. There are forming all over this country some of the most useful societies that I know of in the social uplifting and the industrial uplifting of the country, mainly women, joining together for a laudable purpose now. They find that a department store, for example, makes its employees—women—stand up all day long, and that they work them 16 hours a day. So they publish a list of the people, and they say, "Those people do not treat their employees fairly." Then all the members of that society at once refuse to deal with those people until they do treat their employees fairly.

I think that public opinion invoked in that way is a stronger weapon than any law in the world looking to the uplift of the condition of the industrial labor of the country. I would dislike to see anything in any bill that might possibly be tortured into an interference with that sort of thing.

Mr. CUMMINS. On the contrary, the amendment I read expressly authorizes that.

Mr. WILLIAMS. But that is not a labor organization at all.

Mr. CUMMINS. Oh, no.

Mr. WILLIAMS. I do not know how we could call it a labor organization. They call themselves "consumers' leagues," I believe—just why I do not quite understand.

Mr. CUMMINS. The amendment I shall offer expressly declares that such a proceeding upon the part of laboring men shall not be construed to be a restraint of trade.

Mr. WILLIAMS. If the Senator will excuse me for bothering him one minute more—

Mr. CUMMINS. Certainly.

Mr. WILLIAMS. The Senator said he did not see how this exemption could apply to farmers in a way desired by them. I will give the Senator an illustration in order that he may direct his mind toward it.

Take the cotton crop, for example. America possesses almost a monopoly of cotton production; that is to say, she produces such a great percentage of the cotton crop of the world that the supply of American cotton fixes the price of cotton in the markets of the world. Cotton planters and farmers come together when cotton is very low because of an abnormally large crop and large visible supply, and they agree to decrease the acreage for the next crop, because we frequently get more money for a small crop than for a large one.

If there is no exception of farmers' organizations from the operation of this act and the existing antitrust law, then in my opinion a farmers' union of the South, meeting and passing resolutions and agreeing to curtail the production of cotton is a thing done "in restraint of trade"—there can be no doubt of that—and they would be subject to prosecution unless they were exempted in this bill.

Mr. CUMMINS. They have been, then, for 20 years subject to prosecution.

Mr. WILLIAMS. I know, and the only reason why they have not been prosecuted is because the prosecuting officers were afraid of the farmers' vote. The Senator knows that as well as I. There may be, however, some day some prosecuting officer who will not be afraid, and he might give them a good deal of trouble in a matter of that sort.

Mr. CUMMINS. I rather agree with the Senator from Mississippi that that would be a violation of the antitrust law.

Mr. WILLIAMS. There is not any doubt about it; but it ought not to be prosecuted, because it is a perfectly justifiable means of defending one's self against a positive loss in production, by merely affecting the natural law of supply and demand.

I was very sorry this morning that we struck out the word "consumers." I think the best thing that we could do right now would be to boycott eggs, let us say, for example; to hold meetings and say we would not use any eggs until these miserable robbers reduce the exploitive price they have put on them; and then after we succeeded in bringing them to their knees on eggs—that is, bringing them to a reasonable price—the consumers' league could declare that they will boycott the use of a lot of other things for a while—meat, for example, and fowls—until the robbers concluded to accept reasonable prices. However, that has been passed and settled.

Mr. CUMMINS. May I suggest to the Senator from Mississippi that there may be a great many restraints of trade which for the time being will prove beneficial? But I will ask him this question: The railroads are by far the greatest consumers of iron and steel products. Would the Senator from Mississippi favor such a change in the law as would enable the railroads of the country to combine and dictate the prices of the steel which they might thereafter buy?

Mr. WILLIAMS. I would not have the slightest fear of that.

Mr. CUMMINS. Then the antitrust law is of no value, anyhow.

Mr. WILLIAMS. I have not the slightest fear of that, practically, because they could not refuse to buy steel any longer than a certain length of time. They would be compelled to have rails. They would be compelled to have rolling stock. They would have to go on the market for them. The Steel Trust, upon the other side, moreover, is about as strong as they are. It would be a Kilkenny cat fight, in which I would not be very much interested.

I can imagine cases where the consumer of some product might be so strong that he would have to be curbed in his cunning, in the exercise of his force or power.

But leaving that out, which is a mere offshoot of the argument, it seems to me that the labor organizations and farmers' organizations are not in any sense a commercial or an industrial affair. While this bill was directed in its origin and ought to be directed now and confined to industrial and commercial organizations—to great concentrations of money strength, which owing to their concentration can become dangerous to the public—these other people, farmers and factory hands, can never become dangerous as a money power, being mere voluntary organizations without any profit behind them to drive them to exploitive and tyrannical acts. They are acting in self-defense as a rule. If they use violence, the only way in which they may become dangerous to the liberties or property of society, the criminal law is there to curb and punish them.

Mr. CUMMINS. I think, Mr. President, that there are a great many instances in which cooperation could be employed with great advantage, but the difficulty is, as has been stated here more than once, this is a country of law, and we must describe the offense as certainly as we can, and then it must fall equally upon all who are within its terms.

I have no doubt that if we had an infinitely wise and patriotic and sensible person to administer the affairs of the United States, he could administer them in each individual instance with better advantage than they are administered through general law; but we have no such person. And so long as we are dependent upon general law we ought not to make an exception. Long before the Senator from Mississippi came in I attempted to demonstrate that the legislative declaration, to the effect that labor unions were not restraints of trade, was not an exemption of these unions from the operation of the law because of the difference between labor and a commodity.

I repeat that it disturbs me to hear labor termed a commodity—to hear the power of a man or woman to exercise the strength of mind or body in the production of something useful to the human race confused with the product which is the result of its exercise. It destroys all the distinctions that we ought to preserve. I close as I began with the insistence that when labor unions, with the purpose that I have described, are declared to be without the antitrust law, we are simply recognizing the essential character of things and are making a legislative declaration or interpretation of the law rather than classifying the people of the country and allowing one class to escape and another class to be bound.

Mr. NELSON. I wish the Senator would be good enough to have his amendment offered and printed.

Mr. CUMMINS. I think I will do that, so that it may be seen. I offer it as a substitute for section 7. I intend to discuss it further when we are considering section 18.

The amendment was ordered to lie on the table and be printed and to be printed in the RECORD, as follows:

Amendment intended to be proposed by Mr. CUMMINS to the bill (H. R. 15657) to supplement existing laws against unlawful restraints and monopolies, and for other purposes, viz: Insert as a substitute for section 7 the following:

"SEC. 7. That the labor of a human being is not a commodity or article of commerce, and nothing contained in the antitrust laws shall be construed to forbid the existence and operation of labor organizations having for their objects bettering the conditions, lessenings [sic] the hours, or advancing the compensation of labor, nor to forbid or restrain individual members of such organizations from carrying out said objects in a lawful way; nor shall said laws be construed to prevent or prohibit any person or persons, whether singly or in concert, from terminating any relation of employment or from ceasing to work or from advising or persuading others in a peaceful, orderly way, and at a place where they may lawfully be, either to work or abstain from working, or from withholding their patronage from a party to any dispute growing out of the terms or conditions of employment or from advising or persuading other wageworkers in a peaceful and orderly way so to do, or from paying or giving to or withholding from any person engaged in such dispute any strike benefits or other moneys or things of value, or from assembling in a peaceful and orderly way for a lawful purpose in any place where they may lawfully be, or from doing any act or thing which might lawfully be done in the absence of such dispute. Nothing contained in said antitrust laws shall be construed to forbid the existence and operation of agricultural, horticultural, or commercial organizations instituted for mutual benefit without capital stock and not conducted for the pecuniary profit of either such organization or the members thereof, or to forbid or restrain such members from carrying out said objects in a lawful way."

Mr. KERN. I should like a unanimous agreement that the Senate take a recess not later than 5.45 [sic] until to-morrow morning at 11 o'clock.

The PRESIDING OFFICER (Mr. LEWIS in the chair). Does the Chair hear any objection? The Chair hears none.